## OTHER A TO Z GUIDES FROM THE SCARECROW PRESS, INC.

1. *The A to Z of Buddhism* by Charles S. Prebish, 2001. *Out of Print. See No. 124.*
2. *The A to Z of Catholicism* by William J. Collinge, 2001.
3. *The A to Z of Hinduism* by Bruce M. Sullivan, 2001.
4. *The A to Z of Islam* by Ludwig W. Adamec, 2002. *Out of Print. See No. 123.*
5. *The A to Z of Slavery and Abolition* by Martin A. Klein, 2002.
6. *Terrorism: Assassins to Zealots* by Sean Kendall Anderson and Stephen Sloan, 2003.
7. *The A to Z of the Korean War* by Paul M. Edwards, 2005.
8. *The A to Z of the Cold War* by Joseph Smith and Simon Davis, 2005.
9. *The A to Z of the Vietnam War* by Edwin E. Moise, 2005.
10. *The A to Z of Science Fiction Literature* by Brian Stableford, 2005.
11. *The A to Z of the Holocaust* by Jack R. Fischel, 2005.
12. *The A to Z of Washington, D.C.* by Robert Benedetto, Jane Donovan, and Kathleen DuVall, 2005.
13. *The A to Z of Taoism* by Julian F. Pas, 2006.
14. *The A to Z of the Renaissance* by Charles G. Nauert, 2006.
15. *The A to Z of Shinto* by Stuart D. B. Picken, 2006.
16. *The A to Z of Byzantium* by John H. Rosser, 2006.
17. *The A to Z of the Civil War* by Terry L. Jones, 2006.
18. *The A to Z of the Friends (Quakers)* by Margery Post Abbott, Mary Ellen Chijioke, Pink Dandelion, and John William Oliver Jr., 2006.
19. *The A to Z of Feminism* by Janet K. Boles and Diane Long Hoeveler, 2006.
20. *The A to Z of New Religious Movements* by George D. Chryssides, 2006.
21. *The A to Z of Multinational Peacekeeping* by Terry M. Mays, 2006.
22. *The A to Z of Lutheranism* by Günther Gassmann with Duane H. Larson and Mark W. Oldenburg, 2007.
23. *The A to Z of the French Revolution* by Paul R. Hanson, 2007.
24. *The A to Z of the Persian Gulf War 1990–1991* by Clayton R. Newell, 2007.
25. *The A to Z of Revolutionary America* by Terry M. Mays, 2007.
26. *The A to Z of the Olympic Movement* by Bill Mallon with Ian Buchanan, 2007.
27. *The A to Z of the Discovery and Exploration of Australia* by Alan Day, 2009.
28. *The A to Z of the United Nations* by Jacques Fomerand, 2009.
29. *The A to Z of the "Dirty Wars"* by David Kohut, Olga Vilella, and Beatrice Julian, 2009.
30. *The A to Z of the Vikings* by Katherine Holman, 2009.
31. *The A to Z from the Great War to the Great Depression* by Neil A. Wynn, 2009.
32. *The A to Z of the Crusades* by Corliss K. Slack, 2009.
33. *The A to Z of New Age Movements* by Michael York, 2009.
34. *The A to Z of Unitarian Universalism* by Mark W. Harris, 2009.
35. *The A to Z of the Kurds* by Michael M. Gunter, 2009.
36. *The A to Z of Utopianism* by James M. Morris and Andrea L. Kross, 2009.
37. *The A to Z of the Civil War and Reconstruction* by William L. Richter, 2009.
38. *The A to Z of Jainism* by Kristi L. Wiley, 2009.
39. *The A to Z of the Inuit* by Pamela K. Stern, 2009.
40. *The A to Z of Early North America* by Cameron B. Wesson, 2009.
41. *The A to Z of the Enlightenment* by Harvey Chisick, 2009.
42. *The A to Z Methodism* by Charles Yrigoyen Jr. and Susan E. Warrick, 2009.
43. *The A to Z of the Seventh-day Adventists* by Gary Land, 2009.
44. *The A to Z of Sufism* by John Renard, 2009.
45. *The A to Z of Sikhism* by William Hewat McLeod, 2009.
46. *The A to Z Fantasy Literature* by Brian Stableford, 2009.
47. *The A to Z of the Discovery and Exploration of the Pacific Islands* by Max Quanchi and John Robson, 2009.
48. *The A to Z of Australian and New Zealand Cinema* by Albert Moran and Errol Vieth, 2009.
49. *The A to Z of African-American Television* by Kathleen Fearn-Banks, 2009.

50. *The A to Z of American Radio Soap Operas* by Jim Cox, 2009.
51. *The A to Z of the Old South* by William L. Richter, 2009.
52. *The A to Z of the Discovery and Exploration of the Northwest Passage* by Alan Day, 2009.
53. *The A to Z of the Druzes* by Samy S. Swayd, 2009.
54. *The A to Z of the Welfare State* by Bent Greve, 2009.
55. *The A to Z of the War of 1812* by Robert Malcomson, 2009.
56. *The A to Z of Feminist Philosophy* by Catherine Villanueva Gardner, 2009.
57. *The A to Z of the Early American Republic* by Richard Buel Jr., 2009.
58. *The A to Z of the Russo-Japanese War* by Rotem Kowner, 2009.
59. *The A to Z of Anglicanism* by Colin Buchanan, 2009.
60. *The A to Z of Scandinavian Literature and Theater* by Jan Sjåvik, 2009.
61. *The A to Z of the Peoples of the Southeast Asian Massif* by Jean Michaud, 2009.
62. *The A to Z of Judaism* by Norman Solomon, 2009.
63. *The A to Z of the Berbers (Imazighen)* by Hsain Ilahiane, 2009.
64. *The A to Z of British Radio* by Seán Street, 2009.
65. *The A to Z of The Salvation Army* by Major John G. Merritt, 2009.
66. *The A to Z of the Arab-Israeli Conflict* by P. R. Kumaraswamy, 2009.
67. *The A to Z of the Jacksonian Era and Manifest Destiny* by Terry Corps, 2009.
68. *The A to Z of Socialism* by Peter Lamb and James C. Docherty, 2009.
69. *The A to Z of Marxism* by David Walker and Daniel Gray, 2009.
70. *The A to Z of the Bahá'í Faith* by Hugh C. Adamson, 2009.
71. *The A to Z of Postmodernist Literature and Theater* by Fran Mason, 2009.
72. *The A to Z of Australian Radio and Television* by Albert Moran and Chris Keating, 2009.
73. *The A to Z of the Lesbian Liberation Movement: Still the Rage* by JoAnne Myers, 2009.
74. *The A to Z of the United States–Mexican War* by Edward R. Moseley and Paul C. Clark, 2009.
75. *The A to Z of World War I* by Ian V. Hogg, 2009.
76. *The A to Z of World War II: The War Against Japan* by Ann Sharp Wells, 2009.
77. *The A to Z of Witchcraft* by Michael D. Bailey, 2009.
78. *The A to Z of British Intelligence* by Nigel West, 2009.
79. *The A to Z of United States Intelligence* by Michael A. Turner, 2009.
80. *The A to Z of the League of Nations* by Anique H. M. van Ginneken, 2009.
81. *The A to Z of Israeli Intelligence* by Ephraim Kahana, 2009.
82. *The A to Z of the European Union* by Joaquín Roy and Aimee Kanner, 2009.
83. *The A to Z of the Chinese Cultural Revolution* by Guo Jian, Yongyi Song, and Yuan Zhou, 2009.
84. *The A to Z of African American Cinema* by S. Torriano Berry and Venise T. Berry, 2009.
85. *The A to Z of Japanese Business* by Stuart D. B. Picken, 2009.
86. *The A to Z of the Reagan–Bush Era* by Richard S. Conley, 2009.
87. *The A to Z of Human Rights and Humanitarian Organizations* by Robert F. Gorman and Edward S. Mihalkanin, 2009.
88. *The A to Z of French Cinema* by Dayna Oscherwitz and MaryEllen Higgins, 2009.
89. *The A to Z of the Puritans* by Charles Pastoor and Galen K. Johnson, 2009.
90. *The A to Z of Nuclear, Biological and Chemical Warfare* by Benjamin C. Garrett and John Hart, 2009.
91. *The A to Z of the Green Movement* by Miranda Schreurs and Elim Papadakis, 2009.
92. *The A to Z of the Kennedy–Johnson Era* by Richard Dean Burns and Joseph M. Siracusa, 2009.
93. *The A to Z of Renaissance Art* by Lilian H. Zirpolo, 2009.
94. *The A to Z of the Broadway Musical* by William A. Everett and Paul R. Laird, 2009.
95. *The A to Z of the Northern Ireland Conflict* by Gordon Gillespie, 2009.
96. *The A to Z of the Fashion Industry* by Francesca Sterlacci and Joanne Arbuckle, 2009.
97. *The A to Z of American Theater: Modernism* by James Fisher and Felicia Hardison Londré, 2009.
98. *The A to Z of Civil Wars in Africa* by Guy Arnold, 2009.
99. *The A to Z of the Nixon–Ford Era* by Mitchell K. Hall, 2009.
100. *The A to Z of Horror Cinema* by Peter Hutchings, 2009.
101. *The A to Z of Westerns in Cinema* by Paul Varner, 2009.

102. *The A to Z of Zionism* by Rafael Medoff and Chaim I. Waxman, 2009.
103. *The A to Z of the Roosevelt–Truman Era* by Neil A. Wynn, 2009.
104. *The A to Z of Jehovah's Witnesses* by George D. Chryssides, 2009.
105. *The A to Z of Native American Movements* by Todd Leahy and Raymond Wilson, 2009.
106. *The A to Z of the Shakers* by Stephen J. Paterwic, 2009.
107. *The A to Z of the Coptic Church* by Gawdat Gabra, 2009.
108. *The A to Z of Architecture* by Allison Lee Palmer, 2009.
109. *The A to Z of Italian Cinema* by Gino Moliterno, 2009.
110. *The A to Z of Mormonism* by Davis Bitton and Thomas G. Alexander, 2009.
111. *The A to Z of African American Theater* by Anthony D. Hill with Douglas Q. Barnett, 2009.
112. *The A to Z of NATO and Other International Security Organizations* by Marco Rimanelli, 2009.
113. *The A to Z of the Eisenhower Era* by Burton I. Kaufman and Diane Kaufman, 2009.
114. *The A to Z of Sexspionage* by Nigel West, 2009.
115. *The A to Z of Environmentalism* by Peter Dauvergne, 2009.
116. *The A to Z of the Petroleum Industry* by M. S. Vassiliou, 2009.
117. *The A to Z of Journalism* by Ross Eaman, 2009.
118. *The A to Z of the Gilded Age* by T. Adams Upchurch, 2009.
119. *The A to Z of the Progressive Era* by Catherine Cocks, Peter C. Holloran, and Alan Lessoff, 2009.
120. *The A to Z of Middle Eastern Intelligence* by Ephraim Kahana and Muhammad Suwaed, 2009.
121. *The A to Z of the Baptists* William H. Brackney, 2009.
122. *The A to Z of Homosexuality* by Brent L. Pickett, 2009.
123. *The A to Z of Islam, Second Edition* by Ludwig W. Adamec, 2009.
124. *The A to Z of Buddhism* by Carl Olson, 2009.
125. *The A to Z of United States–Russian/Soviet Relations* by Norman E. Saul, 2010.
126. *The A to Z of United States–Africa Relations* by Robert Anthony Waters Jr., 2010.
127. *The A to Z of United States–China Relations* by Robert Sutter, 2010.
128. *The A to Z of U.S. Diplomacy since the Cold War* by Tom Lansford, 2010.
129. *The A to Z of United States–Japan Relations* by John Van Sant, Peter Mauch, and Yoneyuki Sugita, 2010.
130. *The A to Z of United States–Latin American Relations* by Joseph Smith, 2010.
131. *The A to Z of United States–Middle East Relations* by Peter L. Hahn, 2010.
132. *The A to Z of United States–Southeast Asia Relations* by Donald E. Weatherbee, 2010.
133. *The A to Z of U.S. Diplomacy from the Civil War to World War I* by Kenneth J. Blume, 2010.
134. *The A to Z of International Law* by Boleslaw A. Boczek, 2010.
135. *The A to Z of the Gypsies (Romanies)* by Donald Kenrick, 2010.
136. *The A to Z of the Tamils* by Vijaya Ramaswamy, 2010.
137. *The A to Z of Women in Sub-Saharan Africa* by Kathleen Sheldon, 2010.
138. *The A to Z of Ancient and Medieval Nubia* by Richard A. Lobban Jr., 2010.
139. *The A to Z of Ancient Israel* by Niels Peter Lemche, 2010.
140. *The A to Z of Ancient Mesoamerica* by Joel W. Palka, 2010.
141. *The A to Z of Ancient Southeast Asia* by John N. Miksic, 2010.
142. *The A to Z of the Hittites* by Charles Burney, 2010.
143. *The A to Z of Medieval Russia* by Lawrence N. Langer, 2010.
144. *The A to Z of the Napoleonic Era* by George F. Nafziger, 2010.
145. *The A to Z of Ancient Egypt* by Morris L. Bierbrier, 2010.
146. *The A to Z of Ancient India* by Kumkum Roy, 2010.
147. *The A to Z of Ancient South America* by Martin Giesso, 2010.
148. *The A to Z of Medieval China* by Victor Cunrui Xiong, 2010.
149. *The A to Z of Medieval India* by Iqtidar Alam Khan, 2010.
150. *The A to Z of Mesopotamia* by Gwendolyn Leick, 2010.
151. *The A to Z of the Mongol World Empire* by Paul D. Buell, 2010.
152. *The A to Z of the Ottoman Empire* by Selcuk Aksin Somel, 2010.
153. *The A to Z of Pre-Colonial Africa* by Robert O. Collins, 2010.
154. *The A to Z of Aesthetics* by Dabney Townsend, 2010.

155. *The A to Z of Descartes and Cartesian Philosophy* by Roger Ariew, Dennis Des Chene, Douglas M. Jesseph, Tad M. Schmaltz, and Theo Verbeek, 2010.
156. *The A to Z of Heidegger's Philosophy* by Alfred Denker, 2010.
157. *The A to Z of Kierkegaard's Philosophy* by Julia Watkin, 2010.
158. *The A to Z of Ancient Greek Philosophy* by Anthony Preus, 2010.
159. *The A to Z of Bertrand Russell's Philosophy* by Rosalind Carey and John Ongley, 2010.
160. *The A to Z of Epistemology* by Ralph Baergen, 2010.
161. *The A to Z of Ethics* by Harry J. Gensler and Earl W. Spurgin, 2010.
162. *The A to Z of Existentialism* by Stephen Michelman, 2010.
163. *The A to Z of Hegelian Philosophy* by John W. Burbidge, 2010.
164. *The A to Z of the Holiness Movement* by William Kostlevy, 2010.
165. *The A to Z of Hume's Philosophy* by Kenneth R. Merrill, 2010.
166. *The A to Z of Husserl's Philosophy* by John J. Drummond, 2010.
167. *The A to Z of Kant and Kantianism* by Helmut Holzhey and Vilem Mudroch, 2010.
168. *The A to Z of Leibniz's Philosophy* by Stuart Brown and N. J. Fox, 2010.
169. *The A to Z of Logic* by Harry J. Gensler, 2010.
170. *The A to Z of Medieval Philosophy and Theology* by Stephen F. Brown and Juan Carlos Flores, 2010.
171. *The A to Z of Nietzscheanism* by Carol Diethe, 2010.
172. *The A to Z of the Non-Aligned Movement and Third World* by Guy Arnold, 2010.
173. *The A to Z of Shamanism* by Graham Harvey and Robert J. Wallis, 2010.
174. *The A to Z of Organized Labor* by James C. Docherty, 2010.
175. *The A to Z of the Orthodox Church* by Michael Prokurat, Michael D. Peterson, and Alexander Golitzin, 2010.
176. *The A to Z of Prophets in Islam and Judaism* by Scott B. Noegel and Brannon M. Wheeler, 2010.
177. *The A to Z of Schopenhauer's Philosophy* by David E. Cartwright, 2010.
178. *The A to Z of Wittgenstein's Philosophy* by Duncan Richter, 2010.
179. *The A to Z of Hong Kong Cinema* by Lisa Odham Stokes, 2010.
180. *The A to Z of Japanese Traditional Theatre* by Samuel L. Leiter, 2010.
181. *The A to Z of Lesbian Literature* by Meredith Miller, 2010.
182. *The A to Z of Chinese Theater* by Tan Ye, 2010.
183. *The A to Z of German Cinema* by Robert C. Reimer and Carol J. Reimer, 2010.
184. *The A to Z of German Theater* by William Grange, 2010.
185. *The A to Z of Irish Cinema* by Roderick Flynn and Patrick Brereton, 2010.
186. *The A to Z of Modern Chinese Literature* by Li-hua Ying, 2010.
187. *The A to Z of Modern Japanese Literature and Theater* by J. Scott Miller, 2010.
188. *The A to Z of Old-Time Radio* by Robert C. Reinehr and Jon D. Swartz, 2010.
189. *The A to Z of Polish Cinema* by Marek Haltof, 2010.
190. *The A to Z of Postwar German Literature* by William Grange, 2010.
191. *The A to Z of Russian and Soviet Cinema* by Peter Rollberg, 2010.
192. *The A to Z of Russian Theater* by Laurence Senelick, 2010.
193. *The A to Z of Sacred Music* by Joseph P. Swain, 2010.
194. *The A to Z of Animation and Cartoons* by Nichola Dobson, 2010.
195. *The A to Z of Afghan Wars, Revolutions, and Insurgencies* by Ludwig W. Adamec, 2010.
196. *The A to Z of Ancient Egyptian Warfare* by Robert G. Morkot, 2010.
197. *The A to Z of the British and Irish Civil Wars 1637–1660* by Martyn Bennett, 2010.
198. *The A to Z of the Chinese Civil War* by Edwin Pak-wah Leung, 2010.
199. *The A to Z of Ancient Greek Warfare* by Iain Spence, 2010.
200. *The A to Z of the Anglo–Boer War* by Fransjohan Pretorius, 2010.
201. *The A to Z of the Crimean War* by Guy Arnold, 2010.
202. *The A to Z of the Zulu Wars* by John Laband, 2010.
203. *The A to Z of the Wars of the French Revolution* by Steven T. Ross, 2010.
204. *The A to Z of the Hong Kong SAR and the Macao SAR* by Ming K. Chan and Shiu-hing Lo, 2010.

205. *The A to Z of Australia* by James C. Docherty, 2010.
206. *The A to Z of Burma (Myanmar)* by Donald M. Seekins, 2010.
207. *The A to Z of the Gulf Arab States* by Malcolm C. Peck, 2010.
208. *The A to Z of India* by Surjit Mansingh, 2010.
209. *The A to Z of Iran* by John H. Lorentz, 2010.
210. *The A to Z of Israel* by Bernard Reich and David H. Goldberg, 2010.
211. *The A to Z of Laos* by Martin Stuart-Fox, 2010.
212. *The A to Z of Malaysia* by Ooi Keat Gin, 2010.
213. *The A to Z of Modern China (1800–1949)* by James Z. Gao, 2010.
214. *The A to Z of the Philippines* by Artemio R. Guillermo and May Kyi Win, 2010.
215. *The A to Z of Taiwan (Republic of China)* by John F. Copper, 2010.
216. *The A to Z of the People's Republic of China* by Lawrence R. Sullivan, 2010.
217. *The A to Z of Vietnam* by Bruce M. Lockhart and William J. Duiker, 2010.
218. *The A to Z of Bosnia and Herzegovina* by Ante Cuvalo, 2010.
219. *The A to Z of Modern Greece* by Dimitris Keridis, 2010.
220. *The A to Z of Austria* by Paula Sutter Fichtner, 2010.
221. *The A to Z of Belarus* by Vitali Silitski and Jan Zaprudnik, 2010.
222. *The A to Z of Belgium* by Robert Stallaerts, 2010.
223. *The A to Z of Bulgaria* by Raymond Detrez, 2010.
224. *The A to Z of Contemporary Germany* by Derek Lewis with Ulrike Zitzlsperger, 2010.
225. *The A to Z of the Contemporary United Kingdom* by Kenneth J. Panton and Keith A. Cowlard, 2010.
226. *The A to Z of Denmark* by Alastair H. Thomas, 2010.
227. *The A to Z of France* by Gino Raymond, 2010.
228. *The A to Z of Georgia* by Alexander Mikaberidze, 2010.
229. *The A to Z of Iceland* by Gudmundur Halfdanarson, 2010.
230. *The A to Z of Latvia* by Andrejs Plakans, 2010.
231. *The A to Z of Modern Italy* by Mark F. Gilbert and K. Robert Nilsson, 2010.
232. *The A to Z of Moldova* by Andrei Brezianu and Vlad Spânu, 2010.
233. *The A to Z of the Netherlands* by Joop W. Koopmans and Arend H. Huussen Jr., 2010.
234. *The A to Z of Norway* by Jan Sjåvik, 2010.
235. *The A to Z of the Republic of Macedonia* by Dimitar Bechev, 2010.
236. *The A to Z of Slovakia* by Stanislav J. Kirschbaum, 2010.
237. *The A to Z of Slovenia* by Leopoldina Plut-Pregelj and Carole Rogel, 2010.
238. *The A to Z of Spain* by Angel Smith, 2010.
239. *The A to Z of Sweden* by Irene Scobbie, 2010.
240. *The A to Z of Turkey* by Metin Heper and Nur Bilge Criss, 2010.
241. *The A to Z of Ukraine* by Zenon E. Kohut, Bohdan Y. Nebesio, and Myroslav Yurkevich, 2010.
242. *The A to Z of Mexico* by Marvin Alisky, 2010.
243. *The A to Z of U.S. Diplomacy from World War I through World War II* by Martin Folly and Niall Palmer, 2010.
244. *The A to Z of Spanish Cinema* by Alberto Mira, 2010.
245. *The A to Z of the Reformation and Counter-Reformation* by Michael Mullett, 2010.

# The A to Z of International Law

Boleslaw A. Boczek

*The A to Z Guide Series, No. 134*

The Scarecrow Press, Inc.
Lanham • Toronto • Plymouth, UK
2010

Published by Scarecrow Press, Inc.
A wholly owned subsidiary of
The Rowman & Littlefield Publishing Group, Inc.
4501 Forbes Boulevard, Suite 200, Lanham, Maryland 20706
http://www.scarecrowpress.com

Estover Road, Plymouth PL6 7PY, United Kingdom



British Library Cataloguing in Publication Information Available

**Library of Congress Cataloging-in-Publication Data**

The hardback version of this book was cataloged by the Library of Congress as follows:

Boczek, Boleslaw Adam.
International law : a dictionary / Boleslaw A. Boczek.
p. cm. — (Dictionaries of international law ; no. 2)
Includes bibliographical references.
1. International law—Dictionaries. I. Title. II. Series.

KZ1161.B63 2005
341'.03—dc22

2004017288

ISBN 978-0-8108-7560-9 (pbk. : alk. paper)

To my wife, Annerose;
to our children, Matthew, Andrew, and Barbara;
and to our grandchildren.

# Contents


| | | |
|---|---|---|
| Editor's Foreword *Jon Woronoff* | | xiii |
| Introduction | | xv |
| List of Acronyms and Abbreviations | | xix |
| Glossary | | xxiii |
| Chronology | | xxvii |
| Table of Cases | | xxxiii |
| List of Entries | | xxxix |
| Chapter I | General Problems: Nature and Enforcement of International Law, Sources, Relationship between International and National Law | 1 |
| Chapter II | International Legal Personality, States: Recognition, Jurisdiction, Responsibility, Succession | 37 |
| Chapter III | Individuals, Human Rights | 144 |
| Chapter IV | The Geophysical Context I: Land, Air, Outer Space, International Environmental Law | 201 |
| Chapter V | The Geophysical Context II: The Law of the Sea | 255 |
| Chapter VI | The Law of Treaties | 323 |
| Chapter VII | Peaceful Settlement of Disputes | 349 |
| Chapter VIII | The Use of Force | 391 |
| Chapter IX | International Humanitarian Law | 419 |
| Annex: Bibliography | | 465 |
| About the Author | | 477 |

# Editor's Foreword

It is only on studying a book like this that one realizes what giant strides international law has made over the past few decades. For centuries it inched ahead, rarely moving very fast or very far, and often pushed back while cruder events decided what was "right" and what was "wrong," or at any rate what was tolerated and what not. Indeed, the law of nations was regarded by all but international lawyers and scholars as an illusion if not a joke, something that was certainly commendable but could hardly take root in the world of reality. Then, ever since the end of World War II, and with even more momentum since the end of the Cold War, international law has been moving ahead. Just how far it has gotten only becomes clear when it is all summed up neatly, with everything in its proper place, and we suddenly notice that the old law—the one we studied at school—has been largely displaced by a new law that is being forged even as we read.

One of the reasons we have not realized this sea change is that the movement has been so rapid and, in certain spheres, is not completely assimilated or still open to question. Another is that changes have occurred in so many different sectors and most of us are only aware of what has been going on in one or two. So it is also advantageous that this book delves into all the relevant areas, starting with the sources—of which there are more than ever—and moving on to new fields of activity, such as the law of the sea, then concentrating on what remains of the sovereign use of force and especially how that is being hemmed in by treaties and to some extent at least dulled by resort to more numerous and more effective forms of peaceful settlement. Naturally, there is repeated mention of the growing circle of international organizations, large and small, universal and regional, which adopt resolutions that eventually create more law. This is to say nothing of the international courts, including criminal courts, which adjudicate.

*The A to Z of International Law* is an essential source of information about the world we presently live in. It is useful not only for specialists in international law, scholars and publicists, diplomats and participants at international conferences, and the personnel of many international organizations. It can also be read, or at least consulted, by attorneys, judges, professors and students, journalists, and anyone else interested in how much the world has changed and where it seems to be heading at present. While the treatment of these often complex and even confusing topics is inevitably sober and straightforward, the book is not that hard to read and the facts are not cluttered or hidden by unnecessarily convoluted phrases or technical jargon. Most impressive in one sense is that the advances, considerable and impressive as they are, are not glorified and the occasional reverses are not played down.

Considering the scope, it is quite amazing that this book is the fruit of one person's labor and, in a sense, not years but decades of preparation. It took Boleslaw A. Boczek several years to write this book but prior to that he had spent more than five decades, first studying international law at Jagiellonian University in Cracow and later at Harvard University, then teaching international law and international organization at Kent State University. He was also for some time a consultant for the United Nations and for several years did legal research at Harvard Law School as research associate. He was also a visiting professor and Fulbright senior lecturer at a number of foreign universities and more recently a member of the adjunct faculty of Case Western Reserve University School of Law. All the while Dr. Boczek has been writing, publishing books and numerous articles in professional journals. He coauthored *The International Law Dictionary* and more recently he wrote the *Historical Dictionary of International Tribunals*. His latest offering is thus the culmination of a long and fruitful career and a welcome gift to more of us than he can imagine.

Jon Woronoff
Series Editor

# Introduction

This volume appears at a time when the system of public international law, that is, the law governing relations between states and—to a certain extent—other subjects of international law, has reached a major turning point in its history and is confronting serious challenges generated by a variety of developments unfolding for some time in the structure of the international society and requiring an adjustment of some major rules of international law to the evolving reality of international relations.

From its origins within the context of the early European system of territorial states in the 16th and 17th centuries, the law of nations—as international law used to be called—developed by the 19th century into a system of legally binding customary rules supplemented by a growing network of treaties, and turned, from the "European public law" into the global international law binding states in all regions of the world. Three major features characterized this system. First, states were practically the only subjects of international law; second, the law consisted only of formal rules of coexistence, regulating such problems as recognition of states and governments, diplomacy, jurisdiction, and the like; and third, states enjoyed an extensive freedom of action and resort to war was considered their prerogative under international law. Subject to certain restrictions on the states' right to go to war, introduced by the League of Nations in 1919 and the Pact of Paris of 1928, the basic features of the system of international law continued until 1945. Yet, already in the latter two or so decades of this period a very modest albeit growing network of treaties imposing obligations but also reflecting the need to cooperate in certain non-traditional spheres of law, such as conventions regulating labor drafted by the International Labour Organisation, foreshadowed the future trends of contemporary international law.

The introduction in 1945 by the United Nations Charter of the ban on unilateral resort to force except in self-defense, complemented by the establishment of a multilateral system of collective security centralized in the Security Council, constituted the major turning point in the development of international law. But, in addition to this otherwise revolutionary development, the 60 years since the end of World War II have witnessed a profound transformation and expansion of international law from a relatively narrow system of interstate norms of coexistence into an immense and growing system of rules reaching virtually all aspects of life of the contemporary society. In addition, the system has expanded horizontally by the inclusion, mainly through the process of decolonization, of more than 100 new states which, in principle, accept the major premises and rules of the once European international law, subject to certain demands for change in international economic relations.

The process of the progressive development of international law started already in the Cold War era, from the beginning, has been inseparable from a rapid expansion of international organizations, a major feature of contemporary international law. One can say that—even though largely lacking enforcement powers—international organizations have played a leading and vital role in the transformation of international law from a legal system of mere coexistence of states into a wide-ranging and organized system of cooperation. It is simply impossible within the scope of this introduction to name all the new areas of international law evolved in the past few decades, but most international scholars would agree that the international law of human rights and international environmental law, including the law governing the conservation of species, have emerged as the most vital and growing spheres of public international law. Other areas, for example the law of the sea, which existed in the traditional international law, have expanded into a vast system transcending the narrow limits of jurisdictional rules and encompassing issues of conservation, exploration, and exploitation of natural resources. The traditional "law of war" has grown into a larger area of international humanitarian law, regulated by a number of international agreements, beginning with the Geneva Conventions of 1949. Other new or expanding areas of international law include international labor law, the law of state responsibility, international criminal law, outer space law, international communications law, international river law, and international economic, financial, and trade law, to mention just a few. A striking feature of the past decades or so has been a proliferation of international tribunals and quasi-judicial bodies adjudicating disputes between states. In addition, the World Court (International Court of Justice) an already old institution, has a full docket of cases and is by far more busy at present that in any period of its history. A glance at the chapters in this dictionary addressing, for example, the status of individuals or the spatial aspects of international law gives evidence of the progress that international law has made in a relatively short period of time. A comparable book on international law a few decades ago would have included only a fraction of the number of entries in those chapters, and would have no entries on human rights and the environment. It should be added that in the doctrine and the case law some of the above-mentioned branches of international law are conceptually related to each other. For instance, international humanitarian law is increasingly viewed as an extension of the law of human rights; the law of the sea has affinities to the rules concerning economic development; and the law governing state responsibility has links to international criminal law.

While international law today continues to be predicated on the principle of state sovereignty, the scope of the domestic jurisdiction of states has been shrinking in favor of international concern. This process has been particularly pronounced in the changing status of individuals under international law, who have acquired certain limited, albeit important, rights under this law and are now bound by certain obligations under it, notably those related to international crimes. Accountability of individuals, irrespective of their status, for crimes, directly under international law, is one of the most significant developments in contemporary international law. As a result, the boundary between domestic and international issues has become blurred, with consequent regulation by international law of such issues as, in addition to human rights, the protection of the environment and perhaps even the choice of the domestic political system. Another significant and related development has been the steady growth of transnational non-state actors, such as non-governmental organizations increasingly participating in the shaping of new rules of international law. However, the porous boundaries of today's territorial states also favor the activities of criminal transnational movements, such as terrorist organizations and illicit drug cartels.

In the era of rapid change and globalization international law must flexibly adjust its rules to the evolving reality. In this process of adjustment international law necessarily encounters obstacles and may suffer setbacks. The most urgent and sensitive problems of adjustment of international legal rules to change arise in the sphere of the use of force. Specifically, with regard to humanitarian intervention and self-defense against terrorist attacks, a legitimate question may arise to what extent and in what manner the United Nations Charter rules, which monopolize the decision-making power in the Security Council, can be amended to allow humanitarian intervention by force and similarly to legitimize self-defense against terrorist attacks, without a Security Council's authorization. In this regard, recognition by the Security Council of the United States' right of self-defense against terrorists who perpetrated the attacks in September 2001 (and thereby against states sheltering the terrorists), demonstrates that international law can be adjusted to new situations without the need for a radical restructuring of the system. The United States' preventive war of 2003 against Iraq without a Security Council authorization is interpreted by some as a repudiation by the only superpower of the whole system of collective security and multilateral approach to international problems, especially if viewed in the perspective of the behavioral pattern of the United States reaching back two decades or so. One can mention here withdrawal of the acceptance of the International Court of Justice optional clause jurisdiction; refusal to subscribe to most multilateral treaties, especially in the areas of human rights and the environment, including the Convention on the Law of the Sea of 1982 and the Kyoto Protocol, and open hostility to the first permanent International Criminal Court, an institution endorsed by most countries. The critics of the United States' posture also point out that a selective invocation of international law where it seems convenient reveals double standards in applying the law, thus causing serious damage to the United States' credibility in the world. The United States' ambivalent attitude toward the rule of law today may be only a temporary aberration, but restoring the United States' image as a champion of international law enjoyed in the early decades of the post–World War II era will not be easy. Participation in a continued development of the rule of law on a multilateral basis is indispensable for overcoming the crisis through which international law is undoubtedly passing in the early years of the 21st century.

While public debate over the United States' action in the Iraq crisis stimulated some interest in international law, on the whole—leaving aside professional journals—little time and space has been devoted to the international legal dimension of the Iraqi situation and—even less—other urgent problems in the region. It is significant that the role of international law in shaping the country's foreign policy was totally ignored in the presidential campaign of 2004. More generally, the relevance of international law as a factor that can directly affect the lives of ordinary citizens is not grasped clearly. The media coverage of international legal problems is quite negligible and often biased by extralegal considerations. In addition, the fact that questions of international law are often touched upon by persons not familiar with the subject contributes to misinformation and misunderstanding among the members of the public.

Paradoxically, although scores of excellent international law journals are published by various law schools in the United States, only a tiny portion of law school students selects the optional subject of international law. Most recently, the University of Michigan Law School was the first to introduce the requirement of a mandatory course in international law. As a result of the inferior position of international law in the curriculum of the law schools, only a very small fraction of lawyers has any familiarity with public international law. In fact, this state of affairs prompted the American Society of International Law to prepare, at the request of federal judges, a guide on international law to acquaint them with this—for them—arcane system of law. In most European universities international law is a compulsory part of the curriculum in the law departments. The situation in the teaching of international law in the developing world varies from country to country. Questions of economic development and a corresponding change of the relevant rules of international law occupy a priority in research and teaching.

Considering the need to acquaint legal and other professionals, students, and interested general readers, with the basic tenets of public international law, it is hoped that this volume can be used by them as a source of information on various questions in this sphere of law. The book combines the features of both a brief encyclopedic dictionary and a textbook. It attempts to reconcile the need for articulating ideas with a minimum of legal precision with employing a language understandable to casual readers. The survey of international law is organized in nine chapters with 373 entries consecutively numbered throughout the text. Chapter I contains the usual introductory topics found in international law textbooks: the nature of this law, its sources, the relationship between international and national ("municipal") law, and some other general problems. Chapters II–VIII deal with matters coming within the scope of the "law of peace," organized according to the framework consisting of: states, individuals, spatial context, and interaction. Chapter IX, whose subject unfortunately becomes ever more relevant, describes the rules governing the conduct of warfare, that is, international humanitarian law.

The long chapter II constitutes the central core of the discussion, including, among other topics, states, recognition, jurisdiction, diplomatic and consular law, state responsibility, and state succession (including also entries analyzing the dissolution of the Soviet Union and Yugoslavia, and reunification of Germany). Chapter III focuses on individuals and deals exhaustively with various problems of human rights. Chapter IV reviews various questions relating to the spatial context (land, airspace, and outer space) and contains numerous entries on international environmental law. Chapter V is devoted to the law of the sea. Chapter VI reviews the law of treaties and chapter VII discusses various methods of the peaceful settlement of international disputes. Chapter VIII, which deals with the use of force, includes, in appropriate entries, analyses of the invasion of Iraq, terrorism, and other topical subjects. Finally, chapter IX contains a variety of entries describing, in historical perspective, the rules of international humanitarian law, among others, also the treatments of prisoners of war and other protected persons and war crimes. There are numerous cross references in bold, leading the reader to appropriate entries. A certain amount of repetition and overlap is unavoidable in dealing with such a complex and vast area as international law. In the text there are copious references to primary sources, mostly treaties and court cases; they make it easier for the reader to locate the materials he needs in his research. The text is as of June 2004, but where possible subsequent developments have been taken into account.

The main body of the book is preceded by a list of acronyms and abbreviations; a glossary of mostly Latin phrases; a chronology which offers a historical perspective by listing major developments relating to international law throughout the centuries; a table of cases with references to entries; and a list of the 373 entries. Because of space limitations, the necessarily selective bibliography at the end of the volume includes only books in English, including research aids, textbooks and casebooks as well as recent books on special international law topics.

This dictionary should be a useful addition to both general and university libraries, including in particular libraries of law schools. The format of the book allows it to be used as a reference guide for legal professionals, scholars interested in international law topics, government officials, students, and casual readers. It can also serve as a supplement to casebooks in law schools and be included in reading lists in international law courses.

The author claims sole responsibility for any errors or omissions, and invites the readers to share with him any criticism concerning the contents of this book. He would like to thank Mr. Jon Woronoff, the Series Editor, for encouragement in preparing this book and to express appreciation to the editorial staff of the Scarecrow Press for their assistance and patience. Last but not least, my deepest thanks must be due to my wife, Annerose, and my children, Matthew, Andrew, and Barbara, for their patience, support, and understanding over the years of the preparation of this book.

The author hopes that this book will make a modest contribution to fostering education on international law issues and to a greater awareness of the role of this law in today's world. But the readers should always bear in mind that—to quote from J. L. Brierly's preface to the fifth edition (1954) of his classic *Law of Nations*—international law is "neither a myth on the one hand, nor a panacea on the other, but just one institution among others which we can use for the building of a better international order."

# Acronyms and Abbreviations

| | |
|---|---|
| AC | Appeal Cases, Law Reports |
| ADIZ | Air Defense Identification Zone |
| Adv. Op. | Advisory Opinion |
| AJIL | American Journal of International Law |
| All ER | All England Law Reports |
| ALR | Australian Law Reports |
| ARABSAT | Arab Satellite Communications Organation |
| Art. | Article |
| Arts. | Articles |
| ASEAN | Association of South-East Asian Nations |
| ASIL | American Society of International Law |
| AU | African Union |
| BC | Before Christ |
| Bevans | Bevans, Treaties and Other International Agreements of the United States of America (1776–1949) |
| BFSP | British and Foreign State Papers |
| BIS | Bank of International Settlements |
| BIT | Bilateral Investment Treaty |
| Bull. | Bulletin |
| CAOC | California Asiatic Oil Company |
| CIS | Commonwealth of Independent States |
| CITES | Convention on Trade in Endangered Species |
| COMSAT | Communications Satellite Corporation |
| CPUOS | Committee on the Peaceful Uses of Outer Space |
| Cranch | United States Supreme Court Reports 1801–1815 |
| CRISTAL | Contract Regarding an Interim Supplement to Tanker Liability for Oil Pollution |
| CSCE | Conference on Security and Cooperation in Europe |
| CTS | Consolidated Treaty Series |
| DEA | Drug Enforcement Administration |
| EC | European Community |
| ECHR | European Court of Human Rights |
| ECJ | European Court of Justice |
| ECOSOC | United Nations Economic and Social Council |

| | |
|---|---|
| ECR | European Court Reports |
| ECSC | European Coal and Steel Community |
| EEC | European Economic Community |
| EEZ | Exclusive Economic Zone |
| ELSI | Elettronica Sicula |
| et al. | and others |
| EU | European Union |
| EURATOM | European Atomic Energy Community |
| EUTELSAT | European Telecommunications Satellite Organization |
| F.2d | Federal Reporter, Second Series |
| FAO | Food and Agricultural Organization |
| FRG | Federal Republic of Germany |
| FRY | Federal Republic of Yugoslavia |
| FYROM | Former Yugoslav Republic of Macedonia |
| GA | United Nations General Assembly |
| GATT | General Agreement on Tariffs and Trade |
| GDR | German Democratic Republic |
| IACHR | Inter-American Court of Human Rights |
| IAEA | International Atomic Energy Agency |
| IBRD | International Bank for Reconstruction and Development (World Bank) |
| ICAO | International Civil Aviation Organization |
| ICC | International Chamber of Commerce |
| ICC | International Criminal Court |
| ICCPR | International Covenant on Civil and Political Rights |
| ICESCR | International Covenant on Economic, Social, and Cultural Rights |
| ICJ | International Court of Justice |
| ICJ Rep. | International Court of Justice Reports. |
| ICRC | International Committee of the Red Cross |
| ICSID | International Centre for the Settlement of Investment Disputes |
| ICTR | International Criminal Tribunal for Rwanda |
| ICTY | International Criminal Tribunal for the Former Yugoslavia |
| IFC | International Finance Corporation |
| IFOR | Implementation Force |
| IFRC | International Federation of Red Cross and Red Crescent Societies |
| ILA | International Law Association |
| ILC | International Law Commission |
| ILM | International Legal Materials |
| ILO | International Labour Organisation |
| ILR | International Law Reports |
| IMCO | Intergovernmental Maritime Consultative Organization |
| IMF | International Monetary Fund |
| IMO | International Maritime Organization (formerly IMCO) |
| IMT | International Military Tribunal at Nuremberg |
| INMARSAT | International Maritime Satellite Organization |
| INTELSAT | International Telecommunications Satellite Organization |
| IOC | Inter-Governmental Oceanographic Commission |
| IRO | International Refugee Organization |
| ISA | International Seabed Authority |
| ISAF | International Security Assistance Force |
| ITLOS | International Tribunal for the Law of the Sea |
| ITU | International Telecommunication Union |
| IUCN | International Union for the Conservation of Nature |
| IUSCT | Iran–United States Claims Tribunal |

| | |
|---|---|
| KB | King's Bench Division Law Reports |
| LIAMCO | Libyan American Oil Company |
| LNTS | League of Nations Treaty Series |
| LOS Convention | Convention on the Law of the Sea, 1982 |
| Ltd. | Limited |
| MARPOL | International Convention for the Prevention of Pollution from Ships, 1973 |
| MIGA | Multilateral Investment Guarantee Agency |
| MINURSO | United Nations Mission for the Referendum in Western Sahara |
| MINUSTAH | United Nations Stabilization Mission in Haiti |
| MONUC | United Nations Mission in the Congo |
| NAFO | Northwest Atlantic Fisheries Organization |
| NATO | North Atlantic Treaty Organization |
| NGO | International Non-Governmental Organization |
| NIEO | New International Economic Order |
| OAS | Organization of American States |
| OAU | Organization of African Unity |
| OECD | Organization for Economic Cooperation and Development |
| ONUB | Operation Nations United in Burundi |
| ONUC | United Nations Force in the Congo |
| OPEC | Organization of Petroleum Exporting Countries |
| OPIC | Overseas Private Investment Corporation |
| OSCE | Organization for Security and Cooperation in Europe |
| PCA | Permanent Court of Arbitration |
| PCB | polychlorinated biphenyls |
| PCIJ | Permanent Court of International Justice |
| PLO | Palestine Liberation Organization |
| POLISARIO | Popular Front for the Liberation of Saqia el Hamra and Rio de Oro |
| PREPCOM | Preparatory Commission for the International Seabed Authority and for the International Tribunal for the Law of the Sea |
| PSC | Port State Control |
| QB | Queen's Bench Division Law Reports |
| RIAA | United Nations Reports of International Arbitral Awards |
| RUF | Revolutionary United Front |
| SC | United Nations Security Council |
| SCSL | Special Court for Sierra Leone |
| SFOR | Security Force |
| SFRY | Socialist Federal Republic of Yugoslavia |
| SOLAS | Safety of Life at Sea |
| S.p.A. | società per azioni |
| Stat. | United States Statutes at Large |
| Supp. | Supplement |
| TIAS | Treaties and Other International Acts Series |
| TOPCO | Texas Overseas Petroleum Corporation. |
| TOVAPOL | Tanker Owners' Voluntary Agreement Concerning Liability for Oil Pollution |
| TS | Treaty Series |
| UK | United Kingdom |
| UN | United Nations |
| UNAMIC | United Nations Advance Mission in Cambodia |
| UNAMIR | United Nations Mission in Rwanda |
| UNAMSIL | United Nations Mission in Sierra Leone |
| UNASOG | United Nations Aouzou Strip Observer Group |
| UNAVEM | United Nations Angola Verification Mission |
| UNCITRAL | United Nations Commission on International Trade Law |

| | |
|---|---|
| UNCLOS III | Third United Nations Conference on the Law of the Sea |
| UNCRO | United Nations Confidence Restoration Operation |
| UNCTAD | United Nations Conference on Trade and Development |
| UNDOF | United Nations Disengagement Observer Force |
| UNEF I | United Nations Emergency Force I |
| UNEF II | United Nations Emergency Force II |
| UNEP | United Nations Environment Program |
| UNESCO | United Nations Educational, Scientific, and Cultural Organization |
| UNFICYP | United Nations Force in Cyprus |
| UNGOMAP | United Nations Good Offices Mission in Afghanistan and Pakistan |
| UNHCR | United Nations High Commissioner for Refugees |
| UNIFIL | United Nations Interim Force in Lebanon |
| UNIIMOG | United Nations Iran-Iraq Military Observer Group |
| UNIKOM | United Nations Iraq-Kuwait Observer Mission |
| UNITAF | United Nations Unified Task Force |
| UNMEE | United Nations Mission in Ethiopia and Eritrea |
| UNMIBH | United Nations Mission in Bosnia and Herzegovina |
| UNMIK | United Nations Mission in Kosovo |
| UNMIL | United Nations Mission in Liberia |
| UNMISET | United Nations Mission in Support of East Timor |
| UNMOP | United Nations Mission of Observers in Prevlaka |
| UNMOVIC | United Nations Monitoring, Verification, and Inspection Commission |
| UNOCI | United Nations Operation in Côte d'Ivoire |
| UNOMIG | United Nations Observer Mission in Georgia |
| UNOMIL | United Nations Observer Mission in Liberia |
| UNOMUR | United Nations Observer Mission in Uganda-Rwanda |
| UNOSOM I | United Nations Operation in Somalia I |
| UNOSOM II | United Nations Operation in Somalia II |
| UNPREDEP | United Nations Preventive Deployment Force |
| UNPROFOR | United Nations Protection Force |
| UNRWA | United Nations Relief and Works Agency for Palestinian Refugees in the Near East |
| UNSCOM | United Nations Special Commission |
| UNTAC | United Nations Transitional Authority in Cambodia |
| UNTAET | United Nations Transitional Administration in East Timor |
| UNTS | United Nations Treaty Series |
| UPU | Universal Postal Union |
| US | United States |
| U.S. | United States Supreme Court Reports |
| UST | United States Treaties and Other International Agreements |
| WEU | Western European Union |
| WHO | World Health Organization |
| WIPO | World Intellectual Property Organization |
| WMO | World Meteorological Organization |
| WTO | World Trade Organization |
| YB | Yearbook |

# Glossary

*ad hoc:* For a particular purpose only, as a tribunal established to decide a dispute or a judge appointed by a party to sit on the bench dealing with a case.
*ad initio:* From the beginning.
*ad interim:* In the meantime or temporarily. Used to describe temporary appointments.
*amicus curiae:* Literally: friend of court. A person that can argue before the court, but does not represent the interests of any party to the proceedings.
*animus:* Intention, state of mind.
*aut dedere aut judicare* or *aut dedere aut prosequi:* Either surrender a person suspected of a crime to the state requesting such surrender, or prosecute the suspect. A clause in treaties dealing with terrorist offenses.
*bellum injustum:* Unjust war.
*bellum justum:* Just war.
*bona fide:* In good faith.
*canton:* A constituent territorial unit of Switzerland, corresponding to a "state" in the United States.
*casus foederis:* A situation or event causing an ally to honor the obligations under a treaty of alliance.
*certiorari:* A writ of a higher court to an inferior court calling up the records of a case for review.
*chargé d'affaires ad interim:* A diplomat taking charge of an embassy during a temporary absence of the ambassador.
*collectivité:* A community. Used with respect of some overseas French territories.
*compromis:* An agreement between states to submit a dispute to an international court.
*compromis d'arbitrage:* An agreement between states to submit a dispute to arbitration.
*condominium:* Conjoint sovereignty over a territory.
*culpa:* Negligence or recklessness. A civil-law term used also in international law.
*damnum emergens:* Direct, actual loss.
*de facto:* In fact. Used to distinguish something that actually exists from what may exist only in law.
*de jure:* By virtue of law. Used in contrast to de facto.
*de lege ferenda* (nominative: *lex ferenda*): Relating to the law as it ought to be or is to be adopted.
*de lege lata* (nominative: *lex lata*): According to the law in force.
*debellatio:* Subjugation, conquest, followed by unilateral annexation.
*dictum* (plural: *dicta*). See *obiter dictum.*
*dolus:* Deliberate intention to inflict injury, with guilty knowledge of the consequences of the intended conduct.

*dominium:* A term in civil (Roman) law, meaning "ownership," which, borrowed by the classical writers, acquired the meaning of territorial authority or sovereignty, but is often confused with the term *imperium.*

*droit spontané:* Instant customary law.

*erga omnes:* Valid and opposable against all regardless of others' consent.

*ex aequo et bono:* According to what is equitable, as opposed to what is strictly according to the law in force.

*ex injuria jus non oritur:* The principle that one cannot obtain any legal benefit from an illegal act.

*ex officio:* By virtue of a person's office, in official capacity.

*ex post* or *ex post facto:* After the fact, retroactively.

*exequatur:* Meaning "let him perform," it is a document signed by the head of the host state authorizing a foreign consul-to-be to perform consular functions. It is also sometimes given by means of the word *exequatur* written across the patent or commission issued by the sending state to the appointed consul.

*force majeure:* An unanticipated event or effect beyond human control, including an "act of God" in the form of natural forces. It is one of the circumstances precluding wrongfulness in the law of state responsibility.

*forum:* The place of the court's jurisdiction in a case.

*forum prorogatum:* A doctrine, recognized also by the International Court of Justice, whereby the Court has jurisdiction in a case through an implied consent of the parties given by acts conclusively establishing such consent.

*franchise du quartier:* Historically, a rule whereby the immunity of the residence of the head of a foreign diplomatic mission extended to the whole quarter of the city in which the residence was located. This institution of "exterritoriality" disappeared in the 18th century.

*imperium:* Historically, a rather vague term used in the early doctrine of the law of nations, contrasted to and often confused with *dominium*. Roughly, it corresponded to what is meant by jurisdiction in today's international law, and more generally, the power of state to exercise supreme authority over its citizens as a manifestation of political sovereignty.

*in camera:* In closed session.

*in personam:* Proceedings or a right with reference to or directed against a person, as opposed to *in rem.*

*in rem:* Proceedings or a right with reference to a specific thing, as opposed to *in personam.*

*in statu nascendi:* In the process of being born (nascent) or developing. Sometimes used with respect of an entity that is close to acquiring statehood.

*inter alia:* among other things

*inter se:* Between the parties to an agreement.

*ipso facto:* By the very fact, automatically.

*jure gestionis:* Relating to a state's activities in a non-sovereign capacity, such as commercial activities.

*jure imperii:* Relating to a state's traditional functions in its sovereign capacity, such as administration and defense.

*jus ad bellum:* The right to wage war.

*jus belli* or *jus in bello:* The law of war; international humanitarian law.

*jus civile:* Civil law based on the system of ancient Roman law, as contrasted with the system of common law.

*jus cogens:* Peremptory norms of general international law from which no derogation is permissible and which can be modified only by a subsequent norm. There is no consensus on which norms constitute *jus cogens*, but prohibition of force in international relations and of genocide are universally recognized as such.

*jus dispositivum:* A legal norm that can be derogated from by contrary agreement.

*jus fetiale (feciale*): The ancient Romans' system of religion-based rules, in charge of priests known as "fetiales," on declaring war and making peace.

*jus naturale:* Natural law.

*jus positivum:* Positive law, made by humans, such as customary and treaty law.
*jus sanguinis:* The principle that nationality by birth is acquired by parentage irrespective of the territory where the birth took place.
*jus soli:* The principle that nationality by birth is determined by the territory on which the birth took place.
*Land* (plural: *Länder*): A constituent territorial unit of the Federal Republic of Germany, corresponding to the "state" in the United States.
*legatus a latere:* An ambassador of the Holy See who is a cardinal.
*lettre de créance:* "Letters of Credence" or credentials, that is, the designation of the documents whereby the head of state accredits an ambassador or envoy to a foreign head of state.
*lex fori:* The law of the court's jurisdiction.
*lex posterior derogat priori:* A subsequent rule of law prevails over an earlier one.
*lex posterior generalis non derogat priori speciali:* A subsequent general rule of law yields to an earlier rule of a specific character.
*lex specialis derogat legi generali:* A specific rule of law prevails over a general law.
*locus delicti:* The place or, more generally, the state or jurisdiction within which a wrong was committed.
*locus standi:* The right to apply to a court for a remedy; having sufficient legal interest in the matter at issue.
*lucrum cessans:* Consequential loss.
*mutatis mutandis:* Having made appropriate changes.
*ne bis in idem:* No one should be proceeded against twice over the same offense or, more generally, matter; double jeopardy.
*nemo dat quod non habet:* No one can give what he does not have, no one can transfer a greater interest than that which he has himself.
*nemo judex in causa sua:* No one can be a judge in his own case.
*non liquet:* Invoking by a court of the absence of a clear legal rule as a reason for declining to decide a case. Pronouncing of *non liquet* is, in principle, not permissible in international law.
*nullum crimen sine lege* or *nulla poena sine lege:* No act can be considered to be a crime or no punishment can be imposed unless the act is qualified as a crime punishable under a preexisting law.
*obiter dictum* (plural: *dicta*): An opinion expressed by a tribunal or its individual member on a matter which is not directed to the principal matter at issue.
*opinio juris* or *opinio juris et necessitatis:* The psychological ingredient of customary international law, specifically recognition that a certain practice of states is required by, or consistent with international law.
*ordre public:* Public policy.
*pacta sunt servanda:* The principle that agreements must be observed in good faith.
*pacta tertiis nec nocent nec prosunt:* The principle that agreements (treaties) create neither burdens nor confer benefits upon third parties.
*pactum in favorem tertii:* An agreement (treaty) in favor of a third party.
*par in parem non habet imperium:* Equals have no jurisdiction over each other. This principle illustrates equality of states.
*persona non grata:* Literally "undesired person," this phrase refers to a diplomatic agent who is declared undesirable by the receiving state which has no duty to explain its decision. The sending state must then recall the person concerned or terminate his functions with the diplomatic mission. The corresponding term for a non-diplomatic member of the staff is "not acceptable."
*praetor peregrinus:* In ancient Rome, a judge with jurisdiction over aliens.
*prima facie:* At first sight, presumptively.
*proprio motu:* On one's own initiative.
*quid pro quo:* Something given in return for something else.
*ratione materiae:* With respect of a court's jurisdiction: by reason of the subject matter.
*ratione personae:* With respect of a court's jurisdiction: by reason of the person concerned.

*ratione temporis:* With respect of a court's jurisdiction: by reason of the time reference in the applicable law.

*rebus sic stantibus:* A doctrine recognized in international law in very exceptional situations and under strictly defined conditions whereby a treaty is binding only as long as there is no fundamental change of circumstances which occurred with regard to those that existed at the time of the conclusion of the treaty in question.

*refoulement:* Forced expulsion of a refugee to a state where his life or liberty would be jeopardized.

*res communis:* A thing that belongs to all states and—unlike *res nullius*—cannot be subjected to the sovereignty of any state and whose use is common to all states, such as the high seas and celestial bodies.

*res judicata:* The principle that an issue once definitively adjudicated by a court cannot be reopened.

*res nullius* or *terra nullius:* A thing that belongs to no one or a land territory under no state's sovereignty; it is susceptible to appropriation.

*res transit cum suo onere:* Territory passes to a new sovereign with all burdens connected to it.

*restitutio in integrum:* Specific restitution or restitution in kind, as opposed to pecuniary compensation.

*sensu stricto:* in a narrow or strict sense

*sic utere tuo ut alienum non laedas:* Use your property so as not to cause damage to others. This maxim belongs to general principles of law recognized by civilized nations.

*siège social:* Principal place of business.

*stare decisis:* The principle, which must be followed in common-law countries, that in cases of the same character the courts follow their past decisions and decisions of equal or superior courts. This principle does not apply in international law.

*status quo* or *status quo ante:* The existing state of affairs.

*sui generis:* Unique.

*Thalweg:* The main navigable channel of a river.

*traité contrat:* Contractual treaty, a treaty in its nature analogous to a contract.

*traité loi:* Law-making treaty.

*travaux préparatoires:* Preparatory work relating to the drafting of a treaty, such as drafts and minutes of a conference.

*ultra vires:* Exceeding one's authority.

*uti possidetis* or *uti possidetis juris:* The principle that new states' boundaries should correspond to the administrative boundaries of the predecessor colonial empire or a federal state, as the case may be.

*usus:* General practice.

# Chronology

| | |
|---|---|
| ca. 3100 BC | Treaty between two city states in Mesopotamia |
| 1279 BC | Treaty of Peace and Alliance between Rameses II and Hattusili II of the Hittites |
| 1350 | *Consolato del mare* [Collection of maritime laws] |
| 1492 | Discovery of America |
| 1494 | Treaty of Tordesillas between Portugal and Spain, dividing the newly discovered lands |
| 1513 | Niccolo Machiavelli, *Il principe* [The prince] |
| 1532 | Francisco de Vitoria, *De Indis recenter inventis* [On Indians recently discovered] and *De jure belli Hispanorum in Barbaros* [The law of war of the Spaniards against the Barbarians] |
| 1576 | Jean Bodin, *Six livres de la république* [Six books on the state] |
| 1598 | Alberico Gentili (Gentilis), *De jure belli libri tres* [Three books on the law of war] |
| 1618 | Thirty Years War begins |
| 1625 | Hugo de Groot (Grotius), *De jure belli ac pacis libri tres* [Three books on the law of war and peace] |
| 1648 | Treaties of Westphalia at Münster and Osnabruck ending the Thirty Years War |
| 1650 | Richard Zouche, *Juris et judicii fetialis, sive juris inter gentes et Questionum de eodem explicatio* (Explanation of the law and procedure of the *fetiales,* or the law of nations, and the questions concerning it) |
| 1651 | Thomas Hobbes, *Leviathan* |
| 1672 | Samuel Pufendorf, *De jure naturae et gentium libri octo* [Eight books on the law of nature and nations] |
| 1713 | Abbé de Saint Pierre, *Projet pour rendre la paix perpetuelle en Europe* [Design for perpetual peace in Europe] |
| 1737 | Cornelis van Bynkershoek, *Questionum juris publici libri II* [Two books on questions of public law] |
| 1749 | Christian Wolff, *Jus gentium methodo scientifica pertractatum* [Law of nations treated according to a scientific method] |
| 1758 | Emmerich de Vattel, *Le droit des gens, ou Principes de la loi naturelle appliqués à la conduite et aux affaires des nations et des souverains* [The law of nations, or Principles of natural law applied to the conduct and affairs of nations and sovereigns] |

| | |
|---|---|
| 1776 | United States Declaration of Independence |
| 1787 | United States Constitution adopted |
| 1789 | French Revolution breaks out |
| | *Déclaration des droits de l'homme et du citoyen* [Declaration of the rights of man and citizen] |
| | Jeremy Bentham, *Introduction to the Principles of Morals and Legislation* (first published use of the term "international law") |
| | Georg Friedrich von Martens, *Précis du droit des gens moderne de l'Europe fondé sur les traités et l'usage* [Abstract of the modern law of nations based on treaties and custom] |
| 1791 | Martens' *Recueil des principaux traités* [Collection of principal treaties] begins |
| 1794 | Jay Treaty |
| 1795 | Immanuel Kant, *Zum ewigen Frieden: Ein philosophischer Entwurf* [Toward perpetual peace: A philosophical design] |
| 1815 | Final Act of the Congress of Vienna: Peace Treaty, regulation of diplomatic ranks, condemnation of slavery, recognition of Switzerland's permanent neutrality |
| 1818 | Protocol of Aachen: modification of the rules on diplomatic ranks |
| 1823 | Monroe Doctrine proclaimed |
| 1826 | James Kent, *Commentaries on American Law* |
| 1831 | John Austin's lectures on "The Province of Jurisprudence Determined" |
| 1836 | Henry Wheaton, *Elements of International Law* |
| 1837 | The *Caroline* incident (parameters of self-defense) |
| 1841 | Henry Wheaton, *Histoire des progrès du droit des gens en Europe depuis la paix de Westphalie jusqu'au Congrès de Vienne* [History of the progress of the law of nations in Europe from the Treaty of Westphalia to the Congress of Vienna] (English edition in 1845) |
| 1849 | Treaty of Nanking between Great Britain and China, opening China to the Western system |
| 1851 | François Laurent, *Histoire du droit des gens et des relations internationales* [History of the law of nations and international relations] |
| 1854 | Opening of Japan to the Western system |
| 1854–1861 | Sir Robert Phillimore, *Commentaries on International Law*, 4 volumes |
| 1856 | Treaty of Paris: End of Crimean War, declaration on maritime law, formal acceptance of Turkey into the Western system |
| 1863 | Establishment of the International Committee of the Red Cross by Henry Dunant Francis |
| | Lieber's *Instructions for the Government of Armies of the United States in the Field* in the American Civil War |
| 1864 | Geneva Convention for the Amelioration of the Conditions of the Wounded in Armies in the Field |
| 1865 | Universal Telegraphic Union founded |
| 1868 | US-Mexico Mixed Claims Commission established |
| | Johann Kapar Bluntschli, *Das moderne Völkerrecht als Rechtsbuch dargestellt* [Modern law of nations presented as a code] |
| | Carlos Calvo, *Derecho internacional teórico y práctico de Europa y América* [Theoretical and practical international law of Europe and America] |
| 1869 | Foundation of *Revue de droit international et de législation comparée*, first international law journal |
| 1870–1871 | Franco-Prussian War |
| 1871 | Unification of Germany |
| 1872 | The *Alabama* arbitration (US-Great Britain) |
| 1873 | Foundation of Institut de droit international |
| 1874 | Universal Postal Union |

| | |
|---|---|
| 1884 | Final Act of the Berlin Conference |
| 1887 | Francis Wharton, *Digest of the International Law of the United States,* 3 volumes |
| 1888 | Suez Canal Convention |
| 1890 | Brussels Antislavery Conference |
| 1899 | First Hague Peace Conference |
| | Convention on pacific settlement of international disputes |
| | Permanent Court of Arbitration established |
| | Convention IV with Regulations on laws and customs of war |
| 1905–1906 | F. Lassa Oppenheim, *International Law*, 2 volumes |
| 1906 | J. B. Moore, *Digest of International Law*, 8 volumes |
| | American Society of International Law founded |
| 1907 | Second Hague Peace Conference; adopts 13 conventions on the conduct of war and on neutrality |
| | *American Journal of International Law* begins publication |
| | Central American Court of Justice established (ends in 1917) |
| 1914–1918 | World War I |
| 1917 | United States joins the war |
| | Communist takeover in Russia produces a split in the international system |
| 1919 | Versailles Peace Treaty with Germany; League of Nations and International Labor Organization established |
| | Saint Germain Peace Treaty with Austria |
| 1920 | Trianon Peace Treaty with Hungary |
| 1921 | Permanent Court of International Justice established |
| 1922 | Charles Cheney Hyde, *International law, Chiefly as Interpreted and Applied by the United States* (1st edition) |
| 1923 | Soviet Union established |
| | Academy of International Law at The Hague begins publishing its *Recueil des Cours* [Collection of courses] |
| | Lausanne Peace Treaty with Turkey |
| 1925 | Geneva Protocol on poisonous gases and bacteriological warfare |
| 1926 | Convention on abolition of slavery |
| 1928 | General Treaty on Renunciation of War (Kellogg-Briand Pact or Pact of Paris) |
| | General Act for the Pacific Settlement of International Disputes |
| 1929 | Geneva Convention on prisoners of war |
| | Lateran Treaty (Holy See–Italy) |
| 1930 | Geneva Codification Conference |
| 1933 | Montevideo Convention on the Rights and Duties of States |
| 1936 | Montreux Convention on Turkish Straits |
| | Spanish Civil War begins |
| 1939 | Spanish Civil War ends |
| | World War II begins |
| 1940 | Green Haywood Hackworth, *Digest of International Law*, 8 volumes |
| 1941 | United States enters World War II |
| 1944 | Chicago Convention on International Civil Aviation |
| 1945 | United Nations (UN) established. Resort to force in international relations prohibited |
| | International Court of Justice founded |
| | World War II ends |
| | New Communist states in Eastern Europe become Soviet satellites, division of Germany and Europe |
| | Atomic Age begins |
| | President Truman's Proclamation on continental shelf |
| 1946 | Judgment at Nuremberg |

| | |
|---|---|
| | International Law Commission established |
| 1947 | Peace Treaty with Italy |
| 1948 | Judgment of the Far Eastern (Tokyo) Tribunal |
| | Pact of Bogotá |
| | Charter of OAS |
| | Genocide Convention |
| | Universal Declaration of Human Rights |
| 1949 | Four Geneva Conventions on international humanitarian law |
| | NATO established |
| | Council of Europe established |
| 1950 | European Convention on Human Rights and European Court of Human Rights |
| | Korean War breaks out |
| 1953 | Armistice in Korea |
| 1955 | Austrian State Treaty |
| | Warsaw Pact established |
| 1956 | First UN peacekeeping force, UNEF I, established |
| 1957 | Rome Treaty establishing European Community |
| | Space Age begins |
| 1958 | Four Geneva Conventions on the Law of the Sea |
| 1959 | Antarctic Treaty |
| 1960 | UN GA Declaration on granting independence to colonial peoples |
| | Vienna Convention on Diplomatic Relations |
| 1961 | European Social Charter |
| 1962 | Cuban "Quarantine" |
| 1963 | Partial test ban treaty |
| | Vienna Convention on Consular Relations |
| | Marjorie M. Whiteman, *Digest of International Law*, 15 volumes (1963–1970) |
| 1965 | Convention against racial discrimination |
| | EC Merger Treaty: single Council and single Commission |
| 1966 | International Covenant on Civil and Political Rights |
| | International Covenant on Economic, Social. and Cultural Rights |
| 1967 | Outer Space Treaty |
| 1968 | Convention on non-applicability of statutory limitations to war crimes and crimes against humanity |
| | Nuclear Non-Proliferation Treaty |
| 1969 | J. H. W. Verzijl, *International Law in Historical Perspective*, 12 volumes (1969–1990) |
| | Inter-American Convention on Human Rights |
| | Vienna Convention on the Law of Treaties |
| | Moon landing |
| 1970 | GA Friendly Relations Declaration |
| | GA Seabed and Ocean Floor Declaration |
| 1971 | Convention prohibiting weapons of mass destruction on the seabed |
| 1972 | Bacteriological weapons Convention |
| | Stockholm Declaration on the Human Environment |
| 1973 | Convention against apartheid |
| | MARPOL Convention on preventing pollution by ships |
| 1974 | GA Definition of aggression |
| 1975 | Helsinki Final Act |
| 1977 | Panama Canal Treaties |
| | Protocols I and II to the Geneva Conventions of 1949 on international humanitarian law |
| 1979 | Moon Treaty |

| | |
|---|---|
| | Convention on elimination of discrimination against women |
| | Convention on long-range transboundary air pollution |
| | Peace Treaty between Egypt and Israel |
| 1982 | Convention on the Law of the Sea |
| 1984 | Convention against torture |
| 1985 | Ozone layer Convention |
| 1986 | Single European Act |
| 1988 | Convention for the regulation of Antarctic mineral resources activities |
| 1989 | Convention on the Rights of the Child |
| | Collapse of communism in Eastern Europe |
| 1990 | Charter of Paris for a New Europe |
| | Treaty on the Final Settlement with respect to Germany |
| | Treaty on the establishment of German Unity (Unification Treaty) |
| | Iraq invades and annexes Kuwait |
| 1991 | Dissolution of the Soviet Union, end of Cold War |
| | Yugoslav War erupts |
| | Gulf War, Liberation of Kuwait |
| 1992 | Rio Earth Summit |
| | Biological Diversity Convention |
| | Climate Change Convention |
| | Maastricht Treaty on European Union |
| 1993 | Treaty on the dissolution of Czechoslovakia |
| | Convention on the prohibition of chemical weapons |
| | International Criminal Tribunal for the Former Yugoslavia established |
| 1994 | World Trade Organization established |
| | Treaty of Peace between Israel and Jordan |
| | Implementation Agreement concerning deep seabed |
| | International Criminal Tribunal for Rwanda established |
| 1995 | Dayton-Paris Framework Agreement for Peace in former Yugoslavia |
| 1997 | Treaty of Amsterdam (consolidated EC Treaty ) |
| 1998 | Establishment of the first permanent International Criminal Court |
| 2001 | Terrorist attacks on the United States |
| | UN Security Council recognizes the right of self-defense against terrorists and states sheltering them |
| | United States military action in Afghanistan |
| | Establishment of African Union |
| 2002 | Establishment of the Sierra Leone Special Court to try war criminals |
| | United States proclaims the Preemptive Doctrine of self-defense |
| 2003 | United States invades and occupies Iraq |
| 2004 | Formal termination of US belligerent occupation of Iraq |
| | United Nations publishes the *Report of the High-Level Panel on Threats, Challenges, and Change*, setting out a new vision of collective security for the 21st century |

# Table of Cases

References are to entries.

## PERMANENT COURT OF INTERNATIONAL JUSTICE AND INTERNATIONAL COURT OF JUSTICE

Aegean Sea Continental Shelf, ICJ (Greece v. Turkey) 1978, 205, 302, 309
Aerial Incident, ICJ (US v. Bulgaria) 1955, 294, 323
Ambatielos, ICJ (Greece v. UK) 1952, 74
Anglo-Iranian Oil Co., ICJ (UK v. Iran) 1952, 309, 322
Appeal Related to the Jurisdiction of the ICAO Council, ICJ (India v. Pakistan) 1972, 309
Applicability of Art. VI of the Convention on Privileges and Immunities of the UN, ICJ Adv. Op. 1989, 102
Applicability of the Obligation to Arbitrate, ICJ Adv. Op. 1988, 299
Application for Revision and Interpretation of Judgment in the *Continental Shelf* Case, ICJ (Tunisia/Libya) 1985, 309
Application for Revision of Judgment of 1992, ICJ (El Salvador/Honduras) (judgment) 2003, 309
Application for Revision of Judgment of 1996, ICJ (Bosnia and Herzegovina v. Yugoslavia) 2003, 322
Application of Genocide Convention, ICJ (Bosnia and Herzegovina v. Yugoslavia) 1993 (order), 134
Application of Genocide Convention, ICJ (Croatia v. Yugoslavia) 1999–, 155
Armed Activities, ICJ (Congo v. Uganda) 2000 (Order), 322
Armed Conflict (New application), ICJ (Congo v. Rwanda) 2002–, 322
Arrest Warrant, ICJ (Congo v. Belgium) 2002, 92, 322
Asylum, ICJ (Colombia/Peru) 1950, 39, 64, 309
Avena and Other Mexican Nationals, ICJ (Mexico v. US) 2004, 322
Barcelona Traction (New application), ICJ (Belgium v. Spain) 1970, 22, 95, 155, 159, 174, 180
Certain Expenses of the UN, ICJ Adv. Op. 1962, 84, 334
Certain Norwegian Loans, ICJ (France v. Norway) 1957, 317, 321, 323
Certain Phosphate Lands in Nauru, ICJ (Nauru v. Australia) 1993, 128
Constitution of the Maritime Safety Committee, ICJ Adv. Op. 1960, 241
Continental Shelf, ICJ (Libya/Malta) 1985, 236, 311
Continental Shelf, ICJ (Tunisia/Libya) 1982, 234, 309, 311

Corfu Channel, ICJ (UK v. Albania) 1949, 50, 197, 228, 248, 260, 301, 309
Customs Régime, PCIJ Adv. Op. 1931, 59, 320
Delimitation of the Maritime Boundary in the Gulf of Maine Area, ICJ (Canada/US) 1984, 13, 236, 238, 295
Differences Relating to Immunity of Special Rapporteur, ICJ Adv. Op. 1999, 53, 291
Diversion of Water from the Meuse, PCIJ (Netherlands v. Belgium) 1937, 13
East Timor, ICJ (Portugal v. Australia) 1995, 111, 122, 299
Effects of Awards by UN Administrative Tribunal, ICJ Adv. Op. 1954, 84
Electricity Company of Sofia, PCIJ (Belgium v. Bulgaria) 1939, 299
Elettronica Sicula (ELSI), ICJ (US v. Italy) 1989, 28, 74, 95, 145
Factory at Chorzów, PCIJ (Germany v. Poland) 1927, 118
Factory at Chorzów, PCIJ (Germany v. Poland) 1928, 38, 118
Fisheries, ICJ (UK v. Norway) 1950, 39, 233
Fisheries Jurisdiction cases, ICJ (UK v. Iceland; Fed. Rep. of Germany v. Iceland) 1974, 238, 239
Free Zones, PCIJ (France/Switzerland) 1932, 225, 278
Frontier Dispute, ICJ (Burkina Faso/Mali) 1986, 137, 230, 322
Gabčíkovo-Nagymaros, ICJ (Hungary/Slovakia) 1998, 96, 197, 204, 212, 273, 276, 309
Haya de la Torre, ICJ (Colombia v. Peru) 1951, 64
Interhandel, ICJ (Switzerland v. US) 1959, 321, 347
International Status of South-West Africa, ICJ Adv. Op. 1950, 84
Interpretation of the Agreement between WHO and Egypt, ICJ Adv. Op. 1980, 84
Interpretation of the Treaty of Lausanne, PCIJ Adv. Op. 1925, 38
Jurisdiction of the Courts of Danzig, PCIJ Adv. Op. 1928, 81
Jurisdiction of the European Commission of the Danube, PCIJ Adv. Op. 1927, 204
Kasikili Sedudu Island, ICJ (Botswana/Namibia) 1999, 189
LaGrand, ICJ (Germany v. US) 2001, 55, 322
Land and Maritime Boundary, ICJ (Cameroon v. Nigeria) 1998, 275, 309, 311
Land, Island, and Maritime Frontier Dispute, ICJ (El Salvador/Honduras, with Nicaragua intervening) 1992, 227, 230, 234, 311
Land, Island, and Maritime Frontier Dispute (Request for revision) ICJ (El Salvador/Honduras) 2002, 309
Legal Consequences of Continued Presence of South Africa in Namibia, ICJ Adv. Op. 1971, 98, 122, 227, 289
Legal Consequences of the Construction of a Wall in the Occupied Palestinian Territories, ICJ Adv. Op. 2004, 291, 309, 363
Legal Status of Eastern Greenland, PCIJ (Denmark v. Norway) 1933, 214, 219, 275, 288
Legality of Threat or Use of Nuclear Weapons, ICJ Adv. Op. 1996, 197, 329, 332, 335, 336, 359, 367
Legality of Use of Force, ICJ (Serbia and Montenegro v. Belgium, Canada, France, Germany, Italy, Netherlands, Portugal, and UK) 1999, 134, 322
Legality of Use of Nuclear Weapons in Armed Conflict, ICJ Adv. Op. (denied) 1996, 90, 197, 227, 291, 316, 367
*The Lotus,* PCIJ (France v. Turkey) 1927, 6, 22, 39, 89, 91, 92, 228, 240
Maritime Delimitation and Territorial Questions, ICJ (Qatar v. Bahrain) 2001, 238, 301
Maritime Delimitation in the Area between Greenland and Jan Mayen, ICJ (Denmark v. Norway) 1993, 236, 238
Mavrommatis Jerusalem Concessions, PCIJ (Greece v. UK) 1925, 301
Mavrommatis Palestine Concessions, PCIJ (Greece v. UK) 1924, 95, 299, 316
Military and Paramilitary Activities, ICJ (Nicaragua v. US) 1986, 22, 24, 36, 39, 40, 294, 300, 309, 311, 317, 322, 323, 329, 331, 332, 335, 336
Minquiers and Ecrehos, ICJ (France/UK) 1953, 214, 304
Monetary Gold Removed from Rome in 1943, ICJ (Italy v. France) 1954, 321
Nationality Decrees, PCIJ Adv. Op. 1923, 8, 299

North Sea Continental Shelf, ICJ (Federal Republic of Germany/Denmark; Federal Republic of Germany/Netherlands) 1969, 22, 39, 40, 236, 316
Northern Cameroons, ICJ (Cameroon v. UK) 1963, 321
Nottebohm, ICJ (Liechtenstein v. Guatemala) 1955, 22, 95, 176, 257, 321
Nuclear Tests, ICJ (Australia v. France; New Zealand v. France) 1974, 37, 242, 302, 311
Nuclear Tests (Australia v. France; New Zealand v. France) (Application to intervene) 1996, 311
Oil Platforms, ICJ (Iran v. US) 1996, 321
Oil Platforms, ICJ (Iran v. US) 2003, 321
Passage through the Great Belt, ICJ (Finland v. Denmark) 1992 (removed from the List), 260
Questions of Interpretation and Application of the Montreal Convention (Lockerbie Cases), ICJ (Libya v. UK; Libya v. US) (discontinued in 2003), 322, 327
Readaptation of the Mavrommatis Jerusalem Concessions, PCIJ (Greece v. UK) 1927, 321
Reparation for Injury, ICJ Adv. Op.1949, 22, 37, 84, 85, 274, 291
Request for Interpretation of the Asylum Judgment of 1950, ICJ (Columbia v. Peru) 1950, 64
Reservations to Genocide Convention, ICJ Adv. Op. 1951, 22, 155, 282, 291
Right of Passage, ICJ (Portugal v. India) 1960, 219, 225
Serbian Loans, PCIJ (France/Yugoslavia) 1929, 78
South-West Africa, ICJ (Ethiopia v. South Africa; Liberia v. South Africa) (Second Phase) 1966, 12
Sovereignty over Certain Frontier Land, ICJ (Belgium/Netherlands) 1959, 219
Sovereignty over Pulau Litigan and Pulau Sipadan, ICJ (Indonesia/Malaysia) 2002, 311
Status of Eastern Carelia, PCIJ Adv. Op. 123, 320
Temple of Preah Vihear, ICJ (Cambodia v. Thailand) 1962, 227, 230, 275, 321
Territorial Dispute, (Libya/Chad) 1994, 114, 137, 230
Territorial Jurisdiction of the International Commission of the River Oder, PCIJ (Czechoslovakia, Denmark, France, Germany, Sweden, UK/Poland) 1929, 204
Treaty of Neuilly, PCIJ (Bulgaria v. Greece) 1925, 295
US Diplomatic and Consular Staff in Tehran (US v. Iran) 1980, 53, 58, 67, 300, 309
Western Sahara, ICJ Adv. Op. 1975, 122, 214, 289, 291
The Wimbledon, PCIJ (France, Italy, Japan, UK v. Germany, with Poland intervening) 1923, 125, 252, 311, 320

## OTHER INTERNATIONAL COURTS AND QUASI-JUDICIAL BODIES

Barrios Altos, IACHR (Chumbipuma Aguirre et al. v. Peru) 2001,165
Gallardo et al., IACHR (involving Costa Rica) 1981, 165
Kreil v. Bundesrepublik Deutschland, ECJ 2000, 298
Mox Plant, ITLOS (Ireland v. UK) 2002, 310, 319
The *Saiga*, ITLOS (St. Vincent and the Grenadines v. Guinea) 1997, 246, 257, 309
Simmenthal v. Amministrazione delle Finanze, ECJ 1978, 298
Southern Blue Tuna (Cases 3 and 4), ITLOS (orders) (New Zealand v. Japan) 1999, 310
Van Gend en Loos v. Netherlandse Administratie der Belastingen, ECJ, 298
Velázquez Rodríguez, IACHR (Velázquez Rodríguez v. Honduras) 1988, 165
Yilmaz-Dogan, Human Rights Committee on Racial Discrimination (Yilmaz-Dogan v. Netherlands) 1988, 17

## INTERNATIONAL CRIMINAL COURTS

Akayesu, ICTR 1998, 155, 182, 351
Far East (Tokyo) IMT, major Japanese war criminals judgment, 1948, 151, 335
Furundzija, ICTY (Appeal Chamber) 1998, 182

Kambanda, ICTR 1998, 351
Krstić, ICTY 2001, 352 (in appeal stage in March 2004)
Nuremberg IMT, major Nazi Germany war criminals judgment, 1946, 151, 354
Tadić, ICTY 1995 (Appeal Chamber) 1995, 22, 339

## ARBITRATION TRIBUNALS

Abu Dhabi, (Petroleum Development Ltd.-Sheikh of Abu Dhabi) 1951, 293
Access to Information, (Ireland-UK) 2003, 319
Air Services Agreement, (France-US) 1978, 28, 257, 293
The *Alabama*, (UK-US) 1872, 22, 40, 293
Alaska Boundary, (US-Great Britain) 1903, 189
Ambatielos, (Greece-UK) 1956, 74
Amoco International Finance Corporation, (US-Iran) 1988, 145
Anglo-French Continental Shelf, (UK-France) 1977, 236, 282, 293
Beagle Channel, (Argentina-Chile) 1977, 293
Brćko, (Bosnia and Herzegovina, Croatia-Yugoslavia) 1996, 13, 293
British Petroleum-Libya, 1973, 293
Brown, Robert E. Claim (US v. UK) 1923, 136.
Chamizal (Mexico-US) 1911, 184, 189, 219
Clipperton Island (France-Mexico) 1931, 214
Dispute Concerning Access to Information under Article 9 of the OSPAR Convention (Ireland v. UK), PCA 2003, 319
Dubai-Sharjah Boundary, 1981, 236
EC Arbitration Commission on Yugoslavia, Opinion No. 1, 1991, 134; Opinion No. 2, 1991, 122, 137; Opinion No. 8, 1992, 134; Opinion No. 14, 1993, 136
Home Frontier and Missionary Society (US-UK) 1920, 53
The *I'm Alone*, (UK-US) 1935, 118, 246
Iron Rhine Railway Line, (Belgium-Netherlands) 2004, 145
Lake Lanoux, (France-Spain) 1957, 204
Larsen-Hawaiian Kingdom, 2001, 319
Letelier and Moffit, (US-Chile) 1992, 293
LIAMCO- Libya, 1977, 145, 293
Lighthouses, (France-Greece) 1956, 136
Maritime Border, (Guinea-Guinea Bissau), 1985, 236
Naulilaa, (Portugal-Germany) 1928, 22, 119, 293
Neer Claim, (US-Mexico) 1926, 171
North American Dredging Co., (US-Mexico) 1926, 149
North American Dreyfuss Co., (US-Mexico) 1926, 149
North Atlantic Coast Fisheries, (Great Britain-US) 1910, 225, 319
Palmas Island, (US-Netherlands) 1928, 22, 125, 190, 205, 214, 219, 227, 228
Prisoners of War, (Eritrea-Ethiopia) 2003, 319, 364
The *Rainbow Warrior*, (New Zealand-France) 1990, 78, 87, 104, 118, 128, 293
Rann of Kutch, (India-Pakistan) 1968, 189, 230, 293
The *Red Crusader* (Commission of Inquiry), (UK-Denmark) 1962, 305
Rhine Pollution Convention, (Netherlands-France) 2004, 319
Saint Pierre and Miquelon Delimitation, (Canada-France) 1992, 236, 293
Saluka-Czechoslovakia, 1994, 319
Starret Housing Corporation, (US-Iran) 1984, 145
Taba Area Border, (Egypt-Israel) 1988, 293
Territorial Sovereignty, (Eritrea-Yemen) 2001, 319

Tinoco, (Costa Rica-Great Britain) 1923, 293
TOPCO and CAOC-Libya, 1977, 145, 293
Trail Smelter, (US-Canada) 1941, 50, 197
Youmans Claim, (US-Mexico) 1926, 53

## MUNICIPAL COURTS

Adams v. Adams, 3 All ER 572, 1970
Al Megrahi: Her Majesty's Advocate v. Al Megrahi, Scottish High Court of Judiciary in The Netherlands, 2001, 210
The *Arantzazu Mendi*, AC 256, 1939, 98
Argentine Republic v. Amerada Hess, 488 U.S. 428, 1989, 131
Banco Nacional de Cuba v. Sabbatini, US Sup. Court, 1964, 51
Berizzi Brothers Co v. SS *Pesaro*, 271 U.S. 562, 1926, 131
Blackmer v. US, 284 U.S. 421, 1932, 88
Castioni, Ex parte, 1 QB 149, 1891, 76
Filártiga v. Peña-Irala, 630 F. 2d 876 (2d Circuit) 1980, 92, 159
Foster and Elam v. Neilson, 27 U.S. 253, 1829, 19, 253
Gur Corporation v. Trust Bank of Africa, QB 599, 1987, 98
Joyce v. Director of Public Prosecutions, AC 347, 1946, 90
Meunier, Re, 2 QB 415, 1894, 76
Missouri v. Holland, 252 U.S. 416, 1920, 19
Nulyarimma v. Thompson, 165 ALR 621, 1999, 163
The *Paquete Habana*; The *Lola*, 175 U.S. 677, 1900, 18, 39, 42, 365
Pinochet Ugarte, Ex parte (No. 3), R v. Bow Street Metropolitan Magistrate, 2 All ER 97,160, 160, 182
The *Schooner Exchange* v. MacFaddon, 11 US (7 Cranch) 1812, 116, 1812, 91, 131, 138
Schwarzkopf, US ex rel. v. Uhl, 137 F. 2d, 1943, 136
Sei Fuji v. State of California, 38 Cal. 2d 718, 1952, 19, 156
Underhill v. Hernández, 168 U.S. 250, 1897, 51
US v. Alvarez Machain, 504 U.S. 656, 1992, 25
US v. Aluminum Co. of America, 148 F.2d 416 (2d Circuit), 1945, 91
Victory Transport v. Comisaría General, 336 F 2d 354 (2d Circuit), 1964, 131
West Rand Gold Mining Co. Ltd v. R, 2 KB 391, 1905, 136
Zeiss, Carl, Stiftung v. Rainer and Keeler Ltd, I AC 853, 1967, 98

# List of Entries

## CHAPTER I: ENTRIES 1–49

### General Problems: Nature and Enforcement of International Law, Sources, Relationship between International and National Law

1. Austin, John (1790–1859)
2. Autolimitation Doctrine
3. Bentham, Jeremy (1748–1832)
4. Bynkershoek, Cornelius van (1673–1743)
5. Codification and Progressive Development of International Law
6. Comity
7. Consensual Theory of International Law
8. Critical Legal Studies
9. Domestic Jurisdiction
10. Dualism–Monism
11. Eclectics
12. *Erga Omnes* Obligations
13. *Ex Aequo et Bono* and Equity
14. Friendly Relations GA Declaration, 1970
15. Gentilis (Gentili), Albericus (1552–1608)
16. Grotius (De Groot), Hugo (1583–1645)
17. International Law: Compliance and Enforcement
18. International Law in National (Municipal) Law: Custom
19. International Law in National (Municipal) Law: Treaties
20. International Law: Nature and Characteristics
21. International Law: Theories about
22. Judicial Decisions as Subsidiary Means for the Determination of Rules of Law
23. *Jus Civile*
24. *Jus Cogens*
25. *Jus Gentium*
26. Moser, Johann Jakob (1701–1785)
27. Municipal Law
28. Municipal Law in International Law

29. Natural Law School
30. Policy-Oriented Approach to International Law
31. Positivism
32. Private International Law (Conflict of Laws)
33. Pufendorf, Samuel (1632–1694)
34. Pure Theory of Law
35. Soft Law
36. Sources of International Law
37. Sources of International Law: Binding Acts of International Organizations
38. Sources of International Law: General Principles of Law
39. Sources of International Law: International Custom
40. Sources of International Law: Treaties
41. Suárez, Francisco (1548–1617)
42. Teachings of Publicists as Subsidiary Means for the Determination of Rules of Law
43. Transnational Law
44. Unilateral Acts
45. Vattel, Emmerich de (1714–1767)
46. Vitoria, Francisco (1480–1546)
47. Westphalia, Peace Treaties of, 1648
48. Wolff, Christian (1679–1754)
49. Zouche, Richard (1590–1660)

## CHAPTER II: ENTRIES 50–142

### International Legal Personality, States: Recognition, Jurisdiction, Responsibility, Succession

50. Abuse of Rights
51. Act of State Doctrine
52. Associated State
53. Attribution
54. Confederation
55. Consular Privileges and Immunities
56. Consular Relations, Vienna Convention on, 1963
57. Consuls
58. Countermeasures
59. Customs Union
60. Danzig, The Free City of
61. Diplomat in Transit
62. Diplomatic Agents: Heads of Permanent Missions
63. Diplomatic Agents: Privileges and Immunities
64. Diplomatic Asylum
65. Diplomatic Bag
66. Diplomatic Courier
67. Diplomatic Inviolability
68. Diplomatic Mission
69. Diplomatic Mission: Administrative and Technical Staff
70. Diplomatic Mission: Service Staff
71. Diplomatic Relations, Vienna Convention on, 1961
72. Distress
73. Equality of States
74. Exhaustion of Local Remedies

75. Extradition
76. Extradition and Political Offense
77. Federation
78. *Force Majeure*
79. Government in Exile
80. Holy See—Vatican City
81. Individuals as Subjects of International Law
82. Injured State
83. Intergovernmental Corporation of Private Law
84. Intergovernmental Organizations (Public International Organizations)
85. International Legal Personality
86. International Non-Governmental Organizations
87. Jurisdiction
88. Jurisdiction: Nationality Principle
89. Jurisdiction: Passive Personality Principle
90. Jurisdiction: Protective (Security) Principle
91. Jurisdiction: Territorial Principle
92. Jurisdiction: Universality Principle
93. Mandate System
94. National Liberation Movement
95. Nationality of Claims
96. Necessity, State of
97. Neutralized State
98. Nonrecognition, Legal Effects of
99. Nonrecognition, Obligation of
100. Non-Self-Governing Territory
101. Personal Union
102. Privileges and Immunities of International (Intergovernmental) Organizations
103. Privileges and Immunities of State Representatives to International (Intergovernmental) Organizations
104. The *Rainbow Warrior* Incident and Arbitrations, 1986, 1990
105. Real Union
106. Recognition
107. Recognition, Additional Criteria of
108. Recognition, Collective
109. Recognition, Constitutive and Declaratory Theories of
110. Recognition, *De Facto* and *De Jure*
111. Recognition, Express (Explicit) and Implied (Tacit)
112. Recognition, Legal Effects in Municipal Law
113. Recognition of Belligerency
114. Recognition of Government
115. Recognition of Insurgency
116. Recognition of State
117. Recognition, Withdrawal of
118. Reparation
119. Reprisals
120. Responsibility and Liability
121. Retortion
122. Self-Determination of Peoples, Right of
123. Self-Preservation Doctrine
124. Sovereign Order of Malta
125. Sovereignty
126. Special Missions

127. State
128. State Responsibility
129. State Responsibility, The ILC Draft on, 2001
130. State Responsibility: Objective and Subjective Doctrines
131. State (Sovereign) Immunity
132. State Succession
133. State Succession and the Breakup of the Soviet Union
134. State Succession and the Breakup of Yugoslavia
135. State Succession and the Unification of Germany
136. State Succession in Respect of Matters Other Than Treaties
137. State Succession in Respect of Treaties
138. Status-of-Forces Agreement
139. Taiwan, Legal Status of
140. Transnational Corporation
141. Trieste, The Free Territory of
142. Trusteeship System

## CHAPTER III: ENTRIES 143–183

### Individuals, Human Rights

143. African Charter of Human and Peoples' Rights (Banjul Charter)
144. Aliens
145. Aliens, Expropriation of Property of
146. Aliens, Expulsion of
147. American Convention on Human Rights, 1969
148. Asylum, Territorial
149. Calvo Clause
150. Convention on the Rights of the Child, 1989, with the Protocols
151. Crimes against Humanity
152. Denial of Justice
153. European Convention for the Protection of Human Rights and Fundamental Freedoms, 1950
154. European Court of Human Rights
155. Genocide Convention, 1948
156. Human Rights and the United Nations Charter
157. Human Rights, Concept of
158. Human Rights, High Commissioner for
159. Human Rights, International Customary Law of
160. Human Rights, International Law of
161. Human Rights, United Nations Commission on
162. Human Rights, Universal Declaration of, 1948
163. Indigenous Peoples
164. Individuals in International Law
165. Inter-American Court of Human Rights
166. International Covenant on Civil and Political Rights, 1966
167. International Covenant on Civil and Political Rights, Optional Protocol, 1966
168. International Covenant on Civil and Political Rights, Second Optional Protocol, 1989
169. International Covenant on Economic, Social, and Cultural Rights, 1966
170. International Criminal Court
171. Minimum International Standard of Justice v. National Treatment
172. Minorities
173. Nationality, Dual (Multiple)

174. Nationality of Corporations
175. Nationality of Individuals
176. Naturalization
177. Racial Discrimination, International Convention on the Elimination of All Forms of, 1966
178. Refugees
179. Repudiation and Breach of State Contracts with Aliens
180. Slavery and Slave-like Practices
181. Statelessness
182. Torture: Convention against Torture and Other Cruel and Inhuman or Degrading Treatment or Punishment, 1984
183. Women: Convention on the Elimination of All Forms of Discrimination against Women, 1979

## CHAPTER IV: ENTRIES 184–230

### The Geophysical Context I: Land, Air, Outer Space, International Environmental Law

184. Accretion
185. Air Hijacking
186. Airspace
187. Antarctic Treaty System
188. Biodiversity Convention, 1992, and Cartagena Protocol, 2000
189. Boundary
190. Cession
191. Chicago Convention on International Civil Aviation, 1944
192. Climate Change Framework Convention, 1992
193. Condominium
194. Conquest and Subjugation
195. Desertification Convention, 1994
196. Direct Television Broadcasting
197. Environmental Law
198. Geostationary (Synchronous) Orbit
199. Hague Air Hijacking Convention, 1970
200. Hazardous Waste Transboundary Movement Basel Convention, 1989
201. INTELSAT
202. International Air Services Transit Agreement, 1944
203. International Air Transport Agreement, 1944
204. International River (Fluvial) Law
205. Intertemporal Law
206. Kyoto Protocol, 1997
207. Lease, International
208. Liability for Damage Caused by Space Objects Convention, 1971
209. Long-Range Transboundary Air Pollution Convention, 1979
210. Montreal Sabotage Convention, 1971
211. Moon Treaty, 1979
212. Non-Navigational Uses of International Watercourses Convention, 1997
213. Nuclear Safety IAEA Convention, 1994
214. Occupation
215. Outer Space, International Law of
216. Outer Space Treaty, 1967
217. Ozone Layer Vienna Protection Convention, 1985 and the Montreal Protocol, 1987

218. Persistent Organic Pollutants Convention, 2001
219. Prescription
220. Registration of Objects Launched Out into Space Convention, 1974
221. Remote Sensing
222. Rescue of Astronauts Agreement, 1968
223. Rio Earth Summit, 1992
224. Sector Claims
225. Servitude
226. Stockholm Conference on the Human Environment, 1972
227. Territory, Acquisition of
228. Territory, State
229. Tokyo Convention on Offenses and Certain Other Acts Committed on Board Aircraft, 1963
230. *Uti Possidetis* Doctrine

## CHAPTER V: ENTRIES 231–265

### The Geophysical Context II: The Law of the Sea

231. Archipelagic States
232. Area, The
233. Baselines
234. Bays
235. Contiguous Zone
236. Continental Shelf
237. Enclosed or Semi-Enclosed Seas
238. Exclusive Economic Zone (EEZ)
239. Fisheries, International Law of
240. Flag-State Jurisdiction
241. Flags of Convenience
242. Freedom of the High Seas
243. Geneva Conference on the Law of the Sea, 1958
244. Geneva Conference on the Law of the Sea, 1960
245. High Seas
246. Hot Pursuit
247. Implementation Agreement, 1994
248. Innocent Passage
249. Internal Waters
250. International Seabed Authority
251. Islands
252. Kiel Canal
253. Landlocked and Geographically Disadvantaged States
254. Law of the Sea
255. Marine Pollution
256. Montreux Convention, 1936
257. Nationality of Ships
258. Panama Canal
259. Piracy
260. Straits
261. Suez Canal
262. Territorial Sea
263. Third United Nations Conference on the Law of the Sea, 1973–1982 (UNCLOS III)
264. United Nations Convention on the Law of the Sea, 1982

265. Warships and Other Government-Operated Ships

## CHAPTER VI: ENTRIES 266–288

### The Law of Treaties

266. Acceptance and Approval
267. Accession
268. Adoption of the Text
269. Amendment and Modification
270. Authentication
271. Entry into Force
272. Full Powers
273. Fundamental Change of Circumstances
274. Interpretation
275. Invalidity
276. Material Breach
277. *Pacta Sunt Servanda*
278. *Pacta Tertiis Nec Nocent Nec Prosunt*
279. Peaceful Change
280. Ratification
281. Registration
282. Reservation
283. Signature
284. Successive (Inconsistent) Treaties
285. Supervening Impossibility of Performance
286. Suspension of Operation
287. Termination
288. Treaty

## CHAPTER VII: ENTRIES 289–324

### Peaceful Settlement of Disputes

289. *Ad Hoc* Judge
290. Administrative Tribunals of International Organizations
291. Advisory Jurisdiction
292. Arbitral Tribunals under Annex VII of the Law of the Sea Convention of 1982
293. Arbitration
294. Automatic (Self-Judging) Reservation
295. Chambers
296. Conciliation
297. Contentious Jurisdiction of the International Court of Justice
298. Court of Justice of the European Communities (European Court of Justice)
299. Disputes, International
300. Disputes, International: Justiciability
301. *Forum Prorogatum*
302. General Act for the Pacific Settlement of International Disputes, 1928 (revised in 1949)
303. Good Offices
304. Individual Opinion
305. Inquiry

306. International Adjudication
307. International Centre for the Settlement of Investment Disputes
308. International Commercial Arbitration
309. International Court of Justice
310. International Tribunal for the Law of the Sea
311. Intervention in the Proceedings
312. Iran–United States Claims Tribunal
313. Mediation
314. Mixed Arbitral Commissions and Tribunals
315. Mixed Claims Commissions
316. Negotiation
317. Optional Clause
318. Peaceful (Pacific) Settlement of International Disputes
319. Permanent Court of Arbitration
320. Permanent Court of International Justice
321. Preliminary Objection
322. Provisional Measures
323. Reservation to Acceptance of Compulsory Jurisdiction of the International Court of Justice
324. Special Arbitral Tribunals under Annex VIII of the Convention on the Law of the Sea of 1982

## CHAPTER VIII: ENTRIES 325–338

### The Use of Force

325. Aggression
326. Blockade, Pacific
327. Collective Security System
328. Cuban Quarantine
329. Force, Illegal Threat or Use
330. General Treaty for the Renunciation of War, 1928
331. Intervention
332. Intervention, Humanitarian
333. Just War Doctrine
334. Peacekeeping
335. Self-Defense
336. Self-Defense, Collective
337. Terrorism
338. War

## CHAPTER IX: ENTRIES 339–373

### International Humanitarian Law

339. Armed Conflict, International
340. Armed Conflict, Non-International
341. Blockade, Belligerent
342. Combatants and Non-Combatants
343. Contraband
344. Declaration of Paris, 1856
345. Enemy Alien
346. Enemy Character

347. Enemy Property
348. General Participation Clause
349. Geneva Conventions, 1949
350. Hague Conventions, 1907
351. International Criminal Tribunal for Rwanda
352. International Criminal Tribunal for the Former Yugoslavia
353. International Humanitarian Law
354. International Military Tribunal at Nuremberg
355. International Military Tribunal for the Far East
356. Irregular Forces
357. *Levée en masse*
358. Maritime War Zones
359. Martens Clause
360. Mercenaries
361. Naval Warfare
362. Neutrality
363. Occupation, Belligerent
364. Prisoners of War
365. Prize Courts
366. Prohibited Methods of Warfare
367. Prohibited Weapons
368. Protecting Power
369. Protocols I and II, 1977
370. Reprisals, Belligerent
371. Special Court for Sierra Leone
372. Spy in Wartime
373. War Crimes

# Chapter I
# General Problems: Nature and Enforcement of International Law, Sources, Relationship between International and National Law

**1. Austin, John (1790–1859).** English legal theorist and professor of jurisprudence in the University of London, and the founder of the English "analytical" school of jurisprudence, associated with the doctrine denying the legal nature of international law. In his lectures on *The Province of Jurisprudence Determined*, published in 1831 and 1832 and posthumously edited as *Lectures on Jurisprudence* in 1861, John Austin, following Thomas Hobbes and Jeremy Bentham **(3)**, defined law properly so called as a command of a sovereign **(125)** to his subjects, backed up by threat and ability to enforce obedience. Hence, in Austin's view, international law does not have the quality of true law because states have no superior authority above them to enforce its norms. In Austin's conception, international law, whose value and usefulness he did not otherwise deny, is at best "positive morality" generated by the opinion of the society of nations. Only those rules of international law which have been adopted as part of a country's internal that is, national or—in the international law vocabulary—"municipal" law **(27)**, become law properly so called.

Despite the fact that, contrary to Austin's view, international state practice universally recognizes the legal nature of international law, the unfortunately formulated tenets of the Austinian doctrine have to this day damaged the reputation of international law as a true legal system governing the relations of states. Yet, as cogently argued by a renowned legal theorist, H. L. A. Hart in his *Concept of Law* (1961), the concept of law need not necessarily entail organized sanctions. Furthermore, the perceived system of sovereign **(125)** states **(127)** with no superior above them does not always reflect the reality of the situation. Apart from the vague notion of "morality," one could also argue that claims based on international law are in most cases morally indifferent. More than any other system of social rules, they display analogies to municipal law rather than morality. In fact, the rules of international law are binding because they are accepted and function as law in international society.

**2. Autolimitation Doctrine.** A doctrine on the binding nature of international law **(20)**, advanced by some positivist **(31)** writers toward the end of the 19th century and early 20th century, to the effect that international law is binding because sovereign **(125)** states **(127)** agree to act in the future only in accordance with the rules consented to. Georg Jellinek, the author of *Die rechtliche Natur der Staatenverträge* (The Legal Nature of Treaties), was the major exponent of the autolimitation doctrine asserting, among other propositions, that since international law rules are voluntary creations of the state, the latter may also unilaterally terminate its compliance. Thus international law becomes merely "external public law" (*äusseres Staatsrecht*) binding only as long as the state maintains its consent.

The autolimitation doctrine, whose origins can be traced back to Georg Wilhelm Friedrich Hegel's concept of the autolimitation of sovereignty, has been criticized as basically denying the binding force of international law by asserting the supremacy of municipal law **(27)**. Furthermore, one can argue that on logical grounds a self-imposed limitation cannot be regarded as any limitation at all.

**3. Bentham, Jeremy (1748–1832).** English philosopher, famous for his utilitarian approach to legislation but of interest to historians of international law **(20)** in that he also wrote on this law and in this context is credited, among other linguistic innovations, with inventing the term "international" used in his *Introduction to the Principles of Morals and Legislation* (1789). This felicitous neologism was eventually adopted in other languages, replacing the terms "law of nations" (*jus gentium*) **(25)** and "European public law" (*droit public d'Europe*).

As far as the theory of international law is concerned, Bentham applies his general principle of utility to the conduct of nations which, in his view, should lead to the greatest possible welfare of all of them. According to Bentham, this principle should be observed even in time of war **(338)** when the force inflicted upon the enemy should not exceed that needed to achieve a military objective.

**4. Bynkershoek, Cornelius van (1673–1743).** Dutch jurist and judge, experienced in questions of international commercial and maritime law and practice, Cornelius van Bynkershoek occupies an important place in the history of the doctrine of the law of nations, as a leading representative of the school of legal positivism **(31)**. He became famous through the publication of three works dealing with various aspects of the law of nations and especially the law of the sea **(254)**. In *De dominio maris* (Sovereignty over the Sea) (1702) Bynkershoek upholds the freedom of the high seas **(242)** and expounds his ideas concerning the width of the territorial sea **(262)** based on the so-called cannon-shot rule of three nautical miles (one nautical miles equals 6,080.20 feet, that is 1,853.25 meters). In *De foro legatorum* (Jurisdiction over Ambassadors), 1721, he deals with diplomatic immunity **(63)**. His principal work *Questionum juris publici libri II* (Two Books on Questions of Public Law), 1737, examines the law of war (today known mostly as international humanitarian law) **(353)** in the first book and selected problems of the law of peace and neutrality **(362)** in the second.

Bynkershoek's writings are entirely secularized and based on recent, especially Dutch, state practice which he considered to be more valuable evidence of custom **(39)** than examples borrowed from ancient history so abundantly relied upon by earlier writers, including Hugo Grotius **(16)**. While stressing the role of reason as the ultimate source of the law of nations, Bynkershoek ignored natural law **(29)** and based the law of nations on the common consent of states through treaties **(40)** and international custom **(39)**.

**5. Codification and Progressive Development of International Law.** While both United Nations (UN) Charter and the International Law Commission (ILC) make a distinction between codification and progressive development of international law, the two concepts are overlapping and closely interrelated. Under Art. 15 of the ILC Statute, codification means "the more precise formulation and systematization of rules of international law in fields where there already has been extensive State practice, precedent and doctrine" whereas progressive development is defined as "the preparation of draft conventions on subjects which have not yet been regulated by international law or in regard to which the law has not yet been sufficiently developed in the practice of States." Generally speaking, treaties codifying international law may either restate an already binding rule of customary international law **(39)** or have the effect of crystallizing an emerging rule, or even constitute an element contributing to the formation of customary international law itself.

Ideas of clarifying and systematizing rules of law in an organized way date back to Jeremy Bentham **(3)** in the 18th century and various private codifications in the 19th century, such as those authored by Johann Caspar Bluntschli and Pasquale Fiore, among others. A code of the law of war (international humanitarian law) **(353)** was prepared by Francis Lieber for use by the Union army in the American Civil War. Official codifications started at the two Hague Peace Conferences, 1899 and 1907 **(350)**, when a number of conventions codified various areas of the law of war and of neutrality **(362)**. In the inter-war period, apart from some less important codification attempts, the League of Nations-sponsored codification conference at The Hague in 1930 hoped to codify the laws of nationality **(175)**, territorial sea **(262)** and state responsibility **(128)**, but disappointingly reached agreement only on some aspects of the topic of nationality.

After World War II, in 1949 the General Assembly (GA), acting under Art. 13 of the UN Charter, established the ILC, which was given the task of codifying and progressively developing international law. At this time, the ILC consists of 34 members, elected by the GA for a five-year term and representing the main forms of civilization and the principal legal systems of the world but acting as private individuals and not representatives of their respective governments. The Commission meets in annual sessions of three months but has no permanent organs of its own. The ILC held its 56th session (in Geneva) in 2004.

During 55 years of its activities the ILC has produced the bulk of international law codification in a number of fields. Its procedure has been to prepare, on the basis of reports by a special rapporteur, a set of draft articles which are then discussed by the Sixth (Legal) Committee of the GA and submitted to governments for comments. The adoption of the draft takes place at an international conference convened by the UN. Among the conventions prepared by the ILC and accepted by states have been the four Geneva Conventions dealing with the law of the sea **(254)** adopted by the Geneva Conference in 1958 **(243)**; the Vienna Conventions dealing with diplomatic (1961) **(71)** and consular (1963) **(56)** relations respectively, the Convention on Special Missions, 1969 **(126)**; the Vienna Convention on the Law of Treaties **(288)** of 1969, the Vienna Convention on the Law of Treaties between States and International Organizations or between International Organizations, 1986, and the 1997 Convention on the Law of Non-Navigational Uses of International Watercourses **(212)**. The completion in 2001 after some 40 years of work of a draft dealing with state responsibility **(129)** was one of the most important contributions of the ILC. A related ILC draft, also submitted to the GA, concerned prevention of transboundary harm from hazardous activities. Drafts on jurisdictional immunities of states and their property (state immunity) **(131)** and on diplomatic couriers **(66)** and diplomatic bags **(65)** respectively were also completed. Other topics, on the agendas of the 52d and 53d sessions of the ILC (2000 and 2001), included unilateral acts **(44)**, nationality in relation to state succession **(132)**, diplomatic protection, reservations to treaties **(282)**, and international liability for the injurious consequences of activities not prohibited by international law **(120)**. Among its long-term projects the ILC identified the topics of responsibility of international organizations **(84)**, the effect of armed conflict on treaties, shared natural resources of states, expulsion of aliens **(146)**, and risks ensuing from the fragmentation of international law. At its 54th session, which took place in 2002, the Commission considered or organized its work on the following topics: reservations to treaties, diplomatic protection, unilateral acts of states, international liability for injurious consequences arising out of acts not prohibited by international law (international liability in case of loss from transboundary harm arising out of hazardous activities), responsibility of international organizations, fragmentation of international law, difficulties arising from the diversification and expansion of international law, and shared natural resources. The 55th Session in 2003 continued working on all these topics.

In addition to drafts of potential treaties, the ILC also issues reports submitted to states and the GA and formulates other international instruments, such as the Draft Declaration on the Rights and Duties of States, 1949 and the Nuremberg Principles **(354)** Declaration of 1950. A major achievement of the Commission was the drafting of the Statute of the International Criminal Court **(170)**, eventually adopted in 1998. In sum, the ILC has been by far the most important institution codifying international law. Furthermore, apart from its draft treaties, its commentaries constitute a valuable evidence of international custom **(39)**. Even if not finalized in a treaty, they are at least equivalent to teachings of publicists as subsidiary means for the determination of the rules of law **(42)**.

Despite its status and reputation, the ILC has not been used by the UN to draft certain law-making and politically sensitive treaties whose preparation has been entrusted either to a special conference of states, like the Third United Nations Conference on the Law of the Sea **(263)**, which drafted the Convention on the Law of the Sea of 1982 **(264)**, or to a GA committee, like the Committee on Peaceful Uses of Outer Space (COPUOS), which drafted the treaties concerning the law of outer space **(215)**, or the UN Commission on Human Rights **(161)** responsible for a number of conventions in the area of the law of human rights **(160)**. Treaties concerning international humanitarian law **(353)** have also been drafted outside of the ILC.

Codification has also been undertaken by international organizations other than the UN itself, such as the specialized agencies, especially the International Labor Organization, and other bodies, like the United Nations Commission on International Trade Law. At the regional level codification has proceeded under the auspices of the pertinent regional organizations, such as the Council of Europe and the Organization of American States (OAS). Among international non-governmental organizations **(86)**, the International Committee of the Red Cross stands out as the primary example of such organizations, contributing to drafting international conventions, in particular the four "Red Cross" Geneva Conventions of 1949 **(349)**.

Private institutions, which at one time or another have engaged in codifying various branches of international law, include the Institute of International Law and the International Law Association, both founded in 1873, and Harvard Law School whose Research in International Law produced widely respected drafts. Finally, the *Restatement of the Law (Third) Foreign Relations Law of the United States* (1987), prepared under the auspices of the American Law Institute, constitutes an important and valuable effort at codification, but it must be borne in mind that its work reflects the law as it is interpreted and applied by the United States.

**6. Comity.** Although occasionally courts in England and the United States have used the term "international comity" in the meaning of general international law, the more accepted concept of comity defines it as rules of courtesy or goodwill which states observe in their mutual relations without any sense of legal obligation under international law. Among examples of such behavior are flag salutes between public ships **(265)** of different countries and reciprocal waiver of passport or visa requirement for short-term visits by nationals **(175)** of another country. If used extensively, rules of international comity may eventually evolve into rules of international law, whether customary or conventional. For instance, the rule of international diplomatic law, now endorsed in Art. 36 of the Vienna Convention on Diplomatic Relations, 1961 **(71)**, which grants diplomats exemption from customs duties, used to be a rule of comity.

**7. Consensual Theory of International Law.** A theory which sees the binding force of an international law rule in the consent of states, given expressly as in a treaty **(40)** or by tacit agreement or acquiescence, as in the case of a customary rule of law **(39)**. Among the attempts at providing a theoretical basis for the consent doctrine, perhaps the best known is the work of Heinrich Triepel (1868–1946), a leading representative of the dualist doctrine **(10)**, who in his work *Völkerrecht und Landesrecht* (International Law and Municipal **(27)** Law), 1899, expounded his theory of consent or agreement (*Vereinbarung*). Triepel applied Jean-Jacques Rousseau's social contract theory and looked for the source of obligation in the common will of states. However, his reasoning fails to explain convincingly and definitively the binding force of international law through common consent. As admitted by Triepel himself, in the final analysis the theoretical basis of obligation of international law and for that matter any system of law cannot be explained on merely juridical grounds. In practice, express or tacit consent of states has provided the basis for the emergence of the Western system of international law. As put by the Permanent Court of International Justice (PCIJ) **(320)** in the *Lotus* case (France v. Turkey) (1927 PCIJ, Series A, No. 10), "the rules of law binding upon States . . . emanate from their own free will as expressed in conventions or usages generally accepted as expressing principles of law." However, in a specific dispute **(299)**, it may be difficult to ascertain the existence of consent to an emerging rule of customary international law. In its extreme manifestation, the consensual theory was the accepted doctrine in the former Soviet Union **(133)** whose jurists were eager to uphold their state's sovereign freedom of consent, especially by express agreement through treaty. The consent doctrine also appealed to the post-colonial new states, in particular in the areas of customary law and the law of state succession **(132)**.

While common consent implies the duty to accept the body of international law as such, states, especially new ones, have questioned the universal validity of specific rules of general international law, thus introducing an element of uncertainty, but in some cases eventually influencing the evolution of the law in selected areas. This has been especially the case of the law of the sea **(254)** and international economic law.

**8. Critical Legal Studies.** A controversial movement in the legal theory of the final decades of the 20th century, including also international law, which denies to law any special character that would differentiate it from politics. Originating in Harvard Law School in the United States in the 1970s and 1980s and classically presented by Roberto Unger, the movement has its disciples in Europe as well. While displaying a leftist orientation, the critical studies approach is not a Marxist movement. Actually, it constitutes the most radical manifestation of American legal realism. In international law, the critical legal studies school is represented by, among other scholars, Philip Allott, David Kennedy, and Martti Koskenniemi. Generally speaking, it reflects a frustration with failures to elaborate an all-embracing theory of international law, contending that, since no coherent international legal system exists as such and much of international law is merely an ideological construct, scholars should abandon attempts at developing a general theory of international law and focus instead on exposing the power relationships within specific concepts and issues, such as, for example, the much criticized concept of sovereignty **(125)**, sources of international law **(36)**, and the peaceful settlement of disputes **(318)**. To arrive at their conclusions, the proponents of critical legal studies use concepts and methods borrowed from other disciplines, such as communications theory and literary analysis. The objective would be to "deconstruct" ambiguous international legal concepts and expose their pretensions to objectivity and independence legitimized through the power of the language of the incoherent international law system.

**9. Domestic Jurisdiction.** A concept of fundamental legal and political significance, sometimes referred to as "reserved domain," whereby certain matters may not be regulated by international law and are subject to the exclusive jurisdiction **(87)** of the state which is free to act on them at its discretion. The domain of exclusive jurisdiction reserved to the state is usually contrasted with matters of international concern, meaning those matters which are not solely within the jurisdiction of the state and under international law are susceptible to regulation by that law.

The concept of domestic jurisdiction is necessarily implied in the nature of a decentralized international system; hence it is an essential attribute of sovereignty **(125)**. It is elevated to the rank of the principles governing the Charter of the United Nations (UN) which—like a comparable rule of Art. 5(8) of the League of Nations' Covenant—in Art. 2(7) explicitly precludes the UN from intervening in "matters which are essentially within the domestic jurisdiction of any State" (a limitation which, however, does not apply to the Security Council's (SC) enforcement action within the system of collective security **(327)**) or from requiring the member states "to submit such matters to settlement under the Charter." Hence reservations excluding disputes relating to matters that are "exclusively" or "essentially" within the domestic jurisdiction of the state in question are not uncommon in states' declarations accepting the compulsory jurisdiction **(323)** of the International Court of Justice **(309)**.

However, domestic jurisdiction is an ill-defined and relative concept. As held in 1923 by the Permanent Court of International Justice (PCIJ) **(320)** in its advisory opinion **(291)** on *Nationality Decrees Issued in Tunis and Morocco* (1923 PCIJ, Series B, No. 4), the question whether a certain matter is or is not within the jurisdiction of a state is an essentially relative question: it depends upon the development of international relations. In the opinion in question, the PCIJ denied the quality of domestic jurisdiction to the right of France to apply to British subjects its nationality rules enforced in Tunisia and Morocco. And indeed, notwithstanding Art. 2(7) of the UN Charter, the decades following the adoption of the Charter have witnessed a steady erosion of domestic jurisdiction and a remarkable expansion in the regulation by international law of matters which once used to be firmly within the sphere of the domestic jurisdiction of the states. This process has been particularly significant in the areas of environmental law **(197)** and especially in human rights law **(160)**, both conventional **(40)** and customary **(39)**. In general, the growth of international concern at the expense of domestic jurisdiction was a major trend in the history of international law in the second half of the 20th century. This trend has continued in the new century. As a matter of fact, by now hardly any matter seems to be "domestic" and, within the context of related controversies, the reserved domain of domestic jurisdiction is facing challenges of international legal regulation in an ever increasing number of areas.

**10. Dualism–Monism.** Two contrasting doctrines on the relationship between international law **(20)** and municipal law **(27)**, a topic that has long been a subject of much controversy among international legal scholars, primarily in civil-law **(23)** countries. In general, according to the dualist (or "pluralist") doctrine, international law and municipal law are two intrinsically different and separate systems of law; they operate at different levels, have different subjects, and regulate different matters. As a result, for the rules of international law to have any legal effect in a municipal legal order they must somehow be specifically adopted into the municipal system, by incorporation or transformation by way of a statute, and be applied there not as international law but as part of the domestic system. Moreover, international law thus adopted may be amended or repealed according to the constitutional provisions which apply to all municipal law. Philosophically, the various versions of the dualist doctrine are identified with the consensualist aspects **(7)** of positivism **(31)**, emphasizing the sovereign states as international legal persons **(85)** rather than individuals **(81)**. Dualism in its classical form was elaborated by Heinrich Triepel, a German jurist whose name is also associated with the consensual theory of international law. Dionisio Anzilotti, the best-known Italian scholar in international law, was also an exponent of dualism.

All the varieties of monism postulate the unity of the international and municipal legal orders. In general, while the more nationalistically minded German jurists, active around the turn of the 19th century, in following Johann Jakob Moser **(26)** advocated the superiority of municipal law over international law, regarding the latter as merely an "external state law" of each state serving as guidelines for the conduct of foreign affairs, some more recent scholars, such as Hans Kelsen (otherwise known for his pure theory of law **(34)**), George Scelle, Alfred Verdross, and Hersch Lauterpacht were more internationally inclined since they upheld the primacy of international law. While otherwise representing divergent theoretical approaches, the scholars of the internationalist school proclaimed the unity of all law, hierarchically structured, with the various municipal law systems derived from international law constituting the highest level of legal norms. Kelsen's monism is built up within his conceptual framework unifying all law and grounded in the "basic norm" of international law.

The monist approach is ultimately concerned with the conduct and welfare of individuals; hence—like H. Lauterpacht—its followers uphold the international legal personality of individuals **(81)**. Most monists see municipal law as ultimately deriving its legitimacy from international law. Therefore, in cases of conflict international law must prevail and cannot be subject even to domestic constitutional limitations.

To surmount the dichotomy between dualism and monism, a number of international law scholars have proposed compromise theories of coordination, suggesting that the logical consequences of both doctrines do not fit with the actual conduct of national and international organs. As a matter of fact, in the diverse and complex practice of states, doctrinal controversies do not depend much on national policies in the resolution of conflicts between international and municipal law. On the whole, most states appear to follow a dualist approach, often according primacy to the municipal law over a conflicting rule of international law. Furthermore, a number of national legal systems follow the principle that where fairly possible, municipal law is to be construed so as not to conflict with the international law obligations of the state in question.

It must also be noted that in recent decades the relationship between international and municipal law has undergone a modest but significant evolution whereby the more dualistic approach in the practice of traditional international law has made some concessions to what might be called monism, as illustrated by inroads into the domestic jurisdiction of states **(9)** and the application of some of the rules of international law directly to individuals, to that extent making them subjects of this legal system.

**11. Eclectics.** Sometimes referred to as Grotians, eclectics were those writers of the classical period in the theory about international law **(21)** after Hugo Grotius **(16)** who accepted both natural law **(29)** and positive law **(31)** in their explanation of the basis of the law of nations. Like Grotius, they distinguished between the eternal and universal natural law and the voluntary law of nations or positive law created by man through custom **(39)** and treaty **(40)**. While on the whole the eclectic publicists favored natural law in cases of conflict between the two categories of law, to a greater or lesser extent all of them took account of positive law. Christian Wolff **(48)** and especially Emmerich de Vattel **(45)** were the most prominent representatives of the eclectic approach to the law of nations. By the 18th century the eclectic-type doctrine had become predominant, but with positivist elements steadily gaining ground, until in the 19th century positivism became the prevalent mode of thinking in the doctrine of international law. In turn, in the 20th century, when in some interpretations the general principles of law recognized by civilized nations **(39)** achieved the rank of a source of international law **(36)** reminiscent of natural law, this development was viewed by some scholars as the acceptance of the Grotian point of view combining the two traditional attitudes toward the concept of law.

**12. *Erga Omnes* Obligations.** Obligations *erga omnes* (toward all), that is, owed to or in relation to all, are obligations concerning fundamental values of the international community whose violation by a state constitutes a wrongful act committed not only against the state directly affected by the act but against all members of the international community as a whole. In such cases all states have a legal interest in protecting the rights involved; any state may bring an international claim against the delinquent state without the need to show that it has suffered any injury. Obligations *erga omnes* are an exception to the general rule that only the state to whom the obligation was owed can make a claim for the breach; they resemble the class action (*actio popularis*) of private law. Whereas in the cases of *South West Africa* (Ethiopia v. South Africa; Liberia v. South Africa) (Second Phase) the International Court of Justice (ICJ) **(309)** refused to recognize the existence in international law of an equivalent of *actio popularis* (1966 ICJ Rep. 6), it endorsed the existence in general international law of obligations *erga omnes* deriving from such state conduct as acts of aggression **(325)**, genocide **(155)**, and violations of basic human rights **(157)**, including slavery **(180)** and racial discrimination **(177)**. In addition, in its judgment in the *East Timor* case (Portugal v. Australia) (1995 ICJ Rep. 89) the Court confirmed that the principle of self-determination **(122)** also belonged to the same kind of obligation. However, while there is no agreement on the exact roster of *erga omnes* obligations, their identification tends to overlap with unlawful conduct subject to the related notion of the peremptory norm of international law (*jus cogens*) **(24)**. Obligations *erga omnes* can also arise under a multilateral treaty upholding a fundamental value of the international community. In such cases not only the injured state **(82)** but also other parties to the treaty have the right to take measures designed to make the delinquent state desist from the violation.

At one stage of its work on state responsibility **(129)** the International Law Commission (ILC) first included in, and then removed from its Draft Articles a provision which categorized the internationally wrongful acts into "delicts" and "international crimes," the latter category always constituting a breach of an *erga omnes* obligation. But such an obligation need not necessarily be an international crime. The problem is related to the controversial notion of criminal responsibility of states, once considered by the ILC but—as noted above—abandoned by the Commission, primarily due to opposition by Western states. It may also be added that the concept of the *erga omnes* obligation has not yet been a subject of judicial proceedings before the ICJ or in any other international adjudication **(306)**.

**13. *Ex Aequo et Bono* and Equity.** In international law and adjudication **(306)** *ex aequo et bono* and equity are related but different concepts. *Ex aequo et bono* is a Latin phrase used in civil (Roman) law (*jus civile*) **(23)** meaning "on the basis of what is equitable and fair." In international law it refers to the power of an international tribunal to decide a case, at the request of the parties, not on the basis of the law but according to what, under the circumstances, is equitable, just, and fair regardless of whether or not it departs from the existing rules and principles. Art. 38(2) of the Statute of the International Court of Justice (ICJ) **(309)** confers upon the Court the power to decide a case *ex aequo et bono* if the parties agree thereto, but so far there has never been a case before the ICJ in which parties would make use of this provision. On the other hand, in international arbitration **(293)** in the 19th and 20th centuries, the parties would authorize tribunals to apply justice and equity more often than strictly international law as the basis for arbitral decisions. For example, at least two boundary **(189)** disputes **(299)** in South America were decided on this basis and, as recently as in 1997, the arbitration tribunal, set up under the Dayton-Paris Agreement for Peace in Bosnia and Herzegovina (Bosnia and Herzegovina-Croatia-Yugoslavia) (35 ILM 75 (1996)), applied principles of equity, justice, and reason (36 ILM 396 (1997)) in its Brčko district decision concerning the "inter-entity" boundary, that is, the boundary between Bosnia and Herzegovina itself and the so-called Serbian Republic (*Republika Srpska*).

While occasionally international instruments, for instance the General Act of 1928 **(302)** and some arbitration agreements, have blurred the distinction between *ex aequo et bono* and equity, these two concepts must be differentiated. Moreover, in practice the concept of equity is employed in so many diverse ways, often merging with the notions of justice, fairness, reasonableness, and the like that it is difficult to encompass it precisely in one definition. In addition, *ex aequo et bono* and equity in international law must not be confused with the English-law notion of equity.

In international law, equity is used in the decision-making process not as a formal source of law **(36)**; it means fairness and reasonableness within the confines of the existing law, especially when interpreting or filling gaps in the law. In this sense it could be considered a general principle of law **(38)**, as pointed out by Judge Manley O. Hudson in his concurring individual opinion **(304)** in the Permanent Court of International Justice (PCIJ) **(320)** case *Diversion of Water from the Meuse* (Netherlands v. Belgium) (1937 PCIJ, Series A/B, No. 68). In this dispute, the Netherlands claimed that Belgium had altered the course of the river Meuse by building canals in violation of an agreement of 1863. The Court rejected that claim on the ground of an earlier improper conduct by the Netherlands involving the construction of a lock, invoked in an equally rejected Belgian counterclaim. It is within this context that Hudson referred to the maxim "equality is equity and he who seeks equity must do equity" as a general principle of law.

Equity, equitable principles, and equitable solutions are concepts frequently referred to by the ICJ as an important factor in the Court's decision making, especially in law of the sea **(254)** disputes involving delimitation of maritime zones and boundaries. However, in the case of *Delimitation of the Maritime Boundary in the Gulf of Maine* (Canada /United States of America), (Case referred to a Chamber) **(295)** (1984 ICJ Rep. 246), reliance upon equity was criticized in a dissenting individual opinion as introducing an element of uncertainty into international law.

The notion of equity has also been invoked in General Assembly resolutions and other instruments as a synonym for distributive justice within the context of the demands of Third World countries for redistribution of wealth as part of a New International Economic Order.

**14. Friendly Relations General Assembly (GA) Declaration, 1970.** The Declaration on Principles of International Law Concerning Friendly Relations and Cooperation among States in Accordance with the Charter of the United Nations (UN), annexed to Resolution 2625 (XXV) adopted by consensus in 1970 (9 ILM 1292 (1970)). The Declaration articulated the fundamental principles of international law universally agreed upon by the member states of the UN.

Historically, the notion of fundamental rights and duties of states was recognized by states in the era of traditional international law, that is, before the entry into force **(271)** of the UN Charter in October 1945. Reference to them was made, for example, in the Convention on Rights and Duties of States, adopted by the Pan-American Conference in 1933 (28 AJIL, Supp. 75, (1934)) and in the relevant chapter of the Bogota Charter of the Organization of American States in 1948 (119 UNTS 49). However, no consensus existed on the content of the alleged fundamental rights and, their corollary, the duties of states.

In the very early years of the UN era, the International Law Comission prepared a Declaration on the Rights and Duties of States, 1949 (44 AJIL, Supp. 15 (1950)), but this instrument remained only in a draft form. Eventually, in 1963, the changing composition of the GA, brought about by the process of decolonization, prompted the UN members to establish a special committee charged with the formulation of a Friendly Relations Declaration. The work of this committee provided material for the 1970 Declaration.

The Declaration "solemnly proclaims" and elaborates upon seven basic principles of international law of which five reiterate the principles spelled out in Art. 2 of the UN Charter, namely: 1. prohibition of the threat or use of force in international relations **(329)**; 2. peaceful settlement of disputes **(Ch. 7)**; 3. cooperation in accordance with the Charter; 4. sovereign equality of states **(73)**; and 5. fulfillment in good faith of obligations. Principle 6, the duty of non-intervention in matters within the domestic jurisdiction **(9)**, is a logical corollary of Art. 2(7); and Principle 7 on equal rights and self-determination of peoples **(122)** reiterates the essentials of the GA anti-colonial resolutions and elaborates on the pertinent Charter provisions. The seven principles are declared to be interrelated, each to be construed in the context of the other principles.

The Friendly Relations Declaration is considered to express the universal view (*opinio juris*) shared by all states, and its principles have been invoked and reaffirmed in numerous global and regional instruments.

**15. Gentilis (Gentili), Albericus, 1552–1608.** The most important predecessor of Hugo Grotius **(16)**, at first long forgotten and not rediscovered until toward the end of the 19th century, Albericus Gentilis (in Italian Alberico Gentili) was of Italian birth, but as a Protestant he was forced to flee his native land, eventually settling in England. There he quickly asserted himself as a renowned jurist and expert in civil law (*jus civile*) **(23)** and soon became Professor in the University of Oxford and a practicing lawyer, specializing in the legal aspects of diplomacy **(68)**, war **(338)**, and neutrality **(362)**. His monograph *De legationibus* (On Embassies) is the first exposition of diplomatic law. In it, the author declared himself, in principle, for diplomatic immunity which he had earlier upheld in his opinion in the case of Mendoza, the Ambassador of Spain in England, involved in a plot to assassinate Queen Elizabeth. Gentilis examined various questions of the law of the sea **(254)**, an important area of the law of nations in the era of overseas navigation and discovery, on which he expounded in *Hispanicae advocationis libri duo* (Two Books of the Pleas of a Spanish Advocate), a posthumously published work. But the major treatise of Gentilis is *De jure belli libri tres* (Three Books on the Law of War) (1598). Despite its title, this work contains not only a treatment of the law of war, including an exposition of the just war doctrine **(333)**, but also of a number of issues within the general area of the "law of peace," and especially the law of treaties and the law of the sea. Gentilis is believed to be the first international jurist to have discussed the clause *rebus sic stantibus,* that is, the possibility, under certain circumstances, to terminate a treaty as a result of a fundamental change of circumstances **(273)**. In general, the range of topics treated by Gentilis is wide enough to warrant a claim that his treatise on the law of war can be considered the first textbook of international law.

Like his contemporaries and for quite a long time his successors, Gentilis derived the law of nations from the universal principles of justice and primarily natural law **(29)** discoverable by pure reason. Despite the acceptance of the divine origin of law, Gentilis' writing is characterized by a juridical approach to law. Unlike Grotius, he prefers references to contemporaneous state practice rather than drawing on examples from, and opinions of ancient and medieval writers. It is significant that Gentilis expressly rejected the idea that the law of nations was a preserve of theology. He can be regarded as the first publicist to have separated the law of nations from theology; hence he can be said to have initiated a secular approach to international law.

**16. Grotius (De Groot), Hugo (1583–1645).** The most celebrated classical writer in the law of nations, Grotius was a Dutch Protestant, and jurist, diplomat, historian, poet, theologian, and, in general, a typical Renaissance man and scholar. He was endowed with a cogent and elegant style and owing to this quality and a systematic exposition of his principal work as well as the right time of its publication (the Thirty Years' War, 1618–1648), Grotius soon became recognized as an eminent writer in the law of nature and nations. His major work *De jure belli ac pacis libri tres* (Three

Books on the Law of War and Peace), 1625, rapidly acquired unequalled reputation, enjoying unparalleled success among Europe's intellectuals, diplomats, and politicians. With some exaggeration, Grotius has been proclaimed as the father or founder of international law.

Grotius' work was inspired by his desire to develop rules which would mitigate the horrors that he witnessed during the devastating conflict of the Thirty Years' War. Starting from the sociable nature of man, Grotius proclaimed the need to preserve society as a source of natural law **(29)**. While itself not original, his doctrine is characterized by the author's hypothetical separation of natural law from the traditional concept of its divine origin. Along with repeated disclaimers of any belief in the separation of natural law from such origin, Grotius boldly asserts that natural law, discoverable by reason, would still be valid even if God did not exist. In this way Grotius took a further step in emancipating the doctrine of the law of nations from its medieval theological basis.

In Grotius' conceptual scheme, what today is considered the substance of public international law appears to have a dual nature since, in addition to natural law (*jus naturale*), the command of reason, he recognizes the "law of nations" (*jus gentium*) **(25)** or "voluntary law" (*jus voluntarium*) to which all peoples and states are subject. Unlike Francisco Suárez **(41)**, whose concept of *jus gentium* included only a few rules, Grotius assigned to his law of nations a much wider range of topics, including, *inter alia*, war, treaties, and neutrality. Ultimately, Grotius' law of nations, being based on agreement, conceptually merges with natural law as understood by the author, since common consent must be a deduction from the principles of right reason.

A major part of *De jure belli ac pacis* is taken up by the author's discussion of war **(338)**. In this regard, his rather confused treatment adopts the traditional doctrine of the just war **(333)**. However, his call for a humanization of war (*temperamenta*) is a progressive contribution to the law of war.

Grotius was also involved in the very topical controversy over the freedom of the sea **(242)**. His study *Mare liberum* (The Free Sea), in which he upheld the principle of the freedom of the sea against the claims of the Portuguese, would alone be sufficient to establish his reputation in the history of international law. This short study, published anonymously in 1609, turned out to be authored by Grotius as one chapter in his monograph *De jure praedae* (Prize Law) which was not discovered until 1864.

**17. International Law: Compliance and Enforcement.** Contrary to a widely held belief, most of international law remains unaffected by the weakness of its enforcement system since a great majority of its rules are voluntarily complied with by the states concerned. Every day, national decision makers, such as government officials, diplomats, shipmasters, and customs officials and other state functionaries routinely implement rules in an implied acknowledgment of the need for a legal frame of reference to assure a certain minimum of order and predictability in international relations. Moreover, if an international dispute **(299)** arises, it may turn over uncertainty of fact or law, an unfriendly but legal act, or a demand for a change in the law in force. A deliberate violation of the law in the hope of bringing about a change in a legal rule may, in the long run, turn out to conflict with the interests of the state in question.

Apart from enlightened self-interest, some important considerations contribute to compliance with the rules of international law. One is concern to avoid adverse consequences of a violation, and in particular a reaction by the affected state. Such concern may induce a state to comply with perhaps an inconvenient rule while foregoing short-term gains in the hope of avoiding long-term disadvantages. Fear of retaliation is not necessarily the main reason for observance; expectation of rewards that may accrue from maintaining a state's credit and reputation can also play a role. Moreover, one must not entirely discount the possibility that a routine implementation of international law by national and international officials can contribute to developing a law habit and thereby strengthen voluntary compliance. However, in the final analysis, just as in municipal law **(27)** situations, international law cannot prevent violations, especially if committed by a powerful state.

In traditional international law, that is, before the introduction of the ban on the use of force **(329)** in 1945, in order to enforce their respective perceived rights, states could resort to forcible measures, including military coercion, even without first exhausting peaceful methods of resolving disputes **(318)**. Military reprisals **(119)**, forcible intervention **(331)**, "pacific" blockade **(326)**, and other measures "short of war" were used to enforce alleged rights. Where expedient, states would resort to war **(338)** in the legal sense of the term. However, already in 1907, the Hague Convention II (the Drago-Porter Convention) banned the use of force for the recovery of debt and later, in the inter-war period the Covenant of the League of Nations, 1919, and subsequently the General Treaty for the Renunciation of Force, 1928 (the Pact of Paris or the Kellogg-Briand Pact) **(330)** stipulated more restrictions upon resort to war.

Since the adoption of the prohibition of the use of force in Art. 2(7) of the United Nations (UN) Charter, a rule which soon crystallized into a fundamental principle of general (customary) international law **(39)** eventually acquiring the status of a peremptory rule (*jus cogens*) **(24)**, armed reprisals have been unlawful, with only non-forcible "countermeasures" **(58)** allowed in unilateral enforcement. Thus in contemporary international law, while an injured state **(82)** may attempt to enforce its claim through peaceful means of settling international disputes, self-help (which in municipal law is an exception) is the prevailing method of enforcing a claim against another state for a breach of an international law obligation. Retortion **(121)** and non-forcible reprisals are the two major forms of unilateral self-help countermeasures allowed in today's international law.

The effectiveness of measures designed to enforce international law, especially in reaction to grave violations entailing an *erga omnes* obligation **(12)**, through a collective action of the international community, institutionalized in the collective security system **(327)** of the UN, depends on the complex interplay of political, military, and economic circumstances. The UN Security Council (SC) has the exclusive power to order enforcement action, both in the form of "sanctions" not involving resort to armed force and by the use of armed force. The Council may also authorize UN members to use all available means, including armed force, to enforce international law. However, these powers of the SC are limited to matters under Chapter VII of the UN Charter involving threats to the peace, breaches of the peace, and acts of aggression **(325)**, in all cases to be determined by the Council. Furthermore, the theoretically extensive power of the SC is potentially paralyzed by the institution of veto available in non-procedural matters to each of the five permanent members of the SC (China, France, Russia, United Kingdom (UK), and United States (US)). In fact, the veto, used both during the Cold War, mostly by the Soviet Union, and thereafter, mostly by the United States, has frustrated the enforcement of international law in some important areas of conflict. As a result, the enforcement of international law by the UN in its most dramatic but possibly most effective form, that is by the use of armed force, is possible only in most exceptional cases of a fortunate convergence of, or at least absence of conflict between, the interests of the five permanent members of the SC. The General Assembly, while the most important political forum of the Organization, has no legal power to enforce international law.

The specialized agencies of the UN, such as International Monetary Fund, International Bank for Reconstruction and Development, International Labor Organization, United Nations Educational Scientific and Cultural Organization, World Health Organization, International Civil Aviation Organization, International Maritime Organization, and especially those which can provide essential benefits to member states, can be in a position to exercise pressure for the enforcement of international law rules by depriving an offending state of such advantages. At the regional level, the European Union whose Court of Justice **(298)** has compulsory jurisdiction in wide areas of life of the Union's members, has the power to enforce the Community law against a member state found in breach of its rules. But it must be noted that the European Community constitutes a unique organization displaying features both of international law and municipal law. Whether a collective self-defense organization, such as North Atlantic Treaty Organization, has the right to enforce rules of the international law of human rights **(160)** by resorting to a military "humanitarian intervention" **(332)** without any authorization by the SC, as was the case of Kosovo, is a dubious proposition, especially in view of the extent and intensity of the use of force by the intervening states.

As illustrated by cases involving violations of human rights **(157)**, international law can, under appropriate circumstances, be enforced through national courts which may deny recognition to certain acts attributable to a foreign state or even, more directly, order compensation for injury inflicted upon a national of the forum state. However, there is no definitive answer to the question whether an individual can sue a foreign state in his country's court for damage caused by internationally illegal acts, including in particular illegal use of force or measures taken in an illegally occupied territory.

A discussion of enforcement in international law must not overlook the contribution of international non-governmental organizations **(86)** some of which are playing an increasingly important role in bringing pressure to bear upon governments to comply with their treaty obligations, as is especially the case in the areas of the protection of the environment **(197)** and human rights.

Finally, it must be borne in mind that since in contemporary international law individuals may be criminally responsible for certain offenses directly under international law, international law must also deal with enforcement of the pertinent rules against individuals incurring personal responsibility and to that extent acquiring the quality of subjects of international law **(81)**.

**18. International Law in National (Municipal) Law: Custom.** The relationship between international law and municipal (national) law raises two major questions. First, by what methods is customary law **(39)** implemented in the municipal law **(27)** of the various countries: their respective constitutions (if any), legislative acts, administrative practice, and judicial decisions; and second, which system is granted priority in the state concerned in cases of conflict between international and municipal law **(27)**. However, strictly speaking, from the point of view of international law, the answer is simple: international law shall always prevail over any conflicting rules of municipal law. Yet such an internationalist and monistic **(10)** position, though theoretically true, is unrealistic in view of the rather nationalist stance on this matter of a very large majority of states, let alone general public opinion and the media, in whose view international law still remains marginalized as an element in analyzing international problems.

It is a fundamental principle of international law that a state cannot invoke provisions of its municipal law in justification of its failure to perform a treaty **(288)** (a rule anchored in Art. 27 of the 1969 Vienna Convention on the Law of Treaties) or, for that matter, to comply with a customary or other rule of international law. If there are any discrepancies between municipal law and international law, a state is obliged to bring its law in conformity with international law and—if necessary—to enact pertinent implementing legislation. Otherwise international law does not impose any special rules concerning the methods to be employed by states in making international law legally applicable in their respective domestic systems.

On the whole, the status of customary law in the municipal law systems of states, including both the common-law and civil-law **(23)** systems, is less complex than in the case of treaties. In general, while there exists a tremendous variety in details of implementing general (customary) international law, in virtually all countries this law is automatically incorporated in the domestic system of law (the doctrine of incorporation), either by virtue of a constitutional provision, as in a number of European states (for example, Austria, France, Germany, Greece, and Italy), or through gradual judicial practice, as in the United States and other common-law countries. As far as the United States (US) is concerned, while Art. VI of the Constitution explicitly mentions only treaties as the law of the land, general (customary) law of nations has always been considered as constituting part of the federal law, as eloquently expressed by the US Supreme Court in the celebrated case of *The Paquete Havana; The Lola*, 1900, (175 U.S. 677): "International law is part of our law, and must be ascertained and administered by the courts of justice of appropriate jurisdiction." This fundamental rule is largely overlooked in the perception of international law in the US. In the more recent interpretation, determination of international law by the federal courts is binding on the courts of the component states of the Union.

In the United Kingdom (UK), since the 18th century the rule emerged that the law of nations was part of the law of the land, as stated by Blackstone in his *Commentaries on the Laws of England*, 1769 and reaffirmed in numerous judicial decisions However, in the 19th century, in view of the priority given to Acts of Parliament and the rule of *stare decisis* (following precedents established by higher courts), the doctrine of incorporation underwent some modification in favor of that of transformation or specific adoption of customary international law either by legislation or case law. But the case law has not been quite consistent on the controversial issue whether the doctrine of *stare decisis* in cases involving customary law of nations would have to follow the evolution of this law which does not follow this doctrine. On the whole, however, the doctrine of incorporation appears to prevail.

Concerning the rank accorded by states to the incorporated customary rules of international law, it can be concluded in general that many states treat such rules as ordinary legislative acts, which means that a later law prevails over a conflicting prior customary rule of international law. As a consequence, strictly speaking, the state concerned would incur responsibility under international law. Among the states which do not accord general international law a rank higher than ordinary legislation are the UK, the US, China, and France. In a number of countries, including the US, a principle prevails, however, that a municipal law is to be construed so as not to conflict with international law, a rule much more relevant for treaties than customary law. Whether a newly emerging rule of international customary law supersedes preexisting municipal law is an open question. Unlike the US and other states that do not have provisions granting a superior rank to general international law, some states, in their respective constitutions or in judicial practice, lay down the rule that international customary law prevails over any inconsistent ordinary legislative acts. Among these countries are Germany, Greece, Italy, and Japan as well as some of the new post-Soviet republics.

The general conclusion must be that, while in principle states accept the operation of international customary law in their respective legal systems, the rule appears to be that in cases of unavoidable inconsistency between municipal and international law the former must prevail. Even in such internationally minded countries as the Netherlands and Germany, international customary law cannot override the Constitution, which perhaps reveals a certain distrust of the sometimes uncertain rules of this law even in these states.

**19. International Law in National (Municipal) Law: Treaties.** The relationship between treaties and municipal law raises two questions. First, by what methods are treaties accepted into the municipal law of individual countries: their constitution (if any), legislative acts, administrative practice, and judicial decisions; and second, which system of law prevails in cases of conflict between a treaty and municipal law. But it must be borne in mind that from the point of view of international law it is a matter of indifference by what methods treaty provisions are rendered operative by individual states. Moreover, according to international law, treaty obligations always override any inconsistent provisions of the municipal law of the state concerned. It is a fundamental principle of international law, codified in Art. 27 of the Vienna Convention on the Law of Treaties, that a state may not invoke its municipal law in justification of its failure to perform a treaty **(288)**.

The status of treaties in municipal law varies considerably from country to country. Generally speaking, some states, such as France and the United States (US) among others, use automatic incorporation laid down under the country's law on a standing basis. Treaties may acquire the force of law upon their promulgation in the country's official journal of laws, a practice followed in France, some other European countries, and the states once part of the French colonial empire. In the US, under Art. VI, sec. 2 of the Constitution (the "supremacy clause"), treaties, along with the Constitution and federal statutes, are the supreme law of the land; hence they are superior to the laws of the component states of the US. Technically, by the term "treaty" the Constitution means international agreements made by the President "by and with the Advice and Consent of the Senate, provided two-thirds of the Senators present concur" (Art. II, sec. 2). This "ratification" **(280)** gives effect to the treaty concerned both in the US law and—as far as the US becoming a party is concerned—purposes of international law. However, internationally, the concept of the treaty encompasses not only the treaties made pursuant to Art. II of the Constitution but also "international agreements other than treaties" which do not require the Senate's ratification. More than 90 percent of international agreements entered into by the US are such instruments. The bulk of them is made up of the so-called congressional executive agreements made by the President with the authorization or approval of Congress. Two other categories are "executive agreements pursuant to treaty," and "sole executive agreements" concluded by the President on his own authority without congressional participation. The Presidential authority to make international agreements outside the scope of Art. II of the Constitution has been one of the most controversial political issues in the US. Under the Case Act (11 ILM 1117 (1972)), 1972, the texts of such agreements, including the oral ones, must be submitted to Congress within 60 days of execution.

In the US, the status of treaties has been profoundly affected by the judge-made doctrine of "self-executing treaties" formulated by Chief Justice John Marshall in 1829 (*Foster and Elam v. Neilson* (27 U.S. (2 Pet.) 253)). Briefly, a self-executing treaty (or sometimes only individual provisions) is a treaty that operates automatically without the need for any municipal implementing legislation. On the other hand, if such legislation is mandated constitutionally or is required by the Senate at ratification or—in cases of executive agreements—by virtue of a congressional resolution, or if the need for such legislation results from the treaty itself, then the treaty or executive agreement is non-self-executing. Domestically, the status of a treaty is decided upon by the executive or Congress and is ultimately determined by courts on a case-by-case basis. In general, provisions in treaties of friendship, commerce, and navigation, conferring rights on foreign nationals, are self-executing. On the other hand, in the often quoted case of *Sei Fujii v. State of California*, 1952, involving a claim by an alien, ineligible for citizenship, that the United Nations (UN) Charter provisions referring to human rights **(156)** invalidated a California law barring certain aliens from acquiring ownership of land, the California Supreme Court ruled that the relevant Charter provisions were not intended to supersede existing domestic legislation and were not self-executing. (The California law in question was otherwise declared unconstitutional as a violation of the Fourteenth Amendment to the US Constitution.) Internationally, a treaty is binding irrespective of whether or not it is self-executing, and if it is not self-executing, the country concerned has the obligation to enact pertinent implementing legislation.

A self-executing or legislatively implemented US treaty overrides state law, as illustrated by the celebrated Supreme Court case of *State of Missouri v. Holland* (252 U.S. 416 (1920)) involving the constitutionality of a migratory bird treaty with Canada, 1916, and the congressional Act passed in implementation of the treaty. This decision, rejecting the argument of these instruments allegedly interfering with the constitutionally reserved rights of the states, prompted opponents of a strong federal power to unsuccessfully attempt passing the so-called Bricker Amendment to the US Constitution which would make all treaties effective only through legislation and thus render them non-self-executing. It might be added that in some European countries (France, for example) courts used to construe extensively the concept of non-self-executing treaty provisions in order to prevent undesirable changes in the municipal legislation. The Russian Federal Law on International Treaties, 1995 (34 ILM 1370 (1995)) differentiates between instruments which, in fact, are self-executing and non-self-executing treaties.

The second method of accepting treaties into the domestic system of law is that of transformation, either through reformulating them in the form of a legislative act which makes them legally binding under municipal law (many countries of the civil-law system, the United Kingdom (UK) and many countries of the Commonwealth) or, without any statutory reformulation, on a case-by-case method, through a simple legislative act laying down that the annexed treaty acquires the force of law (Germany and Italy, among other countries).

In the UK the doctrine of transformation is a consequence of the peculiarities of the British political system. Since the Crown, on the advice of the executive, has the prerogative to enter into and ratify treaties, it could, in theory at least, use its treaty-making power to legislate and thereby encroach upon the fundamental principle of Parliament's monopoly of legislative power. Therefore for a treaty to become law it is necessary to pass an enabling Act of Parliament to give it municipal effect. International agreements governing the conduct of war **(339)** or cession of territory **(227)** and less important administrative agreements which do not require ratification are exceptions to this principle. Under the so-called Ponsonby Rule, in order to synchronize the municipal and international entry into effect of treaties **(271)**, the texts of treaties signed **(283)** or scheduled to be acceded to **(267)** are laid before Parliament for adopting enabling legislation at least 21 parliamentary days before the delayed ratification by the Crown and promulgation in the UK Treaty Series.

As far as the rank of treaties within individual municipal systems is concerned, the constitutions of some states, where the method of incorporation is applied, provide for their superior status as against the country's laws. This is the case, among others, of France (subject to reciprocity and the rule that provisions of a treaty incompatible with the Constitution require adoption of a special constitutional law), the successor states **(132)** of the former French colonial empire, Belgium, Greece, Russia and some of the former Soviet republics, and Spain. The same is true of the Netherlands where Art. 91(3) is even construed to accord self-executing treaties a status superior to the Constitution itself. In many countries the Constitution or ordinary law provides for treaties to have the same rank as national laws. As a result, a later law can override an earlier treaty although in a number of countries the law should be so construed as not to conflict with the treaty.

In the US, treaties, including executive agreements, override earlier or later state law, but are, in principle, equivalent in rank to federal statutes. But it is an established principle in the judicial practice that, where fairly possible, Acts of Congress are to be construed so as not to conflict with a treaty, the presumption being that Congress would not violate an international obligation of the US. But if no reconciliation is possible, then the later in time, statute or treaty, prevails. However, as in the case of customary law **(18)**, an Act of Congress supersedes an earlier treaty provision only if the purpose of the Act to have such effect is clearly expressed; it cannot be merely implied. In the early 1970s, during the Rhodesian crisis, (resulting from the unilateral declaration of independence by the white minority regime in Southern Rhodesia and the consequent sanctions imposed by the Security Council (SC)), Congress, in violation of Art. 25 of the UN Charter (enjoining the UN members to accept and carry out the decisions of the SC), adopted the so-called Byrd Amendment, which legalized the importation of Rhodesian chrome specifically prohibited by the SC resolution adopted under Chapter VII of the UN Charter, which sets forth the UN collective security system **(327)**. While finding the Byrd Amendment to be "in blatant disregard" of the US treaty obligations, a federal court recognized its legality under the US law because of the clearly expressed congressional intention.

Treaties, including as a rule executive agreements, supersede earlier Acts of Congress only if they are self-executing. In the case of non-self-executing treaty provisions, a prior congressional Act is superseded upon the implementation by enabling legislation of the provisions. But a treaty provision will never be given effect as law if it is inconsistent with the Constitution, a rule followed in other countries as well.

The Byrd Amendment illustrates the more general problem of implementing decisions of international organizations, in particular the UN, which a state party to the organization's constituent treaty undertook to comply with. Except for a few countries (Greece, the Netherlands, Spain), municipal law does not contain provisions incorporating the contents of such decisions which frequently require specific implementing legislation.

In general, the conclusion concerning the ranking of treaties in municipal law must be that, while some states allow treaties, under certain circumstances, to prevail over conflicting rules of the municipal law (but not the Constitution), the tendency on the whole is to adopt a nationalist attitude of according the municipal law a status superior to that of treaties.

**20. International Law: Nature and Characteristics.** International law or, more precisely, public international law is a body of legal rules governing the conduct of states **(127)** and public or intergovernmental international organizations **(84)** in their mutual relations, as well as—in rather exceptional circumstances—the conduct of other persons, including in particular individuals **(81)** who, for certain specific purposes, may be conferred rights or imposed duties directly under international law. For all practical purposes, however, international law, a term used first by Jeremy Bentham **(3)** in 1789, is primarily the law binding states in ever expanding spheres of international relations and concerns. Hence it is sometimes referred to as public international law to differentiate it from private international law **(32)** or conflict of laws. The law of nations (*jus gentium*) **(25)** is another, more traditional but now less common, term used to denote international law.

A distinction is sometimes made between general and particular international law. The former is meant to apply to the rules found in custom **(39)** and widely accepted multilateral treaties **(288)** tending to encompass all regions of the world. The term "particular international law" is employed to refer to rules which, normally under an agreement, bind two or just a few states only, but do not apply generally among states. If general international law becomes binding upon all states, it is often called universal international law. On the whole, there has been a tendency for the general international law which is considered fundamental to the international community to become universalized. On the other hand, the practice of states of a geographical region may develop, in certain limited areas, rules of regional international law which apply only to the states of the region in question, such as certain rules concerning diplomatic asylum **(64)** accepted or at least acquiesced in by South American states, or the law developed under the auspices of the Council of Europe. The law of the European Union, also a regional type of law, is a unique system displaying the characteristics of both international and municipal law.

In view of the heterogeneity of the states of today's international system and diverse forms of civilization, the issue of adopting regional regulations to take account of the diversity of interests and circumstances of the states in a region, acquires a special significance. On the other hand, the question arises whether, in a long-term perspective, regionalization can pose a challenge to the unity and universality of international law.

Despite the skeptical view, historically associated with the name of John Austin **(1)**, that international law is not a real law because it lacks enforcement sanction, the legal nature of this system of law is taken for granted as such by all states: they create and apply its rules, consider themselves to be bound by them and never question the legal nature of its obligatory force. The misconception about international law arises not only from the widespread lack of familiarity with this system of law but mainly from the fact that international law operates within a loose and decentralized political environment of "sovereign" **(125)** states, without any central legislative body, executive enforcement organs, and compulsory judicial institutions, the features normally associated with the notion of law as understood by legal practitioners, a great majority of whom, especially in the United States, have no training in international law. Misconceptions about international law are also common in the news media and the public in general. It may be added here that inquiry into a law of another country is not, as such, part of research in international law but belongs in the area of "comparative law."

The notion of law for purposes of municipal law **(27)** need not necessarily apply to the law governing relations between and among the members of the society of states ("international community"). International law is still law even if, at least at this stage, it does not meet the qualitative standards of the municipal-law model. While it is common knowledge that there exists no universally agreed upon definition of law as such, international law, to a greater or lesser extent, does meet the criterion of a common-sense conception of law as a recognized body of rules governing relations within a community and provided with some kinds of enforcement mechanism. The decentralized political context within which international law operates could not but produce a system of law in which, in contrast to the highly structured municipal law, the development of enforceable remedies and procedural rights has lagged behind a well-established roster of the substantive rights of sovereign and legally equal **(73)** states. Moreover, by far more than a national system, the international system is subject to power politics and international law suffers from tensions between the need for progressive development and the perceived requirements of national interest. Hence in certain periods of its history, international law may undergo a crisis and be marginalized, especially if a major power or, today, the only superpower, appears to resign its role as the champion of the rule of law in international relations, disregarding, by its policy of unilateralism and double standards, major multilateral efforts of the international community to keep up with grave challenges in human rights, the environment, and the strengthening of the rule and enforcement of law in international relations.

**21. International Law: Theories about.** Prior to the emergence of the system of territorial states in Europe around the 16th century, no theory of international law as such was in existence, but elements of Roman and medieval thought provided a theoretical basis for the eventual building up of a theory of the law of nations in Europe in the eras of the Renaissance and Reformation. The

Roman doctrine of natural law **(29)**, adopted and modified by the Church in the Middle Ages, was the major building block of this theory. Rudiments of a future theory were also found in the Roman *jus fetiale*, the religion-based rules of the *fetiales*, the priests of Jupiter, in charge of ceremonial declarations of war and making peace on behalf of Rome, and the writings of St. Augustine (354–430) whose work implied a conception of a higher legal order with a plurality of states. The concept of just war **(333)** also dates back to Roman philosophers and to the medieval Church doctrine which, among other ideas, dealt with the humanitarian aspects of war **(353)**, a perennial phenomenon in the feudal era. Furthermore, the coexistence of a plurality of political bodies was acknowledged by legal commentators of the late Middle Ages, including Bartolus of Sassoferrato (1314–1357) and Baldus de Ubaldis (1327–1410).

In its formative stage, in the "classical" period, that is, in the 16th to 18th centuries, the doctrine of the law of nations was profoundly influenced by the natural law doctrine. To a greater or lesser degree, the publicists of the period recognized the role of natural law in explaining the obligatory force of the law of nations. In addition, the meaning of the Roman concept of *jus gentium* **(25)** expanded beyond its original scope, limited to legal relations between individuals of different ethnic groups of the Roman Empire, to include relations between states in the meaning of the modern law of nations.

Despite the primacy of natural law of divine origin, even Hugo Grotius **(16)** tended to anchor it in reason and social necessity. Moreover, both he and his predecessor Albericus Gentilis **(15)** admitted the existence of the man-made positive law in the form of custom and treaties. This early legal positivism **(31)**, which stressed the need to examine the actual practice of states as the basis of the law of nations, found its leading exponents in Cornelius van Bynkershoek **(4)** and especially Johann Jacob Moser **(26)** who can be classified as a pure positivist whereas Grotius, Richard Zouche **(49)** and, the most influential of all, Emmerich de Vattel **(45)** combined naturalist and positivist elements; hence they are sometimes referred to as eclectics **(11)**.

With the progressive laicization and intellectual skepticism, the natural law school declined by the onset of the 19th century giving way to positivism which, in the climate of rising nationalism and emphasis on state sovereignty **(125)**, displaced the ethical jurisprudence of the universal natural law of subordination in favor of the positive law of coordination derived exclusively from the will and consent of sovereign states. As a matter of fact, the doctrine of sovereignty dating back to Nicolo Machiavelli (1469–1527) and Jean Bodin (1529–1596) occupied the central stage in the positivist theory of international law through the 20th century. However, no definitive consensus emerged in the doctrine on explaining the reasons for the binding force of international law. In addition, even the very legal nature of this branch of law was questioned either—as was the case of the German nationalist philosopher Hegel—on grounds of the supreme will of the sovereign state not answerable to any external authority or—as was the case of John Austin **(1)**—on the basis of a narrowly defined concept of law. A number of doctrines tried to explain the binding force of international law, such as the doctrine of autolimitation **(2)**, the consensual (common consent) theory **(7)**, or extra-legal assumptions, such as the postulate of the duty to observe treaties, *pacta sunt servanda* **(277)**, put forward by Dionisio Anzilotti. The latter explanation reverts to the tenets of the old school of natural law which otherwise continues to be the official position of the Catholic Church. In fact, the early decades of the 20th century witnessed a revival of the doctrine of natural law in versions more adapted to the modern context. Still other theorists, notably the monists **(10)**, who denied the specific nature of international law as a discrete legal system, dispensed with the need to explain reasons for its binding nature. In this respect, the Vienna school of pure theory of law **(34)**, led by Hans Kelsen, represented perhaps the most influential trend in thinking about the nature of law in Europe. From a completely different point of view, the Marxist doctrine of international law called for the destruction of the whole structure of this "bourgeois" law, but when the doctrine acquired a territorial basis in Russia (the Soviet Union) expedience and pragmatic realism made it imperative for the Soviet state to make an accommodation in coexistence with the capitalist world and use or abuse the institutions of international law, and in particular the principle of sovereignty, for its own interests. Following the collapse of the Soviet Union **(133)**, the Marxist theory of international law lost much of its appeal and even China in fact paid only lip service to its propositions.

On the dawn of the new century and millennium, it appears that positivist approaches are in the mainstream of international law theory competing with other, more internationalist concepts. Actually, a number of schools of thought are challenging the now traditional positivist conception of international law. Among the relatively new developments in the theory of international law, otherwise reflecting trends in legal theory in general, are such unorthodox approaches as the policy-oriented school **(30)** dating back to the Cold War era and the more recent approach known as critical legal studies **(8)**. In addition, some very scanty and tentative attempts by international relations scholars and international jurists to learn more about each others' field of inquiry may perhaps prove useful in enriching the theoretical bases of both disciplines. To what extent any achievements of international legal theory can prove relevant to the actual international political practice continues to remain an open question.

**22. Judicial Decisions as Subsidiary Means for the Determination of Rules of Law.** International judicial **(306)**, including arbitral **(293)**, decisions and even decisions of municipal **(27)** courts are, along with the teachings of publicists **(42)**, the "subsidiary means for the determination of rules of law" (International Court of Justice (ICJ) **(309)** Statute, Art. 38(1)(d)). This means that, while they do not make law since—an essential and often overlooked point—the common-law doctrine of *stare decisis*, that is, the legal duty to follow precedents of higher courts, does not exist in international law, such decisions are among subsidiary means to which sometimes substantial weight is given in order to determine the existence of a rule of international law. The legal effect of the decisions of the ICJ is subject to the express provision of Art. 59 of its Statute to the effect that the Court's decision has "no binding force except between the parties and in respect of that particular case." In fact, however, many decisions in international adjudication, and especially those of the ICJ and its predecessor, the Permanent Court of International Justice (PCIJ) **(320)**, are deemed by international lawyers to have a highly persuasive authority in determining the content of customary law **(39)**, especially if adopted unanimously or supported by a large majority of judges. The ICJ itself has frequently referred to its previous decisions and their reasons in the interests of judicial consistency. Among the landmark decisions of the ICJ have been the judgments in the *North Sea Continental Shelf* cases, (Federal Republic of Germany/Denmark; Federal Republic of Germany/Netherlands) (1969 ICJ Rep. 3) in which the Court elaborated on the formation of customary law; the *Barcelona Traction* case (Belgium v. Spain) (1970 ICJ Rep. 3) in which a Court's *obiter dictum* examined the notion of *erga omnes* obligations **(12)**; and the case of *Military and Paramilitary Activities in and against Nicaragua* (Nicaragua v. United States of America) (1986 ICJ Rep. 14) in which the Court, *inter alia*, analyzed such problems as attribution **(53)** or imputability of an individual's action to a state, self-defense **(335)**, and aspects of international humanitarian law **(353)**. Moreover, while the function of the ICJ is not to make law but to apply and interpret it, some of the Court's decisions in fact turned out to be creative of progressive development of international law. Here belong, *inter alia*, the advisory opinion **(291)** on *Reparation for Injuries Suffered in the Service of the United Nations* (1949 ICJ Rep. 174) in which the Court expounded the doctrine of the implied powers of international organizations **(84)**; another opinion on *Reservations to the Convention on the Prevention and Punishment of the Crime of Genocide* **(155)** (1951 ICJ Rep. 15) which set out the outline of the law governing reservations to treaties; and the judgment on the merits of the *Nottebohm* case (Liechtenstein v. Guatemala) (1955 ICJ Rep. 4) in which the Court ruled for the requirement of a genuine link in cases of diplomatic protection in the circumstances of a single nationality **(175)**. Though highly criticized, this judgment has otherwise influenced the development of the law on nationality, including especially nationality of ships **(257)**. But in the celebrated case before the PCIJ, *The Lotus* (France v. Turkey) (1927 PCIJ, Series A, No. 10) the Court's judgment was subject to severe criticism, especially in shipping circles, and its point of view on jurisdiction **(240)** in cases of collision on the high seas was eventually reversed by a convention in 1952.

A number of arbitral awards have also contributed to interpreting and developing rules of international law. Among the best known cases are: *The Alabama* (United States (US) v. United Kingdom), 1872, in which the tribunal set out certain principles in the area of neutrality **(362)**; *The Isle* *of Palmas* (US v. The Netherlands), 1928, important for the rules governing acquisition of title to territory **(227)**; and the *Naulilaa* Arbitration, 1928, which set out the parameters of the traditional international law for lawful forcible reprisals **(119)** in time of peace. Among other international courts whose decisions contributed to the development of international law are the Iran–United States Claims Tribunal **(312)** and the various mixed arbitral commissions **(314)** and mixed claims commissions **(315)**. One should also include the contribution of the International Tribunal for the Former Yugoslavia **(352)** to the development of international humanitarian law **(353)**, for example, in the *Tadić case* (Appeals Chamber, 1995); and the role of the two regional courts in Europe, the European Court of Justice **(298)** and the European Court of Human Rights **(154)**.

National courts have dealt with large numbers of cases involving various aspects of international law, cumulatively contributing to the growth and clarification of rules, especially in such areas as recognition **(106)**, state immunity **(131)**, and diplomatic **(63)** and consular **(55)** immunities. The weight accorded to a determination by a municipal court depends on the significance of the merits of the case as well as the status, reputation, and perceived impartiality of the court in question. In this respect, decisions of the US Supreme Court and the corresponding judicial organs in England, Scotland, and France, to mention just a few major countries, have been held in high regard. It might be added that because of the federal system **(77)** in the US, decisions of the US Supreme Court involving boundary disputes between component states of the US have also been of relevance for international law.

One should always bear in mind that the evidential value of decisions by national courts must be assessed with caution since they may conceal national bias, occasionally relying on their respective municipal laws rather than on international law.

**23. *Jus Civile*.** As distinct from *jus gentium* **(25)**, *jus civile* in the Roman legal system was the law governing Roman citizens, a duality of law classically stated in the famous *Institutes* of Gajus, a law textbook of the second century AD. Today the term "civil law," as a rule, refers to the ancient Roman private law and especially the legal systems based on it, primarily in the countries of continental Europe and other countries which have followed the features of the system.

Historically, in classical writers, such as Albericus Gentilis **(15)**, Hugo Grotius **(16)** and others, the Roman civil law, regarded as the "written reason," often merged with *jus gentium* and the concept of natural law **(29)**, providing substance for regulating some areas of the law of nations in the emerging system of territorial states in Europe, and especially for the law governing acquisition of territory **(227)**. As a matter of fact, the "reception" of the Roman civil law was a general trend in Renaissance Europe where the early law of nations publicists turned to this legal system to discover the contents of natural law and suggest rules to govern relations between states.

**24. *Jus Cogens*.** Otherwise known as a peremptory norm of general international law, *jus cogens* is defined in Art. 53 of the Vienna Convention on the Law of Treaties (8 ILM 679 (1969)) as "a norm accepted and recognized by the international community of States as a whole as a norm from which no derogation is permitted and which can be modified only by a subsequent norm of general international law having the same character." As a result, a treaty (or possibly a provision in a treaty) in conflict with a peremptory norm is null and void from the very beginning (*ab initio*). If a new peremptory norm emerges, any existing treaty which is in conflict with this norm becomes null and void and terminates (Vienna Convention, Art. 64). Furthermore, the existence of a peremptory norm may have an impact upon a specific area of international law. Thus a state **(127)** that came into being by a violation of *jus cogens*, for example, aggression, cannot lawfully be granted recognition **(99)**; reservations to treaties **(282)** incompatible with it are disallowed; and extradition **(75)** to a state that could reasonably be suspected of inhuman treatment or persecution of the individual to be extradited could be denied.

The notion of *jus cogens* (in contrast to *jus dispositivum* meaning a rule that can be derogated from or modified by contrary agreement of the parties) can be traced back to Roman civil law with respect to private contracts, and to the classical writers in the law of nations for whom a treaty contrary to certain fundamental principles of the law of nations and nature could not be valid. The origin of the contemporary *jus cogens* dates back to the anti-colonialist campaign of developing countries for strengthening those rules of international law which upheld the self-determination of peoples **(122)** and condemned racial discrimination **(177)**. At the Vienna Conference on the Law of Treaties, the Western countries accepted the concept of *jus cogens* on the condition that a state invoking it would agree to submit a dispute over the determination of the peremptory norm in question to adjudication before the International Court of Justice (ICJ) **(309)**.

To qualify as *jus cogens*, a norm must be accepted and recognized by the international community of states *as a whole*, which, reasonably interpreted, means that the norm in question must have achieved consensus among all the essential and important groups of states, and especially of the major powers.

It is not entirely certain which rules of international law belong to peremptory norms of general international law. It is, however, universally accepted that first among them is the United Nations (UN) Charter and customary rule against unlawful use of force **(329)**. As stated by the ICJ in the case of *Military and Paramilitary Activities in and against Nicaragua* (Nicaragua v. United States of America) (1986 ICJ Rep. 14), the prohibition of force is "a conspicuous example of a rule of international law having the character of *jus cogens.*" Other suggested peremptory norms include self-determination of peoples, prohibition of genocide **(155)**, slavery **(180)**, crimes against humanity **(151)**, torture **(182)**, racial discrimination, piracy **(259)**, massive pollution of the environment **(197)**, and violations of the fundamental principles of international humanitarian law **(353)**.

As introduced in 1969, the concept of *jus cogens* could be invoked only by a state party to the Vienna Convention and with respect to a treaty that such state wanted to invalidate because of its alleged conflict with a peremptory norm of general international law. However, eventually the concept of *jus cogens* evolved into a norm of customary international law **(39)** and can now be invoked by a state that is not a party to the Vienna Convention, claiming that a treaty to which it is a party is incompatible with *jus cogens*. Moreover, within the context of the rules on invalidity of treaties **(275)**, any state directly affected by a treaty provision claimed to be in conflict with a peremptory norm may invoke invalidity.

It must be noted that, while peremptory norms have been referred to by courts in *obiter dicta* and have appeared in statements by UN bodies, there has not yet occurred any case of a treaty invalidated on grounds of *jus cogens* and the existence or not of a peremptory norm has not yet been judicially tested. Also, states, including the United States, for their own respective reasons have shown caution and restraint in developing the substantive content of *jus cogens* in the interests of the international community of states as a whole.

**25. *Jus Gentium*.** As distinguished from the civil law (*jus civile*) **(23)** which applied to the Roman citizens, *jus gentium*, roughly translated as the law of ethnic groups or the law of nations, was a major institution of the Roman legal system, governing private law relations of Roman citizens with foreigners and between foreigners themselves. In the Roman legal theory, *jus gentium*, being derived from natural reason, represented the law common to all mankind and in this sense was identified and blurred with natural law **(29)**. In fact, it was a common-sense application of natural law in the legal practice of the multi-ethnic Roman society. As an emanation of reason, it constituted a less formalistic replica of civil law.

*Jus gentium* evolved in the third and second century BC while Rome extended is rule over the whole of Italy, but had not yet granted Roman citizenship to the entire population of the peninsula. A special judge, *praetor peregrinus*, officiated at the head of the administration dealing with litigation among foreigners. In the course of time, the flexible rules of *jus gentium* prevailed over the more "legalistic" civil law, evolving into a common private law of the Roman Empire. Also gradually, because of its cosmopolitan nature, *jus gentium* became associated with something transcending the law of the empire and, expanding into some limited areas of relations with non-Roman political entities, exhibited some features of the future law of nations governing the relations between states.

Writing some 150 years following the fall of the Roman Empire, Isidore of Seville (c. 560–630), a Spanish theologian and encyclopaedist, included in his notion of *jus gentium* wars **(338)**, captivity **(364)**, peace treaties, and diplomatic immunities **(63)**, topics which much later became part of the law of nations as understood by the early publicists in international law in the 16th and 17th centuries. Thus the metamorphosis in the meaning of the term *jus gentium,* from the ancient private law system applied to foreigners to a system of law governing relations between states became accomplished by the time of Francisco Vitoria **(46)**, Francisco Suárez **(41)**, Albericus Gentilis **(15)**, Hugo Grotius **(16)**, and other classics of the early law of nations. One might add that today the term *jus gentium* is the Latin translation for the concept of modern public international law.

**26. Moser, Johann Jakob (1701–1785).** Prolific German writer on the public law of the Empire who also made a noteworthy contribution to the positivist school **(31)** of the law of nations. In his major 12-volume work, written like his other books in German, whose long original title could be briefly rendered as "Essay on the Most Recent European Law of Nations Concerning Peace and War," Moser abandoned natural law as vague and useless to govern relations between states. For Moser, the real law of nations consists of treaties **(40)** and custom **(39)** as gleaned from the actual conduct of states. His rather disorganized and lengthy volumes of the "Essay" lack any meaningful theoretical analysis, but include texts of treaties and other diplomatic instruments of interest to scholars in the history of international law.

By stressing reliance on actual state practice, Moser's work represents a major step in the development of the positivist doctrine. He is also counted among the early exponents of the monistic **(10)** point of view in its variation asserting the supremacy of municipal **(27)** over international law.

**27. Municipal Law.** In the terminology of international law, especially in the English usage, "municipal law" means the same as domestic, internal, or national law, the interchangeable terms which are also used in international law writings and practice. The relationship between international and municipal law has been, more in the past than today, a subject of doctrinal differences **(10)** and is regulated in a variety of ways by the law of each country.

**28. Municipal Law in International Law.** It is a well-established principle of international law that a state may not invoke provisions of its municipal law **(27)**, including even its constitution, or absence of provisions, as an excuse for non-compliance with international law. Endorsed in arbitral **(293)** and judicial **(306)** practice, this principle is also codified in Art. 27 of the Vienna Convention on the Law of Treaties of 1969. As a result, a state which has contracted a valid international obligation has the duty to modify its law in order to bring it into conformity with its obligations under international law. The municipal law of each state decides by what methods customary **(18)** and conventional **(19)** law are integrated into the domestic system In the eyes of international law, a provision of municipal law is merely a question of fact rather than of law, but municipal law is not entirely irrelevant. An international court may have to examine it in order to ascertain a state's position on a subject matter relevant for the case, or use it as evidence of the state's compliance with or breach of an international obligation. The court may also find it necessary to interpret municipal law, as, for example, the International Court of Justice (ICJ) **(309)** did in the case of *Elettronica Sicula S.p.A.(ELSI)* (United States of America v. Italy), (1989 ICJ Rep. 15), where the Court had to consider municipal judicial and administrative procedures for purposes of the requirement of exhaustion of local remedies **(74)**.

**29. Natural Law School.** A very influential school of thought in the doctrine of the early law of nations, prevalent in the classical writings through the 18th century, which taught that, like all law, the law of nations was merely part of the eternal and universally valid natural law (*jus naturale*) governing all men and states. The natural law philosophy has, of course, a very long and venerable tradition dating back to the Greek stoics who believed in the idea of the existence of norms transcending positive, that is, man-made law, and to natural law theories entertained by Roman thinkers. The latter viewed natural law either as a divinely inspired and supreme law, as propounded by Cicero, or, as understood by jurists, as a rational and practical notion which merged with the institution of *jus gentium* **(25)** and was established by natural reason for all mankind. Influenced by all these doctrines in their ancient varieties and by subsequent writings of medieval Church philosophers, especially St. Thomas Aquinas (1225–1274), the early classical writers saw the origin of law in the divine will, discoverable by pure reason and not attributable to any deliberate human action. The most famous of them, Hugo Grotius **(16)**, while not rejecting entirely the religious element in natural law, initiated a secular and rationalist trend which derived the principles of natural law from universal reason and otherwise recognized the existence of "voluntary," that is, positive law.

The natural law school of the law of nations reached its climax in the writings of Samuel Pufendorf **(33)**. This extreme but rationalistic naturalist flatly denied the validity of any positive norms based on custom and treaties, recognizing only natural law devoid of any divine connection and derived from pure reason. By the onset of the 19th century, the naturalist philosophy of the vague and transcendental law of nations had fallen out of vogue and was soon displaced by positivism **(31)**. However, it has remained as the foundation of legal theory for the Catholic Church.

In the formative stages of the law of nations the natural law philosophy played a constructive role in an age of transition from the Middle Ages to the modern state system. However, subjective and incapable of verification, its principles emphasizing reason, morality, and justice provided at least a modicum of restraint for the war-plagued European system of the rising territorial states, badly in need of some international legal foundation. It is significant that the 20th century witnessed a revival of natural law philosophy in various forms. While in general a positivist trend continued in the doctrine of international law, publicists of the naturalist tradition showed more concern for problems of justice and peace as well as the status of the individual in international law **(81)** along lines reminiscent of the classical school of natural law.

**30. Policy-Oriented Approach to International Law.** An outcome of cooperation between international jurists and political scientists in the second half of the 20th century, the policy-oriented approach to, or perspective on international law was developed by Myres S. McDougal (1906–1998) of Yale Law School and Harold D. Lasswell (1902–1978), a political scientist at Yale and a frequent contributor to the work of the "New Haven School," as the policy-oriented jurisprudence is sometimes called.

The policy-oriented approach is an application to international law of a decision-making conceptual framework, a number of which were elaborated in the study of foreign policy when political science in the United States, in its aspiration to be a real science, was going through its "behavioral" stage in the 1950s and 1960s.

The policy-oriented jurisprudence rejects as inadequate the traditional view of law as a static body of rules operating automatically apart from its political and social context and merely discovered to be applied by decision makers. It approaches international law as a constantly evolving and dynamic social process of authoritative decision making in which governments and other participants in this process continually formulate and reformulate policies to maximize their values in a flow of asserted and contested claims and counterclaims. International law is viewed as an instrument of policy for promoting a preferred "world order."

A complex conceptual framework formulated in the terminology of social and behavioral sciences is proposed by the policy-oriented jurisprudence to analyze the "constitutive process of authoritative decision-making." To summarize it briefly, first, both the decision makers and scholars, who deal with international law, should start by establishing and making manifest their observational standpoint which should be as free of bias as possible and ought to reflect the common interests of all people. Second, in order to facilitate the formulation of problems, the policy-oriented approach has developed a comprehensive but not exhaustive set of eight values or preferred events (respect, power, enlightenment, well-being, wealth, skill, affection, and rectitude), each supplemented by additional subcategories designed to assist in a detailed clarification of policy and help perform other intellectual tasks. The delimitation of the focus of inquiry into authoritative decisions constitutes the third element in the policy-oriented approach, incorporating into the inquiry concepts crucial to a viable comprehension of law, namely authority and control. The former includes the normative expectations of relevant social actors in the community about the identity of the decision makers, institutional arrangements, and the projected goals and criteria. The latter refers to the effectiveness in actual practice of the preferred choices. Here the policy-oriented jurisprudence stresses the need to relate decision making to the larger community interests in an interdependent world. The process of authoritative decisions is made up of two kinds of decisions, constitutive and public order. The former refer to the structures and procedures necessary for the process, performing seven decision functions (intelligence, promotion, prescription, invocation, application, termination, and appraisal) essential for maintaining the policy of the community. The latter are decisions resulting from the constitutive process which are designed to protect the community values The explicit postulation of public order goals is the fourth element of the policy-oriented framework. In this regard, the New Haven approach proclaims its stand for the basic values of human dignity and a free society. The fifth and final element of the outline of the policy-oriented approach is the performance of interrelated intellectual tasks, including the clarification of goals, the description of past decisional trends, the analysis of factors affecting decisions, the projection of future trends, and devising and evaluating policy alternatives.

While rather esoteric in the contemporary doctrine of international law, the policy-oriented approach is certainly a unique and most sophisticated though complex approach to law. It offers to international jurists insights into the social science dimensions of the law, providing them with a multifaceted and multidisciplinary framework of inquiry. However, a number of critical points has been raised with regard to the policy-oriented approach. Its complexity and cumbersome superabundance of a multitude of concepts has been a deterrent to international legal scholars not familiar with the behavioral science "metalanguage" which frequently masks propositions that can otherwise be expressed in the "traditional" terminology of international law. A major criticism is that the policy-oriented jurisprudence ignores the reality of the norms as they are recognized and applied in state practice and virtually dilutes the very concept of law in an ocean of interdisciplinary conceptualization. Moreover, despite a call for an objective and bias-free observational standpoint, the policy-oriented approach lends itself easily to a subjective manipulation, considering especially the role of such value-laden concepts as human dignity and free society.

**31. Positivism.** A school of thought in law, including international law, which recognizes as law only those rules (*jus positivum*) by which the states consent to be legally bound either expressly in a treaty **(40)** or tacitly through custom **(39)**. While the term positivism is used in a variety of meanings, in the doctrine of international law, positivists regard the actual behavior of states as the basis of the law. Consequently, positivist publicists reject all metaphysical speculation as useless and vague. They also make a point of distinguishing between what the law is and what it ought to be and to discover the existing law focusing on an empirical analysis of the practice of states.

Historically, certain positivist elements were noticeable already in the early classical writers of the prevalent natural law **(29)** orientation, such as Albericus Gentilis **(15)** and Hugo Grotius **(16)**. Grotius' concept of "voluntary law" (*jus voluntarium*) roughly corresponds to the notion of man-made positive law. Following Grotius, considered by some as the first eclectic **(11)**, the doctrine of the law of nations **(21)** gradually shifted toward a positivist approach away from the natural law perspective whose explanation of the binding force of international law did not accord with the pragmatic facts of state practice and a progressive laicization of intellectual life. Among the early positivists in the law of nations were such writers as Richard Zouche **(49)**, Cornelius van Bynkershoek **(4)**, and especially Johann Jakob Moser **(26)** who expressly denied the existence of natural law. Emmerich de Vattel **(45)**, however, continued the Grotian tradition of combining natural law with a mostly positivist approach. One might add here that in recognition of the importance of state practice for the analysis of international law, Georg Friedrich von Martens (1756–1821) of the University of Göttingen initiated the celebrated collection of treaties continued throughout many decades.

By the onset of the 19th century, positivism had become the dominant approach in the doctrine of international law and had virtually no rivals (apart from isolated survivors of the natural law school) until the 20th century. The ascendancy of positivism logically coincided with the rise of sovereign territorial states in Europe whose political and legal supremacy could not endorse any kind of international legal norms unless they were generated by their sovereign consent. In the 19th century a number of theories was devised by positivists in efforts to provide an explanation for the binding force of international law: the autolimitation theory **(2)**, the consensual or consent theory **(7)**, and, in the early 20th century, the pure theory of law of analytical positivism **(34)**. However, none of the theories advanced could come up with a convincing answer.

The major objective of criticism of the positivist approach to international law has been its claim that for their binding force international law rules depend solely upon the consent of states. This proposition may be true in the case of a new rule which states normally have an option to accept or ignore, but a new state is not considered to have any option to consent to or to turn down the rules of the system of which it becomes a member. Unless an obligation results from an express consent, in practice states do not always regard their obligations as based on their consent, and implied consent is therefore a fiction attempting to fit facts into a preconceived theory. Furthermore, a total negation of any principles and norms transcending the will of states would leave each state as the only judge of ethical standards in international society.

Notwithstanding the criticism leveled against positivism, its doctrines have made a fundamental contribution to international law by advancing the proposition that the rules of this law cannot be discovered by metaphysical speculation confusing reality with the ideal, but by an empirical inquiry into the actual practice of states.

**32. Private International Law (Conflict of Laws).** Private international law or conflict of laws is that branch of municipal law **(27)** which lays down rules in cases between private persons involving a significant foreign element, which are designed to resolve conflicts over the allocation of court jurisdiction **(87)**, the choice of applicable law, and the recognition and enforcement of foreign judgments. The area of conflict of laws, of special significance in the federal United States (US) with a multiplicity of states' jurisdictions, is also important in international relations, typically in cases involving the law of domicile, contracts, torts, personal law, including marriage and divorce, inheritance, nationality **(175)**, recognition and enforcement of judgments, and the like. In such cases, a municipal court must decide which country's court has jurisdiction or which country's law is applicable in a given situation with a significant foreign element. The decision to find the applicable law is made according to the conflict-of-law rules of *lex fori,* that is, the law of the court's jurisdiction.

A diversity of national rules on private international law may lead to hardship for individuals, for example in the area of recognition of marriages and divorces. In order to remedy such situations, states have tried to harmonize their conflict-of-law rules by means of bilateral and multilateral treaties **(288)**, such as those adopted on a regional basis in Latin America and within the European Union. In such cases, if a certain subject matter within the area of private international law has been regulated in a treaty, the adopted conflict-of-law rules acquire the character of public international law. Furthermore, in some circumstances even a municipal conflict-of-law rule, such as, for example, one governing a state's jurisdiction, may by itself affect interests of another state and implicate issues of public international law. The act of state doctrine **(51)** may, in a sense, be viewed as a special principle within the general area of conflict of laws.

**33. Pufendorf, Samuel (1632–1694).** A German publicist on the law of nature and nations and the first professor of the newly founded chair in this subject at the University of Heidelberg and subsequently the incumbent of a similar chair at the University of Lund in Sweden. Pufendorf wrote, among many other philosophical and legal works, a large volume with the title *De jure naturae et gentium libri octo* (Eight Books on the Law of Nature and Nations) (1672). In this work he completely denied the binding force of any voluntary or positive law of nations such as the practice of states **(39)** and treaties **(40)**, basing his system entirely on a moralistic natural law **(29)** which he, however, considered free from any divine connection and based on reason only. Pufendorf's naturalist extremism clearly departed from the general trend, but his ideas on natural equality of states and rejection of all claims to precedence were an important contribution to the history of the law of nations.

**34. Pure Theory of Law.** A general theory of law associated with the name of Hans Kelsen (1881–1973), a Prague-born Austrian jurist and founder of an analytical positivist approach to law which became known as the Vienna school. A professor of law in Vienna, Kelsen eventually moved to the United States where he continued research in legal theory, including in particular international law. Kelsen's pure theory of law, expounded in his *Die reine Rechtslehre* (Pure Theory of Law) (1934) and then in *General Theory of Law and State* (1945) became perhaps the leading legal theory in Europe.

Kelsen's pure legal theory or—as his approach is sometimes known—analytical positivism **(31)** approaches the legal system in a formalistic way as a value-free hierarchical structure of norms in the form of "ought" propositions where every norm depends for its authority on a superior norm, all the way in a step-structure of the law to the constitution and ultimately higher to the initial hypothesis or "basic norm" (*Grundnorm*). From the point of view of international law on which Kelsen published a treatise, *Principles of International Law* (1952), Kelsen's system represents the most radical form of monism **(10)** in which international law occupies the top of the hierarchy of norms, with all the municipal law **(27)** systems deriving their "delegated" binding force from the common root of international law. In this system, international custom **(39)**, with its principle of the duty to observe treaties (*pacta sunt servanda*) **(277)** as the basic norm, reaches a dead end in Kelsen's analysis, in view of his refusal to get involved in the necessarily extra-legal question of the reasons for the binding force of custom in international law.

**35. Soft Law.** A rather controversial but frequently used term in the doctrine and sometimes by practitioners of international law, referring to various categories of legally not binding instruments, such as treaties **(288)** not yet in force, voluntarily observed standards, written guidelines and codes of conduct issued by intergovernmental organizations **(84)** (mainly in international economic, financial, and environmental matters), final acts of international conferences, joint statements, gentlemen's agreements, certain resolutions of intergovernmental organizations, and in general all kinds of provisions in international instruments which are of a merely hortatory nature and, usually because of failure to reach consensus, do not constitute "hard law" clearly stipulating legally binding obligations. Among instances of soft law are such instruments as the Helsinki Final Act of the Conference on Security and Co-operation in Europe, 1975 (14 ILM 1292 (1975)) and the Declaration of the Rio Earth Summit, 1992 **(223)**.

While strictly speaking not binding norms of international law, some categories of soft law, and in particular various guidelines and codes of conduct issued by international organizations, clearly have impact upon the conduct of states which are sometimes hesitant to bind themselves by legally binding rules before testing them in practice. Therefore soft-law rules may eventually harden into legally binding custom **(39)** or be codified **(5)** in a treaty. Whether a given instrument is soft or hard law ultimately depends on the intention of its authors. One should also add that soft law may influence judicial decision making in the interpretation of hard-law rules.

The concept of soft law has been criticized as illogical (something is the law or is not), confusing, misleading, and even dangerous. Critics have charged it with blurring the distinction between the law in force (*de lege lata*) and the law in the process of formation (*de lege ferenda*) and, more generally, between what is actually binding and what is not. However, despite all criticism, international acts encompassed under the rubric of soft law continue to proliferate and, in practice, states tend to rely on soft law as a convenient notion in various areas of international relations.

**36. Sources of International Law.** Sources of international law are methods or ways and procedures by which the rules of international law are created. In this sense, the notion of the source serves to identify a rule as a binding legal norm and differentiate it from other, non-legal rules, for example norms of morality, social behavior, or comity **(6)** and from rules of law as they may or ought to be in the future (*lex ferenda* as opposed to *lex lata*). The notion of the sources of international law as here defined must not be confused with sources in the meaning of the basis of obligation in international law, that is finding an answer to the question why this law is binding, for example because of natural law **(29)**, or what its causes are, with reference to various factors which ultimately may account for the existence of international law, such as reason, expedience, or social needs.

Unlike municipal law **(27)**, where ascertaining a source of law is relatively easy because of a hierarchically structured legal system, with a constitution, statutes, court cases, etc., the identification of the sources of law to govern an international law situation is more complex in the international system of today without a legislature and, in principle, no compulsory adjudication **(306)**.

Historically, as in other, less-developed legal systems, custom **(39)** based on practice has been by far the most common and important category of source, and even today is still the major source in certain areas of international law. However, in the 20th century treaties **(40)** became the major source, with a large number of multilateral "law-making" treaties **(288)** codifying **(5)** and regulating many areas of the law. Since the second half of the 20th century, when the international political system became much more heterogeneous, treaties have had to take into account the concerns of many new states created by overseas decolonization and subsequently a similar process with regard to the break up of the Soviet Union **(133)** and Yugoslavia **(134)**. An important development was the emergence of the hierarchical concept of peremptory norms of international law (*jus cogens*) **(24)** reflecting international consensus on some fundamental values.

A generally accepted list of sources of international law is provided in Art. 38 of the Statute of the International Court of Justice (ICJ) **(309)** which follows the wording of the Statute of the Permanent Court of International Court of Justice **(320)**. Strictly speaking, it is limited to adjudication by the ICJ, but the phrase "in accordance with international law" found in Art. 38 allows one to view it as a general rule transcending the provisions which apply to the Court, especially in view of the fact that the ICJ is universally recognized as the most authoritative judicial body in international law and, practically speaking, all the states are bound by the Statute of the ICJ which constitutes an integral part of the United Nations (UN) Charter. Art. 38 reads as follows:

1. The Court, whose function is to decide in accordance with international law such disputes as are submitted to it, shall apply:
   a. international conventions, whether general or particular, establishing rules expressly recognized by the contesting States;
   b. international custom, as evidence of a general practice accepted as law;
   c. the general principles of law recognized by civilized nations;
   d. subject to the provisions of Article 59, judicial decisions and the teachings of the most highly qualified publicists of the various nations, as subsidiary means for the determination of rules of law.
2. This provision shall not prejudice the power of the Court to decide a case *ex aequo et bono,* if the parties agree thereto.

Art. 59 lays down that "The decision of the Court has no binding force except between the parties and in respect of that particular case."

In doctrinal terms, the formulation of Art. 38 adopts a modified positivist **(31)** approach. While accepting treaties and custom as the primary sources, it does not follow strictly the view that the will of states is the only basis of international law. The definition of custom refers to evidence of a "general" rather than "universal" practice and the general principles of law **(38)** are raised to the same status as the other two sources.

Since the adoption of the Statute, and especially in the decades following World War II, state practice has distilled from treaty and customary rules certain general principles of international law which provide a sort of common denominator of more specific norms of conduct in certain vital areas of international law. Some of these principles are included in Art. 2 of the UN Charter, and a more extensive roster of such principles (which some might regard as a discrete source of international law or treat them as general principles of law under Art. 38(1)(c) of the ICJ Statute), accepted as fundamental standards for the conduct of states, can be found in the General Assembly Friendly Relations Declaration of 1970 **(14)**. General principles of international law have also been abstracted in specific branches of the law, such as, for example, international environmental law **(197)** and international humanitarian law **(353)**.

Legally binding decisions which international organizations are empowered to adopt pursuant to their respective constituent treaties **(37)** could be regarded as separate new sources although they are ultimately generated by consent of the parties and are, in a sense, a kind of secondary treaty law. As stipulated in Art. 38(2), the *ex aequo et bono* principle **(13)** may be used as a source of law in specific cases, but only "if the parties agree thereto." However, judicial decisions **(22)** which are not based on the *ex aequo et bono* principle are not sources of international law but only "subsidiary means for the determination of rules of law." While there may be some doctrinal controversy over their exact nature, they are subsidiary means to be used in proving the existence of a rule of international law. The same is true of the teachings of the publicists **(42)**. Although not listed in Art. 38, unilateral acts of states **(44)** may, in exceptional situations, generate an international legal obligation and to that extent constitute a source of international law.

As far as the ranking of the sources is concerned, in the traditional international law, custom and treaties were of equal status and the relations between them followed the old maxims of civil law **(23)** that a subsequent law prevails over an earlier one (*lex posterior derogat priori*), but that a subsequent general law yields to an earlier law of a special character (*lex posterior generalis non derogat priori speciali*), and that a special rule prevails over a general law (*lex specialis derogat legi generali*). The drafting history of Art. 38, still within the context of the traditional international law, shows that its provisions do not establish any hierarchical order of sources. However, conflicts, especially between custom and treaty, do occur. In principle, custom and treaty have equal authority, with the later in time prevailing. Modification of customary law by treaty has become quite common due to the codification and progressive development of international law **(5)**. Ordinarily, a treaty provision overrides, as between the parties, a prior inconsistent rule of customary law except where that rule has the character of *jus cogens*. Special rules govern relations between successive inconsistent treaties **(284)**, with the privileged status of the UN Charter guaranteed by its Art. 103. A new rule of customary law supersedes any inconsistent provision of an earlier treaty if that is clearly the intention of the parties, as has been the case for a number of provisions of the four Geneva law of the sea conventions adopted at the 1958 Geneva Conference **(243)**. A treaty may also cease to bind by desuetude, that is, fall out of use through a consistent failure to follow its provisions by a party or parties acquiesced in by the other party or parties. As noted in an *obiter dictum* of the ICJ in its judgment in *Military and Paramilitary Activities in and against Nicaragua* (Nicaragua v. United States of America) (1986 ICJ Rep. 14), custom and treaty identically regulating a subject matter may legally coexist and if for jurisdictional reasons (if a state is not a party), a treaty rule cannot be used as a source, the Court can still have jurisdiction based on customary law as incorporated or reflected in the treaty. Hence the customary international law, comprised of rules identical to those of a later treaty, is not superseded but continues to have a further existence of its own. As a source of international law, general principles of law yield to treaty and custom in the case of conflict.

**37. Sources of International Law: Binding Acts of International Organizations.** These acts are rules, decisions, and legal standards which an organ of an intergovernmental organization **(84)** is authorized to adopt, usually by an ordinary or qualified majority, pursuant to the constituent treaty of the organization, and which are legally binding only on the member states of the organization. They are secondary sources **(36)** in the sense that they are derived from a traditional source of international law, namely a treaty **(40)**, and to that extent they are not considered by some scholars, let alone the International Court of Justice (ICJ) **(309)**, as a separate source. Binding acts of international organizations are not listed among the ICJ sources and subsidiary means for the determination of rules of law in Art. 38 of the Statute of the Court which follows the wording of its predecessor, the Permanent Court of International Justice **(320)**. The Statute was drafted at a time when international organizations were only in the incipient stages of their development and their impact upon international law was quite negligible. However, a rapid proliferation of such organizations since 1945 has raised the question of their impact upon the development of international law and in particular the status of their resolutions and other acts in relation to the problem of the sources of this law.

Under express provisions of the United Nations (UN) Charter, the General Assembly (GA) can adopt decisions relating to the internal matters of the organization which are binding on both the members and the organs of the UN; they have a full effect of rules of international law. Here belong, first of all, the budgetary matters (Art. 17); adopting rules of procedure (Art. 21); establishing subsidiary organs (Art. 22); and admission, suspension, and expulsion of members (Arts. 4, 5, 6). Similar provisions exist in other intergovernmental organizations, including the specialized agencies of the UN. Among the latter, the International Monetary Fund and the International Civil Aviation Organization (ICAO), for example, have the power under their respective constituent instruments to adopt, by a majority vote, rules and regulations concerning their respective spheres of activity. The ICAO-adopted standards concerning the safety of air traffic are among the best-known acts in this category. Because of the unique nature of the European Communities, the power of the Council of Ministers to issue various categories of acts (regulations, directives, and decisions), which directly bind the member states, represents a special case of treaty-based power of international organizations to generate sources of international law. Under the universally accepted doctrine of implied powers, endorsed and developed in the advisory opinion (**291**) of the ICJ on *Reparations for Injuries Suffered in the Service of the United Nations* (1949 ICJ Rep. 174), an international organization whose constituent instrument lacks express relevant powers may adopt such measures as are necessary for an effective and efficient performance of its functions.

The most important power to adopt legally binding resolutions is vested in the Security Council (SC) when it acts under Chapter VII of the UN Charter in implementation of the UN collective security system (**327**). Art. 25 of the Charter provides that "The Members of the United Nations agree to accept and carry out the decisions of the Security Council in accordance with the present Charter." Moreover, it is a principle of the UN that it has a duty to "ensure that States which are not Members of the United Nations act in accordance with [the UN] Principles so far as may be necessary for the maintenance of international peace and security" (Art. 2(6)). In view of the virtually universal membership of the UN, this provision appears to be redundant, at least for the time being.

While the above-noted power of the GA to adopt, by virtue of specific Charter provisions, legally binding acts is uncontested, the legal nature of other resolutions has been a matter of controversy. The question is whether many, politically sensitive, resolutions, especially those adopted unanimously, for example, the outer space (**215**) resolutions of the early 1960s, are themselves a source of international law or may only be considered as examples of state practice contributing among other elements to the possible emergence of customary international law according to general rules governing custom as a source of international law (**39**). Despite opinions voiced in Third World countries (which otherwise enjoy a majority of votes in the GA) that such resolutions create international law and thus are one of its sources, the view prevails that they are not and therefore are not legally binding. Such was also the opinion of a great majority of states at the San Francisco Conference on International Organization which was against conferring upon the GA the power to legislate.

Logically, a resolution declaratory of an otherwise existing customary rule can be regarded as evidence of customary law, but its evidentiary value varies depending on the circumstances. While the size and composition of the majority voting for the resolution is a relevant factor, even a unanimous resolution cannot, by itself, be considered as conclusive evidence of customary law if circumstances point to a politically motivated vote. Adopted by consensus or by unanimous or nearly unanimous vote, some resolutions, often known as declarations, have been recognized as reflecting a general *opinio juris*, that is, a sense of legal obligation, of the international community and have acquired the status as authoritative evidence of international law. Examples are: the 1960 Declaration on the Granting of Independence to Colonial Territories and Peoples; the above-noted resolutions concerning outer space; and the Friendly Relations Declaration of 1970 (**14**). On the other hand, a number of resolutions, such as those involving economic interests of Third World countries, for example the Declaration and the Program of Action on the Establishment of a New International Economic Order, 1974 (13 ILM 720 (1974)) and the Charter of Economic Rights and Duties of States, 1974 (14 ILM 251 (1975)), which were adopted against a small but strongly dissenting minority of important countries, are accorded much less weight as evidence of customary law.

However, despite the fact that only a limited number of GA resolutions have been accepted as declaratory of customary law, other resolutions cannot be lightly dismissed as instruments devoid of any legal significance. The votes in the GA are manifestations of a more or less "collective" state practice. Hence GA resolutions which, as such, are not a product of a treaty process can be instrumental in formulating new trends and then generate new rules of customary law if they acquire elements of consistency and uniformity through supportive subsequent resolutions, favorable state practice, and international adjudication **(306)**. Thus, in certain exceptional cases, acts of international organizations, which are otherwise not legally binding but represent a collective expression of state practice, may provide evidence for a gradual evolution of *opinio juris* necessary for the formation of customary law.

**38. Sources of International Law: General Principles of Law.** An independent, albeit secondary and much less used, source of international law, refers to general principles of law, common to the major legal systems of the world. The provision of Art. 38(1)(c) of the International Court of Justice (ICJ) **(309)** Statute on "the general principles of law recognized by civilized nations" as a category of sources of international law is interpreted to mean *all* states.

While the exact meaning of the not entirely clear phrase "general principles of law" has been a matter of some controversy since the very drafting of the Statute of the Permanent Court of International Justice (PCIJ) **(320)** more than 80 years ago, in general the view prevails that the phrase refers to general principles of law, some of them simply a matter of legal logic, common to many municipal **(27)** systems of law, to which recourse can be made if they are compatible with the international law situation involved. In the past, especially in the early period of the formation of the law of nations in the rising system of European territorial states, the less developed system of its rules would prompt jurists and decision makers to resort to principles of civil (Roman) law **(23)** in order to fill in gaps in the law or resolve problems of interpretation **(274)**. Later, in the 19th century, arbitral tribunals **(293)** would make use of general principles, including, *inter alia*, state of necessity **(96)**, *force majeure* **(78)**, and denial of justice **(152)**. More recently, in the 20th century, when international custom **(39)** and conventional, that is, treaty, law **(40)** developed sufficiently, gradually absorbing a number of general principles from municipal laws, the PCIJ occasionally but rather sparingly used the provision on general principles in order to provide supplementary argument to reasoning normally based on custom and treaties. Among the principles resorted to by the PCIJ were, among others, the duty of reparation **(118)** for breach of international obligation, referred to in the often-quoted case (merits) of *Factory at Chorzów* (Germany v. Poland) (1928 PCIJ, Series A, No. 17) and the principle that nobody can be judge in his own case (*nemo judex in causa sua*) invoked in the advisory opinion **(291)** on *Interpretation of Article 3, Paragraph 2 of the Treaty of Lausanne* (1925 PCIJ, Series B, No. 12). Among the few general principles invoked by the ICJ has been the paramount principle of good faith, referred to in the *Nuclear Tests* cases (Australia v. France; New Zealand v. France) (1974 ICJ Rep. 253, 457). This principle is also included in the United Nations Charter (Art. 2(1)) and the Friendly Relations Declaration, 1970 **(14)**, among other instruments.

The emergence of new areas of international law, such as international administrative law and international criminal law, prompted international courts to resort to general principles of law to apply them in the area of international law corresponding to the pertinent branch of the municipal law. For example, the International Criminal Tribunal for the Former Yugoslavia **(352)** referred in a case to the proportionality of penalty to the gravity of the crime, as a general principle of law.

It might be added that in disputes over contracts between a state and a foreign (transnational) **(140)** corporation resort is occasionally made to general principles of law as the law applicable to the merits of disputes concerning such "internationalized contracts."

The inclusion in the ICJ Statute of the rather ambiguous and open-ended provision on the general principles of law as a source of international law independent of custom and treaty can be considered as a potentially significant development in the history of international law which may open a path toward a progressive strengthening of this law in such areas as, for example, human rights **(160)** and international humanitarian law **(353)**.

**39. Sources of International Law: International Custom.** Despite certain conceptual difficulties, custom as international law can, in common sense and in accordance with actual international practice, be defined as general and consistent practice of states followed by them from a sense of legal obligation or, in the case of a permissive rule, the belief that the conduct in question is not prohibited. Until the second half of the 20th century, custom was the principal source of international law. Even in the new century large areas of international law are still guided by custom, complementing the otherwise well-developed treaty law **(40)**. Thus in the area of the law of the sea **(254)** conflicting economic interests of states cannot be promptly accommodated by treaties. As illustrated by the institutions of the continental shelf **(236)** and the exclusive economic zone (EEZ) **(238)**, the practice initiated by some states was eventually joined by others, thus contributing to the creation of new customary rules. Another interesting instance of an emerging customary rule, this time on a sensitive political issue, is the modification of Art. 27(3) of the United Nations Charter concerning the voting in the Security Council whereby abstention of a permanent member is not considered a veto.

Custom in international law is made up of two elements: the material, behavioral element of concordant and general practice (*usus*) of states and the psychological element, known as *opinio juris*, which entails the conviction that the conduct in question is not just habit or usage and stems from a legal obligation under international law and not from other motives, such as courtesy or comity **(6)**, fairness, morality, tradition, or expedience. Unlike treaties, custom is not a product of deliberate creation of international law. As demonstrated by the above examples from the law of the sea, originally the practice in question may evolve under economic, social, or political necessity only among certain states which claim the necessity for such practice (*opinio necessitatis*). Eventually other states join or acquiesce in the practice, with states gradually believing and taking for granted that the practice is enjoined by international law and "that they are conforming to what amounts to a legal obligation," as put by the International Court of Justice (ICJ) in the *North Sea Continental Shelf* cases (Federal Republic of Germany/Denmark; Federal Republic of Germany/Netherlands) (1969 ICJ Rep. 3). This psychological ingredient of customary law is considered crucial by the consensual and other positivist **(31)** doctrines of international law The notion of practice may include not only positive acts but also negative conduct (absence of action, omissions). Where a prohibitory rule of international law applies, it is appropriate to ascertain that a state's abstention from the prohibited conduct results from its recognition of *opinio juris* and not other motivation, as noted by the United States (US) Supreme Court in *The Paquete Habana; The Lola* case, 1900 (175 U.S. 677) and the Permanent Court of International Justice (PCIJ) **(320)** in *The Lotus* case (Turkey/France) (1927 PCIJ, Series A, No. 10).

"Evidence of a general practice accepted as law" can be found in published governmental documentation concerning foreign affairs, such as diplomatic correspondence, statements at international conferences, etc., as well as in indications derived from national legislation, regulations, and instructions, municipal court decisions, and the like. Obtaining relevant information, especially on national conduct may sometimes be difficult. Following the US example of publishing multivolume "Digests" of practice, some other countries record their respective practice in international law in similar volumes. Records of international organizations can also be useful as a source of evidence of custom. Judicial decisions, which under Art. 38(1)(d) are "subsidiary means for the determination of rules of law," can also carry weight in ascertaining whether a certain customary conduct of states has crystallized into a rule of law. Furthermore, a multilateral treaty declaratory of, or otherwise codifying customary law can be invoked as evidence of the existence of the law. In the course of time a multilateral treaty may also be accepted as customary law by the entire community of nations, as demonstrated by the 1856 Declaration of Paris **(344)** on maritime war and neutrality. Whether bilateral treaties habitually including similar or the same rules and widely adhered to in international practice, such as extradition **(75)**, can be considered as evidence of customary law depends on the circumstances and the intention of the parties.

To constitute international law, custom must be general, which, however, does not necessarily mean universal. There exists no formula indicating a precise number of states involved in a certain activity needed for the practice to be qualified as customary law. Existence or absence of protest is an important element in determining the generality of a given practice. Usually, the practice in question reflects wide acceptance among the states that have been involved in the related activity. For example, it is obvious that the practice of maritime nations, especially Great Britain, largely contributed to the emergence and eventual universal adoption of the customary law principle of the freedom of the sea **(242)**. More recently, the United States and the former Soviet Union were the leaders in developing the customary law of outer space **(215)**. A new trend in customary law may originate with a widespread practice of small states, as was the case of the EEZ, but even in such cases failure of a significant number of important states to join the practice may prevent it from becoming a rule of customary law. State practice in a particular region may lead in a certain matter to the emergence of regional or particular law for those states only, but as an exception to general international law it is subject to more rigorous standards of proof of the existence of the law than those applied for general international law, a problem examined by the ICJ in the *Asylum* case (Colombia/Peru) (1950 ICJ Rep. 266).

Since no universality is required for the emergence of customary rules, a state may be bound by such a rule on grounds of acquiescence. But it is a matter of some controversy whether a state, explicitly and consistently dissenting from a practice while the rule is still in its formative stage, is therefore not bound by that rule after it matures into customary law. Among the rare examples of such "persistent objectors" was Norway, which insisted on the use of straight baselines **(233)** in the delimitation of some of its coastal waters, a method that differed from the prevailing practice. The issue was brought to the ICJ by the United Kingdom and became the subject of a celebrated decision in the *Fisheries* case (United Kingdom v. Norway) (1951 ICJ Rep. 116) in which the Court ruled in favor of Norway, subject to certain strict criteria for drawing straight baselines. A persistent objector's point of view may eventually prevail in general international law; otherwise the long-term position of such a state may become untenable against an overwhelming majority of states. Although contested by many new states, the prevailing view is that states newly entering the international system are bound by customary international law as a whole at the time of their birth as new subjects of international law **(85)**, despite the fact that they did not participate in the formation of the law.

Although historically the growth of custom has been a slow process, international law does not lay down any requirements concerning the time span necessary for the formation of customary law. The practice needed to generate it may be of a comparatively short period provided that other, more important, criteria are met, as analyzed by the ICJ in the above-noted *North Sea Continental Shelf* cases. Thus customary law rules governing sovereignty over national airspace **(186)**, and the rules concerning the continental shelf and the EEZ, developed quite rapidly, as did the principles of the law of outer space. In an age of rapid communication, the practice of states becomes more quickly known, thus reducing the time needed to determine their position on a potential rule.

All this, and especially the rule on the freedom of overflight by foreign-registered satellites **(220)** prompted some international jurists to propose the concept of "instant customary law" (*droit spontané*) requiring only a single act and based merely on *opinio juris*. This controversial notion has been criticized as self-contradictory and otherwise inadequate for developing customary law in controversial areas. It was also implicitly rejected by the ICJ in its judgment in the case of *Military and Paramilitary Activities in and around Nicaragua* (Nicaragua v. United States of America) (1986 ICJ Rep. 14) in which the Court reaffirmed the traditional view that for a rule of customary law to exist, *opinio juris* must be confirmed by practice. However, it is argued by some that because of the nature of international humanitarian law **(353)**, where humanitarian considerations dictate an urgent application of measures to protect victims of conflict, the requirement of the practice of states (the behavioral ingredient of customary law) is less important than *opinio juris* justifying the application of international humanitarian rules before a full evolution of the pertinent practice. This reasoning is corroborated by the universally recognized Martens Clause of 1899 **(359)**, according to which principles of general international law are generated not only by state practice but equally by laws of humanity and dictates of public conscience, the latter two sources more relevant in regulating armed conflict.

It may be difficult to discover the real reason for a state's conforming to a certain practice; hence the point in time when a given practice crystallized into law is not easy to determine, as illustrated in the above-noted case of *The Paquete Habana; The Lola* before the US Supreme Court (1900) which examined in detail how the rule of exempting coastal fishing vessels from capture had gradually matured into customary law. In a number of decisions, the ICJ has provided general guidelines concerning the methods used to discover the existence of *opinio juris* as a necessary ingredient of customary law. Normally, in cases of a well-settled rule, parties hardly ever submit evidence of *opinio juris*, but in situations of conflict when the state of the law is at issue, official statements and other explicit evidence are more likely to be adduced. In some cases the ICJ and its predecessor the PCIJ refused to presume the existence of *opinio juris* from the mere repetitiveness of a line of conduct, requiring a more rigorous proof for the recognition of the legal nature of the practice in question (the above-quoted cases of *The Lotus* before the PCIJ and *North Sea Continental Shelf* and *Military and Paramilitary Activities* before the ICJ).

International law needs to be flexible enough to adapt to new developments. If consensus is present, a new rule can emerge quickly, as in the cases of the continental shelf and outer space. On the other hand, as illustrated by the history of the EEZ (and incidentally, in the more distant past, by the very long time needed for the freedom of the sea to assert itself as a legal principle), a new practice, initiated by relatively few states, may initially be condemned and protested against as a violation of the law, but eventually, in a realistic appraisal of the situation, universally accepted and codified. But on such controversial issues as compensation for the expropriation of foreign-owned property **(145)** or the legality of the use of nuclear weapons **(367)** the emergence of *opinio juris* may take a very long time indeed. As noted by the ICJ in its advisory opinion **(291)** on the *Legality of the Threat or Use of Nuclear Weapons* (35 ILM 809 (1996)) the emergence of consensus on a rule of customary international law "is hampered by the continuing tension between the nascent *opinio juris* on the one hand, and the still strong adherence to the practice of deterrence on the other."

**40. Sources of International Law: Treaties.** By whatever label designated, treaties **(288)**, that is, written international agreements between two or more states, or—a much less common occurrence—other subjects of international law, governed by international law, have surpassed custom **(39)** as the most important source **(36)** of this law. The International Court of Justice (ICJ) **(309)** is directed by its Statute (Art. 38(1)(a)) to apply in its decisions "international conventions, whether general or particular, establishing rules expressly recognized by the contesting States." On the dawn of the new century there were approximately 50,000 treaties in force regulating virtually all aspects of international relations. Unlike customary (general) law, they offer a deliberate and, as a rule faster and more precise and convenient method of generating legal rules between and among states. Both bilateral (bipartite) treaties, that is, agreements between two states, and multilateral (multipartite) treaties, that is, agreements concluded by more than two states, are legally binding only on the parties. Private-law contracts between states are normally governed by the municipal law **(27)** of one of the parties; they are not considered treaties under international law. Contracts between a state and a foreign enterprise, for example an oil company, may be "internationalized" by placing them under general principles of law **(38)** or international law. Treaties are not only the major source of international law (the "conventional law" as distinguished from customary law) but themselves constitute an important area of international law, known as the law of treaties.

By far the largest number of treaties belong to bilateral agreements or agreements entered into by a very limited number of states. Such agreements, not unlike contracts in private law, establish mutual rights and obligations of the parties which are of interest only to them and normally of no direct concern to other states for which they are not sources of general international law but merely legal transactions between other subjects of this law. Such agreements, sometimes, perhaps misleadingly, known in the doctrine as "contractual treaties" (*traités-contrats*) are not sources of general international law for the international community as a whole, but still constitute a source of international law for the parties concerned. They are governed by the law of treaties in the same way as the other category of international agreements, often referred to as "law-making treaties" (*traités-lois*) which are multinational treaties very roughly comparable to municipal legislation and sometimes, rather optimistically, are referred to as "international legislation." In practice, there have also been instances of multilateral treaties which contain provisions of both contractual and law-making nature. The Peace Treaty of Versailles with Germany, 1919, (225 CTS 188) is an example. A bilateral treaty, such as for example the Treaty of Washington, 1871, between Great Britain and the United States concerning the settlement of the *Alabama* dispute in an eventual arbitration **(293)** may also generate law-making rules, in this case some rules concerning obligations resulting from neutrality **(362)**.

The law-making treaties are multilateral agreements open to all states which, while formally binding only the states parties, lay down rules of a general character, of interest to all the international community. To the extent that a great many states, including a significant number of important ones, adhere to such treaties or accept their provisions as rules of international law, law-making treaties may become customary law for non-parties except perhaps those that have persistently objected to them. Furthermore, as also recognized by the ICJ (*North Sea Continental Shelf* (Federal Republic of Germany/Denmark; Federal Republic of Germany/Netherlands) (1969 ICJ Rep. 3); and *Military and Paramilitary Activities in and around Nicaragua* (Nicaragua v. United States of America) (1986 ICJ Rep. 14)), treaty rules may become customary law for third parties where a treaty rule is declaratory of an otherwise preexisting custom. As a result of the interrelationship between customary and treaty law, some rules, for example the prohibition of illegal use of force **(329)** or various branches of the law of the sea **(254)** are grounded both in customary and treaty law. This may be relevant if the two categories receive a different treatment under the municipal law.

Apart from such early instruments as the Declaration of Paris of 1856 **(344)** concerning certain maritime matters and neutrality **(362)** and the Hague Conventions of 1899 and 1907 **(350)**, a growing number of multilateral treaties have been adopted in "international legislation," either as part of the trend to codify and develop **(5)** customary law or to create new norms in areas of emerging international concern such as the environment **(197)** and human rights **(160)**, or exhibiting features of both processes.

Among the law-making treaties, the United Nations (UN) Charter, subscribed to by practically all states, occupies the most prominent place. It is paramount among all other treaties in that, under its Art. 103, in the event of a conflict between the members' obligations under the Charter and those under any other international agreement, the obligations under the Charter must prevail. The UN Charter is also the major example of a law-making treaty of a constitutional nature which is the constituent instrument of an international organization.

**41. Suárez, Francisco (1548–1617).** Spanish Jesuit and scholar in the scholastic tradition and professor of theology at the University of Coimbra in Portugal, then under Spanish rule. Among Suárez' prolific scholarly legacy to the early history of the law of nations is, apart from his ideas about just war **(333)**, his *Tractatus de legibus ac de Deo legislatore* (Treatise on Laws and God as Legislator), 1612, in which he provided the conceptual foundations of his theory of the international community of interdependent states governed by the eternal and universal natural law **(29)** supplemented by human usages and custom **(39)**, and changing over time. From a more general concept of *jus gentium* **(25)**, Suárez singled out "the law which all peoples and diverse nations ought to observe among themselves." This definition clearly refers to the law of nations in the meaning of today's public international law.

**42. Teachings of Publicists as Subsidiary Means for the Determination of Rules of Law.** Like judicial decisions **(22)**, "the teachings [in the French text *la doctrine*] of the most highly qualified publicists of the various nations" are under the Statute of the International Court of Justice (ICJ) **(309)** "subsidiary means for the determination of rules of law" (Art. 38(1)(d)). This means that the teachings of scholars in international law are not a source **(36)** of the law but only evidence as to whether a rule followed by states has really achieved the status of a legal norm.

Enormous quantities of publications in international law appear today, a fact that makes it difficult to identify "most highly qualified" publicists in a multicultural world of many nations. Any such identification must necessarily be a subjective one and may be susceptible to bias. The doctrines expounded by the International Law Commission and various private bodies involved in research in the area of international law, such as for example the International Law Association, probably enjoy considerable authority. Individual opinions **(304)** of judges can also be treated as expressions of opinion by most highly qualified publicists.

In making recourse to publicists, caution must be exercised not to confuse evidence of what the law is (*lex lata*) with speculation on what the law ought to be (*lex ferenda*), a distinction eloquently expressed by the United States Supreme Court in *The Paquete Habana; The Lola*, 1900 (175 U.S. 677). Publicists are often referred to in official legal opinions and cited in arbitral **(293)** and municipal **(27)** court decisions, on the whole more frequently in countries of the civil-law **(23)** tradition. The ICJ decisions have very few references to specific names of publicists, but it is obvious that writers are used extensively by the judges, many of whom have been publicists themselves. General references to the teachings of legal authorities and phrases such as "all or nearly all writers" and the like are quite common. References to specific authorities can be found in individual opinions of judges.

In the formative years of the law of nations, when international practice was still rather limited, classical writers, and especially Hugo Grotius **(16)** and Emmerich de Vattel **(45)**, fulfilled a by far more creative role in the development of international law than that played by publicists in modern times. But even today, while providing evidence for the determination of what the law is, the doctrine can play a constructive role in identifying areas requiring international legal regulation and proposing solutions to legal problems confronting international society.

**43. Transnational Law.** A term, advanced by some scholars in international law and coined in the early 1950s by a renowned international jurist, Philip C. Jessup, to encompass in one adjective all branches of law, and legal, especially commercial, transactions, and persons, especially the so-called transnational corporations **(140)**, which in their substance and range transcend national boundaries. The term is used to include both public and private **(32)** international law as well as those rules of municipal law **(27)** which relate to foreign relations. A major objective of introducing the term would be to fill in legal gaps in the regulation of transnational commercial relations by making recourse to universally recognized principles of law **(38)**, in particular in the area of concessions and other contracts between states and foreign corporations.

**44. Unilateral Acts.** A unilateral act is an act performed or conduct followed by a single state **(127)** or several states acting jointly, which produces legal effects with regard to other states. The legal status of unilateral acts belongs to the less-explored areas and their legal effects are not entirely clear in international law. The topic has been on the agenda for codification **(5)** by the International Law Commission which at its 53d session (2001) considered the fourth report of the special rapporteur exploring various aspects of unilateral acts.

Among the most common general unilateral acts are: declaration, notification, protest, renunciation and the related waiver. In addition, various specific categories of recognition **(106)** and certain specific acts performed by states in the process of treaty formation, such as signature **(283)**, acceptance and approval **(266)**, accession **(267)**, reservation **(282)**, and the like can also be included within the concept of the unilateral act.

Whether a unilateral act of a state has legal effects for other states depends on the circumstances and especially the intention of the state performing the act, a problem examined by the International Court of Justice (ICJ) **(309)** in the *Nuclear Tests* cases (Australia v. France; New Zealand v. France) (1974 ICJ Rep. 253, 457). The Declaration of Egypt of 1957 concerning the status of the Suez Canal **(261)** is universally recognized as a unilateral act with direct legal consequences for other states. A unilateral act whereby a state makes a promise toward another state of following a certain course of action gives rise to a binding legal obligation, but, as in other similar cases, cannot be lightly presumed. Sometimes an international instrument styled as a declaration is in fact an agreement governed by the law of treaties or, at least, contains a formal statement, often in the General Assembly, of important principles of international law.

Notification is a unilateral act related to a declaration which may be required by customary law, for example a notification of intended naval exercises on the high seas **(245)**. By notifying certain facts to other states, the state in question precludes other states from subsequently claiming that, lacking knowledge of those facts, they could ignore the legal arguments produced by them. The major objective of a protest by a state is to preserve or reserve its rights involved in a certain situation or express its lack of recognition of, or acquiescence in certain facts. Otherwise if a state fails to protest, its attitude may, under the circumstances, be construed as a tacit renunciation or waiver of the right involved, that is a unilateral act of abandoning a right. But renunciation or waiver, whether tacit or express, must be clear and cannot be inferred from the mere failure to act or passage of time.

**45. Vattel, Emmerich de (1714–1767).** Next to Hugo Grotius **(16)**, the most celebrated classical writer in the law of nations, Vattel was a Swiss who served in the diplomatic service of Saxony and author of a French-language manual of the law of nations with the title *Le Droit des gens ou Principes de la loi naturelle appliqués à la conduite et aux affaires des nations et des souverains* (The Law of Nations or the Principles of Natural Law Applied to the Conduct and Affairs of Nations and Sovereigns) (1758). This treatise, intended by the author to be a popular presentation of the philosophical ideas of Christian Wolff **(48)**, eventually acquired enormous authority in international diplomatic practice, was most copiously cited in courts (despite the author's lack of legal training), appeared in innumerable editions, and was translated into many languages. Vattel's work became especially popular in Great Britain and the United States.

Vattel is usually counted among the eclectic **(11)** or "Grotian" representatives of the doctrine. However, his notion of international law departed from the conception of the earlier classical publicists in that Vattel's idea of natural law follows the doctrine of the state of nature so fashionable in the 18th century. Accordingly he viewed states as free and equal individuals living in the state of nature before the establishment of civil society. States were endowed with certain inherent rights under this "necessary" law of nations or in fact the law of nature. They were accountable for the observance of their duties only to their conscience unless they voluntarily agreed to enforce such duties within the framework of the positive "voluntary" law of nations.

Vattel's overemphasis on the "natural" rights of the states and his unconvincing doctrine of the voluntary law of nations has had a disastrous and as yet unremedied impact upon the doctrine and practice of international law. His natural law supplied a rationale for the legal individualism of states and freedom bordering on anarchy, with overdeveloped substantive" fundamental" rights whereas his voluntary law of nations, based on each state's perceived interests and conscience, provided no reliable method of enforcing duties under international law.

**46. Vitoria, Francisco (1480–1546).** An important predecessor of Hugo Grotius **(16)** and the leading figure in the so-called Spanish school of the law of nations, Vitoria (known by the name of his native city, Vitoria) was a Dominican monk and professor of theology at the University of Salamanca. His posthumously published lectures *De Indis recenter inventis* (On Recently Discovered Indians) and *De jure belli Hispanorum in barbaros* (On the Law of War Made by the Spaniards against the Barbarians), given in 1532, demonstrated, in this otherwise staunch defender of the ecclesiastic authority and expert in the Holy Inquisition, a remarkably progressive and humane attitude on the issue of the Indians in the Spanish-conquered territories of the New World. While, in principle, favoring the conquest itself and the missionary work in the Spanish overseas possessions, Vitoria criticized the abuses of power and inhumane treatment of the Indians by the Spanish conquistadors, putting forward the then-remarkable thesis that according to the principles of natural law the Indian princes had a legitimate right to their lands and were entitled to the protection of the laws of war. He believed that war against the Indians could be waged only in a just cause **(333)**, such as resistance to evangelization or impeding freedom of commerce. In historical perspective, Vitoria must be considered as an early champion of the rights of the indigenous peoples **(163)** and a high-minded thinker in the era of the early colonization. His teaching represents an important step in expanding the binding force of the law of nations beyond the compounds of European Christendom.

**47. Westphalia, Peace Treaties of, 1648.** Two very important treaties, constituting an integrated peace agreement which brought to an end the devastating Thirty Years' War (1618–1648). Because of the disputed precedence problems, the peace was negotiated and signed at two places, Münster and Osnabrück. In the former, a Catholic city, where France was given precedence, peace was signed between Spain and the Netherlands (1 CTS 70) and between France and the Empire (1 CTS 319). In the latter, a Protestant city, Sweden, enjoying precedence, signed the treaty with the Empire (1 CTS 198). France and Sweden were made guarantors of the peace treaty.

The year of the Westphalian peace treaty is usually presented, actually more as a convenient date than for factual reasons, as the birth of the European system of territorial states (not—as sometimes anachronistically claimed—nation-states) and even international law itself. In fact, the major sovereign **(125)** territorial states and the law of nations had existed prior to 1648, but the Peace of Westphalia undoubtedly constitutes a landmark in the history of the European system of states and international law Of significance for the development of international law was the provision granting the more than three hundred members of the Holy Roman Empire, including principalities, duchies, bishoprics, etc. (certainly not "countries" as sometimes these feudal units are called), the right to enter into alliances with foreign powers and to wage war provided that the alliance was not against the Emperor or the Peace of Westphalia. Thus, despite certain surviving limitations, the status of all these German states and "ministates" approximated that of the other sovereign powers of Europe. The Treaty of Westphalia is also important because of its provisions on religious tolerance which were fully implemented despite the papal condemnation. The Treaty constituted a huge step in legitimizing the existence of Protestant states on equal footing with the Catholic ones. Of historical importance only were provisions on peaceful settlement of disputes **(318)**, including even the possibility of collective action against a state in breach of the treaty, which, however, remained a dead letter. In sum, the Peace of Westphalia formalized the balance of power and definitively legalized the existence of the European system of a plurality of independent states.

**48. Wolff, Christian (1679–1754).** A German professor of philosophy in the era of Enlightenment with a theoretical interest in the law of nations who represented the naturalist school of thought **(29)** in its state-of-nature version. Of interest to a student of the history of the doctrines about international law are Wolff's two works: *Jus gentium methodo scientifica pertractatum* (The Law of Nations Treated According to a Scientific Method) (1749) and *Institutiones juris naturae et gentium* (Institutes of the Law of Nature and of Nations) (1750), the latter being an abridgment of a previously published *opus magnum* on the law of nature.

Apart from his minutely and comprehensively elaborated theoretical scheme for the law of nature and nations, much of which was later adopted by Emmerich de Vattel **(45)**, Wolff is remembered for his rather confused hypothesis of *civitas maxima,* a sort of superstate resting on a pact or quasi pact for the promotion of common good. His idea, however, cannot be viewed as an idealistic scheme to ensure peace, such as *Projet pour rendre la paix perpétuelle en Europe* (A Plan to Secure a Perpetual Peace in Europe) (1713) by Abbé de Saint-Pierre or Immanuel Kant's *Zum ewigen Frieden: Ein philosophischer Entwurf* (Toward Perpetual Peace: A Philosophical Design) (1795).

**49. Zouche, Richard (1590–1660).** Albericus Gentilis' **(15)** successor in the chair of civil law **(23)** in Oxford, Zouche is sometimes characterized as the first positivist **(31)** in the doctrine of the law of nations. While not entirely abandoning natural law **(29)** he held custom **(39)** to be the most important source of international law **(36)**. His work *Juris et judicii fecialis, sive juris inter gentes et questionum de eodem explicatio* (Explanation of the *Jus Feciale[or Fetiale]* or the Law among Nations and of the Questions concerning It) (1650) has been called the first manual of positive international law. In this title Zouche used the term *jus feciale,* meaning a system of rules, governing declarations of war and making peace treaties in Rome in the era of the Kings and the early Republic, administered by a special category of Jupiter's priests charged with the administration of religious ceremonies concerning these matters.

An important contribution of Zouche to the development of the doctrine of international law was his division of the law of nations into the law of peace and the law of war, and placing the law of peace as a normal relationship between states, ahead of the exceptional state of war. It might be added here that his major work was published two years after the Treaty of Westphalia **(47)**.

# Chapter II
# International Legal Personality, States: Recognition, Jurisdiction, Responsibility, Succession

**50. Abuse of Rights.** A doctrine proclaiming that any arbitrary exercise of a right by a state in a way causing injury to another state **(127)** and not warranted by any legitimate assessment of the needs of the acting state constitutes a breach of international law. Following the civil-law **(23)** maxim *sic utere tuo ut alienum non laedas* (use your property so as not to do damage to others' property), the doctrine of the abuse of rights starts from the premise that even when undertaking acts that are not prohibited by international law, states ought to avoid acting in an arbitrary manner and exercise their rights with reasonable regard to the interests of other states. Examples of abuse of rights are: arbitrary expulsion of aliens **(146)**; abuse of the state's right to deprive someone of nationality **(175)**; or legitimate activities resulting in transborder pollution, as illustrated by the famous *Trail Smelter* Arbitration **(293)** in 1941 (3 RIAA 1905) where it was ruled that no state had the right to use or permit to use its territory **(228)** in such a manner as to cause injury by fumes in another state. Similarly, in the International Court of Justice (ICJ) **(309)** *Corfu Channel* case (United Kingdom v. Albania) (1949 ICJ Rep. 4) the Court referred to the obligation of every state not to allow knowingly its territory to be used for acts contrary to the rights of other states. The doctrine of abuse of rights is closely related to the topic of international liability **(120)** for injurious consequences arising out of acts not prohibited by international law.

The exact nature of the doctrine, its usefulness, and the extent of its application remain controversial. Some consider it to be a general principle of law recognized by civilized nations **(38)**; others see it as a principle of customary law **(39)**; and for still others it is simply a manifestation of good faith, and one of the general principles in the exercise of states' rights. According to an extreme view, the doctrine of abuse of rights as a general principle does not exist in positive international law.

**51. Act of State Doctrine.** A doctrine proclaiming that the courts of one country will generally refrain from challenging the validity of, or otherwise sitting in judgment on governmental acts of another state **(127)**, done by that state within its territory **(228)** and applicable there. The status and scope of the act of state doctrine in international law are uncertain and controversial. Even in the United States (US), where the doctrine has developed mainly with respect to foreign acts of state expropriating American property and has a long history of judicial support, it is viewed not as a rule prescribed by international law but, at most, as comity **(6)** and an expression of judicial restraint and deference toward the executive in matters of foreign policy as well as a manifestation of the constitutional principle of separation of powers. The act of state doctrine is related to state (sovereign) immunity **(131)** but, whereas under the law of sovereign immunity the commercial (*jure gestionis*) activities of a foreign state are normally carried on or are related to the state of the *forum,* that is, the place where the court has jurisdiction, and concern the jurisdiction of the court, as such, the act of state doctrine pertains to a judicial examination, on the merits, of a foreign state's activities in that state's own territory.

In the US, the act of state doctrine dates back to the statement of the Supreme Court in *Underhill v. Hernández* (168 U.S. 250) in 1897 that "[E]very sovereign State is bound to respect the independence of every other sovereign State, and the courts of one country will not sit in judgment on the acts of the government of another done within its own territory." More recently, in 1964, the doctrine was reexamined in *Banco Nacional de Cuba v. Sabbatino* (376 U.S. 398) where the US Supreme Court held that, subject to certain possible limitations, the judicial branch would not examine the validity of the taking of property **(145)** within its own territory by a foreign government. As long as foreign acts of state raised no fundamental issues of international law and in the absence of any serious conflict situation, the controversy over the status of the doctrine remained rather subdued. However, more recently, against the background of the Cold War and the conflict with Cuba, the Supreme Court refused to examine the validity of the Cuban expropriation even though the complaint alleged that it was in breach of customary international law **(39)**. In the Court's opinion, apart from the controversial nature of the customary rule involved, the Court would not examine the validity of the expropriation decree by a government recognized by the US "in the absence of a treaty or other unambiguous agreement regarding controlling legal principles." In reaction to the Court's strict adherence to the act of state doctrine, Congress enacted an amendment to the Foreign Assistance Act (the so-called Second Hickenlooper or Sabbatino Amendment), 1965, which effectively barred courts in the US from declining on grounds of the federal act of state doctrine to determine, on the merits, cases involving expropriations by a foreign state in violation of international law. To avoid subjecting all claims from acts of foreign states to examination by courts, the amendment provided that the doctrine was to be applied if in a particular case the President determined in a binding suggestion filed with the court that such application was required by US foreign policy interests. On the basis of the Hickenlooper Amendment (and the so-called Bernstein Exception, once enacted to exclude the oppressive acts of Nazi Germany from the scope of the act of state doctrine), in the absence of a presidential communication, the court is required to refrain from applying the doctrine. It may also decline to give effect to a foreign act of state on the grounds that it concerns penal or fiscal laws which under general international law are otherwise denied extraterritorial operation. In any case, the doctrine of the act of state does not apply to the taking by a foreign state of property located outside of its territory. A restrictive view of the doctrine is also taken in connection with war crimes **(373)** and violations of fundamental human rights **(157)**. Private acts of a foreign head of state have also been held to be subject to examination by US courts.

In view of the unclear status of the act of state doctrine there seems to exist no legal duty to apply it in relations between states and, unless barred by its municipal law **(27)**, a state might even give effect to a foreign act of state that is in conflict with international law. In practice, while most states exercise judicial restraint in restricting the application of the doctrine, they do not hesitate to examine the compatibility of foreign acts of state with international law and decline to apply the doctrine if an act fails to meet this test. A state may also ignore the doctrine for other reasons, such as non-enforcement of foreign revenue, penal or confiscatory laws, or conflict with the public policy (*ordre public*) of the *forum* state. Furthermore, although the act of state doctrine covers only official acts, it is closely related to private international law **(32)** and in countries of the civil-law **(23)** tradition municipal law regulating conflicts of law determines to what extent effect is to be given to foreign acts of state that might be in conflict with public international law.

**52. Associated State.** While in a more general sense member states of a confederation **(54)** or of the British Commonwealth could be regarded as associated states, in the United Nations (UN) terminology an associated state is a former non-self-governing territory or a former trust territory **(142)** which has reached a full measure of self-government by a free association with an independent state, usually the former metropolitan power, within the meaning of the General Assembly (GA) decolonization resolutions, such as Resolution 1541 of 1960, and the Friendly Relations Declaration of 1970 **(14)** which, *inter alia,* embodies the principle of self-determination of peoples **(122)**.

Association is one of the three specifically mentioned examples of the modes of implementing the right of self-determination. Although there may be some variations depending on the terms of the association, the associated territory is granted full independence in domestic affairs but continues to depend on the metropolitan power in matters of foreign policy and defense. According to the UN guidelines on the right to exercise the right of self-determination, the association must be freely chosen by the population of the territory, with the people's right of unilateral termination, and must promote the development of the associated state and the well-being of its population. To be legally effective, an association agreement must be approved by a special GA committee and—for trust territories—by the Trusteeship Council (and by the Security Council for strategic trust territories).

There have been very few cases of association because the GA has shown a decisive bias in favor of an early and prompt independence as against the options of association or integration with another state. There were six associated states set up by the United Kingdom in the Lesser Antilles area of the Caribbean in 1967, but they eventually became independent states, with Anguilla's constitution annulled and the island reverting to the status of dependent state. Association agreements are in force between New Zealand and Cook Islands, Niue, and Tokelau, respectively. The Netherlands has arrangements similar to association with Netherlands Antilles and Aruba.

The status of Puerto Rico as a "Commonwealth" since 1952 is in practice a form of association with the United States (US) as is also suggested by its Spanish name *estado libre asociado*. Puerto Rico has its constitution and legal system, and the Puerto Ricans are US citizens although without the right to vote in presidential elections. A Puerto Rican delegate (commissioner) has a voice in the US House of Representatives but can vote only in its committees. The international status of Puerto Rico has been a subject of controversy, with the GA Decolonization Committee raising the question of whether the island was a legitimate case of attaining self-government. However, in three referenda, the Puerto Ricans have voted for a continued association with the US, rejecting the options of independence and the status of a state within the US. The former strategic trust area of the Pacific Islands, once administered in four districts by the US, now includes three independent states, namely Marshall Islands, the Federated States of Micronesia, and Palau, and the former fourth trust territory, Northern Mariana Islands. The three states have compacts of association with the US, in force in 1986, 1986, and 1993, respectively, under which they have the capacity to conduct foreign affairs including the right to make treaties **(288)**, with the US having for at least 15 years responsibility for defense and obligated to provide economic assistance to each of the three states. Marshall Islands and the Federated States of Micronesia joined the UN in 1991, Palau following in 1994.

Under the Covenant of 1976 establishing a Commonwealth in political union with the US (15 ILM 651 (1976)) the Northern Mariana Islands have a status similar to that of Puerto Rico, but without a congressional delegate. Foreign affairs and defense are US responsibility, the islands being a self-governing Commonwealth under the sovereignty of the US. The former self-governing territory of Guam has also achieved the status of a Commonwealth in union with the US.

**53. Attribution.** Attribution or imputability is a legal construct whereby an internationally unlawful conduct of a state organ acting in that capacity is regarded as the conduct of the state itself, making that state responsible **(128)** for it as an internationally wrongful act. Imputability differs from causality in that it is the effect of rules of international law which attribute to the state responsibility for wrongful acts of the state's organs and its other agents. International law rules on attribution have been codified **(5)** by the International Law Commission as part of its Draft Articles on State Responsibility, submitted to the General Assembly in 2001 **(129)**.

A state is internationally responsible for its own acts and omissions, but as an abstract entity it can physically act only through individuals or groups of individuals performing "acts of the state" on its behalf. As recently (1999) noted by the International Court of Justice (ICJ) **(309)** in its advisory opinion **(291)** on *Differences Relating to Immunity from Legal Process of a Special Rapporteur of the Commission on Human Rights* (38 ILM 873 (1999)) "the conduct of any organs of a State must be regarded as an act of that State."

Ordinarily, a state is not responsible for acts committed by its nationals, for example, for an injury caused to an alien within a private context, unless, of course, the state failed to provide the alien reasonable protection or otherwise was to be blamed. State responsibility arises only if an action or omission can be attributed to it as an act of the state, a matter to be determined according to the rules governing attribution. In general, it is not difficult to impute an internationally wrongful act under international law to the state where such conduct results from action or absence of action of members of any state organ acting in that capacity, whether the organ exercises legislative, executive, judicial, or any other function, and regardless of its character as an organ of the central government or of a territorial component of the state. Attribution to the state of a conduct of officials in external relations is relatively easier in view of the fact that their authority to represent their state is well established in international law. In the more complex structure of domestic organs, attribution becomes more difficult. The *Rainbow Warrior* case **(104)** illustrates state responsibility for the conduct of its security organs. Although the status of any individual or an institution as a state organ is determined by municipal law **(27)**, a state is responsible in international law irrespective of any of its constitutional or other domestic rules and regardless of the manner in which it allocates functions to its organs. More generally, the criteria for attributing a conduct to the state according to international law prevail over any conflicting provisions of the municipal law. The conduct of various instrumentalities and other entities empowered by the state to exercise elements of governmental authority is also attributed to the state provided that the entity in question was acting in that capacity in the case in question. Furthermore, conduct by persons, in fact carried out on instructions of the state or under its direction or control, is also attributed to the state as is also conduct by persons exercising elements of governmental authority in the absence of the governmental authorities. Similarly, the conduct of an organ placed at the disposal of a state by another state is attributed to the state. Problems of attribution may become especially controversial where within the context of state responsibility for injury to aliens **(144),** as illustrated by numerous cases before United States (US)–Mexico claims commissions **(315)**, state organs or any other agents of the government cause injury to an alien, acting outside their authority or contrary to instructions. Such *ultra vires* conduct is attributed to the state if the agents in question acted with apparent or manifest authority as competent officials or used powers and methods appropriate to an official capacity. This rule is illustrated by the *Youmans* claim before the US–Mexico General Claims Commission, 1926 (4 RIAA 110) in which the Commission found Mexico responsible for the conduct of a militia unit under the command of an officer, who instead of protecting a group of US nationals, joined the threatening mob and opened fire on the Americans.

Unlawful acts of private individuals are not imputable to the state unless accompanied by the state's internationally wrongful conduct in the form of any of the following actions or omissions: encouraging the criminal conduct of the wrongdoers; failure to apply "due diligence," that is, to take reasonable care to protect the victims; failure to punish the wrongdoers; denial of justice **(152)** by failing to allow the injured alien to obtain just compensation through the local courts; benefiting from the wrongful act; and expressly acknowledging and approving the conduct in question as the state's own act. The responsibility of Iran for the attack upon the US embassy in Tehran and the taking of hostages in 1979 illustrates the principle of responsibility of a state for actions of individuals. In its analysis of the events in the case of *United States Diplomatic and Consular Staff in Tehran* (United States of America v. Iran) (1980 ICJ Rep. 3), the ICJ found that the initial phase of the attack upon the embassy could not be attributable to Iran since—in the Court's view—the attackers were private individuals acting on their own. However, following the approval by the Iranian government of the hostage taking and its decision to maintain the unlawful state of affairs, responsibility had to be attributed to the state of Iran since it endorsed and decided to continue the militants' action as its own act of the state. Otherwise Iran was found responsible for failure to carry out the special obligations under customary law and the Vienna Convention on Diplomatic Relations, 1961 **(71)**, to take appropriate steps to protect the embassy, and failure to do so, apart from failure to punish the wrongdoers, constituted by itself a clear and serious violation of international law.

Whether and to what extent a state bears international responsibility for acts of an insurrectional or similar movement and what would be the responsibility of a successful movement of this kind, raises special problems of attribution. In practice, circumstances often blur the distinction between civil disturbances and mob violence on the one hand and the more extensive and organized action of a rebellious or insurrectional movement **(115)** on the other. Acts of rioters are governed by the rules on attribution to the state of acts committed by private individuals. Concerning insurrectionists, as a general rule, conduct of an insurrectional or similar movement is not attributable to the state unless the government fails to exercise due diligence by preventing the damage caused to aliens by the insurrectionists; fails to punish the guilty individuals; or in compensating for the damage discriminates against nationals of a particular state. These principles are illustrated by the US–Great Britain claims arbitration in the case of *Home Frontier and Foreign Missionary Society* (6 RIAA 42), 1920.

A successful insurrectional movement installed in power as the new government or a secessionist movement establishing a new state in a portion of the state's territory **(228)** is responsible for its conduct prior to the assumption of authority and, under international law, its conduct is considered as an act of the state concerned. Issues concerning attribution of acts by members of an insurrectional movement to its eventually successful new government of the state were considered in some cases before the Iran-US Claims Tribunal **(312).** In one of these cases the Tribunal denied compensation to a US national for his departure from Iran forced by unspecified militants in the turbulent days prior to the installing of the Islamic government on the grounds that his leaving Iran could not be attributed to that government. On the other hand, in another case, the expulsion of a US national by Iranian revolutionary guards who exercised authority with acquiescence by the state, after the establishment of the Islamic regime, was attributed to the state of Iran.

**54. Confederation.** A very loose union of states **(127)**, linked together by a treaty **(288)**, with central organs of its own and vested with certain powers over the member states but not directly over the citizens of these states, each of which retains its individual international legal personality **(85)**. The simplest differentiating criteria between confederation and federation **(77)** are that, unlike a confederation, a federation exercises direct legislative power and jurisdiction over the citizens of the component states and forms one international legal person. Before becoming a federal state, the United States was briefly a confederation under the Articles of Confederation which became effective in 1781. The ratification of the Constitution gave birth to a federation. Other historical examples of confederation include the Netherlands (1579–1798), the Confederation of the Rhine (1806–1813), the German Confederation (1815–1866), and the Swiss Confederation (1201–1798, 1815–1848), which became a federal state in 1848 although the country's formal traditional name in French has retained the term *Conféděration*.

In more recent times, Senegal and the Gambia set up a confederation to be known as "Senegambia" (1981) (21 ILM 44 (1982)). The "Arab-African Union" of Libya and Morocco established in 1984 (23 ILM 1022 (1984)) and soon denounced by Morocco was an example of unions of a rather indeterminate nature agreed upon between Libya and some other Arab states, which proved to be political fictions without much enduring substance. A confederation negotiated between Russia and Belarus and in principle agreed upon in 1999 has not yet become a fact.

**55. Consular Privileges and Immunities.** Unless granted by virtue of a special agreement, privileges and immunities of consular officers **(57)** are less extensive than those of diplomatic agents **(63)**. Customary law **(39)** on the subject is also less certain and uniform although in the past hundred years the right of consuls to an increased measure of immunity has been gradually recognized in bilateral conventions. While many of the provisions of the Vienna Convention on Consular Relations, 1963 **(56)** reflect customary law or at least a widely accepted practice, the Convention as a whole contains more elements of "progressive development" **(5)** than the Vienna Convention on Diplomatic Relations of 1961 **(71)**.

The main difference between the diplomatic and consular immunities under customary law, as codified in the Consular Convention (Art. 43), is that consular officers and employees (meaning administrative and technical staff) enjoy "functional," but not "personal," immunity from civil and criminal jurisdiction **(87)** and from the administrative authorities of the receiving state only in respect of acts performed in the exercise of consular functions. Even performance of diplomatic acts by a consular officer does not confer upon him any right to claim diplomatic privileges and immunities **(63)** (Art. 17). No immunity applies in civil actions arising out of contracts concluded by a consular officer or employee who does not act as an agent of the sending state, or actions by a private third party for damage resulting from accidents in the receiving state and involving consular staff on official business. What exactly are acts performed in the exercise of consular functions has to be determined on a case-by-case basis. In criminal matters, consular officers are not liable to detention or arrest pending trial, except in a case of a grave crime and only pursuant to a court decision, in which case the proceedings must be initiated with the minimum of delay. Any criminal proceedings must be conducted with the respect due to him by reason of his official position and—except for arrest for a grave crime—so as to hamper as little as possible the exercise of consular functions (Art. 41). Under Art. 44 of the Convention a consular officer has no obligation to give expert evidence on the law of his country or official matters and need not produce official documents or correspondence. Otherwise he may be summoned to attend as a witness in judicial or administrative proceedings, but if he declines to do so, no coercive measures or penalties may be applied against him, a rule more liberal than the existing state practice.

Subject to national security of the receiving state, members of foreign consular posts enjoy the freedom of movement (Art. 34), and the receiving state must permit and protect the freedom of communication of the consular post for all official purposes. Of great practical importance is Art. 36 of the Convention which guarantees the right of access, communication, and contact between consular officers and nationals of the sending state who are arrested or in prison and obliges the receiving state to inform the detained individual of all these rights. In the *LaGrand* case (Germany v. United States of America) (2001) the Omtermatopma; Cpirt pf Kistoce (ICJ) **(309)** held in its judgment (40 ILM 1069 (2001)) that the United States (US), *inter alia,* had disregarded its obligations under Art. 36 to inform two German nationals, convicted in Arizona and eventually executed, of their right to consular assistance. In a similar case brought before the ICJ against the US by Mexico in 2002 (*Avena and Other Mexican Nationals* (Mexico v. United States of America)), the ICJ also found, in its judgment in 2004, that the US had breached its obligations under the Vienna Convention to Mexico and to the Mexican nationals involved.

The treatment of consular couriers and bags is similar to that accorded their diplomatic counterparts **(65)**, but the Consular Convention expressly allows the authorities of the receiving state to request that a bag be opened in their presence by an authorized representative of the state; in case of refusal the bag is to be returned to its place of origin (Art. 35(3)). The waiver of privileges and immunities, their termination, the obligations of third states, and the treatment of consular officers of the receiving state's nationality **(175)** largely follow the rules of the Vienna Convention on Diplomatic Relations.

Consular officers and employees and members of their families who form part of their household are entitled to a number of exemptions: from aliens' **(144)** registration, work permits, social security provisions, and all personal and public service, all largely on the same lines as in the case of diplomatic agents. However—unlike their diplomatic counterparts—members of a consular officer's family are not otherwise entitled to immunity. Consular officers and employees are exempt from taxation except for indirect taxes and some other dues and charges. In the area of customs duties, the Convention (Art. 50) allows consular officers exemption of personal use articles only in quantities necessary for direct utilization, but consular employees are entitled to customs exemption only in respect of articles imported at the time of the first installation.

The inviolability of consular archives and documents had been well established in customary law before the Vienna Convention codified this rule in Art. 23. Other aspects of inviolability, such as the exemption of consular premises from taxation, largely follow the rules concerning diplomatic inviolability **(67)**, but (Art. 31) in case of fire or other disaster requiring prompt protective action, the sending state's consent to enter the part of the consular premises used exclusively as offices is presumed. No such provision is found in the Convention on Diplomatic Relations. Residences are not inviolable, but official documents found there are covered by immunity. Concerning asylum in consular premises, the state practice does not essentially differ from that governing diplomatic asylum **(64)**.

Under the Convention (Arts. 58–68), honorary consuls, who are sometimes citizens of the receiving state and otherwise follow their respective professions, enjoy less extensive privileges and immunities. They are entitled to the use of the national flag and the coat-of-arms of the sending state, appropriate accommodations and other facilities needed for the performance of their functions, freedom of movement and communication, and contact with nationals of the sending state. They may also levy consular fees and other charges. On the other hand, they have no personal immunity from arrest or detention pending trial. Since the premises of an honorary consular post are often used also for private purposes, they are not inviolable, but must be protected by the receiving state. The archives and documents are inviolable provided that they are kept separate from the private materials of the honorary consul.

The members of the administrative and technical staff enjoy no personal immunity except for immunity in respect of acts performed in the exercise of their functions. Their families are not entitled to any immunity at all.

**56. Consular Relations, Vienna Convention on, 1963.** A multilateral convention of 79 articles, based on the draft articles prepared by the International Law Commission, adopted by a United Nations–sponsored conference in Vienna in 1963 (596 UNTS 261). The Convention entered into effect **(271)** in 1967 and is in force for a large majority of states, with the United States (US) acceding **(267)** in 1969. In addition to the Convention itself, the Vienna Conference of 1963 also adopted an Optional Protocol concerning acquisition of nationality **(175)** (596 UNTS 469) and another Optional Protocol concerning the compulsory settlement of disputes (596 UNTS 487).

Until the adoption of the Convention, customary law **(39)** governing consuls was regulated by a network of bilateral agreements. There is also a regional agreement, the Havana Convention relating to consular agents, 1928 (15 LNTS 291), with the US a party. A European consular convention was adopted in 1967, already after the entry into effect of the Vienna Convention.

The Vienna Convention was designed to regulate the international law of consular relations in a comprehensive way and on a universal basis. However, as stated in the Preamble, the rules of customary law continue to govern matters not expressly dealt with by the provisions of the Convention. Also, under Art. 73, the Convention does not affect other international agreements in force as between states parties to them. Although many provisions of the Convention reflect customary rules, it does not represent a codification **(5)** to the same extent as the Convention on Diplomatic Relations of 1961 **(71)** and since it includes significant elements of progressive development of the existing law, especially in the provisions which in some respects assimilate the status of career consuls to that of diplomatic agents **(63)**, it cannot entirely be regarded as the conclusive evidence of the current state of customary consular law.

Like the Convention on Diplomatic Relations, the Consular Convention is guided by the principle, articulated in the Preamble, that the purpose of consular privileges and immunities is not to benefit individuals but to ensure the efficient performance of functions by consular posts on behalf of their respective states.

**57. Consuls.** Consuls are officials of a state exercising in the territory of another state a variety of functions consisting in, among other duties, protecting the interests of the sending state and its nationals, furthering commercial, economic, cultural, and scientific relations between the sending state and the receiving state, including supervision of, and assistance to vessels and aircraft of the nationality **(257)** of the sending state, and performing various acts of notarial, civil registry, and administrative nature, including issuing visas to persons wishing to travel to the sending state and passports to its nationals. A detailed list of consular functions can be found in Art. 5 of the Vienna Convention on Consular Relations of 1963 **(56)**.

Traditionally, the origin and functions of consuls differ from those of diplomatic agents, and it must be added that—contrary to a widespread view—consuls are not diplomats. Unlike diplomatic agents, they do not represent their state in the totality of its relations with the receiving state, functioning only for specific tasks and for local purposes. They communicate with the receiving state's government ordinarily through the diplomatic mission **(68)** of their country, to which they are subordinated. Their privileges and immunities **(55)** are much less extensive than those of diplomats;

they are "functional" and not "personal." One should note, however, that misconceptions about the status of consuls are due in part to the fact that in recent times a characteristic feature of the state practice in this area has been a tendency to blur the distinction between consuls and diplomats by organizational arrangements of the foreign service through a partial fusion of the diplomatic and consular services. Thus it may happen that a country's embassy includes a consular section in which diplomatic agents in fact perform functions traditionally associated with consular agents, but formally are listed and treated as diplomats.

An institution similar to modern consuls existed in relations between Greek city-states, but modern consular relations date back to the practice in Spanish and Italian towns, in the early modern era, of electing merchant consuls to arbitrate commercial disputes. The institution was transplanted to the Middle East where under agreements of European states, known as "capitulations," the competence of the merchant consuls expanded to include jurisdiction **(87)** over their respective countrymen. The capitulations regime was later introduced in relations with some Asian and North African states and survived in some of them until the 20th century. Consular relations were established also between a number of states in Western and Northern Europe, but the rise of permanent diplomatic missions reduced their role to protecting the commercial interests of their home states and countrymen. In the 19th and 20th centuries the role of the consuls as agents of their respective states, residing abroad, was institutionalized in many bilateral consular treaties or treaties of friendship, commerce, and navigation, but the legal status of the consuls in general international law remained much less defined than that of the diplomatic agents. In 1963 the Vienna Convention on Consular Relations codified and developed the customary law on the subject.

In general, there are two categories of consular officers: the more important category of career consuls who are regular full-time officials of the sending state performing the consular functions abroad in the receiving country, and the other category of the so-called honorary consuls, often nationals of the host state residing in the consular district in question, appointed on a part-time basis by the sending state.

The Vienna Convention distinguishes four classes of "consular posts" in descending order of importance: consulate-general, consulate, vice-consulate, and consular agency, headed by a consul-general, consul, vice-consul, and consular agent respectively (Art. 9). The head of a consular post and the other persons entrusted with the exercise of consular functions are consular officers, to be distinguished from consular employees and members of the service staff, the kind of status corresponding to the administrative and technical staff **(69)** and the service staff **(70)** of a diplomatic mission. All consular officers, consular employees, and members of the service staff constitute members of the consular post. Whereas a single diplomatic mission of the sending state is headquartered in the capital of the receiving state, there are often, especially in large states, several consular posts located in large cities, often ports, which perform their functions in their respective "consular districts."

The establishment of consular relations between states requires mutual consent, but although there is no duty in international law to admit consuls, practically all states do so out of considerations of national, especially commercial, interests. Consent to establish diplomatic relations implies consent to establish consular relations as well, but a severance of diplomatic relations does not necessarily terminate the consular relations.

To exercise his functions, the head of a consular post must have the authority of the sending state (consular commission or notification of appointment) and an authorization from the receiving state, known as *exequatur* (in Latin "let him carry out"), or at least be admitted provisionally pending its delivery. Other members of a consular post may be freely appointed by the sending state, subject to the requirement of reasonableness, as in the case of diplomatic missions. Other details concerning the establishment and conduct of consular relations, such as precedence, declaring a consular officer *persona non grata* and so on, largely follow the rules concerning diplomatic agents.

Consular functions terminate upon the death of the officer, his recall, withdrawal of the *exequatur*, or an armed conflict **(339)** between the states concerned, in which case the receiving state must—as in the case of the termination of a diplomatic mission—facilitate the departure of the staff of the consular post or posts, as the case may be, and of the families. Even after the severance of consular relations, the receiving state has the duty to protect the consular premises and property and the archives. In 1990 when Iraq's annexation of Kuwait was declared null and void by the Security Council, the termination by Iraq of the appointments of the foreign consuls in Kuwait was not recognized by other states, as was also the case of the diplomatic missions there. Unlike the case of a diplomatic mission, consular functions do not cease upon changes in the head of state in the receiving or sending state.

**58. Countermeasures.** A concept within the general area of state responsibility **(128)** for internationally wrongful acts, referring to nonforcible and proportional unilateral measures which an injured state **(82)** may take in response to another state's wrongful act so as to induce that state to cease its conduct, to make reparation **(118)**, and—where appropriate—to offer assurances and guarantees of nonrepetition.

The term countermeasures, first used in the *Air Services Agreement* Arbitration **(293)** in 1978 (France v. United States (US)) (18 RIAA 411), has largely replaced the term "reprisals" **(119)** which under the traditional international law could include the use of force **(329)** now outlawed by the United Nations (UN) Charter and general international law. Countermeasures may otherwise constitute unlawful acts as such, but if certain conditions are met, they belong to "circumstances precluding wrongfulness" (such as consent, self-defense **(335)**, *force majeure* **(78)** etc.) and do not entail the responsibility of the state resorting in self-help to countermeasures. Such is the conceptual place of countermeasures in the International Law Commission (ILC) Draft Articles codifying **(5)** state responsibility, submitted to the General Assembly in 2001. In practice, however, the terminology is not quite consistent. For example in the International Court of Justice **(309)** case of *United States Diplomatic and Consular Staff in Tehran* (United States of America v. Iran) (1980 ICJ Rep. 3) the Court used the term countermeasures to include also retortion **(121)**. The term "sanctions" is often employed with reference to usually economic measures undertaken collectively by a competent organ of an international organization, such as the Security Council, in response to a serious breach of international law by a state, or similar measures taken by a group of states, independently of the UN.

In traditional international law, states used to apply various unilateral measures, including the use of armed force, without belligerent intent, in retaliation for injury suffered, enforcing perceived legal rights or attaining political or other advantages. Such "coercive (or "forcible") measures short of war" would include retortion, reprisals, pacific blockade **(326)**, and various forms of interference in the affairs of another state, known by the political rather than legal notion of intervention **(331)**. The use of force as a measure short of war served great powers as a rationale for their apparent restraint from exercising their, then legitimate, right of resort to war **(338)**. Whether and to what extent the League of Nations Covenant (1919) and the General Treaty for the Renunciation of War (Kellogg-Briand Pact) (1928) **(330)** affected the legality of forcible measures short of war, such as armed reprisals, is not clear. But a League of Nations–appointed committee of jurists investigating the bombardment of Corfu by Italy in 1923 in reprisal for the murder by Greek extremists of an Italian general, expressed the opinion that the Italian conduct was incompatible with the obligation to settle international disputes by peaceful means **(318)**. Today, as a result of the ban on the use of force, forcible measures short of war are illegal and, though sometimes resorted to, are rationalized in terms of self-defense.

International law imposes certain not entirely well-established conditions for the lawfulness of countermeasures. Apart from the prohibition of force, it requires that the injured state first call upon the delinquent state to desist from its wrongful conduct or make reparation, and if the injured state receives no satisfaction, it must engage in good faith in negotiation **(316)** before resorting to self-help by countermeasures, the latter requirement criticized by some states, including the US. Whether exhaustion of other mechanisms of peaceful settlement, for example arbitration **(293)**, is a prerequisite for lawful countermeasures is a controversial matter. The ILC Draft Articles on Responsibility of States (2001) **(129)** lay down such prerequisite, but this solution has been among those criticized by the US as going beyond the customary rules **(39)** of international law. For example, in the above-mentioned *Air Services Agreement* case the Arbitral Tribunal allowed countermeasures despite the existence of the parties' prior agreement providing for efforts at peaceful methods of settlement.

Certain kinds of countermeasures are prohibited in the interests of the international community as a whole, even if they should comply with the requirement of proportionality. In addition to forcible measures, the list of prohibitions includes countermeasures disregarding the principle of respect for human rights **(157)**, and in particular regard for the fundamental needs of the population of the wrongdoing state, and countermeasures producing extreme economic or political coercion designed to endanger the territorial integrity or political independence of that state. Furthermore, countermeasures must not conflict with peremptory rules of international law (*jus cogens*) **(24)** or infringe upon diplomatic (67) or consular inviolability **(55)**. The question whether a state other than the injured one can lawfully take countermeasures, for example in cases of violation of *erga omnes* obligations **(12)**, is not settled in international law and left open in the ILC Draft of 2001.

**59. Customs Union.** A treaty-based **(40)** substitution of the customs territories of two or more states by a single customs territory, designed to eliminate duties and other restrictions on commerce between the constituent territories. Apart from abolishing customs duties, a customs union establishes a common customs tariff for goods entering from third states. The international legal effects of a customs union, especially for its members, depend on the terms of the treaty and the accompanying circumstances. Thus, for example, the Advisory Opinion **(291)** of the Permanent Court of International Justice **(320)** of 1931 on *Customs Régime between Germany and Austria* (1931 PCIJ, Series A/B, No. 41) found the customs union planned by Austria and Germany incompatible with Austria's treaty obligations not to compromise its economic and political independence. But the customs union of Switzerland and Liechtenstein after World War I and a similar union entered into by Belgium, Luxembourg, and the Netherlands just after World War II were not considered by third states as endangering the independence of the states involved. The member states of the European Union, which in its initial stage was a customs union, continue to be regarded as independent states.

**60. Danzig, The Free City of.** Of historical interest only, the Free City of Danzig (now Gdańsk) was created as a category of protected state with a special status, by Arts. 100–108 of the Peace Treaty of Versailles with Germany, 1919 (225 CTS 188). It was placed under the protection and supervision of the League of Nations, with Poland entrusted with the conduct of foreign affairs and defense. However, treaties **(288)** that applied to Danzig required, as a rule, its consent. The Free City had its own nationality **(175)** laws, its Constitution and legislation, and, in general, exercised jurisdiction **(87)** within its territory in an autonomous way, with Poland having certain reserved rights in the area of postal communications, for example. However, disputes concerning the interpretation of the legal status of the Free City between it and Poland and a discriminatory treatment of Polish nationals and other persons of Polish origin by the German-dominated Danzig authorities, became from the beginning a constant irritant in the relations between Danzig and Poland. Six advisory opinions **(291)** of the Permanent Court of International Justice (PCIJ) **(320)** out of its 27 opinions dealt with various controversial issues relating to Danzig. The PCIJ concluded, *inter alia,* that the Free City of Danzig was invested with international legal personality **(85)**, subject to its special relationship with the League of Nations and Poland under the Treaty of Versailles. Some publicists considered the Free City to be an internationalized territory, but this generic and rather vague term may cover a number of international legal regimes. Among them are not only entities with a degree of international legal personality: Danzig; the Saar Territory, by virtue of Art. 45 of the Treaty of Versailles governed until 1934 by the Council of the League of Nations; and the abortive (similar to the Free City of Danzig) Free Territory of Trieste **(141)**. Also included are territories with a special status but without international legal personality, created within and remaining part of a sovereign state; territories such as Kosovo, administered by an international organization; or East Timor, once also administered by the United Nations.

The Free City of Danzig was occupied by Germany at the outbreak of World War II, ceasing *de facto* to exist. Since 1945, upon the defeat of Germany, it has been part of Poland.

**61. Diplomat in Transit.** A diplomatic agent **(68)** accredited to a state **(127)**, who is passing through or is in the territory **(228)** of a third state while proceeding to take up or to return to his post, or when returning to his own country.

Prior to the adoption of the Vienna Convention on Diplomatic Relations, 1961 **(71)**, the immunities **(63)** of a diplomatic agent in transit were a subject of controversy, especially if they were related to the issues of the recognition of state **(116)** or government **(114)**. Under Art. 40 of the Vienna Convention, a third state which has granted a diplomat in transit a passport visa if such visa was necessary, must accord him inviolability **(67)** and such other immunities as may be required to ensure his transit or return. The same applies to any member of his family, enjoying privileges and immunities whether accompanying the diplomatic agent or traveling separately to join him or to return to their country.

Should a diplomat in transit remain longer than it was necessary for purposes of transit, he could not be entitled to immunity. Abuse of the privilege of transit entitles the transit state to apprehend and try the diplomat involved. A diplomatic agent traveling in a third country *incognito* or for personal reasons is not entitled to the treatment under Art. 40, but the state concerned may, by courtesy ("comity") **(6)**, accord him special consideration.

Official diplomatic correspondence and other official communications in transit, including messages in code or cipher, enjoy the same freedom and protection as are granted by the receiving state. The same applies to diplomatic bags **(65)** and diplomatic couriers **(66)** in transit.

**62. Diplomatic Agents: Heads of Permanent Missions.** In a permanent diplomatic mission **(68)**, the head of mission is its most senior diplomatic agent and, according to the definition in Art. 1(a) of the Vienna Convention on Diplomatic Relations, 1961 **(71)**, is the person charged by the sending state with the duty of acting in the capacity of the head of mission in the receiving state. Under Art. 20 of the Convention, only the mission itself and its head have the right to use the flag and emblem of their state on the premises of the mission, including the residence of the head of the mission, and on his means of transport.

In the early stage of the European diplomacy, by the time that most European states adopted the practice of permanent diplomatic missions in the second half of the 17th century, two classes of major diplomatic agents had emerged: ambassadors, who enjoyed the highest rank and precedence, and ordinary envoys, known as residents. Otherwise the unregulated nature of the diplomatic ranks would often cause disputes by reason of claims to precedence between representatives of rival powers and especially the Emperor and the King of France. Eventually, at the Congress of Vienna, 1815, agreement was reached on the establishment of three classes of heads of mission: 1. ambassadors or—for the Pope—legates or nuncios; 2. envoys, whether styled ministers plenipotentiary or otherwise; (both classes accredited with the head of state); and 3. *chargés d'affaires*, accredited to ministers of foreign affairs. The issue of precedence was resolved (without in any way modifying the position of Papal representatives in some receiving states where they enjoyed special precedence) by ranking the heads of mission in each class in the order of the date and time of taking up their respective functions in the receiving state. In 1818 at the Congress of Aix-la-Chapelle, the great powers added a fourth class of minister residents, intermediate between envoys and *chargés d'affaires.*

In 1961 the Vienna Convention (Art. 14) divided heads of mission into three classes, namely 1. ambassadors or nuncios accredited to heads of state, and other heads of mission of equivalent rank; 2. envoys, ministers, and internuncios, accredited to heads of state; and 3. *chargés d'affaires* accredited to ministers for foreign affairs. Precedence in the respective classes follows the rule of the Congress of Vienna, with an express provision that the general precedence rules are without prejudice to any practice accepted by the receiving state regarding the precedence of the representative of the Holy See **(80)** (Art. 16). Under Art. 17 the precedence of the members of the diplomatic staff of the mission is notified by the head of the mission to the receiving state's minister for foreign affairs or other minister, as may be agreed.

All the heads of diplomatic missions accredited in the same capital together form the diplomatic corps headed by the *Doyen* (Dean) who is a senior diplomat or, in some states, the Papal nuncio. His major function is to represent the common needs and interests of the diplomats in the receiving state and, in particular, watch over the observance of the privileges and immunities **(63)** due to the diplomatic agents.

Historically, ambassadors were accredited only between monarchs, and the United States, for example, did not employ the rank of ambassadors until the end of the 19th century. In the second half of the 20th century, the class of ambassadors became virtually the rule in diplomatic relations, with even the smallest countries, sensitive about the principle of the equality of states **(73)**, adopting the practice.

Considered a personal representative of the head of his state, an ambassador can officially claim the title of Excellency and have the privilege of access to the head of state at all times. Nuncios or—if cardinals—(*legati a latere*) are ambassadors sent by the Holy See. In relations between members of the British Commonwealth ambassadors are known as High Commissioners. Envoys (otherwise a colloquial term often used to denote any diplomatic agent), ministers, and internuncios are heads of mission of the second, now disappearing, class. Although, like ambassadors, accredited to the head of state, they are not considered to be personal representatives of the heads of their respective states and do not enjoy the privilege of requesting a personal audience with the head of the receiving state. The title of Excellency is accorded to them only by courtesy. The rank of minister resident, introduced in 1818 and historically applied to European envoys to overseas states, now belongs to the same class as envoy, but in terms of etiquette is inferior to them. However, this matter has become largely irrelevant as a result of the virtual disappearance of the second class of diplomatic agents from international diplomacy.

The third and lowest class of heads of mission, the *chargés d'affaires,* differs from the other two classes in that such agents are accredited between foreign ministers and enjoy fewer honors. The *chargé d'affaires* as a permanent head of a diplomatic mission (of the third class), sometimes referred to as *chargé d'affaires en titre* (or *en pied*), must be distinguished from the so-called *chargé d'affaires ad interim* who is a senior member of the diplomatic staff provisionally acting as the head of mission in cases where that post is vacant as when he is recalled or unable to perform his functions (Vienna Convention, Art. 19). A *chargé d'affaires ad interim* does not become formally accredited and his name is only notified by the head of the mission or the foreign ministry of the sending state to the foreign ministry of the receiving state. The Convention (Art. 19(2)) allows a member of the administrative and technical staff to be temporarily in charge of the administrative affairs of the mission with the consent of the receiving state.

**63. Diplomatic Agents: Privileges and Immunities.** The twin term "privileges and immunities" is commonly used in general international law and treaties to refer, without distinguishing between the two terms or defining them, to the special status of diplomatic agents **(63)** and to a lesser extent other staff of the diplomatic mission **(68)** in the receiving state, such as various kinds of preferential treatment, special protection, inviolability **(67)**, and exemption from the jurisdiction **(87)** of the receiving state. The head of state, head of government, and minister of foreign affairs also enjoy immunity from jurisdiction in other states, a rule confirmed in the 1969 Convention on Special Missions **(126)**. All these privileges and immunities exist not for the personal benefit of the diplomatic agents, whose duty is to respect the laws and regulations of the receiving state, but in order to ensure the efficient performance of their functions on behalf of the sending state they represent. In the past, diplomatic privileges and immunities were theorized in terms of the "extraterritoriality theory" according to which the premises of the mission constituted a sort of extension of the territory of the sending state or the "representative character theory" under which privileges and immunities were based on the notion that the diplomatic mission personified the sending state. In modern times, however, the prevalent theory is that of "functional necessity" under which diplomatic privileges and immunities are justified by the need to enable the mission efficiently to perform its functions. The Vienna Convention on Diplomatic Relations, 1961 **(71)**, is explicitly guided by this theory while also bearing in mind the representative character of the head of mission and the mission itself.

Under Art. 38 of the Vienna Convention, unless granted additional privileges and immunities by the receiving state, a diplomatic agent who is a national or permanent resident of that state, enjoys only immunity from jurisdiction, and inviolability in respect of official acts performed in the exercise of his functions. Other members of the staff and private servants, who are nationals or permanent residents of the receiving state, have privileges and immunities only to the extent admitted by that state which, however, must exercise its jurisdiction over them in such a manner as not to interfere unduly with the performance of the functions of the mission.

The privileges and immunities of a member of the staff of a diplomatic mission commence from the moment the entitled person enters the territory **(228)** of the receiving state on proceeding to take up his post or, if already in its territory, from the moment when his appointment is notified to the ministry for foreign affairs or other competent ministry of the receiving state. The privileges and immunities normally cease at the moment when the person concerned leaves the country or on expiry of a reasonable period in which to do so, and subsist until that time even in case of armed conflict **(339)**. However, immunity with respect to acts performed by such a person in the exercise of his functions as a member of the mission, continues indefinitely even after the termination of his status. This might possibly extend to such situations as a road traffic accident involving a car on official business.

Apart from inviolability, a diplomatic agent (that is, the head of the mission **(62)** or members of the staff having diplomatic rank) enjoys immunity from the criminal jurisdiction of the receiving state, a well-established principle of customary international law **(39)**, codified **(5)** in Art. 31(1) of the Vienna Convention and illustrated by many incidents and abundant case law. This does not mean, however, that a diplomatic agent may flaunt the laws and regulations of the receiving state. His immunity may be waived by his own state, which may also recall him. In cases of persistent abuse of his immunity he may be declared *persona non grata* by the receiving state. The matter is particularly sensitive insofar as traffic offenses are concerned. It is increasingly recognized that, without infringing on the principle of diplomatic immunity, traffic tickets may be issued to diplomats and forwarded to the diplomatic mission concerned for payment. The receiving state may institute requirements of automobile liability insurance to be met by diplomatic agents and may resort to countermeasures **(58)**, such as, for example, withholding the amount of unpaid traffic fines from the sending state's foreign aid program. Whether a diplomat's driver's license may be withdrawn for flagrant violations of traffic regulations is a controversial issue. In any case, however, police orders and regulations cannot be enforced against diplomatic agents. In many countries regulations provide guidelines for police concerning the treatment of foreign diplomatic and consular personnel in such situations. In the United States there are Department of State Guidelines for law enforcement officers with regard to personal rights and immunities of foreign diplomatic and consular personnel, 1988 (27 ILM 1617 (1988)).

Exemption from civil and administrative jurisdiction of the receiving state with respect to both private and official acts is an important element of diplomatic immunity. The latter category of acts may additionally be subject to the rules governing state (sovereign) immunity **(131)**. Reflecting, in general, the pertinent customary rules, the Vienna Convention (Art. 31(1)) provides for three exceptions from the principle of immunity from the receiving state's civil and administrative jurisdiction, namely with regard to: 1. a real action relating to private immovable property in the territory of that state, unless the diplomatic agent concerned holds it on behalf of his state for the purposes of the mission; 2. an action relating to succession in which he is involved as executor, administrator, heir or legatee as a private person and not on behalf of the sending state; and 3. all actions relating to any professional or commercial activity exercised by him in the receiving state outside his official functions. The third exception is of lesser significance in view of the fact that many sending states bar their diplomats from engaging in such activities, and even some receiving states (for example the US) do not permit them. Since diplomatic immunities exist in the interest of the diplomatic mission and the sending state, the immunity from jurisdiction can be waived only by that state (Art. 32(1)). Waiver must always be express (Art. 32(2)). However, waiver of immunity from jurisdiction in respect of civil and administrative proceedings does not imply waiver in respect of the execution of the judgment, for which a separate waiver is necessary (Art. 32(4)). At least in civil jurisdiction cases, the head of the mission is ordinarily recognized as having the authority to waive the immunity of a member of his staff. In practice, unless withdrawn, waiver in a court of first instance continues in appellate proceedings. If a diplomatic agent or other person enjoying immunity from jurisdiction initiates proceedings, he is precluded from invoking immunity in respect of any counterclaims directly connected with the principal claim, a rule that applies also within the context of state immunity.

Other diplomatic privileges and immunities under Art. 31 include immunity from giving evidence as a witness and from any measures of execution except in the three above-listed cases, but even then such measures cannot infringe on the inviolability of the person of the diplomat or his residence. Of course, in any case, immunity from the jurisdiction of the receiving state does not exempt a diplomatic agent from the jurisdiction of the sending state.

As a general rule, under customary international law, diplomatic agents have been exempt from the obligation to pay dues and taxes of the receiving state, but this exemption has been implemented in municipal law **(27)** in a complex variety of ways, depending on the generosity of the country concerned. Under Art. 34 of the Vienna Convention, the exceptions to the tax exemption include indirect taxes which are normally incorporated in the price of goods or services; dues and taxes on private immovable property in the receiving state unless the property is held on behalf of the sending state for the purposes of the mission; estate, succession, or inheritance duties levied by the receiving state, except (Art. 39(4)) that no such duties are levied on movable property of a deceased member of the mission or a member of his family; dues and taxes levied on private income having its source in the receiving state and capital taxes on investments there in commercial undertakings; charges levied for specific services rendered; registration, court, or record fees, mortgage dues and stamp duty, with respect to private immovable property. Under Art. 23, the sending state and the head of the mission are exempt from all dues and taxes in respect of the mission premises whether owed or leased, other than such as represent payment for services rendered (for example water, electricity, etc.).

Historically, customary law has not granted a clear exemption from custom duties upon goods for a diplomat's private use, but such exemption was frequently granted by courtesy (comity) **(6)**. The Vienna Convention (Art. 36) generously allows exemption from all customs duties, including duties on articles for personal use. The personal baggage of a diplomatic agent is exempt from inspection unless there are serious grounds for suspecting that it contains articles subject to duty (that is, not for official or personal use), prohibited by the law, or controlled by the quarantine regulations. Such inspection, however, may be conducted only in the presence of the diplomatic agent concerned or of his authorized representatives.

Among other miscellaneous diplomatic privileges and immunities is freedom of movement and traveling in the territory of the receiving state, subject to the receiving state's national security regulations (Art. 26), a privilege sometimes construed restrictively (as used to be the practice in the Cold War), but with reciprocal measures of the other state allowed under Art. 47(2)(a) of the Vienna Convention.

Diplomatic agents are exempt from all personal services, all public services, and military obligations such as those connected with requisitioning, military contributions, and billeting (Art. 35). Finally, under Art. II of the Optional Protocol to the Vienna Convention concerning the acquisition of nationality **(175)** (500 UNTS 223), members of the mission who are not nationals of the receiving state and members of their families forming part of their household, do not solely, by the operation of the law of the receiving state, acquire the nationality of that state. In such situations the sending state reserves for itself the right to decide on matters concerning the nationality of its citizens.

**64. Diplomatic Asylum.** Under general international law, there exists no right of the head **(62)** of a foreign diplomatic mission **(68)** to grant asylum in the premises of the mission, that is, to offer shelter to fugitives from justice, political refugees **(178)**, or other individuals requesting refuge on humanitarian or other grounds. The Vienna Convention on Diplomatic Relations **(71)** is deliberately silent on this sensitive political issue and has no explicit provision on diplomatic asylum. The right of diplomatic asylum must be distinguished from the right of political or territorial asylum **(148)** granted by a state within its own territory. It must be stressed here that a state's embassy or other diplomatic mission or a consulate abroad is *not* the sending state's territory; they are not extraterritorial and, while inviolable, form part of the territory of the receiving state.

Unless the right of granting diplomatic asylum is provided for in a treaty or established by local customary law **(39)**, an individual asking for such asylum must be surrendered to the receiving state's authorities at their request. Any decision to grant diplomatic asylum is a derogation from the sovereignty **(125)** of the receiving state and constitutes interference in its domestic affairs. This can be implied from the text of Art. 41 of the Vienna Convention, which prohibits such interference and bans any use of diplomatic premises in any manner incompatible with the functions of the mission. What coercive measures may be taken to force a diplomatic mission to surrender a sheltered fugitive is not clear in view of the principle of inviolability. In practice, however, there have occurred cases of forcible entry into the mission's premises by the enforcement organs of the receiving state in order to apprehend an individual or individuals, usually political opponents, who were sheltered there. For example, in 1980 Liberian troops invaded the French embassy in Monrovia, Liberia, to arrest a political refugee granted asylum in the mission's premises.

Despite the general rule against the right of diplomatic asylum, occasionally various states have granted such asylum in their missions abroad to political and other refugees. This practice is usually associated with Latin America where local usage has long recognized the right of the head of a foreign mission to give asylum in urgent cases and for a limited period of time to political refugees and other individuals on humanitarian grounds. Exercised in certain situations by some Latin American states in times of political upheaval, the practice has been recognized in Latin American conventions on asylum adopted in Havana in 1928, Montevideo in 1933, and Caracas in 1954. The interpretation of these instruments was at issue in the celebrated case before the International Court of Justice **(309)** which produced three judgments of the Court: *Asylum* (Colombia/Peru) (1950 ICJ Rep. 266); *Request for Interpretation of the Judgment* (Colombia v. Peru) (1950 ICJ Rep. 395), (request refused); and *Haya de la Torre* (Colombia v. Peru) (1951 ICJ Rep. 395). The case involved the granting of diplomatic asylum by the Colombian embassy in Lima, Peru, to a Peruvian national who had led an unsuccessful rebellion against the government of Peru.

In exceptional situations countries, including the United States (US), have granted diplomatic asylum in the premises of their embassies to individuals whose life was in imminent jeopardy because of arbitrary action of the authorities in the receiving state in disregard of elementary judicial guarantees, or to shield individuals from mob violence from which the local authorities were not able or willing to offer protection. Sometimes the receiving state has been willing to grant a safe-conduct authorizing the individual granted refuge in an embassy to leave in safety the country in question. Among the most celebrated instances of diplomatic asylum granted by the US was that granted in 1956 during the Hungarian anti-Soviet uprising by the US legation in Budapest to Cardinal Mindszenty who then remained within the premises of the mission for 15 years. In another *cause célèbre,* in 1978, the US embassy n Moscow allowed seven members of a Pentecostal sect seeking emigration to the US to stay at the embassy for some five years.

**65. Diplomatic Bag.** In the International Law Commission (ILC) Draft Articles of 1989 on the status of the diplomatic courier **(66)** and the diplomatic bag not accompanied by the diplomatic courier (ILC YB, 1989, II, 2, 42), the diplomatic bag is defined as "packages containing official correspondence, and documents and articles intended exclusively for official use, whether accompanied by diplomatic courier or not, which are used for the official communication—and which bear visible external marks of their character as a diplomatic bag." This definition is based on, and elaborates the provision of Art. 27(4) of the Vienna Convention on Diplomatic Relations, 1961 **(71)**, and applies also to consular bags and bags of national delegations to international organizations. Despite the term "bag," there are no limits on the size or shape of the diplomatic bag; it may consist of trunks or large containers, the fact which, as demonstrated by various incidents, lends itself to abuse, such as smuggling narcotics, firearms, and even human beings.

Reflecting the state practice in cases of nonconfidential material, the Vienna Convention provides that a diplomatic bag may be entrusted to a captain of a commercial aircraft scheduled to land at an authorized port of entry who, while not being considered to be a diplomatic courier, is provided with an official document indicating the number of packages constituting the bag. The diplomatic mission **(68)** may send one of its members to take possession of the bag directly and freely from the captain (Art. 27(7)). A diplomatic bag in transit through a third state must be accorded the same inviolability **(67)** and protection as the receiving state is bound to accord.

Under the Convention (Art. 27(3)), the diplomatic bag "shall not be opened or detained," a provision that caused some controversy at the Vienna Conference which adopted the Convention. Going beyond the text of the Convention, the proposed ILC Draft Articles (Art. 28(1)) make the diplomatic bag "inviolable wherever it may be" and "exempt from examination directly or through electronic or other technical devices." However, under Art. 28(2) of the Draft Articles, which follows the solution adopted in Art. 35(3) of the Vienna Convention on Consular Relations of 1963 **(56)**, at the request of the competent authorities of the receiving or transit state, consular bags may be opened in their presence by a representative of the sending state and, if the request is refused, the bag must be returned to its place of origin. Since the Vienna Convention on Diplomatic Relations does not explicitly make the diplomatic bag "inviolable" and the controversial ILC draft is as yet only a proposal, states sometimes follow the practice of electronic scanning or sniffing by dogs, and only exceptionally, where they strongly suspect abuse, they ask for permission to inspect the content of the bag according to the procedures with respect to the consular bags.

**66. Diplomatic Courier.** In the International Law Commission (ILC) Draft Articles of 1989 on the status of the diplomatic courier and the diplomatic bag **(65)** not accompanied by the diplomatic courier (ILC YB, 1989, II, 2, 42) the diplomatic courier is defined as "a person duly authorized by the sending State, either on a regular basis or for a special occasion as a courier *ad hoc*, as diplomatic courier within the meaning of the Vienna Convention on Diplomatic Relations of 1961 **(71)**, a consular courier, or a courier of a delegation to an international organization **(84)**" who is entrusted with the custody, transportation, and delivery of the diplomatic bag and is employed by the official communications of the mission. The Convention requires that the diplomatic courier be provided with an official document indicating his status and the number of packages constituting the diplomatic bag. The captain of a commercial aircraft entrusted with a diplomatic bag is not a diplomatic courier.

International law has long recognized the duty of the receiving state to protect the diplomatic courier in the performance of his functions and to afford him personal inviolability and freedom from being liable to any form of arrest and detention, as laid down in the Vienna Convention (Art. 27(5)). Diplomatic couriers who have been granted, in a third state, a passport visa if such visa was necessary, must be accorded the same inviolability and protection as the receiving state is bound to accord (Art. 40(3)).

The ILC Draft Articles codifying and developing **(5)** the customary law **(39)** on diplomatic couriers includes, in addition to the privileges and immunities of a courier specified in the Vienna Convention, inviolability **(67)** of his temporal accommodations and immunity from the jurisdiction **(87)** of the receiving and transit states in respect of all acts performed in the exercise of his functions.

**67. Diplomatic Inviolability.** Inviolability of diplomatic agents **(68)** is universally recognized as a most fundamental rule of both customary **(39)** and conventional (that is, treaty) **(40)** law and an essential prerequisite for the conduct of relations between states. Although the precise meaning of the term "inviolability" evades a clear definition, inviolability as an aspect of the diplomatic privileges and immunities **(63)** means that the person of a diplomatic agent, his residence, and the diplomatic premises and property may not be subject to any kind of interference on the part of the receiving state which is legally bound to afford him special protection. Art. 29 of the Vienna Convention on Diplomatic Relations of 1961 **(71)** reaffirms the rule of customary international law to the effect that the person of a diplomatic agent is inviolable; is not liable to any form of arrest or detention; and that the receiving state must treat him with due respect, and take all appropriate steps to prevent any attack on his person, freedom, or dignity. In this sense, inviolability, while generally included within the general concept of "diplomatic privileges and immunities," is distinct from immunity from criminal jurisdiction of the receiving state. A diplomatic agent's papers, correspondence, and—subject to certain exceptions relating to execution for debts—his property, are also inviolable, and his private residence enjoys the same inviolability and protection as the premises of the mission (Art. 30). The Vienna Convention defines the "premises of the mission" as "the buildings or parts of buildings and the land ancillary thereto, irrespective of ownership, used for the purposes of the mission, including the residence of the head of the mission" (Art. 1(i)).

The principle of personal inviolability applies also to the members of the family forming part of a diplomat's household and not possessing the nationality **(175)** of the receiving state (Art. 37(1)). Members of the administrative and technical staff **(69)** and their families enjoy inviolability to the same extent as the families of diplomatic agents, except that their personal baggage is not exempt from inspection.

In response to a rising incidence of various forms of terrorist **(337)** attacks against diplomats in the 1960s and 1970s, the General Assembly adopted the Convention on the Prevention and Punishment of Crimes against Internationally Protected Persons Including Diplomatic Agents, 1974 (1035 UNTS 167), which provides for various measures to be undertaken by the signatory states to secure a more efficient protection of diplomatic agents against terrorism. This convention belongs to those international agreements which establish a quasi-universal jurisdiction **(92)** for international crimes, and includes the principle of either extraditing **(75)** or prosecuting terrorist suspects. In its objectives, it follows a regional Convention of 1971 of a number of American countries, including the United States, "to prevent and punish the acts of terrorism taking the form of crimes against persons and related extortion that are of international significance" (10 ILM 255 (1971)).

Although the Vienna Convention on Diplomatic Relations does not provide for any exceptions from the rule of inviolability, in emergency situations, when caught committing a violent act, a diplomat may be restrained and briefly detained by the police of the receiving state in order to prevent him from committing further violence. That exceptions are possible in such cases has been noted by the ICJ **(309)** in an *obiter dictum* in *United States Diplomatic and Consular Staff in Tehran* (United States of America v. Iran) (1980 ICJ Rep. 3).

In the early period of European diplomacy, until about the 17th century, the inviolability of diplomatic premises encompassed not just the premises themselves but, under the so-called exemption of the city quarter (*franchise du quartier*), the whole quarter of the city in which a diplomatic mission was located and where, under the then-accepted but now abandoned concept of extraterritoriality, the head of the diplomatic mission could grant diplomatic asylum **(64)**. In today's international law, embassies and other diplomatic premises are *not* foreign territory; what the law accords them is diplomatic inviolability. Under Art. 22 of the Vienna Convention the premises used by a diplomatic mission and private residences of diplomats are inviolable, and agents of the receiving state may not enter them without the consent of the head of the mission **(62)**. This includes such intrusions as introduction into the premises of various listening devices. The receiving state has a special duty going beyond the concept of ordinary due diligence to take all appropriate steps to protect the premises against any intrusion or danger, and to prevent any disturbance of the peace of the mission or impairment of its dignity. Diplomatic premises and the property in them as well as the means of transport of the mission are immune from search, requisition, attachment, or execution.

The Convention lacks any provisions relating to emergency cases where the organs of the receiving state, on grounds of *force majeure* **(78)** would force entry into diplomatic premises without an express consent of the head of the mission. Such action might, however, occur as a last resort not only in cases of fire or other accidents but also within a political context such as seizing control of the premises and taking hostages by a group opposing the sending state's government or even because of the use of the mission's premises by the staff itself for unlawful purposes. It might be added that at the Vienna Conference, which adopted the Convention, a proposed amendment requiring the head of mission to cooperate with the local authorities in case of fire, epidemic, or other extreme emergency, was rejected by the Conference, thus leaving unaffected the principle of absolute inviolability of diplomatic premises.

It is a rule of international law, as laid down in Art. 41 of the Vienna Convention, that diplomatic agents must respect the laws and regulations of the receiving state and that the inviolability of diplomatic premises may not be abused in any manner incompatible with diplomatic functions. It is uncertain to what extent a receiving state may apply coercive measures designed to put an end to abuse of the inviolability of diplomatic premises by the sending state. Rare instances of forcible entry into diplomatic premises have been recorded, the receiving state not hesitating to act in breach of the principle of inviolability if perceived vital national interest was at stake. Other, less extreme but more common, measures include surrounding the premises and cutting off the mission's communications. Whether forcing entry into diplomatic premises could be justified on grounds of self-defense **(335)**, for example in cases when shots have been fired from an embassy building, endangering the lives of innocent passers-by, is not clear. When in 1984 during an anti-Qaddafi demonstration in London shots were fired from the Libyan diplomatic mission (the "People's Bureau" as its embassies are called by Libya), killing a local policewoman, the British security organs did not force entry into the embassy, but the United Kingdom severed diplomatic relations with Libya.

Inviolability also covers the diplomatic mission's archives and documents at any time and wherever they may be (Art. 24) as well as the official correspondence of the mission (Art. 27(2)). Furthermore, the receiving state must permit and protect free communication on the part of the mission for all official purposes, including communication with nationals of the sending state residing in the receiving state. In communicating with the government and other missions and consulates of the sending state, a diplomatic mission may employ all appropriate means, including diplomatic couriers and messages in code or cipher, but it may install and use a radio transmitter only with the consent of the sending state (Art. 27(1)). The monitoring, intercepting, and decoding of messages sent to, and received by a diplomatic mission, seem to be common practice permitted by international law unless such activity jams the messages themselves.

**68. Diplomatic Mission.** In relations between states **(127)**, a diplomatic mission is a duly accredited representation of a state, sent by mutual consent to the receiving state either on a permanent and reciprocal basis to carry out as a permanent diplomatic mission, normally from the capital of the receiving state, the totality of functions within the context of the diplomatic relations between the two states, or a temporary *ad hoc* mission sent to another state for the performance of a certain specific and limited, ceremonial or political, tasks **(126)**. Permanent and *ad hoc* representations of states to international (intergovernmental) organizations **(84)** are a 20th-century addition to the institution of diplomatic missions.

While in practice, the distinction between diplomatic missions and consular posts often tends to be blurred, consuls **(57)** as such are not diplomatic agents.

Codifying **(5)** the long-established practice, the Vienna Convention on Diplomatic Relations of 1961 **(71)** sums up the functions of diplomatic missions as consisting, *inter alia,* in representation; protection of the interests of the sending state and its nationals; negotiation **(316)**, a function much more important in the past era of primitive transportation and communication; lawful collection of information on the receiving state and reporting such information to the sending state; and promotion of friendly relations between the two states and developing cultural, economic, and social relations. The Convention expressly allows diplomatic agents to perform consular functions (Art. 3). It is universally recognized that a member of a foreign diplomatic mission must not interfere in the internal affairs of the receiving state or, for that matter, any third state. Apart from clear cases of espionage, the line between legitimate reporting on the political life of the receiving state and reporting that goes beyond a normal function of diplomats may sometimes be difficult to draw. State practice has recorded numerous instances of conduct by diplomatic agents perceived by the receiving state as abuse of the diplomatic status for purposes of interfering in the domestic affairs of that state.

Temporary diplomatic missions are an old institution dating back to antiquity and known also in non-European state systems. However, it was not until in the early period of the territorial state system in Europe that permanent diplomatic missions became a common feature of diplomatic relations, with the first permanent missions established between Italian states in the 15th and 16th centuries. The practice of permanent embassies and legations gradually became a general institution of the European system following the Peace Treaties of Westphalia in 1648 **(47)**. Since then a body of customary diplomatic law has accumulated, focusing primarily on privileges and immunities of diplomatic agents on the one hand and the receiving states' rights to counter any abuse of their status by diplomatic missions on the other. This law was to a large extent codified by the Vienna Convention on Diplomatic Relations of 1961.

Although references to the "right of legation" (both "active," that is, the right to send, and "passive," that is the right to receive diplomatic missions) can be found in the literature on diplomatic law, under international law there exists no right of legation in the strict sense of the word. All independent states have the capacity both to send and to receive diplomatic missions, but in the absence of any treaty obligations incur no international responsibility **(128)** for refusing to receive or send them. Under Art. 2 of the Convention, the establishment of diplomatic relations as well as of permanent diplomatic missions takes place by mutual consent. It must be noted that while mutual recognition **(116)** is a condition for the establishment and existence of diplomatic relations between states (and the existence of such relations always implies recognition) recognition is not necessarily followed by diplomatic relations. In practice, all states maintain diplomatic relations with at least a minimum of countries; absence of diplomatic relations is often due not to politics but simply to no perceived need to maintain them, or economic necessity. Absence or withdrawal of the mission may also be due to compliance with a Security Council binding resolution on nonmilitary enforcement measures as part of the United Nations collective security system **(327)**. It is possible, as recognized in the Vienna Convention (Art. 5), to accredit a head of mission or assign a member of the diplomatic staff to more than one state, unless there is an express objection by any of the receiving states. In addition, unless so objected, two or more states may accredit the same person as head of mission **(62)** to another state (Art. 6).

In the terminology of the Vienna Convention (Art. 1) the head of mission and the members of the staff of the mission are referred to as "members of the mission," the latter expression including the diplomatic staff, the administrative and technical staff **(69)**, and the service staff **(70)** of the mission. Only the head of mission and the members of the diplomatic staff have diplomatic rank; they are diplomatic agents. The distinction between diplomatic staff and other staff members is important mainly for purposes of privileges and immunities **(63)**. Members of the diplomatic staff of a mission ordinarily include such officials as counselors, secretaries (first, second, third), and often a separate category of the so-called *attachés* (cultural, commercial, military, naval, air, etc.) who are seconded to the mission by their state to function in their respective specialty. As a general rule, in the case of military, naval, and air *attachés,* the receiving state may require their names to be submitted beforehand for approval (Art. 7).

Unless otherwise agreed, the receiving state may, at its discretion, require that the size of a mission be kept within reasonable and normal limits (Art. 11(1)). This rule was an outcome of the Cold War climate when for security reasons Western countries were concerned about the size of diplomatic missions of the Soviet Union and other Communist states, which exceeded the bounds of reasonable needs. The Convention (Art. 11(2)) also allows the receiving state, within similar bounds and on a discriminatory basis, to refuse to accept officials of a particular category.

To avoid situations where a sending state's candidate for the head of a diplomatic mission should be objectionable to the receiving state (which otherwise need not give reasons for its refusal), the sending state must in advance make certain that the person in question is acceptable to the receiving state. The acceptance of a proposal to accredit an individual as the head of mission is known as *agrément* or *agréation*. The official accreditation of the head of mission takes place through the ceremonial of handing by him the sealed original of the letter of credence (*lettre de créance*) from the head of the sending state to the head of the receiving state. The head of mission with the rank of *chargé d'affaires* presents his credentials in an audience with the receiving state's foreign minister (in the United States (US), Secretary of State). The head of mission is not considered as having taken up his functions until he has presented his credentials or—in the case of a *chargé d'affaires*—has notified his arrival and presented a copy of the credentials to the foreign minister of the receiving state or other appropriate official. However, special powers are necessary for the head of a mission if he is to undertake extraordinary duties, and in particular negotiate **(316)** a treaty **(288)**. Appointments of diplomatic agents other than the head of mission are merely notified to the receiving state whose failure to object implies acceptance of the agent concerned. As noted, special rules apply, under the Convention, to military, naval, and air *attachés.*

At any time, for any or no reason and without any explanation, the receiving state may notify the sending state that its diplomatic agent is *persona non grata*, or that a member of the nondiplomatic staff is "unacceptable." In such cases the sending state must, within a reasonable period of time, either recall the individual in question or terminate his functions in the mission; otherwise the receiving state would refuse to recognize him as a member of the mission. It is common practice in such, not infrequent, situations for the sending state to reciprocate the expulsion by singling out for an identical treatment freely selected members of the mission of the other state.

The termination of a diplomatic mission as a whole brings the diplomatic relations to a close. It must be distinguished from the termination of the mission of the head of mission himself, in which case the mission itself continues to function under a *chargé d'affaires ad interim*, sometimes for a prolonged period of time. Apart from death, resignation, transfer or, sometimes, expiration of temporary credentials, the head of mission may be recalled "for consultation," a step reflecting a serious tension in the relations between the two states. He may also be asked to leave by the receiving state as *persona non grata* if the sending state has declined to recall him. Breaking off diplomatic relations implies a very serious deterioration of the relations between the states concerned, but does not signify withdrawal of recognition. Normally, outbreak of war **(338)** brings the diplomatic missions of the belligerents to a close, but in some more recent armed conflicts **(339)**, which amounted to regular warfare, such as the China-India war of 1962, the Indo-Pakistani War of 1965, and throughout much of the bloody and long war between Iran and Iraq (1980–1988), the diplomatic missions in the relations between the belligerents continued, albeit subject to various restrictions and breaches of inviolability **(67)**. Under the Vienna Convention (Art. 45(a)), if diplomatic relations are broken off or if a mission is recalled, the receiving state must, even in case of armed conflict, respect and protect the premises of the mission, together with its property and archives. Furthermore, in case of armed conflict, it must facilitate the departure of the other party's mission at the earliest possible moment (Art. 44). The sending state, for its part, if diplomatic relations are broken off or the mission is recalled, may entrust the custody of the premises of the mission and the protection of its interests and those of its nationals to a third state acceptable to the receiving state (Art. 45 (b)(c)). In such cases some diplomatic agents of the states in question may, with the permission of the respective receiving state, continue necessary functions in the" special interests section" of the embassy of the third state which undertook the custody of the respective sending state's mission. Such an arrangement was, for example, agreed upon in the US-Cuba relations, with Switzerland and (now) the Czech Republic offering the premises of their respective missions to accommodate the US and Cuban interest sections, respectively. Similarly, upon the severance of diplomatic relations between Iran and the US in 1980, a US interests section was established in the embassy of Switzerland in Tehran and an Iranian section in the Algerian embassy in Washington.

A constitutional change in the head of state in the sending or receiving state does not affect the continued order of precedence or produce any substantial changes in the diplomatic relations of the states concerned, except perhaps for the issuance of new credentials. On the other hand, an unconstitutional change of the political regime, replacing the head of state in the sending or receiving state, normally terminates the appointments of the heads of mission. Otherwise, the status of the missions depends on the political relations between the two states and especially, if relevant, their respective positions on the issue of recognition of the new government **(114)**.

Voluntary extinction of a state as, for example, the absorption of the German Democratic Republic into the Federal Republic of Germany **(135)**, terminates the diplomatic missions involved. On the other hand, unlawful annexation, such as resulting from unlawful use of force **(329)**, as was the case of annexation of Kuwait by Iraq, does not affect the status of the diplomatic missions of the occupied **(363)** or annexed country, accredited to third states. An interesting historical example of continued existence of diplomatic missions of annexed states is offered by the missions of the three Baltic republics subjugated **(194)** by the former Soviet Union, which, in principle, continued to be accredited in the US, a country that did not recognize their annexation into the Soviet Union.

**69. Diplomatic Mission: Administrative and Technical Staff.** Art. 1(b) of the Vienna Convention on Diplomatic Relations, 1961 **(71)**, defines the "members of the administrative and technical staff" of a diplomatic mission **(68)** as the members of the staff of the mission employed in the administrative and technical service of the mission. Included are such employees as administrative officers, typists, mail and file clerks, and the like. They do not belong to the diplomatic staff of the mission and do not have diplomatic rank **(63)**. Although historically they enjoyed considerable privileges and immunities, the practice of states was not uniform in this area. Hence the nature of their status and the extent of their privileges and immunities were not clearly defined in customary law **(39)**. As a result, they became a subject of some controversy at the Vienna Conference which adopted the Convention of 1961 and the pertinent provisions of the Convention, in particular Art. 37(2) on privileges and immunities, can be considered as an example of progressive development of international law **(5)**.

Under the Convention, the sending state may freely appoint the members of the administrative and technical staff of a diplomatic mission, subject—as in the case of the diplomatic staff—to the right of the receiving state to require that the size of the mission be kept within reasonable limits and the right to declare any member of the administrative and technical staff as "not acceptable" (corresponding to *persona non grata,* used only in the case of a diplomatic agent) (Arts. 7, 9, 11)). Like in the case of diplomats, the appointment, arrival, and final departure of members of the administrative and technical staff must be notified to the ministry for foreign affairs of the receiving state.

Concerning the crucial question of privileges and immunities, Art. 37(2) accords members of the administrative and technical staff of the mission, together with members of their families forming part of their respective households if they are not nationals or permanent residents of the receiving state, all the privileges and immunities enjoyed by diplomatic agents specified in Articles 29 to 35 of the Convention (inviolability **(67)**, immunity from criminal and civil jurisdiction **(87)**, exemption from social security provisions, taxation, and personal and public service). However, immunity from civil and administrative (but not criminal) jurisdiction does not extend to acts performed outside the course of their duties. Furthermore, they enjoy immunity from customs duties only in respect of articles imported at the time of first installation. Under Art. 40(2), third states must not hinder their passage and that of the members of their families through their territories in circumstances similar to those applicable to diplomats in transit **(61)**.

Like other nondiplomatic staff and private servants, members of the administrative and technical staff of a diplomatic mission who are nationals or permanent residents of the receiving state enjoy privileges and immunities only to the extent admitted by the receiving state which, however, must exercise its jurisdiction over them in such a manner as not to interfere unduly with the performance of the function of the mission (Art. 38).

**70. Diplomatic Mission: Service Staff.** Art. 1(g) of the Vienna Convention on Diplomatic Relations, 1961 **(71)**, defines the "members of the service staff" of a diplomatic mission **(68)** as the members of the mission in domestic service. Such members of the staff, who include chauffeurs, butlers, maids, gardeners, etc., are to be distinguished from "private servants" who are in the domestic service of a member of the mission and are not employees of the sending state.

The provisions of the Vienna Convention on the administrative and technical staff, including those concerning transit through a third state, apply to the service staff except that—as far as privileges and immunities are concerned—members of the service staff who are not nationals or permanent residents of the receiving state have immunity only in respect of acts performed in the course of their duties (Art. 7(3)), as might be the case of an embassy chauffeur involved in a traffic accident during a business trip. They are exempt from dues and taxes on the emoluments they receive by reason of their employment, and from social security provisions of the receiving state, the exemptions enjoyed also by private servants. In other respects private servants may enjoy privileges and immunities only to the extent admitted by the receiving state. However, that state must exercise its jurisdiction over them in such a manner as not to interfere unduly with the performance of the functions of the mission.

**71. Diplomatic Relations, Vienna Convention on, 1961.** A multilateral convention **(288)** of 53 articles, based upon the Draft Articles prepared by the International Law Commission and adopted by a United Nations–sponsored international conference in Vienna in 1961 (500 UNTS 95). The Convention entered into force **(271)** in 1964 and by the end of the century virtually all states had become parties. The United States joined in 1972 and implemented the Convention by the Diplomatic Relations Act of 1978. In addition to the Convention itself, the Vienna Conference adopted the Optional Protocol Concerning the Acquisition of Nationality **(175)** (500 UNTS 223) and the Optional Protocol Concerning the Compulsory Settlement of Disputes **(299)** (500 UNTS 241).

While not specifying to what extent it is declaratory of customary law **(39)**, the Vienna Convention is primarily a codification **(5)** of the customary rules **(39)** of international diplomatic law. In certain respects, however, such as for example the more restricted treatment of the immunities of the administrative and technical staff **(69)** and the even more constrained scope of the immunity of the service staff **(70)**, it constitutes a progressive development of the law, establishing rules in an area of uncertain and inconsistent practice. But, as declared in the Preamble to the Convention, "the rules of customary international law should continue to govern questions not expressly regulated by the provisions of the Convention." The Convention expressly forbids discrimination in the application of its rules, but a restrictive, that is, less favorable application of a provision on grounds of reciprocity or a more favorable treatment extended by custom or agreement are allowed (Art. 47).

In codifying and progressively developing the crucial subject of privileges and immunities, the Convention is guided by the functional necessity theory whereby—as declared in its Preamble—"the purpose of such privileges and immunities is not to benefit individuals but to ensure the efficient performance of the functions of diplomatic missions **(68)** as representing States."

**72. Distress.** Art. 25 of the International Law Commission Draft Articles on state responsibility **(129)** precludes the wrongfulness of an act of a state in violation of that state's international obligation if the author of the conduct in question had no other reasonable way, in a situation of distress, of saving his life or the lives of other persons entrusted to his care. However, the act remains wrongful if the conduct of the state in question has contributed to the situation of distress or if the act in question was likely to create a comparable or greater peril.

In theory, unlike the case of *force majeure* **(78)**, it is materially possible for a person in distress to comply with the international law obligation involved. For example, a warship **(265)** in distress may have a choice between compliance with the law but risking inevitable loss on the one hand and entering foreign territorial sea **(262)** or other foreign waters and saving lives, on the other. The 1982 Convention on the Law of the Sea **(264)** takes into account distress and *force majeure* in that it includes exculpatory provisions in such situations as vessels in distress and marine pollution **(255)**.

The *Rainbow Warrior* Arbitration, 1990 **(104)**, elaborates in more detail on the conditions which have to be met for the plea of distress to be acceptable in a case of extreme urgency involving elementary humanitarian considerations affecting state agents.

**73. Equality of States.** One of the fundamental principles of international law whereby all states **(117)**, notwithstanding the obvious inequalities in various respects, are equal before the law, with equal rights and obligations under international law. The principle of the equality of states dates back to the early doctrine of the law of nations and nature. Samuel Pufendorf **(33)** saw equality as a natural condition of states and Emmerich de Vattel's **(45)** statement that "a small republic is no less a sovereign State than the most powerful kingdom" is often quoted to illustrate the principle of the equality of states. However, in actual state practice the principle of the equality of all states before the law was not recognized until much later. In the contemporary era, the United Nations (UN) Charter (Art. 2(1)) proclaims that "the Organization is based on the principle of the sovereign equality of all its Members." This principle was reaffirmed in numerous international instruments, including in particular the General Assembly Friendly Relations Declaration of 1970 **(14)**. As elaborated by the Declaration, sovereign equality, as regards each state, includes juridical, that is legal equality; enjoyment of the rights inherent in full sovereignty **(125)**; the duty to respect the personality of other states; inviolability of the territorial integrity and political independence; the right freely to choose and develop its political, social, economic, and cultural systems; and the duty to comply fully and in good faith with international obligations and to live in peace with other states.

Among the major legal consequences of the principle of the legal equality of states, which in themselves are a corollary of the very fact of the independence of states, are: the right to a vote when decision making is based on consent, but to one vote only, unless otherwise freely accepted and agreed upon (as in the case of "weighted voting" differentiated according to certain power elements, for example in the International Monetary Fund and the World Bank); equal treatment before international law irrespective of whether a state is powerful or weak; sovereign immunity **(131)** from the jurisdiction **(87)** of other states according to the maxim *par in parem non habet imperium* (a peer (an equal) has no jurisdiction over another peer); and the right of the state not to have the validity of its official acts questioned by courts in another state insofar as they are not contrary to international law and purport to take effect within its jurisdiction (the "act of state doctrine" **(51)**).

Despite the fundamental nature of the principle of equality, in practice the great powers have always been realistically recognized not only for their role in creating and developing international law but also have been, albeit reluctantly, accorded a special legal status. This was the case in the League of Nations in which the principal allied powers secured for themselves permanent seats on the organization's Council, and is the case now in the UN where the five permanent members of the Security Council (China, France, Russia, United Kingdom, United States) have a privileged legal status in the UN and in particular in the working of its collective security system **(327)**. It must also be borne in mind that legal equality does not exclude differentiation in the treatment of other states in terms of both preferential and discriminatory treatment; it is only when discrimination becomes so arbitrary as to constitute abuse of rights **(50)** that, under the circumstances, the principle of legal equality may be infringed upon.

**74. Exhaustion of Local Remedies.** A well-established rule of customary international law **(39)** concerning an aspect of admissibility of claims in international adjudication **(306)** whereby an injured alien **(144)**, whether an individual or a corporation or other juridical persons, must first exhaust all effective and reasonable local remedies available in the state in which the injury occurred, before the state of the injured alien's nationality **(175)** may exercise its right of diplomatic protection and bring an international claim before an international tribunal on behalf of its national, that is, "espouse" its national's claim. Among the reasons for the existence of the rule of the exhaustion of local remedies, the following are usually invoked: to reduce the number of potential international claims by giving, first, the state concerned an opportunity to deal with an alleged injury to the alien under its own municipal law **(27)** system, something that a resident alien should in any case do according to the general principles of territorial jurisdiction **(91)**; to ascertain the basis for the international claim of the alien's national state; to make it possible for the state concerned to avoid breaching an international obligation by redressing the consequences of the injurious conduct; and, more generally, to uphold respect for sovereignty **(125)** as a fundamental principle of international law. Whether exhaustion of local remedies is a substantive or procedural rule of international law has been a subject of debate in the doctrine for some time. In 2001 the International Law Commission (ILC) Rapporteur concluded that it might be substantive if it formed part of the wrong inflicted, or procedural if it originated in a subsequent separate act, such as denial of justice **(152)**.

Under the rule of exhaustion of local remedies, an injured alien should seek recourse in the whole system of legal protection available in the state in question, including, in addition to administrative remedies, courts and tribunals as well as the available procedural facilities. Whether remedies of an extraordinary nature should also be exhausted is not a settled issue.

The rule of exhaustion of local remedies does not apply to disputes **(299)** between states; there, injury is inflicted directly on the state which in such cases itself protects its sovereign rights. Nor does the rule apply if no appropriate remedies are available or are known to be in practice ineffective and, in general, if it is obvious that recourse to local remedies would be futile under the circumstances. There is no requirement of exhausting local remedies if it is dispensed with by waiver of the state where the remedies exist or by a treaty as, for example was agreed between the United States and

Mexico with respect to claims before the Mexican Claims Commission **(315)**. However, dispensing with the requirement of local remedies must be stated in express terms and not merely implied.

The rule of exhaustion of local remedies has been applied by the International Court of Justice (ICJ) **(309)** in the *Interhandel* case (Switzerland v. United States) (1959 ICJ Rep. 6) in which Switzerland's claim was rejected because of non-observance of this rule, held by the Court to be "a well established principle of customary international law." The rule was also at issue in the case of *Elettronica Sicula S.p.A.* (*ELSI*) (United States of America v. Italy) (1989 ICJ Rep. 15), which was decided by a Chamber **(295)** of the ICJ. As far as arbitral tribunals **(293)** are concerned, the *Ambatielos* Arbitration (12 UNRIAA 83) between Greece and the United Kingdom, 1956, which followed the ICJ judgments in the *Ambatielos case* (1952 ICJ Rep. 28; 1953 ICJ Rep. 10), is often invoked to illustrate the rule of exhaustion of local remedies. In this arbitration it was held that, by failing to call a vital witness and to appeal from the Court of Appeal to the House of Lords, the alien (Ambatielos) had not met the requirement of exhausting the local remedies available under the English law.

As part of its codification **(5)** work, the ILC has dealt with the topic of exhaustion of local remedies within the context of diplomatic protection. This work was resumed in 1997 and in 2001 the Rapporteur submitted proposals on the topic to the 53d session of the Commission.

**75. Extradition.** A form of international judicial assistance designed to deny criminals safe haven abroad, extradition is a formal procedure whereby an individual accused or convicted of a crime under the laws of one state, is arrested in another state and handed over to the former state, at that state's request, for trial or punishment. Ordinarily the alleged offense was committed in the territory of the "requesting" state or aboard a vessel or aircraft flying its flag **(240)**, and the offender has fled to the territory of the state asked to surrender him, the "requested" state.

A legal right to demand extradition and a duty to extradite do not exist in customary **(39)** international law. As provided for in the laws of many countries, extradition is based on treaty **(288)** arrangements, usually bilateral, and is circumscribed by certain requirements. Whether even in the absence of a treaty a state has the duty to extradite a suspected terrorist **(337)**, foregoing the alternative to prosecute him itself which is available to it under a treaty, such as the Montreal Sabotage Convention of 1971 **(210)**, was an issue arising in connection with the Lockerbie disaster involving the destruction of an American airliner over Scotland in 1988, and a consequent Security Council resolution ordering Libya to surrender the suspects for trial under the law of Scotland.

Although certain general international law principles, such as those of double criminality and specialty, can be derived from the vast network of bilateral (and a few multilateral regional) treaties, such treaties have not crystallized into a customary rule of international law that would require a state to "extradite" in the absence of a treaty obligation. However, while many states extradite only if bound by a treaty, states are free, subject only to certain limitations motivated by human rights **(157)** (such as the prohibition of *refoulement,* that is, forced expulsion of a refugee to a state where his life or liberty would be jeopardized, found in the 1951 Convention on refugees **(178)**), to informally hand over an individual even if no extradition treaty exists with the requesting state, or hand him over to a third state from which he can be formally extradited.

The practice of concluding multilateral extradition treaties, known for about a hundred years, is of relatively limited importance, with perhaps the most notable exceptions the Council of Europe European Convention on Extradition, 1957 (359 UNTS 273) and the Inter-American Convention on Extradition of 1981 (20 ILM 723 (1981)). In addition, a number of multilateral treaties dealing with offenses of special concern to international community, such as genocide **(155)**, air hijacking **(185)** and other terrorist crimes, which in a quasi-universal manner establish a multiple basis for national jurisdiction **(87)**, oblige the parties either to extradite or otherwise surrender individuals wanted for trial by another treaty party for the offense in question, or to try such suspected offenders themselves (the principle of *aut dedere aut judicare*).

Since 1833, when the newly born state of Belgium became the first country to adopt a national extradition law, many states, including the United States (US), have enacted similar laws which list the extraditable offenses and provide for rules governing extradition and its procedure. Subject to contrary treaty provisions, any individual, in the common-law countries irrespective of his nationality **(175)**, may be extradited. On the other hand, countries of the civil-law **(23)** tradition on the whole follow the principle of non-extradition of nationals, but many of them apply the nationality principle of jurisdiction **(88)** more extensively than it is done in the common-law countries.

In general, extradition is granted only in cases of serious offenses. Traditional extradition treaties list the extraditable offenses, but the more recent treaties, including the multilateral ones, define the extraditable offenses in terms of acts subject to a certain minimum level of punishment, one year for example, and considered as crimes in both the requesting and the requested state. Under this requirement of "double criminality," widely accepted in international practice as a principle of international extradition law, a fugitive will not be extradited unless the offense involved is punishable as a serious crime in both countries at the time of the commission of the offense. But for the extradition to proceed, the offense in question need not be defined in equivalent terms in the two countries as long as there is similarity in the substance between the definitions. On the other hand, the principle of double criminality is not satisfied if the offense is listed in both states among extraditable offenses but is understood differently in its substance. This is illustrated by the incident in 1948 involving Eisler, a German national and a Communist Party member who, having made false statements before a US congressional committee in his application to leave the US, jumped bail and fled aboard a ship bound for Poland, then under Communist rule. When the ship stopped in England, Eisler was arrested pursuant to the US request that he be extradited to the US for perjury, as provided in the United Kingdom–US extradition treaty. However, the English court refused to allow extradition on the grounds that while perjury under the US law was defined as swearing falsely before a government official or a legislative hearing, Eisler's offense was not perjury as defined by the English law according to which only a charge of swearing falsely in a judicial proceeding would meet the test of double criminality for purposes of extradition. As a result, Eisler was released and eventually arrived in Communist East Germany.

As required by most extradition treaties and municipal legislation **(27)** (but not necessarily by customary law), a request for extradition submitted to the state of refuge through diplomatic channels must be preceded by some kind of judicial inquiry in that state to examine whether the evidence submitted by the requesting state provides a *prima facie* case against the alleged offender to allow the extradition. However, in many countries decisions on extradition are made in administrative proceedings and may even be a mere formality.

State practice and treaties generally recognize that a fugitive may not be subject to double jeopardy, that is be prosecuted more than once for the offense which was the basis for extradition. As a rule, treaties preclude extradition if prosecution or, in some treaties, also enforcement of the sentence, has been barred by the appropriate period of limitation.

Even though the conditions for extradition may have been met and the proceedings completed, the executive branch of the requested state still has the discretion to decline surrendering the fugitive, for example because of concern that he would not receive a fair trial in the requesting state or would be subject to other violations of human rights. In this context, the general tendency in recent extradition treaties has been to allow extradition or otherwise surrender the fugitive on the condition that he will not face death penalty in the requesting state.

To protect extradited individuals and preclude open-ended requests for extradition, most extradition treaties provide for, and the practice follows the doctrine or principle of specialty whereby, unless the state of refuge waives the requirement, the requesting state may not try the extradited individual for any pre-extradition offense other than the one for which the extradition was asked and granted, or to punish him more severely than was stipulated by the law of the requesting state at the time of the extradition request. A re-extradition by the requesting state to a third state also requires the consent of the state of refuge. Difficult issues arise in connection with the principle of non-extradition of fugitives charged with or convicted of the so-called political offenses **(76)**.

Since surrender of fugitives is allowed also in the absence of any treaty provisions, states may hand over such individuals by comity **(6)** or resort to various methods of informal *de facto* extradition, including summary deportation to the requesting country, However, in the prevailing international legal opinion and contrary to the highly criticized US Supreme Court's decision in the *United States v. Machain* case, 1992 (31 ILM 900 (1992)), good faith requires that if an extradition treaty exists between the countries involved, the country seeking prosecution of an alleged offender present in the other country, is in breach of international law not only by abducting him forcibly from that country but also by prosecuting him and thus exercising personal jurisdiction over the abducted individual. In the *Machain* case a Mexican national suspected by the US of involvement in the murder in Mexico of a US government (Drug Enforcement Agency) agent, was abducted by agents of the US government from Mexico and taken to the US to face charges there, over Mexico's protests and demands for his return for trial in Mexico. While admitting the illegality of the abduction, the US Supreme Court held that it could legally exercise jurisdiction over Machain without breaching the US-Mexico extradition treaty (1978) (17 ILM 1058 (1978)) because the treaty did not expressly forbid trial of abducted offenders. As it turned out, Machain was eventually acquitted of all charges and the US assured Mexico that it would respect its sovereignty **(125)** in accordance with international law.

**76. Extradition and Political Offense.** The concept of political offense, like that of political offender, is ordinarily relevant within the context of the international law of extradition **(75)** in which the principle of non-extradition of political offenders, while not a norm of customary **(39)** international law, is found in virtually all extradition treaties since 1834 when, in a politically more liberal era, it was first adopted in the Franco-Belgium treaty of 1834. In municipal law, **(27)** it was Belgium (which owed its statehood to a political rebellion) that became the first country to enact a law prohibiting extradition of political offenders in 1833. Prior to that, in the largely homogeneous European system of absolutist regimes, extradition had, as a rule, been used to secure the surrender of political offenders viewed as a common menace to the political systems of the day.

While widely accepted both in the municipal laws and in extradition treaties, in its application the concept of political offense has caused insurmountable difficulties and has so far evaded a universally acceptable and precise definition. The concept encounters similar problems within the context of the related area of territorial asylum **(148)**. The major reason for these problems lies in the necessarily subjective view of the very existence and scope of the political element of an offense, in particular when elements of a common crime and political motivations and objectives are closely intertwined. What in the eyes of one state is a band of common criminals or terrorists to be extradited for punishment may be viewed by another state as a political movement aspiring to laudable ends and deserving support rather than punishment. Hence under customary law it may still be permissible to refuse surrender of an individual regarded as a terrorist suspect by the requesting state but as a non-extraditable political offender by the state sheltering him.

Relatively simple are what is sometimes referred to as pure political offenses, traditionally proscribed by all states: sedition, treason, espionage, conspiracy to overthrow the government, and purely military offenses. Much more controversial are the so-called relative political offenses, that is, common crimes with a political motivation, objective, or some other political coloring, depending on the circumstances. For example, murder and manslaughter, crimes typically subject to extradition, may not lead to the surrender of the fugitives to the requesting state if committed for political motives.

Two leading cases before English courts in the late 19th century illustrate the distinction between a relative political offense and an extraditable common crime. In the case *Ex parte Castioni* (1891, 1 QB 149) the court refused extradition to Switzerland of Castioni who had taken part in an armed attempt by a group of other citizens in the canton of Ticino to overthrow the cantonal government, in the course of which a cantonal official was shot dead by Castioni. The court determined that since the shooting was incidental to a political disturbance and the perpetrator was part of a political movement involved in an assault upon a governmental authority, the offense was of a political character as against Switzerland (the requesting state) and therefore extradition had to be denied. In contrast, in *Re Meunier* (1894, 2 QB 415) the court granted France's request for extradition of Meunier, a fugitive French anarchist who, in revenge for the execution of another conspirator, had set off two lethal explosions in Paris resulting in the death of two individuals and was under a death sentence in France. The English court held that Meunier's acts in Paris did not constitute a political offense but individual acts of promoting chaos, the anarchist group with which he identified aiming at an abolition of government rather than taking political control of it, and being directed primarily against the general body of private citizens.

In the second half of the 20th century, at the height of the Cold War, courts in Western countries, including the United States (US), the United Kingdom (UK), and Germany, relaxed the *Castioni* test in cases involving fugitives from Communist states, refusing to surrender such individuals even where the offense in question (hijacking a ship or an aircraft) **(185)** was in itself a common crime and no contention for political power in the traditional sense was taking place in the Communist state in question. The major reason for refusing to surrender the fugitives from Communist rule was to protect them from excessive punishment and repression by a totalitarian state on account of their political opinions.

In another political context, courts in the US would for some time refuse, on grounds of political offense exception, to extradite to the UK members of the Provisional Irish Republican Party charged in Northern Ireland and in England with crimes of violence. Subsequently, in 1985, in order to exclude terrorist **(337)** crimes from the political offense exception in the UK-US extradition treaty of 1972 (1049 UNTS 167), the two countries signed a Supplementary Treaty (24 ILM 1104 (1985)) which excluded the application of that exception to certain specified terrorist offenses, including aircraft hijacking and sabotage, hostage taking, abduction, murder and manslaughter, offenses relating to the use of explosives or firearms, and damage to property with intent to endanger life.

In any case, war crimes **(373)** and crimes against humanity **(151)** are excluded from the concept of political offenses, a rule expressly stated in the Genocide Convention, 1948 **(151)**, and endorsed in a number of General Assembly resolutions. Furthermore, in reaction to a rising incidence of terrorist acts in the 1970s and 1980s a perception grew that perpetrators of such acts should be denied refuge in a foreign country and be subject to extradition as common criminals.

Historically, international cooperation to restrict the notion of political offense for purposes of extradition dates back to the enactment by Belgium of the so-called *attentat* clause (*attentat* meaning in French successful or unsuccessful attempt on someone's life) in 1856, following an assassination attempt on the life of Emperor Napoleon III and Belgium's refusal to extradite the would-be assassin to France because of the Belgian law barring extradition of political offenders. Under the *attentat* clause, an attempt on the life of a head of a foreign state or a member of the family is not considered a political offense and consequently the perpetrator is subject to extradition. In the course of time the clause was widely, albeit not universally, adopted in national law and extradition treaties, including the Council of Europe European Convention on Extradition, 1957 (359 UNTS 273).

Certain multilateral treaties explicitly exclude from the concept of political offense specific acts of violence (hijacking **(185)**, hostage taking, etc.) which are usually encompassed within the concept of terrorist acts. Among the relatively few such instruments are, in addition to the Genocide Convention, the above-noted European Convention on Extradition of 1957, the Inter-American Convention on Extradition of 1981 (20 ILM 723 (1981)) and the European Convention for the Suppression of Terrorism adopted by the Council of Europe in 1976 (15 ILM 1272 (1976)). It might be added that the Convention on the Status of Refugees **(178)** of 1951 excludes from its scope any person that committed a serious common crime prior to entering the country of refuge. Exceptions to the concept of political offense can be more readily found in bilateral extradition treaties, such as, *inter alia,* the US-Brazil treaty of 1961 (532 UNTS 177) providing for the exception of anarchism; the above-noted Supplementary Treaty between the UK and US of 1985; the Protocol of 1988 (27 ILM 422 (1988)) amending the US-Canada Extradition Treaty of 1971; and the US-Federal Republic of Germany Supplementary Extradition Treaty of 1986 (81 AJIL 935 (1987)) to the Extradition Treaty of 1978 (1220 UNTS 269).

As part of international cooperation in combating acts of terrorism (and certain other universally condemned crimes) a number of multilateral treaties incorporate the policy of denying shelter to offenders by requiring the parties either to surrender or to prosecute them (*aut dedere aut judicare*). The crimes involved cannot be considered as political offenses. These treaties, which otherwise establish a wide quasi-universal multiple jurisdictional basis **(92)** for the states parties include, *inter alia* (in addition to the Genocide Convention **(155)**, the four Geneva Conventions of

1949 **(349)** and the Protocols of 1977 **(369)**; the Tokyo Convention dealing with offenses on board aircraft **(229)**; anti-narcotic Conventions of 1961 (520 UNTS 521), 1971 (976 UNTS 3, and 1988 (1019 UNTS 175); the Hague hijacking **(199)** and the Montreal civil aviation sabotage **(210)** Conventions of 1970 and 1971, respectively; the Convention on the prevention and punishment of crimes against internationally protected persons, including diplomatic agents, 1973 (1035 UNTS 17); the International Convention against the taking of hostages, 1979 (18 ILM 1456 (1979); the Convention against torture **(182)**; the Convention to Suppress Acts against the Safety of Maritime Navigation, 1988, with a Protocol relating to the continental shelf, (27 ILM 672, 685 (1988)); the Convention against mercenaries **(360)**; and the above-mentioned European Convention of 1976 for the Suppression of Terrorism.

**77. Federation.** Federation or federal state is a union of states into a single composite state which becomes the only international legal person **(85)**, the constituent territorial units ("states," provinces, cantons, and the like) having permanently surrendered the control of foreign affairs and some other important powers to the federal government while authority in internal matters is divided by the constitution between the federal government and the member units of the federation. One clear, distinguishing feature of a federation, as contrasted with a confederation **(54)**, is the fact that a federal government possesses, side by side with the governments of the component units, a direct authority and jurisdiction over the citizens of these units. Furthermore, while in practice there may be some variations in the division of competences between the federal government and the component units, a federal state differs from a confederation also in that it is the only subject of international law, that is, the only international legal person responsible under international law for any violation of international obligations by any of its component units. In this regard, the division of powers between the federal government and the component units may create problems in the implementation of treaty **(288)** provisions, for example, International Labour Organisation conventions, which regulate certain matters constitutionally reserved to these units, such as the states of the United States (US). A "federal clause" in treaties to which a federal state is a party, whereby such state may be somewhat relieved from treaty obligations in matters within the domain of the component units, is sometimes used but, as a matter of principle, conflicts with the requirements of effectiveness and reciprocity in treaty relations.

Under some federal constitutions, the component units possess a very limited personality in international law allowing them, with the consent of the federal government, to enter into agreements with a neighboring state or its territorial unit on matters of common local concern such as transborder traffic, maintenance of bridges and roads, and the like. Provisions to this effect are found, for example, in the Constitution of Switzerland (Art. 7 and 9), a federation since 1848 (despite its official name in French, *Confédération*), and that of the Federal Republic of Germany (Art. 32).

Under Art. I, sec. 10 of the Constitution of the US, a federation since 1787, the federal government has exclusive treaty-making power, but a component state may, with the consent of Congress, enter into an agreement or compact with a foreign state, including that state's territorial unit, but in practice agreements involving local transborder issues have not required congressional consent. A state of the US may not exchange diplomatic missions **(68)** but may send agents to foreign countries in matters concerning its commercial and similar interests of a local nature.

Today, while most members of the international community are unitary states, a considerable number of states in all parts of the world are federations. In addition to the US, they include: Argentina, Australia, Austria, Belgium, Bosnia-Herzegovina, Brazil, Canada, Ethiopia, Germany, India, Malaysia, Mexico, Federated States of Micronesia, Nigeria, Pakistan, Russia, Switzerland, United Arab Emirates, Venezuela, and a rather loose federation known as "State Union of Serbia and Montenegro."

***78. Force Majeure.*** This term applies to one category of "circumstances precluding wrongfulness" of an act of state, namely a situation where the act was due to an irresistible force or an unforeseen event beyond the control of the state, which made it materially impossible in the circumstances to perform the obligation in question. However, a state cannot disclaim responsibility **(128)** on grounds of *force majeure* if the occurrence of *force majeure* results from the conduct of the state invoking it or if the state has assumed the risk of that occurrence. *Force majeure* has long been recognized in international law as absolving the state concerned from responsibility for an otherwise wrongful act. The International Law Commission Draft Articles on State Responsibility of 2001 **(129)** include it among the other circumstances precluding wrongfulness, namely, self-defense **(335)**, distress **(72)**, necessity **(96)**, the need to comply with *jus cogens* **(24)**, and countermeasures **(58)**, all of them situations where a state does not incur responsibility and an otherwise unlawful act becomes permissible. For example, *force majeure* occurs in case of violation by an aircraft of foreign airspace **(186)** due to bad weather or malfunction of the equipment, which made such diversion from the course unavoidable or of which the pilot was unaware. As illustrated by the shooting down by a Soviet military aircraft of a South Korean airliner in 1983 (23 ILM 937 (1984)), it may be very difficult to verify whether an act in question was indeed due to *force majeure*. In 1929 the Permanent Court of International Justice **(320)** in the case of *Serbian Loans* (France/Yugoslavia) (PCIJ, Series A, No. 20) rejected Serbia's argument that World War I had made it materially impossible to repay loans. The Court required a high standard of proof for Serbia's plea of *force majeure* which it declined to accept. More recently, the pleas of *force majeure* and distress were invoked by France in the arbitration between New Zealand and France over the *Rainbow Warrior* case **(104)**.

**79. Government in Exile.** Government in exile or exile government is a government that lacks its territorial base **(228)** and for political reasons had to establish itself abroad in a friendly country. A typical case of exile government is represented by a government forced to flee its own country or one established abroad, as a result of enemy occupation, as was the case of a number of exile governments (Czechoslovakia, Poland, Norway, Netherlands, Yugoslavia, among others) set up first in France and then in the United Kingdom, following the occupation of their respective countries by Germany during World War II until the defeat of Germany allowed them (in most cases) to return to their respective territories.

An exile government which fled its country or its successor in exile continues to be recognized *de jure* **(110)** by other states, generally on the assumption that the displacement of the government was caused by an illegal and temporary occupation which did not terminate the existence of the affected state **(127)**. An exile government continues to be the legal representative of the state without in fact exercising effective control over its territory and population, although it can perform some state functions through an underground network of clandestine authority, as was, for example, the case in German-occupied Poland.

A government in exile may lawfully sign treaties on behalf of its state; has control of its assets in recognizing states; exercises authority over its citizens abroad; and certain of its absentee laws applicable to events in the occupied homeland may be given effect and continue to be recognized by subsequent *de jure* governments.

Another type of exile government emerged after World War II during the era of decolonization when some "national liberation movements" **(94)** (unlike others that preferred simply to be accredited to friendly international organizations **(84)**), proclaimed and established "provisional" governments in friendly countries well before gaining control of their respective claimed territories, that is, before the aspired state was created, as was the case of the provisional government of Algeria set up in Tunisia in 1952 and recognized **(114)** before the actual independence was achieved in 1962. From the point of view of the idea of self-determination of overseas colonial peoples **(122)** such recognition was perfectly legal, while under the rules of the traditional international law it was certainly premature and could be regarded as intervention in the affairs of the metropolitan state.

**80. Holy See—Vatican City.** A unique international legal person **(85)** possessing a sovereign territorial base **(228)** in the form of the Vatican City and universally recognized as a subject of international law by the international community. Historically, the Holy See has for centuries enjoyed a special position as a subject of international law not only because of the Pope's status as the head of a once relatively large state in central Italy ("the Papal States") but primarily because of his position as the Head of the Catholic Church. In 1870, following the absorption, on the tide of Italian nationalism, of the remainder of the Papal States into the united Kingdom of Italy, the Papacy lost its territorial basis and its status became regulated—against the protests by the Pope—by the Italian municipal **(27)** Law of Guarantee of 1871. However, internationally the Holy See continued to be recognized by most states as a *sui generis* subject of international law.

Almost sixty years following the annexation of the last papal territory by Italy, the conflict between the Holy See and the Italian state was finally resolved by the Lateran Treaty in 1929 (23 AJIL 216 (1929)) between the two parties, which formally recognized the Holy See as an international legal person and created for the Papacy a territorial basis **(228)** in the form of the State of the Vatican City under the sovereignty **(125)** of the incumbent Supreme Pontiff and pledged to permanent neutrality **(97)**. A concordat and a financial convention, revised in 1984 (24 ILM 1589 (1985)), regulated the position of the Church in Italy and provided for a financial compensation of the Holy See.

Although not a state in the normal sense of the word and with Italy performing for it a number of state functions, the State of the Vatican City, an enclave of 109 acres (44 hectares) within Rome and with some 900 inhabitants, almost exclusively church functionaries and Vatican employees, is widely recognized as a subject of international law, with a treaty-making capacity and the right to send and receive diplomatic missions **(68)**. However, theoretically the question of distinguishing, for purposes of personality under international law, between the Holy See as a religious organ and the Vatican City as a state, is a difficult and controversial one, with some jurists even suggesting the existence of two distinct international legal persons. But the fact of the Holy See possessing a sovereign territorial basis in the form of the State of the Vatican City allows to avoid implications of the religious aspects of international personality, such as possibly similar claims of heads of other religions.

In practice the designation of the Holy See is used for more important political and diplomatic treaties and accreditation of diplomatic agents **(62)**, whereas that of the Vatican City is found in more technical agreements specifically applicable to the Vatican City. The Holy See participates in major international conferences and, apart from bilateral concordats dealing with the status of the Church in the contracting state, is a party to other agreements and especially a number of important multilateral treaties, such as, for example, the two Vienna conventions on diplomatic **(71)** and consular **(56)** relations respectively; the Vienna Convention on the Law of Treaties, 1969 (1155 UNTS 331); the United Nations (UN) Convention on the Law of the Sea **(264)**; and even (with statement) the Treaty on the Non-Proliferation of Nuclear Weapons, 1968 (729 UNTS 161), and the Convention on the Prohibition of Bacteriological (Biological) Weapons of 1972 (1015 UNTS 163). While not yet a member of the UN (but maintaining a permanent observer mission at the UN), the Holy See is a member of such UN specialized agencies as the International Atomic Energy Agency; International Labour Organisation; International Telecommunications Union; United Nations Educational, Scientific, and Cultural Organization; Universal Postal Union; World Health Organization; and World Intellectual Property Organization. Regionally it has membership in the Organization for Security and Cooperation in Europe. Some 100 states maintain diplomatic relations with the Holy See and many grant the Papal nuncio special precedence. While for reasons unrelated to international law the United States had only a personal presidential representative to the Holy See for some time following 1939, full diplomatic relations were established in 1984.

**81. Individuals as Subjects of International Law.** It is a key question in international law whether individuals **(164)** are endowed with international legal personality **(85)**, that is, whether and to what extent they have rights and obligations derived directly from international law, independently of, and sometimes even contrary to their respective national legislation.

In the conception of the law of nations of the early doctrine, dominated by natural law **(29)**, all persons, states **(127)** and individuals alike, were considered to be subject to a universal jurisprudence based on natural law **(29)** which did not make a clear distinction between municipal law **(27)** and the law of nations, that is, international law. Gradually, however, in practice, with the progressing strengthening of the territorial states, there followed, in international perspective, a parallel submergence of the individual within the personality of the state. In the 19th century, when legal positivism **(31)**, reflecting the ascendant assertions of sovereignty **(125)** by territorial states, came to dominate the legal thinking, the legal personality of individuals would become restricted to the municipal sphere of law. Individuals, as it were, became invisible at the international level.

Whereas states constituted subjects of international law, individuals, not as human beings as such but only certain categories of individuals, such as aliens **(144)**, were merely objects of possible treaty regulation between states which might or might not agree to grant them certain benefits according to their discretion. But, as stated by the Permanent Court of International Justice (PCIJ) **(320)** in its advisory opinion **(291)** on the *Jurisdiction of the Courts of Danzig* in 1928 (PCIJ, Series B, No. 15), treaties as such "did not create direct rights and obligations for private individuals." Similarly an injury to an alien was considered to be an offense against the state of his nationality **(175)**, and after he had exhausted the local remedies **(74)** his claim against the foreign state became a claim negotiated **(316)**, at the discretion of the state of nationality **(95)**, on a state-to-state basis, or possibly adjudicated **(306)** by an international tribunal. Private corporations **(173)** and other private juridical persons received similar treatment. However, as also noted in the above-mentioned advisory opinion of the PCIJ, states may at their discretion confer upon individuals direct rights by a treaty, enforceable in municipal courts irrespective of municipal legislation.

The latter decades of the 20th century witnessed an increasing trend in state practice as well as the doctrine of international law toward discarding the legal fiction that states were the exclusive subjects of international law and accepting the view that individuals might, for certain purposes, be governed directly by international law, both in terms of their obligations to follow certain conduct and not to commit acts considered criminal under that law and consequently entailing individual criminal liability (the earlier focus in the evolution of the status of individuals), and in terms of specific rights (subsequent focus) which individuals could pursue, in cases of alleged violation by their respective states, before some kind of international body, perhaps obtaining direct access to an international tribunal independently of the municipal legal system of their respective states.

The evolution of international law with regard to the international legal personality of individuals in terms of their obligations initially focused on their criminal responsibility for grave violations of the laws of war, the "war crimes" **(373)**, and then also on "crimes against humanity" **(151)** and genocide **(155)**. Insofar as their rights are concerned, the quality of individuals as subjects of international law was shaped mainly within the context of the expanding international law of human rights **(160)** in the latter half of the past century.

In general international law, apart from piracy **(259)**, traditionally considered a crime against the law of nations for which individuals were personally responsible, responsibility of individuals for war crimes was recognized already prior to World War I. But it should be added that even with regard to piracy, a doctrinal controversy developed whether individuals were responsible for the crime directly under international law and punishable by states which were authorized by that law to seize and try them, or instead, international law only obligated states to criminalize piracy in their respective national laws and authorized them to prosecute and punish guilty individuals.

Though unsuccessful in enforcing its pertinent provisions, the Peace Treaty of Versailles (225 CTS 188) recognized the right of the Allies to try individuals accused of war crimes and establish the personal responsibility of the German ex-emperor for offenses against "international morality and the security of treaties." However, it was not until following World War II, after the unprecedented crimes against humanity and violations of the laws of war by Nazi Germany, that the International Military Tribunal at Nuremberg **(354)** firmly established the principle that responsibility for certain grave offenses against international law could be directly attributed to individuals who, to that extent, acquired the quality of subjects of that law. In an often-quoted ruling, the Tribunal pointed out that "international law imposes duties and liabilities upon individuals as well as upon states" since "crimes against international law [crimes against peace, crimes against humanity, and war crimes] are committed by men, not by abstract entities, and only by punishing individuals who commit such crimes can the provisions of international law be enforced" (41 AJIL 220 (1947)). The principles of the Nuremberg Charter (82 UNTS 274) and the judgment of the Tribunal were followed by the International Military Tribunal for the Far East **(355)** in its judgment in 1948, and numerous national tribunals trying other war criminals of the defeated states. The Nuremberg principles were unanimously reaffirmed by the General Assembly in 1946 as forming part of general international law and adopted in a number of major international instruments in the second half of the past century. These instruments further developed the responsibility of individuals, whether private persons or state officials of any rank, for certain crimes directly under international law which otherwise became subject to punishment under the so-called universality principle of jurisdiction **(92).** Among the major instruments have been the Genocide Convention, 1948 **(155)** and the four Geneva Conventions, 1949 **(349)** with the two Protocols of 1977 **(369)**, which codified and developed various aspects of international humanitarian law **(353)** on the protection of the victims of armed conflict **(339)**. All these treaties provide for individual responsibility of individuals for grave breaches of their respective provisions, the principle recognized also by the Security Council (SC), *inter alia,* with regard to violations by Iraq during the occupation **(363)** of Kuwait in 1990 of the Fourth Geneva Convention of 1949 Relative to the Protection of Civilian Persons in Time of War. A most significant development in the past decade has been the creation under the authority of the SC of *ad hoc* international criminal tribunals for the prosecution of individuals responsible for serious violations of international humanitarian law in armed conflicts in former Yugoslavia **(352)** and Rwanda **(351)**, followed more recently by the establishment of a similar court in Sierra Leone **(371)**. These tribunals, and especially the first two, have firmly put into practice their statutory rule of individual criminal responsibility irrespective of the position of the individual concerned. This principle also provides the basis for the newly (1998) established International Criminal Court (ICC) **(170)** (Statute of the ICC, Art. 25), a landmark in the evolution of international criminal responsibility of individuals and in that sense their position as persons directly subject to international law.

The exact list of international crimes entailing individual criminal responsibility is not settled in international law. The best guidance in this respect is provided by the Statute of the ICC which constitutes a detailed and comprehensive exposition of the principles of international criminal law, listing a large number of most serious crimes of concern to the international community as a whole within the four general categories of genocide, crimes against humanity, war crimes, and—subject to the adoption of a definition—the crime of aggression **(325)**. The trend in contemporary international law points toward an expansion of the criminal responsibility of individuals to include also such crimes as various categories of terrorist acts **(337)**, torture **(182)**, and perhaps potentially some other offenses, such as illicit traffic in narcotic drugs, cases of massive and serious pollution of the environment, and other suggested offenses, all to be qualified as international crimes irrespective of the position of municipal law and the status of the individual concerned as a private person or a state official of whatever rank.

Prosecution and punishment of individuals for international crimes may take place, as the practice of states has already amply illustrated, either before national courts or international *ad hoc* tribunals and the newly established ICC. National courts may prosecute individuals for international crimes on the basis of the traditional jurisdictional principles: territorial **(91)**, nationality **(88)**, protective **(90)**, possibly passive nationality **(89)**, and, less common, universality. Concerning the last mentioned principle, it is not clear whether a state may be entitled to exercise its jurisdiction, including jurisdiction *in absentia,* on the basis of customary law and without any authorization in municipal law. However, practice shows that states are on the whole reluctant to initiate prosecution of individuals and crimes without any clear link to the state in question. At any rate, although states are not yet obliged under customary international law **(39)** to prosecute or extradite an alleged perpetrator of an international crime, they have an obligation, in the interests of the international community, to cooperate in the prevention and punishment of such crimes.

The international legal personality of individuals by reason of certain specific rights that may accrue to them directly under international law and not as benefits which their state is obligated to provide them because of an international law obligation (mainly a treaty), raises conceptually more difficult issues than those related to individuals' international legal personality founded upon their obligations and consequently criminal responsibility imposed by international law. This question arises primarily within the context of the international law of human rights. While many treaties stipulate substantive rights to be enjoyed by individuals, such rights or perhaps, rather, benefits are normally derived indirectly from a state's treaty obligation to implement them within its municipal legal system. Furthermore, for practical purposes, only an individual's access to an international judicial body, provided for by the pertinent treaty for the purpose of obtaining a legally binding judgment and enforcing the individual's right in his own name and even against his own state, can constitute the test of the individual's international status. However, as noted below, such situations are exceptions in international legal regulations, being limited to the advanced system of protecting human rights in Europe and to a lesser degree in the Western Hemisphere.

Historically, the capacity of individuals to bring claims against their own states for international adjudication dates back to the short-lived Central American Court of Justice (1908–1918) and various arbitration tribunals **(293)** and claims commissions **(314)** set up in the aftermath of World War I to settle claims against Germany and its allies, such as some 96 mixed arbitral tribunals set up under the peace treaties; the German–United States (US) and the US-Austria-Hungary mixed claims commissions; and the German-Polish Upper Silesian Arbitral Tribunal set up in 1922 (9 LNTS 466), which conferred upon members of ethnic minorities a capacity to make direct claims to vested interests against their own and the other state. Following World War II individuals were granted access to submit claims to the Arbitral Commission on Property Rights and Interests in Germany set up by the "Settlement Convention" (322 UNTS 219) (a part of Agreements with Germany of 1952 and 1954) in order to decide cases concerning recovery and restitution of property and rights of nationals of the allied countries. More recently, individuals obtained standing in arbitrations before the International Center for the Settlement of Investment Disputes **(307)** and under certain circumstances before the Iran–United States Claims Tribunal **(312)**. In addition, individual victims of Iraq's aggression against Kuwait in 1990 could submit their claims directly before the quasi-arbitral United Nations (UN) Compensation Commission established by the SC in 1991. It may also be noted that an amendment to the rules of the Permanent Court of Arbitration **(319)**, adopted in 1993, allows nonstate parties, including individuals, to engage in arbitration with states (32 ILM 572 (1993)). Nonstate parties have also access to the International Tribunal for the Law of the Sea **(310)** established by the UN Convention on the Law of the Sea of 1982 **(264)**.

The most significant development in the evolution of the concept of individuals as subjects of rights accrued directly under a treaty and enforceable by them before an international tribunal, even against the state of their nationality **(175)**, has taken place within the European Communities where individuals and companies may enforce their directly binding treaty rights before the Court of Justice of the European Communities (European Court of Justice) **(298)**. But this is a special case in view of the unique nature of the organization in question and the "supranational" features of its legal system.

In the area of human rights at the regional level, in Europe applicants have the capacity to bring their complaints directly before the European Court of Human Rights **(154)** whose jurisdiction has been accepted by the states parties to the Convention **(153)** which established the Court. In the less-advanced Western Hemisphere's system for the protection of human rights individuals have, under certain conditions, direct access to the Commission and the Inter-American Court of Human Rights **(165)**. In both the European and the American systems individuals have a certain capacity as subjects of international law and their complaints are decided primarily according to that system of law regardless of the provisions of the municipal legislation involved.

Apart from the above-noted exceptional cases, individuals have, as a rule, only a procedural right to lodge complaints to international bodies established under a pertinent agreement. Historically, following World War I, ethnic and other minorities in central Europe obtained the right to lodge petitions to the Council of the League of Nations in cases of alleged violations of their treaty rights and—a system still continuing—International Labour Organisation (ILO) rules allow workers' and employers' unions to lodge complaints about violations of ILO conventions. In contemporary international law the system of complaints and petitions applies mainly in the area of the law of human rights. However, the treaty-established international bodies concerned are not judicial in nature and, apart from the fact that the complaining individual ordinarily has no right to participate in the proceedings, the decision of the body has no legally binding force and any enforcement depends on the goodwill of the state involved. In addition, the international procedural right of complaint is based on a treaty to which the state concerned need not necessarily be a party or need not have accepted an optional treaty provision allowing complaints to be filed against that state.

In summary, while states still remain the primary subjects of international law, the status of individuals has changed significantly in the several decades following World War II. They have international legal personality by reason of their individual responsibility directly under general international law with regard to international crimes and, insofar as their rights are concerned, they have achieved certain limited procedural rights allowing them to expose violations of human rights before international bodies but, except for the European system for the protection of human rights and the less-advanced American system, making them dependent on their respective states for any enforcement of their rights. Still, compared with what the status of individuals was in relatively not too distant past, their position in international law has undergone a remarkable transformation which appears to have a tendency to continue in the foreseeable future, at least in certain regions of the world.

**82. Injured State.** Generally speaking, an injured state is a state whose right has been infringed through a breach of obligation by another state's internationally wrongful act. The breach gives rise to the right of the injured state to invoke responsibility **(128)** of the delinquent state, which may arise either from a bilateral treaty relationship or from a binding international adjudication **(306)**, or even from a right that might exceptionally arise for the injured state from a treaty between third parties **(278)**.

Defining an injured state becomes more complex and controversial within the context of a right under a multilateral treaty or general international law. Here the question may arise whether and under what circumstances a state may be regarded as an injured state if not itself but another state has been the victim of a breach of obligation. Because of the vital importance of the rights involved, state practice recognizes such *erga omnes* obligations **(12)**, as with respect of human rights **(157)** and significant and massive damage to the environment **(197)**. For example, a state may have a legal interest in demanding compliance with provisions of a human rights treaty even without showing that it has suffered any particular injury itself. Thus, the European Convention for the Protection of Human Rights and Fundamental Freedoms, 1950 **(153)**, allows any state party in such cases to bring a breach of the Convention before the Court **(154)** established by the Convention (subject to acceptance by the states concerned of an optional clause to that effect). However, this rule does not necessarily imply that a state has the right to seek reparation **(118)** if it has not suffered injury itself.

The originally proposed definition of injured state in the International Law Commission (ILC) Draft Articles on State Responsibility **(129)** was criticized by a number of states, including the United States, as giving too broad a meaning to the concept of injured state. Especially controversial was the provision that all states may be considered injured if the internationally wrongful act in question constitutes an international crime (in the sense of state crime), which would allow all states to assert injury and pursue remedies, including reparation, without any primary rule of law specifically granting such right of action.

The definition of the injured state was modified in its next version, and the latest ILC Draft Articles on State Responsibility, 2001, reformulated the concept, arriving at a narrower definition for situations where the obligation breached is owed to a state as part of a group of states (including the injured state to which the obligation is owed individually) or the international community as a whole. In such cases, in conformity with Art. 60(2)(c) of the Convention on the Law of Treaties (1155 UNTS 331) on termination or suspension of the operation of a treaty as a consequence of its breach **(276)**, the requirement in the ILC Draft is that the breach of the obligation either specially affects a state or is of "such a character as radically to change the position of all the other states to which the obligation is owed with respect to the further performance of the obligation" (ILC Draft, Art. 42). However, states other than the injured state also have a legal interest in compliance with multilateral obligations by all the parties and are also entitled to invoke the responsibility of another state to the extent that the obligation breached either is owed to a group of states including that state and is established for the prosecution of a collective interest or is owed to the international community as a whole.

**83. Intergovernmental Corporation of Private Law.** Known also as multinational public enterprises or international public corporations or consortia, intergovernmental corporations vary in their constitutional elements and powers and, unlike intergovernmental organizations in the strict sense of the term **(84)**, do not constitute a clear and distinct category of entity operating on the international plane. Generally speaking, in their nature, intergovernmental corporations are intermediate between intergovernmental organizations and private business (transnational) **(140)** corporations. An intergovernmental corporation is ordinarily established by states for some economic purpose by a treaty providing for cooperation between states in order to deal, in a joint action of governmental agencies and private enterprises, with matters beyond the scope of a single state. Their status is normally governed by the municipal law **(27)** of one or more treaty parties, but they may enjoy considerable independence from the municipal law, the treaty-based statute of the corporation prevailing over any contrary provisions of that law.

The Bank of International Settlements, established by a convention (104 LNTS 443) between five states and Switzerland as a Swiss corporation in 1930 is an early example of a multinational public enterprise in the financial field. A number of intergovernmental corporations of private law emerged in Europe in the early post–World War II period. Perhaps the best known is EUROFIMA, the European Company for Funding Railway Equipment, founded by a convention of 14 states parties (378 UNTS 225) in 1955. It was established as a corporation under Swiss law to function as an intergovernmental company whose capital was subscribed by the national railway administrations of the parties. Intergovernmental corporations were also created in other fields, such as air navigation and economic development. INTELSAT **(201)**, the International Telecommunications Satellite Organization, was founded in 1973 as an important enterprise in space communications.

Whether an intergovernmental corporation of private law contains any elements of international legal personality **(85)** can be determined in the light of the particular circumstances. Generally speaking, if the statute stipulates considerable independence of the entity from the municipal laws of the treaty parties and especially if the entity's organs are endowed with significant decision-making powers, an intergovernmental corporation of private law may acquire some attributes of an international organization with a limited extent of rights and obligations as an international legal person.

**84. Intergovernmental Organizations (Public International Organizations).** Sometimes referred to as public international organizations, international organizations are permanent associations of states **(127)**, created by states on the basis of a treaty **(288)**, a constituent instrument variously known as charter, constitution, statute, or covenant, for the performance of certain goals of common interest spelled out in the constituent instrument, and governed by public international law. Although international organizations are, as a rule, limited to states, they may, in exceptional cases, such as for example the Universal Postal Union (UPU), accept dependent territories as members or, like the International Labour Organisation (ILO), include a tripartite representation of government, employers, and labor. Whether a certain cooperative arrangement of states is an organization or only a standing conference is a matter of degree but, as illustrated by the case of the General Agreement on Tariffs and Trade, the feature of permanence, as reflected in the headquarters, staff, and budget are important indications for the existence of an international organization. As a rule, an international organization has a permanent secretariat, an assembly of all members, and a governing body (a council) of a limited number of members.

In rudimentary form, international organizations emerged in the 19th century following the Congress of Vienna, 1815, which heralded a multilateral approach to international cooperation in a variety of areas. The first one was the management of international rivers **(204)** through permanent river commissions. Subsequently, new developments in technology and industrial and commercial cooperation prompted states to create a number of "public international unions," such as the International Telecommunication Union (ITU), 1865 (the predecessor of the present ITU); the UPU, 1874, and a number of other "unions" and "institutes" for a collective management of specific technical tasks.

The inter-war period and, even more, the years following World War II witnessed a rapid growth of international organizations in many dimensions of international interaction, thus reflecting recognition by states of the need to approach problems transcending borders on a permanent institutional basis. The establishment of the League of Nations in 1919 was an important turning point in that the League was the first international organization of a political nature and universal in scope, designed to prevent war through a collective security system **(327)**, and thus a significant development in international law. Another international organization established along with the League but, unlike the League of Nations, continuing its activities until today, is the ILO.

The year 1945 is a turning point in the history of international law and organizations in that the foundation of the United Nations (UN) highlights the role of international organization in the prohibition of the use of force **(329)** in international relations and the development of international law. In addition to the UN, a large number of international organizations in various fields of activity have been established since 1945, with some 500 such institutions existing in the international system in the early 21st century.

According to their membership and geographical scope, international organizations are either global, that is, accepting members from all parts of the world, or—the prevalent category—regional, that is, limiting its membership to a geographical region, in principle defined by geography but in some cases subject to other considerations. Classified according to the criterion of their function, international organizations are either general, that is, in principle, competent under their respective instruments to deal with any international problem, or—the case of a great majority of organizations—specialized, that is, possessing a limited competence in a specific field, as defined by the member states in the constituent instrument. The UN is the only universal and general international organization. The most important organizations specializing in specific tasks, the so-called specialized agencies of the UN, such as ILO, the United Nations Educational, Scientific, and Cultural Organization, the World Health Organization (WHO), etc. are global, but the bulk of organizations specializing in specific fields of action have only a regional scope. Regional organizations include political organizations in Europe and other regions, envisioned by Chapter VIII of the UN Charter where they are known as "regional arrangements." Here belong, *inter alia,* the Organization for Security and Cooperation in Europe and the Organization of American States, but not the North Atlantic Treaty Organization, which is not a regional organization in the UN Charter sense but a collective defense **(336)** organization based on the self-defense Art. 51 of the UN Charter and a survival of the Cold War in search of new tasks and its very *raison d'être.*

Unlike the traditional international organizations, the European Communities (European Economic Community, European Coal and Steel Community, and European Atomic Energy Community or EURATOM) represent a new and unique category of organization, often described as "supranational." This is not a precise term, but in essence it implies, as against a traditional international organization, a more extensive transfer of sovereign powers by the member states to the organs of the Communities in a process of a progressive integration of states into a future federal union **(77)**. Consequently, the laws of the Communities constitute a legal system in its nature intermediate between national and international law. It should be noted that the "European Union" established by the Maastricht Treaty in 1992 (31 ILM 247 (1992)), in force in 1993, and encompassing the three Communities, is generally considered as lacking its own international legal personality **(85)**, constituting an association of the states members of the three Communities.

The emergence and spread of international organizations has raised a number of legal issues related to their nature and various dimensions of their activities, thus leading to the rise of a specialized area of study in international relations. There exists consensus in the doctrine on the preliminary issue of the very nature of international organizations as entities distinct from states, the traditional subjects of international law. As noted by the International Court of Justice (ICJ) **(309)** in its Advisory Opinion **(291)** on the *Interpretation of the Agreement of 25 March between the WHO and Egypt* (1980 ICJ Rep. 73), international organizations are not superstates; like states, they are bound by general international law, and—in addition—by their respective constituent instruments and by any international agreement to which they become parties. However, not all international organizations are automatically international legal persons, and the notion that they can be endowed with international legal personality entailing a capacity to have rights and obligations under, and perform legal acts governed by international law rather than just a capacity within a domestic system of law, is a relatively recent idea. The legal status of the League of Nations was never a subject of judicial assessment and was controversial in the doctrine. What the tests are for determining whether an international institution does have personality under international law was analyzed by the ICJ in its Advisory Opinion on *Reparation for Injuries Suffered in the Service of* *the United Nations* (1949 ICJ Rep. 174). Generally speaking, the original member states had to have the intention to endow the organization with all the competences required for an effective exercise of its functions and the performance of its purposes as an entity separate from its members and, in addition, the organization must in fact exercise its functions and rights in a way that can only be accounted for by its possessing "a large measure of international personality."

Whereas the international legal personality of the state is general and all embracing, and as it were, absolute, all states, in principle, automatically being endowed with it in equal measure, the personality of an international organization is not an absolute but a relative concept: it exists only for specific purposes and with regard to specific rights, attributes, and obligations which vary from organization to organization. Furthermore, this personality is also relative in a sense that, as argued by some publicists, non-members are, in principle, under no obligation to recognize it, especially insofar as less important non-universal organizations are concerned. On the other hand, as also held by the ICJ in the above-mentioned Advisory Opinion, the UN is vested with international legal personality not only in relation to its members but also *erga omnes* **(12)**.

There are, in general, three methods whereby an international organization can acquire personality under international law. In some cases, the Statute of the International Criminal Court **(170)** for example, the constituent instrument itself expressly confers international legal personality upon the organization in question. However, as far as the UN is concerned, the Charter lacks such an express provision. The purpose of its Art. 104 (and similar articles in some other instruments) is to secure for the Organization legal capacity merely under municipal law of each of its members "as may be necessary for the exercise of its functions and the fulfillment of its purposes." Second, the constituent instrument may confer upon an organization specific international capacities, to that extent implying attributes of international legal personality for the organization in question. For example under Art. 43 of the UN Charter, the Security Council (SC) shall negotiate agreements with members concerning contributions of armed forces and other assistance within the framework of the collective security system **(327)** of the Organization. Trusteeship **(142)** agreements are another category of international agreements that the UN has been empowered to conclude. In this context, the ICJ ruled in its Judgment on preliminary objections **(321)** in the case of *Certain Phosphate Lands in Nauru* (Nauru v. Australia) (1992 ICJ Rep. 240) that the administrative authority established by virtue of such an agreement did not constitute a separate international legal person. Under another provision of the Charter (Art. 63), the UN may enter into agreements with other international organizations, specifically, specialized agencies established for purposes of economic, social, cultural, educational, health, and related fields. Third, as analyzed by the ICJ in its Advisory Opinion on *Reparation for Injuries* with regard to the UN, the capacity of being an international legal person, including the right to bring an international claim for reparation **(118)** for damage caused by a state to the UN or its officials acting on its behalf, need not be expressly conferred in the constituent instrument; the possession of such personality is implied to the extent that it is necessary for the most efficient performance of the organization's functions or purposes. Also, even if not expressly authorized by its constituent instrument, an international organization has jurisdiction over its finances, employment, and similar internal matters.

The Advisory Opinion of the ICJ of 1949 contributed to a wide recognition of the international legal personality of public international organizations within the limits set out by the Court. But it remains controversial whether their rights and duties depend on the functions of the organization concerned or are within a precise category derived from the attributes of international legal personality, and more specifically, whether such personality, like that of a state, is an inherent and objective feature of international organizations and should be recognized by third states. Under express authorization of their respective constituent instruments and possibly other treaties as well as under the doctrine of implied powers, as set out by the ICJ, international organizations can perform a variety of legal acts which are otherwise associated with states. However, unlike states, they cannot exercise sovereign rights over territory **(228)** but, as demonstrated by the UN experience in such places as the Free City of Trieste **(141)**, West Irian, and more recently Kosovo and East Timor, administration of a territory by an international organization is not incompatible with incapacity to exercise territorial sovereignty. Constituent instruments do not ordinarily grant international organizations a general treaty-making capacity but—as example in the UN

Charter—refer to specific categories of agreements that the organization in question may conclude. The treaty-making capacity may also be based on implied powers as well as resolutions and an established practice of the organization. As formulated in Art. 6 of the Vienna Convention on the Law of Treaties between States and International Organizations or between International Organizations, 1986 (25 ILM 543 (1986)), the "capacity of an international organization to conclude treaties is governed by the rules of the organization."

Following the ICJ *Reparation* Opinion of 1949, a number of other advisory opinions of the Court have interpreted the doctrine of implied powers essential to the performance of the constitutional duties or appropriate to the fulfillment of the purposes of international organizations. Such powers were affirmed in the Advisory Opinion on *Effects of Awards of Compensation Made by the United Nations Administrative Tribunal* **(290)** (1954 ICJ Rep. 47) and *Certain Expenses of the United Nations (Article 17, paragraph 2, of the Charter)* (1962 ICJ Rep. 161). But in its Opinion for the WHO concerning *Legality of the Use by a State of Nuclear Weapons in Armed Conflict* (1996 ICJ Rep. 66) the ICJ concluded that the WHO was not competent to request an advisory opinion on the legality of the use of nuclear weapons, on the grounds that that was not a question arising within the WHO competence or the scope of its activities, as required by Art. 96(2) of the UN Charter on the right to request an advisory opinion. In rejecting the WHO request, the ICJ pointed out that, unlike states, international organizations do not have general competence but only specific powers and, like the WHO, relatively narrow and technical areas of concern spelled out in their respective constituent instruments.

International organizations are entitled to privileges and immunities **(102)** to the extent that they are necessary for the fulfillment of the purposes of the organization in question. The rule on the implied right to bring a claim against a state for direct injury to the organization, recognized by the ICJ in its *Reparation* Opinion, may also, under the circumstances, apply to other international organizations endowed with international legal personality. However, it is not certain that the UN right to espouse claims for injury to its agents, based on functional protection, could be invoked by other international organizations if involvement in maintenance of peace and security is not within their statutory functions. Whether an international organization has *locus standi,* that is, a capacity to sue and be sued in international adjudication **(306)** proceedings, depends on the statute of the tribunal or the arbitration **(293)** agreement, as the case may be. Only states may be parties in contentious cases **(297)** before the ICJ, but the General Assembly (GA) and the SC and—if authorized by the GA—other UN organs and specialized agencies may request advisory opinions. Logically, international organizations should be responsible for an injury to a state arising from a breach of an international obligation by the organization involved. The issue has arisen mainly within the context of UN peacekeeping (and similar) operations **(334)** when members of the forces acting under the authority of the Organization have committed wrongful acts causing injury to third persons. In such cases the liability of the UN for financial compensation depends on the particular circumstances of the case, and in particular the relevant agreement between the Organization on the one hand and the host state or the state contributing personnel to the UN action in question, on the other. In a number of cases the UN has assumed responsibility for damage and injury by members of the forces acting under its authority.

In the prevailing opinion, it cannot be presumed that member states of an international organization are concurrently or secondarily liable to third parties for debts of the organization, the view affirmed by English courts in the extensively litigated case of *International Tin Council*, 1988, an international organization that had failed to meet its liabilities arising from contracts with third parties. It might be added that the topic of responsibility of international organizations had been included for codification **(5)** in the long-term program of work of the ILC.

Succession between international organizations is possible, but as demonstrated by the dissolution of the League of Nations by its members in 1946 and the transfer of the League's property and certain of its functions to the UN, the succession was not automatic and required the consent of the UN. On the other hand, as opined by the ICJ in its Advisory Opinion on the *International Status of South West Africa* (1950 ICJ Rep. 128), in certain circumstances succession may be implied, as in the case of the UN succeeding to the League of Nations' supervisory functions concerning the mandate of South-West Africa **(93)**.

**85. International Legal Personality.** International legal personality is a concept referring to the status of having personality under international law, that is, possessing rights and duties governed directly by this law, and, in general, a capacity to act on the international plane, including, among other rights, the capacity to enter into treaties **(288)** with other international legal persons, to bring in international claims, and to be entitled to privileges and immunities according to the rules of international law **(131)**. The status of being an international legal person is alternatively known as being a "subject' of international law, but in the opinion of some publicists the latter terminology suggests more restrictive implications which limit an entity in question to possessing rights and obligations only, but not other capacities and attributes possible under international law. But, subject to this reservation, the terms "subject of international law" and "international legal person" tend to be used interchangeably.

The concept of legal personality is, of course, central in contemporary municipal **(27)** systems of law which confer it, as a general rule, on individuals as well as corporations and other juridical (legal) entities. In international law, states **(127)** remain the only subjects of this law to possess a general competence as international legal persons, and not just a specific competence or specific competences merely for certain purposes. States had achieved the fullness of this status by the 19th century when positivist doctrines **(31)** and practice based on the notion of state sovereignty **(125)** replaced the natural law **(29)** jurisprudence applicable to states and individuals **(164)** alike. However, apart from the unique status of the Holy See **(80)**, as late as the first half of the 19th century the British East India Company was in many respects treated as a subject of international law, waging wars and making treaties, among other activities associated with states. Insurgents **(115)**, sometimes granted the status of belligerency **(113)**, possessed international legal personality for certain specific purposes only. The case of pirates **(259)**, responsible directly under international law, was a *sui generis* phenomenon from the point of view of international legal personality.

While states remain the only subjects of general competence in international law in the sense of institutions possessing *the* totality of rights and duties, with the unique status as repositories of legitimate authority over sovereign territory and people and the capacity to create and develop international law by custom **(39)** and treaty **(40)**, the 20th century, and especially its latter half, witnessed the rise of new categories of subjects endowed by states with various limited degrees of international legal personality As pointed out by the International Court of Justice in its Advisory Opinion on *Reparation for Injuries Suffered in the Service of the United Nations* (1949 ICJ Rep. 174), the concept of the subjects of law in any legal system is a dynamic one, depending on the needs of the community. In international relations, the rapidly growing interaction across national borders and a desire to restrain international violence prompted states to create intergovernmental organizations (public international organizations) **(84)** whose state-produced constituent instruments conferred on them a limited degree of international legal personality with respect to specifically named rights and obligations, with additional attributes possibly accorded by, or implied from agreements. National liberation movements **(94)**, a product of anti-colonialist ideology of self-determination of peoples **(122)**, emerged as another category of subjects of international law with certain specific but limited rights and obligations.

However, by far the most remarkable and potentially significant phenomenon in the expansion of certain features of international legal personality has been the change in the status of individuals **(81)**. This development has been in progress in two dimensions: initially with reference to their obligations and individual responsibility, directly under international law, for especially grave international crimes, and soon thereafter with respect to their limited but expanding array of human rights protected by international law **(159)**.

**86. International Non-Governmental Organizations.** International non-governmental organizations (NGOs) are private, non-profit organizations established by individuals and national associations in order to coordinate their cooperation on the international level in a given field of activity. The existence of NGOs dates back to the 19th century, but the decades following World War II witnessed a proliferation of such private organizations in virtually all areas of human activity. More than 2,000 NGOs of varying importance are listed in the latest *Yearbook* published since

1907 by the Union of International Organizations in Brussels. Apart from the International Committee of the Red Cross (ICRC), an organization closely related to international humanitarian law **(353)**, the best-known NGOs whose activities affect the development of international law are those promoting the cause of human rights **(157)**, such as Amnesty International and *Médecins sans frontières* [Doctors without borders], both winners of the Nobel Peace Prize, and NGOs involved in advancing the protection of the environment, including in particular Greenpeace and Friends of the Earth.

While not international legal persons **(85)** themselves, NGOs have emerged as influential actors in international relations, disseminating information on a wide range of subjects and acting, sometimes with great determination, as pressure groups in national legislative processes and in the lobbies of international conferences drafting new rules of international law. This role of the NGOs was well demonstrated by their lobbying activities at the Rio World Summit in 1992 **(223)** and the Johannesburg World Summit for Sustainable Development in 2002.

NGOs are not subjects of international law and their legal status is governed by the municipal law **(27)** of the state in which they are registered. In the European region, under the Council of Europe–sponsored European Convention on the Recognition of the Legal Personality of International Non-Governmental Organizations, 1986, the states parties agree to recognize the legal personality of NGOs, acquired in any other state party to the Convention. Although NGOs are not subjects of international law, the role of many such organizations is recognized in Art. 71 of the United Nations (UN) Charter providing for consultative arrangements between the United Nations Economic and Social Council (ECOSOC) and non-governmental organizations. In this regard, the ECOSOC has established three categories of consultative status for NGOs. Category I includes organizations with demonstrable capability of making contribution to economic and social purposes of the UN. In the more limited Category II are organizations concerned with special areas of ECOSOC activity. Category III on the so-called Roster lack consultative status, but may be able to make occasional contributions to the work of UN bodies. Altogether more than 1,000 NGOs have obtained consultative status under Art. 71 of the Charter. Similar arrangements are possible within the framework of specialized agencies of the UN. Representatives of NGOs with consultative status may sit as observers and take the floor in ECOSOC meetings; they may also have their memoranda circulated as UN documents. The highest category of NGOs may submit proposals for the agenda of the Council.

The status of the ICRC, which is incorporated under Swiss law, is rather unique. Although not a subject of international law, the ICRC, founded in 1873 by Henri Dunant and known until 1880 as "International Standing Committee for Aid to Wounded Soldiers," plays a formal role under the four Geneva Conventions ("Red Cross Conventions") **(349)** as "an impartial humanitarian body" and may serve in the same role as a protecting power **(368)**. The ICRC also played a crucial formal role in the drafting of the two Protocols of 1977 **(369)**. Some 11,000 ICRC workers are posted in numerous zones of international **(339)** and civil **(340)** armed conflict in the world, performing often dangerous international humanitarian tasks in an independent and neutral manner.

The ICRC must be distinguished from the closely related International Federation of Red Cross and Red Crescent Societies (IFRC), the world's largest humanitarian organization, supporting its 176 independent national societies. While the ICRC functions within the context of the political conflict, the IFRC and its national members are involved in natural disaster preparedness and emergency relief assistance.

Despite its recognized independence and neutral posture, the Red Cross organizations have not been able to avoid political challenges related in particular to their emblem (the Swiss flag with colors reverse), the reason why Israel (which uses a red star as the emblem for its equivalent national organization, the Magen David Adom (MDA)), has not joined the world Red Cross movement.

**87. Jurisdiction.** In its most common international legal meaning, jurisdiction means a state's authority over persons, property, events, and circumstances. In this sense the term must be distinguished from the special notion of "domestic jurisdiction" **(9)** of the UN Charter and the rather free use of the term as synonymous with territory. Although derived from sovereignty **(125)** of which it is a corollary and the central aspect, the concept of jurisdiction is not always linked to the territorial aspect of sovereignty, as shown, for example, by the states' right in certain circumstances to exercise jurisdiction over offenses committed abroad and by immunity from territorial jurisdiction **(91)** under the rules of state (sovereign) **(131)** and diplomatic **(63)** immunity. However, whereas prescriptive jurisdiction, that is jurisdiction to make laws, may be based on grounds other than territoriality, for example on the nationality principle **(88)**, jurisdiction to enforce is based exclusively on territoriality.

While municipal law **(27)** determines the extent of a state's jurisdiction, this discretion is limited by certain prohibitive rules placed by international law upon the exercise of jurisdiction by states. Such rules have been developed primarily through the case law of national courts applying their respective municipal rules of law. As a result, there exists no comprehensive set of international legal rules governing jurisdiction by states. In general, restrictions upon the jurisdictional reach of states apply to criminal matters rather than to civil cases. With respect to the latter, apart from situations involving immunity, states are allowed a much wider scope in their jurisdictional powers. But even there, excessive and unreasonable claims to jurisdiction, for example over an alien **(144)**, without any sufficiently close connection between the subject matter of the civil case and the state of the *forum,* could result in protests by a foreign state with a competing jurisdictional claim. In addition, where enforcement in civil cases ultimately involves criminal sanctions, the differences between the exercise of civil and criminal jurisdiction tend to be reduced. Moreover, as illustrated by the controversy over an extraterritorial application of United States (US) anti-trust and securities legislation within the context of the so-called effects doctrine used as a sort of extension of the territorial principle **(91)**, a formally civil process may in substance assume features of a coercive, basically penal, procedure.

According to a general principle, the *forum* state has the right to exercise jurisdiction in respect of an act considered criminal under its law, if there exists between that state and the matter in question a link or contact sufficiently close to warrant jurisdiction and possibly override a competing jurisdictional claim of another state. Since the latter part of the 19th century, state practice has generated several principles upon which states have based their criminal jurisdiction, but even if one of the below-named bases for jurisdiction were to be present, the exercise of jurisdiction might still be unlawful if it proved to be unreasonable under the circumstances.

The principles of jurisdiction include: 1. territorial (or territoriality) principle which is by far the most common basis of jurisdiction; 2. nationality principle; 3. protective principle **(90)**; 4. passive nationality principle **(89)**, once opposed but now increasingly invoked in connection with terrorist offenses; and 5. universality principle **(92)**, applied in cases of international crimes. The so-called effects principle or doctrine is in its essence an aspect of the principle of territoriality ("objective" territoriality principle), but is sometimes regarded as a distinct category.

Jurisdiction has three aspects or categories. First, there is jurisdiction to prescribe (prescriptive jurisdiction), meaning the authority of a state to make laws. Since it is viewed mainly as a function of legislation, it is sometimes referred to as legislative jurisdiction, but it also encompasses rules issued by an executive authority, and prescriptions emanating from the exercise of, or even determined by a judicial authority. Second, jurisdiction to adjudicate (adjudicative jurisdiction) denotes a state's authority to subject persons or things to the process of its courts whether or not the state is a party to the proceedings. And third, jurisdiction to enforce (enforcement jurisdiction) refers to the authority of a state to induce or compel compliance with its law or to punish noncompliance through courts (in which case it constitutes an aspect of adjudication) or resort to executive action, including physical interference, seizure of property, and similar actions.

Prescriptive jurisdiction may extend its reach beyond a state's borders, as in the case of tax laws applying to nationals abroad. But exorbitant, let alone extravagant and broadly speaking unreasonable extension of such jurisdiction, would be an unlawful encroachment upon a foreign state's legislative jurisdiction. Adjudicative jurisdiction represents the most common aspect of jurisdiction in situations involving a foreign element. It is based primarily but not exclusively on the principle of territoriality, but again, except—and this is controversial—for jurisdiction under the principle of universality, the judicial authority of a state may be challenged under international law if the person or thing has no reasonable link to the state seeking to exercise jurisdiction. Of course, a state is not permitted to exercise its adjudicative jurisdiction in the territory of another state without that state's consent. Such consent was granted by the Netherlands to the United Kingdom to allow the trial of the two suspects in the Lockerbie case in the territory of the Netherlands by a Scottish court according to Scotland's law. Among the criteria for determining the reasonableness of the exercise of adjudicative jurisdiction by a state are such facts as, for example, a more than transitory presence in the state's territory, nationality **(175)**, residence, conducting regular business, and owning or possessing assets in the state.

A state may exercise its enforcement jurisdiction provided it has jurisdiction to prescribe in the matter in question, but it is a universally recognized principle of international law that a state's officials may not exercise their functions in the territory of another state without the latter's consent. If such breach of another state's territorial sovereignty does occur, the injured state **(82)** is entitled to protest and, under the circumstances, to reparation **(118)** from the offending state. If the unauthorized action consists in abducting by a foreign state's agents of a person, as was in 1960 the abduction from Argentina for trial in Israel of the Nazi war criminal Eichmann by agents of the Israeli government, the state whose territorial sovereignty was violated may demand return of the abducted person, and international law requires that such person be returned. In a number of such abductions the individuals involved were indeed returned. However, in the absence of a demand for the return of the abducted person or—as in the Eichmann case—if the states concerned reach a settlement that does not call for such return, the state which carried out the abduction may proceed to try the accused criminal under its law. While criticized by some, this principle of criminal law, known as *male captus bene detentus* (meaning that a person improperly seized may nevertheless be properly tried) has been upheld by courts in a number of countries. The abduction by US agents from Mexico of Machain, a Mexican national, tried in the US—as it turned out wrongly—for involvement in the murder of a US anti-narcotics agent (31 ILM 902 (1997)), a case of interest also in extradition law **(75)**, and the sinking in New Zealand by agents of the French government of the *Rainbow Warrior* **(104)** are two other notorious instances involving unlawful exercise by a state of enforcement jurisdiction in another country.

Jurisdiction to prescribe and enforce rules of law in the territory under the sovereignty of another state may be conferred by an agreement, as is for example the case of Guantánamo lease **(207)** over which, under an agreement of 1903 with Cuba, the US has complete control and jurisdiction, with Cuba continuing to have "ultimate sovereignty" over the area. Agreements concerning the status of forces **(138)** stationed in another country provide another example of jurisdiction conferred by agreement.

**88. Jurisdiction: Nationality Principle.** A principle whereby a state **(127)** may exercise jurisdiction **(87)** over its nationals **(175)**, including entities **(173)**, even if they are physically outside the state's territory. Universally recognized as a basis for jurisdiction, the nationality principle is justified on the grounds that a national owes allegiance to his country irrespective of wherever he may be and that his state has responsibility for its nationals as well as an interest in them and the right to protect them while they are outside its territorial jurisdiction **(91)**.

While a state has the right to prescribe laws with regard to activities, interests, status, or relations of its nationals abroad, its power of enforcement depends on the national's physical presence in its territory or the location of assets there against which the state can enforce its laws. The scope of the nationality principle may be extended to links other than nationality, such as for example an extended residence in the state concerned. The nationality principle necessarily provides the main basis for jurisdiction in exceptional situations where the territorial principle is simply not suitable, as in Antarctica **(187)**.

The extent to which states assert jurisdiction on the basis of the nationality principle, especially in criminal cases (including imposition of penalties in technically civil cases), varies from state to state. Countries of the civil-law **(23)** tradition assert a substantially more comprehensive jurisdiction over crimes committed by their nationals abroad than the countries whose legal systems are derived from the common-law tradition of England. The latter, including the United States (US), ordinarily restrict jurisdiction based on nationality to very serious crimes, some of which, such as treason, can also be based on the protective principle of jurisdiction **(90)** or rationalized by the effects doctrine. In addition, the United Kingdom claims jurisdiction over murder and bigamy committed by nationals abroad. Under the law of the US, the application of the nationality principle is limited, apart from some less serious offences, to treason, illicit drug trafficking, violation of the selective service law, trading with the enemy, and interference with the US foreign policy by unlawful contact with a foreign government. As ruled in 1932 by the US Supreme Court in *Blackmer v. United States* (284 U.S. 421), a US citizen abroad has the obligation to obey a subpoena requiring him to return to the US to testify as a witness in criminal proceedings. There has not been much state practice concerning the grounds upon which a state may assert jurisdiction in civil law matters, but under the general principle governing jurisdiction there must be a sufficiently close and real connection between the matter involved and the state claiming jurisdiction.

Because of the concurrence of the otherwise primary territorial jurisdiction and jurisdiction based on nationality, an individual may be exposed to double jeopardy. The resulting hardship can only be remedied by treaty **(288)** in the same way as in a case of double taxation, or by one of the states concerned showing restraint in enforcing the law for humanitarian reasons.

As a basis for jurisdiction, the nationality principle applies also to corporations and other juridical persons, the nationality of such entities **(173)** being determined by the state of incorporation, the principal place of business, or the registered office (*siège social*). The exercise of jurisdiction in cases of intercorporate affiliations of transnational corporations **(140)** raises controversial issues in international law. Generally speaking, while a state has jurisdiction over corporations of its nationality, it may not ordinarily regulate activities of corporations organized under the law of a foreign state, on the basis of a claim that they are owned or controlled by nationals of the claiming state. Assuming that such regulation is, for limited purposes, permitted under international law, the extent of jurisdiction by that state is not clear. This is related to the controversial issue of the extraterritorial reach of a state's law and the effects doctrine, as adopted by the US and some other countries, but strongly objected by other states.

Activities aboard vessels, aircraft, and spacecraft are subject to the jurisdiction of the state of registration, the "flag state" in the law of the sea **(240)**, subject to concurrent territorial jurisdiction over vessels and aircraft in the internal waters **(249)** and the territorial sea **(262)** of the coastal state according to the jurisdictional provisions of the relevant treaties.

**89. Jurisdiction: Passive Personality Principle.** A controversial jurisdictional principle under which a state applies its laws, and in particular, its criminal law, to try an alien for an act committed outside its territory where its national was the victim of the act. In the past, though accepted by some countries (for example Brazil, France, Mexico), this principle was considered a basis for jurisdiction of dubious legal validity and used to be consistently opposed by the United Kingdom and the United States (US), as illustrated, *inter alia,* by the *Cutting* incident in 1886 in which a US national was arrested in Mexico and brought to trial there (but eventually released after US protests) for an alleged libel against a Mexican, published in a newspaper in the US. The passive personality principle was also criticized as contrary to international law by all six dissenting judges in their opinions **(304)** in the *Lotus* case (Turkey/France) before the Permanent Court of International Justice (PCIJ) **(320)** in 1927 (PCIJ, Series A, No. 10), but in its judgment the PCIJ refused to enter into the theoretical argument over this principle and approached this case of a collision on the high seas **(242)** from the viewpoint of the "objective" territorial principle of jurisdiction **(91)**.

More recently, while the passive personality principle had not been accepted in cases of common crimes, it has become since the 1970s one of the several elements of the approach adopted in a dozen or so multilateral conventions, most of them designed to combat terrorist offenses **(337)**, following a treaty-based "universality" principle **(92)** of jurisdiction. A number of countries adopted the passive personality principle for cases of terrorist-related injury to nationals abroad in their respective national legislations. In 1984 the US extended the special maritime and territorial jurisdiction to include any place outside the jurisdiction of any state, that is, practically speaking the high seas with respect to offenses by or against a national of the US, and in 1986, following the terrorist incident involving the seizure of the *Achille Lauro* in the Mediterranean with a related murder of a US national on board and the interception by the US Air Force of an Egyptian airliner over the high seas, the US adopted the passive personality principle to cases of killing or causing serious bodily harm to US nationals abroad if, as certified by the US Attorney General, the offense in question was intended to coerce, intimidate, or retaliate against a government or a civilian population. A number of convictions of terrorists, some of them apprehended abroad by US agents, have taken place under these provisions.

**90. Jurisdiction: Protective (Security) Principle.** A generally recognized jurisdictional principle whereby a state may assume jurisdiction **(87)** over, and punish foreign nationals for certain conduct outside its territory, which is directed against its security, territorial integrity, and political independence, or against a limited number of certain other vital state interests, such as counterfeiting the state's currency, falsification of official documents, perjury before a consular **(57)** or diplomatic **(68)** official, conspiracy to violate immigration or customs law, and illicit drug trafficking. However, the concept of protecting a state's interests must not be abused by being interpreted too broadly, to include, for example, criticism of the affected state or government by foreign newspapers or other publications among the offenses warranting the application of the protective principle of jurisdiction. Otherwise, this principle is believed to be justifiable in view of the fact that national laws concerning prosecution for offenses committed within the territory of the state concerned against the security and other vital interests of foreign states, are either nonexistent or inadequate.

The English case of *Joyce v. Director of Public Prosecutions*, 1946 (15 ILR 91), involving the notorious radio announcer, broadcasting from Nazi Germany to England in the service of the enemy during World War II and popularly known as Lord Haw-Haw, is an interesting example combining the protective principle with a "constructive" nationality principle **(88)** as the bases for conviction of Joyce by the House of Lords and his eventual execution. Although born in the United States, Joyce fraudulently obtained a United Kingdom passport and in 1939 left Britain for Germany to work for the Nazi government.

In a way, since the prejudicial acts are committed outside the territory of the affected state but generate effects within it, the protective principle can also be viewed as an application of the effects principle or the objective territorial principle **(91)**.

**91. Jurisdiction: Territorial Principle.** The by far most common basis for jurisdiction **(87)** whereby a state has complete and exclusive jurisdiction in its territory **(228)** with respect to all persons, transactions, and things for virtually all purposes. As noted by the United States (US) Supreme Court in the case of *The Schooner Exchange v. MacFaddon* in 1812 (7 Cranch 116), except for its consent, "the jurisdiction of the nation within its own territory is necessarily exclusive and absolute." Of course, the territorial jurisdiction of the state is subject to exceptions under the international law rules governing immunities of foreign states **(137)**, diplomatic **(63)** and consular **(55)** privileges and immunities, and any other exceptions agreed to by the state concerned.

Under the territorial or territoriality principle the state has jurisdiction over all crimes committed in its territory, extending to the superjacent airspace **(186)** and including internal waters **(249)**, the territorial sea **(262)** and—for certain purposes reaching beyond the territorial sea to adjacent maritime areas which are not under the coastal state's sovereignty.

Subject to the general requirement of reasonable exercise of jurisdiction and, in particular, taking account of the interests of other states, the territoriality principle may also provide a basis for jurisdiction in criminal cases when a crime is—as it were—made up of two elements: it is initiated in the territory of one state but completed or consummated in another's, as illustrated by the usually quoted case of a lethal shot across a border. In such a case of concurrent jurisdiction, the state where the criminal act was initiated has jurisdiction under the "subjective" territorial principle and the state in which the offense was consummated under the "objective" territorial principle. The latter principle can also provide a basis for jurisdiction when a crime is consummated in cases of conspiracy and violation of immigration law, for example. The application of the objective territorial principle to a case of collision on the high seas **(245)** was upheld by the Permanent Court of International Justice (PCIJ)

**(320)** in its controversial judgment in the *Lotus* case (Turkey/France) (1927 PCIJ, Series A, No. 10) in which the Court upheld Turkey's right to exercise criminal jurisdiction over an officer of the French vessel, *The Lotus,* involved in a collision with a Turkish-flag vessel, because—as held by the Court—among other grounds, the act committed on board the French vessel produced "effects" on board the other vessel which the PCIJ made equivalent to Turkish territory. This decision, endorsing a state's discretionary power to extend the reach of jurisdiction beyond its territorial limits, subject only to any prohibitive rules of international law, was widely criticized in the doctrine and in shipping circles. Eventually, its impact, as far as collisions on the high seas are concerned, was reversed by a subsequent treaty regulation. More recently, however, the *Lotus* decision has been suggested as an argument for extending the reach of jurisdiction under the universality principle **(92)**.

While the objective territorial principle allows a state to exercise jurisdiction over offenses even if not begun in its territory, claims under this principle, which extend such jurisdiction over conduct abroad to cases where such conduct produces effects in the *forum* state, are highly controversial. In particular, the US, more than any other country, has sought to apply its legislation (in matters of antitrust and securities as well as embargo legislation) to situations abroad, thus precipitating jurisdictional conflicts with other states. This approach dates back to the case of *US v. Aluminum Co. of America* before a federal court in 1945, subsequently reaffirmed in a number of other cases before US courts. Strictly speaking, while associated with the territorial principle, this extraterritorial reach of US jurisdiction is not an application of the objective territorial principle in that, unlike the case of the pure physical consequences of a shot across the border, the economic effects involved are not an ingredient of one offense that commenced abroad but was completed in the US. The effects doctrine is also closely related to the controversial US claims, based on the nationality principle **(88)**, to exercise jurisdiction over foreign-incorporated subsidiaries of American corporations, which subsidiaries are considered as nationals **(173)** by the foreign state of incorporation. While broadly speaking, the extraterritorial reach of jurisdiction in all these situations represents an aspect of jurisdiction based on territoriality, such reach, having or intended to have substantial effects within the forum state, is sometimes conceptualized in terms of the so-called effects principle and viewed as a distinct basis of jurisdiction to prescribe.

The application of the effects principle has become a major source of controversy when invoked by the US to support an extraterritorial reach of its legislation to activities in a foreign country which are lawful there but otherwise are believed by the US government to have an adverse economic impact in the US. However, some European states and the European Community itself have also adopted an equivalent of the effects doctrine in their own regulations of restrictive business practices.

Foreign countries have regarded the extraterritorial application of US economic laws under the effects principle as an infringement of their respective powers of legislative jurisdiction under general international law and pertinent trade agreements. As a result, a number of them have lodged protests and adopted a variety of defensive legal measures ("blocking legislation") which, *inter alia*, prohibited production of documents required by the US and even made illegal compliance with extraterritorial laws in conflict with the jurisdiction of the state concerned. In the US, the position of the courts has not been entirely consistent. The case law follows the principle that the US economic legislation applies to foreign conduct which was meant to produce or did in fact produce substantial effects within the US, but the idea of minimizing any possible jurisdictional conflicts with other countries by applying the judicial principle of reasonableness to balance any conflicting interests has not been consistently resorted to by the courts. At the same time, agreements have been concluded in order to reduce jurisdictional conflicts in the enforcement of antitrust laws. Thus the US and the Commission of the European Communities entered into agreements in 1991 (30 ILM 1487 (1991)) and 1998 (37 ILM 1070 (1998)) committing the parties to cooperate rather than seeking to apply their anti-competition laws exterritorially. These agreements introduced the principle of the so-called positive comity **(6)** designed to reduce the possibility of conflicting decisions by different authorities, whereby a party, for example the US, adversely affected by the anti-competitive conduct in the territory of the other party, may request that other party (the European Communities) to take enforcement measures in accordance with the requesting party's laws. In addition, the agreement of 1998 created a presumption that a party (the Communities) would normally defer or suspend its enforcement in cases where the conduct at issue did not have a direct, substantial, and reasonably foreseeable impact on the requesting party's (the US) consumers or where it occurs principally in, and is directed principally toward the other party's (the Communities') territory.

Controversies over an excessive assertion of US legislative jurisdiction have arisen also for international political reasons. During the Cold War, in 1981, the US made an attempt to regulate extraterritorially the conduct of foreign companies abroad, seeking in particular to impose its boycott regulations with respect to exports from third states to the Soviet Union of materials for the construction of a pipeline from Siberia to Europe (21 ILM 855 (1982)). Apart from this episode, hopefully of historical interest only, more recently, in 1996, the tightening of anti-Cuban sanctions by the US Cuban Liberty and Democratic Solidarity (Libertad) Act of 1996, the so-called Helms-Burton Act (35 ILM 357 (1996)), *inter alia*, threatening legal proceedings in the US against foreign nationals "trafficking in confiscated US-claimed property," and the adoption of the US Iran and Libya Sanctions Act of the same year, the so-called D'Amato Act (35 ILM 1273 (1996)) designed to impose sanctions on persons engaged in developing oil resources in these two countries, led to diplomatic protests and protective measures by numerous countries, including the United Kingdom, Canada, Mexico, Russia, and by the European Community (35 ILM 397 (1996); 36 ILM 111, 125, 133, 213 (1997)), bringing about a partial suspension by the US of the sanctions, as specified in the European Union–US Memorandum of 1997 (36 ILM 529 (1997). In addition to the above-mentioned protests, the Organization of American States Inter-American Juridical Committee adopted a resolution (35 ILM 1322 (1996)) which found the Helms-Burton Act to be in violation of international law governing jurisdiction because neither the foreign nationals involved nor the conduct in question had any connection with the US territory and there was no apparent connection between the acts at issue and the protection of US essential sovereign interests. Concerning the extraterritorial application by a state of its law, the Committee generalized that it was justified only insofar as an act occurring outside a state's territory had a direct, substantial, and foreseeable effect within its territory, and the exercise of such jurisdiction was reasonable.

The issue of the extraterritorial reach of a country's laws, especially in the economic area, on grounds of the effects doctrine, remains controversial, with no consensus apparent on the limits which international law places on the exercise of such jurisdiction.

**92. Jurisdiction: Universality Principle.** There is no generally agreed upon definition of universality principle for purposes of national criminal or civil jurisdiction **(87)**. Understood in its most extensive sense, in criminal matters it would mean jurisdiction whereby a state would be entitled to claim the right to prosecute and punish offenses irrespective of where they had occurred, whoever the offender and victim, and regardless of the state where the offender was found. Such a range of jurisdiction with respect to any offense is not allowed in international law since it would conflict with the principle of sovereign equality of states **(73)**, would constitute unlawful interference in other states' affairs, and in general would lead to intolerable judicial chaos. On the other hand, eventually even those countries that once opposed universality jurisdiction as contrary to international law, have in the past few decades accepted the lawfulness of such jurisdiction over offences recognized as a grave threat to the international community as a whole, and in particular serious war crimes **(373)**, genocide **(155)**, crimes against humanity **(151)**, torture **(182)**, and certain terrorist crimes **(337)**.

Traditionally, international law recognized universal jurisdiction only with respect to piracy **(259)**, the rationale being that this crime, condemned by all, is committed in an area beyond the territorial sovereignty of any state. However, unlike in the case of piracy, universal jurisdiction was not recognized under the anti-slavery **(180)** Conventions of 1926 and 1956 and the 1961 and 1971 Conventions on narcotic drugs and psychotropic substances respectively, even though the crimes involved could also be committed on the high seas **(245)**.

International measures to broaden national jurisdiction took place in the early post–World War II period in the area of war crimes when each of the four Geneva Conventions of 1949 **(349)** (Convention I: Art. 49; II: Art. 50; III: Art. 129; and IV: Art. 146) obligated each state party to search out alleged offenders suspected of having committed grave breaches of the Conventions and bring them, regardless of nationality **(175)**, before its own courts unless the state in question preferred to hand them over for trial to another party to the Convention concerned. This early instance of the principle *aut dedere aut prosequi* (or *aut dedere aut judicare*), that is, either to extradite or to prosecute (try), adopted by the Conventions (and later by Protocol I of 1977) **(369)**, was designed to ensure that offenders should not go unpunished and was an important step toward universal jurisdiction even though it limits the obligation to search for offenders to the territory of the state concerned.

A significant advance toward universal jurisdiction took place in the latter decades of the past century in reaction to a rising threat of all kinds of terrorist activity, beginning with aircraft hijacking **(185)**. In this regard, the Hague air hijacking Convention of 1970 (10 ILM 133 (1971)) **(199)** was a turning point in that it initiated an innovative system of other multilateral conventions establishing a treaty-based quasi-universal or subsidiary jurisdiction (loosely referred to as universal) over the crimes specified in the respective instrument. With certain variations, in the next three decades this system was adopted in such agreements as: 1. Montreal "Sabotage "Convention, 1971 (10 ILM 1151 (1971)) **(210)**; 2. Its Protocol of 1988 Concerning Acts of Violence at Airports (27 ILM 627 (1988)); 3. Convention on the Prevention and Punishment of Crimes against Internationally Protected Persons, Including Diplomatic Agents, 1973 (1035 UNTS 167); 4. Convention against the Taking of Hostages, 1979 (18 ILM 1456 (1979)); 5. Convention on the Physical Protection of Nuclear Materials, 1979 (18 ILM 1419 (1979)); 6. Convention against Torture and Other Cruel and Inhuman or Degrading Treatment or Punishment, 1984 (23 ILM 1027 (1984), 24 ILM 535 (1985)); 7. Convention for the Suppression of Unlawful Acts against the Safety of Maritime Navigation, 1988 (27 ILM 668 (1988)); 8. Its Protocol Concerning the Safety of Fixed Platforms Located on the Continental Shelf **(236)**, 1988 (27 ILM 685 (1988)); 9. Convention against Illicit Traffic in Narcotic Drugs and Psychotropic Substances, 1988 (28 ILM 493 (1989)); 10. Convention for the Suppression of Terrorist Bombings, 1997 (37 ILM 249 (1998)); 11. Convention for the Suppression of the Financing of Terrorism, 1999 (39 ILM 270 (2000)). Additional agreements, including a comprehensive convention on the elimination of terrorism, were being drafted in 2003. Generally speaking, each of the contracting states of these conventions has to establish, on the basis of multiple links, its jurisdiction over the offense covered by the convention in question, and if the alleged offender is found in its territory, the state concerned has an obligation to arrest him and then either extradite or prosecute him. However, none of the conventions contemplates total universal jurisdiction, including jurisdiction *in absentia*, that is, when the alleged offender is not in the territory of the state concerned. But in the free use of the term, the system of jurisdiction adopted by the conventions is often referred to as universality principle.

The jurisdictional rules of municipal laws **(27)** in general follow the rules of the multilateral conventions, referring in some countries (for example Austria, France, Germany, the Netherlands) to their provisions. However, like the treaties themselves, they do not seem, with two or three exceptions, to explicitly assert a total universal jurisdiction that would provide for the right to try offenders without any link whatever with the *forum* state, and in particular if the alleged offender is not present in the state's territory. In the area of war crimes and crimes against humanity, apart from the special case of Israel, the Belgian Act Concerning the Punishment of Grave Breaches of International Humanitarian Law of 1993, as amended in 1999 (38 ILM 918 (1999)), granted total universal jurisdiction over such breaches and over genocide and crimes against humanity. However, more recently the law became a subject of bitter legal controversy and pressures by the United States (US) and the United Kingdom concerned about various criminal complaints filed against American and British high governmental officials (including the US President and British Prime Minister) for illegal use of force against Iraq and alleged war crimes committed there. As a result of American and British pressures, the Belgian law of 1993 as amended in 1999 was further amended twice in 2003 (42 ILM 749, 1258 (2003)) to restrict even more the scope of Belgium's jurisdiction, limiting it to situations where the alleged offender was a Belgian national or resident or in which the victim was Belgian or had resided in Belgium for at least three years. In addition, the federal prosecutor was granted discretion to decline prosecution if in the interest of administration of justice and in respect of Belgium's international obligations, it resulted that the matter should be brought either before an international tribunal or before a competent, independent, impartial, and fair tribunal in the state where the acts were committed, or the state of the suspect's nationality, or the state where he may be found. Moreover, the amended law precludes filing complaints against sitting heads of state and foreign ministers, and individuals enjoying diplomatic immunity in Belgium. The Spanish Organic Law of the Judicial Power of 1985 (which provided the basis for attempts to prosecute the former Chilean dictator Augusto Pinochet when Spain requested his extradition), which applies to the same crimes and to torture, still allows jurisdiction *in absentia*. This also seems to be the position of the pertinent law of New Zealand of 2000. On the whole, however, state practice, including the case law, is not consistent, and there is also a profound difference of opinion on the subject in the doctrine, as illustrated by contrasting individual opinions **(304)** in the International Court of Justice (ICJ) *Case Concerning the Arrest Warrant of 11 April 2000* (2002) (Democratic Republic of the Congo v. Belgium) (41 ILM 536 (2002)). Although in its *dispositif* (that is, the judgment itself), the ICJ did not deal with the issue of the legality of the Belgian law on universal jurisdiction; that issue remains alive in view of the Court's statement that immunity from jurisdiction, which the Court upheld, does not mean impunity. It must be pointed out here that the ICJ judgment ruled that state practice did not allow to deduce that "there exists under customary international law **(39)** any form of exception to the rule according immunity from criminal jurisdiction and inviolability to incumbent ministers for foreign affairs, where they are suspected of having committed war crimes or crimes against humanity." The Court also found that the rules concerning the immunity or criminal responsibility of persons having an official capacity contained in the statutes of international tribunals likewise did not enable the Court to conclude that "any such exception exists in customary international law in regard to national courts." However—as also stated by the ICJ—immunity from jurisdiction does not mean impunity from individual responsibility and from prosecution, either in the alleged offender's own country, or as a result of waiver of immunity by his government, or after he ceases to hold the office of (as in this case) foreign minister. Finally, an incumbent foreign minister (or presumably any state official) may be tried before the International Criminal Court **(170)** whose Statute (Art. 27(2)) provides that the official capacity of a person is not a bar to prosecution.

Among the multilateral conventions providing for a broad extraterritorial jurisdiction only the Hague and Montreal Conventions on air hijacking and air sabotage, respectively, have been ratified by a very large majority of states; the other conventions bind a more limited, albeit growing, number of states. This raises the question whether the jurisdictional rules of these agreements are legally binding only for the parties or perhaps have become obligations under customary law or, at least, belong to permissive rules of the law. As far as the gravest international crimes are concerned, namely, serious war crimes, genocide, crimes against humanity, torture, and probably serious cases of terrorism, universal jurisdiction proper, including jurisdiction *in absentia*, is certainly not considered unlawful although it may not be an obligation. Whether such universal jurisdiction with respect to other offenses as contemplated by the conventions, and specifically jurisdiction *in absentia,* is in accordance with international law, is still a controversial issue. However, even though state practice does not lead to any definitive conclusions, it does not necessarily mean that such exercise of jurisdiction is unlawful. Subject to safeguards against any abuse that a broad exercise of criminal jurisdiction may involve, it may be exercised on a voluntary basis, as is even provided for in relevant conventions. The "Princeton Principles on Universal Jurisdiction," a set of guidelines drafted by 30 international law experts in 2001, suggests applying a very broad scope of universal jurisdiction to offenders accused of grave crimes against humanity and war crimes, subject to the observance of safeguards of international due process.

The general trend in contemporary international practice indicates a gradual evolution toward widening national jurisdiction. Although the rule *aut dedere aut judicare* logically implies the offender's presence in the territory of the *forum* state, there exists no prohibition in international law for a state to enact municipal legislation allowing universal jurisdiction *in absentia*. In this respect Belgium (and some international jurists) have rationalized universal jurisdiction by seeking its basis in an extensive construction of an *obiter dictum* of the Permanent Court of International Justice **(320)** in the *Lotus* case (Turkey/France) (1927 PCIJ, Series A, No. 10), involving jurisdiction in a case of collision on the high seas **(245)**, to the effect that in the exercise of extraterritorial jurisdiction states have "a wide measure of discretion which is only limited in certain cases by prohibitive rules."

Trends toward broadening the basis of jurisdiction beyond the territorial principle have also emerged in matters other than criminal jurisdiction. Apart from the effects doctrine, regarded also as part of the territorial principle **(91)**, the US has asserted jurisdiction over violations of international law, including in particular violations of human rights committed by and against non-nationals in other countries, such as Argentina, Chile, Guatemala, Haiti, Paraguay, and Ethiopia, among others. In one of the best-known cases, *Filártiga v. Peña-Irala* (19 ILM 966 (1980)) a US Court of Appeals provided a remedy in tort to an alien invoking the Alien Torts Act of 1790 (enacted as part of the Judicial Act of 1789), which allows foreign nationals to sue in a US court for a private tort committed abroad in violation of the law of nations or a treaty of the US. In this case, the Court, rejecting the act of state **(51)** defense, awarded punitive damages to nationals of Paraguay against a former Paraguayan police officer for acts of torture and death committed in Paraguay. In some other cases considerations of state immunity **(131)** prevented bringing claims in human rights litigation in the US, a difficulty which special legislation and amendments to the Foreign Sovereign Immunities Act of 1976, denying immunity in suits involving torture and certain terrorist offenses, were designed to overcome.

**93. Mandate System.** Now of historical interest, the mandate system, a predecessor of the United Nations (UN) trusteeship system **(142)**, was established under Art. 26 of the Covenant of the League of Nations, whereby the colonies and certain other territories lost in World War I by defeated enemy powers, Germany and Turkey, were placed under the tutelage of some of the victorious states ("mandatory states") to be administered by such states, on the basis of written agreements ("mandates") between the League and each mandatory state, on behalf of the League of Nations but in the interests of the inhabitants of the territory concerned, with the implied right of self-determination to be exercised some time in the future. The guiding principle of the mandate system was that the well-being of "peoples not yet able to stand by themselves" was a "sacred trust of civilization" to be carried out by the mandatory powers, responsible to the League's Council assisted by the Permanent Mandates Commission, in order to prepare the people of the mandatory territory for eventual independence.

The mandated territories were of three categories: A, B, and C, in descending order of their political development. The A mandates (former Turkish territories), namely Iraq, Palestine, and Transjordan, under Great Britain, and Syria and Lebanon under France, were the territories most advanced on the road to independence and even possessed some treaty-making capacity. Iraq became independent in 1932, followed by Lebanon in 1941 and Jordan and Syria in 1946. The former mandate of Palestine, abandoned by Great Britain, became the state of Israel in 1948, with the question of a state for the Palestinians still unresolved. The type B mandates, some former German colonies in Africa, (British Cameroon, British Togoland, and Tanganyika under Great Britain; French Cameroun and French Togoland under France; and Rwanda-Urundi under Belgium) required a longer period of tutelage. The type C mandates, the other former German colonies in Africa and the former German colonies in the Pacific (South-West Africa under the Union of South Africa; Samoa under New Zealand; Nauru under the joint mandate of Great Britain, Australia, and New Zealand; other Pacific islands south of the equator under Australia; and Pacific islands north of the equator under Japan), were the least advanced areas and were administered as virtual colonies of the mandatory power.

The administering power did not acquire sovereignty **(125)** over the mandated territory. Nor did the native inhabitants acquire the nationality **(175)** of the administering power concerned, but the inhabitants of the A-type mandates became nationals of their respective territories. In the doctrine of international law, there was no agreement on the precise legal status of the mandated territories, but in a majority of views sovereignty over them was in abeyance or, vested in the people of the territory but temporarily in suspense, was exercised by the mandatory power.

After World War II the mandatory system was replaced by its UN successor, the trusteeship system **(142)**, except for the South African mandate over South-West Africa, which the mandatory state refused to place under the trusteeship system, precipitating a prolonged conflict lasting for several decades.

**94. National Liberation Movement.** In the terminology of the decolonization policy of the United Nations (UN), the term "national liberation movement" refers to an organization leading, as a rule, by force of arms, the struggle for independence of peoples under colonial, alien, or racist domination, as reaffirmed by numerous General Assembly (GA) resolutions pertaining to the right of self-determination of peoples **(122)**. The phenomenon of national liberation movements in this sense virtually disappeared from the international stage upon the near completion of the decolonization process. By the beginning of the new century, apart from the special case of the Palestine Liberation Organization (PLO), there seemed to be in existence only two national liberation movements worth mentioning. First, there was the POLISARIO Front (Popular Front for the Liberation of Saquia el Hamra and Río de Oro), still engaged in the manifestly hopeless struggle against Morocco for the liberation of the self-proclaimed Saharan Arab Democratic Republic in the territory of the former Spanish Sahara unilaterally taken over by Morocco. The other, much less known, liberation movement was the Kanak Socialist National Liberation Front in New Caledonia, under French rule. By contrast, in the early 1970s there had existed about a dozen national liberation movements sponsored by the former Organization of African Unity (OAU) and the League of Arab States. Under the OAU rules the movements were expected to be united (which was not always the case; example: Southern Rhodesia) and to conduct effective military operations against the colonial power. However, in most cases, the status of the movements rested not on the control of the territory but on the international political support of the anti-colonial forces for the principle of self-determination of peoples.

The international legal status of national liberation movements has been a controversial issue. While at least some of them could be classified as insurgents **(115)**, there were pressures by Third World countries for recognizing them as belligerents **(113)**, as was done in Art. 96(3) of Protocol I of 1977 **(369)** to the Geneva Conventions of 1949 **(349)**, or even as full subjects of law with international legal personality **(85)**. In practice, national liberation movements with an official status in the OAU and the League of Arab States, were granted by the GA certain rights, such as participation as observers in the proceedings of the 4th Committee of the GA and attendance, with signing the Final Act as a separate group, at international conferences, including the Third United Nations Conference on the Law of the Sea, 1973–1982 **(263)** and the Geneva Conference on International Humanitarian Law, 1974–1977, which adopted the two Protocols to the Geneva Conventions of 1949. National liberation movements have also participated in the work of some specialized agencies of the UN, including International Civil Aviation Organization, International Labour Organisation, United Nations Educational, Scientific, and Cultural Organization, and the World Health Organization.

The PLO, the best-known national liberation movement, has been granted by some states diplomatic privileges and immunities **(63)** and has participated in the Security Council (SC) debates with the status under the UN Charter (Art. 31) equivalent to a state **(127)** which is not a member of the SC but which participates, without vote, in the discussion of any question before the Council whenever the latter considers that the interests of that state are specially affected. In 1988 the PLO proclaimed the "State of Palestine," but without any claim that such a state existed in fact.

In 1974 the GA granted the PLO the permanent observer status in the UN, a right nominally granted only to states and international organizations **(84)**. This status led to conflict with the host state when the US closed the PLO mission, invoking US anti-terrorist laws, an action subsequently ruled by a US court (27 ILM 712, 1055 (1988)) to be a breach of the Headquarters Agreement of the US with the UN. The position of the PLO changed after the 1993 Washington Israel-PLO Declaration of Principles on Interim Self-Government Arrangements (32 ILM 1525 (1993)) and the subsequent creation of the Palestinian Authority, accompanied by negotiations for a permanent solution of the Palestinian problem. The *sui generis* status of the Palestinian Authority exhibits some features of a state *in statu nascendi* (for example, the treaty-making power), but on the threshold of the 21st century its prospects for achieving statehood were as bleak as ever.

The numerous and proliferating secessionist movements active in various parts of the world at the beginning of the 21st century are denied by the UN the status of national liberation movements.

Hence, they do not possess the special rights enjoyed in the colonial era by the anti-colonial national liberation movements. Because of their image of international "political incorrectness," due to their objective of disrupting the territorial stability of the existing states, especially in the Third World, and their sometimes terrorist methods of achieving their goals, the status of such contemporary secessionist (and sometimes perhaps justifiable) movements is, at least for now, governed merely by the rules pertaining to insurgency, possibly belligerency, and by the international humanitarian law **(353)** applicable in non-international armed conflicts **(340)**.

**95. Nationality of Claims.** The concept of nationality of claims refers to the rule of international law whereby a state may not present a claim for reparation **(118)** in respect of an injury suffered by a private person (individual or juridical person) as a result of an internationally wrongful act of a foreign state unless the injured person was its national **(175)** at the moment when the injury was caused and retains its nationality continually (the rule of continuous nationality) at least until the claim is decided by a competent international tribunal **(306)** or other method of claim settlement chosen by the parties. An additional condition is that the injured person should not have the nationality of the state against which the claim is brought. The rule on continuity of nationality came on the agenda of the International Law Commission in 2001 as part of its work on codifying **(5)** the rules on diplomatic protection.

The basic principle governing a state's right to submit an international claim in cases of injury to individuals was articulated by the Permanent Court of International Justice **(320)** which in its Judgment (jurisdiction) in *Mavrommatis Palestine Concessions* (Greece v. Great Britain) (1924 PCIJ, Series A, No. 2) pointed out that "by taking up the case of one of its subjects and by resorting to diplomatic action or international judicial proceedings on his behalf, a State is in reality asserting its own rights, its rights to ensure, in the persons of its subjects, respect for the rules of international law." Despite progress achieved since in the matter of the status of individual in international law **(81)**, this principle still obtains today: individuals can pursue claims against a foreign state only through the intermediary and protection of the state of their nationality. Apart from rare departures from this rule by virtue of a treaty **(288)**, the exceptions to the rule of the nationality of claims include the state's right to protect foreign nationals in its armed forces and serving as crew members on ships of the state's nationality **(257)**. A state may also undertake protection of foreign nationals upon severance by their state of diplomatic relations with a third state. In addition, under some human rights treaties **(160)** any contracting party may institute proceedings against another party for a violation of human rights irrespective of the nationality of the victim.

In most cases the determination of the nationality of claims does not present problems. On the other hand, the fact that the granting of nationality is within the exclusive jurisdiction **(87)** of the state, a state's right to protect its national may be challenged by the wrongdoing foreign state on the grounds that in reality the nationality bond between the claimant state and its alleged national is not genuine and so tenuous as in effect not to warrant the claimant state's right to diplomatic protection. In the celebrated (but, of course, legally not binding for other cases) and much criticized judgment in the *Nottebohm* case (Liechtenstein v. Guatemala) (1955 ICJ Rep. 4) the International Court of Justice (ICJ) **(309)**, without questioning the right of states to grant nationality, held that a state might not legally espouse a claim on behalf of its national in the absence of a real and genuine link between the individual and the claimant state, at least in cases of claims against a state to which the individual is tied by such link. As formulated by the ICJ in the *Nottebohm* case, the requirement of genuine link for purposes of exercising the right of diplomatic protection over nationals, constituted in effect an extension of the concept of effective nationality, applied to resolve problems of dual nationality **(174)**, to the right of diplomatic protection in general. The rules governing nationality of claims in situations of dual (or multiple) nationality are to a large extent based on the principles developed in the Convention on Certain Questions Relating to the Conflict of Nationality Laws, 1930 (179 LNTS 89). On the whole, state practice gives priority to the effective or dominant nationality, an approach adopted also by the Iran–United States (US) Claims Tribunal (IUSCT) **(312)** (where individuals did have the right of direct access). This Tribunal adjudicated a number of politically sensitive cases in which claimants possessing both Iranian and US nationality sought compensation from Iran. Residence, family connections, business interests, and participation in public activities at the relevant period of time were among the criteria selected by the IUSCT to substantiate the existence of the dominant and effective nationality for purposes of the admissibility of claims for compensation by Iran.

Insofar as corporations are concerned, nationality of claims may raise controversies because of a rather flexible concept of nationality of corporations **(173)** accepted for purposes of international law and complexities in the structure of transnational corporations **(140)**, especially where a corporation and its shareholders (subsidiaries and individuals) are tied by the bond of nationality to different states. Although no absolute test is accepted, a corporation is ordinarily considered to have the nationality of the state of incorporation where its registered office is located. As ruled by the ICJ in the case of *Barcelona Traction, Light and Power Company, Limited* (Belgium v. Spain) (New Application-Judgment on the Merits: 1970 ICJ Rep. 3), the state of a corporation's nationality has the right to make claims on the corporation's behalf even if it is controlled by foreign shareholders and conducts its operations abroad. Thus, normally, to avoid further confusion in the already complex international intercorporate relations, the state of the shareholders' nationality may not present claims on their behalf in respect of losses suffered by them as a result of an internationally wrongful act committed against the corporation itself. However, in the case of *Elettronica Sicula S.p.A.* (*ELSI*) (United States of America v. Italy) (1989 ICJ Rep. 15), in which the US instituted proceedings against Italy on behalf of ELSI (a subsidiary company incorporated in Italy but wholly owned by two American corporations) in respect of losses inflicted upon ELSI by the seizure of its assets by Italy, allegedly in breach of certain treaty provisions, the Chamber **(295)** of the ICJ ruled for Italy, but otherwise did not question the right of the US to espouse the claims of the two American corporations.

Exceptionally, and apart from any treaty provisions, diplomatic protection of shareholders is possible if a corporation has gone into liquidation, in which case the respective state or states of the shareholders' nationality may find it appropriate to espouse claims on behalf of the shareholders. Furthermore, the national state may take up the claims of the shareholders whose right has been directly infringed, for example by a discriminatory expropriation of shares.

In adjudicating large claims of American corporations against Iran, the IUSCT developed certain criteria which, by piercing the corporate veil, established a presumption of American nationality of a corporation by such tests as a US address of a majority of the shareholders, proof of incorporation in the US, and certain relevant data on the principal American shareholders, including those enjoying voting rights in the corporation concerned.

**96. Necessity, State of.** According to the International Law Commission (ILC) Draft Articles on State Responsibility of 2001 **(129)**, the state of necessity is a circumstance that may be invoked by a state **(127)** as a ground for precluding the wrongfulness of an otherwise unlawful act of that state which consequently entails no international responsibility **(128)** on the conditions, first, that such act is the only means for the state of safeguarding an essential interest against a grave and imminent peril and, second, that it does not seriously impair an essential interest of the state or states toward which the obligation exists, or of the international community as a whole. Furthermore, in any case, necessity may not be invoked by a state as a ground for precluding wrongfulness if the international obligation in question arises from a peremptory rule of general international law (*jus cogens*) **(24)**, or excludes the possibility of invoking necessity (for example a human rights treaty) **(160)**, or if the state itself has contributed to the situation of necessity.

Unlike *force majeure* **(78)**, the defense of necessity constitutes a deliberate act of not conforming to an international obligation. Among "essential interests of the state" warranting the plea of necessity may be the existence of a serious danger to the whole state or its population as such or part of it, preservation of essential services, keeping domestic peace, or defense against a serious ecological disaster, the last mentioned situation, under the circumstances, involving an essential interest of the international community as a whole. In this regard, the ILC found the sinking in 1967 on orders of the British government of the Liberian oil tanker the *Torrey Canyon*, which ran aground off the coast of Cornwall, polluting large areas of the coastline, to be a legitimate case of the state of necessity. Whether a serious case of failure to meet financial obligations justifies invoking necessity is not a settled issue. More recently, in 1997, the International Court of Justice (ICJ) **(309)** found the prerequisites for necessity listed by the ILC as reflecting customary international law **(39)**. In the *Case Concerning the Gabčikovo-Nagymaros Project* (Hungary/Slovakia) (37 ILM 162 (1998)) the ICJ ruled that the perils invoked by Hungary on account of the alleged state of ecological necessity were not sufficiently established; neither were they imminent nor could they not be responded to by means other than the suspension and abandonment by Hungary of the treaty obligation of the joint construction with Slovakia (succeeding Czechoslovakia) of a dam on the Danube.

Since the plea of necessity can lend itself to abuse as a pretext for breaching an international obligation, its validity as a rule of international law is considered by some to be controversial, with some publicists even denying its existence as a rule of international law. A violation of the territorial integrity of another state to rescue or protect life and property on the ground of necessity has been an especially sensitive issue. The doctrine of military necessity is a different problem which arises within the context of an armed conflict, international **(339)** or non-international **(340)**.

**97. Neutralized State.** A neutralized or permanently neutral state is a state which in return for a permanent guarantee of its territorial integrity by third powers is obligated to maintain permanent neutrality, except for situations of its own defense. Unlike neutrality **(362)**, which is relevant only during an ongoing war **(338)** (international "armed conflict") **(339)**) between third countries, the status of a permanently neutral or neutralized state entails an obligation to be neutral both in war and in peace. As a result, a permanently neutral state is barred from participating in military alliances. On the other hand, it has a duty to defend itself and maintain reasonably strong armed forces. Other modalities of the status of permanent neutrality depend on the provisions of the relevant treaty and the particular circumstances. However, neutralization in no way impairs the state's sovereignty and independence.

In the post–Cold War era neutrality appears to have lost its traditional *raison d'être*. Historically, the rather rare cases of neutralization, a diplomatic device mainly in the European balance-of-power system of the 19th century, include first of all Switzerland, the classical model of permanent neutrality, the neutralization of which by the Congress of Vienna in 1815, reaffirmed by the Treaty of Versailles in 1919, has been successfully maintained ever since and is even considered by some as part of customary international law **(39)**. On the other hand, Belgium and Luxembourg, neutralized by the treaties of London, 1831 (renewed in 1839) and 1867, respectively, lost their permanently neutral status as a result of World War I, as confirmed in the Treaty of Versailles. The permanently neutral status of Albania, which was neutralized upon its creation in 1913, ended as a result of fundamental changes of circumstances **(273)**. The abortive Free Territory of Trieste **(141)** was also intended to be a neutralized entity.

Austria has been a permanently neutral state since 1955 when in return for a guarantee of its integrity under the State Treaty for the Reestablishment of an Independent and Democratic Austria, 1955 (217 UNTS 223), of which France, the United Kingdom, the United States, the Soviet Union and several other states are parties, it undertook to follow the permanent neutrality of the Swiss type. Austria's neutrality was subsequently anchored in Art. 1 of its Constitution.

The permanent neutrality of Laos is based on the Declaration and Protocol on the Neutrality of Laos, signed at the Geneva Conference of 1962 (456 UNTS 301) by the five permanent members of the Security Council (SC) and several other states. However, subsequent developments in the Indochina peninsula made it impossible to preserve Laos' status of permanent neutrality although the Paris Act of the International Conference on Vietnam, 1973 (935 UNTS 405), reaffirmed this status. Formally, it continues to bind Laos, but it has lost much of its practical significance.

Neutralization is a legal status under international law and in this regard it must be distinguished from self-neutralization whereby a country follows a policy of permanent neutrality without any legal obligation, as it was once practiced by the old Swiss Confederation before 1815, or by Finland and Sweden during the Cold War. A state may also unilaterally declare **(44)** itself permanently neutral, as in the historical cases of Honduras in 1907 and Iceland in 1918. Such declarations by Vatican City **(80)** in 1929, Malta in 1981 (21 ILM 396 (1981)), and Costa Rica in 1983 are still in force.

The neutralization of a state must not be confused with the "neutralization," also known as "demilitarization," of such areas as Antarctica **(187)** or parts of a state's territory, such as border areas, rivers **(204)**, and canals: Kiel **(252)**, Panama **(258)**, and Suez **(261)**. Such arrangements prohibit maintenance of military installations and conduct of hostilities in the area concerned. The term "neutralization" is also used to denote areas set up by agreement during an armed conflict for maintaining certain non-combatant establishments.

In 2003, for all practical purposes, Austria and Switzerland were the only permanently neutral countries. Switzerland, which after World War I joined the League of Nations on the condition that it would not take part in the League's military actions or permit the passage of foreign troops over its territory, did not become a member of the United Nations (UN) for more than a half century, concerned about a potential conflict between its permanent neutrality obligations and the duties of UN membership. It finally joined the UN as its 190th member in 2002. But even before that, it had become a party to the Statute of the International Court of Justice **(309)** and a number of UN specialized agencies, subject in certain cases to reservations protecting its permanent neutrality status.

Prior to its admission to the UN in 2002, Switzerland formally refused to take part in UN collective security **(327)** measures, such as the sanctions against Southern Rhodesia and Iraq and arms embargo against South Africa, but took unilateral measures in substance equivalent to those ordered or called for by the SC. In the post–Cold War period, Switzerland's interpretation of its permanent neutrality status gradually has grown more liberal. More significantly, the Swiss parliament overwhelmingly approved the country's association with the North Atlantic Treaty Organization's (NATO) Partnership for Peace program, and negotiations **(316)** with the European Union (EU) for entry into the European Economic Area, a halfway house to EU membership, were concluded successfully in 1998, with Switzerland joining the Area as of 2001.

Although on the threshold of the new century Austria maintained its constitutionally mandated and popular policy of permanent neutrality, the status of neutrality was a subject of a heated national debate and discord among the major political parties. As a member of the UN, Austria has complied fully with UN enforcement measures and during the Gulf War of 1991 even permitted overflights of its territory by Allied aircraft. In 1995 Austria became a member of the EU and, like Switzerland, joined NATO's Partnership for Peace program. However, Austria continued to emphasize its neutral status, and its public opinion has been overwhelmingly opposed to NATO membership, especially as a result of NATO's intervention in Kosovo. In the course of time, Austria will have to confront the issue of participating in the European security arrangements and reconcile it with its neutralization or formally terminate this status, a step that would require the consent of the guarantee powers under the State Treaty of 1955.

**98. Nonrecognition, Legal Effects of.** Legal effects of nonrecognition of a state **(127)** or government depend in general upon whether the nonrecognition is due to an obligation under international law or to other reasons. Nonrecognition in pursuance of an obligation under international law **(99)** results in a situation where the entity in question does not, in principle, enjoy any rights flowing from recognition **(106)** or implied in the treatment as a state **(127)** or government, as the case may be. It is not entirely clear what obligations such an entity would have under international law, being suspended in a sort of international legal vacuum, but the very fact of having physical control of a territory may provide a basis for liability for acts affecting states. Ideally, the legal effects of nonrecognition in such cases, including enforcement measures against the entity in question, should be authoritatively determined by the Security Council, as was done in the case of the measures against the illegal regime of Southern Rhodesia in the 1960s, the "bantustans" created by South Africa, and with respect to South Africa's illegal presence in South-West Africa (Namibia), as elaborated in the ICJ **(309)** Advisory Opinion **(291)** on the *Legal Consequences for States of the Continued Presence of South Africa in Namibia* (*South West Africa*) *Notwithstanding Security Council Resolution 276* (*1970*) (1971 ICJ Rep. 16). As a practical matter, however, it is doubtful whether in the long run an internationally illegal state or government can be regarded as a legal nullity. For example, it would be contrary to common sense and humanitarian considerations not to recognize the validity of the acts of an illegal entity affecting the private rights and interests of its inhabitants. Hardship resulting from nonrecognition is well illustrated by a court case in England (*Adams v. Adams*) in 1971 in which a Rhodesian divorce decree was not recognized by the court because it was an act of an illegal regime, a situation subsequently rectified by an English law recognizing Rhodesian decrees dealing with personal matters.

In cases of nonrecognition due to causes other than obligation under international law, an unrecognized state or government is not, as a rule, accorded all the rights and prerogatives granted to a recognized entity under the municipal law **(27)** of the recognizing state. Thus, while much depends also on the extent to which national courts are bound by the executive policy, in the United States (US) an unrecognized entity is ordinarily denied access to courts except that corporations owned by such an entity have been allowed to sue. But in 1923 the then-unrecognized Soviet government in control of its territory was granted state immunity **(131)** in a New York court. The same approach was followed in England by the House of Lords in the *Arantzazu Mendi* case in 1939 where the insurgent nationalist government in Spain, unrecognized *de jure* but treated as a government *de facto* **(110)**, was found entitled to immunity from suit in an English court. An unrecognized government does not enjoy state immunity and is not entitled to property belonging to its predecessor, located in the US. Official acts and court judgments of an unrecognized entity are given effect in the interests of common sense and justice to the extent that they deal solely with day-to-day private, local, and domestic matters, but not to acts with respect to matters extending beyond the borders of the unrecognized entity.

Exceptionally, giving effect to acts of an unrecognized state can be accomplished by employing a pragmatic legal device of treating such acts as those of a subordinate body acting under the authority of an otherwise recognized state. This approach is illustrated by the case of *Carl Zeiss Stiftung v. Rayner and Keeler* [1967] AC 853, which involved the validity of acts of the then-unrecognized East German state, held by the House of Lords to be legally acts of the occupying power, the Soviet Union, a recognized state. Similarly, in the case of *GUR Corporation v. Trust Bank of Africa Ltd* [1986] 3 All ER 449, the English Court of Appeal found the unrecognized "bantustan" of Ciskei to be capable of access to court as a subordinate body of South Africa, the creator of such puppet states. Generally speaking, courts will give effect to the laws of an unrecognized entity if this is indicated by a suggestion from the executive authority.

Apart from the incapacity in treatment of non-recognized entities under the municipal law of the non-recognizing state, nonrecognition does not mean that the entity in question exists in a total legal vacuum, entirely outside the bounds of international law. Since statehood as such does not depend on recognition **(116)**, non-recognizing states must observe toward such an entity certain most fundamental duties under international law, and in particular maintain respect for its territorial integrity and property, its right to use the high seas **(242)**, and so on. Similarly, unrecognized states have obligations under international law and must bear responsibility for its violations **(128)**. State practice shows that claims against such states are raised even by the very states that withhold recognition, as for example in the case of US claims against North Korea related to the sinking of the *Pueblo* in 1968.

While the breaking of diplomatic relations does not automatically imply derecognition, nonrecognition excludes diplomatic relations. However, occasionally states enter into unofficial contacts with unrecognized entities and may even conclude agreements with them, valid under international law, such as for example the armistice agreement with North Korea in 1953 or US negotiations with that state concerning nuclear matters in the 1990s.

On the whole, the rules of international law on the legal effects of nonrecognition are not well settled, but generally speaking nonrecognition does not fundamentally affect the rights and duties of an unrecognized state *vis à vis* states that do not recognize it, but in everyday practice the ability of an unrecognized state or government to function on the international plane and especially to enforce its rights and protect its interests, and the ability of third states to enforce obligations, may be seriously handicapped.

**99. Nonrecognition, Obligation of.** While recognition **(106)** is a unilateral political act within the discretion of the recognizing state, there are occasionally situations where states are obligated under international law to withhold recognition. Apart from any treaty obligations to that effect, states have the duty not to recognize any new situation (state, government, insurgency, territorial claim) that originated in a violation of international law. This is a corollary of the general principle of law known in its Latin form as *ex injuria jus non oritur* meaning, in its application to the duty of nonrecognition, that an internationally wrongful act cannot generate a legal right.

Historically the doctrine of nonrecognition is associated with a unilateral United States (US) declaration articulated by Secretary of State Henry Stimson in 1932 (hence "Stimson Doctrine"). This declaration, addressed to Japan and China and relating to Japan's intention to set up a puppet state of Manchuria, proclaimed that the US would not recognize any situation or treaty **(288)** contrary to the obligations under the Pact of Paris of 1928 **(330)**. At the international level, the Assembly of the League of Nations adopted a similar resolution of a more general character and invoked not only the Pact of Paris but also the Covenant of the League, presumably its Art. 10 guaranteeing the existing territorial integrity and political independence of the League's members. Similar undertakings were included in the Montevideo Convention on the Rights and Duties of States, 1932 (165 LNTS 19), and a resolution of the Conference of American States in 1938. However, the state practice pertaining to the nonrecognition of the consequences of the illegal acts by the aggressor states in the inter-war period (Germany, Italy, the Soviet Union) opportunistically did not conform to the principle of nonrecognition. Thus, the Italian conquest of Abyssinia (Ethiopia) was recognized *de jure* **(110)** by many states, albeit this recognition was later withdrawn after Italy joined Germany in World War II. The incorporation of Austria (*Anschluss*) by Germany was widely recognized *de jure* but subsequently declared null and void upon the outbreak of the war. Despite some initial protests, the incorporation of the Czech part of Czechoslovakia into Germany as a "protectorate" and the creation of the German puppet state of Slovakia were also recognized by many states, but then derecognized following the outbreak of the war. The Soviet annexation in 1940 of the three Baltic republics of Lithuania, Latvia, and Estonia (which regained their independence in 1991) as well as other Soviet territorial acquisition by force in Eastern Europe in the early stages of the war at the expense of Finland, Poland, and Romania were also recognized by a number of states.

Since 1945, with the introduction of the ban on the use or threat of force in international relations **(329)**, as anchored in Art. 2(40) of the United Nations (UN) Charter, states have had the obligation not to recognize or treat as a state an entity that was created in violation of the Charter. More recently, this principle was reaffirmed by the European Community (EC) in connection with the question of recognition of the new states emerging from the breakup of the former Yugoslavia **(134)** and the Soviet Union **(133)**. The relevant provisions of the EC Guidelines state that the Community and its members will not recognize entities which are the result of aggression. There is also an obligation under international law not to recognize a government imposed by a state upon another state in violation of the prohibition of force. A premature recognition of an insurgent regime **(115)** or recognizing it as a successor government while the established government is still in control constitutes an illegal intervention **(331)** in the internal affairs of another state or, if accompanied by military support, may be even considered a violation of the ban of the use of force in international relations. Furthermore, the Friendly Relations Declaration of 1970 **(14)**, which expresses the fundamental principles of international law, expressly states that "[n]o territorial acquisition resulting from the threat or use of force shall be recognized as legal."

Strictly speaking, the Security Assembly (SC) is the organ with the authority to determine whether a controversial recognition situation originated in a violation of the ban on the threat or use of force or some other fundamental rule of international law and ought to be subject to the obligation of nonrecognition. Thus the obligation not to recognize the unilateral declaration of independence by the minority regime of Southern Rhodesia was based on the SC mandatory resolutions under Chapter VII in 1965, which called upon all states not to recognize this "illegal act." As a result, only South Africa recognized Southern Rhodesia as a state and it was not until the change of the regime in 1980 that Zimbabwe's statehood was universally recognized. The creation of the bantustans by South Africa in the years 1976–1981 was condemned by General Assembly (GA) resolutions calling for their nonrecognition, a call endorsed by SC statements and complied with by the members of the international community, even though the obligation not to recognize was based on non-binding resolutions of the GA **(37)**. The question of nonrecognition arose again in 1983 following the

Turkey-inspired establishment in the Turkish-controlled area of Cyprus of the "Turkish Republic of Northern Cyprus." Having previously deplored the division of the island, the SC declared in Resolutions 541 and 550, in 1983 and 1984, respectively, the creation of the Turkish Republic to be legally invalid and asked all states not to recognize any Cyprus state other than the Republic of Cyprus. Except Turkey, no other state has recognized the Turkish entity created on Cyprus as a state. Again, during the first Gulf crisis, Iraq's annexation of Kuwait in 1990 was also declared null and void by the SC, which called upon all states not to recognize it. On the other hand, while India's intervention during the East Pakistan's secession from Pakistan in 1971, rationalized by India on humanitarian grounds, and the resulting creation of the state of Bangladesh, could be and initially was considered as illegal by a vast majority of the international community, no authoritative determination could be forthcoming from the SC. Due to the power realities of the situation, an exception was in fact made to the paramount prohibition of disrupting the national unity of a country, incompatible with the purposes and principles of the UN Charter, and Bangladesh, the entity resulting from the secession, was accepted as an accomplished fact: it was universally recognized as a state and admitted to the UN.

**100. Non-Self-Governing Territory.** A non-self-governing territory is the term used in the United Nations (UN) system for territories "whose peoples have not yet attained a full measure of self-government" (UN Charter, Art. 73), that is all categories of dependent territory, whatever its name (dependency, overseas *département,* overseas territory, territorial *collectivité,* self-governing territory, etc.). In traditional international law, before the onset of decolonization, sovereignty over a colonial territory was vested in the metropolitan power, but each case had to be considered on its own merits, as some of the dependent territories possessed a degree of autonomy and in some cases acted for the metropolitan power on the international scene, for example, by making treaties **(288)**. Some territories had even the right to join public international organizations **(84)**, but the case of India, which was a member of the League of Nations and then an original member state of the UN, is rather exceptional as is the case of the Philippines, which became an original member of the UN before becoming independent in 1946.

Art. 73 of the UN Charter calls upon the states administering non-self-governing territories to recognize the principle that the interests of the inhabitants of the territories are paramount and to this end ensure their advancement, develop self-government, taking due account of the political aspirations of the people, and assist them in the progressive development of their free political institutions, according to the particular circumstances of each territory and its peoples and their varying stages of advancement. The administering states were to transmit to the Secretary-General "for information purposes" statistical and other information of a technical nature relating to economic, social, and educational conditions of the administered territories. A special UN body, now known as the Committee of 24, has been considering the information submitted under Art. 73(e). Separate, more intrusive, provisions on reporting duties applied to territories under the trusteeship system **(142)**. In 1946 as many as 74 territories were classified by the UN as falling within the purview of Art. 73.

Very soon, on the tide of the rising anti-colonial ideology, the General Assembly (GA), in a series of resolutions, began to interpret Art. 73 in an extensive manner in the name of the right of self-determination of peoples **(122)**, asserting to itself the competence to supervise the implementation of its provisions and in particular to decide, against the position of administering states, whether or not a territory has reached the stage of "self-government" envisaged in Art. 73(b). Furthermore, the GA defined the concept of the non-self-governing territory by adopting a presumption that the obligation to transmit information applied in respect of a territory which "is geographically separate and distinct ethnically and/or culturally from the country administering it," this presumption being further strengthened if the territory was arbitrarily placed in a position or status of subordination to the metropolitan state. Practically speaking, the GA definition limited the concept of the non-self-governing territories to the overseas possessions of Western powers, acquired in the era of the overseas expansion since the 15th century. But interestingly, the two Spanish enclaves in Africa, Ceuta and Melilla, totally surrounded by Morocco, are excluded from the GA definition.

Following the adoption (by a vote of 89–0, with 9 abstentions) by the GA in 1960 of the Declaration on the Granting of Independence to Colonial Countries and Peoples (Res. 1514) the self-government under Art. 73 of the UN Charter became in practice identified with complete independence. At the same time, the rapidly decreasing category of the dependent territories (and even more the trusteeship territories) was no more to be considered as mere parts of the respective metropolitan powers, but—as articulated in the Friendly Relations Declaration of 1970 **(14)**—became invested with "a status separate and distinct from the territory of the State administering it" until the people of the colony or other non-self-governing territory exercised their right of self-determination.

With decolonization as understood by the GA virtually accomplished, the list of the self-governing territories on which information was to be submitted under Art. 73, has shrunk to a dozen or so, mostly little islands and archipelagoes of which the United Kingdom's (UK) Falkland Islands (Malvinas) are perhaps politically the most sensitive. The largest territory is the former Spanish Sahara (Western Sahara) still occupied by Morocco and awaiting, with little chance of success, the implementation of a UN settlement plan for a repeatedly postponed referendum on self-determination. Gibraltar is another controversial territory, still considered a "colonial situation" by the GA, over which negotiations between the UK and the claimant state, Spain, have been in progress for some time. Otherwise, by the beginning of the 21st century, the question of the non-self-governing territories had largely lost its erstwhile significance. But the differences between administering states claiming that their respective territories had reached self-government and the GA not accepting such assertions, still continued.

**101. Personal Union.** Largely of historical interest, the personal union is a union of states **(127)** occurring when two or more states share an individual as their monarch. A personal union does not acquire its own international legal personality **(85)**; each member state retains its separate personality in international law. Historically, personal unions existed, for example, between Poland and Lithuania (1385–1569), a connection which subsequently became a real union **(105)**; Spain and Portugal (1580–1640); Great Britain and Hanover (1714–1837); the Netherlands and Luxembourg (1815–1890); and Belgium and the Congo Free State (1885–1908). There are no personal unions of this kind today, but one could venture to say that a personal union of sorts exists between the United Kingdom and those few member states of the Commonwealth for which formally the English monarch is still their Head of State.

**102. Privileges and Immunities of International (Intergovernmental) Organizations.** This is a phrase referring to a variety of special rights and exemptions from jurisdiction **(87)** which are accorded by states **(127)** to intergovernmental organizations (public international organizations) **(84)**, their officials, premises, assets, and archives and other documents. Privileges and immunities of representatives of states to international organizations **(103)** constitute an additional and separate category. As in their traditional application to diplomatic **(63)** and consular **(55)** agents, the terms "privileges" and "immunities," as applied to international organizations, are not clearly distinguished from each other in the doctrine or in practice.

The general principle is that the privileges and immunities of international organizations have a functional basis, that is an organization enjoys such privileges and immunities as are necessary for the fulfillment of the purposes of the organization without interference from state authorities and with a guarantee of a certain minimum of freedom and security for its headquarters, property, and staff, and, in addition, for representatives of member states. Although applied to a certain extent by analogy to the immunity of states **(131)** and diplomatic agents, the privileges and immunities of international organizations are not claimed or granted on the basis of reciprocity but are claimed by an organization from a state, ordinarily where the organization conducts its activities. Furthermore, albeit it is not entirely settled, the restrictive theory applied to sovereign (state) immunity does not apply to the United Nations (UN), its specialized agencies, and major regional organizations; but it is not clear whether other international organizations are also entitled to absolute immunity.

The privileges and immunities of international organizations are set out in their respective constituent instruments which are often supplemented by special multilateral conventions and in some cases by bilateral "headquarters agreements" between the organization concerned and the host state which usually grants additional privileges and immunities. In a number of states all these international agreements have been implemented in municipal law **(27)** by special international organizations acts. Insofar as the UN is concerned, Art. 105(1) of the Charter stipulates that "[t]he Organization shall enjoy in the territory of each of its members such privileges and immunities as are necessary for the fulfillment of its purposes," a principle complemented and developed by the Convention on the Privileges and Immunities of the United Nations, 1946 (1 UNTS 16). The relevant provisions of the constituent instruments of the specialized agencies are developed by the Convention on Privileges and Immunities of the Specialized Agencies, 1947 (33 UNTS 261) with draft annexes adapted to each specialized agency. The United States (US) is not a party to this Convention. There are also agreements regulating the privileges and immunities of the Council of Europe, 1949, and the European Communities, 1965, to mention just two. A special Convention on the Safety of the United Nations and Associated Personnel was adopted in 1994, with 33 parties in 2000, to prevent and punish attacks upon the UN and its personnel.

The UN has headquarters agreements with a number of host states, first of all an agreement of 1947 with the US (11 UNTS 11), with supplemental agreements of 1966, 1969, and 1980, and agreements with Switzerland (1947) and Austria (1979) concerning the UN offices in Geneva and Vienna, respectively. Similar agreements are in force with Kenya, 1975, and Japan, 1976. Furthermore, the International Court of Justice (ICJ) **(309)**, its judges, and its staff are accorded privileges and immunities in The Hague under a UN agreement with the Netherlands of 1947 (80 UNTS 61). The Statute of the International Criminal Court (ICC) **(170),** which also has its headquarters in The Hague, provides for privileges and immunities to be granted to the Court and its judges. The US, which hosts the headquarters of the Organization of American States in Washington, has a bilateral agreement of 1975 with the Organization relating to privileges and immunities (26 UST 1025; TIAS 8089).

The precise extent of the privileges and immunities of international organizations under customary international law is not certain, the case law of national courts varying from a strictly functional necessity approach to a more liberal analogy to diplomatic immunities. The matter is of less importance for the UN and its affiliated organizations whose membership is virtually universal and their treaty-based privileges and immunities can even be regarded as part of general international law. Thus for example, the US did not cease to grant privileges and immunities to the United Nations Educational, Scientific, and Cultural Organization during its absence from that organization in the years 1985–2002. On the other hand, organizations outside the UN system do not, in principle, enjoy privileges and immunities in non-member states unless they are provided under municipal law (like the organizations designated in the US under the International Organizations Immunities Act) or are upheld in court.

The rules of the 1946 General Convention, as complemented by the Headquarters Agreement, are typical for privileges and immunities of the UN organizations, but there are some departures as, for example, in the charters of the UN financial-type organizations which allow certain categories of lawsuits against the organization concerned. Under the 1946 Convention, which in general provides a model for similar instruments, the UN and its property enjoy immunity from every form of legal process, except in cases of waiver. However, no waiver may extend to any measures of execution. The Organization is also exempt from financial, monetary, and currency controls, from all direct taxes, customs duties, and restrictions on imports and exports in respect of articles for its official use and its publications. The premises, archives and other documents, and communications are immune and inviolable **(67)** from any exercise of jurisdiction **(87)** by a member state that would interfere with their official use. This rule is reaffirmed by the Headquarters Agreement according to which the UN headquarters district, while of course not "extraterritorial" since the US, New York state, and local law apply there, is inviolate, and US and state and local officials may enter it only with the consent of the UN Secretary-General. The UN has the authority to issue regulations necessary for the performance of its functions, such as those pertaining to its staff and retail sales establishments, for example its bookstores.

The host state has the obligation to protect the UN headquarters district against any disturbances from outside, and the UN is obliged to prevent the district from becoming a refuge for fugitives from law. The principles governing the so-called diplomatic asylum **(64)** appear to apply equally to international organizations.

Under the applicable international agreements, officials of international organizations are, as a general rule, entitled only to privileges and immunities necessary for the independent exercise of their functions in connection with the organization, a general rule, laid down for the UN system in Art. 105(2) of the UN Charter, developed in more detail in the General Convention and in the Convention concerning the specialized agencies. Under these Conventions only the senior executive officials, namely, the Secretary-General and the Assistant Secretaries-General of the UN and their counterparts in the specialized agencies, are entitled to full diplomatic immunity for themselves and their families. Under special provisions of the ICJ Statute (Art. 19) the members of the Court, when engaged on the business of the ICJ, enjoy diplomatic privileges and immunities as do the judges of the ICC.

Among the major immunities listed in the General Convention are immunity from legal process, taxes on official salaries, customs duties, and immigration regulations. Experts on missions for the UN are also accorded such privileges and immunities as are necessary for the independent exercise of their functions, a rule upheld by the ICJ in its Advisory Opinion **(291)** on *Applicability of Article VI, Section 22, of the Convention on the Privileges and Immunities of the United Nations* (1989 ICJ Rep. 177). However, persons invited by the UN to its headquarters are not entitled to any privileges and immunities. In addition, host states sometimes make reservations concerning the right to immunity of international officials who are their nationals **(175)** or permanent residents. Under the US law, such officials are subject to taxes and military service obligations, but while the US reserves the right to levy taxes on their salaries (but not on US permanent residents working for the International Monetary Fund or the World Bank), they are compensated for the tax amounts from a special fund financed by the contributions of the staff.

Privileges and immunities of international officials are subject to waiver. Under the two basic conventions on the immunities of the UN and the specialized agencies, respectively, the chief executive of the organization concerned must waive the immunity of any official in any case where, in his opinion, the immunity would impede the course of justice and can be waived without prejudice to the interests of the UN. For example, the UN does not claim immunity in respect of traffic violations by its chauffeurs or members of the staff driving on official business. In the case of the Secretary-General, the Security Council has the right to waive immunity. If the immunity of an official with respect to his official acts is waived by the organization, he may be tried and convicted for such acts as any private individual. Abuse of the privilege of residence by acts outside his official capacity may lead to deportation by the host state after consultation with the Secretary-General.

**103. Privileges and Immunities of State Representatives to International (Intergovernmental) Organizations.** These are privileges and immunities which under the applicable international agreements are accorded by the host state to various kinds of representatives of states in their relations with international organizations **(84)**, such as heads of permanent missions to the United Nations (UN) or delegates sent by states to participate in the proceedings of an organ of the organization or in an international conference.

Members of states' representations to the UN and the specialized agencies are the major categories of persons entitled to privileges and immunities. Under Art. 105(2) of the UN Charter, representatives of the members enjoy, like officials of the Organization, such privileges and immunities as are necessary for the independent exercise of their functions. Based on this provision, the Convention on the Privileges and Immunities of the UN of 1946 (1 UNTS 16), as supplemented—as far as the United States (US) is concerned—by the Headquarters Agreement with the UN of 1947 (11 UNTS 11), provides that the permanent missions to the UN and the members' representatives of diplomatic rank (as agreed upon between the UN and the US and the state concerned) are entitled essentially to the same privileges and immunities as diplomatic agents **(63)**. Rules corresponding to those applying to representatives to the UN are found in the respective constituent instruments and other agreements governing the specialized agencies of the UN. Concerning representatives of members whose governments are not recognized **(114)** by the US, the Headquarters Agreement provides that the US must extend them privileges and immunities only within the UN district, at their residences and offices outside the district, and when they are in transit **(61)**. It is a controversial matter whether a host state, such as the US may, on grounds of national security, restrict the movements of members' representatives, as has been done by the US with respect to some member states whose movements were limited to a 25 miles radius from the UN Headquarters.

Staff members of non-diplomatic rank may be granted some immunities under the law of the host country, such as the US International Organizations Immunities Act. Members of permanent observer delegations are not entitled to any privileges or immunities. The status of representatives to organizations other than those of the UN system are based either on their charters or agreements with the host state, or may be guaranteed under the law of the host state concerned.

In view of the uncertainties over the status of state representations to international organizations, a UN-sponsored conference adopted the Vienna Convention on the Representation of States in Their Relations with International Organizations of a Universal Character, 1975 (69 AJIL 730 (1975)) drafted by the International Law Commission and closely patterned after the Vienna Convention on Diplomatic Relations of 1961 **(71)**. However, the Convention of 1975 met with opposition by the major host countries, including the US, which criticized it as going too far beyond the existing customary law and, while unduly expanding the obligations of the host states with respect to the privileges and immunities of the representations, and especially the administrative and technical staff, failed to take into account and adequately protect reasonable interests of the host states concerned. The 1975 Convention created a serious division between sending and host states and appeared to be a failure as a product of codification and progressive development of international law **(5)**. It was not yet in force as late as 25 years following its adoption.

**104. The *Rainbow Warrior* Incident and Arbitrations, 1986, 1990.** This *cause célèbre* resulted from the blowing up in 1985 in the Auckland harbor by two clandestine agents of the French government of the British-registered Greenpeace vessel, the *Rainbow Warrior.* As part of the Greenpeace anti-nuclear campaign, the vessel was to sail into the French-prohibited waters of the Mururoa Atoll in Polynesia, the site of French nuclear tests. France requested the release of its two agents convicted to prison terms in New Zealand and refused to extradite **(75)** to New Zealand other officials involved in the operation. Eventually, both countries agreed to arbitration **(293)** by the Secretary-General of the United Nations (first ever by such official) who handed down his award in 1986. Without giving reasons, the award required France to pay a reparation **(118)** of $7 million and offer apologies for the violation of New Zealand's sovereignty, and desist from interfering with the European Community imports from New Zealand. The two agents were required to be transferred to French custody to be confined by France in a military facility on an isolated island in French Polynesia for a period of three years and not to leave without the mutual consent of the two countries. However, before the expiration of the term of confinement the two agents were unilaterally repatriated to France, allegedly for health reasons and before obtaining any consent from New Zealand which itself—as part of the ensuing negotiation **(316)**—sent a physician to France to monitor the medical condition of one of the agents. The agent in question eventually stayed in France for "health reasons" notwithstanding the finding by the New Zealand physician that he could return to the place of confinement. However, the physician did not examine the other French agent, a pregnant woman whom the French authorities, in a *fait accompli,* had flown to France before obtaining New Zealand's consent, justifying her repatriation on the humanitarian ground of the need to see her dying father in France.

New Zealand demanded that France acknowledge its breach of obligation under the 1986 agreement by unilaterally repatriating the two agents from the island of confinement, and that it return the agent there to serve the remaining time of confinement. Invoking *force majeure* **(78)** and distress **(72)**, France denied any international responsibility **(128)**. In its 1990 decision, the tribunal of three arbitrators condemned France for violating the agreement of 1986, but made a distinction between the circumstances surrounding the repatriation of the two agents. On grounds of extreme urgency, involving distress and humanitarian considerations, France was not held responsible for breaching its obligation under the 1986 agreement by transferring one agent to Paris in December 1987, but was found responsible for failing to return him to the confinement island in the Pacific by February 1988 when distress was no more a relevant factor since the state of his health no longer required his continued stay in France. Concerning the other agent, the tribunal found France in breach of its international obligation by failing to obtain in good faith New Zealand's consent to her departure for France on 5 May 1988, and, instead of sending her back to the confinement island, keeping her in France following her father's death on 16 May 1988. In addition, the tribunal made an unusual condition that France should contribute the sum of $2 million to a fund promoting friendly relations between the two countries.

Concerning the private claims, a settlement had been reached with the family of the victim. Furthermore, France admitted its liability to Greenpeace, but the amount of the indemnity due to it had to be determined by an arbitration in 1987 which awarded it $8.152 million.

The *Rainbow Warrior* arbitrations of 1986 and especially 1990 touched upon a number of issues relating to state responsibility, such as the relationship between the customary law **(39)** of state responsibility and the primary rules of international law in the matter; the nature of material breach of a treaty **(276)**, and the nature of reparation, and in particular the principle that monetary compensation may also be paid for non-material damage; and the nature of appropriate satisfaction for such damage in the form of public condemnation of a state, as was done by the tribunal in 1990 with respect to France's breach of a treaty obligation. Of interest is also the tribunal's reasoning, based on the International Law Commission Draft on State Responsibility **(129)**, on the concepts of *force majeure* and distress as circumstances precluding the wrongfulness of an act of state **(51)** in breach of an international obligation.

**105. Real Union.** Largely of historical interest, a union of states **(127)** created by treaty **(288)**, whereby two states are linked together under the same head of state (historically a monarch), creating one single composite international person **(85)** with common organs, especially for purposes of defense, finances, and the conduct of foreign policy. Otherwise, the two states continue to exist as separate units, and to what extent they can act on the international scene as legal persons is determined by the treaty of union. However, the concept of real union lacks any more precise legal meaning and each, otherwise historical, case must be analyzed on its own merits. Past examples of what is generally regarded as real union include Poland and Lithuania (1569–1795) (succeeding a personal union); Sweden and Norway (1814–1905); Austria-Hungary (1867–1918); and—according to some opinions—Denmark and Iceland (1918–1943). More recently, the short-lived (1959–1961) union of Egypt and Syria could also be considered a real union. Attempts by some Arab states, such as Libya, to set up some kind of union resembling a real union have proved to be political fictions without much substance, as was, for example, the union between Libya and Morocco in 1984 (23 ILM 1022 (1984)).

**106. Recognition.** A unilateral and discretionary act of political decision making by the government of a state **(127)** acknowledging the existence of a certain set of facts, with a parallel commitment to apply to this factual situation the relevant legal consequences envisaged by international law. Governed to a large extent by customary law **(39)**, recognition is relevant primarily in cases of entities claiming statehood **(116)** and—in practice the most frequent situation—governments **(114)** coming to power by unconstitutional means. However, recognition may also apply to insurgency **(115)** and belligerency **(113)** and to specific rights of other states, such as the title to territory **(227)** or the validity of other states' legislative and administrative acts.

It is essential to bear in mind the distinction between recognition of state and recognition of government. For example, in the now largely historical prolonged conflict over the so-called recognition of the Chinese People's Republic, the existence of China as a state was obviously not at issue: nobody could question the statehood of China or, for that matter, any other long-established state. At issue was which of the two regimes claiming to be the government of China was to be treated by the United States or other individual countries as *the* government of the state of China. Logically, the recognition of a government automatically implies recognition of the statehood of the entity which the regime claims to be governing. However, recognition of a state need not necessarily entail recognition of its government, although normally it has such effect. Ultimately, the nature of recognition depends on the actual circumstances and the intent of the recognizing state.

As to its form or mode, recognition can be either explicit (express) or implied (tacit) **(111)**. It is ordinarily granted on an individual basis, but may also be collective **(108)**. As far as its scope is concerned, recognition of a state may be unconditional or conditional **(107)** in the sense of the recognizing state's adding certain political conditions to the standard legal requirements traditionally prescribed by international law. The distinction between recognition *de jure* and recognition *de facto* **(110)**, once quite common, especially in the doctrine, has now become virtually obsolete in recent diplomatic practice. While there is no principle of retroactivity in international law, in general, recognition once given is treated as retroactive, that is, the acts of the recognized state or government are considered as valid, dating back to the time when the state or government, as the case may be, established its control as an effective authority in a given area, a date which may sometimes be difficult to ascertain.

While recognition is a discretionary act, often governed by political expediency, it has important consequences both in international and municipal **(27)** law. The legal consequences of recognition on the international plane have generated a doctrinal controversy between the declaratory and constitutive theories **(109)**. Unless barred by the obligation of nonrecognition **(99)**, a state is free to exercise its right to recognize a state or government (or other relevant situations) if the minimum factual conditions prescribed by international law are present. If these conditions meet the standards of international law, the recognition cannot be regarded as an illegal intervention into the affairs of other states.

**107. Recognition, Additional Criteria of.** Additional criteria of recognition **(106)**, sometimes referred to as conditional recognition, are applied when a recognizing state makes the recognition in question subject to conditions additional to those required by general international law to be present for recognizing a state **(116)** or a government **(114)**. State practice does not know conditions in the strictly technical legal sense of the term, attached to recognition, where failure to fulfill a condition would result in a withdrawal of recognition. As stated in the Montevideo Convention of 1933 on the Rights and Duties of States (165 LNTS 19), "recognition is unconditional and irrevocable." However, in view of the political nature of recognition, states have occasionally made recognition dependent on the acceptance of certain conditions by the state or government seeking recognition. For example, at the Berlin Congress in 1878 certain European powers recognized the statehood of Bulgaria, Montenegro, Romania, and Serbia on the condition of the guarantee of freedom of religion, and the United States (US) required written assurances of safeguarding American interests and securing trade advantages when recognizing a new government in Haiti in 1918, and the statehood of Albania and Lebanon in 1922 and 1942, respectively. The recognition of the Soviet government by the US in 1933 (the "Litvinov Agreement") was also conditional in this sense. However, while nonfulfillment of such conditions can be considered a breach of an international obligation, it does not provide legal grounds for withdrawal of recognition (derecognition) **(117)**.

In the early 1990s, the breakup of the Soviet Union **(133)** and the former Yugoslavia (SFRY) **(134)** raised a number of questions pertaining to recognition of the statehood of the emergent states in South-Eastern Europe and in the former Soviet Union, including in particular the application to those new states by the European Community (EC) and some states of additional criteria of recognition in excess of the traditional standards of general international law. In substance, despite certain inconsistencies found in the pertinent EC instruments, the EC Guidelines on the Recognition of New States in Eastern Europe and in the Soviet Union, 1991 (31 ILM 1486 (1992)) and the EC Declaration on Yugoslavia issued on the same date (31 ILM 1485 (1992)) contain political criteria designed to achieve certain otherwise progressive objectives. Reaffirming the Principles of the Helsinki Final Act of 1973 (14 ILM 1292 (1975)) and the Charter of Paris for a New Europe of 1990 (30 ILM 190 (1991)), the EC Guidelines require, in addition to the traditional international law standards for recognition, the fulfillment of several generally formulated conditions: commitment to democracy and human rights **(157)**, including guarantees for the rights of ethnic and national groups and minorities **(172)**; respect for the inviolability of all frontiers **(189)**; acceptance of all relevant commitments with regard to disarmament and nuclear non-proliferation (a condition that applies in particular to those post-Soviet republics which had nuclear weapons in their respective territories) as well as to security and regional stability; and commitment to settle by agreement all questions concerning state succession **(132)**, and regional disputes. Commitment to these principles was stipulated in agreements and opened the way to recognition by the EC and its member states and to the establishment of diplomatic relations with the post-Soviet states. The US adopted a similar approach to the recognition of these states. The three Baltic republics (Lithuania, Latvia, and Estonia) had been recognized already before the adoption of the EC Guidelines.

The conditions for the recognition of the new post-Yugoslav republics were set out in the EC Declaration on Yugoslavia, which developed a common position of the EC and its members, based on the Guidelines in their specific application to the Yugoslav situation. In the Declaration, its authors took the unusual step of inviting the new post-Yugoslav republics to declare by a set deadline whether they wished to be recognized as independent states, and promised recognition if they met all the conditions specified in the Declaration. One condition, addressed to "a Yugoslav republic" (presumably Macedonia), was a commitment prior to recognition to adopt constitutional and political guarantees ensuring that it had no territorial claims toward a neighboring Community state (presumably Greece, concerned that the adoption of the name "Macedonia" and the use of a flag with a symbol questioned by Greece would imply a claim to the northern Greece province of Macedonia) and that it would not conduct any hostile propaganda activities against "a neighboring Community state" (Greece), including the use of a denomination which implied territorial claims. Following applications for recognition by all the republics except the newly formed Federal Republic of Yugoslavia (now "Serbia and Montenegro"), the five-member Arbitration Commission, established in 1991 by the Peace Conference on Yugoslavia to advise the EC on legal matters pertaining to the Yugoslav question and made up of the Presidents of the Constitutional Courts of Belgium, France, Germany, Italy, and Spain (known as the Badinter Commission after its French Chairman), held in Opinions 4, 5, 6, and 7 that Slovenia and Macedonia had met the EC conditions while Croatia still had to amend its Constitution to incorporate clauses on the protection of its (mostly Serbian) minority, and Bosnia was required to determine its population's will in a referendum on independence. Eventually, the four republics were recognized by the EC (Germany having already unilaterally recognized Croatia and Slovenia) although Croatia apparently had not fully complied with the human rights and minorities requirements. The recognition of Macedonia in 1993 under the provisional name of the "Former Yugoslav Republic of Macedonia" was implied from the support of its application for United Nations membership by the EC states. However, the dispute with Greece over the name of the new state was not settled until 1995. It should be added that in 2004 the US, against protest by Greece, recognized FYROM simply as Republic of Macedonia. The last state of the former Socialist Federal Republic of Yugoslavia (SFRY) at that time, namely, the new Federal Republic of Yugoslavia (now "Serbia and Montenegro"), was recognized by the European Union and its members in 1996 on the condition that all the successor states of the SFRY would recognize one another.

At least some of the criteria articulated by the EC in its Guidelines for recognition of the states emerging from the break-up of the Soviet Union and the SFRY were purely political conditions transcending the traditional qualifications for statehood required by international law. However, it appears that the standards devised by the EC, especially those pertaining to democracy, human rights, and treatment of minorities, have been rapidly evolving into legal criteria acquiring the nature of general standards of international law used in the recognition of states and governments.

**108. Recognition, Collective.** Collective recognition of a state **(116)** means recognition of the statehood of an entity by a group of states issuing a joint declaration to that effect or by adherence of the entity in question as a party to an important multilateral treaty **(288)**, such as a peace treaty. A rather rare occurrence, recognition of a number of states was effected in this way in the 19th century: Greece in 1830; Belgium in 1831; and Montenegro, Romania, and Serbia in 1878. After World War I, Poland and Czechoslovakia were recognized by a joint declaration of the Allied Supreme Council and the signing of the Treaty of Peace of Versailles (225 CTS 188) between the Allied and Associated Powers and Germany. There have been very few instances of a collective recognition of government; historically one such case occurred in 1975 when the Association of South East Asian Nations jointly recognized the new Communist government of Cambodia.

Voting in the General Assembly of the United Nations (UN) (but not in the corresponding organs of the specialized agencies) for admission of new members, which under Art. 4 of the UN Charter must be "states," while certainly providing a strong *prima facie* evidence of statehood (though not always, as shown by the instances of Byelorussia and the Ukraine before the collapse of the Soviet Union) **(133)**, in no way constitutes a collective recognition by the UN, as illustrated by the example of Israel which shares membership in the UN and other organizations with Arab states that do not recognize it as a state. Like participation in a multilateral treaty, membership in an international organization is not inconsistent with continued nonrecognition of a state by other parties or members respectively. On the other hand, a decision of the GA or another UN organ, taken in the routine performance of its functions and regarding an entity as a state, is a collective act binding even the dissenting states. Considerations applying to states in international organizations are also pertinent to the question of state representations which—as clarified by the UN Secretariat in 1950 in connection with the credentials of the Chinese representation (from the Nationalist government located in Taiwan **(139)** until 1971 when the Beijing government representation took China's seat in the UN)—should not be linked to that of recognition. Thus, a member state could vote to accept the credentials of the representation of a government which it did not recognize, and such positive vote would not imply recognition of the government in question. The question of collective nonrecognition by an international organization relates to a separate situation concerning the illegality of recognition of state under certain circumstances **(99)**. Although the conditional recognition **(107)** of statehood by the European Community in the post–Socialist Federal Republic of Yugoslavia **(134)** situation is regarded by some as an instance of collective recognition, it could rather be described as a common position on the additional criteria to be applied with regard to the recognition of states.

**109. Recognition, Constitutive and Declaratory Theories of.** These are two opposing theoretical views concerning the consequences of recognition **(106)** in international law. They apply mainly to recognition of states **(116)** and are hereafter discussed in this sense, but their propositions may also be incidentally relevant to recognition of governments **(114)**, especially where the recognition of a state takes on the form of the recognition of its government.

According to the declaratory theory, dating back to Vattel **(45)** and represented by such 20th-century writers as J. L. Brierly, Herbert Briggs, Charles Rousseau, and Georges Scelle, among others, statehood **(127)** in international law does not depend on recognition. Once an entity meets the factual criteria of statehood, it automatically becomes a state irrespective of whether it has been recognized as such by other states. Recognition is merely declaratory of the existing fact of an entity's meeting the criteria of statehood and its existence as a state with all its rights and duties under international law. Recognition does not bring a pre-existing state into existence; it is solely an acknowledgment by the recognizing state of the status of an entity as a state and expressing the intention and willingness to treat it as such.

The adherents of the constitutive theory, including such 20th-century publicists as Paul Fauchille, Dionosio Anzilotti, Hersch Lauterpacht, and the founder of the school of the pure theory of law **(34)**, Hans Kelsen, regard the act of recognition by individual states, in a system lacking a central organ to decide on questions of statehood, as creative or constitutive of personality under international law **(85)**. An entity purporting to be a state does not acquire statehood until it is recognized as a state by the will and consent of the already existing members of the international community. Brought to its logical conclusions, the constitutive theory faces two awkward questions. First, for those states that have not recognized an entity as a state, such an entity claiming statehood is largely a legal nullity with hardly any rights or obligations and, second, the theory must admit of a high likelihood of creating a legal anomaly of a state with a split international personality, being a subject of international law for the recognizing states, but not for the others. To remedy this problem, some publicists of the constitutive school (and in particular Hersch Lauterpacht) proposed an ingenious but not practical compromise suggesting the obligation to recognize the statehood of an entity once it has met the necessary qualifications. While state practice is not entirely conclusive, in general it tends to support, with certain modifications, the declaratory view of recognition, but it also demonstrates that the gap between the two approaches to recognition is not so wide in the practice of states as in the doctrine. The declaratory approach to recognition of states was adopted in Art. 3 of the Montevideo Convention of 1933 on the Rights and Duties of States (165 LNTS 19) and in substance reiterated in Art. 12 of the Organization of American States Charter of 1948 (119 UNTS 3) as amended by a Protocol in 1967. Essentially the same position was adopted by courts adjudicating matters related to the recognition of states in the aftermath of World War I. More recently, within the context of the recognition of the new states following the breakup of the former Yugoslavia **(134)**, the Arbitration Commission, set up in 1991 by the Peace Conference on Yugoslavia (Badinter Commission) as an advisory body of the European Community, held in its Opinion No. 1, 1991, that "the existence or disappearance of the State is a question of fact" and that "the effects of recognition by other States are purely declaratory." The practice of states clearly supports the view that, subject to the obligation of nonrecognition in certain exceptional cases **(99)**, an entity that meets the criteria of statehood is a state even if it is not recognized as such by other states. It cannot evade certain obligations under international law and is accorded certain basic rights owed to recognized states. All these considerations have somewhat reduced the relevance of the constitutive theory while narrowing the differences between the two approaches to recognition. Furthermore, even in the logic of the declaratory theory it is the other states individually or collectively **(108)** that as a practical matter subjectively determine the fulfillment of the criteria for statehood by the entity in question, especially in borderline cases, thus adding a certain constitutive element to the process of recognition. Also the fact that a recognized state (or government) can claim a better treatment in the councils of the recognizing state than that available to an unrecognized entity **(98)**, points to a constitutive element in the act of recognition. In any case, while being declaratory of the factual conditions of statehood, recognition of statehood is certainly constitutive of the rights and duties acquired by a new state through the bilateral relationship with the recognizing state, including the capacity (but not necessarily the obligation) to establish diplomatic relations **(68)** and make treaties **(288)** with the recognizing state.

**110. Recognition, *De Facto* and *De Jure*.** A rather confusing distinction, recently becoming obsolete but once commonly used in the international practice of recognition of governments **(114)** and in rare cases of states **(116)**, and in recognition of territorial changes, whereby states would qualify either the character of the government to be recognized or the nature of the recognition **(106)** itself by resort to otherwise inconsistent and uncertain attributes *de jure* or *de facto*. However, for all practical purposes, the *de jure* recognition or the recognition of a *de jure* government signified a definitive and complete kind of recognition with all the diplomatic and legal relations under international law. On the other hand, the *de facto* recognition or the recognition of a *de facto* government was a provisional kind of recognition; hence it could be withdrawn and did not entail any diplomatic relations or courtesies otherwise followed in relations with a recognized government. Recognition *de facto* suggested a reluctance to recognize a government fully and with all the consequences under international law even if that government was in effective control of the state in question. It implied lingering doubts about its long-term viability and/or its willingness to fulfill international obligations. The technical legal meaning of the term *de facto* must be distinguished from its loose use in colloquial phrases referring to a *de facto* government or state as in fact existing though not granted any *de facto* recognition, or *de facto* contacts with unrecognized entities and communities which may or may not amount to recognition. It is in the nature of an explicit recognition **(111)** that it is meant to be *de jure* whereas an implied recognition **(111)** may raise doubts concerning the nature and the very existence of recognition.

The use of the *de facto* and *de jure* attributes has been a source of occasional confusion in international practice. In a particular case, such attribute could be construed as attached to the government itself and its constitutional legitimacy, *de jure* meaning a government which was legitimate under the constitutional order of the state whereas a *de facto* government would be one that came to power through a revolutionary change or other violation of the constitutional rule. Or the term *de jure* might be considered to qualify a government that ought to be in power but was displaced from power whereas the *de facto* government was in real but constitutionally wrongful possession of power.

Historically, the United States (US) opposed the doctrine of dynastic legitimacy and in its early period followed the Jeffersonian policy of disregarding the distinction between the two forms of recognition throughout much of the 19th century. Other states, despite occasional exceptions, based their policy of recognition mainly on the effectiveness of the new regime and its ability to comply with international obligations. Leaving apart the Wilsonian policy of withholding recognition from governments which came to power by unconstitutional means (the doctrine of legitimacy or the Tobar Doctrine), the use of the *de facto–de jure* distinction reemerged after World War I, with the motives of disapproval of ideologically hostile *de facto* governments, such as the Soviet regime, added to the traditional criteria concerning stability and compliance with international obligations. Thus in 1921 the United Kingdom (UK) recognized the Soviet regime *de facto.* "H. M. Government recognize the Soviet Government as the *de facto* Government of Russia," was the official declaration. This was followed three years later, in 1924, by a recognition *de jure*. A similar approach was adopted by a number of other countries, but not the US, which did not recognize the Soviet government *de jure* until 1933.

The Spanish Civil War (1936–1939) provided an interesting instance of a concurrent recognition by the UK of two Spanish governments, namely the incumbent government recognized *de jure* and the nationalist insurgents' government recognized *de facto* in the areas under its control. After the nationalists' victory, the UK recognized their government *de jure.* Similarly, in 1937 the UK recognized *de facto* the conquest **(194)** of Abyssinia (Ethiopia) while still recognizing *de jure* the government of that country. This recognition terminated upon the *de jure* recognition of the Italian annexation which was subsequently declared null and void by the UK in 1940.

In the post–World War II period the *de facto–de jure* distinction was applied for example, by the UK when in 1949 it first recognized the Communist government of China *de facto*, and then *de jure* in 1950. The US applied a *de facto* recognition to the provisional French government in 1944 and to the government of Israel, with a concurrent recognition *de jure* of the state of Israel.

Resort to the *de facto–de jure* forms of recognition is largely due to political considerations of the situation rather than any legal reasons. In both cases the government is, as a rule, entitled to jurisdictional immunities **(131)**; is subject to the rules on state responsibility **(128)**; and governmental acts are given the same effects in the courts of the recognizing state. But the ambiguities inherent in the distinction between the two forms of recognition eventually led to the distinction losing much of its relevance in contemporary state practice.

**111. Recognition, Express (Explicit) and Implied (Tacit).** Recognition **(106)** may be either express (explicit) or implied (tacit), but in any case it must conclusively indicate the intent of the recognizing state. Express recognition is effected through an official declaration or a formal notification, also in a treaty **(288)** clause, unconditionally and unambiguously stating the intention of recognizing a state **(116)**, a government **(114)**, or a territorial situation, to mention the most important cases of recognition. Implied or tacit recognition results from any act or conduct which, in the absence of any indication to the contrary, can reasonably and conclusively be construed as recognition. In the matter of recognition of state, the following actions are widely considered to imply recognition: establishment of diplomatic relations **(68)**; conclusion of a bilateral treaty comprehensively regulating the relations between the two states (such as, for example, the France–United States (US) Treaty of Amity and Commerce of 1778); and, in the practice of some states, authorization to perform consular functions **(57)** in the recognizing state. Voting for the admission of a candidate to the United Nations or other organizations **(84)** of which only states may become members also implies recognition. In the case of recognition of belligerency **(113)**, the proclamation of neutrality **(362)** or a similar unambiguous act would point, at least in the traditional international law, to according such status to insurgents **(115)**. Insofar as recognition of territorial changes is concerned, an official communication to a state, treating a territory **(228)** as one under that state's sovereignty **(125)** implies recognition of a territorial claim. When in 1989 Australia agreed with Indonesia by a treaty creating a "Zone of Cooperation" to allocate the continental shelf **(236)** between Australia and the non-self-governing territory **(100)** of East Timor, formally under Portugal's administration but illegally annexed by Indonesia in violation of the prohibition of the use of force **(329)** and Security Council and General Assembly resolutions, Australia thereby implicitly recognized the unlawful incorporation of East Timor into Indonesia. The issue came before the International Court of Justice (ICJ) **(309)** in the *East Timor* (Portugal v. Australia) case (1995 ICJ Rep. 90), but the Court found that in the specific circumstances of the case it could not exercise jurisdiction.

It is essential for governments to be on their guards lest their conduct in sensitive situations be, against their intent, construed as at least a *de facto* recognition. Among the acts which do not by themselves imply recognition are: initiation of unofficial contacts through agents without diplomatic status; various kinds of negotiations **(316)**; participation in a multilateral treaty to which the unrecognized entity is also a party (in which case, just to be sure, the non-recognizing party attaches a special declaration); participation in an international conference in which the entity in question also takes part; and, with regard to states opposing it, admission to an international organization. Where the recognition of the authority of one of the competing regimes to represent a state is involved, even a visit of the highest-ranked official does not necessarily imply recognition, as illustrated by President Richard Nixon's visit to Beijing in 1972 (11 ILM 443 (1972)). Similarly, the visit of Egypt's President Anwar Sadat to Israel in 1977 did not imply recognition of Israel's statehood or its claim to the whole of Jerusalem, and President JimmyCarter's visit to Jerusalem in 1979 did not imply recognition of the latter claim.

As far as recognition of government is concerned, implied recognition has assumed more significance since the latter decades of the last century when many states adopted a new policy of de-emphasizing the institution of recognition, in effect reverting to the Estrada Doctrine on the recognition of governments.

**112. Recognition, Legal Effects in Municipal Law.** Recognition of a state **(116)** or a government **(114)** results not only in the recognized entity's acquiring the fullness of rights and obligations under international law, but also produces effects under the municipal law **(27)** of the recognizing state. Since recognition is a political act of the executive, the courts of the recognizing state as a rule defer to the executive's decision as to whether a particular state or government, as the case may be, has been accorded recognition. The exact scope of the effects of recognition in the municipal law of the recognizing state depends on the law concerned, but, in general, the recognized state (government) acquires the right to sue in the courts of the recognizing state; becomes entitled to state immunity **(131)**; and, where appropriate, its executive and legislative acts are given effect in those courts. In addition, a recognized government becomes entitled to the property of the preceding government located in the territory **(228)** of the recognizing state.

**113. Recognition of Belligerency.** Recognition of belligerency is an acknowledgment by a third state that an organized insurgent group in a civil war ("non-international armed conflict") **(340)**, attempting to overthrow the established government or secede from the state, possesses a limited measure of international legal personality **(85)**, known as the status of belligerency, which allows it to exercise certain belligerent rights and imposes upon it the duty to observe the rules of the law of war (international humanitarian law) **(353)**. As a result, not only the established government but also the insurgents, now—for those states that have recognized this status—belligerents, are to be treated as a legitimate armed force of lawful combatants. On the other hand, states that recognize their status of belligerency have the rights and obligations of neutrality **(362)** in the ongoing conflict.

As a rule, recognition of belligerency is not expressed by any explicit proclamation, but is implied from certain acts of third states, mainly proclamations of neutrality, or may even be assumed from the conduct of the established government. During the American Civil War, in 1861, the United States (US) protested, without a legal foundation, against Great Britain's proclamation of neutrality, an act that implied recognition of the status of belligerency of the Confederacy, but the US itself had already unwittingly recognized it by instituting a belligerent blockade **(341)** of the rebel ports. On the whole, in the 20th century, recognition of belligerency in a civil-war situation became very rare. Even the contending parties in the Spanish Civil War (1936–1939) were not recognized as belligerents for a variety of reasons, but mainly because of intervention in the conflict by other powers, even though the practice pointed to the obligation of recognizing the belligerency of the established government.

Whether recognition of belligerency is within the political discretion of the state or is mandated by international law is a controversial matter. For such recognition to be justified, the civil conflict must have reached the magnitude of an actual war, with the insurgents controlling a considerable part of the state territory **(228)** and maintaining a reasonably orderly and effective government administration, and enforcing observance of the laws of war. Another condition is that the course of war has reached a point where third states cannot simply afford standing aside from the conflict. They must take some action, but are confronted by the dilemma brought about by the civil war, especially if it extends to maritime operations. Thus, if a third state allows the parties to a civil conflict to exercise belligerent rights against its shipping, such as those relating to contraband **(343)**, then by implication it recognizes the fact of a regular war. On the other hand, if it refuses to do so and resorts to force in self-defense **(335)**, then it is drawn into the ongoing armed conflict. While a hasty recognition of belligerency granted by a third state to an insurgent group may be considered by the established government as an unfriendly act of interference in its domestic affairs, it relieves that government, for the time of the conflict, from responsibility **(128)** for injuries inflicted by the insurgents upon nationals of third states.

It should be added that, as part of the United Nations decolonization policy, national liberation movements **(94)** engaged in wars of national liberation received a strongly preferential treatment. Such, basically non-international, wars were granted the status of international armed conflicts under Protocol I of 1977 **(369)** and the movements enjoyed a unique measure of international legal personality.

**114. Recognition of Government.** Recognition of government is a political decision at the discretion of a state's government acknowledging that a particular regime in another state **(127)** meets the criteria of effective government and implying a commitment to treat that regime as the legitimate authority representing the state with all the consequences that such status entails under international law. Recognizing a government automatically implies the recognition of the statehood **(116)** of the (as a rule new) entity governed by the recognized regime, but the recognition of a state may take place without recognizing its government. Changes of government and their recognition or nonrecognition **(98)** do not affect the legal identity and continuity of the state itself.

When a new government assumes power in accordance with the constitutional provisions of the state or with only very minor departures from the rules, no problems arise and recognition is assumed as a matter of course. It is only when a new head of state or a new government comes to power by unconstitutional, often violent, methods, such as a *coup d'état* and the like, that other states decide whether to recognize the new regime as the government of the state in question. Like recognition of state, recognition of a new government is not mandatory under international law, but states are required to treat as government a regime that is in effective control of the state, with all the legal consequences of recognition of state being applied correspondingly. A rule also applies that states have the obligation not to recognize **(99)** or treat as government a regime that was established in violation of international law, such as a government imposed on a state by threat or use of force **(329)**.

While political considerations have always played a major role in recognition of governments, the doctrine of effectiveness, followed especially by Great Britain in the 19th century, emerged as the most important guide albeit not an absolute principle in according recognition. Recognition would normally be forthcoming if the new regime was on its own in effective control of the state, with reasonable prospects of permanence and apparent popular assent or at least acquiescence, along with the regime's ability and willingness to discharge the international obligations of states. The United States (US) policy of recognition, which on the whole prevailed in the 19th century (associated with the name of Secretary of State Thomas Jefferson), was also based on the criterion of effective control but was complemented by an assumption of democratic legitimacy manifested by "the will of the nation substantially declared." However, toward the end of the 19th century and especially in the early 20th century, the US, in an aberration from its traditional policy, would refuse recognition to some Latin American governments which had come to power through unconstitutional means, until a government, resting upon the consent of the governed expressed in free elections, assumed power in the state. This doctrine of constitutional legitimacy, known as the Tobar Doctrine after Carlos R. Tobar, the foreign minister of Ecuador, was anchored in treaties of Central American states in 1907 and 1923, but on the whole was not followed by Latin American states. Eventually, in 1965 the Organization of American States accepted as valid recognition of non-elected regimes (5 ILM 155 (1966)). On the other hand, the doctrine of constitutional legitimacy found support in the US in the early decades of the past century, especially under President Woodrow Wilson's administration (hence the "Wilson Doctrine"). President Wilson's refusal to recognize the regime of General Victoriano Huerta in Mexico in 1913 is usually quoted as the most notorious example of the Wilsonian policy of nonrecognition of "revolutionary" governments in the hope of undermining their power and thus restore the democratic legitimacy. However, this US policy led to a belief in some Latin American states that recognition implied approval, even if no such intent was present, and came to be viewed as unlawful intervention in the domestic affairs of the countries concerned. It is in reaction to the doctrine of legitimacy and, more generally, to the institution of explicit recognition **(111)** as such that in 1930 Genaro Estrada, Mexico's Secretary of Foreign Relations, announced a doctrine, subsequently known as the Estrada Doctrine (2 Whiteman 85 (1963)) proclaiming that an effective control of the state by the new regime should be the only test of recognition and that the explicit act of recognition should be abandoned as "an insulting practice" offending the sovereignty **(125)** of other states and implying judgment passed by foreign governments upon their the internal affairs. Earlier, in 1923, the award in the *Tinoco* Arbitration **(293)** between Great Britain and Costa Rica (1 RIAA 369) had confirmed the effective control doctrine of recognition by ruling that the obligations of Costa Rica under contracts of certain British companies with the Tinoco government, which in 1917 had seized power unconstitutionally, could not be repudiated by the successor government since the Tinoco government, though unrecognized by Great Britain, had been in actual and peaceful control of the country at the time the rights at issue were acquired.

Following the rise to power of Communist governments, in Russia toward the end of the World War I and in China after World War II, a number of countries initially refused, basically for ideological reasons, to recognize these new regimes, invoking their failure to live up to international obligations. The US did not recognize the Soviet government until 1933. The Beijing Communist government was recognized by the US in 1979 while concurrently the Nationalist government in Taiwan **(139)** was derecognized **(117)**.

It is important to bear in mind that in the last few decades of the 20th century most states, among them virtually all the Western countries, adopted what in its substance is equivalent to the Estrada Doctrine of recognition, indicating that in order to avoid recognition by them to be construed as approval of the new regime concerned, they would henceforth de-emphasize or completely cease to grant recognition to governments, choosing only to establish or not to establish diplomatic relations with whatever government was in effective control of the state concerned. The US essentially adopted this edition of the Estrada Doctrine in the 1970s. Such policy separated the issue of approval or disapproval of a new regime from recognition. By avoiding the use of the latter concept in cases of a change of government in another state, the US and other countries following such policy, including the United Kingdom (UK) since 1980, had to concern themselves only with the question of whether to have diplomatic relations with the new regime. Effective control appears to be the sole criterion for qualifying a new regime as the government of the state in question. However, in situations where, as in the case of China, two political groups compete for power, an express recognition may be necessary, especially for reasons of legal repercussions under the municipal law **(27)**.

Yet, although recognition as such was discontinued, the tests of effective control and expectation of permanence have remained the same as before, determining the dealings with regimes that achieved power by unconstitutional means. For all practical purposes, the abandonment of the traditional institution of recognition of government simply means the substitution of an explicit recognition by the equally traditional implied recognition through a variety of dealings with the new regime, the establishment of diplomatic relations constituting the most reliable act to show the intention of recognition. But, under the circumstances, a state may recognize a new regime in another country without establishing diplomatic relations. Nor does a breaking off of such relations constitute a withdrawal of recognition of government, as in the case of the US-Cuban relations severed in 1961. Moreover, diplomatic relations may in such cases be somehow maintained at a minimum level through diplomatic missions **(68)** of friendly states.

It is worth noting that states professing adherence to the effective control—Estrada Doctrine—have not been consistent in their policy of recognition of governments, occasionally resorting to political considerations. For instance, Mexico, the country where the Estrada Doctrine was enunciated, refused to recognize the Nationalist government of Franco in Spain despite the fact that it was in full control of the Spanish territory **(227)**, and in 1979 the UK granted recognition to the Ugandan government installed by the Tanzanian troops still present in Uganda, but withheld recognition from the government of Cambodia on the ground that it was supported by the Vietnamese troops. All this again points to the fact that for reasons of perceived national interest, states are not yet ready to abandon recognition as a political tool in international relations.

**115. Recognition of Insurgency.** A rather vague form of recognition **(106)**, the term refers to an implicit acknowledgment by a third state that an insurgent movement striving by force of arms either at overthrowing the established government or at seceding from a state, while not warranting recognition of belligerency **(113)**, has enough territory under control and organization not to be treated as common criminals but as a potential government deserving, as against the recognizing state, to be accorded the status of insurgency.

Recognition of insurgency originated in the unstable political conditions of Latin American states in the 19th century. It does not involve any formal explicit act by the recognizing state; it is implicit in contacts that a third state may maintain with the insurgents controlling part of the state territory **(228)**, such as the limited dealings of British agents sent to the Confederate States during the American Civil War, and is motivated by the desire to protect the nationals and interests of the recognizing state. Despite the continued existence of the established government, the insurgents have the competence to perform routine administrative functions, including collecting taxes. Under the circumstances, it is possible to recognize their authority as a *de facto* government **(110)** in the area under their control. But recognition of insurgency relieves the established government of responsibility **(128)** for wrongful acts committed by the insurgents in the territory under their control. Representing a potentially nascent state power, insurgent authorities are also competent to make agreements with third states, including those concerning cessation of hostilities, as was the case of the insurgent Laotian and Cambodian forces which signed the Geneva Agreements of 1954.

The institution of recognition of insurgency became quite rare in the many civil wars of the 20th century. Recognition accorded by Great Britain to the Nationalists in the Spanish Civil War (1936–1939) was a major instance of such recognition. In the period following World War II the insurgents forming part of the anti-colonialist national liberation movements **(94)** were considered a special privileged category of insurgents and their armed struggle with the colonial powers was treated as an international armed conflict **(339)**.

**116. Recognition of State.** A unilateral discretionary act of political decision making by the government of a state **(127)** acknowledging that an entity meets the qualifications for statehood required by international law, with parallel commitment to treat that entity as a state with all the consequences envisaged by international law for the status of international legal person **(85)**.

It is obvious that for a great majority of the long-established states, recognition has been of no consequence and the origin of their statehood goes back to the remote and murky past. Still, for example, the statehood of the Netherlands was not officially recognized by Spain until 1648 and the recognition of the United States (US) as a sovereign state after the Revolutionary War at the end of the 18th century was a subject of major controversy involving Great Britain and France. It might be noted that the Ottoman Empire (Turkey) was not formally admitted to the system of states until the Treaty of Paris ending the Crimean War in 1856.

Historically, the present-day "international community" of states originated in Europe, with gradual admission, first of the US, and then by the 19th century of the very few then existing extra-European states (such as Japan) and in the aftermath of the disintegration of the Spanish and Portuguese colonial empires new independent states in the Western hemisphere. Finally, the worldwide expansion into more than 190 states in the international community of today was a result of, first, the collapse of empires in Europe in the aftermath of World War I (1914–1918), and then, after World War II (1939–1945), the decolonization of Western overseas possessions in the second half of the 20th century and the disintegration of the Soviet multinational state **(133)** and Yugoslavia **(134)** (and Czechoslovakia) in the last decade of the century. All these developments, and especially those of the 1990s, generated a variety of problems relating to recognition of states, contributing to a further development of the customary rules of international law in this area.

Recognition of an entity as a state is an optional act of individual states. Contrary to some views in the doctrine, there exists no duty to recognize the statehood of an entity claiming it or the entity's right under international law to be automatically recognized. However, as a general rule, recognition is granted if in the judgment of the recognizing state's government the entity in question satisfies the criteria of statehood, subject to the obligation of nonrecognition **(99)** where an entity has attained the qualifications for statehood in violation of the United Nations (UN) Charter. But if the qualifications for statehood do not conflict with international law, recognition is permissible and other states may not regard it as intervention **(331)**.

Ascertaining the presence of the factual criteria of statehood may in some cases be difficult, leaving individual states enough latitude for political expediency. Hence an entity may be recognized as a state by some states, but not by others, a situation that long prevailed during much of the Cold War with respect to the nonrecognition for fundamental ideological and political reasons of the former German Democratic Republic by major Western powers. But after 24 years this policy had to yield to political realities, leading to recognition of this otherwise eventually extinct state. In another case, Israel, a state and member of the UN since 1948, has not been recognized by Arab states (except for Egypt and Jordan in 1979 and 1995, respectively).

Strictly speaking, leaving aside the theoretical controversy over the constitutive or declaratory significance of recognition **(109)**, an entity recognized as a state is regarded as such and fully enjoys all the benefits of statehood only with regard to the recognizing states. Therefore the more states, especially important ones, recognize its statehood, the more fully will such a new state be able to benefit from its status as an international legal person. Thus, for example, the fact that the Turkish Republic of Northern Cyprus, set up by Turkey in 1983, was recognized only by that state while all the other members of the international community complied with the UN call for nonrecognition, meant that the international status of that entity was limited to the relations with Turkey. In another case, during the civil war in Nigeria the secessionist state of Biafra set up in 1967 was recognized—as it turned out, prematurely—by only five minor states (Côte d'Ivoire, Gabon, Haiti, Tanzania, and Zambia), a recognition that did not help much the insurgents to establish themselves as an internationally viable state. The contrast between Biafra and Bangladesh, the latter's secession from Pakistan and recognition as a state initially disapproved by most countries but enjoying support by India and the Soviet Union, illustrates the crucial importance of major powers strongly perceiving a recognition in question to be in their national interest.

If an unrecognized entity meets the requirements of statehood compatible with the UN Charter, the non-recognizing states are still required to observe toward it certain fundamental duties under international law and treat it as a state albeit without according it the same rights and privileges to which a recognized state is entitled.

The traditional criteria of statehood are fairly strict in order to prevent premature or precipitate recognition, especially in cases of a secessionist civil war where recognition of a breakaway entity as a state is withheld because of doubts persisting concerning the likelihood of its viability as a state. A precipitate recognition of such an entity, especially if it is not in effective control of territory, is contrary to international law in that it constitutes an improper interference in the affairs of an established state and a violation of its territorial integrity. If combined with military aid to the secessionists, recognition in such circumstances may even be considered as an illegal threat or use of force in violation of the UN Charter **(329)**. However, the dividing line between a legitimate recognition and unlawful interference may be rather blurred in actual practice. Among the historical instances of premature recognition, otherwise soon legalized in the course of time, are: the recognition of the US by France in 1778; of Panama by the US in 1903; and of Bangladesh by India in 1971. The already mentioned recognition of Biafra by five states proved to be premature, as confirmed by the eventual defeat of the insurgent province. However, it must be added that in the name of the right of self-determination of peoples **(122)** many states, in disregard of the criterion of effective control, recognized as states dependent territories (such as Algeria and Guinea-Bissau) while they were still under an effective control of their respective colonial powers. The Sahrawi Arab Democratic Republic, proclaimed in 1976 by the Popular Front for the Liberation of Saqia el Hamra and Rio de Oro, the national liberation movement **(94)** of Western Sahara, is a case in point, considering that it was recognized by the OAU and a number of African states although its territory was under an effective, albeit unlawful, control of Morocco.

More recently, in 1992, in the aftermath of the breakup of Yugoslavia (Socialist Federal Republic of Yugoslavia (SFRY)), Croatia was recognized by the European Community (EC) and its member states (as well as by Austria and Switzerland) and was admitted as a state to the UN in conditions of civil war when it was not yet in control of a considerable part of its territory and did not meet the additional criteria of recognition **(107)** articulated in the EC Guidelines of 1991. The recognition of Bosnia-Herzegovina and its admission to the UN was even more premature in view of the continued civil war, with the Bosnia-Herzegovina government controlling less than a half of the state's territory as defined by the pre-civil war borders of the republics. However, in both cases, by its constitutive effects, recognition could have contributed to a certain stabilization of the situation in both republics. One can add that the EC was right in its decision not to recognize the statehood of Kosovo, an autonomous, demographically mostly Albanian, region of Serbia, and also to reject an application for recognition as a state of Krajina, a part of Croatia, with mostly Serbian population.

On the threshold of the 21st century, apart from the claims to statehood of the Sahrawi Arab Democratic Republic and the uncertain status of Palestine, specific controversial issues of recognition of states were increasingly related to secessionist movements, some of which have managed to secede from existing states, establishing themselves in a limbo status of nonrecognized states. Among such entities were (in addition to the Turkish Republic of Northern Cyprus whose nonrecognition was mandated by the UN): Somaliland, which in 1991 declared its independence from Somalia within the borders of the former British protectorate; another breakaway entity in the northeast of Somalia, known as Puntland; Abkhasia, a Black Sea, mostly Moslem, province which seceded from Georgia but was later reunited with that country; Azaria and South Ossetia seceded from Georgia; Transdniester (Transdniestria), an ethnically mostly Russian and Ukrainian region which seceded from Moldavia (Moldova); and Nagorno-Karabakh, an ethnically mostly Armenian separatist enclave within Azerbaijan, functioning as a *de facto* ostensibly independent republic.

Recognition of state entails consequences in international law which in doctrinal terms are approached within the conceptual frameworks of the constitutive and declaratory theories of recognition. It also has important effects in the municipal law **(27)** of the recognizing state.

**117. Recognition, Withdrawal of.** In principle, as stated in the Montevideo Convention of 1933 on the Rights and Duties of States (165 LNTS 19) (of which the United States (US) is a party), "recognition [of states] is, unconditional and irrevocable." However, withdrawal of a specific recognition of statehood of an entity, that is, derecognition of a state, is not necessary because if an entity ceases to meet the requirements of statehood **(127)**, it automatically ceases to be a state. Situations of this kind usually occur when a state is incorporated into another state, as when the German Democratic Republic was incorporated into the Federal Republic of Germany in 1990 **(135)** or when the Soviet Union became extinct in 1991 **(133)**. However, incorporation into another state in violation of the United Nations Charter, as authoritatively determined by a Security Council resolution, may not be recognized **(99)** by states since the statehood of the incorporated entity continues under international law **(98)**, as was the case of the illegal annexation of Kuwait by Iraq in 1990.

Derecognition of a government is ordinarily effected by recognizing *de jure* **(110)** the rival regime. Instances of an express withdrawal of recognition of government have been quite rare, and, if not accompanied by the recognition of another government, virtually nonexistent. The express derecognition by the US of the Taiwan **(139)** regime, accompanied by the concurrent recognition of the Beijing Communist government as "a sole legal government of China," is perhaps the best-known example of derecognition of government. Severance of diplomatic relations **(68)** does not necessarily entail withdrawal of recognition of government.

**118. Reparation.** Reparation is a comprehensive term to denote remedies which an injured state **(82)** is entitled to obtain from the state that caused it injury by an internationally wrongful act. The obligation to pay full reparation to the injured state is a fundamental and well-established principle of international law, recognized and reaffirmed in international practice and in particular in numerous judicial and arbitral decisions **(306)**. In an often quoted *dictum,* the Permanent Court of International Justice (PCIJ) **(320)** stated in the case of *Factory at Chorzów* (Germany v. Poland) that "it is a principle of international law and even a general conception of law that the breach of an international engagement involves an obligation to make reparation" (1927 PCIJ, Series A, No. 9). The delinquent state must, of course, cease the violation in question, for example, repeal the wrongful act of the state's authority.

In its judgment on the merits of the *Factory at Chorzów* case (1928 PCIJ Series A, No. 17), the PCIJ laid down the guiding principle to govern reparation, emphasizing that "reparation must, as far as possible, wipe out all the consequences of the illegal act and reestablish the situation which would, in all probability have existed if that act had not been committed." In its Draft Articles on State Responsibility of 2001 **(129)** the International Law Commission (ILC) upholds this principle of making full reparation and lists the forms which reparation by the responsible state may take. In what form and measure reparation is due depends on the merits of the case in question, but the redress must, to the extent possible, undo the effects of the violation. As also codified in the ILC Draft Articles, reparation may consist, singly or in combination, of restitution in kind, compensation, and satisfaction. In addition, if circumstances so require, the delinquent state must offer appropriate assurances and guarantees of non-repetition. Awarding penal damages, in addition or unrelated to the damage inflicted, has not been common in state practice and is considered by some to be contrary to the notion of reparation.

Restitution in kind (*restitutio in integrum*) has long been recognized as an important form of remedy in cases of material damage, especially in situations of an illegal possession of territory or objects of historical or cultural significance, but such specific restitution has recently become rather exceptional because of practical difficulties involved. According to the ILC Draft Articles (Art. 36) the purpose of restitution in kind is "to re-establish the situation which existed before the wrongful act was committed, provided and to the extent that restitution: (a) is not materially impossible; (b) would not involve a burden out of all proportion to the benefit deriving from restitution instead of compensation." The latter situation takes into account hardship for, or jeopardy to the economic stability or political independence of the responsible state. Although restitution in kind remains, in principle, the main form of reparation in cases of material damage, monetary compensation, also known as indemnity, is the more usual form. But two major arbitrations in the 1970s, concerning reparation due from Libya for breaches of oil concession agreements with Texaco and BP, respectively, reached contrary conclusions on the form of reparation. In the *TOPCO & CAOC* Arbitration, 1977 (17 ILM 1 (1978)), the arbitrator ruled that Libya was bound to perform the contracts by restitution in kind whereas in an earlier BP Arbitration of 1973 (53 ILR 297) another sole arbitrator had adopted the monetary compensation approach.

As provided in the ILC Draft, compensation is payable for "financially assessable loss," a formulation which includes also compensation for moral damage and, in addition to the actual direct loss (*damnum emergens*), also consequential damages for the loss of profits (*lucrum cessans*) insofar as it is established. However, gains based on highly problematic and speculative prospects have not been allowed in state practice. The rules on calculating monetary compensation, and especially those on direct and indirect damage, interest, and loss of profit are not clear in international law. The ILC Draft does not deal with these matters in any detail. In addition, in cases arising from nationalization or expropriation of foreign property **(145)**, reparation is based not only on the law but in practice is also influenced by political and economic considerations. In general, indemnity should compensate the injured state for all damage sustained because of the wrongful act. Reparation for a wrong committed deliberately (with the element of *dolus,* in civil-law **(23)** terminology) is ordinarily calculated higher than that due merely to culpable negligence (*culpa*).

State practice has frequently awarded interest payable in addition to the principal amount of the indemnity, calculated from the date the obligation to make reparation arose or from the date of the judicial or arbitral decision, as recently confirmed by the case law of the Iran–United States Claims Tribunal **(312)** and the United Nations Compensation Commission deciding claims arising from Iraq's invasion of Kuwait. The ILC Draft devotes a separate article to payment of interest, providing that it shall be payable on any principal sum "when necessary to ensure full reparation." The article also provides that interest runs from the date when the principal sum should have been paid until the date the obligation to pay is fulfilled.

Under the fiction that it is the state itself that suffers a loss when one of its nationals suffers injury, the injured state is free, in state-to-state relations, to settle the compensation claim at the measure it chooses and, under international law, has no obligation to pay the compensation received to its injured national. As noted by the PCIJ in the above-mentioned *Factory at Chorzów* case, the damage to the rights of an individual and that caused to the state are always on a different plane even though the rights have been infringed upon by the same act. As put by the PCIJ, "The damage suffered by an individual is never therefore identified in kind with that which will be suffered by a State: it can only afford a convenient scale for the calculation of the reparation due to the State." Hence, in practice, compensation is usually calculated by the loss to the national concerned, arising from the original injury, including, under the circumstances, also damages for mental pain and anguish, that is, moral damages. As illustrated by the *I'm Alone* Arbitration, 1935 (3 RIAA 1609) between the United Kingdom (UK) (Canada) and the United States (US), involving the sinking on the high seas **(245)** in 1929 by the US Coast Guard of a UK-registered (but American-owned) vessel on suspicion of smuggling liquor to the US, monetary compensation (in this case $25,000) may be awarded as a material amends for the indignity suffered by a country's flag. In the *Rainbow Warrior* **(104)** Arbitration monetary compensation was also awarded for non-material damage.

Satisfaction is the third form of reparation. It is appropriate in cases where an injury cannot be made good by restitution or compensation, typically for non-material damage and moral injury to the personality of the state. According to the ILC Draft, satisfaction may consist in "an acknowledgment of the breach, an expression of regret, a formal apology or another modality," but it must not be "out of proportion to the injury and may not take a form humiliating to the responsible State." For example, in 2001 the US apologized to China for the intrusion of a US military aircraft landing on Hainan without prior authorization. Punishment of the guilty individuals by the national authorities of the responsible state or—as in the *Rainbow Warrior* arbitral award—a formal declaration of the unlawful character of the act involved, are among other modalities of satisfaction. Assurances and guarantees of non-repetition are, strictly speaking, a *sui generis* remedy rather than a form of reparation.

Whether punitive (penal) damages, that is, measures going beyond making the responsible state cease the wrongful act or exceeding the limits of compensation for the damage actually suffered, may be awarded against a state is a matter of debate in the doctrine. Punitive damages could be awarded if the concept of state crimes and criminal responsibility of states became part of international law, something that is not likely to take place in the foreseeable future. In practice, international tribunals have in some cases held penal damages to be inadmissible against states, but in a number of cases the reparation awarded amounted in its substance to such damages albeit formally no punitive damages were specifically articulated. For example, in 1925 the Council of the League of Nations awarded Bulgaria, as against Greece, a monetary sum in addition to compensation to damage to movable property. A similar "material amends" was awarded to Canada in the above-noted *I'm Alone* Arbitration. Under the Foreign Sovereign Immunity Act, governing state immunity **(131)**, the US excludes punitive damages against a foreign state but allows them against such state's agency or instrumentality.

**119. Reprisals.** Reprisals are unilateral measures taken by an injured state against the offending state, which might otherwise, as such, be unlawful, but are rendered legal as a response to a prior illegal act of the offending state. In traditional international law, armed reprisals in time of peace were considered lawful, but as a result of the prohibition of the use of force in international relations **(329)**

introduced by the United Nations Charter (Art. 2(4)), they are illegal in contemporary international law. The Friendly Relations Declaration **(14)** adopted by consensus in Resolution 2625 of the General Assembly in 1970 expressly states that "States have a duty to refrain from acts of reprisal involving the use of force." Consequently, only those kinds of reprisals that do not involve the use of force are permitted. To distinguish the now prohibited armed reprisals from the lawful reprisals, that is, those that do not involve the use of force, the latter are now referred to as countermeasures **(58)**. Reprisals differ from retortion **(121)** in that the retributive measures taken as retortion are generally legal whereas acts of reprisal by themselves would be illegal. Reprisals in time of peace must not be confused with belligerent reprisals **(370)**, that is, reprisals in war, an institution of the law of war, governed by the rules of international humanitarian law **(353)**.

In the past, under the traditional rules, states, and especially great powers, would resort to armed reprisals to punish a weak state or force it to desist from an alleged wrongdoing, occasionally by such methods as a "pacific" blockade **(326)**. But even more recently, despite the ban on the use of force, including armed reprisals, states have found it unavoidable to resort to what, in fact, could be qualified as armed reprisals, but rationalizing such action by the right of preventive self-defense **(335)**. This has not been uncommon within the context of the Middle East conflict, especially in the Israel-Lebanon relationship. The United States armed reprisals against Libya and the Sudan were also justified by the right of self-defense. All these and other similar situations in the gray zone between reprisals and self-defense reveal a weak spot in the rules of international law governing resort to force. The problem is that the borderline between reprisals and possibly legal anticipatory self-defense is often blurred in situations where armed reprisals, while illegal, may be the only methods of protecting a state from external threats to its security. The chances of acquiescing by third states in reprisals in such situations will be stronger if they are clearly reasonable under the circumstances, especially if they observe the principle of proportionality.

Even under the traditional law, to be lawful, reprisals, and especially those involving armed force, had to meet certain conditions, as formulated in 1928 in the often quoted *Naulilaa* Arbitration by a Mixed Arbitral Tribunal **(314)** between Portugal and Germany (2 RIAA 1013), resulting from a border incident in Portuguese Angola in 1914 while Portugal was still neutral **(362)** in the war. In this incident, following the killing, through a misunderstanding, of three Germans in the Portuguese territory, Germany, without requesting amends, retaliated with excessive force against Portugal by destroying some frontier stations in Angola (including Naulilaa). Deciding for Portugal, the Tribunal formulated the following conditions necessary for lawful reprisals: existence of a prior illegal act by the delinquent state; unsatisfied demand for redress in negotiations **(316)** before resorting to reprisals; the need for the reprisals not to be excessive, that is, the need to be reasonably proportionate to the offense; and observance of good faith and considerations of humanity. The *Naulilaa* principles are still applicable in today's international law, subject to their interpretation in the light of the ban on the use of force in international relations.

**120. Responsibility and Liability.** These related concepts are sometimes used interchangeably, but whereas in English terminology state responsibility **(128)** involves liability to make reparation for a breach of an international legal obligation by a wrongful act, the term liability or strict liability refers to the obligation to pay compensation for injurious consequences even if no international obligation has been breached. Liability may arise especially under international environmental law **(197)** in cases of damage caused by harmful consequences of hazardous activities which, as such, are not prohibited by international law but may produce deleterious consequences for the environment. Whereas responsibility arises from an internationally wrongful act, liability is predicated purely on damage. Incidentally, in the French terminology, the same term, *responsabilité*, is used for both responsibility and liability.

In recognition of the fact that preclusion of wrongfulness by such circumstances as, in particular, consent, *force majeure* **(78)**, distress **(72)**, state of necessity **(96)**, compliance with *jus cogens* **(24)**, countermeasures **(58)**, and self-defense **(335)**, does not necessarily prejudice any questions that may arise in respect of compensation for damage caused by an act that is not wrongful, the International Law Commission (ILC) has, since 1978, studied the topic of international liability for injurious consequences arising out of acts not prohibited by international law, with emphasis of the codification **(5)** work resting on liability for environmental transboundary harm from hazardous activities. The ILC completed its work on this particular aspect of international liability in 2001. Its proposal adopted the principle of strict liability, based on a test designed to balance the interests of states carrying on activities likely to cause transboundary harm and subject to the duty of due diligence, with the rights of states desiring to protect themselves against the injurious consequences of such activities and entitled to appropriate compensation.

The theoretical problems concerning the distinction and separation of problems of liability from the main body of rules governing state responsibility are not entirely resolved. In some doctrinal formulations, the concept of state responsibility includes also that of strict liability, as proposed, for example, in 1997 in a resolution of the Institut de droit international on formulating the law on responsibility and liability for environmental damage (37 ILM 1473 (1998)). In any event, civil liability of operators for environmental damage (apart from possible criminal responsibility) can be engaged under municipal law **(27)** or international law, irrespective of the lawfulness of the activity concerned.

**121. Retortion.** A self-help retaliatory measure of an injured state **(82)** in the form of an unfriendly though otherwise lawful act, in response to an injurious legal or possibly unlawful act of the offending state. A common category of retaliation in relations between states, retortion includes such actions as severance of diplomatic relations **(68)**, limiting or cutting off trade or economic aid, curbing fishing rights in the injured state's exclusive economic zone **(238)**, canceling landing rights of the offending state's aircraft, closing the ports to ships of its nationality **(257)**, and denial of various kinds of rights to the nationals of the offending state. Retortion is often applied as an "equivalent" act of retaliation, as in the case of expulsion of diplomats **(68)** where the state of the expelled diplomatic agent normally declares as *persona non grata* a diplomat of equivalent rank sent by the expelling state.

In principle, an act of retortion cannot be questioned under international law unless in certain, sometimes not easily apparent, situations the aggrieved state takes advantage of the circumstances to achieve an unlawful objective, such as for example coercing the offending state into surrendering its sovereign rights. Under general rules, the retaliatory act must be proportionate to the injurious conduct of the offending state and must be discontinued as soon as that state ceases the conduct in question.

**122. Self-Determination of Peoples, Right of.** The key concept in the United Nations (UN) decolonization practice, referring to the right of the trust **(142)** and non-self-governing territories **(100)** or any other territory which has not yet attained independence, to freely and without external interference determine their political status and pursue their economic, social, and cultural development. The right of self-determination of peoples, as understood by the UN, is limited to such colonial and similar overseas non-self-governing territories of Western states, and may be exercised by a territory only as a unit, within the administrative boundaries inherited from the colonial power concerned, without any disruption of the territorial integrity of the new state. In view of the fact that the decolonization process has virtually achieved its objective, with only a fraction of the former colonial territories still remaining, it can be concluded that the right of self-determination, as postulated in the decades following World War II, had lost much of its relevance by the end of the past century, becoming largely of historical interest. Whether a more widely and inclusively conceived right of self-determination of "peoples" in the real sociocultural sense of the term (not just inhabitants of a colonial administrative unit) will emerge in the future, is a matter of conjecture. However, on the threshold of the 21st century the prospects for such development were not promising. Paradoxically, for example, Pitcairn Island with a population less of than fifty, had a legal right to self-determination whereas large ethnic minorities numbering millions of members, some possessing a well-developed national identity, such as Kurds, among other similar groups, had no right of political determination involving creation of an independent sovereign state.

In the absence of any treaty provisions, such as for example some stipulations of the Versailles Peace Treaty with Germany, 1919 (225 CTS 188), pertaining to a plebiscite in the German-Polish border areas, the principle of self-determination, as a rule of universal application, has always been a political concept in the Wilsonian sense rather than a right under international law. In 1920, such was the finding of the International Commission of Jurists in its report to the League of Nations on the Aaland Islands case otherwise dealing with the demilitarized status of these islands in the Baltic Sea, under Finland's sovereignty but demographically Swedish. However, self-determination was vaguely implied in the provisions on the League of Nations' mandate system **(93)**. The UN Charter (Arts. 1(2) and 55)) includes references to self-determination of peoples, but these provisions are too vague to allow a conclusion that they recognize the application of this principle to the non-defined concept of "people." There is no explicit mention of self-determination in the provisions on non-self-governing and trust territories, but self-determination is implicitly the basic objective of the trusteeship system.

In the early decades of the UN, the principle of self-determination for the colonial territories became the cornerstone of the General Assembly (GA) decolonization policy and was given expression in numerous resolutions upholding this principle which by the 1960s achieved the quality of a right. The 1960 Declaration on the Granting of Independence to Colonial Territories and Peoples (Resolution 1514), adopted by 80 votes to none, with nine abstentions, complemented by Resolution 1541 of the same year, became the major point of reference in the accelerating decolonization process, with calls for taking immediate steps to transfer all power to the "peoples" of the territories concerned. In 1961, a Decolonization Committee was established to assist the GA in the implementation of the 1960 Declaration and—since 1963—to consider the information regarding the non-self-governing territories, transmitted under Art. 73(e) of the UN Charter to the Secretary-General. The right of self-determination was incorporated and further elaborated as one of the seven basic principles of international law articulated in the Friendly Relations Declaration of 1970 **(14)** which, adopted by consensus, is considered to be the authoritative interpretation of the UN Charter.

Concerning the substantive content of the right of self-determination, however, apparently under the Western influence, an opening appeared in its elaboration, which could provide a basis for moving the right of self-determination beyond its original anti-colonial direction. First, apart from independence, association **(52)**, and integration, "the emergence into any other political status freely determined by a people" was declared to be a mode of implementing the right of self-determination, which possibly might even legitimize the status of such territories as, for example, Gibraltar whose population prefers continued links to the United Kingdom (UK), and Mayotte which chose to stay with France rather than be a part of the independent Comoros. Second, while disclaiming any intent of authorizing or encouraging dismemberment or impairment of the territorial integrity or political unity of states, the Declaration adds that this disclaimer is meant for states "conducting themselves in compliance with the principle of equal rights and self-determination of peoples . . . and thus possessed of a government representing the whole people belonging to the territory without distinction as to race, creed or color." More recently, in 1993 the Vienna Declaration of the UN World Conference on Human Rights **(157)** (33 ILM 1661 (1993)) reformulated the phrase to "without distinction of any kind." While legally not binding, such formulation could be one step further toward recognizing the right of an undefined "people" to secede from a state whose government persistently excludes the members of that group from participating in the governance of the state.

A number of additional resolutions of the GA and the Security Council (SC), designed to intensify efforts to end colonialism, dealt with specific instances of colonialism, but the attention of the UN focused primarily on the apartheid regime of South Africa. The right of self-determination in its UN conception was also reaffirmed in a number of decisions of the International Court of Justice (ICJ) **(309)**, and in particular its advisory opinions **(291)** on *Legal Consequences for States of the Continued Presence of South Africa in Namibia* (1971 ICJ Rep. 16) and *Western Sahara* (1975 ICJ Rep. 12), and the judgment (Chamber) in the *Frontier Dispute* (Burkina Faso/Republic of Mali) (1986 ICJ Rep. 554). More recently, in its *obiter dictum* in the *Case Concerning East Timor* (Portugal v. Australia) (1995 ICJ Rep. 90) the ICJ found that the right of self-determination had an *erga* *omnes* **(12)** character as "one of the essential principles of contemporary international law." However, the peremptory nature of this right is denied in much of the doctrine **(42)** of international law.

From the perspective of the international law of human rights **(160)**, intended to be of universal validity, the right of self-determination is articulated in its UN phraseology in the relevant identical articles (Art. 1(1)) of the two Covenants of 1966: on civil and political rights **(166)** and on economic, social, and cultural rights **(169)**. However, the right expressed in these two instruments is generally not believed to refer to "external" self-determination of a people within a state, the interpretation **(274)** confirmed by India's reservation **(282)** to the Covenants. On the other hand, the concept of self-determination under the Covenants may, without any conflict with the GA concepts, be interpreted as a collective human right to democratic government ("internal" self-determination). But as analyzed in 1984 by the Human Rights Committee in its general comment on self-determination, this is not an individual right enforceable through the petition procedure under the (First) Optional Protocol **(167)** to the International Covenant on Civil and Political Rights. The formulation in the Friendly Relations Declaration of the GA, 1970, also seems to continue upholding the internal aspect of self-determination. It must be pointed out that the concept and term "people" as the holder of the right of self-determination is not used in its normal sociopolitical meaning but only in the demographic sense of all the population of the self-determination territorial unit as such, without taking into account any racial, ethnic, religious, or other distinctions and differences.

The only two cases expressly endorsed by the GA as legitimate self-determination units outside the colonial context have been the now historical case of the apartheid regime in South Africa and the still unresolved case of the Palestinians, the latter within undefined political boundaries. Rather inconsistently, the GA refused to include the "peoples" of the Falkland Islands (Malvinas) and Gibraltar among those entitled to self-determination, in the latter case even disregarding the outcome of free referenda whereby the inhabitants voted for the continued UK sovereignty.

The right of self-determination must be exercised by each territorial unit in question within the existing boundaries of the colonial administration units, converted into international boundaries **(189)** in accordance with the overriding principle of *uti possidetis* **(230)**. While potentially conflicting with aspirations of "subnational" ethnic groups for independence, this principle is rationalized in terms of the need to maintain the territorial integrity of states and prevent internal destabilization. As a matter of fact, according to the Friendly Relations Declaration of 1970, states are prohibited to undertake or encourage any action aimed at the partial or total disruption of the national unity and territorial integrity of any other state or country. Thus the now historical "bantustans" set up within South Africa were declared illegal by the GA not only as a manifestation of the regime's apartheid policy but also as an attempt to disrupt the territorial unity of South Africa in violation of the right of self-determination of the South African people. It remains to be seen whether the concept of "internal" self-determination of the Friendly Relations Declaration, implied in the stated link between representative government and disclaimer of secession, will contribute to a widening of the scope of self-determination under international law.

It appears that whereas secession as such (and suppression of it) is not contrary to international law, assistance by other states offered to a secessionist movement (which, in the UN conception, is not a "national liberation movement") **(94)** contravenes the principle of self-determination as circumscribed by the UN and endorsed by its members. However, as demonstrated by the cases of Bangladesh on the one hand and Biafra on the other, the prohibition of disrupting national unity of a state in the name of self-determination may fail to have any effect if confronted by third powers determined to support a secessionist movement where such support is dictated by their perceived national interest.

The right of self-determination implies a free determination by the people of the territory of their future political status. The Friendly Relations Declaration names four possible modes of implementing this right: 1. establishment of a sovereign independent state (a pattern normally followed in practice); 2. free association with another state; 3. integration with another state; and 4. any other political status freely determined by the people of the territory in question (a clause absent in GA Resolution 1541 of 1960), an option whose potential implications were noted above.

Integration with a contiguous state without consulting the population is considered a legitimate mode of implementing the right of self-determination for very small territories, but not for Western Sahara, forcibly integrated into Morocco and for decades awaiting a referendum to decide the status of the territory. In the case of East Timor, illegally occupied by Indonesia, it took 24 years to achieve independence in 2002 after the withdrawal of the Indonesian troops in 1999 followed by the establishment by the SC of the Transitional UN Administration for the territory.

The disintegration of the Soviet Union **(133)** and Yugoslavia **(134)** with the resulting emergence of new states raised the question whether the right of self-determination, largely implemented by the 1990s, was a universally applicable concept going beyond the traditional colonial context. At least for the time being, this question must be answered in the negative. There is virtually no evidence in state practice to suggest that international law recognizes the right of self-determination of peoples in such situations or, to put it more cautiously as stated by the Arbitration Commission of the European Community (EC) Conference on Yugoslavia in Opinion No. 2, "international law, as it currently stands, does not spell out all the implications of the right of self-determination." The dissolution of the Soviet Union in 1991, with its constituent republics becoming independent states within the boundaries based on the principle of *uti possidetis,* proceeded relatively peacefully. While the right of self-determination was invoked in the special cases of the three Baltic republics, the breakup of the federation was eventually accomplished on the basis of the members' consensus without any reference to the right of self-determination. On the other hand, the independence of the republics which seceded from the Socialist Federated Republic of Yugoslavia (SFRY) was largely the result of a successful armed struggle within the context of a civil war ("non-international armed conflict") **(340)** exhibiting also features of an international armed conflict **(339)**. When declaring independence preceded by referendum, Slovenia and Croatia invoked the "inalienable" right of self-determination, including the right of dissociation, but the Arbitration Commission of the EC Conference on Yugoslavia did not examine the international law aspects of this justification. Referenda on independence were also held in Macedonia and Bosnia and Herzegovina. Thus the disintegration of the three East European federations (the Soviet Union, SFRY, and Czechoslovakia) was purely a question of fact: either consent, as in Czechoslovakia and the Soviet Union, or a *fait accompli* and armed struggle, as in the SFRY. In the last mentioned situation, self-determination was achieved not because it was a recognized right, which it is not in the case, but because it was an outcome of a successful secession which is legal in international law unless it is a result of an illegal intervention **(331)** by third states.

It is to be noted that the principles pertaining to the territorial *status quo* as applied in the colonial context, and in particular the principle of *uti possidetis*, were recognized as legally binding also in the non-colonial context; hence, the inter-republican boundaries within the former federations became international frontiers in terms of international law. Like in colonial situations, the principle of *uti possidetis*, in some cases resulting from fortuitous circumstances, prevails over that of self-determination so that for example the Serbian minority **(172)** in Croatia has no right of self-determination and is entitled only to treatment by Croatia as an ethnic minority under international (human rights) law **(160)**, as ruled in Opinion No. 2 of the Arbitration Commission of the EC Conference on Yugoslavia. One might add that, theoretically, no rule of international law would prevent such minorities from seceding by means of their own armed struggle. A growing number of separatist movements within existing states, resorting to armed force in the name of self-determination, poses difficult problems in contemporary international law whose rules on self-determination originated in a different era of international relations.

**123. Self-Preservation Doctrine.** A doctrine of traditional international law, asserting that in the name of an alleged fundamental right of self-preservation a state **(127)** is allowed to violate by force the sovereignty **(125)** and territorial integrity of another state. The doctrine of preservation was invoked at the time when resort to force was not yet illegal under international law and the doctrine occasionally offered powerful states a convenient pretext for using force in the defense of perceived vital interests even against innocent states on the assumption that the supreme right of survival prevailed over any conflicting duties under international law. Among the most notorious instances of such situations was the bombardment of Copenhagen with the seizure of Denmark's fleet by Great Britain in 1807 and the violation by Germany of the permanent neutrality **(97)** of Belgium and Luxembourg in 1914.

In contemporary international law, peremptorily **(24)** banning the threat or use of force in international relations **(329)**, the old doctrine of self-preservation, can no longer be validly invoked to justify forcible action by a state even in vindication of its legal rights. But the doctrine of self-preservation must not be confused with such circumstances as distress **(72)**, *force majeure* **(78)**, and the state of necessity **(96)** which, in strictly defined circumstances, may be invoked by a state to safeguard its essential interests against a grave and imminent peril. Conceptually, this not entirely settled issue forms part of the rules governing state responsibility **(128)**, and specifically circumstances precluding wrongfulness and, otherwise as such, giving rise to international responsibility.

In a decentralized legal system, still in fact largely lacking an effective machinery of international law enforcement **(17)**, unilateral self-help (otherwise also known but rare and strictly circumscribed in municipal law) **(27)** in one form or another, remains the ultimate method for an injured state to enforce its legal rights against the wrongdoing state. The use of armed force in self-defense **(335)** is the most pronounced form of self-help, as defined in Art. 51 of the United Nations Charter, and the otherwise very controversial resort to it, preventively or preemptively could, under the circumstances, be viewed as in fact an exercise of the right of self-preservation. Other kinds of self-help, known as countermeasures **(58)**, may be applied only by methods other than armed force, and are subject to strict limitations.

**124. Sovereign Order of Malta.** A curious survival from the time of the Crusades, the "Sovereign Military Order of St. John of Jerusalem, of Rhodes, and of Malta" is not a state **(127)** but a unique humanitarian organization whose international legal personality **(85)** is recognized **(106)** for very limited purposes by a small number of states. Historically, a charitable and relief but military brotherhood, the Order was established during the Crusades and eventually conquered Rhodes in 1309 where it ruled under a treaty with the Emperor until 1522. Subsequently, it moved to Malta in 1530 where it stayed until evicted by Napoleon in 1798. In 1834 the Order established its headquarters in Rome, retaining close links with the Holy See **(80)** but more recently renewing its traditional connection with Malta.

While ruling in Rhodes and Malta, the Order had international legal personality. Even having lost its territorial basis, it exchanged diplomatic missions **(68)** with most European states, enjoying special ceremonial treatment. As recently as the 20th century, Italian courts upheld the Order's personality in international law and some 40 states maintained diplomatic relations with this *sui generis* entity. Basically, however, the Order is a humanitarian non-governmental organization that can be active in an armed conflict **(339)** as a relief society under Art. 129 of the 1949 Geneva Convention on the Prisoners of War **(364)**. It might be added that the Sovereign Order of Malta has a standing invitation to the United Nations (UN) to attend the sessions of the General Assembly and maintains a permanent office at the UN headquarters.

**125. Sovereignty.** A fundamental concept underlying the system of public international law which implies the state's **(127)** lawful and essentially exclusive control of its territory **(228)**, with the authority to govern it and enact and enforce its laws with respect to all persons, property, and events within this territory. As noted by the eminent arbitrator in the *Island of Palmas* Arbitration **(293)**, 1928 (2 RIAA 829) involving a dispute between the United States (US) and the Netherlands concerning the acquisition of sovereignty **(227)** over an island, sovereignty is tantamount to independence, that is, the right to exercise in a territory the functions of a state to the exclusion of any other state, and with no other authority over the state than that of international law.

Theoretically conceived by Jean Bodin, the author of *Six livres de la République* (Six Books on the State) (literally "Commonwealth"), 1576, as a legal rationalization of the absolutist power of the French monarchy, the idea of sovereignty was at that time essentially a concept applicable to the internal political situation in France and was well suited to the goal of integrating the country into a centralized territorial state under an absolutist king, himself above the law, yielding unlimited and undivided authority over his subjects. In the course of time, and especially in the 19th century and the early decades of the past century, the concept of sovereignty in the meaning of the unlimited authority of the state in internal affairs was transposed into the external, international context in the sense of "external" sovereignty of the state's relationship toward other states. This distortion of the original concept of sovereignty has been a source of much confusion in the doctrine. Moreover, with sovereignty automatically associated with independent states, the concept has been used and abused as a catchword invoked by states to cover their reluctance to comply with inconvenient rules of international law. Otherwise, the doctrine of absolute and indivisible sovereignty simply could not be applied in actual state practice since by their consent **(7)** and in their own interest states have accepted limitations on their sovereign power under customary law **(39)** and treaties **(40)**. As pointed out by the Permanent Court of International Justice **(320)** in the *SS Wimbledon* case (Great Britain, France, Italy and Japan v. Germany) (with Poland intervening) **(311)** (1923 PCIJ, Series A, No. 1), restrictions imposed by a treaty were not to be considered as abandonment of sovereignty; on the contrary, the right to enter into international engagement was "an attribute of state sovereignty." Furthermore, with the emergence of federal states **(77)** with divided sovereignty, and occasional blurring of the line between sovereign and non-sovereign states, it has become apparent that, in reality, it is the possession of specific rights and duties under international law and not sovereignty as such that determines the existence of international legal personality **(85)**.

By the end of the 20th century, the growing interdependence of states facing all kinds of challenges that transcended their territorial boundaries **(189)**, had brought about a progressive depreciation of the concept of sovereignty in the views of some representatives of the doctrine of international law in the West. Some publicists even wrote about sovereignty as a relic of an earlier era and not a normative principle of international law. However, all these now still utopian views of sovereignty as "an idea whose time has come and gone" do not correspond to international reality where sovereignty still remains a central concept for all states, including the US, and especially for the newly independent and the Third World states which represent a great majority in the international community and whose impact upon the development of international law is certain to be significant. Today "sovereign equality" **(73)** remains the fundamental principle under the United Nations Charter (Art. 2(1)), subsequently reaffirmed for all states in the Friendly Relations Declarations of the General Assembly of 1970 **(14)**. Various manifestations of sovereignty, such as exclusive territorial jurisdiction **(91)**, state immunity **(131)**, immunity of diplomatic agents **(63)**, and so on, are always resolutely upheld by all states. On the other hand, a growing emphasis on the protection of human rights **(157)** and the environment **(197)** as a common value transcending the boundaries of territorial sovereignty, may in the long run contribute to an erosion of sovereignty as a basic concept of international law.

**126. Special Missions.** In addition to permanent diplomatic missions **(68)**, states **(127)** often send abroad official *ad hoc* representations, including temporary missions for various purposes such as attending a conference, represent the sending state on a ceremonial occasion, or to negotiate a specific issue. Recent proliferation of all kinds of special missions, in their nature reminiscent of the era prior to the emergence of permanent diplomatic missions, reflects a growing complexity and specialization of transnational issues, often requiring expert individuals to perform the tasks assigned to the mission by the government of the sending state.

Customary international law **(39)** governing the status of the members of such *ad hoc* missions is not entirely clear and may depend on the category of the mission in question. If they are heads of state or members of government, individuals sent on a special mission, such as delegates to an international conference, enjoy full diplomatic immunity **(63)** under the principle of state (sovereign) immunity **(131)**. Other members of special missions are granted by the receiving state, either expressly or by implication, at least inviolability **(67)** and immunity in respect of official acts.

In order to codify and develop a legal regime to govern special missions, in 1969 the General Assembly adopted the International Law Commission–drafted Convention on Special Missions (9 ILM 127 (1970)) which entered into effect in 1985. The Untied States is not a party to this Convention, however. For the purposes of the Convention, a "special mission" is defined as "a temporary mission, representing the State, which is sent by one State to another State with the consent of the latter for the purpose of dealing with it on specific questions or of performing in relation to it a specific task" (Art. 1(a)). This formulation excludes from the scope of the Convention missions sent to congresses and conferences. While adopting a general principle that a special mission should have at its disposal all the necessary facilities and immunity essential for the performance of its task, the Convention is essentially based on the Vienna Convention on Diplomatic Relations of 1961 **(71)**, with appropriate modifications.

The status of missions sent by states to international organizations **(84)** of a universal character, such as the United Nations, and of delegations participating in conferences convened by such organizations, is the subject of the Vienna Convention on the Representation of States in Their Relations with International Organizations of a Universal Character of 1975 **(103)**.

**127. State.** A state, the by far most important international legal person **(85)**, is an entity with a defined territory **(228)** with a permanent population, under the control of its own government which engages in or has the capacity to engage in formal relations with other states. This definition follows in general that of Art. 1 of the often quoted Montevideo Convention on the Rights and Duties of States of 1933 (165 LNTS 19) of which the United States (US) and some 15 Latin American states are parties. One should add that to be a state under international law, an entity must claim statehood, a requirement that perhaps should be borne in mind when examining the status of Taiwan **(139)**.

It should be pointed out that the term "state," as used in international law and in most countries other than the US, must not be confused with the American usage of the term in the meaning of a constituent unit of the federal US. In the American usage the otherwise basically sociological term "nation" is ordinarily used. The term "nation-state" refers to a sociopolitical concept invented to denote the prevailing type of state in the continuing era of nationalism, which exists or is aspired to in the world today. This term is sometimes used inappropriately in the meaning of "state' in international law literature. It is important to bear in mind the distinction between state and government, which is essential for purposes of recognition **(106)**. The identity of the state as a subject of international law continues unaffected by changes in its government. For example, in the early 21st century the German government was still paying compensation to victims of crimes committed by the Nazi government of the state some sixty years before.

Questions of statehood do not arise with respect to old, established states, but are generated by rather unusual political developments and upheavals such as a breakup of an existing state into several states, secession of a territory becoming independent, or merger of states. Following the era of decolonization in the first decades after World War II, resulting in the creation of many new states, the last decade of the past century witnessed new statehood-related issues generated primarily by the breakup of the former Soviet Union **(133)**, Yugoslavia **(134)** and Czechoslovakia, and by the reunification of Germany **(135)**. As a result of all these events, the number of states grew from 74 in 1946 to 192 in 2003 (including the *sui generis* state of Vatican City) **(80)**. At the same time, the circumstances surrounding the emergence of new states succeeding to the Soviet Union and Yugoslavia raised the question of whether the traditional requirements for statehood under customary international law **(39)** should not be complemented by additional criteria **(107)**, such as those spelled out by the European Community (EC) Declaration on the Guidelines on the Recognition of New States in Eastern Europe and the Soviet Union and in the EC Declaration on Yugoslavia, 1991 (31 ILM 1485 (1992)).

The capacity to exercise sovereignty **(125)** over territory ("territorial sovereignty") is the very essence of statehood, involving "the exclusive right to display the activities of the State," as expressed by the sole arbitrator in the *Island of Palmas* Arbitration of 1928 (2 RIAA 829) between the US and the Netherlands involving the issue of acquisition of territory **(227)**. A state's territory includes also the superjacent airspace **(186)** and—if any—internal waters **(249)** and territorial sea **(262)** and archipelagic waters **(231)**. There is no required minimum area of territory for an entity to claim statehood, and states differ enormously in the size of their respective territories. A state territory may be split into distinct, noncontiguous parts with outlying enclaves, as for instance in the case of Russia or Timor-Leste. There are also numerous states consisting exclusively of islands **(251)**. Although a state's territory must be more or less defined, the territorial requirement for statehood is met even if the boundaries **(189)** are in dispute or not finally defined. Even a total military occupation **(363)** by another state does not necessarily terminate the statehood of the entity, especially if the territory was annexed in violation of the United Nations (UN) Charter.

There is no minimum population requirement as a prerequisite of statehood or any required minimum of citizen residents, as demonstrated by some Persian Gulf states or Andorra, the latter state's population including 80 percent foreign nationals. As in the case of territory, there is a very vast range in the size of population between the largest state, China, numbering 1, 275 billion and such states as Nauru and Tuvalu, with the population of 12,100 and 11,000, respectively, let alone the unique case of the Vatican City **(80)**. As a result of decolonization, the number of demographically very small states, popularly referred to as "ministates," has increased considerably so that on the threshold of the new century out of the existing 192 states 58 numbered less that 2.5 million inhabitants each, with 35 states having, each, population not exceeding 500,000. As long as an entity has a significant number of permanent inhabitants, it meets the test of statehood in terms of population even if large numbers of nomads move in and out of the territory. Ethnic, linguistic, religious, racial, and other criteria are virtually irrelevant as tests of statehood in international law.

The existence of a government exercising a reasonably effective control over its territory and population, both internally and—in terms of independence of any other authority—externally, is the third essential element of statehood. However, exceptionally, the required standard of effective government has not been observed, as was the case of some newly independent former colonial territories such as Algeria, Burundi, Guinea-Bissau, and Rwanda where in the name of the right of self-determination **(122)** statehood was recognized despite absence of an effective government and virtual anarchy. More recently, Croatia and Bosnia and Herzegovina were recognized as states and admitted to the UN in the conditions of the still raging civil war while the respective governments were not yet in control of sizable portions of territory. As shown by state practice in such cases as Lebanon during the civil war in the 1970s and Somalia in the 1990s and early 2000s, where no effective government existed in conditions of anarchy and disintegration, the requirement of a stable political organization in control of the territory is not applied too strictly with respect to already existing states, and the state affected by anarchy, even for a rather prolonged period of time, continues to be recognized as a state by the international community. Furthermore, even if a state's government suffers interference from without, being in reality politically and economically subordinated to, and dependent on another state, it does not cease to be treated as an "independent" state under international law so long as it appears to perform the state functions in an ostensibly independent and effective manner. However, there is no clear rule to this effect so that in extreme cases of subordination to another state a "puppet state" may be treated as not meeting the requirement of government for purposes of recognition of statehood. Thus, in the early Cold War years subordination to the Soviet Union was cited by some Western powers as a ground for denying the quality of state to the German Democratic Republic.

While the existence of an effective government is an essential requirement of statehood, as a general proposition international law does not inquire into the nature of the internal political system of the state or the legitimacy of its government. Violations of fundamental human rights **(157)** do not put into question the statehood of an already established state. However, as noted above, criteria concerning human rights, including even the right to democratic government, can play a role as additional conditions for recognizing new states and governments.

The standard of an effective government, in itself a question of fact, is closely related to the requirement of the capacity to enter into relations with other states, which, however, is not always considered as necessary. Whether or not an entity, otherwise competent and capable of conducting formal international relations, can demonstrate such qualities by actually engaging in foreign relations, depends on the will of other states to establish relations with it, in other words to recognize the entity in question as a state This aspect of statehood is related to the doctrinal controversy over the legal effects of recognition (constitutive or declaratory) **(109)** and recognition of states in general.

A state does not lose its statehood by voluntarily turning over to another state some of or even all control of its foreign relations. This is the case of the European "ministates," which have largely entrusted the conduct of defense and foreign relations to other states, but are states and members of the UN. Liechtenstein, which otherwise has been joined to Switzerland by a customs and monetary union **(59)** since 1923, has an agreement with Switzerland, 1919, whereby that country conducts Liechtenstein's foreign relations, with all guarantees of Liechtenstein's sovereign rights, including the right to appoint its diplomatic agents **(62)**. Monaco's status is based on a treaty of 1918 with France, recognized in Art. 436 of the Treaty of Versailles (225 CTS 188). It is united with France in a customs and monetary union and France is responsible for its defense. Under the 1918 treaty with France, which guarantees Monaco's independence and sovereignty, in the event that the male dynasty of Monaco should become extinct, the state would become a French protectorate. San Marino conducts its foreign relations independently, subject to certain exceptions under agreements with Italy. Andorra, a co-principality, with the president of France and the bishop of Urgell, Spain, as joint heads of state ("co-princes"), was ruled for more than 700 years (1278–1993) under a system of semi-feudal suzerainty. Under a democratic constitution adopted in 1993, the system of co-princes was retained but greatly reduced. Andorra has the right to conduct its diplomatic relations, but France and Spain are still responsible for its external security and its police force is assisted in alternate years by either French or Spanish police.

In another part of the world, in the Pacific region, the foreign relations of Samoa (formerly Western Samoa, which changed its name despite protests by American Samoa) are conducted by New Zealand under a Treaty of Friendship of 1962. However, Samoa is an independent country, and a member of the UN since 1976.

The so-called protectorates or protected states, common in the colonial era under arrangements between local rulers and Great Britain, France, or Spain, respectively, are now an extinct category of dependent state. The legal status of such entities depended on the terms of the agreement with the protecting power, but generally the latter was responsible for the defense and conduct of foreign relations of the protectorate. Today, perhaps the only example of entity approximating the status of protected state is Bhutan whose defense and foreign relations are in charge of India under a treaty of 1949 (157 BFSP 214). However, Bhutan maintains diplomatic relations with some countries and joined the UN in 1971.

It may be added that the creation of the European Communities (EC), where the member states turned over to the EC some of the matters previously under their control, in no way terminated the statehood of the EC members or endowed the Community itself with the attribute of statehood.

**128. State Responsibility.** State responsibility is a fundamental principle of international law whereby a state **(127)**, either by an act or omission, has breached an international obligation in force and incurs, in the absence of circumstances precluding wrongfulness of its conduct, certain legal consequences for the internationally wrongful act attributable **(53)** to it, including the obligation to cease the wrongful conduct and make such full reparation **(118)** of any material and moral damage to the injured state or states **(82)** as is reasonably adequate depending on the merits of the case in question. As a general rule, responsibility arises regardless of the intention or fault of the state officials involved. While ordinarily international law is concerned with responsibility of states as the, by far, primary international legal persons, that is, subjects of international law **(85)**, public international organizations **(84)** may in exceptional cases bear responsibility for violating their obligations. The topic of responsibility of international organizations under international law is on the codification **(5)** agenda of the International Law Commission (ILC). State responsibility must be distinguished from international liability for injurious consequences arising out of acts not prohibited by international law **(120)**, a topic also under study by the ILC.

State responsibility is different from individual criminal responsibility of individuals **(81)**. Whereas state responsibility arises only if it can be attributed (imputed) to it and it does not entail any punishment of the delinquent state, its objective being to bring about cessation of the wrongful act and/or reparation, individual criminal responsibility rests on the premise that any individual committing a crime against international law, whether acting as a state organ or as a private individual, is subject to criminal liability and may be prosecuted and punished in the interests of the international community by a domestic court on very broad jurisdictional grounds **(87)** or by an international criminal tribunal. However, it must be added that in such cases as war crimes **(373)** and crimes against humanity **(151)** including genocide **(155)**, perpetrated by state officials, both state responsibility and individual criminal liability of the individual officials find their application.

Whether in addition to the breach of an obligation ("legal injury"), material or moral damage is to be regarded as a distinct, objective element of the wrongful act or omission is not an entirely settled theoretical issue. But in actual international judicial practice in state-to-state cases based on customary law **(39)**, courts have as a rule taken for granted the presence of damage as an inherent element of responsibility. In its Draft Articles of 2001 **(129)** the ILC found that damage was not a necessary element of state responsibility, reasoning that since the legal injury is logically inherent in any breach of international obligation, material or moral damage does not constitute a distinct element which triggers responsibility, but may be used for purposes of determining the form and amount of reparation.

The law of state responsibility is sometimes referred to as "secondary" rules of international law in the sense that it deals with determining the legal consequences of violations of substantive "primary" rules which define and determine the legality of states' conduct. As noted in the *Rainbow Warrior* arbitral award **(104)**, "the legal consequences of a breach of a treaty, including the determination of the circumstances that may exclude wrongfulness . . . and the appropriate remedies for breach are subjects that belong to the customary law of state responsibility." Specific legal consequences of an internationally wrongful act are frequently spelled out in the primary law dealing with the particular substantive matter and specifying the remedies available to the injured state. Under the circumstances, joint responsibility of two or more states is possible, but state practice has not yet sufficiently developed the principles governing such situations, as admitted by the International Court of Justice **(309)** in the case concerning *Certain Phosphate Lands in Nauru* (Nauru v. Australia) (1992 ICJ Rep. 240). As listed by the ILC in its Draft Articles, the circumstances precluding wrongfulness of the act involved include: valid consent given by the injured state; countermeasures **(58)**; *force majeure* **(78)**; distress **(72)**; state of necessity **(96)**; obligation to comply with *jus cogens* **(24)**; and self-defense **(335)**.

In general, in ordinary cases involving a bilateral situation, injury which gave rise to state responsibility may have been suffered either directly by the state itself (for example, violation of its territorial integrity, failure by the other state to fulfill an international obligation in force for that state at the time when the injurious act was committed) or by its national whose claim, taken over by the state of his nationality, becomes a claim of the state itself. The rules governing the nationality of claim **(95)** apply here and the exhaustion of effective local remedies **(74)** is ordinarily needed before a state can espouse its national's claim as against another state. In exceptional cases, individuals have a treaty-based right of access to an international tribunal **(306)** to pursue their claims, thus acquiring a certain measure of international legal personality in confronting a state.

Traditionally, the law of state responsibility has been made up almost exclusively of rather rudimentary and not quite settled customary rules applied in a bilateral relationship between the injured and the wrongdoing state. The focus has been primarily on the law of state responsibility for injury to aliens **(144)**. However, the last decades of the 20th century witnessed significant developments in the law of state responsibility which were also stimulated by the work of the ILC. The Commission was engaged throughout much of the latter part of the past century in codifying and progressively developing this area of public international law, a truly monumental task completed in 2001. In its substance, the scope of the law of state responsibility expanded beyond matters dealing with injury to aliens, and its rules emerged as a more inclusive and separate branch of international law. Furthermore, a trend has emerged, at least in the doctrine, related to the concept of *erga omnes* obligations **(12)**, to the effect that in the interests of the world community, responsibility for wrongful acts amounting to serious breaches of essential obligations toward all parties to multilateral treaty or constituting violations of customary law obligations protecting fundamental values of the international community, should be owed not just to the state directly affected but also to the parties to the treaty or all the members of the intentional community, as the case may be. This distinction between ordinary and special responsibility became a controversial issue in the work of the ILC on state responsibility. Initially, the Commission adopted a distinction between delicts, entailing ordinary responsibility, and crimes (such as aggression, crimes against humanity, slavery, colonial domination, among others), giving rise to responsibility to the international community as a whole. However, confronted with a strong opposition against the notion of state crime, alien to international law and with implications for the duty of reparation and the concept of the injured state, the ILC deleted the controversial article and removed any references to state crimes as a distinct category of the most serious wrongful acts. In principle, the ILC included all internationally wrongful acts in a single category, with the rules on attribution and circumstances precluding wrongfulness applying to all. On the other hand, the Commission adopted the concept of serious breaches of obligations under peremptory norms of general international law. Such breaches entail consequences for the international community as a whole and in substance correspond to the concept of crimes in the earlier version of the ILC Draft Articles on State Responsibility.

The major difference in the ILC Draft of 2001 between ordinary wrongful acts and serious breaches of obligations to the international community as a whole lies in the consequences of the wrongful act. In the latter category of acts, the delinquent state has obligation toward all other states and the latter have an obligation not to recognize **(99)** the situation brought about by the serious breach and not to render assistance to the responsible state. In addition, reparation claimed should be proportionate to the gravity of the wrongful act, reflecting the serious nature of the breach and seeking to deter any repetition of the breach. The claim is instituted by the injured state or by any other state for the injured state's benefit, or—in cases of gross violations of human rights **(157)**—by any state acting on behalf of the individuals injured by such violations. As already demonstrated by international practice, in cases of failure to cease the wrongful act or provide adequate reparation, any state may bring the matter before a competent international organization which may adopt collective sanctions. Subsequently, if need be, individual states may adopt appropriate countermeasures.

It remains to be seen whether the ILC rules on special responsibility, if adopted in the form of a binding treaty, will be made use of in the interests of the international community. So far, however, on the whole, states are reluctant to take action in the community interest, invoking the principles of state responsibility as a rule only when their perceived interests are directly at stake.

**129. State Responsibility, The ILC Draft on, 2001.** The draft articles on "Responsibility of States for Internationally Wrongful Acts" were submitted to the General Assembly (GA) by the International Law Commission (ILC) in 2001 after some fifty years of the ILC work to codify and progressively develop **(5)** this area of public international law. The topic of state responsibility **(128)** was included in the original list of fourteen topics selected for codification by the ILC. In confronting its task, in 1955 the ILC initially focused only on responsibility of states for injury to aliens **(144)**, the area of international law from which the contemporary law of state responsibility has largely developed, but subsequently, in 1963, the Commission shifted to a more inclusive approach of tackling the subject comprehensively. The focus of the ILC was on the rules and procedures governing state responsibility ("secondary" rules) rather than on the enormous task of dealing with the substantive ("primary") rules, the violation of which could give rise to state responsibility.

The work of the ILC proceeded throughout the years in preparing parts of the prospective draft until in 1996 it provisionally adopted a complete set of Draft Articles at first reading, on which states were invited by the GA to provide comments (37 ILM 440 (1998)). For its part, the United States in its comments (37 ILM 468 (1998)) expressed concern about provisions of the Draft which, it claimed, were not supported by state practice and went beyond the current state of customary international law **(39)**, questioning especially the introduction of the highly controversial notion of international criminal responsibility of states. Eventually the ILC reached a compromise on the issue of "state crimes." The concept of crime was deleted and instead the Draft adopted the notion of serious breaches of obligations under peremptory norms **(24)** of general international law. The final text of the draft articles was approved at the 53d session of the ILC in 2001 and referred to the GA for adoption of a GA resolution with the text of the draft articles annexed, and an eventual adoption of a convention on the law of state responsibility.

The ILC Draft of 2001 consists of four parts. Part 1, dealing with the internationally wrongful act of a state, includes, in addition to general provisions, the rules concerning: acts of state, and in particular those governing attribution **(53)**; breach of international obligation; responsibility in respect of acts of another state; and circumstances precluding wrongfulness, namely, consent of the injured state, compliance with peremptory norm, self-defense **(335)**, countermeasures **(58)** in respect of the wrongful act, *force majeure* **(78)**, distress **(72)**, and state of necessity **(96)**. Part 2 spells out the rules on the content of the international responsibility of a state, dealing mainly with the legal consequences of an internationally wrongful act and forms of reparation **(118)**. It is this part that recognizes the existence of the category of "serious breaches of obligations under peremptory norms of general international law" which entail consequences for the international community as a whole. Here the text of the Draft reflects the formulation of Art. 53 of the Vienna Convention on the Law of Treaties, 1969 (1155 UNTS 331) on invalidity of treaties **(275)** conflicting with a peremptory norm. Part 3, the implementation of state responsibility, includes provisions on invocation of responsibility, elaborating especially on countermeasures and the concept of the injured state **(82)**. The rules on the latter issue reflect the formulation of Art. 60(2)(c) of the Vienna Convention on the Law of Treaties concerning termination **(287)** or suspension **(286)** of the operation of a treaty **(288)** as a consequence of its breach. The Draft recognizes the rule whereby states other than the one to which a breach of obligation was owed individually may also, under the circumstances, be included within the concept of injured state as part of a group of states or international community as a whole. Part 4, general provisions, deals with certain rules and principles which, like the rule concerning *lex specialis* (prevailing over a general rule), relation to the United Nations Charter, and the principle of individual responsibility **(81)** are relevant to the law on state responsibility. Overall, the ILC Draft on the complex and difficult topic of state responsibility can be counted among the most outstanding achievements of the Commission in the field of codification and progressive development of international law.

**130. State Responsibility, Objective and Subjective Doctrines.** These are two contrasting doctrines concerning the basis of state responsibility for internationally wrongful acts **(128)**. First, responsibility may be subjective, that is, based on fault, where a state is responsible only if the commission of a wrongful act is accompanied by some degree of proven psychological attitude of the wrongdoer: negligence or recklessness, *culpa* in civil (Roman) law **(23)**, or—worse—intention or guilty knowledge (*dolus*). The rules on attribution **(53)** apply to all these situations. Second, responsibility may be objective or strict, that is, based, on the premise of creating a risk, purely on the commission of the wrongful act by a state's organ or other agent irrespective of whether or not negligence or recklessness, intent or bad faith were involved. In addition to responsibility for injury to other states caused by an unlawful activity ("internationally wrongful act"), there are, of course, problems brought about by responsibility or—in the current terminology—"liability" **(120)** for injurious consequences arising out of acts not prohibited by international law.

General international law, as reflected in arbitral **(293)** and judicial decisions **(306)**, is not clear or consistent on the question of the basis of state responsibility, with support for both approaches available in state practice as well as international legal doctrine. In recent decades the doctrinal debate on fault versus objective or strict responsibility has lost much of its practical importance, considering that in view of the expansion and growing complexity of state organs and activities, the application of the subjective fault principle has become more difficult and less practical. Ordinarily, unless a state intentionally directs and controls a wrongful act of another state or coerces it to commit such act, international tribunals do not inquire whether a state's agent acted with intent to perform an internationally wrongful act. Intent or fault is not regarded as a discrete element of state responsibility but is taken into account in the assessment of compensation or within the context of circumstances precluding wrongfulness. Furthermore, the adequacy of the fault doctrine has been questioned in cases of state responsibility for transnational pollution damage and damage resulting from particularly dangerous activities involving nuclear and other ultrahazardous materials. On the whole, unless regulated by treaty, responsibility in the area of international environmental law **(197)** is not governed by any firmly settled rules, but the general trend is to follow the objective approach, irrespective of any fault or negligence considerations, especially since the borderline between lawful and unlawful acts causing injurious environmental consequences may not be clearly drawn in particular cases. Liability for such consequences arising out of acts not prohibited by international law is on the codification agenda of the ILC which in its work focused first on liability in cases of loss from transboundary harm arising out of hazardous activities.

**131. State (Sovereign) Immunity.** An established principle of customary international law **(39)** whereby a state **(127)** or its instrumentality is, as a general rule, immune from the jurisdiction **(87)** of the courts of another state (the *forum* state). While a state may claim immunity from all forms of jurisdiction, immunity from judicial and enforcement jurisdiction has traditionally been considered of primary importance. Historically, sovereign immunity, first vested in the person of the monarch (and now applying to head of state), was justified on the basis of "perfect equality and absolute independence of sovereigns," as argued by the United States (US) Supreme Court in the case of *Schooner Exchange v. McFaddon* (7 Cranch 116(1812)). In the facts of this classical case, a French warship **(265)** the *Balaou*, put into Philadelphia for repairs after a storm. Even though the ship turned out to be in reality a renamed private American-owned schooner, the *Exchange,* which had been seized by France on the high seas **(245)** in 1810, the Court held the ship to be exempt from US jurisdiction as property of France.

Until about the 1920s, under the maxim *par in parem non habet imperium* (equals have no jurisdiction over each other), sovereign immunity from the jurisdiction of foreign courts was virtually absolute irrespective of the nature of a state's activity. Thus, in 1926, like courts in many other countries, the US Supreme Court reaffirmed the doctrine of absolute immunity of a foreign state and its property in the case of *Berizzi Brothers Co. v. SS Pesaro* (271 U.S. 562), overturning the decision of a lower court which argued that international law did not require granting immunity to states with respect to their commercial activities because such immunity deprived private parties of judicial remedies and provided an unfair advantage to states in competition with private enterprises.

With a growing engagement of states in trade and other commercial activities, including especially operation of state-owned seagoing vessels for commercial purposes, a trend soon emerged in national judicial practice, first in civil-law **(23)** countries (especially Belgium and Italy) and then in the United Kingdom (UK), US, and other common-law jurisdictions, toward the doctrine of restrictive immunity, that is, granting state immunity only with respect to claims arising out of activities traditionally associated with the functions of states (activities *jure imperii*), such as activities in the exercise of the state's administration, acts concerning diplomatic missions and armed forces, legislative acts such as nationalization, and—a more controversial area—public loans. On the other hand, more and more states of *forum* would deny foreign states immunity from jurisdiction in respect of claims arising out of activities that could otherwise be carried on by private persons, that is, commercial activities (*jure gestionis* or *jure commercii*). Already in 1926 the Brussels Convention on the Immunity of State-Owned Vessels (176 LNTS 199) adopted the restrictive principle of immunity to state-owned merchant vessels and their cargoes. But it was following World War II in reaction to the spreading of state trading and other commercial activities, mainly by the Communist states and some Third World countries with socialized type of economies, which claimed absolute immunity with respect to such activities, that many states adopted a restrictive approach to state immunity so that by the 1980s a great majority of states, including especially Western states, favored the restrictive principle. For pragmatic reasons, even Communist states had to accept this principle in agreements with Western states. The US adopted the restrictive principle in 1952, a move associated with a letter to the Acting Attorney General of the Acting Legal Advisor of the Department of State, known after the name of its author as the "Tate Letter" (26 Department of State Bulletin 984 (1952)), which set forth the restrictive approach to be taken by the US on the issue of sovereign immunity.

The abandonment of the rule of absolute immunity by many states was reflected in municipal **(27)** legislation codifying the national approach to the problem, including the US Foreign Sovereign Immunities Act (FSIA) of 1972 (15 ILM 1388(1976)) and similar acts in the UK, 1978 (17 ILM 1123 (1978)), Canada, 1981 (21 ILM 798 (1982)), and Australia, 1985 (25 ILM 715 (1986)). The US Act also shifted the responsibility of deciding pleas of immunity by foreign states from the State Department to the courts. In addition to municipal legislation, a number of bilateral agreements and a multilateral European Convention on State Immunity, 1972 (11 ILM 470 (1972)) reflected the new approach to state immunity. A Protocol to this convention provided for a tribunal (consisting of judges of the European Court of Human Rights (ECHR)) **(154)** with the function of adjudicating disputes between states over the application of the 1972 Convention. The restrictive approach to state immunity was also adopted in the International Law Commission (ILC) Draft Articles of 1991 on Jurisdictional Immunities of States and Their Property (30 ILM 1554 (1991)).

More recently, with the dissolution of the Soviet Union **(133)** and the collapse of Communism in Europe as well as transition to market economy in a number of Third World countries, the absolute immunity approach has been followed only by a handful of developing countries, China, and the remaining few Communist regimes. Thus, while states are still entitled to immunity from judicial process of foreign states as a general principle, that immunity applies in most states only with respect to governmental activities *jure imperii,* but not to a government's activity *jure gestionis*, but—as discussed below—this distinction is not entirely clear and considerable difficulties of interpretation arise in the manifold and large practice of states.

Although the restrictive approach applies primarily to commercial and contractual claims, state practice has long, even under the absolute theory of immunity, admitted exceptions from immunity, such as for example in cases to immovable property owned or possessed by a foreign state in the *forum* state, property rights arising by way of succession or gift, or—a more controversial exception—public loans contracted abroad which in some states are held to be subject to the law of the *forum* state. It has also been a recognized rule of international law that a foreign state is ordinarily not immune with respect to claims in tort due to death or injury to persons or damage to property in the state of *forum,* attributable **(53)** to that state. Under the FSIA, courts have jurisdiction with respect to property of a foreign state present in the US in connection with commercial activity, but taken by that state in violation of international law. Under an amendment to the FSIA in 1996, immunity is denied to foreign states designated as sponsors of terrorism **(337)** or practicing official torture **(182)**. Generally speaking, the number and variety of exceptions from immunity point to a considerable shrinking of the concept of sovereign immunity in contemporary international law.

States are free to grant immunity beyond the limits prescribed by international law. On the other hand, a foreign state may voluntarily waive its immunity, either by explicit consent given for a specific claim or actual submission to the proceedings, or by a prior waiver in a contract with a private party or in a treaty **(288)**. Waiver of immunity in cases of activities *jure gestionis* is provided in numerous bilateral agreements. Waiver continues for any subsequent appeal proceedings in a case but, as noted below, does not extend to measures of execution. If a foreign state institutes proceedings in the *forum* state or intervenes in proceedings, it is ordinarily deemed to have waived immunity with respect to any counterclaims arising out of the matter in dispute or concerning a matter for which it would in any event not be entitled to immunity if such claim had been brought against it in a separate action. Municipal law provides for further situations of implied waiver of sovereign immunity of foreign states.

Immunity from jurisdiction to adjudicate must be distinguished from immunity from various measures of constraint against a foreign state's property, such as pre-judgment attachment, that is, seizure and execution for the purpose of enforcing a forthcoming judgment. Due to the sensitivity of states to any measures of actual forcible constraint against their assets, international law recognizes immunity from execution, and even if a foreign state consents to the exercise of jurisdiction by the *forum* state, such waiver does not imply its consent to any measures of attachment, arrest, or execution. Such measures of constraint require a separate, usually explicit, waiver, but under the FSIA explicit waiver is needed only for pre-judgment attachment.

Execution and similar measures may be levied only upon state property which is not used for governmental, *jure imperii*, purposes and is connected with the claim that is the object of the proceedings. Under the US FSIA, immunity is not granted also if it concerns immovable property located in the US, property taken in violation of international law, or acquired by gift or succession. Details concerning immunity from attachment or execution vary from state to state.

Apart from theoretical and policy science arguments on the role of the state in modern society, the application of the principle of sovereign immunity encounters complex legal problems of interpretation, sometimes inconsistently resolved by national courts even within the same state of the *forum*. Among major problems are: identification of the entity benefiting from immunity (the meaning of "state"), especially where a state's instrumentality is involved; the question of indirect impleading, that is, a situation where proceedings are brought against a person other than the foreign state concerned but which involve property in which that state has an interest; and—last but not least—the most common problem of differentiating between acts *jure imperii* and acts *jure gestionis*.

While the matter is not quite settled and, broadly speaking, for purposes of sovereign immunity, the concept of the foreign state includes, in addition to the state's government, the constitutional units of a federal state **(77)** (but not under the European Convention of 1972) and the state's political subdivisions to the extent that they perform functions in the exercise of the sovereign authority of the state. Lower-level administrative units, such as counties, cities, and towns, are ordinarily not entitled to immunity. The status of semi-governmental agencies and instrumentalities may raise difficult problems, as in the case of a nationalized branch of economy of a foreign state, commercially active in the *forum* state. On the whole, even if an economically active entity is endowed with a distinct legal personality, with possible autonomous *juris gestionis* activities in the forum state, it is still entitled to sovereign immunity if in effect it is closely linked to the organization of the foreign state concerned. Effective control by the state is often the decisive test, as it is provided in the FSIA according to which immunity extends to foreign agencies and instrumentalities in which a foreign government or its subdivision has a controlling interest.

With regard to indirect impleading, the general rule is that proceedings relating to property in the possession of a state or in which a state claims to have an interest supported by *prima facie* evidence, may not be instituted against another person if that state were immune if the proceedings had been brought against it. Under the FSIA, this rule applies only with regard to suits in admiralty brought to enforce a maritime lien against a vessel or cargo of a foreign state where activity *jure gestionis* is involved.

The emergence of the restrictive immunity approach has introduced a good deal of complexity into the law of state immunity in view of the fact that the distinction between acts *jure imperii* and those of *jure gestionis* is not sufficiently clear in actual international practice and no definite generalizations can be arrived at. In the case of *Victory Transport, Inc v. Comisaría General de Abastecimientos y Transportes* (35 ILR 110), 1964, a US Circuit Court held that a chartering of a vessel to transport grain from the US to Spain for distribution to the population was a commercial act, denying the defendant agency of the Spanish government immunity from suit to compel commercial arbitration **(308)**. In this case the Court identified five categories of acts *jure imperii:* internal administrative acts; legislative acts, including nationalization; acts concerning armed forces; those concerning diplomatic activities; and public loans. In 1989 the US Supreme Court found a clear instance of an act *jure imperii* in the case of *Argentine Republic v. Amerada Hess Shipping Corp*. (109 U.S. 683 (1989)) in which it granted sovereign immunity to Argentina against a claim brought by a company whose tanker had been damaged by the Argentine air force during the Falklands War of 1982.

To distinguish between the two categories of activity may be especially difficult where a foreign state engages in commercial activities for public purposes. As defined, for example, in the FSIA, a commercial activity means either a regular course of commercial conduct or a particular commercial transaction or act. In addition, under the due process rule concerning the jurisdictional reach **(91)** of US courts requiring a minimum of contacts of the defendant with the *forum* state, claims against a foreign state must be derived out of commercial activities in the US, or an act performed in the US in connection with a commercial activity carried on outside the US, or an act performed outside the US in connection with a commercial activity carried on outside the US if the act causes a direct effect in the US.

While, under the circumstances, courts in some countries look to the ultimate purpose of the activity in question, the more common test for determining a *jure gestionis* character of an activity is to look to its nature, as is done especially in the common-law countries. The US FSIA provides that "the commercial character of an activity shall be determined by reference to the nature of the course of conduct of particular transaction or act, rather than by reference to its purpose." The 1991 ILC Draft on Jurisdictional Immunities of States and Their Property, which in principle also adopts a restrictive approach to state immunity, includes the following commercial transactions: commercial contract or transaction of sale of goods or supply of services; loans and other financial transactions; and any other contract or transaction of a commercial, industrial, trading, or professional nature, but not contracts of employment of persons. In countries where—like in the US—the courts look to the nature of the transaction as the test for immunity, examples of commercial activity have included purchases of food for the population; of cement for military purposes; even of a truck for an embassy; issuance of governmental bonds; artistic performances by foreign state-operated companies, but with an impresario from the *forum* state; a contract for repairing a diplomatic residence (but the treatment of embassies' bank accounts varies); and claims for wages by seamen aboard vessels owned by a foreign state and calling at the *forum* state's ports in pursuance of commercial activities. The US courts follow in general the rule that unless related to a government service by a national of a foreign state, claims arising out of contracts for performance of services are also considered to be claims of a commercial nature.

**132. State Succession.** One of the most uncertain and controversial areas of international law, state **(127)** succession means both an actual occurrence of "the replacement of one state by another in the responsibility for the international relations of territory," as defined in Art. 2 of the Vienna Convention on Succession of States in respect of Treaties of 1978 (17 ILM 1488 (1978), reiterated in the Vienna Convention on Succession of States in respect of State Property, Archives and Debts of 1983 (22 ILM 298 (1983)), and the legal consequences which arise concerning the extent to which the replacing (successor) state assumes the capacities, rights, and duties of the replaced (predecessor) state in respect of the territory **(228)** concerned. The succession of states must be distinguished from the succession of governments. Whereas changes in government, even truly revolutionary ones, do not affect the legal identity and continuity of the state itself, state succession implies a discontinuity in statehood, that is, replacement of one state by another in respect of a part or the whole of the territory of the replaced state.

State succession has been an endemic feature of international relations for centuries, frequently occurring in the aftermath of wars, with the consequent redistribution of territories and the creation and extinction of states. In modern times, the rise and consolidation of a number of national states in Europe in the 19th century produced a series of succession issues. In the past century, perhaps the most complex succession problems associated with the aftermath of World War I (1914–1918) were brought about by the disintegration of four empires and the creation of a number of new or revived states in Europe. Similar, though not so extensive and complex, problems of succession resulted from World War II (1939–1945). A long series of succession issues was caused by massive decolonization throughout the latter half of the 20th century, with the consequent creation of some one hundred new states. This development prompted the United Nations (UN) to codify and progressively develop **(5)** the law of state succession in the two above-noted conventions of 1978 and 1983, respectively. However, these not widely accepted instruments, not yet in force, reflected the drafters' preoccupation with and bias for the circumstances and interests of the "newly independent states" (that is, former colonies), apparently dismissing the likelihood, let alone a possibility, of any future wave of new states emerging within a noncolonial context, for which the drafters' codification might not necessarily be entirely appropriate. However, that is exactly what happened in the early 1990s upon the end of the Cold War, resulting in the unification of Germany **(135)**, and the dissolution of the Soviet Union **(133)**, the former Yugoslavia (Socialist Federated

Republic of Yugoslavia (SFRY)) **(134)**, and Czechoslovakia. With a number of secessionist entities already claiming the right to statehood and separatist movements on the rise, new succession problems are likely to arise in the near future.

State practice and judicial decisions have not been consistent enough so that the still customary law **(39)** of state succession cannot provide sufficiently clear and well-established principles and rules in this area. However, in any case, state practice follows neither the misleading municipal law **(27)** analogy of universal succession to all rights and obligations of the predecessor, which is inappropriate within the context of sovereign states, nor the opposite doctrine of extreme positivism **(31)** which denies any transmission of rights and obligations between the predecessor and successor states. Hence, in rejecting these two polar doctrines, international law requires each particular case to be examined on its own merits depending on the succession event (whose very nature may be at issue) and the rights and obligations involved, although—as found by the Arbitration Commission of the European Community Conference on Yugoslavia in its Opinion No. 13—the two codifying conventions can offer some guidance on the subject. Concurrence or acquiescence of other states is an important element, but no succession may be recognized if incompatible with international law.

In view of the complexity of the subject, it is no wonder that, ordinarily, succession situations have been dealt with in international agreements, either multilateral peace treaties, such as for example the Treaty of Peace with Austria of St. Germain of 1919 (226 CTS 8) which, *inter alia,* regulated the extremely complex issues of succession to the debts of the Habsburg monarchy or, as part of the decolonization process, the bilateral "devolution" agreements between a metropolitan power and individual newly independent states. In the opinion of the above-mentioned Arbitral Commission (Opinion No. 9) (31 ILM 1523 (1993)) and the Security Council (Resolution 1022 of 1995), all aspects of succession should be settled by the successor states by agreement. The Agreement on Succession Issues between the Five Successor States (Bosnia and Herzegovina, Croatia, Macedonia, Slovenia, and the newly reconstituted Federal Republic of Yugoslavia) of the former state of Yugoslavia, 2001 (41 ILM 3 (2002)) is a recent major example of such agreements.

A transfer of territory from one state to another entails a number of legal problems, the foremost of which is the question whether and to what extent the successor state acquires the treaty rights and obligations of its predecessor **(137)**. Other succession issues include the effect of the transfer of sovereignty upon the predecessor state's property and archives; property rights of private persons; debts owed by the predecessor state to other states and international organizations **(84)** and to private persons; succession to other states' contracts and to obligations resulting from torts (or delicts) of the predecessor state; and the effect of the change of sovereignty upon the nationality **(175)** of the persons in the territory involved.

State succession problems arise as a result of a variety of events. First, part of the territory of a state may be transferred to and absorbed by another (successor) state (partial absorption or transfer of territory, or partial succession). Second, a state, ordinarily a federation **(77)**, may absorb all of the predecessor state, without creating a new state, with the predecessor state assimilated into it and becoming extinct (total absorption). Third, two existing states may merge into a single new state with a new name (merger). Fourth, a part of the predecessor state separates, forming one or more independent states (secession). Separation of dependent territories from colonial powers belonged in principle to this category, but under the influence of the UN principle of self-determination **(122)** the successor states ("newly independent states") enjoyed a separate and privileged legal status in such succession situations. Finally, fifth, a state splits up or—if a federation—dissolves into two or more states, itself becoming extinct (dismemberment or dissolution). The terms concerning these five situations are not necessarily clearly differentiated in practice and are not terms of art in international law. Furthermore, special intermediate situations are possible, as illustrated by India's evolution toward independence, during which that country enjoyed a considerable degree of international personality before full independence in 1947. In addition, the same set of events may, depending on the point of view, be classified as one or another form of succession event, as was at one time the case of the succession to the former Yugoslavia. Vagaries of history may also have a state pass through several events involving complex questions of succession, as shown by the history of Austria in the 20th century: from the dissolution of the Austro-Hungarian Empire in 1918 to a much smaller and possibly new Austria; then to a forced incorporation (*Anschluss*) into Germany in 1938; and finally to a reborn Austria following the end of the Third Reich in 1945 and the State Treaty of 1955.

As far as absorption of an entire state is concerned, as was, *inter alia*, the case of the admission of Texas into the United States (US) in 1845, the unification of Germany in 1990 provides a unique recent instance of this kind of succession event brought about, in legal terms, by agreement of the parties concerned and full acceptance of other states. The unification of Yemen in 1990 occurred in the form of a merger whereby the Yemen Arab Republic and the People's Democratic Republic of Yemen agreed to merge into a single new state to be known as the Republic of Yemen, with the international personalities of each predecessor state to be integrated in the new state (30 ILM 820 (1991)). Apart from early cases of unification through the formation of a federation (example: the creation of the federal US), more recent instances of merger include the unification of Tanganyika and Zanzibar into Tanzania in 1964 and the ephemeral union of Egypt and Syria in a United Arab Republic created in 1958 but discontinued by Syria's secession in 1961. Other cases of union proclaimed by some Arab states were purely symbolic acts without much substance and did not give rise to any succession problems. Instances of secession include: the separation of Pakistan from India in 1947; of Singapore from Malaysia in 1965; of East Pakistan from Pakistan, with the creation of the state of Bangladesh in 1971; and of Eritrea from Ethiopia in 1993, after thirty years of nationalist rebellion and a UN-sponsored plebiscite. Minor cases of dissolution of states in recent history had occurred before the 1990s, as exemplified by the breakup of the short-lived Federation of Mali into Mali and Senegal in 1960 and the already noted dissolution of the United Arab Republic in 1961. However, it was the dissolution of the Soviet Union and the SFRY and the split-up of Czechoslovakia that raised numerous issues of succession and continuity of states, demonstrating again the uncertainties prevailing in this area of public international law.

**133. State Succession and the Breakup of the Soviet Union.** The dissolution of the Soviet Union in 1991 provides a good example of the proposition that some factual situations involving the issue of state succession **(132)** cannot be easily subsumed under any specific legal form of succession.

When analyzing the problem of succession and continuity of states with regard to the Soviet Union one must first deal with the special case of the three Baltic republics, Estonia, Latvia, and Lithuania, which, absorbed by force into the Soviet Union in 1940 (annexations that were not recognized by some states), fifty years later reasserted themselves in the conditions of a deepening crisis in the Soviet state, declaring independence in 1990 (Lithuania) and 1991 (Estonia and Latvia). These three republics had effectively seceded from the Soviet Union even before its dissolution at the end of 1991 and their case must be treated as restoration of independence and statehood **(127)** which soon gained universal recognition **(116)**, including by the Soviet Union itself, and admission to the United Nations (UN). For those states which, like the United States (US), had never recognized the annexation of the Baltic republics into the Soviet Union in 1940, the three republics legally never lost statehood and therefore, following their rebirth, such states as the US simply resumed full diplomatic relations (which otherwise had continued in rather symbolic form after 1940) with each of the Baltic republics. Although some states have treated the restoration of the Baltic republics within the context of secession or dissolution, the republics do not regard themselves as successor states to the Soviet Union and consequently refused to be bound by Soviet treaties **(137)** and take over any debts and other international obligations **(136)** of the Soviet Union. However, some kind of final settlement of reciprocal claims between Russia and each of the Baltic republics must be agreed upon in the future. Whether the three republics should be treated as "newly independent states" under the 1978 Vienna Convention on Succession of States in respect of Treaties (17 ILM 1488 (1978)) and the 1983 Vienna Convention on Succession of States in respect of State Property, Archives and Debts (22 ILM 298 (1983)) is a debatable issue.

Insofar as the extinction of the Soviet Union is concerned, the agreement of 1991 (8 December) (the "Minsk Agreement") establishing the Commonwealth of Independent States (CIS) by the Russian Federation, Belarus and Ukraine declared that "the Union of the Soviet Socialist Republics as a subject of international law and a geopolitical reality no longer exists" (31 ILM 143 (1992)). Open for accession by all states members of the former Soviet Union, thirteen days later the Minsk Agreement was supplemented by the Alma Ata Protocol (31 ILM 147 (1992)) whereby eight more former Soviet republics joined the CIS. Georgia followed them in 1993, but the three Baltic republics remained outside of the Commonwealth. A Declaration (31 ILM 148 (1992)) accompanying the Protocol reiterated that with the establishment of the CIS which—as explicitly stated in the Declaration—is "neither a State nor a super-State entity," the Soviet Union ceased to exist. All these developments would indicate a case of dissolution or dismemberment. A state, the Soviet Union, becomes extinct, having entirely broken up into parts which become separate states themselves; hence all of them, including the Russian Federation, become the successor states of the Soviet Union, with none of them being a continuation of the extinct Soviet state. However, the Alma Ata Declaration on the extinction of the Soviet Union was complemented on the same day by a decision of the Council of Heads of State of the CIS, expressing those states' support for "Russia's continuance of the membership of the USSR in the United Nations, including permanent membership on the Security Council and other international organizations" (31 ILM 151 (1992)). Three days later, the President of the Russian Federation informed the UN Secretary-General in a letter about Russia's continuing the membership of the Soviet Union in the UN, including the Security Council (SC) and all other organs and organizations of the UN system, pledging to maintain "full responsibility to all the rights and obligations of the USSR under the Charter of the United Nations, including the financial obligations." In response, no formal action was forthcoming from the UN or its members, and in the euphoric atmosphere of the time Russia's continuance of the Soviet Union's membership was rather casually but pragmatically accepted by the UN without going through the proper admission procedure otherwise required of the other post-Soviet states, except that Ukraine and Byelorussia, original members of the UN, continued their respective membership status. As a result, while Art. 23 of the UN Charter remains unamended, still listing the Soviet Union as one of the five permanent members of the SC, the Russian Federation occupies the permanent seat as the continuation of the Soviet Union. In this regard, the Vienna Convention of 1978 on succession to treaties, while not in all respects declaratory of customary law, does reflect this law, leaving the issue of membership to the rules of the organization concerned.

The continuity between the Soviet Union and Russia was explicitly accepted only in respect of the latter's membership in international organizations. However, a concordant attitude of the successor states and recognition by the international community of this, internationally most important, element of the continuity of states, as well as the impact of Russia's status as the core and by far most important successor state, combined with Russia's assurances concerning honoring the Soviet debts and treaties, allow by implication to conclude that the Russian Federation is the legal continuation of the Soviet Union in general. Therefore the dissolution of the Soviet Union can be regarded as a unique case of dismemberment of a federal state, but with a universal acquiescence in the core state's claim as a continuation of the dissolved federation.

Upon the breakup of the Soviet Union, the issue of the continued maintenance in force by Russia and the other successor states of various arms control and security treaties became a major concern for the Western powers. The states participating in the CIS, including Russia, undertook in the agreement founding this organization and in the Alma Ata Declaration, to discharge the international obligations incumbent on them under treaties and agreements entered into by the former Soviet Union. In addition, for its part Russia reiterated this promise ("unilateral act") **(44)** to the heads of diplomatic missions **(62)** in Moscow, informing them also that it would perform the functions of depositary for the multilateral treaties of the former Soviet Union, and requesting that the Russian Federation be considered as a party to all international agreements in force in place of the Soviet Union.

Notwithstanding all the guarantees offered, it was not entirely certain to what extent the successor states would succeed to the treaty obligations of the extinct Soviet Union, an issue particularly relevant with regard to the nuclear successor states Belarus, Kazakhstan, and Ukraine. Following the conceptual framework of the above-mentioned 1978 Vienna Convention, if the successor states of the Soviet Union were treated as separating (seceding) states, the Soviet treaties would continue to bind them, but if, in addition, they were to be regarded as "newly independent states" (a term applied so far within the context of decolonization), they would not be bound by their predecessor's treaty obligations, entering statehood with a "clean state." As a matter of fact, some publicists, including those of the Restatement (Third) of 1987, reject the distinction of the 1978 Convention, believing that the clean slate approach should be applied to any new state.

Acceptance of all relevant commitments with regard to disarmament and nuclear non-proliferation as well as to security and regional stability was one of the requirements stipulated by the 1991 European Community (EC) Declaration on the Guidelines on the Recognition of New States in Eastern Europe and in the Soviet Union (31 ILM 1486 (1992)) **(107, 116)**. The three nuclear successor states undertook to honor the Soviet treaty commitments and, in a joint agreement (31 ILM 152 (1992) with the Russian Federation, adopted at the time of the official dissolution of the Soviet Union, agreed to accede **(267)** to the 1968 Treaty on the Non-Proliferation of Nuclear Weapons (729 UNTS 161) as non-nuclear states and to withdraw their tactical nuclear weapons to central bases for dismantling under joint control.

As far as succession to bilateral treaties is concerned, they became a subject of treaty-by-treaty review between the successor states and the third state concerned, as was for example the case of the validation of such treaties in relations between the US and Ukraine. Some of the treaties were declared no longer applicable while the continuance in force of others was confirmed by the two countries.

The dissolution of the Soviet Union gave rise to a number of succession problems in the areas other than treaties. According to the above-noted EC Guidelines, recognition of the successor states of the Soviet Union was made dependent on the fulfillment by them of the obligation to settle by agreement or—where appropriate—by arbitration **(293)** all questions concerning state succession and regional disputes. The EC members recognized these states on the assumption that that obligation would be met. In fact, Russia and the successor states signed agreements apportioning the state property and liabilities of the former Soviet Union, including its debts, with the Russian Federation's share amounting to 61.34 percent, that of Ukraine 16.37 percent, and the remainder to be paid by the other republics. However, the implementation of these agreements encountered resistance on the part of the successor republics which refused to assume their respective shares of the Soviet debts. Eventually, it appears that the Russian Federation became solely responsible for the debts while in return claiming all Soviet state property situated outside the former Soviet Union instead of dividing it in equitable proportion among all the republics.

**134. State Succession and the Breakup of Yugoslavia.** The breakup of the former Yugoslavia (Socialist Federated Republic of Yugoslavia (SFRY)) generated complex succession problems **(132)**, including a controversy concerning the legal nature of the event: was it a process of secession from the SFRY, with the continued existence of the former Yugoslavia in a rump form of only two republics (Serbia and Montenegro), or of dissolution of the SFRY whereby all its six republics would be equal successor states to the extinct SFRY?

In 1991 a series of ethnic civil wars broke out in the SFRY, setting in motion the process of disintegration of this federal state of six constituent republics: Bosnia and Herzegovina, Croatia, Macedonia, Montenegro, Serbia, and Slovenia, This process, noted in Opinion No. 1 of the Arbitration Commission set up by the European Community (EC) Conference on Yugoslavia in 1991 and consisting of five members chosen from the Presidents of Constitutional Courts in EC members states (named "Badinter Commission" after its French Chairman), was found by the Commission to have been completed by the time it issued Opinion No. 8 in July 1992 (31 ILM 1488, 1490–1526 (Opinions 1–10) (1992)). In the latter opinion it was stated that "the SFRY no longer exists." Specifically, in 1991 Slovenia and Croatia declared independence, followed by Bosnia and Herzegovina, and eventually Macedonia. The independent statehood of these four republics was recognized by other states, including, eventually, also by the state proclaimed in 1992 under the name of the Federal Republic of Yugoslavia (FRY), made up of two former republics of the SFRY: Serbia and Montenegro and now known as "Serbia and Montenegro." However, for several years no agreement on succession issues could be reached by the now five successor states because of the position of the FRY claiming that it was not a new state but the exclusive legal continuation of the SFRY from which—it asserted—the other four republics had seceded. Consequently, the FRY laid claims to all state property of its alleged predecessor, expressing willingness to share some of this property only on grounds of equity and goodwill. Also, in an agreement in 1996 the FRY and

Croatia "noted" the historical fact of the continuity of their respective state organizations (35 ILM 1220 (1996)). A similar agreement between the FRY and Macedonia promised to respect each other's state continuity (35 ILM 1247 (1996)).

The claim of the FRY was rejected both by the other four republics and the Arbitration (Badinter) Commission. In its Opinion No. 8, reaffirmed by Opinions 9 and 10, the Commission ruled that the breakup of the SFRY resulted in its dissolution as a result of which all the five post–Yugoslav states and not just the FRY were to be considered equal successors to the SFRY, continuing, under the principle of *uti possidetis* **(230)**, within the boundaries which they had had as the constituent republics of the former Yugoslavia. Following the same approach, but in a striking inconsistency with its position on the issue of Russia's succession to the Soviet Union **(133)**, the Security Council in Resolution 777 (1992) (31 ILM 1473 (1992)) "considered" that the FRY could not continue automatically the membership of the former SFRY in the United Nations (UN) and recommended to the General Assembly (GA) that it decide that the FRY should apply for membership in the UN and that "it shall not participate in the work of the General Assembly." However, until—after the Kosovo intervention and the change of the regime in the FRY—the FRY finally relinquished its claim to be the sole successor to the SFRY, applied for membership in the UN and was admitted in October 2000, the status of the FRY in the UN had rested in a rather indeterminate legal limbo, considering that the UN never terminated or suspended the membership of the former Yugoslavia. As noted by the UN Legal Counsel and by the International Court of Justice (ICJ) in the below-noted Order, its seat and nameplate in the GA remained as before, but in the GA bodies representatives of the FRY could not sit behind the sign "Yugoslavia." The status of Yugoslavia in the other organs of the UN was also not entirely clear. When in 1993 the ICJ **(309)** considered the request of Bosnia and Herzegovina for the indication of provisional measures **(322)** against Yugoslavia in the case of *Application of the Convention on the Prevention and Punishment of the Crime of Genocide* (Bosnia and Herzegovina v. Yugoslavia) in its Order (1993 ICJ Rep. 3) it did not consider it necessary or appropriate to determine Yugoslavia's status, finding the GA treatment of the Yugoslav question "not free from legal difficulties." Again in 1999 a majority of the ICJ held that it did not need to consider the question of Yugoslavia's status for the purpose of deciding on request for provisional measures in the cases concerning *Legality of Use of Force* brought by the FRY against ten North Atlantic Treaty Organization (NATO) states as a result of NATO's bombing of Yugoslavia (38 ILM 950 (1999)).

Efforts to achieve agreement on the issues of Yugoslav succession proceeded slowly, mainly because of the continued armed conflict and a fundamental disagreement on the nature of the succession event in question. In any event, the UN/EC International Conference on Former Yugoslavia (replacing the EC Conference) stressed the principle that any resolution of the succession questions should be based on the parties' agreement or arbitration. For its part, in 1993 the Arbitration Commission, in its Opinions Nos. 13 and 14 (32 ILM 1591, 1593 (1993)) endorsing the principle of agreement, previously stressed in the EC Guidelines of 1991 on the Recognition of new States in Eastern Europe and in the Soviet Union (31 ILM 1486 (1992)), recommended observance of the principle of equity and drawing on the solutions adopted in the Vienna Convention of 1983 which codified **(5)** state succession in respect of matters other than treaties **(136)**. Following the conclusion in 1995 of the Dayton Agreement on Implementing the Federation of Bosnia and Herzegovina (35 ILM 170 (1996)) and of the related Paris General Framework Agreement for Peace (35 ILM 75 (1996)), the London Peace Implementation Conference in its conclusions, 1995, decided, *inter alia*, that the succession issues concerning Yugoslavia would be among the functions of the designated High Representative (35 ILM 223 (1996)). The High Representative appointed a special negotiator to mediate **(313)** the succession issues of the five states, which eventually, in 2001, after the Kosovo War and the regime change in the FRY, brought, first, an agreement on the distribution of the assets of the former SFRY held at the Bank for International Settlements (BIS) and then the Agreement on Succession Issues between the Five Successor States of the Former State of Yugoslavia, 2001 (41 ILM 3 (2002)) which also incorporated the BIS agreement. However, certain succession issues had been resolved outside of the main process. Thus all the five states accepted the International Monetary Fund (IMF) apportioning of the SFRY assets and liabilities in the Fund according to a key later adopted for purposes of the BIS; various financial liabilities of the SFRY had been dealt with by the successor states (except the FRY) in bilateral agreements with Western creditors; nationality questions **(174, 175)** became subject to regulation by the municipal law **(27)** of each successor state; and succession to the treaties of the SFRY was decided by each of these states, with special emphasis on the obligation to confirm the multilateral human rights of the predecessor state.

The 2001 Agreement definitively and finally settles the rights and obligations of the five states which are "in sovereign equality" the successors states to the former SFRY, covering, in seven annexes to the body of the Agreement, the following issues: movable and immovable property; diplomatic and consular properties, with a detailed list of properties allocated to each of the five states; financial assets and liabilities; archives; pensions; other rights, interests, and liabilities, such as, *inter alia*, patents, royalties, and debts owed to the former SFRY; and private property and acquired rights. The provisions of the Agreement rely in general on the principles articulated in the 1983 Vienna Convention on Succession of States in Respect of State Property, Archives and Debts (22 ILM 306 (1983)) which otherwise has been signed and ratified only by a handful of states. The Agreement recognizes equity **(13)** as a guiding principle for the distribution of assets and liabilities, stressing in particular nondiscriminatory protection of private and acquired rights. It also includes provisions on the protection of the national cultural heritage of the states involved. Its rules on the distribution of financial assets and liabilities reflect the influence of international organizations **(84)**, such as the IMF, in the shaping of the international law governing important succession issues.

**135. State Succession and the Unification of Germany.** The unification of Germany in 1990 represents a case of absorption or incorporation of one state **(127)**, the German Democratic Republic (GDR), into another, the Federal Republic of Germany (FRG). Following the integration of the GDR into the monetary, economic, and social system of the FRG by a treaty in May 1990 (29 ILM 1108 (1990)), the FRG-GDR Treaty on the Establishment of German Unity (the Unification Treaty) signed in August of the same year (30 ILM 457 (1991)) explicitly stipulated the assimilation of the GDR into the FRG in accordance with Art. 23 of the Basic Law (Constitution) of the latter, which provides for the application of the law of the FRG to other parts of Germany upon their joining the FRG. As a result, on 3 October 1990, the GDR became extinct, while the FRG has continued its identity, with its territory enlarged to include the provinces of the former GDR as new *Länder* of the Federal Republic of Germany. A separate Treaty on the Final Settlement with Respect to Germany (29 ILM 1186 (1990)), previously signed (in Moscow) in September of the same year by the two German states and the four Powers (France, Soviet Union, United Kingdom, and the United States (US)), settled all the problems still remaining in the aftermath of World War II, including the finality of the borders **(189)**, questions of weapons and armed forces, renunciation by Germany of weapons of mass destruction, termination of the responsibilities of the four allied Powers, and restoration of full sovereignty **(125)** of the united Germany over its internal and external affairs.

As a result of the absorption of the East German state into the FRG, the treaties **(288)** of the former were terminated and those of the latter became applicable to the territory of the former GDR (the "moving treaty frontier"), as provided by Art. 11 of the Unification Treaty. However, Annex I to the Treaty excluded from this extension certain agreements relating primarily to North Atlantic Treaty Organization activities. The future status of certain other agreements of the former GDR was to be determined following a review in consultation with the parties concerned and—if necessary—the EC. In the matter of treaties establishing international organizations **(84)**, such as the United Nations Charter, the FRG simply continued as Germany, but refused to assume responsibility for the outstanding contributions of the GDR to some peacekeeping operations **(334)**. The succession in respect of matters other than treaties **(136)** was regulated in detail in the Unification Treaty. Of special interest is the assumption by the FRG of the East German national debt to be served by a special fund. Numerous claims for compensation or return of property became a subject of international agreements, including also an agreement between the FRG and the US of 1992 concerning claims filed by US nationals **(95)**.

**136. State Succession in Respect of Matters Other Than Treaties.** The legal consequences of state succession **(132)** in respect of matters other than treaties **(288)**, such as the title to state property, responsibility for the public debts and other obligations of the predecessor state, its archives, and the nationality **(175)** of the population concerned, are normally settled by agreement between the parties involved. As stated in Opinion No. 14 of the Arbitration Commission of the Conference on Peace in Yugoslavia, 1993 (32 ILM 1593 (1993)), "the first principle applicable to state succession is that the successor states should consult each other and agree on a settlement of all questions relating to the succession." Such agreements were recently concluded for example by the Czech Republic and Slovakia after their split in 1993 and by the five successor states (including the Federal Republic of Yugoslavia) of the Socialist Federal Republic of Yugoslavia, which regulated most matters of succession in their agreement in 2001 **(134)**. On the merits, such agreements should be based on the principle of equitable distribution of assets and liabilities. If no treaty solution has been reached, the succession questions are governed by the rather unsettled rules of customary international law **(39)**. The controversial Vienna Convention on Succession of States in Respect of State Property, Archives and Debts of 1983 (22 ILM 306 (1983)) is not yet in force (by 2002 it was signed and ratified by only a handful of states) and is not likely to enter into effect in the foreseeable future. Otherwise, its provisions would for the most part be applied only in the absence of an agreement of the parties concerned.

It is an established rule of international law that state property belonging to the predecessor state passes without compensation to the successor state or states as the case may be. The distinction between immovable and movable property is a basic one in the allocation of the predecessor state's property. Immovable property of the predecessor state, defined as public property by its law, passes to the successor state concerned. Immovable property located abroad remains with the predecessor state, but in case of its extinction it passes to the successor or to the successors in equitable proportions. Without referring to the possibility of an agreement, the 1983 Vienna Convention establishes a special regime for "newly independent states," going beyond existing customary law. Its controversial rules provide that such states (in practice, former overseas colonies of Western powers) acquire not only the immovable state property located in the territory but also such immovable property as belonged to the territory but is situated outside it and had become state property in the colonial period, and in addition, external immovable property of the predecessor state if the dependent territory in question had contributed to its creation, in which case such property passes to the newly independent state in proportion to the dependent territory's contribution.

Movable property connected with the activity of the predecessor state, such as state funds, passes to the successor state. In practice, only agreement can establish the identity of such property in borderline cases. In general, external assets pass in their entirety to the successor state only in case of absorption, as happened in the unification of Germany **(135)**. In cases of secession from, or dissolution of the predecessor state into new states, the external assets are to be divided in equitable proportions.

State archives represent an important asset reflecting a state's past and the community's heritage. In cases of succession their fate would normally be regulated by treaties dealing with the transfer of territorial sovereignty **(227)**. However, archives clauses were not common in agreements concluded within the context of succession involving newly independent states. Under the 1983 Convention, state archives exclusively or principally relating to the transferred territory and those needed to a normal administration of the newly independent state pass to it without any compensation.

Succession to public debt, including the debt owed by the state as such, localized debt contracted by the central government in a local interest, and local debt incurred by an administrative subdivision of the state, belongs to the most unsettled and uncertain issues in the law of state succession. Thus, it is a controversial matter whether the rules governing succession to public debt apply to debts held by private persons as well as by other states and international organizations, such as the World Bank or the International Monetary Fund. Whereas in the prevailing view of the doctrine, including a majority of the International Law Commission (ILC), private debts are transferable, under the 1983 Convention (Art. 33) state debts are debts owed by the predecessor state to a state, an international organization **(84)** or any other subject of international law. There is only a negative formulation (Art. 6) that nothing in the Convention "shall be considered as prejudging in any respect any question relating to the rights and obligations of natural and juridical persons." The implicit exclusion of debts owed to private persons has been a major reason for many Western states' refusal to sign the Convention. Generally speaking and always considering the element of equitable distribution, in cases of a transfer of a part of the territory of a state, local public debt is taken over by the successor state. In cases of total absorption (such as the unification of Germany) the entire public debt passes to the absorbing state. Likewise, upon a merger of states the debt of the predecessor states passes to their successor. Similarly upon dissolution or secession (separation), the debt is expected to be taken over in equitable proportion. However, under the 1983 Vienna Convention, a succeeding "newly independent state" is privileged in that it does not acquire the state debts of its predecessor, and any agreement to the contrary must not infringe the principle of permanent sovereignty of every people over its natural resources or endanger the new state's economic equilibrium. It is interesting that in drafting this provision the ILC invoked the fact of the United States (US) refusal to succeed to any indebtedness of Great Britain after the Revolutionary War of Independence. In fact, state practice provides a number of historical instances of similar refusal, such as Panama's refusal to succeed to debts of Colombia from which it seceded in 1903 and Germany's refusal to take over the debt of Austria upon the *Anschluss* in 1938. On the other hand, in some other cases, liabilities of the predecessor were taken over by the successor states and apportioned by agreement according to equitable principles, for instance, the debts of the Habsburg Empire in the aftermath of its disintegration, the debts of Great Britain assumed by the Irish Free State by agreement in 1921, and—more recently—the debts of the SFRY taken over by the five successor states under the Agreement of 2001. It should be noted that state practice tends to recognize the right of a successor state to refuse taking over the so-called odious debts, that is, debts contracted by the predecessor state contrary to the fundamental interests of the successor state which in all fairness cannot be expected to take them over. For example, a state born through a secessionist war **(340)** cannot be bound to assume liabilities contracted by the hostile "parent" state for the purpose of financing an armed conflict against it. The 1983 Convention does not deal with this issue of non-transferability of odious debts.

Whether a successor state is obligated to take over and recognize private claims resulting from contracts or concessions or liabilities for delicts (torts) of the predecessor state, is also an unsettled issue, related to the concept of "acquired rights," presuming the continuation of the rights of foreign nationals acquired from the predecessor state in the territory transferred to a successor state. The doctrine of acquired rights was endorsed by the Permanent Court of International Justice **(320)** in a series of decisions, and in particular its Advisory Opinion **(291)** on the *German Settlers in Poland* (1923 PCIJ, Series B, No. 6) where it held that "private rights acquired under existing law do not cease on a change of sovereignty." However, the doctrine of acquired rights, mainly in respect of debts and concessions granted by a predecessor state to individuals or companies to operate an enterprise or providing a public utility, has not been universally accepted in state practice. The old (1905) case of *West Rand Central Gold Mining Co., Ltd. v. The King* (1905 2 K.B. 391) is usually quoted in support of the thesis that a successor state is under no international law obligation to respect contractual obligations of the predecessor state entered into with private persons. But this case, concerning refusal by Great Britain to respect a gold mining concession granted by the South African Republic subsequently succeeded (by conquest) **(194)** by Great Britain, involved a British company and to that extent—apart from the court's comments on the international law aspects of the matter—pertains more to determining municipal law **(27)** rather than international. The recent Western practice and doctrine tend to support the view that concession contracts made in good faith and involving substantial investments by a foreign company should be binding on the successor state. On the other hand, newly independent states have often repudiated contracts and concessions **(179)** of their respective colonial powers on the grounds of the clean slate approach applied in succession to international agreements **(137)**. The 2001 Agreement on succession to the former Yugoslavia, which obligates the five successor states to respect acquired rights of private persons, made an important contribution to the emergence of a rule of customary international law **(39)** on respecting the contractual rights acquired by private persons under the law of the predecessor state.

Whether the successor state is liable for obligations of the predecessor state arising out of international torts (delicts) is controversial in international law. Arbitration decisions in cases that originated in the colonial era, such as the *Robert E. Brown Claim* (US v. United Kingdom (UK)) (6 RIAA 120

(1923)), involving the issue of the succession of the UK to a denial of justice **(152)** claim of a US national against the South African Republic, held that the extinction of the state involved terminated such claims; hence a successor state was not liable for unliquidated damages for the torts (delicts) of the extinct state and other wrongful acts, including breaches of contract. However, in a more recent case (1956), the *Lighthouses Arbitration* (France v. Greece), an arbitral tribunal, set up within the framework of the Permanent Court of Arbitration **(319)**, held Greece liable for payments resulting from the breach of a concession contract of the predecessor state (12 RIAA 155 (1956)), expressing doubts concerning the existence of any general rule of international law denying succession to liability for wrongs inflicted upon individuals. The contemporary doctrine in the West tends to follow the view that fairness requires that a successor state should be liable for the wrongs of its predecessor at least to the extent of preventing the successor state's unjust enrichment by a wrongful act of the predecessor.

Concerning expropriation **(145)**, under traditional international law state succession does not affect the property rights of private persons. If the owner adopts the nationality **(175)** of the successor state, the right of that state to expropriate his property is limited only by the rules of the international human rights law **(160)**. In cases of property owned by a national of the predecessor state or of a third state, the right to expropriate is subject to the relevant rules of international law governing the treatment of aliens **(144)**. However, in both situations, a number of Third World states, such as Zimbabwe, claiming colonial exploitation, affirm the right to expropriate private property inherited from the colonial era in disregard of the international law rules governing compensation **(118)**.

There are no clear rules on international law concerning acquisition and loss of nationality of individuals upon state succession. The topic was on the agenda of the ILC, which emphasized the right of individuals to nationality as a human right **(157)** and the obligation of states to prevent statelessness **(181)** and other potentially detrimental effects that may arise upon the transfer of sovereignty over a territory. In practice, the matters relating to nationality are frequently dealt with by agreements of the states concerned. Otherwise, as a general rule, the nationality of the inhabitants of the affected territory changes to that of the successor state. Thus in cases of separation (secession) and transfer of a part of a state's territory, the succeeding state normally confers its nationality upon the residents and possibly other persons specifically defined in its law, but, as a rule, there must be some genuine link between the individuals concerned and the territory. A successor state may also give the inhabitants an option to retain their original nationality, which under the circumstances may result in dual nationality **(174)**. In case of absorption or merger the nationality of the extinct predecessor state ceases to exist and it is up to the domestic law of the successor state to determine the conditions for acquiring its nationality by the inhabitants. The successor state is probably bound under international law to provide for the possibility of acquiring its nationality by those individuals who reside in the territory in question or have some other genuine link with it. However, nationality may not be imposed upon those who are not willing to be subject to the sovereignty **(125)** of the absorbing state. In this regard, a US Circuit Court of Appeals ruled in 1943 (*US ex rel. Schwarzkopf v. Uhl*) (1943, 137 F (2d) 898) that an Austrian national residing in the US during Nazi Germany's *Anschluss* of Austria in 1938 had not, against his will, acquired German nationality imposed upon Austrians by a German collective naturalization **(176)** decree.

Following dissolution (dismemberment) of a state, its nationality ceases to exist and—as in cases of absorption and merger—each successor state determines, in its sovereign territory, the nationality of the former nationals of the dismembered state.

**137. State Succession in Respect of Treaties.** Subject to any contrary agreement of the states involved, succession **(132)** to treaty **(288)** rights and obligations upon a change in territorial sovereignty is governed by customary law **(39)**. As of 2003, the 1978 Vienna Convention on the Succession of States in Respect of Treaties (17 ILM 1488 (1978)) was not yet in force. Except for a few controversial points, in particular the dubious distinction between "newly independent states" and states resulting from separation, the Convention is generally regarded as declaratory of the existing customary international law on the subject. While, except as otherwise agreed, the Convention applies only with respect to successions taking place after its entry into force **(271)**, there is a possibility to apply it in earlier cases with the agreement of the states involved (Art. 7). A so-called devolution agreement, that is, an agreement between the predecessor state and the successor state providing for the obligations and rights of the former to pass ("devolve") on to the latter, does not by itself affect the rights of third parties (Art. 8). A similar rule applies to a unilateral declaration by a successor state regarding treaties of its predecessor, providing for the continuance in force of the treaties in respect of the territory in question (Art. 8).

In the interests of international stability, the so-called dispositive or localized treaties which establish special territorial regimes are not affected by a succession of states. Here belong treaties establishing boundaries **(189)** and their regimes, and other international legal regimes which are permanently attached to a specific territory, such as those concerning demilitarization, transit, or river navigation. Treaties establishing such regimes continue in force for the successor state or states, except for treaty obligations of the predecessor state providing for the establishment of foreign military bases on the territory in question (Art. 12). However, whereas the Convention does not mandate in positive mandatory "shall" terms the continuance of dispositive treaties, Art. 13 provides that nothing in the Convention shall affect the principles of international law affirming the permanent sovereignty of every people and every state over its natural wealth and resources. This rule, adopted in the interests of the newly independent states, seems to make it possible for such states to override the obligation to continue the application of any localized treaty.

The principle that localized treaties bind successor states is of fundamental significance with respect to treaties establishing boundaries and is related to the principle of *uti possidetis* **(230)** mandating the obligation to respect pre-existing international borders in succession cases. Initially applied in settling territorial disputes in the aftermath of decolonization, first in Latin America and then, more recently, in Africa, this principle has been recognized as binding by the International Court of Justice **(309)** in such cases as *Frontier Dispute* (Burkina Faso/Republic of Mali) (1986 ICJ Rep. 554), a case referred to a Chamber **(295)**, and *Territorial Dispute* (Libya/Chad) (1994 ICJ Rep. 37). In the 1990s the principle was extended beyond the decolonization situations to the creation of new states as a result of the breakup of the Soviet Union **(133)**, the former Yugoslavia **(134)**, and Czechoslovakia. In all these cases these federal successor states agreed to continue the boundaries of the previous constituent republics, transformed into international frontiers. In this connection, the European Community Arbitration Commission of the Conference on Yugoslavia in its Opinion No. 2 stressed the need to respect the territorial *status quo* according to the principle of *uti possidetis* whereby, "whatever the circumstances, even the right of self-determination **(122)** must not involve changes to existing frontiers at the time of independence" (31 ILM 1497 (1992)), a position further developed by the Commission in its Opinion No. 3 (31 ILM 1499 (1992)).

Unless otherwise agreed by the parties and subject to the continued validity for successor states of the dispositive treaties, and—according to the contemporary trends—human rights treaties **(160)**, as well as subject to consistency of the succession event with international law, succession with respect to treaties in various types of the succession situation is governed by the following rules. If only a part of a state's territory **(228)** changes sovereignty (**125**) the treaties of the predecessor state cease to have effect in respect of that territory and those of the successor state enter into effect there (the "moving treaty frontier") unless the application of the successor state's treaties would be incompatible with the object or purpose of the treaty or would radically change the conditions for their operation. In cases of absorption, as illustrated by the reunification of Germany **(135)**, the treaties of the absorbed state are terminated while those of the absorbing state are extended to the territory of the absorbed state. Following a merger of two or more states which produces one successor state, possibly a federation **(77)**, the treaties of the predecessor states continue within the respective parts of the successor state.

The legal consequences of succession in case of secession (separation) are more controversial. Whereas state practice has traditionally tended to follow the clean slate approach whereby a newly created state need not succeed to the treaties of its predecessor, the Vienna Convention of 1978 makes a distinction between "newly independent states," that is, successor states, in practice former overseas colonies, "the territory of which immediately before the date of the succession of States was a dependent territory for the international relations of which the predecessor State was responsible" (Art. 2(1)), and states separated in a non-colonial context. Under the Convention, the clean slate principle applies only to newly independent states (Art. 16). On the other hand, successor states in a noncolonial situation must normally follow the principle of the continuity of treaties (Art. 34), being bound by the treaties of their predecessor states, a rule that does not reflect the existing customary law.

During the decolonization era the newly independent states followed a variety of paths in the matter of succession to treaties. Some applied the clean slate principle; others, and especially former British territories, would explicitly assume the rights and obligations under the predecessor state's treaties in a devolution agreement. A number of African countries allowed the treaties to continue for an interim period pending a revision (the "Nyerere formula," named after Tanganyika's President). Some states unilaterally declared which of the predecessor colonial power's treaties they would continue, and still others would defer the decision, preferring to deal with the problem on a case-by-case basis. Under the Vienna Convention of 1978 (Art. 17), a newly independent state may succeed to a multilateral treaty by notifying its decision to the depositary of the treaty, but the application of the treaty in question by that state may not be incompatible with the object and purpose of the treaty or cause a radical change in the conditions for its operation. Succession to a bilateral treaty requires consent of the other party and, of course, of the successor state.

State practice is not consistent on the issue of succession to treaties following a break-up of a state into two or more states, except that ordinarily treaties of a political nature are terminated. The Convention of 1978 (Art. 38) provides for the predecessor's treaties to continue in force in respect of each of the successor states, subject to the consent of the states concerned and the above-mentioned conditions concerning compatibility and possible radical change. When in 1992 the Czech and Slovak Federal Republic decided to split up as of 1993, the two successor states undertook each to continue all treaties to which their predecessor was a party and, where appropriate, to negotiate on the fate of specific treaties with third parties.

One aspect of state succession with respect to treaties pertains to the question whether a successor state becomes a member of an international organization **(84)** by virtue of the predecessor state's membership or must apply for admission as a new member according to the rules in force. The Vienna Convention of 1978, which also applies to treaties creating such organizations, leaves the problem to the decision of the organization concerned. In practice, international organizations, including the United Nations (UN), require new states resulting through secession or dissolution to apply for membership, as was required by the UN of Pakistan in 1947 when it split from India which, however, retained its legal identity and membership. When Singapore withdrew from Malaysia in 1965, it also had to go through the regular UN admission procedure. The same approach was followed with respect to the states resulting from the dissolution of Yugoslavia. However, inconsistent with this practice, upon the dissolution of the Soviet Union, Russia was accepted by all international organizations as a continuation of the Soviet Union whereas the other former Soviet republics (except Belarus and Ukraine, which are the original members of the UN and other organizations) had to undergo the regular admission procedure. When in 1958 Egypt and Syria merged to form the United Arab Republic, the UN treated the new entity as a single member, with Syria disappearing from the UN membership roster. Upon the dissolution of this short-lived union in 1961, Syria resumed its membership without any new admission procedure. The merger of the two Yemens in 1990 resulted in the replacement of the two predecessor states in international organizations by one Republic of Yemen as their successor.

**138. Status-of-Forces Agreement.** A bilateral or multilateral international agreement **(288)** allocating the right to exercise jurisdiction **(87)** between the receiving and the sending state over the latter's military forces present in the receiving state during peacetime. In customary international law **(39)**, the status of a state's armed forces present for various reasons in the territory **(228)** of another state in peacetime, whether in passage or on a long-term basis, is not an entirely settled issue. Historically, the United States Supreme Court's decision in the case of *Schooner Exchange v. McFaddon* (8 Cranch 116 (1812)) was used by some publicists in support of the sovereign immunity **(131)** of foreign land forces exercising the right of passage granted by a state or stationed in a specific base area, or even foreign armed forces stationed in a state in general. But such views of extraterritoriality allowing a sending state wide powers of jurisdiction over its military forces in the receiving state is rejected in the contemporary doctrine and state practice as conflicting with the fundamental principles of territorial jurisdiction **(91)**. Whereas a receiving state may exercise jurisdiction over offenses committed by members of foreign armed forces outside their bases, it appears to be generally recognized that the sending state has exclusive jurisdiction over internal disciplinary matters of the forces, including offenses committed by a member of the forces against another member and offenses by the forces' members committed in the performance of their official duties. However, in some situations, for example breaches of the local law in the base area by members of the foreign armed forces, it is not clear whose jurisdiction applies in the case, and frequently the right to exercise jurisdiction is concurrent. But the exercise of civil jurisdiction in most situations belongs to the receiving state.

To avoid uncertainties of customary law, states have frequently relied on treaty arrangements regulating the legal status of foreign forces, and in particular the allocation of jurisdiction between the receiving and the sending state. Among many agreements of this kind the multilateral North Atlantic Treaty Organization (NATO) Status of Forces Agreement of 1951 (139 UNTS 67) has been the most important in influencing the contents of other similar agreements, perhaps even contributing to an eventual emergence of the customary law on this subject.

The NATO Agreement of 1951 follows the general scheme of granting the sending state exclusive criminal jurisdiction over all persons subject to its military law who commit offenses punishable by the law of the sending state but not by that of the receiving state. On the other hand, the latter state has exclusive jurisdiction to punish any offenses committed by a member of the visiting force or its civilian personnel which are breaches of its law but not of the law of the sending state. In the large area of concurrent jurisdiction, the Agreement provides rules to decide which of the states has a primary right to jurisdiction. Thus, the sending state has primary jurisdiction if the act concerned constitutes an offense solely against its property or security or against a person or property of another member of the force or civilian component of the sending state, or an offense arising out of any act or omission done in performance of an official duty. The receiving state has the primary right to exercise jurisdiction over any other offenses. However, both states may waive their respective right to exercise the primary right of jurisdiction. Special provisions of the Agreement regulate the question of the settlement of claims arising out of the presence of foreign troops in the receiving state.

The United Nations (UN) has concluded a number of agreements regulating the status of UN forces present in a country. National contingents engaged in various kinds of "peacekeeping" operations **(334)** are under the command of the UN in whose name they act, but for certain purposes, such as internal discipline, continue to be subject to their respective national laws and regulations. Under the UN status of forces agreements, the territorial state concerned has limited jurisdiction in civil matters, but in criminal matters jurisdiction over members of the UN forces is allocated to the home state concerned. Under the Military Technical Agreement of 2002 (Annex A) between the International Security Assistance Force (ISAF), which, though endorsed by the Security Council, is not a UN operation, and the Interim Administration of Afghanistan (41 ILM 1032 (2002)) the ISAF and its personnel were made subject in respect of any criminal or disciplinary offenses to the exclusive jurisdiction of their respective national elements, enjoying also the status of experts on mission under the 1946 Convention on the Privileges and Immunities of the UN **(102)**.

**139. Taiwan, Legal Status of.** A political entity resembling a *de facto* state **(127)**, whose government is not claiming statehood for the entity as such under international law but (at least still in 2003) considers itself the government of the whole of China. The island of Taiwan (formerly known as Formosa) was ceded by China to Japan in 1895. Following World War II Japan renounced all rights to the island in the San Francisco Treaty of Peace of 1951 (136 UNTS 45) to which, however, neither the Soviet Union nor China were parties. As a result of the victory of the Communist regime in mainland China, the People's Republic of China claims Taiwan as part of the Chinese territory, but in fact the island is still governed by the competing nationalist regime which, as the "Republic of China," exercises full control over Taiwan and a few small islands off the Chinese coast. Both the government established in Taiwan and the Beijing government agree that the island constitutes part of China, a position either recognized or acquiesced in by other states. Thus, in the prevailing view, Taiwan is legally a Chinese province, although a minority opinion believes that the legal status of Taiwan remains unclear even following the renunciation by Japan of all claims to the island in 1952.

The nationalist government in Taiwan, which still lays no official claim to a separate statehood for the island, continues to be recognized **(114)** by a small number of states (about two dozen), some of them lured by financial incentives offered by this government. However, a great majority of states recognize the Beijing government as the government of the whole of China, especially since 1971 when its representatives replaced the nationalists in the United Nations and all its bodies and agencies. The United States (US), which for years had been the main supporter of the "Republic of China," recognized the Beijing government as the sole legal government of China, withdrawing its recognition of the nationalist government as of January 1979 (18 ILM 272 (1979)). The US also gave notice of termination **(287)** of its mutual defense treaty of 1954 with the nationalist government, an action unsuccessfully challenged in a US court (19 ILM 239 (1980)). However, in order to spare the government in Taiwan the adverse consequences of derecognition **(117)**, the US has continued to maintain economic and cultural relations with the Taiwan regime through an arrangement involving a nonprofit corporation known as the American Institute in Taiwan. Under the pertinent US legislation, the Taiwan Relations Act, 1979 (18 ILM 873 (1979)), the government in Taiwan is allowed to own property in the US, to sue and be sued in the US, and, in the application of US laws referring or relating to foreign countries, to be treated as before 1979. For its part, Taiwan maintains an agency in the US, known as the Taipei Economic and Cultural Representative, with offices in Washington, DC and some other cities in the US.

**140. Transnational Corporation.** Also known as multinational corporations, the so-called transnational corporations or TNCs (strictly speaking, not a legal term) are profit-making enterprises, as a rule, private entities, established under municipal law **(27)**, which conduct business in two or more countries through foreign subsidiaries or branches loosely linked together by ties of ownership, integrated policy, and managerial control by a parent corporation. Transnational corporations own and/or control production or service facilities outside the state of incorporation, but their foreign activities may be limited to investments in enterprises abroad. A transnational corporation does not have a special status in international law. Like an ordinary corporation **(174)**, each corporate unit is treated according to the domestic law either of the state of incorporation or the state where the corporate management has its headquarters (*siège social*).

Although enterprises of the TNC category have been known for some time, it is the decades following World War II that witnessed a rapid proliferation of such entities in numerous branches of industry, services, and other areas of economic life. This phenomenon, on the one hand, contributed to the internationalization of the world economy and the spread of technical know-how but, on the other hand, made the TNCs a focus of criticism and controversy because of their tremendous economic assets, surpassing the wealth of many a developing country, and the related possibilities of political influence.

The complexity and flexibility of the intercorporate arrangements and operations of TNCs make it difficult both for the home and the host state to monitor their activities and, in general, exercise an effective legal authority over such enterprises. Especially during the Cold War era the perception of the TNCs in the developing countries was often rather negative, such enterprises being charged with interference in the politics of their host countries, tax evasion, pollution of the environment, and corrupt business practices. It is primarily for all these reasons that a number of attempts were made to regulate the conduct of TNCs and define their rights and duties in relation to their respective host and home states. Foremost among such recommendatory soft law **(35)** acts was the proposed Draft Code of Conduct on Transnational Corporations, negotiated for some fifteen years under the auspices of the United Nation's Commission on Transnational Corporations (22 ILM 177 (1983); 23 ILM 602 (1984)).

With the end of the Cold War and a decline of socialist-type economies, the political controversy surrounding the TNCs lost much of its significance as various developing states adopted a more favorable attitude toward them and foreign private direct investment in general. The Guidelines on the Treatment of Foreign Direct Investment, prepared in 1992 by the World Bank Group (International Bank for Reconstruction and Development, International Finance Corporation, International Center for Settlement of Investment Disputes (ICSID) **(307)**, and Multilateral Investment Guarantee Agency) and the International Monetary Fund (31 ILM 1379 (1992)) reflected this more positive attitude toward the treatment of the TNCs. Efforts to develop some kind of code of conduct for such entities are likely to continue. Should eventually a code be adopted that, in a treaty **(288)** form, directly conferred upon the TNCs rights as against the host state and imposed duties upon such corporations, they would to that extent be endowed with a limited international personality **(85)**. However, states are reluctant to upgrade the TNCs to such an internationally elevated status, preferring to treat them like other private-law corporations. The conclusion of an "internationalized" contract between a state and a foreign corporation, whereby the parties agree that the transaction in question should be governed by public international law or general principles of law **(38)** rather than municipal law, does not necessarily result in the creation of international legal personality for the corporation involved. Granting a TNC (or an individual for that matter) access to an international tribunal or a similar body is possible under a treaty, as in the case of the ICSID or the Iran–United States Claims Tribunal **(312)**. The legal standing of corporations and individuals before the European Court of Justice **(298)** is a special case in view of the unique nature of the European Community law.

**141. Trieste, The Free Territory of.** Of historical interest, the Free Territory of Trieste was envisaged as a solution to the territorial dispute between Italy and Yugoslavia in the aftermath of World War II. Under Articles 21 and 22 of the Peace Treaty with Italy (49 and 50 UNTS) Italy's sovereignty over the Trieste area was terminated and a Free Territory with a permanent statute approved by the Security Council (SC) was established. The Territory was demilitarized and declared permanently neutral, with no armed forces allowed without the approval of the SC. Due to Cold War tensions the Statute was never implemented, the SC being unable to agree upon the appointment of the Territory's governor. However, following the outbreak of an open feud between Tito's Yugoslavia and Stalin's Soviet Union, a possibility opened up for a peaceful agreement between Italy and Yugoslavia. In 1954 these two countries adopted a "practical arrangement" whereby the disputed Territory was divided between them, with endorsement by the United States and the United Kingdom and the post-Stalin Soviet Union acquiescence. The partition of the Territory was eventually finalized by a treaty between Italy and Yugoslavia. Like the Free City of Danzig **(60)**, to which it bore resemblance, the proposed Free Territory of Trieste is sometimes counted among "internationalized" territories which historically included in the 19th century "the Republic of Cracow" (1815–1846) under the protectorate of the three powers which had partitioned the former Kingdom of Poland (Austria, Prussia, and Russia), and in the 20th century the Saar Territory (1920–1924, 1947–1954), the Memel Territory (1920–1924), and the International Zone of Tangier (1923–1953). The abortive General Assembly plan of 1947 for an internationalization of Jerusalem could also be regarded as an attempt to create an international regime for a territory.

**142. Trusteeship System.** The successor of the League of Nations' mandate system **(93)**, whose motivations and objectives it followed, the international trusteeship system was a United Nations (UN) institution under Chapters XII and XIII of the UN Charter, whereby certain categories of territories were placed under this system by means of General Assembly (GA)–approved trusteeship agreements for the administration and supervision of specific trust territories in order to promote the inhabitants' human rights **(157)** and their political, economic, social, and educational advancement, and the development of the territories toward self-government or independence according to the freely expressed wishes of the inhabitants.

The legal status of the trust territories was very much like that of the League of Nations' mandates. The trusteeship system was applicable to: former mandates; territories detached from the defeated states as a result of World War II; and any territory (practically speaking, a colony) voluntarily placed under the system by the administering power, an event that never occurred. Under the UN Charter, one or more states or even the UN as such (an arrangement that never happened) could be the administering authority of a trust territory. Except for South Africa (the mandatory state for the former German South-West Africa), all mandatory states placed their respective mandated territories under the trusteeship system, with Nauru administered by Australia in accordance with an agreement with the three former mandatory states (United Kingdom, Australia, and New Zealand). The Somaliland, detached from the defeated Italy, was entrusted to Italy, at the time a non-member of the UN. Exceptionally, this trusteeship agreement specified a definite period for the duration of the trusteeship (10 years).

A unique feature of the international trusteeship system was the establishment, for reasons of defense as viewed in the early post-war period, of a strategic trust area under the supervision of the Security Council (SC) and not the GA as was the case of the other trust territories. The strategic trust area included the formerly Japanese mandated islands in the Pacific, administered in four districts (Northern Mariana Islands, Federated States of Micronesia, the Marshall Islands, and Palau) by the United States under an agreement approved by the SC in 1947.

The supervision of the ordinary trust territories was in the hands of the Trusteeship Council (one of the six principal organs of the UN), acting under the authority of the GA and consisting of member states administering trust territories, those members of the SC that did not administer any of them, and as many states elected by the GA for a period of three years as was necessary to ensure equal membership number between the administering and non-administering members, a provision of the Charter that became inapplicable already in 1968 with the diminishing number of the administering states. Eventually, by the early 1990s all the trust territories became independent states and the Trusteeship Council lost—at least for now—its *raison d'être* and became *de facto* extinct.

The issue of South-West Africa, now of historical interest, was a unique and lengthy chapter related to the history of the League of Nations' mandates and the UN trusteeship system, which for decades absorbed the attention of the principal organs of the UN, including innumerable resolutions of the SC and the GA and the involvement of the International Court of Justice **(309)**, which handed down four advisory opinions **(291)** and two judgments **(297)** pertaining to South-West Africa (Namibia). This long-drawn conflict between South Africa and the UN was caused by the former mandatory power's persistent refusal to place South-West Africa under the trusteeship system, eventually leading to the termination of the mandate by the GA and condemnation of the illegal presence of South Africa in the former mandated territory. The conflict was not resolved until 1990 when after prolonged negotiations South-West Africa, renamed Namibia, became an independent state and a member of the UN.

# Chapter III
# Individuals, Human Rights

**143. African Charter of Human and Peoples' Rights (Banjul Charter).** A treaty adopted in 1981 (21 ILM 58 (1982)), in force 1986, under the aegis of the former Organization of African Unity (OAU), which provides the legal basis for the African system for the protection and promotion of human rights **(157)**. Virtually all African states are parties to this treaty, commonly known as the Banjul Charter. In 1990 the OAU complemented the 1981 Charter by adopting a Charter on the Rights and Welfare of the African Child, which stipulates the obligation of the states parties with regard to the protection of the rights of children, otherwise governed by a global Convention of 1989 **(150)**.

The Banjul Charter lists a number of protected rights, largely following other human rights instruments, but it also includes some distinctive features. It specifies not only rights but also duties of individuals toward family, society, and state, which in practice may lead to a restrictive interpretation of the rights. The Charter also stipulates rights of "peoples," apparently to be interpreted according to the prevailing ideology of the developing states. Such "third generation" rights as the right to development, self-determination **(122)**, and national natural resources are listed among other rights.

Unlike the European **(154)** and inter-American **(165)** systems, the Banjul Charter does not provide for a judicial or even quasi-judicial organs for the enforcement of the rights. It creates an African Commission on Human and Peoples' Rights, made up of eleven persons, with the mandate to investigate inter-state complaints and make attempts at reaching an amicable solution. If supported by a majority of its members, the Commission may also consider individual complaints and in the case of serious or massive violations must submit the matter to the OAU Assembly. States are required to submit biennial reports on their measures to implement the Banjul Charter, but this procedure has not been successful in that many states have failed to meet this requirement. However, it must be added that after the launching of the African Union (AU) to replace the OAU in 2002, one of the organs of the AU is to be a Court of Justice competent to rule on violations of human rights in Africa. Hopefully, the new AU will live up to the challenge of protecting and promoting human rights in Africa more effectively than its predecessor, the OAU.

**144. Aliens.** From the viewpoint of a state **(127)**, an alien is a person present in its territory **(228)** who is not a national **(175)** of that state. The term is used with respect to legal entities as well as individuals, but is more commonly used in the latter sense. In municipal law **(27)** aliens are ordinarily classified as permanent residents of the host country or individuals present there for a relatively short period of time for purposes of tourism, study, business, and the like. Individuals granted diplomatic immunity **(63)** represent a special category.

Traditionally, the admission and conditions of stay and departure of aliens have been within the competence of the host state. In principle, a state, albeit required to allow entry to returning nationals, has no obligation to admit aliens unless it undertook to do so by treaty **(288)**. Special agreements with respect to the freedom of movement and establishment within the territories of the member states, with virtual elimination of all border controls for nationals of these states, exist within the context of the integration of political communities, as is the case in the European Community (EC).

Normally an alien entering a host country is required to possess a passport (or an equivalent travel document such as special documents issued for seamen or stateless persons), with a visa of the host country entered into it. However, in relations between friendly states, waiver of visa requirements for non-permanent foreign visitors is quite common, usually on conditions of reciprocity.

Under the now historical treaty regimes of the so-called capitulations between certain European powers and some Levantine and oriental states, such as the Ottoman Empire, Persia, China, and Japan, the subjects of the European power concerned who resided in these states enjoyed a form of extraterritoriality, whereby they were exempt from the jurisdiction **(87)** of the state of residence, continuing to be subject to the jurisdiction of their respective states of origin, exercised by a special system of consular **(57)** courts established in the state of residence. All such capitulatory regimes had been terminated by the early decades of the 20th century.

While a state may exercise considerable discretion in its treatment of aliens and their property, it is subject to any treaty obligations providing special protection to foreign nationals and, more generally, is circumscribed by the internationally recognized human rights law **(160)** which grants rights and freedoms to aliens as well as nationals. However, the substantive content of the international minimum standard of justice in the treatment of aliens, as championed by the traditional Western states, is challenged by other states following the national treatment principle **(171)**. In any case, aliens must be offered an equal protection under the law, and subject to any treaty-based advantages, a state may not discriminate between aliens of different nationality.

International law allows states to impose certain restrictions and burdens upon the residing aliens. Apart from the generally recognized principle of excluding aliens from the exercise of political rights and restricting their political activities, they include, *inter alia*, and depending on the state in question, ineligibility for public office, exclusion from certain professions and occupations, denial of access to certain facilities and advantages, prohibition of acquiring real property, the duty of registration, and the possibility of expulsion. Otherwise, aliens are subject to the state's law and jurisdiction and, if granted the status of permanent residence, may even be subject to certain police and public service duties, including military service which, however, may not be directed against an alien's national state.

More recently the growing concern for an international protection of human rights **(157)** has made some inroads into the traditional exclusive competence of states to admit and expel **(146)** aliens. The Universal Declaration of Human Rights, 1948 **(162)**, proclaims everybody's right to freedom of movement and residence and the right to leave any country and return to one's country of origin, the freedoms confirmed in treaty form in Articles 12 and 13 of the International Covenant on Civil and Political Rights **(166)** which specifically guarantee the aliens' freedom from arbitrary expulsion. However, except for some agreements on the rights of migrant workers, agreements under the auspices of the EC and the Council of Europe, and the Convention between the American Republics regarding the status of aliens in their respective territories, 1928 (132 LNTS 301), limited to 15 states including the United States (US) (which, however, does not consider the Convention to be in force between the US and Mexico), the legal status of aliens has not been a subject of general codification **(5)**.

**145. Aliens, Expropriation of Property of.** Expropriation means a compulsory deprivation of an alien **(144)** of his property by the state **(127)**. It may take the form of an outright transfer of an alien's legal title to the property or a unilateral taking of possession, or it may be carried out by the state in a disguised form of all kinds of deliberate legal subterfuges, in fact depriving the alien of his property. As formulated in Art. 10(3)(a) the 1961 Harvard Draft of Responsibility of States, a constructive or creeping expropriation may be achieved by "any such unreasonable interference with the use, employment or disposal of property as to justify an inference that the owner thereof will not be able to use, enjoy or dispose of the property within a reasonable period of time after the inception of such interference" (55 AJIL 548 (1961)). Whether such interference goes beyond the bounds of reasonable regulation and in fact amounts to constructive expropriation depends on the particular circumstances. It must be distinguished from a state's conduct interfering with the alien's property but constituting a lawful and reasonable exercise of the state's regulatory power in matters of public order, safety or health, planning, increase in taxation, and the like.

What precisely is meant by property is not an entirely settled question. The 1961 Harvard Draft defines property as including "all movable and immovable property, whether tangible or intangible, including industrial, literary and artistic property, as well as rights and interests in any property" (Art. 10(7)). Contractual rights are excluded. On the other hand, in the *Anglo-Iranian Oil Co.* (United Kingdom v. Iran) case before the International Court of Justice (ICJ) **(309)**, in which the Court declined jurisdiction (1952 ICJ Rep. 93), the United Kingdom pleaded that concession contracts were property rights, a view confirmed with respect to contractual rights closely related to the physical property in question in the more recent (1983) case law of the Iran–United States Claims Tribunal (IUSCT) **(312)** in *Starrett Housing Corp. v. Islamic Republic of Iran* (23 ILM 1090 (1984)) and more generally in 1987 in *Amoco International Finance Corp. v. Islamic Republic of Iran* (reported in 82 AJIL 358 (1988)).

Expropriation of a major national resource, to be managed in national interest and carried out as part of a state's program of economic and social reform, is known as nationalization. It applies to nationals as well as aliens and encompasses categories of property, such as coal mining, oil, railroads, and the like, rather than a specific item of property. It is through various kinds of nationalization by a number of countries in the 20th century that the subject of expropriation became one of the most controversial areas of international law. Confiscation has become a term usually applied to a situation where the taking of alien property is unlawful and no appropriate compensation is provided to the injured alien. But certain kinds of expropriation are unlawful in themselves and not just in the absence of compensation. Examples of such unlawful expropriation are: taking property of an international organization **(84)**; illegal countermeasures **(58)**; taking property as part of crimes against humanity **(151)**; or property of another state used for official purposes. On the other hand, expropriation for public purposes in the exercise of legitimate police power, including seizure of property as penalty of the law within the limits of the minimum international standard of justice **(171)**, and as a defense measure in an armed conflict **(339)**, are considered to be lawful even in the absence of appropriate compensation.

There is general consensus that expropriation of alien property is not in itself contrary to international law provided that it conforms to certain rules of this law. Apart from the generally accepted requirement that it must not be arbitrary, that is, in a "willful disregard of due process of law; an act which shocks, or at least surprises, a sense of juridical propriety" (ICJ in the case of *Elettronica Sicula S.p.A.* (*ELSI*) (United States of America v. Italy) (1989 ICJ Rep. 15), expropriation must be for public purposes (public utility), that is, must not be undertaken for purely extraneous political reasons or for private interests, for example enrichment of public officials of the expropriating state. Considering the dynamic nature of the concept of public purpose, ranging from the rather narrowly circumscribed notion of public utility in the practice of states following the traditional *laissez-faire* ideology, to the more recent broader concept of public utility as a crucial element of economic development and even national sovereignty **(125)**, international jurisprudence has been reluctant to pronounce on what international standards of public utility meet the tests of international law. As a result, this requirement remains an open and rather ambiguous question. The 1962 General Assembly (GA) Resolution 1803 on Permanent Sovereignty over National Resources in sec. 4 lists it as a requirement for lawful expropriation. But there is no mention of it in the 1974 GA Charter of Economic Rights and Duties of States (14 ILM 251 (1975)). Also, rather exceptionally, in the award in the *LIAMCO* Arbitration **(293)** in 1981 (20 ILM 1 (1981)), involving nationalization by Libya of an American oil company, the sole arbitrator held that there existed no separate public purpose requirement in international law, at least in cases of nationalization.

The next condition for a lawful expropriation, insisted upon by the developed countries, is nondiscrimination against or between aliens. However, in concrete cases challenges to expropriation on grounds of discrimination may be difficult to prove, especially where there is no comparable enterprise owned by nationals of the taking country or of another state. In addition, a certain degree of discrimination related to public purpose need not necessarily make an expropriation illegal under international law. Neither the 1962 GA Resolution nor the 1974 Charter mention nondiscrimination as a condition for expropriation. In practice the argument of discrimination has not been a major challenge, especially if the expropriating state meets the crucial requirement of compensation. But it was resorted to, among other reasons, by United States (US) courts with regard to Cuban nationalizations of American-owned property and in some arbitral awards in the aftermath of nationalization by Libya of foreign oil companies in 1971 and 1973, especially the arbitral award in the *TOPCO & CAOC* case in 1977 (translated in 17 ILM 1 (1978)).

The most important and by far most contentious requirement for a lawful expropriation is compensation. Disagreement over an appropriate standard of compensation has been one aspect of the conflict between the industrialized capital-exporting countries and the developing states, which reached its peak in the 1970s and '80s within the context of the debate over the demands of the latter for a New International Economic Order (NIEO). However, by the onset of the last decade of the 20th century the controversy seemed somehow to have subsided, following the end of the Cold War and a tendency in many developing countries toward a reappraisal of the old "socialist"-style policies and embracing a more realistic and more "capitalist" approach to their respective economies and international economic relations in general and foreign investment in particular.

The principle that a state's right to expropriate alien property is conditioned by the payment of compensation is of long standing. The position of the developed countries in this respect still essentially (but often for bargaining purposes) follows the traditional "Hull formula" asserted in 1938 in a note from the US Secretary of State to the Mexican government concerning Mexican expropriations, to the effect that under the international minimum standard of justice the legality of expropriation depends on the observance by the taking state of the obligation to make adequate, prompt, and effective compensation. On the other hand, following the national treatment principle, Mexico asserted that aliens should be compensated to the same extent as nationals. The two contrasting approaches continue to underlie the positions of the developed and developing countries, respectively.

Various articulations of the lawful standard of compensation in substance express the same idea. The Restatement (Third) of 1987 (sec. 712) refers to "just compensation" which must be "in the amount equivalent to the value of the property taken," ordinarily fair market value, and must "be paid at the time of taking, or within a reasonable time thereafter with interest from the date of taking and in a form economically usable by the foreign national," normally in a convertible currency or—exceptionally—economically reasonable bonds. But the Restatement concedes that exceptional circumstances might warrant a different standard of compensation. As suggested in the doctrine and asserted by Latin American countries, exceptional circumstances include in particular expropriation as part of a national program of land reform, on the grounds that the state cannot afford full payment, not the least because unlike the case of mineral resources, the taking of farmland does not produce sufficient funds for compensation.

The issue of expropriation of foreign investors became a subject of heated debates in the GA as part of the campaign for the NIEO waged by Third World countries invoking the right to dispose freely of their sovereign resources. However, in the matter of compensation, the important abovementioned GA Resolution 1803 of 1962, adopted by a vote of 87 (including the US) to 2, with 12 abstentions, evaded the issue, using a deliberately general question-begging phraseology in order to create the appearance of reaching a solution acceptable to both the industrialized nations and the Third World countries alike. The Resolution declared, *inter alia*, in para. 4 that expropriation, nationalization, or requisition should be based on grounds of public utility, security, or national interest, and required that the owner be paid "appropriate" compensation in accordance both with the municipal law **(27)** of the taking state and international law. Accepting this formulation, the US and other industrialized countries declared their understanding of the term "appropriate" as equivalent to the "prompt, adequate and effective" formula whereas the developing states claimed that compensation in accordance with the national treatment principle satisfied the standards of "appropriate" compensation. Subsequently, in the 1970s, pressures by the developing states resulted in a number of NIEO resolutions, culminating in the above-mentioned Charter of Economic Rights and Duties of States of 1974 (14 ILM 251 (1975), adopted by a vote of 120 in favor to 6 against (including the US), with 10 abstentions. In Art. 2 the Charter reflected the view of the developing world and did not mention any limitation upon the right to expropriate alien property. While adopting the standard of "appropriate" compensation, it based it exclusively on pertinent national law and regulations of the expropriating state, without any obligation of compensation according to international law. Of course, it could be argued that even if this view, embraced by a numerical majority of states, should eventually crystallize into customary law **(39)**, it would not bind the states persistently objecting to the position of this majority.

Whereas the 1962 GA Resolution 1803 was referred to with approval in the above-mentioned *TOPCO &CAOC* arbitral award of 1977 as reflecting the customary international law on compensation, the formula in the 1974 Charter was found in most arbitral awards to have no standing as evidence of custom and to express merely a *de lege ferenda* program of action.

It appears that neither the traditional "adequate, prompt, and effective" formula of the industrialized nations, based on the minimum international standard of justice for aliens, nor the "appropriate" standard, based only on the municipal law and championed by developing countries (some of which, however, entered into treaties with industrialized nations that uphold the traditional formula), can be regarded as the customary law on the subject supported by the international community as a whole. That is why the "appropriate" compensation principle based on international law and applied in a flexible manner in the light of the particular circumstances of each case and all the factors bearing directly upon the value of the asset involved, has found favor in numerous international settlements of disputes, such as the *AMINOIL* Arbitration of 1982 between Kuwait and the American Independent Oil Company (21 ILM 976 (1982)) and more recently in the case law of the IUSCT. The interpretation of the appropriate compensation standard by the IUSCT, though in general favoring the traditional position, varied depending on the circumstances. It has been suggested in the doctrine that the traditional Hull formula could be replaced by the standard of appropriate compensation, especially in cases of large-scale nationalizations, but not to the point of an unjust enrichment of the expropriating state.

Concerning the method of valuating the assets subject to expropriation, the fair market value rather than the book value is used in practice, as was for example done in the above-mentioned *Starrett* case before the IUSCT. Whether in a case of a going concern the alien should be compensated not only for the direct loss (*damnum emergens*) but also for the consequential loss of expected profits (*lucrum cessans*) is a controversial matter, as it is in reparation **(118)** questions under international law in general, but the tendency is to award both in cases where the expropriation is unlawful *per se* under international law and thus provides no valid title.

The conclusion must be that there is no clear consensus on the rules of international law to govern expropriation of alien property, but virtually all states accept that some compensation is payable. The prompt, adequate, and effective formula is still upheld as a principle by most industrialized countries, but it is often subject to economic realities affecting the amount of compensation and certain exceptional situations involving nationalization of major national resources and land reform. At the same time, judging by the fact that, as a rule, quite a large number of developing countries have signed bilateral investment treaties stipulating the traditional principle of compensation, it appears that at least some developing states are willing to compromise in the matter of compensation and acknowledge the role of foreign capital in their economic development. Many cases have been settled by agreements providing for a lump-sum payment in respect of all pending claims of a state's nationals, usually amounting to a small part of the traditional standard. Subsequently, the state of the investor's nationality (in the US the Foreign Claims Settlement Commission) settles individual claims. Investment disputes are also settled by the International Center for Settlement of Investment Disputes **(307)** and claims of US nationals against Iran and those of Iranian nationals against the US were adjudicated by the IUSCT. The capital-exporting countries obtained legal protection in the form of bilateral investment treaties and similar agreements concluded with many developing countries since 1959. On the multilateral level the Multilateral Investment Guarantee Agency, established by the World Bank–sponsored Convention of 1985 (24 ILM 1598 (1985)), provides insurance coverage to investors against non-commercial risks, including expropriation. In addition, the US and other capital-exporting countries administer special insurance program against such risks. The US program, the Overseas Private Investment Corporation, is a government corporation functioning on a commercial basis, which insures investors in foreign countries, without prejudice of their right to resort to international remedies such as arbitration **(293)**.

The proliferation of many bilateral lump-sum agreements providing for compensation which falls far short of the traditional Hull formula as well as bilateral investment protection treaties that uphold this formula, raise the question of their value as evidence of state practice potentially leading to customary law. However, as noted in one of its cases by the IUSCT, such international agreements are often influenced by political and other nonjudicial considerations; hence caution is required in drawing any conclusions on their evidentiary value as *opinio juris* creative of customary international law.

**146. Aliens, Expulsion of.** Expulsion means removal, forcible if need be, of an individual alien **(144)** from the territory of a state **(228)** by a unilateral order of its government, ordinarily the judicial authority. Expulsion, itself not a technical legal term, is sometimes used interchangeably with deportation. It differs from extradition **(75)** in that the latter involves a degree of international cooperation in handing over the individual in question. In its strict meaning, deportation differs from expulsion in that it applies to an alien who stays in the state in violation of its law whereas expulsion may affect also a legally residing alien. In addition, the primary purpose of deportation is just to remove an alien from the territory of the deporting state to any other state willing to receive him whereas under international law the state of his nationality **(175)** is obliged to admit him, at least if he has nowhere to go. Expulsion of aliens in time of an armed conflict **(339)** and deportation from a territory under belligerent occupation **(363)** is governed by special rules.

While a state has the right to expel aliens, international law imposes certain restrictions on the circumstances and manner of expulsion. In any case, expulsion may not be arbitrary, but customary law **(39)** concerning limits to states' discretion in the process of expulsion is not well established. It is not clear whether a state must give reasons for expelling an alien. Generally speaking, state practice accepts that expulsion is justified in cases of deportation of an alien who entered the country illegally or in breach of the terms of admission; aliens involved in criminal activities; and on grounds of security and political considerations, taking account of the threat the alien poses to the so-called public order (*ordre public*), a rather vague general legal concept whose content depends on the municipal law **(27)** of the expelling state, leaving it a considerable scope of discretion. As a general rule, it can be suggested that the demands of public order should be balanced against the basic standards of human rights **(157)** and legitimate interests and expectations of the individual concerned. In any event, the expelling state must act in good faith, a consideration that also applies to the manner of expulsion itself. Expulsion of long-settled aliens may be carried out only with an advance notice to allow them sufficient time to wind up their affairs. The Iran–United States Claims Tribunal (IUSCT) **(312)** dealt with a number of cases of the expulsion of aliens by Iran during the turbulent time of the Islamic revolution and the hostage crisis. The Tribunal held that a state might bear responsibility for the so-called constructive expulsion, that is, a seemingly voluntary departure of an alien, if under the circumstances the alien had no other choice but to depart and the state of residence failed to exercise due diligence in protecting the alien against threats of violence (by revolutionary guards in this case) and to give him adequate time to wind up his interests, the government thus in fact indirectly showing its intention to eject the alien. However, the IUSCT also held that an alien's departure as a result of general anti-foreigners acts and attitudes of supporters of the revolutionary movement which came to power following the alien's departure did not amount to constructive expulsion.

The right to expel aliens and the manner of expulsion may be subject to treaty **(288)** obligations, such as the International Covenant on Civil and Political Rights **(166)**, *inter alia*, stipulating certain procedural guarantees for the lawfulness of expulsion; the 1951 Convention on refugees **(178)** prohibiting the expulsion of refugees except on grounds of national security or public order and banning the so-called *refoulement,* that is, forcing a refugee to return to a country where his life or freedom would be at risk; and the Convention against torture **(182)** which prohibits returning a refugee to a state where he would be in danger of being subjected to torture. Regionally, certain restrictions on the manner of carrying out expulsion are implied in the 1950 European Convention on human rights **(153)**. Under the European Community Treaty the free movement and freedom of establishment may be limited only on grounds of public policy, security, and health.

Mass expulsion of aliens, motivated by racial, ethnic, religious, or similar discrimination, may constitute a violation of human rights **(157)**, especially if carried out at short notice without observing fundamental humanitarian considerations, as illustrated by the expulsion by Uganda of the Asian community in 1972, the expulsion of foreign workers by Nigeria in 1981, and of nationals of Sub-Saharan states by Libya in 2000. Collective expulsion of aliens is prohibited in Europe under Art. 4 of Protocol No. 4 of 1963 to the European human rights Convention of 1950.

**147. American Convention on Human Rights, 1969.** A regional Organization of American States (OAS)–sponsored convention signed in 1969 in San José, Costa Rica (1144 UNTS 123), in force **(271)** 1978, which sets forth the rules governing the protection of human rights and freedoms **(157)** in the Western Hemisphere, constituting the principal mechanism to this effect in the region. In 2000, 25 Latin American and Caribbean states (but not the United States) were parties. In 1998 Trinidad and Tobago was the first country to withdraw from the Convention. Earlier, in 1948 the OAS had proclaimed a non-binding American Declaration of the Rights and Duties of Man and in 1959 created the Inter-American Commission on Human Rights, an autonomous organ of the OAS with the function to promote the observance and defense of human rights and to serve the OAS in an advisory capacity in this area. The Commission's procedure is now governed by the Rules adopted in 2001 (40 ILM 752 (2001)). The Commission has no power to make decisions on individual complaints, but its competence to examine them and make recommendations to governments as well as to investigate on its own the human rights condition in member countries of the OAS is recognized by this organization.

The American Convention on Human Rights lists some 22 civil and political rights and freedoms more or less along the lines drawn by the European Convention of 1950 **(153)**. The rights guaranteed by the Convention were extended by a Protocol in 1988 to cover a number of economic, social, and cultural rights, on the basis of the standards spelled out in the Protocol amending the OAS Charter. A Protocol on abolition of death penalty was adopted in 1990 (29 ILM 1447 (1990)) but is in force only for a very limited number of states.

Modeled largely on the old pre-1998 European system, the American Convention established two seven-member organs: an Inter-American Commission on Human Rights, which actually is the same as the already mentioned OAS Commission, thus acting both as an OAS organ with powers *vis à vis* all OAS members and a new institution under the Convention of 1969; and the Inter-American Court of Human Rights **(165)**. Apart from its powers within the context of the OAS, namely receiving and examining petitions alleging violations of the human rights set forth in the above-mentioned American Declaration in relation to the member states of the OAS that are not parties to the American Convention, the main function of the Commission under the Convention is to hear petitions from individuals alleging violation by a state party of any of the civil or political rights guaranteed in various hemispheric instruments, namely the American Declaration; the Convention itself; the Additional Protocol of 1988 in the Area of Economic, Social and Cultural Rights (28 ILM 156 (1989); the Protocol of 1990 to Abolish the Death Penalty (29 ILM 1447 (1990)); the Inter-American Convention of 1985 to Prevent and Punish Torture; the Inter-American Convention of 1994 on Forced Disappearance of Persons (33 ILM 1529 (1994)); and the Inter-American Convention of 1994 on the Prevention, Punishment and Eradication of Violence against Women (33 ILM 1534 (1994) **(183)**. While the right of the Commission to hear individual, group, and non-governmental organization **(86)** petitions against state violations arises automatically upon the domestic ratification of the Convention by a state party, and hundreds of such petitions have been processed by the Commission, in inter-state complaints the

Commission may deal with a matter only if both states concerned have made a declaration recognizing the Commission's jurisdiction to receive such complaints. If the Commission fails to secure a friendly settlement, it transmits its report with conclusions and possibly recommendations to the state concerned. Within three months following such transmittal the Commission or a state concerned may submit the case to the Inter-American Court of Human Rights.

**148. Asylum, Territorial.** Territorial or political asylum is refuge granted by a state **(127)** in its territory **(228)** to an alien **(144)** fugitive fleeing another state for reasons of genuine fear of persecution for political, racial, ethnic, or religious reasons. The concept of territorial asylum is closely related to that of the refugee **(178)** and to the question of surrendering fugitives and more specifically extradition (or rather nonextradition) of political offenders **(76)**.

Although states have always upheld the right to grant asylum and some have even anchored such a right in their respective constitutions, there is no right of asylum under international law, and the state to which a fugitive has fled is under no obligation to grant it to him. In any event, states are barred from granting asylum to fugitives who are war criminals **(373)** or have committed other crimes under international law **(151)**.

While the Universal Declaration of Human Rights of 1948 **(162)** makes a reference to asylum in other countries from persecution, it proclaims only the right to "seek and enjoy" but not to receive asylum (Art. 14). No right of asylum is stipulated in the International Covenant on Civil and Political Rights **(166)**, and the General Assembly Declaration of 1967 on Territorial Asylum is too general in its content, apart from being only recommendatory and legally not binding **(37)**. The 1993 Vienna Declaration and Program of Action of the United Nations World Conference on Human Rights (32 ILM 1661 (1993)) reaffirmed the right to seek asylum but did not establish any legally binding rules for states to grant it. In general, efforts to introduce a treaty right, on the global level, to receive asylum have not succeeded, primarily because of political considerations and difficulties related to the definition of the concept of the political offense. On the regional level and especially in Latin America a number of multilateral agreements, such as the Montevideo Treaty of 1939 on Political Asylum and Refuge (37 AJIL Supp. 99 (1943)) and the American Convention on Human Rights of 1969 **(147)**, refer to the right to seek and receive asylum, but these agreements are in force only for a limited number of states.

**149. Calvo Clause.** Named after Carlos Calvo, a renowned Argentinian jurist and diplomat of the 19th century who is said to be responsible for this legal device, it is a clause in contracts between a host state and an alien whereby the latter agrees to submit any claim or dispute arising from the contract exclusively to the jurisdiction of the host state, waiving his right to seek diplomatic protection of the state of his nationality **(95)** after the exhaustion of the local remedies **(74)** in the host state. In its theoretical foundations the Calvo Clause, once widely practiced by Latin American states in concessions and other contracts with aliens and in national legislations and even anchored in some states' constitutions, was based on the principle of the freedom of a sovereign state from interference by other states and on the doctrine of national treatment **(171)** providing for a host state to accord aliens essentially the same extent of rights as granted by the state to its nationals. The Calvo Clause was reaffirmed in 1933 in a resolution of the Montevideo Conference of Latin American states as a principle of international law. However, most publicists **(42)** and decisions of international adjudication **(306)** have denied the validity of the clause under international law on the grounds that it cannot deprive the alien's national state of the right to espouse his claims if his rights under this law were violated. It has been argued that a private claimant cannot renounce a right, in this case the right of diplomatic protection, which does not belong to him but is conferred upon his state by international law (*North American Dredging Co.,* United States (US). v. Mexico, General Claims Commission, 4 RIAA 26 (1926)). This has been the position of the US and other developed countries which assert their right to raise a claim against the state involved, especially in cases of denial of justice **(152)** or where a claim was not based on a contract.

While in the past several decades the Calvo Clause has not been a subject of significant international litigation, its underlying theoretical and ideological assumptions continue to be endorsed in

Latin America and other developing countries and are articulated there in national legislation and international instruments concerned with the status of foreign investments in international law and, more generally, to the demands of the developing countries for the so-called New International Economic Order. Furthermore, the fact that most Latin American countries have not joined the 1965 Convention on the Settlement of Investment Disputes between States and Nationals of Other States (575 UNTS 159), which reflects the viewpoint of the developed nations, points to the continued attachment in Latin America to the principles underlying the Calvo Clause.

The Calvo *Clause* must not be confused with the Calvo *Doctrine,* also associated with Calvo, propounding the view that a state cannot be responsible **(128)** for acts of insurrectionists against aliens irrespective of whether or not the state in question undertook all reasonable measures of due diligence to protect the aliens.

**150. Convention on the Rights of the Child, 1989, with the Protocols.** This Convention (1577 UNTS 3), which stands out as the most rapidly and widely ratified international human rights agreement **(160)**, entered into force **(271)** in 1990 and had virtually all the states as its parties in 2003. However, the United States (US), which had signed it in 1995, was not a party. The Convention of 1989 is the first treaty to deal comprehensively with the norms and standards concerning the protection and promotion of the rights of the child. The child is defined (Art. 1) as a human being below the age of 18 years, unless under the law applicable to the child, majority is attained earlier. In its approach the Convention displays the need to recognize the interdependence of all human rights in their application to the child. Nondiscrimination, best interests of the child, the right to life and development, and attention to the views of the child are the general guiding principles of the Convention.

Among a variety of rights named in the Convention are the traditional human rights, such as, apart from the right to life, the right to a name and nationality **(175)** from birth and the right to freedom of thought and expression. The Convention also sets out standards in such areas as the rights of disabled and refugee **(178)** children, protection from an illicit use of drugs, the administration of juvenile justice and social reintegration of children victims of neglect and abuse and armed conflict, international **(339)** or non-international **(340)**. The primary role of the family and especially the parents in the care of children is emphasized along with the duty of the state to help them carry out this task.

The implementation of the Convention is in the hands of the Committee on the Rights of the Children, a monitoring treaty body of ten independent experts with the competence to hear periodic state reports and make suggestions and general recommendations. The Committee in turn reports every two years to the General Assembly through the United Nations Economic and Social Council. However, like other human rights committees of this kind it has no legal power to enforce decisions upon the state party concerned.

The Convention on the Rights of the Child is complemented by two Optional Protocols of 2000 (39 ILM 1285 (2000)). These Protocols in turn develop further certain provisions of the International Labour Organisation Convention No. 182 of 1999 on the Prohibition and Immediate Action for the Elimination of the Worst Forms of Child Labor (38 ILM 1215 (1999)).

The Optional Protocol on the Involvement of Children in Armed Conflict had more than 100 signatures in 2000, including the US, and under Art. 10 entered into force in February 2000, three months after the deposit of the tenth instrument of ratification. The Protocol is open for signature by any state that is a party to the Convention or has signed it. Moreover, it is open to accession **(267)** by any state. It might be added that a number of Security Council resolutions has raised the problem of children in armed conflict, the latest being Resolution 1379 (2001) (41 ILM 507 (2002). The Optional Protocol on the Sale of Children, Child Prostitution and Child Pornography was to enter into force according to the same rules as the Protocol on the involvement of children in armed conflicts and may be ratified by any state party or signatory to the Convention, which in effect means that a state may ratify either Protocol without becoming a party to the Convention itself.

At the negotiations on the Protocol concerning children in armed conflict, virtual consensus existed that the minimum age for compulsory military service should be set at 18 years. But voluntary recruitment below this age (allowed by about half of the existing states, including the US) and participation of children in hostilities, widely practiced in Africa and some other domestic armed conflicts, were the most controversial issues. The Protocol stipulates (Art. 3) that the states parties must declare upon ratification their consent to raise the minimum age limit for voluntary recruitment from the currently quite common standard of 15 years mandated by the Convention (Art. 38(3)) and some other international instruments, including the Geneva Protocol I of 1977 **(369)**, and explicitly sets forth the minimum age at which it will permit voluntary recruitment, with a description of the safeguards adopted to ensure that such recruitment is not forced or coerced. Thus, while in principle allowing voluntary recruitment under the age of 18, the Protocol requires states to establish safeguards, and especially informed consent of the recruit's parents or the legal guardian. Such consent and reliable proof of age are required by law in the US, which ratified the Protocol in 2002 and which recruits some 50,000 volunteers at the age of 17 each year. Concerning participation in hostilities by individuals under the age of 18, the Protocol in Art. 1, following the language of Art. 38(20(1) of the Convention and Art. 77(2) of Protocol I of 1977, established an obligation for the parties to take all "feasible" measures to prevent "direct" participation, a formulation that lends itself to circumventing the protection of children in armed conflict.

The Protocol also deals (Art. 4) with the problem of various "armed groups that are distinct from the armed forces of a State" which use persons under the age of 18 in hostilities. It is a proven fact that this practice takes place in some 28 countries. The Protocol mandates states parties to take all "feasible" measures to prevent such recruitment and use and criminalize them by appropriate legal measures. States are also obligated to cooperate internationally in preventing such and any other activity contrary to the Protocol (Art. 7). They also have the obligation to report periodically to the Committee on the Rights of the Child on the implementation of the Protocol (Art. 8). It should be noted here that under Art. 8(2)(e)(vii) of the Rome Statute of the International Criminal Court **(170)**, conscription or enlistment of children under the age of 15 years in armed forces or groups or using them to participate actively in hostilities is considered a war crime **(373)**.

The other Protocol supplements the Convention on the Rights of the Child by setting out rules for the criminalization of violations of the rights of children in the context of the sale of children, child prostitution, and child pornography, crimes closely related to slavery and similar practices **(180)**. The term "sale of children" is defined (Art. 2(a)) as "any act or transaction whereby a child is transferred by any person or group of persons to another for remuneration or any other consideration." The Protocol specifies (Art. 3) a number of acts and activities which states are obliged to criminalize in their respective national legislations, including, *inter alia*, sexual exploitation, transfer of organs for profit, forced labor, and improperly inducing consent, as an intermediary, for the adoption of a child in violation of international legal instruments on adoption. It is understood that the Convention of 1993 on Protection of Children and Cooperation in Respect of Intercountry Adoptions is the relevant instrument. The Protocol defines child prostitution as "the use of a child in sexual activities for remuneration or any other form of consideration" (Art. 2(b)) and child pornography as "any representation, by whatever means, of a child engaged in real or simulated explicit sexual activities or any representation of the sexual parts of a child" (Art. 2(c)). Such activities are to be criminalized, but the Protocol fails to name the age of consent, a controversial issue in the negotiations on the Protocol. Other provisions deal with measures of protection of victims and preventive efforts as well as international cooperation in the prosecution of suspected offenders. The grounds for jurisdiction **(87)** under the Protocol are broad enough to ensure that an offender can be extradited **(75)** or tried regardless of where apprehended.

**151. Crimes against Humanity.** While there exists no single, universal, authoritative definition and roster of crimes against humanity, accepted for all purposes, one can describe them in a general working definition as certain inhumane acts which are not just ordinary offenses but crimes of the gravest nature directed on a large scale in a course of conduct against civilian population and consciously pursued in an armed conflict **(339)** or in peace time as part of a systematic policy of a government or some form of non-state organization. Crimes against humanity are subject to universal jurisdiction **(92)** and involve responsibility of individuals **(164)** directly under international law. For purposes of judicial determination, the definition of crimes against humanity by an international tribunal, such as the International Military Tribunal (IMT) at Nuremberg **(354)**, the Tokyo Tribunal **(355)**, the International Criminal Tribunal for Rwanda (ICTR) **(351)**, the International Criminal Tribunal for the Former Yugoslavia (ICTY) **(352)**, and the International Criminal Court (ICC) **(170)**, may vary in details circumscribing this category of crime.

Historically, while general references to "laws of humanity" are found in the Hague Conventions of 1899 and 1907 **(350)**, denunciations of enemy powers in World War I, and declarations and reports in the aftermath of this war, crimes against humanity were first recognized and defined in reaction to Nazi atrocities committed in World War II, in the Charter of the IMT and its Judgment of 1946, and in substantially the same formulation in Law No. 10 of the Control Council for Germany 1946 which provided the basis for trying other war criminals charged with crimes against humanity, and—in reaction to Japanese atrocities in the war—in the Tokyo Charter of 1946 setting up the International Military Tribunal for the Far East (the Tokyo Tribunal).

The IMT distinguished three major categories of crime within its jurisdiction, namely, crimes against peace, war crimes **(373)**, and crimes against humanity. The latter were defined as "murder, extermination, enslavement, deportation, and other inhumane acts committed against any civilian population before or during the war or persecution on political, racial, or religious grounds in execution of or in connection with any crime within the jurisdiction of the Tribunal, whether or not in violation of the domestic law of the country where perpetrated." Two of the accused major war criminals were found by the IMT guilty of crimes against humanity alone.

The concept of crimes against humanity (and incidentally also crimes against peace) was criticized by some as victors' retroactive legislation creating a new crime in international law heretofore unknown in customary law **(39)**. But whatever doubts may have existed about the legality of the concept of crimes against humanity, they became irrelevant following a unanimous reaffirmation by the General Assembly (GA) in 1946 of the principles of international law of the Charter and Judgment of the IMT. Furthermore, the concept of crimes against humanity led to the adoption of the Genocide Convention **(155)** in 1948. However, efforts undertaken throughout the next few decades by the International Law Commission (charged with codifying **(5)** international law) to codify comprehensively "offenses against the peace and security of mankind," including crimes against humanity, did not produce any internationally binding instrument. On the other hand, the Convention on the Non-applicability of Statutory Limitations to War Crimes and Crimes against Humanity, 1968 (754 UNTS 73) and a similar Convention adopted in 1974 under the auspices of the Council of Europe (13 ILM 540 (1974)) ensured that statutory or other limitations would not apply to such crimes. Furthermore, some additional acts were added to the roster of crimes against humanity by special treaties. In 1973 the GA adopted the Apartheid Convention (1015 UNTS 243) which, reaffirming a previous resolution of 1971, condemned apartheid as a crime against humanity and in 1982 a GA Declaration on the Protection of All Persons from Enforced Disappearance (32 ILM 903 (1993)) recognized the same with respect to enforced disappearance. On the regional level, this position was confirmed in the Inter-American Convention on the Forced Disappearance of Persons, 1994 (33 ILM 1529 (1994)).

While local armed conflicts, not devoid of atrocities and amounting to crimes against humanity, were fought in the post-war decades, prosecution for such crimes largely remained a dead letter. It was not until the early 1990s, following the end of the Cold War, that prosecution for crimes against humanity became possible in the wake of the disintegration of Yugoslavia in the midst of a civil, but through specific circumstances partially internationalized armed conflict, and in order to deal with the genocide and other grave crimes committed on a large scale in the civil war in Rwanda. Acting under Chapter VII of the United Nations (UN) Charter, dealing with the enforcement of the collective security system **(327)** of the UN, the Security Council (SC) established two special international criminal courts: the ICTY in 1993 and the ICTR in 1994. In addition to genocide, the respective statutes of these two tribunals include, in the category of crimes against humanity, murder, extermination, enslavement **(180)**, deportation, imprisonment, torture **(182)**, rape, persecution on political, racial, and religious grounds, and "other inhumane acts directed against any civilian population." However, the prosecutory powers of the ICTY extend only to crimes against humanity when committed in an armed conflict, whether international or domestic, but—unlike the provision of the Statute of the ICTR—its definition of such crimes does not require the presence of a discriminatory motive. However, when commenting on crimes against humanity, the UN Secretary-General's report submitted to the SC in 1993 (32 ILM ILM 1159 (1993)) does include national, political, ethnic, racial, or religious grounds as an element in the definition of crimes against humanity. In any event, in cases of persecution the mental element of the crime does include a special intent of the perpetrator to persecute or discriminate against members of a group on the above-mentioned grounds.

It is reasonable to assume that the definition of crimes against humanity adopted in 1998 in the Statute of the ICC (37 ILM 999 (1998)) through a difficult and prolonged negotiating process and with the participation of most members of the international community, is the most accurate reflection of the current state of international law on the subject. Under Art. 7(1) of the Statute, "crime against humanity" means "any of the following acts when committed as part of a widespread or systematic attack directed against any civilian population, with knowledge of the attack: murder; extermination; enslavement; deportation or forcible transfer of population ["ethnic cleansing"]; imprisonment or other severe deprivation of physical liberty in violation of fundamental rules of international law; torture; rape, sexual slavery, enforced prostitution, forced pregnancy, enforced sterilization, or any other form of sexual violence of comparable gravity; persecution against any identifiable group or collectivity on political, racial, national, ethnic, cultural, religious, gender as defined in paragraph 3 [of Art. 7], or other grounds that are universally recognized as impermissible under international law, in connection with any act referred to in this paragraph or any crime within the jurisdiction of the Court; enforced disappearance of persons; the crime of apartheid; [and] other inhumane acts of a similar character intentionally causing great suffering, or serious injury to body or to mental or physical health." The concepts of "attack," "extermination, "enslavement," "deportation or forcible transfer of population," "torture," "forced pregnancy," "persecution," "the crime of apartheid," and "enforced disappearance of persons" are defined in Art. 7(2).

It is important to bear in mind that the ICC definition of crimes against humanity does not require that the crime be committed during armed conflict and that, except for persecution, which in itself implies a crime by reason of the identity of the group or collectivity, discriminatory motive, which otherwise may be difficult to prove, is not a general element of the crime. Concerning the threshold test of the attack beyond which an act becomes a crime against humanity, the Statute of the ICC employs the terms "widespread or systematic," also used in the jurisprudence of the ICTY and the ICTR, but to reduce the extension potential of this test, Art. 7(2) clarifies that attack directed against any civilian population means a course of conduct involving the multiple commission of acts against any civilian population, pursuant to or in furtherance of a state or organizational policy to commit such attack. Isolated inhumane acts committed by individuals as such need not be regarded as crimes against humanity, but if perpetrated as part of a course of conduct involving multiple commission, then even a single such act constitutes a crime against humanity. Two elements of the ICC definition are essential: the policy and planning element attributable to a government or a non-state actor or group, implied in the term "directed against," and the element of the perpetrator's knowledge of the attack, which means that, while not necessarily responsible for the overall attack, he must at least be aware that his act forms part of such attack. This mental element as a rule exists in attacks amounting to crimes against humanity. Under Art. 9 of the Rome Statute of the ICC, the interpretation and application of the crimes within the ICC jurisdiction is to be assisted by an elaboration of the so-called Elements of Crimes dealing in more detail with the principles and structure of the mental elements of such crimes, including crimes against humanity. A special Preparatory Commission for the ICC completed a draft of such Elements, to be eventually adopted by a two-thirds majority of the members of the Assembly of states parties.

**152. Denial of Justice.** A rather imprecise term, denial of justice was defined at the Hague Codification **(5)** Conference of 1930 in its abortive draft on state responsibility **(128)** (Art. 8(2)) as a fact that "in a manner incompatible with the international obligation of the State, the foreigner has been hindered by the judicial authorities in the exercise of his right to appear in Court, or has encountered in his proceedings unjustifiable obstacles or delays implying a refusal to do justice." In this sense the term refers to a deficient conduct of the authorities of the host state, mainly its judicial branch, which results in an injury to an alien **(144)** entailing responsibility of the host state. Sometimes, however, the term denial of justice is used in a very general meaning of any unjust treatment of an alien by any organ of the host state.

In its essence, the concept of denial of justice is an application of an appropriate international standard **(171)** to the administration of justice in respect of an alien, an issue on which no consensus exists in international practice. In general, Latin American and other developing states, which follow the national treatment standard, interpret the concept of denial of justice in a restrictive procedural sense, limiting it to the duty of the host state to allow an alien access to the courts, without entering into the question of the quality, effectiveness, and impartiality of the administration of justice by that state. In the more extensive interpretation, championed by states in the developed world, a minimum international standard of justice is denied not only by denial of access to courts, including failure to resort to an arbitral tribunal **(293)**, if arbitration has been agreed upon in the contract with the alien, but also by absence of procedural fairness and due process, and in general serious inadequacies in the administration of justice toward the alien. In this regard, the Harvard Research Draft on state responsibility of 1929 includes such instances of denial of justice as unwarranted delay and obstruction of access to court, gross deficiency in the administration of the judicial or remedial process (for example corruption, intimidation, flagrant abuse of procedure), and failure to provide those guarantees which are generally considered indispensable to the proper administration of justice. To what extent an error of the court may amount to denial of justice is a controversial matter, but the opinion prevails that if made with intent to discriminate against an alien, an error of law violates the international standard of justice, especially if it results in manifest injustice. Over the past few decades, with the growing impact of human rights **(157)** upon international law, certain kinds of injury to aliens, historically classified within the concept of denial of justice, such as various kinds of denial of due process in criminal proceedings, have since been accepted as violations of human rights which a state must respect for all persons regardless of their nationality.

**153. European Convention for the Protection of Human Rights and Fundamental Freedoms, 1950.** A regional convention adopted under the auspices of the Council of Europe in 1950, in force **(271)** in 1953 (213 UNTS 221), which sets out the system of observance and promotion of human rights and fundamental freedoms **(157)** to be followed by the states parties. Sponsored by the Council of Europe, an organization created in 1949 (87 UNTS 103) and not to be confused with the European Community (European Union), the Convention is now in force for 44 countries, virtually all the European states including the former Communist states. The European Court of Human Rights (ECHR) **(154)** in Strasbourg is the central institution of this by far most active and advanced system for the protection of human rights. A European Commissioner for Human Rights, an office analogous to the United Nations High Commissioner for Human Rights **(158)**, was established in 1999.

The European Convention, supplemented by a number of Protocols, comprehensively covers a variety of civil and political rights, in substance analogous to those stipulated in the International Covenant on Civil and Political Rights (ICCPR) **(166)** of 1966. A derogation from most obligations of the Convention (but not from the article guaranteeing the right to life and those prohibiting torture, slavery, and retroactive criminal legislation) is possible "in time of public emergency threatening the life of the nation." A separate treaty, adopted by the members of the Council of Europe in 1961 (529 UNTS 89) and known as the European Social Charter, deals with economic, social, and cultural rights and is supplemented by two protocols of 1991 (31 ILM 155 (1991)), and 1995 (34 ILM 1453 (1995)), respectively. In addition, the Council of Europe system for the protection of human rights includes a number of agreements dealing with specific human rights problems. One should mention here the European Convention for the Prevention of Torture and Inhuman and Degrading Treatment or Punishment, 1987 (27 ILM 1152 (1988)), with a Protocol of 1993 made open for accession to new member states of the Council of Europe at the invitation of the Committee of Ministers of the Council. The rights of national minorities **(172)** are protected by the Framework Convention of 1995 (34 ILM 351 (1995)).

Among the rights and fundamental freedoms guaranteed by the European Convention to everyone within a state party's territory and implemented in the municipals laws **(27)** of the parties are: the right to life, liberty and security, fair trial and no punishment without the law, the right to marry, to respect for private and family life, freedoms of thought, conscience, and religion, freedom of expression, assembly and association, prohibition of slavery and forced labor **(180)**, torture **(182)**, retroactive criminal legislation, and discrimination. More rights and freedoms have been added by (so far 13) Protocols, including the right to property (not mentioned in the ICCPR), education, and free elections, the right to appeal in criminal matters, prohibition of double jeopardy, equality between spouses, the right to be compensated for wrongful conviction, freedom of movement, prohibition of imprisonment for debts, of expulsion of nationals and of collective expulsion of aliens **(146)**. The death penalty, which had been abolished by Protocol No. 6 of 1983, except in respect of acts committed in time of war **(338)** or of imminent threat of war, was completely abolished in all circumstances by Protocol No. 13 of 2002 (41 ILM 515 (2002)).

In the first period of the European human rights regime (1953–1998) the observance of the rights and freedoms protected by the Convention and the Protocols was ensured by three organs: the European Commission of Human Rights, the ECHR, and the Committee of Ministers of the Council of Europe. Under this system all complaints went to the Commission for initial screening. Any state party could refer an alleged breach of the Convention to the Commission. In addition to this rarely used system of interstate complaints, individuals, groups of individuals or non-governmental organizations, having exhausted local remedies **(74)**, had the right of petition, but only if the state concerned had recognized the competence of the Commission by an express declaration. This option was exercised by all states parties. However, it was a fundamental jurisdictional principle of the ECHR that it could deal with a case, among other conditions, only after the Commission had found a claim admissible, had established the facts of the case, and acknowledged the failure of efforts at a friendly settlement. Furthermore, the Committee of Ministers of the Council of Europe had the power to decide whether a breach of the Convention had taken place.

As a result of a greatly increasing backlog of applications and the steadily growing membership of the Council of Europe in the 1990s due to the accession **(267)** of Eastern European states, the Council found it urgently necessary to restructure the whole machinery established by the Convention system in order to improve the efficiency of its protection of human rights and fundamental freedoms in Europe. This was achieved by Protocol No. 11 of 1994 (33 ILM 943 (1994)) which entered into effect in November 1998, and the new system began to operate following the necessary transition period. The major elements of the restructuring have been the abolition of the Commission and transformation of the ECHR into a full-time permanent court.

**154. European Court of Human Rights.** The European Court of Human Rights (ECHR) is the judicial body established within the framework of the Council of Europe pursuant to the European Convention for the Protection of Human Rights and Fundamental Freedoms, 1950 **(153)** and subsequently fundamentally restructured by Protocol No. 11 to the Convention (33 ILM 943 (1994)) adopted in 1994 and in force on 1 November 1998. As a result, apart from the abolition of the Commission, the original semi-permanent Court, which was active (since 1959) for more than three decades, was transformed into a new full-time permanent Court with a new structure and additional competences. The role of the Committee of Ministers, which in the old system had the power to decide whether a breach of the Convention had taken place, became limited to receiving the final judgment of the Court and supervising its execution.

The ECHR is composed of a number of judges equal to that of the states parties to the European Convention, which in 2004 amounted to more than 40. There is no longer any requirement that no two judges may be nationals of the same state. The judges are elected on a staggered schedule by a majority of votes by the Parliamentary Assembly of the Council of Europe from national lists of three candidates each, for a six-year, renewable term, but the term of office of judges expires when they reach the age of 70. The plenary Court sets up Chambers, elects its President and one or two Vice-Presidents for a renewable period of three years, elects the Court's Registrar and two Deputy Registrars, and adopts the Rules of the Court. To consider cases the ECHR may sit in Committees of three, in Chambers of seven, or a Grand Chamber of 17 judges. The institution of an *ad hoc* judge, known in the International Court of Justice (ICJ) **(289)**, is also used in the ECHR. A Committee may, by a unanimous vote and with final authority, declare inadmissible or strike out of its list an individual application in cases where such decision could be made without further examination. Otherwise a Chamber decides on admissibility and merits of all applications. Unless objected by a party to the case, a Chamber may relinquish its jurisdiction in favor of the Grand Chamber if a case raises a serious question affecting the interpretation of the Convention or its Protocols or where the resolution of the question might result in inconsistency with an earlier judgment of the Court.

The jurisdiction of the ECHR extends to the interpretation and application of the Convention and its Protocols and covers both the very rare inter-state complaints and individual applications by an individual, a group of individuals or a non-governmental organization claiming to be a victim of a breach by a state party of rights and freedoms set forth in the Convention or its Protocols. Unlike the old system, applicants are allowed to bring their cases directly without any restriction or hindrance by the state involved. They participate in the proceedings confronting that state on an equal footing. The ECHR has also advisory jurisdiction **(291)**, but—unlike in the ICJ **(309)**—this kind of jurisdiction has not been made use of in the Court.

Exhaustion of local remedies **(74)** according to the generally recognized rules of international law is a major criterion of admissibility of a claim and only within a six-month period from the date on which the final domestic decision was made. Other grounds of inadmissibility for individual applications include filing an anonymous application or an application that is in substance the same as a matter already examined by the Court or that has been submitted in another international investigative procedure. In addition, applications found incompatible with the Convention or a Protocol, or manifestly unfounded or abusive of the right of application, are to be declared inadmissible. In practice, a large proportion of individual complaints are rejected as unfounded. Furthermore, the Court may at any stage of the proceedings decide to strike out an application if the matter has been resolved or the applicant fails to pursue his case or due to any other reason established by the Court. A third party intervention (as in the ICJ) **(311)** is possible under the Convention itself in cases before a Chamber or the Grand Chamber.

The number of individual applications has been growing each year but only a small proportion of initial individual complaints are registered and even much smaller reach the judgment stage. In 2001 some 31,000 individual complaints were sent to the Court, out of which only some 13,800 were registered, with the Court deciding on less than 10,000 complaints and handing down judgments in 888 cases. Of course, the number of individual applications by far exceeds that of interstate complaints.

Except for the friendly settlement process, hearings are public and documents accessible unless in exceptional circumstances the Court decides otherwise. A judgment by a Chamber becomes final if no referral to the Grand Chamber is requested by the parties, if the Grand Chamber rejects such request, or if no request has been made within three months following the date of the judgment. A panel of five judges considers a referral case if it raises a serious question affecting the interpretation or application of the Convention or a Protocol, or a serious issue of general importance. Judgments of the Grand Chamber are final. All judgments and decisions of the ECHR must be accompanied by reasons and any judge is entitled to deliver a separate opinion **(304)**, a rule also known in the ICJ.

A state found by a Court's judgment to have committed a breach of its human rights obligations under the Convention or a Protocol is legally bound to afford satisfaction to the injured person under its municipal law system **(27)**, but if it is not fully possible under this law, the Court affords the injured person just satisfaction by ordering the state involved to pay a determined sum of money as reparation to the injured person.

The state involved undertakes to abide by a final judgment of the Court, the Committee of Ministers supervising its execution. There exists no formal enforcement mechanism, but except for a very few cases political considerations have dissuaded states from openly defying the Court's decisions. Ultimately, under Art. 8 of the Statute of the Council of Europe, any member state defying the rule of law may be suspended in its membership rights and requested to withdraw. Failure to comply with such request may result in expulsion from the organization, that is, the Council of Europe.

In applying the European Convention and its protocols the ECHR has developed by far the most effective international human rights regime. Its decisions have brought about important changes in the municipal laws of the states parties concerned, contributing to a progressive harmonization of the law of human rights, first in Western Europe and then positively influencing the state of human rights in the new states parties which joined the system following the end of the Cold War. A landmark of sorts in the jurisprudence of the ECHR occurred in 2002 when the Court handed down its first decision involving Russia in a case brought against that country by a victim of the Chernobyl nuclear disaster of 1986.

**155. Genocide Convention, 1948.** The Convention on the Prevention and Punishment of the Crime of Genocide (78 UNTS 277) adopted by the General Assembly (GA) in 1948, in force in 1951. Originally signed by 42 states, it had more than 130 states parties in 2003, including the United States which had signed it in 1966 but did not ratify until 1988. The nine articles of the Convention, the first human rights–related **(157)** treaty to be adopted under the auspices of the United Nations (UN), envisages genocide as a subcategory of the crimes against humanity **(151)**, previously encompassed within this category of crimes albeit not as a discrete offense. The term "genocide" itself had been first used by Raphael Lemkin in his book, *Axis Rule in Occupied Europe*, published in 1944.

The Convention declares genocide a crime under international law irrespective of whether committed in international **(339)** or internal conflict **(340)** and whether in time of peace or war. It is noteworthy that by condemning genocide as a crime under international law the Convention codified the already crystallized law to this effect. This results from the wording of Art. I where the contracting parties "confirm" genocide as a crime. Both the Convention and GA Resolution 96 (I), upon which the Convention is based, were accepted unanimously. The acts constituting genocide under the Convention were subsequently included in the Draft Code of Offenses against the peace and Security of Mankind in 1954, and genocide was listed among the crimes against humanity in the consideration of the topic by the International Law Commission. The qualification of genocide as a crime under customary international law **(39)** was also affirmed by the International Court of Justice (ICJ) **(309)** in its Advisory Opinion **(291)** on *Reservations* **(282)** *to the Convention on the Prevention and Punishment of the Crime of Genocide* (1951 ICJ Rep. 15) (where the Court noted that "principles underlying the Convention are principles which are recognized by civilized nations as binding upon States, even without any conventional obligation") and reaffirmed in the ICJ Judgment in the case of *Barcelona Traction, Light and Power, Limited* (Belgium v. Spain) (1970 ICJ Rep. 3). That genocide is a crime under customary law was also stressed by the UN Secretary-General in his Report on the Establishment of the International Criminal Tribunal for the Former Yugoslavia (ICTY) **(352)** in 1993. The rule on the prohibition of genocide cannot be derogated from: it is a peremptory norm of general international law (*jus cogens*) **(24)**.

The Convention (Art. II) defines genocide as any of a number of acts committed with the intent to destroy, in whole or in part, a national, ethnic, racial or religious group; killing members of the group; causing serious bodily or mental harm to members of the group; deliberately inflicting on the group conditions of life calculated to bring about its physical destruction in whole or in part; imposing measures intended to prevent births within the group; and forcibly transferring children of the group to another group.

In defining genocide, the statutes of the ICTY **(352)**, the International Criminal Tribunal for Rwanda (ICTR) **(351)**, and the International Criminal Court (ICC) **(170)** follow the Genocide Convention.

As noted by the ICTR in the first case of finding an individual guilty specifically of genocide, the *Akayesu* case of 1998 (37 ILM 1399 (1998)), the crime of genocide does not necessarily imply the actual extermination of a group in its entirety; it exists once a genocidal act is committed with the specific intent to destroy in whole or in part a group in question. This special intent, *dolus specialis* in civil law **(23)**, is a unique constitutive element of the crime of genocide; victims are selected specifically because of their being members of the targeted group and not because of their individual identity. In practice, the determination of an offender's intent may not be possible and in the absence of a confession such intent must be inferred from certain presumptions of fact within the context of other culpable acts perpetrated against the targeted group, the scale of the atrocities, the fact of excluding non-members of the group from the genocidal acts, and the like.

The Convention (Art. III) declares as punishable not only the act of genocide itself but also conspiracy to commit this crime, direct and public incitement to commit it, attempts to commit genocide and—a rather vague concept—complicity in genocide In addition, the Convention expressly states that any person committing the crime shall be punished irrespective of whether they are constitutionally responsible rulers, public officials, or private individuals. The definition of genocide in the Convention does not include extermination of a group on social or political grounds. Thus, contrary to common opinion, from the point of view of the Convention the crimes of the Pol Pot Communist regime in Cambodia were not genocide but other crimes against humanity in the form of mass murder, enslavement, deportation, torture, imprisonment, persecution on political grounds, and other inhumane acts. The Preparatory Committee on the ICC adopted the same position on the definition of genocide in response to proposals by some state delegations to add political and social groups to the list of the groups named with reference to this definition. Another gap in the definition of genocide is the absence among the listed genocidal acts of deliberate destruction of the cultural life of the targeted group.

Concerning implementation, the Convention provides that the states parties (and of course all states because of the customary law character of the crime) must legislate to give effect to its provisions and, in particular, criminalize the genocidal acts named in the Convention by laying down penalties for persons guilty of such acts. The accused shall be tried by a competent tribunal of the state in whose territory the act was committed or by such international penal tribunal as may have jurisdiction with respect to those contracting states which have accepted its jurisdiction. However, it must be borne in mind that, more inclusively, as a most serious crime under general international law, genocide is covered by universal jurisdiction **(92)** in its most widely conceived range. The Convention stipulates (Art. VII) that genocide shall not be considered as a political offense for purposes of extradition **(75)**.

Unlike other subsequently adopted human rights agreements, the Genocide Convention does not set up any monitoring body or committee. Under Art. VIII any contracting party may call upon the competent organs of the UN (primarily the Security Council) to take such action under the UN Charter as considered appropriate for the prevention and suppression of acts of genocide. Moreover (Art. IX), disputes **(299)** relating to the interpretation and application of the Convention, including those relating to the responsibility of a state **(128)** for genocide shall be submitted to the ICJ at the request of any of the parties to the dispute, which implies the possibility of the ICJ ordering provisional measures **(322)**. A number of states, including those of the Soviet bloc, made reservations **(282)** not accepting the compulsory jurisdiction of the ICJ under Art. IX, an issue that eventually led to the Advisory Opinion of the Court concerning *Reservations to the Convention on the Prevention and Punishment of the Crime of Genocide* (1951 ICJ Rep. 15).

The enforcement of the rules against genocide has been the weakest aspect of the Convention. Apart from the GA qualifying the massacre in the Palestinian Sabra and Shatila refugee camp in Lebanon in 1982 as an act of genocide, the issue of state responsibility for genocide did not come up before international adjudication **(306)** until the 1990s within the context of genocide charges by Bosnia and Herzegovina against Yugoslavia. The large-scale genocide in Rwanda, as described in the Organization of African Unity Report of 2000 of the International Panel of Eminent Personalities of 2000 (40 ILM 141 (2001)), was committed within the context of a civil war and—like the conflict in the former Yugoslavia—resulted in trials of individuals before the special tribunals, the ICTY and the ICTR.

As far as the responsibility of a state for genocide is concerned, in 1993 Bosnia and Herzegovina, under Art. IX of the Genocide Convention, brought a case against Yugoslavia before the ICJ, alleging, *inter alia*, breaches of the Convention by Yugoslavia (*Application of the Convention on the Prevention and Punishment of the Crime of Genocide* (Bosnia-Herzegovina v. Yugoslavia, 1993–). In its Order of 1993 the ICJ indicated provisional measures **(322)** requesting the government of Yugoslavia to take all measures to prevent commission of genocide. Following rejection of Yugoslavia's preliminary objections **(321)** in the Court's Judgment in 1996, the case proceeded to the merits stage, but in the meantime the rump Yugoslavia (the Federal Republic of Yugoslavia) brought preliminary objections against that judgment, resulting in a new case of Yugoslavia v. Bosnia-Herzegovina. In addition, in 1999 charges under the Genocide Convention were also raised by Croatia against Yugoslavia (*Application of the Convention on the Prevention and Punishment of the Crime of Genocide* (Croatia v. Yugoslavia, 1999–)). However, the cases may not even come to judgment because of changed political circumstances. In any event, while responsibility of a state for acts of genocide by individuals might arise, it would not be responsibility of criminal nature which—as yet—is not accepted in international law.

**156. Human Rights and the United Nations Charter.** The crucial question in this context is whether and to what extent the United Nations (UN) Charter imposes upon its member states a legal obligation to observe human rights and fundamental freedoms **(157)**. The Charter refers to human rights in a number of articles (Preamble and Arts. 1(3); 13(1)(b); 55; 56; 62(2); 68; and 76(c)), but only in general terms and without expressly providing for a legal obligation to observe them or giving any definition of the concept of such rights, let alone listing the rights themselves. The Preamble reaffirms the founders' faith in "fundamental human rights, in the dignity and worth of the human person, [and] in the equal rights of men and women." Promoting and encouraging "respect for human rights and fundamental freedoms for all without distinction as to race, sex, language, or religion" is declared to be one of the purposes of the UN (Art. 1(3). In order to assist in the realization of these rights and freedoms the General Assembly (GA) must initiate studies and make recommendations. Furthermore, in the sphere of economic and social cooperation the UN is obliged to promote universal respect for, and observance of, human rights and fundamental freedoms for all with a view to the creation of conditions of stability and well-being among nations (Art. 55(e)). For these purposes the UN Economic and Social Council may make recommendations (Art. 62(2)) and is required to set up commissions for the promotion of human rights (Art. 68), an obligation met in 1946 by the creation of the Commission on Human Rights **(161)**. Encouraging respect for human rights is also one of the principal objectives of the now historical international trusteeship system (Art. 76(c)) **(142)**.

Central to the problem of human rights is Art. 56 whereby the "members pledge themselves to take joint and separate action in cooperation with the Organization for the achievement of the purposes set forth in Article 55," that is, respect for, and observance of, human rights. This rather general and vague provision, reaffirmed in the Friendly Relations declaration of the GA in 1970 **(14)**, is usually not interpreted as directly conferring any rights under the UN Charter upon individuals **(164)**, but is viewed as an obligation of states to make reasonable efforts, without any specific time period, in support of the human rights purposes of the UN. But if a state deliberately adopted a retrogressive posture in its human rights policy then it would be violative of Art. 56 of the UN Charter.

In view of the above, it is controversial whether the human rights provisions of the Charter are directly binding and enforceable under municipal law **(27)** although, exceptionally, in some countries, for example Canada, courts have occasionally treated these provisions as binding, self-executing treaty obligations However, in the often quoted case of *Sei Fuji v. State of California* (1952) the Supreme Court of California held that the relevant provisions of the UN Charter were not self-executing and did not purport to create directly any rights for individuals, requiring further legislative action by a state (that is, the United States) to turn them into an enforceable domestic law **(19)**.

It is essential to bear in mind that from the very beginning UN organs have increasingly followed the view that consideration by the UN of human rights violations by member states is a legitimate concern of the Organization and its members; it cannot be regarded as intervention in their domestic affairs, in no way conflicting with the domestic jurisdiction **(9)** limitation of the UN powers stipulated in Art. 2(7) of the Charter.

**157. Human Rights, Concept of.** While there exists no universal consensus on, or an authoritative definition of, human rights and fundamental freedoms, they are those fundamental and inalienable rights and freedoms essential to all human beings which every individual should enjoy as of right and which all states have the duty to recognize, respect, and promote. Some of these rights are considered so fundamental that, as stipulated in some human rights treaties, they cannot be derogated from even in time of public emergency threatening the life of the nation. Under Art.

4(2) of the International Covenant on Civil and Political Rights **(166)** such rights and freedoms include the rights to: life, recognition as a person before the law; freedom of thought, conscience, and religion; freedom from torture **(182)** or cruel, inhuman or degrading treatment or punishment; from slavery and servitude **(180)**; from imprisonment merely on grounds of inability to fulfill a contractual obligation; and from retroactive application of criminal law. Under Art. 15 of the European Convention for the Protection of Human Rights and Fundamental Freedoms of 1950 **(153)** such rights include the right to life; freedom from torture or cruel or inhuman or degrading treatment or punishment; from slavery or servitude; and from retroactive application of criminal law. Whether human rights obligations should also apply to non-state actors is a rather controversial issue. In principle, such actors should also be bound by fundamental human rights rules, but this position cannot divert the focus of human rights protection from the conduct of states toward their own citizens and residents.

Because of the cultural, economic, and political diversity among the states of the world, it is obviously more difficult to arrive at a consensus on the meaning and content of human rights at the universal level than within a region of the world, often characterized by a more or less homogeneous cultural tradition. That is the major reason why the European system for the protection of human rights **(153)**, now encompassing the whole continent (and actually even part of Asia) is by far more advanced and effective than the global system. In addition, the very concept of "the right" may refer either to a state's obligations toward individuals which are ordinarily of a negative character (prohibitions) and are capable of immediate implementation by the state, such as civil and political rights, or to rights that require positive action by the state and can be fully realized progressively only in the future, such as human rights of an economic, social, and cultural nature **(169)**, or the postulated "third generation" rights, such as the right to democratic governance. Finally, there is the fundamental problem of the legal personality of individuals under international law **(81)** entailing the need to distinguish an individual's right conferred directly by international law from a benefit that an individual is entitled to receive from the state which is legally bound to grant it to the individual under an international agreement.

Historically, the conceptual foundations of the human rights movement in international law date back to the 18th-century natural law **(29)** philosophy of John Locke, Jean-Jacques Rousseau, and others within the context of the social contract hypothesis and the natural and inalienable rights and fundamental freedoms of men and citizens. Designed to restrict the power of the government over the citizens, such rights were proclaimed, *inter alia*, in 1776 in the American Declaration of Independence and the Bill of Rights and in France in the Declaration of the Rights of Man and the Citizen in 1789. Eventually, such basic rights and freedoms were anchored in the constitutions of many countries, especially in Western Europe. They included primarily the right to life, liberty, equality before the law, fair trial, freedom of speech, assembly, and religion, and so on, and became known as civil and political rights. Rather misleadingly, and to the prejudice of the notion of the universal and indivisible human rights, they are often referred to as the first generation of human rights, as distinguished from the second generation which, under the impact of socialist and welfare state ideologies, encompasses various economic, social, and cultural rights increasingly recognized in the 20th century as valid claims of individuals to various benefits to be provided by the state. While the civil and political rights have been emphasized by the Western states, the less-developed countries claim that priority should be given to the other category, considering the major economic and social challenges facing them in these areas. Furthermore, going beyond the "second generation" rights, there emerged an idea of the "third generation" of human rights which, unlike the other two, would be vested not in individuals but in the aggregate. This idea of group or solidarity rights was largely but not exclusively associated with the Third World countries' demands for a New International Economic Order and included, in addition to the right of self-determination **(122)**, the right to development endorsed by the Rio Earth Summit in 1992 **(223)** and the General Assembly (GA) in 1986 and 1993. Other suggested third generation rights included the right to a clean environment, the right to peace, and the right to a democratic system of governance, the latter championed by democratic countries in the United Nations (UN) Commission on Human Rights **(161)** where in 1999 they sponsored a resolution, adopted by a vote of 50 with two abstentions (China and Cuba), affirming the right to democracy as a human right. Ultimately, however, the third generation group rights are too vague in their nature and the identity of their subjects as well as the entity responsible for their implementation. Thus far they have not yet achieved recognition as rights under international law.

The UN concept of human rights is based on the premise that ultimately all human rights are of equal priority and mutually interdependent. In reaction to cultural relativism voiced in 1993 in the Bangkok Declaration of Asian states, which challenged the concept of universal human rights as based on the Western values and declared the need to differentiate the approach to human rights according to the national and regional context of the culture and historical tradition, the 1993 Vienna Declaration and Program of Action of the UN World Conference on Human Rights, attended by 171 states and adopted by acclamation (32 ILM 1661 (1993)), reaffirmed the universal nature of all human rights. It emphasized that they must be promoted and protected in an equal measure and with the same emphasis despite national and regional particularities and various historical, cultural, and religious backgrounds. Also, in 1993 in creating the post of the High Commissioner for Human Rights **(158)**, the GA decided that the Commissioner "be guided by the recognition that all human rights—civil, cultural, economic, political and social—are universal, indivisible, interdependent and interrelated and that, while the significance of national and regional particularities and various historical, cultural and religious background must be borne in mind, it is the duty of States, regardless of their political, economic and cultural systems, to promote and protect all human rights and fundamental freedoms" (para. 3(b)). Furthermore, the UN Educational, Scientific, and Cultural Organization Universal Declaration on Cultural Diversity, 2002 (41 ILM 57 (2002)), while acknowledging cultural diversity, stressed that no one may invoke it to infringe upon human rights guaranteed by international law, nor to limit their scope. The problem of the content and scope of human right remains acutely relevant, being highlighted by such matters as discrimination against women **(183)**; child labor **(150)**; excessive use of the death penalty; and torture and inhuman punishment, still officially practiced in some countries on grounds of religious laws. In the new century there is as yet no consensus on the substance of human rights in the multicultural world and while the idea of the international legal protection of human rights as such seems to be accepted by all states, there is a continued tension between claims of domestic jurisdiction on the one hand and international concern on the other.

**158. Human Rights, High Commissioner for.** A post at the rank of Under-Secretary-General of the United Nations (UN) created by consensus by a Resolution of the General Assembly (GA) in 1993 on the High Commissioner for the Promotion and Protection of All Human Rights (33 ILM 303 (1994)). The creation of this office had been recommended by the Declaration and Program of Action of the UN World Conference on Human Rights, 1993 (32 ILM 1661 (1993)). The main Office of the High Commissioner is in Geneva, where its Secretariat maintains the Center for Human Rights, with a liaison office at the UN Headquarters in New York. The first High Commissioner, an Ecuadorian diplomat, was succeeded in 1997 by Mary Robinson, former President of Ireland, succeeded in turn by Sergio Vieira de Mello of Brazil in 2002, after whose tragic death in a bombing in Baghdad in 2003 Louise Arbour, former prosecutor of the International Criminal Tribunal for the Former Yugoslavia (ICTY) became the Commissioner. The High Commissioner is appointed by the UN Secretary-General and approved by the GA, with due regard to geographical rotation, for a fixed term of four years with a possibility of one renewal for four years.

The High Commissioner has principal responsibility for the UN human rights activities. Functioning within the framework of the UN Charter, the Universal Declaration of Human Rights **(162)**, and other international instruments of human rights and international law, the High Commissioner faces the daunting task, spelled out in the constituent Resolution, of reconciling respect for domestic jurisdiction **(9)** of sovereign states with the legitimate concern of the international community in the protection of all human rights. At the same time the Commissioner must recognize the importance of promoting a balanced and sustained development for all people and of ensuring realization of the right to development. The Commissioner must be guided by the principle of universality, indivisibility, and interdependence of all human rights **(157)**. A long list of responsibilities of the office in the Resolution specifies in detail the various tasks and functions to be performed by the Commissioner.

**159. Human Rights, International Customary Law of.** It is now recognized that a state's obligations with respect to certain human rights and fundamental freedoms have achieved the status of customary law **(39)**. This means that if a state as a matter of state policy practices, encourages, or condones a certain conduct violating a treaty-protected human right or fundamental freedom, for example, freedom from torture **(182)**, that state violates international law regardless of whether or not it is a party to the treaty, if the protection of the right or freedom in question is otherwise part of customary international law. Furthermore, violation of a human right protected by customary law entails a state's responsibility **(128)** toward all other states, *erga omnes* **(12)**, and any state may pursue remedies for the violation irrespective of the nationality **(175)** of the victim. The question is, however, which human rights and freedoms are so important that their violation is proscribed even by customary law. Although there is universal consensus that at least some human rights rules, such as for example prohibition of slavery **(180)** and genocide **(155)**, are already part of customary law, there is no agreement on precisely which other human rights and freedoms have achieved such status. While the protection of some rights may be in the process of crystallizing into a rule of customary international law, it is a difficult and controversial task to determine that the process has been completed. The essence of customary law is constituted by two elements: the behavioral element of general and consistent practice of states and the psychological element of *opinio juris* entailing the conviction of a state's authoritative representatives that the behavior in question is followed by them from a sense of legal obligation and is expected by other states to be followed as enjoined by international law. In the area of human rights the practice of states leading to the emergence of a customary rule of law includes the virtually universal membership in the United Nations (UN) whose Charter proclaims respect for human rights among its principles, and adherence of a very large number of states to human rights instruments drafted under the auspices of the UN, and specifically the Universal Declaration of Human Rights of 1948 **(162)** and other resolutions explicitly or by implication recognizing certain human rights rules as international law as well as certain human rights treaties which have gained practically universal acceptance, such as the Genocide Convention **(155)** or the Convention on the Rights of the Child **(150)**. Additional elements of state practice can be found in national constitutions and legislation which incorporate certain human rights rules in municipal law **(27)**. The emergence of customary international law of human rights has been recognized by the International Court of Justice **(309)** in the case of *Barcelona Traction, Light and Power Company, Limited* (Belgium v. Spain) (1970 ICJ Rep. 3) where the Court held that some of the human rights had entered into the body of general international law. That human rights may be governed by customary law has also been recognized in national courts, as in the case of *Filártiga v. Peña-Irala* before the United States (US) Court of Appeals for the Second Circuit in 1980 (19 ILM 966 (1980)) involving liability for torture by a Paraguayan official, committed in Paraguay, where the Court found that prohibition of state-sponsored torture had become part of customary international law, and as such part of the law of the US **(18)**.

While there may occasionally arise doubt as to the scope and content of standards applicable to the human right or fundamental freedom in question (for example, in case of torture or inhuman treatment or punishment), it is universally recognized and would not be denied by any government that if practiced, encouraged, or condoned by a state as a matter of its policy, the following types of conduct (as listed in secs. 702 (a)–(g) of Restatement (Third)) constitute violations of customary international law or, perhaps, also general principles of law **(38)**, even if not consistently practiced or not part of a pattern: genocide, slavery or slave trade, murder or causing disappearance of individuals, torture or other cruel, inhuman, or degrading treatment or punishment, prolonged arbitrary detention, systematic racial discrimination **(177)** (one might add also systematic religious discrimination), and a consistent pattern of gross violations of internationally recognized human rights. The last-mentioned phrase derives from resolution 1503 of the UN Economic and Social Council in 1971 empowering a subcommittee of the UN Commission on Human Rights **(161)** to deal with individual petitions appearing to reveal such a pattern. As argued in Restatement (Third), the conduct in the form of the pattern refers to other violations of human rights and fundamental freedoms which, while constituting no breaches of customary law if committed in an isolated case or sporadically, do conflict with customary law if part of a consistent pattern of violations of a right as state policy. Of course, they are breaches if committed by a state party to the relevant treaty. In practice, because of disagreements over the definition and scope of some rights and freedoms in a multicultural world, it would sometimes be difficult to prove a consistent pattern of violations recognized universally by all states.

The general trend in the international law of human rights is for additional rights and freedoms to be absorbed into customary law. Among the suggested rights and freedoms have been, in addition to the above-mentioned, freedom from religious discrimination, freedom from gender discrimination, equality before the law, the right to leave and return to one's own country, and the prohibition of *refoulement* of refugees **(178)**. Notwithstanding Art. 17 of the Universal Declaration of Human Rights proclaiming everybody's right to own property, this right or, at least its scope, is too controversial to be considered as part of customary law. In the era of decolonization, the right of self-determination of peoples **(122)** articulated in the human rights Covenants of 1966 on civil and political rights **(166)** and on economic, social, and cultural rights **(169)**, became, in its restrictive anti-colonial context, a part of general (customary) international law. Whether a new post-colonial right of self-determination involving the right of secession can assert itself as a right in customary international law is rather doubtful for the foreseeable future. On the other hand, the right to democratic governance (internal self-determination) has a much better chance in this respect, in particular with respect to new states.

**160. Human Rights, International Law of.** The branch of public international law which governs the obligations and responsibilities of states with regard to recognition, respect for, and observance of human rights and fundamental freedoms **(157)** of all individuals **(164)**. The international law governing human rights comprehensively and protecting all human beings as such has developed largely since the end of World War II. However, certain aspects of what today belongs in this branch of international law were raised already in the 16th century by Francisco Vitoria **(46)** who questioned the unjust treatment by Spaniards of the native inhabitants of the newly discovered America. Other early instances of concern with the treatment of individuals by their states included treaties in the 17th century, including the Peace Treaty of Westphalia **(47)**, stipulating freedom of religion to Catholics and Protestants as the case might be. Much later, in the 19th century, freedom from slavery and suppression of slave trade **(180)** was recognized in customary international law and subsequently reaffirmed by treaties in the 20th century. However, until the emergence of the law of human rights following World War II the treatment by a state of its nationals was regarded as remaining within the domestic jurisdiction **(9)** of sovereign states and only occasionally some publicists would suggest that the law of nations should guarantee all individuals a certain minimum of "rights of mankind." In exceptional situations where atrocities against religious or other minorities **(172)**, as they occurred in the Ottoman Empire against Christians, shocked the conscience of mankind, it was considered justifiable to resort to the otherwise controversial humanitarian intervention **(332)** practiced in the latter half of the 19th century. What now is known as international humanitarian law **(353)** and applies in armed conflict, international **(339)** or not **(340)**, also dates back to that period.

Unlike the case of individuals as such, one category of them, namely, aliens **(144)**, enjoyed unique protection even before the emergence of the modern law of human rights. A body of rules in customary international law **(39)** governing state responsibility **(128)** for injury to aliens according to a minimum international standard of justice **(171)**, championed by the Western states, had emerged already by the turn of the 19th century. Although it protected only foreign nationals, this branch of public international law made a significant contribution to the eventual development of a body of human rights law applying to all individuals regardless of nationality **(175)**. Along with the principle of natural and inalienable human rights proclaimed in the latter decades of the 18th century in the newly created United States (US) and in the Revolutionary France, and later affirmed in many national constitutions and bills of rights, the standards of international law governing the status of aliens can be regarded as precursors of the contemporary law of human rights.

In the aftermath of World War I (1914–1918) the peace treaties and other international instruments instituted provisions designed to protect the rights of three specific categories of individuals. First, there were treaty clauses protecting national minorities **(172)** in central and eastern Europe. Second, the mandate system **(93)** was created specifically in the interests of the inhabitants of the former enemy overseas possessions. While the arrangements created for the protection of minorities and the inhabitants of the mandated territories proved to be (except for the continuation of the mandate idea in the form of the now also extinct trusteeship system) **(142)** rather short-lived experiments, the third category of provisions, namely the many conventions and other international instruments, drafted by the International Labour Organisation (ILO) and designed to protect and enhance the standards of treatment of labor, have continued until today, making a lasting contribution to the international protection of human rights in the economic and social spheres.

The lessons of World War II (1939–1945), and especially the atrocities committed by Nazi Germany, provided a powerful stimulus for generating a more comprehensive approach to the protection of the rights of all individuals as human beings. The signing in 1945 of the United Nations (UN) Charter which, *inter alia*, stipulates the promotion and protection of human rights as a purpose of the Organization **(156)**, marks the beginning of the contemporary international law of human rights based on the principle that, subject to the rule of exhaustion of local remedies **(74)**, the treatment of all human beings, including a state's citizens, is no longer within the state's domestic jurisdiction but a matter of international concern which may be regulated by international law.

The main body of the law of human rights is constituted by a growing number of international agreements **(288)**, but the protection of certain fundamental rights and freedoms has acquired the status of customary law **(159)** which has a tendency to expand into additional areas of human rights. Since provisions protecting such human rights and freedoms are anchored in constitutions of many countries and protected by legislation they could arguably also be evidence of general principles of law recognized by civilized nations **(38)**.

Apart from a limited number of pre-1945 agreements, the bulk of the treaty law of human rights has resulted from action taken at the global level by the UN. Regionally, the European system for the protection of human rights is the most advanced and effective one, encompassing virtually all the European states now bound by the Council of Europe-sponsored European Convention of 1950 for the Protection of Human Rights and Fundamental Freedoms **(153)** which provides for a permanent European Court of Human Rights **(154)**. Another international instrument upholding human rights in Europe is the Final Act of the Conference on Security and Cooperation, adopted (with Canada and the US also taking part) in Helsinki in 1975 (14 ILM 1292 (1975)). While not a treaty, this "soft law" **(35)** instrument, dealing, *inter alia*, with human rights, has provided a major forum for discussing human rights in Europe and played a useful moral and political role especially in the Cold War era. The inter-American system is based on the Charter of the Organization of American States (119 UNTS 3) and the American Convention on Human Rights of 1969 **(147)** providing for an Inter-American Court of Human Rights **(165)** which, however, despite some progress in the promotion of human rights in the Western hemisphere, has been much less active than its European counterpart. In Africa the Banjul Charter on Human and Peoples' Rights **(143)** is the major human rights instrument, but it has not been able to make any significant contribution in this area. However, the newly created African Union provides for an international court with a competence to deal with human rights violations in the region.

The Universal Declaration of Human Rights of 1948 **(162)**, although not a treaty itself, is the principal and fundamental international instrument elaborating on the UN Charter's concept of human rights. It was largely the work of the UN Commission on Human Rights **(161)** which, established as an organ of the UN Economic and Social Council (ECOSOC) in 1946, constitutes the crucial political organ of the UN in the area of human rights. The rights and freedoms listed in the Universal Declaration were articulated in more detail and converted into two separate legally binding instruments in 1966: the International Covenant on Civil and Political Rights (ICCPR) **(166)** with two Optional Protocols of 1966 **(167)** and 1989 **(168)** respectively and the International Covenant on Economic, Social, and Cultural Rights (ICESCR) **(169)**. The division into two distinct human rights treaties, each with its own measures of implementation, had been decided upon by the General Assembly in 1952 at the insistence of the Western states arguing for a separate treatment because of the difference between economic, social, and cultural rights which were in essence aspirations for the future and the traditional civil and political rights whose observance, unlike the former category of rights, could be implemented by states relatively promptly without the need for any far-reaching economic and social investments. The Universal Declaration, the ICCPR with its Protocols, and the ICESCR constitute what is known as the International Bill of Human Rights, dealing comprehensively with human rights at the universal level. In addition, a large number of multilateral conventions deal with the protection of specific rights, focusing either on specific categories of individuals or treating a specific human rights problem. A number of such agreements were concluded before the adoption of the two Covenants of 1966, with some of them, such as slavery and slave trade and related conventions, dating back to the turn of the 19th century. Problems of nationality and statelessness **(181)** were subjects of conventions already in the inter-war period. While the protection of labor had been a subject of a limited number of international agreements before World War I, the ILO, since its creation in 1919, has been involved in drafting a large number of conventions dealing with various aspects of the rights of workers: freedom of association, employment, and social conditions of labor.

Among the major global human rights conventions with focus on specific issues are: 1. A number of conventions on prevention of discrimination, the major ones being the International Convention on the Elimination of All Forms of Racial Discrimination of 1966 **(177)** and the International Convention on the Suppression and Punishment of the Crime of Apartheid of 1973 (13 ILM 50 (1974). There are also conventions against apartheid in sports; discrimination in employment and occupation; a convention against discrimination in education, with a protocol; and a convention on equal remuneration; 2. Slavery, servitude, forced labor and similar institutions and practices are proscribed in five conventions, most of them predating the contemporary era of the human rights law; 3. In the area of human rights and the administration of justice the major and only treaty is the Convention against Torture and Other Cruel, Inhuman or Degrading Treatment or Punishment of 1984. There are, however, numerous other international instruments concerning the administration of justice which are in the nature of soft law (guidelines, principles, rules, declarations, etc.); 4. The Convention on the International Right of Correction deals with an aspect of the fight to freedom of information; 5. Freedom of association, employment and other aspects of labor relations have been largely covered since the establishment of the ILO in 1919 by conventions drafted by this specialized agency of the UN. Of interest here is the relatively recent Convention (No. 169) of 1989 concerning Indigenous and Tribal Peoples **(163)** in Independent Countries; 6. Concerning crimes against humanity **(151)**, there exists no general substantive treaty, but there is the Convention of 1968 on the Non-Applicability of Statutory Limitations to War Crimes and Crimes against Humanity (754 UNTS 73).

Among treaties focusing on the protection of the rights of specific categories of individuals are: 1. Conventions dealing with the rights of women **(183)**, namely, the Convention of 1979 on the Elimination of All Forms of Discrimination against Women (1249 UNTS 13) with a Protocol (not yet in force), and the Convention of 1952 on the Political Rights of Women. One could also include here the Convention on the Nationality of Married Women, 1957, designed to protect married women's right to nationality; 2. The rights of children are the subject of the Convention of 1989 on the Rights of the Child, with two Optional Protocols on the involvement of children in armed conflict and on the sale of children, child prostitution, and child pornography (not yet in force), respectively **(150)**; 3. In the area of social welfare the Convention of 1990 on the Protection of the Rights of All Migrant Workers and Members of Their Families is not yet in force; 4. Refugees **(178)** are covered by the Convention of 1951 (189 UNTS 137) and the Protocol of 1967 (606 UNTS 267) which incorporates its substantive provisions. The related problem of statelessness is addressed in two conventions: the Convention of 1954 relating to the Status of Stateless Persons and the Convention of 1961 on the Reduction of Statelessness; and 5. International humanitarian law **(353)** protects specific categories of victims of armed conflict, international **(339)**, or civil **(340)**. The four Geneva "Red Cross" Conventions of 1949 **(349)** focus respectively on: wounded and sick in armed forces in the field; wounded, sick, and shipwrecked members of armed forces at sea; prisoners of war **(364)**; and civilian persons in time of war. The two Protocols of 1977 **(369)** deal with the protection of victims of international and non-international conflict, respectively.

The body of human rights conventions is complemented by numerous other international instruments entitled declarations, proclamations, principles, rules, codes of conduct, guidelines, safeguards, recommendations, and "model treaties" suggested for specific aspects of human rights. While technically not legally binding, such soft law instruments may eventually provide the basis for widening the conventional (or customary) law of human rights into heretofore legally not regulated areas of common positions and consensus.

The emergence and expansion of the international law of human rights has been perhaps the most remarkable development in public international law since 1945. However, the adoption of effective remedies to induce compliance with the human rights law has largely lagged behind the adoption of substantive rules and in many countries the rights proclaimed in the basic human rights instruments remain little more than a paper promise. Although obligations under the treaties and any customary rules are binding like any other obligations under international law, international concern over violations of human rights (which in their nature injure individuals in the states involved) is not so strong as breaches of international law directly affecting states. While any state party to a human rights treaty has in principle the right *erga omnes* **(12)** to demand remedies for a violation by any other party, states are reluctant to do so for political considerations. As a result, enforcement of the human rights rules remains the weakest point in the system, except at the regional level in Europe (and, to a certain degree, in the Western Hemisphere) where, unlike at the global level, international adjudication **(306)** has become an accepted method of ensuring compliance.

At the global level, the persistence of domestic jurisdiction arguments allows international supervision only through resort to monitoring mechanisms, in the form of committees created under the treaty concerned or special procedures established by the UN, both of which types of monitoring lack the usual attributes of judicial settlement. Committees ("treaty bodies") set up by treaty exist under the Conventions dealing with: the rights of the child; civil and political rights (Human Rights Committee); torture; economic, social, and cultural rights; elimination of racial discrimination; and elimination of discrimination against women. The monitoring mechanism under these conventions consists of periodic reports; inter-state complaints (possible only if the state involved accepted the procedure in an optional clause), a procedure which however has not been used in practice; and, also optionally, as in the first Optional Protocol **(167)** to the ICCPR, the complaint procedure initiated by individuals or groups of individuals filing complaints on breaches of their rights by a state. The UN-established monitoring mechanisms include, first, those set up by the ECOSOC in Resolution 1235 in 1967 and Resolution 1503 in 1970, as amended in 2000, which involve investigation by the UN Commission on Human Rights and some other bodies and deal only with such individual and group complaints as involve "a consistent pattern of gross violations." Second, generally speaking, the Commission operates using working groups or rapporteurs and focusing either on certain human rights problems, or themes or on specific countries. However, fact-finding missions to a country are possible only with that country's consent. Finally, the Office of the High Commissioner for Human Rights **(158)** was created in 1993 to undertake the challenging task of overseeing the whole UN system of protecting and promoting human rights.

The UN receives more than 100,000 complaint communications about human rights violations, but only a very minute fraction reaches the stage of resolution agreed by the rather politicized Commission on Human Rights, and the more legally conceived system of petitions before the treaty bodies, for various reasons (procedural requirements, shortage of legal staff, and the like) reviews only some 100 complaints out of the above-mentioned total of the communications filed.

In general, in the highly sensitive human rights issues the monitoring bodies of the UN system must avoid confrontation with governments and their effectiveness resides more in focusing world opinion on major human rights violations and mobilization of shame pressuring delinquent governments to improve their human rights record. Their function has also been to clarify, interpret, and develop in more detail the standards to be observed in complying with the human rights conventions. An effective international system of enforcing these standards remains the major task of the law of human rights in the 21st century.

When discussing enforcement of international human rights standards, one must not overlook the possibility of victims of human rights violations pursuing their claims before a municipal court of a country that may be willing to exercise its jurisdiction on a "universal principle" **(92)** even if the violation occurred outside its territory and did not involve its national. The US has been the country that has provided a venue for civil litigation by aliens on the basis of an old statute of 1789 (Alien Torts Claims Act) under which US district courts have "original jurisdiction of any civil action by an alien for a tort only, committed in violation of the law of nations or a treaty of the United States." Beginning with the landmark case of *Filártiga v. Peña-Irala* in 1980, involving nationals of Paraguay suing an official of that state for state-sponsored torture and death of their relative in Paraguay, US courts have exercised jurisdiction under the 1789 statute in cases brought by victims against high officials accused of torture and other human rights violations in such countries as Argentina, Bosnia and Herzegovina, Chile, East Timor, Ethiopia, Guatemala, Haiti, and the Philippines. One must bear in mind, however, that these suits were all civil actions against specific individual officials of a foreign state, as a rule physically not present in the US, and not criminal trials for violations that otherwise could be regarded as crimes under international law **(151)**. On the other hand, some European countries, such as Belgium and Spain allowed criminal prosecution for such violations. In addition, the celebrated case (1998–1999) of extradition **(75)** request brought in the United Kingdom (UK) by Spanish prosecutors for extradition to Spain, under the European Convention on Extradition, of the former president of Chile, Augusto Pinochet, for violations, primarily in Chile, of the Torture Convention, ended after a prolonged legal battle (38 ILM 68 (1999); 37 ILM 1302 (1998); 38 ILM 489 (1999); 38 ILM 430 (1999)) with the judgment of the UK Bow Street Magistrates' Court (*The Kingdom of Spain v. Augusto Pinochet Ugarte*) (39 ILM 135 (2000)) which ruled, following the opinion of a new seven-member panel of the Lords of Appeal (38 ILM 581 (1999)), that Pinochet had no immunity from extradition to be tried in Spain. Thus, legally, the idea of human rights was vindicated in the UK, but later the Home Secretary, with whom the final decisions on extradition rest in the UK, declined to extradite Pinochet on grounds of ill health, and allowed him to return to Chile.

**161. Human Rights, United Nations Commission on.** A subsidiary body of the United Nations Economic and Social Council (ECOSOC) set up in 1946 pursuant to Art. 68 of the United Nations (UN) Charter, charged with the promotion of human rights in implementation of the principles set forth in Arts. 55 and 56 of the Charter. The Commission is a political body composed of representatives of 53 UN member states chosen in secret vote, with the right of reelection, to a three-year term on the basis of equitable geographical distribution. The Commission meets in annual six-week sessions in March and April. In addition to the 53 states represented there, over 3,000 other participants, such as delegates of observer states, non-governmental organizations **(86)** and UN specialized agencies and other organizations are allowed to attend public sessions. In urgent situations a special session can be convened with the agreement of a majority of states members of the Commission. For the first time since the establishment of the Commission, in 2001 the United States (US) failed to be elected as a member but regained its seat a year later. The chairmanship of the Commission is selected by consensus under a rotating system whereby a candidate is nominated by the regional group whose turn it is to propose the chairman for the annual session. For the 2003 session the African grouping nominated Libya, whereupon the US, motivated by that country's poor human rights record, insisted on a vote (an unprecedented move) which resulted in favor of Libya (33 against 3, with 17 abstentions). The above-mentioned two episodes highlighted the need for a reform of the membership rules of the Commission which would take into account the observance of human rights of the states aspiring for a seat on the Commission, excluding those with questionable records.

In general, the Commission adopts about a hundred resolutions and decisions during an annual session, assisted by working groups, experts, representatives, and rapporteurs reporting to it on specific issues. The Commission monitors both specific countries (country mechanisms or mandates) and certain aspects of human rights violations worldwide (thematic mechanisms or mandates). For example, in early 2003 mandates to monitor specific countries chaired by special rapporteurs or UN experts existed on situations in 11 countries (Afghanistan, Bosnia and Herzegovina, Federal Republic of Yugoslavia [now Serbia and Montenegro], Burundi, Cambodia, Congo [former Zaire], Haiti, Iraq, Myanmar, Somalia, Sudan) and the Palestinian territories occupied **(363)** since 1967. At the same time there were 16 thematic mandates on a variety of human rights problems.

Initially, the Commission had no authority to hear individual complaints addressed to the UN and in the first two decades focused its work on drafting human rights instruments and related activities. In 1967, mainly as part of the anti-apartheid campaign, the Commission obtained, under ECOSOC Resolution 1235, the competence to "examine information relevant to gross violations of human rights" originating from complaints communicated by individuals and groups of individuals and to study "situations which reveal a consistent pattern of violations of human rights." On this basis the Commission undertakes public investigation against specific states, operating either on an *ad hoc* basis or through a standing group. A resolution deploring or condemning a state's violations may be adopted, but such result is rather rare since in this highly politicized organ of the UN its members are reluctant directly to criticize ideologically close countries, and voting alliances often bloc attempts of other members to single out a country for condemnation by the Commission. In 1970 the ECOSOC Resolution 1503 authorized the Commission's Subcommission on the Prevention of Discrimination and the Protection of Minorities **(172)**, since 2000 known as the Subcommission on the Promotion and Protection of Human Rights, to examine, in a confidential procedure by a special working group, individual complaints. The working group then reports to the Subcommittee on complaints which appear to reveal a "consistent pattern of gross and reliably attested violations of human rights," even by states which are not parties to the agreement involved. Ultimately, the Commission may undertake a more thorough study of the situation and make a recommendation to the ECOSOC. It may also decide to set up an *ad hoc* committee to investigate the situation with the express consent of the state concerned. Although many states have been its subject, this procedure, essentially concerned with situations, proved to be rather ineffective because of the confidentiality and politicized nature of the Commission, otherwise handicapped by the lack of enforcement power and of the competence to hear witnesses or to enter a state's territory without an invitation in order to conduct investigations. However, as of early 2003, 42 countries had extended a standing invitation to the thematic procedures of the Commission

In its 2002 session the Commission was able to adopt a resolution, sponsored by Latin American states, urging Cuba to grant its citizens more political rights, a decision which precipitated a strong, hostile reaction by Cuba and led to a serious diplomatic dispute. Unlike some of the past sessions, China avoided censure for the suppression of religious freedom of Tibetans and other minorities. There was also no criticism of Iran, once subject to the Commission's condemnation, and a resolution condemning Russia for violations of human rights in Chechnya was narrowly defeated. Iraq, Myanmar, and Sudan were among the countries whose human rights abuses were deplored, as was also Israel, for many years a target of the Commission which has criticized it for breaches of international humanitarian law **(353)**, devoting to Israel a disproportionate amount of time (15 percent) and a third of the Commission's country-oriented resolutions. A new theme for the Commission to examine has become the question whether combating terrorism **(337)** can be an excuse for restricting human rights, but so far the Commission has not taken any definite stand on this issue.

The UN Commission on Human Rights certainly needs reforming, especially insofar as the problem of selecting its membership is concerned. Nevertheless, its reports and public discussions have alerted international public opinion to human rights abuses. Apart from its valuable work on drafting international human rights standards, it has made a positive contribution to the principle that the question of human rights is no longer within the domestic jurisdiction of states **(9)** but within the domain of international law.

**162. Human Rights, Universal Declaration of, 1948.** A General Assembly (GA) resolution adopted in 1948 by 48 votes to none with eight abstentions (by the Communist states, Saudi Arabia, and South Africa), containing in 30 articles a comprehensive list of human rights **(157)** including both civil and political as well as economic, social, and cultural rights. As agreed by the adopting governments, the Declaration is not a legally binding instrument but—in the words of its preamble—"a common standard of achievement for all peoples and all nations" which the member states are recommended to keep constantly in mind, in striving to secure, by progressive measures, the universal and effective recognition of the rights and freedoms listed in the Declaration.

The rights proclaimed by the Declaration, eventually known as civil and political rights **(166)** and in their substance very much influenced by Western values, include, *inter alia*, the rights to life, liberty, and security; to nationality **(175)** and asylum **(148)**; to marry; to own property; freedom from slavery and servitude **(180)**; from torture and cruel and inhuman or degrading treatment or punishment **(182)**; freedom of movement and residence; freedom of thought, opinion, conscience, and religion; the right to peaceful assembly and association; equality before the law and fundamental judicial safeguards; and the right to free elections and equal opportunity and access to take part in the government and public service of the country. Among the rights which became known as economic, social, and cultural rights **(169)** the Declaration mentions the rights to: social security, equal pay for equal work, the right to join trade unions, to an adequate standard of living; favorable conditions of work; protection against unemployment; the right to rest and leisure; the right to education at least in the elementary stage; and the right freely to participate in the cultural life of the country. All these rights are to be enjoyed without any distinction as to race, color, sex, language, religion, political or other opinion, national or social origin, property, birth or other status. They cannot be curtailed except by legally determined limitations solely for the purpose of securing respect for the right of others and of meeting the just requirements of morality, public order, and the general welfare in a democratic society.

While legally not binding at its adoption as a resolution of the GA, the Declaration was designed as a blueprint for the future treaty codification of human rights, providing at the same time an authoritative guide to the pertinent provisions of the United Nations Charter **(156)**. In the decades following its adoption the standards set by the Declaration have had a considerable impact upon the process of drafting many human rights treaties **(160)**. It has been referred to in national constitutions and legislation as well as in international and municipal law judicial decisions and innumerable invocations by national and international public organs and by individuals complaining of violation of their rights. At least insofar as certain fundamental human rights and freedoms are concerned, the widespread endorsement of the Universal Declaration can arguably be evidence of its binding force under international customary law **(39)** or general principles of law recognized by civilized nations **(38)**.

**163. Indigenous Peoples.** Over the last three decades of the 20th century the concept of indigenous population or in more recent (since 1988) terminology "indigenous peoples" has acquired a considerable significance in transnational **(43)** and international relations, but its meaning and implications have been a subject of controversy. It is arguable that as an international legal concept it is redundant since indigenous peoples are simply a special category of minority **(172)**. As a matter of fact, while indigenous peoples are relatively clearly differentiated from the dominant majority in European-colonized areas, it may be difficult to distinguish an "indigenous people" from a minority in tribal societies in Africa or in South and Southeast Asia. In any case, in international law indigenous peoples, like minorities, do not possess international legal personality **(85)** and are not subjects of international law.

The special rapporteur in a United Nations (UN) 1983 study of the problem of discrimination against indigenous population, within the Working Group on Indigenous Populations established in 1982, defined "indigenous communities, peoples and nations" as "those which, having a historical continuity with pre-invasion and pre-colonial societies . . . consider themselves distinct from other sectors of the societies now prevailing in those territories . . . or parts of them. They form at present non-dominant sectors of society and are determined to preserve, develop and transmit to future generations their ancestral territories, and their ethnic identity, as the basis of their continued existence as peoples, in accordance with their own cultural patterns, social institutions and legal systems." On the other hand, the International Labour Organisation (ILO) Convention No. 169 of 1989 concerning Indigenous and Tribal Peoples in Independent Countries (28 ILM 1382 (1989)), a revision of the original Convention No. 107 of 1957 (328 UNTS 247), still in force for some states, which incidentally used the term "populations," not "peoples," applies not only to indigenous peoples in post-colonial societies and those who inhabited the area at the time of the establishment of present state boundaries, but also to the category of "tribal peoples" in independent countries, socially, culturally, and economically distinguished from the other sectors of the national society and whose status is regulated by their own customs and traditions or by special laws and regulations (Art. 1(1)). A directive of the World Bank, a UN specialized agency with some interest in indigenous affairs, included under the collective concept of indigenous peoples such groups as "indigenous peoples" themselves, "indigenous ethnic minorities," "tribal groups, and "scheduled tribes," all of them groups socially and culturally distinct from the dominant society and vulnerable to being disadvantaged in the development process. The indigenous peoples' movement, initially focusing on various groups in the Europeanized areas, such as aborigines in Australia, Maoris in New Zealand, Indians, Aleutians, and Inuit (Eskimo) in North America, and the Saami (Lapp) in Europe, acquired momentum in the 1980s and '90s to rally numerous organized groups in Asia, including the Ainus in Japan, hill tribes in Thailand, the Karen in Myanmar, various native groups in India, such as the Naga, the aborigines of Taiwan **(139)**, the native tribes of Sarawak and Sabah in East Malaysia (North Borneo), and indigenous peoples of Indonesia, including West Papua, the Moluccas, and other groups, in Africa (the Berbers in North Africa, and various Subsaharan tribes) and in South America (the Amazon Indians). It is estimated that the total number of members of indigenous groups amounts to about 300 million. The movement got organized in a transnational network of organizations headquartered either in home countries or—for political reasons—abroad. The foundation in 1975, on the initiative of the Canadian Indians movement, of the World Council of Indigenous Peoples (WCIP) was an important turning point in the organizational development of the indigenous peoples' movement, which became a major factor in voicing the demands of the increasingly assertive indigenous peoples from all regions. In this action the Working Group on Indigenous Populations within the UN, created in 1982, constituted the major form of expression for indigenous peoples. Furthermore, some 15 indigenous organizations have obtained a consultative status with the UN Economic and Social Council. In 1994 the Subcommission on the Prevention of Discrimination and Protection of Minorities (now known as Subcommission on the Promotion and Protection of Human Rights) of the UN Commission on Human Rights **(161)** adopted a Draft UN Declaration on the Rights of Indigenous Peoples (34 ILM 541 (1995)). At the same time the General Assembly proclaimed the years 1995–2005 as the International Decade of the World's Indigenous Peoples. Although legally not binding, the 1994 Draft Declaration was a groundbreaking international instrument which recognized the group rights of indigenous peoples, contributing in this sense to developing a body of customary international law **(39)** on the subject.

So far, in practice, claims involving indigenous rights are instituted within the ambit of an already established area of international law such as, for example, the law of the sea **(254)**, environmental law **(197)**, the law of treaties, and especially the law of human rights, including rights of minorities and the right of self-determination **(122)** in the meaning of internal autonomy of the group concerned. As articulated in more detail in the 1994 Declaration, the body of human rights law applying specifically to indigenous peoples rests on the fundamental principles of the right of self-control of the indigenous land and the requirement for the national state to obtain indigenous consent in all maters affecting the indigenous people. It is generally understood that the right of self-determination of indigenous peoples, articulated in the two Covenants of 1966 and in the Declaration of 1994, is limited to internal self-determination in the sense of a people's right to pursue its political, legal, economic, social, and cultural development within the framework of an existing state, without any threat to the state's territorial integrity. This proviso is implied, *inter alia*, in Art. 1(3) of ILO Convention No. 169 of 1989 concerning indigenous and tribal peoples in independent countries and in a footnote to sec. 2 of the Declaration on the Establishment of the Arctic Council, adopted by the eight states of the Arctic region (Canada, Denmark, Finland, Iceland, Norway, Russia, Sweden, and the United States (US)) in Ottawa in 1996 (35 ILM 1382 (1996)). The right to recognize and observe treaties between an indigenous people and a state is included in the right to self-government, but the status of such agreements which are not treaties in the sense of international law is not entirely clear.

The right of political participation of indigenous peoples involves their right to control their own process of development and the right to be consulted and participate in the decision-making process of the state when matters affecting them are considered. This right has been upheld in a number of national judicial decisions and constitutes an important element in the cooperation of the Arctic states within the Arctic Council in which up to seven organizations representing indigenous communities may participate, albeit without vote, in the work of the Council. Among the organizations recognized by the Council are: the Inuit Circumpolar Conference, the Saami Council, the Russian Association of Indigenous Peoples of the North, and the Aleut International Association.

The special collective relationship of indigenous peoples to their ancestral lands and territories is of crucial significance for their respective culture and identity, It entails an inalienable right to own and control their traditional land and territories, including the total environment and resources which they have traditionally used. Hence they have the right to their restitution and, where this is not possible, the right to fair and just compensation, preferably in the form of equal lands, territories, and resources. The states concerned are required to protect indigenous peoples against encroachments and environmental degradation, as is also emphasized in Principle 22 of the Declaration on Environment and Development of the Rio Earth Summit **(223)** in 1992. The indigenous peoples' right of ownership and possession over their traditional lands is recognized in Art. 14(1) of ILO Convention No. 169 of 1989 (36 ILO 775 (997)), but this Convention is only in force for a limited number of states, including Denmark and Norway.

Self-identification as indigenous or tribal is to be regarded as a fundamental criterion for determining membership in an indigenous group, a principle laid down in ILO Convention No. 169 and a Draft American Declaration on the Rights of Indigenous Peoples of 1997. Self-identification as indigenous, as opposed to certain "objective" criteria laid down by states, is stressed in the Draft Declaration of 1994 as the basis for defining an indigenous group: "Indigenous peoples have the collective and individual right to maintain and develop their distinct identities and characteristics, including the right to identify themselves as indigenous and to be recognized as such" (Art. 8). The right to exist as a distinct people implies the right to be free from genocide **(155)**, including removal of indigenous children from their communities, and from acts of cultural genocide and dispossessing indigenous peoples from their lands and imposing integration.

At the dawn of the new century, the Draft Declaration on Indigenous Peoples of 1994 still remained a draft of the UN Commission on Human Rights concerning the rights of a special category of minority, but pressures by various transnational organizations promoting the rights of indigenous peoples produced at least a partial improvement in their position along the lines spelled out in the Declaration. However, a distinction must be made between states of the past European colonization, where indigenous groups are clearly differentiated from the dominant majority (Canada, the US, Australia, and New Zealand), and the European Arctic states (with regard to the 80,000 Saami) on the one hand, and states in Africa and especially South Asia, on the other, which are in general opposed to applying the concept of the indigenous people to their "tribal" minorities.

In the states of European settlement, including to a certain extent Latin America, the original policy of assimilation and eventual integration shifted toward recognition of the special rights of indigenous peoples. Aside from the US, where more than 500 Indian tribes have, to a varying degree, self-government, other countries granted special rights to indigenous groups. Thus, in 1997, New Zealand agreed to make a compensation settlement to a major South Island Maori tribe and apologized for the dispossession of tribal land dating back to the Treaty of Waitanga of 1840. In Australia the process of recognizing the rights of aborigines started in the 1990s, but was complicated by their potential claims to as much as 78 percent of the land under a decision of the High Court in 1996 and by painful memories of tens of thousands of mixed-race children (the "stolen generation") removed from their parents in the period of 1910–1970. In a more general context, the question whether the past conduct of European settlers toward the aborigines should be qualified as genocide has been examined in Australian courts and especially in the case of *Nulyarimma v. Thompson* before the Federal Court of Australia in 1999 (39 ILM 20 (2000)).

The most visible progress in the status of indigenous peoples has been achieved in Canada, as demonstrated by the Nisga'a Agreement of 1998 (37 ILM 1258 (1998)) between the Canadian government and an Inuit tribe of 6,000, reached after years of litigation, whereby the members of the tribe obtained a collective ownership of a valley in British Columbia with the right of self-government. In spite of some controversial issues, the settlement is likely to be followed by similar arrangements.

The most dramatic instance of implementing the principles of the 1994 Draft Declaration is offered by the creation in 1999 of Nunavat ("our land" in Inuit), an autonomous territory of some 733,000 square miles (nearly as large as Alaska and California combined) with a population of 25, 000 (85 percent Inuit) receiving absolute ownership and control of 18 percent of the Nunavat territory, a compensation for the remaining land to be paid within 14 years.

Like Canada, a number of Latin American states incorporated provisions guaranteeing the rights of indigenous peoples in their respective constitutions. In Latin America the indigenous population is estimated at 45 million, with high concentrations in Bolivia (71.1 percent), Peru (47 percent), and Ecuador (38 percent). However, although such countries as Brazil, Colombia, and Venezuela recognized the distinctive identity of such groups, no real internal self-determination was granted. In Asia most states, and especially India and China, are opposed to applying the concept of the indigenous people to their various "tribal" groups, arguing that it should apply only in states of past European colonization and not to the Asian states' tribal minorities who otherwise share their ethnic origin with the non-tribal population. Even Japan is reluctant to accept the Ainus as a distinct indigenous group. Only the Philippines accept it with respect to various tribal minorities. The treatment of indigenous tribes in Myanmar, Bangladesh, let alone Indonesia, departs far from the principles expressed in the Draft Declaration of 1994.

**164. Individuals in International Law.** Although in the several decades following the end of World War II individuals have increasingly acquired rights under international law for specific limited purposes and have in rather rare cases been found criminally responsible for crimes directly under international law, such situations of individuals as subjects of international law **(81)** belong to exceptions from the general rule that individuals are not endowed with legal personality under international law. Even as far as rights are concerned, in particular human rights **(157)**, they are still, as a rule, conferred upon individuals by the state **(127)** through the linkage of nationality **(175)** pursuant to the state's treaty **(288)** obligations.

Yet the traditional positivist **(31)** dichotomy between states as subjects and individuals as objects of international law is being blurred in practice and rejected by a sizable part of the doctrine mindful of the fact that in the final analysis individuals are the ultimate actors, both beneficiaries and injured persons, in international law and relations. Although treaty rules concerned with individuals were not unknown in the more distant past, as in the case of aliens **(144)** and minorities **(172)**, the treatment of individuals by their respective governments was within the domestic jurisdiction **(9)** of the state. The emergence of human rights law and individual criminal responsibility initiated a new trend in the approach to the status of individuals in international law, placing them within the bounds of international law concerns. Both in respect of rights and of duties, the tendency is to expand the legal personality of individuals on the international plane.

**165. Inter-American Court of Human Rights.** The Inter-American Court of Human Rights (IACHR) is a judicial body established in 1969 under the American Convention on Human Rights **(147)** whose function is to supervise, along with the Inter-American Commission on Human Rights, the observance of the rights and freedoms listed in the Convention. Effectively set up in 1979 with headquarters in San José, Costa Rica, the Court operates on the basis of the Convention and the Statute approved by the Organization of American Studies (OAS) General Assembly in 1978. The Court adopted its Rules of Procedure in 1980.

The IACHR is made up of seven judges, nationals of OAS states, not necessarily parties to the Convention. The judges, who otherwise may follow other careers, are elected by the states parties to the Convention for six-year, once-renewable terms from a panel of candidates proposed by these states. The United States is not a party to the Convention.

Like the International Court of Justice (ICJ) **(309)**, the IACHR has contentious and advisory **(291)** jurisdiction. Only the Commission and states parties have the right to submit cases. Although individuals activate proceedings they do not have direct access to the Court. Petitions from individuals have first to go through proceedings before the Commission which examines their admissibility, verifies exhaustion of local remedies **(74)**, and carries out procedure on the merits, with the possibility of on-site investigation. A friendly settlement procedure is possible on the basis of the consent of the parties. The Rules of Procedure of the Commission of 2001 (40 ILM 752 (2001)) also provide for a Commission's report taking account of information that is a matter of public knowledge. If within three months following the transmittal of the report to the state concerned the matter has not been solved, the Commission may refer the case to the Court. Otherwise, it issues a final report with its opinion and recommendations. It also appears before the Court in all cases.

As in the case of the ICJ, the jurisdiction of the IACHR is based on the consent of the state in question in accordance with Art. 62 of the American Convention. A state party to the American Convention may accept the Court's jurisdiction either for a specific case or—a method analogous to the ICJ optional clause **(317)**—by a declaration recognizing as binding the jurisdiction of the Court in all matters relating to the interpretation and application of the Convention. As of 2000, 17 states had filed declarations to this effect.

The judgments of the IACHR are final and not subject to appeal. They must be accompanied by reasons. Individual opinions **(304)** are allowed and provisional measures **(322)**, first granted in 1988, are also possible. States must comply with the judgment in any case to which they are parties. While the Convention refers to the possibility of executing a judgment's clauses stipulating compensatory damages in the state concerned in accordance with the domestic procedure, the paucity of contentious cases before the Court has so far not allowed to test the execution possibilities in actual practice.

The IACHR has not only contentious but also advisory **(291)** jurisdiction, but in this regard its competence to deliver advisory opinions is more extensive than that of the ICJ or the European Court of Human Rights (ECHR) **(154)** inasmuch as not only an organ of the OAS but also any OAS member state may consult the Court on questions concerning the interpretation of the American Convention or any other treaty dealing with the protection of human rights in the Western Hemisphere. In addition, any OAS member state may seek an advisory opinion on the compatibility of its law with the Convention or any such treaty.

Compared with the vast jurisprudence of the ECHR, the achievements of the IACHR have been rather modest. It has handed down only four judgments. In the *Viviana Gallardo et al.* case, 1981 (20 ILM 1424 (1981)) it refused to take jurisdiction, in a case involving the death of a Costa Rican national in a Costa Rican prison, because the matter had not been first submitted to the Commission. In the *Velásquez Rodríguez* case, 1988 (28 ILM 291 (1989)) and another, identical, case in 1989, the Court found Honduras responsible for forced disappearance and death of its nationals in violation of the American Convention and ordered the government to pay pecuniary compensation and to try and punish the state agents responsible for the violations. In the latest case, *Barrios Altos* (*Chumbipuma Aguirre et al. v. Peru*), 2001 (41 ILM 840 (2002)), involving a killing in 1991 by members of the armed forces of Peru of 15 innocent people mistaken for terrorists, with a subsequent cover-up and adoption of an amnesty law which exonerated all state agents from responsibility for human rights violations, the Court ruled that the amnesty law was incompatible with the American Convention and hence null and void, and ordered the state to pay compensation to the next of kin of the victims and identify and punish the guilty individuals. The judgment was complied with by the national authorities of Peru.

The IACHR has delivered nine advisory opinions, three at the request of the Commission and six requested by states. Its latest opinion was delivered in 1999 at the request of Mexico and concerned a prisoner's right to be informed of consular assistance, stipulated in the Vienna Convention on Consular Relations **(56)** and relevant especially because of its implications for prisoners on death row. The Court held that imposition of the death penalty was arbitrary and impermissible if a detained foreign national was not informed of his right to such consular assistance.

In general, the IACHR, while less successful than the ECHR, mainly because of the legacy of authoritarian regimes in Latin America, has made a modest contribution to the protection and promotion of human rights in the Western Hemisphere.

**166. International Covenant on Civil and Political Rights, 1966.** The major global treaty which articulates in greater detail and transforms into legally binding norms the civil and political rights and freedoms proclaimed by the Universal Declaration of Human Rights of 1948 **(162)**. The International

Covenant on Civil and Political Rights (ICCPR) (999 UNTS 171) was originally drafted by the United Nations (UN) Commission on Human Rights **(161)** and reported to the General Assembly in 1954. It was finally adopted in 1966, along with the other major human rights treaty, the International Covenant on Economic, Social and Cultural Rights **(169)**. Signed by 60 states, the ICCPR entered into force **(271)** in 1976, with the below-noted special Art. 41 entering into effect in 1979. As of June 2000, the ICCPR had 144 contracting parties, including the US which did not ratify it until 1992. The United States (US) ratification was accompanied by a number of reservations designed to limit the scope of the rights to the extent of the constitutional protection in the US. In addition, the US does not regard the rights under the Covenant as self-executing, that is, directly enforceable by US law, an issue within the context of the relationship between treaties and domestic law **(19)**. The Covenant is not subject to denunciation, a rule confirmed by the Human Rights Committee in its General Comment No. 26 in 1997. Hence the withdrawal of the North Korean state from the Covenant in that year was illegal.

Like its twin instrument, the Covenant in its substance largely follows the Universal Declaration, but also borrows from the European Convention of 1950 **(153)**. While it generally elaborates on the rights proclaimed in the Declaration, it departs from it in certain respects. Thus it does not include the right to own property and the prohibition of arbitrary deprivation of property. However, these omissions are not interpreted as rejection of these rights. Unlike the Declaration, the Covenant does not include the right to political asylum **(148)**, the right to nationality **(175)** (except, that is, it affirms the right of every child to acquire nationality) and the right not to be arbitrarily deprived of it. On the other hand, the ICCPR lists rights which are not found in the Declaration, such as the right of peoples to self-determination **(122)**, freedom from imprisonment for inability to fulfill contractual obligations, procedural protection of aliens **(144)** against expulsion **(146)**, freedom from double jeopardy, and protection of the rights of minorities **(172)**.

The Covenant consists of six parts. In Part I, like the other Covenant, it reaffirms the right of self-determination of all peoples. Part II stipulates general obligations of the state parties, including implementation of the Covenant in municipal law **(27)**, effective remedies for victims of human rights abuses, and equal rights of men and women **(183)**. Derogation in time of public emergency is possible, except for certain fundamental rights, such as the right to life; freedom of thought, conscience, and religion; recognition as a person before the law; freedom from torture **(182)**, slavery and servitude **(180)**; freedom from imprisonment for inability to fulfill contractual obligations, and from retroactive application of criminal law.

The classical civil and political rights ("first generation rights") are spelled out in Part III which lists, *inter alia*, the right to life, liberty, privacy, and security; equality before the law; prohibition of torture; freedom of thought, conscience, expression, movement, religion, peaceful assembly; the right to family life; the right of children **(150)** to special protection; the right to participate in public affairs; and special rights of persons belonging to ethnic, religious, or linguistic minorities. Part IV deals with the implementation of the Covenant, which centers upon the institution of the Human Rights Committee, a body of 18 members elected for four-year terms from among the nationals of the contracting parties. Unlike the UN Commission on Human Rights **(161)**, which is a political body, the Committee is a legal panel whose members are expected to interpret the law and do not represent their respective governments. The members of the Committee are supposed to be chosen on the basis of equitable geographical distribution and represent different forms of civilization and the principal legal systems. In practice, the Western members constitute a majority. Meeting for three sessions a year, the Committee operates by way of consensus The Committee has additional powers under the provisions of the Optional Protocol of 1966 **(167)**. The brief Part V stipulates that nothing in the Covenant shall be interpreted as impairing the inherent right of all peoples to enjoy and to utilize fully their national resources. Part VI contains final provisions governing ratification **(280)**, entry into force, amendment procedures **(269)**, and the like, specifically laying down that the Covenant shall extend to all parts of federal states **(77)** without any limitations or exceptions.

The system set up in Part IV to monitor the compliance with the Covenant is rather weak and made even less effective by numerous reservations entered by the parties. The only compulsory mechanism is a reporting system requiring the states parties to submit periodic, five-year interval, reports (Art. 40) to the UN Secretary-General who transmits them to the Human Rights Committee for consideration at public hearings, with the attendance of representatives of the state involved. The states' reports are prepared on the basis of 28 general comments formulated by the Committee. States' response to the reporting system has varied, but inadequacy of and failure to submit reports has been a problem for the Committee. In the practice of the Committee, specialized agencies are not invited to comment on the reports but may submit information to individual Committee members who can also receive it from non-governmental organizations **(86)** such as Amnesty International or the International Commission of Jurists. The reports are examined by the Committee and, accompanied by comments, transmitted to the states concerned. Since the 1990s the Committee has been able to prepare, according to a common format, collective comments reviewing the human rights record of specific states. It also produces general comments on various issues such as, *inter alia*, in addition to the comments assisting states in the preparation of reports, the comments on the rights of the child, minorities, and reservations **(282)** to the Covenant. Among the comments, there has been one on the right to life, 1984, in which the Committee expressed the view that the production, testing, and possession, let alone the use, of nuclear weapons should be prohibited and condemned as a crime against humanity **(151)**.

In addition to the reporting mechanism, the ICCPR (Art. 41) provides for an optional system of state applications whereby a state party may, on conditions of reciprocity, recognize the right of another state party to bring a claim to the Committee alleging a violation of the Covenant, a procedure subject to a prior failure at a bilateral attempt at an adjustment of the complaint in question and the exhaustion of local remedies **(174)**. The Committee may investigate the matter and, if no settlement is reached, may submit it, with the states' consent, to a five-member conciliation commission **(296)** which then issues a non-binding report. However, this optional procedure of interstate complaints has been accepted by only a handful of states and in practice has not been used.

Finally, there is the procedure of individual communications to the Human Rights Committee from individuals claiming to be victims of a violation by a state of rights stipulated by the Covenant. This procedure is set out in the (First) Optional Protocol to the ICCPR **(167)**.

**167. International Covenant on Civil and Political Rights, Optional Protocol, 1966.** This first Optional Protocol to the International Covenant on Civil and Political Rights (ICCPR) (999 UNTS 171) was signed by 25 states along with the Covenant **(166)** itself, and entered into force **(271)** with it in 1976. As of June 2000 it had 95 contracting parties. The United States is not a party. The Protocol contains a denunciation clause allowing withdrawal following a three-month denunciation period. Jamaica and Trinidad and Tobago availed themselves of this provision, denouncing and withdrawing from the Protocol in 1997 and 1998, respectively.

The Protocol provides states parties to the ICCPR with the option to recognize an additional competence of the Human Rights Committee (the "treaty body" set up to monitor compliance with the ICCPR) to receive and consider "communications," that is complaints from individuals under their respective jurisdiction who claim to be victims of a violation by the state in question of any of the rights set forth in the Covenant and who have exhausted all available domestic remedies **(74)**. The communications must not be anonymous or relate to a matter being examined under another procedure of international investigation or settlement, for example before the European Court of Human Rights **(154)**, the Inter-American Court on Human Rights **(165)** or the Inter-American Commission on Human Rights acting either as an organ of the Organization of American States or under the American Convention on Human Rights **(147)**.

In dealing with the complaints under the Protocol, the Human Rights Committee is neither a court nor a quasi-judicial body. It has no power to hand down binding decisions and in case of noncompliance lacks any enforcement mechanism or sanctions against the offending state. Its function is only to examine the communications from individuals and the explanation received from the state in question (within the prescribed time limit of six months), including any remedies that may have been taken, and subsequently forward its legally non-binding, recommendatory decision, known as a "view," to the state and the individual concerned. By June 2000 the Committee had registered more than 930 cases, dealing with about a third of them by adopting views and finding violations of the Covenant in 261 of them. In response to the Committee's recommendation some states have taken correcting action, such as commuting death sentences, releasing prisoners, paying compensation, and amending their legislation. The Committee has also conducted visits to states to assist governments in the implementation of its views. However, many countries have ignored the Committee's view, and in practice the individual complaints procedure has been most effective with respect to countries with an otherwise good human rights record. On the other hand, the Committee must include a summary of its activities under the Protocol in the annual reports to the General Assembly envisaged by Art. 45 of the ICCPR and in addition, may follow up cases of noncompliance by publicizing them to promote transparency and exercise pressure upon delinquent states for changes in their human rights conduct.

Since 1977 the periodically published decisions of the Human Rights Committee have produced a considerable body of interesting "case law" on the interpretation and application of the ICCPR which is increasingly quoted by domestic and international judicial bodies, thus making a contribution to the development of the international law of human rights.

**168. International Covenant on Civil and Political Rights, Second Optional Protocol, 1989.** The Second Optional Protocol to the International Covenant on Civil and Political Rights (ICCPR) **(166)**, aiming at the abolition of the death penalty, was adopted in 1989 by a General Assembly resolution with 59 votes in favor and 26 against, and 48 abstentions. It entered into force **(271)** in 1991, and as of June 2000 had 44 contracting parties. The United States (US) is not a party to the Protocol.

While Art. 6 of the ICCPR guaranteeing "the inherent right to life" does not prohibit the death penalty, it considers its abolition desirable as progress in the enjoyment of the right to life. In any case, under the Covenant, states parties are obliged to limit resort to the death penalty and to abolish it for other than the "most serious crimes," making capital punishment a most exceptional measure. Furthermore, death sentences shall not be imposed for crimes committed by persons below 18 years and shall not be carried out on pregnant women. At its sessions in the years 1997–2000, the United Nations (UN) Commission on Human Rights **(161)** adopted resolutions calling for a moratorium on executions with a view to the complete abolition of the death penalty. In 2000 the vote to condemn capital punishment was 27 in favor to 13 against such condemnation. Among the countries casting negative vote were China (where more executions take place annually than in all other countries combined), Cuba, India, Indonesia, Japan, Pakistan, and Rwanda. A number of "communications" to the UN Human Rights Committee, which monitors compliance with the ICCPR, have dealt with death penalty cases involving extradition **(75)** by Canada to the US, but a majority of the Committee was of the opinion that such extradition did not infringe upon Art. 6 of the ICCPR. A majority also considered that, in contrast with gas asphyxiation, execution by lethal injection of cyanide was not in violation of Art. 7 of the ICCPR, which prohibits cruel, inhuman, or degrading punishment. When ratifying the Covenant in 1992, the US, where some of its component states make minors of 16 or 17 liable to capital punishment, made a reservation **(282)** to safeguard such legislation.

The Second Optional Protocol abolishes the death penalty and disallows reservations **(282)** except for those made at the time of ratification or accession **(267)** that provide for the application of the death penalty in time of war pursuant to a conviction for a most serious crime of a military nature committed during wartime (Art. 2(1)). The states parties to the Second Optional Protocol are obliged to include, in the reports to the Human Rights Committee, information on the measures that they have adopted to give effect to the Protocol (Art. 3). The competence which the Committee has under the First Optional Protocol **(167)** of the ICCPR to receive and consider communications from individuals is extended to matters concerning the death penalty, unless the state concerned has made a statement to the contrary at the moment of ratification or accession. The still not applied procedure under Art. 41 of the ICCPR concerning the option of interstate complaints is also extended to the provisions of the Second Protocol, subject to the above-noted statement to the contrary.

It should be added that in Europe the death penalty, first abolished except for wartime cases by Protocol No. 6 of 1983 to the European Convention for the Protection of Human Rights and Fundamental Freedoms **(153)**, is now completely and in all circumstances abolished by Protocol No. 13 of 2002 (41 ILM 515 (2002)). In the Western Hemisphere the death penalty was abolished, except for extremely serious wartime crimes of a military nature, by the Protocol of 1990 (29 ILM 1447 (1990)) to the American Convention on Human Rights **(147)**. However, the Protocol is not yet in force. Altogether, by June 2000 the death penalty had been abolished by the law or in actual practice in 118 countries.

**169. International Covenant on Economic, Social, and Cultural Rights, 1966.** The major global treaty **(40, 288)** which articulates in greater detail and transforms into legally binding norms the economic, social, and cultural rights and freedoms proclaimed by the Universal Declaration of Human Rights of 1948 **(162)**. Like its twin instrument, the International Covenant on Civil and Political Rights (ICCPR) **(166)**, the International Covenant on Economic, Social, and Cultural Rights (ICESCR) (993 UNTS 3) was originally drafted by the United Nations (UN) Commission on Human Rights **(161)**, reported to the General Assembly in 1954, and eventually adopted in 1966 along with the other major human rights treaty, the ICCPR. It entered into effect **(271)** in 1976 and as of June 2000 had 142 contracting parties. The United States (US) signed the Covenant in 1977 but has not ratified it, its main points of objection being the guarantees of the right to work, unionization, social security, and maternity leaves.

The main difference between the two covenants is that, due to the nature of its rights, the ICESCR cannot be formulated in terms of obligations directly binding the parties and can be implemented only progressively depending on the availability of economic and other necessary resources. On the other hand, the ICCPR deals with rights which in principle do not require such resources and can, by and large, be carried out immediately upon ratification **(280)**. Under Art. 2(1) of the Covenant each state party merely undertakes "to take steps . . . to the maximum of its available resources, with a view to achieving progressively the full realization of the rights recognized in the . . . Covenant by all appropriate means, including particularly the adoption of legislative measures." Exceptionally, some obligations must be met immediately. Here belong, *inter alia*, the obligations to guarantee and ensure non-discrimination and equal treatment under Art. 22(2)(3), to ensure trade union rights (Art. 8), to respect parental choice of school (Art. 13(3)), and scientific freedom (Art. 15(3)). To what extent such immediate obligations under the Covenant are justiciable, that is, capable of being settled by a court, is an open question. With respect to discrimination, the Covenant contains a qualification in favor of developing countries to the effect that such countries, with due regard to human rights and their national economy, may determine to what extent they would guarantee the economic rights recognized in the Covenant to non-nationals (Art. 2(3)).

In view of the fact that, despite global economic growth and development, well over one billion people live in conditions of extreme poverty, illiteracy, and chronic ill health, the ICESCR provides the major, global, international standards for protecting human rights at the basic level of human existence. Proclaiming the right of self-determination **(122)**, identical to that articulated in Art. 1 of the ICCPR, and equal rights for men and women, the Covenant proceeds to list such other rights as the right to work in just and fair conditions; to form trade unions; to strike; to social security and protection of, and assistance to the family; to maternity leaves; adequate food, clothing, and housing; to the highest attainable standards of physical and mental health; to education and to enjoyment of the benefits of cultural freedom and scientific progress. However, like the other covenant, the ICESCR does not mention the right to property.

The machinery to supervise compliance by the states parties with the obligations under the ICESCR is even weaker than the otherwise not very effective implementation provisions under the other covenant. There are no provisions for inter-state complaints or individual petitions, with reliance placed on a system of periodic reports to be submitted to the UN Economic and Social Council (ECOSOC) (Arts. 16–22) which considers them through a subsidiary body whose composition and competence has changed over the years. Originally, the reports were considered by a working group of the ECOSOC, composed of representatives of the states parties. Having proved ineffective, this body was followed in 1985 by a committee of 18 experts which, unlike the ICCPR Human Rights Committee and other similar bodies, is responsible not to the states parties but to the ECOSOC. This Committee on Economic, Social and Cultural Rights (established by the ECOSOC against the lonely vote of the US) began its operations in 1987. It meets every year at the UN Geneva headquarters, its major task being to examine the sometimes long overdue state reports and submitting annual reports to the Council. The reporting states are given a chance to express their views at the Committee's meetings. In addition to state reports, the Committee's sources of information include data received from UN specialized agencies and other UN bodies as well as information provided by non-governmental organizations **(86)**. The so-called General Comments prepared by the Committee on various topics relating to the Covenant, such as, for example, adequate housing, persons with disabilities, and the rights of the elderly, can be considered as authoritative interpretations of the obligations under the ICESCR, and are designed to assist states parties in fulfilling their reporting obligations.

**170. International Criminal Court.** The first permanent international criminal court (ICC), established in 1998 by the Rome Statute of the ICC (37 ILM 999 (1998)) to try individuals **(164)** for the most serious crimes of concern to the international community as a whole. Under Art. 1 the ICC has the power to exercise jurisdiction over "persons," by which the Statute means (Art. 25(1)) "natural persons," that is, individuals. Originally drafted by the International Law Commission, the Statute of the ICC, an instrument consisting of a preamble and 128 articles, was adopted by a United Nations (UN) conference with the participation of 160 states **(127)** and a large number of intergovernmental organizations **(84)** and non-governmental organizations (NGOs) **(86)**. The Statute entered into force **(271)** in 2002 and the Court became effective in 2003. By March 2003 it had been ratified by 89 states and even before the election of the Prosecutor the ICC received some 200 complaints on alleged crimes within the Court's jurisdiction.

At the Rome Conference, which adopted the ICC Statute by a vote of 120 to 7, the United States (US) voted against the Statute along with China, Iran, Iraq, Israel, Libya, and Sudan. Although the US eventually signed the Statute on the last day it was open for signature **(283)** (31 December 2000), the signature was accompanied by a statement expressing concern about certain provisions of the treaty and a recommendation that the successor administration should not ratify it until the US concerns were satisfied. In April 2002 the new administration, in a move unprecedented in the history of treaty making, repudiated the signature, notifying the UN that it did not intend to become a party to the ICC Statute and had no legal obligations arising from its signature (41 ILM 1014 (2002)). At the same time, the US adopted an extremely hostile attitude to what a US senator called a "rogue court" but which in reality was recognized by the international community as the most important international judicial body **(306)** since the establishment of the International Court of Justice (ICJ) **(309)** in 1945. The major objection to the ICC, raised by the US, was that US nationals, in particular soldiers or civilian leaders, could be prosecuted by the ICC without the US consent, in possibly politically motivated or frivolous trials, a situation that—as claimed by the US—in cases of major national security decisions by high US officials, brought before the ICC, would be tantamount to bypassing the Security Council (SC) as the only international organ authorized to pass judgment upon the legality of such decisions under international law. To prevent such alleged contingencies, the US sought bilateral agreements with as many countries as possible, designed to exempt US nationals from the Court's jurisdiction and—as far as any states parties to the ICC Statute are concerned—taking advantage of (or—as claimed by some—misusing) Art. 98(2) of the ICC Statute which provides that the Court "may not proceed with a request for surrender which would require the requested State to act inconsistently with its obligations under international agreements pursuant to which the consent of a sending State is required to surrender a person of that State to the Court, unless the Court can first obtain the cooperation of the sending State for the giving of consent for the surrender." By March 2003, 21 countries had agreed to grant such immunity to US nationals. Furthermore, the US pressured some states parties to the Statute, especially recipients of US aid, to opt for the transitional provision of the Statute (Art. 124) allowing a state, on becoming a party, to declare nonacceptance of the Court's jurisdiction for a period of seven years after the entry into force for that state. In another move in 2002 and 2003 but not 2004, the US made the SC agree to exempt the US members of peacekeeping forces **(334)** in Bosnia and Herzegovina, and Croatia, and subsequently other peacekeeping **(334)** operations, from prosecution by the ICC.

It appears that the fears and concerns of the US over possible threats of prosecution of US nationals by the ICC are unfounded. As a matter of fact, by joining the ICC Statute the US would provide greater protection to its citizens because of the below-noted principle of complementarity.

Double jeopardy (Art. 20) and trial *in absentia* are prohibited by the Statute (Art. 63) and cases of not sufficient gravity are inadmissible (Art. 17(1)(d)). Moreover, contrary to US claims, the ICC guarantees due process protection at least to the extent of the US Constitution Bill of Rights and spells out the pertinent rights in more detail than the Constitution.

The ICC is designed to deal only with the most serious crimes committed after the entry into force of the Statute, that is, after 1 July 2002. In cases of states joining after the entry into force, the ICC may exercise its jurisdiction only with respect to crimes committed after the entry into force of the Statute for the state concerned, unless that state declares its willingness to accept the Court's jurisdiction (Art. 11). It is essential to bear in mind that the Court is "complementary to national criminal jurisdictions" (the principle of complementarity) (Arts. 1, 17–18), which means that the ICC is not intended to supersede national jurisdiction; it may act only if the state concerned is unable or unwilling to genuinely prosecute or if the situation has been referred to it by the SC. Thus, unlike the jurisdiction of the International Criminal Tribunal for the Former Yugoslavia **(352)** and the International Criminal Tribunal for Rwanda **(351)**, national jurisdiction is primary, prevailing over the residual jurisdiction of the ICC. In terms of its approach to criminal law, the Statute of the ICC combines the common-law adversarial principle with the inquisitorial principle followed in the civil-law **(23)** countries.

In the matter of the politically sensitive problem of preconditions to the exercise of jurisdiction in specific cases, the Statute provides (Art. 12) that the Court may exercise jurisdiction with the consent of the state party on the territory **(228)** of which the conduct in question occurred, or the consent of the state party of the accused person's nationality, a requirement strongly insisted upon by the US at the Rome Conference but objected to by many states. A state which is not a party to the Statute may also accept the jurisdiction of the ICC on a case-by-case basis. The Court may exercise jurisdiction with respect to a crime through a referral by a state party of a "situation" (a general term which avoids naming the specific suspect) to the Prosecutor of the Court (Arts. 13(a) and 14) or—a provision strongly lobbied for by NGOs—by the Prosecutor himself who may initiate investigation at his own initiative (*proprio motu*) but subject to the authorization of the Pre-Trial Chamber of the Court (Arts. 13(c) and 15). As proposed by the US, in both cases the Prosecutor must notify all states parties and those states which would normally exercise jurisdiction **(87)** over the crimes concerned (Art. 18(1)). However, the ICC may exercise its jurisdiction without the consent of the states concerned if a situation is referred to it by the SC under the collective security **(327)** Chapter VII of the UN Charter (Art. 13(b)), even if the crime was committed in the territory of a non-party state by a national of such party. In any case brought before it, the Court must satisfy itself that it has jurisdiction. Detailed provisions govern the procedure of challenging the Court's jurisdiction by the state or states concerned and by the accused individual himself (Art. 19). To minimize conflicts between the Court's jurisdiction and the powers of the SC, a compromise formula bars any investigation or prosecution for a period of 12 months following the SC resolution under Chapter VII, requesting deferral of an investigation or prosecution, with the possibility of renewing such request at 12-month intervals (Art. 16).

Consistent with the principle of complementarity, the Court determines a case inadmissible (Art. 17) if it is already investigated or prosecuted by a state which has jurisdiction over it; if such state has decided not to prosecute; or if the person concerned has already been tried for conduct which is the subject of the complaint. Inadmissibility on any of these three grounds is subject to certain guidelines concerning the determination of a state' unwillingness or inability to carry out investigation or prosecution in a particular case. Insufficient gravity of the case is an additional ground for inadmissibility. The general principle of law **(38)** prohibiting double jeopardy (*ne bis in idem*) is expressly stipulated in Art. 20, subject to certain reservations concerning the impartiality and independence of the other court.

Insofar as the sources of the applicable law **(36)** are concerned, Art. 21 of the ICC Statute (comparable, as it were, to Art. 38 of the ICJ **(309)**) provides that the Court shall apply, in the first place, the Statute; the so-called Elements of Crime which pursuant to Art. 9 are to be adopted by a two-thirds majority of the members of the Assembly of States Parties (an organ established pursuant to Art. 112 of the Statute, in which each state party has one representative and which oversees the operations of the ICC and meets in annual sessions) and are to assist the Court in the interpretation **(274)** and application of the articles defining the crimes within the Court's jurisdiction; and the Court's Rules of Procedure and Evidence. Second, the Court applies, where appropriate, applicable treaties **(40)** and the principles and rules of international law, including the established principles of the international law of armed conflict, both international **(339)** and non-international **(340)**, that is, international humanitarian law **(353)**. Third, failing that, the ICC applies general principles of law derived by the Court from national laws of legal systems of the world including, as appropriate, the national laws of states that would normally exercise jurisdiction over the crime, provided that those principles are not inconsistent with the Statute and with international law and internationally recognized norms and standards. The Statute states that the Court may apply principles and rules of law as interpreted in its previous decisions (Art. 21(2)). The implication is that—like the ICJ—the ICC is not legally bound to observe the doctrine of *stare decisis,* that is, binding precedent. The Statute also expressly lays down that all law must be applied and interpreted in consistence with internationally recognized human rights **(157)** and without any discrimination. Under Art. 10 (the only article without a title), nothing in the provisions of the Statute on the Court's jurisdiction, admissibility, and applicable law may be interpreted as limiting or prejudicing in any way existing or developing rules of international law for purposes other than the Statute.

Although at the Rome Conference there was some support for including also the crimes of terrorism **(337)**, illicit drug trafficking, and offenses against UN personnel among the crimes within the Court's jurisdiction, there emerged a wide consensus on including (Art. 5) within the ICC jurisdiction only the crime of genocide **(155)**, defined in Art. 6; crimes against humanity **(151)**, defined in detail in Art. 7; war crimes **(373)**, dealt with extensively in Art. 8; and the crime of aggression **(325)**. However, since no agreement could be reached on the divisive issue of defining aggression and especially the role of the SC in such determination, a compromise solution was reached whereby, even though the crime of aggression was incorporated in the Statute in Art. 5(1)(d) as within the Court's jurisdiction, under Art. 5(2) the Court shall not exercise jurisdiction over this crime until it is defined in a new provision of the Statute in accordance with the amendment and review procedures of the Statute spelled out in Arts. 121 and 123, and until the conditions are set out under which the Court is to exercise its jurisdiction with respect to this crime. Moreover, amendment and review procedures may not be initiated until after the expiry of seven years from the entry into force of the Statute, that is, not until after 2 July 2009. The Statute adds the otherwise obvious proviso that any provisions on aggression must be consistent with the relevant provisions of the UN Charter.

Part III of the ICC Statute (Arts. 22–33) sets out general principles of criminal law to be followed by the Court: *nullum crimen sine lege*, meaning that responsibility does not arise unless the conduct in question constitutes, at the time it takes place, a crime within the jurisdiction of the Court; *nulla poena sine lege*, referring to the principle that punishment shall be only in accordance with the Statute; the principle of non-retroactivity *ratione personae*, meaning that no person shall be responsible for conduct prior to the entry into force of the Statute; the principle of individual criminal responsibility, the elements of which are spelled out in detail in the Statute, including no jurisdiction over persons under the age of 18 at the time of the alleged commission of a crime, irrelevance of official capacity, responsibility of commanders and other superiors, non-applicability of statutes of limitations, the need of knowledge and intent as required mental elements, and grounds excluding criminal responsibility, namely, mental disease or defect, innocent intoxication, self-defense or the defense of others, duress, mistake of fact or law, and, subject to certain conditions, superior orders. Such orders and prescriptions of the law do not relieve a person of criminal responsibility unless that person was under a legal obligation to obey orders, did not know that the order in question was unlawful, and the order was not manifestly unlawful. Orders to commit genocide or crimes against humanity are presumed to be manifestly unlawful.

The composition and administration of the ICC are set out in detail in Part 4 of the Statute (Arts. 34–42). Briefly, the Court is composed of the Presidency; an Appeals Division, a Trial Division and a Pre-Trial Division; the Office of the Prosecutor; and the Registry. The 18 judges, of whom at least 9 must have criminal law competence and at least 5 must be competent in relevant areas of international law, such as human rights **(160)** and international humanitarian law, are elected by ballot by the Assembly of States Parties, as full-time members of the Court, but if the workload allows, some judges (but not the President and the Vice-President) may be part-time. The membership of the Court must take into account the principal legal systems of the world, equitable geographical representation, and a fair representation of female and male judges. No two judges may be nationals **(175)** of the same state. The judges hold office for a term of nine years but, by lot, at the first election one-third were selected for three years, another third for six years, and the remaining six for nine years. In the first election (in February 2003) the membership of the Court included judges from Bolivia, Brazil, Canada, Costa Rica, Cyprus, Finland, France, Germany, Ghana, Ireland, Italy, Korea (Republic of), Latvia, Mali, Samoa, South Africa, Trinidad and Tobago, and the United Kingdom. Among them there were seven female judges. The judge from Canada was selected as President of the Court. The Prosecutor, who, unlike the judges, need not be national of a state party, is elected by the Assembly. A national of Argentina, a state party, was elected as the first Prosecutor of the Court. The Registrar is elected by the judges. Other matters concerning the composition and administration of the ICC and regulated by the Statute deal, *inter alia*, with the Presidency of the Court, the Chambers, the independence of judges, the authority and composition of the Offices of the Prosecutor and the Registrar, privileges and immunities **(102)** of the Court and its officials, salaries, expenses, official and working languages, the Rules of Procedure and Evidence, and regulations of the Court.

The rules governing investigation and prosecution are detailed in Part 5 of the Statute (Arts. 53–61). Included are the duties and powers of the prosecutor; the rights of persons during an investigation; the role of the Pre-Trial Chamber in relation to a unique investigative opportunity; the functions and powers of the Pre-Trial Chamber, the organ which, if satisfied that there are reasonable grounds for prosecution, issues, on the application of the prosecutor, arrest warrants and summons to appear; the arrest proceedings in the custodial state and the surrender of persons to the ICC; initial proceedings before the Court, and confirmation of the charges before trial. Unless exceptional circumstances are present, hearings to confirm charges must take place in the presence of the person charged. Upon request of the Prosecutor, who considers an investigation to present a unique opportunity to take testimony or collect evidence which may not be available subsequently for the purposes of the trial, the Pre-Trial Chamber may take such measures as may be necessary to ensure the efficiency and integrity of the proceedings and, in particular, to protect the rights of the defense.

The Statute's provisions of Part 6 (Arts. 62–76) (the trial) guarantee, in detail, due process and fair trial for the accused in compliance with the generally accepted standards of human rights. Apart from the rights of the accused, the Statute regulates the conduct of the trial (which must take place in the presence of the accused, normally at the seat of the ICC); the protection of the victims and witnesses, and their participation in the proceedings; evidence; offenses against the administration of justice; sanctions for misconduct in the Court; protection of national security information; third-party information or documents; requirements for the decision; sentencing; and reparation to victims, with a provision on setting up a Trust Fund for this purpose. There are also provisions on compensation for victims of unlawful arrest or detention, or clear miscarriage of justice. The judges must attempt to achieve unanimity in their decision, failing which the decision is taken by a majority of the judges. The deliberations of the Trial Chamber remain secret. The sentence is pronounced in public and, wherever possible, in the presence of the accused.

The negotiations on Part 7 on penalties (Arts. 77–80) reflected the conflict between supporters and opponents of the death penalty. The Statute does not provide for the death penalty, envisaging imprisonment up to 30 years, or life imprisonment when justified by the extreme gravity of the crime and the individual circumstances of the convicted person. In addition, the Court may order a fine and/or a forfeiture of proceeds, property, and assets derived from the crime, without prejudice to the rights of *bona fide* third parties. It should be noted that, while there is no death penalty under the ICC Statute, a person convicted by the ICC may still be sentenced to death by a national court. Art. 80 of the Statute provides that nothing in its Part governing penalties affects the application by states of penalties prescribed by their national law.

Pursuant to Part 8 (Arts. 81–85) on Appeals and Revision, appeals to the Appeal Chamber against decisions of the Trial Chamber of acquittal or conviction or against a sentence may be made by the prosecutor on the grounds of procedural error, error of fact, or error of law, and by the convicted person or the Prosecutor on that person's behalf also on any other ground that affects the fairness or reliability of the proceedings or decision. Appeals are also possible against decisions other than sentences, for example, decisions with respect to jurisdiction or admissibility. The Appeals Chamber may reverse or amend the decision or sentence or order a new trial before a different Trial Chamber.

Elaborate provisions of Part 9 of the Statute (Arts. 86–102) regulate international cooperation and judicial assistance, dealing, *inter alia*, with such matters as requests for cooperation, surrender of persons to the Court, provisional arrest, postponement of execution of a request for arrest and surrender, and cooperation with respect to waiver of immunity and, the above-noted provision of Art. 98(2) on consent to surrender.

Enforcement (Part 10) of sentences of imprisonment is largely in the hands of states. A sentence is served in a state designated by the Court from a list of states which have indicated their willingness to accept sentenced persons, but among other factors the Court must take into account the views and nationality of the sentenced person. At any time the Court may decide to transfer a prisoner to a prison of another state and in general supervises the enforcement of sentences and conditions of imprisonment.

Parts 11 and 12 deal with the Assembly of States Parties and the financing of the ICC, respectively. Part 13 includes the final clauses of the Statute. In this Part, pursuant to Art. 119, disputes concerning the judicial functions of the Court are settled by the Court itself. Any other dispute **(299)** between states parties relating to the interpretation or application of the Statute and not settled through negotiations within three months is referred to the Assembly which may itself seek to settle it or make recommendations on further means of settlement, including referral to the ICJ. No reservations are allowed to the Statute (Art. 120), but—as noted above—Art. 124 on transitional provisions allows a state not to accept the Court's jurisdiction for a period of seven years when a war crime is alleged to have been committed by its nationals or on its territory. Amendments to the Statute may be proposed by any state party seven years after its entry into force and adopted according to the detailed rules of the Statute (Art. 121). A Review Conference is required to be convened at that time by the UN Secretary-General to consider any amendments. Thereafter, another Review Conference will be held, at the request of any state party, upon approval by a majority of the states parties (Art. 123). Under Art. 127, withdrawal from the Statute is possible, taking effect one year following the date of receipt of the notification, unless the notification specifies a later date.

**171. Minimum International Standard of Justice v. National Treatment.** Two contrasting approaches to the treatment of aliens **(144)** by the host state which are relevant for purposes of determining state responsibility **(128)** for injury to aliens. The states advocating the international minimum (or minimum international) standard of justice argue that in international law there is a certain minimum standard of treatment which must be accorded to aliens by all states irrespective of how they treat their own nationals, whereas the states supporting the national treatment (or equality of treatment) principle claim that aliens are entitled, without discrimination, to no more and no less than the treatment equal to that granted by the state to its own nationals. However, all states, regardless of the standard of treatment of aliens, agree that customary international law allows a degree of differential discriminatory treatment of aliens in such matters as their political rights, exercise of certain professions, ownership of real property, and the like.

The two approaches to the treatment of aliens have clashed since the latter half of the 19th century when the United States (US) and a number of European powers upheld the minimum international standard against Latin American states championing the equality of treatment principle. As early as 1868 the equality of treatment was advocated in his famous treatise on international law by a renowned international lawyer, the Argentinian Carlos Calvo, whose name is mainly associated with the "Calvo Clause" **(149)**. The Latin American position was later adopted by the Communist states in the 20th century and has become the position of a great majority of the developing countries today.

The contrasting stands of the two approaches was vividly highlighted in the 1930s in the diplomatic correspondence between the US Secretary of State Cordell Hull and the Mexican ministry of foreign affairs in connection with the compensation of US nationals **(175)** for expropriation **(145)** of their landed property by Mexico. In international arbitration **(293)** of the 20th century a great majority of awards favored the international minimum standard even though a number of leading representatives of the doctrine favored the national treatment doctrine. In 1930 the balance of forces on the issue was well illustrated by the vote at the Hague Codification Conference where a draft favoring national treatment was rejected by 23 votes to 17 and the text in favor of international minimum standard was adopted by 21 votes to 17 (24 AJIL 500 (1930)). On the other hand, in the Western hemisphere Art. 9 of the Montevideo Convention on Rights and Duties of States (165 LNTS 19) endorsed, with US reservations, the national treatment principle to the effect that "nationals and foreigners are under the same protection of the law and the national authorities, and the foreigners may not claim rights other or more extensive than those of the nationals." In the 1950s, in the early stages of its codification work on state responsibility **(129)**, the International Law Commission made an unsuccessful attempt to devise a new, compromise, standard based on national treatment but living up to the minimum standards of the fundamental human rights **(157)**.

It is difficult to determine in specific cases what elements are included in the minimum international treatment standard. In its often quoted *Neer Claim* decision (4 RIAA 60) in 1926, the US-Mexican General Claims Commission expressed the view that "the treatment of an alien, in order to constitute an international delinquency, should amount to an outrage, to bad faith, to willful neglect of duty, or to an insufficiency of governmental action so far short of international standards that every reasonable and impartial man would readily recognize its insufficiency." It is obvious that the content of the international minimum standard may prove controversial in such areas as expulsion of aliens **(146)**, deportation, the measure of penalty, and especially in cases of alleged violations of aliens' economic rights, with a fundamental disagreement on the appropriate compensation for expropriation of aliens' property.

On the threshold of the 21st century there was still no consensus on the standards of treatment to be accorded to aliens under international law. On the other hand, the developing law of human rights **(160)**, which protects individuals as such regardless of their nationality **(175)**, has the potential of generating common standards for the rights of foreign nationals.

**172. Minorities.** With literally thousands of various, numerically inferior, groups within states in all parts of the world, there is no precise definition of what constitutes a minority for purposes of international law. Among national minorities, international instruments usually include ethnic, religious, or linguistic groups. As tentatively defined in 1977 by the Special Rapporteur of the Subcommission on the Prevention of Discrimination and the Protection of Minorities of the United Nations (UN) Commission on Human Rights **(161)**, the term "minority" refers to "a group inferior to the rest of the population of a state, in a non-dominant position, whose members—being nationals of the State—possess ethnic, religious or linguistic characteristics differing from those of the rest of the population and show, if only implicitly, a sense of solidarity, directed towards possessing their culture, traditions, religion or language." This definition combines the objective feature differentiating the group from the majority population with the subjective element present in the members of the group to preserve and foster these characteristics of the group's culture and identity. An essentially the same though more elaborate definition of "national minority" is used for purposes of the Council of Europe's Framework Convention for the Protection of National Minorities of 1995 (34 ILM 351 (1985)). The problem of defining a minority has recently been compounded by a growing emphasis on the promotion and protection of the human rights **(157)** of indigenous peoples **(163)** who, while logically constituting a specific category of minorities, are increasingly subsumed under a separate legal category.

Historically, isolated treaty **(288)** provisions guaranteeing religious freedom to minorities were known already before World War I (1914–1918). However, it was in the aftermath of that war that a network of treaties with special minority clauses (special minority treaties, chapters in peace treaties, and special treaties concerning the rights of minorities in Upper Silesia and the Memel

Territory) was set up for the protection of minorities in Central Europe. These clauses were placed under the guarantee of the League of Nations and could not be changed without the consent of its Council. Any breaches of the obligations under the minority clauses could be brought to the attention of the Council which was authorized to take appropriate action, but only a German-Polish convention of 1922 (9 LNTS 466) provided for the right of individual petitions before an arbitral tribunal **(293)** whose function was to adjudicate disputes involving claims to vested rights by members of an ethnic minority in Upper Silesia against their own government or the government of the other party to the 1922 Convention. During its existence (1922–1937) the Upper Silesia Arbitral Tribunal decided 3,726 cases. International disputes **(299)** involving minority issues were also brought before the League's Council and submitted to the Permanent Court of International Justice **(320)** which dealt with a number of contentious cases and advisory opinions **(291)** dealing with minority rights violations. Ultimately, however, the whole system of the protection of minorities fell victim to the decline of the League of Nations and the rise of Nazi Germany for which the alleged mistreatment of German minorities provided a pretext for aggression.

After World War II, with the abuse of minority clauses by Nazi Germany fresh in mind, there was no willingness to deal with the problems of minorities in the fluid conditions in the aftermath of the war while such problems were simply solved by mass transfers (today called "ethnic cleansing") of millions of people, as was especially the case in Central and Eastern Europe. Only exceptionally, as in the relations between Italy and Yugoslavia, the problem of minorities was dealt with in a treaty, specifically the Treaty of Peace with Italy, 1947 (49 and 50 UNTS).

Eventually, the problem of minorities became part of the general trend to deal with the protection of human rights as a whole. In this context, the UN Commission on Human Rights set up the above-mentioned special subcommission for minority problems. While the UN Charter **(156)** and the Universal Declaration of Human Rights **(162)** do not mention the problem of minorities, Art. 27 of the International Covenant on Civil and Political Rights (ICCPR) **(166)** stipulates that "in those States in which ethnic, religious or linguistic minorities exist, persons belonging to such minorities shall not be denied the right, in community with the other members of their group, to enjoy their own culture, to profess and practice their own religion, or to use their own language." Consequently, the Human Rights Committee, the "treaty body" of the ICCPR, has investigated the problem of minorities both within the context of the annual national reports and in its general comments on Art. 27. The interpretation **(274)** adopted by the Committee can, in general, be regarded as representing the state of international law on the question of minorities. First of all, on the politically sensitive issue of the relationship between national minorities and the right of self-determination of peoples **(122)**, the Committee has taken the position, implied in Art. 27 of the ICCPR, that minorities, even ethnic minorities on a relatively clearly defined territorial basis, do not have the right of secession, such right being reserved only to "people" in the meaning of the anti-colonial self-determination policy of the UN. Thus, for example, in 1990, with regard to a claim involving the German speaking minority in South Tirol, Italy, the Committee explicitly declared inadmissible the right of this minority to self-determination and in its general comments on Art. 27 of the ICCPR made it quite clear that the right under this article could not prejudice the sovereignty and territorial integrity of states; this right, as ruled by the Committee, was vested in individual members of a minority and did not constitute any collective right.

Under current international law minorities are not endowed with international legal personality **(85)** and consequently are not subjects of this system of law, a legal status reaffirmed by such international instruments as the General Assembly (GA) Friendly Relations Declaration of 1970 **(14)** and the GA Declaration of 1992 on the Rights of Persons Belonging to National or Ethnic, Religious and Linguistic Minorities (32 ILM 911 (1993)). On the other hand, while minorities, as such, have no right to secede from a state, there is no rule of international law that would prohibit them from seeking secession even by force of arms unless the secession is a result of unlawful military intervention **(331)**. Whether in extreme situations, where a national minority is persistently denied fundamental human rights binding states even under customary international law **(159)**, the minority in question would acquire the right of secession under international law, is a controversial issue. Today international law reaches a dead end in this respect. As stated in Opinion No. 2 of the Arbitration Commission of the European Community (EC) Conference on Former Yugoslavia **(134)**, "international law, as it currently stands, does not spell out all the implications of the right of self-determination."

Action to protect ethnic and national minorities has been undertaken at the regional level in Europe, primarily under the auspices of the EC, the Council of Europe and the Organization for Security and Cooperation in Europe (OSCE) (formerly known as the Conference on Security and Cooperation in Europe). In the early 1990s, within the context of the rise of new states in Eastern Europe resulting from the disintegration of the Soviet Union **(133)** and the former Yugoslavia, the EC Guidelines of 1991 on the Recognition of New States in Eastern Europe and the Soviet Union (31 ILM 1486 (1992)) made the recognition of these new states conditional on their "guarantees for the rights of ethnic and national groups," a condition reiterated in the above-noted Opinion No. 2. In a more general context, while national minorities are mentioned in Art. 14 of the European Convention for the Protection of Human Rights and Fundamental Freedoms **(153)** only with reference to nondiscrimination, the problem of minorities, especially the linguistic ones, became a major item on the agenda of the Council of Europe. In 1992 the Council's Committee on Minorities adopted the European Charter for Regional and Minority Languages, followed in 1995 by the Framework Convention for the Protection of National Minorities (34 ILM 351 (1995)), the major European instrument for the protection of minorities. For its part, the OSCE, which is a regional arrangement in Europe in the meaning of Chapter VIII of the UN Charter, has dealt, *inter alia*, with the question of minorities. It established the post of High Commissioner on National Minorities, designed to alert the Organization to minority issues with a potential of conflict between member states.

**173. Nationality, Dual (Multiple).** As a result of the diversity of municipal laws **(27)** concerning acquisition and withdrawal of nationality **(175)**, an individual **(164)** may find himself simultaneously to be a national of two (dual nationality) or more than two (multiple nationality) states **(127)**. Such a situation has both advantages, for example protection by, and access to more than one state, and disadvantages, as in the area of taxation or military service and in general subjection to nationality-based jurisdiction **(88)** of more than one state. Moreover, dual nationality may cause problems in connection with diplomatic protection when a dual national has the nationality both of the claimant and the respondent state.

Dual nationality may arise both at birth, for example, for a child born in a *jus soli* state (that is, a country in which the place of birth is the decisive test of citizenship) to parents who are nationals of a *jus sanguinis* country (that is, a country where the nationality of the parents determines citizenship), and subsequent to birth, as by legitimation, naturalization **(176)** in the strict sense of the term, or marriage, if an individual acquires a new nationality without losing his original one.

International efforts to limit the occurrence of dual nationality and its effects led, apart from bilateral agreements, to the adoption at the 1930 Hague Conference for the Codification **(5)** of International Law of the Convention on Certain Questions Relating to the Conflict of Nationality Laws (179 LNTS 89) which, however, had only a limited effect upon reducing the incidence and consequences of dual nationality. The United States is not a party to this Convention, but is a party to the Hague Protocol of 1930 Relating to Military Obligations in Certain Cases of Double Nationality (178 LNTS 227). The regional Convention on the Reduction of Cases of Multiple [including dual] Nationality and Military Obligations in Cases of Multiple Nationality, adopted under the auspices of the Council of Europe in 1963, aims at reducing cases of multiple nationality and military obligations in such circumstances, and its application is not prejudiced by the 1997 European Convention on Nationality (37 ILM 44 (1998)).

Under the Convention of 1930, a dual or multiple national may be regarded as a national by each of the states involved, but a state may not afford diplomatic protection to its national against a state whose nationality he also possesses. The Convention adopted the principle of effective or dominant nationality whereby a dual national is treated as the national of the state in which he is habitually and principally resident or the state to which he appears to be most closely connected. The Convention provides for the right of an individual whose dual nationality was acquired involuntarily, to renounce one nationality with the authorization of the state from which he intends to be expatriated. Such authorization must be granted if the individual has his habitual or principal residence outside of this state.

**174. Nationality of Corporations.** A concept employed by analogy to the nationality of individuals **(175)**, whereby a corporation or some other legal person of private law is attributed to a state for purposes of applying to the entity in question the appropriate rules of law. However, due to the obvious differences between individuals and legal entities, the analogy to nationality of individuals can be applied only to a limited extent, as noted in 1970 by the International Court of Justice **(309)** in its judgment on the merits in the *Barcelona Traction, Light and Power Company, Limited* (Belgium v. Spain) (1970 ICJ Rep. 3). Corporate nationality under international law is relevant primarily for purposes of the right to exercise diplomatic protection within the context of the nationality of claim **(95)** principle, but also when claiming treaty **(288)** rights and in the area of a state's legislative jurisdiction **(87)** where the acts of its corporate "nationals" are concerned. Subsidiaries incorporated in different countries, as in the case of transnational corporations **(140)**, acquire different nationalities depending on the municipal law **(27)** in question.

Unlike the relatively fixed notion of nationality of individuals, nationality of corporations is not, as a rule, defined by municipal law, and the attribution by states of nationality to a corporation may differ depending on the purpose of jurisdiction involved. A *prima facie* assumption in many countries, including the United States, is that a corporation has the nationality of the state under whose law it is organized, that is, the law of the state that created it. On the other hand, many European countries refer to the principal place of management or administrative center (*siège social*) as the basis of nationality under international law, constituting a connection additional to incorporation which must be effected in the same state. Ordinarily, the French concept of *siège social* means the administrative center of the entity, where the shareholders' meetings take place, but occasionally conventions insist that it is not just a nominal concept but that it should in fact be the actual center of business activity of the entity in question.

Depending on the circumstances, formal requirements of incorporation constitute only a *prima facie* presumption of nationality and international courts may pierce the corporate veil in order to determine which state in reality controls the entity, by using such substantive links as the location of the *siège social*, the principal place of business, and nationality of major shareholders. A variety of criteria can be found in definitions of corporate nationality in international conventions, such as those dealing with double taxation, air transport, and settlement of claims in cases of nationalization of foreign-owned property **(145)**. Some treaties, for example the 1982 Convention on the Law of the Sea **(264)** in its provisions on the sponsorship of deep seabed operations **(250)**, specifically depart from the criterion of the place of incorporation, referring to the test of foreign control as the criterion of attributing nationality. In any event, where national security is involved, as in the matter of defining an enemy alien **(345)** corporation, the nationality of the individuals actually controlling the entity or owning its stock is the overriding criterion.

**175. Nationality of Individuals.** Nationality is the principal legal link between an individual **(164)** and a state **(127)**. It results in his quality of being a national ("citizen" in the terminology of municipal law) **(27)** of the state in question and establishes a bond of allegiance of the individual to this state. While essentially an institution of municipal law, nationality is relevant in international law for a number of reasons. It provides a basis for the exercise of jurisdiction **(87)** over nationals abroad under the nationality principle **(88)**; it allows a state (however, without any obligation under international law) to accord diplomatic protection to its nationals and make claims on their behalf if their rights have been infringed by a foreign state; it makes it possible for a national to benefit from the rights conferred by a treaty concluded by the state of nationality; it may exempt an individual from extradition **(75)** as a national of the requested state; and it provides an individual, expelled from a state, with the right of repatriation to his state of nationality.

As a concept for purposes of international law, nationality does not refer to a person's ethnic origin. Furthermore, its municipal law counterpart, "citizenship," implies full political rights and benefits under the law of the state of citizenship and in this respect may differ from the concept of nationality. Thus in United States (US) law a distinction is made between citizens and nationals of the US. A US citizen is *ipso facto* a national for purposes of international law, but inhabitants of certain outlying possessions of the US (American Samoa and Swain Island) are not citizens for purposes of the US Constitution and laws, while owing allegiance to the US and being US nationals for external purposes.

Under general principles concerning nationality, each state determines under its law who its nationals are, a principle codified in Art. 1 of the 1930 Hague Convention on Certain Questions Relating to the Conflict of Nationality Laws (179 LNTS 89). However, a question arises whether there are any limits that international law sets upon the freedom of states concerning acquisition or loss of nationality with respect to whomsoever it pleases. There exists an international consensus that states need not accept a nationality law that is not consistent with applicable treaties **(40)** customary international law **(39)**, and the principles of law generally recognized **(38)** with regard to nationality. First among the latter is the principle that everyone has a right to nationality, a principle proclaimed in the Universal Declaration of Human Rights **(162)** and included in such treaties as, *inter alia*, the International Covenant on Civil and Political Rights **(166)**, the Convention on the Rights of the Child **(150)**, and, more recently, in the Council of Europe European Convention on Nationality of 1997 (37 ILM 44 (1998)). The last mentioned treaty may be regarded as the most recent articulation of the contemporary international law of nationality, encompassing such matters as the guiding general principles relating to nationality, rules relating to acquisition, loss, and recovery of nationality, relevant procedures, questions relating to multiple (two or more) nationality **(173)**, state succession **(132)** and nationality, and military obligations in cases of multiple nationality. Other principles governing nationality rules are that statelessness **(181)** must be avoided, arbitrary depriving of nationality is unlawful, and the nationality of a spouse may not be automatically affected by marriage or the dissolution of a marriage between an individual and an alien **(144)**, or the change of nationality by one of the spouses during marriage.

According to generally accepted practice, nationality is acquired at birth, the by far most common case, or subsequent to birth, by naturalization **(176)**. In granting nationality by birth, municipal laws in general apply, in modified form and in combination, either the principle of *jus soli* or that of *jus sanguinis*. Under the principle of *jus soli* (the law of the territory), historically favored by the countries of the common-law tradition, including the US, a child born on the state's territory **(228)** automatically becomes its national. The few exceptions include, first of all, children born to persons with diplomatic immunity **(63)**. Many states extend the principle of *jus soli* to include children born on ships and aircraft beyond the territorial sea **(262)**, registered in the state in question. Foundlings found in a state's territory are presumed to have its nationality unless proven to the contrary, a rule found in Art. 1 of the Convention on the Reduction of Statelessness of 1961 (989 UNTS 175). Under the principle of *jus sanguinis* (the law of the blood), favored by the civil-law **(23)** countries of Europe, the nationality of a child is determined, irrespective of its place of birth, by the nationality of its parents or, in some countries, one of its parents. Children born out of wedlock usually follow the nationality of their mother.

International law does not, in principle, deny a state's right to terminate the nationality of its national. In addition, voluntary renunciation of nationality at the initiative of the individual belongs to fundamental human rights. Withdrawal of nationality by a state may take place by virtue of the law or at the initiative of the state, but may not be arbitrary or motivated by discrimination, or used as an instrument of political repression, as was the case of the Soviet and other Communist states' denationalization decrees and the Nazi German decrees used as part of the state's racist policy. In today's international law, denationalization may not result in the statelessness of the person concerned. Voluntary acquisition of another nationality, public renunciation of nationality, voluntary service in a foreign military force, voting in a political election abroad, or conduct prejudicial to the vital interests of the state, fraudulent conduct in the naturalization proceedings, are listed, *inter alia*, as circumstances warranting withdrawal of nationality. Protracted habitual residence abroad, especially of a naturalized citizen, may in some countries (but not the US) be a ground for denationalization in the absence of some genuine link other than residence in the state in question. Voluntary expatriation, that is, loss of nationality at the initiative of the individual, is included among the fundamental human rights **(157)** in the Universal Declaration of Human Rights and the American Convention on Human Rights of 1969 **(147)**. However, in a number of countries it is subject to various legal and administrative barriers, for example, under the municipal law of some countries renunciation of nationality may be effected only by nationals who are habitually resident abroad, a rule also found in the above-mentioned European Convention on Nationality of 1997 (Art. 8(2)). Some states follow the doctrine of "indelible allegiance" whereby an individual acquiring the nationality of another state continues to be regarded as a national of the original state unless the latter itself terminates the bond of nationality. In other states, an individual's nationality automatically terminates upon his naturalization abroad, but in some states he is given the option of renouncing his original nationality. In a number of countries an individual born as a dual national is allowed, upon coming of age, to make a declaration renouncing his nationality acquired by virtue of *jus soli*, but according to the Convention on the Reduction of Statelessness of 1961, renunciation of nationality may not result in statelessness.

**176. Naturalization.** In its broadest sense, the term naturalization encompasses any change of nationality **(175)** subsequent to birth, including the acquisition of nationality as a result of state succession **(132)**, marriage to a foreign national, legitimation or adoption of children, naturalization of a minor as a result of the naturalization of the parents, acquisition of nationality through exercise of an option, obtaining appointment as a civil servant or joining the armed forces, and redintegration as a national. In its more narrow, but much more common, meaning naturalization or—as it is sometimes referred to—"voluntary naturalization" is the grant of nationality to an alien through a formal procedure upon the alien's application. Under general international law aliens have no right to be naturalized, each state being free to determine eligibility to naturalization. Under the European Convention on Nationality of 1997 (37 ILM 44 (1998)) the states parties are bound to provide in their respective internal laws for the possibility of naturalization of persons lawfully and habitually resident on their respective territories and are obliged to facilitate naturalization of such persons as spouses and children of nationals, persons born on their respective territories, stateless persons, and refugees **(178)**.

A naturalized alien need not be accorded the same rights as a native-born national, as demonstrated for example by Art. II of the United States (US) Constitution requiring the President to be a native-born citizen. Compulsory naturalization of aliens on such grounds as land ownership or residence in the state, as attempted by some Latin American states in the 19th century, met with protests by some countries and refusal to recognize such naturalization as contrary to international law. As a general rule, however, naturalization acts are presumed to be valid and granted in good faith.

The effect of marriage on nationality is regulated in a variety of ways, the principle of the unity of the family and the more recent approach emphasizing the wife's freedom to choose her nationality competing in the municipal laws **(27)**. The latter approach is followed in the pertinent treaty **(288)** law concerning the status of women **(183)**.

The conditions for naturalization found in municipal laws vary from country to country. Residence for a certain period of time is the most common requirement. The above-mentioned European Convention on Nationality of 1997 provides that such period of residence shall not exceed ten years before the lodging of an application. The US law requires, as a general rule, a five-year period of residence.

In certain cases it is possible for a state not to recognize some effects of a naturalization granted by another state. As held by the International Court of Justice **(309)** in its judgment in the *Nottebohm* case (Liechtenstein v. Guatemala) (1955 ICJ Rep. 4), largely influenced by the analogy to the principle of effectiveness in cases of dual nationality **(173)**, Guatemala was under no obligation to recognize, for purposes of diplomatic protection, the effects of naturalization granted by Liechtenstein to Nottebohm in the absence of a genuine link between that individual and Liechtenstein. The Court's decision has been criticized in the doctrine as dissociating the right of diplomatic protection from nationality and using a vague and relative notion of genuine link. Depending on the circumstances, the bonds constituting a genuine link may include, apart from birth, such factual ties as habitual residence, the center of interests, family ties, participation in public life, and the like. The existence or not of a genuine link may be one of the elements taken into account in the granting or the retention of nationality in cases of state succession.

**177. Racial Discrimination, International Convention on the Elimination of All Forms of, 1966.** A convention (660 UNTS 195) drafted by the United Nations (UN) Commission on Human Rights and adopted by the General Assembly (GA) in 1965, open for signature in 1966 and in force in 1969, committing the states parties to eliminating racial discrimination and promoting racial equality. In 2000 the Convention had 156 contracting parties, including the US. The adoption of the Convention was largely due to a determined action in the UN of the developing countries, designed to outlaw discrimination based on color and put an end to the apartheid regime practiced at that time in South Africa. The Convention defines the term "racial discrimination" rather extensively as "any distinction, exclusion, restriction or preference based on race, color, descent, or national or ethnic origin which has the purpose or effect of nullifying or impairing the recognition, enjoyment or exercise, on equal footing of human rights and fundamental freedoms **(157)** in the political, economic, social, cultural or any other field of public life." However, the Convention does not apply to distinctions, exclusions, restrictions or preferences made by a state between citizens and non-citizens. The language of the definition ("effect") suggests that the Convention aims not only at achieving *de jure* racial equality but at prohibiting indirect, *de facto*, discrimination. Certain discriminatory measures in favor of racial or ethnic groups needing special protection (known in the US as "affirmative action") shall not be considered racial discrimination so long as they are not continued after the objectives for which they were taken have been achieved (Art. 1). The Convention (Art. 20) requires the states parties, *inter alia*, to eliminate racial discrimination and to this end change any laws and policies which create and perpetuate such discrimination, and to prohibit any private conduct amounting to racial discrimination. Affirmative action when circumstances so warrant is another mandatory rule of the Convention. The provision of Art. 3, which particularly condemns racial segregation and apartheid, has not been significant in practice since the abolition of the apartheid regime in South Africa. The interpretation **(274)** of Art. 4, which condemns all propaganda and all organizations based on theories of racial superiority or promoting racial hatred and discrimination, and obliging the states parties to criminalize and punish the dissemination of such ideas irrespective of their effect or intention, has been a subject of international controversy in that a number of Western states have made reservations **(282)** or interpretative statements expressing concern that the full application of Art. 4 may jeopardize freedom of opinion and expression and of peaceful assembly and association, otherwise recognized as fundamental human rights. However, in 1986 the Committee for the Elimination of Racial Discrimination, the UN "treaty body" monitoring compliance with the Convention, held in its report on Art. 4 that "the rights of free speech and of free association are not absolute but subject to limitations." But whether the Committee has the power of authoritative interpretation is questionable since under Art. 22 of the Convention disputes between states parties with respect to the interpretation and application of the Convention are to be referred to the International Court of Justice **(309)**. The possibility of such referral is largely undermined by reservations submitted by a number of states.

Under Art. 5 the parties to the Convention are required to guarantee equality before the law in the enjoyment of a long but not exhaustive list of rights and freedoms, including certain rights not proclaimed by the Universal Declaration of Human Rights **(162)**, such as the right to inherit and to access to any place or service intended for use by the general public as well as rights in regard to which racial discrimination is prohibited, such as the right to work, to join trade unions, and the right to housing.

Compliance with the provisions of the Convention is monitored by the above-mentioned Committee, the first treaty body created by the UN to oversee the implementation by states of human rights agreements. Consisting of 18 independent experts, the Committee has the mandate to review the steps taken by individual states to fulfill their obligations to combat racial discrimination. First, all states parties must submit periodic reports to the Committee, which in turn is itself required to report annually to the GA on its activities, with suggestions and recommendations. In this respect the Committee, like its counterparts under the two Covenants, has encountered problems of late or even unsubmitted state reports as well as financial difficulties. The second procedure, thus far not resorted to, provides for a system of interstate complaints which, however, lacks any legally binding force for the state concerned. Third, an individual or a group of persons, who claim to be victims of racial discrimination, may lodge a complaint before the Committee against the allegedly responsible state, but here as well, the Committee has no power to make legally binding decisions. Furthermore, the procedure can be applied only if the state concerned has made a declaration recognizing the competence of the Committee to receive such complaints. As of June 2000, 30 states have used this option. The case of *Yilmaz-Dogan v. Netherlands*, 1988, involving a Turkish guest worker's complaint over the termination of her employment contract and her employer's objectionable remarks about foreign workers, belongs with the most interesting cases of using the right of petition under the Convention. The competence of the Committee to receive petitions from trusteeship **(142)** and non-self-governing territories has not been of much practical significance.

The provisions of the Convention against racial discrimination were complemented by the 1973 Convention on the Suppression and Punishment of the Crime of Apartheid (1015 UNTS 244) and the Convention against Apartheid in Sport of 1985. It must also be borne in mind that the prohibition of racial discrimination now forms part of customary international law **(39)**. Furthermore, provisions against a widely conceived discrimination, including not only discrimination based on race, color, and language but also on grounds of sex, religion, political or other opinion, national or social origin, property, birth or other status, as well as provisions guaranteeing equality before the law, are part of the International Covenant on Civil and Political Rights **(166)**. The Committee set up under this Covenant found non-discrimination to be "a basic and general principle relating to the protection of human rights." It may be added that a special convention deals with the elimination of discrimination against women **(183)** and with regard to religion, in 1981 the GA adopted by consensus the Declaration on the Elimination of All Forms of Intolerance and Discrimination Based on Religion or Belief (21 ILM 205 (1982)).

**178. Refugees.** The refugee is an individual who "owing to well-founded fear of being persecuted for reasons of race, religion, nationality [presumably ethnic origin], membership of a particular social group of political opinion, is outside the country of his nationality **(175)** and is unable or, owing to such fear, is unwilling to avail himself of the protection of that country, or who, not having a nationality and being outside the country of his former habitual residence as a result of such events, is unable or, owing to such fear, is unwilling to return to it." This definition in the Convention Relating to the Status of Refugees of 1951 (189 UNTS 137), originally applying to events in Europe prior to 1951 and in force for 141 countries, was extended to all refugees without any temporal and geographical limitations, by Art. 1(2) of the Protocol Relating to the Status of Refugees of 1967 (606 UNTS 267) which by virtue of its Art. 1(1) incorporates the substantive articles of the Convention of 1951. Some 140 countries, including the United States (US), were parties to the Protocol in 2000. Certain refugee problems are also covered by a number of regional agreements.

There are analogies and similarities between the status of refugees fleeing their home country and that of *de facto* stateless individuals **(181)**, both categories lacking the protection of their home government. Many refugees also fit in the category of stateless persons; hence the Convention Relating to the Status of Stateless Persons of 1954 is modeled on the Convention Relating to the Status of Refugees of 1951. Migrant workers from less-developed regions of the world, in search of economic opportunity abroad, represent a growing category of individuals residing outside the country of their birth. The International Convention on the Protection of the Rights of All Migrant Workers and Members of Their Families, 1991 (30 ILM 1517 (1991), defines various categories of migrant workers and provides for the duties of the receiving states with regard to the protection of the rights of the migrants. However, this Convention has been ratified only by a limited number of countries (19 in early 2003). Supplementing the United Nations (UN) Convention against Transnational Organized Crime, 2000 (40 ILM 335 (2001)), the Protocol of 2000 against the Smuggling of Migrants by Land, Sea and Air (40 ILM 384 (2001)) aims at combating such smuggling, but reaffirms the need for the protection of migrants.

International efforts undertaken in the 20th century to protect and safeguard the rights of refugees date back to agreements of 1926 and 1928 relating to the protection of Russian and Armenian refugees in the aftermath of the war and political upheavals in Russia. These early agreements culminated in the Convention of 1933 Relating to the International Status of Refugees which, *inter alia*, granted refugees the right to use an international travel document, the "Nansen passport," named after the head of the League of Nations' International Office for Refugees (1936–1939), an agency succeeded in 1939 by an organization under the High Commissioner for Refugees under the Protection of the League of Nations. International agreements to help refugees from Germany and Austria were also concluded in 1936 and 1938, respectively.

Following World War II the General Assembly established the International Refugee Organization to deal with the daunting task of helping and resettling a million and a half refugees and other "displaced persons." This organization functioned until 1951 when its functions and the supervision of the implementation of the 1951 Convention (and then also the Protocol of 1967) were taken over by the Office of the United Nations High Commissioner for Refugees (UNHCR), formally established in 1950. The second half of the 20th century was characterized by large-scale movements of refugees due to war and political upheavals on all continents, a phenomenon that has continued into the new century. In more than 50 years of its existence the UNHCR has helped some 50 million refugees. At this time its staff of around 5,000 in more than 120 countries helps an estimated 20 million persons who fall under its mandate. This figure includes some 12 million refugees within the meaning of the Convention as well as about one million of asylum **(148)** seekers and more than five million "internally displaced persons" who, while in principle not protected in international law as refugees, are granted help at the request of the UN. In 2002 the total number in this category exceeded 20 million persons. It must be added that, except for about 350,000 Palestinians residing outside the Near East, some three million Palestinians do not fall under the mandate of the UNHCR, but are covered by a special organization known as the United Nations Relief and Works Agency for Palestinian Refugees in the Near East (UNRWA).

While international law does not require states to admit refugees, states parties to the Convention or its Protocol are obliged to provide them favorable treatment: national treatment with regard to such matters as access to elementary education, courts, social security, and labor legislation; most favored nation treatment with regard to such matters as employment, the right of association, and education above the elementary level; and treatment no less favorable than that accorded to aliens **(144)** in such areas as acquisition of property, self-employment, and exercise of a liberal profession. Furthermore, refugees are guaranteed freedom of movement within the state and are entitled to travel documents for foreign travel. However, it appears that a refugee who obtains a passport or other travel document from his original country ceases to be regarded as a refugee.

The Convention (and the Protocol) includes a rule that eventually became the basis for what is known as the "first-asylum" principle whereby a person entering a state of refuge "directly" from his home country, that is, reaching the very first state territory **(228)** after fleeing the state where his life or freedom was threatened, cannot be penalized by that first state for illegal entry. This means that while the first state must accept a refugee or find him another state of refuge, any subsequent country where a refugee arrives in order to reside there may disqualify him from the status of refugee and expel him from its territory. The rationale of the first-asylum principle is to reduce the number of would-be applicants for refugee status by denying such status to individuals who in reality left their home country for economic reasons and not because of fear of political persecution.

The state of refuge may not expel a refugee save on grounds of national security or public order, but expulsion or return of a refugee to a state where his life or freedom would be threatened, the so-called *refoulement*, is prohibited unless the individual involved is a security threat or a danger to the community. The interdiction in 1981 and 1992 by the US of Haitian vessels suspected of bringing illegal aliens to the US and subsequent return of the individuals concerned to Haiti, without any inquiry, was criticized by some as being in violation of the principle of non-*refoulement* or, at least of the spirit of this rule, assuming that it was not intended to have extraterritorial effect. In 1994 the US instituted a policy of shipboard inquiry by the Coast Guard to determine which individuals had legitimate grounds for fleeing Haiti.

The refugee agreements do not apply to persons for whom there are serious reasons for considering that they have committed a crime against peace **(325)**, a war crime **(373)** or a crime against humanity **(151)**, or a serious non-political crime outside the country of refuge, or persons guilty of acts contrary to purposes and principles of the UN.

**179. Repudiation and Breach of State Contracts with Aliens.** A breach or any outright disclaimer by a state **(127)** of liability under a contract with an alien **(144)** which, under the circumstances, may constitute a violation of international law entailing the state's responsibility **(128)** for injury sustained by the alien. It is normal for states to enter into all kinds of contract with nationals **(175, 173)** of another state and ordinarily, unless the parties designate another proper law for the contract, the validity, interpretation, and performance of the contract is governed by the municipal law of the state concerned. Contracts involving public loans, including the issue of state bonds, and other contractual arrangements, especially concession or development agreements concerning exploitation of natural resources of the state concerned, have engendered more international controversy than any other forms of contract between states and foreign nationals.

In principle, a repudiation or breach by a state of a contract with an alien, attributable to *bona fide* commercial reasons, entails liability for damage according to the municipal law **(27)** of the state. State responsibility under international law arises only if, as is the case of expropriation **(145)**, the violation in question is motivated by non-commercial considerations and the state commits an arbitrary act or omission that impairs any economic interest of the alien, fails to pay compensatory damage, or is responsible for denial of justice **(152)**. As a rule, disputes concerning delivery of goods or loans by a foreign lender are resolved in international commercial arbitration **(308)**. Most cases of failure to pay interest in loan agreements are settled by negotiation, the agreement often providing for a waiver of the debtor state's immunity **(131)** from being sued in the other state. Repudiation by the host state of a concession contract may often be tantamount to expropriation, especially if the right conferred under the concession involves ownership by the alien of assets or equipment. In this sense, concessionary rights are sometimes considered as a category of proprietary rights. In a number of arbitrations **(293)** involving nationalization by Libya of foreign oil companies, such as for example the *Texaco Overseas Petroleum Co.& California Asiatic Oil Co.* (*TOPCO & CAOC*), decided by a sole arbitrator in 1977 (17 ILM 1 (1978)), repudiation of concession agreements was treated as expropriation. A state may also breach or repudiate its obligations under a contract with an alien by changing its tax laws, imposing a new exchange rate, or issuing other regulations adversely affecting the value of the contract for the foreign national concerned. Anticipating any such developments, foreign investors sometimes include in concession contracts the so-called stabilization clause stipulating that the contract will be governed by the municipal law in force at the time of the conclusion of the contract, thus barring the state from annulling the contract or enacting any laws or regulations that would in effect modify its terms. While some developing countries oppose stabilization clauses as derogating from their sovereignty, a number of arbitral decisions have found them not to be contrary to international law.

The foreign investor and the host country are free to choose the law to govern their contract, but the determination of which body of law governs the valuation, performance, and interpretation **(274)** of the contract may pose a difficult task for the tribunal. While the principle of observing agreements, *pacta sunt servanda* **(277)**, underlies any system of law governing agreements, the resulting decision may be significantly affected by a more specific identification of the substantive contents of both the law and the modalities of compliance. Occasionally concession agreements are governed not by the municipal law of the host country but by some other body of law as indicated in the choice of law clause of the contract, which may often strengthen the position of the foreign investor as against the host state, preventing the latter from effecting changes in its municipal law, detrimental to the alien, and in general "internationalize" the contract by removing it from the sphere of this law. Although some jurists favor the idea of a body of law that would, like the Roman *jus gentium* **(25)**, handle the issue of internationalized contracts, the opinion prevails that a choice of law clause cannot convert a concession contract into an international agreement **(288)**. Internationalized contracts have been strongly opposed by developing countries as derogating from their sovereign rights over natural resources; hence their contracts with aliens designate the municipal law of the host country as the law governing the contract.

**180. Slavery and Slave-like Practices.** The prohibition of slavery and the slave trade and slave-like practices as international crimes, both in customary law **(39)** and on grounds of general principles of law common to major law systems **(38)**, is firmly established as a fundamental norm of public international law. It has also been articulated in a variety of international instruments, such as declarations and treaties specifically dealing with the slave trade and slavery as well as agreements concerning human rights and other matters where legal prohibition of slave trafficking and slavery is pertinent to the subject matter of the instrument in question. Historically, international opposition to the slave trade and slavery, both still legal at the beginning of the 19th century, followed national anti-slavery measures led by Great Britain, which abolished the slave trade in 1807 and largely contributed to the condemnation of the practice in principle at the Congress of Vienna, 1815, and in a series of treaties in the 19th century aimed at international cooperation in combating the slave trade, the most important of which was the General Act of the Brussels Conference Relative to the African Slave Trade of 1890. The British Royal Navy played a crucial role in enforcing the anti-slavery provisions of these international instruments so that by the end of the 19th century prohibition of slavery and the slave trade had been recognized as a rule of customary international law. However, slavery continued to exist in certain parts of the world, both in its traditional form and as various slave-like practices, despite the virtually universal acceptance by states of treaties stipulating the obligation to bring about a complete suppression of slavery. The major international acts in this respect were the Convention adopted under the auspices of the League of Nations in 1926 (60 LNTS 253), with a Protocol of 1953, and the Supplementary Convention on the Abolition of Slavery, the Slave Trade, and Institutions and Practices Similar to Slavery of 1956 (266 UNTS 3). Under Art. 99 of the United Nations (UN) Convention on the Law of the Sea **(264)**, every state shall take effective measures to prevent and punish the transport of slaves in ships flying its flag **(240)** and to prevent the unlawful use of its flag for that purpose. Any slave taking refuge on board any ship, whatever its flag, shall *ipso facto* be free. Furthermore, under Art. 110(1)(b) warships **(265)** and other vessels on government service have the right to stop, visit, and search any merchant vessel on the high seas **(245)** when there is reasonable ground for suspecting that the vessel in question is engaged in the slave trade. Special international agreements were concluded for the suppression of traffic in women and children as early as 1904 (1 LNTS 83) and 1910 (3 LNTS 278). More recently, freedom from slavery and slave-like practices became part of the protection of human rights in general. It is guaranteed in Art. 4 of the Universal Declaration of 1948 **(162)**; Art. 8 of the International Covenant on Civil and Political Rights **(166)**; Art. 6 of the American Convention on Human Rights **(147)**; and Art. 5 of the African Charter of Human and Peoples' Rights **(143)**. Conventions designed to protect the rights of women **(183)** and children **(150)**, *inter alia*, oblige the states parties to take all appropriate measures to suppress all forms of traffic in women and children, respectively. The Protocol of 2000 to Prevent, Suppress and Punish Trafficking in Persons, Especially Women and Children (40 ILM 377 (2001)) (ratified by 18 countries), supplementing the UN Convention of 2000 against Transnational Organized Crime (40 ILM 353 (2001)), is a major recent instrument designed to meet these objectives. Slavery and the slave trade are also banned under Art. 4(2)(f) of Protocol II of 1977 **(369)** Additional to the 1949 Geneva Conventions **(349)**, which relates to the protection of victims of non-international armed conflicts **(340)**.

Resulting in complete destruction of an individual's legal personality, slavery constitutes the gravest offense against the freedom of human beings. Art. 1 of the Slavery Convention of 1926 defines slavery as "the status or condition of a person over whom any or all the powers attaching to the right of ownership are exercised." Similarly, the Rome Statute of the International Criminal Court (ICC) **(170)**, which in Art. 7(1)(c) includes "enslavement" among crimes against humanity **(151)**, defines it as "the exercise of any or all of the powers attaching to the right of ownership over a person and includes the exercise of such power in the course of trafficking in persons, in particular women and children." In the early 21st century, some 27 million human beings were estimated to be in conditions of enslavement, primarily through practices similar to the traditional slavery such as the below-noted debt bondage and forced labor under the threat of violence.

There is universal consensus that, like piracy **(259)**, slavery is a crime under international law. Consequently, states have the duty to prevent slavery and to punish individuals engaging in it. Any state that as a matter of state policy practices slavery or fails to exercise due diligence to prevent or punish violations by private persons commits a violation of international law. This is still the case of a number of countries in Africa, especially Sudan, the Middle East, and South Asia. Private persons and other non-state actors engaging in slavery incur criminal responsibility directly under international law and under the principle of universality of jurisdiction **(92)** may be tried and punished by any state that obtains the custody of the suspect. As held by the International Court of Justice **(309)** in an *obiter dictum* in its judgment on the merits in the case of *Barcelona Traction, Light and Power Company, Limited* (Belgium v. Spain) (1970 ICJ Rep. 3), protection from slavery constitutes a state's obligation toward the international community as a whole, that is, *erga omnes* **(12)**. Following the view of the International Law Commission, it can also be argued that the prohibition of slavery belongs to the peremptory rules of international law (*jus cogens*) **(24)**.

It is not entirely settled which acts of enslavement constitute crimes against humanity. Under the Statute of the ICC, enslavement, as defined above, is a crime against humanity if "committed as part of a widespread or systematic attack directed against any civilian population, with the accused being aware of the attack" (Art. 1). Pursuant to this definition the criminal conduct need not be linked to an international or internal armed conflict and there is no requirement for the presence of a discriminatory motive. According to overwhelming (but denied by the government) evidence by human rights non-governmental organizations, exiles, traders, and former slaves, slave traders from the Northern Sudan have been carrying out armed raids in the South, with the connivance of the government, abducting into enslavement women and children of the local black tribes. Such acts qualify as crimes against humanity under the Statute of the ICC. Otherwise, albeit denied by governments, the institution of the traditional slavery (apart from practices similar to slavery) continue in some other African countries. In Mauritania, slavery was officially abolished three times, most recently in 1980, but "chattel slavery," the owning of and trading in human beings, persists in remote rural areas of the country.

Practices similar to slavery, such as forced labor, debt bondage and serfdom, and child prostitution have long been on the agenda of international bodies, and especially the International Labour Organisation (ILO), and are prohibited in a number of anti-slavery conventions and various human rights and fundamental freedoms instruments. The practice of debt bondage, the most common form of contemporary slavery, whereby a debtor pledges his personal service or frequently that of his children, as a collateral security for debt, without a reasonable application of the value of the otherwise undefined and temporally unlimited services toward the liquidation of the debt, is quite common in South and South-East Asia, with more than 10 million persons living in bondage in India alone. The practice also persists in remote regions of Brazil and Peru. The debts of the bonded workers, including their children, toiling in manufactures, brick kilns, and mines, are often passed on to the next generation. Failure to pay a debt often results in outright selling to another landlord or into marriage. These practices are still condoned even in states which are parties to slavery conventions. As a matter of fact, a United States (US) government study released in 2000 revealed that in the US transnational criminal syndicates effectively sold 50,000 women and children into *de facto* slavery in 1997. Altogether it is estimated that worldwide at least 700,000 individuals are trafficked in this way each year. While a special UN working group, set up in 1974, reports to the UN Commission on Human Rights **(161)** on contemporary forms of slavery, the pertinent conventions have no monitoring bodies to oversee state compliance with their provisions.

Forced labor, which frequently is nothing but a form of slavery, is condemned or banned in a number of international agreements drafted under the auspices of the ILO, including Convention No. 29 of 1930 (39 UNTS 55) and Convention No. 105 of 1957 (320 UNTS 291). Art. 2 of the widely ratified Convention No. 29 defines "forced or compulsory labor" as "all work or service which is exacted from any person under the menace of any penalty and for which the said person has not offered himself voluntarily." Under the 1930 Conventions the parties undertook to suppress forced or compulsory labor "within the shortest possible period," but it was not until 1957 that Convention No. 105, to which the US has been a party since 1992, formally abolished this slave-like practice for certain specific purposes, namely, as a means of political coercion; labor discipline; punishment for striking; racial, social, national, or religious discrimination; or as a method of using labor for purposes of economic development. However, in reality, the Convention had little effect upon the practice of nondemocratic states. As recently as 1999, the widespread use of forced labor by the government of Myanmar prompted condemnation in an ILO resolution and adoption of certain sanctions against that country (38 ILM 1215 (1999)). Forced labor is also banned in global and regional human rights instruments. Arguably, this ban can be considered as a norm of general international law.

**181. Statelessness.** As a result of diversity of municipal laws **(27)** concerning acquisition and withholding of nationality **(175)**, an individual **(164)** may find himself to have no nationality at all, that is, to be a stateless person. Statelessness entails serious disadvantages for the individual concerned since, among other handicaps, he has no state **(127)** to protect him and his freedom of movement across international borders **(189)** may be severely limited and, if expelled **(146)** from a country, he has no state that would be obliged to accept him in its territory **(228)**. For these reasons, contemporary international law tends to limit the incidence of statelessness as much as possible, viewing this phenomenon within the context of promoting human rights and fundamental freedoms **(157)** for all individuals.

Statelessness may arise both at birth, as illustrated by the example of a child born in a *jus sanguinis* country of parents of a strict *jus soli* state, and subsequent to birth, when an individual loses his nationality without acquiring another one. Statelessness resulting from a conflict of nationality laws (statelessness *de jure*) must be distinguished from statelessness *de facto*, which results from displacement due to war, civil strife, or other serious political upheaval. A *de facto* stateless individual, in practice a refugee **(178)**, may still formally hold his nationality but, refused a passport (or renewal thereof) by the government of his homeland, is in fact exposed to all the disadvantages of a *de jure* stateless person.

In the aftermath of World War I the so-called Nansen passport (named after the head of the League of Nations' International Office for Refugees), which was a document issued to refugees by the state of residence, contributed in some measure to ameliorating the legal position of *de facto* stateless persons, many of them finding refuge in the West to flee the political upheavals in Soviet Russia. The issue of statelessness was also raised at the Hague Conference for the Codification **(5)** of International Law in 1930 which, apart from the Convention on Certain Questions Relating to the Conflict of Nationality Laws and some other instruments mitigating the status of statelessness, adopted a special Protocol Concerning Statelessness (24 AJIL Supp. 211 (1930)). Efforts to reduce the incidence of statelessness and its effects were resumed after World War II when, often closely related to the problem of refugees, statelessness reemerged as a serious humanitarian issue. The right of every individual to nationality was included in the Universal Declaration of Human Rights **(162)** and statelessness was brought on the agenda of the International Law Commission and the United Nations Economic and Social Council. Eventually, a number of international agreements were drawn up designed to reduce statelessness and its effects. The Convention of 1954 Relating to the Status of Stateless Persons (360 UNTS 117), patterned on the Convention Relating to the Status of Refugees of 1951 (189 UNTS 150), reflected in its provisions the close relationship between these two categories of persons. The main instrument dealing in detail with the problem of statelessness is the Convention on the Reduction of Statelessness of 1961 (989 UNTS 175). Unfortunately, this convention has only a limited number of parties. The United States has not subscribed to either convention.

Asserting the right of every individual to nationality, the Convention of 1961 contains numerous provisions designed to eliminate statelessness. For example, it requires the contracting parties to grant nationality to persons born in their respective territories who would otherwise be stateless; with certain exceptions (such as individuals with criminal records), commits the parties to granting nationality on the basis of residence; makes loss of nationality contingent upon acquiring another nationality; and prohibits denationalization as an instrument of discrimination on racial, ethnic, religious, or political grounds.

**182. Torture: Convention against Torture and Other Cruel and Inhuman or Degrading Treatment or Punishment, 1984.** This Convention of 1984 (1465 UNTS 85), briefly known as the Torture Convention, in force in 1987, had 129 parties, including the United States (US), in May 2002. It defines torture in Art. 1 as "any act by which severe pain or suffering, whether physical or mental, is intentionally inflicted on a person for such purposes as obtaining from him or a third person information or a confession, punishing him for an act he or a third person has committed or is suspected of having committed, or intimidating or coercing him or a third person, or for any reason based on discrimination of any kind, when such pain or suffering is inflicted by or at the instigation of or with the consent or acquiescence of a public official or other person acting in an official capacity. It does not include pain or suffering arising only from, inherent in or incidental to lawful sanctions." The concept of torture for purposes of the Convention is limited to the intentional inflicting of severe pain or suffering for the purposes listed in this definition. However, unintentional inflicting of pain or suffering or its imposition as a lawful sanction may qualify as "other cruel, inhuman or degrading treatment or punishment." In this connection, the Committee against Torture, the treaty body charged with overseeing compliance with the Convention, has held with respect to Saudi Arabia's penal law based on the Shariah (Islamic law) that flogging (used as penalty for certain sexual offenses and drinking alcohol) and amputation (applied in cases of theft) constitute breaches of the Convention. As indicated by the Human Rights Committee, the body which interprets the International Covenant on Civil and Political Rights (ICCPR) **(166)**, in its general comment on Art. 7 of the Covenant, dealing with torture, the distinction between the various forms of mistreatment depends on the kind of purpose and severity of the particular treatment. Regionally, the European Court of Human Rights (ECHR) **(154)**, in trying to differentiate torture from other forms of prohibited treatment, found the level of pain and suffering to be the distinguishing factor, with torture characterized by a very severe and aggravated form of suffering deliberately inflicted upon a victim. For purposes of the 1984 Torture Convention, the distinction between torture and other forms of prohibited conduct may be important in that certain provisions of the Convention, for example, the procedure of the Committee against Torture under Art. 20, apply only to torture.

If practiced, encouraged, or condoned by a state, torture and other cruel, inhuman, or degrading treatment or punishment constitute violation of customary international law **(39)**. Anchored in constitutions and laws of many countries (in the US by the Eighth Amendment), prohibition of torture has arguably become a general principle of law common to major legal systems **(38)**. It is banned in a number of major global human rights instruments, including the Universal Declaration of Human Rights **(162)** (Art. 5) and the ICCPR (Art. 7), and regional human rights treaties and other instruments, such as the European Convention for the Protection of Human Rights and Fundamental Freedoms **(153)** (Art. 3), the American Convention on Human Rights **(147)** (Art. 5), and the African Charter of Human and Peoples' Rights **(143)** (Art. 4). There are also regional conventions prohibiting torture: the European Convention for the Prevention of Torture and Inhuman and Degrading Treatment and Punishment of 1987 (27 ILM 1153 (1988)) and the Inter-American Convention to Prevent and Punish Torture of 1985 (24 ILM 519 (1985)).

The main elements of the definition of torture in the 1984 Convention (Art. 1) are now generally accepted as reflecting the notion of torture in customary law. They are also in line with the definitions of torture in other conventions and international jurisprudence, including the case law of the ECHR. The definition has also been adopted for purposes of international humanitarian law **(353)** in the relevant decisions of the International Criminal Tribunal for the Former Yugoslavia **(352)**, for example, in the *Furundzija* case (38 ILM 317 (1999)), and the International Criminal Tribunal for Rwanda **(351)**, as in the *Akayesu* case (37 ILM 1399 (1998)).

Under the Torture Convention (Art. 2) prohibition of torture is absolute and no exceptional circumstances whatever, including state of emergency, war, or an order from public authority, may be invoked as a justification of torture. As illustrated by the case of Augusto Pinochet, held in the United Kingdom on demand for extradition by Spain on charges of having violated the Convention while in office as president of Chile, even an individual in the highest public office may not in principle avoid criminal liability by invoking the plea of sovereign immunity. Prevention of torture is an obligation *erga omnes* **(12)** and has acquired the status of a peremptory norm of international law, *jus cogens* **(24)**. States parties have the obligation to prevent and punish acts of torture as defined in the Convention which lists a variety of measures to be taken by states in order to prevent acts of torture from occurring on their respective territories under control. The same obligation applies to mistreatment other than torture when the acts involved are committed by or at the instigation of, or with the consent or acquiescence of, a public official or other person acting in an official capacity. Torture is to be made an extraditable offense **(75)** and states parties are to take measures to establish jurisdiction **(87)** over torture committed on their respective territories by any of their nationals. The Convention provides for a quasi-universal jurisdiction **(92)** whereby for a state's jurisdiction to be established it is sufficient that the alleged offender be present within its territory and is not extradited to another state. States parties may not expel, return (*refouler*), or extradite an individual if the individual would be in danger of being subjected to torture in the other country.

The Convention provides for four procedures designed to monitor its implementation. First, the states parties have the obligation to submit periodic reports to the Committee against Torture, a body of ten experts serving in their personal capacity. Following the examination of a report, the Committee may make appropriate comments which are transmitted to the state concerned. Subsequently the Committee adopts its conclusions and makes recommendations to be published in its annual report. Each year more than 20 countries are reviewed in this way by the Committee. Second, the Committee may decide to institute a confidential inquiry if it receives reliable information indicating that torture is being systematically practiced in a state party, but under the Convention, country visits require consent of the state concerned. However, the Optional Protocol to the Convention, adopted in 2003 (42 ILM 26 (2003)), established a system of regular prison visits undertaken by independent international and national bodies and functioning under the mandate of a special Subcommittee of the Committee against Torture. The US opposed the adoption of the Protocol as too intrusive and difficult to be applied in the conditions of a federal country. It might be added here that under the European Torture Convention of 1987, its Committee has the power to visit prisons in any place within the territory of any party to the Convention. Third, the Convention provides for an optional system of individual complaints, modeled on that of the Optional Protocol to the ICCPR **(167)**. This system applies, of course, only if the state concerned has declared that it recognizes the competence of the Committee to receive and examine such complaints. As of June 2000, 44 states had made such declarations. Fourth, under a procedure modeled on Art. 41 of the ICCPR the Convention envisions, on condition of reciprocity, an optional procedure for state-to-state complaints, a method which, however, has not been resorted to by any state.

As in the case of other global human rights conventions, lack of legally binding enforcement powers remains the weakest point of the Torture Convention in a world where, according to reports of such non-governmental organizations **(86)** as Human Rights Watch and Amnesty International a third of the world's governments are routinely engaged in practicing torture and other cruel, inhuman, or degrading treatment or punishment.

**183. Women: Convention on the Elimination of All Forms of Discrimination against Women, 1979.** This Convention (1249 UNTS 13), adopted in 1979, entered into effect **(271)** in 1981, with 165 contracting parties in June 2000. The United States signed **(283)** the Convention in 1980 but has not ratified it. The Convention is the major and most comprehensive treaty **(288)** on women's rights, providing for equality between the sexes in the enjoyment of civil, political, economic, social, andcultural rights, and requiring the states parties to end all forms of discrimination against women in political and public life with regard to nationality **(175)**, education, employment, health, and economic and social benefits. The Convention (Art. 1) defines discrimination as "any distinction, exclusion or restriction made on the basis of sex which has the effect or purpose of impairing or nullifying the recognition, enjoyment or exercise by women, irrespective of their marital status, on a basis of equality of men and women, of human rights and fundamental freedoms in the political, economic, social, cultural, civil or any other field." The Convention also provides for elimination of discrimination against women in marriage and family life and for ensuring equality of treatment before the law. It also obliges the states parties to take all appropriate measures to suppress all forms of traffic in women and their exploitation for purposes of prostitution. In this connection, the Convention against Transnational Organized Crime, adopted by the General Assembly (GA) in 2000 (40 ILM 353 (2000)) was supplemented by Protocol (of the same year) to Prevent, Suppress and Punish Trafficking in Persons, Especially Women and Children (40 ILM 377 (2000)). Regionally, in America women are protected by the Inter-American Convention of 1994 on the Prevention, Punishment and Eradication of Violence against Women (33 ILM 1434 (1994)).

The Convention of 1979 urges the parties to take into account the particular problems of women in rural areas and their special roles in the economic survival of the family. Furthermore, it affirms the reproductive rights of women and, more generally, imposes upon the parties the daunting task of modifying the social and cultural patterns of conduct of men and women with a view to achieving the elimination of prejudices and customs and all other practices which are based on the idea of the inferiority or the superiority of either of the sexes or on stereotyped roles for men and women. Discrimination is to be eliminated through appropriate constitutional and other legal as well as policy measures, and through temporary special measures, such as affirmative action and preferential treatment of women, aiming at accelerating *de facto* women's equality with men, but such measures shall not be considered as discrimination.

The monitoring of compliance with the Convention rests with the Committee on the Elimination of Discrimination against Women, a treaty body of 23 independent experts which considers annual reports submitted by the states parties and makes recommendations to them and to the relevant United Nations (UN) organs. Furthermore, the Optional Protocol to the Convention, 1999 (39 ILM 281 (2000)) allows individuals or groups of individuals who have exhausted national remedies to submit complaints ("communications"), directly to the Committee, about violations of the Convention by their government. The Protocol permits the Committee to conduct inquiries into grave or systematic violations in countries which are parties to the Convention and the Protocol, but a visit to the territory of the country involved requires the consent of its government. The right to complain and the inquiry procedures follow, in general, those under the Torture Convention of 1984 **(182)**. The Optional Protocol entered into force in 2000, but had only ten parties in January 2001. The Protocol allows no reservations **(282)** but a state party may opt out of the inquiry procedure at the time of signature, ratification, or accession **(267)**. As part of its monitoring functions, the Committee adopted a number of recommendations on various issues relating to the status of women, such as, *inter alia*, women and health, equality in marriage and family relations, violence against women, and female genital mutilation still widely practiced in large areas of Africa, Yemen, and Oman.

Unlike the movement for the protection of human rights, which can be traced to the early post—World War II years, the question of women's rights did not emerge as a major publicized human rights concern until the 1970s. However, even earlier, in 1946 the UN Economic and Social Council established a Commission on the Status of Women and in 1952 the GA adopted a Convention on the Political Rights of Women (193 UNTS 3) providing for equal voting rights to women and the right to seek and hold public office. References to ensuring equal rights for women can be found in the two human rights Covenants of 1966 **(166, 169)** and other relevant conventions, including those drafted under the auspices of the International Labour Organisation, and conventions dealing with problems of nationality **(175)**. More recently, following the adoption of the 1979 Convention, international concern with women's rights moved on the agenda of the UN and became the focus or a major item of a number of international conferences and declarations, beginning with the Vienna Declaration and Program of Action adopted at the World Conference on Human Rights in 1993 and the GA Declaration on the Elimination of Violence against Women in 1994 (33 ILM 1049 (1994)). Subsequent World Conferences on Human Rights, namely the International Conference on Population Development in Cairo, 1994; the Fourth World Conference on Women in Beijing, 1995 (35 ILM 401 (1996); and the World Conference against Racism, Racial Discrimination, Xenophobia and Related Intolerance in Durban, 2001, all acknowledged that women's rights are an inalienable part of universal human rights. A Special Session of the GA in 2000 adopted a document entitled "Women 2000: Gender Equality, Development and Peace for the Twenty-first Century" which dealt in particular with the concerns of women relating to armed conflict **(339, 340)**. In this regard in 2000 the Security Council adopted Resolution 1325 on Women and Peace and Security (40 ILM 500 (2001)) which dealt with all the major aspects of the impact of armed conflict on women and girls.

# Chapter IV
# The Geophysical Context I: Land, Air, Outer Space, International Environmental Law

**184. Accretion.** Accretion means addition of new land to the existing territory of a state **(228)** by operation of nature and without the need of any formal acts on the part of the state; there is a presumption of occupation **(214)**, theoretically at least, subject to challenges. An example of a slow and gradual enlargement of territory is offered by the formation of alluvial deposits (alluvium) on shorelines, river banks, and especially in river deltas, continually building up through the operation of water currents. Alluvial deposits can significantly add to a state's territory through such alluvions and thereby push forward the baselines **(233)** of the territorial sea **(262)**. Such deposits on the banks of a boundary **(189)** river lead to an alteration in its course, adding to or subtracting from the territory of the riparian states. The imperceptible and gradual process of accretion must be distinguished from avulsion, a phenomenon of a significant, sudden, and violent shift in the course of a river, removing land from the territory of one state to that of another. Whereas accretion taking place on a boundary river results in the alteration of the boundary, avulsion has no effect upon the existing boundary lines, as illustrated in international river law **(204)** by the *Chamizal* Arbitration of 1911 between Mexico and the United States (US) and a number of other boundary disputes **(299)**. A special case of accretion may take place, due to volcanic activity, through a sudden emergence in the internal waters **(249)** or the territorial sea of a state of a new island **(251)**, as was the case of the island of Surtsey born in the territorial sea of Iceland in 1963 or an islet off the Japanese island of Iwo Jima in 1986. A newborn island rising on the high seas **(245)** is a *res nullius* belonging to no state, but if it emerges in an exclusive economic zone (EEZ) **(238)**, it falls under the sovereignty **(125)** of the coastal state concerned, a proposition that can be inferred from Art. 60 of the United Nations Convention on the Law of the Sea of 1982 **(264)** whereby the coastal state has the excusive right to construct artificial islands within its EEZ. Accretion may also occur as a result of building artificial structures, for example, airfields, adding to the shoreline. In general, although accretion is a continually ongoing natural phenomenon, it is relatively negligible in international law. On the other hand, it has been of interest in a number of disputes between the component states of the US.

**185. Air Hijacking.** A separate offense established by the Hague Convention for the Suppression of Unlawful Seizure of Aircraft of 1970 **(199)**, air hijacking is an unlawful seizure or exercise of control of an aircraft in flight by a person on board of that aircraft, through force, threat of force, or any other form of intimidation. The offense is also committed if a person attempts to undertake any such acts or is an accomplice of a person who performs or attempts to perform them. Air hijacking is a specific category of offenses within the general concept of the international crime of terrorism **(337)**. A new lethal dimension was added to the terrorist offense of air hijacking by terrorists' use of civil aircraft for an armed attack upon civilized society, as it occurred in the United States (US) on 11 September 2001. In its Declaration of 5 October 2001 on misuse of civil aircraft as weapons of destruction and other terrorist acts involving civil aviation (41 ILM 501 (2002)), the International Civil Aviation Organization condemned such acts as grave offenses in violation of international law.

Seizure of aircraft in flight, popularly known as hijacking (a term derived probably from the call "Hi Jack" used during the Prohibition era in the US by customs agents seizing illegal liquor from bootleggers), became a problem with a wave of air hijackings that started in the 1960s and eventually made governments on both sides of the Cold War divide realize that air hijacking posed a serious international threat that should not be overridden by any alleged political considerations motivating the offender. Governments also became more aware of the inadequacy of extradition **(75)** conventions and gaps in the customary international law **(39)** on criminal jurisdiction **(87)**. The already adopted Tokyo Convention of 1963 on Offenses and Certain Other Acts Committed on Board Aircraft **(229)** was a modest attempt to deal with the problem of hijacking within the general context of all offenses, but the Hague Convention deals specifically with the offense of hijacking. The Montreal Sabotage Convention of 1971 **(210)** with its Protocol of 1988 concerning violence at airports, pertains to a related offense of unlawful acts against the safety of civil aviation, other than hijacking.

Because of the political dimension of most hijackings and in the absence of full cooperation by states, international agreements and condemnation of the offense by the General Assembly could not suffice as an effective weapon against hijacking. On the other hand, a number of states undertook action at national, bilateral, and regional levels. Nationally, states enacted appropriate stringent legislation and adopted security measures. Occasionally, radical, unilateral, self-help measures were resorted to, as demonstrated by the Entebbe raid in 1976 by Israeli commandos (15 ILM 1224 (1976)) who, against the protests of the Ugandan government, rescued mostly Jewish passengers of an Air France airliner held hostage at a Ugandan airport. In a similar incident, but with the consent of the local sovereign, German agents successfully recaptured a hijacked Lufthansa plane in Mogadishu, Somalia. National measures eventually led to a significant reduction of air hijacking incidents since the 1980s. At the regional level, the 1977 European Convention on the Suppression of Terrorism (1137 UNTS 93) introduced the rule excluding terrorist acts, including aircraft hijacking, from the definition of political offenses, thus allowing extradition of hijackers between the states parties **(76)**. In another action, in the Bonn Declaration on International Terrorism, 1978 (17 ILM 1285 (1978)) seven major Western powers, including the US, agreed to cease all flights to and from a country that refused extradition or prosecution of hijackers, and banned its airliners from their airspace **(186)**.

Though not so frequent as in the 1960s and 1970s, aircraft hijackings still occasionally take place. While it appears that the return of the hijacked aircraft and the persons on board is required by customary international law **(39)**, it is not entirely certain that air hijacking belongs, like piracy **(259)**, to crimes subject under customary international law to universal jurisdiction **(92)**. The September 2001 terrorist acts against the US involved hijacking, but in addition, raised more general and fundamental issues of the scope of the notion of armed attack **(325)** and self-defense **(335)** in international law.

**186. Airspace.** Airspace is the air pillar above the subjacent territory **(228)**. It is a fundamental and firmly established rule of international law that national airspace, including also the airspace above the internal waters **(249)** and the territorial sea **(262)**, is under complete and exclusive sovereignty **(125)** of the subjacent state **(127)**. There is, however, no rule of international law establishing a legal boundary between the airspace and the superjacent outer space **(215)**. The airspace above the sea beyond the territorial sea and—a very rare case—above territory which is not subject to any state's sovereignty is free for use by all states' aircraft without any control by the coastal state. The so-called air defense identification zones (ADIZ), established during the Cold War by the United States (US) in 1950 and Canada in 1951, and similar zones extending off the coasts hundreds of miles beyond the territorial sea are of dubious validity in international law. Using the concept of such a zone, a coastal state, such as the US, would require all aircraft entering the ADIZ to identify themselves, file flight plans, and report their position to ground control even though such aircraft were still above the high seas **(245)**, far from the US territory.

Although various doctrines were proposed in the early era of air navigation, the rule of exclusive sovereignty quickly emerged, primarily for reasons of national security, as the guiding principle of international air law. It was reaffirmed, first, in Art. 1 of the 1919 Paris Convention on the Regulation of Aerial Navigation and subsequently in Art. 1 of the Chicago Convention on International Civil Aviation of 1944 **(191)**, which still today provides the basic framework of rules governing the international use of airspace in civil aviation. This widely ratified convention established a specialized agency of the United Nation (UN) for purposes of civil aviation, the International Civil Aviation Organization (ICAO), with headquarters in Montreal.

Entry of national airspace by a foreign-registered aircraft may take place only with the authorization of the territorial state, the basic rule confirmed in Art. 3(c) of the Chicago Convention. Violation of this rule constitutes a serious breach of international law, justifying that state to take appropriate measures. As a consequence of the rule of national sovereignty over the superjacent airspace, operations in international civil air traffic are legally based primarily upon a complex network of mainly bilateral agreements, regulating "scheduled" air services according to the basic principles of international air law as set out in the Chicago Convention. Transit rights and landing for non-traffic purposes are the subjects of the Chicago International Air Service Transport Agreement, 1944 **(202)**. Of much less significance for scheduled air services is the Chicago Air Transport Agreement, 1944 **(203)**. It might be added that the 1982 Law of the Sea Convention **(264)** provides for transit rights for aircraft through straits used in international navigation **(260)** and through archipelagic **(231)** waters.

Since 1945, and especially during the Cold War, many incidents have occurred in which foreign aircraft, both civilian and military, have made incursions into foreign airspace. In a number of cases the trespassing aircraft was destroyed by the military force of the subjacent state. Among the most publicized incidents have been: the shooting down of an Israeli airliner by Bulgaria in 1955; of a US military reconnaissance aircraft U-2 by the Soviet Union in 1960; of a Libyan airliner by Israel in 1973; and—perhaps the most celebrated case—the shooting down by Soviet fighter planes of a South Korean airliner in 1983 (23 ILM 864 (1984)). In a more recent incident, in 2001, the emergency landing at a Chinese military airfield of a US surveillance plane, badly damaged in a collision with a shadowing Chinese jet fighter (whose pilot was killed in the collision) over the high seas off the South China coast, was certainly an unauthorized entry of the Chinese airspace, but could be justified in international law by such exculpatory reasons as distress **(72)** or *force majeure* **(78)**. In the case in question, after an ambiguously worded statement by the US, which China could interpret **(274)** as an apology (denied by the US), the US crew of 24 was released by China after 11 days of detention and the disassembled damaged spy plane was eventually returned to the US.

It is not entirely clear what measures a state may undertake against an unauthorized aerial intrusion. At a minimum, the foreign aircraft may be ordered to leave or ordered to land at a designated place, but the affected state may not expose the intruder to danger or resort to disproportionate forceful measures. However, a distinction must be made between military and civilian aircraft. In cases where intrusion by a former can reasonably be regarded as an immediate and serious threat to national security, the foreign military aircraft disobeying orders to change course or land may ultimately be attacked. On the other hand, in the prevailing view and as recommended by the ICAO in 1983, intercepting aircraft should refrain from the use of weapons in all cases of interception of civil aircraft (22 ILM 1185 (1983)). Detailed provisions to be followed in cases of interception are included in Annex II to the Chicago Convention **(191)**. In the aftermath of the shooting down of the South Korean airliner, a Security Council (SC) draft resolution confirming the prohibition of the use of weapons against intruding civilian aircraft was vetoed by the Soviet Union (22 ILM 1148 (1983)). An ICAO investigation, with which the Soviet Union refused to cooperate, concluded in its report in 1984 (23 ILM 864 (1984)) (confirmed in a subsequent investigation in 1994 (33 ILM 310 (1994)) that the fateful airliner's deviation had been due to the negligence of the crew and, with regard to the Soviet response, concluded that the intercepting fighters had mistaken the airliners for a US military intelligence aircraft, interpreting its climb as an evasive action confirming the Soviet assumption. Subsequently, an ICAO resolution condemned the Soviet Union for the "use of armed force" against the airliner (23 ILM 937 (1984)) and the ICAO Assembly amended **(269)** the

Chicago Convention, adding Art. 3 bis (not yet in force) which, *inter alia,* provided that every state, in the exercise of its sovereignty **(125)**, was entitled to require the landing at some designated airport of a civil aircraft flying above its territory without authority, an order with which every civil aircraft must comply, but that every state must refrain from resorting to the use of weapons against civilian aircraft and that in case of interception the lives of persons on board and the safety of the aircraft must not be endangered. This rule, recalled by the President of the SC following the downing in 1996 by Cuban military aircraft in international airspace of two US-registered civilian planes, can be regarded as part of customary international law **(39)**. It also applies to civilian airliners suspected of breaking UN sanctions. However, the new Art. 3 bis adds that its provisions should not be interpreted as modifying in any way the obligation of states under the UN Charter, which implies that in unusual circumstances the right of self-defense **(335)** by use of weapons might still be invoked in cases of intrusion by a foreign civilian aircraft clearly involved in an act of aggression **(325)** or terrorism **(337)**. The invocation of the right of self-defense would logically involve a lower burden of proof in cases of intrusion by a military aircraft.

The case of the Iranian civilian airliner shot down by the USS *Vincennes* over the Persian Gulf in 1988 (in the mistaken belief that it was an attacking Iranian military plane) did not involve any aerial intrusion into another state's airspace, but still was contrary to the rule expressed in the newly added article of the Chicago Convention, which reflects the existing customary law. The US offered to pay an *ex gratia* compensation to Iran but the case was brought by Iran to the International Court of Justice **(309)** (28 ILM 842 (1989); 29 ILM 123 (1990)). Eventually, the case was discontinued following a settlement agreement between Iran and the US in 1996 (35 ILM 553 (1996)).

**187. Antarctic Treaty System.** An international cooperative legal regime, based on the Antarctic Treaty adopted in Washington, DC, in 1959, in force **(271)** in 1961 (402 UNTS 71), and complemented by associated separate international instruments in force and the measures in force under the Treaty and such instruments. Under Art. VI of the Treaty, territorially the Antarctic system applies to the area south of 60 degrees South latitude including all ice shelves, but without prejudice to the rights or exercise of the rights of any state **(127)** (including non-parties) under international law with regard to the high seas **(245)**.

With an area of 5.4 million square miles (14 million square km) the continent of Antarctica constitutes the central part of the treaty area. However, the continent is covered in more than 98 percent by ice averaging 7,085 feet (2,160 m) in thickness, with permanently frozen ice shelves adjoining the landmass at certain points. It has no indigenous human population, the human activity consisting mainly of scientific research centered on a number of national stations and occasional, mostly seaborne, tourists, 11,588 in the 2000–2001 Antarctic summer. While animal life inland is extremely poor, the coastal areas provide ample ground for millions of seabirds, including various species of penguin which feed on the plentiful marine organisms, especially krill, a small shrimp-like crustacean which is the basis of the Antarctic food chain. Various species of seal thrive in Antarctica, and the surrounding ocean is rich in krill and fish, including the Patagonian toothfish ("Chilean sea bass"), and is host to a variety of whales. The environmental protection of Antarctica against pollution and the need to conserve its living resources under strain of overexploitation, especially because of illegal fishing and whaling, are the major concerns in the management of the Antarctic treaty system.

The Antarctic treaty system was adopted following the International Geophysical Year of 1957, in the interest of freedom of scientific research and information and in order to ensure that Antarctica shall continue forever to be used exclusively for peaceful purposes. By early 2004 the number of states parties to the Antarctic Treaty had grown, from the original 12 states (Argentina, Australia, Belgium, Chile, France, Japan, New Zealand, Norway, South Africa, United Kingdom (UK), United States (US), and the Soviet Union) to 45, adding Austria, Brazil, Bulgaria, Canada, China, Colombia, Cuba, Czech Republic, Denmark, Ecuador, Finland, Germany, Greece, Guatemala, Hungary, India, Italy, Japan, North Korea, Netherlands, Papua New Guinea, Peru, Poland, Romania, Slovakia, South Korea, Spain, Sweden, Switzerland, Turkey, Ukraine, Uruguay, and Venezuela. Thus, membership in the system includes the major developed and developing countries of the world. However, as explained below, the making of the Antarctic policy is in the hands of only those states parties which are endowed with the "consultative status." Amendments and modifications **(269)** of the Antarctic Treaty are possible at any time by unanimous agreement of the consultative parties. Failure of a party to ratify a modification or amendment is deemed to be a withdrawal from the Treaty. The Treaty provides for no time limits, but at the expiration of 30 years following its entry into force **(271)** any consultative party could call for a conference of all contracting parties to review the operation of the Treaty, with a possibility of adopting by a majority of all the parties, including a majority of the consultative parties, modification or amendment of the Treaty (Art. XII). No such conference has been called for.

Under Art. IV of the Treaty, the previously asserted rights of or claims to territorial sovereignty in Antarctica are held in abeyance ("frozen"), but not eliminated for the duration of the Treaty, in the sense that the Treaty shall not be interpreted **(274)** as meaning that any party renounces previously asserted rights or claims; renounces or diminishes a basis of claims which it may have as a result of its activities or activities of its nationals in Antarctica or otherwise; or has its position prejudiced as regards its recognition or nonrecognition **(106)** of any other state's territorial right or claim. Further provisions of Art. IV, apparently applying to nonparties as well, stipulate that no acts or activities taking place while the Treaty is in force shall constitute a basis for asserting, supporting, or denying a claim to territorial sovereignty **(125)** in Antarctica, or create any rights of sovereignty there. No new claims, or enlargement of any existing claim to territorial sovereignty in Antarctica shall be asserted while the Treaty is in force. Incidentally, it is of interest to mention that in the 1951 Peace Treaty (136 UNTS 45), that is, prior to the adoption of the Antarctic Treaty, Japan renounced any territorial claims in connection with any part of Antarctica.

By freezing all territorial claims without entering into an examination of their legitimacy under international law, the Treaty defuses, at least for its duration, the outstanding territorial claims and disputes concerning Antarctica. At the time the Treaty was signed, that is, in 1959, seven states (Argentina, Australia, Chile, France, New Zealand, Norway, and the UK) claimed titles to sovereignty over pie-like sectors of the continent on various, mostly dubious, grounds, such as discovery followed by a long and peaceful display of sovereignty or the so-called sector principle **(224)**, with the claims of Argentina, Chile, and the UK overlapping with one another. A small sector of Antarctica (Marie Byrd Land) is not claimed by any state. The US, for which Admiral Richard Evelyn Byrd claimed this area, refrained from asserting a claim and refused to recognize any territorial claims in Antarctica. On the other hand, some claimant states have recognized each other's claims to sectors of the continent. One could argue that consistent with the premise of freezing all territorial claims in Antarctica for the duration of the Treaty, no territorial sea **(262)** or other maritime zones, such as the exclusive economic zone (EEZ) **(238)**, could be claimed off the Antarctic coast. Nonetheless, in 1994 Australia raised, against US protest, a claim to an EEZ off its Antarctic sector.

Jurisdiction **(87)** in Antarctica raises special problems. Jurisdiction over official observers carrying out inspection pursuant to the Treaty and over exchange scientists is governed only by the nationality principle **(88)** in respect of acts occurring while they are in Antarctica for the purposes of exercising their functions (Art. VII (1)). On the other hand, because of the difference of opinion in this respect at the Washington Conference in 1959, the Treaty has no provisions on what jurisdictional principles apply to other persons. In practice, all non-claimant states resort to the nationality principle. For the claimant states the territoriality principle **(91)** is easy and welcome but some of them (New Zealand and the UK) in general purport to regulate the conduct of their nationals **(175)** throughout the Antarctic area, which may result in jurisdictional conflicts with other states.

Perhaps the most significant provision of the Antarctic Treaty is that Antarctica shall be demilitarized and used for peaceful purposes only. However, the use of military personnel or equipment for scientific research or for any other peaceful purpose is allowed (Art. I). Nuclear explosions and disposal of radioactive waste material are prohibited, subject to any international agreement concerning nuclear energy to which all the states with the consultative status are parties. The Treaty provides for freedom of scientific investigation and cooperation, including exchange of scientific information and personnel (Arts. II and III). There are also provisions for mutual inspections through designated observers to verify compliance with the Treaty (Art. VIII).

Under Art. IX of the Treaty, the Antarctic Treaty system is managed by a select group of states parties with "consultative status," consisting of the original 12 signatories and those of the acceding **(267)** states that have demonstrated interest in Antarctica "by conducting substantial scientific research activities there, such as establishment of a scientific station or the dispatch of a scientific expedition." In 2002 there were 15 such states (Brazil, China, Ecuador, Finland, Germany, India, Italy, Japan, Republic of Korea, Netherlands, Peru, Poland, Spain, Sweden, and Uruguay) which, together with the original 12 signatories, in essence formulate the Antarctic policy, participating in periodic, mainly biennial, Antarctic Treaty Consultative Meetings. The major legal instrument through which they develop the Antarctic system are the so-called Recommendations adopted by the Consultative Meetings, which in fact are treaties **(288)**. In order to be binding they must be approved by representatives of all the Consultative Parties, a rule that also governs any amendments **(269)** to the Treaty (Art. XII(1)(a)). More than 150 Recommendations on a variety of concerns have been adopted by the Consultative Meetings (35 ILM 1165 (1996) (listing the measures adopted in 1961–1995). The largest number of them pertains to the protection of the Antarctic environment and ("Agreed Measures") conservation of its fauna and flora. In addition to the recommendations, the legal regime of the Antarctic environmental law **(197)** includes the Convention of 1972 for the Conservation of Antarctic Seals (1080 UNTS 175), in force 1978, and the Convention of 1980 on the Conservation of Antarctic Marine Living Resources (19 ILM 837 (1980)), in force 1982, which set up a special Commission to promote the conservation of such resources.

The Antarctic Treaty contains no provision on mineral resources, a matter too controversial to be included. On the assumption that the Antarctic Treaty does not bar mineral exploration and exploitation, in the 1980s the Consultative Parties initiated negotiations for a regime governing such activities, with the environmental implications a major consideration. However, the proposed Convention of 1988 on the Regulation of Antarctic Mineral Resource Activities (27 ILM 859 (1988)), which envisaged a limited mining activity, met with a strong opposition on environmental grounds and never entered into force. This development led to the adoption **(268)** in 1991, at a special session in Madrid, of the Protocol on Environmental Protection to the Antarctic Treaty (30 ILM 1460 (1991)) which, after ratification by all the Consultative Parties, entered into force in 1998. The Protocol of 1991, with its four Annexes, constitutes a most comprehensive agreement on environmental protection. It designates Antarctica as a natural reserve devoted to peace and science, spelling out detailed rules to govern the protection of its environment. It also established the Committee for Environmental Protection to function as an advisory body to the Consultative Meetings. Under the key Art. 7, "any activity relating to mineral resources, other than scientific research, shall be prohibited," a ban that cannot be lifted until 50 years have lapsed following the entry into force of the Protocol in 1998, that is, not until 2048.

The Antarctic Treaty has proved to be a successful arrangement for the management of the Antarctic region. Yet the consultative parties could not avoid charges, leveled at them especially by some less-developed states, of the exclusive nature and secrecy of the Antarctic system. Suggestions were made by Malaysia and some other countries to replace the current system by one based on the concept of the "common heritage of mankind" and managed for the benefit of all, especially the less developed states, within the context of a "new international economic order." However, the consultative parties skillfully disarmed such ideas by admitting key Third World countries, such as China, India, and Brazil, to the consultative status and allowing observers from the non-consultative parties to the Antarctic Treaty to participate in the consultative meetings. While a detailed report considering the question of Antarctica was issued by the United Nations in 1984, any action against the Antarctic Treaty system was successfully resisted by the consultative parties. By expanding its membership to all groups of states the Antarctic system strengthened the argument that it represented an objective international legal regime binding on the non-parties as well as the parties to the Treaty. However, even though the consultative parties have operated in a manner implying exclusive competence and responsibility for Antarctica, it is controversial whether the rules of the Antarctic system can, under international law, be enforced against third parties, considering that a treaty cannot be binding upon nonparties **(278)**. As a matter of fact, Art. X of the Antarctic Treaty and analogous provisions found in the Recommendations to the effect that the consultative parties undertake (not the mandatory "shall undertake") to exert appropriate efforts to the end that no one engages in any activity in Antarctica contrary to the principles or purposes of the Antarctic Treaty, can arguably be construed as admission by the parties to the Treaty of legal incompetence to regulate the conduct of non-parties in Antarctica. On the other hand, third parties may otherwise be bound to comply with certain rules of the Antarctic system either on the grounds of general (customary) international law **(39)** or by virtue of extra-Antarctic international agreements, such as those adopted in international environmental law **(197)** or the law of the sea **(254)**. In practice, with the gradual widening of the adherence of states to the Antarctic Treaty the issue of the binding force of the Treaty with respect to the nonparties appears to lose its relevance.

**188. Biodiversity Convention, 1992, and Cartagena Protocol, 2000.** The Convention on Biological Diversity (31 ILM 818 (1992)) was drafted by the United Nations Environmental Program and adopted at the Rio Earth Summit **(223)**. It entered into force **(271)** in 1993 with a great majority of states becoming parties. In Rio the United States (US) refused to sign the Convention because of concerns about protecting US patents on products developed from materials obtained in tropical countries, but subsequently it signed it on the last day open for signature **(283)**. However, it has not yet ratified the Convention.

The Biodiversity Convention was prompted by concern over threats to the survival of species and integrity of habitats and ecosystems. The objectives of the Convention (Art. 1) are the conservation of biological diversity, the sustainable use of its components, and the fair and equitable sharing of the benefits arising out of the utilization of genetic resources. Biological diversity is defined (Art. 2) as "variability among living organisms from all sources, including, *inter alia*, terrestrial, marine and other aquatic systems and the ecological complexes of which they are part." The Convention recognizes that the conservation of biological diversity is a "common concern of humankind" and an integral part of the development process. The parties are committed to conserve and sustainably use biodiversity according to national strategies and action plans, integrating these into broader national environmental planning, especially in such sectors as forestry, agriculture, fisheries, energy, transportation, and urban planning. The important components of biological diversity are to be identified and monitored. The Convention provides for establishing protected areas, rehabilitating degraded ecosystems, and promoting the recovery of endangered species. At the same time it emphasizes the need to respect the traditional knowledge of indigenous peoples **(163)**. Control and eradication of threatening alien species and risks posed by organisms modified by biotechnology are also stressed.

The various national measures of conserving biodiversity are kept under review by the Conference of the Parties to which states are obligated to submit periodic reports. Like many other environmental conventions, the Biodiversity Convention establishes its own institutional arrangements which, in addition to the Conference, include a subsidiary body on scientific, technical, and technological advice and a secretariat.

Where mutually agreed, access to and transfer of technology is to be provided under fair and favorable terms. The transfer of patents must respect the effective protection of intellectual property rights, but such rights must not conflict with the goals of the Convention. On mutually agreed terms, countries of origin of a resource are to be granted priority access to benefits arising from biotechnologies based on their genetic resources. The provisions on the financial mechanism of the Convention enjoin the developed states parties to offer financial resources in order to fund the costs of implementing the Convention by less-developed countries. The whole financial mechanism is placed under the authority of the Conference of the Parties.

While the Convention is the first global treaty addressing all aspects of biodiversity, its provisions are not formulated in specific and determined language. Like the Climate Convention **(192)**, the Biodiversity Convention is a framework agreement requiring protocols regulating specific areas of concern, as provided for in Art. 28 of the Convention. The first protocol is the Cartagena Protocol on Biosafety, 2000 (39 ILM 1027 (2000)). Named after Cartagena, Colombia, where earlier, inconclusive negotiations on the subject of biosafety had taken place, the Protocol had 68 signatories in June

2000. In accordance with the precautionary approach contained in Principle 15 of the Rio Declaration, the objective of the Protocol is "to contribute to ensuring an adequate level of protection in the field of the safe transfer, handling and use of living modified organisms resulting from modern biotechnology that may have adverse effects on the conservation and sustainable use of biological diversity, taking also into account risks to human health, and specifically focusing on transboundary movements" (Art. I). In other words, the Protocol is designed to regulate trade in living modified organisms. "Living modified organisms" are defined as "any living organism that possesses a novel combination of genetic material obtained through the use of modern biotechnology," and the term "living organism" refers to "any biological entity capable of replicating genetic material, including sterile organisms, viruses and viroids" (Art. 3 (g)(h)). The Protocol spells out detailed rules to govern a variety of aspects of the transboundary movement of living modified organisms, including, *inter alia*, transit and contained use; notification of import; procedures for living modified organisms intended for direct use as food or feed, or for processing; risk assessment and risk management; unintentional transboundary movements and emergency measures; handling, transport, packaging, and identification; information sharing; public awareness and participation; and illegal transboundary movements. The Protocol designates the institutional arrangements of the Biodiversity Convention as serving also the purposes of the Protocol.

**189. Boundary.** International boundaries are imaginary lines which separate the territory of a state **(228)** from territories of other states, thus determining the reach of the state's territorial sovereignty **(125)**. Maritime boundaries delimiting various maritime zones are subject to special rules under the law of the sea **(254)**. The so-called natural boundaries are only a geophysical concept and normally require a more precise definition like other land frontiers. This is especially important where a mountain range forms a boundary between states. Delimitation on boundary lakes and inland seas is often effected by a treaty, such as the 1909 Treaty Relating to the Boundary Waters and Questions Arising along the Boundary between the United States and Canada (12 Bevans 319). Otherwise—but this is not a rule of international law—the boundary runs along the median or equidistance line of a lake. Special doctrines and principles of equity **(13)**, otherwise not mandatory under international law, apply to boundary rivers **(204)**. For non-navigable rivers, the midline of a river as a rule constitutes the boundary. Unless otherwise provided by treaty, navigable rivers are governed by the *Thalweg* principle, a German term referring to the main navigable or principal channel of a river. The middle of this channel is usually accepted as the boundary. Details concerning the criteria for determining the *Thalweg* were analyzed by the International Court of Justice (ICJ) **(309)** in 1999 in its judgment in the case concerning *Kasikili/Sedudu Island* (Botswana/Namibia) (39 ILM 310 (2000)).

In accordance with the general principle concerning the effects of accretion **(184)**, a gradual change in the course of a boundary river will alter the boundary in that the *Thalweg* or—in case of non-navigable rivers the midline—will shift with the change. On the other hand, the boundary remains unaffected by avulsion, that is a sudden change in the course of a river. As a result, the boundary remains in the old dried up riverbed while the river flows in its new bed within the territory of the other country. The difficulties of resolving boundary disputes in such situations are compounded where the changes in the course of the river over a long period of time are attributable to both accretion and avulsion. The *Chamizal* Arbitration **(293)** between Mexico and the United States (US) of 1911 illustrates the problem. Briefly, the dispute, which had arisen in 1895, concerned a tract of land of about 600 acres, the Chamizal Tract, between the old bed of the Rio Grande and the new bed which in the course of time and especially following the floods of 1864 moved progressively to the South, decreasing Mexico's territory. The two countries had accepted the principles governing the legal effects of accretion and avulsion in a treaty concluded in 1884 (164 CTS 337) but, apart from the US claims on grounds of prescription **(219)** and Mexico's questioning the application of the 1884 convention, the US contended that the changes in the riverbed had occurred through accretion whereas Mexico attributed them to avulsion and consequently continued to consider the abandoned bed of the Rio Grande as the legitimate boundary. The arbitrators agreed with Mexico's position, awarding it a major part of the disputed tract. The US member of the arbitration commission dissented from the award and the US rejected it. The dispute was finally settled by a treaty in 1963 (505 UNTS 185) which divided the Chamizal Tract, awarding Mexico more than two-thirds of the area.

The process of determining a boundary commonly consists, first, of delimitation, that is, a detailed description in a treaty or a judicial or arbitral decision, and then the procedure of demarcation, usually by a joint boundary commission, that is, an actual marking of the frontier on the ground by means of posts, pillars, and other visible signs. The use of maps is a standard procedure, discussed in such ICJ cases as the *Temple of Preah Vihear* (Cambodia v. Thailand) (1961 ICJ Rep. 17) and more recently (2000) in the already mentioned case concerning *Kasikili/Sedudu Island* (Botswana/Namibia). But, as noted by the Court, maps merely constitute information which varies in accuracy from case to case and they cannot, by themselves, constitute a territorial title; only exceptionally they acquire legal form as when they are annexed to an official text (such as a treaty) of which they form an integral part. Any discrepancy between a map and the text must be resolved in the light of all relevant circumstances.

A boundary that is not precisely determined may still be accepted as legal for some purposes. Boundary treaties belong to the category of "dispositive" treaties passing on succession **(132)** to the successor state. They are an exception to the operation of the principle of fundamental change of circumstances in the law of treaties **(273)**. Apart from disputes involving delimitation of maritime boundaries, numerous arbitration decisions have dealt with land boundary disputes, including the arbitral decision on the *Alaska Boundary* dispute between the US and the United Kingdom, 1903, and the *Rann of Kutch* Arbitration between India and Pakistan, 1968 (17 RIAA 1), concerning sovereignty over a border area known as the Rann of Kutch. An increasing number of disputes involving international boundaries, especially in Africa and Latin America, has come on the agenda of the ICJ in the past decade or so.

**190. Cession.** Cession is a transfer of sovereignty **(125)** over state territory **(228)** by agreement, normally a treaty **(288),** from one state **(127)** to another, and in this sense constitutes a "derivative" mode of acquisition of territory **(227)** by a state through a formal procedure for changing the title to territorial sovereignty. Historically, there have been two categories of cession: first, the cession resulting from the use of force against the state ceding the territory in question, in which case the treaty of cession merely formalized military coercion; and second, the cession effected by sale, gift, exchange, or other voluntary transaction. The former category of cession, that imposed by coercion between states and frequently formalized in a peace treaty, was a standard feature of international relations and law until the adoption of the United Nations (UN) Charter in 1945 when international law banned the threat or use of force **(329)** in international relations and thus made illegal the acquisition of territory by conquest **(194)**. In this regard, Art. 52 of the Vienna Convention on the Law of Treaties **(288)** of 1969 makes a treaty void if its conclusion has been procured by the threat or use of force in violation of the principles of international law embodied in the UN Charter. However, under the principles of intertemporal law **(205)** this rule does not apply retroactively to coercive cessions of the pre-Charter era. The other category of cession, the voluntary cession, was once relatively common in international relations. Examples of cession by sale include the purchase by the United States (US) from France of the Louisiana Territory in 1809; of Florida from Spain in 1819; the Gadsden purchase from Mexico in 1853; the purchase of Alaska (for $7.2 million) from Russia in 1867; and of the Danish Virgin Islands from Denmark in 1916. The cession in 1890 of Helgoland by Great Britain to Germany in exchange for Zanzibar is an example of acquisition of territory by exchange. In the more recent period, exchanges of very minor pieces of territory for purposes of the frontier **(189)** rectification have taken place, *inter alia,* between the German Federal Republic and Switzerland, and between Poland and the then Soviet Union. Otherwise, cession of territory has become a rather rare phenomenon unless the transfer of territories to new states within the context of decolonization is to be regarded as a form of cession. The relinquishment of a claim to a territory, coupled with recognition of the successor state's sovereignty over the territory, is tantamount to cession, as in the case of the US ceding Swan Island to Honduras in 1972 and certain Pacific islands, including Canton and Endenbury, to Kiribati in 1975. An interesting case of cession occurred when South Africa ceded by treaty Walvis Bay to Namibia in 1994 (33 ILM 1526 (1994)).

Whether to be in force a cession requires the taking of actual possession of the territory by the successor state must be decided on a case-by-case basis, but as a rule the date of the treaty's entering into force **(271)** is taken as the date on which the title to the territory in question is transferred. Internal waters **(249)** and territorial sea **(262)** cannot be objects of cession by themselves; they can be ceded only as appurtenance of the land involved.

As illustrated by the famous *Island of Palmas* Arbitration **(293)** between the US and the Netherlands, 1928, cession of territory follows the civil law **(23)** maxims *nemo dat quod non habet*, that is, nobody can give something that he does not have himself, and *nemo plus juris transferre potest quam ipse habet*, meaning that nobody can transfer more rights than he has himself. Therefore, any defects in the ceding state's title are passed on to the acquiring state. Furthermore, following the principle of *res transit cum suo onere*, the ceded territory passes to the new sovereign with any burdens and obligations that may be locally connected with the territory.

**191. Chicago Convention on International Civil Aviation, 1944.** The principal multilateral agreement (15 UNTS 295), concluded at the Chicago Conference in 1944 and replacing the 1919 Paris Convention on Regulation of Aerial Navigation (11 LNTS 173) and some other inconsistent agreements, which lays down the fundamental rules and principles governing international civil aviation. In addition, the Convention created the International Civil Aviation Organization (ICAO), eventually a United Nations (UN) specialized agency. In force **(271)** since 1947, the Convention has been accepted by virtually all the countries of the world. The Chicago Convention applies only to civil aviation. It does not apply to "state aircraft" by which it means aircraft used by military, customs, and police services. But it appears that aircraft on non-scheduled services carrying heads of state are treated as state aircraft. The Convention provides that state aircraft shall not fly over the territory of another state or land there without authorization.

The Chicago Convention reaffirms the fundamental rule of complete and exclusive sovereignty **(125)** of states **(127)** over their respective airspace **(186)**, including the territorial sea **(262)**. It establishes a not entirely clear distinction between scheduled and unscheduled services. Generally speaking, in the ICAO terminology scheduled services are those scheduled in a published timetable or those with flights so regular or frequent that they constitute recognizable systematic services. The crucial Art. 6 provides that no scheduled international air service may be operated over or into the territory of a contracting state, except with a special permission or other authorization of that state and in accordance with the terms of such permission or authorization. This means that the Chicago Convention by itself does not provide a legal basis for the operations of international scheduled airline traffic. Since the "Two Freedoms Agreement" **(202)** deals only with transit rights and the "Five Freedoms Agreement" **(203)** is in force only for a very limited number of states and otherwise its freedom to carry passengers includes merely through services on a direct route out from and back to the state of the airliner's nationality, Art. 6 of the Convention generated, in the conditions of an enormous expansion of the airline industry, hundreds of bilateral, usually reciprocal, agreements covering routes, traffic volume, and other matters relating to air traffic. The so-called Bermuda Agreement of 1946 (3 UNTS 253) relating to air services between the United Kingdom and the United States, replaced by another Bermuda Agreement in 1977 which largely eliminated the fifth freedom guaranteed under the Five Freedoms Agreement, became a model for the drafting of many bilateral agreements regulating air traffic between the parties.

On the other hand, as an exception to the general rule, the states parties to the Chicago Convention agreed in Art. 5 to grant aircraft not engaged in scheduled international air services the right to fly into or in transit non-stop across their respective territories and to make stops for non-traffic purposes, without obtaining prior permission of the state concerned, subject to the right of the state to order immediate landing and impose various restrictions, such as routes and off-limits areas. The right of cabotage, that is, reserving to national carriers the traffic between airports of a state's territory, is a general rule.

The Chicago Convention also deals with the problem of nationality of aircraft. Like ships **(257)**, aircraft have the nationality of the state in which they are registered and, if engaged in international air navigation, must bear appropriate nationality and registration marks. An aircraft cannot be validly registered in more than one state. The practice of the flags of convenience **(241)** does not seem to have affected the air navigation. Information concerning registration and ownership must be supplied on demand from any state party of the ICAO.

Part 2 of the Convention deals with the ICAO, now a specialized agency of the UN with headquarters in Montreal. It consists of an Assembly of all members and a Council of 21 states. The organization may establish other bodies necessary for the performance of its tasks. Its aims and objectives under the Convention are to develop principles and techniques of international air navigation and air transport. Since its establishment the ICAO has played a central role in developing international air law. It performs crucial regulatory functions in the area of air navigation, including quasi-law-making functions of adopting international standards and recommending practices in the nature of "soft law" **(35)**. As demonstrated, *inter alia*, by the South Korean airliner incident in 1983, the ICAO Council possesses investigatory and quasi-judicial powers in deciding disputes relating to the application and interpretation **(274)** of the Convention, but the states involved retain the right of appeal to an arbitral tribunal **(297)** or the International Court of Justice **(309)**. The ICAO is among the most active specialized agencies of the UN. It has drafted a number of important international agreements in the field of air transport, including the amendment **(269)** protocols to the 1929 Warsaw Convention for the Unification of Certain Rules Regarding International Air Transport (137 UNTS 11; 500 UNTS 31), the Rome Convention of 1952 on Damage Caused by Foreign Aircraft to Third Persons on the Surface (52 AJIL 593 (1958)), and the Hague **(199)** and Montreal **(210)** conventions dealing with hijacking **(185)** and sabotage of aircraft, respectively.

**192. Climate Change Framework Convention, 1992.** A global UN-sponsored framework convention (1771 UNTS 108) signed in 1992 in Rio de Janeiro by 154 states and the European Community on the eve of the Rio Earth Summit **(223)** in 1992. It entered into force **(271)** in 1994, with most of the states, including the United States (US), becoming parties to this treaty. No reservations **(282)** may be made to the Convention (Art. 24), but withdrawal, which automatically also applies to protocols, is possible on one-year notice.

The Convention was prompted by concerns voiced in the scientific community, non-governmental organizations **(86)**, and the general public as well as in the General Assembly and other international bodies that human activities had been substantially increasing, in the Earth's upper layers of its atmosphere the concentration of carbon dioxide and other heat-trapping greenhouse gases, thus enhancing the otherwise natural "greenhouse effect." This situation resulted in an additional warming of the planet's surface and atmosphere, with potentially disastrous impact of such climate change upon natural ecosystems and human population, including raising sea levels and threatening the very existence of small island nations. Various aspects of this global warming trend have been studied by the Intergovernmental Panel on Climate Change, established by the United Nations Environment Program and the World Health Organization in 1988.

The Convention (Art. 1(1)) defines the adverse effects of climate change as "changes in the physical environment or biota resulting from climate change which have significant deleterious effects on the composition, resilience or productivity of natural and managed ecosystems or on human health and welfare." By "climate change," the Convention (Art. 1(2)) means "a change of climate which is attributed directly or indirectly to human activity that alters the composition of the global atmosphere and which is in addition to natural climate variability observed over comparable time periods." The ultimate objective of the Convention is to stabilize greenhouse gas concentrations in the atmosphere at a level that would prevent dangerous interference by man with the climate system, which should be achieved within a time frame sufficient to allow natural adaptation of ecosystem to climate change, ensure food production, and enable sustained economic development. The Convention spells out certain guiding principles relating to: the leading role of the developed countries; consideration of special circumstances of the developing states; precautionary measures; promotion of sustainable development; and international cooperation. However, because of the resistance of the members of the Organization of Petroleum Exporting Countries and the US, there are no quantitative restrictions on the greenhouse gas emissions. But, all states parties, taking into account their specific priorities and concerns (but with differentiated responsibilities), are committed to developing national inventories of emissions by sources and removals by the so-called sinks (meaning any process, activity, or measure that removes a greenhouse gas from the atmosphere, for example, forestation) of the greenhouse gases not covered by the 1987 Montreal Protocol to the 1985 Vienna Convention concerning the protection of the ozone layer **(217)**. Furthermore, they have committed themselves to implementing programs which mitigate climate change; promoting exchange of relevant information, cooperation and transfer of technology; and taking climate change considerations into account in their policies. Following the principle of "common but differentiated responsibilities," detailed and not entirely clear provisions of the Convention (Art. 4(2–10)) call upon the developed countries and states with economy in transition (referring mainly to the successor states of the Soviet Union **(133)** and the Baltic states) to undertake special actions mitigating the adverse effects of climate change, with the duty to submit periodic reports to the Conference of the Parties, the supreme body established by the Convention. The ultimate aim of the Convention was to return by the year 2000 to the 1990 levels of emissions (Art. 4(2)). The developed states and states with economies in transition have the obligation to provide financial resources to less-developed countries to enable those countries to meet their treaty obligations and to cope with the adverse effects of climate change, with full consideration of especially vulnerable developing countries, such as small island states, states with low-lying coastal areas, and the like. Institutional arrangements of the Convention provide for the Conference of the Parties as the supreme body, the Secretariat (eventually set up in Bonn), and two subsidiary bodies: for scientific and technological advice and for the implementation of the Convention.

Despite some progress (in Western Europe), the national, otherwise not strictly mandatory, measures to reduce emission of greenhouse gas proved inadequate, the fact realized by the subsequent sessions of the Conference of the Parties. As a matter of fact, it was eventually found that in the last decade of the past century the global emissions of carbon dioxide had risen 10 percent, with the emissions originating in the US reaching 16 percent. To cope with this trend, the parties to the Convention initiated a series of difficult and contentious negotiations for establishing legally binding, quantified limitations and reductions of emissions to be achieved within specified time frames. As a result, the third conference of the parties to the Convention in Kyoto in 1997 adopted the much-publicized Kyoto Protocol **(206)** to the framework Convention of 1992.

**193. Condominium.** Resembling the institution of *condominium* in civil law **(23)**, condominium, or more precisely co-imperium, is an international arrangement whereby two or possibly more states **(127)** have conjoint sovereignty **(125)** over a territory **(228)** administered jointly or in some other form of agreed divided administration. The legal institution of condominium is largely of historical interest. The British-French condominium of New Hebrides (1887–1980) in the Pacific, in which, under a treaty of 1906, each party retained sovereign powers over its nationals **(175)** without either of them exercising separate sovereign authority over the islands, and the British-French condominium over the Sudan (1889–1956), are perhaps the best-known examples of this type of arrangement. The Sudan became independent in 1956 and New Hebrides, as Vanuatu, in 1980. In the Pacific, during the 40-year period (1939–1979) the disputed islands of Kanton and Enderbury (part of the Phoenix Islands) were, by agreement, under the "joint control" of the United Kingdom and the United States, prior to becoming part of the independent state of Kiribati in 1979. In Europe, Andorra, a survival of the medieval feudal institution similar to condominium, was for centuries (1278–1993) under a joint sovereignty of France (the head of the state of France), succeeding to the count of Foix, and the bishop of Urgel. In 1993 Andorra, while nominally still remaining a co-principality, declared its sovereignty in a constitution which in fact terminated the authority of the two "princes." Also in Europe, under special arrangements of 1856 and 1901, the Île des Faisans (the Pheasants Island), an island situated on a river forming a common border between France and Spain, still remains a Franco-Spanish condominium. One can also mention the case of conjoint sovereignty over a defined territory established by treaty between Saudi Arabia and Kuwait in 1922, eventually divided by agreement between the two states in 1965 (4 ILM 1134 (1965)), with a reservation of undivided interest in mineral resources.

The institution of condominium can also apply to rivers **(204)** and gulfs and bays **(234)**. Thus, a joint sovereignty of Nicaragua, El Salvador, and Honduras over the waters of the Gulf of Fonseca beyond the three mile limit was recognized by the International Court of Justice **(309)** in its judgment (merits) in 1992 (1992 ICJ Rep. 351). The relevance of the institution of condominium has until recently been an issue in the controversy over the division of sovereignty over the Lake Constance (Bodensee) among the three riparian states.

**194. Conquest and Subjugation.** Historically, prior to the proscription of the threat and use of force **(329)** in international relations, institutionalized in the United Nations (UN) Charter in 1945, conquest, that is, acquisition by force by a state **(127)** of title to another state's territory **(228)**, ordinarily effected through war **(338)**, was recognized as a legal mode of acquiring territory **(227)** under international law. The fact of conquest was usually formalized in treaty provisions on cession **(190)** whereby the coerced state would transfer the title to the new sovereign. However, even under traditional international law, a belligerent occupying a territory, did not acquire title as long as the war was not formally terminated by a treaty of cession or, even without any treaty, where there was clear evidence that all resistance by the enemy and its allies had ceased and the former sovereign was left without any realistic chance of regaining the territory. In the latter case the conquest of the whole territory was tantamount to the destruction of the defeated state and followed by annexation by the conqueror, a development known as subjugation (*debellatio*). In any event, the intention to annex the conquered territory was crucial for the legitimacy of the title.

In the first half of the past century, after World War I (1914–1918), a movement began in international diplomacy to limit resort to war, as stipulated in the Covenant of the League of Nations, 1919, and the General Treaty for the Renunciation of War, 1928 **(330)**. This legal trend culminated in 1945 with the provisions of the UN Charter (Art. 2(4)) on the ban of the threat and use of force **(329)**. A corollary of this is the rule that international law no longer permits states to acquire territory by threat or use of force. However, under the doctrine of intertemporal law **(205)** and pursuant to the general principle of non-retroactivity of the law, the title to territory conquered and annexed at a time when international law allowed acquisition of title by a conqueror, remains legally valid.

The principle of inadmissibility of acquiring territory by force has become part of general international law, endowed with the character of a peremptory rule of international law (*jus cogens*) **(24)**. It has been confirmed in such international instruments as, *inter alia*, the Friendly Relations Declaration of the General Assembly (GA) in 1970 **(14)** and reaffirmed in a series of Security Council (SC) resolutions concerned with specific cases, including Resolution 242 of 1967 dealing with the Israeli occupation of Arab territories, and more recently Resolutions 660 and 662 of 1990 condemning Iraq's annexation of Kuwait as null and void and without any legal validity (29 ILM 1323, 1927 (1990)). The fact that a conquest has been formalized in a treaty of cession does not cure the invalidity of the title. Under Art. 52 of the 1969 Vienna Convention on the Law of Treaties, a treaty **(288)** is void "if its conclusion has been procured by the threat or use of force in violation of the principles of international law embodied in the Charter of the United Nations." The illegality of acquisition of territory by force is interpreted extensively to encompass also acquisition of the aggressor's territory by the victim state acting in the exercise of the right of self-defense **(335)**. In this regard the Friendly Relations Declaration, making a distinction between military occupation and acquisition of territory, provides that the territory of a state shall not be the object of military (that is, belligerent) occupation **(363)** in contravention of the provisions of the Charter (thus by implication permitting military occupation by a state acting in self-defense) and the territory of a state shall not be the object of acquisition by another state "resulting from the threat or use of force." This is a general formulation denying legal validity of any acquisition of territory, including acquisition by a victim state. The rule is premised on the need to keep the right of self-defense within the limits of necessity and proportionality and to prevent possible abuses of this right by states engaged in otherwise legitimate self-defense.

It would be logical to conclude that since acquisition of territory by a breach of a peremptory rule of international law concerning the use of force did not give rise to a valid title, third states have no discretion with respect to such title and are legally bound to deny its recognition **(99)**. This position, designed to deny potential violators the fruits of their aggression **(325)**, has its historical antecedent in the so-called Stimson Doctrine proposed in 1932 following the seizure of Manchuria by Japan, by the United States (US) Secretary of State Henry L. Stimson, to the effect that states should refuse to recognize any situation or treaty brought about by a violation of the General Treaty for the Renunciation of War of 1928 and relevant other agreements. The League of Nations Assembly also passed a resolution to this effect but unfortunately international practice largely failed to live up to the requirements of these instruments. Still, the Stimson Doctrine received strong support among Latin American states which strongly condemned conquest as a mode of territorial acquisition in international law.

Following World War II (1939–1945) the nonrecognition principle reappeared in the International Law Commission Draft Declaration on Rights and Duties of States of 1949 and subsequently in the Friendly Relations Declaration of 1972 which reaffirmed that "[n]o territorial acquisition resulting from the threat or use of force shall be recognized as legal." Applying this principle to Iraq's briefly lasting conquest of Kuwait in 1990, the SC in its Resolution 662 unanimously called upon all states and international organizations not to recognize the annexation of Kuwait and to refrain from any action or dealing that might be interpreted as an indirect recognition of the annexation. All states complied with this call. On the other hand, Indonesia's now historical annexation of East Timor was recognized by some states, including indirectly by Australia, despite a unanimous SC resolution in 1975 (Resolution 384). In this context Australia argued that there existed no duty under international law not to recognize acquisition of territory by force.

In situations involving the anti-colonial ideology, international "political correctness" has favored seizure of territory by conquest, as was the case of India's conquest of Goa in 1961, without any censure by the SC, let alone the GA, and with eventual recognition by Portugal, itself the victim of this, strictly speaking, illegal use of force. Again, following Morocco's seizure of the Spanish Western Sahara in 1975, the principle of nonrecognition has not been upheld with real determination even though the issue also involved self-determination **(122)** as conceived by the UN. Some states expressly recognized the Moroccan conquest while others acquiesced in the accomplished fact, limiting their reaction to mild diplomatic protests. The reaction to Indonesia's 25 years of Indonesian rule over the now independent East Timor was also very half-hearted.

In the Middle East, Israel's seizure of Arab territories in 1967 gave rise to complex questions of international law governing acquisition of territory. Following Israel's peace treaties with Egypt in 1979 (18 ILM 362 (1979)) and Jordan in 1994 (35 ILM 43 (1995)), apart from the Gaza Strip, Israel still held Syrian territory (part of Golan Heights) and the West Bank, including East Jerusalem, with respect to which Jordan waived all its rights in favor of a future Palestinian state. It is generally recognized that Israel is still in belligerent occupation **(363)** of all these territories, with all the rights and duties of the occupying power under the Regulations of the relevant Hague Convention of 1907 **(350)** and the Fourth Geneva Convention of 1949 Relative to the Protection of Civilian Population in Time of War **(349)**, and other pertinent rules of international humanitarian law **(353)**. The *de facto* annexation of East Jerusalem has been declared as illegal by a series of SC and the GA resolutions, but calls upon Israel to rescind the annexation measures have remained ineffective. Similarly, the *de facto* annexation of the Golan Heights was protested by a number of states and declared null and void by resolutions of the SC and the GA, but a draft SC resolution calling for voluntary sanctions against Israel failed to be adopted because of a US veto.

The outstanding territorial issues involving acquisition of territory by conquest reflect the discrepancy between the political and military reality and the law. Ultimately, in the interests of effectiveness and legal stability, international law may have to take account of political compromise which would recognize or acquiesce in certain consequences of past illegalities.

**195. Desertification Convention, 1994.** The UN Convention to Combat Desertification in the Countries Experiencing Serious Drought and/or Desertification in Particular in Africa (1954 UNTS 3) was adopted **(268)** in 1994 and entered into force **(271)** in 1996, with more than 100 parties in 2000. The United States is a signatory but has not ratified the Convention. The Desertification Convention translates into a treaty form a plan formulated at the Rio Earth Summit of 1992 **(223)** to combat desertification defined by the Convention (Art. 1(a)) as "land degradation in arid, semi-arid and dry sub-humid areas resulting from various factors, including climatic variations and human activities." While there is still disagreement on the precise contribution of man to desertification, there is evidence that overgrazing, deforestation, and poor irrigation, along with an increasing population pressure, are among significant factors aggravating the erosion of land and water supply. The situation is particularly serious in Africa, with up to 75 percent of land already degraded. Hence the Convention (Art. 7) obligates the parties to give special priority to the affected African states. Central Asia is another area threatened by desertification. Overall, arid and semi-arid areas make up some 25 percent of the earth's landmass, with a population of about 900 million.

The objective of the Convention is to "combat desertification and mitigate the effects of drought in countries experiencing serious drought and /or desertification, particularly in Africa, through effective action at all levels, supported by international cooperation and partnership arrangements within the framework of an integrated approach which is consistent with Agenda 21 [of the Rio Summit], with a view to contributing to the achievement of sustainable development in affected areas." As stated in the Convention, this objective will involve long-term integrated strategies that focus simultaneously on improving productivity of the land and water resources, leading to improved living conditions, in particular at the community level. Among its principles, the Convention stresses the need for local communities and non-governmental organizations **(86)** to be involved in decisions concerning the designing and implementing of programs (Art. 3). The parties have an obligation to adopt an integrated approach, addressing the physical, biological, and socioeconomic aspects of desertification and drought. Affected countries, that is, those whose lands include, in whole or in part, arid, semi-arid, and/or sub-humid areas affected or threatened by desertification, undertake to give priority to combating desertification and mitigating the effects of drought by establishing strategies and priorities within the framework of sustained development plans and policies. For their part, developed states parties commit themselves to provide substantial financial resources and other assistance to the efforts of the affected countries, such resources to be channeled through the already existing fund, known as the Global Environment Facility. However, it appears that only a modest portion of the needed $10–20 billion per year has been pledged by the developed states parties, most of which oppose creating a new special fund to combat desertification.

The Convention is to be implemented through national action programs identifying the factors which contribute to desertification and through practical measures to combat it and to mitigate the effects of drought. National programs are to be supplemented by programs at regional and sub-regional levels. Further provisions of the Convention call for scientific and technical cooperation and transfer of technology.

Like other multilateral environmental agreements, the Desertification Convention sets up an institutional structure made up of the Conference of the Parties, the Permanent Secretariat, and the Committee on Science and Technology. Four regional Implementation Annexes, which provide guidelines for implementation, constitute an integral part of the Convention, with Africa given particular attention in Annex I. The other annexes deal with Asia; Latin America and the Caribbean; and the Northern Mediterranean. All the annexes contain, *inter alia*, detailed rules concerning commitments and obligations of the parties, national, sub-regional, and regional programs, finances, technical assistance and transfer of technology.

**196. Direct Television Broadcasting.** This kind of television broadcasting refers to broadcasting programs through space satellites directly to individual dish antennas linked to receivers. What the international law status of such broadcasts should be has been on the agenda of the legal subcommittee of the United Nations (UN) Committee for Outer Space **(215)** for the past three decades or so. The matter is controversial, primarily because of a fundamental divergence of view between developed Western states which favor freedom of information proclaimed in the Universal Declaration of Human Rights **(162)** and most of the less-developed countries contending that direct broadcasting requires prior consent of the state where the broadcast is to be received. Thus, the direct television broadcasting dimension of the international telecommunication law became part of the general North-South conflict. At its 1982–1983 session, the General Assembly adopted, by a vote of 107 to 13 with 13 abstentions, the Resolution on the Principles Governing the Use by States of Artificial Earth Satellites for International Direct Television Broadcasting (22 ILM 451 (1983)), providing that a state intending to establish a direct television broadcasting system must first notify the proposed receiving state and seek its prior consent. The Resolution stresses the duty to conduct the broadcasting activities "in a manner compatible with the sovereign rights" and "due respect to the political and cultural integrity of States." Thus, while there is consensus that direct television broadcasting should be regulated by international law and subject to the pertinent rules of the Outer Space Treaty of 1967 **(216)** and regulations of the International Telecommunication Union (ITU), there still persists a fundamental disagreement concerning the notion of the freedom of direct broadcasting. Any future agreement would be under the auspices of the ITU, a specialized agency of the UN with headquarters in Geneva, including more than 180 states, whose origins date back to 1932 and which is the successor of the Bureau of International Telegraph Union set up in 1865. Reorganized by a number of conventions, the ITU is now governed by the Geneva Constitution and Convention of 1992, in force in 1994, which restructured this agency to respond more effectively to the rapidly changing telecommunications technology.

**197. Environmental Law.** International environmental law is the branch of public international law which governs the rights and obligations of states **(127)** with respect to the natural environment, including especially the environment of other states and areas beyond the limits of national jurisdiction **(87)**, and thereby the planet's environment as a whole. Considering the interdependence of all elements in the earth's natural balance, the concept of environment is being understood increasingly as meaning the entire natural and physical environment and the relationship of people with this environment. In this sense, international environmental law also encompasses rules on conservation, that is, management of the human use of the planet's natural resources, such as soil, water, fauna and flora, and preservation of endangered wildlife species. The bulk of international environmental law is in the form of treaty **(288)**, often a framework agreement, developed in more detail in subsequent protocols. However, as noted below, there are also certain emerging principles which, though controversial, are acquiring increasing validity as part of general (customary) **(39)** international law.

Like the law of human rights **(160)**, international environmental law is a relatively recent field of international law, but it has been rapidly growing in the past three decades or so, with the heightened awareness of, and concern over the progressive degradation of the environment by various forms of pollutants attributable to human activity, and with the growing realization of the insufficiency of unilateral state action and consequently of the need of international cooperation to protect, preserve, and improve the environment. Although a very limited number of international agreements concerning the protection of the environment, especially in the area of marine pollution **(255)**, had been concluded prior to the 1970s, the Stockholm Conference on Human Environment, 1972 **(226)**, is generally regarded as the major landmark in, and a stimulus for the development of international environmental law. The creation in 1972 by the General Assembly (GA) of the United Nations (UN) Environment Program (UNEP), a new UN specialized agency (with headquarters in Nairobi), and establishing various bodies in the environmental area, both globally, regionally, and subregionally, provided an international organizational structure for building up a body of environmental law. Of major importance is the establishment by the GA in 1992 of the UN Commission on Sustainable Development whose main purpose is to achieve sustainable development while maintaining a balance between the needs of economic development and the protection of the environment and not compromising the ability of future generations to cope with their needs. In addition, a number of nongovernmental organizations **(86)** kept under review and monitored the environmental situation and implementation of an ever-growing number of international agreements dealing with the environment. As a matter of fact, even exposure to tobacco smoke became a subject of international regulation when in 2003 the World Health Organization (WHO) adopted the Framework Convention on Tobacco Control (42 ILM 518 (2003)), the first international agreement adopted by this specialized agency since its establishment 55 years before. Environmental concerns have also been taken into account in the drafting of the rules of international humanitarian law governing armed conflict **(353)**.

The Rio Earth Summit, 1992 **(223)**, was the second major landmark in the development of international environmental law. By the time the Summit convened, this branch of international law had grown into a major area. Private international institutions, such as the International Law Association and Institut de droit international had become engaged in studying various aspects of the protection of the environment. It is also significant that in 1993 the International Court Justice ICJ **(309)** deemed it appropriate to establish a seven-member Chamber **(295)** for Environmental Matters.

Human activities with a potential for transboundary environmental harm are wide-ranging. A harm may occur by accident but ordinarily it is from pollution resulting from everyday economic activities, especially in industry, transportation, exploitation of resources, use of international watercourses **(204)**, and disposal of waste. A commonly used definition of pollution, dating back to a formulation by the Organization for Economic Cooperation and Development (OECD) in 1977 (16 ILM 977 (1977)), states that pollution is "any introduction by man, directly or indirectly, of substance or energy into the environment resulting in deleterious effects of such a nature as to endanger human health, harm living resources and ecosystems, impair amenities or interfere with other legitimate uses of the environment." As defined in 1987 by the Experts Group on International Environmental Law of the UN-sponsored World Commission on Environment and Development, environmental interference in a more extensive sense may occur not only through polluting substances but also due to ionizing radiation, explosions, vibrations, or other forms of energy, flooding, and similar means.

Pollution occurs in various forms depending on the environment affected, the source where it originated, and the medium through which it spreads, but a clear separation and identification of the specific form of pollution may not be possible in practice. Marine pollution is the first form of pollution to become an object of treaty regulation and the protection of the marine environment is covered by more treaties than in any other area of environmental concern. Atmospheric or air pollution, caused by emissions of pollutants into the atmosphere, is covered, first, by the Long-Range Transboundary Air Pollution Convention of 1979 **(209)** with Protocols which, though regional in scope, is subscribed to by most of the countries of the industrialized North, and, second, by the global Persistent Organic Pollutants Convention of 2001 **(218)**. More localized air pollution problems are sometimes regulated subregionally or bilaterally as, for example, is the case of the United States (US)–Mexico Agreement of 1983 (22 ILM 1025 (1983)). Pollution by emission of chlorofluorocarbons and some other substances causing depletion of the ozone layer which protects the Earth from harmful ultraviolet radiation is one dimension of atmospheric pollution but, because of its fundamental implications for the environment, can be treated as a special form of pollution. Protection of the ozone layer is the subject of the Ozone Layer Protection Vienna Convention of 1985 **(217)**, complemented by the Montreal Protocol of 1987 and subsequent amendments and modifications **(269)**. Similar considerations apply to atmospheric pollution by the so-called greenhouse gases, with potentially disastrous consequences for the Earth's climate. This aspect of pollution is governed by the Climate Change Framework Convention of 1992 **(192)** and the US-criticized Kyoto Protocol of 1997 **(206)**. The protection of rivers and lakes against pollution is governed by the global framework Convention on Non-Navigational Uses of International Watercourses of 1997 **(212)**. Regionally, the problem is addressed in Europe by a special convention; there are also agreements designed to protect specific rivers. Pollution associated with the transboundary movement and disposal of hazardous waste is the subject of the global Basel Convention of 1989 **(200)**. Certain kinds of industrial accidents resulting from activities involving hazardous materials are dealt with in a special convention. Among regional agreements, the Bamako Convention of 1991 bans import and transboundary movement of hazardous waste within Africa. The transboundary movement and disposal of radioactive waste is governed by more stringent rules. Movement of hazardous waste from OECD countries is regulated by resolutions of the Organization's Council and guidelines of the UNEP. Apart from the Code of Practice adopted on this subject by the International Atomic Energy Agency (IAEA) in 1990 (30 ILM 556 (1991)), disposal of such ultrahazardous waste is banned under the Antarctic Treaty **(187)** and the above-noted Bamako Convention. Dumping at sea is regulated by conventions within the area of the law of the sea **(254)** dealing with the protection of the marine environment **(255)**.

In the aftermath of the Chernobyl nuclear power station accident in 1986, two international agreements drafted in record time under the auspices of the IAEA addressed the problem of radioactive pollution, especially as a consequence of an accident: Convention on Early Notification of a Nuclear Accident, 1986 (25 ILM 1369 (1986)) and Convention on Assistance in the Case of a Nuclear Accident or Radiological Emergency, 1986 (25 ILM 1377 (1986)). The major agreement dealing with such emergencies and hazards is the IAEA Convention on Nuclear Safety of 1994 **(213)**. There are also bilateral agreements addressing such problems. A number of multilateral conventions govern liability in the field of nuclear energy, *inter alia*: Convention on Third Party Liability of 1960 (956 UNTS 251), with a supplementary Convention of 1963 (2 ILM 685 (1963)); and the Vienna Convention on Civil Liability for Nuclear Damage of 1963 (1063 UNTS 265). Measures to improve the security of nuclear and other radioactive materials have been a major concern of IAEA resolutions (41 ILM 737, 743 (2002)).

The Treaty of 1963 Banning Nuclear Weapons Tests in the Atmosphere, in Outer Space and Under Water (Test Ban Treaty) (480 UNTS 43) is also of relevance for the environmental law. This partial test ban treaty was followed in 1996 by the UN Comprehensive Test Ban Treaty (35 ILM 1439 (1996)) designed to ban all nuclear weapon test explosions or any other nuclear explosions. The Treaty established an elaborate institutional framework, including an organization to ensure its implementation. Signed by a great majority of states (but not by India, Pakistan, and North Korea), the Treaty was to enter into force 180 days after the deposit of instruments of ratification by all the 44 nuclear and potentially nuclear states specifically listed in its Annex 2. France and the United Kingdom (UK), followed by Russia, were among the first to ratify, but the US, alleging lack of effective verification provisions, refused to ratify. As of 2004 the Treaty was not yet in force.

Habitat and species protection has been an aspect of international environmental law for some time, with wildlife protection conventions dealing with specific endangered species and habitat protection concluded in the past century. As early as 1940 countries of the Western Hemisphere, including the US, concluded the Convention on Nature Protection and Wildlife Preservation (161 UNTS 193). A similar agreement, the African Convention on the Conservation of Nature and Natural Resources, 1968 (1001 UNTS 3) concern the African continent. The Convention on Wetlands of International Importance of 1971 (996 UNTS 245) and the World Heritage Convention of 1972 are important multilateral instruments in the protection of habitat and species. Two agreements deal specifically with Antarctic wildlife, forming part of the Antarctic treaty system **(187)**: the Convention for the Conservation of Antarctic Seals, 1972, and the Convention on the Conservation of Antarctic Marine Living Resources, 1980. In the Arctic, polar bears (some 7,000 in 2000) are protected under the Agreement on the Conservation of Polar Bears of 1973 (13 ILM 13 (1974)) to which the five Arctic states are parties. In addition, more recently, in 2000 Russia and the US signed the Agreement on the Conservation and Management of the Alaska-Chukotka Polar Bear Population (some 4,000 bears) (40 ILM 397 (2001)). In the area of environment and trade the Convention on International Trade in Endangered Species of Wild Fauna and Flora of 1973 (993 UNTS 243) is the major international legal instrument setting forth the rules and standards to govern the protection of wildlife against overexploitation through trade. The principles and rules of this relatively successful treaty (for example, with respect to elephant poaching in Africa) have been replicated in a number of other agreements.

While specific rules and standards are spelled out in treaty form, obligations and responsibilities of states in respect of transboundary pollution are governed by, and are grounded in, certain general principles relating to state responsibility **(128)** which find their application also to environmental harm. Historically, first and foremost is the customary law obligation of states to ensure that activities within their jurisdiction or control do not cause damage to the environment of other states or of areas beyond the limit of national jurisdiction. This principle, associated with the *Trail Smelter* Arbitration **(293)** (second decision, 1941) between the US and Canada (3 RIAA 1938), was subsequently reaffirmed in a number of decisions of the ICJ, including the judgment of 1949 (1949 ICJ Rep. 4) in the *Corfu Channel* case between the UK and Albania and the 1997 judgment of the ICJ in the case concerning the *Gabčíkovo-Nagymaros Project* between Hungary and Slovakia. It was most explicitly stated in the ICJ Advisory Opinion **(291)** of 1996 on the *Legality of the Threat or Use of Nuclear Weapons* (35 ILM 809 (1996)) where the principle was held to be "part of the corpus of international law relating to the environment." Furthermore, the obligations of states in this regard were articulated in Principle 21 of the Stockholm Declaration **(226)** and in a number of international instruments, for example in Art. 194 of the Law of the Sea Convention of 1982 **(264)**. More generally, it can be concluded that the contemporary international environmental law rejects the principle of states' unlimited exercise of sovereignty in exploitation of their natural resources without regard to potential adverse consequences for other states and upholds states' conduct according to the maxim of using one's property so as not to injure another person (*sic utere tuo ut alienum non laedas*), a maxim that can be considered a general principle of law recognized by civilized nations **(38)**. But achieving a just balance in specific cases between the two principles is a task lying in the center of international environmental law.

Environmental conventions and other pertinent instruments, including those adopted at Stockholm in 1972 and Rio de Janeiro in 1992, point to additional emerging general principles of customary environmental law: the states' obligation to cooperate in order to protect the environment; the obligation to notify exposed states in advance and in good faith of possible risks to their environment, caused by an accident in the notifying state's territory; and to refrain from causing massive transboundary pollution of air or marine spaces. To a large extent these principles also apply in international river law to upstream states. Emergence of specific customary law rules can be observed especially in the area of the protection of the marine environment and conservation of marine living resources. Whether the so-called precautionary principle is only an "approach," and otherwise impedes economic growth (for example, in biotechnology), as claimed by the US, or has already become a general Principle, if not a customary rule, is not yet clear. However, it was already articulated in Principle 15 of the Stockholm Declaration and is increasingly gaining support in the texts of environmental conventions, such as the Ozone Layer Protection Convention **(217)**, Biodiversity Convention **(188)**, Climate Change Convention, and the regional (European) Convention on the Protection of Transboundary Watercourses and Lakes of 1992. The precautionary principle, expressing the common sense attitude of "better safe than sorry," requires that before starting a potentially harmful course of action a state should take into account the environmental risks involved and undertake all the possible measures to avoid damage to the environment. The problem is closely related to the obligation of states to make an environmental impact assessment prior to embarking on a potentially harmful activity. Guidelines and directives of international institutions, especially the UNEP, suggest that the "soft law" **(35)** pertinent to such situations expresses new emerging customary rules of law. Furthermore, a special agreement, namely, the Convention on the Environmental Impact Assessment in a Transboundary Context, was adopted in Espoo, Finland, in 1991 (30 ILM 800 (1991)). Another evolving principle, related to the still controversial right to a healthy environment as a human right **(157)**, is the public's right of access to information, as proclaimed in Principle 1 of the Stockholm Declaration, Principle 10 of the Rio Declaration, GA Resolution of 1990 on the need to ensure a healthy environment for the well-being of individuals, and the WHO-sponsored European Charter on Environment and Health of 1989, and articulated in treaty form in the Convention on Access to Information, Public Participation in Decision-Making and Access to Justice in Environmental Matters of 1998 (38 ILM 517 (1999). Whether the above-noted concept of sustainable development will evolve into a legal principle is not certain, but it has been articulated in guidelines and other soft-law pronouncements of international institutions. In 2002 the World Summit on Sustainable Development in Johannesburg adopted a declaration supporting the leadership role of the UN in promoting sustainable development. Considerations similar to those relating to sustainable development also apply to the concept of common but differentiated responsibilities proclaimed in Principle 7 of the Rio Declaration.

The polluter-pays doctrine is specifically referred to in some environmental conventions, such as the 1992 Convention on the Transboundary Effects of Industrial Accidents, as a general principle of international environmental law. It is recommended by the OECD and the European Union, especially in cases of civil liability for damage caused by ultrahazardous activities. However, the exact scope of the doctrine as a legal principle is not yet clear.

It can be added that a draft framework convention on the prevention of transboundary damage from hazardous activities, prepared by the International Law Commission (ILC) in 1998, adopts a number of the above-mentioned emerging principles of international environmental law. Drawing, *inter alia,* on the already drafted Convention of 1997 on Non-Navigational Uses of International Waterways, the draft articulates the principles of: consultation, prior authorization, impact assessment, exchange of information, notification, and emergency preparedness.

In addition to rules governing prevention of transboundary environmental harm, international environmental law includes principles and rules applicable to the responsibility and liability **(120)** of states within the context of environmental damage, without, of course, any prejudice to the principles which govern state responsibility as such. Treaty law with regard to liability for compensation of persons who suffered environmental damage is rather sketchy. International agreements setting forth liability rules for pollution damage exist only in certain areas, in particular ship-generated marine pollution by oil; pollution by noxious and hazardous substances; nuclear materials; and offshore activities. At the regional level, the Council of Europe sponsored the Convention on Civil Liability for Damage Resulting from Activities Dangerous to the Environment of 1993 (32 ILM 1228 (1993)). Of interest here is also the Nordic Convention for the Protection of the Environment of 1974 (13 ILM 591 (1974)), which allows nationals of each of the contracting states (Denmark, Finland, Norway, and Sweden) to bring an action before a court of another state party to challenge the permissibility of a pollution-causing activity and claim compensation for damage suffered.

The need for developing international law regarding liability and compensation for environmental damage was stressed both at Stockholm (Principle 22) and Rio (Principle 13). The issue of liability for injurious consequences arising out of acts not prohibited by international law is among the most controversial issues. Most environmental conventions addressing specific forms of pollution call upon the parties to develop special liability regimes for the pollution damage involved. In this regard, the model conceptual framework on "Responsibility and Liability under International Law for Environmental Damage," prepared by the Institut de droit international in 1997 (37 ILM 1473 (1998)) has proved a valuable aid in formulating the law on the matter. It largely reflects the current legal situation, but also takes into account the emerging trends in international environmental law.

As a general rule, a breach by a state of an obligation of environmental protection under international law engages the responsibility of that state for both its own activities and those of private persons under its jurisdiction and control. This entails an obligation to eliminate or mitigate the harm caused and, where appropriate, to pay compensation if a causal link exists between the activity involved and the damage and injury suffered. On the whole, a state is not held responsible if it has taken the necessary and practicable measures to prevent or minimize the harm. The due diligence test for engaging responsibility, adopted expressly in a number of conventions, is to be measured objectively by generally accepted international rules and standards, and the criteria of conduct to be expected of a "good government," as expressed in 2001 by the ILC in its draft concerning the prevention of transboundary harm from hazardous activities. But in practice such tests afford a good deal of flexibility and their application varies depending on the circumstances.

As expressly provided in most conventions, the requirement for engaging a state's responsibility is that the environmental harm be "significant," "serious," or "substantial," but there is no need of proving the impact of transboundary environmental interference if it is caused by highly dangerous substances, ordinarily listed in the agreement in question. Whether a state's responsibility for an alleged breach of an environmental obligation arises before any actual damage has occurred, that is, whether there is responsibility for risk, is not a settled issue, at least for situations which do not involve ultra-hazardous activities. In environmental law, responsibility raises particularly complex problems in view of the sometimes gradual and insidious progression of pollution and difficulties in proving the definite threshold of damage and in determining liability in cases of pollution originating in several states.

Whereas international responsibility based on fault is the prevailing type of responsibility, international environmental law recognizes strict responsibility irrespective of fault **(130)**. It is adopted in international agreements governing ultra-hazardous, especially nuclear, activities. Otherwise, determination of environmental activities that engages responsibility for harm alone may be controversial. The Convention on International Liability for Damage Caused by Space Objects of 1972 **(208)** adopts strict liability for damage caused by space objects on the surface of the earth or to aircraft in flight, but otherwise follows the subjective approach of fault-based responsibility.

In the matter of civil liability for environmental damage, international agreements follow the approach of strict liability of operators as the normal standard, but in certain cases exceptionally allow for appropriate upper limits. The primary liability applies also to states engaged as operators. In addition to treaty regulation of liability for oil and other noxious substances pollution damage in the area of marine pollution, special treaty-based liability regimes exist for radioactive pollution, all of them following the principle of strict liability of operators in a way amounting to the application of the polluter-pays doctrine. However, the number of states parties is rather limited and the US is not a party. International agreements include, *inter alia*, the OECD Paris Convention of 1960 (956 UNTS 251); the 1977 IAEA Vienna Convention (1063 UNTS 265); and conventions dealing with liability resulting from nuclear accidents at sea. These instruments require operators to have adequate financial capacity to pay possible compensation through insurance schemes, compensations funds, and other safeguards. However, states are internationally responsible for failure to comply with the obligation to establish and implement such mechanisms under their respective laws. Subsidiary state liability is recognized as a backup system of liability if the operator is unable to pay the required compensation. Subject to rules of international law, civil liability conventions ordinarily provide that such circumstances as armed conflict, whether international **(339)** or internal **(340)**, terrorism **(337)**, a grave natural disaster, intentional or grossly negligent conduct of a third party, or compulsory measures by the government, release the operator from liability.

The modalities of compensation and reparation **(118)** of damage are on the whole not elaborated upon in environmental conventions, but it is obvious that in accordance with the general rules of international law governing claims and remedies, the concept of reparation entails the obligation to cease the harmful activity, desist from further violations, pay compensation and, if necessary, give satisfaction to the injured party.

A state's claim for reparation of damage to the environment is independent of any claim of its nationals **(175)** resulting from death, personal injury, or loss of property. The right of equal access on a non-discriminatory basis to municipal **(27)** courts and remedies in cases of transboundary pollution is not clearly established in international environmental law, but is recognized in relations between member states of the OECD by virtue of an OECD Council recommendation of 1977, by the parties to the already mentioned Nordic Convention of 1974; and—incidentally—also in relations between the component states of the US and the provinces in Canada. Jurisdictional and enforcement provisions to ensure compensation for persons who suffered damage caused by nuclear accidents are found in the conventions on liability in the field of nuclear energy: the already noted 1960 Paris and 1977 Vienna conventions. However, the fact that only a limited number of states and not all the states with nuclear capabilities subscribe to these conventions is a serious handicap.

International environmental law has made tremendous strides in the past three decades or so. Yet despite all the progress in developing legal rules, a number of factors have increasingly contributed to a deterioration of the earth's environment including the conservation of wildlife, and improvement has taken place only in limited areas. Leaving apart the problem of ensuring compliance with the treaty law in force, there are mainly substantive reasons for the deterioration in the state of the environment. According to the 2002 report of the UNEP on global environment outlook, since 1972 environmental improvement in air and water quality has taken place in Europe and North America but overall there has been a steady environmental deterioration, especially in developing countries. The rapid development of industry and technology, especially in the industrialized states, has been the major factor contributing to this situation. But environmental degradation is noticeable also in less-developed regions, where not just the growing industrialization but mainly demographic and economic pressures, progressing deforestation and urbanization, poverty, domestic instability, and environmental destruction due to armed conflicts, continue to bring damage to the natural environment. Hence, environmental problems have become part of the North-South conflict, the developing countries claiming the need to receive large financial support from the industrialized nations if any improvement in the environmental conditions is to be achieved. In another dimension, the rules of free trade can work to the detriment of environmental protection and while some attempts have been made in international trade agreements and decision making in trade dispute settlement to take account of environmental considerations and allow some restrictions of trade activities in favor of the need to protect the environment, this difficult issue still awaits a more determined international regulation.

**198. Geostationary (Synchronous) Orbit.** A circular orbit, 22,300 miles (36,000 km) above the equator, at which a satellite turns on the polar axis of the earth in the same direction and at the same speed as that of the rotation of the earth so that in effect it appears to remain stationary above a particular point on the earth. The geostationary orbit is the only orbit to provide continual relay of signals from a station on earth to a single satellite in orbit and back to a wide area on the earth, and for this reason it is the most valuable segment of the outer space finite resources used in telecommunication and broadcasting.

While there is consensus that—as otherwise provided for in Art. 1 of the Outer Space Treaty **(216)**—the outer space resources should be used "for the benefit of and in the interests of all countries, irrespective of their degree of economic or scientific development," the allocation of wave bands in the geostationary orbit on a first-come first-served basis has become controversial because of the growing congestion in the spectrum of the orbit and concerns of technologically less-advanced states that they will be deprived of equal rights to this finite resource. In 1976, taking advantage of the fact that there is no agreed legal boundary between airspace **(186)** and outer space, eight of the equatorial states (Brazil, Colombia, the Congo [Brazzaville], Ecuador, Indonesia, Kenya, Uganda, and Zaire [now Dem. Rep. of the Congo]) issued a declaration **(44)** in Bogotá asserting that the individual segments of the geostationary orbit were part of their respective national territories **(228)** and that placement of satellites in them required prior authorization of the state concerned. These exorbitant claims, difficult to reconcile with the principle of outer space law **(215)** which forbids national appropriation in outer space, prompted vigorous protests and opposition from most countries and the United Nations Committee on the Peaceful Uses of Outer Space. The International Telecommunication Union, which controls the allocation in the orbit of frequencies utilized by the satellites, also disregarded claims of the equatorial states in question. Eventually, the latter lessened their emphasis on sovereignty **(125)** but did not formally abandon their claims, pressing—like other less-developed countries—for preferential rights in the utilization of the geostationary orbit and space technology in general.

**199. Hague Air Hijacking Convention, 1970.** The Hague Convention for the Suppression of Unlawful Seizure of Aircraft of 1970 (860 UNTS 105) is the first multilateral treaty **(288)** dealing with aircraft hijacking as a discrete offense. Drafted by the International Civil Aviation Organization, the Convention entered into force **(271)** in 1971 and binds more than 160 states, including the United States. After defining the offense (without using the term hijacking), the Convention obligates the states parties to make it punishable by severe penalties. As a result, the crime of air hijacking is now included in the legislation of a great majority of states which must take such measures as may be necessary to establish their respective jurisdiction **(87)**. The resulting quasi-universal jurisdiction **(92)** is exercised by a state if one or more of the following grounds apply: 1. commission of the offense on board an aircraft registered in that state; 2. landing of the aircraft in the territory of the state with the alleged offender still on board; 3. commission of the offense on board an aircraft leased by the state without crew to a lessee with the principal place of business or permanent residence in that state. As a safety net the Convention provides for the jurisdiction to apprehend an offender who escapes from, or is allowed to leave a state which has jurisdiction on grounds of registration. Any state party on whose territory the offender is present must take him into custody and either prosecute him if so provided in its law or extradite **(75)** him according to Art. 8 of the Convention which makes hijacking an extraditable offense in present and future extradition treaties or in reciprocal practice. However, there is no obligation to extradite in the absence of a treaty or such practice. Hence, if an existing extradition treaty allows a state to refuse extradition in a case of political offense **(76)** or if the hijacker is its national **(175)**, then extradition may not take place. Ultimately there exists no effective international legal mechanism to enforce the law against a state sheltering a hijacker. It may be noted here that the European Convention on the Suppression of Terrorism, completed at Strassbourg in 1977 (15 ILM 1272 (1976)), explicitly excludes terrorist activities, including air hijacking, from the concept of the political offense.

**200. Hazardous Waste Transboundary Movement Basel Convention, 1989.** This Convention (28 ILM 657 (1989)) was adopted in response to concerns over indiscriminate disposal of hazardous toxic waste from the state of their generation to another state, thus creating risk of damage to human health and the environment. The Basel Convention was supplemented in 1999 by the Protocol on Liability and Compensation for Damage Resulting from Transboundary Movement of Hazardous Wastes and Their Disposal. The wastes governed by the Convention are listed in its Annex I, with hazardous characteristics specified in Annex III. In addition, any wastes considered to be harmful under the law of the export, import, or transit state are also subject to the rules of the Convention. Within six months of becoming a party, each state is required to inform the Secretariat of the Convention of any waste considered hazardous under its national legislation. However, radioactive waste is subject to special international regulation as are also discharges from ships and dumping of waste at sea governed by special global and regional conventions dealing with marine pollution **(255)**.

The parties to the Basel Convention undertake, *inter alia*, to reduce to a minimum generation and transboundary movement of hazardous waste; criminalize illegal traffic in such waste; and ban dumping waste in Antarctica **(187)**. The export of waste to states parties which have banned their import and have so informed the other parties is prohibited. The state of export must notify the states concerned of any proposed transboundary movement of hazardous waste. A written consent of the state of import and any transit state is required before an export of such waste can be allowed to commence the transboundary movement. Provisions are also made for the duty of the state of export to take back the waste if the movement cannot be completed. If not in conflict with the Convention, special agreements regarding transboundary movement of waste are allowed, but must be notified to the Secretariat of the Convention. The regional Bamako (Mali) Convention of 1991 on the Ban of the Import into Africa and the Control of Transboundary Movement and Management of Hazardous Wastes within Africa (30 ILM 773 (1991)) is such an agreement. In general, its provisions are modeled on the global Basel Convention.

Under the Basel Convention the parties are obligated to transmit to each other any relevant information, in particular information on accidents occurring during a transboundary movement; on any changes in national definition concerning hazardous waste; and designation of competent authorities. The parties are also required to submit to the Secretariat annual reports on various aspects of the transboundary movement of waste. The Convention envisions the need to establish centers for training and technology transfer, and a revolving fund for emergencies resulting from accidents. The institutional structure consists of the Conference of the parties and the Secretariat.

The Convention does not allow any reservations **(282)** or exceptions, but withdrawal on one year notification is possible at any time after three years from the date on which the Convention entered into force for the party concerned. A United Nations (UN) convention, namely, the Convention on the Transboundary Effects of Industrial Accidents, adopted in Helsinki in 1992 (31 ILM 1330 (1992)), applies to industrial accidents with transboundary effects, including those occurring during installation or transportation of hazardous substances. It does not apply to nuclear accidents and oil spills. A special program for managing toxic substances was set up jointly by UN specialized agencies in 1995 (34 ILM 1311 (1995)).

**201. INTELSAT.** International Telecommunications Satellite Organization (INTELSAT) is the principal institution engaged on a commercial and non-discriminatory basis in cooperative management of the use and service of communications satellites. At the turn of the century more than 37 percent of the world satellite capacity was managed by INTELSAT.

The origins of INTELSAT date back to 1964 when the United States (US) and some other countries established the International Telecommunications Consortium which acquired an international satellite communications system previously set up by COMSAT (Communications

Satellite Corporation), a private corporation set up by Congress and subject to federal control. COMSAT became the US representative to INTELSAT, the operating manager of its system, and the exclusive lessor of space segments in the INTELSAT facilities. The other member states were represented either by governments or governmental telecommunications instrumentalities.

With increasing demand for satellite technology, the membership in INTELSAT grew rapidly along with pressures to reorganize it and limit the influence of the US in the system. As a result, the original, loose INTELSAT consortium was transformed into an international organization with competence to conclude agreements with states and international organizations. The operations of INTELSAT are now based on the INTELSAT Agreement (10 ILM 909 (1971)) and Operating Agreement Relating to INTELSAT (10 ILM 946 (1971)), both completed in Washington in 1971. The former is a treaty of which eventually most states of the world, members of the International Telecommunication Union (ITU), became members and the latter is an agreement open both for states and public or private telecommunications entities designated by governments in accordance with the provisions of the INTELSAT treaty. COMSAT has been so designated by the US.

Under the INTELSAT Agreement membership in the organization is open to all member states of the ITU, the ultimate goal being the creation of a single global satellite telecommunications system. The members participate in the organization by way of investment shares determined by the percentage of utilization of the INTELSAT space segments. The institutional structure includes the Assembly of Parties, the Meeting of Signatories, the Board of Governors, and an executive organ headed by the Director General. The decision making in the Board is based on a weighted voting system depending on the amount of shares held by each government, but no government may cast more than 40 percent of the total vote. Decisions on substantive matters require either the support of at least four governors representing at least two-thirds of the investment shares or the support of all but three governors regardless of the total of the investment shares that they may represent.

The US has played the major role in the satellite system from its beginning. The creation of a separate, private satellite communications system in competition with the INTELSAT has been a controversial issue within this organization and a number of states have argued against the US position that any authorization to set up a separate system would conflict with the goal of achieving a truly global system. However, the 1971 INTELSAT Agreement provides (Art. XIV(d)) for the possibility of a state party or a person within its jurisdiction of setting up a separate system, subject to its technical compatibility with the INTELSAT system and avoidance of significant economic harm to the Organization.

At one time satellite communications systems were established under the aegis of the USSR by communist states: INTERSPUTNIK and INTERCOSMOS (16 ILM 1 (1977)). Today, regional communications systems in existence include the European Telecommunications Satellite Organization, set up by an agreement in 1977, in force **(271)** 1985, and Arab Satellite Communications Organization established by the Arab League in 1976. An important satellite communications system was created in 1976 in the area of global maritime communications. It is based on the Convention on the International Maritime Satellite Organization (INMARSAT) (15 ILM 1051 (1976)), drafted on the initiative of the International Maritime Consultative Organization (now International Maritime Organization) (15 ILM 219 (1976).

The technological and organizational development of satellite communications have raised a number of legal problems, such as those related to the regulation of radio frequency spectrum, a matter within the competence of the ITU; the controversial issue of direct television broadcasting **(196)**; and responsibility of international organizations under Art. 6 of the Outer Space Treaty **(216)** for activities carried out in outer space.

**202. International Air Services Transit Agreement, 1944.** A multilateral agreement (84 UNTS 389), otherwise known as the "Two Freedoms Agreement," adopted **(268)** at the 1944 Chicago Conference on International Civil Aviation and in force **(271)** in 1945. In this Agreement the states parties grant each other only two freedoms for scheduled air services: 1. to fly across their territory without landing; and 2. to land for non-traffic purposes, that is, mainly for refueling and repairs. Adopted as a compromise following the failure of the Chicago Conference to reach agreement on more extensive rights of scheduled flights, the Two Freedoms Agreement fills to an extent a gap in the Chicago Convention of 1944 which spells out the general principles governing airspace **(186)**, but otherwise does not provide any rights beyond the two freedoms. Because of its modest scope the Transit Agreement has gained much more acceptance by states than the accompanying (more generous but less acceptable) International Air Transport Agreement **(203)**.

**203. International Air Transport Agreement, 1944.** A multilateral agreement (171 UNTS 387), otherwise known as the "Five Freedoms Agreement," adopted **(268)** at the 1944 Chicago Conference on International Civil Aviation, which, in addition to the two freedoms under the Transit Agreement **(202)** (overflight without landing and landing for non-traffic purposes), guaranteed three more privileges to scheduled international air services of the contracting parties, namely: 1. to put down passengers, mail, and cargo taken in the state of the nationality of the aircraft; 2. to take on passengers, mail, and cargo destined for the territory of that state; and 3. to take on passengers, mail, and cargo destined for the territory of any state party and to put down passengers, mail, and cargo coming from any such territory. The Five Freedoms Agreement received only limited support at the Chicago Conference. Originally signed **(283)** by 19 states, it is now in force for 11 states of which only Greece and the Netherlands are of significance for international air transport. Hence, the Air Transport Agreement is of little importance, and the United States, which once sponsored it, denounced it already in 1946 (84 UNTS 389).

**204. International River (Fluvial) Law.** International river, or fluvial, law or, in the more recent terminology, the law of international watercourses, is the law governing the use and utilization of rivers, lakes, and other surface and underground waters hydrographically constituting a unitary system parts of which are situated in different states. The terminology concerning rivers, the major element of watercourses, is not uniform. A national river is one whose entire course flows within the territory of one state. An international river traverses the territories of two or more states (successive river) or forms an international boundary (contiguous river). Rivers, whether national or international, whose legal status is subject to a special regime by virtue of a treaty **(40)** or customary law **(39)** are sometimes referred to as internationalized rivers. Such regimes for purposes of navigation have governed a number of rivers in Europe and other continents.

In the past, navigation was the primary use of international rivers. More recently, generation of hydroelectric power and other industrial uses as well as irrigation, waste disposal, and flood control have become more prominent. However, for purposes of legal analysis and in the treaty practice, a distinction between navigational and non-navigational uses of international rivers and watercourses in general is still widely used.

Unless otherwise regulated by treaty, there is no general (customary) rule of international law allowing foreign-registered vessels navigation on a riparian state's river. Since the beginning of the 19th century there has been a trend to recognize free navigation on certain important international rivers. Thus in 1815 the Final Act of the Congress of Vienna (64 CTS 454), *inter alia*, proclaimed the principle of free navigation on the international rivers of Europe by private vessels, including even those of non-riparian states, a principle reaffirmed by the Peace Treaty of Paris in 1856 (114 CTS 409), especially in respect of the Danube for which a European Commission of the Danube was created to regulate free navigation on the river. Following World War I, the peace treaties with Austria, Hungary, Germany, and Bulgaria confirmed this arrangement, extending the internationalization of the Danube upwards to Ulm in Germany. Subsequently, the Convention on the Definitive Statute of the Danube of 1921 (26 LNTS 174) reaffirmed the unrestricted freedom of navigation on the river and created (in addition to the 1856 Commission) another body, the International Commission with jurisdiction over the upper Danube from Ulm to Brăila in Romania, with the original European Commission assigned the supervision of the navigation in the estuary from Brăila to the Black Sea. The powers of the latter Commission were the subject of an advisory opinion **(291)** of the Permanent Court of International Justice (PCIJ) **(320)** of 1927 on the *Jurisdiction of the European Commission of the Danube* (1927 PCIJ, Series B, No. 14). Eventually, by agreements of Romania with the United Kingdom (UK) and France in 1936, the powers of the European Commission were reduced largely to advisory capacity, and upon the outbreak of World War II the International Commission was in fact dissolved in 1940. In the aftermath of the war, when much of the Danube found itself under the control of the Soviet

Union and its satellite states, the Belgrade Conference, 1948, dominated by the Soviet Union and its satellites, voted through, against the opposition of the United States (US), UK, and France, a new Danube legal regime (33 UNTS 181) in a single Danube Commission, which rejected the principle of international control and in practice legalized the Soviet monopoly of regulating navigation on the Danube. The Western powers refused to recognize the new regime, contending that the 1921 Statute was still in force. However, in 1960 the neutralized **(97)** Austria acceded to the decision of the Belgrade Conference. Some three decades later, the collapse of communism in Europe restored in practice the freedom of navigation on the Danube, as guaranteed by the Convention of 1921.

The principle of free navigation applied also to some other European rivers, such as the Rhine for which the Convention of Mannheim established a Commission in 1868, revised in 1963. A similar commission, now extinct, was created for the river Oder. The territorial jurisdiction of this international body was the subject of a judgment of the PCIJ in 1929, namely *Territorial Jurisdiction of the International Commission of the River Oder* (Czechoslovakia, Denmark, France, Germany, Sweden, UK/Poland) (1929 PCIJ, Series A, No. 23). Treaties stipulating freedom of navigation for specific river systems were concluded also in other continents at the end of the 19th and early 20th centuries. A major example of the treaty regime for an international watercourse is offered by the Canada-US Washington Treaty of 1909 Relating to the Boundary Waters (12 Bevans 319) of the Great Lakes, which set up an International Joint Commission administering the regime and deciding disputes.

In 1921 the Barcelona Convention and Statute on the Regime of Navigable Waters of International Concern (7 LNTS 35), negotiated **(316)** under the auspices of the League of Nations, granted the freedom of navigation on conditions of perfect equality to vessels of the signatory states, without distinction as to riparian or non-riparian states, on navigable waterways, apparently including lakes, of international concern, which flow through each other's territory. Although the Barcelona Convention was designed to provide a global regime of freedom of navigation on international rivers, only a minority of states, but not some major states such as the US, became parties, and an additional Protocol providing for the possibility of extending the right of free navigation to all navigable rivers and lakes received minimal acceptance and had little practical effect.

The limited endorsement of the Barcelona Convention, which is still in force for less than 20 countries, highlighted the fact that the principle of free navigation on rivers was not yet recognized as a rule of general international law in the first half of the 20th century. The so-called Helsinki Rules, a private codification drafted by the International Law Association in 1966, did suggest free navigation, but only for riparian states, excluding other states. However, the Helsinki Rules provided that each "basin state" has the right to a reasonable and equitable share in the uses of the waters of an "international drainage basis." Non-navigational uses of international watercourses are at this time still largely governed by treaties dealing with specific watercourses. The 1997 Convention on the Law of Non-Navigational Uses of International Watercourses **(212)** was not yet in force in 2004. However, as reflected also by provisions of the United Nations Economic Commission for Europe Convention on the Protection and Use of Transboundary Watercourses and International Lakes of 1992 (31 ILM 1312 (1992)), in addition to treaty regulation, certain general principles governing such waters are increasingly being recognized in practice. The most basic is the principle of equitable utilization of international watercourses, entailing the obligation of each state to take reasonably into account the interests of other watercourse states in accordance with the principle *sic utere tuo ut alienum non laedas* (use your property so as not to harm another person). Among international judicial decisions upholding this principle, the most prominent are the arbitral award **(293)** in the case of *Lake Lanoux* (France v. Spain) in 1957 (12 RIAA 281) and the International Court of Justice judgment in the case of *Gabčíkovo-Nagymaros Project* (Hungary/Slovakia) in 1997 (1997 ICJ Rep. 7). Other general principles being accepted in general international law refer to the obligation of riparian states to prevent and reduce any transboundary harm, particularly water pollution; to notify states concerned about planned activities with potentially significant adverse effects such as diversion of waters; consult with such states and, if necessary, negotiate to arrive at an equitable resolution of the problem; and, in general, cooperate with one another in mitigating transboundary environmental hazards. Rejecting the doctrine of unlimited sovereignty **(125)** (the "Harmon Doctrine," formulated by US Attorney General Judson Harmon in 1895), allowing states unlimited rights to utilize the waters of an international watercourse flowing through their respective territories, contemporary international law increasingly embraces the principle of equitable sharing of such waters. But as demonstrated by continuing international river disputes, such as the dispute between Israel and Palestinians over the Jordan aquifer and the dispute in the Euphrates and Tigris basin involving Turkey, Iraq, and Syria, "hydropolitics" still interferes with a progressive development of law in the area of international watercourses.

**205. Intertemporal Law.** The term intertemporal law refers to the principles of international law dealing with the problem of which of the different rules of international law prevailing in succeeding periods are to govern a specific situation. Issues of this kind occasionally arise because of the dynamic nature of the rules of law which in the course of time may change, raising the question whether to apply, to a situation, the rule in force in the sometimes distant past when the situation arose, or the rule of a successive period at the time when states confront a dispute **(299)** over the legal solution of the situation. The matter is of particular relevance in the law governing acquisition of title to territory **(227)**, and especially acquisition by conquest or subjugation **(194)**. In the past, title to territory acquired by force, a rather common occurrence, was legal in international law, but in contemporary law, based on the United Nations (UN) Charter's prohibition of the threat or use of force in international relations **(329)**, conquest cannot confer title. However, this does not mean that as a result of this otherwise positive and progressive evolution of international law all the titles based on pre-1945 conquests become null and void; such an operation of intertemporal law would run counter to the well-established general principle of non-retroactivity of the law and, by jeopardizing many titles, would lead to chaos and instability in international relations. For these reasons such unrealistic application of intertemporal law is rejected by states. The 1970 Friendly Relations Declaration of the General Assembly **(14)**, adopted by consensus and reflecting the *opinio juris* of the international community, explicitly declares that the contemporary rule of international law prohibiting acquisition of territory by conquest should not be construed as affecting, *inter alia*, any international agreement prior to the Charter regime and valid under international law.

Yet, the argument that titles based on conquests in the colonial era, though acceptable at their time, were no longer valid in today's international law, was used by India in its conquest of Portuguese Goa in 1961. This action was acquiesced in by most UN members as politically correct within the context of anti-colonialism, and eventually even recognized by Portugal. But this line of reasoning may turn out to be a double-edged weapon, as demonstrated by China's similar argument in its border war with India in 1962 when China raised the issue of the border whose line could ultimately be traced to a British conquest of Chinese territory in the colonial era.

The principle of non-retroactivity of the law in the sense of the intertemporal rule that the validity of the acquisition by states of territorial title is to be governed by the contemporaneously prevailing rule, that is, the rule as accepted at the time of conquest, seemed to be placed in doubt by the arbitrator (an eminent Swiss jurist) in the *Island of Palmas* case between the United States and the Netherlands (2 RIAA 829) in 1928. In this case, the arbitrator made a distinction between, on the one hand, the creation of a right which is governed by the law then in force and, on the other, the continued existence of the right, which should follow the conditions required by the evolution of the law. Thus, Spain gained title to the island by mere discovery in the 16th century when discovery was sufficient for a valid title, but subsequently the Netherlands acquired sovereignty **(125)** through a new, evolving rule of effective control and peaceful display of authority, in this particular case at least since 1700. While in a way logical, such an unrealistic prerequisite would oblige states concerned to continually re-examine and update titles of their territorial acquisitions in order to maintain them in keeping with the ever stricter requirements of the law. But, as noted, this extreme approach to intertemporal law is rejected by most states, and even in the *Palmas* award the arbitrator himself ruled out its application in cases of territories with an "established order of things." Still, the matter is not entirely crystal clear, at least in cases other than the validity of acquisitions of the past era. Thus, in 1978, in the case of *Aegean Sea Continental Shelf* (Greece v. Turkey) (1978 IJC Rep. 3), the International Court of Justice (ICJ) **(309)** followed, in a general sense, the thinking of the *Palmas* arbitrator in its interpretation **(274)** of a 1931 reservation **(282)** of Greece to the General Treaty for the Renunciation of War (Kellogg-Briand Pact) **(330)**, which exempted from the provisions of the Treaty "disputes relating to the territorial status of Greece." The Court held that the phrase "territorial status" had to be appraised in accordance with the rules of international law "as it existed today," that is, in the current period of the evolution of international law, and not as they had been in 1931. In this interpretation of the ICJ, the operation of intertemporal law included the continental shelf **(236)** within the concept of "territorial status" even though the concept of the continental shelf was still unknown in the law of the sea **(254)** when the reservation was made in 1931.

**206. Kyoto Protocol, 1997.** The Protocol (37 ILM 22 (1998)) to the 1992 United Nations Framework Convention on Climate Change **(192)** adopted in 1997 at Kyoto by the Third Conference of the Parties and subsequently further elaborated and implemented in detail in complex and contentious negotiations of successive Conferences of the Parties, in particular the Sixth Conference in Bonn (the Bonn Agreements) and the Seventh Conference in Marrakesh (the Marrakesh Accords), both in 2001.

Under the Protocol, as finally hammered out in Bonn and Marrakesh, 38 industrialized countries (listed in Annex B), including 13 countries undergoing the process of transition to market economy, to which the Protocol grants a certain degree of flexibility in choosing their respective base year, are committed in the period 2008 to 2012 to cut their combined emissions of the heat-trapping carbon dioxide and other five greenhouse gases (listed in Annex A) by an average of more than 5 percent below the 1990 levels, but each party must, by 2005, have made demonstrable progress in achieving its commitments. Annex B lists differentiated targets for the industrialized countries. For example the European Union (EU) and Switzerland agreed to reduce emissions by an average of 8 percent and Japan by 6 percent. No binding commitments are required for the developing countries, but, reaffirming the commitment under the Framework Convention, the Protocol mandates that the industrialized states provide them additional financial resources. It can be added here that in terms of metric tons per capita the United States (US) emits 5.5 tons, followed by Norway, Czech Republic, Netherlands, Belgium, Germany, Russia, Japan, Poland, and the United Kingdom. However, in absolute terms the US, with about 4 percent of the world's population, is the largest emitter, producing 25 percent of the world's greenhouse gases, including 50 percent of such gases released by the industrialized countries.

To facilitate the parties fulfillment of their respective commitments, the Protocol allows them to include the net changes in the emissions since 1990 due to activities in agriculture and forestry which, acting as the so-called sinks, remove carbon dioxide from the atmosphere through photosynthesis. Generally speaking, the Protocol provides for four mechanisms designed to help a committing state to reduce the costs of meeting its emission targets: 1. emissions trading; 2. clean development mechanism; 3. emissions "banking"; and 4. joint implementation. Emissions trading, favored by many developed countries but opposed by developing countries, including China, is a mechanism whereby instead of carrying out a reduction of emissions themselves, a country would find it more cost-effective to "buy" part of emission credit from another country with emissions below the 1990 level. In this regard Russia would benefit by a surplus of billions of tons of carbon dioxide credit because a sharp decline in its industrial production in the 1990s resulted in emissions falling below the 1990 levels. However, under the Protocol such trading may be only supplemental to a country's positive domestic action. The clean development mechanism refers to credit that a country could get by investing in emission reduction projects in developing countries. Emissions banking would allow a country to add, to its assigned amount for subsequent periods, the difference between the assigned amount of emissions and the actual emissions in a commitment period. Joint implementation refers to the right of parties to transfer to, or acquire credit from each other for emissions reduction resulting from projects aimed at reducing emissions or enhancing removals by sinks in any sector of the economy.

The Kyoto Protocol does not lay down any mandatory system for implementing the parties' commitments; each state implements them "in accordance with its national circumstances." During the first years of the commitment period, that is up to 2008, the developing countries are required to establish a national system for estimates of emissions and removal of greenhouse gases by sinks, and to incorporate supplementary information necessary to demonstrate compliance with their commitments under the Protocol. The Protocol itself is to be reviewed periodically in the light of the best available scientific information and assessment on climate change and its impact. Procedures to address cases of noncompliance remain to be determined by the Conference of the Parties.

Considering the complexity of the problem of climate change itself and the clash of interests on a number of issues, it is not surprising that seven years following the Kyoto Conference the Protocol was not yet in force. For entry into force the Protocol required ratification (acceptance, approval **(266)** or accession **(267)**) by at least 55 states, including the industrialized countries that in total accounted for at least 55 percent of the total carbon dioxide emissions in 1990. The first requirement, namely 55 states, was met already in 2002. Despite the rejection of the Protocol by the new US administration in 2001, which believed that the climate science remained too uncertain to justify economically harmful mandatory measures and which therefore favored voluntary reductions in greenhouse emissions and cooperative international research into the problem of climate change, the Protocol was ratified by the EU, Japan, and other industrialized states (but not Australia, which refused to support the Protocol on economic grounds). Prompt ratification by Russia was optimistically expected so that the Kyoto Protocol would meet the other requirement (that is, 55 percent of total emissions from industrialized states), for entry into force in 2003. However, it was not until late 2004 that Russia ratified the treaty, thus allowing it to enter into force in 2005. It should be noted that China ratified the Protocol even though as a developing country it was not subject to emissions reductions.

Without the participation of the US, the impact of the Kyoto Protocol in force for 126 countries in October 2004 will be greatly reduced. Moreover, it is not certain that the industrialized states parties will meet their Kyoto targets. According to the International Energy Agency, even if all the required policies were implemented, the total emissions would not fall by 5.2 percent between 2008 and 2012 and would not stabilize until 2030. Still, the significance of the Kyoto Protocol as the first detailed, legal implementation of the Framework Convention on Climate Change should not be entirely discounted.

**207. Lease, International.** Largely of historical interest, an international lease is an agreement, formalized in treaty **(288)** form, whereby a state **(127)** (lessor) leases part of its territory **(228)** to another state (lessee), granting it, for a specified or non-specified period, more or less extensive rights, possibly including even the exercise of all sovereign rights, short of transfer of territorial sovereignty **(125)** as such. The term "lease" is conveniently borrowed from private law, but it covers a variety of rights exercised by the lessee, the exact nature of which depending on the terms of the treaty. In any case, however, the "residual" sovereignty of the lessor must be presumed even though the rights of the lessor state may, in fact, be reduced to a purely nominal status. An international lease by virtue of a treaty and governed by international law must, in principle, be distinguished from a lease of land under the municipal law **(27)** in which land, for example, a site for diplomatic premises in the receiving state, is granted in lease by the government or a private person in the host state without any transfer of the exercise of sovereign rights to the sending state. The wartime leases, granted by the United Kingdom (UK) to the United States (US) for naval and air bases in the western hemisphere (204 LNTS 15), belonged to this type of lease as well, despite granting the US the exercise of criminal jurisdiction **(87)** in certain limited situations. However, it may not be always entirely clear whether a lease belongs to the "political" category, involving the lessee's exercise of sovereign powers, or is governed by a private-law contract.

International law leases are mainly associated with the colonial policy of western powers as a method of gaining *de facto* control of important, often strategic, points without need for formal annexation. In this sense leases were frequently in essence disguised cessions **(190)** resulting from an unequal power relationship. Most leases were effected at the end of the 19th and in the early 20th centuries and belonged to the "unequal treaties" between on the one hand China and on the other the UK, France, Germany, Austria-Hungary, and Russia, the latter country transferring its lease to Japan after losing the war in 1905. All these leases of territory were eventually restored to China. The best known is the 1898 lease to the UK for 99 years of the Hong Kong "New Territories" which constituted 92 percent of the whole territory under British control, the remaining area including Hong Kong Island and some small areas which had been ceded in perpetuity to the UK in 1842 and 1860, respectively. In 1997 the leased area and the remaining territory reverted to China as a Special Administrative Region according to an agreement of 1984 between China and the UK (23 ILM 1366 (1984)).

The lease of Guantánamo by Cuba to the US remains a survival of the old era. Dating back to an agreement between the two countries in 1903, the lease was later, in 1934, limited to a 4.5 square mile area of the Guantánamo Bay in the eastern tip of Cuba. Under the terms of these agreements the US, while recognizing Cuba's sovereignty over the area, exercises complete jurisdiction and control over this "coaling and naval station" for an indefinite period of time for an annual payment of $4,085 which the Castro government, after it came to power, has refused to accept.

The case of the Panama Canal Zone **(258)**, transferred by Panama to the US in 1903, was unique in that it was neither a cession nor a lease or servitude **(225)**, but a "grant in perpetuity of the use, occupation and control" of the area, with Panama retaining only nominal sovereignty. This regime, of course, ended upon the adoption of the Panama Canal treaties in 1977.

**208. Liability for Damage Caused by Space Objects Convention, 1971.** The Convention on International Liability **(120)** for Damage Caused by Space Objects (961 UNTS 187) was drafted by the UN Committee on the Peaceful Uses of Outer Space and, approved by the General Assembly in 1971, was opened for signature **(283)** and entered into force **(271)** in 1972. The Convention elaborates upon the responsibility and liability provisions of Art. 7 of the Outer Space Treaty of 1967 **(216)**. It provides for absolute ("no fault") liability of the launching state for damage caused by its space objects to persons or property on the earth or to aircraft in flight (Arts. II and VI). On the other hand, only fault liability applies to damage caused to other space objects in flight and persons in them (Art. III). Joint and several liability applies in cases of a joint launching (Art. V). However, the Convention does not cover any damage to nationals of the launching state or foreign nationals participating in the operation (Art. VII). Presentation of a claim does not require the prior exhaustion of local remedies **(74)** but a claimant is barred from pursuing his claim in the courts or administrative tribunals or other agencies of the launching state (Art. XI). Claims may be presented by the state suffering damage or by the state on behalf of its nationals **(175)**; by the state in whose territory **(228)** damage has occurred; or by a state whose permanent residents have suffered damage (Art. VIII). Claims are presented through diplomatic channels **(68)** (Art. IX) within one year following the occurrence of the damage or the identification of the responsible launching state, or the date on which the claimant state became aware of the facts. Compensation is to be determined "in accordance with international law and the principles of justice and equity" **(13)** so as (if possible) to restore the person injured to the condition which would have existed if the damage had not occurred (Art. XII). If no settlement is reached within a year since the submission of the documentation of the claim, the issue is to be resolved by a claims commission **(315)** established at the request of either party. The decision of the commission is final and binding if the parties so agreed. This means that if there is no such agreement, the procedure is conciliation **(296)** rather than arbitration **(293)**. The Convention's procedure of dispute **(299)** settlement has never been used, but in one case a claim was brought, namely, in 1978 by Canada against the Soviet Union, following the breakup of a malfunctioning Soviet nuclear-powered satellite which disintegrated over Canada and fell to earth in its territory, depositing hazardous radioactive debris (18 ILM 809 (1979)). The case was eventually settled in 1981 by an agreement (20 ILM 689 (1981)) whereby the Soviet Union paid Canada C $3 million in full and final settlement of the claim.

**209. Long-Range Transboundary Air Pollution Convention, 1979.** This Convention (1302 UNTS 217) is a regional instrument adopted in 1979 in Geneva under the auspices of the United Nations Economic Commission for Europe. In force since 1983, it is binding upon virtually all European states, Canada, and the United States. The Convention is supplemented by a 1984 Protocol dealing with long-term financing of the co-operative program for monitoring and evaluation of the long-range transmission of air pollution in Europe (24 ILM 484 (1985)).

The goal of the Convention is to limit and, as far as possible, gradually reduce and prevent air pollution, including in particular the long-range pollution from sulfur and nitrogen dioxide. The Convention defines air pollution (Art. 1) as "the introduction by man, directly or indirectly, of substances or energy into the air resulting in deleterious effects of such a nature as to endanger human health, harm living resources and ecosystems and material property or impair or interfere with amenities and other legitimate uses of the environment." Long-range transboundary air pollution in the meaning of the Convention is "air pollution whose physical origin is situated wholly or in part within the area under the jurisdiction of one State and which has adverse effects in the area under the jurisdiction of another State at such a distance that it is not generally possible to distinguish the contribution of individual emission sources or groups of sources." Such pollution is associated primarily with emissions of so-called acid rain, that is, pollution by sulfur from industrial sources which causes damage to natural resources, such as forests and water, through the process of acidification.

The states parties are obligated to develop policies and strategies to combat the discharges of air pollution, by means of exchanges of information, consultations, research, and monitoring. The Convention does not deal with the issue of liability. Since it is basically a framework agreement, specific obligations to reduce particular air pollutants are included in protocols: on sulfur emissions, 1985 (27 ILM 701 (1988)) and 1994 (33 ILM 1540 (1994)); nitrogen oxide emissions, 1988 (28 ILM 212 (1989)); and on volatile organic compounds, 1991 (31 ILM 568 (1992)). The above-noted Protocol on sulfur emissions of 1994 specified emissions ceilings for the years 2000, 2005, and 2010, and established a committee to review the implementation of these rules and compliance by the parties. It should be added that the members of the European Union are subject to special rules. In 1998 the Convention was supplemented by the Protocol on Persistent Organic Pollutants (37 ILM 505 (1998)) which later provided the United Nations Environment Program useful guidance for drafting a convention in 2001 addressing the same problem on the global level.

**210. Montreal Sabotage Convention, 1971.** This is the International Civil Aviation Organization–drafted Montreal Convention for the Suppression of Unlawful Acts against the Safety of Civil Aviation, 1971 (10 ILM 1151 (1971)). It is supplemented by the Protocol for the Suppression of Unlawful Acts of Violence at Airports Serving International Civil Aviation of 1988 (27 ILM 627 (1988)), adopted following terrorist **(337)** attacks at the Rome and Vienna airports. In force **(271)** since 1973, the Convention has more than 160 parties, including the US. The Protocol, in force since 1989, has some 60 parties, with the United States (US) joining in 1994.

Commonly known as the Sabotage Convention, the Montreal Convention in general follows the principles of the Hague Hijacking Convention of 1970 **(199)** which it complements in that it covers sabotage and other offenses against civilian aircraft, other than hijacking an aircraft in flight. It includes: 1. violence against a person on board an aircraft in flight if it is likely to endanger the safety of that aircraft; 2. destruction of, or damage to an aircraft; 3. placing explosive devices on an aircraft in service; 4. destruction of, or damage to air navigation facilities or interfering with their operations; 5. bomb hoax extortion and similar acts; and, added by the Protocol of 1988, 6. violence against persons or facilities of an airport serving international civil aviation. Attempts of, and complicity in committing any of these acts are also included in the concept of the offense.

The Convention applies to civil aircraft only and only if the place of takeoff or landing is outside the territory of the state of registry or if the offense is committed in a non-registry state or if the offender is found in the territory of such state. With regard to jurisdictional rules **(87)**, the Montreal Convention follows the pattern of the Hague Air Hijacking Convention, obligating the contracting states to make the listed offenses punishable by severe penalties and to take the necessary measures to establish their respective jurisdiction over the offense if committed in the territory of the state concerned as well as in circumstances largely the same as those envisioned in the Hague Convention so as to provide the widest possible jurisdictional basis. Provisions concerning extradition **(75)** also follow those in that instrument. As a result, in this respect the Montreal Sabotage Convention suffers from the same weaknesses of enforcement as its predecessor covering air hijacking.

The obligation to prosecute or extradite the alleged offenders was at issue in the case of the sabotage in 1988 of a PanAm airliner on its way from Frankfurt to New York which exploded over Lockerbie, Scotland, with a loss of 270 lives, including nationals **(175)** of 21 states. The US, United Kingdom (UK), and France called upon Libya to hand over for trial two Libyan nationals, suspected of the sabotage of the airliner and another similar act against a French airliner over Africa, against whom warrants had been issued in Scotland and the US. Libya (like the UK and US, a party to the Montreal Convention), invoking the pertinent provisions of the Convention, established its jurisdiction to investigate the case for purposes of possible prosecution and asked the UK for assistance in the proceedings. However, it refused to hand over the two suspects to the UK. Incidentally, there was no extradition treaty between Libya and the UK, and the law of Libya forbids extradition of nationals. In 1992 the Security Council (SC) adopted a resolution urging Libya to respond to the request for extradition, whereupon Libya, acting under Art. 14 of the Montreal Convention, took the case to the International Court of Justice (ICJ) **(309)** claiming a breach by the UK of obligations under the Convention and seeking interim measures of protection **(322)**, a request eventually denied by the Court because of the SC action in the case. For their part, the UK, US, and France brought the case back to the SC which, acting under Chapter VII of the United Nations (UN) Charter **(327)**, adopted Resolution 748 holding that Libya's engagement in terrorism was a threat to peace and ordering it to return the alleged offenders. Libya's initial failure to comply resulted in economic sanctions against that country, but eventually, in 1999, Libya surrendered the two suspects for trial by a Scottish High Court of Judiciary especially set up in Kamp van Zeist in the Netherlands, which acquitted one accused but found the other guilty of the terrorist charge (Scottish High Court of Judiciary at Camp Zeist (The Netherlands): *Her Majesty's Advocate v. Al Megrahi* (2001) (40 ILM 582 (2001)). The sanctions against Libya were lifted by the SC, and the cases of *Questions of Interpretation and Application of the 1971 Montreal Convention arising from the Aerial Incident at Lockerbie* (Libyan Arab Jamahiriya v. United Kingdom and Libyan Arab Jamahiriya v. United States of America) were discontinued and removed from the ICJ's General List in 2003. While the Court had ruled that it had jurisdiction and the cases were admissible, the whole matter was of great interest, not the least because it raised fundamental problems of jurisdictional conflict between the ICJ and the SC. As far as the Lockerbie case itself is concerned, it was not until 2003 that Libya acknowledged responsibility for the downing of the PanAm airliner and agreed to pay compensation to the survivors of each victim, whereupon the SC lifted the UN sanctions. Libya agreed to transfer $2.7 billion into an escrow account at the Bank for International Settlements, from which the compensation was to be paid to each family of the victims in three installments: the first $4 million following the lifting of the UN sanctions; then another $4 million after the US lifted its sanctions; and a final $2 million after the US removed Libya from its list of states supporting terrorism. A much smaller reparation **(118)** ($30 million for 170 persons killed) for the 1989 sabotage of the French airliner over Africa had been paid to France in 1999, but France later demanded and received from Libya additional compensation comparable to that granted in the Lockerbie case.

**211. Moon Treaty, 1979.** This is the Agreement Governing the Activities of States on the Moon and Other Celestial Bodies (18 ILM 1434 (1979)), drafted by the United Nations (UN) Committee on the Peaceful Uses of Outer Space and approved without vote by the General Assembly (GA) in 1979. It entered into force **(271)** in 1984 but—unlike the other multilateral treaties concerning outer space—it was signed by a limited number of states and ratified only by nine states which otherwise have no experience in outer space activities. The Moon Treaty elaborates upon the general principles and rules of the Outer Space Treaty of 1967 **(216)** pertinent to celestial bodies and introduces the concept of the common heritage of mankind into the law governing the moon. It applies to the moon and its orbits and other celestial bodies without prejudice to any specific future treaties governing such bodies. Meteorites and similar extraterrestrial materials reaching the earth are not covered by the Agreement.

The Moon Treaty deals with two major problems: demilitarization, and exploration and exploitation of the resources of the moon. But first, it declares that all activities there are to be carried out in accordance with international law, including the UN Charter and the Friendly Relations Declaration of the GA of 1970 **(14)**. The moon is to be used exclusively for peaceful purposes; it is to be demilitarized, with prohibition of nuclear and other weapons of mass destruction. The vague term "for peaceful purposes" is not defined, but surveillance for purposes of military defense is not named among the prohibited activities. Still, the legality of such use is potentially controversial.

The provisions regarding exploration and use of the moon's resources largely reflect the ideology of the New International Economic Order promoted by the developing countries. Art. 11 declares the moon and its natural resources to be the common heritage of mankind, a concept otherwise adopted by the Third UN Conference on the Law of the Sea **(263)** for purposes of the "Area" (deep seabed) **(232)** and its resources. The treaty declares the moon to be exempt from any appropriation, national or otherwise. It prohibits any claims to rights of ownership over any part of the moon and its resources in place. In order to operationalize the concept of common heritage of mankind, the Treaty calls for the parties to negotiate **(316)** an "international regime" to govern any future exploitation of the natural resources of the moon. The purpose of such regime would be a rational management and orderly development of the resources, with special emphasis on an equitable sharing by all states parties of the benefits derived, whereby the interests and needs of the developing countries as well as of the countries contributing to the exploration of the moon, shall be given special consideration. How this provision would be reconciled with the principle of the Outer Space Treaty of free and equal exploitation is not clear.

Other provisions of the Moon Treaty declare freedom of scientific investigation without discrimination, with the right to collect and remove from the moon samples of minerals and other substances; protection of the moon's environment; safeguarding the life and health of persons on the moon; and a mutual right of inspection. It is still a moot question whether unilateral exploitation would be allowed under the Treaty if no agreement were reached on the establishment of the international regime envisioned by its rules. It appears that unless the concept of common heritage of mankind becomes part of general international law, a non-party state, for example, the United States, would be entitled to undertake a unilateral exploitation of the moon's resources. However, in the early 21st century the provisions of the Moon Treaty continue to remain in the realm of theory, considering that the exploitation of the moon is still a matter for the remote future.

**212. Non-Navigational Uses of International Watercourses Convention, 1997.** The Convention on the Law of Non-Navigational Uses of International Watercourses (36 ILM 700 (1997), an example of codification and progressive development of international law **(5)** was adopted **(268)** by an overwhelming majority of the General Assembly, following negotiations in the 6th (Legal) Committee of the Assembly on the basis of a draft prepared by the International Law Commission (ILC). The Convention defines "watercourse" (Art. 2(a)) as "a system of surface waters and groundwaters constituting by virtue of their physical relationship a unitary whole and normally flowing into a common terminus." "International watercourse" means a watercourse, parts of which are situated in different states (Art. 2(b)). This broad definition applicable to international rivers, lakes, glaciers, and other hydrographic components, follows the terminology of the ILC which in its later work adopted it after abandoning the previously used term "international drainage basin," developed earlier by the International Law Association in its Helsinki Rules in 1966. Traditionally, international law makes a distinction between two kinds of use of international watercourses and their waters: for navigation and for purposes other than navigation. The Convention applies only to the latter uses, such as human consumption, production of energy, irrigation, industrial processes, and the like. It also applies to measures of protection, preservation and conservation, and management related to such uses (Art. 1(1)). It is understood that the Convention does not apply to fishing and other living resources, except to the extent provided for by its rules concerning the above-noted measures and insofar as other uses affect such resources.

As a framework agreement, the Convention allows parties to enter into "watercourse agreements" which may apply and adjust its provisions to the particular characteristics of the international watercourse in question. Furthermore, the Convention makes it clear that it does not affect the rights and obligations of states parties arising from already existing agreements, but harmonization of such agreements with the principles of the Convention is possible. In any case, watercourse agreements may not adversely affect, "to a significant extent," the use by other watercourse states of the waters of the watercourse without their express consent. All watercourse states have the right to participate in agreements applying to the entire watercourse. A riparian state significantly affected by the implementation of a proposed agreement applying only to a part of the watercourse or to a particular project, program, or use, has the right to participate in consultations on the agreement and, where appropriate, in negotiations in good faith with a view to becoming also a party (Art. 4). The Convention on the Protection and Use of Transboundary Watercourses and International Lakes, adopted by the United Nations Economic Commission for Europe in Helsinki, 1992 (31 ILM 1312 (1992)) (with a protocol of 1999), is the major regional convention concerning watercourses. This regional framework agreement requires its parties to enter into bilateral and subregional agreements. One can mention here the 1994 Agreement on Cooperation for the Protection and Sustainable Use of the Danube and two conventions of 1994 for the protection of the Meuse and the Scheldt, respectively. The protection of the Rhine against noxious chemical pollution is the subject of two conventions of 1976. A further convention banning discharge of waste from boats was adopted in 1996. There is also an international agreement on Action Program for the Rhine of 1987. In South Asia, three water sharing agreements are worth mentioning: the India-Nepal Treaty Concerning the Integrated Development of the Mahakali River, 1996 (36 ILM 531 (1997)); the Bangladesh-India Agreement on Sharing of the Ganges' Waters, 1977 (17 ILM 103 (1978)); and the Bangladesh-India Treaty on Sharing of the Ganges Waters at Farakka, 1996 (36 ILM 519 (1997)). There is also the Israel–Jordan–Palestine Liberation Organization Declaration on Cooperation on Water-Related Matters of 1996 (36 ILM 761 (1997)).

Among the general principles to govern non-navigational uses of international watercourses under the Watercourses Convention of 1997, the principle of equitable and reasonable utilization (Art. 5), emphasized by the International Court of Justice **(309)** in its judgment of 1997 on the merits in the case of *Gabčíkovo-Nagymaros Project* (Hungary/Slovakia) (37 ILM 162 (1998)), lies at the foundations of international fluvial law. Following trends in contemporary international environmental law **(197)**, the Convention calls for the use of international watercourses with a view to attaining not just optimal but sustainable utilization, taking into account the interests of the watercourse states and consistent with adequate protection of the watercourse in question. Riparian states have the obligation to participate in the use, development, and protection of an international watercourse in an equitable and reasonable manner, which means that they have both the right to utilize a watercourse and the duty to cooperate with each other (Art. 5). Among the factors relevant to equitable and reasonable utilization the Convention (Art. 6) lists, *inter alia*, geographic, hydrographic climatic, ecological, and other factors of a natural character; social and economic needs of the states concerned; the population dependent on the watercourse in each watercourse state; effects of the use of the watercourse in one state on the other states; conservation, protection, development, and economy of the use and the costs involved; existing and potential uses; and the availability of alternatives. Each factor must be assessed in its relative weight compared with that of other relevant factors, and all factors are to be considered in order to determine what constitutes a reasonable and equitable use. Concerning the controversial problem of how to formulate the obligation not to cause harm, the Convention (Art. 7) mandates that "watercourse States should, in utilizing an international watercourse in their territories, take all appropriate measures to prevent the causing of significant harm to other watercourse States." Furthermore, as a compromise between the downstream and upstream states concerned about any potential harm from the utilization of the watercourse in question, the Convention, striking a balance between the equitable utilization rule and the obligation not to cause harm, adds that if significant harm does occur, the state causing it must take all appropriate measures in consultations with the affected state, to eliminate or mitigate such harm and, where appropriate, to discuss the question of compensation **(118)**. The relationship between different kinds of use is governed by the general principle (Art. 10) that, in the absence of agreement or custom to the contrary, no one use enjoys inherent priority over another use, and in the event of a conflict it is to be resolved observing the principle of equitable and reasonable utilization and participation, considering all relevant factors and the obligation not to cause significant harm, with special regard being given to the rather general requirement of "vital human needs." One of the "statements of understanding" attached to the Convention articulates the view that providing sufficient water to sustain human life is to be paid special attention. Obligations to cooperate (Art. 8) and regularly exchange data and information (Art. 9) are also included among the general principles governing the utilization of international watercourses.

Part III of the Convention elaborates on the duties to exchange information and consult each other on possible effects of a planned measure, and sets forth procedures to observe before a watercourse state implements or permits to implement the measure (for example, building a dam) which may have a significant adverse effect upon other watercourse states. Included are rules on timely notification; reply to it; the rights of the notifying state in absence of reply to the notification; consultation and negotiation; procedure in the absence of notification; and immediate implementation of the planned measure of the "utmost urgency."

In Part IV the Convention spells out provisions governing the protection and preservation of the ecosystems of international watercourses, and to this extent forms part of international environmental law. Mandating a due diligence standard on watercourse states, the Convention calls upon them to prevent, reduce, and control the pollution of an international watercourse that may cause significant harm to other watercourse states or to their environment. On request, watercourse states are to consult on such measures as setting joint quality objectives and criteria; establishing techniques and practices to address pollution; and prepare a list of prohibited, limited, investigated, or monitored substances (Art. 21). In this context, pollution of an international watercourse is defined as "any detrimental alteration in the composition or quality of the waters of an international watercourse which results directly or indirectly from human conduct" (Art. 21(1)). Watercourse states must take all measures necessary to prevent the introduction of species, alien or new, into an international watercourse, which may cause significant harm to other watercourse states (Art. 22). They must also take steps to protect and preserve the marine environment **(255)**, including estuaries, taking into account generally accepted international rules and standards (Art. 23). Thus prevention of marine pollution from land-based sources becomes a duty of the watercourse states. Watercourse states have the duty, at the request of any of them, to enter into consultations concerning the management of an international watercourse, which may include the establishment of a joint management mechanism (Art. 24). The Convention means here joint international river commissions, a mechanism already used with respect to some international rivers and lakes. The International Joint Commission established in 1909 by the United States and Canada for the management of the Great Lakes is a major example of arrangement dealing, *inter alia*, with the complex problem of pollution in these inland waters. Further duties of the watercourse state concern cooperation in the flow of water and the maintenance and protection of installations (Art. 26). Moreover, in time of armed conflict, both international **(339)** and non-international **(340)**, such installations and other facilities and works (for example, dams) shall enjoy protection accorded by international law applicable to such conflict **(353)** (Art. 29). In case of emergency situations resulting from both natural causes and human conduct, the state concerned must immediately notify other potentially affected states and competent international organizations **(84)** and take all practicable measures to deal with the emergency (Art. 28). Watercourse states must otherwise take all appropriate measures to prevent and mitigate conditions that may be harmful to other watercourse states, resulting from natural causes and human conduct, such as flood, ice conditions, drought, siltation, erosion, waterborne diseases, and the like (Art. 27). Among miscellaneous provisions, the Convention includes, in addition to the above-noted protection of works in an armed conflict, exemption of data and information vital to national defense and security (Art. 31); non-discrimination (Art. 32); indirect procedures applicable to watercourse states maintaining no direct contacts with each other (Art. 30); and settlement of disputes (Art. 33) **(318)**. Here the Convention provides for optional arbitration **(293)** and /or judicial settlement, and the possibility of other methods of peaceful settlement, such as good offices **(303)**, mediation **(313)**, conciliation **(296)** and resort, at the request of any party to the dispute **(299)**, to a mandatory fact-finding by a commission of inquiry **(305)** to act after negotiations **(316)** have failed to settle the dispute within six months, a provision strongly objected to by some states, including China, India, and a number of upstream countries.

The International Watercourses Convention of 1997 promises to become the major international instrument codifying and developing **(5)** the law of non-navigational uses of such watercourses. While some of its general principles, such as that of equitable utilization, the duty not to cause significant harm, and the obligation to notify other affected states of potentially harmful planned measures, reflect the already existing customary law **(39)**, other rules of the Convention have a good chance of eventually crystallizing into customary law, considering the very great majority voting for the Convention (103 in favor, 3 against, and 27 abstaining). It remains to be seen whether the Convention, when in force **(271)** (entry into force requiring at least 35 instruments of ratification **(280)**, acceptance or approval **(266)**, or accession **(267)**), will contribute to a peaceful settlement of international disputes over non-navigational uses of international watercourses.

**213. Nuclear Safety IAEA Convention, 1994.** The Convention on Nuclear Safety (33 ILM 1514 (1994)), adopted **(268)** in Vienna under the auspices of the International Atomic Energy Agency (IAEA), with the objective of achieving a high level of nuclear safety, establishing effective defenses against radiological hazards, and preventing and mitigating accidents with radiological consequences (Art. 1). Unlike most other environmental agreements **(197)**, the Nuclear Safety Convention is not a framework agreement to be supplemented by protocols. Reaffirming the rule that responsibility **(128)** for nuclear safety rests with the state having jurisdiction **(87)** over a nuclear installation, the Convention (Art. 4) mandates that the parties take all necessary measures for implementing their obligations under its provisions and submit reports on such measures to periodic review meetings of the contracting parties to be convened at intervals not exceeding three years. It is these review meetings that constitute the main method for monitoring compliance. Each party is obligated to designate a special regulatory body entrusted with the implementation, separate from any other regulatory body concerned with the promotion or utilization of nuclear energy. The parties must ensure that primary responsibility for the safety of nuclear installations rests with the holder of the relevant license (Art. 9). The Convention provides for a number of general safety considerations and specific procedures for the safety of nuclear installations. Due priority must be given to nuclear safety; ensuring adequate financial resources and qualified staff and quality insurance programs; comprehensive and systematic assessment and verification of safety; radiation protection; and appropriate emergency preparedness, including providing information for emergency planning to its own population likely to be affected by a radiological emergency and to the authorities of other states in the vicinity of the nuclear installation involved. States parties which do not have a nuclear installation on their territory must also take appropriate steps insofar as they are likely to be affected by an emergency. Specific safety considerations (Arts. 17–19) that must be taken into account in the operation of nuclear installations include, *inter alia*, considerations with regard to the siting of installations, design and construction, and operation. There is no obligation to follow the IAEA standards, but adoption of different standards would have to be justified at the review meeting of the parties. The Convention establishes a system of accountability which may eventually develop necessary safety standards and even provide a basis for international liability for failure to abide by its rules. The review meetings and a secretariat constitute the necessary institutional arrangements, and are treated in detail in Chapter 3 (Arts. 20–26) of the Convention.

In view of the fact that almost 500 nuclear plants were operating or being built at the turn of the century, the chances of safety risks, especially in the aging Soviet era nuclear reactors, are considerable and a number of reactors which did not live up to the Convention's standards were shut down.

There are other IAEA-sponsored agreements in the area of nuclear safety dating to the period prior to the adoption of the 1994 Convention. Among them are: the Convention on Physical Protection of Nuclear Material of 1979 (18 ILM 1419 (1979)) and two agreements adopted together in the aftermath of the 1986 Chernobyl nuclear disaster: the Convention on Early Notification of a Nuclear Accident, 1986 (25 ILM 1369 (1986)) and the Convention on Assistance in the Case of a Nuclear Accident or Radiological Emergency, 1986 (25 ILM 1377 (1986)). In addition there are bilateral agreements dealing with cooperation in cases of such emergencies

**214. Occupation.** Not to be confused with belligerent occupation **(363)**, occupation is a mode of acquisition **(227)** by a state **(127)** of title to a territory which at the time in question is not under the sovereignty of any other state, that is, is *terra nullius*. By now there is hardly any such territory except for some very small rock islands, and a sector **(224)** in Antarctica **(187)** which in any case may not be appropriated by virtue of Art. IV of the Antarctic Treaty. Notwithstanding all these facts, the knowledge of the nature and modalities of occupation as a historical mode of acquiring territory, resorted to by analogy to civil (Roman) law **(23)** of property, may still be of use considering that some contemporary territorial disputes **(299)** can be traced back to their legal roots centuries ago when occupation of overseas territories was a fairly common mode of acquisition of territory by European states.

Unlike prescription **(219)**, a mode of acquisition which is often not easy to distinguish from occupation, occupation must relate to *terra nullius* that either has never been under the sovereignty **(125)** of any state or is a derelict territory formally belonging to a state but in fact once abandoned with the intention of giving up sovereignty. In past centuries of overseas exploration, European jurists and governments would consider a newly discovered inhabited territory (for example, Australia and New Zealand) as *terra nullius* even if the territory was inhabited by indigenous peoples, and sometimes were unwilling to treat organized societies as legitimate states under the law of nations. But in retrospect, it is difficult to identify in specific cases the nature of the innumerable and manifold dealings of Europeans with native societies, related to acquisition of territory: whether it was a case of a unilateral occupation of *terra nullius* or—as it appears in most cases in Africa and Asia—a derivative acquisition through some kind of cession **(190)** agreement with a local tribal chief or ruler, or a combination of both. However, as found by the International Court of Justice (ICJ) **(309)** in 1975 in its advisory opinion in the case of *Western Sahara* (1975 ICJ Rep. 12), by the time of the Spanish colonization of Western Sahara in 1884, "territories inhabited by tribes or peoples having a social and political organization were not regarded as *terra nullius*," and acquisition of such territories by colonial powers was not generally considered as effected by occupation but through agreement with local rulers. Hence, it was regarded not as an original title obtained by occupying a territory belonging to no state but as a derivative root of title. The recent movement in support of the rights of indigenous peoples **(163)** constitutes another chapter in the history of this issue.

As evolved by the early 19th century in the practice of European states engaged in overseas expansion throughout the previous three or so centuries, to create a valid title to territory, occupation required the presence of two elements: effective control and intention and will to act as the sovereign. As stated by the Permanent Court of International Justice (PCIJ) **(320)** in its judgment in the case of *Legal Status of Eastern Greenland* in 1933 (1933 PCIJ. Series A/B, No. 53), a claim to a valid title to territory based on occupation must be accompanied by the intention or will to act as sovereign, and some actual exercise or display of such authority. This means that the claiming state had to take actual possession of the territory and within reasonable time establish some kind of administration exercising governmental functions attributable to sovereign states. Historically, with the passage of time the requirement of such effective control became increasingly stricter. Initially, discovery alone, while not sufficient to create title, was nonetheless given some weight in that the state whose explorers discovered a territory was conceded a temporary right ("inchoate" title), an option as against other states, to proceed to an effective occupation within a reasonable period of time, failing which the discovering state's option would lapse and any other state could acquire title by effective occupation, as illustrated in the *Island of Palmas* Arbitration (2 RIAA 829) between the United States and the Netherlands in 1928. Another case, the *Clipperton Island* Arbitration between France and Mexico in 1931 (2 RIAA 1104), illustrates the rule that, unlike a mere discovery, claims based on symbolic annexation through a declaration or a ceremonial act of taking possession, such as flag raising authorized by the state, were given more weight in practice, in particular in exceptional circumstances of uninhabited regions and remote islands **(251)** where the requirement of effectiveness could be met by symbolic acts of possession. A more recent instance of such annexation occurred in 1955 when a party of four British soldiers, sent by the United Kingdom (UK) Ministry of Defence, landed by helicopter on a tiny (less than 0.06 square miles) uninhabited *terra nullius* Atlantic islet of Rockwell, some 250 miles west of the Outer Hebrides, and formally annexed it to the UK, erecting a flagstaff with a Union Jack and cementing a brass plaque which recorded this unique case of occupation. But it must be remembered that otherwise, by the 19th century, with the proliferation of claims based on symbolic annexation, the requirement of actual taking possession had become necessary and international law came to require effective control for a valid title to territory.

The requirement of intention and will to act as sovereign (*animus occupandi*) means that occupation can be effected only by a state and for a state, and that ordinarily the activity undertaken must constitute acts normally performed by sovereign states. As ruled in the above-noted judgment by the PCIJ in the *Eastern Greenland* case, "the independent activity of private individuals is of little value unless it can be shown that they have acted in pursuance of a licence or some other authority received from their government or that in some other way their governments have asserted jurisdiction through them." Thus, in the *Island of Palmas* Arbitration, 1928, the arbitrator found that from the end of the 16th until the 19th century the Dutch East India Company was fully authorized by the Netherlands to exercise public powers for the acquisition and administration of Dutch colonies. In practice it may be difficult to find out how the intention to act as sovereign is to be inferred and how to identify the judgments of individuals involved; hence the intention must be determined on a case-by-case basis. Thus in the *Eastern Greenland* case the PCIJ was satisfied on the evidence that at any rate after 1721, Denmark's intention to claim title to the whole of Greenland was firmly established.

The concept of effective control, analyzed and refined in the first half of the 20th century in such major international decisions as the *Island of Palmas* and *Clipperton Island* arbitrations, and in the PCIJ leading judgment in *the Eastern Greenland* case, was subsequently further discussed by the ICJ in its 1953 judgment in the *Minquiers and Ecrehos* case (France/United Kingdom) concerning a dispute over the sovereignty over two groups of islets situated between the island of Jersey and the French coast (1953 ICJ Rep. 47), and the already mentioned ICJ advisory opinion in the *Western Sahara* case. A major refinement of these decisions in the second half of the past century concerns the view that in special geographical circumstances, state activity and not actual settlement of the territory constitutes the decisive test of effective control. Effective control in the sense of actual display of state authority, reasonably sufficient to produce a valid title to territory, is a relative concept which depends not only on the geographical features of the territory but also on the extent of any competing claims. For example in the *Eastern Greenland* case the polar and desolate nature of the uninhabited territory in question made it unreasonable to require a continuous and intensive display of state authority. In this case, the PCIJ found that legislative and administrative acts of Denmark purported to apply to the whole of Greenland, and clauses in certain treaties provided sufficient evidence for a title to the entire island. At the "critical" date of 1931, when Norway laid claims to certain parts of Eastern Greenland, those parts had already been occupied by Denmark and were no more *terra nullius*. As also pointed out by the PCIJ, the extent to which other states laid claims to the same territory—a common occurrence in territorial disputes—was an important consideration, with very little actual exercise of sovereign rights sufficing for a claimant state to establish its title, especially in barren and uninhabited areas, provided that no other state could show a superior claim.

It is not a settled issue to what extent the legal effect of occupation may extend beyond the effectively occupied area. Although in practice, for security reasons, states have claimed title to such wider areas on grounds of continuity, contiguity, watershed, hinterland, and other geographical doctrines, there is no rule of international law recognizing the legality of such claims. Thus, in the *Island of Palmas* case, the arbitrator denied the legal validity of the contiguity argument with regard to the island, as a basis for title to territorial sovereignty. However, it must be noted that, barring extravagant and unreasonable geographical doctrines, geographical arguments could, under the circumstances, be accepted in international law as subsidiary and reinforcing support in the process of establishing title by occupation.

**215. Outer Space, International Law of.** These are the rules of international law governing space beyond the air surrounding the earth. However, it remains undetermined in international law at what altitude the airspace **(186)**, and thereby the sovereignty **(125)**, of the subjacent state **(127)** ends, and outer space begins. But all states agree that state sovereignty does not extend without any limits and obviously ends at some altitude. The issue whether it is possible or useful to establish a legal boundary between airspace and outer space has been debated in the doctrine for quite a long time. Proposals concerning the upper limit of national airspace are based on various scientific and technological criteria, such as the limits of the gravitational pull of the earth, the flying capability of air-breathing aircraft (about 50 km), or the lowest safe altitude for orbiting artificial satellites (about 100 km). According to a functional approach, no fixed line is necessary and the legal status of activities in space would depend on the nature of the activity. The question of the legal airspace–outer space boundary has been on the agenda of the United Nation (UN) Committee for the Peaceful Uses of Outer Space (CPUOS), a subsidiary organ of the General Assembly (GA) composed of 61 states, established in 1958 and made permanent in 1959, whose debates revealed both doubts about a clear scientific basis for a precise demarcation of such boundary and reluctance to adopt such a line in the first place. The space powers believe that a fixed delimitation would be premature and impede progress of space technology. Moreover, an undefined upper limit of the airspace serves better national security considerations of states concerned about surrendering potential sovereign rights to the airspace when future technology allows the attainment of higher altitudes.

Originally in the realm of legal science fiction, since 1957 the law of outer space has had to keep pace with the rapid progress in space technology, beginning with the launching by the Soviet Union of the first artificial satellite in that year and the first manned flight in 1961; followed eight years later by the first successful landing on the moon and a safe return to the earth of United States (US) astronauts, an achievement subsequently repeated several times; the flight of the first re-usable spacecraft, the US space shuttle, in 1980; and the collaborative Russian–US construction of a space station, to mention only the major milestones in the development of space technology.

While no agreement exists on a fixed airspace–outer space boundary, consensus was quickly reached on some fundamental principles of outer space law. First, acquiescence in overflights of foreign satellites and space vehicles over national territory has given rise to a permissive rule of customary international law **(39)** that states have the right to place such objects in space orbit and fly them over other states' territory, and to implied recognition that states' sovereignty over airspace does not extend infinitely into space. Second, a rather ambitious view was adopted by the GA in 1961 and reaffirmed in the Outer Space Treaty of 1967 **(216)**, that (human) "international law, including the Charter of the United Nations, applies to outer space and celestial bodies." Third, there is consensus that outer space and celestial bodies are not susceptible to appropriation and are free for exploration and use by all states. Finally, there is a generally phrased principle that outer space and celestial bodies are to be used exclusively for peaceful purposes. In this regard the Test Ban Treaty of 1963 (480 UNTS 343) bans nuclear weapons tests not only in the earth's atmosphere and water but also in outer space. The 1977 Convention on the Prohibition of Military or Any Other Hostile Use of Environmental Modification Techniques (1108 UNTS 151) applies also to the protection of outer space. Issues related to peaceful uses of outer space are studied by the CPUOS. The above-listed basic principles of outer space law, as articulated by the GA, especially in its 1963 Declaration on Legal Principles Governing the Activities of States in the Exploration and Use of Outer Space, as well as the Outer Space Treaty, 1967, may now be considered part of general international law.

The general principles and rules of outer space law are further developed and implemented by numerous international agreements, the major of them being the Rescue of Astronauts Agreement of 1968 **(222)**; the Convention on Liability for Damage Caused by Space Objects of 1971 **(208)**; the Registration of Objects Launched out into Space Convention of 1974 **(220)**; and the Moon Treaty, 1979 **(211)**. Other, more controversial, matters for a possible codification **(5)** are on the agenda of the CPUOS. They include remote sensing **(221)**; direct television broadcasting **(196)**; geostationary orbit **(198)**; space debris; and the use of nuclear power sources in outer space. Detailed regulations related to outer space are also developed by competent specialized agencies of the UN, such as the International Telecommunication Union and the World Meteorilogical Organization, and, in satellite communication, by the International Telecommunications Satellite Organization **(201)**. On the regional level, the European Space Research Organization, established in 1975 and replacing two earlier agencies, issues rules and regulations to govern the European cooperation in space activities. Cooperation in such activities is also the subject of numerous bilateral agreements.

However, some major gaps in international outer space law still remain. The problem of the boundary between airspace and outer space remains unsolved, and in the area of telecommunications the controversial issues of direct television broadcasting and remote sensing await some kind of solution.

**216. Outer Space Treaty, 1967.** Drafted by the United Nations Committee for the Peaceful Uses of Outer Space, the Treaty on Principles Governing the Activities of States in the Exploration and Use of Outer Space, Including the Moon and Other Celestial Bodies, 1967 (610 UNTS 205), with more than 120 states **(127)** parties, incorporates the principles spelled out in the General Assembly Declaration of Principles on this subject in 1963 (31 ILM 157 (1964)). The Treaty proclaims the principle of exploration and use of outer space **(215)** for the benefit of all countries as "the province of all mankind" without discrimination and on the basis of equality **(73)** in accordance with international law (Art. I) and in the interest of maintaining international peace and security (Art. III). Exploration of outer space must be guided by the principle of cooperation and assistance and with due regard to interests of other states and without any harmful contamination of the celestial bodies and the earth itself. The Treaty also proclaims (Art. II) that outer space, including the moon **(211)** and other celestial bodies are not subject to national appropriation **(227)** by claims of sovereignty **(125)**. Unlike the Declaration, the Treaty includes provisions concerning the military uses of outer space. Under Art. IV the states parties undertake not to place in orbit around the earth any weapons of mass destruction or install such weapons on celestial bodies, or station them in outer space in any other manner. This demilitarization provision, analogous to that in the Antarctic Treaty of 1959 **(187)**, implies that the orbit of the earth may be used for other military purposes. As demonstrated by state practice, such use may include launching military reconnaissance satellites, for example, to verify compliance with arms control agreements. Furthermore, the moon and other celestial bodies are to be used exclusively for peaceful purposes; military bases and installations, testing of any type of weapons, and conduct of military maneuvers are prohibited. However, the use of military personnel for peaceful purposes is allowed as well as the use of any equipment or facility necessary for peaceful exploration. Adding to the Declaration, the Treaty provides for mutual inspection of stations, equipment, and facilities on the moon and other celestial bodies (Art. XII). Activities of non-governmental entities require authorization and supervision by the states parties which otherwise bear international responsibility **(128)** for national activities in outer space. Responsibility for activities of intergovernmental organizations **(84)** is to be borne both by the organization and by its members (Art. XI). A state that launches or procures the launching of an object into space, as well as the state from whose territory the launching takes place, are liable for damage caused by such object (Art. VII), a rule subsequently elaborated upon in the Liability Convention of 1971 **(208)**. The state of registration retains jurisdiction **(87)** and control over objects launched by it into outer space, and ownership of such objects is not affected by their presence in outer space or by their return to earth. If found beyond the limits of the state of registry, they must be returned to that state (Art. VIII). Registration of objects launched out into space is governed by a special convention **(220)**. Astronauts, as "envoys of mankind in outer space" must be rendered all possible assistance in the event of distress **(72)** or emergency landing on the territory of a state party and must be safely and promptly returned to the state of registry (Art. V). This provision was further developed in 1968 in a special agreement on the rescue of astronauts **(222)**.

**217. Ozone Layer Vienna Protection Convention, 1985 and the Montreal Protocol, 1987.** The framework Vienna Convention for the Protection of the Ozone Layer (1515 UNTS 293), in force **(271)** in 1988, complemented by the Montreal Protocol on Substances That Deplete the Ozone Layer of 1987 (26 ILM 1541 (1987)) in force in 1989, have the objective to protect the ozone layer, a veil of ozone a few millimeters thick, some 30 km above the earth, against depletion by certain harmful, human-emitted, chemical substances. The "layer of atmospheric ozone above the planetary boundary layer" (Art. 1(1) of the Convention) must be distinguished from ozone found near the earth's surface, a harmful pollutant which is not covered by the Convention.

The major substances regulated by the Convention are chlorofluorocarbons (CFC) and halons, which are used for refrigeration, air conditioning, aerosol propellants, and other applications, but some other chemicals, for example, methyl bromide used in pesticides, are also contributors. The Vienna Convention was adopted in response to the discovery by scientists of gaping holes in the ozone layer, especially in Antarctica, which shields the earth from excessive ultraviolet radiation from the sun, a phenomenon that can impair the immune system, cause skin cancer, and have other deleterious effects upon human health and the environment. There is evidence that chlorine gases and some other ozone-depleting substances also belong to greenhouse gases leading to global warming and climate change **(192)**.

As a framework instrument, the Vienna Convention deals mainly with institutional arrangements typical of many multilateral environmental agreements, such as the rules concerning the Conference of the Parties and the Secretariat, and with such problems as general obligations of the parties with respect to protecting the environment and human health from adverse effects of the ozone depletion; research and systematic observations; cooperation and exchange of information; adoption of protocols; amendments; and settlement of disputes. More specific details on eliminating or reducing the ozone-depleting substances are set forth in the Montreal Protocol (the "Protocol on Chlorofluorocarbons").

The Montreal Protocol provided for a phased reduction in the consumption of CFCs and imposed a freeze on halons. Soon, however, the original reduction rates were found insufficient and the parties, resorting to a rather unusual procedure, adopted, in Helsinki, a Declaration on the Protection of the Ozone Layer (28 ILM 1335 (1989) which called for phasing out the production and consumption of CFCs not later than 2000; phasing out halons; reducing other ozone-depleting substances; and developing environment-friendly substituting technologies. Further adjustments and amendments to the Protocol, necessitated by the need to move up the consumption and production targets, were made first by the Conference of the Parties in 1990 (30 ILM 537 (1991)) and subsequently in 1992 (32 ILM 874 (1993)). More recently, the Vienna session of the Conference of the Parties added the already mentioned methyl bromide to the list of the ozone-depleting chemicals. It called for a reduction of production of this powerful but short-living chemical in industrialized countries by 25 percent by 2001; 50 percent by 2005; with a complete phasing out by 2010. However, exemptions to the ban on methyl bromide are possible at the recommendation of a panel of experts. Thus in 2003 such exemptions were granted for the United States (mainly for strawberry and tomato growers) and some other countries. The developing countries were to stabilize the use of this pesticide at the average 1995–1998 levels by 2002. The timetable for eliminating the production of the less harmful hydro-CFCs was moved from 2030 to 2020. The production of such chemicals in developing countries was to be eliminated by 2016.

All these and other international legal measures against the ozone depletion seem to have been at least partially effective. Satellite data have shown a slowing down in the depletion starting in 1997. Thus in 2002 the Antarctic ozone hole decreased and in 2003 further monitoring of the ozone layer pointed to a further reduction in the destructive effect of the CFCs and other harmful chemicals. However, it is not yet entirely clear whether the improvement in the ozone layer represents a decisive reversal in the process of depletion.

**218. Persistent Organic Pollutants Convention, 2001.** The United Nations Environment Program–sponsored Convention on Persistent Organic Pollutants (40 ILM 532 (2001)) whose text was agreed on in Johannesburg by representatives of 122 countries, including the United States (US), in 2000, and which was opened for signature **(283)** in Stockholm 2001. The Convention was to come into force **(271)** once 50 countries had ratified it, which was expected to take place in 2003 or 2004. The objective of the Stockholm Convention is to ban completely or, in some cases, reduce production and use of 12 toxic pesticides and industrial chemicals (the "dirty dozen"), including DDT, dioxin, PCBs (polychlorinated biphenyls), and other substances, otherwise already banned in the US and some other countries. They are "persistent" because they tend to accumulate in living tissue with significant health hazards, resist degradation, and are transported through air, water, and migratory species across international boundaries and deposited in terrestrial and aquatic ecosystems. Among these toxic substances, the status of DDT, which is banned in 34 countries and restricted in 34 more, but still used in such countries as Mexico, China, India, and in many African states, was the most controversial issue in drafting the Convention. Some health experts, including those in the World Health Organization, backed the use of DDT for malaria control, while environmental groups, such as the Worldwide Fund for Nature, insisted on a total ban. The Convention allows tropical countries to use DDT for malaria control until a suitable substitute can be developed to combat this disease.

Upon entry into effect (probably in 2003 or 2004) the Stockholm Convention, modeled on the analogous but essentially regional Long-Range Transboundary Air Pollution Convention of 1979 **(209)**, is expected to eliminate eight of the persistent chemicals, including DDT. However, specific countries are granted the exemption for five pesticides. The use of DDT was permitted as an anti-malarian insecticide and PCBs were allowed for reduced use in electrical equipment, but new production was banned. In addition, incidence of two pollutants which are unintentional by-products from waste incineration and industry was to be reduced and minimized. The Convention obligates developed countries to provide $150 million a year for ten years to developing countries to help them phase out the use of the banned persistent organic pollutants.

**219. Prescription.** A controversial concept, derived from civil (Roman) law **(23)** and referring to acquisition **(227)** by a state **(127)** of sovereignty **(125)** over a territory **(228)** at one time under the sovereignty of another state, through uninterrupted and uncontested peaceful exercise of state authority which has persisted for an undefined period of time, sufficiently long to legitimize the status of the territory in the eyes of the international community as based on a valid title acquired under international law by the possessor state. However, this general definition has not been consistently applied in the doctrine and judicial practice. Moreover, while many publicists accept prescription as a mode of acquisition, a considerable number of authorities does not believe it has much utility in today's international law. In 1960 a judge of the International Court of Justice (ICJ) **(309)** in his individual (dissenting) opinion **(304)** in the *Right of Passage over Indian Territory* (Portugal v. India) (1960 ICJ Rep. 6) expressed the opinion that "prescription, a private law institution . . . finds no place in international law." The term "prescription" is also used with regard of situations, such as in the *Island of Palmas* Arbitration, 1928 (2 RIAA 829), where, by the test of effective control, the court decides on competing claims to a territory, or where a title is acquired through acquiescence or consent. Whether prescription belongs to the general principles of law recognized by civilized nations **(38)** is doubted by most authors. Still, as demonstrated by the United Kingdom arguments in its dispute with Argentina over the Falkland Islands, prescription, along with conquest **(194)**, is invoked to establish a title acquired at a time when these modes of acquisition were undoubtedly recognized. It can be added that in its judgment in the case of *Sovereignty over Certain Frontier Land* (Belgium/Netherlands) (1959 ICJ Rep. 209) the ICJ accepted the possibility of acquiring title to territory by prescription. However, international judicial practice has not been consistent in its appraisal of prescription, primarily because of the fact that—as noted further—although prescription is theoretically distinct from occupation **(214)**, the two concepts are very much entangled with each other and often indistinguishable in actual practice. In theory, prescription differs from occupation in that it applies to a territory which once belonged to another state or possibly was part of *res communis*, whereas occupation refers to acquisition of *terra nullius*, that is territory under no state's sovereignty. Therefore, a claim based on prescription requires a larger extent of exercising effective control than in the case of occupation. But effective control is a common and essential requirement for both occupation and prescription, and for that matter for all acquisition of territory. In reality the theoretical distinction between prescription and occupation is often blurred. It may not be clear whether a case involves an original occupation of *terra nullius* by a prior state, followed later by dispossessing acts of another state or whether from the very beginning both states have been competing in developing their respective cases for a valid title of occupation. In any event, international courts, as in the *Island of Palmas* and *Eastern Greenland* cases, have tended to base their decisions not on the theoretical categories of occupation or prescription, which frequently are not even specified by the court, but rather on the test of balancing the validity of arguments on the effectiveness of the display of state authority by the claimants over the disputed territory.

Acquisitive prescription in its standard meaning covered by the definition must be distinguished from the concept of immemorial possession which refers to titles to territory, frequently of unknown origin and presumed legal simply because they have existed *de facto* for a very long time and are recognized as the foundation of the territorial *status quo* in the contemporary international system. Apart from the concept of immemorial possession, prescription is derived from the more or less equivalent civil-law **(23)** institution of *usucapio.* However, whereas the Roman-law *usucapio* required good faith of the displacing possessor, an element also stressed by some publicists as essential for prescription in international law, most writers do not require the existence of good faith for purposes of prescription in international law. The suggested controversial concept of consolidation by historic titles differs from prescription in that it can also be applied to territories that are *terra nullius.*

The conditions for acquisitive prescription are similar to those required to be present for effective occupation, but in cases of prescription, possession must be clear and unequivocal and made public to the state concerned. It may be added that contemporary international law does not recognize the doctrine of the so-called adverse holding ("negative prescription") whereby the dispossessing state acquires a valid title by prescription simply through mere passage of time lasting a definite period, even without acquiescence of the dispossessed state but without any forcible self-help of the dispossessed state to regain the possession of the territory concerned. What kind of conduct indicates lack of acquiescence and thereby interrupts prescription is a matter of controversy. Some publicists regard diplomatic protests by the dispossessed state as sufficient to deny its acquiescence while others believe that protests **(44)** must be followed by some such steps as severance of diplomatic relations **(68)**, or referring the dispute **(299)** to the United Nations, to arbitration **(293)** or judicial settlement. Resort to force is not allowed in today's international law. In the *Chamizal* Arbitration (11 RIAA 309), 1911, involving the US-Mexico dispute in the area of international river law **(204)**, the commission ruled that Mexico's diplomatic protests sufficed to interrupt the prescriptive claim of the US. The length of time required for an eventual creation of a title to territory by prescription is a matter of fact depending on the circumstances of the case. Apart from the mere passage of time, manifold factors can contribute to the legitimization of the possessor's title. Among all those circumstances, acquiescence and recognition **(106)** by third states play a most significant role.

**220. Registration of Objects Launched Out into Space Convention, 1974.** The Convention on Registration of Objects Launched Out into Space (1023 UNTS 15) was adopted **(268)** by the General Assembly in 1974 and opened for signature **(283)** in 1975. It entered into force **(271)** in 1976, with more than 50 states parties at the turn of the century, including all the launching states. The Convention established a compulsory system of registration with the United Nations (UN) of objects launched into outer space, thus making it possible to keep a complete and open record of all satellites and other objects launched and authorized to be launched by any state party. The United States space shuttles are among the registrable space objects. The registration procedure is spelled out in detail in 22 articles of the Convention. It requires each state of registry to keep a national register and provide the UN with detailed information concerning the space object, including its registration number, date and location of launch, and technical information concerning the orbit and functions of the object, subsequently recorded on the central register of the UN. However, the Convention does not specify any deadline for registration of a launching. In cases of a joint launching, the states concerned are to determine, without prejudice to any agreements on jurisdiction **(87)**, which of them shall register the object.

**221. Remote Sensing.** The term "remote sensing" refers to the gathering of information from artificial satellites in outer space which are fitted with sensors enabling the launching state to acquire all kinds of data about the location and nature of the earth's natural resources. While remote sensing has the potential to bring enormous benefits in a number of areas, it raises various controversial technical, legal, and primarily political issues, and its status in international law is rather uncertain. Among the major disputed international law issues concerning this aspect of the outer space law **(215)** are: whether the principle of the free use of outer space implies the right to obtain data through remote sensing without a prior consent of the "sensed" state; who should be allowed access to data obtained from sensing without authorization of that state; and whether the "sensing" state is legally bound to give the sensed state access to such data and their analysis.

The United Nations (UN) Committee on the Peaceful Uses of Outer Space has been studying problems of remote sensing since 1971 and in 1975 established a working group on this subject. However, so far no agreement has been reached on the legal regime of remote sensing that would be acceptable to both industrialized and developing countries. Invoking the Outer Space Treaty's **(216)** principle of freedom of exploration and use of outer space, most industrialized nations, and especially the United States, have insisted on the freedom to sense and disseminate information at their discretion. On the other hand, many developing states have raised the arguments of permanent sovereignty of states over their respective natural resources and of exclusive sovereignty over the national airspace **(186)** which might allegedly be compromised by remote sensing. National security considerations also obviously contribute to reluctance to endorse the principle of the freedom of sensing by foreign-launched satellites.

In 1986 the General Assembly (GA) adopted a resolution on the principles of remote sensing based on the work of the UN Committee for the Peaceful Uses of Outer Space (25 ILM 1334 (1986)). Among its 15 principles the Resolution affirmed the right of free access to the use of outer space for purposes of remote sensing without prior consent, but at the same time upheld the sensed state's right of access, on reasonable and nondiscriminatory terms, to primary and processed data and analyzed information concerning the sensed state's territory. It also upheld the sensing state's right to disseminate information to third parties. The Resolution emphasized that remote sensing should be carried out for the benefit of all states, taking into particular account the needs of developing nations. The need to disclose information capable to avert harm to the environment was particularly stressed. The 15 principles adopted by the GA are not legally binding, but have the potential of contributing to the development of customary international law **(39)** governing the legal status of remote sensing.

**222. Rescue of Astronauts Agreement, 1968.** The Agreement on the Rescue of Astronauts, the Return of Astronauts and the Return of Objects Launched into Outer Space (627 UNTS 119) implements and develops Art. V of the Outer Space Treaty **(216)** concerning assistance to astronauts in distress and Art. VIII on return of objects launched into outer space to the state of registry. The Agreement regulates in detail the duties of states parties with regard to assistance to, and return to the state of registry of the personnel of a spacecraft in emergency and spacecraft landing outside the territory of that state. States have the duty immediately to notify, to the launching authority (a state or an international organization) **(84)** and the United Nations (UN), accidents in their respective territories and on the high seas **(245)** or other places outside the jurisdiction **(87)** of any state. They are also obligated to disseminate the news of accidents and to undertake all possible search and rescue operations when a spacecraft lands in their territory. If landing occurs on the high seas or another place not subject to the jurisdiction of any state, assistance is to be rendered if necessary by states in a position to do so. The obligation to return astronauts to representatives of the launching authority is absolute and unconditional. The astronauts involved remain under the jurisdiction of the state of registry. The Agreement also regulates the duties of states with regard to the return of space objects and procedures concerning recovery of such objects or any debris of a hazardous or dangerous nature. So far there has not occurred a contingency of astronauts landing in distress in a foreign territory. However, there have been cases of debris from space objects falling in such territory. In 1962 the United States returned a part of a Soviet satellite found in its territory to representatives of the Soviet Union at a meeting of the UN Committee for the Peaceful Uses of Outer Space.

**223. Rio Earth Summit, 1992.** The United Nations Conference on Environment and Development, held in Rio de Janeiro 20 years following the Stockholm Conference on Human Environment **(226)** and convened by a 1989 resolution of the General Assembly (GA) in order "to promote the further development of international environmental law **(197)**, taking into account the [Stockholm] Declaration of the United Nations Conference on Human Environment, as well as the special needs and concerns of the developing countries, and to examine, in this context, the feasibility of elaborating general rights and obligations of States, as appropriate, in the field of the environment, taking into account relevant existing international instruments."

The Rio Summit was the culmination of 20 years of a remarkable development of the environmental agenda by various international bodies, encompassing a plethora of international, global and regional, agreements, resolutions of the GA and other public international bodies, the work of the International Law Commission, the Helsinki Final Act of the Conference on Security and Co-operation in Europe, 1975 (14 ILM 1292 (1975)), as well as contributions by international non-governmental organizations (NGOs) **(86)** and other private bodies, such as the International Union for the Conservation of Nature (IUCN), engaged in developing international environmental law. Many NGOs were present at Rio in 1992 and organized their own global forum in order to publicize their views on environmental matters.

The Rio Earth Summit approved three documents: 1. Rio Declaration on Environment and Development of 27 non-binding principles (31 ILM 874 (1992)); 2 equally non-binding, the so-called Agenda 21 included in a very large (some 800 pages) and detailed action plan designed to guide the environment and development policies of states through the 21st century; and 3. a legally non-binding "Statement of Principles for a Global Consensus on the Management, Conservation and Sustainable Development of All Types of Forests." (31 ILM 881 (1992)). In addition, the Earth Summit witnessed the signing **(283)** of two international agreements: 1. United Nations (UN) Framework Convention on Climate Change **(192)** and 2. Convention on Biological Diversity **(188)**.

The concept of the so-called sustained development, found in the 1987 report of the World Commission on Environment and Development, was endorsed by a majority of states as the guiding principle in solving the environmental problems of the planet. As stated in Principles 3 and 4 of the Rio Declaration, sustained development is understood as development that equitably meets the needs of the present generations, especially the needs of the developing countries, without compromising the ability of the future generations to meet their own needs. But in order to achieve the goal of sustainable development, environmental protection must constitute an integral part of the development process and cannot be considered in isolation from it. Hence (Principle 6) all states and people must cooperate in eradicating poverty, as an indispensable requirement for sustainable development. Because of such understanding of the potentially legal concept of sustainable development, there was no wonder that the North-South conflict over this concept—apart from other differences—was a major feature of the negotiations **(316)** at the Earth Summit.

Most of the principles of the Declaration are in the nature of a program for future action. But there are some rules that have already been accepted in customary international law **(39)**: Principle 2 (reiterating Principle 21 of the Stockholm Declaration) concerning states' responsibility for transboundary environmental harm; Principle 7 on international cooperation in environmental matters; Principle 18 of the states' duty of immediate notification in cases of emergency likely to produce harmful transboundary effects; and Principle 19 on timely notification and relevant information on activities that may have a significant adverse transboundary environmental effect. Principle 17 on the states' duty to prepare an environmental impact assessment for proposed activities likely to have such effect may be an emergent rule of international environmental law, as reflected in a number of treaties and other international instruments. The same applies to Principle 15 on the precautionary approach whereby in cases of threat of serious or irreversible damage the lack of full scientific certainty of the danger cannot be used as a reason for postponing cost-effective measures to prevent environmental depredation. Whether the polluter-pays Principle 16, applied in cases of hazardous activities and endorsed by the European Union and the Organization for Economic Cooperation and Development, and referred to in some environmental conventions as a general principle of international environmental law, has crystallized into general international law, is not yet quite certain.

The optimistic expectations voiced at the Rio Earth Summit failed to materialize. A special session of the GA in 1997 (36 ILM 1639 (1997), convened to review progress achieved toward meeting the objective of the Earth Summit, concluded that the less-developed countries had not benefited from the globalization of the economy and still needed international assistance in achieving sustainable development. Moreover, despite some small progress in certain areas, the state of the global environment had continued to deteriorate. The 1997 Session found the major reasons for this state of affairs in failure to provide adequate financial resources by the Global Environment Fund (an international fund designed to support environmental projects in developing countries);

in a sharp decrease in the aid from rich countries; an inadequate transfer of appropriate technology; and the rising indebtedness of the developing states. Still, the Special Session formulated detailed proposals for making progress toward sustainable development and prepared a five-year program of work for the Commission on Sustainable Development in the years 1998–2002. However, no agreement could be reached on the major objective of the Session, namely, a political statement that would indicate how the objectives of the Rio Summit could be realized. The World Summit on Sustainable Development in Johannesburg, 2002, reviewed the implementation of the Agenda 21 plan of the Rio Summit and adopted a declaration on the action plan containing a number of objectives, but in essence the 2002 Summit failed to reach agreement on specific targets and commitments concerning social and environmental responsibility in international economic relations.

**224. Sector Claims.** Sector claims are assertions of claims or at least bases of claims to territorial sovereignty **(125)** in polar regions over all land and islands **(251)**, whether discovered, effectively occupied or not, enclosed within a triangular sector defined by a baseline or the contiguous land mass of the claiming state and two lines of longitude traced, in some cases, from the Eastern and Western extremities of the claiming state's territory **(228)** to the point at which they converge at the Pole. By itself, the sector doctrine does not constitute a valid basis for claims of title to territory. Furthermore, in practice the assertions of sector claims have been largely determined by the contrasting geopolitical features of the two polar regions. The North Pole region is not a landmass like Antarctica but an ocean area covered mostly by ice pack which, due to currents, is in constant motion, allowing research stations to drift on ice islands for up to two years. More importantly, sector claims in the Arctic are a method of expressing the doctrine of continuity or contiguity of the peripheral state since the Arctic Ocean is surrounded by land areas crossing the Arctic circle and under the sovereignty of the directly adjacent states: the United States (US), Canada, Denmark (because of Greenland), Iceland, Norway, and Russia. Among these states Canada and Russia, the main beneficiaries of the sector doctrine, claim the title to all land and islands (but not the sea beyond the territorial waters) **(262)** to the North, within sectors delimited by their respective Arctic coastlines within the meridian lines drawn to the North Pole from the Eastern and Western extremities of the contiguous landmass of each state. Neither state has claimed sovereignty over the ice shelves beyond the territorial sea. The legal status of this ice shelves area is not clear in international law. Some of the states bordering on the Arctic Ocean, and especially the US, Denmark, and Norway, do not accept the sector approach, but it appears that, since there are no outstanding disputes over land and island territories in the Arctic, the substance of the sectors claims there has been recognized either by treaty or simply by acquiescence.

In Antarctica **(187)**, unlike in the Arctic, there are no directly adjacent states whose territory could provide a geographical basis for raising sectors claims. Still, except for an unclaimed sector (90 to 150 degrees West longitude) political maps show that the Antarctic territory is "divided' into sectors: the largest, Australian, sector split by a narrow sliver of the French sector (Adélie Land); the three sectors of new Zealand, all with the 60 degrees latitude base; the Norwegian sector, 20 to 45 degrees East longitude, actually not reaching the Pole and with the Antarctic Circle as its baseline; and the sectors of the United Kingdom (UK), Argentina, and Chile. Under an Order in Council of 1962 the "British Antarctic Territory" consists of the land territory, mainly the Palmer Peninsula, and the islands (including also the Falkland Islands), situated between 20 and 80 degrees longitude West, with the base reaching north of the legal boundary under the Antarctic treaty. The sectors of Argentina (74 to 25 degrees West longitude) and Chile (90 to 53 degrees West longitude) overlap each other as well as the claim of he UK.

Unlike the situation in the Arctic, most of the Antarctic claims are based on the grounds of discovery. Against claims by Argentina and Chile, the British claim invokes a "long-continued and peaceful display of British sovereignty." Argentina and Chile apply the sector theory on grounds of proximity of the Antarctic Palmer Peninsula to their respective territories. The extent of the Argentine claim is drawn in its Eastern-most meridian by a projection that includes the British Falkland Islands (Islas Malvinas) as well as a Chilean island in the Beagle Channel. Generally speaking, the application of the sector doctrine to Antarctica cannot be regarded as providing, by itself, a valid basis for title to territory. In any case, under the Antarctic Treaty the territorial claims in Antarctica are held in abeyance for the duration of the Treaty.

**225. Servitude.** State or international servitude is a controversial legal concept, referring to an alleged existence in international law of servitude, by analogy to the civil-law **(23)** institution of servitude, in its substance similar to the common-law institution of easement. International servitude is a right *in rem* whereby by treaty or otherwise a part or the whole territory of one state (the "servient territory") is made liable to ordinarily permanent use by another state (the "dominant territory") for some specified purpose. A servitude can never involve an obligation of positive acts, but only a duty to endure something or to abstain from performing some action. Among the former category of servitude (assuming that this concept may apply to a burden on a state's territory) are, for example: the obligation to allow passage of foreign troops; the presence of foreign military or civilian personnel; and the use of the servient territory for such purposes as mining, water diversion, or free use of port facilities. The other category of servitude may involve an obligation to abstain from fortifying a certain part of the territory; maintaining armed forces there; levying duties in a certain area; or alienating a specific part of the territory.

On the analogy to private law, to be a servitude the right over territory must be a right *in rem*, which means that the ordinarily permanent legal relationship between the territories in question remains unaffected by a change in the sovereignty over either the servient or dominant territory; it must, so to speak, "run with the land" and can terminate only by mutual consent of the states concerned, by express or tacit renunciation of the state of dominant territory; merger or other consolidation of the territories under one sovereign; or—if the right is for an agreed term—by expiry of the term of servitude. Assuming the existence of an international servitude established by treaty, it is an open question whether such servitude can be terminated on grounds of fundamental change of circumstances **(273)**, an issue before the Permanent Court of International Justice (PCIJ) **(320)** in the case of *Free Zones of Upper Savoy and the District of Gex* (France/Switzerland), 1932 (PCIJ Series A/B, No. 46).

The major problem with international servitude is that this concept, being borrowed from private law rules governing land property, has been used rather extensively to encompass not only the rather rare cases of burdens on state territory, which in their substance and especially their legal effects can reasonably be compared to servitudes under private law, but also other kinds of rights that a state may acquire over a foreign territory. This includes not just rights *in rem* but also rights *in personam* to be in force between particular contracting states and not surviving a change in the sovereignty of one or the other state. In its award, within the framework of the Permanent Court of Arbitration **(319)**, in the *North Atlantic Coast Fisheries* case between Great Britain and the United States (US), 1910 (11 RIAA 173) involving the disputed extent of the British competence unilaterally to regulate fishing by US nationals exercising, under a 1818 treaty between Great Britain and the US, the right to fish "forever" in British waters off the southern coast of Newfoundland (the "treaty coast"), the arbitral tribunal **(293)** had to deal with the existence or not of the concept of servitude in international law. The US argued that the liberty of fisheries, including the right to use the coast itself for shelter and other purposes, granted to its fishermen, constituted an international servitude in favor of the US. Thereby, as further argued by the US, this grant resulted in a derogation from Great Britain's sovereign right over the territory and consequently a division of sovereignty which deprived Great Britain of the independent right to regulate the fisheries in the area involved. While not completely denying the possible existence of international servitudes, the tribunal rejected the US contention on the grounds that the right in question was not a sovereign right, but merely an economic one, and that the doctrine of international servitude was unknown to the drafters of the 1818 treaty, found little, if any, support in the modern doctrine, and was otherwise little suited to the system of modern sovereign states.

Leaving aside the controversial nature of the concept of servitude in international law, one can distinguish a number of situations involving some kind of permanent charge on state territory which are not treated as servitudes, in some cases not even in private law. First, there are certain universally recognized standards of behavior in customary law **(39)** which are not viewed as exceptional legal burdens. They involve certain rights and duties in relations between neighboring states, such as for example those applying in the utilization of water courses. Second, the customary institution of innocent passage **(248)** through foreign territorial sea and the treaty-based right of transit of landlocked states **(253)** also in fact constitute rights over another state's territory. Third, certain limitations concerning the use of national territory which apply not just to specific areas but the whole territory, for example, obligatory demilitarization, constitute general restrictions on a state's exercise of territorial sovereignty **(125)** and cannot be regarded as servitudes. Finally, as illustrated by the below-noted Aaland Islands case, a multilateral treaty may establish a special objective legal regime of permanent charges on a specific portion of a state's territory in the interests of not just a specific state but of the international community or a region as a whole. Although some authors refer to a servitude attached to the Aaland Islands (Finnish: Ahvenanmaa), this qualification is controversial in the doctrine. With regard to these islands in the Baltic Sea off the Swedish coast, but historically under the Russian sovereignty by virtue of a treaty of 1809 (60 CTS 457), Russia agreed by a convention annexed to the Treaty of Paris of 1856 ending the Crimean War (114 CTS 405) not to fortify the islands, an obligation to which—according to the decision of the Commission of Jurists, appointed by the Council of the League of Nations in 1920—Finland succeeded upon gaining independence in 1918. While expressing doubts concerning the existence of international servitudes, especially in the Aaland Islands situation where Sweden, not a party to the agreement of 1856, could not be regarded as the "dominant" state in relations to the "servient" territory of the Aaland Islands, the Commission ruled that, beyond purely Swedish interests, the provisions of 1856 had established a special objective regime of demilitarization in the interests of "European public policy." In the Commission's view, this regime, initially binding only the parties to the 1856 arrangement, was eventually extended to non-party but directly interested states, including Sweden, which acquired the right to insist upon compliance with the obligation not to fortify the islands. This obligation became binding upon any state that had sovereignty over the islands, now Finland. One must add that the existence of an objective treaty regime must not be easily presumed. It appears that such regime exists with respect to the operations of the Suez Canal **(261)** (referred to by a US Secretary of State as a "sort of easement" on the Egyptian territory), the Panama Canal **(258)**, and the Kiel Canal **(252)**. The objective nature of the Antarctic Treaty system **(187)** remains a controversial issue.

The issue of local charges, persisting irrespective of changes in sovereignty over the territory concerned, came up in 1932 before the PCIJ in the above-noted case of *Free Zones of Upper Savoy and the District of Gex* (France/Switzerland) and before the International Court of Justice (ICJ) **(309)** in the Court's judgment (1960) in the case of *Right of Passage over Indian Territory* (Portugal v. India). The former case involved the customs-free zones south of Geneva in the territory once under Sardinia's sovereignty, established for the benefit of Switzerland by the Final Act of the Congress of Vienna in 1815 (64 CTS 454). After Sardinia had ceded this Upper Savoy servient territory to France in 1859, France continued the territorial obligation of its predecessor in favor of Switzerland. However, eventually in 1919 Art. 435 of the Versailles Treaty of Peace (225 CTS 188) called upon France and Switzerland to negotiate the status of the territories in question found in the Treaty to be no longer consistent with the "present circumstances." But the Treaty did not make any statement to the effect that the territorial burden of 1815 had legally lapsed. On the other hand, Art. 435 expressly abolished the "servitude" concerning the neutralization (demilitarization) of certain French provinces bordering Switzerland. After failing to achieve agreement on the issue of the free zones, France and Switzerland brought the case before the PCIJ, asking the Court to declare whether Art. 435 in effect had abrogated the regime of the free zones. In its judgment of 1932 (PCIJ Series A/B, No. 46) the PCIJ, while refraining from getting involved in the doctrinal controversy over international servitude, decided for Switzerland by upholding the continued existence of the free zones purely on the basis of interpreting **(274)** Art. 435. The matter was eventually resolved by an arbitration **(293)** between the two countries in 1933 which still governs the regime of the zones. In its judgment on the merits in the *Rights of Passage* case (1960 ICJ Rep. 6) the ICJ recognized the existence of Portugal's right of passage over Indian territory with respect to non-military personnel. The Court found this right to be based on a consistent and uniform practice in local custom, dating back to the British rule and unaffected by the change in the sovereignty over the territories concerned. However, the ICJ judgment involved a special case of localized customary law **(39)** and the Court refrained from making any reference whatever to the controversial question of servitudes in international law.

**226. Stockholm Conference on the Human Environment, 1972.** An international conference held in 1972 in Stockholm on the recommendation of the United Nations (UN) Economic and Social Council, which is considered as a landmark in and the starting point for the development of international environmental law **(197)**. The Stockholm Conference unanimously adopted a seminal Declaration including 26 Principles to guide states in building up the law governing the protection and improvement of the human environment (11 ILM 1416 (1972)), and an Action Plan providing a framework for future international action in this regard (11 ILM 1421 (1972)). In addition, on the recommendation of the Conference, in 1972 the General Assembly established the UN Environment Program, a UN specialized agency with Headquarters in Nairobi, and created an Environmental Fund to be financed by voluntary contributions.

Among the 26 Principles of the Stockholm Declaration, Principles 21 and 22 are of special significance for international environmental law. While reaffirming the sovereign right of states under international law to exploit their own resources pursuant to their environmental policies, Principle 21 emphasizes their responsibility to ensure that activities within their jurisdiction **(87)** and control do not cause damage to the environment of other states or of areas beyond the limits of national jurisdiction. In a shift to the general global perspective, this formulation is broader than the rules already upheld in international arbitral awards **(293)** in such cases as the *Trail Smelter*, 1938, 1941, (3 RIAA 1911, 1938) and other United States–Canada cases (8 ILM 118 (1969)), and the *Lake Lanoux*, 1957 (12 RIAA 281) involving a dispute **(299)** between France and Spain. These awards focused only on specific physical harm to the environment and interests of particular states. Principle 21 has now become a universally recognized principle of international environmental law. In addition, Principle 24 called upon states to cooperate through treaties or other appropriate means in order to protect and improve the environment. Such cooperation has become a recurring theme and requirement in many conventions dealing with environmental matters. Principle 22 calls upon states to cooperate in developing further the international law regarding liability and compensation for victims of pollution and other environmental damage. There exists universal agreement that such cooperation is necessary, but in practice the development of consensus with regard to the law of states' liability for environmental damage has proved a difficult task.

The Stockholm Declaration formulated a number of other principles to govern the international management of the human environment. Some of them give expression to generally accepted propositions, such as Principle 8 that "economic and social development is essential for ensuring a favorable living and working environment for man." The right balance between development and environment has become a major theme in shaping international environmental law, as subsequently reflected in the work of the Rio Earth Summit in 1992 **(223)**. Whether the right to a healthy environment, affirmed in the Preamble and Principle 1 of the Stockholm Declaration, has actually become a legal right under international law is not certain.

**227. Territory, Acquisition of.** Acquisition of territory means acquisition by a state **(127)** of title to sovereignty **(125)** over this territory. The concept of title refers to all factual and legal evidence required under international law as the source and basis for a change in sovereignty over a territory. The traditional classification in the law of nations of the modes by which a title to territorial sovereignty could be transferred is a result of the historical feudal law view which tended to regard the state territory as a private estate of the ruler. Hence, in the 16th and 17th centuries the legal doctrine borrowed the civil (Roman) law **(23)** conceptualization of the rules governing acquisition of land property, adapting them to acquisition of territory in relations between states, with the now illegal mode of conquest (subjugation) **(194)** added to accretion **(184)**, occupation **(214)**, prescription **(219)**, and cession **(190)**. These five modes are categorized in civil law—but without much practical use in international law—according to whether the title is derived from that of a prior sovereign or not. Thus, in the traditional law of nations a title derived by cession was "derivative" whereas accretion, occupation, prescription, and conquest were considered "original" titles. These five modes of acquiring title to territory had their reverse image in the rules governing the loss of title: by accretion or other operation of nature; dereliction or abandonment, corresponding to occupation, which required actual relinquishment plus intention to give up sovereignty; prescription; cession; and loss of territory through conquest. Secession became another mode of losing title to territory, without a corresponding mode of acquisition. Although no longer wholly appropriate in the conditions of the modern world, the scheme of discrete modes of acquisition of territory, based on the civil law, is still essential to be acquainted with in order to understand and explain contemporary territorial issues and disputes **(299)** whose roots may go centuries back in history, as demonstrated by the reasoning in judicial decisions which often traces the relevant rules back to a distant past.

The rather rigid civil-law-based classification of the modes of acquiring territory by states was intended to apply to acquisition by occupation and "acquisitive" prescription of newly discovered territories, ordinarily regarded as *terra nullius* (under no sovereignty), and by—now illegal—conquest, on the one hand, and transfers by cession between already existing states on the other. In contemporary law, cases of cession have occurred, but there have been hardly any cases of occupation of *terra nullius,* the Rockwell situation being a rather unique case of occupation. Furthermore, beginning with the *Island of Palmas* Arbitration **(293)** between the United States (US) and the Netherlands in 1928 (2 RIAA 829), arbitral and judicial decisions have on the whole ignored the theoretical distinction between occupation and prescription, focusing rather on assessing the relative intensity of the continuous and peaceful display of state functions in the disputed territory by the competing claimants to sovereignty, which in the *Palmas* Arbitration was found to be "the constituent element of territorial sovereignty." In their appraisals, courts have tended in most cases to focus on the situation prevailing on the so-called critical date or dates. Generally speaking, the concept of critical date refers to the date on which the territorial sovereignty of a state must have existed in order to render invalid a competing claim or claims, and following which the legal situation is deemed to remain legally frozen. For example, in the *Palmas* case the year 1898, the date of the Treaty of Paris whereby Spain ceded the Philippines to the US, was found by the arbitrator to be such a date. Similarly, in the case of *Land, Island and Maritime Frontier Dispute* (El Salvador/Honduras) the International Court of Justice (ICJ) **(309)**, (Chamber) **(295)**, in its Judgment of 1992 (1992 ICJ Rep. 351) ruled that the year 1821, the date on which the colonies in question seceded from Spain, was the critical date.

As illustrated in major leading cases and expressed in the *Palmas* Arbitration "the establishment of sovereignty may be the outcome of a slow evolution, of a progressive intensification of state control." Normally, unlike title to land in municipal law **(27)**, title to territory in international law is a result of gradual growth where, if contending claims are involved, initially the title is often only relative, with the claimants aspiring to transform it into an absolute title and the court appraising the relative intensity of their state functions in the disputed territory. In this process of historical consolidation of title, the title is perfected through a variety of constituent elements, among which recognition by third parties and lack of protests or acquiescence play major roles. Estoppel, or its virtual equivalent, the civil-law concept of preclusion, in the sense of a legal bar preventing a state from asserting a claim or fact which is inconsistent with its previously taken position, often has the effect of acquiescence, but may hold a state to a position that in reality conflicts with its intentions. An example of estoppel in a territorial dispute is provided by the case of *Legal Status of Eastern Greenland* (Denmark v. Norway) decided by the Judgment of the Permanent Court of International Justice **(320)** in 1933 (1933 PCIJ, Series A/B, No. 52, 22). In this case, Norway, having in the past accepted treaties recognizing Denmark's sovereignty over the whole of Greenland, debarred itself from subsequently contesting Denmark's sovereignty in Eastern Greenland. The ICJ invoked estoppel in a few cases, including that of *Temple of Preah Vihear* (Cambodia v. Thailand) (1962 ICJ Rep. 6). In general, a multiplicity of factors and considerations may contribute to a decision on title to territory in a particular case. In contemporary international law, such elements as, *inter alia*, recognition, acquiescence, historical and geographical considerations (unity, contiguity, and continuity), and the principle of *uti possidetis* **(230)**, must be complemented by the overriding requirements of the claimant's compliance with the United Nations (UN) Charter's ban on the use of force **(329)** and by the principle of the right of self-determination of peoples **(122)**. However, by themselves historical or geographical arguments alone cannot create a valid title, but in cases of uncertainty and doubt over the extent of effective control by the claimants, may provide supporting evidence for the title.

Perhaps more than in other areas of international law, the rules governing acquisition of territory have been influenced by exercise of power and force. Territorial disputes arouse more passions than other kinds of international disagreements, with legal and political arguments invoked side by side, blurring the distinction between law and politics. It might be added that while border disputes are sometimes distinguished from disputes over the very title to sovereignty over a territory, the two are often intertwined and the distinction becomes blurred and not important in practice. While territorial disputes abound in many regions of the world, more serious is a situation where the whole territory of a state and its very existence are at issue.

The inadequacy of the traditional scheme of the modes of acquisition of territory was exposed in practice in the second half of the past century, primarily with respect to the decolonization process and, more recently, within the context of the disintegration of the Soviet Union **(133)** and Yugoslavia **(134)**. Here, acquisition of territory by an already existing state was not a typical form of transfer of territory; by far the most common case involved the acquisition of territory by a newly born state. While the question of title to territory as an essential element of statehood does not arise in the case of the well-established traditional members of the international community whose territorial component of statehood is universally recognized on grounds of immemorial possession, new states pose a theoretical problem with regard to acquisition of their territory since until a new state comes into existence there is no entity capable of acquiring title, a difficulty that cannot be resolved by resort to the traditional modes of acquisition of territory. On the whole, this problem is approached in the doctrine by reference to the criteria of statehood applied for the recognition of states **(116)**, and apart from any issues related to the succession of states **(132)** and the delimitation of disputed boundaries **(189)**, recognition of statehood automatically entails recognition of the territory under the sovereignty of a new subject of international law **(85)**. A distinction can be made here between the birth of a state by peaceful and constitutional means on the one hand, and—sometimes violent—secession on the other. In the former case the new state emerges by agreement with the previous territorial sovereign, a typical case in actual international practice, whereby the entity in question is granted independence by a legal act of that sovereign, automatically entailing the cession of the title to the territory involved. Where a new state comes into being against the opposition of the previous sovereign over the territory involved, the recognition of title to the new entity's territory will depend on recognition of its statehood by other states and ultimately by the dispossessed sovereign itself. The dilemma of acquiring a title to territory in the absence of an already existing state is resolved by various theoretical constructs, such as the constitutive theory of recognition **(109)** extended to acquisition of territory or treating the people of the seceding territory as acquiring sovereignty pending the establishment of a state. But this last-mentioned theory, which relies on the principle of the Friendly Relations Declaration of the General Assembly **(14)** proclaiming that a colony or other non-self-governing territory has a status separate and distinct from the state administering it and bestowing the status of legal entity upon the people of such territory, as also ruled by the ICJ in its Advisory Opinion **(291)** on *Legal Consequences for States of the Continued Presence of South Africa in Namibia (South West Africa) notwithstanding Security Council Resolution 276* (1971 ICJ Rep. 16), suffers from the limitations of the narrow UN conception of the right of self-determination **(122)** of peoples. In 2001 it could still, however, apply to East Timor.

**228. Territory, State.** State territory, one of the essential elements of statehood **(127)**, is a definite portion of the earth which is subject to the sovereignty **(125)** of a state. The spatial framework within which the state exercises its territorial sovereignty encompasses land with any inland waters, and—if it is a coastal state—internal waters **(249)** and the territorial sea **(262)** with their seabed and subsoil. Like the territorial sea, archipelagic waters are under the sovereignty of the archipelagic state **(231)**. State territory extends to the superjacent airspace **(186)**. The concept of territory also includes islands **(251)**, rocks, and reefs. Territorial sovereignty is not affected by the configuration of a state's territory or the fact that the territory is made up of parts that are separated from one another or constitute enclaves within other states (exclaves from the viewpoint of the state concerned).

Virtually all land territory is under the sovereignty of some state; isolated rocks in the ocean and a small sector **(224)** of Antarctica **(187)** are the only areas outside of the sovereignty of any state (*terra nullius* or, more generally, *res nullius*). In principle, subject to any treaty rules, they are open for acquisition by any state by occupation **(214)**. The concept of *res nullius* must be differentiated from that of *res communis* signifying a thing that belongs to all and—in contrast to *res nullius*—cannot be appropriated by a state or be subjected to any state's sovereignty. As a matter of fact, since the high seas **(245)** are the major instance of such common area, most of the surface of the earth constitutes *res communis.* Outer space **(215)** also belongs to this category. The concept of the so-called common heritage of mankind is derived from that of *res communis*, but has its own features related primarily to deep seabed (the "Area") **(232)** and outer space.

Despite the rise of transnational forces, territorial sovereignty remains the crucial and central concept in contemporary international law. Defined in the *Island of Palmas* Arbitration of 1928 (2 RIAA 829) as the "right to exercise [in a territory] to the exclusion of any other state the functions of a state," it constitutes the fullest and most complete rights over territory known to international law. As noted by the Permanent Court of International Justice **(320)** in the *Lotus* case (France/Turkey) (1927 PCIJ, Series A, No. 10), "the first and foremost restriction imposed by international law upon a State is that—failing the existence of a permissive rule to the contrary—it may not exercise its power in any form in the territory of another State." It is the fundamental principle of international law, as enshrined in the United Nations (UN) Charter (Art. 2(4)) that all members are required to "refrain in their international relations from the threat or use of force against the territorial integrity or political independence of any State." On the other hand, as stressed in the International Court of Justice Judgment in the *Corfu Channel* case (United Kingdom v. Albania) (1949 ICJ Rep. 4), every state must not allow knowingly its territory to be used for acts contrary to the rights of other states.

Although there may be some inconsistency in the use of the terms, the concept of territorial sovereignty implies a totality of a state's rights as such, whereas that of jurisdiction **(87)** refers to specific rights and claims. It must be added that the exclusive right of territorial sovereignty, including the right to transfer a territory, may be limited by treaty or even custom.

In the feudal era, the territory was considered to be owned as a private estate to be ruled by the monarch of the patrimonial state. Hence in modern times, although this notion has obviously become obsolete, the concept of territorial sovereignty bears a certain resemblance to ownership (*dominium*) in private law, as demonstrated by the concept of eminent domain (as in the government's right to expropriate private property) lingering in the legal language up to the present day. But the notion of modern territorial sovereignty encompasses the aggregate totality of the powers of a state's government over the territory and its inhabitants, sometimes referred to as *imperium*. However, there is a lot of confusion, inconsistency, and overlapping in the doctrine of international law concerning the use of and distinction between the terms of *dominium* and *imperium.*

Territorial sovereignty over a single territory may be divided, as in the case of condominium (or rather co-imperium) **(193)** or a federation **(77)**. Legally, sovereignty may be vested in one state, but exercised by another, as historically in the case of Bosnia-Herzegovina, in the years 1878–1908 still nominally under Turkish sovereignty, but administered by Austria-Hungary. More recently, the UN-administered Kosovo and East Timor illustrate administration of a territory by an international organization. In the former case, the territory, though administered by the UN, still remained under the nominal sovereignty of Yugoslavia (now the state of Serbia and Montenegro). In the case of East Timor before independence, the territory was notionally, according to the principle of self-determination **(122)**, first under the sovereignty of the Timorese people but administered by the UN, and subsequently became a fully-fledged state of Timor-Leste. Separation between nominal sovereignty and actual exercise of control over a territory may occur in the case of certain kinds of leased territory **(207)**.

**229. Tokyo Convention on Offenses and Certain Other Acts Committed on Board Aircraft, 1963.** An International Civil Aviation Organization–drafted Convention (704 UNTS 219), in force

1969 and with more than 160 states parties, including the United States, which provides for jurisdictional rules **(87)** to govern offenses and other acts which may or do jeopardize the safety of civilian aircraft or of persons and property on board or which jeopardizes good order or discipline on board. The Tokyo Convention is the first international multilateral agreement **(288)** to ensure that individuals committing criminal offenses and through their conduct jeopardizing the safety of the aircraft or persons on board in flight do not escape state jurisdiction for their acts. The Convention provides for jurisdiction of the state of registration while the aircraft is in flight or on the surface of the high seas **(245)** or on any other area outside the territory of any state. A non-registry state, such as the state in whose airspace **(186)** or on whose territory the aircraft is in flight when the offense is committed, or any other state, may not interfere with an aircraft in flight in order to exercise its criminal jurisdiction unless the offense has effects in its territory; or has been committed against its national **(175)** or permanent resident; or against its security; or constitutes a breach of any rule relating to the flight in that state; or where exercise of jurisdiction is necessary to meet any obligation under a multilateral treaty. The Convention grants extensive powers to the aircraft commander who, outside the airspace of the state of registration, has the power, if need be, to restrain persons on board; disembark them; or deliver them to the competent authority of a contracting state. The Convention does not provide for any obligation to extradite **(75)** offenders. In the case of a hijacking, contracting states must take all appropriate measures to restore lawful control over the aircraft and, where an unlawfully seized aircraft lands, must permit its passengers and crew to continue their journey, and to return the aircraft and its cargo to persons lawfully entitled to possession. Under the Tokyo Convention, hijackers are treated just like any other offenders on board. Hijacking and other offenses against the safety of aircraft are governed by the Hague Convention **(199)** and the Montreal Convention **(210)**, respectively.

**230. *Uti Possidetis* Doctrine.** In civil (Roman) law **(23)** the term *uti possidetis* referred to a judicial edict whose purpose was to preserve, pending litigation over immovable property, the existing state of possession by the parties. In the early 19th century, at the time of the disintegration of the Spanish colonial empire in Latin America, succession **(132)** states of this empire agreed to apply the principle of *uti possidetis* in their territorial disputes **(299)** with each other and later also with Brazil. Under this principle they agreed to base their territorial claims upon the borders of the administrative divisions (provinces, vice-royalties, captaincies general) of the Spanish colonial empire, as they were presumed to exist at the time of the declaration of independence, thus in effect transforming these internal administrative boundaries into international frontiers **(189)**. This principle was adopted by the successor states in the interests of stability and peace. However, since the boundaries between the old Spanish colonial provinces were often ill-defined and uncertain, a series of boundary disputes ensued, leading to military clashes and fiercely fought border wars between successor states. On the other hand, a number of arbitral **(293)** and judicial decisions involving various border disputes clarified and further developed the modalities of the principle of *uti possidetis* in contemporary international law. As a result, the principle applies not only to the transformation of administrative boundaries of a colonial empire into international frontiers but, more generally, in the absence of contrary treaty **(288)** arrangements, implies respect for the continuity of treaty-based borders in cases of succession. In the *Territorial Dispute* case (Libyan Arab Jamahiriya/Chad) (1994 ICJ Rep. 6) the International Court of Justice (ICJ) **(309)** stressed the principle of the continuance of such borders even if the treaty itself is terminated **(287)**. Two principles of the international law of treaties are relevant in this context: first, that a boundary established by treaty is not affected by a succession of states and, second, that the principle of fundamental change of circumstances **(273)** may under no circumstances be invoked as a ground for termination of a treaty if the treaty in question establishes a boundary. The doctrine of *uti possidetis* has also been adopted by governments and international tribunals with respect to boundaries in Africa. In 1964 a resolution of the Organization of African Unity (OAU) concerning border disputes pledged its members to respect the borders existing on achieving independence. Moreover, as noted by the ICJ (Chamber) **(295)** in the case of *Frontier Dispute* (Burkina Faso/Republic of Mali) (1986 ICJ Rep. 554), this principle prevails even over the right of self-determination of peoples **(122)**, which must be exercised without any disruption of the inherited colonial boundaries transformed into international frontiers. Arguments based on *uti possidetis* were also raised in disputes between Asian states, as illustrated by the case of *Temple of Preah Vihear* (Cambodia v. Thailand) before the ICJ (1962 ICJ Rep. 6) and in the *Rann of Kutch* Arbitration between India and Pakistan in 1968 (17 (RIAA 1). Finally, it is significant that, beyond a purely post-colonial situation, the principle of *uti possidetis* was applied to the boundaries of the successor states of the former Yugoslavia **(134)** and apparently also the Soviet Union **(133)**.

Where an *uti possidetis* line cannot be conclusively identified and no clear legal title is in existence, boundaries must be determined by an inquiry into the evidence of effective control (*effectivités*) over the disputed territory in the colonial period and in the post-independence practice, and ultimately by recourse to equity **(13)** as extensively analyzed by the ICJ Chambers in the abovementioned *Frontier Dispute* case and the *Land, Island and Maritime Frontier Dispute* (El Salvador/Honduras, with Nicaragua intervening) **(311)** (1992 ICJ Rep. 351).

# Chapter V
# The Geophysical Context II: The Law of the Sea

**231. Archipelagic States.** Under Art. 46 of the 1982 United Nations Convention on the Law of the Sea **(264)** (LOS Convention), an archipelagic state is a state constituted wholly by one or more archipelagoes and may include other islands **(251)**. An archipelago is defined as "a group of islands including parts of islands, interconnecting waters and other natural features which are so closely interrelated that such islands, waters and other natural features form an intrinsic geographical, economic and political entity, or which historically have been regarded as such." Under the pressure of archipelagic states, led by Indonesia, Philippines, Fiji, and Mauritius, the Convention establishes a special legal regime permitting straight "archipelagic baselines" **(233)** to be drawn around the outermost islands of the archipelagic state, thus creating for the waters included there a new legal concept of archipelagic waters. In fact, a number of archipelagic states had already claimed an archipelagic status, with some states even going beyond the innovation provided for in the Convention. As of the end of October 2003, 19 states had claimed archipelagic status.

The right to draw archipelagic baselines is granted only to those states which are made up exclusively of an archipelago or archipelagoes and islands. Thus, for example Spain is not an archipelagic state despite the fact that the archipelago of the Canary Islands is part of its territory. On the other hand, such states, as for example, the United Kingdom (UK) and Japan, are, in fact, archipelagoes, but do not normally consider themselves as such. Were it not for certain rules governing the drawing of the baselines, they could, in theory, be archipelagic states in the meaning of the Convention.

Under Art. 47 of the LOS Convention, an archipelagic state may draw archipelagic baselines joining the outermost perimeter of the islands and drying reefs of the archipelago, which serve as baselines from which the breadth of the territorial sea **(262)**, the contiguous zone **(235)**, the exclusive economic zone (EEZ) **(238)**, and the continental shelf **(236)** is measured (Art. 48 of the LOS Convention). The archipelagic waters with the superjacent airspace **(186)** and their bed and subsoil with the resources contained in them, are under the sovereignty **(125)** of the archipelagic state (Art. 49). The drawing of archipelagic baselines, which otherwise must be clearly indicated on charts, is subject to a number of conditions (Art. 47), in general following those governing the straight baselines: the need to include the main islands; not to depart to any appreciable extent from the general configuration of the archipelago; not to draw baselines to and from low-tide elevations, unless the elevation is situated wholly or partly at a distance not exceeding the breadth of the territorial sea from the nearest island or unless lighthouses or similar installations which are permanently above sea level have been built on such elevations; and the need not to cut off the territorial sea of another state from the high seas **(245)** or its EEZ. In addition, the Convention lays down certain precise quantitative rules. First, in the enclosed area the ratio of land to water must not be more than one to one, a rule designed to prevent archipelagic baselines from being drawn by states, such as, for example, the UK or New Zealand, which consist mainly of one large island or several large islands close together. However, some of the states in this category, for example Iceland, can draw their baselines according to the general rules governing straight baselines. Second, in order to prevent archipelagic states from drawing baselines around very distant islands in an archipelago or around the whole of a widely spreading archipelago of small islands, the ratio of land to water must not be less than one to nine, as is the case of Kiribati and Tuvalu, for example. Furthermore, the length of the baselines cannot exceed 100 nautical miles (one nautical mile equals 6080.20 feet or 1853.25 meters), except that up to 3 percent of the total number of baselines enclosing any archipelago may exceed that length, up to a maximum length of 125 nautical miles.

Within its archipelagic waters, the archipelagic state may draw closing lines for the delimitation of internal waters **(249)**, according to the general rules of the law of the sea (Art. 50). Existing agreements with other states, traditional fishing rights, and other legitimate activities of the immediately adjacent neighboring states, existing (not new) submarine cables (but not pipelines), and the right of innocent passage **(248)** through archipelagic waters must be respected (Art. 51). Perhaps the most important navigational right is the right of foreign ships and aircraft to expeditious passage over archipelagic waters and the adjacent territorial sea. This right of "archipelagic sea lanes passage" (Art. 53) is exercised on, under, and over the waters, in designated sea lanes and air routes, up to 50 nautical miles wide and approved by a competent international organization **(84)**, in this case the International Maritime Organization. If none are designated, the right is exercised through routes normally used in international navigation, a provision which is interpreted **(274)** to include aircraft as well. The archipelagic state concerned may prescribe traffic separation schemes for the safe passage in narrow lanes. In its essence, the archipelagic sea lanes passage is the same as the "transit passage" through straits used in international navigation **(260)**. As a matter of fact, the LOS Convention refers to a number of matters regulating transit passage as applying *mutatis mutandis* to archipelagic sea lanes passage (Art. 54).

As a result of the extensive scope of rights granted by the LOS Convention to foreign ships and aircraft in archipelagic waters, such ships and aircraft enjoy—at least in theory—more rights there than in the archipelagic state's territorial sea. But in practice, the municipal law **(27)** of some of these states has not yet conformed to the provisions of the Convention. Still, the innovative legal regime concerning archipelagic states strikes a balance between the aspirations of such states and naval and commercial interests of maritime nations. Generally speaking, at least the major features of this regime have crystallized into customary rules **(39)** of the law of the sea **(254)**.

**232. Area, The.** For purposes of the United Nations (UN) Convention on the Law of the Sea of 1982 **(264)** (LOS Convention) and the Implementation Agreement of 1994 **(247)** the term "Area" refers to "the seabed and ocean floor and subsoil thereof, beyond the limit of national jurisdiction" **(87)** (LOS Convention, Art. 1(1)(1)), that is, beyond the limits of the continental shelf **(236)** in the legal sense, as defined in the Convention. Approximately 60 percent of the total seabed belongs to the Area. However, the legal status of the waters superjacent to the Area and that of the airspace **(186)** above them remains unaffected. Under Art. 141 of the Convention the Area shall be used exclusively for peaceful purposes, a provision that is generally interpreted **(274)** in the same way as the analogous provision of Art. 88 that the high seas **(245)** "shall be reserved for peaceful purposes." It must be added that the widely accepted Seabed Treaty of 1971 (955 UNTS 115) prohibits the emplacement of nuclear weapons and weapons of mass destruction on the seabed and the ocean floor and in the subsoil. Under Art. 149 of the LOS Convention all objects of an archeological and historical nature found in the Area must be preserved or disposed of for the benefit of mankind as a whole, particular regard being paid to the preferential rights of the state or country of origin, or the state of cultural origin, or the state of historical and archeological origin. This provision may be relevant for the salvage of wrecks found on the deep sea floor. The matter is regulated in detail in the UN Educational, Scientific, and Cultural Organization (UNESCO) Convention on the Protection of the Underwater Cultural Heritage of 2001 (41 ILM 40 (2002)) which also governs such heritage in the exclusive economic zone (EEZ) **(238)** and on the continental shelf **(236)**. Under this Convention, states have a responsibility to protect underwater cultural heritage in the Area and require their nationals **(175)** and vessels flying their respective flags **(240)** to report any discovery or intended activity directed at such heritage. Any discoveries and activities must be reported by the states parties to the International Seabed Authority (ISA), **(250)**, which then makes available such information to all states parties, any of which may declare its interest in being consulted on how to ensure the effective protection of the underwater cultural heritage involved. Such declarations are based on a verifiable link to such heritage, with particular regard to be paid to the preferential rights of states of cultural, historical, or archeological origin (Art. 11). A number of states, including France and the United States (US) refused to sign the underwater heritage Convention because it failed to include the rule that, unless expressly abandoned, title to sunken warships remains vested in the state flag.

While not the most important issue at the Third United Nations Conference on the Law of the Sea (UNCLOS III) **(263)**, the legal status of the deep seabed was politically the most controversial one, primarily because of the possibility of mining minerals there. The question of deep-sea mining can be traced back to the events which eventually led to the convening of UNCLOS III. The famous address of Ambassador Arvid Pardo (Malta) in 1967 before the General Assembly (GA), proposing a declaration and a treaty concerning the reservation of the seabed and ocean floor beyond national jurisdiction to exclusively peaceful purposes and the use of their resources in the interests of mankind, introduced the topic. It was followed by the setting up of the Seabed Committee; the "Moratorium" Resolution of the GA in 1969, passed by a vote of 62 to 28, with 28 abstentions, barring any exploitation of the seabed resources pending the establishment of an international regime (10 ILM 419 (1970)); and the important 1971 GA Declaration of Principles Governing the Seabed and the Ocean Floor, and the Subsoil Thereof, beyond the Limits of National Jurisdiction (10 ILM 220 (1971)), passed by 108 votes to 0, with 14 abstentions. The Declaration declared these parts of the oceans to be the "common heritage of mankind" exempt from appropriation by any state or persons and to be governed by an international regime to be established under UN auspices. The less-developed countries hoped to benefit greatly from the exploitation of the resources of the deep seabed, primarily manganese nodules (found already in 1873 by the British explorer ship, the HMS *Challenger*), rich in high-grade manganese, iron, nickel, copper, and cobalt. A commercial exploitation of the manganese nodules was believed to be a real possibility in the 1970s after various technologies had been developed for this purpose by private seabed consortia.

Although the concept of common heritage of mankind was endorsed by all countries, there was a fundamental divergence of views on the interpretation of the concept between the developed and developing nations. Both agreed that the seabed and the ocean floor of the Area were not *res nullius*; they were not things without any owner, subject to national appropriation **(227)**. Hence, all agreed that no state could claim or exercise sovereignty **(125)** over any part of these marine spaces or its resources. However, most industrialized nations, including especially the US, regarded the deep seabed as *res communis*, in the sense of things that, in this case, under the principle of the freedom of the seas **(242)** were under international law, though not subject to sovereign appropriation, open to use and utilization by any state technologically able to mine the seabed. On the other hand, a majority of states, mainly less-developed countries, concerned that under this interpretation the technologically advanced Western nations would be the main beneficiaries of the optimistically expected exploitation of the manganese nodules, promoted the meaning of the common heritage of mankind as an undivided asset to be shared by all nations, irrespective of technological capabilities, under the management of an international regime to be established by the UN.

The contrasting approaches to the interpretation of the concept of common heritage of mankind were reflected at UNCLOS III, which, despite certain concessions to the developed countries, in essence introduced, in Part XI of the LOS Convention, the idea of the common heritage as promoted by the Group of 77 (the developing countries whose number had grown to some 120 by the opening of UNCLOS III). Under this scheme, access to the seabed and recovery of its minerals was to be controlled by the ISA, which itself was to engage in the mining operations through its "Enterprise," under the so-called parallel system of exploitation devised as a concession to the developed states. Generally speaking, under this system, a state or a company would submit to the ISA a proposal on exploiting a site in the seabed with commercial possibilities, and the ISA would allow half of it to the prospective miner, under a contract with the Authority, while the other half would be reserved for use by the Enterprise and by developing countries. Contractors would be obliged to transfer the necessary technology on commercial terms, and production limitations were provided for to minimize harm to land-based producers of the minerals in question. In addition to Part XI (Arts. 133–191) of the Convention itself, an elaborate and complicated system of rules of Annex III governed in detail the conditions for prospecting, exploration, and exploitation of the Area.

Part XI of the LOS Convention proved to be unacceptable to the US and a number of other industrialized nations, which refused to ratify the LOS Convention, objecting, *inter alia*, that—as it stood—the structure of the seabed-mining regime failed to secure them influence commensurate with their interests; displayed features inconsistent with the free market principles; created a cumbersome bureaucratic structure; and in general impeded access by the industrialized countries to the resources of the deep seabed. Even Resolution II of UNCLOS III, adopted at its 11th session in 1982, which as a last compromise offered a privileged preferential treatment to so-called pioneer investor companies which had made considerable investments in deep-seabed mining, could not induce adherence to the Convention of the Western states possessing appropriate mining technology. Some of these states (including the US, United Kingdom (UK), France, Italy, and Japan) adopted analogous seabed mining legislation enabling them to coordinate regulation of seabed mining in their mutual relations. This "Reciprocating States Regime" was internationally institutionalized in an Agreement of 1982 between the US, UK, France, and the Federal Republic of Germany (21 ILM 950 (1982)) which recognized mining authorizations in the parties' mutual relations, but the parties stressed the interim nature of the Agreement which was to apply only pending the entry into force **(271)** of the LOS Convention. Another agreement, joined by some other Western states and known as Provisional Understanding Regarding Deep Seabed Matters, 1984 (23 ILM 1365 (1984)) dealt with procedures to follow in order to avoid overlapping claims to seabed sites. An Agreement of 1987 (26 ILM 1503 (1987)) between non-signatory states and states recognizing the Convention's deep-seabed regime dealt with the same matters.

The Group of 77 and the Preparatory Commission for the ISA and for the International Tribunal for the Law of the Sea, briefly known as PrepCom, criticized the unilateral legislation of the reciprocating states as allegedly contrary to customary law **(39)** of the sea as evidenced by the 1970 Seabed and other GA resolutions, and the PrepCom ruled that any claims that were not based on the Part XI regime were illegal. However, suggestions for referring this controversial issue for an advisory opinion **(291)** of the International Court of Justice **(309)** were not followed. The PrepCom proceeded to implement the deep-seabed regime after four pioneer investors (France, India, Japan, and the Soviet Union) applied for registration of their claims in 1986. Departing from various provisions of the Convention, the PrepCom adopted an Understanding on new procedures which granted far-reaching concessions to the applicants. As a result, the applications of the four countries were approved. Another Understanding concerning pioneer investors was adopted by PrepCom in 1990, but failed to attract the US, UK, and the Federal Republic of Germany to accede **(267)** to the Convention.

By the early 1990s, the political and economic changes related to the end of the Cold War as well as a marked decline in commercial interest in deep-seabed mining, brought the developing countries to the realization that an exploration of the Area was highly unlikely in the near future, but that adherence to the LOS Convention of the developed countries was indispensable in order to fund the institutions created by the Convention. All these factors facilitated the adoption by the GA of the Implementation Agreement of 1994 which substantially revised Part XI and Annex III in a way meeting the objections of the industrialized countries. As a result, the deep-seabed regime is now governed by Part XI of the LOS Convention, as modified **(269)** by the 1994 Agreement **(247)**. A necessarily brief outline of this revised but still rather complex legal regime is as follows.

Under Art. 134(2) of the Convention the deep-seabed regime governs "activities in the Area" defined in Art. 1(3) as all activities of exploration for and exploitation of the mineral resources. Prospecting does not require prior authorization, subject to environmental regulations; a notification to the ISA is sufficient to engage in prospecting. The principle of the common heritage of mankind is reaffirmed in the GA resolution which adopted the Implementation Agreement of 1994, but subsequent revisions carried out in the Convention indicate that the developed nations' understanding of this principle is now accepted for the legal regime of the Area. However, considering the decision-making structure of the ISA, as thoroughly reformed in their favor by the Agreement of 1994, the industrialized countries could afford making all mining activities subject to the authorization by the ISA and accept the principle of Art. 137(2) to the effect that "[a]ll rights in the resources of the Area are vested in mankind as a whole, on whose behalf the Authority shall act."

The parallel system of exploitation is now significantly affected by the diminished status of the Enterprise, originally conceived as the operating arm of the Authority. Mining rights can be acquired by states parties or qualified state-sponsored entities (Art. 153 of the Convention; Annex III, Arts. 3, 4). The application fee is reduced (Agreement, sec. 8(3)) from the original $500,000 to $250,000 for each phase of operations (exploration or exploitation). Applications are reviewed by the Legal and Technical Committee which makes recommendations to the Council of the ISA on the approval of applicants' plans of work and their qualifications. The 1994 Agreement introduces provisions designed to deal with any applications in a timely manner (Sec. 3(1)). It also requires the ISA to approve plans of work for exploration for a period of 15 years, following which an applicant must apply for approval of a plan of work for exploitation, but a four-year extension may be granted under the circumstances. Approval of plans of work accords exclusive rights in respect of a specific resource in the area in question (Convention, Annex III, Art. 16). Approval of an exploration plan confers a priority right for approving the exploitation plan; the latter may be withdrawn for reasons of unsatisfactory performance. Pioneer investors which have already registered mining sites with the PrepCom under Resolution II of the Final Act of UNCLOS III enjoy special treatment (Annex III, sec. I(6)(a)(ii)) which was accorded pioneer investors from China, India, France, Japan, Russia, South Korea, and a joint consortium of Eastern European states and Cuba, to which contracts were issued in 1998. Consortia licensed by Germany, US, and UK were to be approved under certain conditions, such as, *inter alia*, spending at least $30 million on relevant research, but arrangements with them must be no less favorable than with those with the first group of pioneer investors (Convention, Annex III, sec. 1(6)(a)(i)(iii)). The provisions of Annex III to the Convention, which envision setting aside "reserved sites" for the Enterprise, remain in principle in force, subject to conditions imposed by the 1994 Agreement on this temporarily inactive organ of the ISA: initial operations through joint ventures; sound commercial principles; plans of work in contract form as in the case of other miners; and no mandatory transfer of technology. Special provisions of the Agreement modify Arts. 8 and 9 of the Convention's Annex III concerning reservation of areas for the Enterprise.

The Agreement of 1994 eliminates or simplifies the extremely complex and rigid terms of the contracts envisioned by the Convention in Art. 13 of Annex III. It requires the system to be fair to both the ISA and the miners with rates comparable to those prevailing in land-based mining. The $1 million annual fee under the Convention is eliminated, the fee to be fixed by the ISA Council during the commercial production. The fee can then be credited against payments due under royalty or profit-sharing arrangements.

In its original text, Part XI of the Convention called for production limitations to protect land-based producers and for mandatory transfer of technology by national investors to developing nations and the Enterprise. The Agreement of 1994 (Annex, secs. 5(2) and 6(7)) explicitly eliminates these provisions and bases the production policy of the ISA on sound commercial principles. Bringing the seabed-mining regime up to the rules of the General Agreement on Tariffs and Trade/World Trade Organization system, it prohibits any contrary subsidization of activities in the Area and any discrimination in access to markets between sea-based and land-based minerals (Annex, sec. 6(1–6)). The provision of Art. 151(10) of the LOS Convention on compensating developing countries for adverse economic effects of seabed mining is implemented (Agreement, sec.

7) by a provision contemplating the establishment of an economic assistance fund which, however, may be financed only from revenues from seabed mining and voluntary contributions. Acquisition of technology (Annex, sec. 5) by developing countries and the Enterprise must take place on the open market on fair and reasonable commercial terms and conditions, consistent with the effective protection of intellectual property rights.

The Agreement of 1994 introduced an important revision of the LOS Convention by meeting the concerns of the US and other industrialized countries over the provisions relating to the Review Conference for Part XI, which would have enabled such Conference to adopt key modifications in the otherwise unacceptable rules governing deep-seabed mining, over the objections of states parties. The Agreement (Annex sec. 4) eliminates the provisions of Art. 155 of the Convention requiring a Review Conference to be convened 15 years after the beginning of the commercial production. On the other hand, the Agreement allows a review at any time, but only on the recommendation of the Council of the Authority and subject to the amendment procedures of Arts. 314–316 of the Convention, which in view of the decision-making system in the Authority's organs, and especially the Council, ensures the US a veto over any unacceptable amendments. In addition, rights acquired under mining contracts and the fundamental principles governing the Area, referred to in Art. 155(2) (such as, *inter alia*, the concept of common heritage of mankind; the exclusion of claims of sovereignty; the protection of the marine environment; the legal status of the superjacent waters; and the use for peaceful purposes only), must be preserved in any amendment.

By the turn of the century a legal regime for regulating the exploration and exploitation of the deep-seabed resources was already in place. However, there has been realization that a commercial mining of the Area is a matter for the distant future in view of the more than adequate reserves of minerals on land, and manganese nodules found on the ocean floor of exclusive economic zones and even the territorial sea of some countries.

**233. Baselines.** Baselines are the lines from which the breadth of the territorial sea **(262)** and other maritime zones of a state **(127)**, such as the contiguous zone **(235)**; the exclusive economic zone (EEZ) **(238)**; if still existing, fishery zone **(239)**; and, in some circumstances, the continental shelf **(236)**, are measured. A baseline forms the boundary between internal waters **(249)** on its landward side and territorial sea on its seaward side. The tracing of baselines along the coast is important because a state's baseline claim can extend the state's sovereignty **(125)** and maritime jurisdiction **(87)** seaward, to the detriment of other states navigational, overflight, and other interests. The rules for drawing baselines are codified **(5)** in Arts. 5–11, 13, and 14 of the United Nations (UN) Convention on the Law of the Sea, 1982 (LOS Convention) **(264)** which, in general, reflect customary rules **(39)** of the law of the sea **(254)**.

The law of the sea differentiates between normal baseline and straight baselines. The normal baseline is the low-water line along the coast as marked on large-scale charts officially recognized by the coastal state in question (Convention Art. 5). As noted by the International Court of Justice (ICJ) **(309)** in the celebrated *Fisheries* case (United Kingdom v. Norway) (1951 ICJ Rep. 116), under this method the baseline either follows all the curves, bends, and sinuosities of the coast (*tracé parallèle*) or is established by drawing arcs of circles from points along the low-water line (*courbe tangente*). In the case of islands **(251)** situated on atolls or islands having fringing reefs, the baseline is the seaward low-water line of the reef, as shown by the appropriate symbol on charts officially recognized by the coastal state (Art. 6). However, the Convention does not deal with the question of the distance of the reef from the coast. Low-tide elevations, that is, naturally formed areas of land (for example, sandbars), which are surrounded by and above water at low tide but submerged at high tide, may be used as baselines for measuring the breath of the territorial sea if they are situated wholly or partly at a distance not exceeding the breadth of the territorial sea from the mainland or an island. If they are wholly situated beyond that distance, they generate no territorial sea of their own (Art. 13). The outermost permanent harbor works which form an integral part of the harbor system (but not off-shore installations and artificial islands) are regarded as forming part of the coast and can be used for delimiting the territorial sea (Art. 11). Examples are jetties, wharves and quays, and breakwaters before a harbor.

The purpose of the other category of baselines, the straight baselines, is to allow the coastal state, if it so desires, to enclose waters which, because of their closeness to the coast, have the character of internal waters, or to eliminate a complex pattern of coastal configuration that would otherwise result if normal baselines were to be used. The initial rationale of straight baselines, namely, protection of the coastal state's interests, has lost much of its relevance; hence, they should be used sparingly to avoid interference with the navigational interests of other users of the sea. Under the LOS Convention (Art. 7), straight baselines joining appropriate points of the coast may (but need not) be used only in localities where the coastline is deeply indented and cut into or if there is a fringe of islands along the coast in its immediate vicinity. In case of rivers flowing directly into the sea without forming an estuary, the baseline is formed by a straight line drawn across the mouth of the river between points on the low-water line of its banks (Art. 9). If a river does not flow directly into the sea, but via an estuary, baselines are governed by the provisions on bays **(234)**. As shown by the 120-mile wide line drawn in 1961 by Argentina and Uruguay across the mouth of the River Plate, the concept of the river flowing directly into the sea may be used (or abused) quite liberally.

The use of straight baselines is subject to specific criteria (Art. 7). First, they must not depart to any appreciable extent from the general direction of the coastline, and the sea area within the lines must be sufficiently closely linked to the land domain to be subject to the regime of internal waters. Second, the lines may not be drawn to and from low-tide elevations, unless they contain lighthouses or similar installations which are permanently above sea level, or except in instances where the drawing of baselines to and from such elevations has received general international recognition **(106)**. Third, the system of straight baselines may not be applied by a state in such a manner as to cut off the territorial sea of another state from the high seas **(245)** or an EEZ. This provision applies to exceptional situations where a small state is located within a larger one, for example, Monaco and France, or where small islands of a state are situated close to the territory **(228)** of another state, as is the case in the Aegean Sea. There, by using straight baselines, Turkey could cut off the territorial sea of Greek islands very near its coast. In addition (Art. 8(2)), where the establishment of straight baselines has the effect of enclosing as internal waters areas which had not previously been considered as such, a right of innocent passage **(248)** shall exist in those waters, a provision that also applies with respect to the transit passage through straits **(260)**. Finally, the fourth requirement is (Art. 16) that straight baselines must be clearly indicated on duly publicized charts. While economic interests as such are not a valid reason for the location of particular straight baselines, the Convention (Art. 7(5)) allows taking account of economic interests peculiar to the region concerned, the reality and the importance of which are clearly evidenced by usage.

The LOS Convention introduces a special provision (Art. 7(2)) governing the exceptional situation of straight baselines along coastlines which are "highly unstable" because of the presence of a delta and other natural conditions. In such cases the appropriate points may be selected along the furthest seaward extent of the low-water line and, notwithstanding subsequent regression of this line, the straight baselines shall remain effective until changed by the coastal state. Among other contested aspects of this provision, it is not clear whether it requires that the coastline should be indented or fringed with islands under the general rules governing straight baselines. In this connection, it may be noted that the unique case of the baselines drawn by Egypt in 1990 around the Nile delta, parts of whose waters retreat at the rate of 40 meters a year, was objected to by the United States (US) on grounds that the coastline there fails to meet the criterion of deep indentation or fringe of islands.

The straight baselines method, applied by Norway since the 19th century to parts of its island-fringed coastline (*skjaergaard*), was the subject of the above-noted *Fisheries* case before the ICJ between the United Kingdom (UK) and Norway. Against the UK objection that the Norwegian decree of 1935, which delimited straight baselines along the northern part (north of 66 degrees) of Norway's coast, was contrary to international law, the ICJ, in its judgment of 1951 upheld the validity of straight baselines under the conditions which were subsequently followed in the Convention on the Territorial Sea and the Contiguous Zone, adopted by the Geneva Conference on the Law of the Sea in 1958 **(243)**, and eventually also in the LOS Convention of 1982.

In view of the fact that the relatively imprecise rules of the LOS Convention regarding the use of straight baselines, which on the whole reflect the customary law on the subject, allow states sufficient latitude in drawing such lines, this method, in principle designed to be applied in exceptional geographical circumstances, has been used and abused by a number of states. As of the end of October 2003 the legislation of 89 countries provided for straight baselines, including straight lines across the mouths of rivers and across the mouths of bays. Thus, *inter alia*, straight baselines have been drawn along coasts that are not "deeply indented," for example the cases of Albania, Cuba, Italy, Senegal, and Columbia. The 131-mile long baseline in the Caribbean of the last-mentioned state is drawn along a coast lacking any island fringe. Incidentally, the position of the US is that a straight baseline segment should not exceed 24 miles in length and that the "general direction of the coast" should be assessed by reference to general direction lines not exceeding the length of 60 miles in each locality. Some states, for example Iceland, Iran, Italy, Malta, Thailand, and especially Vietnam, have drawn straight lines along coasts which, while having some offshore islands, lack any fringe of islands "in immediate vicinity." Other states, especially Ecuador and Myanmar, have drawn straight baselines that appreciably depart from the "general direction of the coast." In the case of Myanmar, the enclosure of a sea area by a 222-mile long straight baseline, some 75 miles from land, also conflicts with the criterion of close link to the land domain, enclosing large areas of the ocean as internal waters. Still some other countries disregard the rule concerning disallowing basepoints on low-tide elevations (Saudi Arabia, Syria); cut off territorial seas of another country from the high seas or EEZ (Morocco with regard to cutting off Spain's territorial sea in respect of the Spanish territories of Ceuta and Melilla); simply locate basepoints for straight baselines in the sea (Bangladesh) or even in another state's territory (Colombia); or have not given due publicity (Art. 16) to baseline charts or lists of coordinates and failed to deposit them with the Secretary-General of the UN (Haiti, North Korea, Malaysia). Some of the extravagant applications of straight baselines have prompted objections by other states. On the other hand, some doubtful cases may have been acquiesced to or tolerated even though the abuse of the straight baseline method has pushed the sovereignty of the coastal states involved further seaward and enclosed considerable marine spaces on the landward side of the straight baselines as internal waters of such states.

**234. Bays.** There are three kinds of bays under the law of the sea **(254)**: 1. bays the coast of which belongs to a single state **(127)** ("juridical bays"); 2. the so-called historical bays; and 3. bays bordered by more than one state. Only the rules governing the status of the first kind of bay have been codified **(5)**, first, in Art. 7 of the Convention on the Territorial Sea **(262)** and the Contiguous Zone **(235)** (Art. 7), adopted by the Geneva Conference on the Law of the Sea of 1958 **(243)**, and then, in virtually identical terms, in Art. 10 of the United Nations (UN) Convention on the Law of the Sea of 1982 (LOS Convention) **(264)**. The legal status of the other two kinds of bay continues to be governed only by customary law **(39)**.

The 1982 LOS Convention uses the term "bay," but the term "gulf," often referring to an ocean inlet larger than a bay, is in practice used interchangeably with the term "bay." For the purposes of the Convention, which—it must be borne in mind—deals only with bays the coasts of which belong to a single state (the first kind of bay), a bay is defined as "a well-marked indentation whose penetration is in such proportion to the width of its mouth as to contain land-locked waters and constitute more than a mere curvature of the coast." Furthermore, an indentation shall not be regarded as a bay unless its area is as large as, or larger than, that of a semi-circle whose diameter is a line drawn across the mouth of that indentation. For the purposes of measurement, the Convention provides that the area of an indentation is that lying between the low-water mark around the shore of the indentation and a line joining the low-water mark of its natural entrance points. If any islands **(251)** produce more than one mouth, the semi-circle is drawn on a line as long as the sum total of the lines across the different mouths. Islands with an indentation are included as if they were part of the water area of the indentation. The Convention fixes 24 nautical miles (one nautical mile equals 6080.20 feet, that is 1853.25 meters) as the maximum distance between the low-water marks of the natural entrance points of a bay. The waters enclosed thereby are considered as internal waters **(249)**. Where the distance between the low-water marks of the natural entrance points exceeds 24 miles, a straight baseline of 24 miles is drawn within the bay in such a manner as to enclose the maximum area of water that is possible with a line of that length. The Convention provides that all these foregoing rules do not apply to "historic" bays, or in any case where the system of straight baselines **(233)** is applied.

While a progress compared with customary law, the Convention's provisions on juridical bays are not free of uncertainties. For example, it may sometimes not be clear where the "natural entrance points" of an indentation are located in the case of estuaries, or to what extent lagoons (a maritime area of shallow water between the coast and sandy dunes) should be included for the purposes of measurement.

The status of historic bays is rather controversial. It is governed by customary law, but—as ruled by the International Court of Justice (ICJ) **(309)** in the cases of *Continental Shelf* (Tunisia/Libyan Jamahiriya) (1982 ICJ Rep. 18) and (Chamber) **(295)**, *Land, Island and Maritime Frontier Dispute* (El Salvador/Honduras, with Nicaragua intervening) **(311)**, (1992 ICJ Rep. 351)—each case of a claimed historic bay is subject to a legal regime determined by its specific circumstances. Certain general standards for establishing a valid claim to a historic bay were suggested by a UN Secretariat study in 1962. According to this study, to meet the standards of customary law a claimant state must, for a considerable period of time, have claimed the bay as internal waters and must demonstrate its open, effective, long-term, and continuous exercise of authority over the bay with acquiescence of other states. There seem to exist no limits as to the maximum permissible length of the closing lines of an historic bay. When that length was still in doubt, prior to the adoption of the 24-mile rule, the United States (US) claimed the Delaware and Chesapeake Bays as historic bays, but now these two inlets of the Atlantic Ocean, in any case, satisfy the 24-mile criterion of measuring the entrance to a bay under the contemporary law of the sea; they are simply juridical bays. Some 20 states claim historic bays, with the validity of some claims contested by other states. Thus, for example, the US denies the status of historic bay to Canada's Hudson Bay, Italy's Bay of Taranto, and Russia's Peter the Great Bay, the last two claims not accepted as historical bays by the United Kingdom as well.

Among the most extravagant claims to historic bays is Libya's claim to the Gulf of Sidra (Sirte) proclaimed by that state in 1973, with the resulting closing line as wide as 296 miles across the Gulf. This claim which, because of failure to meet the fundamental criteria under customary international law, prompted protests from a number of countries and led to armed incidents in the Gulf of Sidra between Libya and the US in 1981 and 1986.

The third kind of bay, the bays bordered by more than one state, for example, the Passamaquoddy Bay, an inlet of the Bay of Fundy between Canada and the US, are not dealt with by the LOS Convention. The existing more than 40 such bays are governed by customary, rather unsettled and controversial, rules. Generally speaking, unlike juridical bays, bays bordered by more than one state cannot be closed by a line joining the entrance points of their mouth; hence, the low-water mark around the coast of the bay seems to constitute the baseline unless the circumstances warrant a different solution. Thus the Fonseca Bay, bordered by El Salvador, Honduras, and Nicaragua, once on the agenda of the short-lived Central American Court of Justice (1908–1918), was held by the ICJ in the above-noted complicated case of *Land, Island and Maritime Frontier Dispute* to be a *sui generis* body of internal waters treated as a historic bay, with the right of innocent passage **(248)** of third states. The ICJ found the Gulf of Fonseca to be a pluri-state historic bay subject to a special kind of threefold sovereignty **(125)** of the three coastal states, with a three-mile belt along the littoral of each of them under the exclusive sovereignty of the state concerned. With regard to the waters outside the Gulf, the ICJ ruled that the closing line of the Gulf constituted the baseline for the territorial sea, the exclusive economic zone **(238)**, and the continental shelf **(236)** of the three countries, all of these zones to be held by them in joint entitlement in the same way as the Gulf itself.

**235. Contiguous Zone.** According to the United Nations Convention on the Law of the Sea of 1982 (LOS Convention) **(264)**, contiguous zone is a zone contiguous to the territorial sea **(262)** in which the coastal state **(127)** may exercise the control necessary to prevent infringement of its customs, fiscal, immigration or sanitary laws and punish infringement of the above laws and regulations committed within its territory **(228)** or territorial sea (Art. 33(1)). This means that under this provision the coastal state has merely enforcement jurisdiction **(87)**, and only with respect to offenses committed in its territory, including its territorial sea. However, under a general provision of the Convention (Art. 303(1)) the coastal state's enforcement jurisdiction in the contiguous zone is extended to a new subject matter whereby, in order to control traffic in archeological and historical objects, the coastal state may, in applying the provisions of Art. 33, presume that removal of such objects from the seabed of the contiguous zone without its approval would, presumably by virtue of a legal fiction, result in an infringement within its territory or territorial sea of the laws and regulations referred to in that article. The matter of archeological and historical objects found on the seabed, including the contiguous zone, is regulated in detail by the Convention on the Protection of Underwater Cultural Heritage of 2001 (41 ILM 40 (2002)). Unlike the territorial sea, which is, as it were, an automatic appurtenance to the coastal state's land domain and, as such, must be maintained by it, a contiguous zone must, but need not, be specifically claimed by the state.

Historically, the institution of contiguous zone can be traced back to the 18th-century British "hovering acts" enacted against smugglers hovering in their vessels within 24 miles (eight leagues) offshore. Eventually, after a three-mile-wide territorial sea under the coastal state's sovereignty **(125)** became established, the United Kingdom (UK) repealed the hovering acts legislation in 1876. However, the doctrine of "hot pursuit" **(246)** and "constructive" presence whereby the offender ship's boats present beyond the three-mile limit were treated as the ship itself, allowed to a certain degree to enforce jurisdiction beyond the width of the territorial sea. Other states (for example, Belgium and Spain), without as yet establishing a territorial sea, claimed either a variety of offshore zones for various purposes, such as fishing **(239)**, customs, neutrality **(362)**, and security or, like some Latin American states, established nine-mile customs and security zones beyond their respective territorial seas. The United States (US) Tariff Act of 1922, which subjected foreign vessels within a 12-mile zone to enforcement of US prohibition of alcohol (introduced in 1919), prompted a good deal of foreign opposition on the part of such countries as, for example, the UK, Canada, Germany, Sweden, and Japan. But, as the 20th century wore on, an increasing number of states made claims to various zones of jurisdiction beyond the generally accepted zone of territorial sea. Such special zones, mainly for customs and security purposes, became known as contiguous zones, a term devised in the inter-war period by Gilbert-Charles Gidel, a renowned French international jurist, whose idea contributed to acceptance in international law of such universally proclaimed zones, distinct from fishery zones which required international agreement.

With opposition to the idea of contiguous zone having all but disappeared, the Convention on the Territorial Sea and the Contiguous Zone (516 UNTS 205), adopted by the Geneva Conference on the Law of the Sea of 1958 **(243)**, included a provision (Art. 24) establishing a contiguous zone up to 12 miles beyond the baselines **(233)**. This provision was reproduced almost *verbatim* in Art. 33(1) of the LOS Convention of 1982, but in view of the widely claimed territorial sea of 12 miles the limits of the contiguous zone were moved seaward to a maximum of 24 (nautical) miles (about 27.4 standard miles) from the baselines. Unlike the 1958 Convention, the LOS Convention is silent on the question of the delimitation of the contiguous zone, now part of the exclusive economic zone (EEZ) **(238)**. The US, which in 1988 extended its territorial sea from 3 miles to 12 miles, proclaimed extension of its contiguous zone to 24 miles in 1999. The jurisdiction claimed by the US in the zone in substance follows the rules of the LOS Convention.

In the early 21st century, there existed a wide variety of claims to zones contiguous to the territorial sea. Among other claims, as of the end of October 2003, 63 states had a zone of 24 miles (including 12 miles of the territorial sea) for the purposes of the LOS Convention, but some of them, going beyond the Convention, included security as one of the purposes in establishing a contiguous zone, while others claimed a zone for unnamed purposes. A small number of states claimed a zone below the maximum allowed under the Convention and going only six miles beyond the territorial sea (Bangladesh, Gambia, Norway, Saudi Arabia, Sudan) or—in the case of Finland—only two miles. Syria's 41-mile claim included 35 miles for the territorial sea and 6 miles for the contiguous zone for purposes listed in the LOS Convention and for security. For its part, North Korea proclaimed a 50-mile military security zone. Canada's 100-mile zone declared in the Arctic for reasons of environmental protection in 1970 exists apart from the standard contiguous zone adopted in 1996. Generally speaking, the legal status of the contiguous zone remained rather uncertain both because of divergence in states' practice and jurisdictional complications resulting from the position of the zone as part of the EEZ **(238)**.

**236. Continental Shelf.** As defined in the United Nations (UN) Convention on the Law of the Sea of 1982 (LOS Convention) **(264)**, the continental shelf of a coastal state **(127)** in its legal meaning comprises the seabed and subsoil of the submarine areas that extend beyond its territorial sea **(262)** throughout the natural prolongation of its land territory **(228)** to the outer edge of the continental margin, or to a distance of 200 nautical miles from the territorial sea baselines **(233)** where the outer edge of the continental margin does not extend to such distance (Art. 76(1)). One nautical mile equals 6080.20 feet or 1853.25 meters. It is clear that the definition of the continental shelf in the meaning of international law is different from its geological definition. Geologically, the shelf forms only the first section of the continental "margin," constituting some 20 percent of the total seafloor, which—as stated in the Convention (Art. 76(3))—comprises the submerged prolongation of the land mass of the coastal state, and consists of the seabed and subsoil of "shelf," "slope," and "rise." The first section, the shelf, is a rather gently descending platform of submerged land which is adjacent to the coast and on an average reaches 130 meters depth at its outer limit. It is followed by a sharply falling continental slope extending to a depth of 1,200 to 3,000 meters, and then, in many marine spaces, by the continental rise which gradually falls into the deep seabed at the depth of approximately 3,500 to 5,500 meters, depending on the configuration of the seafloor. Under the LOS Convention, the continental margin does not include the deep ocean floor with its oceanic ridges and its subsoil.

As defined in the LOS Convention, the "legal" continental shelf differs from the geological notion of the shelf in that, first, it includes not just the geological shelf (whose width varies from only five miles, as off the coast of California, to as much as 750 miles below the Barents Sea), but the whole margin and, second, it may include an area of the seabed that is not a natural prolongation of the land territory at all, in which case the sovereign **(125)** right of the coastal state over the legal continental shelf extends 200 miles seaward, the limit following that adopted by the Convention for the exclusive economic zone (EEZ) **(238)**. Wherever the margin extends beyond 200 miles from the baselines of the territorial sea, the outer edge of the legal continental shelf is established by one of the prescribed two complex formulas, but the resulting line of the outer limit must be either within 350 miles from the baselines or, subject to the below-noted Convention's rules on submarine ridges and elevations (Art. 76(6)), within 100 miles from the 2,500 meter isobath, that is, a line connecting the depth of 2,500 meters. In the interests of equity **(13)**, Annex II to he Final Act of the Third United Nations Conference on the Law of the Sea (UNCLOS III) **(263)** allows a special method of establishing the outer edge of the continental margin by the coastal states of the Bay of Bengal.

On submarine ridges the limits of the continental shelf may not exceed the 350 miles from the baselines, but this rule does not apply to submarine elevations that are natural components of the continental margin, such as its plateaux, rises, caps, banks, and spurs (Art. 76(6)). This means that the more shallow depths due to submarine ridges rising from the deep seabed, which geologically are not natural components of the continental margin, cannot be used to extend the margin into the deep-seabed areas. The coastal state has the obligation to delimit the outer limits of the continental shelf where it extends beyond 200 miles from the baselines, by straight lines up to 60 miles in length, connecting fixed points, defined by coordinates of latitude and longitude (Art. 76(7)). Furthermore, the coastal state must notify the outer limits of such shelf to a special Commission on the Limits of the Continental Shelf set up by Annex II to the Convention, elected (in 1997) on the basis of equitable geographical representation. The coastal state must also deposit all charts and relevant data with the Secretary-General of the UN (Art. 76(8)(9)).

The LOS Convention's rules on the continental shelf (Part VI) were arrived at after difficult and protracted negotiations **(316)** and were a major landmark in the evolution of the state practice in this area since 1945 when President Harry Truman's Proclamation (40 AJIL (Supp.) 47 (1946)) was issued as the first clear assertion of the coastal state's exclusive sovereign rights to the living and non-living resources of the continental shelf to the subsequently defined depth of 100 fathoms (one fathom equals 6 feet or 1.8 meters). Though running counter to the fundamental rule of the law of the sea **(254)** that no state has exclusive right to any part of the seabed and subsoil beneath the high seas **(245),** the United States (US) move proved very attractive to other states motivated by prospects of potential benefits from the exploitation of their offshore oil and gas and other resources. Already at that time the rapidly advancing technology made it possible to explore and exploit ever deeper offshore areas of the seabed. Currently, the continental shelf is estimated to contain, apart from other mineral and living resources, a quarter of the total oil and 15 percent of the gas resources of the world. A number of states followed the US example, and some Latin American states, especially those of the Pacific coast where the continental shelf is very narrow, extended their respective claims even to the resources of the superjacent waters to a distance of 200 miles, prompting protests by the US and other countries.

The coastal state's exclusive right to the resources of the continental shelf rapidly developed into a rule of customary international law **(39)**, endorsed in the Convention on the Continental Shelf (499 UNTS 311) adopted by the Geneva Conference on the Law of the Sea of 1958 **(243)**, which, without prejudice to the legal status of the superjacent waters, fixed the limits of the shelf on the basis of the criterion of ocean depth: up to 200 meters (approximately the US claim) or beyond to "where the depth of the superjacent waters admits of exploitation" (Art. 1). The possibility that under this exploitability criterion ever deeper areas of the seabed and subsoil could legally acquire the status of continental shelf with benefits mainly to industrialized countries controlling the necessary technology, caused considerable but legally unfounded concerns among less-developed states. It was unfounded because the 1958 Geneva Convention on the Continental Shelf defined the continental shelf as an area "adjacent to the coast," conceiving the continental shelf as a prolongation of the land territory. However, less developed states called for declaring the deep seabed as a "common heritage of mankind," and eventually the whole issue provided a stimulus for convening UNCLOS III which—as already noted—in fixing the limits of the shelf dropped the criterion of depth of the 1958 Convention, adopting a definition according to the criterion of the 200-mile distance from the baselines or, for countries favored by nature, determined by the continental margin.

In considering the rights and duties of the coastal state in the continental shelf, the LOS Convention differentiates between the shelf within the 200-mile limit, a zone governed by the regime of the EEZ (if claimed by the state concerned) and that of the continental shelf on the one hand, and the outer continental shelf, that is, the shelf beyond 200 miles governed only by the regime of the continental shelf, on the other. Where appropriate in the changed circumstances, other provisions of the LOS Convention concerning the continental shelf follow those of the 1958 Convention.

Within a 200-mile zone the coastal state has "sovereign rights" to the natural resources of the shelf. These rights are exclusive in the sense that no other state may undertake exploration or exploitation of such resources without the coastal state's consent. Furthermore, the coastal state's sovereign rights are, so to speak, automatic and do not depend on effective or notional occupation **(214)** or on any express proclamation. The natural resources consist of 1. the mineral and other non-living resources of the seabed and subsoil, and 2. the living resources, meaning "living organisms belonging to sedentary species, that is to say, organisms which, at the harvestable stage, either are immobile on or under the seabed or are unable to move except in constant physical contact with the seabed or subsoil" (Art. 77). At the Geneva Conference of 1958, which adopted the same rule, sedentary species were said to include, *inter alia*, corals, sponges, oysters, pearls, and clams, but not shrimps and prawns or, of course, bottom fish. The exact legal nature of crabs, lobsters, and scallops has been a subject of some controversy. Subject to Art. 303 which allows the coastal state certain rights with regard to archeological and historical objects in the contiguous zone **(235)**, wrecks lying on the continental shelf are not natural resources and therefore are not included within the concept of the sovereign rights of the coastal state. Otherwise, questions relating to the status of specific wrecks resting on the continental shelf require regulation by agreement of the states directly concerned. In 2001 the UN Educational, Scientific, and Cultural Organization adopted the Convention on the Protection of the Underwater Cultural Heritage (41 ILM 40 (2002)) (not yet in force) which, generally speaking, reserves to the coastal state the right of issuing authorizations to other states for conduct of research on underwater cultural heritage on its continental shelf (and the EEZ). Underwater cultural heritage refers to vessels, aircraft, and their content, as well as sites, structures, artifacts, and human remains, which have been partially or totally, periodically or continuously under water for at least 100 years. But no activity directed at warships **(265)** and other state vessels and aircraft may be conducted without the agreement of the flag state and the collaboration of the "coordinating state," normally the coastal state concerned. The underwater heritage Convention of 2001 cannot prejudice the rights, jurisdiction, and duties of states under the LOS Convention of 1982 and must be interpreted **(274)** and applied in a manner consistent with that Convention and other rules of international law. The US (and France) voted against the adoption of the underwater heritage Convention because it did not recognize the principle that, unless expressly abandoned, title to sunken state ships remains vested in the ship's sovereign.

It is essential to bear in mind that the LOS Convention does not grant the coastal state sovereignty over the continental shelf, but only the exercise of specific sovereign rights. Moreover, such rights of the coastal state do not affect the legal status of the superjacent waters or of airspace **(186)** above these waters (Art. 78(1)). The right of the coastal state to exploit the subsoil by means of tunneling, irrespective of the depth of water above the subsoil, is expressly reserved (Art. 85). The coastal state may not unjustifiably interfere with navigation and other rights and freedoms of other states (Art. 78(2)) and may not impede the laying or maintenance by other states of submarine cables and pipelines on its continental shelf (Art. 79). The right of the coastal state to construct and operate and authorize construction of artificial islands, installations, and structures within the EEZ applies *mutatis mutandis* to the continental shelf. Subject to certain conditions, establishing safety zones up to 500 meters is allowed (Arts. 60 and 80). Any abandoned or disused installations or structures must be removed to ensure safety of navigation.

The rights of the coastal state over the continental shelf that continues beyond the 200-mile zone differ slightly from those within the 200-mile zone, considering that the superjacent waters are high seas **(245)**. Apart from certain differences relating to scientific research, the major difference is that as a compensation for reducing the Area **(232)**, that is, the deep seabed subject to the special regime of the common heritage of mankind, the coastal state has to pay to the International Seabed Authority (ISA) **(250)** annual payments or contributions in kind in respect of the exploitation of the non-living resources of the portion of the shelf beyond the 200-mile limit. The payments would start following five years of exploitation of a site and would be in proportion to the value of volume of production, rising from 1 percent in the sixth year to 7 percent in the twelfth and following years. However, developing countries that are net importers of the minerals involved would be exempt from this obligation. The ISA would distribute the payments to the states parties of the Convention on an equitable **(13)** basis, but taking into account the interests and needs of the developing states, particularly the least developed and the landlocked **(253)** among them (Art. 82).

Legal problems, unique to the area of the legal continental shelf, if it reaches beyond the 200-mile limit, can arise over whether some organisms are in the nature of sedentary species. Since fishing on the high seas is governed by a free fishing regime, a controversial species may become a subject of a jurisdictional dispute **(299)**, as was the case of a US-Canada dispute over scallops, if the coastal state (Canada) considers scallops as sedentary and the other state (US) regards them as non-sedentary species.

Delimitation of the continental shelf between states with opposite or adjacent coasts was one of the most difficult issues faced by UNCLOS III, with some states favoring in principle the equidistance method and others stressing only the element of equitable solution. Ultimately, the Convention provides (Art. 83) that, unless otherwise agreed between the states concerned, delimitation shall be effected by agreement on the basis of international law in order to achieve an equitable solution, a provision analogous to that governing delimitation of the EEZ. It is believed by commentators that

Art. 83 merely implies the obligation to enter into meaningful negotiations in good faith, but does not provide any clear guidance if no agreement is reached. It does, however, oblige the parties involved to resort to peaceful settlement **(318)** provisions of Part XV of the Convention and, without prejudice to a final delimitation, to enter into provisional agreements without jeopardizing the reaching of the final agreement. While most delimitation disputes have been settled by agreement, in practice the problem generated a good deal of litigation leading to some important judicial and arbitral **(293)** decisions.

The landmark judgment of the International Court of Justice (ICJ) **(309)** in the joint proceedings of the *North Sea Continental Shelf* cases (Federal Republic of Germany/Denmark; Federal Republic of Germany/Netherlands) (1969 ICJ Rep. 3) was followed by the judgments in: *Continental Shelf* (Tunisia/Libyan Arab Jamahiriya) (1982 ICJ Rep.18); *Continental Shelf* (Libyan Arab Jamahiriya/Malta) (1985 ICJ Rep.13); and *Maritime Delimitation in the Area between Greenland and Jan Mayen* (Denmark v. Norway) (1993 ICJ Rep. 38). The case of *Delimitation of the Maritime Boundary in the Gulf of Maine* (Canada/United States of America), decided by a Chamber **(295)** of the Court (1984 ICJ Rep. 246) and some other cases, dealt with the delimitation of a single maritime boundary, including that of the continental shelf. Arbitration has included, *inter alia*, two important cases: the *Anglo-French Continental Shelf*, 1977 (18 ILM 397 (1979)) and the *Dubai-Sharjah Border* case, 1981 (91 ILR 543). The *Guinea/Guinea Bissau Maritime Boundary* Arbitration of 1985 (25 ILM 251 (1986)) and the arbitration in the *Saint Pierre and Miquelon* case between Canada and France (31 ILM 1145 (1992)) concerned the delimitation of a single maritime boundary. It can be added that in the above-noted *Anglo-French* Arbitration of 1977 and the ICJ cases of *Gulf of Maine* and *Jan Mayen,* both parties to the dispute were bound by the 1958 continental shelf Convention whose provisions, at least formally, applied in these cases but, as found by the tribunals, this fact led in substance to much the same result as the customary law on the subject, namely achieving an equitable solution to the problem of delimitation.

The Truman declaration of 1945 called for applying equitable principles in delimiting continental shelf boundaries. Under the 1958 Geneva Convention on the Continental Shelf (Art. 6), the parties first have to seek agreement in the absence of which and, unless another boundary line is justified by special circumstances, the boundary is to be determined by application of the principle of equidistance, that is, by a median line, every point of which is equidistant from the nearest point of the baselines. Special circumstances exist for example if offshore islands **(251)** are present or where a specific configuration of the coast could distort the median line, with consequent inequity for a party or parties. It must be noted that after the entry into force **(271)** of the LOS Convention in 1994, for a case to be decided on the basis of the Geneva 1958 Convention, all parties to the dispute must be parties to it, but not to the 1982 LOS Convention. Under Art. 311(1) of the latter Convention, the Convention shall prevail, as between states parties, over the Geneva 1958 Convention. In the early 21st century only a few countries, including a few that signed **(283)** but did not ratify the LOS Convention, were parties only to the1958 Geneva Convention. In practice, irrespective or whether or not the parties to a dispute are bound by Art. 6 of the Geneva Convention, tribunals have, at their own discretion, to apply or rather develop **(5)** the customary law on the subject of delimitation. They need to achieve an equitable result, taking into account all relevant circumstances of the particular cases. This has become the guiding principle underlying all pertinent decisions, such as the already mentioned ICJ decision of 1969 in the *North Sea Continental Shelf* cases. At the same time, as noted by the ICJ in its judgment in the Tunisia/Libya case of 1982, an equitable result must be within the limits of the law and not in fact dispense distributive justice through a decision *ex aequo et bono* **(13)**. Among relevant circumstances, judicial decisions identified configuration of the coast, relative lengths of the coastline, presence of islands, prior conduct, such as granting offshore concessions, and even security and socioeconomic factors. While the concept of natural prolongation of land was emphasized by the ICJ in 1969, subsequent decisions tended to discount it. Delimitation of the outer continental shelf, that is, the shelf beyond the 200-mile limit, a situation that exists in at least 30 cases with more than 50 claiming states involved, had by the end of 2002, taken place by agreement between neighboring states. The US signed two such agreements: with Mexico in 2000 and, with respect to the Bering Sea, the Chukchi Sea, the Arctic Ocean, and the North Pacific Ocean with Russia. However, certain aspects of delimitation between the US and Russia (inclusion by Russia of oceanic ridges and insufficient information submitted to the Commission on the Limits of the Continental Shelf) were still awaiting solution.

At the beginning of the 21st century a great majority of continental shelf claims followed the provisions of Part VI of the LOS Convention. Its major features appear to have crystallized as part of customary law although the old-type modest claims based on the 1958 Geneva Convention's criterion of 200-meter depth plus exploitability were still followed by a small number of countries, mainly in areas deprived of a wide continental margin. With regard to the delimitation of the shelf between states, in some cases the states concerned do not draw a boundary, but settle the problem by establishing a joint development zone or adopt some other cooperative arrangement which may also include management of the living resources of the EEZs involved.

**237. Enclosed or Semi-Enclosed Seas.** Art. 122 of Part IX of the United Nations Convention on the Law of the Sea of 1982 (LOS Convention) **(264)** defines "enclosed or semi-enclosed sea" as "a gulf **(234)**, basin or sea surrounded by two or more States **(127)** and connected to another sea or the ocean by a narrow outlet or consisting entirely or primarily of the territorial sea **(262)** and exclusive economic zones of two or more coastal States." It should be stressed that this concept has nothing in common with the doctrine of the "closed sea" excluding certain seas from the high seas **(245)** rules, once promoted by the Soviet Union for political and strategic reasons. Among the major marine spaces that meet the criteria of the LOS Convention are the Baltic, Bering, Black, Caribbean, East China, Mediterranean, Red, Solomon, and South China Seas, the Gulf of Mexico, the Gulf of Oman, and the Persian Gulf.

Without imposing any mandatory mechanisms upon states bordering an enclosed or semi-enclosed sea, the LOS Convention (Art. 123) provides in a less-binding language that states bordering an enclosed or semi-enclosed sea "should" cooperate with each other in the exercise of their rights and in the performance of their duties under the Convention, but they have the duty ("shall") to endeavor, directly or through an appropriate organization **(84)**, to coordinate the management, conservation, exploration, and exploitation of the living resources of the sea; coordinate the implementation of their rights and duties with regard to the protection and preservation of the marine environment **(255)**; and coordinate their scientific research policies. As appropriate, states bordering an enclosed or semi-enclosed sea shall also endeavor to invite cooperation of other states or regional organizations in furtherance of these tasks.

Cooperation of the kind meant by the Convention had already taken place for some time, especially in the area of the conservation of the living resources and the protection and preservation of the marine environment. The Gdańsk Convention on Fishing and Conservation of the Living Resources of the Baltic Sea and the Belts, 1973, (1090 UNTS 54) is a major example of cooperation in the area of fisheries. But cooperation of the littoral states of an enclosed or semi-enclosed sea has taken place primarily in the area of the protection of the marine environment of such seas, particularly vulnerable to the effects of pollution. The Helsinki Convention of 1974 on the Protection of the Marine Environment of the Baltic Sea Area (13 ILM 544 (1974)), subsequently replaced by a new convention of the same name in 1992 (LOS Bull. January 1993, 54), was a pioneering case of a comprehensive approach of states bordering an enclosed sea to the challenge of combating marine pollution. It was followed by a series of regional environmental conventions focusing on specific marine areas, including enclosed and semi-enclosed seas, and concluded under the Regional Seas Program of the United Nations Environment Program (UNEP). Chronologically, first among such arrangements focusing on enclosed and semi-enclosed seas is the Convention for the Protection of the Mediterranean Sea against Pollution, 1976 (1102 UNTS 27). It was followed by the Kuwait Regional Convention for Cooperation on the Protection of the Marine Environment from Pollution, 1978 (1140 UNTS 13), which focuses on the Persian Gulf and the Gulf of Oman; Regional Convention for the Conservation of the Red Sea and Gulf of Aden Environment, 1982; Convention for the Protection and Development of the Marine Environment of the Wider Caribbean Region, 1983 (22 ILM 227 (1983)); and Convention for the Protection of the Black Sea against Pollution, 1992 (LOS Bull. January 1993, 31). These conventions were followed by protocols dealing with specific sources of pollution.

**238. Exclusive Economic Zone (EEZ).** A revolutionary development in the modern law of the sea **(254)**, the exclusive economic zone (EEZ) is, under the United Nations Convention on the Law of the Sea of 1982 (LOS Convention) **(264)**, the marine area, including the subjacent seabed and subsoil beyond and adjacent to the territorial sea **(262)** extending up to 200 nautical miles (one nautical mile is equal to 6,080.20 feet or 1,853.20 meters) from the baselines **(233)** of the territorial sea, in which the coastal state has sovereign rights for the purpose of exploring and exploiting, conserving and managing the living and non-living resources of the waters and the seabed and its subsoil, and with regard to other activities for the economic exploitation and exploration of the zone, such as the production of energy from the water, currents, and winds (LOS Convention, Arts. 55–57). The sovereign rights of the coastal state to the non-living resources of the continental shelf **(236)** in its EEZ are exercised in accordance with Part VI of the LOS Convention, governing the regime of the continental shelf, whose rules with respect to some uses (artificial structures, delimitation of boundaries, publishing charts), are the same as those concerning the EEZ.

The sovereign rights of the coastal state in the EEZ fall short of sovereignty **(125)**. All other states enjoy there the high seas freedoms **(242)** of navigation and overflight, laying submarine cables and pipelines and other internationally lawful uses of the sea related to these freedoms (Arts. 58(1), 87)). In this sense, as made clear by the LOS Convention (Arts. 55 and 56), the EEZ is a separate *sui generis* maritime zone between the territorial sea and the high seas **(245)**, which is subject to a specific legal regime of its own, codified and developed **(5)** in Part V (Arts. 55–75) of the LOS Convention of 1982. Much of this part of the Convention deals with the utilization of the living resources of the EEZ, mainly fisheries, and forms part of what one might call international law of fisheries **(239)**.

In addition to the above-listed sovereign economic rights, the coastal state has jurisdiction **(87)** with regard to the establishment and use of artificial islands, installations, and structures; marine scientific research; and the protection and preservation of the marine environment (Art. 56(b)) **(255)**. The Convention also assigns to the coastal state "other rights and duties provided for by the Convention" (Art. 56(1)(c)), such as the rights resulting from the contiguous zone **(235)** (which overlaps with the first 12 miles of the EEZ), and the right of hot pursuit **(246)**. With regard to its rights and duties, the coastal state is bound by the general clause of "due regard" to the rights and duties of other states (Art. 56(2)). It also has specific duties in relation to certain specific rights in the EEZ, primarily with regard to its living resources.

Art. 58(1) of the Convention guarantees all third states all the high seas freedoms and "other internationally lawful uses of the sea related to these freedoms, such as those associated with the operation of ships, aircraft, and submarine cables and pipelines, and compatible with the other provisions of this Convention." Like the other rights, navigation by foreign ships in the EEZ is explicitly subject to the general "due regard" clause (Art. 58(3)) and various regulations governing navigation on the highs seas as well as regulations pertaining to prevention of pollution and possibly artificial islands and similar installations erected in the EEZ by the coastal state. Whether the coastal state is allowed to exercise its enforcement jurisdiction in its EEZ pertaining to illegal traffic in narcotics is a controversial matter. Such jurisdiction appears to be more readily allowed in combating terrorism **(337)**. The municipal laws **(27)** of a number of countries conflict in certain respects with the navigational rights of foreign ships in the EEZ and, in general, there exists potential for conflict between the rights of the coastal states and those of third countries.

The right of warships **(265)** to conduct military exercises in a foreign EEZ without the coastal state's consent has been a subject of considerable controversy. Whereas the United States (US) and some other naval powers insist on such a right as an internationally lawful use of the sea related to the freedom of navigation and compatible with the reservation of the high seas for "peaceful purposes," stipulated in Art. 88, a number of less-developed countries (Brazil, Cape Verde Islands, Malaysia, Pakistan, Uruguay) made declarations when signing or ratifying the LOS Convention to the effect that in their view the Convention did not authorize military exercises or deployment of military installations in a foreign EEZ. The municipal law of some states, for example Iran, prohibits all foreign military activities in their respective EEZs. The controversial issue of operating military devices and conducting intelligence gathering in the airspace **(186)** of a foreign EEZ is illustrated by the incident of a collision between US and Chinese military aircraft over China's EEZ in 2001.

Conflicts between the interests of the coastal state and any other state regarding the attribution of rights and jurisdiction in the EEZ that are not attributed by the Convention to either of the states, must be resolved on the basis of equity and in the light of all the relevant circumstances, taking into account the respective importance of the interests involved to the parties as well as to the international community as a whole (Art. 59). This provision means that the Convention does not establish any presumption in favor of either party.

The historical evolution of the EEZ can be traced back to the then extravagant claims of some Latin American countries to a 200-mile exclusive fishery zone in the decade following 1945. In 1946 Argentina claimed not only its continental shelf but also the epicontinental sea above it. Claims over a 200-mile zone, including the shelf and the sea above were proclaimed by Chile and Peru in 1947, and Ecuador in 1950. Though considered as illegal by many developed countries, such claims formally announced in international declarations (Santiago, 1952; Lima, 1970), often motivated by concern over conservation of fishery resources in the face of exploitation by foreign fishermen in the rich waters of the Humboldt Current off the Pacific coast of Peru, Chile, and Ecuador, gained support of an increasing number of less-developed states, especially in Africa. Moreover, the failure of the First **(243)** and the Second **(244)** Geneva Conferences in 1958 and 1960, respectively, to resolve the issues of the width of the territorial sea and offshore fishery zones, initiated a general and, as it turned out, irreversible trend toward extension of fishery jurisdiction beyond the territorial sea from the initially modest claims of 12 miles (upheld in 1974 by the International Court of Justice (ICJ) **(309)** in the *Fisheries Jurisdiction* cases (United Kingdom v. Iceland; Federal Republic of Germany v. Iceland) (1974 ICJ Rep. 3, 75)) to rapidly extending distances, soon reaching 200 miles. By 1978, 23 states claimed a 200-mile fishery zone. Moreover, 38 states laid claims not just to a fishery zone of such width, but to a more inclusive "exclusive economic zone," an idea originally proposed by Kenya in 1971 and similar to the concept of the "patrimonial sea" promoted by certain Latin American countries. By the time of the Third United Nations Conference on the Law of the Sea (UNCLOS III) **(263)** the concept of a 200-mile zone, in most cases an EEZ, had received widespread approval and was accepted even by states which had originally opposed it as curtailing the traditional freedom of the seas. The US, which introduced a 200-mile exclusive fishery zone in 1976, converted this zone into an EEZ in 1982 (but without requiring consent for foreign marine scientific research in its zone). By the 1980s the basic legal framework of the EEZ as adopted in Part V of the LOS Convention became part of customary international law **(39)**, a conclusion reached by the ICJ in a number of cases, for example in *Continental Shelf* (Libyan Arab Jamahiriya/Malta) (1985 ICJ Rep. 13).

While strictly speaking there is no legal obligation to claim an EEZ, by the turn of the century such a zone of 200 miles was claimed by a very large majority of states (apart from ten states' extravagant claim of a 200-mile territorial sea). There were still less than ten states, including Finland, Ireland, Netherlands, Peru, and the United Kingdom, which saw no advantage in having an EEZ and claimed a 200-mile exclusive fishery zone only. For geographical reasons, a few states bordering a semi-enclosed sea **(237)** claimed exclusive fishery zones less than 200 miles wide. France did not include the Mediterranean Sea in its 200-mile EEZ. The LOS Convention has no rules on fishery zones. Whether and to what extent the Convention's rules on fisheries in Part V (EEZ), especially those concerning access to the zone by other states, apply to states with fishery zones only, is not entirely clear.

Where, because of geographical circumstances, states cannot claim a full 200-mile zone, a delimitation is to be effected by agreement on the basis of international law in order to achieve an equitable solution (Art. 74(1)), a rule similar to that concerning delimitation of the continental shelf. In practice, delimitation of the EEZ usually follows the equidistance principle which may be modified by taking into account special circumstances. Some 150 EEZ delimitation disputes have been settled by states. Judicial and arbitration practice **(318)** in the matter of principles governing delimitation of an EEZ or fishery zone has been much the same as in the delimitation of the continental shelf. In a number of cases the tribunal delimited a single maritime boundary for both the EEZ and the continental shelf. Examples are: the *Gulf of Maine* case (Canada/US) (1984 ICJ (Chamber) **(295)** Rep. 246)) the ICJ *Case Concerning Maritime Delimitation and Territorial Questions between Qatar and Bahrain* (Qatar v. Bahrain) (40 ILM 847 (2001)) and, more recently, the case concerning the maritime boundary between Romania and Ukraine in the Black Sea (2004– ). In the *Greenland/Jan Mayen Maritime Delimitation* (Denmark v. Norway) (1993 ICJ Rep. 38) the Court applied rules of customary international law **(39)** with regard to the delimitation of the fishery zone while basing its decision concerning the continental shelf on Art. 6 of the 1958 Geneva Convention on the Continental Shelf.

As in the case of the continental shelf, instead of delimiting the EEZ area, states may decide to set up some kind of cooperative arrangement for the exploitation and management of the living resources of the zone at issue. An Agreement of 1978 between Norway and the then Soviet Union on joint development of an overlapping area in the Barents Sea is an example of such joint development.

The virtually universal adoption of the EEZ (apart from a small number of cases of a fishery zone) has had a profound impact upon marine affairs and the law of the sea. It subtracted from the high seas area some 38 million square nautical miles, that is, more than one-third of ocean space, containing more than 90 percent of fishing grounds and about 87 percent of all known and estimated hydrocarbon reserves, apart from mineral resources, mainly manganese nodules and metallic crusts. As far as navigation is concerned, since most major shipping routes must cross some foreign EEZ, the extension of the coastal states' jurisdiction according to the EEZ rules must have impacts upon international navigation.

As a result of the introduction of the EEZ the system of managing marine resources shifted largely to the jurisdiction by coastal states, many of them less developed and newcomers to marine affairs. But, contrary to expectations of less-developed states which promoted the adoption of the EEZ in the name of the New International Economic Order, the emergence of the EEZ has not resulted in any fundamental redistribution of the oceans' resources in favor of the less-developed states. Although some of them (for example China, India, Indonesia, Brazil, Mexico, Pacific island states, and some states off the coast of Africa) have gained sizable areas of the EEZ and others have benefited from licensing fees on foreign fishing, seven developed nations (most of all, the US, and—because of its Pacific territories—France, followed by New Zealand, Australia, Russia, Japan, and Canada) are among the ten largest beneficiaries of the EEZ.

The introduction of the EEZ has in general resulted in decline in the catches of distant water fishing states, but with some states successfully continuing this kind of fisheries. Still, almost 99 percent of the world's fisheries fall under some country's jurisdiction. Coastal states which gained exclusive sovereign rights in their respective EEZs have in general either increased their catches or benefited from license fees paid by foreign fishing vessels. However, many developing countries have not been able to develop their fishing industries enough to derive significant benefits from the EEZ.

**239. Fisheries, International Law of.** International law of fisheries is that part of the law of the sea **(254)** which regulates marine fisheries, and more inclusively, the exploitation, management, and conservation of the living resources of the sea. Marine fisheries account for approximately 20 percent of protein supply, but some 30 percent of the world's catch is processed for use in nonhuman consumption as animal feed and fertilizers. The extraordinary growth of the total marine catch in the past 50 years or so is mainly due to advances in marine fishing technology, a rising investment of developing countries in the fishing industry, and mounting demand for fish. From a traditional cottage industry, still practiced by fishermen plying the seas close to shore in small, often sailing, boats, fishing has become a modern industry using large trawlers dragging their wide nets along the sea floor and scouring much of the living resources in their path, including unintended marine life, such as porpoises and dolphins. Some of these vessels are large, long-distance, factory-fishing vessels which stay for months far from their country's shores and catch mass amounts of fish with the help of ever more sophisticated equipment. The huge increase in the world catch of ultimately finite fishing resources led to depletion of important fish stocks, collapse of fisheries in certain regions as was the case of Californian sardines and, more recently, North Atlantic cod, and a real prospect of extinction of several species of fish. The Food and Agriculture Organization (FAO) estimated that 35 percent of the fish stocks which were underexploited a decade before were in decline in the 1990s. The total world marine catch grew from about 20 million metric tons in 1948 to 94.8 million in 2000. In 2000 China was the leading fishing state, followed by Peru, Japan, United States (US), Chile, Indonesia, Russia, India, Thailand, and Norway. China was also leading in aquaculture, accounting for approximately two-thirds out of the total 35.6 million metric ton of this booming branch of the fish industry.

The nature of fish as a common property resource with open access by all to fishing grounds has been historically the major factor influencing the international legal regulations of fisheries. However, open access to fishing grounds eventually led not only to overfishing but also inevitably to overcapacity, with the resulting economic inefficiency and costly governmental subsidies where returns for fishing investment were falling below the maximum economic yield. It is estimated by the FAO that 53 percent of the world fishing fleet has become superfluous.

Since marine fisheries are an international industry they must be regulated by the law of the sea through such measures as, *inter alia*, setting the total allowable catch (TAC) with the guidance of scientifically obtained data on the maximum sustainable yield for interdependent stock, that is, a level at which the loss from fishing and natural causes is compensated by increase from reproduction; regulating gear and minimum size of fish permitted to be caught; and establishing closed areas and closed seasons.

Until the mid-1970s the international legal framework of fisheries was based on the coastal states' exclusive fishery jurisdiction **(87)** only in their respective internal waters **(249)** and the territorial sea **(262)**. Beyond the territorial sea, fishing was open to all under the principle of the freedom of the high seas **(242)**. However, as early as the late 1940s and early 1950s Peru, Chile, and Ecuador, concerned about protecting the rich waters adjacent to their territorial sea, proclaimed 200-mile exclusive zones, claims subsequently joined by some other Latin American states. The 1958 Convention on Fishing and Conservation of the Living Resources of the High Seas, adopted by the Geneva Conference on the Law of the Sea of 1958 **(243)**, was an early, though modest, recognition of the special interest of coastal states in the conservation and management of fisheries on the high seas adjacent to the territorial sea. But its rather vague provisions on unilateral measures of the coastal states were never implemented and soon overtaken by events, namely, a general trend toward expansion of the coastal states' territorial sea and their exclusive fishery jurisdiction in adjacent waters. The next Geneva Conference on the Law of the Sea of 1960 **(244)**, convened to resolve the issue of the width of the territorial sea and the fishing rights of the coastal states in the high seas waters adjacent to it, ended in failure.

The progressing depletion of fishing grounds, due largely to foreign distant-waters vessels, led to a number of international disputes **(299)**: over anchovies, cod, tuna, and other species of fish between, *inter alia*, Morocco and Spain, the US and Peru, and the most publicized "cod wars" between Iceland and the United Kingdom (UK) (as well as the Federal Republic of Germany). As demonstrated by the last-mentioned dispute, the trend toward extending coastal states' fisheries jurisdiction was irreversible. In these cod wars between 1958 and 1976 the UK failed to prevent Iceland from enforcing its jurisdiction, first up to 12 nautical miles, then 50 miles, and finally 200 miles. In 1974 the International Court of Justice (ICJ) **(309)** itself ruled in the *Fisheries Jurisdiction* cases (UK v. Iceland; Federal Republic of Germany v. Iceland) that a 12-mile exclusive fisheries zone had become part of customary international law **(39)** (1974 ICJ Rep. 3, 175). Of course, sedentary species were under an exclusive control of the coastal state as part of its sovereign rights over the continental shelf **(236)** under the 1958 continental shelf Convention, a rule that promptly became part of customary law. High seas **(245)** fisheries continued to be governed by the principle of free access for all, a rule which certainly favored the distant-water fishing states but caused resentment of coastal states, especially those which, like Iceland, were dependent on fishing for their livelihood. Conservation of the living resources in national waters (internal waters and territorial sea) was within the competence of the coastal state and possible on a bilateral basis between such state and a third state allowed to fish there. Any conservation measures with respect to vessels on the high seas could be enforced only by the flag state **(240)** which, as a rule, had little incentive to apply them. Hence, the management and conservation of fisheries beyond the territorial sea was largely a function of some 20 international commissions set up either to manage a specific species or to regulate all fisheries in a particular region, for example, the North East Atlantic Fishery Commission. In general, these commissions were not endowed with sufficient law-making and enforcement powers. As noted above, the 1958 Convention on Fishing and Conservation of the Living Resources of the High Seas was of little practical importance for the conservation of fisheries.

The international law of fisheries underwent a radical transformation with the almost universal acceptance of a 200-mile fishery jurisdiction as part of the coastal state's sovereign rights in its exclusive economic zone (EEZ) **(238)**. Since some 90 percent of world fishing resources are caught within this 200-mile zone (due to concentration of phytoplankton, the basic food of fish, brought from the deep by currents and the upwelling of cold waters), the coastal state must play a key role in the management of marine living resources.

Part V (EEZ) of the United Nations (UN) Convention on the Law of the Sea (LOS Convention) of 1982 **(264)** devotes most of its provisions to the regulation of the living resources of the zone. However, as already noted, Part V does not apply to sedentary species as defined for purposes of the continental shelf. Fisheries on the high seas are regulated in Arts. 116–120 of Part VII (High Seas). The rules concerning highly migratory species, and anadromous and catadromous stocks, are included in Part V in Arts. 64, 66, and 67, respectively, but have relevance for their status on the high seas as well. Mammals are the subject of Art. 65 of Part V, which, by the explicit provision of Art. 120 in Part VII, also applies to their conservation and management in the high seas.

The coastal state, which under Art. 56(1)(a) of the LOS Convention has "sovereign rights" over the living resources in its EEZ, is subject to a number of generally formulated duties, but has a broad discretion in performing them and in exercising its rights under the Convention. The conservation duties of the coastal state in its EEZ are spelled out in Art. 61. They include: determining the TAC; preventing overexploitation; and maintaining the maximum sustainable yield, taking into account fishing patterns, the interdependence of stocks, and generally recognized standards. Using available scientific evidence and cooperation with international organizations **(84)** are mandatory for this purpose. Otherwise, subject to these duties, the coastal state must promote the objective of optimum utilization of the living resources in the EEZ (Art. 62(1)). Access of other states to such resources is regulated in Art. 62(2)(3)(4), but special rules (Arts. 69 and 70) apply to landlocked and geographically disadvantaged states **(253)**. If a coastal state does not have the capacity to harvest the entire allowable catch, it must, through agreements or other arrangements, allow other states access to the surplus, having particular regard to developing landlocked and geographically disadvantaged states and taking into account such factors as the significance of the living resources to its economy, the needs of developing states of the same subregion or region, the rights of landlocked and geographically disadvantaged states, and the need to minimize economic dislocation in states whose nationals have habitually fished in the zone or that have made substantial efforts in research and identification of stocks. Under the continental shelf rules, exploitation of sedentary species is not subject to the conservation and sharing duties. The LOS Convention contains detailed provisions concerning conditions which the coastal state can prescribe to foreign nationals fishing in its EEZ (Art. 62(4)). It may enforce them by measures including boarding, inspection, arrest and judicial proceedings (Art. 73(1)). However, under Art. 297(3) of the Convention, disputes concerning a coastal state's rights over fisheries in its EEZ are not subject to compulsory arbitration **(293)** or adjudication, and only exceptional cases are subject to compulsory (but not binding) conciliation **(296)**. For coastal states with large EEZs, especially developing countries, such as the South Pacific island states in whose zones foreign vessels represent a large majority of fishing vessels, enforcement of fishery regulations constitutes a challenging task. To improve surveillance of foreign fishing vessels in the EEZ, states enter into cooperative agreements **(288)**, such as for example the 1993 Niue Treaty on Cooperation in Fisheries Surveillance and Law Enforcement in the South Pacific Region (32 ILM 136 (1993)). In state practice, agreements concerning access of foreign fishermen to the EEZ have been entered into for some time, displaying a variety of terms concerning compensation of the coastal state. The number of such agreements is estimated to exceed 300.

The management of stocks shared by two or more coastal states within their respective EEZ is governed by Art. 63(1) whereby states are required to seek to agree upon measures necessary to coordinate and ensure the conservation and development of such stocks. There are more than 20 agreements of this kind. They may be in the form of a framework treaty, with specific annual or other periodic regulations; a bilateral commission; a regional fisheries organization, or some other arrangement.

Special problems of management and catch allocation arise in the regulation of the so-called straddling stocks, that is, stock or stocks of associated species that occur both within the EEZ and in an area beyond and adjacent to the zone. The Convention regulates such stocks in a brief provision (Art. 63(2)) requiring the coastal state and the state fishing for such stock in adjacent waters of the high seas to agree upon the conservation of these stocks in the area of the high seas (not in the EEZ). One of the relatively few areas where straddling stocks occur is the area of the Grand Banks in the Northwest Atlantic off Newfoundland, managed by the Northwest Atlantic Fisheries Organization (NAFO) established in 1978. This straddling stock area of turbot (also known as "Greenland halibut") became the subject of a serious dispute (the "turbot war") between Canada and Spain over the arrest in 1995 by Canada, in this area but on the high seas, of the Spanish trawler the *Estai*. The vessel was seized on charges of violating the conservation rules of NAFO, in the enforcement of a Canadian law of 1994 which prohibited non-Canadian vessels from fishing for straddling stock on the high seas in contravention of NAFO rules, thus extending Canada's legislation to foreign ships on the high sea. Spain instituted proceedings against Canada before the ICJ, but the dispute was eventually settled by agreement between Canada and the European Community (EC) whereby Canada repealed the application of its regulations to Spanish (and Portuguese) vessels and discontinued its legal proceedings against the Spanish trawler (34 ILM 1260 (1995)). Incidentally, the ICJ rejected Spain's application on the ground of lack of jurisdiction because of a Canadian reservation **(323)**. In another part of the oceans, the conflict over fishing for pollock by distant-water states in the straddling area of the so-called doughnut hole in the Bering Sea, surrounded by the EEZs of Russia and the US, was resolved by a Convention of the parties concerned in 1994 (34 ILM 67 (1995)). Charges of overfishing straddling stock by distant-water fishing states were also raised by Russia with respect to the "peanut hole," an area in the Sea of Okhotsk which is entirely surrounded by the Russian EEZ, and jointly by Russia and Norway with regard to the straddling stock area (the "loophole") in the Barents Sea, surrounded by the EEZs of these two states. In an effort to deal comprehensively with the management of straddling stocks, a UN-sponsored conference, convened in implementation of Agenda 21 of the Rio Earth Summit of 1992 **(223)**, adopted in 1995 the "Agreement for the Implementation of the Provisions of the UN Convention on the Law of the Sea of 10 December 1982 Relating to the Conservation and Management of Straddling Fish Stocks and Highly Migratory Stocks," briefly, the "Straddling Stock Agreement" (34 ILM 1542 (1995)), which entered into force **(271)** in 2001.

Highly migratory species, anadromous and catadromous stocks, and marine mammals are governed by specific rules of the LOS Convention (Arts. 64–67). Highly migratory species are the 17 species, listed in Annex I of the Convention, including, *inter alia*, eight species of tuna, marlins, swordfish, oceanic sharks, and cetaceans. Conservation and optimum utilization of such species throughout a region, both within and beyond the EEZ, is the duty of the coastal states concerned and other states whose nationals fish in the region. For this purpose states are required to cooperate directly or through appropriate international organizations which already exist or—if non-existent—must be established. Set up by a convention in 1949 (80 UNTS 3), the Inter-American Tropical Tuna Commission is the oldest institution of this kind, but it has not been very effective in the era of a 200-mile EEZ. Other major organizations active under Art. 64 of the LOS Convention include the Commission for the Conservation of Southern Bluefin Tuna, established under a convention of 1993 by Australia, New Zealand, and Japan (26 LOS Bull. 57 (1994)); Convention for the Conservation of Atlantic Tuna, 1966 (673 UNTS 63); Agreement for the Establishment of the Indian Ocean Tuna Commission of 1993; the Commission set up in 2001 under the Convention on the Conservation and Management of Highly Migratory Fish Stocks in the Western and Central Pacific Ocean (40 ILM 277 (2001)); and the Commission as an organ of the South East Atlantic Fisheries Organization established in 2001 by the Convention on the Conservation and Management of Fishery Resources in the South-East Atlantic Ocean (41 ILM 257 (2001)).

Anadromous species, such as salmon and sturgeon, that is, species which spawn in fresh waters but subsequently live in the ocean, are governed by Art. 66 of the LOS Convention. States in whose rivers such species originate have the primary responsibility for managing and conserving such stocks and need not grant other states access to any surplus. Fishing for anadromous species beyond the 200-mile limit is not allowed unless this would cause economic dislocation for a state other than the state of origin. A number of international organizations (commissions) have been established by a convention in implementation of Art. 66, *inter alia*: Convention for the Conservation of Salmon in the North Atlantic, 1982; Convention for the Conservation of Anadromous Stock in the North Pacific Ocean, 1992 (22 LOS Bull. 21 (1993)). Under a bilateral treaty between Canada and the US concerning Pacific salmon, 1985, a commission was established whose purpose is to recommend conservation measures and allocating principles. However, the two countries soon, and especially following the expiration of the treaty **(287)**, became engaged in a protracted dispute **(297)** (the "salmon war") over the quotas and conservation measures, which was not settled until 1999 when an agreement was reached setting new reduced quotas and establishing a $150 million fund to help restore the depleted salmon population.

Catadromous species, that is, species like eels, which spawn in the ocean but spend the greater part of their life cycle in fresh waters, are governed as a general rule by the provisions of Part V (EEZ) of the LOS Convention, but fishing for such species in the high seas is not allowed. Management of catadromous species migrating through the EEZ is to be regulated by agreement (Art. 67).

The conservation of marine mammals, including cetaceans (whales, dolphins, and porpoises), seals, and sirenians (manatees and dugongs) has been among the most controversial and publicized issues in the international law of fisheries. Marine mammals are addressed in Part V of the LOS Convention in a brief article (Art. 65) which—under Art. 120—also applies to the conservation and management of marine mammals on the high seas. Art. 65 explicitly allows coastal states and international organizations to regulate the exploitation of marine mammals more strictly than is provided for in Part V. As a general rule, states are required to cooperate with a view to the conservation of such mammals but, in addition, in the case of cetaceans states must work through appropriate international organizations for their conservation, management, and study. A number of countries, including Australia, UK, and US, have prohibited whaling in their respective EEZs. As early as 1931, a convention for the regulation of whaling was adopted in Geneva (155 LNTS 349). After World War II an International Whaling Commission (IWC), established in 1948 under the 1946 International Convention for the Regulation of Whaling with Schedule of Whaling Regulations (161 UNTS 72) and complemented by a protocol in 1956 (338 UNTS 366) is the organization supervising the management and conservation of whales. In 2001 it had 43 states parties. Initially the IWC was not successful in preventing excessive whaling by some countries, especially the Soviet Union and Japan, a situation that led to near extinction of some species. Eventually, the adoption of new management methods in 1974 whereby, except for five species, whaling was prohibited, and the mounting pressures of environmental and conservation non-governmental organizations **(86)** led to a total moratorium on all commercial whaling, imposed by the IWC as of 1986. However, on pretexts of scientific research some countries, such as Iceland, Japan, and Norway, continued to carry on whaling, thus circumventing the moratorium which they eventually promised to observe. Despite proposals by Japan and Norway to ease restrictions on whaling, the moratorium continued into the new century. In addition, a Southern Ocean Whale Sanctuary, closing the Antarctic Ocean to whaling in 1994 remained in force along with the Indian Ocean sanctuary declared already in 1970. Yet, Iceland, Japan, and Norway continued hunting minke whales, insisting that that species was not endangered at all. Between them, Japan and Norway were estimated to catch some 1,000 minke whales annually under self-issued "scientific permits." In 2001 an IWC meeting expressed concern that the minke whale population had declined to half of what it had been in 1990. But Japan notified the IWC that it planned to kill 50 more minke whales in 2002 in addition to 50 sei whales considered to be an endangered species. When the IWC forbade Japan to carry on commercial whaling, that country, in reaction, succeeded in leading the IWC to a resolution that denied whaling rights to indigenous communities depending on whale as food, and at the 2004 IWC meeting, threatened withdrawal from the organization unless it gained whaling concessions.

Apart from protection under protocols to regional seas marine pollution **(255)** conventions, small cetaceans are protected in some regions by special agreements, such as the 1992 Agreement on the Conservation of Small Cetaceans of the Baltic and North Seas, and a similar Agreement of 1995 on the Conservation of Cetaceans of the Black Sea, Mediterranean Sea and Contiguous Atlantic Area (36 ILM 777 (1997)). Small cetaceans may also be protected in a region under a general wildlife convention, such as the Convention on the Conservation of European Wildlife and Natural Habitat of 1979. The plight of dolphins, captured and killed in purse-seine nets drawn around schools of tuna, has been well publicized. Apart from unilateral measures undertaken by some countries to protect dolphins, the Agreement on the Reduction of Dolphin Mortality in the Eastern Pacific Ocean of 1992 (33 ILM 925 (1994)), sponsored by the Inter-American Tropical Tuna Commission, sets progressively diminishing limits on dolphin catches and deals with the problem of the fishing technology in order to reduce the dolphin mortality.

Among international measures to protect seals, the most important is the Convention for the Conservation of Antarctic **(187)** Seals of 1972 (11 ILM 251 (1972)). Apart from unilateral measures by Canada, the conservation of Arctic seals in waters under Norwegian and Russian jurisdiction is regulated by a bilateral fisheries commission established by Norway and Russia. Sea turtles in the Western Hemisphere are protected by the Inter-American Convention for the Protection and Conservation of Sea Turtles, adopted in 1996, the first multilateral instrument setting standards for the protection of these animals.

Freedom of fishing is one of the freedoms of the high seas codified in Art. 87 of Part VII (High Seas) of the LOS Convention, but—apart from any treaty obligations—is subject to provisions in Part V dealing with straddling stocks (Art. 63(1)), highly migratory species (Art. 64), marine mammals (Art. 65), and anadromous (Art. 66) and catadromous (Art. 67) species. It is also subject to the conservation and management provisions of Arts. 116–120. States must cooperate in the management and conservation of high-seas fishing resources, establishing, as appropriate, subregional and regional bodies to this end. At the turn of the century four such treaty-based commissions were active in their respective regions: the Northwest Atlantic Fisheries Organization established under the Convention on Future Multilateral Cooperation in the Northwest Atlantic Fisheries, 1978; a similar commission created by the Convention on Future Multilateral Cooperation in the Northeast Atlantic Fisheries; the General Fisheries Council for the Mediterranean set up by an agreement to this effect in 1949 (126 UNTS 237), as subsequently amended; and the Commission for the Conservation of Antarctic Marine Living Resources established under the 1980 Convention on the Conservation of Antarctic Marine Living Resources (1329 UNTS 47). The last-mentioned instrument is perhaps the most significant. It encompasses a vast ocean area south of 60 degrees South which, because of the absence of an EEZ off the Antarctic continent, includes also waters within 200 miles off land. The above-noted North Pacific Anadromous Fish Commission also belongs to regional ocean commissions for management and conservation of fisheries.

As a result of the phasing out of most distant-water fishing from foreign EEZs the high seas fisheries have increased significantly, using fish gear such as drift nets many miles in length, which often cause indiscriminate loss of fish and mammals, in particular dolphins. Concern about such methods led to the 1989 Tarawa Declaration on Driftnet Fishing (14 LOS Bull. 29 (1989)) by the states members of the South Pacific Forum, followed in the same year by the Convention for the Prohibition of Fishing with Long Drift Nets in the South Pacific of 1989 (29 ILM 1449 (1990)), with two protocols, and a number of UN General Assembly resolutions recommending cessation of drift net fishing. In the North Pacific, drift net fishing was largely reduced by measures imposed on Japanese fishing by the International North Pacific Fisheries Commission and unilateral measures by some countries, threatening sanctions against states whose fishing industry practices long drift net fishing.

All these actions contributed to a substantial reduction in this practice on the high seas. The more general concerns, including activities undermining the effectiveness of international conservation and management measures, such as the resort to flags of convenience **(241)** to circumvent them, led to adoption under the auspices of the FAO of the Agreement to Promote Compliance with International Conservation and Management Measures by Fishing Vessels on the High Seas of 1993 (33 ILM 968 (1994)) and a "soft law" **(35)** Code of Conduct for Responsible Fisheries in 1995. It remains to be seen whether and to what extent all these measures will contribute to remedying the problems challenging international conservation and management of fisheries on the high seas, the task that must be addressed parallel with the more general problems of dealing with over-capacity in world fisheries and improving linkages between the relevant scientific knowledge and a more rational exploitation of marine living resources.

**240. Flag-State Jurisdiction.** Jurisdiction **(87)** of the flag state is the fundamental principle of jurisdiction on the high seas **(245)**, codified in Art. 92(1) of the United Nations (UN) Convention on the Law of the Sea of 1982 (LOS Convention) **(264)**, whereby, save in exceptional cases, a ship on the high seas is subject only to the jurisdiction of the flag state, that is, the state which granted it the right to sail under its flag, also known as the state of registry or the state of the ship's nationality **(257)**. This "law of the flag" is a natural consequence of the principle that no state can claim sovereignty **(125)** over the high seas and of the need to avoid a state of anarchy in that part of the oceans. Thus, in principle, the state of the ship's nationality has the exclusive right to exercise legislative and enforcement jurisdiction over persons and events aboard the ship, which prevails over any concurrent jurisdiction of other states.

The issue of jurisdiction in cases of collision on the high seas is historically associated with the celebrated *Lotus* case in 1927 before the Permanent Court of International Justice (PCIJ) **(320)** (France v. Turkey) (1927 PCIJ, Series A. No. 10) in which the Court, applying the "objective" territorial principle of jurisdiction **(91)** to the collision on the high seas between a French vessel, the *Lotus,* and a Turkish vessel, upheld the right of Turkey to prosecute the responsible crew member of the French ship. The PCIJ judgment, which under Art. 59 of the Statute of the PCIJ had of course a binding force only between the two parties and in respect of that particular case, gave rise to much criticism and its substance was eventually reversed by the Brussels Convention of 1952 for the Unification of Certain Rules Relating to Penal Jurisdiction in Matters of Collision or Other Incidents of Navigation (439 UNTS 233). The Brussels Convention's solution was followed by the Geneva Convention on the High Seas (Art. 11) adopted by the 1958 Conference **(243)** and by the LOS Convention of 1982 (Art. 97). As a result, in the event of a collision or any other incident of navigation on the high seas (and under Art. 58(2) of the Convention also in the exclusive economic zone (EEZ) **(238)** beyond the territorial sea **(262)**), penal or disciplinary proceedings may be initiated against a crew member only before the judicial or administrative authority either of the flag state or the state of which the individual concerned is a national **(175)** (LOS Convention, Art. 97(1)). Since, as elaborated in detail in Art. 94 of this Convention, the flag state is responsible for the safe operation of its ships, its jurisdiction is likely to have priority over the concurrent jurisdiction of the state of nationality. The flag state has also an obligation to enact laws with respect to penalizing and making responsible its ships and persons under the state's jurisdiction for breaking or injury of a submarine cable or pipeline (Art. 113); make its nationals bear the cost of repairs in such cases (Art. 114); and ensure that foreign owners of ships that have sacrificed an anchor or a fishing gear in order to avoid damage to a submarine cable or pipeline, be indemnified by the owner of the cable or pipeline (Art. 115). Every state must also require masters of ships under its flag to render assistance at sea (Art. 98) and cooperate in the repression of piracy **(259)** (Art. 100), illegal traffic in narcotics (Art. 108), and unauthorized broadcasting from the high seas (Art. 109).

As a general rule every state must effectively exercise its jurisdiction and control in administrative, technical, and social matters over ships flying its flag (Art. 94(1)). The particulars of such exercise are relevant for the purposes of the institution of nationality of ships **(257)**, especially with respect to flags of convenience **(241)**. The most important consequence of the exclusive jurisdiction by the flag state is that on the high seas and—subject to the coastal state's rights—in the EEZ beyond the territorial sea, a merchant vessel can be stopped, boarded, or otherwise interfered with only by a warship **(265)** or other authorized governmental ship or aircraft of the vessel's nationality. However, subject to complete immunity **(131)** of warships (Art. 95) and such authorized ships and aircraft (Art. 96), and apart from the coastal state's right to exercise its jurisdiction over foreign vessels in its EEZ or contiguous zone **(235)** which infringe upon its legitimate rights in these zones, there are exceptional situations in which a warship or other public ship or aircraft clearly marked and identifiable as being on government service, has the right to board a foreign vessel on the high seas in the exercise of the so-called right of visit codified in Art. 110 of the LOS Convention.

The right of a warship or other governmental ship to board a foreign vessel on the high seas is justified if there is reasonable ground for suspecting that: 1. the vessel is engaged in piracy; 2. it is engaged in slave trade **(180)**; 3. it is engaged in unauthorized broadcasting (an unlawful procedure practiced in the North Sea in the 1960s, but largely suppressed after the adoption in 1965 of the European Agreement for the Prevention of Broadcasting Transmitted from Stations outside National Territory (634 UNTS 239); 4. the vessel is without nationality; or 5. though flying a foreign flag or refusing to show its flag, is in reality of the same nationality as the warship. In all these five situations the warship may proceed to verify the ship's right to fly its flag, and to this end it may send a boat under the command of an officer to the suspected ship. If suspicion remains after the documents have been checked, it may proceed, with all possible consideration, to a further examination on board the ship. If the suspicions prove to be unfounded and not justified by any acts of the ship boarded, the ship must be compensated for any loss or damage sustained.

In addition to the five situations justifying the right of visit, the other exceptions to the flag state's jurisdiction include: 6. hot pursuit **(246)**; 7. intervention as a measure to avoid pollution from maritime casualties, probably lawful in customary law **(39)** and otherwise recognized in Art. 221 of the LOS Convention and the Convention Relating to Intervention on the High Seas in Cases of Oil Pollution casualties of 1969 (9 ILM 25 (1969)) and the Protocol of 1973 applying to substances other than oil (1313 UNTS 3); 8. action against foreign vessels authorized by the Security Council as an enforcement measure under Art. 41 of the UN Charter; and 9. interference with foreign vessels under an international agreement to enforce certain rules, such as joint inspection schemes established to protect submarine cables under the 1884 Convention for the Protection of Submarine Cables (163 CTS 391); similar schemes for purposes of the conservation and management of fisheries **(239)**; or—last but not least—arrangements to combat illicit drug trafficking. In the last-mentioned situations, under customary international law, as also stipulated in Art. 108 of the LOS Convention, states have the obligation to cooperate in suppressing such trafficking. But it appears that—unlike the case of piracy or slave trade, and possibly terrorism **(337)**—foreign vessels suspected of being engaged in drug trafficking may not—or at least not yet—be interfered with on the high seas. Therefore, in practice such interference is based on treaties dealing with combating illicit drug traffic. A bilateral agreement on cooperation to combat narcotic traffic by sea exist, for example, between the United Kingdom (UK) and the United States (US), 1981 (1285 UNTS 197). This agreement facilitates interdiction by the US of vessels under the UK flag, suspected of trafficking in drugs, without any additional authorization. On the other hand, Art. 17 of the widely accepted UN Vienna Convention against Illicit Traffic in Narcotic Drugs and Psychotropic Substances of 1988 (28 ILM 493 (1989)) requires a permission of the flag state to board a suspected vessel which can be granted on an *ad hoc* basis for a specific case or, more generally, on the basis of an agreement. The Council of Europe implemented Art. 17 of this Vienna Convention by an agreement in 1995 which, while still requiring the flag state's authorization for boarding a suspected vessel, widens the scope of enforcement jurisdiction for purposes of prosecuting any offenders. Interception of foreign ships on grounds of self-defense, such as the large-scale searches of ships by French warships during the Algerian war in the late 1950s and early1960s, and interdiction of ships during the Cuban quarantine of 1963 **(328)** are highly controversial from the viewpoint of international law.

**241. Flags of Convenience.** Flags of convenience or open registry states **(127)** are states whose laws allow foreign ship owners without any real connection to them to register their ships under the flags of such states and thereby benefit from the very low taxation and greatly reduced operating costs, and especially, low wages paid to the crews of open-registry vessels. More recently, in less typical situations, fishing vessels owned by nationals of states parties to a high seas fisheries conservation regime have in a number of cases been registered in non-party open-registry states in order to avoid compliance with restrictions in fishing and other measures of the conservation regime involved.

Flag-of-convenience states claim that they allow foreign-owned vessels registration under their flags in the exercise of their sovereign **(125)** powers and in accordance with the international law rules governing nationality of ships **(257)**. On the other hand, ship owners of the traditional European maritime nations and their governments have opposed the practice of open registry, claiming that it gives an unfair competitive advantage to ship owners operating under flags of convenience over shipping registered under flags of traditional maritime nations. International labor unions in the West have also fought flags of convenience since the open-registry practice allows ship owners to avoid jurisdiction **(87)** in the area of labor and other legislation of maritime nations and deprives seamen in those nations of job opportunities. More recently, international trade unions intensified their demands concerning wages paid seamen on open-registry vessels. There have also been charges against flags of convenience of laxity in crew standards, failure to comply with anti-pollution regulations of international law **(255)**, and jeopardizing safety of navigation, especially because of old vessels and obsolete equipment and failure to comply with the requirement to submit reports on casualty investigations to the International Maritime Organization (IMO). While it is true that on the whole the flag-of-convenience ships account for a disproportionately higher share of losses at sea as compared to the traditional merchant fleets (with Cyprus, Malta, Panama, and the Philippines accounting for the highest share of losses per 1,000 ships in the period 1990–1995), some open-registry fleets have a relatively larger number of modern tankers and other cargo carriers than those under traditional maritime flags. A more recent concern with respect to the flags of convenience has been that the secrecy surrounding the ownership structure of vessels might allow terrorist organizations to register ships under an open registry flag and use them as weapons in, for example, American ports. It is for this reason that the United States (US), which in a way was a creator of the flags of convenience and so far their major supporter, has made proposals at the IMO to make the beneficial ownership of open registry ships more transparent.

The modern history of the flags of convenience dates back to the 1920s when American shipping companies began to use the flag of Panama to avoid Prohibition regulations in their cruise ships just outside the then three-mile-wide territorial sea **(262)**, and then helped Liberia to set up its open registry to accommodate American oil companies under its flag. Honduras and, for some time, Costa Rica, also offered their respective flags in a policy of open registry. For economic reasons, the practice of flags of convenience continued after World War II when Liberia and then Panama, rapidly grew to become the leading flag-of-convenience states and, formally, the world's by far largest "ship-owning nations" in terms of gross registered tonnage (GRT) (the total volume of a ship within the hull and above deck, with one GRT equaling 100 cubic feet). The adoption of the "genuine link" requirement for purposes of nationality of ships in the Convention on the High Seas produced by the Geneva Conference on the Law of the Sea in 1958 **(243)** had no impact upon the continued expansion of the open registry practice. Furthermore, the International Court of Justice (ICJ) **(309)**, in its advisory opinion **(291)** on the *Constitution of the Maritime Safety Committee of the Intergovernmental Maritime Consultative Organization* (IMCO) (now International Maritime Organization, IMO) (1960 ICJ Rep.150), indirectly upheld Liberia's and Panama's right to open registry, by ruling that the concept of genuine link was irrelevant for determining the meaning of the phrase "the largest ship-owning nations" for purposes of IMCO's Maritime Safety Committee, as formulated in the Convention establishing this specialized agency of the United Nations (UN). The ICJ held that the phrase simply meant nations with the largest shipping tonnage, irrespective of any link between ships and the state of nationality. The Court implied that ownership was also an irrelevant factor.

By the turn of the century the number of open-registry states had multiplied significantly. According to the International Transport Workers Federation there were 27 states that could be qualified as offering flags of convenience. In addition to the well-established flags of Liberia and Panama, they included, *inter alia*, Bahamas, Belize, Cambodia, Cyprus, Honduras, Malta, Marshall Islands, Philippines, Vanuatu, Saint Vincent and the Grenadines, and even the landlocked Bolivia. The fact that the 1982 UN Convention on the Law of the Sea (the LOS Convention) **(264)** reiterated and further developed the genuine link rule has not had a negative effect upon the growth of flags of convenience. In 1998, out of the total of 532 million GRT of ships over 100 tons, 273 GRT (16,000 ships) were registered in 27 open-registry countries, with Panama, Liberia, Bahamas, and Malta having by far the largest merchant fleets in terms of foreign-owned tankers and other merchant cargo ships registered under their respective flags. Shipping companies from the US, United Kingdom (UK), Greece, Japan, and, more recently, Russia and China, are the major users of flags of convenience. It must be noted, however, that because of complex international corporate arrangements it may sometimes be difficult to determine whether a ship flies a flag of convenience or has a real beneficial ownership connection to its state of registry. A new type of flags of convenience was resorted to during the Iran-Iraq War (1980–1988) when the US (and less so the UK), without any concern over the genuine link requirement, agreed to register under its flag ("reflag") a number of Kuwaiti tankers in order to protect them from Iranian attacks.

It is believed that, strictly speaking, in case of an international armed conflict **(339)** or other national emergency the state of registry has the right to requisition ships flying its flag. On the other hand, the state of ownership may requisition national-owned vessels within its internal waters **(249)** or territorial sea **(262)**. Requisition on the high seas **(245)** and in ports of third states could be justified by the need to offer protection which, unlike the state of ownership, the open-registry states are, as a rule, not able to provide. Some open-registry states have agreed to such arrangement with the state of ownership (for example, the UK with Liberia and Vanuatu, 1989). Under traditional rules of naval warfare **(361)**, while the enemy or neutral character **(362)** of a merchant ship is determined by its flag, prize courts **(365)** have looked behind a neutral flag, regarding ownership as the test of the enemy character **(346)** of a vessel. In fact, the same position was taken by the Security Council in its resolution on sanctions against the new Yugoslav state **(134)** in 1992: ownership and control by Yugoslav nationals and not the flag was the test of a ship's nationality.

The expansion of open-registry fleets raised a serious concern of the UN Conference on Trade and Development (UNCTAD) that not only did this practice have a negative impact upon the interests of traditional ship-owning nations but on the whole was also detrimental to the competitiveness and, in general, the economy of the less-developed countries. As a result, as part of international action against flags of convenience, in 1984 UNCTAD convened a diplomatic conference of 106 states which in 1986 adopted the UN Convention on Conditions for Registration of Ships (26 ILM 1229 (1987)). However, by 2004 this Convention had not yet entered into force **(271)**, requiring for this end ratification **(280)** by 40 states the combined GRT of which amounts to at least 25 percent of world tonnage. The UNCTAD Convention developed the requirements on the duties of the state of the ship's nationality, laid down in Art. 91 of the LOS Convention of 1982, adding some provisions designed to strengthen the required link between a ship and its state of registry not only with regard to effective jurisdiction but also in respect to including in the state's register of shipping relevant information concerning participation of nationals in the ownership and manning of ships. The Convention also stipulated standards for a competent maritime administration and identification of owners, operators, and agents in a state register as well as their accountability.

The above-noted issue of the use of flags of convenience by fishing vessels has been on the agenda of the Food and Agricultural Organization. More generally, on the national level, some maritime nations, such as Norway, succeeded in diverting significant portions of open-registry vessels owned by their nationals to a special "international register" providing for more liberal conditions of operating ships than those in the general national register. One might also note the practice of registering ships in dependent territories. For example, many British-owned vessels are registered in the Isle of Man, Bermuda, and some other dependent territories.

The general conclusion must be that the practice of open registry is allowed under international law, subject to a general rule that every state, whether a flag-of-convenience state or a traditional maritime nation, must fulfill the duties of flag state spelled out in Art. 94 of the LOS Convention.

**242. Freedom of the High Seas.** A fundamental principle of the law of the sea **(254)**, codified in Art. 87 of the United Nations (UN) Convention on the Law of the Sea (LOS Convention) **(254)**, whereby the high seas **(245)** are open to all states **(127)**, whether coastal or landlocked **(253)**, and all states have the right to exercise certain freedoms there, with due regard for the interests of other states.

As an accepted institution of international law, the principle of the freedom of the high seas did not assert itself universally until the beginning of the 19th century. Earlier, some states had laid claims to large portions of the oceans, denying foreign fishermen the freedom of fishing, claiming for their warships **(265)** the right of salute by foreign ships and, in some cases, disallowing passage through vast areas of the sea off their coasts without payment of tolls. For example, in the 15th and 16th centuries Venice claimed sovereignty **(125)** over the Adriatic; Sweden and Denmark each claimed the Baltic; and England laid such claims to vast areas of the surrounding ocean.

As overseas exploration and trade increased, opposition to the notion of the "closed sea" would steadily mount and in legal terms was reflected in the debate between the advocates of maritime sovereignty and champions of the free sea. The debate is commonly associated with the name of Hugo Grotius **(16)** whose pamphlet *Mare Liberum* (The Free Sea)—as discovered in the 19th century, one chapter of his treatise *De Jure Praedae* (On the Law of Prize and Booty) not published until 1868—defended the principle of the freedom of the seas against Portuguese encroachments. However, Alberico Gentili (Gentilis) **(15)**, one of Grotius' predecessors, had been an earlier advocate of this principle. Grotius' defense of the freedom of the seas prompted the appearance of pamphlets advocating the legality of claims to sovereignty over the sea, of which *Mare Clausum* (The Closed Sea) authored by John Selden, an English jurist and antiquarian representing England's claims to maritime sovereignty, is the best known. However, even England, which had originally advocated the idea of a closed sea, eventually discontinued its claims, realizing the advantages of the freedom-of-the seas regime. Thus, with the growing importance of free navigation as an essential element of overseas trade, the extravagant claims to sovereignty over marine spaces were abandoned in the 18th century, subject to recognition of some kind of coastal maritime belt which later developed into the concept of territorial sea **(262)**.

In the second half of the 20th century the regime of the high seas underwent a fundamental modification due to a universal acceptance of the institution of the exclusive economic zone (EEZ) **(238)** and—with a less general impact—archipelagic waters **(231)**. In the new century, despite isolated, extravagant claims to wide territorial seas and ideas asserting priority in the utilization of high seas fisheries **(239)**, like Chile's notion of *mar presencial*, the new regime for the oceans, in principle upholding the freedom of the seas, is likely to continue in the foreseeable future.

Both the 1958 Convention on the High Seas (Art. 2), a product of the first Geneva Conference on the Law of the Sea **(243)**, and the LOS Convention of 1982 (Art. 87) give non-exhaustive examples of high seas freedoms: navigation and overflight; laying submarine cables and pipelines ("right of immersion"), subject to certain rights of states on the continental shelf **(236)** within the 200-mile EEZ; fishing (subject to rules on conservation and management of fisheries); and—as added by the LOS Convention—constructing artificial islands and other installations permitted under international law (subject to the rules on the continental shelf) and conducting scientific research (subject to the rules on the continental shelf and (Part XIII) provisions on marine scientific research). However, there remains potential for conflicts in that the freedoms are not listed in an exhaustive manner and the existence of requirement that they be exercised by all states with due regard to the interests of other states on the high seas and in the deep-seabed "Area" **(232)**. Thus certain activities exercised on grounds of the freedom of the high seas may be controversial. Naval maneuvers and conventional weapons testing are allowed on prior notification to all third states which are free to monitor and observe such activities, but the lawfulness under customary international law **(39)** of testing nuclear weapons on the high seas by a state which is not a party to the 1963 Partial Test Ban Treaty (480 UNTS 43), is a highly controversial issue. In instituting proceedings before the International Court of Justice (ICJ) **(309)** against France, which closed a large area of the Pacific Ocean to shipping to conduct nuclear tests there in 1974, Australia and New Zealand argued that France's action unreasonably interfered with shipping and polluted the sea with radioactive fallout, thus constituting lack of due regard for the interests of other states and abuse of the freedom of the high seas. The ICJ did not rule on the legality of the testing after France had announced its intention to disregard further underwater testing (1974 ICJ Rep. 253). It is arguable, however, that by the end of the 20th century a ban on nuclear testing at sea had emerged in customary international law.

Art. 88 of the LOS Convention states briefly that "[t]he high seas shall be reserved for peaceful purposes." This "peaceful purposes reservation" (and the analogous reservation of Art. 149 with regard to the Area) cannot reasonably be interpreted **(274)** as imposing restraints on all naval activities on the high seas (including the EEZ beyond the territorial sea), the more so as the LOS Convention itself contains some dozen provisions governing warships. In conjunction with the general provision of Art. 301 on "Peaceful Uses of the Sea," the peaceful purposes reservation must simply be construed to mean that on the high seas states shall refrain from any threat or use of force contrary to Art. 2(4) of the UN Charter **(329)**. Military uses of the seas may, of course, be restricted by treaty **(288)**, such as for example the US-Soviet Treaty on the Limitations of Anti-Ballistic Missile Systems of 1972 (the First Strategic Arms Limitation Treaty, SALT I) (944 UNTS 13) which, *inter alia*, imposes limits upon strategic nuclear missile submarines. There are also bilateral agreements designed to avoid incidents at sea, such as the US-Soviet Agreement on the Prevention of Incidents on and over the High Seas of 1972 (852 UNTS 151), and a number of similar agreements entered into by the former Soviet Union **(133)** with Western states.

Navigation on the high seas of nuclear-powered ships (all of which are warships at this time) and warships carrying nuclear weapons belongs to activities allowed under the freedom of navigation. The regional treaties on "nuclear-free" zones apply only to areas under the sovereignty of the states parties. Among such treaties are: the Tlatelolco Treaty of 1967 (634 UNTS 281) for Latin America; the Rarotonga Treaty of 1985 (24 ILM 1440 (1985)) for South Pacific; the Treaty on African Nuclear-Free Zone of 1995 (35 ILM 705 (1996)); and the Bangkok Treaty of 1995 establishing such a zone in South-East Asia (35 ILM 635 (1996)).

**243. Geneva Conference on the Law of the Sea, 1958.** An international conference convened in 1958 under the auspices of the United Nations (UN) in Geneva with the participation of 86 states **(127)** and designed to codify and develop **(5)** the law of the sea **(254)** on the basis of drafts prepared by the International Law Commission (ILC). This Conference is sometimes referred to as the First UN Conference on the Law of the Sea since it was followed by a conference in 1960 **(244)** and in 1982 by the most important and comprehensive Third UN Conference on the Law of the Sea (UNCLOS III) **(263)**.

The 1958 Conference produced four conventions which constituted the first major codification of the law of the sea in modern international law: 1. Convention on the Territorial Sea **(262)** and the Contiguous Zone **(235)** (516 UNTS 205); 2. Convention on the High Seas **(245)** (450 UNTS 11); 3. Convention on the Continental Shelf **(236)** (499 UNTS 311); and 4. the soon outdated Convention on Fishing and Conservation of the Living Resources of the High Seas **(239)** (559 UNTS 285). In addition, there was an Optional Protocol of Signature Concerning the Compulsory Settlement of Disputes **(318)** (450 UNTS 162).

As declared in its preamble, the high seas convention was generally declaratory of established principles of international law. The other three conventions are silent on their nature but, in general, at the time of their adoption, they were a mixture of codification and development of the law of the sea. In 2004 the 1958 conventions were still in force for the few of the states parties that had not ratified **(280)** or acceded to **(267)** the comprehensive regime of the UNCLOS III Convention on the Law of the Sea (LOS Convention) of 1982 **(264)**. Under Art. 311 of the LOS Convention, this Convention shall prevail, as between states parties, over the Geneva Conventions of 1958.

While the 1958 Geneva Conference resulted in a considerable codification achievement, the participating states could not reach agreement in the territorial sea convention on the then controversial issue of the breadth of the territorial sea and, in the fishing convention, on the related issue of the fishing rights of the coastal states in the area of the high seas adjacent to the territorial sea. It was to deal exclusively with these two questions that another conference was convened for 1960.

In the years following 1959, technological developments in offshore drilling and other seabed exploration and exploitation made it necessary to revise the continental shelf regime and perhaps even develop a new approach to the utilization of the resources of the deep seabed. Moreover, concerns of coastal states over progressive depletion by other states of fishing resources in the high seas close to the territorial sea of these states induced coastal states to claim wider territorial sea and expand their fisheries jurisdiction **(87)** at the expense of the high seas, thus making the fishing convention of 1958 virtually meaningless. Politically, many new, mostly less-developed, states which had not existed at the time of the 1958 Geneva Conference, pressed for a completely new regime for the law of the sea that would take account of their concerns and demands. With the 1958 Conventions largely overtaken by events, all these pressures eventually led to the convening of UNCLOS III in 1973.

**244. Geneva Conference on the Law of the Sea, 1960.** An international conference in Geneva under the auspices of the United Nations (UN) in 1960, with the participation of 87 states **(127)**, convened specifically to resolve the outstanding issues of the 1958 Conference on the Law of the Sea **(243)**, namely, the breadth of the territorial sea **(262)** and the fishing rights of states in the areas of the high seas **(245)** adjacent to the territorial sea. The 1960 Conference, sometimes known as the Second UN Conference on the Law of the Sea, failed to achieve its objectives. A joint United States–Canada compromise proposal for a territorial sea of six nautical miles (one nautical mile is equal to 6080.20 feet or 1853.25 meters) plus a six-mile exclusive fisheries jurisdiction **(87)** zone failed by one vote needed for the necessary two-third majority. However, as it soon turned out, even if a compromise on the two controversial issues had been reached at the 1960 Conference, it would not have meant much in practice because of the irreversible trend of expanding coastal states' jurisdiction, including claims of the territorial sea wider than six miles (mostly 12 miles) and fisheries zone extending up to 200 miles, which was far beyond the modest limits proposed in 1960. Eventually, the two issues became only a small though important part of the overall codification and development **(5)** of the law of the sea by the Third UN Conference on the Law of the Sea (UNCLOS III) **(263)**.

**245. High Seas.** As a result of the emergence in the past few decades of the institution of the exclusive economic zone (EEZ) **(238)**, the concept of the high seas, as codified in Art. 86 of Part VII of the United Nations (UN) Convention on the Law of the Sea of 1982 (LOS Convention) **(264)**, applies to all parts of the sea that are not included in the EEZ, in the territorial sea **(262)**, or in the internal waters **(249)** of a state, or in the archipelagic waters of an archipelagic state **(231)**. Historically, as a relatively simple law of the sea **(254)** regime more or less stabilized by the end of the 18th century, the high seas encompassed all parts of the sea beyond the limits of a narrow belt of territorial sea. However, this traditional legal framework, eventually codified in the Convention on the High Seas adopted by the Conference on the Law of the Sea in 1958 **(243)**, had to yield to economic and political pressures in the latter decades of the 20th century. As a result, the coastal states' jurisdiction extended seawards at the expense of the high seas. Specifically, the emergence of the EEZ removed approximately one-third of the ocean space from the regime of the high seas. Initially, the traditional maritime powers, concerned about a potential conversion of the reluctantly accepted EEZ into the territorial sea ("creeping jurisdiction") would prefer to treat the EEZ merely as a part of the high seas, subject to certain economic rights of the coastal state, rather than a legally separate marine zone. However, eventually all states acquiesced in the new order of the oceans, as codified by the Third UN Conference on the Law of the Sea of 1982 (UNCLOS III) **(263)**, and accepted the new legal concept of the high seas in its diminished geographical scope, subject, however, to the rights of all states to exercise in a foreign EEZ (beyond the territorial sea), the freedoms of navigation and overflight, of laying submarine cables and pipelines, and other internationally lawful uses of the sea, as provided for in the pertinent EEZ provisions of the LOS Convention.

The concept of the high seas extends also to the superjacent airspace **(186)** and to the seabed and subsoil subject, for the area beyond the EEZ, to the law governing any continental shelf **(236)** and, in the case of the Area **(232)**, that is, the deep seabed beyond national jurisdiction, to the provisions of Part XI of the LOS Convention, as revised by the Implementation Agreement of 1994 **(247)**.

It is a fundamental rule of international law, as codified in the LOS Convention, that "[n]o State may validly purport to subject any part of the high seas to its sovereignty" **(125)** (Art. 89). However, this principle did not assert itself until the early 19th century. In the early centuries of the territorial states system some states had laid claims to large portions of the oceans. In legal theory, the conflict over such claims was debated within the context of the principle of the freedom of the seas **(242)**. It might be noted here that while there is no specific provision in the LOS Convention to the effect that no part of the EEZ may validly be subjected to any state's sovereignty, Art. 89 on invalidity of claims of sovereignty over the high seas and other articles governing various problems of the high seas (Arts. 88 and 90–115) also apply to the EEZ "in so far as they are not incompatible" with Part V dealing with the EEZ (Art. 58(2)).

**246. Hot Pursuit.** An exception to the rule of exclusive jurisdiction **(87)** of the flag state **(240)** over its ships on the high seas **(245)**, the right of hot pursuit is the right of a warship **(265)** or military aircraft, or other authorized ship or aircraft on government service to pursue and arrest a foreign ship suspected with good reason by a coastal state of having violated the coastal state's laws and regulations while in that state's internal waters **(249)** or territorial sea **(262)**.

The right of hot pursuit, alluded to by Cornelius van Bynkershoek **(4)**, evolved in the maritime practice of the 19th century, and by the 20th century became an established rule of the law of the sea **(254),** eventually codified in the Convention on the High Seas (Art. 23) adopted by the Geneva Conference on the Law of the Sea of 1958 **(243)** and in the United Nations (UN) Convention on the Law of the Sea (Art. 111) of 1982 (LOS Convention) **(264)**. One of the most celebrated historical cases in which the right of hot pursuit was at issue was the *I'm Alone* Arbitration **(293)** (3 RIAA 1609) between the United Kingdom, (Canada), and the United States (US) in 1935, involving the sinking on the high seas by the US Coast Guard of the *I'Alone*, a British-flag but American-owned schooner pursued on suspicion of smuggling liquor during the Prohibition in the US. A more recent case (Case No. 2), which also involved problems of circumstances excluding state responsibility **(128)** and the issues of genuine link and nationality of ships **(257)**, is that of an oil tanker, *M/V Saiga* before the International Tribunal for the Law of the Sea (ITLOS) **(310)** (Saint Vincent and the Grenadines v. Guinea) in 1999 (38 ILM 1323 (1999)).

Hot pursuit must meet certain conditions, all of which must be met for the pursuit to be lawful under international law, as also ruled by the ITLOS in the above-noted *M/V Saiga* judgment. First, the hot pursuit may be undertaken when the competent authorities of the coastal state have good reason to believe that the foreign ship has violated the laws and regulations of that state. Second, the pursuit must be commenced when the foreign ship or one of its boats is in the internal waters, the territorial sea, or the archipelagic waters **(231)** of the pursuing state, or—in case of violation of customs, fiscal, immigration, or sanitary laws—within the contiguous zone **(235)**. To begin hot pursuit, the pursuing ship must first satisfy itself that the pursued ship or one of its boats or other craft working as a team and using the ship pursued as a mother ship, is within the territorial sea or other zone as the case may be. The right of hot pursuit applies *mutatis mutandis* to violations in the exclusive economic zone **(238)** or on the continental shelf **(236)** of the laws and regulations applicable to them, including those on safety zones around continental shelf installations. Third, the pursuit may only commence after a visual or auditory signal to stop has been given at a distance which enables the pursuing ship to be seen or heard by the foreign ship, but it is not necessary that the ship giving order to stop should likewise be within the territorial sea or the contiguous zone at the time. It appears that a radio signal, especially at a great distance, is not sufficient to order the ship to stop. Fourth, the hot pursuit must be uninterrupted. However, a pursuit commenced by an aircraft may be taken over by another aircraft or ship, but the aircraft giving order to stop must itself actively pursue the fleeing vessel until a ship or another aircraft of the coastal state, summoned by the aircraft, arrives to take over the pursuit, unless the aircraft is itself able to arrest the fleeing vessel. It is not entirely clear whether a ship may also take over the pursuit from another ship. Fifth, the right of hot pursuit ceases as soon as the ship pursued enters the territorial sea of its own state or of a third state. Finally, stopping or arresting a foreign vessel outside the territorial sea in circumstances that do not justify the exercise of the right of hot pursuit entails the duty to compensate that ship for any loss or damage sustained, as was, *inter alia*, decided by the ITLOS in the above-noted case of *M/V Saiga* where the Tribunal found that Guinea was in violation of Art. 111 on hot pursuit of the LOS Convention and had no legal basis for the exercise of the right of hot pursuit against the Saint Vincent and the Grenadines vessel. Concerning the use of force in arresting a ship, the ITLOS observed that considerations of humanity require that it should be avoided if at all possible and, when force is unavoidable, it should not go beyond what is reasonable and necessary under the circumstances.

Apart from the right of hot pursuit codified in the LOS Convention, customary international law **(39)** recognizes the doctrine of the so-called constructive presence allowing arrest of a foreign vessel which, while remaining on the high seas, violates the coastal state's law by its own boat. In a liberal interpretation of the right of hot pursuit under Art. 111 of the Convention, the doctrine of constructive presence is already implied in that right.

**247. Implementation Agreement, 1994.** This is the Agreement relating to the Implementation of Part XI of the United Nations (UN) Convention on the Law of the Sea of 1982 (LOS Convention) **(264)**, adopted by a resolution of the UN General Assembly (GA) in 1994 (33 ILM 1309 (1994)) and in force **(271)** in 1996, with 117 states parties in early 2004. The Agreement was adopted without any opposing vote by a vote of 121, including the United States (US), with seven abstentions. Its overwhelming approval testifies to the successful compromise achieved between the industrialized and the less-developed countries over the issue of the legal status of the deep seabed (the Area) **(232)**.

The Agreement was adopted in order to achieve universal participation in the LOS Convention, by modifying its Part XI dealing with the regime of the Area, whose provisions were found unacceptable by the US and some other industrialized states. The need to secure acceptance of the Convention by those states led the UN Secretary-General in 1990 to initiate consultations aimed at reforming Part XI, which eventually led to the adoption by the GA of the Resolution on the Agreement. This was made possible because of a marked decline in commercial interest in deep-seabed mining and a general recognition that the cumbersome bureaucratic structure of the Area's regime, as devised by the LOS Convention, was unnecessary. In addition, political and economic changes in the post–Cold War world, including a growing reliance on free market principles among the politically weakened Group of 77 (the less-developed states), created conditions favoring a reform of Part XI to meet the concerns of the industrialized countries, especially in view of the prospect of the impending entry into force of the LOS Convention in November 1994, following the 60th ratification **(280)** in November 1993.

The Agreement consists of two parts. First, the short, ten-article main text deals only, without entering into the substance of the problem, with the legal relationship between the LOS Convention and the Implementation Agreement and the various means whereby states may consent to be bound by the Agreement. Second, the Annex, which is an integral part of the Agreement, spells out in detail, in nine long sections, provisions thoroughly reforming Part XI of the LOS Convention on the Area, dealing with: the costs to states parties and institutional arrangements; the Enterprise (an organ of the International Seabed Authority); decision making; review conference; transfer of technology; production policy; economic assistance; financial terms of contracts; and the Finance Committee.

An unusual agreement from the point of view of treaty **(288)**-making practice, the 1994 Agreement is styled as an "implementation" agreement, but in reality it constitutes a thorough revision of the part of the LOS Convention that it purports to implement. This ingenious approach was chosen to avoid the protracted amendment **(269)** procedure of the Convention, otherwise open solely to the parties of the Convention. The Agreement and Part XI of the Convention are to be interpreted **(274)** and applied together as a single instrument, but—understandingly enough—in the event of any inconsistency the provisions of the Agreement prevail. Arts. 309–319 of the LOS Convention (reservations **(282)** and exceptions, declarations and statements, relations to other agreements, amendments, denunciation, status of annexes, and the UN Secretary as the depositary) apply to the Agreement as they apply to the Convention. Furthermore, to ensure that the Convention after its entry into force should already include the modifications introduced by the Agreement, the Agreement provides that any ratification, confirmation of, and accession **(267)** to the Convention shall also represent consent to be bound by the Agreement. Any state that wishes to be a party to the Agreement must have, previously or at the same time, ratified or acceded to the LOS Convention. Thus, any future ratification or accession to the Convention automatically implies consent to the Agreement and, in the interests of universal adherence to the Convention, no state may consent to the Agreement without consent to the Convention whose scope otherwise by far transcends the less important provisions on any future—and uncertain—activities in the deep-seabed Area.

The Agreement allows states to choose among a number of alternative means of expressing consent to be bound by it (Art. 4(3)), including a simplified procedure under Art. 5 which, in principle, enabled a state that had become party to the Convention before the date of the adoption of the Agreement (28 July 1994) to become party to the Agreement without further action unless it otherwise notified the depositary within a year following that date. But such a state is still eligible to accede to the Agreement by a subsequent accession. The Agreement flexibly provided (Art. 7) for a provisional application (possible under the Vienna Convention on the Law of Treaties) pending entry into force, which on 16 November 1994 allowed the Convention to enter into effect already in its revised form. The provisional application terminated upon the date of entry into force of the Agreement, that is, 28 July 1996.

**248. Innocent Passage.** The right of innocent passage is the right of ships of all states **(127)**, whether coastal or landlocked **(253)**, to pass through another state's territorial sea **(262)**. The right of innocent passage does not, however, include the right of overflight. Codified in Arts. 17–32 of the United Nations (UN) Convention on the Law of the Sea of 1982 (LOS Convention) **(264)**, which significantly developed the provisions of the Convention on the Territorial Sea and the Contiguous Zone **(235)**, adopted at the 1958 Geneva Conference on the Law of the Sea **(243)**, the customary law **(39)** right of innocent passage is a fundamental and firmly established rule of the international law of the sea which **(254)** evolved along with the institution of the coastal states' territorial sea.

Innocent passage includes two components: "passage" and "innocent." As defined in the LOS Convention (Art. 18), passage means navigation through the territorial sea for the purpose of traversing the sea without entering internal waters **(249)** or calling at a roadstead (an area of water in the internal waters or territorial sea, normally used for the loading, unloading, or riding at anchor of ships (Art. 12)) or port facility outside internal waters or—an innovation of the LOS Convention—proceeding to or from internal waters or a call at such roadstead or port facility. Passage includes stopping and anchoring, but only insofar as this is incidental to ordinary navigation or is rendered necessary by *force majeure* **(78)** or distress **(72)** or—a situation added by the LOS Convention—for the purpose of rendering assistance to persons, ships, or aircraft in danger or distress. It is an essential requirement that passage shall be continuous and expeditious; hovering is not allowed. Under Art. 20, submarines and other underwater vehicles are required to navigate on the surface and to show their flag. Incidentally, this requirement has been waived in relations between the members of the North Atlantic Treaty Organization. It must be added that foreign ships have the right of innocent passage through internal waters in cases where the establishment of straight baselines **(233)** has the effect of enclosing as internal waters areas not previously considered as such. Furthermore, the right of innocent passage exists through archipelagic waters of archipelagic states **(231)** and—in certain situations—as unsuspendable innocent passage in straits used for international navigation **(260)**.

Passage is "innocent' as long as it is not prejudicial to the peace, good order, or security of the coastal state, a rule already stated in the 1958 Geneva Convention on the Territorial Sea and the Contiguous Zone (Art. 14(4). This rule is further developed in Art. 19(2)) of the LOS Convention which adds an all-inclusive list of activities, engaged in by a foreign ship in the territorial sea in question, which deprive a passage of innocent character. The fact that the Convention refers to "activities" that occur "in the territorial sea" means that facts other than such activities, for example, the ship's cargo, flag, means of propulsion, destination, purpose of the voyage, and the like, cannot be used as criteria for determining lack of innocence. This is of major national security significance for the United States (US) in whose navy some 40 percent of ships use nuclear propulsion. The list of activities automatically depriving the passage of a foreign ship of innocent character includes (Art. 19(2)): threat or use of force **(329)** against the coastal state in violation of the UN Charter; exercise or practice with weapons of any kind; collecting intelligence to the prejudice of the coastal state's security; hostile propaganda; launching, landing, or taking on board any aircraft or any military device; loading or unloading any commodity, currency, or person contrary to the customs, fiscal, immigration, or sanitary laws and regulations of the coastal state; willful and serious pollution; fishing; carrying out research or survey activities; interfering with the coastal state's communication systems or other facilities or installations; and—a general but rather vague criterion which may in practice restrict the right of innocent passage—"any other activity not having a direct bearing on passage." In 1989 a Joint Statement by the Soviet Union and the US on uniform interpretation **(274)** of rules of international law governing innocent passage (28 ILM 1444 (1989)) confirmed the substance of Art. 19(2) of the LOS, stating that "a ship passing through the territorial sea that does not engage in any of these activities is in innocent passage."

The coastal state may take the necessary steps in its territorial sea (including use of force apparently even against a warship) **(265)**, to prevent passage which is not innocent (Art. 25(1)). Without any discrimination in form or in fact among foreign ships, the coastal state may suspend the right of innocent passage in specified areas for reasons of security, including weapons exercises, but such suspense shall take effect only after giving due publicity (Art. 25(3)). In the exercise of its legislative jurisdiction **(87)** the coastal state may enact laws and regulations relating to innocent passage and designate sea lanes and traffic separation schemes, but it may not thereby hamper innocent passage or discriminate against ships of any state or against ships carrying cargoes to, from, or on behalf of any state. On the other hand, the coastal state has the duty to give publicity to dangers of navigation (Art. 24(2)). As held by the International Court of Justice **(309)** in 1949 in the *Corfu Channel* case (United Kingdom v. Albania), there exists a customary law duty to warn ships of the danger of mines (1949 ICJ Rep. 4).

Whether and under what conditions warships enjoy the right of innocent passage has long been one of the most controversial issues in the law of the sea. Like the relevant 1958 Geneva Convention, the LOS Convention contains no provisions expressly allowing or denying such right to foreign warships. Evading the issue, it simply grants the right of innocent passage to "ships" of all states (Art. 17). Thus, it seems obvious that logically such formulation includes warships the more so as Art. 20 requires submarines, a type of ship that ordinarily is a warship, to navigate on the surface. At the Geneva Conference on the Law of the Sea in 1958 and at the Third UN Conference on the Law of the Sea (UNCLOS III) **(263)** the Western powers insisted, against a number of less-developed countries and the then Soviet bloc, that warships enjoyed the right of innocent passage without any need for authorization of the coastal state involved or prior notification. Eventually, the Soviet position shifted to the Western view and in the above-noted Joint Statement with the US in 1989 expressly recognized the right of innocent passage of warships without any notification or authorization. Still, the issue continues to be controversial as a sizable minority of coastal states, including mainly but not exclusively developing states (for example Brazil, China, and India), claim the right to control entry of warships into their territorial sea by means of the requirement of prior notification, authorization, or placing limits on the number of foreign warships allowed at any time. The right of innocent passage of foreign nuclear-powered ships and ships carrying nuclear or other inherently dangerous or noxious substances has also been questioned by some states, but such right is anchored in Art. 23 of the LOS Convention which only requires such ships to carry documents and observe special precautionary measures established for such ships by international agreements.

**249. Internal Waters.** Internal waters (sometimes referred to as interior waters) are waters on the landward side of the baselines **(233)** of the territorial sea **(262)**. They usually comprise bays **(234)**, estuaries, and ports, and waters enclosed by straight baselines. Special rules govern the status of internal waters of archipelagic states **(231)**. Internal "seas," actually saltwater lakes, such as the Caspian Sea, are not governed by the law of the sea **(254)** and are subject to special treaties of the littoral states. The legal status of inter-oceanic canals is also regulated by special treaties.

The law of the sea codifications **(5)**, including the United Nations (UN) Convention on the Law of the Sea (LOS Convention) of 1982 **(264)**, do not devote much space to the problem of internal waters; hence, their legal status is based mainly on customary law **(39)**. Art. 2 of the LOS Convention confirms the well-established rule of customary law that the coastal states' sovereignty **(125)** extends to internal waters. As a result, the right of innocent passage **(248)** of ships through foreign territorial sea does not, as a rule, exist so far as internal waters are concerned. The only exception to the right of the coastal state to deny foreign ships entry into or passage through its internal waters is stipulated in Art. 8(2) of the LOS Convention, providing that innocent passage exists in internal waters when the establishment of straight baselines has the effect of enclosing as internal waters areas which had not previously been considered as such. It is not clear whether such right exists also in customary law.

Two aspects of the legal status of internal waters are of major interest in state practice: the right of access of foreign ships and jurisdiction **(87)** over such ships by the coastal state. Although asserted by some writers **(42)**, there exists in principle no general right of access by foreign ships to ports and other parts of internal waters of the coastal state. At its discretion, a coastal state has the right to designate ports open to international shipping or it may close its ports on grounds of national interest. Access to navigable rivers and other national waterways is governed by special treaties **(204)**. Coastal states have the right to prescribe conditions for access and exit of foreign ships, a right stipulated in a number of treaties **(288)** such as those on maritime safety and prevention of pollution and implicit in a number of provisions of the LOS Convention, for example in Arts. 25(2) and 211(3) (rights of protection of the coastal state to prevent any breach of the conditions of admission to a port including measures against marine pollution). Numerous bilateral treaties of commerce, friendship, and navigation and the multilateral Convention and Statute on the International Regime of Maritime Ports of 1923 (50 LNTS 287), ratified by some 40 states, regulate the problem of access of foreign ships. The port state may arrest a foreign ship in port or take it as security in civil action *in rem,* but ships of the parties to the Brussels Convention on the Arrest of Sea-Going Ships of 1952 (439 UNTS 193) may be detained only in cases of maritime claims. Warships **(265)** and other governmental ships on non-commercial service are governed by special rules. In general, despite the port state's rights, a clearly arbitrary or discriminatory closure or such conditions of access to ports may justify diplomatic protests and even international responsibility **(128)** of the coastal state. Under an ancient customary rule of international law, ships in distress **(72)** have the right of entry to a port or other internal waters, but this right appears to apply only if human life is at risk and not in order to save the ship's cargo.

As to jurisdiction, the general rule is that, subject to state **(131)** and other **(67)** immunities, foreign vessels in internal waters are under complete civil and criminal jurisdiction of the coastal state. However, in practice, for reasons of comity **(6)** and expediency, that state asserts its jurisdiction only when it perceives that its interests are at stake. Matters of the "internal economy" of the foreign ship are usually left to the jurisdiction of the flag state. A distinction is often made between the Anglo-American and the French positions in the matter of jurisdiction in internal waters. According to the former a state may, as a matter of policy, choose to forego the exercise of jurisdiction to which it is fully entitled under international law whereas in the French doctrine the coastal state's jurisdiction does not extend to purely internal affairs of the foreign ship. But the actual practice of states does not reveal any essential differences between the two approaches. Apart from exercising jurisdiction in such routine matters as pilotage, safety of navigation, and pollution, the coastal state's intervention takes place if it is perceived to be necessary for reasons of national security. To sum up states' practice, the coastal state normally asserts its jurisdiction if an offense committed on board a foreign ship (for example, homicide) disturbs the peace and good order of the port; or if intervention is requested by the captain or a consul **(57)** of the flag state; or in cases where an individual who is not a crew member is involved. However, attempts by a port state, as for example, by the United States with regard to labor and anti-trust legislation, to impose upon a foreign ship the obligation to comply with the law of the port state even after that ship has left its jurisdiction, have been opposed by the states concerned as contrary to the fundamental principle of jurisdiction in international law.

Ships driven into foreign internal waters by distress or *force majeure* **(78)** are usually granted a certain degree of immunity. For example, they are exempt from any harbor fees and import duties and are not liable to arrest, but otherwise are expected to comply to a reasonable extent with the laws and regulations of the state of shelter.

**250. International Seabed Authority.** An autonomous United Nations (UN) organization **(84)** with its seat in Kingston, Jamaica, established at the Third UN Conference on the Law of the Sea (UNCLOS III) **(263)** under the UN Convention on the Law of the Sea (LOS Convention) (Arts. 156–168) of 1982 **(264)** and the 1994 Implementation Agreement **(247)**, through which states parties, in accordance with the legal regime for the Area **(232)**, that is, the deep seabed and subsoil beyond national jurisdiction **(87)** established in Part XI of the LOS Convention and the Implementation Agreement of 1994, shall organize and control activities in the Area, in particular with a view to administering the resources of the Area. But activities in the deep seabed unconnected with administering the resources, such as, for example, laying cables and pipelines or conducting scientific research relative to the superjacent water, are beyond the competence of the International Seabed Authority (ISA) (LOS Convention, Art. 135). Under Resolution I of Annex I to the Final Act of UNCLOS III, the Preparatory Commission for the ISA and for the International Tribunal for the Law of the Sea (ITLOS) **(310)**, commonly referred to as PrepCom, was charged with making the necessary arrangements for the commencement of the functions of the ISA. The ISA came into existence on 16 November 1994 upon the entry into force **(271)** of the LOS Convention and became operational in 1996. The PrepCom had been formally wound up in 1994. The relationship between the ISA and the UN is regulated by the Agreement to this effect of 1997 (36 ILM 1492 (1997)).

While the basic framework of the ISA is set forth in Part XI of the LOS Convention, the Implementation Agreement of 1994 substantially revises its structure, powers, and decision making in order to meet the objections of the United States (US) and other industrialized nations, and guarantee their paramount position in the ISA, commensurate with their interests and investments. Funded until 1997 from the regular UN budget, since 1998 the ISA has received its financial means from assessed contributions of its members, but when adequate revenue from any seabed mining is available, it is expected to be a self-financing organization.

The Authority has three principal organs: the Assembly consisting of all states parties to the LOS Convention; the Council, made up of 36 states, and the Secretariat. There are three subsidiary organs. The Legal and Technical Commission and the Finance Committee, which was added by the Implementation Agreement (Annex sec. 9), were established upon the entry into force of the LOS Convention in 1994, but the establishment of an Economic Planning Commission, envisaged in Art. 163 of the LOS Convention, was made conditional upon a future decision of the Council for reasons of efficiency and economy and in accordance with the evolutionary approach adopted. For the time being, the functions of the Commission were delegated to the Legal and Technical Commission (Agreement, Annex sec. 1(4)). In addition, there is an operating arm of the Authority, called "Enterprise" (LOS Convention Art. 170), which is retained by the Agreement of 1994 but deprived of its independence and subjected to the Council, the most powerful organ of the ISA. A major concern of the industrialized countries in reforming the ISA was to make it cost-effective and to make the whole system operate according to a functional and evolutionary approach. Hence, the Agreement (Annex sec. 1(2) and (3)) provides that the establishment of the Authority and its organs and meetings are to be governed by the objective of minimizing costs while allowing the Authority to develop in keeping with its functions according to an evolutionary approach.

The powers of the Assembly, which under the LOS Convention was envisaged as the supreme organ of the Authority, were considerably reduced by the Implementation Agreement in favor of the Council conceived there as the executive body primarily responsible for the administration of the seabed mining regime. A complex formula on the composition of the Council seeks to balance the various groups and interests involved. Under sec. 3(15) of the Annex to the Agreement, which revised Art. 161(1) of the Convention in order to take account of the new political and economic developments and secure the US a seat in the 36-member Council, that crucial organ is to be made up of: 1. four members from the major consumers of the categories of minerals to be derived from the Area; 2. four members from among the eight largest investors in deep-seabed mining; 3. four members from among the major net exporters including at least two developing states; 4. six members from among developing states parties, representing special interests (states with large populations; landlocked and geographically disadvantaged states **(253)**; island **(251)** states; major importers of the categories of minerals to be derived from the Area; potential producers of such minerals; and least developed states); and 5.18 members elected in a way ensuring an equitable geographical distribution. The seats for the US and Russia are guaranteed under the provision on major consumers, which expressly lays down that the membership shall include the state with the largest economy in terms of gross domestic product (GDP) in 1994, that is the US, and one state from the Eastern European region, having the largest economy in the region, that is the Soviet Union (now Russia) **(133)**. For purposes of voting, each of the first three groups (1, 2, and 3) plus the developing states of the other two groups (4 and 5) taken together as a single voting unit, will be treated as a "chamber" (Annex sec. 3(9)(a)).

As the chief executive body of the Assembly, the Council supervises the implementation of the deep-seabed mining regime, approves plans of work, adopts rules and regulations, and performs a variety of other functions listed in Art. 162 of the LOS Convention as modified by the Agreement of 1994. The 15-member Finance Committee, established by the Agreement (Annex sec. 9) in response to proposals by the industrialized states, includes members from the five largest contributors to the budget until the ISA can generate sufficient funds (other than assessed contributions) for its administrative expenses. All the decisions of the Council and the Assembly having financial or budgetary implications must be based on a recommendation of the Finance Committee, adopted by consensus.

Conceived under the LOS Convention as the principal mining operator, the Enterprise (Agreement Annex sec. 2) is retained by the 1994 Agreement, but for the time being made inactive, with its otherwise only preparatory functions performed by the Secretariat. It can become operational only by virtue of the Council's decision, and any of its operations will have to conform to sound commercial principles. Furthermore, initially it may operate only in joint ventures with commercial enterprises until the Council—where the industrialized countries have the power of blocking decisions—decides that it may operate independently like other contractors, and without any obligations by states to finance its operations either in a joint venture or as an independent operator. In addition, the Agreement (Annex sec. 5(2) and sec. 6(7)) eliminated the provisions of the LOS Convention on compulsory transfer of technology. By increasing the powers of the Council at the expense of the Assembly the 1994 Agreement assured a predominant role of the US and other industrialized nations.

As a general rule, decision making in the organs of the ISA should be by consensus (Agreement Annex sec. 3(2)), by which term the LOS Convention (Art. 161(8)(e)) means the absence of any formal objection. When consensus cannot be reached, the Assembly's decisions in procedural matters require a simple majority of votes, and those on substantive questions need two-thirds of members present and voting. Although the Assembly has the right to shape general policies, it must do so in collaboration with the Council, in the sense that the Assembly's decisions on any matter in which the Council has also competence or on any administrative, budgetary, or financial matter, must be based on a recommendation of the Council. If a recommendation is not accepted, the matter must be returned to the Council for further consideration. When consensus cannot be reached in the Council, under the general rules in the ISA, procedural questions require a simple majority and substantive ones are subject to a two-third majority, provided that the decision in question is not opposed by a majority in any of the above-noted chambers representing various interests groups. As a result, three members of a chamber, for example, the US and two other consumer countries, can block any substantive decision of the Council. Four categories of substantive decisions must, under the retained provision of Art. 161(8)(d) of the LOS Convention, be made only by consensus, which in effect is tantamount to a veto. These four categories involve: protection of land-based producers of the developing countries; recommendations on rules on seabed revenue sharing; adoption and application of provisional rules implementing the seabed mining regime; and amendments **(269)** of the regime. To help overcome a decision-making deadlock, the LOS Convention (Art. 161(8)(e)) provides for the possibility of setting up a conciliation **(296)** committee and the Agreement envisages deferring the taking of a decision in order to facilitate further negotiations **(316)** whenever all efforts at achieving consensus on a question appear not to have been exhausted (Annex sec. 3(6)). It should also be added that the LOS Convention provides for a Seabed Dispute Chamber of ITLOS (Arts. 186–191 and Annex VI, Statute of the ITLOS) which has jurisdiction in disputes with respect to activities in the Area, including also disputes involving the ISA as a party.

**251. Islands.** The United Nations (UN) Convention on the Law of the Sea (LOS Convention) of 1982 **(264)** defines an island as a "naturally formed area of land, surrounded by water which is above water at high tide." (Art. 121(1)). The legal status of islands, once governed exclusively by customary law **(39)**, is now regulated in a number of aspects by the LOS Convention. Irrespective of size, every island, including islets and rocks, has a territorial sea **(262)**. In addition, except for "rocks which cannot sustain human habitation or economic life of their own" (Art. 121(3)), islands can serve as baselines **(233)** for all other maritime zones: the contiguous zone **(235)**, the exclusive economic zone (EEZ) **(238)**, and the continental shelf **(236)**. However, since they generate the territorial sea, rocks also can have a contiguous zone. The provision on rocks does not define the meaning of this feature and the description of inhabitable rocks is rather vague, which has made it possible for some states to claim an EEZ around islets that could not reasonably meet the test of Art. 121(3). In the best-known case of this kind, in 1976 the United Kingdom (UK) proclaimed, against protests by Ireland and Denmark, a 200-nautical mile fishing zone (one nautical mile equals 6080.20 square feet or 1853.25 meters) around Rockall, a rock of less than 0.01 square miles in area, situated 180 miles northwest of the Hebrides. Eventually however, after acceding **(267)** to the LOS Convention, the UK gave up its claim to the zone.

The LOS Convention includes special rules for drawing baselines in cases of islands situated on atolls or islands having fringing reefs (Art. 6). In such cases the baseline is the seaward low-water line of the reef, as shown on official charts. Within the context of straight baselines the Convention also deals with a fringe of islands along the coast in its immediate vicinity. Islands are also taken into account in measuring the area of a bay **(234)** and within the context of the transit passage in straits **(260)** and waters of archipelagic states **(231)**.

Artificial islands, installations, and structures (for example, oil drilling rigs) do not possess the status of islands and may not be used to establish baselines, to enclose internal waters **(249)**, or to establish or measure the breadth of a maritime zone (LOS Convention Arts. 60(8), 147(2)(e), and 259). The coastal state has an exclusive right to construct artificial islands in its EEZ and its continental shelf, but construction of such installations on the high seas **(245)** is recognized as one of the freedoms of the high seas.

**252. Kiel Canal.** A major international maritime waterway in northern Germany, 61 miles (98 kilometers) long, connecting the Baltic with the North Sea. Also known as the North Sea–Baltic Canal, it was constructed for strategic reasons by the German Empire, and until the end of World War I was not recognized by it as an international waterway such as the Suez Canal **(261)** and the Panama Canal **(258)**. Unlike these two inter-oceanic waterways, the legal status of the Kiel Canal is not based on any international agreement specifically governing the Canal. However, Art. 380 of the Treaty of Peace between the Allied and Associated Powers and Germany, Versailles 1919 (225 CTS 189) provides that "[t]he Kiel Canal and its approaches shall be maintained free and open to the vessels of commerce and of war of all nations at peace with Germany on terms of entire equality."

In 1920 a dispute arose between Poland, then at war with Soviet Russia, and Germany over Germany's refusal to grant a request for the passage through the Canal of the *Wimbledon*, a British ship chartered to a French company, carrying a cargo of munitions for Poland to the Free City of Danzig **(60)**. Justifying its refusal (and thereby indirect assistance to Soviet Russia), Germany contended that the passage would constitute a breach of neutrality **(362)** on its part. As a result, the *Wimbledon* had to take a longer route around the Jutland Peninsula, with a 13-day delay. Following the end of the Poland–Soviet Russia war the issue came before the Permanent Court of International Justice **(320)** in its first contentious case, SS *Wimbledon* (Great Britain, France, Italy, and Japan, with Poland intervening **(311)** v. Germany) (1923 PCIJ, Series A, No. 1). In its judgment the Court decided against Germany, holding that by virtue of Art. 380 of the Peace Treaty of Versailles the Kiel Canal had ceased to be an internal waterway, becoming an international waterway open to states at peace with Germany "in the sense that even a passage of a belligerent man-of-war **(265)** does not compromise the neutrality of the sovereign **(125)** state **(127)** under whose jurisdiction **(87)** the waters in question lie."

In 1936 Germany unilaterally denounced the articles of the Versailles Treaty governing the Kiel Canal, making passage of warships subject to prior permission of Germany. A majority of the signatories of the Treaty acquiesced in this illegal act of Nazi Germany. After World War II the Federal Republic of Germany did not reinstate the relevant provisions of the Versailles Treaty, but declared the Canal, otherwise internal waters **(249)** of Germany, to be open to ships of all nations, with foreign ships requiring prior notification and authorization for the passage from the foreign office of the Federal Republic. However, ships of the members of the North Atlantic Treaty Organization (NATO) are exempt from these restrictions, being governed by special arrangements applying to the members of NATO.

**253. Landlocked and Geographically Disadvantaged States.** As stated in Art. 124(1)(a) of the United Nations Convention on the Law of the Sea (LOS Convention) of 1982 **(264)**, "landlocked" states are states **(127)** which have no seacoast whereas "geographically disadvantaged" states, a much less precise term, are defined (but only for purposes of Part V of the LOS Convention, dealing with the exclusive economic zone (EEZ) **(238)**) as "coastal States, including States bordering enclosed and semi-enclosed seas **(237)**, whose geographical situation makes them dependent upon the exploitation of the living resources of the exclusive economic zone (EEZ) of other States in the subregion or region for adequate supplies of fish for the nutritional purposes of their populations or parts thereof, and coastal States which can claim no exclusive economic zones of their own." In a more inclusive sense, geographically disadvantaged states are states which, while having access to the sea and being coastal states, have a coastline that is very short in proportion to the area of their land territory (for example, the Democratic Republic of Congo, Iraq, and Bosnia and Herzegovina), or because of the close vicinity to another state or states, cannot claim an EEZ or a continental shelf **(236)** of their own that would be commensurate with the length of their coastline or the size of their territory (such as, for example, Germany and Singapore), or whose EEZs are poor in marine resources (such as, for example, Jamaica and Nauru).

Landlocked states, which in the early 21st century numbered as many as 42 (13—or 14 if one includes Vatican City **(80)**—in Europe; 15 in Africa, 12 in Asia, and 2 in South America), raise, first, the question of their rights of access to and navigation on the sea. Second, there is the problem of the right of such states and geographically disadvantaged states to participate in the exploitation of marine resources, including also deep-seabed minerals of the Area **(232)**.

It is still a controversial issue whether under customary law **(39)** landlocked states have a right of transit to the coast through the territory of a neighboring state. In treaty **(40)** form (apart from the LOS Convention, as below), such right is guaranteed in a number of agreements, such as the Convention and Statute on Freedom of Transit of 1921 (7 LNTS 13) to which, however, less than 50 states, including 12 landlocked ones, are parties, and Art. V of the General Agreement on Tariffs and Trade (GATT) of 1947 (55 UNTS 18) reiterated in the GATT Agreement of 1994 (33 ILM 1154 (1994)) to which some 130 states are parties. The Convention on the High Seas, adopted at the Geneva Conference on the Law of the Sea of 1958 **(243)**, provides that rights of access to seaports and transit are to be granted to landlocked states by agreement (Art. 3). There are numerous bilateral agreements to this effect and some multilateral conventions of which the Convention on

Transit Trade of Landlocked Countries of 1965 (597 UNTS 3) is the most important although it also suffers from a low number of ratifications **(280)** (36 in 1998). Other multilateral agreements include the 1921 Convention and Statute on the regime of Navigable Waterways of International Concern (7 LNTS 36); the Convention and Statute on the International Regime of Railways of 1923 (47 LNTS 55); and the Convention on Road Traffic of 1968. Conventions on freedom of navigation on specific international rivers **(204)** and civil aviation agreements also grant, to a various extent, the right of transit to landlocked states.

Notwithstanding a large number of transit agreements, the landlocked states pressed for a clear guarantee of the right of transit at the Third United Nations Conference on the Law of the Sea (UNCLOS III) **(263)**. Such right is stipulated in Art. 125 of the LOS Convention in Part X on the right of access of landlocked states to and from the sea and freedom of transit. However, the Convention's provisions did not fully meet the expectations of the landlocked countries because, first, the exercise of the right of transit depends on agreement between the landlocked and the transit states and, second, transit states, that is, states (with or without a seacoast) situated between a landlocked state and the sea, through whose territory traffic in transit passes (Art. 124(1)(b)), have the right to take all measures necessary to ensure that the rights and facilities provided for landlocked states in no way infringe their legitimate interests (Art. 125 (3)).

Although historically there had been some doubts whether vessels of landlocked countries had the right to navigate on the high seas **(245)**, the peace treaties ending World War I recognized such right, as for example stipulated in Art. 273 of the Peace Treaty of Versailles with Germany (225 CTS 189). The right in question has been firmly established since the adoption in 1921 of the Declaration Recognizing the Right to a Flag of States Having No Seacoast (7 LNTS 73). Reaffirmed by the 1958 Geneva Convention on the High Seas and the LOS Convention of 1982, it can be regarded as part of customary international law. As laid down in Art. 87(1) of the LOS Convention, "[t]he high seas are open to all States, whether coastal or landlocked." As a matter of fact, a dozen or so landlocked states maintain a merchant fleet plying the high seas under their respective flag.

There is no universal right of access to ports and other internal waters **(249)**, available to foreign vessels in customary law. Hence, the use by a landlocked state of ports of another state is based on bilateral agreements, and—for six signatory landlocked states—on the Convention and Statute on the International Regime of Maritime Ports of 1923 (58 LNTS 287) to which altogether 40 states are parties. Under Art. 131 of the LOS Convention ships flying the flag of landlocked states enjoy treatment equal to that accorded to other foreign ships in maritime ports. However, the exact meaning of this provision is not entirely clear.

Access to marine resources is relevant to both landlocked and geographically disadvantaged states. Their access to high seas resources and the use of the high seas for other lawful purposes is ensured under the general principle of the freedom of the high seas **(242)**, codified in Art. 87 of the LOS Convention. The projected deep-seabed regime of the Area grants developing landlocked and—to a lesser extent—geographically disadvantaged states special consideration and representation in the Council of the International Seabed Authority **(250)**. The interests and needs of developing landlocked countries are also to be taken into account in distributing any revenues from the exploitation of the continental shelf beyond the 200-mile limit.

The LOS Convention provides (Arts. 69(1) and 70(1)) for a limited right of landlocked states and geographically disadvantaged ones (as defined in Art. 79(2)), to participate on an equitable basis in the exploitation of an appropriate part of the surplus, that is, the part of the total allowable catch (TAC) which the coastal state is not capable of harvesting, of the living resources of the EEZs of coastal states of the same subregion and region (terms not defined in the Convention). Account must be taken of the relevant economic and geographical circumstances of all the states concerned, with the terms of such participation to be established through agreements, taking into account various factors specified in Arts. 69(2)(a)(b)(c)(d) and 70(3)(a)(b)(c)(d) for landlocked and disadvantaged states respectively.

When a coastal state's harvesting capacity approaches a point where it is able to harvest the entire TAC in its EEZ, it must make arrangements on a bilateral, subregional, or regional basis to allow developing landlocked states and developing geographically disadvantaged states of the same subregion or region to participate in the exploitation of the living resources of the EEZs of coastal states of the subregion or region "as may be appropriate in the circumstances and on terms satisfactory to all parties" (Art. 69(3) and 70(4)). This means that the coastal states have a wide discretion in allocating the surplus fisheries in their respective zones, let alone because of the vague concepts of "subregion" and "region." Developed landlocked and developed geographically disadvantaged states are entitled to participate in the exploitation of the living resources only in EEZs of developed coastal states under conditions spelled out in Arts. 69(4) and 70(5).

The right of neighboring landlocked and geographically disadvantaged states to conduct marine scientific research is addressed in Art. 254 of the Convention. States and international organizations **(84)** undertaking a research project in an EEZ must, whenever feasible, give neighboring landlocked and geographically disadvantaged states an opportunity to participate in it and in any case must give an assessment of its results to such states.

The landlocked and geographically disadvantaged states, which despite wide disparities in economic and political development, formed a large group of more than 50 states at UNCLOS III, were not entirely satisfied with the treatment accorded them in the Convention. Their rights of transit to the seacoast and of benefiting from the surplus in the EEZ are not formulated precisely and still depend on the discretion of the coastal state in question. In addition, lack of adequate fishing technology does not allow many less-developed states to take advantage of their rights under the LOS Convention to benefit from exploitation of fisheries in the EEZs of other countries.

**254. Law of the Sea.** The law of the sea is the part of public international law which governs states **(127)** and possibly other international legal persons **(85)** in their international relations concerning the use and utilization of the oceans. Marine spaces cover some 140 million square miles, that is, 72 percent of the earth's surface. This fact, plus the role that the oceans play in shaping the planet's climate and weather, in providing nourishment for a sizable portion of the world's population and other vital resources, and in facilitating international communication, trade, and commerce, point to the crucial position of the law of the sea as part of international law.

The law of the sea must be distinguished, first, from private maritime law or admiralty law, which is concerned with rights and obligations in maritime matters of private persons and deals with such problems as carriage of goods, marine insurance, and the like. However, the law of the sea can be of significance for private persons when they happen to get involved in violations of municipal law **(27)** pertaining to laws and regulations concerning maritime matters, such as fisheries **(239)**, navigation, prevention of marine pollution **(255)**, and the like, which are enacted by states in accordance with the public international law of the sea. Second, the law of the sea regulates maritime matters between states only in time of peace; rules governing naval warfare **(361)**, maritime neutrality **(362)**, and other issues of warlike relations at sea form part of the international law covering conduct of warfare and more generally "international humanitarian law" **(353)**.

While the law of the sea evolved as an important part of the law of nations in the early centuries of the modern territorial state system in Europe coinciding with the age of overseas discoveries, some of its rules had their antecedents in various medieval compilations of maritime law for use by merchants, ship owners, and seamen in the Mediterranean, the North Sea, and the Baltic. Among such codes, the best known are: the Rhodian Law (*Lex Rhodia*) compiled between the 7th and 9th centuries; *Tabula Amalfitana*, 10th century; laws of Oléron, a 12th-century collection made in France; *Consolato del Mare*, perhaps the most famous compilation prepared in Barcelona in the 14th century; and the Laws of Wisby, put together on the island of Gotland, Sweden, in the 14th century, a maritime law collection for use in the Baltic area.

The origins of the modern law of the sea are associated with the name of Hugo Grotius **(16)**, a Dutch jurist and the major champion of the principle of the freedom of the seas **(242)**. Like other areas of the law of nations in the early modern era, the rules of the law of the sea relied heavily on civil (Roman) law **(23)** and the ancient natural law doctrine **(29)**. Gradually, however, with expanding overseas trade and exploration, maritime matters increasingly came to be governed by customary rules of law **(39)** developed in state practice and based on consent. The 18th-century Dutch jurist Cornelius van Bynkershoek **(4)** best reflects this trend which by the early

19th century resulted in a body of customary law of the sea of relative simplicity, based on the existence of two kinds of maritime zones: the by far larger zone of the high seas **(245)** governed by the principle of the freedom of the seas, and various narrow offshore belts of coastal jurisdiction which eventually consolidated into the territorial sea **(262)**. At the same time some problems of the law of the sea were increasingly subject to a treaty **(40)**, mostly bilateral, regulation.

Codification **(5)** of the law of the sea dates back to the 19th century and modest attempts by private organizations **(86)**, such as the International Law Association and the Institut de droit international. In the inter-war period the private codification work of Harvard Law School also included some problems of the law of the sea, but the first official international endeavor at codifying one area of this law, namely the law of territorial sea, is associated with the League of Nations. However, the League of Nations-sponsored Hague Conference of 1930 failed to reach agreement on the matter.

Following World War II the basic framework of the law of the sea (supplemented in the early 20th century by a narrow "contiguous" zone **(235)** of special jurisdiction on the high seas adjacent to the territorial sea for specific purposes only) continued to be anchored in customary law. Hence it was a major topic selected for codification by the International Law Commission whose drafts of four conventions (territorial sea and contiguous zone, fishing, continental shelf **(236)**, and high seas) were discussed and adopted as treaties **(288)** by the Geneva Conference on the Law of the Sea of 1958 **(243)**. But these four conventions, apart from the fact that the Convention on the Territorial Sea and the Contiguous Zone and then the 1960 Geneva Conference **(244)** failed to resolve the then controversial issue of the width of the territorial sea and fishery jurisdiction beyond that zone, were soon overtaken by events which—as it turned out—amounted to a revolutionary sea change in the law of the sea. The major development was the trend to extend the coastal states' sovereignty seaward by claiming a wider territorial sea and expanding their jurisdiction for fishing to ever wider areas. At the same time, claims to offshore sovereign rights in the continental shelf, initiated by the United States (US) in 1945, raised, under the pretext of the exploitability criterion, the possibility of extending sovereign rights to the resources of the deep seabed. Less-developed countries, aspiring to reform the traditional law of the sea by redistributing marine resources in the name of a New International Economic Order, played a major role in the trend to expand coastal jurisdiction, in reality amounting to the shrinking of the high seas. All these developments led to a major transformation of the law of the sea and to required an international action to adopt new rules keeping up with the changes in states' practice and to elaborate some kind of legal code to govern the oceans. That was the task of the Third United Nations (UN) Conference on the Law of the Sea, 1973–1982 (UNCLOS III) **(263)** which in 1982 adopted the UN Convention on the Law of the Sea (LOS Convention) **(264)**, comprehensively codifying and progressively developing this large and complex branch of public international law. Supplemented by the "Implementation Agreement" of 1994 **(246)**, in force **(271)** in 1996, which met the objections of the industrialized states concerning the LOS Convention's approach to deep-seabed mining, the Convention entered into force in 1994. Another agreement, which gave effect to an important but—unlike the seabed mining—currently urgent problem, was the Agreement for the Implementation of the Provisions of the UN Convention on the Law of the Sea of 10 December 1982 Relating to the Conservation and Management of Straddling Fish Stocks and Highly Migratory Fish Stocks, 1995 (34 ILM 1542 (1995)), not yet in force.

In the early 21st century the LOS Convention (with the Implementation Agreement) provided the basic framework for a comprehensive regulation of maritime matters governing states. By the end of 2004 the LOS Convention was in force for 145 and the Agreement for 117 states, that is, a fairly large majority of states. A sizable minority (some 30 states) had not yet ratified the LOS Convention. Under the law of treaties **(288)**, as stipulated in Art. 18 of the Vienna Convention on the Law of Treaties of 1969 (8 ILM 679 (1969)), such states, if parties to the Vienna Convention, were obliged not to defeat the subject and purpose of a treaty (in this case the LOS Convention) prior to its entry into force unless they had made their intention clear not to become parties. A small number of states, including the US, are still parties only to one or more Geneva Conventions of 1958. Formally, unless denounced, these conventions will continue to bind them until the state in question ratifies **(280)** or accedes to **(267)**, as the case may be, the LOS Convention. Under Art. 311 of the latter, the LOS Convention prevails over any of the four Geneva conventions of 1958.

It is not unusual that in such a large area of international law as the law of the sea there is need, in addition to the comprehensive LOS Convention, to regulate by special conventions a number of issues: fisheries **(239)**, navigation and maritime safety, protection of the marine environment against pollution **(255)**, and questions of liability **(120)** and compensation **(118)**, to mention only a few major problems. An important role in producing this body of rules and thus contributing to further development of the law of the sea has been played by public international organizations **(84)**, both global, such as especially the International Maritime Organization and the UN Environment Program, and numerous regional organizations, especially in the area of fisheries and the protection of the marine environment.

Considering the fact that many provisions of the LOS Convention reflect customary law and some other rules of the Convention which progressively develop the law of the sea have, on the whole, been accepted and are gradually acquiring the status of customary law, a great majority of states recognize the same rules as binding either under the Convention or as customary law of the sea. Despite uncertainty with regard to some sensitive and controversial issues, such as doubts whether certain of the Convention's provisions, for example, the right of transit through international straits **(260)**, really reflect customary law, and notwithstanding some questions left unanswered by the Convention, for example, historic and some other categories of bays **(234)**, the process of gradual consolidation of the body of rules governing the oceans is likely to continue.

**255. Marine Pollution.** A large portion of the conventional (that is, treaty-based) **(40)** law of the sea **(254)** is designed to combat marine pollution and to protect and preserve the marine environment. At the same time, these rules of the law of the sea form part of international environmental law **(197)** in general whose fundamental principles apply also to the marine environment. Awareness of the dangers posed by pollution of the oceans grew in the latter decades of the 20th century, and especially following the Stockholm Conference on Human Environment of 1972 **(226)**. As a result, a network of international agreements produced a variety of legal regimes for the protection of the marine environment, both in terms of functional scope and geographical domain. As a matter of fact, marine pollution was the first form of pollution to be subject to treaty regulation even before the Stockholm Conference. Modest, unsuccessful efforts in this area date as far back as the 1920s.

Protection and preservation of the marine environment forms a major part of the United Nations (UN) Convention on the Law of the Sea of 1982 (LOS Convention) **(264)**. Its Part XII (Arts. 192–237) is, of course, not intended by itself to regulate all problems of marine pollution. It sets forth some fundamental principles which in many respects correspond to those governing international environmental law **(197)** as such, including, *inter alia*, the general obligation of states to protect and preserve the marine environment and to take individual or joint measures necessary for this purpose; to adopt the precautionary approach; not to transfer damage or hazards or transform one type of pollution into another; to prevent pollution resulting from the use of technology; not to introduce potentially harmful alien or new species in the marine environment; and to notify of imminent or actual damage. The provisions on global and regional cooperation impose the duty to develop joint contingency plans; to cooperate for the purpose of promoting studies, research programs, and exchange of information and data; and cooperate in establishing scientific criteria for elaboration of rules, standards, and practices for the prevention, reduction, and control of pollution of the marine environment (Arts. 192–201). Section 3 of Part XII mandates developed countries to provide the developing states scientific and technical assistance and accord them preferential treatment. General rules on monitoring the risks or effects of pollution, publication of reports, and assessment of potential effects of activities are set forth in Section 4. Through all these general provisions, the LOS Convention offers an unprecedented overarching framework for the vast and growing number of global and regional treaty law relating to combating marine pollution in all its forms. However, the Convention focuses in more detail on one form of marine pollution, namely, vessel-source pollution. It elaborates relatively detailed rules on a system of legislative and enforcement jurisdiction with regard to this form of pollution, making an attempt to balance the interests of port, coastal, and flag states. Art. 237 of the Convention lays down that specific objectives assumed under the anti-pollution agreements should be carried out by states in a manner consistent with the general principles and objectives of the Convention.

Following UN experts, the LOS Convention (Art. 1(1)(4)) defines pollution of the marine environment as "the introduction by man, directly and indirectly, of substances or energy into the marine environment, including estuaries, which results or is likely to result in such deleterious effects as harm to living resources and marine life, hazards to human health, hindrance to marine activities, including fishing and other legitimate uses of the sea, impairment of quality for use of sea water and reduction of amenities." Generally speaking, there are six sources of marine pollution, a classification adopted also in the Convention (Arts. 207–212): 1. from land-based sources, the most serious threat to the oceans; 2. from or through the atmosphere, essentially a form of pollution from land-based sources; 3. from offshore drilling, that is, from seabed activities subject to national jurisdiction; 4. from dumping waste and toxic substances, the dumping of nuclear waste being the most hazardous procedure; 5. from vessels; and 6. a potential problem, from activities in the deep seabed beyond national jurisdiction, that is the "Area" **(232)**.

Action to prevent and control marine pollution has been taken, apart from national measures, on global, regional, subregional, and bilateral levels. Much of the international environmental law protecting the sea has been generated by regional and lower-level cooperation which takes account of the local peculiarities of the marine environment. In regional arrangements, the approach can be a piecemeal one where specific types of marine pollution are tackled by special conventions; or it may be derived from a framework umbrella convention setting forth general principles of combating pollution but leaving a more detailed regulation of specific sources of pollution to special protocols, as has been the practice in the Regional Seas Program of the UN Environment Program (UNEP); or, finally, a single convention may comprehensively regulate all pollution in a marine region, as was done in the pioneering Helsinki Convention on the Protection of the Marine Environment of the Baltic Sea Area of 1974 (13 ILM 546 (1974)), replaced by a new Convention of the same name in 1992 (22 LOS Bull. 54 (1993)). There are also subregional conventions, such as the Nordic Agreement Concerning Cooperation in Measures to Deal with Pollution of the Sea by Oil, 1971 (822 UNTS 311) and a general, all-inclusive Nordic Convention on the Protection of the Environment of 1974 (13 ILM 591 (1974)). In addition, a number of bilateral agreements deals with pollution questions of a more localized nature.

Pollution from land-based sources (by waste effluents, rivers, and the like) accounted for approximately 44 percent of all marine pollution in 1990, but some 33 percent was contributed by atmospheric pollution derived from land-based sources, such as fumes, sewage, vehicle exhausts, and pesticides. Art. 207 of the LOS Convention requires national laws to apply internationally agreed standards to control land-based pollution. Apart from Arts. 207 and 213 of the Convention which lay down general rules for combating pollution from land-based sources, there is no global convention dealing specifically with this type of marine pollution. There are, however, more specific "soft-law" **(35)** Guidelines adopted in 1985 by the UNEP, and, as a by-product of the Rio Earth Summit **(223)**, a Declaration was adopted in Washington in 1995 on a global program of action to protect the marine environment from pollution derived from land-based activities. Pollution of rivers, the main contributor to marine pollution from land-based sources, is regulated by the Convention on the Protection and Use of Transboundary Watercourses and International Lakes of 1992 (31 ILM 1312 (1992)) and the Convention on Non-Navigational Uses of International Watercourses of 1997 **(212)**, and by specific river regimes **(204)**. As a rule, this type of pollution is more amenable to regional action; hence numerous regional conventions dealing with this problem. The Paris Convention of 1974 (14 ILM 352 (1975)), which applied to the North-East Atlantic and the North Sea, was replaced by the Paris Convention of 1992 for the Protection of the Marine Environment of the North-East Atlantic (32 ILM 1069 (1993)), an instrument which also succeeded the below-noted Oslo Dumping Convention of 1972. Like its predecessor, the Paris Convention of 1992 has a Commission which assesses the parties' complaints on the basis of periodical reports on the implementation of the Convention. Under the comprehensive approach of the above-noted Helsinki Baltic area Convention of 1974 and its successor Convention of 1992, states are subject to various obligations concerning control and reduction of land-based pollution. A Commission carries on studies and adopts recommendations, and receives obligatory national reports on compliance with the provisions of the Convention. The 1992 Helsinki Convention adopts recent principles of international environmental law, including the precautionary principle.

The UNEP Regional Seas framework agreements, adopted for a number of enclosed and semi-enclosed seas **(237)**, also covers some other marine regions. A framework agreement for a region is followed by protocols dealing with specific sources of marine pollution. Apart from enclosed and semi-enclosed seas, the UNEP Regional Seas Program includes conventions (with protocols, including in most cases a protocol on land-based pollution) on: West and Central Africa, 1981 (20 ILM 746 (1981)); South-East Pacific, 1981; East Africa, 1985; and South Pacific, 1986 (26 ILM 41 (1987)). Land-based sources of marine pollution are also addressed within the context of the Antarctic Treaty system **(187)**.

Pollution from or through the atmosphere is treated in the LOS Convention as a separate type of marine pollution (Art. 212). The Convention mandates that states adopt anti-pollution legislation applicable to the airspace **(186)** under their sovereignty **(125)** and to vessels flying their flag or vessels or aircraft of their registry, taking into account internationally agreed rules, standards and recommended practices and procedures, and the safety of air navigation. However, it is the rules of conventions designed to reduce and control pollution from atmospheric emissions with respect to land that have contributed more to reduce pollution of the sea than agreements applying specifically to marine pollution. Among the former, the Convention on Long-Range Transboundary Air Pollution of 1979 **(209)**, designed to combat acid rain, is the major international instrument in this regard. Other relevant conventions are: the Vienna Convention for the Protection of the Ozone Layer of 1985 **(217)** with the Montreal Protocol of 1987; the UN Framework Climate Change Convention of 1992 **(192)** with the Kyoto Protocol of 1997 **(206)**, finally in force in January 2005 **(271)**; and the Convention on persistent organic pollutants of 2001 **(218)**. The 1963 nuclear test ban Treaty (480 UNTS 43) is also relevant here as are resolutions of the International Civil Aviation Organization concerning reduction of exhaust emissions from aircraft. Among the rules of international instruments designed to control atmospheric pollutants within the specific context of the marine environment, are provisions in some of the already noted conventions on land pollution, and especially the 1992 Paris Convention and the Helsinki Baltic convention of 1992. The contribution of the UNEP Regional Seas agreements to combat atmospheric pollution of the oceans has so far been of less importance.

Pollution from dumping was estimated to contribute 10 percent to overall marine pollution in 1990. The LOS Convention (Art. 1(1)(5)) defines dumping as "any deliberate disposal of wastes or other matter from vessels, aircraft, platforms or other man-made structures at sea" and "any deliberate disposal of vessels, aircraft, platforms or other man-made structures at sea," but dumping does not include disposal of matter incidental to or derived from normal operations or placed for a purpose other than mere disposal.

Apart from a general provision of Art. 210 of the LOS Convention, requiring, *inter alia*, that national standards shall be no less effective than global standards, dumping is globally regulated by the London Convention of 1972 on the Prevention of Marine Pollution by Dumping of Wastes and Other Matter (12 ILM 466 (1973)). The rules of the London Convention have been gradually tightened up by a number of amendments adopting a more stringent policy under the precautionary principle of environmental law whereby preventive measures are to be taken where there are reasonable grounds for concern that a substance introduced into the environment may cause pollution even if there is no conclusive evidence of a causal relationship between such introduction and the effects thereof. Ultimately the purpose of the Convention has been to phase out and ban completely all substances except dredged material, sewage sludge, fish processing waste, vessels and continental shelf oil and gas installations.

Regional agreements concerning dumping include, first of all, the above-noted 1992 Paris Convention for the Protection of the Marine Environment of the North-East Atlantic which also applies to land-based pollution. The already mentioned Baltic Convention of 1992 provides, under its comprehensive approach, for rules against dumping at sea which, in certain of its aspects, are stricter than the global London Convention of 1973 or the regional Paris Convention of 1992. Dumping is also regulated in protocols to a number of the UNEP Regional Seas Program conventions (Mediterranean, Black Sea, South Pacific). In addition, dumping of nuclear waste is banned under treaties that proclaim nuclear-free zones in their respective marine regions. It is estimated that the restrictions on dumping at sea introduced by all these above-mentioned treaty regulations have contributed to a significant decline in the amount of harmful waste dumped at sea.

Pollution from offshore drilling for oil and gas, and other, less-common activities in the seabed subject to national jurisdiction (LOS Convention, Art. 208), contributes only about 1 percent to the world marine pollution, but, locally, accidental pollution of this kind may cause considerable harm. Such accidental pollution must be distinguished from operational pollution which is unavoidable in drilling operations. The LOS Convention has general provisions in Art. 208 concerning prescribing and enforcing pollution from seabed activities in waters under national jurisdiction and calls upon states to develop global and regional standards, requiring at the same time that the coastal states' laws be no less effective than international rules and standards. While there is no global treaty establishing them, there are the UNEP guidelines to that effect. In addition, the below-noted International Convention for the Prevention of Pollution from Ships, 1973 (1340 UNTS 61), as modified by the Protocol of 1998 (MARPOL 73/78) and the London Dumping Convention of 1973 (and the 1992 Paris Convention on the North-East Atlantic) regulate some aspects of operational pollution arising from continental shelf installations. Regionally, pollution from offshore seabed activities is covered by the already noted Paris Convention of 1992; the Helsinki Baltic Convention of 1992; and protocols to some of the UNEP Regional Seas conventions. Special guidelines on this kind of marine pollution were adopted by Arctic states in 1997.

Art. 194, which forms part of the general provisions of Part XII (Protection and Preservation of the Marine Environment) of the LOS Convention, *inter alia*, requires states to minimize to the fullest possible extent pollution from offshore installations and in particular to take measures for preventing accidents and dealing with emergencies, ensuring the safety of operations at sea, and regulating the design, construction, equipment, and operations and manning of such installations. There are no internationally binding standards in this respect. Regionally, under the relevant protocols to the Mediterranean and Persian Gulf conventions, a state authorization for seabed operations can be issued only if the installations meet international standards.

Provisions on preventing collisions between ships and installations in the exclusive economic zone (EEZ) **(238)** and the continental shelf are laid down in Arts. 60 and 80 of the LOS Convention and are further developed by the International Maritime Organization (IMO), a UN specialized agency with (as of 31 October 2003) 163 contacting states accounting for 98.44 percent of the world tonnage. The IMO is the nerve center of international maritime matters, responsible for drafting more than 40 conventions on maritime safety, marine pollution, liability and compensation, and other subjects. Major emergencies, such as oil blowouts, are governed by the rules of the International Convention on Oil Pollution Preparedness, Response and Cooperation of 1990 in force in 1995 (30 ILM 733 (1991)), with 73 contracting states representing 58.84 percent of the world tonnage, which also applies in cases of vessel-source pollution. The Baltic Convention of 1992 and the protocols to the Mediterranean and Persian Gulf conventions provide for the obligation of persons operating offshore installations to be ready with oil pollution emergency plans.

Like most environmental agreements, the LOS Convention (Art. 235) and the UNEP guidelines call for developing special regimes to cover liability and compensation for damage caused by marine pollution in general, including damage caused by offshore activities. However, while such regimes exists with respect to damage caused by vessel-source pollution, there are no international conventions in force to implement this provision with regard to offshore activities. In 1977 an International Convention on Civil Liability for Oil Pollution Damage Resulting from the Exploration for, or Exploitation of Submarine Mineral Resources was signed but never came into force because of lack of ratifications **(280)** by states. For North-Western Europe, its functions are performed by a private scheme set up under the Offshore Pollution Liability Agreement of oil companies operating in the area of the North Sea.

As far as the pollution from mining in the deep seabed (the Area) is concerned, the LOS Convention includes provisions to prevent such pollution. The 1994 Implementation Agreement also calls for taking account of the potential environmental impact of such activities. In addition, the Draft regulations on prospecting and exploration in the Area, prepared by the legal and technical commission of the International Seabed Authority **(250)**, include environmental provisions to be applied in case of any future deep-seabed mining activity.

Pollution from ships was the first form of marine pollution to lead to international legal regulation, and today it is the most developed part of the law for the protection and preservation of the marine environment. The Convention of 1954 for the Prevention of Pollution of the Sea by Oil (327 UNTS 3), now mainly of historical interest, was the first international instrument on the global level. It was designed to combat deliberate discharges of oil by vessels in certain sensitive zones of the oceans. In the latter decades of the 20th century the rising demand for oil greatly increased the danger of oil pollution due to accidents at sea resulting in spillage of oil or other noxious cargo by the ever-growing tonnage of tankers and other cargo vessels in international traffic. A series of spectacular accidents began with the *Torrey Canyon*, a Liberian-registry **(241)** tanker which foundered off the Cornwall coast in 1967, polluting large stretches of the English and French coastlines, and had to be destroyed by the Royal Air Force (6 ILM 480 (1967)). The resulting International Convention Relating to Intervention on the High Seas in Case of Oil Pollution Casualties (known as Intervention Convention) of 1969 (9 ILM 25 (1970)), in force 1975, as of 31 October 2003 with 78 contracting parties representing 71.28 percent of the world's tonnage, will be discussed later in connection with the rights of coastal states. Other, ever more serious accidents involved, *inter alia*, the tanker *Amoco Cadiz* off Brittany in 1978; the much-publicized case of the *Exxon Valdez* off the Alaskan coast in 1989; and more recently, in 2002, the *Prestige*, a Bahama-registered oil tanker, which, carrying twice the amount of fuel that had been spilled by the *Exxon Valdez*, split in two and, towed away from the coast, sank some 130 miles (200 kilometers) off the coast of Galicia, Spain, causing one of the worst oil spills in history. Various international instruments to avoid accidental vessel-source pollution have been adopted under the auspices of the IMO, including some provisions in the major and widely ratified International Convention for the Prevention of Pollution from Ships, 1973, modified by the Protocol of 1978 (1340 UNTS 61). This large and complex agreement, accompanied by detailed (separately ratified) annexes, commonly known as MARPOL 73/78, succeeded the 1954 Convention and is largely designed to deal with all forms of accidental and operational pollution from ships other than dumping. However, it must be borne in mind that the by far major share (80 percent) of all vessel-source pollution, which is estimated to account for some 12 percent of all marine pollution, is attributable to deliberate operational spillage at sea by tankers discharging oil with seawater used for cleaning tankers or serving as ballast.

An amendment of 1992 to the MARPOL Convention calls for the introduction on tankers of double hulls in order to somehow limit as far as possible the effects of any spillage of oil. The *Prestige* disaster off the Spanish coast prompted governments of the states concerned and the European Union (EU) to impose stricter tanker inspections and phase in a ban on single-hull tankers after 2005. Such tankers carrying heavy fuel oil were to be banned in the waters of the EU. In addition to these measures, there are a number of IMO conventions whose main purpose is securing safety at sea through improving seaworthiness of ships, avoiding collisions and establishing traffic separation schemes in congested areas, and improving crewing standards, and thus avoid potentially dangerous spillage accidents. The list of major maritime safety conventions which are almost universally accepted by states (also the United States (US)) includes: the International Convention for the Safety of Life at Sea of 1974 (1184 UNTS 2), in force 1980, with 147 contracting states accounting for 98.40 percent of the world tonnage; the International Convention on Load Lines of 1966 (640 UNTS 133), in force 1968, with 151 parties representing 98.38 percent of the world tonnage; the Convention on the International Regulations for Preventing Collisions at Sea of 1972 (28 UST; TIAS 8587) in force 1977, with 142 parties accounting for 97.39 of the world tonnage; the International Convention on Oil Pollution Preparedness, Response and Cooperation of 1990 (30 ILM 733 (1991), in force 1995, with 73 states parties accounting for 58.84 of the world tonnage (its Protocol of 2000 on Preparedness, Response and Cooperation to Pollution Incidents by Hazardous and Noxious Substances was not yet in force as of 2004); and the International Convention on Standards of Training, Certification and Watchkeeping for Seafarers of 1978, in force 1984, with 144 contracting states accounting for 98.38 percent of the world tonnage. A similar convention of 1995 for fishing vessel personnel is still far from entering into force. Of relevance are also: Convention on Facilitation of International Maritime Traffic of 1965 (591 UNTS 265), in force 1967, with 95 states parties accounting for 61 percent of the world tonnage; the International Convention on Tonnage Measurement of Ships of 1969 (TIAS 10490), in force 1982, with 137 states parties accounting for 98.14 percent of the world tonnage; the International Convention on Salvage of 1989 (14 LOS Bull.77 (1990)), in force 1996, with 44 states parties accounting for 34.32 percent of the world tonnage; the International Convention for Safe Containers of 1972, in force 1977, with 75 states parties accounting for 60.26 percent of the world tonnage; the International Convention on Search and Rescue of 1979 (TIAS 11093) in force 1985, with 79 parties accounting for 51.64 percent of the world tonnage; the Convention on the International Maritime Satellite Organization of 1996, in force 1979, with 89 states parties accounting for 92.34 of the world tonnage; and—an agreement dealing with terrorist acts **(337)** against ships—the Convention for the Suppression of Unlawful Acts against the Safety of Maritime Navigation of 1988 (27 ILM 668 (1988)) in force 1992, with 95 contracting states accounting for 76.70 percent of the world tonnage. A Protocol to this Convention, concerning the safety of fixed platforms on the continental shelf **(236)**, entered into force in 1992 and was binding 87 states with 76.39 percent of the world tonnage. A number of conventions awaits entry into force, for example the 2001 International Convention on the Control of Harmful Anti-Fouling Systems on Ships. There are also numerous IMO "soft law" regulations, which may apply to accidental spillages at sea. As discussed later on, there are a number of liability and compensation conventions.

The MARPOL 73/78 Convention covers accidental and operational pollution by oil as well as pollution by chemicals, goods in packaged form, sewage, garbage and air pollution. Its six annexes dealing with these various forms of vessel-source pollution spell out in detail complex regulations which are further complemented by IMO resolutions and in some cases (for example, carriage of nuclear material by ships) by special IMO codes. Annexes I and II on oil and noxious liquid substances in bulk, respectively, in force in 1983, constitute the main part of the Convention which must be accepted by any state that wishes to subscribe to it. As of 31 October 2003, 127 states with 96.92 percent of the world tonnage were parties. Optional Annexes were accepted as follows: Annex III on harmful substances in packaged form was in force for 110 states (84.37 percent of world tonnage); Annex IV on sewage for 94 states (52.47 percent); and Annex V on garbage for 115 states (90.57 percent). The MARPOL Protocol of 1997 containing Annex VI on air pollution is not yet in force. It is estimated that, despite the still continuing lack of adequate reception facilities in the ports of many countries, significant progress has been made in reducing operational pollution by oil. The effect of the other annexes is not yet quite clear due to failure by some states to submit the required reports. In addition to the MARPOL Convention, other IMO conventions, as listed above, which are indirectly relevant for accidental pollution, apply largely to operational pollution. Regional conventions do not, on the whole, deal in detail with vessel-source pollution and refer the contracting states to generally recognized international standards, that is, in practice, the MARPOL 73/78 Convention. A number of regional conventions contain contingency plans for responding to pollution emergency, similar to the above-noted global Convention of 1990. The 1983 Agreement for Cooperation in Dealing with Pollution of the North Sea by Oil and Other Harmful Substances, in force 1989, succeeded an earlier agreement of 1969 and preceded the global Convention of 1990. One might add that the1991 Protocol on Environmental Protection to the Antarctic Treaty also provides for contingency plans in case of major disasters.

Legislative and enforcement jurisdiction **(87)** in matters of marine pollution largely depends on whether the state claiming jurisdiction is the flag state **(240)** of the ship; the coastal state, that is, a state in whose maritime zone, such as the territorial sea **(262)** or the EEZ, the vessel is found; or the port state. In customary law, the flag state has jurisdiction over ships flying its flag irrespective of where they are, but enforcing anti-pollution agreements may in practice be difficult. The port state may prescribe and enforce pollution standards against all vessels, but not in respect of violations committed before the ship entered that state's territorial sea. The coastal state may enact and enforce pollution legislation binding foreign vessels in its territorial sea provided that it does not impede the right of innocent passage **(248)**. However, the boundaries of the coastal state's jurisdiction in pollution matters are not clearly settled in customary law.

The LOS Convention codifies in considerable detail and in important respects progressively develops the legal framework governing legislative and enforcement jurisdiction with respect to the vessel-source pollution. The traditional legislative jurisdiction of the flag state is confirmed, with such states required to adopt anti-pollution standards for their respective vessels, which must have at least the same effect as that of generally accepted international rules and standards established through the competent international organization or general diplomatic conference (Art. 211(2)). The coastal state's legislative jurisdiction over foreign vessels in its territorial sea includes measures to reduce and control marine pollution from such vessels, but such measures shall not require foreign vessels to observe design, construction, manning, or other than generally accepted international rules and equipment standards (Art. 211(6)(c)). In transit passage through straits **(260)** the bordering states' legislative jurisdiction is limited to publicizing rules concerning discharges of oil and other noxious substances in the straits (Art. 42(1)(b)). The pollution-related legislation of coastal states in their respective EEZs must conform to, and give effect to generally accepted international standards (Art. 211(5)). The LOS Convention also sets forth circumstances under which a coastal state may establish, with the approval of the IMO, special anti-pollution measures in sensitive areas of the EEZ. A provision of the Convention (Art. 234) on ice-covered areas within the limits of the EEZ allows coastal states to adopt and enforce special non-discriminatory laws and regulations in areas where particularly severe climatic conditions and the presence of ice for most of the year create hazards to navigation, and pollution could cause major harm to, or irreversible disturbance of the ecological balance. As far as the legislative jurisdiction of the port state is concerned, the LOS Convention recognizes the authority of such states to establish their own requirements relating to vessel-source pollution as a condition of entry of foreign ships into their ports or internal waters **(249)**, but such conditions must be given due publicity and be notified to the competent international organization **(84)**, that is, in practice, the IMO (Art. 211(3)).

Enforcement of anti-pollution standards and regulations is the most sensitive and challenging aspect of the rules governing the protection and preservation of the marine environment. In this respect the relevant provisions of the LOS Convention (Arts. 213–222) are designed to strengthen the powers of states to enforce such rules against foreign vessels. The flag state has, of course, the duty to ensure that its ships are in compliance with the pertinent international rules and standards and must provide for immediate investigation and punishment of violations (Art. 217). The Convention (Art. 220) deals in detail with the enforcement of international rules and standards by coastal states. Foreign vessels in the territorial sea suspected of a violation may be inspected and the coastal state may institute legal proceedings against the operators involved and detain the vessel, but arrest ("appropriate enforcement measures") of a foreign ship exercising the right of transit passage through straits is permitted only in case of major environmental damage in the straits (Art. 233). Foreign vessels navigating in the EEZ or the territorial sea, suspected "on clear grounds" of violating international standards in the EEZ may be required to give relevant information to the competent authorities of the coastal state. Where there are clear grounds for suspecting a violation resulting in a "substantial discharge causing or threatening significant pollution" the coastal state may, where justified by the circumstances, inspect the vessel if it has refused to provide the necessary information. Violations resulting in a discharge causing major damage or threat of major damage to the coastline or related interests of the coastal state, or to any resources in the territorial sea or its EEZ, justify institution of proceedings and detention of the vessel, subject to any existing arrangements on appropriate financial security (Art. 220(5)(6)(7)).

The LOS Convention (Art. 218) strengthens considerably the enforcement powers of the port states. It grants them not only the well-established competence to arrest and prosecute foreign violators in its own territorial sea and EEZ but also vessels alleged to have discharged pollutants outside the coastal state's jurisdiction in violation of international rules and standards. However, it may not institute proceedings if a discharge violation occurred within the jurisdiction (including the EEZ) of another state unless that state or the flag state so requests. In order to prevent pollution, the port state must take administrative measures to prevent vessels which are not seaworthy from leaving its port unless the vessel removes the causes of the violation. It may also permit the vessel to proceed only to the nearest appropriate repair yard (Art. 219).

In any proceedings instituted against foreign vessels the actions of the port and coastal states are subject to a number of safeguards in the interests of due process and to prevent undue delays, including, *inter alia*, measures to facilitate proceedings; avoiding adverse consequences (for example, danger to navigation) in the exercise of enforcement powers; non-discrimination; observance of recognized rights of the accused; limitation of penalties to monetary penalties; and notification of other states concerned. In addition to the LOS provisions, various IMO conventions and the International Labour Organisation Convention No. 147 of 1976 Concerning Minimum Standards in Merchant Ships in force 1981, give port states additional powers of control. Moreover, as part of "port state control," a number of European states, joined later by Canada, Japan, Russia, and the US signed in 1982 the Memorandum of Understanding on Port State Control (21 ILM 1(1982)) which coordinates these states' policy in the matter of controlling, in their ports, the foreign ships' compliance with pollution and safety regulations irrespective of the ship's status *vis à vis* the convention concerned. Subsequently, many other regions adopted systems of port state control based on the Memorandum of 1982. All these arrangements must have contributed (apart from improving safety at sea), at least to a modest extent, to increased compliance with international environmental law protecting the oceans.

What measures a coastal state may take against a foreign vessel, a pollution casualty beyond the state's territorial sea, is the subject of the already noted Convention Relating to Intervention on the High Seas in Cases of Pollution Casualties, the so-called Intervention Convention (9 ILM 25 (1969)), in force 1975, with 78 parties accounting for 71.28 percent of the world tonnage. This Convention was extended by a protocol of 1973 (13 ILM 605 (1974)), in force in 1983, with 44 parties accounting for 45.06 percent of the world tonnage, to cover substances other than oil. With the introduction of the EEZ the geographical scope of application of the Intervention Convention widened to include the EEZ. Under the Convention (whose adoption was prompted by the *Torrey Canyon* disaster of 1967) a state may take measures reasonably necessary to prevent, mitigate, or eliminate grave and imminent danger to its coastline or related interests from actual or threatened pollution related to a maritime casualty. Of course, in its territorial sea a coastal state may take any measures it considers appropriate to prevent pollution from a stricken foreign vessel.

Issues concerning responsibility for damage caused by pollution, the liability basis, and the amount of compensation are among the most important and difficult in the environmental law of the sea. Unlike claims resulting from collisions at sea, marine pollution, especially in cases of oil spillage disasters, may result in enormous damage and involve third parties. Following the *Torrey Canyon* disaster the IMO sponsored a conference which in 1969 adopted the International Convention on Civil Liability for Oil Pollution Damage (9 ILM 45 (1970)) whose purpose was to ensure that victims of pollution received adequate compensation and the ship owner was, as a rule, subject to strict liability. Because of the concern of some states that compensation under the Convention might prove inadequate, another conference was convened which resulted in the adoption of the International Convention on the Establishment of an International Fund for Compensation for Oil Pollution Damage, 1971 (11 ILM 284 (1972)), in force 1978, under which oil importers were to contribute to the Fund to pay additional compensation to victims if the compensation for the pollution damage exceeded that available under the 1971 Convention. However, the amount of the maximum limits of liability and thereby the compensation to be paid became a matter of controversy during subsequent negotiations on protocols to the 1969 and 1971 conventions. Briefly speaking, the limits of liability in the two conventions were increased by a considerable amount in 1992 and again in 2000, and the two protocols, in fact new conventions, entered into force in 1996 and 2003, respectively, for the parties which were required to denounce the original conventions of 1969 and 1971. Some 90 percent of the world tonnage is covered under the two 1992 protocols. In addition, in 2003 a Protocol on the Establishment of a Supplementary Fund for Oil Pollution Damage was established, open on an optional basis to all states parties to the 1992 agreement. When the Protocol enters into force, the amount of compensation to be paid for any one pollution incident will be limited to the total amount of 750 million special drawing rights (SDR, the accounting unit in the International Monetary Fund), that is, approximately US $1 billion, an amount including also the compensation paid under the 1969 and 1971 conventions. More recently, in 2001 the IMO adopted a convention on liability and compensation for oil spills carried as fuel in ships' bunkers. Complementing the 1969 civil liability Convention, this Bunkers Convention (not yet in force) covers bunker oil spills from vessels other than tankers. The next area under consideration for codification **(5)** by the IMO's Legal Committee (which drafts all IMO conventions) is removal of wrecks, the subject of a conference in 2004.

Tanker owners established their own compensation schemes: the Tanker Owners' Voluntary Agreement Concerning Liability for Oil Pollution, 1969 (8 ILM 497 (1969)) and the Contract Regarding an Interim Supplement to Tanker Liability for Oil Pollution, 1971 (10 ILM 137 (1971)).

Civil liability in the field of maritime carriage of nuclear material is regulated by the pertinent Convention of 1971 (974 UNTS 255), in force 1975 for only 16 states accounting for 19.78 percent of the world tonnage. Like other similar conventions concerning nuclear energy, this Convention is based on the exclusive liability of the operator. A separate convention deals with the complex problem of liability for hazardous and noxious substances. This International Convention on Liability and Compensation for Damage in Connection with the Carriage of Hazardous and Noxious Substances by Sea, 1996 (35 ILM 1406 (1996)) is not yet in force (only four states had ratified it by 2004). It provides for a maximum of 250 million SDR payable to victims of accidents at sea involving such substances. Finally, it should be borne in mind that there exists a general treaty limit for maritime claims, including those arising from pollution at sea. In 1976, replacing a convention of 1957, the IMO adopted the Convention on Limitation of Liability for Maritime Claims (16 ILM 606 (1977)), in force 1986, with so far 41 contracting parties accounting for 44.26 percent of the world tonnage, followed in 1996 by a protocol, not yet in force, which considerably raised the compensation limits for the Convention's two categories of claim: for loss of life and personal injury and for damage to property.

**256. Montreux Convention, 1936.** A multilateral convention (173 LNTS 213) signed at Montreux in 1936 which governs the regime of the Turkish Straits, including the Dardanelles (41 miles long) and the Bosphorus (19 miles long and at its narrowest only 600 yards wide), separated by the Sea of Marmara (125 miles long). The Montreux Convention is the latest of a series of international agreements **(288)** since 1774 dealing with these very important international straits **(260)** which are located entirely within Turkey's territory **(228)** but for two centuries were a major issue in European diplomacy. The Montreux Convention, which at Turkey's request replaced the Lausanne Convention of 1923 (28 LNTS 115), guarantees complete freedom of transit and navigation to all merchant vessels in time of peace and war, subject only to certain sanitary regulations and Turkey's right to refuse passage to vessels of states at war with Turkey. The passage of warships **(265)** is regulated in more detail and requires prior notification. While only minor restrictions (prior notification and only daytime entry) apply to light surface vessels, limitations are placed on the tonnage, size, and length of stay of other foreign warships. In time of peace, warships of Black Sea states may pass without any tonnage restrictions provided that they pass singly and are escorted by no more than two torpedo boats. Warships of a non-Black Sea state are subject to tonnage restrictions: the aggregate tonnage of ships entering the Straits must not exceed 30,000 tons or, in certain circumstances, 45,000 tons, but never more than two-thirds of the aggregate tonnage of the Black Sea states. Single warships are limited to 15,000 tons. Passage of submarines is prohibited except for submarines of Black Sea states constructed, purchased, or sent out for repairs outside. Friendly visits by foreign warships of limited duration and at Turkey's invitation are exempt from restrictions.

In time of war, when Turkey is not a belligerent, warships of belligerents are allowed passage unless such passage conflicts with the obligations under Art. 16 of the Covenant of the League of Nations (sanctions against aggressor states), now presumably under Art. 41 of the United Nations (UN) Charter on non-military enforcement measures within the UN collective security system **(327)**; or if the ship in question renders assistance to an attacked state on the basis of a treaty binding Turkey and in conformity with the Covenant (now presumably the UN Charter). Neutral **(362)** warships are subject to the same conditions, but otherwise are treated as in peacetime. When Turkey is a belligerent or believes to be threatened by imminent danger of war, no warships enjoy the right of passage through the Straits except with Turkey's permission.

The Montreux Convention belongs to the "long-standing international conventions" envisaged by Art. 35(c) of the UN Convention on the Law of the Sea of 1982 (LOS Convention) **(264)** according to which nothing in Part III (Straits Used for International Navigation) of the LOS Convention affects the legal regime of straits regulated by long-standing conventions. Hence, despite the entry into force **(271)** of the LOS Convention in 1994 (to which Turkey—for other reasons—is not a party), the restrictions under the Montreux Convention continue to apply. In the Cold War era, and recently as late as 1991, the former Soviet Union tested Turkey's resolve to uphold the rules of the Convention, *inter alia*, by sending through the Straits the warship *Kiev*, classified by the Soviet Union as an anti-submarine cruiser but in reality an aircraft carrier, a type of ship that is not expressly authorized for the passage through the Straits and which in Annex II of the Convention is specifically excluded from the category of "capital ships." This and other similar categories of ship were allowed by Turkey to pass. Although after the breakup of the Soviet Union in 1991 **(133)** the issue has lost much of its urgency, there is need to revise the Montreux Convention and adapt it to the general LOS Convention regime governing straits used for international navigation, a daunting task in view of Turkey's continued refusal to become a party to the LOS Convention.

**257. Nationality of Ships.** A fundamental institution in the law of the sea **(254)**, linking a ship to a state **(127)** and creating the right of the ship to fly the flag of that state which is variously known as the state of nationality, the flag state, or the state of registry or registration. As stated in Art. 5(1) of the Convention on the High Seas adopted in 1958 at the Geneva Conference on the Law of the Sea **(243)**, and reiterated in Art. 91 of the United Nations (UN) Convention on the Law of the Sea of 1982 (LOS Convention) **(264)**, "ships have the nationality of the State whose flag they are entitled to fly." Every state, whether coastal or landlocked, has the right to sail ships flying its flag on the high seas **(245)**. The terms "ship" and "vessel" are equivalent; the LOS Convention uses these terms interchangeably, even when referring to warships **(265)**. In general, the term "state of registration" is used in the sense of state of nationality or flag state, as it is, for example, in the Convention on Conditions for Registration of Ships of 1986 (26 ILM 1229 (1987)). However, in many states ships below a certain tonnage (for example 20 or 50 tons) are not required to register like large ocean-going vessels and carry documents applying to such ships. As stated in Art. 94(2)(a) of the LOS Convention, "every State shall . . . maintain a register of ships containing the names and particulars of ships flying its flag, except those which are excluded from generally accepted international regulations on account of their small size." But even small vessels are issued some documents as evidence of nationality of the state of issuance and have the right to fly the flag of that state.

Nationality indicates that the flag state has the right (and duty) to exercise jurisdiction over the ship, is responsible for it under international law, and has the right to exercise diplomatic protection on its behalf. The institution of nationality of ships is indispensable for orderly and safe navigation on the high seas and for attribution **(53)** to states of the rights and obligations of ships in international traffic.

A ship may sail under the flag of one state only and may not change its flag during a voyage or while at a port of call, save in the case of real transfer of ownership or change of registry. Furthermore, a ship which sails under the flag of two or more states, using them according to convenience, may not claim any of the nationalities in question with respect to any other state, and may be assimilated to a ship without nationality (LOS Convention, Art. 92). A ship may become stateless if its right to fly a flag has been revoked by the state of nationality. In principle, a stateless ship as such does not normally enjoy protection of any state unless protection is exercised by the state of the owner's nationality or by the state of which the crew or passengers are nationals **(175)**. Under the right of visit a ship suspected of statelessness may be boarded by any warship or other authorized ship on governmental service. In 1999 in the M/V *Saiga* case (Saint Vincent and the Grenadines v. Guinea) (38 ILM 1323 (1999)) the International Tribunal for the Law of the Sea (ITLOS) **(310)** rejected Guinea's argument that at the time of arrest the *Saiga* was stateless because its provisional certificate of registration under the St. Vincentian flag had expired while a permanent certificate was not yet issued by St. Vincentian authorities. The ITLOS based its ruling that the *Saiga* was entitled to fly the flag of Saint Vincent and the Grenadines, *inter alia*, on certain indirect indications of St. Vincential nationality found on the ship or carried on board. It also ruled that the ship's previous registration under Malta's flag had been closed.

A ship may also fly the flag of an intergovernmental organization **(84)**. Art. 93 of the LOS Convention expressly grants ships employed on the official service of the UN, its specialized agencies, or the International Atomic Energy Agency the right to fly the flag of the organization. It is not entirely clear what would, for example, be the legal status of a ship (but not a warship) flying the flag of another organization, such as the European Union or the North Atlantic Treaty Organization.

Subject to any treaty commitments, conditions for granting nationality to ships, for the registration of ships in a state's territory **(228)**, and for the right to fly a state's flag are determined exclusively by the law of each state. This general rule is articulated in Art. 5 of the 1958 Convention on the High Seas and Art. 91(1) of the LOS Convention. States vary greatly as to the conditions and requirements for the granting of nationality to ships, such as the requirement found in the laws of many traditional maritime nations that all or a certain proportion of the ship's owners or crew must be nationals of the state in question, or that the ship must have been built in that state's shipyards. However, some countries' laws lack any such requirements, with the resulting severance of the link between the ownership of, and control over a ship on the one hand and the ship's merely formal nationality and flag, on the other. These are the so-called flag-of-convenience or open registry **(241)** states whose vessels ply the oceans without, as a rule, ever visiting their respective ports of registry whose names are inscribed on their sterns. It is because of the growth of the flags of convenience that the 1958 Geneva Convention on the High Seas appeared to limit the traditional principle of each state's freedom to fix the conditions for granting its nationality to ships, by adding in the pertinent article (Art. 5(1)) a proviso that "[t]here must exist a genuine link between the State and the ship; in particular the State must effectively exercise its jurisdiction and control in administrative, technical and social matters over ships flying its flag." The inclusion of the requirement of a "genuine link" was inspired by the judgment of the International Court of Justice (ICJ) **(309)** in the *Nottebohm* case (Liechtenstein v. Guatemala) (1955 ICJ Rep. 4) in which the ICJ ruled that for Liechtenstein to have the right to protect an individual claimed to be its national, there must exist a genuine link between that individual and Liechtenstein. However, the 1958 Convention did not specify concrete criteria for determining whether or not in a particular case a genuine link exists. Nor did it spell out what legal consequences the absence of such link would entail under international law. The genuine link clause of 1958 is reiterated in Art. 91 of the LOS Convention of 1982, but, unlike the 1958 formulation, it is not connected directly in the same article to a provision on effective exercise of jurisdiction over ships by the state of nationality. On the other hand, a separate article (Art. 94: Duties of the Flag State) repeats in its first section the 1958 formulation on the duty to exercise effective control and follows it by a detailed list (Art. 94(2)–(5)) of the duties that the flag state is required to fulfill to meet the requirement of effective control: to maintain a register of ships, except those which are excluded from generally accepted regulations on account of their small size; and to assume jurisdiction under its internal law over each ship flying its flag and its master, officers, and crew in respect of administrative, technical, and social matters concerning the ship. Furthermore, every state must take measures necessary to ensure safety at sea with regard, *inter alia*, to the construction, equipment, and seaworthiness of ships; manning, labor conditions, and training; the use of signals, the maintenance of communications and the prevention of collisions. Such measures must include those necessary to ensure periodic surveyance by qualified surveyors of ships and possession of appropriate charts and other necessary navigational equipment; measures necessary to ensure that the master and officers possess appropriate qualifications and that the crew is appropriate in qualification and numbers for the type, size, machinery, and equipment of the ship; and that the master, officers and, to the extent appropriate, the crew are fully conversant with safety regulations, prevention of collisions, prevention, reduction, and control of marine pollution **(255)**, and maintenance of communications by radio. All these measures must conform to generally accepted international standards. In addition—a crucial provision—Art. 94(6) sets out the procedure to be followed by a state other than the flag state that has "clear grounds to believe that proper jurisdiction and control with regard to a ship have not been exercised." In such cases that state may report the facts to the flag state which is required to investigate the matter and, if appropriate, take any action necessary to remedy the situation. It must be stressed that the LOS Convention lacks any provisions permitting the state that has discovered evidence of the absence of effective jurisdiction and control by a flag state over a ship to refuse to recognize the national character of the ship and its right to fly the flag in question. As concluded by the ITLOS in the above-mentioned *Saiga* case in 1999, the purpose of the genuine link provision in the LOS Convention is "not to establish criteria by reference to which the validity of the registration of ships in a flag State may be challenged by other States," but "to secure more effective implementation of the duties of the flag State." But it is worth noting that in his individual opinion **(304)** a judge noted that since the adjective "genuine" contains an element of good faith, the requirement of genuine link may have some relevance for the grant of nationality. Still, it must be concluded that it is not clear what exactly constitutes genuine link. In state practice the link between a state and a ship flying its flag is often rather tenuous, apart from the fact that it may sometimes be difficult to determine the real nature of the link behind the international complexities of corporate and maritime law. It is also not clear whether the genuine link requirement is part of customary law **(39)**, and such character of the rule is denied by some in the doctrine of international law. Finally, it must be added that in an armed conflict **(339)** a ship's flag constitutes only a *prima facie* evidence of its nationality. Thus to determine the enemy character **(346)** of a ship in wartime the beneficial ownership of the ship is, as a rule, decisive.

**258. Panama Canal.** A major interoceanic, international waterway running across Panama, which connects the Atlantic with the Pacific Ocean. Since the termination **(287)** on the last day of 1999 of the Panama Canal Treaty of 1977 (1280 UNTS 3), in force 1979, which governed the transition from the United States (US) to Panamanian control of the Canal, the legal status of the Panama Canal has been regulated by the US-Panama Treaty Concerning the Permanent Neutrality and Operation of the Panama Canal, 1977 (1161 UNTS 177), in force **(271)** in 1979 and subject to numerous and detailed US amendments **(269)**, conditions, "reservations," and understandings (17 ILM 817 (1978)) and to a brief understanding and declaration by Panama (17 ILM 834 (1978)).

The two treaties of 1977 replaced two prior international instruments adopted before the construction of the Canal and its opening in 1914: the so-called Hay-Pauncefoote Treaty between the US and Great Britain of 1901 which superseded an agreement of 1850 and projected the international legal regime of the future canal along the lines of the regime governing the Suez Canal **(261)**; and the so-called Hay-Varilla Convention of 1903 between Panama and the US for the Construction of a Ship Canal (194 CTS 263) whereby for a guarantee of the independence of the newly born Republic of Panama and monetary consideration, the US obtained the monopoly to construct, manage, and protect a canal across the Isthmus of Panama, and for this purpose was granted in perpetuity the right to act as if it were sovereign in a zone ten miles (16 kilometers) wide along the two sides of the Canal.

Following World War II a prolonged period of tension ensued between Panama and the US, with Panama no longer prepared to suffer US restrictions over its sovereignty **(125)** in the Canal Zone.

Eventually, lengthy and difficult negotiations **(316)** led to the conclusion of the two already mentioned treaties of 1977, but their entry into force could not be secured until Panama accepted various amendments and other conditions and reservations added by the US Senate in the ratification **(280)** process.

The first treaty, the Panama Treaty, abrogated all previous treaties between Panama and the US; provided for reintegration of the Canal Zone into Panama; and reestablished full sovereignty of Panama over its territory **(228)**. The US agreed to a gradual withdrawal of its forces, but was to have primary responsibility for the defense, management, and operation of the Canal through a governmental agency called the Panama Canal Commission. However, pursuant to the Treaty, Panama was to become increasingly involved in the Canal work, with the Treaty objective of phasing out US personnel and Panama's assuming full responsibility for the management, operation, and maintenance of the Canal upon the termination of the Treaty, that is, 31 December 1999.

Pursuant to the other agreement, that is, the Treaty Concerning the Permanent Neutrality and Operation of the Panama Canal, which now governs the legal regime of the canal, Panama recognized the international character of this waterway and its—as the Treaty states—"permanent neutrality" both in time of peace and war so that the Canal shall remain open for all ships on terms of full equality. Warships **(265)** of all states are entitled to transit the Canal, irrespective of their internal operation, means of propulsion, origin, destination, or armament, without being subject to any search or surveillance.

Both Panama and the US agree to maintain the neutrality regime of the Canal (Art. IV). According to an amendment and an understanding added at the insistence of the US Senate, this has to be interpreted as giving either party a unilateral right to act against any aggression or threat directed against the Canal or a peaceful transit through it, as determined by the party taking such unilateral action (17 ILM 832 (1978)). In addition, although under Art. V of the Treaty only Panama operates the Canal and maintains military forces in its territory, a condition added by the US Senate stipulates that in cases of closure or interference with the operation of the Canal the US may also take unilateral action, including the use of military force in Panama to reopen the Canal or restore the operations, respectively. Moreover, a condition added by the US Senate admits of a possibility of stationing, with Panama's consent, US military forces in Panama, deemed necessary for maintaining the neutrality regime. Under Art. VI warships of both parties are entitled to transit the Canal "expeditiously." To this provision, the US Senate added an interpretative amendment to the effect that the provision is intended to assure the transit as quickly as possible, without any impediment and with expedited treatment. In case of need or emergency, a warship has the right to go to the head of the line of vessels in order to transit the Canal as rapidly as possible. As added by a US Senate's understanding, the existence of such need or emergency is to be determined by the party operating the warship in question (17 ILM 828 (1978)). It is noteworthy that the additions by the US Senate were made following a Panamanian "plebiscite" on the Treaty pursuant to the Constitution of Panama, but were treated by the president of that country as an elaboration of the ratified text, which approach avoided the need for another "plebiscite" with an unpredictable outcome.

**259. Piracy.** In international law, as defined in Art. 101 of the United Nations Convention on the Law of the Sea (LOS Convention) **(264)**, piracy consists of "any illegal acts of violence or detention, or any act of depredation, committed for private ends by the crew or the passengers of a private ship or a private aircraft, and directed: (i) on the high seas **(245)** [or in an exclusive economic zone (EEZ) **(238)** beyond the territorial sea **(262)**], against another ship or aircraft, or against persons or property on board such ship or aircraft; (ii) against a ship, aircraft, persons or property in a place outside the jurisdiction of any State." Voluntary participation in the operation of a pirate ship or aircraft, and inciting or intentionally facilitating piratical acts also constitute piracy. Thus, to be piracy under international law—and the definition of piracy may differ in municipal law **(27)**—an act requires the presence of all of the following elements: 1. private ship or aircraft; 2. illegal violence, detention, or depredation; 3. private ends; 4. location on the high seas or an EEZ beyond the territorial sea, an area to which, under Art. 58(2), the high seas rules of the LOS Convention apply, or—a rare possibility—in an area outside the jurisdiction of any state (*terra nullius*), for example—as suggested by some writers—in the unclaimed sector of the Antarctic **(187)** continent; and 5. involvement of a pirate ship or aircraft against *another* ship or aircraft, or persons or property on board such ship or aircraft. Under Art. 103, if a ship or aircraft is intended to be or has been used by the persons in dominant control for piratical purposes, it is considered a pirate ship or aircraft. In addition, acts of piracy committed by a warship, government ship, or government aircraft whose crew has mutinied and taken control of the ship or aircraft are assimilated to acts committed by a private ship or aircraft (Art. 102). Whether a pirate ship or aircraft retains or loses its nationality **(257)** is determined by the law of the state from which such nationality was derived (Art. 104).

Piracy is the oldest crime under customary law of nations **(39)**, and a pirate has always been considered an outlaw and "enemy of mankind" (*hostis humani generis*) who may be brought to justice by any state. In this sense, piracy is sometimes considered to be a crime under international law in respect of which all states have jurisdiction **(87)**, but in another view piracy is not an international crime but a crime under municipal law with respect to which states are authorized by international law to exercise criminal jurisdiction on the basis of the principle of universal jurisdiction **(92)**.

It is essential to bear in mind that the definition of piracy in international law may differ from that adopted by a state in municipal law. For example, in the United Kingdom slave trading **(180)** on the high seas and certain offenses committed in the territorial sea are piracy whereas they do not fall within the definition of piracy under international law. Moreover, the term "piracy" is commonly used in a loose sense to include acts which are not piracy in the meaning of international law. Thus, in international law attacks on ships in the territorial sea, archipelagic **(231)** or internal waters are not piracy. From the international viewpoint they are just as any similar acts on land even though they may be included within the legal concept of piracy in the municipal law concerned (statutory piracy). In addition to the geographical element (the high seas as the locale of the crime) the concept of piracy in international law requires involvement of at least two ships: the target ship and one or more piratical craft. Acts such as the taking over by Henrique Galvão of the Portuguese-flag vessel, the *Santa Maria* in 1961 to dramatize his opposition against the then authoritarian government of Portugal, did not constitute piracy *jure gentium*, that is, piracy according to international law, because: 1. only one vessel was involved; and 2. the hijacking of the vessel was not for private ends. The same applies to the 1985 hijacking by terrorists on board the *Achille Lauro*, an Italian-flag cruise ship. Such acts are subject under the law of the flag **(240)** to the jurisdiction of the state of the ship's nationality. In response to the *Achille Lauro* incident, the International Maritime Organization drafted the Convention for the Suppression of Unlawful Acts against the Safety of Maritime Navigation, 1988, in force 1992, with 95 states parties accounting for 76.70 percent of the world tonnage as of the end of October 2003. The Convention is accompanied by the Protocol (of the same year) for the Suppression of Unlawful Acts against the Safety of Fixed Platforms Located on the Continental Shelf **(236)**, in force 1992, with 87 states parties accounting for 76.39 percent of the world tonnage. Applying to non-governmental vessels in any maritime zone, the Convention lists a number of offenses against shipping, including seizure of ships, violence against persons on board, placing explosives on a ship, damage or destruction of a ship or its cargo, and other acts endangering safe navigation. Like other international instruments against acts of terrorism **(337)**, the Convention includes provisions designed to close jurisdictional gaps with respect to the listed offenses, and requires the states parties to criminalize them and either prosecute or extradite **(75)** the offenders found in their respective territories.

Although piracy had largely been eradicated by the 19th century, it has recently reemerged as an increasingly alarming and serious problem. According to the International Maritime Bureau of the International Chamber of Commerce, 445 piratical acts were reported in 2003, which exceeded by four times the number of piracies in 1991. Ninety-two crew members were killed, 359 taken hostage, and about 100 injured. Most deadly attacks occurred in the waters of South-East Asia, with one-third in or around Indonesian waters. Other dangerous marine areas are off the West African coast and near Brazil. However, one must take into account the fact that since most piratical acts take place in territorial seas or even internal waters **(249)**, strictly speaking, many incidents included in the statistics do not qualify as piracy in international law. On the other hand, attacks beyond the limits of a territorial sea do occur and may be left unreported.

Cooperation in the repression of piracy is a duty of all states (LOS Convention, Art. 100), but only warships and military aircraft, or other ships or aircraft on governmental service are entitled to seize vessels on account of piracy (Art. 107). As an exception from the law of the flag, ships reasonably suspected of piracy can be boarded and subject to the right of visit, in which case the warship (or other governmental vessel) may proceed to verify the ship's right to fly its flag. To this end, it may send a boat under the command of an officer to the suspected vessel and check its documents. If suspicion remains it may proceed, with all possible consideration, to a further examination on board the ship, arrest the suspects, and seize the property on board, but if the suspicions prove to be unfounded, the ship boarded must be compensated for any loss or damage (Art. 110). The courts of the state whose ship carried out the seizure may try pirates according to the state's penal law and may also determine the action to be taken with regard to the seized pirate ship and property, subject to the rights of third parties acting in good faith (Art. 105). This means that under the principle that a pirate cannot acquire legal title to his booty (*pirata non mutat dominium*), ships and goods must be restored to their owners. Under Art. 106, seizure of an alleged pirate ship or aircraft without adequate grounds makes the state making the seizure liable to the state, the nationality of which is possessed by the ship or aircraft, for any loss or damage caused by the seizure.

**260. Straits.** In its geographical meaning a strait (or straits) is a narrow, natural, sea passage connecting two large bodies of water. There is no legal definition of the strait in any of the conventions dealing with problems of the law of the sea **(254)** since it is the legal status of the waters of a strait that matters insofar as the rights and duties of the coastal and flag states are concerned for purposes of passage through "straits used for international navigation," and more than one legal regime exists for passage through straits, depending on various criteria: transit passage, archipelagic **(231)** sea-lanes passage, non-suspendable innocent passage **(248)**, and a regime based on a "long-standing international convention."

The right of free and unimpeded navigation through straits used for international navigation has been of paramount importance to maritime states, especially great powers, not just for commercial reasons but mainly for national security considerations. The United States (US) has always maintained the position that this right must be explicitly guaranteed in the United Nations (UN) Convention on the Law of the Sea of 1982 **(264)**.

Historically, when the three-mile breadth of the territorial sea **(262)** was still prevalent, there arose no major problems of passage in many international straits because their waters left a sufficiently wide corridor of the high seas **(245)** in which the principle of the freedom of the seas **(242)** guaranteed free navigation. If, however, a strait was totally overlapped by the territorial sea of one or more states, foreign ships had the right of innocent passage which, as held in 1949 by the International Court of Justice (ICJ) **(309)** in the *Corfu Channel* case (United Kingdom v. Albania) (1949 ICJ Rep. 4), was unsuspendable and applied to warships **(265)** as well. This unsuspendable right of innocent passage by ships, but not overflight, through straits used for international navigation between parts of the high seas was codified in the Convention on the Territorial Sea and the Contiguous Zone **(235)** (Art. 16(4)), adopted by the Geneva Conference on the Law of the Sea of 1958 **(243)**, but the Convention expressly provided that this non-suspendable passage also includes innocent passage through straits between the high seas and the territorial sea of a foreign state. This innovation in the law of the sea was introduced mainly to secure Israel's passage through the Straits of Tiran in the Red Sea leading to the Gulf **(234)** of Aqaba bordered by Egypt, Israel, Jordan, and Saudi Arabia. Because of the already then existing claims by Egypt and Saudi Arabia to a 12-mile territorial sea, both of which border the mouth and most of the length of the Gulf of Aqaba, the whole of the Gulf constitutes territorial sea. Israel joined the 1958 Convention, but the other three states (and for that matter all the other Arab states) in protest refused to become parties. Subsequently, the threatened closure of the Straits of Tiran to Israeli and other vessels carrying military supplies to Israel became the *casus belli* of the Six Day War in 1967. In that same year Security Council Resolution 242, setting out a basis for the settlement of the Arab-Israeli conflict, affirmed the necessity for guaranteeing freedom of navigation in the waters of the area, subsequently reaffirmed in the Treaty of Peace between Egypt and Israel in 1979 (18 ILM 362 (1979)).

Serious concern over passage through international straits, especially for warships, was expressed by major maritime powers following the widening by many states of their territorial sea up to 12 miles in the 1960s and 1970s, as a result of which some 100 straits, including, *inter alia*, Dover, Gibraltar, Hormuz, and Bab-el-Mandeb, which previously had a high seas corridor, fell within the territorial sea of the coastal states. Hence, at the Third UN Conference on the Law of the Sea (UNCLOS III) **(263)** the major maritime powers pressed for creating a special regime for straits used for international navigation which could meet their economic and, mainly, security interests in a manner more favorable than the right of a mere innocent passage. They also made their endorsement of a 12-mile territorial sea contingent upon the adoption of such regime. Eventually a compromise was reached at UNCLOS III, resulting in the creation of two completely new legal rights: the "transit passage" through international straits, established in Part III of the LOS Convention, and the analogous right of "archipelagic sealanes passage" through archipelagic waters and international straits within such waters, regulated separately in Part IV.

While falling short of the scope of the right of navigation existing in the high seas (and the exclusive economic zone, EEZ **(238)**, beyond the territorial sea), the transit passage goes a long way toward meeting the essential demands of the maritime powers for securing, as a matter of right, an unimpeded transit of ships through international straits and thus to maintain a balance of interests between the straits states and other countries concerned.

The general provisions of Part III of the LOS Convention (Straits Used for International Navigation) ensure that the provisions of Part III do not affect the legal status of the waters forming the straits or the exercise by the states bordering the straits of their sovereignty **(125)** or jurisdiction **(87)** over such waters and their airspace **(186)**, bed, and subsoil (Art. 34(1)). Nor does Part III affect the legal status of the waters beyond the territorial seas of such states as EEZs or high seas; or any areas of internal waters within a strait, except where as a result of straight baselines **(233)** areas which had not previously been considered internal waters were enclosed within such waters. In addition, the regulation of international straits in Part III does not affect the legal regime in straits in which passage is regulated in whole or in part by "long-standing international conventions" in force specifically relating to such straits (Art. 35). It is not explained what "long-standing" means; hence, the mostly general provisions of such conventions may cause problems of interpretation **(274)** in specific cases. The straits regulated by long-standing conventions certainly include: 1. Straits of Bosphorous and the Dardanelles (the Turkish Straits) governed by the Montreux Convention of 1936 **(256)**; 2. Danish Straits (Great Belt and Sound or Øresund) with regard to which unimpeded freedom of passage is guaranteed by the 1857 Treaty of Copenhagen for the Redemption of Sound Dues (116 CTS 357); 3. Aaland Straits in the Baltic between Sweden and Finland (Aaland Islands), governed by the Convention Relating to the Non-Fortification and Neutralization of the Aaland Islands of 1921 (9 LNTS 212); and 4. Straits of Magellan in respect of which the Boundary Treaty between Argentina and Chile of 1881 (159 CTS 45) guarantees in general terms freedom of navigation for ships of all nations.

Since in practice problems of straits passage arise as a rule with respect to straits made up of territorial sea, Part III does not apply to broad or "corridor" straits through which there exists a route through the high seas or an EEZ, of similar convenience with respect to navigational and hydrographical characteristics (Art. 36). Of course, in such straits foreign ships and aircraft enjoy the high seas freedoms of navigation and overflight, respectively, according to other relevant provisions of the LOS Convention. They are also entitled to innocent passage through the belts of territorial sea on both sides of the straits. The Florida Straits between Cuba and the US is an example of such a situation.

The new legal regime of the right of "transit passage" applies to straits which are used for international navigation between one part of the high seas or an EEZ and another part of the high seas or an EEZ (Art. 37). A great majority of strategically important straits fall within this category. However, in addition to the exception of straits regulated by long-standing conventions under Art. 35(c)) and the broad "corridor" straits under Art. 36, two categories of straits are excluded from the transit passage regime and instead are governed by the regime of unsuspendable innocent passage. First, in a provision drafted with the Straits of Messina (between the Italian mainland and Sicily) in sight, under the island exception of Art. 38(1)), transit passage does not apply to international straits, as defined in the Convention, where the strait is formed by an island of a state bordering the strait and its mainland, if there exists seaward of the island a route through the high seas or through an EEZ of similar convenience with respect to navigational and hydrographical characteristics. Second, excluded from the transit passage are straits connecting an area of the high seas or an EEZ with the territorial sea of another state (Art. 45(1)(b)). Such "dead end" straits include, *inter alia*, the straits of Tiran, otherwise also regulated in the above-noted Peace Treaty between Egypt and Israel of 1979, and Head Harbour Passage leading through the territorial sea of Canada to the US Passamaquoddy Bay, an inlet of the Bay of Fundy.

Unlike innocent passage, transit passage is more inclusive since it applies to both ships and aircraft and cannot be suspended. It means "the exercise . . . of the freedom of navigation and overflight solely for the purpose of continuous and expeditious transit of the straits," including also passage for the purpose of entering, leaving, or returning from a state bordering the strait. The right of transit passage extends both to civil vessels and military ships and aircraft in "their normal modes of . . . transit," which—as interpreted by maritime states—implies that submarines may transit submerged and military aircraft may overfly in combat formation. Whether the right of transit passage includes the right of oil rigs and other special ships to pass through the Great Belt, the only deep-water strait among the Danish Straits, and whether that right could be unilaterally curtailed by a straits state by building a fixed bridge over the straits, under which a very high Finnish-built oil rig could not pass, was at issue between Denmark and Finland. In 1991 Finland instituted proceedings against Denmark before the ICJ, but in 1992 the case was removed from the Court's list by an order (1992 ICJ Rep. 348) after the two countries had reached a compromise whereby Denmark agreed to pay a sum of money (90 million Danish kroner, that is approximately US $11.25 million at the time) regarded by Finland as "compensation" **(118)** for a violation of its right by Denmark, but denied such characterization by that country.

Although there is no requirement of "innocence," all ships and aircraft have the obligation to proceed without delay through or over the straits, respectively, and restrain from any activities threatening a straits state in violation of the principles of international law embodied in the UN Charter and from any activities other than those incident to their normal modes of "continuous and expeditious" transit unless rendered necessary by *force majeure* **(78)** or by distress **(72)** (Art. 39(1)(a)(b)(c)). Any activity in the straits that is not an exercise of the right of transit passage remains subject to the other applicable provisions of the Convention (Art. 38(3)). This raises the possibility of applying to a ship or an aircraft the less generous regime of innocent passage with consequent denial of passage on grounds of lack of innocence or, in extreme cases, even self-defense **(335)**. However, it appears that a mere passage of an unusually large number of warships does not give a straits state the right to hamper or suspend the transit passage. Under Art. 44, states bordering straits are not permitted to suspend or hamper transit passage and must give appropriate publicity to any danger to navigation or overflight of which they have knowledge. Foreign ships may not carry out any research or survey activities without the prior authorization of the states bordering the straits (Art. 40).

Ships in transit are required to comply with pertinent international regulations for preventing collision at sea and other regulations for safety at sea and pollution control **(255)**. Aircraft in transit must at all times monitor the appropriate radio frequency and observe the International Civil Aviation Organization rules of the air as they apply to civil aircraft. It is assumed that state aircraft will normally comply with such safety measures and will operate with due regard for the safety of navigation (Art. 39(2)(3)). States bordering straits may designate sea lanes and prescribe traffic separation schemes (Art. 41). They are authorized to adopt non-discriminatory and duly publicized laws and regulations relating to transit passage in respect of safety of navigation and pollution control, fishing, and loading or unloading of any commodity, currency, or persons in contravention of the customs, fiscal, immigration, or sanitary laws and regulations of states bordering straits (Art. 42).

Jurisdiction **(87)** of straits states over foreign ships in transit passage is less extensive than that applying to ships in innocent passage. While Part III has no specific provisions on their jurisdiction over ships in transit passage, Art. 34(2) provides that the jurisdiction of the states bordering the straits is exercised subject to rules of international law, which would imply the application of the rules governing jurisdiction in the territorial sea. However, most commentators believe that a state bordering straits may take enforcement measures against a foreign ship only in cases of violation of safety at sea or pollution control laws and regulations of states bordering straits referred to in Art. 42(1)(a)(b) if such violation has caused or threatens major damage to the marine environment of the straits (Art. 233).

The LOS Convention has been in force since 1994, with a great majority of states being parties, but in view of the fact that some states, and in particular the US, are not parties, the question arises whether the right of transit passage as it is laid down in the LOS Convention is in any case part of customary law **(39).** The United Kingdom (UK), which recognized such right with regard to the Dover Straits in a joint UK-France declaration in 1988, had regarded the right of unimpeded transit passage through international straits as reflecting customary law even before the LOS Convention entered into force. The matter remains most controversial, especially with respect to warships, and is rather ambivalent in practice, but on the whole, most commentators believe that, contrary to the position of the US, a general right of transit passage through international straits does not form part of customary international law.

**261. Suez Canal.** A major man-made, international transit waterway under Egypt's sovereignty **(125)** which connects the Mediterranean Sea with the Red Sea, opened in 1869 and governed by the Constantinople Convention of 1888 (171 CTS 241). The building of the Suez Canal was financed by a Franco-Egyptian company in accordance with concession agreements between the company and the Ottoman Empire, then having sovereignty over Egypt. In 1876 Great Britain became the largest shareholder in the company and at that country's initiative an international conference was convened with the participation of Great Britain, Austria-Hungary, France, Germany, Italy, Netherlands, Russia, Spain, and Turkey, which adopted the Convention Respecting Free Navigation on the Suez Canal. In practice, non-parties have also benefited from the internationalization provisions of the Constantinople Convention. This right of non-parties has been variously rationalized in the doctrine as a servitude **(225)**, a "dispositive" treaty creating an objective legal regime for the Canal, or the dedication of a waterway by a state's unilateral declaration **(44)**, a treaty **(288)**, or even a concession, to international use which, if relied upon, creates legally enforceable rights in favor of international shipping. The Constantinople Convention stipulates that the Suez Maritime Canal shall always be free and open, in time of war **(338)** as in time of peace, to every vessel of commerce or of war **(265)**; its use shall never be interfered with, and it shall never be subjected to the exercise of the right of blockade **(341)**. The Canal was demilitarized and no warships were to be stationed in it, but in the harbors of Port Said and Suez each party might station two warships; no belligerent state was allowed to station warships in those harbors. In wartime, even if Turkey (at that time the sovereign of Egypt) was a belligerent, no hostilities were allowed in the Canal and within three miles from its ports. Belligerent warships were to be free to pass without delay but, except for absolute necessity, could not stay longer in the two harbors than 24 hours. A belligerent warship could not enter them until 24 hours following the departure of hostile warships. No troops and war matériel were allowed within the Canal and its harbors.

After the defeat of Turkey in World War I its rights and titles with respect to Egypt were transferred, under the peace treaties with Germany and Austria, to Great Britain, which for some time in any case had already been in *de facto* control of Egypt. In 1922, when declaring Egypt's independence, Great Britain reserved for itself the right of negotiating **(316)** with Egypt for the defense of the Canal. In 1936, under a treaty of alliance with Great Britain, Egypt agreed to the stationing of British troops in its territory for a joint defense of the Canal. This arrangement was tested in World War II when Great Britain justified its measures inconsistent with the Constantinople Convention as necessary **(96)** to prevent the destruction of the Canal. After the war the treaty of 1936 was replaced by another agreement which provided for a withdrawal of the British forces within 20 months, but with certain rights of Great Britain to defend the Canal. The agreement reaffirmed the internationalization of the Canal and upheld the Constantinople Convention. Navigational restrictions in the Canal against Israel were justified by Egypt in terms of the right of self-defense **(335)**. However, in 1956, against United Kingdom, United States, and French protests, Egypt nationalized the Suez Canal, compensating the shareholders according to the current value of their shares, and assumed control and management of the Canal, but did not question its international status. Efforts to resolve the dispute **(299)** ended in failure. After Israel had attacked Egypt, a joint Franco-British force invaded the Canal area but was soon withdrawn after the General Assembly adopted a resolution which established a peacekeeping **(334)** force (first of its kind), the United Nations (UN) Emergency Force, to supervise the ceasefire.

In 1957, after rescinding previous agreements with Great Britain, Egypt unilaterally assured all interested states in a declaration deposited with the UN Secretary-General (265 UNTS 299) that it would respect the terms and the spirit of the Constantinople Convention and would continue to implement its provisions, a promise that Egypt has on the whole met satisfactorily. Egypt accepted the compulsory jurisdiction **(297)** of the International Court of Justice (ICJ) **(309)** under the optional clause **(317)** of the ICJ Statute, with respect to any differences arising between the parties to the Constantinople Convention regarding the application of its provisions. The Suez Canal, blocked by the hostilities of 1967, was reopened in 1977 and opened to Israel-bound cargoes in accordance with Art. V(1) of the Peace Treaty between Egypt and Israel of 1979 (18 ILM 362 (1979)).

**262. Territorial Sea.** Territorial sea is a belt of sea adjacent to the coast, over which, subject to the right of innocent passage **(248)** by foreign ships, the coastal state **(127)** has full sovereignty **(125)** which also extends to the airspace above **(186)** the territorial sea as well as to the seabed and subsoil. The coastal state sovereign rights in its territorial sea also include the exclusive right of cabotage, that is, the right to transport goods and passengers between its ports. The exercise by the coastal state of sovereignty in its territorial sea is subject to the law of the sea **(254)** and other rules of international law **(20)**; in this respect the right of innocent passage constitutes the most fundamental limitation upon the coastal state's sovereignty. It should be noted that in view of various responsibilities in the territorial sea, imposed upon the coastal states by the law of the sea, in such areas as policing the sea, safety of navigation, rescue services, and the like, the opinion prevails and is implicit in the United Nations (UN) Convention on the Law of the Sea of 1982 (LOS Convention) **(264)** that coastal states have not just the right but an obligation to have a reasonably minimum belt of coastal marine space as their territorial sea.

Historically, the distinction between the high seas **(245)** governed by the freedom of the sea and some kind of maritime belt, adjacent to the coast, under the coastal state's control, crystallized by the early 18th century, and is usually associated with the name of Cornelius van Bynkershoek **(4)** who in his *De dominio maris* (Sovereignty over the sea), 1702, propounded the principle that a coastal state's sovereignty extended as far seaward as the range of the coastal artillery. But originally this doctrine did not necessarily imply the existence of a continuous maritime belt along the coast. Such concept eventually evolved in the course of the 18th century, parallel with claims by some states to maritime zones for special purposes, such as defense, fishing, or customs enforcement. In addition to the "cannon shot" rule prevailing along the Mediterranean coasts and applying to protection from capture of merchant ships found within the cannon range of a neutral **(362)** coast, a trend in state practice toward establishing a continuous territorial sea along the coast was stimulated by the practice of Denmark. By the mid-18th century that state had gradually reduced its exorbitant claims to sovereignty over northern waters to one "league," a unit of distance which—unlike the English league of roughly three nautical miles—corresponded to four such miles, a rather accidental difference that in the future adversely affected chances for a generally acceptable breadth of the territorial sea. A nautical mile is a unit of distance at sea equal to 6080.20 feet or 1,853.25 meters. The three-mile limit (one league) recognized in most European states and the United States (US) was first applied for purposes of neutrality by the US in 1793 and in fishery treaties **(288)** since

1818. Generally speaking, while disagreement over the exact legal nature of the coastal state's rights in its maritime belt persisted throughout the 18th century, claims for specific purposes invariably turned into assertions of sovereignty. Thus, a general trend emerged toward a universal recognition of a territorial sea under exclusive sovereignty of the coastal state, subject to the right of innocent passage of foreign ships. However, the fundamental distinction between the territorial sea under the coastal state's sovereignty and a special jurisdiction **(87)** zone in the high seas adjacent to the territorial sea, subsequently known as the "contiguous zone" **(235)**, was not recognized clearly until the early decades of the 20th century. The institution of the territorial sea itself had become firmly established in the customary law **(39)** of the sea by the time of the 1930—otherwise unsuccessful—Hague Codification **(5)** Conference. Following World War II it was codified (along with the contiguous zone) in the Convention on the Territorial Sea and the Contiguous Zone, adopted by the 1958 Geneva Conference on the Law of the Sea **(243)**, and then in the LOS Convention adopted by the Third UN Conference on the Law of the Sea of 1982 (UNCLOS III) **(263)**.

Until the very last decades of the 20th century the breadth of the territorial sea was one of the most widely debated and controversial issues in the law of the sea. By the 19th century the three-mile (one league) width, supported by the United Kingdom (UK), US, most Latin American countries, China, and Japan, had been accepted by many coastal states, with relatively few exceptions. For the Scandinavian countries one league meant four miles, and Spain and Portugal traditionally claimed two leagues, that is, six miles. However, the problem was compounded by the fact that various coastal states claimed jurisdiction to control certain activities in the high seas adjacent to their territorial sea. Claims to a territorial sea exceeding three miles and assertions of certain jurisdictional rights beyond this limit often resulted in protests and disputes **(299)**. No agreement on the breadth of the territorial sea was reached at the Hague Codification Conference in 1930, with 20 states following the three-mile limit; 12 states claiming six miles; and the Scandinavian states continuing to apply a four-mile limit.

The post–World War II decades witnessed a steady trend in favor of a wider territorial sea, reflecting the demands of the newly independent states to expand their control over the resources of the coastal waters. At the Geneva Conference on the Law of the Sea in 1958 only about a quarter of the participating states favored the traditional three-mile limit. No agreement could be reached on an acceptable solution although the adopted rule that the contiguous zone could not extend beyond 12 miles from the baselines **(233)** implied that the territorial sea itself could not be wider than that distance. The Geneva Conference on the Law of the Sea of 1960 **(244)** failed by only one vote to reach agreement on a proposed six-mile limit for the territorial sea along with a contiguous zone of the same width. By the time of UNCLOS III, which convened in 1973, a shift toward adopting a 12-mile territorial sea had become dominant although some exorbitant claims to a wider distance, including as much as 200 miles, were not unknown.

Taking account of the emerging practice, the LOS Convention (Art. 3) sets the limit of the territorial sea at 12 miles, a rule eventually accepted even by the US and UK, the two countries that had in the past rejected claims exceeding the three-mile limit and in general opposed the "creeping" jurisdiction of many coastal states. Art. 12 of the Convention recognizes that roadsteads, that is, areas near a shore in which vessels may ride at anchor and which are normally used for the loading and unloading of ships, and which would otherwise be situated wholly or partly outside the outer limit of the territorial sea, are included in the territorial sea. The LOS Convention entered into force in 1994, and by the early 21st century (as of early 2004) 132 states followed the 12-mile rule; 3 claimed 6 miles (but Turkey claimed 12 miles in the Black Sea and Greece had a civil aviation zone of 10 miles in the Aegean Sea). Norway continued its 4-mile claim; and 3 states still followed the traditional 3-mile limit (Jordan, Palau, Singapore). Extravagant assertions of territorial seas included: 200 miles by Benin, Congo (Brazzaville), Ecuador, El Salvador, Liberia, Peru, and Somalia; 35 miles by Syria; and 30 miles by Togo. Such claims beyond 12 miles are not recognized except if "opposable" to one another, that is, in relations between states making such claims. In general, one can venture the proposition that—at least for the foreseeable future—the maximum breadth of the territorial sea under international law is 12 nautical miles.

Like delimitation of other maritime boundaries, delimitation of the territorial sea between states must aim at an equitable solution. Under the provisions of Art. 15 of the LOS Convention, which in general follow the state practice, delimitation between states with opposite or adjacent coasts is carried out, failing agreement to the contrary, by the equidistance method whereby in case of opposite coasts, states draw as a boundary a median line equidistant from the nearest points of the opposite states' baselines, and in case of adjacent territorial seas delimit the boundary by drawing a median line outwards from the baseline on the coast. However, in special circumstances, such as the presence of offshore islands or the configuration of the coast, or by reason of historic title, it is possible to depart from the median line methods by agreement between the states concerned.

The practice of states in the matter of jurisdiction over foreign ships in the territorial sea has not been consistent and there are some differences in this respect between the common-law and civil-law **(23)** countries. In principle—and this is especially the view of the common-law countries—a coastal state could claim plenary jurisdiction, but normally states show self-restraint in exercising jurisdiction for reasons of expediency and comity **(6)**. The civil-law countries tend to follow the view that the coastal state has only such legislative powers as agreed by states in matters relating to innocent passage. Appearing to favor this approach, with regard to the innocent passage, Art. 21 of the LOS Convention allows the coastal state to adopt laws and regulations relating to innocent passage through the territorial sea, in respect of safety of navigation, protection of cables and pipelines, conservation of the living resources of the sea; fishing regulations, preservation of the marine environment **(255)**; marine scientific research and hydrographic surveys; and prevention of breaches of customs, fiscal, immigration, or sanitary laws and regulations of the coastal state, the matters within the purview of jurisdiction in the contiguous zone. However, with a view of balancing coastal and flag state interests, the Convention provides that such laws and regulations of the coastal state shall not apply to the design, construction, manning, or equipment of foreign ships unless they are giving effect to generally accepted international rules or standards. Foreign ships must also comply with regulations concerning safety at sea and (Art. 22) must observe regulations on the use of sea lanes and traffic separation schemes designated by the costal state. In practice, all these provisions bind not only ships in innocent passage but also any ships present in the territorial sea. It is consistent with the concept of innocent passage that the coastal state is not allowed to legislate so as to deny or impair, levy charges upon, and, in general hamper such passage or apply discrimination (Art. 24), but charges as payments for specific services are allowed.

The practice of coastal states concerning enforcement jurisdiction has been fairly uniform. Although they could assert their jurisdiction upon foreign ships in the territorial sea, they restrain from it for reasons of comity and expediency. In general, Art. 27 of the LOS Convention on criminal jurisdiction on board a foreign ship follows the practice of states, providing that such jurisdiction by the coastal state "should" (not the mandatory "shall") not be exercised on board a foreign ship passing through that state's territorial sea to arrest any person or conduct any investigation in connection with any crime on board the ship during its passage, save only in cases where the consequences of the crime extend to the coastal state (for example, in cases of pollution or smuggling); the crime disturbs the peace of the country or the good order of the territorial sea; the assistance of the local authorities has been requested by the master of the ship, or by a diplomatic agent **(62)** or consular officer **(57)** of the flag state; or the measures are necessary for the suppression of illicit traffic in narcotic drugs or psychotropic substances. However, the coastal state has the right to arrest a person or investigate a criminal offense on board a foreign ship passing through the territorial sea after leaving internal waters. In any case, if the master so requests, a diplomatic agent or consular officer of the flag state must be notified and his contact with the ship's crew facilitated. Except for certain provisions concerning the protection against pollution of the marine environment **(255)** or with respect to violations of the laws and regulations relating to the exclusive economic zone (EEZ) **(238)**, the coastal state has no jurisdiction with respect to crimes committed before a ship entered the territorial sea, if the ship, proceeding from a foreign port, is only passing through the territorial sea without entering internal waters **(249)**.

In matters within the ambit of civil jurisdiction over foreign ships passing through the territorial sea the coastal state "should" not stop or divert a foreign ship in its territorial sea to exercise civil jurisdiction in relation to a person on board a ship. Execution against or arrest of the ship may take place only in respect of obligations or liabilities assumed or incurred by the ship itself in the course or for the purpose of its voyage through the waters of the coastal state, but such action may be taken against a ship lying in the territorial sea or passing through it after leaving internal waters (Art. 28). The formulation used in the Convention ("should") creates uncertainty, compounded by differences in approach between common-law countries, which interpret **(274)** "should" as implying a rule of comity, and civil-law countries, which regard it as imposing a binding obligation. Government ships operated for commercial purposes enjoy no state (sovereign) immunity **(131)**, but warships **(265)** and other government ships operated for non-commercial purposes enjoy immunity from the coastal state's jurisdiction.

**263. Third United Nations Conference on the Law of the Sea, 1973–1982 (UNCLOS III).** A landmark United Nations (UN)-sponsored international conference which, first convened for an organizational session in New York in 1973, after eight years of substantive sessions, first in Caracas in 1974 and then alternately in Geneva and New York, produced the UN Convention on the Law of the Sea **(264)**, signed **(283)** in Montego Bay, Jamaica, in 1982, comprehensively codifying and developing **(5)** the rules of the public international law of the sea **(254)**. Apart from being a milestone in the history of the law of the sea, the Third UN Conference on the Law of the Sea (UNCLOS III) was at the time the largest diplomatic conference in history, with representatives of more than 160 participating states **(127)** and observer entities participating at sessions of the Conference, including states and territories; national liberation movements **(94)**; UN specialized agencies and other global and regional intergovernmental organizations **(84)**, such as, *inter alia*, the European Communities and Council of Europe; and many international non-governmental organizations **(86)**.

UNCLOS III had its origin in the decision of the UN General Assembly (GA) in 1967 to address the problem of the seabed and ocean floor beyond national jurisdiction **(87)** and for this purpose created a 35-member *ad hoc* committee to study this problem. The action was largely inspired by the famous address before the First Committee of the GA of Malta's ambassador to the UN, Arvid Pardo, calling for an effective regime for these marine spaces as the "common heritage of mankind." After the *ad hoc* committee had grown to 41 members, it was renamed Committee on the Peaceful Uses of the Seabed and Ocean Floor beyond the Limits of National Jurisdiction. In 1970, as a result of the Committee's work, the GA adopted a Declaration endorsing the concept of the common heritage of mankind, and decided to convene a conference to elaborate an appropriate legal framework. While originally the conference as planned by the Committee (enlarged to 91 members) was to deal only with the problem of the deep seabed, a GA declaration in 1971 decided on a comprehensive review of the entire law of the sea in an international conference, UNCLOS III.

The work of UNCLOS III was organized into three main committees. Committee One dealt with the regime of the deep seabed; Committee Two focused on the traditional problems of the law of the sea, such as, *inter alia*, territorial sea **(262)**, straits **(260)**, high seas **(245)**, continental shelf **(236)**, and on more recent developments in the law of the sea such as the exclusive economic zone (EEZ) **(238)** and archipelagic states **(231)**. Committee Three worked on the protection of the marine environment **(255)**, scientific research, and transfer of technology. There were also the General Committee, the Drafting Committee, and the Credentials Committee. The Conference elected as its president Hamilton Sherley Amerasinghe of Sri Lanka, and on his death in 1980, Tommy T. B. Koh of Singapore was elected as president in 1981. In addition, working groups within each committee were set up to consider specific issues. The major difference between UNCLOS III and the 1958 Geneva Conference **(243)** was, first, that UNCLOS III did not have any International Law Commission drafts as a basis and starting point for negotiations **(316)** and, second, it was conceived not just as a legal codification undertaking, but primarily as a political enterprise dealing with a host of interrelated complex legal, but politicized, issues in which conflicting and crisscrossing interests of various groups of states required resort to all kinds of "package deals," thus delaying the adoption of the final text until 1982. The most prominent group was the so-called

Group of 77, a loose pressure group of less-developed countries, originally formed within the UN Conference on Trade and Development in 1964, but by the time of UNCLOS III had grown to some 120 states of rather diverse background, which pressed for inclusion of ideas of a "New International Economic Order" in the new law of the sea. The Western nations and the Communist bloc were the other two major groups, but on some issues, for example, straits, the interests of states transcended membership in the grouping. In addition to the three major groups, there were a number of smaller, but still fairly large and vocal interest groups on specific issues, such as, *inter alia*, archipelagic states, landlocked and geographically disadvantaged states **(253)**, and straits states, whose membership encompassed countries with diverse economic background and overlapped with their membership in one of the three major groupings.

Unlike the Geneva Conference of 1958 and that of 1960 **(244)**, the decision making at UNCLOS III followed the consensus procedure when adopting a series of informal negotiating texts of the three committees, then a "single negotiating text," followed by a "revised single negotiating text" and subsequently an "informal composite negotiating text," later revised to produce an "informal text" of Draft Convention and finally an official text of Draft Convention in 1981, later amended, also by voting, at the 11th session. But at the end, after all efforts at reaching general agreement on a final text had been exhausted, the Conference had to proceed to voting, and at the request of the United States the Convention was adopted in April 1882 as a whole package on the law of the sea by a recorded vote (130 in favor, 4 against, with 17 abstentions). The 11th session of the Conference approved the Drafting Committee changes, adopted a draft Final Act, and selected Jamaica as the site of the signing session. The final meetings of UNCLOS III were held in Montego Bay, Jamaica, in December 1982 when, after closing statements by delegations, the Final Act was signed by all 119 delegations which signed the Convention and 23 delegations of other states which were full participants at the Conference but did not sign the Convention. The Final Act was also signed by two territories with observer status, the European Economic Community, and four national liberation movements **(94)**. Annex I to the Final Act established the Preparatory Commission (PrepCom) for the International Seabed Authority **(250)** and for the International Tribunal for the Law of the Sea **(310)**. The official records of UNCLOS III were published by the UN in 17 volumes.

**264. United Nations Convention on the Law of the Sea, 1982.** The United Nations (UN) Convention on the Law of the Sea of 1982 (LOS Convention) (1833 UNTS 397) comprehensively codifies and progressively develops **(5)** the international law of the sea **(254)** in time of peace. The LOS Convention is the culmination of 14 years of work, first within the UN Seabed Committee and subsequently by the Third UN Conference on the Law of the Sea, 1973–1982 (UNCLOS III) **(263)**. Although UNCLOS III followed the principle of consensus, at the request of the United States (US) the final text of the Convention was adopted by a recorded vote of 130 votes to 4 against, with 17 abstentions. Four states **(127)** did not "participate" in the vote and 13 were absent. The official signing ceremony took place at Montego Bay, Jamaica, on 10 December 1982. Signed by the delegations of 119 states, the LOS Convention was opened for signature **(283)** for two years (Art. 305(2)), but thereafter remained indefinitely open for accession **(267)**. When closed for signature in December 1984, the Convention had been signed by 159 states and some other entities, including the European Community, an organization **(84)** to which its member states had transferred competence over matters governed by the LOS Convention and to which the Convention is open for signature under Art. 305(1)(f) and Annex IX, Art. 1. However a number of industrialized countries, including the US, refused to sign the Convention because of their concern over many provisions of its Part XI regulating the regime of deep-seabed (the "Area") mining **(232)**.

Pursuant to Art. 308(1) the Convention entered into force **(271)** on 16 November 1994, that is, 12 months after the date of deposit of the sixtieth instrument of ratification **(280)** or accession. Guyana happened to be the state in question. Incidentally, Fiji was the first state to ratify the LOS Convention, an action that took place on the day of the signature. For each state ratifying or acceding after the deposit of the sixtieth instrument of ratification, the Convention enters into force on the thirtieth day following the deposit of either of these instruments, subject to the general rule on the entry into force of the Convention (Art. 308(2)).

Although in the early 1990s the number of ratifications gradually increased with the entry of the Convention into force, it was obvious at the time that participation in the Convention of major industrialized nations was hampered by the deep-seabed provisions of Part XI, found by them to be too cumbersome and conflicting with the principles of the free-market economy. To secure the widest possible participation of the industrialized nations in the Convention, steps were undertaken within the UN, prior to the entry into force of the Convention, to amend **(269)** the objectionable Part XI by adopting a special agreement to this effect. The chances for such agreement improved considerably as a result of the significant changes in the international economic and political situation and a growing acceptance of free-market principles in all parts of the world. The resulting Agreement Relating to the Implementation of Part XI of the Convention of 1994 **(247)**, in force 1996, largely met the concerns of the industrialized nations and accelerated the process of ratification and subsequently accession by states to the Convention. As of 18 November 2003, the LOS Convention was in force, by ratification, accession, or succession **(137)**, for 144 states and the European Community. It is an irony that the US, which had pressed so hard for a revision of the deep-seabed mining regime, was virtually the only state among the industrialized and maritime nations to continue refusing to accede to the Convention. Another agreement that supplemented the LOS Convention was the Agreement for the Implementation of the Provisions of the Convention, Relating to the Conservation and Management of Straddling Fish Stocks and Highly Migratory Fish Stocks, 1995 (in force 2001). As of 18 November 2003 this Implementation Agreement, part of the international law of fisheries **(239)**, was in force for 36 states, including this time also the US. The two Implementation Agreements can in substance be treated as an integral part of the LOS Convention.

As an outcome of a package deal balancing a variety of interests and forming an integral system of rights and duties, the LOS Convention (Art. 309) does not allow any reservations or exceptions **(282)** unless expressly permitted by a provision of the Convention. Declarations and statements made when signing, ratifying, or acceding to the Convention may be made provided that they do not purport to exclude or to modify the legal effect of the provisions of the Convention in their application to the state in question (Art. 310). However, in practice such declarations and statements expressing a state's interpretation of a specific provision or its dissatisfaction with it can sometimes be hardly distinguishable from a reservation.

The LOS Convention has been universally acclaimed as an unprecedented achievement in codification and the major milestone in the history of the law of the sea. In its 320 articles in 17 parts, and nine annexes, the Convention comprehensively covers a highly complex and vast subject matter dealing both with traditional jurisdictional issues, such as the territorial sea **(262)**, the high seas **(245)**, and the like, and new areas in the use and utilization of marine resources, including protection of the marine environment and conservation of the living resources of the oceans. The substantive problems covered include: territorial sea and contiguous zone **(235)**; straits used for international navigation **(260)**; archipelagic states **(231)**; exclusive economic zones (EEZ) **(238)**; continental shelf **(236)**; high seas; islands **(251)**; enclosed and semi-enclosed seas **(237)**; rights of landlocked and geographically disadvantaged states **(253)**; deep seabed beyond the limits of national jurisdiction **(232)**; protection and preservation of the marine environment **(255)**; marine scientific research; development and transfer of marine technology; and settlement of disputes **(318)**. While many of the provisions, especially those relating to traditional jurisdictional issues with respect to the territorial sea and the high seas, reiterate the rules of the pertinent Geneva Conventions, adopted by the Geneva Conference on the Law of the Sea of 1958 **(243)**, and largely reflect the customary law **(39)** of the sea, important areas of the law of the sea in the Convention can be classified as progressive development of international law, in some respects crystallizing evolving state practice and in others setting forth new rules. The most significant are: the endorsement of the 12-mile territorial sea; the 200-mile EEZ; the transit passage through international straits; rights of archipelagic and landlocked states; a new approach to the continental shelf; and—the most controversial issue at the time of UNCLOS III—the regime of the deep seabed beyond the limits of national jurisdiction, revised by the Implementation Agreement of 1994.

The adoption by the LOS Convention of certain provisions became a stimulus for states, even non-signatory ones, to adjust their marine policies and national legislation to the rules of the Convention. Extension of the territorial sea to 12 miles and the adoption of a 200-mile EEZ are examples of such adjustment. In addition, by contributing to the harmonization of state practice in important areas, the Convention has had a stabilizing effect upon the law of the sea. Most of its provisions actually reflect customary law, but there still remain some controversial questions, such as, for example, whether the right of transit passage through international straits exists in customary law as well.

**265. Warships and Other Government-Operated Ships.** "Warship" is defined in Art. 29 of the United Nations (UN) Convention on the Law of the Sea of 1982 (LOS Convention) **(264)** as "a ship belonging to the armed forces of a State **(127)** bearing the external marks distinguishing such ships of its nationality **(257)**, under the command of an officer duly commissioned by the government of the State and whose name appears in the appropriate service list or its equivalent, and manned by a crew which is under regular armed forces discipline." The major category of government-operated ships, warships enjoy complete sovereign immunity **(131)** from the jurisdiction **(87)** of any state other than the flag state **(240)**, irrespective of whether they are in foreign internal waters **(249)** or territorial sea **(262)**, or on the high seas **(245)** (Art. 95). Unless the flag state waives its immunity, crew members are immune from prosecution by the coastal state for crimes committed on board the ship, and non-crew members taking refuge there cannot be forcibly removed from the ship. Warships and other ships operated exclusively on government non-commercial service also enjoy sovereign immunity from the enforcement provisions of the LOS Convention regarding the protection and preservation of the marine environment against pollution **(255)**, but each state must "ensure, by the adoption of appropriate measures not impairing operations or operational capabilities of such vessels or aircraft owned or operated by it, that such vessels or aircraft act in a manner consistent, so far as is reasonable and practicable, with [the] Convention." (Art. 236).

The title to wrecks of warships lost at sea remains with the flag state as long as that state has not abandoned any claim to them in an express renunciation, for example, in a treaty. It is arguable that customary law **(39)** requires that the immunity of warships wrecked at sea be respected and (without the permission of the flag state) not subject to exploration or exploitation by private treasure-seeking parties. This view was reaffirmed in 2000 by United States (US) courts and the US *amicus curiae* in a suit by Spain seeking to prevent a marine salvage company (Sea Hunt, Inc.) from recovering artifacts from the wrecks of two Spanish warship, *La Galga* and *Juno* which had sunk off Virginia in 1750 and 1802, respectively. It should be added that the UN Educational, Scientific, and Cultural Organization Convention on the Protection of the Underwater Cultural Heritage of 2001 (41 ILM 40 (2002)) (not yet in force) provides with respect to recovery of underwater cultural heritage including vessels and aircraft, that no recovery activity may be undertaken without the consent of the flag state. However, a number of countries, including France and the US, refused to sign this Convention because it failed to include the principle that, unless expressly abandoned, title to sunken warships and other state ships operated for non-commercial purposes, remains vested in the state of the ship's flag.

While foreign warships are expected to comply with the laws and regulations of the coastal state concerning passage through its territorial sea **(248)** (and the archipelagic **(231)** sea lanes passage and transit passage through straits **(260)**), and the authorities of that state are not allowed to set foot on board such ships or carry out any act on board without the permission of the captain or other competent authority of the flag state, in case of non-compliance the coastal state may require the warship to leave the territorial sea immediately (LOS Convention Art. 30). It appears that the coastal state may resort to a reasonable use of force for this purpose. The flag state must bear international responsibility **(128)** for any loss or damage to the coastal state resulting from the non-compliance with the coastal state's laws and regulations by a warship or other government ship operated for non-commercial purposes (Art. 31). The legal status of the crew on land is not entirely clear. In customary law a distinction is usually made between a stay on land in the service of the vessel and a private stay. In the former case, a crew member remains immune from local jurisdiction even with respect to crimes committed on land. In the latter situation, a crew member is subject to local jurisdiction like other aliens, but becomes immune once he reaches the ship. In any case, as a matter of comity **(6)**, the coastal state may surrender to the flag state a crew member who committed a crime while on shore.

Although it is contested by some states, especially many developing ones, warships enjoy the right of innocent passage applying to vessels in general. Under the LOS Convention, the right of transit passage through straits used for international navigation and the right of archipelagic sea lanes passage extend to all ships. Special regimes govern passage of warships through the Turkish Straits under the Montreux Convention of 1936 **(256)**, and through the Panama **(258)**, Suez **(261)**, and Kiel **(252)** Canals. According to the general rules concerning the high seas, warships, like other vessels, enjoy freedom of navigation and other relevant rights which are in no way limited by the reservation of the high seas for peaceful purposes under Art. 88 of the LOS Convention. Warships (or military aircraft, or other authorized ships or aircraft on government service) have an exclusive right to enforce order on the high seas in such matters as combating piracy **(259)**, hot pursuit **(246)**, and the right of visit in cases of suspicion of piracy, slave trade **(180)**, unauthorized broadcasting, or to verify the flag of a non-government vessel. Only officials and warships, as well as military aircraft and authorized government vessels, may exercise powers of enforcing measures to control pollution (Art. 224).

As far as government ships other than warships are concerned, customary law and the LOS Convention distinguish between government ships operated for non-commercial purposes and those operated for commercial purposes. In many respects the status of the former is expressly assimilated to the status of warships as, *inter alia*, in the provisions of the LOS Convention governing immunity in the territorial sea (Art. 32); responsibility for loss or damage caused to the coastal state by non-compliance with its laws and regulations concerning innocent passage (Art. 31); the transit passage (Art. 42(5)); or archipelagic sea lanes passage (Art. 54); immunity on the high seas (Art. 96); the right to enforce order on the high seas (Art. 110(5)); and enforcement of measures to protect the marine environment (Art. 224). Government ships operated for commercial purposes are, under the prevailing doctrine of restrictive state immunity, subject to the same rules as applied to non-government vessels. However, it must be added that the practice with respect to government ships operated for commercial purposes (activities *jure gestionis*) is not quite uniform.

# Chapter VI
# The Law of Treaties

**266. Acceptance and Approval.** Acceptance and approval are terms denoting international acts which establish a state's **(127)** consent to be bound by a treaty **(288)** on the international plane and in their substance are virtually the same as ratification **(280)** or accession **(267)** (Art. 2(1)(b) of the Vienna Convention on the Law of Treaties of 1969 (Vienna Convention) (1155 UNTS 331)). The procedures of acceptance and, more recently, approval have become common in international practice in the past 50 years or so and were introduced in order to provide a simplified form of ratification allowing a state to avoid going through the internal procedure of ratification. If a treaty itself declares to be open to acceptance or approval without prior signature **(283)**, acceptance or approval are practically the same as accession, but where acceptance or approval follows a state's signature, they are in their function synonymous with ratification. In general, there is some confusion in this respect in the matter of multilateral treaties drawn up by international organizations **(84)**, which are not consistent in their terminology, using several terms to describe the same means of expressing consent to be bound by a treaty. The Vienna Convention states only that acceptance or approval are expressed as consent "under conditions similar to those which apply to ratification" (Art. 14(2)).

**267. Accession.** Accession is a formal act of acceptance of a treaty **(288)** by a state **(127)** which did not take part in the drawing up and adoption **(268)** of the treaty. It is a traditional method allowing a state to become a party to a multilateral treaty of which it was not a signatory **(283)**, and in this sense it encourages wider acceptance and universality of treaty arrangements. However, a state is not free to accede to any treaty that it chooses. Under Art. 15 of the Vienna Convention on the Law of Treaties of 1969 (Vienna Convention) (1155 UNTS 331) accession is possible if: 1. the treaty provides that consent may be expressed by means of accession; 2. it is otherwise established that the negotiating states were agreed that such consent may be expressed by that state by means of accession; or 3. all the parties have subsequently agreed that such consent may be expressed by that state by means of accession. Unless otherwise provided by the treaty, as in the cases of ratification **(280)** and acceptance or approval **(266)**, an instrument of accession becomes legally effective only upon the exchange, deposit, or notification (Art. 16). It was once controversial whether a state could accede to a treaty that was not yet in force, but in the more recent practice accession is not made dependent upon the treaty having entered into force **(271)**.

In modern practice, multilateral treaties, especially those negotiated under the auspices of an international organization **(84)**, are normally open for signature for a period of time up to two years for states which may not have participated in negotiating the treaty. This results in blurring the distinction between accession on the one hand, and signature and ratification on the other. In addition, the text of a treaty may be adopted or approved by the United Nations General Assembly by a resolution, and then submitted to states for accession without prior signature. One can add that, compounding the terminological confusion, "adhesion" or "adherence" are occasionally employed in the meaning of accession.

**268. Adoption of the Text.** The adoption of the text of a treaty **(288)** is a procedure followed by the negotiating **(316)** states **(127)** which agree upon the form and content of the treaty by drawing up its provisions. However, adoption does not yet mean that the negotiating states have expressed consent to be bound by the treaty or, in a major codification **(5)** conference, even signed it, as was, for example, the case of the United Nations (UN) Convention on the Law of the Sea of 1982 (LOS Convention) **(264)** where a text was "adopted" in April 1982, but was not signed until December of that year. Formerly, the adoption of the text always required unanimous consent of the negotiating states, a rule which, of course, is natural in case of bilateral treaties, but is not realistic for large international conferences. In multilateral negotiations, the adoption of the text is normally effected by a vote. In this respect, Art. 9(2) of the Vienna Convention on the Law of Treaties of 1969 (Vienna Convention) (1155 UNTS 331), in force 1980, to which a majority of states are parties (but not the United States and France, among others), provides that the adoption of the text of a treaty at an international conference takes place by the vote of two-thirds of the states present and voting, unless by the same majority they decide to apply a different rule. However, under Art. 5, adoption of treaties which are charters ("constituent instruments") of international organizations, and treaties adopted within an international organization, for example, by the UN General Assembly, may follow the relevant rules of the organization. Unanimity still remains a rule for treaties establishing close cooperation among the states involved, as may be the case of treaties on regional economic or political integration which normally require unanimity for entry into force **(271)** as well as for admission of new members.

**269. Amendment and Modification.** Amendment of a treaty **(288)** means an alteration of the treaty, adopted through a formal treaty-making procedure. An amendment is intended to be binding upon all parties to the treaty and requires their consent. Amendment of a bilateral treaty, that is, a treaty between two states **(127)**, raises no special problems in that the parties may agree to alter it at any time even if the treaty expressly rules out any amendments. Therefore, in practice, it is only amendment of multilateral treaties, that is, treaties involving more than two parties, that—apart from political problems—raises a variety of procedural questions. Unlike an amendment, a "modification" is a term used to denote an alteration in a multilateral treaty agreed upon only between certain two or more parties.

Amendments of multilateral treaties are a very common occurrence in international relations. Such treaties normally include detailed provisions to govern adoption of any future amendments, as a rule by consent of a qualified majority of the parties. For example, the Charter of the United Nations (UN) provides in Art. 108 that its amendments shall come into force **(271)** for all members upon adoption **(268)** and ratification **(280)** by two-thirds of the members, including all the permanent members of the Security Council. Three amendments, otherwise politically not controversial, have been adopted by the UN in its history. Oral or tacit agreement to amend a treaty is not to be ruled out, but it must be clear and unambiguous.

Apart from an amendment procedure, multilateral treaties often provide for periodic general conferences designed to review the operation of the treaty. Such conferences, envisaged, for example, in the UN Charter (Art. 109) and the Antarctic **(187)** Treaty (Art. XII(2)(a)) may generate an amendment procedure that may not be clearly separate from a review conference.

The Vienna Convention on the Law of Treaties, 1969 (Vienna Convention) (1155 UNTS 331) stipulates only general rules concerning amendments (Art. 40) and modifications (Art. 41) of multilateral treaties to govern the practice of states unless the treaty in question provides otherwise. Proposals to amend a treaty must be notified to all the contracting parties which have the right to take part both in decisions as to the action to be taken in regard to such proposals and the negotiation and conclusion of any agreement for the amendment of the treaty. Every state entitled to become a party to the original treaty is also entitled to join the treaty as amended, but the amending agreement will not bind any state already a party to the original treaty which does not become a party to the amending agreement. This provision prevails over the rule concerning the application of successive treaties **(284)** applying in relation to such state.

Unless it expresses a different intention, a state which becomes a party to a treaty after the amendments have entered into force, will be considered: 1. as a party to the treaty as amended; and 2. as a party to the unamended treaty in relation to any party of the original treaty not bound by the amending agreement.

Modification (Art. 41) of a multilateral treaty may be agreed upon by two or more of the parties if such procedure is provided for by the treaty or if the modification in question is not prohibited by it. However, in order to prevent an agreement between only certain parties from affecting the treaty arrangements as they apply to other states parties, a modification is allowed only if it does not affect the enjoyment by the other parties of their rights under the treaty or the performance of their obligations, and does not relate to a provision, derogation from which is incompatible with the effective execution of the object and purpose of the treaty as a whole. In addition, the parties intending to modify a treaty are required to notify the other parties of their intention to conclude the agreement and of the modification to the treaty for which it provided.

A treaty may also be modified by a successive agreement or by the emergence of a peremptory rule of international law (*jus cogens*) **(24)**. Moreover, although the Vienna Convention does not include any rules on modification of multilateral treaties by subsequent practice, on the ground that such rules would create instability in treaty relations, cases of such modification have occurred in practice.

**270. Authentication.** Authentication is a procedure in the formation of a treaty **(288)** whereby the text of a treaty is established by the negotiating **(316)** states **(127)** as authoritative and definitive. Authentication is necessary in order that the states should know definitively the content of the treaty so as to avoid any misunderstanding as to its exact terms. The text of a treaty may sometimes be authenticated in two or more languages but adopted only in one. In the past, authentication was not a distinct procedural phase in the formation of treaties, with signature **(283)** serving as the general method of authenticating a text. While this is still the case of bilateral treaties, authentication of multilateral treaties constitutes a separate step in treaty formation. What the procedure is to be in a given case is often provided for in the text itself or agreed upon by the states participating in the drawing up of the treaty. In the absence of any such procedure, authentication is effected by signature; signature *ad referendum* (meaning a signature given provisionally and subject to confirmation by the governments in question); initialing of the text by state representatives; or the "Final Act" of the conference in question, incorporating the text (Vienna Convention on the Law of Treaties of 1969 (Vienna Convention) (1155 UNTS 331) (Art. 10)). The last-mentioned method has been used in concluding a number of important multilateral treaties. Authentication may also take place by a resolution of the international organization **(84)** sponsoring the negotiations or by a competent authority of the organization, such as, for example, the Director of the International Labour Office.

**271. Entry into Force.** The entry into force or effect of a treaty **(288)** normally constitutes the commencement of the time period of the binding force of the treaty for the contracting states **(127)**, that is, the coming into operation of the treaty. In the terminology of the Vienna Convention on the Law of Treaties of 1969 (Vienna Convention) (1155 UNTS 331), a "contracting state" means a state which has consented to be bound by the treaty, whether or not the treaty has entered into force (Art. 2(1)(f)). Art. 24(1) of the Vienna Convention states the general rule that a treaty enters into force "in such manner and upon such date as it may provide or as the negotiating States may agree." The agreement on the date of entry into force of a treaty is essential for ascertaining the rights and obligations of the parties with regard to the treaty. The date of entry into force is normally named in one of the final provisions of the treaty. Typically, where ratification **(280)** or an equivalent procedure is required, multilateral treaties normally provide for entry into force after an exchange or deposit of the pertinent instruments by a specified number of states. For example, Art. 84 of the Vienna Convention provides that it "shall enter into force on the thirtieth day following the date of deposit of the thirty-fifth instrument of ratification or accession **(267)**." A number of treaties simply name the date of signature **(283)** as the date of their entry into force.

In the case of multilateral treaties with the participation of a large number of states it would be unreasonable to wait for ratification by all the parties. Even with a provision on the minimum number of ratifications necessary for their entry into force, multilateral treaties are notorious for a very slow rate of adherence and sometimes a very long time gap between signature and ratification. Hence, treaties usually provide for entry into force either on a specific fixed calendar date or in a specific number of days or months following the date of deposit of a specified minimum number of instruments of ratification, as was, for example, the case of the Vienna Treaty itself. Some treaties provide for their entry into force on a specific date irrespective of the number of ratification by states, or upon the occurrence of a certain event. It is essential to bear in mind that, unless otherwise provided by the treaty, a treaty that is in force is binding only upon those states which have ratified or otherwise definitively accepted it. For a state joining an already operative treaty, the treaty enters into force on the date of deposit of the instrument of consent to be bound (Art. 24(3)). Where—rather exceptionally—a treaty lacks any provision on the date of its entry into force and in the absence of any agreement of the negotiating states, the treaty enters into force as soon as all the negotiating parties have consented to be bound by it. Concerning the territorial scope of treaties, a treaty is binding upon each party in respect of its entire territory unless a different intention appears from the treaty or is otherwise established (Art. 29). A state party may, for example, specify the territory to which the treaty is not to apply.

It is naturally assumed and stated in the Vienna Convention (Art. 24(4)) that matters arising necessarily before the entry into force of a treaty, namely authentication **(270)**, signature **(283)**, ratification, the establishment of consent to be bound, the functions of the depositary, the manner or date of entry into force, reservations **(282)**, and other similar matters which must be dealt with before the treaty is in force, have to apply from the time of the adoption of its text **(268)**.

It is a general principle of the law of treaties, codified **(5)** in Art. 28 of the Vienna Convention, that, unless a different intention appears from the treaty or is otherwise established, its provisions are not retroactive, that is, do not bind a party in relation to any act or fact which took place or any situation which ceased to exist before the date of the entry into force of the treaty with respect to that party. One must add that if a treaty provision reflects an otherwise binding customary rule of law **(39)**, it is of course applied retroactively. In addition, following the general principle of intertemporal international law **(205)**, concepts are to be interpreted **(274)** as understood at the time when a treaty provision was drafted, and any fact, act, or situation must be assessed in the light of the contemporaneously existing rules of law.

Because of lengthy delays in obtaining a minimum of ratifications necessary for entry into force (due not only to doubts on the merits of the treaty but also to technical and administrative problems), combined with urgent need to deal with the issues regulated by the treaty, treaties increasingly provide for resort to the so-called provisional application, a practice recognized in Art. 25 of the Vienna Convention. A treaty or its part may be applied provisionally pending entry into force if the treaty itself so provides or if the negotiating states have in some other manner so agreed, for example in a separate protocol or exchange of notes. It is understood that states which have not yet ratified or otherwise definitively approved a treaty, may also apply the treaty provisionally even if the treaty is in force for other states. Unless otherwise provided by the treaty or agreed by the negotiating states, a state may terminate the provisional application if it notifies other states between which the treaty is being applied provisionally of its intention not to become a party to the treaty.

It is a contested issue in customary law whether a state that has signed a treaty subject to ratification or already ratified, or definitively accepted it in the interval prior to its entry into force, has a legal obligation to refrain from acts which would defeat the object and purpose of the treaty. The position of the Vienna Convention is (Art. 18) is that a state does have such an obligation when it has signed or ratified (accepted or approved) **(266)** a treaty, until it shall have made its intention clear not to become a party to the treaty or has expressed its consent to be bound by it, pending the entry into force of the treaty and provided that such entry into force is not unduly delayed.

**272. Full Powers.** The term "full powers" refers to a formal document from the competent authority of a state **(127)**, designating a named person or persons ("plenipotentiary" or "plenipotentiaries") to represent that state for the purposes of adopting **(268)** or authenticating **(270)** the text of a treaty **(288)**, or for expressing the consent of that state to be bound by the treaty. Under Art. 7(1) of the Vienna Convention on the Law of Treaties of 1969 (Vienna Convention) (1155 UNTS 331) a person is considered such representative if he produces appropriate full powers or if it appears from the practice of the states concerned or from other circumstances that their intention was to consider that person as representing the state for such purposes and to dispense with full powers. However, following international practice, the Vienna Convention declares that, in virtue of their functions, certain persons considered as representatives of their state do not have to produce full powers. There are three categories of such persons. First, heads of state (who otherwise rarely act in person), heads of government, and ministers for foreign affairs are considered as representing their state for the purpose of performing all acts relating to the conclusion of a treaty. Second, heads of diplomatic missions **(62)** are so considered only for the purpose of adopting the text of a treaty between the accrediting state and the state to which they are accredited. Third, representatives accredited by states to an international conference or to an international organization **(84)** or one of its organs are also considered such representatives, but only for the purpose of adopting the text of a treaty in that conference, organization, or organ (Art. 7(2)). The major consequence of performing without authority, on behalf of a state, an act relating to the conclusion of a treaty is that the act in question is without legal effect unless afterwards confirmed by that state (Art. 8). It appears from the practice of states that such confirmation may be implied from the conduct of the state in question. There have been very few cases in diplomatic history of representatives signing a treaty text without authority to do so. The issue of whether persons authorized to act without full powers (heads of state, etc) are presumed to be entitled to perform, in a treaty-making process, acts in violation of their municipal law **(27)** rules regarding competence to conclude treaties, is a matter of controversy and is related to the question of rules governing invalidity of treaties **(275)**.

In the distant past, the institution of full powers was much more consequential than in modern times, and the authority of plenipotentiaries was circumscribed by their sovereign in all details. In modern times, the importance of full powers has been reduced due to ease in communications and the tendency to simplify the process of treaty formation by such methods as, for example, an exchange of notes where full powers are not so relevant.

**273. Fundamental Change of Circumstances.** A most exceptional ground for terminating or withdrawing **(287)** from a treaty **(288)**, which may be invoked by a state party if a fundamental change of circumstances, not foreseen by the parties, has occurred with regard to those existing at the time of the conclusion of the treaty. However reluctantly, this rule, commonly known by the Latin phrase as the clause of *rebus sic stantibus* meaning "as long as things remain the same," has been recognized by many publicists and invoked by states in international practice. The rule that a party to a treaty, due to a fundamental change in a situation, may unilaterally repudiate its obligations under that treaty, reflects the tension between the principle of the sanctity of treaties (*pacta sunt servanda*) **(277)** and the fact that treaties involving outdated and burdensome duties for a party or parties need to be brought into line with the changing circumstances. In past centuries classical publicists propounded a doctrine that every treaty allegedly always contained an implied clause that the treaty should remain in force only so long as the circumstances remained the same as at the time of the conclusion of the treaty. In modern international law this doctrine is considered a dangerous fiction which could be used as a pretext for evading inconvenient or onerous treaty obligations and, in general, would entail grave dangers to international peace as a source of insecurity of obligations among nations. On the other hand, in extreme cases when a fundamental change of circumstances frustrates the object and purpose of a treaty, transforming completely the invoking state's obligation, the doctrine of *rebus sic stantibus* formulated as an objective rule of law might be invoked by a party under certain rigorously defined conditions on grounds of equity **(13)** and justice as a ground for the termination or suspension of a treaty with respect to that party.

A fundamental change of circumstances as a ground for termination of a treaty was invoked in certain cases before the Permanent Court of International Justice **(320)** which, while recognizing the validity of the principle, generally avoided giving it effect in specific cases. The International Court of Justice (ICJ) **(309)** considered the application of the principle in the *Fisheries Jurisdiction* cases (United Kingdom (UK) v. Iceland and Federal Republic of Germany v. Iceland) (1974 ICJ Rep.3, 107) in which Iceland claimed against the UK that a fundamental change of circumstances had terminated a clause in its agreement with that country concerning acceptance by Iceland of the Court's jurisdiction. In another case, namely the *Gabčíkovo-Nagymaros* Project (Hungary/Slovakia) (1997 ICJ Rep. 7), Hungary invoked a number of political, economic, and environmental events which—in its view—cumulatively warranted invocation of a fundamental change of circumstances as a ground for terminating in 1992 (32 ILM 1260 (1993)) the Treaty with Czechoslovakia (succeeded **(132)** by Slovakia) concerning the construction and operation of a system of locks on the Danube at Gabčíkovo-Nagymaros, 1977 (1109 UNTS 235). In both of the above-noted cases the ICJ found that Art. 62 (Fundamental Change of Circumstances) of the Vienna Convention on the Law of Treaties of 1969 (Vienna Convention) (1155 UNTS 331) reflected the existing customary law **(39)** on the subject, but—at the same time—rejected arguments invoking a change of circumstances, as not meeting the below-listed prerequisites for valid grounds for terminating the treaties in question.

The principle of fundamental change of circumstances has been invoked in the political organs of the United Nations (UN) and the UN Secretariat. In a study of the validity of minority **(172)** treaties concluded in the aftermath of World War I, they accepted the existence of this principle while stressing the exceptional and limited nature of its application. The termination of these minority treaties on grounds of *rebus sic stantibus* provides a clear and manifest example illustrating the overpowering and massive political, social, and demographic change of circumstances wrought by World War II in the region involved. There have been very few other, more appropriate, instances in actual international practice where the principle of *rebus sic stantibus* could be invoked as a ground for terminating a treaty. It should be borne in mind that termination of treaties within the context of the so-called "peaceful change" **(279)** may take place under Art. 14 of the UN Charter.

The Vienna Convention formulates the principle of fundamental change of circumstances in a negative and conditional language, implying that in the interests of stability of treaty relations this plea shall be invoked and applied only in exceptional circumstances. In addition, to avoid any associations with the discredited old doctrine of an implied *rebus sic stantibus* clause the Convention does not use this Latin phrase in the text of the title of the relevant Art. 62. In principle, a fundamental change of circumstances may not be invoked as a ground for terminating or withdrawing from a treaty. Exceptions to this rule are allowed only if all the following prerequisites are met: 1. the change must be of the circumstances existing at the time of the conclusion of the treaty; 2. the change must have been "fundamental"; 3. it must have been unforeseen by the parties; 4. the existence of the circumstances that have changed must have constituted an essential basis of the consent of the parties to be bound by the treaty; 5. the effect of the change is radically to transform the extent of obligations of the party invoking the change; and 6. the obligation has still to be performed under the treaty, which implies that fully executed treaties are not included. A fundamental change of circumstances may also be invoked as a ground for suspending **(286)** the operation of a treaty.

Under no circumstances may a fundamental change of circumstances be invoked as a ground for terminating or withdrawing from a treaty if the treaty establishes a boundary **(189)** or if the fundamental change is the result of a breach by the party invoking it either of an obligation under the treaty or of any other international obligation owed to any other party to the treaty. The latter exception is simply an application of a general principle of law **(38)** that no one may derive benefit from his own wrong. The exclusion of boundary treaties is motivated by the desire to prevent destabilizing international relations through re-opening already executed international agreements.

**274. Interpretation.** Interpretation of treaties **(288)** is a thought process of clarifying and elucidating unclear and ambiguous provisions of a treaty. Under Art. 31 of the Vienna Convention on the Law of Treaties of 1969 (Vienna Convention) (1155 UNTS 331), which article reflects the customary law **(39)** on the subject, interpretation must be carried out "in good faith in accordance with the ordinary meaning to be given to the terms of the treaty in their context and in the light of its object and purpose." Because of imperfections of language as a medium of expressing legal rules, uncertainties in treaty texts are a common phenomenon and are compounded by the fact that, especially in treaties dealing with important but controversial subjects, the wording used may be deliberately general, vague, and ambiguous. As a result, interpretation of treaties is the most frequent focus of disputes **(299)** arising with respect to treaties, as demonstrated even by the history of such international instruments as the Charter of the United Nations (UN). In international adjudication **(306)**, the task of the courts and arbitral tribunals **(293)** has been largely to interpret treaties.

A treaty may explicitly grant the competence to interpret its provisions to an international court, as is, for example, the case of the Treaty of Rome of 1957 which established the European Community. In the UN, each of its six principal organs interprets the Charter. In addition, each of them, except the Secretariat, and all the specialized agencies of the UN, except the Universal Postal Union, may ask the International Court of Justice (ICJ) **(309)** for an advisory opinion **(291)** interpreting provisions of their respective charters, a task that may in some organizations **(84)** also be performed by the competent organ of the organization in question.

Except for obvious rules of logic, there exist in international law no mandatory principles or canons to govern the process of interpretation which in its nature cannot be a science and is only an art whose various principles, maxims, canons, and rules have developed in the practice of international adjudication and diplomacy, and in the doctrines of publicists **(42)**. Historically, many of them have been borrowed from private law dating back to the Roman (civil) law **(23)**, but have been adapted to the context in which public international law operates in relations between states **(127)**. It must be remembered that interpretation of international law by municipal **(27)** courts may differ in its emphases and nuances from the approach followed by international tribunals. These differences, often attributable to the existence of diverse systems of law, and in particular common law as against international law, the latter largely following the tradition of civil law, must not be in the final analysis exaggerated.

In general, there are three main approaches or schools on the subject of interpretation of treaties: 1. the plain or ordinary meaning of words, or textual school, whose primary objective is to ascertain the ordinary meaning of the text; 2. the intention of the parties school, for which the primary objective is to ascertain this intention; and 3. the aims and objects, or teleological school, which emphasizes the general purpose of the treaty, construing its particular provisions in the light of this purpose. This approach is common in interpreting multilateral law-making treaties in economic, social, and similar areas. It must be borne in mind that the ideas of these three schools of thought are not necessarily mutually exclusive; interpretation of a treaty usually includes elements of these three approaches and, as a rule, leads to the same result albeit in special cases it may produce divergent interpretations of the text.

In any case, the text of the treaty must provide the basic starting point for its interpretation. Terms should be construed according to their ordinary meaning unless this would result in absurdity or if it is established that the parties intended a special meaning to a term. Terms used should be given the meaning in their context, and words and phrases should be understood in their reasonable and consistent meaning in the light of international law. According to Art. 31(2) of the Vienna Convention, the context comprises, in addition to the text itself (including its preamble and annexes), any agreement relating to the treaty which was made between all the parties in connection with the conclusion of the treaty, and any instrument made by one or more parties in connection with the conclusion of the treaty and accepted by the other parties as an instrument related to the treaty. Under Art. 31(3), subsequent agreement regarding the interpretation or application of the treaty, and subsequent practice in its interpretation, as well as any relevant rule of international law applicable in the relations between the parties, must also be taken into account, together with the context.

Other general canons of interpretation (but not specified in the Vienna Convention) call for construing ambiguous provisions of a treaty in a way least restrictive of a party's sovereignty **(125)**, a rule that is considered controversial in the doctrine. Following civil law, a specific rule prevails over a general one (*lex specialis derogat legi generali*). It is also a general principle that past events and situations should be assessed by contemporaneous rules of their time (intertemporal law) **(205)**. Under the so-called principle of effectiveness, a treaty should be interpreted in a way that would render it most effective and useful. This is of particular significance in the interpretation of constituent instruments of international organizations, as evidenced by the recognition of implied powers of the UN in the Advisory Opinion **(291)** of the ICJ on *Reparation for Injuries Suffered in the Service of the United Nations*, 1949 (1949 ICJ Rep. 174). The principle of effectiveness is also very relevant in the interpretation of treaties for the protection of human rights **(160)**.

Resort to "supplementary means of interpretation" (Art. 32) was a disputed issue at the Vienna Conference which adopted the Vienna Convention of 1969. The United States argued for permitting the preparatory work of the treaty *(travaux préparatoires)* to be used equally with the text in determining the parties' intention, but under Art. 32, recourse may be had to such supplementary means of interpretation and the circumstances of its conclusion only to confirm the meaning resulting from the application of the general rule of interpretation spelled out in Art. 31, or to determine the meaning when that general rule leaves the meaning ambiguous or obscure; or leads to a result which is manifestly absurd or unreasonable.

Special problems arise in the case of treaties authenticated in two or more languages, a situation quite common in treaty-making. Many multilateral treaties, and especially those concluded under UN auspices, are drafted in Chinese, English, French, Russian, Spanish, and (since 1970) Arabic. As a rule, a provision determining the status of the different language versions is included in the treaty. In the absence of such provision, each version is to be considered authoritative for purposes of interpretation. Under Art. 33 of the Vienna Convention, when a treaty has been authenticated **(270)** in two or more languages, the text is equally authoritative in each language unless the treaty provides or the parties agree that, in case of divergence, a particular text should prevail. A version in a language other than one of those in which the text was authenticated, is considered an authentic text only if the treaty so provides or the parties so agree. The terms of the treaty are presumed to have the same meaning in each authentic text. Except where a particular text prevails, the meaning which best reconciles the texts, having regard to the object and purpose of the treaty, shall prevail.

**275. Invalidity.** Invalidity of a treaty **(288)** means the nullity of the treaty as a whole or of some of its provisions because of the presence or absence of certain facts or circumstances affecting the legal status of the treaty. The rather controversial rules of customary law **(39)** concerning invalidity of treaties were codified and developed **(5)** in the Vienna Convention on the Law of Treaties of 1969 (Vienna Convention) (1155 UNTS 331). For the parties to the Vienna Convention, the grounds set forth in Arts. 46–53 are the only grounds on which the validity of a treaty or of the consent of a state **(127)** to be bound by it, may be impeached (Art. 42(1)). The Convention also states explicitly that the fact that a treaty is invalid does not in any way impair the duty of a state to fulfill any obligations embodied in the treaty, to which the state would in any case be subject under customary law (Art. 43). Under Art. 45 a state loses its right to invoke a ground for invalidating as well as suspending **(286)**, terminating **(287)**, and withdrawing from a treaty, involving the following grounds: incompetence to conclude treaties; *ultra vires* action of representatives; error; fraud; corruption; material breach **(276)**; and fundamental change of circumstances **(273)**. But this loss of the right to exercise one of the above-named options applies in cases where the aggrieved party, after becoming aware of the facts, has expressly agreed that the treaty is valid or continues in operation, or by its conduct must be considered as having acquiesced in the validity of the treaty or its continued operation.

With regard to the unsettled question of whether a treaty provision may be struck out without invalidating the entire treaty, the Vienna Convention follows the principle of limited separability of treaty provisions. As a general rule—which also applies to terminating or withdrawing from or suspending the operation of a treaty—the grounds for invalidity of a treaty may be invoked only with respect to the whole treaty (Art. 44(2)). This rule of inseparability always applies in cases of coercion and conflict with *jus cogens* **(24)**. Otherwise, under Art. 44(3) only specific clauses are voided where they are separable from the remainder of the treaty with regard to their application; their acceptance was not an essential basis of the consent of the other party or parties to be bound by the treaty as a whole; and where continued performance of the remainder of the treaty would not be unjust. However, under Art. 44(4)) in cases of fraud or corruption the state entitled to invoke them has a choice of invalidating the entire treaty or only a particular clause, subject to the condition of reciprocity. To avoid possible abuse, a state loses the right to invoke a ground for invalidating a treaty if, after becoming aware of the facts, it has expressly agreed that the treaty is valid or acquiesced in the continued validity of the treaty (Art. 45). Apart from the situation where an act relating to the conclusion of a treaty was performed without proper authorization and full powers **(272)** and, as a result is without legal effect, the Vienna Convention lists (Arts. 46–53) eight grounds for invalidating a treaty.

First, while as a general rule a state may not invoke its municipal law **(27)** as justification for failure to comply with a treaty provision (Art. 27 of the Vienna Convention), the Convention permits a state to invoke as a ground of invalidity the fact that its consent to be bound has been expressed in violation of its law concerning competence to conclude treaties, but only if the violation was "manifest" and concerned a rule of its law of fundamental importance. Manifest violation is defined as one that "would be objectively evident to any state conducting itself in the matter in accordance with normal practice and in good faith" (Art. 46). In practice, as illustrated, *inter alia*, by the distinction in the United States between treaties and executive agreements, constitutional competence to conclude treaties is often not entirely clear. But otherwise, there have been no treaties invalidated on grounds of constitutional incompetence. In 2002, in its judgment in the case of a boundary dispute between Cameroon and Nigeria, the International Court of Justice (ICJ) noted in an *obiter dictum* that states have no legal obligation to keep themselves informed of constitutional developments in other states, that may become important for the international relations of these states (*Land and Maritime Boundary between Cameroon and Nigeria* (Cameroon v. Nigeria, with Equatorial Guinea intervening **(311)**).

Second, as stipulated in Art. 47, if the authority of a representative to express the consent of a state to be bound by a particular treaty has been made subject to a specific restriction, his *ultra vires* action, that is, his omission to observe that restriction, may not be invoked as invalidating the consent expressed by him unless the restriction was notified to the other negotiating **(316)** states prior to his expressing such consent.

Third, under Art. 48, an error may be invoked by a state as a ground for invalidating its consent if it relates to a fact or situation which was assumed by that state to exist at the time when the treaty was concluded and which formed an essential basis of its consent to be bound by the treaty. However, a state that contributed to the error by its own conduct or was put on notice of a possible error is not allowed to invoke the error as a ground for invalidating its consent. Error is a rare occurrence in treaty making. Most errors invoked as an invalidating ground have concerned errors in geographical data. If such data, for example maps, are deliberately falsified, the error must be qualified as "fraud." The effect of errors on treaties has been discussed, *inter alia*, by the Permanent Court of International justice in its judgment in *Legal Status of Eastern Greenland* (Denmark v. Norway) (1933 PCIJ, Series A/B, No. 53); and by the ICJ in its judgment in *Temple of Preah Vihear* (Cambodia v. Thailand) (1962 ICJ Rep. 6), in which case the Court expressed its view as subsequently formulated in Art. 48 of the Vienna Convention. An error in the treaty must be distinguished from one relating only to the wording of the text of the treaty, which does not affect its validity. Such errors in treaty texts are corrected according to the rules spelled out in Art. 79 of the Vienna Convention on the correction of errors in texts or in certified copies of treaties.

Fourth, fraud may be invoked by a state as invalidating its consent to be bound by a treaty if such consent was induced by the fraudulent conduct of another negotiating state (Art. 49). The Convention does not define fraud, and there is not sufficient international practice in this regard. In the opinion of the International Law Commission's (ILC) *travaux préparatoires* for the Convention, 1966, the expression "fraudulent conduct" includes any false statements, misrepresentations, or other deceitful proceedings by which a state is induced to give its consent to a treaty that it would not otherwise have given.

Fifth, corruption of a representative as a ground for invalidating a treaty, intermediate in gravity between fraud and coercion, has been uncommon in the practice of the law of treaties. Art. 50 of the Vienna Convention includes the corruption of a state's representative "directly or indirectly" by another negotiating state as a ground for invalidating its consent. In its comments of 1966 the ILC noted that only acts calculated to exercise a substantial influence on the disposition of a representative to conclude the treaty may be invoked. A small courtesy or favor shown to a representative in connection with the conclusion of a treaty would not amount to corruption and become a pretext for invalidating the treaty.

Sixth (Art. 51), consent to a treaty procured by a coercion of a state's representative through acts or threats directed against him shall be without any legal effect. Coercion against a representative personally, that is, duress, must be distinguished from coercing him through a threat of force against his state. The concept of personal coercion of a representative also includes threats of blackmail and threats against his family. While very rare, cases of personal coercion of representatives of a state have occurred in the past. The most notorious case of personal coercion, which also displays features of the coercion of a state, took place in 1939 in Berlin when ministers of Nazi Germany, by pressure and intimidation, extracted form President Emil Hacha and the foreign minister František Chvalkovsky of the by then already rump Czechoslovakia, their signature to a treaty establishing Germany's "protectorate" over Bohemia and Moravia, the remaining (Czech) part of Czechoslovakia.

Seventh, as laid down in the much debated Art. 52, a treaty is void if its conclusion has been procured by the threat or use of force **(329)** in violation of the principles of international law embodied in the UN Charter. This provision of the Vienna Convention codifies a now generally accepted rule of customary international law. Under traditional, pre-Charter, international law, when resort to force in the settlement of international disputes **(299)** was considered legal, the validity of a treaty was not vitiated by the fact that it was brought about by the threat or use of force. However, the Covenant of the League of Nations, 1919, and the General Treaty for the Renunciation of War, 1928 (Pact of Paris or Kellogg-Briand Pact) **(330)** initiated a trend which culminated in the UN Charter proscribing illegal threat or use of force in international relations, with the logical consequence of considering treaties imposed by force as void from the beginning (*ab initio*). This rule has become a peremptory norm of international law (*jus cogens*) **(24)**. Concerning the date from which the ban on the threat or use of force should be considered in force for purposes of vitiating a treaty, the ILC concluded that the rule was to be applied at any rate to treaties concluded since the entry into force **(271)** of the UN Charter, that is, 24 October 1945. But, since according to the rule of intertemporal law **(205)** judicial facts must be assessed in the light of contemporaneous law, that is, the law in force at the time of the conclusion of the treaty, the rule concerning the vitiating effects of coercion upon the validity of treaties, codified in Art. 52 of the Vienna Convention, has no retroactive effect on the validity of treaties procured by coercion prior to the outlawry of force in 1945. This interpretation of the future Art. 52 was also confirmed by the ILC in its comments of 1966 on the draft law of treaties. It should also be stressed that the vague and controversial doctrine of "unequal treaties," once inconsistently and selectively championed by Communist and many Third World countries, is of dubious validity in international law. This doctrine alleges that treaties concluded between Western powers and overseas developing states under excessive economic and political pressures of those powers were to be considered as invalid. Questions relating to this doctrine were on the agenda of the ILC and the Conference which adopted the Vienna Convention, within the context of the contested issue of whether the notion of force for purposes of invalidating a treaty included—as argued by many Third World countries and the then Soviet Union—not only armed force but also economic and political pressures. As a compromise, it was agreed to include a "Declaration on the Prohibition of Military, Political and Economic Coercion in the Conclusion of Treaties" in the Final Act of the Vienna Conference. But this declaration is not a treaty and therefore is not legally binding. Under the Vienna Convention only coercion by threat or use of armed force against a state in violation of the UN Charter makes a treaty void in international law. However, the matter is not so simple, considering that in international relations, states, and especially weak ones, are often subject to indirect and subtle political, economic, and other pressures inducing them to enter into "freely concluded" lawful treaties which they would otherwise prefer to eschew.

Finally, eighth, a treaty is void if at the time of its conclusion it conflicts with a peremptory norm of general international law (*jus cogens*) defined for purposes of the Vienna Convention as "a norm accepted and recognized by the international community of States as a whole as a norm from which no derogation is permitted and which can be modified only by a subsequent norm of general international law having the same character" (Art. 53). In addition, if a new norm of *jus cogens* emerges, any existing treaty which is in conflict with that norm becomes void and terminates (Art. 64), a wording making it clear that the emergence of a peremptory norm of international law has no retroactive effect upon the validity of a treaty. However, because of lack of consensus, the Vienna Convention does not specify which norms exactly belong to the *jus cogens* category and how they are generated. Because of the special position of the peremptory norms within the context of the validity of treaties, Art. 66(a) provides for a mandatory submission of disputes over the interpretation **(274)** and application of Arts. 53 and 64 to the ICJ unless the parties agree to submit the dispute to arbitration **(293)**.

The consequences of invalidity of a treaty (and its termination and suspension), spelled out in Art. 69 of the Vienna Convention, depend on the nature of the ground for voiding the treaty, but in any event a treaty whose invalidity is established under the Convention is void, that is, its provisions have no legal force. However, the Convention makes a new distinction, namely, between treaties which do not become void *ipso facto* but are voidable at the discretion of the party invoking the ground in question and treaties which are automatically void. The former ("relative") grounds of invalidity include: manifest violation of municipal law; *ultra vires* acts of representatives; error; fraud; and corruption. They can be invoked only by the state that has suffered injury because of these acts; may invalidate only some provisions of a treaty; and render the treaty or certain of its provisions void as of the date of the conclusion of the treaty. The other category of grounds ("absolute grounds"), which also results in voiding the treaty as of the date of its conclusion, includes, apart from lack of full powers, coercion of a representative; coercion of the state; and conflict with a peremptory norm of international law. Any party to the treaty may invoke its invalidity and each of these grounds entails invalidity of the treaty as a whole. Whether a non-party concerned state has the same right is not clear. In case of incompatibility with *jus cogens* the parties are obliged (Art. 71(1)) to eliminate as far as possible the consequences of any act performed in reliance on any provision in conflict with *jus cogens* and must bring their mutual relations into conformity with the peremptory norm. In case of a treaty becoming, under Art. 64, void and terminating because of an emerging rule of *jus cogens*, the termination of the treaty releases the parties from any obligation to perform the treaty, but does not affect any right, obligation, or legal situation of the parties created through the execution of the treaty prior to its termination, provided that their maintenance is not in itself in conflict with the new peremptory norm.

If some acts were performed in reliance on a voided treaty, each party may require any other party to establish as far as possible in their mutual relations the position that would have existed if the acts had not been performed. Acts performed in good faith before the invalidity was invoked are not rendered unlawful by reason only of the invalidity of the treaty. However these two provisions do not apply with respect to the party to which the fraud, the act of corruption, or the coercion is imputable. In multilateral treaties, a state may assert invalidity against each of the other parties even though a ground for invalidity of the treaty is imputable to only one of the parties.

The procedure to be followed with regard to invalidity of treaties is set forth in detail in Arts. 65–68 of the Vienna Convention. Generally speaking, a state challenging the validity of a treaty must notify the other party or parties so that any dispute can be resolved peacefully. If no solution is reached within 12 months, the dispute is to be submitted to a special conciliation **(296)** commission or—as mentioned above—to the ICJ. The Annex to the Convention governs the composition and procedure of the conciliation commissions established under Art. 66 of the Convention.

**276. Material Breach.** Under Art. 60(3) of the Vienna Convention on the Law of Treaties (Vienna Convention) (1155 UNTS 331) material breach is a repudiation of a treaty **(288)** by a party, not sanctioned by international law, or a violation of a provision essential to the accomplishment of the object or purpose of the treaty, which entitles the other party or parties to invoke the breach as a ground for terminating **(287)** the treaty or suspending **(286)** its operation as a whole or in part. It is generally recognized, codified **(5)**, and further elaborated upon by the Vienna Convention that only a "material" breach justifies the termination or suspension of a treaty, but a breach, however serious, does not *ipso facto* rescind the treaty. It only gives the party or parties affected by the breach the right to invoke it as a ground for terminating or suspending the treaty. Customary law **(39)** is uncertain with respect to the precise circumstances in which a state party may exercise the right to terminate a treaty, especially a multilateral one, because a breach by one state cannot entitle another state party to rescind it *vis à vis* innocent parties. It may also be a difficult task to determine what constitutes a "material" breach, but in any case a breach cannot be trivial.

The Vienna Convention (Art. 60) lays down the rules to govern the problems of material breach arising within a bilateral treaty and multilateral treaties. When a material breach occurs in a bilateral treaty, the party claiming the breach has the option of terminating the treaty or suspending its operation in whole or in part. As noted by the International Court of Justice **(309)** in the *Gabčíkovo-Nagymaros* (Hungary/Slovakia) case (1997 ICJ Rep. 7), the breach must have already occurred for the termination to be legal. A material breach of a multilateral treaty by one of the parties may, depending on the circumstances, result in a joint response of the other parties or a response of the state specially affected by the breach. In the former situation, the parties are entitled by unanimous agreement to suspend the operation of the treaty in whole or in part, or to terminate it in relations between themselves and the defaulting state, or altogether as between all the parties. In the latter situation, a party specially affected is entitled to invoke the breach as a ground for suspending (but not terminating) the operation of the treaty in whole or in part in relations between itself and the defaulting state. In addition, where a material breach by one party is of such character that it radically changes the position of every party with respect to the further performance of its obligations under the treaty, for example, in arms control treaties, any party other than the defaulting state is entitled to invoke the breach as a ground for suspending the operation of the treaty in whole or in part with respect to itself in relations with all the other parties. Prior agreement of the other parties is not required.

To ensure that the rules on termination or suspension of treaties as a consequence of a material breach by a party do not prejudice individuals, the Convention states that these rules do not apply to provisions relating to the protection of individuals under treaties of a humanitarian **(353)** character, in particular to provisions prohibiting any form of reprisals **(370)** against persons protected by such treaties.

**277. *Pacta Sunt Servanda.*** Perhaps the most famous and fundamental Latin maxim in international law, *pacta sunt servanda* means that treaties shall be observed. It gives expression to the principle of the sanctity of treaties **(288)** which underlies the entire system of the law of treaties and is believed to be the very foundation of the legal relations among nations, as in particular propounded by Hans Kelsen's pure theory of law **(34)**. The doctrine of the sanctity of treaties is considered by some to be a principle of natural law **(29)**; by others a general principle of law recognized by civilized nations **(38)**; and by yet others a principle of customary international law **(39)**. But whatever its philosophical origin, it is indispensable to predictability and stability in international relations, allowing states to expect that their mutual treaty commitments will be fulfilled in good faith. Dating back in the doctrine to the ancient traditions of the law of nature and of nations, the principle of *pacta sunt servanda* has been upheld by publicists **(42)** writing on the law of nations since the early centuries of the modern state system. It has also been referred to in countless decisions reaffirming it in international jurisprudence **(22)**. While not necessarily consistently observed in actual practice, it has always been asserted by those in power as the fundamental principle of international law. The United States (US) has historically been, in general, faithful to treaty obligations, but international publicists have cast doubt upon the more recent US posture in this regard. One of the best-known articulations of the principle of *pacta sunt servanda*, the Declaration of London of 1871 subscribed to by the major European powers, stated, *inter alia*, that "it is an essential principle of the Law of Nations that no Power can liberate itself from the engagements of a treaty nor modify the stipulations thereof, unless with the consent of the Contracting parties by means of an amicable understanding." The Charter of the United Nations enshrines "respect for the obligations arising from treaties" in its Preamble and the principle of *pacta sunt servanda* in its Latin form is noted in the Preamble to the Vienna Convention on the Law of Treaties (Vienna Convention) (1155 UNTS 331) as "universally recognized." Art. 26 of the Vienna Convention codifies the principle of *pacta sunt servanda* providing that "[E]very treaty in force is binding upon the parties to it and must be performed by them in good faith." Art. 27 codifies the well-established customary law principle that "[A] party may not invoke the provisions of its internal law as justification for its failure to perform a treaty." This is without prejudice to the rule expressed in Art. 46 that, while it is presumed that a treaty was entered into without any violation of internal law, a "manifest" violation concerning a rule of internal law of fundamental importance may justify non-observance on grounds of invalidity.

The principle of *pacta sunt servanda* is the foundation of the law of treaties, but—as shown by experience—to function successfully it must be complemented by appropriate procedures for peaceful change **(279)** and the rule allowing termination of treaty obligations in very exceptional cases of a fundamental change of circumstances **(273)**.

**278. *Pacta Tertiis Nec Nocent Nec Prosunt.*** A maxim of civil (Roman) law **(23)**, which in its application to international law means that a treaty **(288)** creates neither obligations nor rights for a third state **(127)** without its consent. Codified **(5)** in Art. 34 of the Vienna Convention on the Law of Treaties of 1969 (Vienna Convention) (1155 UNTS 331) this maxim expresses a firmly established rule of general international law and is a corollary of the principle of consent inherent in the system of sovereign **(125)** and equal **(73)** states. Many treaties expressly declare that they are to be binding on the parties only. The principle has also been reaffirmed in international adjudication **(306)** of which the judgment of the Permanent Court of International Justice (PCIJ) **(320)** in the case of the *Free Zones of Upper Savoy and the District of Gex* (France/Switzerland) (1932 PCIJ Series A/B, No. 46) is perhaps the best known in this regard. In this judgment the PCIJ held that Art. 435 of the Peace Treaty of Versailles (225 CTS 188) was not binding upon Switzerland which is not a party to that treaty except to the extent to which it accepted it.

It is controversial whether and to what extent the rule of *pacta tertiis nec nocent nec prosunt* admits of any exceptions both with regard to creation of obligations for, and conferment of rights upon a third state that is not a party to the treaty. The Vienna Convention makes it clear that "third State" means a "State not a party to the treaty" (Art. 2(1)(h)). Under Art. 35 of the Vienna Convention, a third state may be bound by a provision of a treaty under two conditions. First, the parties to the treaty must intend the provision to be the means of establishing the obligation and, second, the third state must expressly accept that obligation in writing. In effect, these strict requirements constitute a collateral agreement between the parties and that third state. It is that agreement that provides the legal basis for the third state's obligation, especially since under Art. 37(1) of the Vienna Convention, unless otherwise agreed, the obligation may be revoked or modified only with the consent of the parties to the treaty and of the third state.

There are a few exceptions to the general principle regarding third states in respect of obligations. First, a treaty rule may in any case become binding upon non-parties if it becomes a customary **(39)** rule of international law, recognized as such (Art. 38). For example, the agreement on neutralization **(97)** of Switzerland of 1815 and the Hague Convention **(350)** IV Respecting the Laws and Customs of War on Land, with an Annex and Regulations, 1907, have achieved the status of customary law and are recognized as such by non-party states. Second, a treaty may deal with lawful enforcement measures of the collective security system **(327)**, ordered by the Security Council of the United Nations (UN) against an aggressor state, a situation envisaged in Art. 75 of the Vienna Convention (Case of an Aggressor State). Finally, there is the now not so significant exception under Art. 2(6) of the UN Charter which, by providing that the UN shall ensure that non-members act in accordance with the principles of the Charter "so far as may be necessary to the maintenance of international peace and security" seems to conflict with the principle that a treaty is not binding on third parties. However, apart from the fact that the UN Charter is practically universally subscribed to, its principles involved here (peaceful settlement of disputes **(318)**, outlawry of force) are in any event binding all states as customary law.

The question of rights that may arise for a third state from a provision of a treaty is more controversial than the question of obligations. As noted by the PCIJ in the above-mentioned *Free Zones* case, the existence of such rights must not be lightly presumed and must be decided and ascertained in each particular case. The Vienna Convention takes the position (Art. 36(1)) that a right arises for a third state from a provision of a treaty if two conditions are met. First, the parties must intend the treaty provision to accord a legal right, and not a mere benefit, either to a particular third state, or to a group of states to which that state belongs, or to all states. Second, the third state must assent to the conferment of the right. Unless otherwise stipulated by the treaty, its assent must be presumed so long as the contrary is not indicated. Failure to exercise the right conferred may be taken by the parties for lack of assent. In any case (Art. 36(2)), a third state exercising the right must comply with the conditions for its exercise provided for in the treaty or established in conformity with the treaty. If intended to be irrevocable or not subject to modification **(269)**, a third state's right may not be revoked or modified by the parties without the consent of the third state.

Diplomatic practice provides numerous instances of treaties containing stipulations in favor of a third state, *pactum in favorem tertii* in civil (Roman) law terminology. Among them are: the Convention of 1856, an annex to the Treaty of Paris (France, Great Britain, Russia) (114 CTS 405), concerning the non-fortification of the Aaland islands then under Russian rule, whose provisions were invoked by Sweden; certain provisions of the above-mentioned Treaty of Versailles, in favor of Denmark and Switzerland; provisions of the Constantinople Convention of 1888 (171 CTS 241) guaranteeing all third states freedom of transit for ships through the Suez Canal **(261)**; and similar provisions of the Treaty of Versailles concerning the Kiel Canal **(252)**. The Vienna Convention does not include any rules concerning the so-called dispositive treaties creating "objective" regimes valid for all states, *erga omnes* **(12)**, such as, in addition to the Suez and Kiel Canals, provisions of the Antarctic Treaty of 1959 **(187)** on demilitarization of Antarctica; or the stipulations in the Treaty of Versailles reaffirming the permanent neutrality of Switzerland. The International Law Commission (which prepared the draft of the Vienna Convention) took the position that such *erga omnes* treaties are simply an application of the rule of Art. 36 of the Vienna Convention on treaties providing for rights for third states, which constitutes a sufficient legal basis for the establishment of such rights.

**279. Peaceful Change.** The concept of "peaceful change" refers to the pacific methods of resolving international disputes **(318)** arising out of demands for changing the existing legal *status quo* which was once established by a treaty **(288)** perceived by a state **(127)** party or parties to be a serious burden and a potential threat to international peace and security. While itself not a concept in international law, the notion of peaceful change is of paramount importance for international law in that it aims at peaceful alteration of treaties in a system of law that forbids forcible change but lacks effective peaceful mechanisms for changing a treaty based on sovereign **(125)** consent of the parties. In the inter-war period the League of Nations made an unsuccessful attempt to set up procedures for securing peaceful change in treaty relations. Art. 19 of the Covenant of the League of Nations (225 CTS 188), forming part of the Treaty of Versailles and the other peace treaties with the defeated states, provided for the right of the League's Assembly to advise members to reconsider treaties which have become "inapplicable." However, caught between the states satisfied with the existing *status quo* of treaties and the "revisionist" states, especially Nazi Germany, the League of Nations was unable to make much use of Art. 19.

For its part, subject to the rights of the Security Council, the United Nations Charter (Art. 14) authorizes the General Assembly (GA) to "recommend any measures for the peaceful adjustment of any situation, regardless of origin, which it deems likely to impair the general welfare or friendly relations among nations, including situations resulting from violation of the provisions of the present Charter setting forth the Purposes and Principles of the United Nations." The term "situation" arguably includes burdensome treaty relationships, but the limited, recommendatory only, powers of the GA would not allow it to make any legally binding decisions on adjusting such treaties.

The concept of peaceful change is absent in the Vienna Convention of 1969. However, apart from the possibility of amendments and modifications **(269)**, problems of peaceful change arise within the purview of the institution of the fundamental change of circumstances **(273)** as a ground for terminating or withdrawing **(287)** from a treaty. In this context the Vienna Convention provides for a variety of peaceful procedures, such as conciliation **(296)** and adjudication **(306)**, and to that extent application in good faith of such procedures may contribute to peaceful change in international treaty relationships.

**280. Ratification.** According to Art. 2(1)(b) (Use of Terms) of the Vienna Convention on the Law of Treaties **(288)** of 1969 (Vienna Convention) (1155 UNTS 331), ratification is an international act "whereby a State **(127)** establishes on the international plane its consent to be bound by a treaty." "Acceptance," "approval" **(266)**, and "accession" **(267)** perform substantially the same function as ratification. Ratification on the international plane must be differentiated from ratification in the meaning of a procedural act performed on the domestic plane by the constitutionally authorized organ or organs of state, such as the national parliament. In the United States (US) this function is carried out by the president with the "advice and consent of two-thirds of senators present and voting" (US Constitution Art. II). As elaborated below, in bilateral treaties this domestic "ratification" becomes internationally effected by the exchange of pertinent instruments between the states parties. In multilateral treaties it is accomplished by depositing the instrument of ratification with one of the parties or—a common practice—with the United Nations (UN) Secretary-General.

The institution of ratification has undergone substantial transformation in the history of European international law and diplomacy. Prior to the 19th century, it was in substance not an approval of a treaty itself but a formal act whereby the sovereign **(125)** confirmed his plenipotentiaries' full powers **(272)** to negotiate **(316)** the treaty and was obliged to approve it unless they exceeded his secret instructions. In the 19th century, ratification developed its contemporary significance as a formal declaration of a state on the international plane of its definitive consent to be bound by a treaty. At the same time, the progressive democratization of governments entailed the need and ordinarily a constitutional duty to submit the treaty-making powers of the executive authority to parliamentary scrutiny. Since in the 19th century treaties were still, as a rule, formal instruments dealing primarily with territorial and other "high politics" issues, a rule developed that ratification was necessary to render a treaty binding. Eventually, in the 20th century, with the gradual extension of treaty relations to virtually all aspects of international relations, many less formal treaties would become, with the contracting states' agreement, binding on signature **(283)** alone. But ratification, if required, allows states to reexamine the provisions of a treaty before undertaking a formal obligation and, in the period between signature and ratification, enable them to pass the necessary implementing legislation. In general, most international agreements do not require ratification, but this method of expressing consent to be bound by a treaty is still prevalent with respect to more important agreements.

Treaties normally state expressly either that ratification is necessary for the entry into force **(271)** or that they enter into effect upon signature or upon a specified date or event. In exceptional cases, where a treaty is silent on the matter, the intention of the parties must be ascertained. For cases where there is no mention of ratification in a treaty, the Vienna Convention establishes no legal presumption in favor of ratification as a means of expressing consent to be bound and leaves the matter to the intention of the parties. Under Art. 14(1), ratification is necessary for a state to be bound by a treaty if: a. the treaty itself provides for consent to be expressed by means of ratification; b. if it is otherwise established that the negotiating states were agreed that that ratification should be required; c. if the representative of the state has signed the treaty subject to ratification; or d. if the intention of the state to sign the treaty subject to ratification appears from the full powers of its representative or was expressed during the negotiation. A state may agree to or withhold ratification at its own discretion without conveying to the other state or states the reasons for refusal to ratify. But the fact that a certain category of international agreements, in particular the so-called "executive agreements" in the US (and some other countries), does not, under US law, require ratification, is irrelevant for purposes of international law. Whether delays in carrying out the internal act of ratifying a signed treaty (as illustrated by the practice persisting in the US in this regard) may amount to a violation of international law is not clear.

Unless specifically provided by the treaty, there is no special form of ratification in international law. It usually takes the form of acts signed by the head of state or foreign minister, which in unambiguous terms refer to the treaty in question as ratified by the state concerned. Conditional ratification is not legally effective, and if attempted—as was the case of the US with regard to the Panama Canal treaties **(258)** in 1976—must be considered as refusal of ratification requiring a renegotiation of the treaty if the other party so agrees. Without prejudice to the institution of reservations **(282)**, partial ratification is possible under the Vienna Convention only if the treaty so permits or the other contracting states so agree, but the consent of a state to be bound by a treaty permitting a choice between differing provisions is effective only if it is made clear to which of the provisions the consent relates (Art. 17).

Unless the treaty otherwise provides, instruments of ratification, acceptance, approval, or accession must, in order to have their intended effect of establishing a state's consent to be bound by a treaty on the international plane, be exchanged between the contracting states; deposited with the depositary; or notified to the contracting states or to the depositary, if so agreed (Art. 16). Ratification instruments for bilateral treaties are exchanged by the contracting states and each instrument is filed in the archives of both states. Since this method would be too cumbersome in cases of multilateral treaties, such treaties normally provide for the deposit of all instruments of ratification with a single state acting as depositary notifying all the other contracting parties of each incoming deposit. For example, the US is the depositary of the UN Charter (UN Charter Art. 110(2)). In rare cases, more than one state is designated as a depositary, for example in the Nuclear Test Ban Treaty of 1963 (480 UNTS 43) and the Non-Proliferation of Nuclear Weapons Treaty of 1968 (729 UNTS 161). It is now quite common that an international organization **(84)** involved in the drafting of the treaty or its chief administrative officer may be designated as depositary. For example, the UN Secretary-General performs this function for treaties adopted under the auspices the UN. Over 500 major multilateral instruments were deposited with the UN Secretary-General as of May 2003. Rules relating to depositaries of treaties and their functions are spelled out in more detail in Arts. 76 and 77 of the Vienna Convention.

**281. Registration.** Registration of treaties **(288)** takes place through public recording by the United Nations (UN) of treaties submitted to it by members of the organization. Reiterating in somewhat different terms an analogous provision of Art. 19 of the Covenant of the League of Nations (225 CTS 188), introduced into the Covenant to discourage secret diplomacy, Art. 102(1) of the UN Charter mandates that "[E]very treaty and every international agreement entered into by any members of the United Nations after the . . . Charter comes into force shall as soon as possible be registered with the Secretariat and published by it." The Regulations Concerning the Registration and Publication of Treaties and International Agreements, adopted by the UN General Assembly in 1946 (76 UNTS xviii) provide more detailed rules on the matter. Registration does not take place until a treaty has come into force; registration by a party relieves all other parties of the obligation to register. Among the registrable instruments are not only treaties between members but also between members and non-members or international organizations **(84)**; treaties between international organizations; declarations accepting the compulsory jurisdiction **(297)** of the International Court of Justice (ICJ) **(309)** under the optional clause **(317)**; declarations by new UN members accepting membership; and even unilateral engagements **(44)** of an international character which have been accepted by other states. The Declaration by Egypt of 1957 on the Suez Canal **(261)** and arrangements for its operations is an example of such engagements. However, registration by the UN Secretariat does not imply its judgment on the nature of the instrument. An instrument, such as the Helsinki Final Act of 1975 or the Charter of Paris for a New Europe, 1990, may expressly state that it is not eligible for registration under Art. 102 of the UN Charter, with the implication that legally it does not have the binding force of a treaty. In the practice of the UN Secretariat, non-member states have been allowed to "file and record" their treaties. The Vienna Convention on the Law of Treaties of 1969 (Vienna Convention) (1155 UNTS 331) reaffirms in Art. 80 the obligation of states to transmit treaties, after their entry into force **(271)**, to the UN Secretariat or—a phrase that applies to non-members—"filing and recording," and for publication. The designation of a depositary constitutes authorization for it to perform registration or recording, as the case may be. Among the functions of a depositary, the Vienna Convention lists the registration (Art. 77(1)(g)) and—by implication—(Art. 77(1)(h)) filing and recording of treaties.

There is an essential difference between the provisions on registration in the Covenant of the League of Nations and in the UN Charter insofar as the legal effects of failure by a state to register a treaty are concerned. Whereas under the Covenant no treaty was binding until registered, under the UN Charter a non-registered treaty remains valid but no party (including a non-member) may invoke it before any organ of the UN. This means that a non-registered treaty or international agreement may not be invoked as evidence, for example, before the ICJ, but apparently may be invoked before other international tribunals. In a case of this kind, the unregistered Treaty Establishing the Organization of Eastern Caribbean States of 1981 (20 ILM 1166 (1981)) could—apart from other reasons—not be invoked to justify the invasion by the United States of Grenada in 1984. Whether an unregistered treaty not invoked by a party may be relied upon by the ICJ or other UN organ on that organ's own initiative is not entirely clear.

The publication by the UN Secretariat of treaties and other international agreements in the UN Treaty Series (UNTS) is the continuation of the League of Nations Treaty Series (LNTS). The LNTS reported, in 204 volumes, 4,827 instruments registered under Art. 18 of the Covenant. The UNTS includes the texts of treaties in their original language or languages, along with translations into English and French, as appropriate. To facilitate reference the UN Secretariat publishes a Cumulative Index (in English and French) for every 50 volumes of the UNTS. As of January 2004 the collection contained over 50,000 treaties and a similar number of related subsequent actions, published in over 2,000 volumes. However, there had been a time lag between the entry into force of instruments and their publication in the UNTS. More recently the UN Secretariat has started enhancing the collection to include the latest desktop published volumes.

**282. Reservation.** As defined in Art. 1(1)(d) of the Vienna Convention on the Law of Treaties of 1969 (Vienna Convention) (1155 UNTS 331), reservation means "a unilateral statement **(44)** however phrased or named, made by a State **(127)**, when signing **(283)**, ratifying **(280)**, accepting, approving **(266)** or acceding **(267)** to a treaty **(288)**, whereby it purports to exclude or to modify the legal effect of certain provisions of the treaty in their application to that State." A reservation must be distinguished from a mere interpretative statement or declaration of national policy concerning the manner of applying the treaty in relations with the other states parties. But caution must be exercised because, despite its designation, such a "conditional" declaration or statement may in substance and its legal effects be a pretext for a disguised reservation in treaties prohibiting them. The International Law Commission (ILC), in connection with its codification **(5)** of the topic of reservations to treaties, prepared special guidelines expressing concern about such conditional interpretative declarations. The distinction between them and reservations has been analyzed in international adjudication **(306)**, including, *inter alia*, the arbitral **(293)** award in the *Anglo-French Continental Shelf* case of 1977 (18 ILM 397 (1979)) involving a French reservation to Art. 6 of the Geneva Convention on the Continental Shelf, 1958 which—as contended by the United Kingdom (UK)—was only an interpretative declaration and thus did not constitute a condition attached by France on its acceptance of the delimitation method under Art. 6. The arbitration tribunal (called "court") ruled that Art. 6 was binding upon the two countries only to the extent that it was not modified by what it found to be a French reservation which included both elements of interpretation and a specific condition. The distinction between an interpretative declaration and a reservation was also at issue before the European Court of Human Rights (ECHR) **(154)** in the *Belilos* case in 1988 in which the Court ruled that Switzerland's "declaration" made upon the ratification of the European Convention for the Protection of Human

Rights and Fundamental Freedoms of 1950 **(153)** was in substance a general reservation and therefore invalid in a treaty prohibiting such reservations.

The problem of reservations arises only with regard to multilateral treaties where they are very common. In bilateral treaties any reservation by a party is merely a counteroffer of the reserving state which the other state may either accept, thus agreeing to the text of the treaty modified by the reservation, or reject whereupon the negotiations **(316)** either continue or end without concluding the treaty. The general rationale of reservations is to reconcile the objective of as wide participation in a treaty as possible, with the need to avoid uncertainty and complexity in treaty relations and to preserve the integrity of the treaty as one multilateral instrument. From a practical point of view, the institution of reservation makes it possible for a state wishing to join an otherwise attractive treaty arrangement to be exempt from one or more undesirable provisions of the treaty. In this way the state concerned may become a party to a treaty which it might reject entirely if no reservations were possible.

The issue of reservations exhibits a number of complex and controversial aspects, not the least of which is the possibility of some states' objecting, for various reasons, to another state's attempt to become a party to a treaty subject to one or more reservations. In particular, the question arises whether a reservation, to be valid, has to be accepted by all of the parties and, if not, what legal relationship exists between the reserving and objecting states. In view of such eventualities the legal rules concerning acceptance of and objections to reservations and their legal effects are not settled. On the whole, however, the solution adopted by the Vienna Convention (Arts. 19–23) corresponds to the position of a great majority of states. Historically, two approaches have evolved in international practice relating to the admissibility of reservations. The first approach, adopted by the League of Nations in 1927, followed the principle of absolute integrity of the multilateral treaty whereby a reservation was valid only if accepted by all the contracting parties. If opposed, a reserving state had to forego its reservation if it wanted to be considered a party to the treaty. In the other approach, in 1932 the Governing Board of the Pan American Union (later known as the Organization of American States), proposed a more flexible approach whereby, if some parties might be willing to accept a reservation and others might not, the treaty would enter into force **(271)**, as negotiated between the states accepting it without any reservations, but would not come into force between the reserving states and those that did not accept the reservation The approach of the Pan American Union was criticized as fragmenting the integrity and uniform application of multilateral treaties to the detriment of any advantages that might accrue to the parties

Following the adoption of the Genocide Convention in 1948 **(155)**, which is silent on the matter to reservations, the question was raised of the legal effect of reservations formulated with respect to that Convention by the states of the Soviet bloc, an issue that eventually led to the Advisory Opinion **(291)** of the International Court of Justice (ICJ) **(309)** of 1951 on *Reservations to the Convention on the Prevention and Punishment of the Crime of Genocide* (1951 ICJ Rep. 15). While tending to prefer the Pan American approach, essentially the Court's principal ruling was that a state making a reservation to the Genocide Convention, to which reservation some but not all the parties objected, was to be regarded as being a party to the Convention if its reservation was "compatible with the object and purpose of the Convention." Although originally the ILC, a subsidiary organ of the General Assembly (GA), charged with the codification and development of international law **(5)**, rejected the compatibility test as too subjective, the GA requested the UN Secretary-General in his capacity as depositary of treaties to follow, in UN-sponsored treaties, the principles applied by the ICJ to the Genocide Convention unless the treaty contained provisions to the contrary, to which position the ILC itself eventually adhered in tune with the general trend toward a wider acceptance of multilateral treaties and majority decision making in international organizations **(84)**.

In its approach, the Vienna Convention (Art. 19) basically follows the principle of the freedom to formulate a reservation except in three cases: first, if the reservation is prohibited by the treaty; second, if the treaty provides that only specified reservations, which do not include the reservation in question, may be made; and third, in cases not falling under the above two situations, if the reservation is incompatible with the object and purpose of the treaty, a formula of the ICJ expressing the incompatibility test applied to the Genocide Convention.

Since there is, as a rule, no appropriate decision-making mechanism, each state must subjectively decide for itself whether a reservation is or it not compatible with the object and purpose of the treaty. As a result, the test of compatibility can be subjected to diverse interpretations **(274)** by individual contracting states. However, in human rights treaties **(160)** the Human Rights Committee considers itself to be the only body able to decide on the compatibility test in individual cases. Exceptionally, some treaties provide for special procedures to determine whether a reservation is admissible. For example, the International Convention on the Elimination of All Forms of Racial Discrimination of 1966 **(177)** considers a reservation to be incompatible if at least two-thirds of the contracting states object to it, a rather high proportion not likely to be met in practice. Concerning acceptance of and objection to reservations, under Art. 20 of the Vienna Convention a reservation expressly authorized by a treaty does not require any subsequent acceptance by the other parties unless the treaty so provides. As a concession to the traditional rule of treaty integrity, the Convention stipulates that if it is clear from the object and purpose of a treaty negotiated by a limited number of states that the application of the treaty in its entirety is an essential condition of the consent of each one to be bound by the treaty, a reservation requires acceptance by all the parties. In addition, unless the treaty provides otherwise, reservations to treaties establishing an international organization require acceptance by the competent organ of that organization. In other cases a more flexible approach applies whereby a reserving state may become a party to the treaty in relation to an accepting state, while an objection to a reservation does not preclude the entry into force of the treaty as between the objecting and reserving states unless a contrary intention is expressed by the objecting state. The Vienna Convention recognizes tacit or implied acceptance of a reservation by a state if it has raised no objections within a year of the notification of the reservation or its expressing to be bound by the treaty, whichever is later.

In its legal effects, a reservation modifies certain provisions of the treaty in the reserving state's relations with another party, without, however, modifying the provisions of the treaty for those parties in their relations with each other (*inter se*) (Art. 21(1)(2)). The other party is affected to the same extent in its relations with the reserving state. For example, in respect of the 1961 Vienna Convention on Diplomatic Relations **(71)**, since the UK accepted Libya's reservation concerning the search of the diplomatic bag **(65)**, it could treat Libya's diplomatic bag in the same manner. If an objecting state has not opposed the entry into force of the treaty between itself and the reserving state, its treaty relationship *vis à vis* the reserving state is modified by the reservation (Art. 21(3)), a rule applied in the above-noted *Anglo-French Continental Shelf* Arbitration in 1977.

It is not clear what the legal effects are of an inadmissible reservation, that is, one conflicting with the requirements of Art. 19 of the Vienna Convention. The question has arisen especially with regard to reservations to human rights treaties. In such cases, the jurisprudence of the ECHR, taking account of the special nature of the human rights treaties, has favored "severing" an inadmissible reservation so as to make the reserving state bound by the treaty, as illustrated by the above-noted case of *Belilos* and the *Loizidou* case of 1995 involving Turkey's otherwise disguised reservations. Against contrary views of the United States and the UK, the Human Rights Committee followed the same approach in respect to inadmissible reservations to the International Covenant on Civil and Political Rights **(166)**. The issue remains controversial even for reservations to treaties other than human rights conventions. However, on the whole, the problem of reservations has not proved to be as troublesome as had been expected at the negotiations on the Vienna Convention. Despite the frequency of reservations, many treaties do not have them, and reservations on substantive matters are not common. Those concerning the dispute settlement are the most frequent category. In addition, problems relating to the interpreting of the legal effects of reservations are largely remedied by a careful drafting of reservation provisions in international agreements.

Unless otherwise provided by the treaty, withdrawal of reservations and of objections to reservations may be effected at any time. In both cases, a withdrawal becomes operative after notice of the withdrawal has been received by another contracting state (withdrawal of a reservation) or when notice has been received by the state which formulated the reservation (withdrawal of an objection) (Art. 22). A reservation as well as an express acceptance of a reservation, and an objection to a reservation, must be formulated in writing and communicated to the contracting states and other states entitled to become parties to the treaty (Art. 23(1)). Communication through the depositary appears to be acceptable. Reservations made when signing a treaty must be formally confirmed upon ratification, acceptance, or approval.

**283. Signature.** One of the several methods of expressing consent to be bound by a treaty **(288)**, or an expression of provisional consent subject to ratification **(280)**, acceptance, or approval **(266)**, signature is the official affixing of names to the text of a treaty by the negotiating states representatives. As stated in Art. 12(1) of the Vienna Convention on the Law of Treaties of 1969 (Vienna Convention) (1155 UNTS 331), the signature of a treaty by a representative of a state expresses his state's consent to be bound by the treaty in three cases: 1. when the treaty itself provides that signature shall have that effect, a common practice in many bilateral treaties; 2. when it is otherwise established that the negotiating states were agreed that signature should have that effect; and 3. when the intention of the state to give that effect to its signature appears from the full powers **(272)** of its representative or was expressed during the negotiation. In addition, a signature *ad referendum*, that is, one given provisionally and subject to confirmation by the representative's government, if confirmed by his state constitutes a full signature of the treaty. The initialing of a text constitutes a signature of the treaty when it is established that the negotiating states so agreed (Art. 12(2)).

If a treaty is subject to ratification, acceptance, or approval by the signing state, the signature legally means only that the text of the treaty has been authenticated **(270)** and the representatives will refer it to their respective governments for definitive acceptance or rejection as the case may be, but in the absence of an express agreement by the state concerned, there is no obligation to submit the text of the treaty to the appropriate national authority for action. However, even in cases where signature does not signify consent to be bound by a treaty, a state is obliged to refrain from acts which would defeat the object and purpose of the treaty until it shall have made its intention clear not to become a party to the treaty (Art. 18(a)). Whether this provision reflects a customary rule of law **(39)** is not quite certain.

**284. Successive (Inconsistent) Treaties.** These are treaties **(288)** successive in time and relating to the same subject matter, whose provisions are mutually incompatible by creating conflicting obligations for one or more parties. A state party to a treaty has the obligation not to conclude, with third states, treaties whose provisions conflict with the obligations contracted by it in an earlier treaty. Occasionally global, regional, and subregional treaties relating to the same subject matter may produce overlapping provisions which create conflicting obligations for one or more parties. A case in point is the area of the law of human rights **(160)** where two sets of major treaties coexist: one adopted regionally, as exemplified by the European Convention for the Protection of Human Rights and Fundamental Freedoms of 1950 **(153)**, and the other, on the global level, namely, the International Covenant on Civil and Political Rights, 1966 **(166)**, and the International Covenant on Economic, Social and Cultural Rights of the same year **(169)**.

Treaties frequently contain a clause designed to regulate the relationship of a treaty with an earlier or future treaty. The United Nations (UN) Convention on the Law of the Sea of 1982 **(264)** provides in Art. 311(1) that it shall prevail, as between states parties, over the Conventions on the law of the sea adopted by the Geneva Conference of 1958 **(243)**. The UN Charter, 1945, occupies a special position in the law of treaties. In Art. 103, it regulates its relationship to other treaties, establishing the paramount position and status of the Charter in the whole system of conventional international law. This article provides that "in the event of a conflict between the obligations of the Members of the United Nations under the present Charter and their obligations under any other international agreement, their obligations under the present Charter shall prevail."

It is generally recognized that this rule applies to all treaties, past and future, concluded between member states and with non-members. Whether a treaty incompatible with the UN Charter is voidable or *ipso facto* null and void is not clear. However, within the context of invalidity of treaties **(275)** a treaty is void if at the time of its conclusion it conflicts with a peremptory norm of general international law (*jus cogens*) **(24)**. On the other hand, a treaty overrides other treaties if it represents such norm.

In its provisions on the application of successive treaties relating to the same subject matter, the Vienna Convention on the Law of Treaties of 1969 (Vienna Convention) (1155 UNTS 331) recognizes the paramount status of the UN Charter (Art. 30(1)), otherwise approaching the problem of incompatible treaties as one of priorities. However, its rules apply only in the absence of express treaty provisions regulating priority. Thus, under Art. 30(2), when a treaty specifies that it is subject to an earlier or later treaty, the provisions of that other treaty prevail. The same rule applies when a treaty specifies that it is not to be considered as incompatible with such an earlier or later treaty. For example, the 1958 Geneva Convention on the High Seas provided that its provisions shall not affect conventions already in force, as between states parties to them (Art. 30).

All the parties to a treaty may, of course, adopt a later treaty on the same subject matter. Normally such later treaty is presumed to prevail over an earlier one. If it is established by an express provision or otherwise that the earlier treaty is not terminated **(287)** or suspended **(286)**, the earlier treaty applies only to the extent that its provisions are compatible with those of the later treaty (Vienna Convention Art. 30(3)). The same rule applies as between states parties to both treaties even when the parties to the later treaty do not include all the parties to the earlier one (Art. 30(4)(a)). However, as between a party to both treaties and a party to only one of them, the treaty to which both states are parties is to govern their mutual rights and obligations (Art. 30(4)(b)). But this rule is without prejudice to any agreement on modification **(269)** of multilateral treaties, or termination or suspension of a treaty as a consequence of its breach **(276)**, or any responsibilities **(128)** that may arise for a state from conclusion or application of a treaty in conflict with its obligations toward another state under an earlier treaty (Art. 30(5)).

**285. Supervening Impossibility of Performance.** This is a ground for terminating or withdrawing **(287)** from a treaty **(288)** due to the impossibility resulting from the permanent disappearance or destruction of an object indispensable for the execution of the treaty. There are very few examples in state **(127)** practice of termination of a treaty on this ground. Among grounds that may be invoked, the International Law Commission, a subsidiary organ of the United Nations General Assembly, charged with codification and progressive development **(5)** of international law, mentions such events as the submergence of an island, the drying up of a river, or the destruction of a dam or hydroelectric installation indispensable for the execution of a treaty. Whether a supervening impossibility of performance automatically terminates a treaty is an unsettled issue in customary international law **(39)**. Under Art. 61 of the Vienna Convention on the Law of Treaties of 1969 (Vienna Convention) (1155 UNTS 331), such an event merely gives a party the option of terminating or withdrawing from a treaty. If the impossibility is temporary, it may be invoked only as a ground for suspending **(286)** the operation of the treaty. A party may not invoke impossibility of performance if the impossibility is the result of a breach by that party either of an obligation under the treaty or of any other obligation owed to any other party to the treaty.

**286. Suspension of Operation.** This is temporary discontinuance of the operation of a treaty **(288)** in regard to all the parties or to a particular party. Treaties occasionally provide for the possibility of suspension of the entire treaty or some of its provisions. Like termination **(287)**, suspension may take place only according to the provisions of the treaty or at any time by consent of all the parties after consultation with the other contracting states, a rule codified **(5)** in Art. 57 of the Vienna Convention on the Law of Treaties of 1969 (Vienna Convention) (1155 UNTS 331).

Suspension of the operation of a multilateral treaty by agreement between certain of the parties only is also possible. For this purpose, parties may conclude an agreement to suspend the operation of provisions of the treaty, temporarily and as between themselves alone, on the condition that such suspension is provided for by the treaty; or is not prohibited by the treaty and does not affect the enjoyment of the other parties of their rights under the treaty or the performance of their obligations, and is not incompatible with the object and purpose of the treaty. Notification of the other parties of the intention to suspend the treaty is required unless the possibility of such suspension is stipulated by the treaty (Vienna Convention Art. 58(1)). Suspension of a treaty may be implied by the conclusion of a later treaty if such was the intension of the parties (Art. 58(2)). Material breach **(276)**, fundamental change of circumstances **(273)**, and supervening impossibility of performance **(285)** also entitle a party to suspend the operation of a treaty. Unless otherwise agreed, the suspension of the operation of a treaty releases the parties concerned from the obligation to perform the treaty in their mutual relations during the period of suspension, but it does not otherwise affect the legal relations between the parties, established by the treaty. During the period of the suspension, the parties must refrain from acts tending to obstruct the resumption of the operation of the treaty.

**287. Termination.** As distinguished from suspension **(286)**, termination of a treaty **(288)** means bringing its operation to a permanent end. In terms of concepts, a further distinction must be borne in mind. A multilateral treaty terminates only for a particular party upon that party's "withdrawal" from the treaty, the concept and term of withdrawal being used within the context of multilateral treaties. In such cases, the treaty itself continues in force for the other parties. In bilateral treaties, the term "denunciation" is, as a rule, used to denote withdrawal from a bilateral treaty and *ipso facto* entails the termination of the treaty. But the terminology is not entirely consistent, and occasionally the term "denunciation" is used with reference to a multilateral treaty.

While the principle *pacta sunt servanda* **(277)** is the foundation of security in treaty relations, international law recognizes the need for rules on termination of treaties in force, taking account of the fact that in the absence of a possibility for legal termination the law would become too rigid and would fail to ensure a right balance between security and flexibility of treaty obligations. Customary law **(39)** relating to termination of treaties developed a number of rules on this subject, but they were not entirely clear on the issue under which circumstances a party to a treaty was legally entitled to terminate a treaty. The Vienna Convention on the Law of Treaties of 1969 (Vienna Convention) (1155 UNTS 331) codifies and progressively develops **(5)** the relevant rules, clarifying a number of points and—if possible—filling in loopholes existing in the customary law on the subject of termination of treaties. However, the Convention does not deal with the problem of the legal effects of war **(338)** on treaties, discussed below.

The Vienna Convention stipulates, among its general provisions on invalidity, termination, and suspension of operations **(286)** of treaties, the cardinal principle that the termination (and suspension) of a treaty, its denunciation or the withdrawal of a party, may take place only as a result of the application of the provisions of the treaty or of the Convention (Art. 42(2)). The termination of a treaty or a withdrawal of a party may take place only in conformity with the provisions of the treaty or, at any time by consent of all the parties after consultation with the other contracting states (Art. 54). A multilateral treaty may provide that it will terminate if the number of parties is reduced below the number necessary for its entry into force **(271)**, but, unless a treaty so provides, it does not terminate by reason only of that diminution (Art. 55). Most treaties contain provisions fixing the duration of the treaty or the date of its termination, or an event or condition which will bring about its termination. As a rule, treaties also provide for denunciation or withdrawal after a certain period of notice. A treaty may be concluded for a limited fixed period, for example five or ten years, with a possibility of continuance thereafter for a period of time or indefinitely, subject to the right of denunciation or withdrawal. Some treaties assign no specific period of duration, providing only for the right of denunciation or withdrawal either with or without a period of notice.

The termination of a treaty by consent may result from either explicit or implicit consent. A situation of termination by implicit content occurs when a treaty has fallen into "desuetude," that is, it is no longer applied and it is clear from the conduct of the parties that they no longer consider the treaty to be in force. But the mere passage of time does not necessarily mean that this is in fact the case. The issue whether the General Act for the Pacific Settlement of International Disputes of 1928, revised in 1949 (71 UNTS 101) had fallen into desuetude was raised before the International Court of Justice (ICJ) **(309)** in a few cases, but the ICJ did not find it necessary to decide the matter.

A treaty is also considered terminated if all the parties conclude a later treaty relating to the same subject matter, intended to replace the earlier treaty, or if the later treaty is so incompatible with the provisions of the earlier one that the two cannot be applied at the same time. However, the earlier treaty is considered as only suspended in operation if it appears from the later treaty or is otherwise established that such was the intention of the parties (Art. 59). Emergence of a new peremptory norm of international law (*jus cogens*) **(24)** voids and terminates any existing treaty which is in conflict with that norm, but the voiding has no retroactive effect (Art. 64).

Denunciation of or withdrawal from a treaty containing no provision regarding termination depends on the intention of the parties. This is a question of fact to be determined by reference to all the circumstances of the case, including the character of the treaty. Treaties of peace, boundary, and other territorial agreements are presumed to be permanent since by their very nature they have already been executed. Subject to contrary treaty provisions, treaties of alliance and commercial agreements are presumed to be concluded with an implied right to denunciation or withdrawal. On the other hand, with respect to the International Covenant on Civil and Political Rights, 1966 **(166)** which has no termination clause, the Human Rights Committee ruled in 1997 that, as a major codification of human rights, the Covenant did not by its nature belong to treaties implying a right of withdrawal, and such right was deliberately not intended to be included in the Covenant. Because of the principle of non-retroactivity (Vienna Convention Art. 4), the United Nations Charter (which has no provisions on withdrawal), formally is not subject to the rules of the Vienna Convention, but because of its nature also belongs to treaties which by customary law do not imply any right of withdrawal.

The Vienna Convention (Art. 56) provides that a treaty which contains no provision regarding its termination and which does not provide for denunciation or withdrawal, is not subject to denunciation or withdrawal unless it is established that the parties intended to admit such possibility; or if such right may be implied by the nature of the treaty. The Convention requires of a party not less than 12 months' notice of its intention to denounce or withdraw from a treaty.

Special circumstances that may give a party an option to terminate (or suspend) a treaty arise in cases of material breach **(276)**, supervening impossibility of performance **(285)**, and fundamental change of circumstances **(273)**. The rules regarding the loss of a party's right to invoke a ground for terminating, withdrawing from, or suspending the operation of a treaty, follow those governing invalidating **(275)** a treaty (Art. 45). The severance of diplomatic **(71)** or consular **(56)** relations between parties does not affect the legal relations established by the treaty between them except insofar as the existence of such relations is indispensable for the application of the treaty (Art. 63).

To what extent a treaty is terminated by the outbreak of war or, more generally, in modern terminology, international armed conflict **(339)** between the parties, is a complex and unsettled problem. It is not covered by the Vienna Convention which in Art. 73 only states that its provisions shall not prejudge any question that may arise in regard to a treaty from the outbreak of hostilities between states, state succession **(132)**, and international responsibility **(128)**. Hence, the question of the effect of war on treaties is governed only by the customary rules of law, otherwise not entirely settled. The more general opinion is that the outbreak of war does not automatically abrogate treaties between belligerents. Such was the view of the Institut de droit international expressed in its resolution of 1985 on the effects of armed conflict on treaties. The issue is compounded by the formal outlawry of force **(329)** in today's international law, which makes it less clear to what extent illegal resort to armed force affects the right to regard a treaty as terminated or suspended. In general, the practice in post–World War II armed conflicts has been for states to maintain a treaty between *de facto* belligerents in force unless in practice the outbreak of hostilities should bring about the termination or suspension of the treaty on grounds of fundamental change of circumstances or supervening impossibility of performance. It is obvious that treaties which by their very nature begin to be operative during an armed conflict, in particular the various international humanitarian law **(353)** conventions regulating the conduct of hostilities, do not terminate. The same is true of treaties establishing international organizations **(84)**; they are not considered to be affected by the existence of an armed conflict between any of the parties. Historically, upon the outbreak of war treaties were often suspended and, after the war, peace treaties included clauses regulating the status of pre-war treaties between belligerents, revising some and declaring other treaties not specifically named as abrogated. This was the case after World War I with regard to the Treaty of Versailles with Germany, 1919 (225 CTS 188); the Treaty of St. Germain with Austria, 1919 (226 CTS 8); the Treaty of Trianon with Hungary, 1920 (6 LNTS 188); the Treaty of Neuilly with Bulgaria; 1919 (226 CTS 332); and the Treaty of Lausanne with Turkey, 1923 (128 LNTS 11) and—after World War II—in respect to, *inter alia*, the peace treaties with: Italy, 1947 (49 and 50 UNTS); Romania, 1947 (42 UNTS 3); Bulgaria, 1947 (41 UNTS 21); Hungary, 1947 (41 UNTS 135); and Japan, 1951 (136 UNTS 45).

Unless otherwise agreed by the parties, the termination of a treaty releases them from any obligation further to perform the treaty, but does not affect any right, obligation, or legal situation of the parties created through the execution of the treaty prior to its termination. For a state denouncing or withdrawing from a multilateral treaty, the same legal consequences follow in its relations with each of the other parties from the date when such denunciation or withdrawal takes effect (Vienna Convention Art. 70). In addition, if a treaty becomes void and terminates because of the emergence of a new rule of *jus cogens*, the legal position of the parties prior to the termination may be maintained only to the extent that it is not itself in conflict with the new peremptory norm.

The rules governing separability of treaty provisions for purposes of invalidity of a treaty apply also to termination and withdrawal. The procedure to be followed with respect to termination, withdrawal from, or suspension of a treaty is governed by the rules of Arts. 65–68 which regulate cases involving invalidity of a treaty.

**288. Treaty.** According to the definition in the Vienna Convention on the Law of Treaties of 1969 (Vienna Convention) (1555 UNTS 331) in force in 1980 and with 96 parties as of 20 January 2004, a treaty means "an international agreement concluded between States **(127)** in written form and governed by international law, whether embodied in a single instrument or in two or more related instruments and whatever its particular designation" (Art. 2(1)(a)). While ordinarily treaties are concluded between states, other subjects of international law **(85)**, such as intergovernmental organizations **(84)** and insurgent movements **(115)**, have a limited competence to enter into written international agreements under international law. A Convention on the Law of Treaties between States and International Organizations or between International Organizations (25 ILM 543 (1986)) was adopted in 1986 but was not yet in force in 2004. It should be added that, as expressly stated in Art. 3 of the Vienna Convention, the fact that the Convention does not apply to international agreements between states and other subjects of international law or between such other subjects, or to international agreements not in written force, shall not affect the legal force of agreements which are not regulated by the Vienna Convention.

There is no legal significance attached to the appellation employed. Although the term "treaty" is used in the Vienna Convention and often in everyday international practice as a convenient generic term for all written international agreements, such labels as "convention," "agreement," "protocol" (ordinarily used for agreements supplementing or implementing a framework treaty), "pact," "accord," "covenant," "charter," "arrangement," "act," "general act," "statute," "*modus vivendi*," "declaration," "exchange of notes," and "agreed minutes" are used, *inter alia*, to denote what comes within the all-embracing term "international written agreement," known in the Vienna Conventions as a "treaty." With respect to one category, exchange of notes, the Convention (Art. 13) provides that the consent of states to be bound by a treaty constituted by instruments exchanged between them is expressed by that exchange when the instruments so provide or it is otherwise established that those states were agreed that the exchange of instruments should have that effect. A special term, the "concordat," is used for bilateral agreements of the Holy See **(80)**, governing the status of the Church in the other party. Occasionally there is no consistency in the use of a term in one instrument. For example, the Statute of the International Court of Justice **(309)** refers to "treaties" in Art. 36 but to "conventions" in Art. 38.

The term "treaty" tends to be employed with regard to major political or solemn agreements, such as a peace treaty or treaty of alliance, whereas "convention," more often than not, will imply a more technical, but sometimes very important, subject matter, such as the United Nations (UN)

"Convention" on the Law of the Sea of 1982 **(264)**. It is also normally used for agreements relating to specific human rights. The designations "covenant" and "charter" are often applied to constituent instruments of international organizations, such as "Covenant" of the League of Nations and "Charter" of the UN. Occasionally, as in the case of treaties establishing a UN specialized agency, the terms "statute" or "constitution" are also used. The "Final Act" is a term adopted for an instrument which records the winding up of an important international conference, for example the Final Act of the UN Conference on the Law of Treaties, 1969, or the Final Act of the Third UN Conference on the Law of the Sea **(263)**. However, a final act is normally not a legally binding instrument, that is, it is not a treaty unless the parties intend it to be so. Thus, the Final Act of the Helsinki Conference on Security and Cooperation in Europe of 1975 (14 ILM 1292 (1975)) is not a treaty.

As far as national terminology is concerned, in the United States (US) there are two categories of written international agreements: 1."treaties," which under Art. II of the US Constitution are agreements made ("ratified") **(280)** by the President with the advice and consent of the Senate by a vote of two-thirds of senators present and voting; and 2. the so-called "executive agreements" which do not require such a procedure albeit, for domestic purposes, the Case Act of 1972 requires executive agreements to be transmitted to Congress within 60 days following the execution of the agreement. However, it is essential to understand that in terms of international law there is no difference between US "treaties" and "executive agreements." This distinction is irrelevant on the international plane; both are equally valid and must be performed in good faith.

Historically, treaties, now the major source **(40)** of international law, have been negotiated **(316)** and concluded on behalf of heads of state. Today states are contracting parties, but treaties may also be cast as agreements between governments or their departments (ministries), or—as in the case of armistice agreements—between commanders in chief. All such agreements have equal force in international law. Component units of federal states **(77)** may possess treaty-making capacity within the limits admitted by the federal constitution. States may also agree that their border regions may make agreements with each other on matters of local concern. Non-self-governing territories **(100)** and similar entities have also been occasionally granted treaty-making powers, as was, for example, the case of some British territories, including India, which was invited to sign the Treaty of Versailles (225 CTS 188) and become a founding member of the League of Nations in 1919. India was also a signatory of the UN Charter as an original member in 1945.

Whether or not an agreement between states is to be governed by international law and is to be considered a treaty is determined by the intention of the parties involved. Various purely commercial agreements, such as those for the acquisition of premises for diplomatic missions **(68)**, are contracts governed by the municipal law **(27)** of one of the parties or some other municipal system of law chosen by them. Concession agreements between states and private companies are not treaties although it is possible that a state may agree to "internationalize" the contract by applying general principles of law **(38)** to such a contract. Individuals do not possess the capacity to make treaties.

Oral international agreements are most exceptional in international practice, but are valid if concluded between authorized agents of government. This rule was upheld by the Permanent Court of International Justice **(320)** in the case of the *Legal Status of Eastern Greenland* (Denmark v. Norway) (1933 PCIJ Series A/B. No. 53). In this case, Denmark successfully argued, *inter alia*, that its claim to the whole of Greenland had been recognized (as a *quid pro quo* in which Denmark in return had recognized Norway's claim to Svalbard) in an oral declaration of Norway's foreign minister ("Ihlen declaration"), made to his Danish counterpart. The scope of the Vienna Convention is limited to written agreements in the interests of clarity and simplicity, but, as provided in Art. 3, this restriction is not intended to deny the legal force of oral agreements under international law or to imply that any rules of the Convention would not apply to such agreements. A unilateral, oral or written, declaration **(44)** may create a binding international obligation if the state making it clearly intended to be bound by it in international law. Intention to undertake a legal, and not just political, obligation by the declaring state is not lightly to be presumed, especially if the declaration is directed not to a specific state but to the entire international community as was, for example, the case in 1957 of Egypt's unilateral declaration concerning freedom of navigation through the Suez Canal **(261)**, communicated to the UN Secretary-General and registered by the UN Secretariat as an international instrument. In addition, to be valid under international law, a unilateral declaration requires acceptance by other states.

Typically, a treaty, following its title, consists of a preamble invoking the names of the contracting parties and their motivation for concluding the treaty, followed in numbered articles by substantive (dispositive) provisions, sometimes supplemented by an annex or annexes to the treaty, and then the final provisions, usually including such miscellaneous matters as the opening for signature **(283)**, ratification **(280)**, accession **(267)**, the matter of reservations **(282)**, declarations and statements, amendments **(269)**, entry into force **(271)**, denunciation, depositary, authentic text **(270)**, and the like.

The formation of a treaty, that is, its conclusion, goes through several stages: establishing full powers **(272)**; negotiation **(316)**, either directly between states concerned or—for major multilateral treaties—at a diplomatic conference (or within the UN General Assembly); adoption **(268)** and authentication **(270)**; signature **(283)**; often ratification, acceptance, or approval **(266)**, or—for non-negotiating states—accession **(267)**, sometimes known as adhesion or adherence; and entry into force.

Until the entry into force of the Vienna Convention in 1980 the law concerning conclusion of treaties, their validity, termination, etc. was based on customary rules **(39)**. Adopted by 79 votes to 1 (France), with 19 abstentions, the Convention is primarily a codification of the existing customary rules, but in some important respects, for example, the introduction of the concept of *jus cogens*, it constitutes a progressive development of the law. It is not retroactive (Art. 4) and applies only to treaties concluded after its entry into force. However, this is without prejudice to the continued application of any rules of customary law and general principles of law set forth in the Convention, to which treaties would be subject independently of the Convention. In force for approximately half of the existing states, the Vienna Convention is widely recognized as an authoritative guide to the law of treaties despite the fact that some important countries, including France and the US are not parties. As a result, treaties made by non-party states are governed only by customary law, and the rules of the Convention apply to them only if in a particular case they happen to be declaratory of customary law, which occurs in many legal situations.

While both bilateral and multilateral treaties are subject to the rules of international law governing treaties, the latter, because of often numerous contracting parties, give rise to special problems in such matters as entry into force, reservations, termination, and so on. Some important multilateral treaties ("law-making treaties") which transcend their formal validity for the parties only and, by virtue of their vital subject matter of interest to other states, may evolve into generally binding rules of customary international law.

# Chapter VII
# Peaceful Settlement of Disputes

**289.** ***Ad Hoc* Judge.** The *ad hoc* judge or judge *ad hoc*, is a common term for a judge whom a state **(127)** before an international tribunal **(306)**, such as the International Court of Justice (ICJ) **(309)** (but not the European Court of Justice **(298)**), may choose when it does not have a judge of its nationality **(175)** on the bench, a frequent occurrence before the ICJ. Under Art. 31 of the Statute of the ICJ, an *ad hoc* judge (a designation not used in the Statute) may be appointed by either of the parties if the Court includes no judge of their nationality. Where there are several parties to a dispute, the parties acting in the same interest may choose only one judge *ad hoc*. If one of the parties already has a judge of its nationality on the bench, it is not entitled to appoint a judge *ad hoc*. An *ad hoc* judge need not be of the same nationality as the appointing state and may have the nationality of an elected member of the Court. An *ad hoc* judge may also be appointed where the ICJ sits in a chamber **(295)**. *Ad hoc* judges participate in the case in which they sit on terms of complete equality with their colleagues, but they take precedence after the elected members of the Court in order of seniority. As a result of the provision on *ad hoc* judges, the normal 15-judge bench of the ICJ may increase to 17 judges.

In the ICJ, an *ad hoc* judge may also be appointed in advisory proceedings **(291)**. In particular, under the ICJ Rules (Art. 102), if an advisory opinion is requested upon a legal question pending between two or more states, each state may be allowed, at the Court's discretion, to appoint an *ad hoc* judge. The Permanent Court of International Justice **(320)** agreed to the appointment of such judges in six cases. The ICJ has received two requests of this kind: it turned down the request in the case concerning the *Legal Consequences for States of the Continued Presence of South Africa in Namibia (South West Africa) Notwithstanding Security Council Resolution 276* (1971 ICJ Rep. 16), and in the *Western Sahara* case accepted Morocco's request but rejected that of Mauretania (1975 ICJ Rep. 12).

The institution of *ad hoc* judges in the ICJ system has been criticized as detracting from the need for impartiality in an international tribunal. As a rule, *ad hoc* judges have voted in favor of the state appointing them, in most cases the state of their nationality. No *ad hoc* judge has ever dissented from a majority decision favoring that judge's country, and judges *ad hoc* have typically appended individual (dissenting) opinions **(304)** if the majority on the bench decided against their vote. On the other hand, it has been contended that the *ad hoc* judges, a survival of the institution of national members of *ad hoc* arbitration tribunals **(293)**, are a concession to the political context in which an international court operates but—at the same time—this institution allows to include on the bench a person that is more familiar with the views of a party than are the elected members of the Court.

**290. Administrative Tribunals of International Organizations.** These are tribunals of international organizations **(84)** whose function is to adjudicate, mainly according to the internal law of the organization, labor disputes between members of the staff and the organization. The first permanent administrative tribunal was established by the League of Nations. The United Nations (UN) founded its own Administrative Tribunal in 1949. It hears applications alleging breach by the UN of terms of employment of staff members. Its competence may be extended to UN specialized agencies, as was done with respect to the International Civil Aviation Organization and International Maritime Organization, but most of the specialized agencies use the services of the International Labour Organisation (ILO) Tribunal established in 1946. The International Bank for Reconstruction and Development (World Bank) has its own tribunal created in 1980. In other international organizations staff disputes are heard either by a tribunal, such as the Inter-American Development Bank Administrative Tribunal created in 1981 and the Administrative Tribunal of the Organization of American States established in 1976, or an equivalent body (Appeal Board) used by the organization concerned: Organization for Economic Cooperation and Development (1950); Council of Europe (1965); North Atlantic Treaty Organization (1965); European Space Agency (1975); Intergovernmental Committee for Migration (1972); and Western European Union (1956). In the European Union, disputes with staff members are within the jurisdiction of the Court of Justice of the European Communities (European Court of Justice) **(298)**, which adjudicates them in accordance with its statute and other laws and regulations governing the service of its staff.

While the decisions of administrative tribunals are final, they may be reviewed by the International Court of Justice (ICJ) at the request of the executive body of the organization concerned or by a screening committee, depending on the organization. In response to an application for review, the ICJ may give an advisory opinion **(291)**. Three such opinions for review of judgments of the UN Administrative Tribunal and one for review of judgments of the Administrative Tribunal of the ILO were handed down by the ICJ. Whether such advisory opinions are legally binding depends on the rules of the organization in question. In the UN the Secretary-General may implement an opinion if it agrees with the decision of the administrative tribunal, or he may request the tribunal to confirm its judgment or reconsider it in accordance with the advisory opinion.

**291. Advisory Jurisdiction.** This is the competence of an international tribunal, including especially the International Court of Justice (ICJ) **(309)**, to give legal opinions at the request of an authorized organ of an international organization **(84)** or of an international organization as such. Under Art. 96 of the Charter of the United Nations (UN) and Art. 65 of the Statute of the ICJ, the ICJ may give an advisory opinion on "any legal question" at the request of the UN General Assembly (GA). In commenting on the otherwise rejected request of the World Health Organization (WHO) for an advisory opinion on the *Legality of the Use by a State of Nuclear Weapons in Armed Conflict* (1996 ICJ Rep. 66), the ICJ expressed the view that there were three conditions which must be satisfied in order to found the advisory jurisdiction of the Court at the request of a specialized agency. First, the agency must be duly authorized under the UN Charter (that is, by the GA) to request opinions; second, the opinion must be on a legal question; and third, this question must be one arising within the scope of the activities of the requesting agency, a condition not met by the WHO in the case in question. The advisory jurisdiction of the ICJ dates back to the Permanent Court of International Justice (PCIJ) **(320)** which was competent to give advisory opinions under Art. 14 of the Covenant of the League of Nations.

Although primarily associated with the ICJ, advisory jurisdiction is also known in a number of regional tribunals, such as, *inter alia*, the European Court of Human Rights **(154)** (a rather strictly circumscribed jurisdiction); the Inter-American Court of Human Rights **(165)** (which has delivered some important opinions and in which states may also request advisory opinions); the Benelux Union Court of Justice, established in 1965; and the European Court of Justice (ECJ) **(298)**. In addition, under Art. 191 of the UN Convention on the Law of the Sea of 1982 **(264)**, the Seabed Disputes Chamber of the International Tribunal for the Law of the Sea gives advisory opinions at the request of the Assembly or the Council of the International Seabed Authority **(250)**. Advisory opinions may also be given within the context of an arbitration body, for example, the Arbitration Commission of the International Conference on the Former Yugoslavia **(134)** which gave a number of such opinions at the request of the Steering Committee of the Conference (32 ILM 1572, 1577 (1993)).

Having received a request for an advisory opinion, the ICJ first decides which states and international organizations should be invited to submit written or oral statements. Otherwise, where applicable, the procedure in advisory jurisdiction is modeled on that for contentious proceedings **(297)** (ICJ Statute Art. 68). While commanding a strong persuasive force as an interpretation **(274)** of the law by a prestigious international court, an advisory opinion lacks the legal binding force of a judgment, even for the organ or agency that requested it, unless states have in advance undertaken to be legally bound by the opinion of the ICJ, as in the General Convention on the Privileges and Immunities of the UN of 1946 **(102)** which provides, *inter alia*, that in cases of a difference between the UN and a member state, the parties shall accept as decisive the Court's opinion. This happened as a result of the Court's advisory opinion of 1999 in the case of *Difference Relating to Immunity from Legal Process of a Special Rapporteur* (1999 ICJ Rep. 62). It can be added that under Arts. 228 and 236 of the Treaty of Rome establishing the European Community (298 UNTS 3) the so-called "opinions" of the ECJ have legally binding consequences for the organs of the Community.

The use of advisory jurisdiction of the ICJ has been rather modest as compared with that of its predecessor. Whereas the PCIJ delivered 27 advisory opinions during its relatively short experience (and all of them within 13 years), the ICJ had handed down, by the end of 2004, only 25 advisory opinions in 58 years of its existence. The most recent advisory opinion requested by the GA in 2003 (by a vote of 90 against 8, with 74 abstentions) on *Legal Consequences of the Construction of a Wall in the Occupied Palestinian Territory* (43 ICM 1009 (2004)) was delivered in July 2004 (finding the wall illegal under international law). Most (15) opinions were delivered at the request of the GA; one at the request of the Security Council; two originated in the UN Economic and Social Council; one was requested by the Intergovernmental Maritime Consultative Organization (now International Maritime Organization); one by the UN Educational, Scientific and Cultural Organization; one by the WHO; and three by the Committee on Applications for Review of Judgments of the UN Administrative Tribunal. A request by the WHO to give an advisory opinion on the legality of the use by a state of nuclear weapons in armed conflict was refused by the ICJ by a vote of 11 to 3 on the ground that the question asked was not one arising within the scope of the activities of WHO whose responsibilities are necessarily restricted to the sphere of public "health" and cannot encroach on those of other parts of the UN system. However, unlike the PCIJ, the ICJ did not hesitate to exercise its advisory jurisdiction in cases, such as *Western Sahara* (1975 ICJ Rep. 12), where the request for an opinion originated in an actual international dispute and an advisory opinion might be considered as the exercise of a disguised contentious jurisdiction **(297)**.

Most of the requests for an advisory opinion of the ICJ involved issues concerning the functioning of the body requesting the opinion; five were delivered within the context of reviewing decisions of the UN and ILO administrative tribunals. Three opinions in the 1950s concerned matters connected with the Cold War, such as admission of states to the UN. Five dealt with decolonization: four concerned South-West Africa (Namibia), and one dealt with Western Sahara. Other opinions concerned reparation for injuries suffered in the service of the UN; applicability of the UN Headquarters Agreement; immunity of a special rapporteur of the UN Commission on Human Rights **(161)**; and—an advisory opinion delivered at the request of the GA—the legality of the threat or use of nuclear weapons in armed conflict.

Although politically the advisory opinions of the ICJ have not been an effective tool in influencing states' policies, the advisory jurisdiction of the Court has contributed to clarifying and developing international law on such issues as the capacity of the UN to advance an international claim in respect to the damage suffered (*Reparation for Injuries Suffered in the Service of the United Nations* (1949 ICJ Rep. 174)) and reservations **(282)** to multilateral treaties (*Reservations to the Convention on the Prevention and Punishment of the Crime of Genocide* (1951 ICJ Rep. 15)). However, the above-noted opinion of the ICJ on nuclear weapons did not reach any definitive conclusions on this most difficult and controversial issue.

**292. Arbitral Tribunals under Annex VII of the Law of the Sea Convention of 1982.** These arbitral tribunals **(293)** are one of the four categories of compulsory procedures for the settlement of disputes **(299)** concerning the interpretation **(274)** or application of the United Nations (UN) Convention on the Law of the Sea (LOS Convention) **(264)** (Art. 287). The other three options available, under Art. 287 of the LOS Convention, to parties which have not reached settlement by means of their own choosing are: the International Tribunal for the Law of the Sea (ITLOS) **(310)**; the International Court of Justice **(309)**; and special arbitral tribunals under Annex VIII of the LOS Convention **(324)**. The choice of one or more of these four procedures is made by a party, when signing **(283)**, ratifying **(280)**, or acceding **(267)** to the LOS Convention or at any time thereafter, by means of a revocable written declaration deposited with the UN. A party that has not selected any of the four available procedures is deemed to have accepted arbitration under Annex VII. Declarations under Art. 287 shall not affect or be affected by the obligation to accept the jurisdiction of the Seabed **(232)** Disputes Chamber **(295)** of the ITLOS.

According to Annex VII (Arbitration) of the LOS Convention any party to a dispute, whether a state **(127)** or an international organization **(84)**, may submit a dispute to arbitration by a tribunal constituted in accordance with the Convention. Under the complex and detailed provisions of Annex VII, an arbitral tribunal is to be composed of five members, one to be chosen by each party and the remaining three chosen jointly by the parties from a panel of individuals with experience in maritime affairs, maintained by the UN, to which each state party to the LOS Convention is entitled to nominate four potential arbitrators. If no agreement is reached on choosing the three arbitrators, they are appointed by the President of the ITLOS. Like the other three bodies, the arbitral tribunals under Annex VII apply international law, but the parties may agree to request a decision *ex aequo et bono* **(13)**. Unless otherwise agreed by the parties, the award of the tribunal is final. The "compulsory" nature of the Annex VII tribunals is subject to the same exclusions of certain categories of disputes (Arts. 297 and 298) that apply to the ITLOS.

**293. Arbitration.** A method of legally binding peaceful settlement of disputes **(318)** between states **(127)** by one or more arbitrators of the parties' choice, according to procedures—and sometimes even to a certain extent the law—set forth by the parties, and on the basis of voluntary submission to and respect for the law. In a more inclusive sense, arbitration is a method of judicial settlement **(306)** of international disputes **(299)** but differs from adjudication in the strict sense of the term in that the parties normally are free to select arbitrators and decide upon the procedure to be followed and occasionally the law to be applied. Conceptually, arbitration must be differentiated from conciliation **(296)** in that, unlike a conciliation report, an arbitral award is legally binding upon the parties. A "conciliation agreement" in which the parties undertake to be legally bound by the conciliators' award would therefore in fact constitute a *compromis d'arbitrage*, that is, an agreement submitting the dispute to arbitration.

Arbitration between states concerns matters governed by public international law. As demonstrated by the final arbitral award of 1999 in the dispute over inter-entity boundary in *Brćko* (The Federation of Bosnia and Herzegovina v. The *Republika Srpska* (Serbian Republic)) (38 ILM 534 (1999)), in which the tribunal applied "relevant legal and equitable principles," "substates" can also be parties to international arbitration. Arbitration between states and private persons, as a rule, entities, is governed by the law chosen by the parties. The so-called international commercial arbitration **(308)** involves disputes between enterprises from different states.

The parties' consent required for arbitration (unless arbitration is mandatory under a treaty) and the terms of reference to the tribunal are usually formulated in an international agreement (*compromis* or *compromis d'arbitrage*), but the tribunal is competent to decide upon matters not addressed in the *compromis*, including the competence to determine its jurisdiction, a principle dating back to the arbitration commission established by the Jay Treaty of 1794 between the United States (US) and Great Britain (52 CTS 243) whose purpose was to resolve the outstanding issues between the two countries in the aftermath of the American War of Independence.

Consent to submit to arbitration of any future dispute is expressed either in a general arbitration treaty or in a clause in some other treaty providing that disputes arising in regard to the interpretation and application of the treaty, shall be settled by arbitration. In practice, however, in case of an actual dispute a *compromis* is ordinarily required.

An arbitral tribunal (or court, commission, or whatever term is used) may consist of a single arbitrator, sometimes head of a state who delegates his charge to experts, or it may be a collegiate body of odd number, often known as mixed arbitral commission **(314)** or mixed claims commission **(315)**, made up of arbitrators or commissioners who are selected in equal number by each party, and an umpire appointed by the parties or selected by the arbitrators.

In the early cases of arbitration in the 19th century, tribunals decided on principles of justice and equity **(13)**, but by the end of that century arbitral awards were mostly decided on the basis of international law although some agreements occasionally directed the tribunal to decide in accordance with "law and equity." On the whole, the distinction between arbitration and judicial settlement *sensu stricto* has eventually become formal rather than substantive.

Arbitration procedure follows generally used rules, such as those formulated in the Hague Convention of 1899 (revised in 1907) for the Pacific Settlement of Disputes; model rules drafted by international organizations, such as those in the General Act for the Pacific Settlement of International Disputes of 1928 (93 LNTS 345), revised in 1948 (71 UNTS 101) **(302)**; the European Convention for the Peaceful Settlement of Disputes of 1957 (320 UNTS 243); the widely accepted Convention on Conciliation and Arbitration of the Organization for Security and Cooperation in Europe of 1993 (32 ILM 55 (1993)); the Arbitration Rules of the United Nations (UN) Commission on International Trade Law of 1976 (15 ILM 701 (1976); the Rules of the International Centre for the Settlement of Investment Disputes **(307)**; the Optional Rules of the Permanent Court of Arbitration (PCA) **(319)** of 1992 (32 ILM 572 (1993)); PCA Optional Rules for Arbitration of Disputes Relating to Natural Resources and/or the Environment of 2001 (41 ILM 202 (2002)); and other PCA Rules for disputes between states and international organizations; and the Model Rules of the International Law Commission (ILC) of 1958.

An arbitral award is normally final, but in exceptional cases it may be revised because of discovery of new decisive facts. However, what precisely the grounds for a challenge by a party may be is not a settled issue. Among the very few instances of repudiating an arbitral award are rejection by the US in 1911 of the award in the US-Mexico *Chamizal* case (11 RIAA 309) concerning effects of avulsion upon state boundaries **(189)** and rejection by Argentina (17 ILM 738 (1978)), on the ground of alleged excess of jurisdiction (*excès de pouvoir*) by the tribunal, of the 1977 arbitral award in the Beagle Channel case between Chile and Argentina, which involved claims to three islets at the entrance to the Beagle Channel (17 ILM 638 (1978)). In its Model Rules of 1958, the ILC listed the following grounds for invalidating an arbitral award:1. invalidity of the *compromis*; 2. *excès de pouvoir* by the tribunal; 3. failure to set forth the reasons or a serious departure from a fundamental rule of procedure; and 4. corruption or fraud on the part of a member of the tribunal.

Although in a limited sense arbitration was already practiced between city-states of ancient Greece and to a certain extent in medieval Europe, the history of arbitration is usually traced back to the above-mentioned Jay Treaty of 1794 which, *inter alia*, provided for arbitration of claims for war **(338)** damage suffered by British and US nationals and inaugurated a widespread practice of inter-state arbitration in the 19th century. State responsibility **(128)** for injury to aliens **(144)** was the most common subject matter treated by these "mixed claims commissions" **(315),** the forerunner of a variety of the post–World War I "mixed arbitral tribunals" or "commissions" **(314)**. The famous *Alabama* Arbitration award of 1872 (1 Moore, International Arbitrations 653 (1898)) in a dispute between the US and Great Britain (won by the US) over violation by Great Britain of its neutrality **(362)** obligations during the American Civil War by permitting the vessel *Alabama* and some other ships to be built in Great Britain for use by the Confederate States, was a turning point in the history of international arbitration. In a departure from the model of mixed claims commissions, it initiated the system of a truly third-party collegial arbitral body made up, preferably, of jurists familiar with international law. The next landmark in the history of arbitration was the codification at the First Hague Peace Conference, 1899, of the methods of pacific settlement, including arbitral procedure, in the Convention for the Pacific Settlement of Disputes (187 CTS 410), revised by the

Second Hague Peace Conference in 1907 (205 CTS 277). The Convention created a roster of potential arbitrators within the framework of what was called the "Permanent Court of Arbitration" and codified procedures for the pacific settlement of disputes. However, attempts to create a real permanent arbitral tribunal ended in failure. Moreover, since the first standing arbitration treaty between France and Great Britain of 1903 non-legal, "political," disputes were not arbitrable ("non-justiciable") **(300)** under arbitration treaties. Such treaties contained "special clauses" excluding from the obligation to arbitrate disputes affecting "vital interests, the independence, or the honor of the two contracting Parties." In addition, various reservations **(282)** in effect eliminated the parties' obligation to submit their disputes to arbitration. One might add that in the relations between the US and Canada, a permanent arbitral tribunal to deal with various boundary problems, known as International Joint Commission, was established under a treaty in 1909 (36 Stat 2448; TS 548).

The establishment of the Permanent Court of International Justice **(320)** after World War I overshadowed the institution of arbitration, but various mixed arbitral tribunals settling disputes resulting from claims of individuals affected by the war were quite common. Among the mixed claims commissions of the 19th-century type, nine such bodies dealing with US-Mexico claims are the best known. Of special historical interest is the Upper Silesia Arbitral Tribunal set up by Germany and Poland in 1922 (9 LNTS 466) whose function was to adjudicate disputes involving claims to vested rights by members of an ethnic minority **(172)** in Upper Silesia against their own and the other government. During its existence (1920–1937) this tribunal dealt with 3,726 cases. The League of Nations, within the framework of its codification efforts, adopted the General Protocol for Pacific Settlement of International Disputes (19 AJIL Supp. 9 (1925)) which provided for referral of political disputes to conciliation **(296)** and arbitration, and in 1928 drafted the above-noted General Act for the Pacific Settlement of International Disputes. In the Western Hemisphere, the General Treaty of Inter-American Arbitration of 1929 (130 LNTS 132) followed a similar path, as did a number of other, including bilateral, agreements. Among the few inter-state arbitrations, the *Tinoco* Arbitration between Costa Rica and Great Britain of 1923, involving the issue of recognition of government **(114)** (1 RIAA 369); the US-Netherlands *Isle of Palmas* case of 1928 (2 RIAA 829) involving the issues of acquisition of territory **(227)** and intertemporal law **(205)**; and the *Naulilaa* Arbitration of 1928 (2 RIAA 1013) between Portugal and Germany, which interpreted **(274)** the rules governing military reprisals **(119)** under the then existing law, were perhaps the most important arbitral decisions of the inter-war period.

The UN Charter (Art. 33) endorses arbitration as one of the methods of pacific settlement of disputes. Arbitration ("compromissory") clauses were included in numerous post–World War II bilateral and multilateral instruments, including the Convention on Conciliation and Arbitration, 1992 (32 ILM 557 (1993)) of the Organization for Security and Cooperation (OSCE) (formerly Conference on Security and Cooperation in Europe). In 1949 the UN General Assembly revised the 1928 General Act for the Pacific Settlement of International Disputes and adopted optional Model Rules of Arbitral procedure.

Unlike international commercial arbitration, arbitration of disputes between states in the post–World War II decades was not very common. More recently, there has been a modest revival of inter-state arbitration, including some cases within the framework of the PCA. Major arbitrations worth mentioning, in the last few decades, include *Rann of Kutch* (India v. Pakistan), 1968, (17 RIAA 1), concerning determination of a section of their border **(189)**; the *Anglo-French Continental Shelf* Case, Award of 1977 (18 RIAA 3), with an interpreting award of 1978 (18 RIAA 271); the *Air Services Agreement* case (France v. US) (18 RIAA 416); the *Delimitation of Maritime Areas between Canada and France (St. Pierre and Miquelon),* 1992 (31 ILM 1145 (1992)); The *Taba Area Boundary* Arbitration between Egypt and Israel, 1988 (27 ILM 1421 (1988)); the *Rainbow Warrior* **(104)** Arbitration (second) between France and New Zealand, 1990 (82 ILR 499), involving problems of state responsibility; and the case of 1992 between Chile and US, *Letelier and Moffitt* (31 ILM 1 (1992)). The dispute between Argentina and Chile over the determination of their maritime boundary in the Beagle Channel was first decided by an arbitral award (17 ILM 631 (1977)) of the Queen of England as nominal arbitrator, the actual tribunal being made up of five judges of the International Court of Justice (who incidentally may serve as arbitrators). However, after the repudiation of the award by Argentina (17 ILM 738 (1978)) the two countries agreed to mediation **(313)** by the Pope (18 ILM 1 (1979)) whose proposals eventually led to an agreement resolving the dispute in 1994 (24 ILM 10 (1985)).

Arbitration of international commercial disputes between states and private companies has been a significant phenomenon in international arbitration of the recent decades. The *Abu Dhabi* Arbitration of 1951 between Abu Dhabi and Petroleum Development (Trucial Coast) Ltd. (18 ILR 144); the *ARAMCO* Arbitration of 1958 between Saudi Arabia and the Arabian American Oil Company (27 ILR 117); and the three major arbitrations resulting from nationalization by Libya of foreign oil companies, namely the *British Petroleum* Arbitration of 1973 (53 ILR 297); the *LIAMCO* Arbitration of 1977 (20 ILM 1 (1981)); and the *TOPCO & CAOC* Arbitration of 1977 (17 ILM 1 (1978)) are the best-known instances of this kind of arbitration. There is also a number of permanent arbitral tribunals and other dispute settlement bodies, such as, *inter alia*, the International Centre for the Settlement of Investment Disputes **(307)**; the OSCE Court on Conciliation and Arbitration (32 ILM 557 (1993); the Tribunal established under the North American Free Trade Agreement (32 ILM 289, 605 (1993)); and the arbitral panels established under the Canada-Mexico-US North American Agreement on Environmental Cooperation of 2003 (32 ILM 1480 (1993); and arbitration tribunals of the Association of the Southeast Asian Nations. The Iran–United States Claim Tribunal **(312)** must also be mentioned as perhaps the most important bilateral arbitration body in recent decades. Finally, because of its flexibility and less formal nature, international commercial arbitration has become a popular method of resolving international investment and commercial disputes between private enterprises.

**294. Automatic (Self-Judging) Reservation.** A kind of reservation **(323)** to acceptance of compulsory jurisdiction of the International Court of Justice (ICJ) **(309)** under the optional clause **(317)** of Art. 36(2) of the ICJ Statute, whereby the reserving state unilaterally claims the right to determine the scope of this reservation, such as the reservation exempting from the Court's jurisdiction **(297)** all matters of domestic jurisdiction **(9)**. The history of such reservations dates back to 1946 when the United States (US), at the initiative of Senator Thomas Connally of Texas (hence "Connally Reservation" or "Connally Amendment"), restricted its acceptance of the Court's jurisdiction under the optional clause by excluding from that jurisdiction "disputes with regard to matters essentially within the domestic jurisdiction of the United States" and—what is the essence of the self-judging reservation—adding the phrase "as determined by the United States of America" (1 UNTS 9). At the present time, this reservation is of historical interest only in view of the fact that in 1985, with effect in 1986, the US terminated its acceptance of the optional clause as a whole (24 ILM 1742)) because of its dissatisfaction with the 1984 ICJ judgment on jurisdiction in the case *Military and Paramilitary Activities in and against Nicaragua* (Nicaragua v. United States of America) (1984 ICJ Rep. 392). A few other countries, including Liberia, Malawi, Mexico, Philippines, and Sudan, still uphold the self-judging reservation.

The self-judging reservation operates automatically, enabling a state to determine subjectively and unilaterally whether or not a case brought against it falls within the scope of acceptance of the contentious jurisdiction of the ICJ under Art. 36(2) of the Statute. The reservation has the potential of limiting the Court's optional system of compulsory jurisdiction inasmuch as by virtue of reciprocity a reservation filed by a party to a dispute may be invoked by the other party or parties, thus depriving the Court of jurisdiction in the case. Thus, in 1957 Norway, against which France had instituted proceedings before the ICJ in the case of *Certain Norwegian Loans* (1957 ICJ Rep. 9), invoked the automatic domestic jurisdiction reservation contained in the French optional clause declaration, as a result of which the ICJ declined jurisdiction without considering the validity of the reservation on which Norway so successfully relied. In another case, the *Aerial Incident of 27 July 1955* (United States v. Bulgaria), the defendant state, Bulgaria, invoked the Connally reservation whereupon the US, whose nationals, passengers on board an Israeli airliner, had been killed in the incident in the Bulgarian airspace **(186)**, withdrew its suit. In the event, the Court declined jurisdiction in its judgment in 1960 (1960 ICJ Rep.146).

The legality of the automatic reservation has been questioned by many writers and ICJ judges who in their individual opinions **(304)** argued that it contradicted the power of the Court under Art. 36(6) of the Statute to determine its own jurisdiction. Some judges expressed the opinion that since a reservation could not be detached from the remaining text of the acceptance of compulsory jurisdiction, the entire optional clause declaration must be null and void. Others believed that only the automatic reservation was invalid whereas the other parts of the declaration remained unaffected.

**295. Chambers.** As an exception to the rule that the number and composition of permanent international tribunals do not depend on the parties, statutes of some tribunals provide for the possibility of forming a chamber to deal with a particular case or cases. The Statute of the International Court of Justice (ICJ) **(309)** provides for three categories of chamber in contentious (but not advisory) **(291)** proceedings. First (Art. 29), with a view to a speedy dispatch of business, the ICJ annually forms a Chamber of Summary Procedure of five judges, with President and Vice-President always members *ex officio* (ICJ Rules Art. 15) which, at the request of the parties, may hear and determine cases. The Chamber of Summary Procedure has never been called to meet in the ICJ, but the Permanent Court of International Justice **(320)** did use summary procedure in its two judgments in the case of *Treaty of Neuilly, Art. 179, Annex, Paragraph 4 (Interpretation)* (Bulgaria/Greece) (1925 PCIJ, Series A, No. 3 and No. 4). Second, the ICJ may from time to time form one or more chambers of three or more judges for dealing with particular categories of cases. These chambers hear and determine cases only if the parties so request (ICJ Statute Art. 26(1)). The ICJ has not yet had occasion to use such chambers, and the only one established is the Chamber for Environmental Matters of seven members elected for three years and set up in 1993. Third, under Art. 26(2) of the Statute the ICJ may form a chamber dealing with a case, the number of judges in the chamber to be determined by the Court with the approval of the parties. Hence, to a certain extent, as in arbitration **(293)**, the parties may influence the choice of the judges in a chamber. Normally, five judges, including where appropriate *ad hoc* judges **(289)**, form a chamber. Except for *ad hoc* judges, the chamber is elected by secret ballot. Cases are heard and determined only at the request of the parties. Used for the first time in the case of *Delimitation of the Maritime Boundary in the Gulf of Maine* (Canada/United States) (1984 ICJ Rep. 246), the procedure has so far been resorted to in six cases. One might add that the institution of chambers is also known, *inter alia*, in the European Court of Justice **(298)** and the International Tribunal for the Law of the Sea **(310)**.

**296. Conciliation.** Conciliation is a diplomatic method of third-party peaceful settlement **(318)** of an international dispute **(299)**, whereby a dispute is referred by the parties, with their consent, to a permanent or *ad hoc* commission, or—in rare cases—a single conciliator whose task is impartially to examine the dispute and to prepare a report with the suggestion of a concrete proposal. However, and this is crucial for the definition of conciliation, the parties to the dispute are under no legal obligation to accept it. If they were under such obligation, the procedure would be arbitration **(293)**.

As such, conciliation combines elements both of inquiry **(305)** and mediation **(313)**. Parties to a dispute appoint one or two of their nationals **(175)** each, and add a certain number of nationals of a third state or states, sufficient to provide a "neutral" majority. Compared with mediation, conciliation is a more formal and less flexible method for settling disputes between states **(127)**. A mediator whose suggestion is turned down by the parties may still continue mediation by reformulating his proposal whereas a conciliation commission (or a single conciliator), occasionally known as "commission of investigation and conciliation," having investigating the facts and confidentially discussed the case with the parties, issues a single formal report with conclusions and legally non-binding terms of settlement. Unlike mediation, conciliation is a task of a commission. It differs from arbitration in that a conciliation report only suggests the terms of settlement whereas an arbitral award is legally binding upon the parties. However, in practice the terminology may be rather confusing since a strict distinction between conciliation and arbitration is not always observed, and an agreement may refer to a "conciliation" commission which is otherwise expected by the parties to deliver a binding decision. Such a conciliation commission would in fact be an arbitral tribunal. Conciliation commissions set up under the Peace Treaty with Italy, 1947 (49 and 50 UNTS), were in reality bilateral arbitral tribunals.

Historically, conciliation commissions can be traced back to provisions in the Hague Conventions for the Pacific Settlement of International Disputes of 1899 (187 CTS 410) and 1907 (205 CTS 277), with the first such commission being established between the United States (US) and Great Britain by the so-called "Bryan Treaties" 1913/1914, named after the US Secretary of State, William Jennings Bryan. Altogether, the US entered into 48 such treaties, stipulating submission of disputes of any kind and without the honor and vital interests exception, to standing "peace commissions" for investigation and report, but without the competence to make legally binding decisions. Between the two World Wars, hundreds of conciliation and arbitration agreements were concluded on compulsory conciliation as a procedure preceding, if need be, arbitration or adjudication **(306)** of legal disputes. The General Act for the Pacific Settlement of International Disputes of 1928 (93 LNTS 345), revised after the war in 1949 (71 UNTS 101), was the major, though unsuccessful, multilateral treaty providing for compulsory methods of peaceful settlement, including conciliation. The League of Nations employed the procedure of conciliation in an imaginative way, but few cases were actually submitted to conciliation. Under Art. 33(1) of the United Nations (UN) Charter, conciliation is one of the methods for the peaceful settlement of disputes, and Draft Rules on Conciliation of Disputes between States were proposed by the UN in 1990 (30 ILM 231 (1991)). As part of attempts to revive the institution of conciliation, numerous multilateral treaties **(288)** provided for this technique of settling disputes. Among them are: the American Treaty of Pacific Settlement of 1948 (Pact of Bogotá) (30 UNTS 55); the European Convention for the Pacific Settlement of Disputes of 1957 (320 UNTS 243); the Vienna Convention on the Law of Treaties of 1969 (1555 UNTS 331); the 1982 UN Convention on the Law of the Sea **(264)**; and the Convention on the Protection of the Ozone Layer of 1985 **(217)**. The establishment of a Conciliation Commission in a dispute between Iceland and Norway over the delimitation of the continental shelf **(236)** between Iceland and Jan Mayen Island was a successful application of the conciliation technique as a flexible and relatively informal method of settling disputes. Both countries accepted the recommendations of the Commission's report in 1981 (20 ILM 797 (1981)) and proceeded to implement it by an agreement on the disputed continental shelf (21 ILM 1222 (1982)). In general, however, conciliation has been resorted to in rather minor legal disputes, mostly in situations where the parties would otherwise be obliged to settle their dispute by arbitration or adjudication.

**297. Contentious Jurisdiction of the International Court of Justice.** This kind of jurisdiction means the competence of the International Court of Justice (ICJ) **(309)** to render a legally binding decision in disputes **(299)** submitted to it on the basis of consent by states **(127)** in adversary proceedings before the Court. The existence of a genuine international dispute is a necessary prerequisite for the exercise of contentious jurisdiction by the ICJ. Only a state may be a party in contentious proceedings. International organizations **(84)** and individuals **(164)** have no standing, and in this respect the ICJ differs from some other international tribunals, such as the International Tribunal for the Law of the Sea **(310)**, or some regional courts such as the European Court of Justice (ECJ) **(298)** where organs of the European Union may institute proceedings against a member state and *vice versa*, and even individuals may pursue their alleged rights before that Court, as they also may do so under the rules of the European Court of Human Rights **(154)**. The contentious jurisdiction of the ICJ must be differentiated from its jurisdiction to give advisory opinions **(291)**.

Unless a case is settled by the parties at any stage of the proceedings or discontinued by the applicant state with subsequent removal of the case from the Court's List by an order of the Court or—in cases of discontinuance—of the Court's President, the proceedings are brought to a conclusion by a judgment. As far as the states entitled to be parties before the ICJ are concerned (jurisdiction *ratione personae*), the Court's jurisdiction covers: 1. members of the United Nations (UN); they are automatically parties to the ICJ Statute which is an integral part of the UN Charter; 2. non-member states which have become parties to the Statute only, on conditions determined in each case by the UN General Assembly upon recommendation of the Security Council (SC). This category, as well as category 3, any another state that accepted the Court's jurisdiction are, practically speaking non-existent today in view of the virtually universal membership in the UN.

It should be borne in mind that the mere fact of a state being a party to the Charter, with the ICJ Statute as its integral part, does not necessarily mean that the state in question is *ipso facto* subject to the Court's jurisdiction. Unlike the case of the ECJ, the jurisdiction of the ICJ is not automatically compulsory. It is optional and based on the fundamental principle of each party's consent, either express or implied from its conduct (*forum prorogatum*) **(301)**. In general, express consent can be manifested in one of the three below-described ways.

First, under Art. 40(1) of the Statute and Art. 39 of the Rules, the parties may by means of a "special agreement" bring an already existing dispute before the ICJ. In such cases of the notification of the special agreement to the Court, there is formally neither an applicant nor a respondent state; hence, in the official designation of the case brought to the ICJ by the notification, the names of the parties are separated not by "v" (*versus*, against) but by an oblique stroke, for example, Benin/Niger, or Malaysia/Singapore. By the end of 2004, 15 cases had been brought to the ICJ by the notification of a special agreement. Second, the same article of the ICJ Statute and Art. 38 of the Rules provide for bringing a case by means of a written application addressed to the Registrar of the Court. Here the ICJ has jurisdiction over a dispute if the parties happen to be bound by a "compromissory clause" of a prior treaty **(288)** in force, obligating them to refer to the Court the category of dispute which includes the dispute that has arisen between them. Except for the 15 cases that were brought before the ICJ by the notification of a special agreement, all contentious cases have been brought before the Court by a written application. When proceedings are instituted by application, the name of the applicant state is listed first in the official designation of the case and is separated from the name of the respondent state by the abbreviation "v" (*versus*), for example Mexico v. United States of America, or Republic of the Congo v. France. Compromissory clauses referring any future disputed matters to the ICJ are found both in treaties dealing specifically with the problem of peaceful settlement of disputes **(318)** and—much more frequently—in treaties addressing all kinds of subjects of interest to the parties. The treaties contain a provision on referring to the ICJ any dispute between the parties relating to the interpretation **(274)** and application of the treaty. Clauses in the treaties which conferred jurisdiction upon the Permanent Court of International Justice **(320)** remain in effect provided such a treaty is still in force and the states concerned are parties to the ICJ Statute. There are more than 250 treaties adopted since 1933 which grant jurisdiction to the ICJ by their respective compromissory clauses. However, although Art. 36(1) of the ICJ Statute refers to "all matters specially provided for in the Charter of the United Nations" as a basis for the Court's jurisdiction, it is generally accepted that no such matters exist since recommendations of the SC—unlike its decisions—are not legally binding. This apparent contradiction is due to the fact that the relevant Statute provision was drafted at a time when it was expected that the Charter would provide for compulsory jurisdiction of the ICJ. The third method whereby a contentious case may be brought under the jurisdiction of the ICJ, of course always with the parties' consent, is through the so-called "optional clause" **(317)** of Art. 36(2) of the ICJ Statute whereby a state may accept in advance, on conditions of reciprocity, the compulsory jurisdiction of the ICJ in all legal disputes concerning any question of international law, interpretation of a treaty, existence of a breach of international obligations, or the nature or extent of the reparation **(118)**. Historically, this clause is a compromise between the states advocating and those opposing the principle of compulsory jurisdiction of the Court. In cases where Art. 36(2) provides the basis of consent, the proceedings are instituted either through notification to the Registrar of the Court of the special agreement or by a written application.

It should be noted that the contentious jurisdiction of the ICJ pursuant to a special agreement or provided for in a treaty stipulation is not limited in terms of the nature and scope of the dispute; it may also include political disputes. However, since under Art. 38(1) of its Statute the function of the ICJ is to decide disputes "in accordance with international law," a political dispute would have to be decided, if the parties agree, *ex aequo et bono* **(13)** rather than according to the legal rules in force. Under the optional clause, contentious jurisdiction is expressly limited to "legal disputes." The UN Charter (Art. 36(3)) provides that in making recommendations within the context of a dispute, the SC should (not "shall") take into consideration that legal disputes should as a general rule be referred by the parties to the ICJ. It is a controversial issue what criteria should govern the distinction between "justiciable" legal and "non-justiciable" political disputes **(300)**.

The jurisdiction of the ICJ can also be incidental, that is, the Court has the authority to decide, in the event of a dispute, whether it has jurisdiction with respect to a particular case (Statute Art. 36(6)). The Court also has the competence to allow intervention in the proceedings **(311)**; to indicate provisional measures **(322)**; and to interpret a judgment at the request of any party (Statute Art. 60). In addition, the ICJ may admit proceedings in revision at the request of a party to a past dispute on the basis of discovery of decisive factors unknown, without the party's negligence, at the time of the judgment (Statute Art. 61). The application must be made within six months since the discovery and not later than 10 years since the date of the judgment. Three applications for revision have been made in the history of the ICJ, but have been rejected in each case.

**298. Court of Justice of the European Communities (European Court of Justice).** Along with the European Parliament, the Council, the Commission, and the Court of Auditors, the Court of Justice of the European Communities, briefly known as the European Court of Justice (ECJ), is a major institution and the principal judicial body of the European Union (EU). Originally in existence since 1952 as an institution of the European Coal and Steel Community, it became the common organ of the three Communities upon the foundation of the European Economic Community and the European Atomic Energy Agency (Euratom) in 1957. The ECJ has its seat in Luxembourg. It must not be confused with the European Court of Human Rights (ECHR) **(154)** in Strasbourg established under the auspices of the Council of Europe.

Following the adoption of the treaty **(288)** establishing a Constitution for Europe, drafted by the European Convention in the years 2002 to 2004, and ratification **(280)** by the 25 member states (including, since May 2004, 10 new members) of the EU, the Court is expected to be known as the Court of Justice of the European Union, and will exercise its functions under the Constitution of the Union and pertinent legislation. The current Court is expected to undergo a number of reforms, but—for the time being—as of December 2004, the ECJ continues its functions as part of the single institutional framework of the EU pursuant to the treaties establishing the three communities and other treaties and acts modifying them as well as by the provisions of the Maastricht Treaty on European Union of 1992 (31 ILM 247 (1992)) as amended in 1997. Arts. 220–245 of the consolidated version of the Maastricht Treaty and the Treaty of Rome establishing the European Council (37 ILM 56 (1998)) spell out the principal rules governing the ECJ at this time. They are complemented by the ECJ Statute and the Rules adopted by the Court. The Maastricht Treaty, as amended, granted the ECJ some additional jurisdiction in the area of police and judicial cooperation in criminal matters.

The ECJ is composed of 15—and since May 2004—25 members, one from each member of the European Union, appointed on a staggered schedule by common accord of the member states for a renewable term of six years. The Court is assisted—at this time—by officials modeled after the French procedure and called advocates-general whose role is to assist the Court by making, in open court, non-binding "reasoned submissions" on cases before the ECJ. Such submissions are often followed by the Court. The ECJ normally sits in plenary sessions, but it may also form small chambers **(295)** of three, five, or seven judges. However, cases brought by a member state or a major Union organ and particularly important cases must be heard in plenary session. Unlike the International Court of Justice (ICJ) **(309)**, no individual opinions **(304)** are allowed. A registrar is in charge of the administration of the Court.

In its decisions, the ECJ applies "primary legislation" which includes the Community constitutive treaties; "secondary legislation" consisting of the law generated by the Community institutions pursuant to the constitutive treaties; "regulations" (directly binding legislative measures enacted by the Commission or the Council); "directives" (binding orders); "decisions" (binding designating states or private persons); and international agreements of the Community. In addition, the ECJ resorts to non-written sources: general principles of law **(38)**, customary law **(39)**, and—as a supplementary source—general rules of international law. In certain situations, in particular for purposes of enforcement, the Court applies the internal (municipal) **(27)** law of member states. Like the ICJ, the ECJ does not recognize the mandatory nature of the doctrine of *stare decisis* known in the common-law countries; yet, in many cases it follows precedents while citing its past cases only sparingly.

It is a fundamental principle, established by the ECJ, that Community law prevails over the laws of the member states and is directly applicable in disputes between private parties and national authorities. This supremacy of the Community law is illustrated in such landmark cases as *Van Gend en Loos v. Nederlandse Administratie der Belastingen* (1963) and *Amministrazione delle Finanze dello Stato v. Simmenthal S.p.A* (1978).

The jurisdiction of the ECJ is broad and rather complex. The major task of the Court is to ensure observance of the law in the interpretation **(274)** and application of the constitutive treaties, the matters over which no other international court has jurisdiction. Economic and social issues have been the most common subject matter before the Court. Apart from judgments, on rare occasions the ECJ delivers opinions. Decisions may either originate in direct actions resulting in a final judgment or may be preliminary rulings requested by a national court which then must decide in accordance with the ECJ interpretation of the law. Apart from a less important category of direct actions where jurisdiction is conferred upon the Court by the consent of the parties, the most important categories of direct action are those in which the Court's jurisdiction is anchored directly in the Community law providing for action against the Community or a member state. Actions against a Community institution (Council or Commission) include, first, actions for judicial review which can be brought by a member state, another Community institution (a rare case), or a private person. Second, the ECJ has the so-called plenary jurisdiction for non-contractual liability (delicts or tort) resulting from damage caused by a Community institution or its officials; appeals by individuals against penalties for violation of the Community law; and jurisdiction as an administrative tribunal in staff cases **(290)**. Finally, there are enforcement actions brought by the Commission or a state member against a member state for alleged failure to fulfill an obligation under the Community law. Most Court time is spent on preliminary rulings interpreting the law of the Community, delivered at the request of a national court. They have been very important in the process of European integration, contributing to the furthering of uniform application of the Community law and establishing the doctrine of supremacy of this law over the laws of the member states. The ECJ does not have a general advisory jurisdiction **(291)**, but in special circumstances it may deliver an opinion at the request of the Community or a member state. Provisional measures **(322)**, preliminary objections **(321)**, and intervention in the proceedings **(311)** are possible. Enforcement of judgments against persons other than states is governed by the rules of the state where the enforcement takes place. There are no express provisions on enforcing judgments against defaulting member states, but political or economic pressures can force a member into compliance. In practice, there have not been many cases of persistent refusal by states to comply with decisions of the Court.

The ECJ is the most active permanent international tribunal. Compared with the still modest, albeit recently growing caseload of the ICJ, the docket of the ECJ has always been full. With the number of cases growing annually by 10 percent, the workload of the Court reached more than 1,000 cases pending in 2000, and the average time needed to decide on a preliminary ruling amounted to more than 20 months. The decisions of the ECJ have covered a wide variety of issues relating not only to the law of economic integration, freedom of movement and establishment, and the like, but also to matters ranging into the jurisdictional competence of the ECHR, such as the treatment of aliens, workers' rights, social security, and discrimination on grounds of sex or age. This was recently demonstrated by the preliminary ruling of the Court in *Kreil v. Bundesrepublik Deutschland* (39 ILM 531 (2000)) in which the ECJ upheld the right of women to have access to military posts in the German armed forces.

In 1988 the EC Council created a Court of First Instance to relieve the ECJ of the pressure of its heavy workload (EC Treaty, consolidated text, Art. 225). Commencing its operations in 1989, the Court of First Instance has taken over jurisdiction in some of the routine but time-consuming classes of action, such as, *inter alia*, staff disputes, competition policy and tariff cases, but not actions brought by EC institutions or member states and requests for preliminary rulings submitted by national courts. The right of appeal to the ECJ from the Court of First Instance is possible. The composition and procedure of the Court of First Instance in general follows the pattern of the ECJ, but there are no advocates-general.

Various proposals to reform the ECJ have recently been debated to allow the Court to focus only on cases of fundamental importance for the European Union. This might lead to the creation of specialized tribunals for various categories of cases, with the evolution of the Court of First Instance into a major Community court. At the same time, as proposed by some, the ECJ would evolve into a supreme court of the European Union in the manner of the United States Supreme Court. In 2004, the whole issue of the European judiciary was under consideration as part of the work on reforming the structure of the EC and drafting a Constitution for the new European Union.

**299. Disputes, International.** The concept of "dispute" has no precise connotation for purposes of international adjudication **(306)**. As defined by the Permanent Court of International Justice (PCIJ) **(320)** in the case of *Mavrommatis Palestine Concessions* (Greece v. Great Britain) (1924 PCIJ Series A, No. 2), a dispute, as a prerequisite for resorting to an international tribunal, means "disagreement on a point of law or fact, a conflict of legal views or of interests between two persons." For the International Court of Justice (ICJ) **(309)** to be seised of a case, a dispute must genuinely exist between the states **(127)** involved, a principle reaffirmed in a number of cases before the Court, for example, in the Advisory Opinions **(291)** on the *Interpretation of Peace Treaties with Bulgaria, Hungary and Romania* (1950 ICJ Rep. 65) and on the *Applicability of the Obligation to Arbitrate under Section 21 of the United Nations Headquarters Agreement of 26 June 1947* (1988 ICJ Rep. 12); and in contentious cases, such as the case of *East Timor* (Portugal v. Australia) (1995 ICJ Rep. 89). While a dispute need not necessarily be manifested by diplomatic negotiation **(316)**, it would be desirable for a state filing an application to the ICJ to make it quite clear that a difference of view existed with another state, which could not be otherwise overcome, as was stressed by the PCIJ in *Electricity Company of Sofia and Bulgaria* (Belgium v. Bulgaria) (1939 PCIJ Series A/B, No. 77) in which case the Court rejected a claim on the ground that the applicant state had not established the existence of a dispute.

What is meant by "international" dispute is a difficult question to which no general answer can be given. Under international law, as stipulated in Art. 2(3) of the United Nations Charter and in other treaties **(288)**, only "international" disputes must be settled by peaceful means **(318)**, a principle constituting a peremptory norm of general international law (*jus cogens*) **(24)**. Non-international disputes are disputes whose subject matter is essentially within the domestic jurisdiction **(9)** of a state; under international law they need not, in principle, be settled by peaceful means. The reservation to the acceptance of compulsory jurisdiction of the ICJ **(323)**, including the automatic (self-judging) reservation **(294)**, has been a device whereby states exclude from the jurisdiction of the ICJ disputes which potential adversary states would otherwise like to raise to the level of "international" disputes. No clear definition of the "international" element of a dispute seems to be possible, but—as held by the PCIJ in its advisory opinion on *Nationality Decrees Issued in Tunis and Morocco* (1923 PCIJ Series B, No. 4)—the scope of a state's domestic jurisdiction is essentially relative and depends upon the development of international law. The contemporary trend toward expanding international versus domestic jurisdiction in such matters as human rights **(157)** and protection of the environment **(197)**, to name only the most prominent areas, is likely to be reflected in the widening scope of the concept of "international" disputes before international tribunals.

**300. Disputes, International: Justiciability.** The concept of justiciability of an international dispute **(299)** refers to the quality of the dispute to be suitable for submission under international law to arbitration **(293)** or adjudication **(306)**. While states have a legal duty to settle their disputes by peaceful means, they are under no obligation to submit them to arbitral or judicial settlement unless they are bound to do so by virtue of a prior obligation, normally contracted under an international agreement such as a bilateral or multilateral treaty **(288)**.

International practice has long made a distinction between "justiciable" or "legal" disputes, which lend themselves to legal settlement, and "non-justiciable" or "political" disputes, which can be resolved only by non-judicial methods: diplomatic negotiation **(316)**, good offices **(303)**, mediation **(313)**, conciliation **(296),** possibly aided by an impartial inquiry **(305)**. Thus in the pre–World War I arbitration treaties, disputes perceived by a party to concern vital interests, honor, or independence, or interests of a third state were excluded from arbitration. After World War I, the Covenant of the League of Nations (Art. 13(2)) assumed that only some categories of international disputes were suitable for submission to arbitration or judicial settlement. Among them, the Covenant listed "disputes as to the interpretation **(274)** of a treaty, as to any question of international law, as to existence of any fact which, if established, would constitute a breach of any international obligation, or as to the extent and nature of the reparation **(118)** to be made for any such breach." This list was subsequently adopted in the optional clause **(317)** of Art. 36(2) of the Statute of the Permanent Court of International Justice **(320)** and then the Statute of the International Court of Justice (ICJ) **(309)**. Other treaties, following the Hague Convention of 1899 for the Pacific Settlement of International Disputes (187 CTS 410), revised in 1907 (215 CTS 233), also referred to legal disputes, including, *inter alia*, questions of interpretation and application of treaties. The General Act for the Pacific Settlement of International Disputes of 1928 (93 LNTS 345), revised in 1949 (71 UNTS 101), made a distinction between legal and non-legal disputes, and Art. 36(3) of the United Nations (UN) Charter itself refers to "legal" disputes which should "as a general rule" be referred to the ICJ, the implication being that there are other, "non-legal" disputes to be settled, normally by diplomatic methods. In more general terms of "questions," the ICJ, in its advisory opinion on *Western Sahara* (1975 ICJ Rep. 12) made an attempt to elucidate the nature of "legal questions," defining them as questions that are by their very nature susceptible to a reply based on law. On the regional level, under the European Convention on Peaceful Settlement of Disputes of 1957, all international legal disputes are susceptible to judicial settlement.

As a body deciding "in accordance with international law" (ICJ Statute Art. 38(1)), the ICJ may hear only disputes that are essentially legal. However, as held by the Court, *inter alia*, in such cases as *Military and Paramilitary Activities in and against Nicaragua* (Nicaragua v. United States) (1986 ICJ Rep. 14); and *United States Diplomatic and Consular Staff in Tehran* (United States v. Iran) (1980 ICJ Rep. 3), the fact that a legal dispute has a political context or is only one aspect of a political dispute does not deprive it of a legal character, that is, it does not make it non-justiciable, even if at the same time it is an object of a diplomatic attempt at solution within a political organ, such as the UN Security Council. In addition, while the cases brought to the ICJ under the optional clause **(317)** of Art. 36(2) of the Court's Statute are limited to "legal disputes," under Art 36(1) "all cases" are admissible to the ICJ. This means that a political dispute can also be justiciable, but in such a case the Court would in effect decide not according to international law but, if the parties agree, *ex aequo et bono* **(13)**.

The issue of justiciability of international disputes has long preoccupied the doctrine, but what criteria should govern the distinction between justiciable and non-justiciable disputes is still an open question. In the most common view of the problem, which adopts a less vague criterion than the other approaches, a dispute is legal and justiciable if it concerns an existing legal right, the parties accepting the legal norms that currently govern their mutual relations as the basis for a settlement of the dispute. On the other hand, if a state party to a dispute seeks a change of the existing law, normally a treaty, the dispute is political and non-justiciable. However, one can argue that justiciability is determined by the parties' attitude toward the dispute; hence any international dispute is justiciable regardless of its subject matter.

**301. *Forum Prorogatum.*** This Latin phrase, loosely translated as "deferred or postponed jurisdiction of the court" refers to a doctrine relied upon in practice by international tribunals, including the International Court of Justice (ICJ) **(309)**, whereby the court founds the consent of a state to its jurisdiction **(297)** not on an express declaration but on that state's tacit consent inferred from the whole of its conduct in arguing the case on its merits subsequent to the institution of the proceedings, without raising the question of jurisdiction. This informal way of expressing, with the agreement of the parties, consent to the Court's jurisdiction, does not apply in advisory proceedings **(291)** although its application in such proceedings is propounded by some representatives of the doctrine.

The doctrine of *forum prorogatum* was accepted in the Permanent Court of International Justice (PCIJ) **(320)** and subsequently by the ICJ because ultimately the exercise of the Court's contentious jurisdiction depends on the parties' consent. The ICJ Statute and the Rules do not contain any specific mandatory rules concerning the way in which such consent can be expressed, but the Rules require that the basis of the Court's jurisdiction should be specified "as far as possible" (Art. 35(2)).

The doctrine of *forum prorogatum* was first relied upon by the PCIJ in the case of *Mavrommatis Jerusalem Concessions* (Greece v. Great Britain) (1925 PCIJ Series A, No. 5). In this case, the reply of Great Britain in its written argument to an issue raised by Greece that was not within the Court's jurisdiction was found by the PCIJ to be sufficient to confer jurisdiction upon the Court in respect of that issue. The ICJ has also relied on the doctrine of *forum prorogatum*. Thus, in *Corfu Channel-Preliminary Objection* (Great Britain v. Albania) (1947–1948 ICJ Rep. 15) the Court inferred Albania's assent to the Court's jurisdiction from a letter that Albania had sent to the ICJ following the initiation of proceedings, in which it stated that it was prepared to appear before the Court. *Forum prorogatum* was also applied by the ICJ in the case of *Maritime Delimitation and Territorial Questions between Qatar and Bahrain* (Qatar v. Bahrain) (1994 ICJ Rep. 12). In its interpretation of the doctrine of *forum prorogatum* the ICJ has been careful to stress that assent, if inferred, must be clearly present; otherwise the Court will not accept jurisdiction and the case cannot be entered in its Court's List. This occurred in 1999 when Eritrea made an unsuccessful attempt to employ the technique of *forum prorogatum* in its abortive suit against Ethiopia.

**302. General Act for the Pacific Settlement of International Disputes, 1928 (Revised in 1949).** This is an unsuccessful multilateral treaty **(288)** adopted by the Assembly of the League of Nations in 1928 (93 LNTS 345), which consolidated the rules and procedures governing the peaceful settlement of disputes **(318)** between states **(127)**. The Act was a major but disappointing attempt to introduce a legal obligation to settle international disputes **(299)** exclusively by peaceful means. A revised text of the General Act was approved by the United Nations General Assembly in 1949 (71 UNTS 101). Formally, the Act still has eight parties.

The General Act made a distinction between, on the one hand, legal disputes which, if conciliation **(296)** failed, were to be compulsorily decided by arbitration **(293)** or the Permanent Court of International Justice **(320)**, and non-legal or political disputes, on the other, to be settled by conciliation or arbitration, with the possibility of deciding a dispute *ex aequo et bono* **(13)**. Although the General Act of 1928 seems, at least formally, to have outlived the League of Nations, and in its revised form was signed by seven states, the validity of the 1928 text is a subject of controversy, also between parties in some cases before the International Court of Justice (ICJ) **(309)**, such as the *Aegean Sea Continental Shelf* (Greece v. Turkey) in which the Court found itself lacking jurisdiction (1978 ICJ Rep. 3); the *Nuclear Tests* cases (Australia v. France and New Zealand v. France) (1974 ICJ Rep. 253); and the *Trial of Pakistani Prisoners of War* case of 1973 which was removed from the Court's List. But the ICJ itself preferred not to get involved in determining the legal status of the General Act of 1928.

**303. Good Offices.** The term good offices refers to a diplomatic method of peaceful settlement **(318)** of international disputes **(299)** whereby a third party, whether a representative of a third state **(127)**, an organ of an international organization **(84)**, or even a private individual, acting with the consent of the disputing states but not necessarily offering them substantive suggestions of settlement, serves as a friendly go-between in an effort to persuade the parties to negotiate by themselves a satisfactory solution of their dispute. The most restrained kind of third-party, friendly intercession in a dispute, good offices are often confused with mediation **(313)**, but strictly speaking they differ from mediation in that a mediator actually participates in the negotiations **(316)** and often suggests terms of settlement, whereas a third party proffering good offices only serves as a channel of communication between the disputing states, sometimes even after the outbreak of hostilities. The person offering good offices attempts to persuade the parties to enter into direct negotiations, but meets with them separately in a "shuttle diplomacy" manner. However, in actual practice, good offices and mediation are often difficult to differentiate, tending to merge with each other. Thus, a good offices intermediary may not only transmit messages between the disputing states but may also make suggestions concerning the merits of the dispute and terms of settlement. The disputing states themselves may invite the intermediary to continue as a mediator. In no case may good offices be regarded as an unfriendly act, a rule stated already in the Hague Conventions for the Pacific Settlement of International Disputes of 1899 (187 CTS 410) and 1907 (205 CTS 277).

The institution of good offices, codified in the Hague Conventions of 1899 and 1907, became a standard feature in treaties, along with other techniques of peaceful settlement. While there is no express mention of good offices in Art. 33(1) of the Charter of the United Nations (UN) which lists various methods of peaceful settlement, the competence of the General Assembly (GA) and the Security Council (SC) to recommend good offices is implied in the provisions of the Charter on the competence of the GA and in Chapter VI on the Peaceful Settlement of International Disputes. The UN Secretary-General has on numerous occasions exercised good offices with variable success, both on his own initiative and at the recommendation of the SC. Diplomatic history records numerous instances of good offices at least since a hundred years ago: The United States (US) President offered them to help end the Russo-Japanese War of 1904–1905. More recent examples of good offices include the role of Algeria in the US–Iran hostage crisis of 1979–1980, leading to the Algerian Accords and the establishment of the Iran–United States Claims Tribunal **(312)**, and the good offices of the US Secretary of State in the United Kingdom–Argentina Falklands crisis in 1982.

**304. Individual Opinion.** This is an opinion that an individual judge of an international court may attach to the Court's judgment, order, or advisory opinion **(291)**, in which he states and explains his position with regard to certain points in the Court's decision. Usually associated with the International Court of Justice (ICJ) **(309)**, individual opinions may also be given by judges in other international courts such as the European Court of Human Rights **(154)**, the Inter-American Court of Human Rights **(165)**, but not in the European Court of Justice **(298)**.

In the ICJ, an individual opinion can take the form of a "dissenting opinion," a "separate opinion," or a "declaration." A dissenting opinion is one given by a judge who disagrees with the decision of the majority. It states the reasons for the disagreement with the Court's decision on one or more points and why, in consequence, the judge voted against the majority. A separate opinion is one given by a judge who, while voting in favor of the Court's decision, disagrees with some or all of its reasoning, which means that a separate opinion may be given even if the Court's decision is unanimous. This happened in the case of *Minquiers and Ecrehos* (France v. United Kingdom) (1953 ICJ Rep. 47). Two or more judges may write a joint dissenting or separate opinion. A declaration is a brief indication by the declaring judge recording concurrence or dissent without stating the reasons.

Until the entry into force of the revised Rules of the ICJ in 1978, the Court's decisions had provided only the number of judges voting for and against each point of the operative sections of the decision, but did not reveal who voted which way. Under the new Rules each decision indicates the names of the judges constituting the majority. The number of individual opinions attached to the decisions of the ICJ is relatively high: on an average there are seven such opinions for a decision.

The right to attach individual opinions is not known in the European continental judicial systems, but is frequently used in the common-law jurisdictions. Within the ICJ system, this right has become a controversial issue. In one view, it could weaken the authority and cohesion of the Court, but in another view, the judges' right to express their opinions freely is an essential safeguard of their independence in the interest of international justice. Moreover, many individual, including dissenting, opinions have been frequently quoted because of the prestige of their authors. In this sense, individual opinions occupy the position midway between judicial decisions **(22)** and the teaching of publicists **(42)**, that is, scholars in international law.

**305. Inquiry.** Inquiry is a method of ascertaining facts, whereby an impartial investigative body elucidates the facts relating to a dispute **(299)** between states **(127)** in order to produce a finding on the disputed facts for the purpose of a successful peaceful settlement of the dispute. Inquiry or—as it is sometimes called "fact-finding"—may be either an independent procedure terminating in the issuance of a report, as it was understood in the 1899 Hague Convention for the Pacific Settlement of International Disputes (187 CTS 410), or it may be a preliminary phase in a procedure of dispute settlement by means of conciliation **(296)**, arbitration **(293)**, or adjudication **(306)** by a tribunal. However, the parties are not obliged to accept the findings of the inquiry.

As an independent procedure designed merely to ascertain the disputed facts, inquiry has not been a common procedure in diplomatic practice; usually it involves a clarification of "points of law" as well. The commissions of inquiry set up under the Hague Convention of 1899 proved their usefulness in several cases, the best known of which is the first use of such a commission in the British-Russian dispute over the Dogger Bank incident in 1904. It concerned an accidental sinking and damage to British fishing boats in the North Sea by Russian warships on their fateful voyage to the Far East during the Russo-Japanese War. The mandate of the commission of inquiry appointed by the parties was not only to establish the facts but also to make findings concerning the responsibility of the party at fault. This—at that time—dangerous dispute was settled successfully on the basis of the Commission's report.

Following the success of the commission of inquiry in the Dogger Bank incident, the rules of inquiry were further developed in the Hague Convention of 1907 (205 CTS 277), and the procedure was used in a number of cases. Each of the 48 "Bryan treaties" of conciliation in the period of 1913 to 1940, named after United States Secretary of State William Jennings Bryan, and treaties between Latin American states made provisions for a permanent commission of inquiry. In the inter-war period, the League of Nations whose Covenant, 1919, included a reference to inquiry as a useful technique in the process of resolving disputes, employed inquiry in six cases, of which the task of the so-called Lytton Commission investigating the facts concerning Japan's role in the Manchurian crisis of 1931 is a major example.

The Charter of the United Nations (UN), 1945, includes inquiry in its Art. 33(1) which lists various means of peaceful settlement of disputes **(318),** and the UN and various regional organizations **(84)** have on numerous occasions employed fact-finding missions within the framework of their respective constituent instruments. However, the use of commissions of inquiry as a discrete technique, as envisaged in the Hague Conventions of 1899 and 1907, was very rare. An exception was the 1962 incident of the *Red Crusader* (35 ILR 485) involving the seizure in the North Sea by Denmark of a British trawler, but even in this case the report of the commission included a legal opinion going beyond a mere clarification of the disputed facts. In 1967, the UN General Assembly adopted a resolution upholding the institution of impartial fact-finding, separate from conciliation, and requested the Secretary-General to set up a register of experts to be used in specific disputes, but no permanent commission of inquiry was established. In general, states have not been willing to obligate themselves in advance to compulsory inquiry procedures. Despite that, resort to inquiry has increased within the UN and specialized agencies, for example, the International Labour Organisation. Inquiry is also stipulated among special procedures of dispute settlement, as in the Special Arbitral Tribunals under Annex VIII **(324)**of the Law of the Sea Convention of 1982 **(264)**.

**306. International Adjudication.** International adjudication is a general term referring to settlement of inter-state disputes **(299)** by all sorts of international judicial bodies variously known as courts, tribunals, commissions, or committees, and in particular permanent global and regional courts of general or specialized jurisdiction established pursuant to a treaty, in which independent judges render legally binding decisions on the basis of international law, following previously laid down rules and procedures usually articulated in the statute of the judicial body in question. Although in its strict meaning, international adjudication implies the existence of an international judicial body displaying the above-mentioned features, the term is frequently used more inclusively to encompass also settlement of disputes **(318)** by other international judicial and quasi-judicial bodies, such as arbitration **(293)** tribunals, including, *inter alia*, the International Centre for the Settlement of Investment Disputes **(307)**; arbitration tribunals envisaged by the 1982 Convention on the Law of the Sea (LOS Convention) **(264)** under Annex VII **(292)** and Annex VIII **(324)**; and—despite its special nature—also the Permanent Court of Arbitration **(319)**. In addition, the concept of international adjudication includes a variety of now mostly historical mixed arbitral commissions **(314)** and mixed claims commissions **(315)**. The Iran–United States Claims Tribunal **(312)** has been perhaps the most important bilateral adjudicatory body in recent times. International administrative tribunals and inspection panels set up by the World Bank in 1994 and by some regional banks as well as the quasi-judicial bodies verifying compliance with environmental conventions **(197)** are also included within the more extensive concept of international adjudication, as are also various human rights-related bodies, such as the United Nations (UN) Commission on Human Rights **(161)** and committees verifying compliance with specific human rights conventions, such as, *inter alia*, the International Civil and Political Rights **(166)** Committee, 1976; the Committee on Economic, Social and Cultural Rights **(169)**, 1987; the Committee on the Elimination of Racial Discrimination **(177)**, 1969; the Committee against Torture **(182)**, 1987; the Committee on the Elimination of All Forms of Discrimination against Women **(183)**, 1981; and the Committee on the Rights of the Child **(150)**, 1990.

Historically, adjudication in the strict sense in the form of settling or determining disputes by institutionalized permanent judiciary developed from the much longer experience of arbitration. Apart from the short-lived Central American Court of Justice (1908–1918) regarded as the first permanent international court and whose jurisdiction covered also cases between individuals and foreign states, the Permanent Court of International Justice (PCIJ) **(320)**, functioning in the League of Nations period as a court of general (but, of course, not criminal) jurisdiction, was the first global, permanent tribunal to decide disputes between states. The International Court of Justice (ICJ) **(309)**, one of the six principal organs of the UN, is essentially a continuation of the PCIJ. Two recently created regional international courts are the only other judicial bodies of general jurisdiction: the Central American Court of Justice, 1994 (34 ILM 921(1995)), and the Caribbean Court of Justice, created in 2000 (39 ILM 945 (2000)). A global UN-sponsored international judicial body of specialized jurisdiction, the International Tribunal for the Law of the Sea **(310)**, established under the UN Convention on the Law of the Sea of 1982 **(264)**, started its operations in 1996.

The latter part of the 20th century, and especially its last decades or so, witnessed a remarkable proliferation of international courts. Some of them eventually terminated their functions, others turned out to be abortive non-starters or practically idle bodies, but many continued to function in various areas of jurisdiction. An important international tribunal in the area of trade and commerce started its functions in 1996. It was the World Trade Organization's (WTO) Appellate Body, a permanent organ created to hear appeals against WTO in *ad hoc* panels, set up in 1995 under the WTO Dispute Settlement Understanding.

The idea of international judiciary found an unprecedented application on the regional level, beginning early in Western Europe where broad consensus on fundamental social and political values contributed to the success of the Court of Justice of the European Communities, currently known as the European Court of Justice (ECJ) **(298)**, complemented since 1988 by the Court of First Instance of the European Communities. After the admission in 2004 of 10 new states, mostly from eastern Europe, the ECJ jurisdiction now encompasses 25 European states. Of lesser importance are: the European Free Trade Association Court, 1994 and the Benelux Economic Union Court of Justice, created in 1965 and active since 1974. In Africa, international tribunals were established in various regions, but either terminated their activities or proved to be abortive attempts. Whether some more recently created courts, for example, the Court of Justice of the Common Market for Eastern and Southern Africa, 1997, will be successful, remains to be seen. In Latin America, in addition to the already mentioned Central American Court of Justice created in 1994, the major regional court is the Court of Justice of the Cartagena Agreement (18 ILM 1203 (1979)) established in 1979. This judicial body is similar to the ECJ and constitutes an integral part of the Andean Community set up in Cartagena (Colombia) in 1969 (8 ILM 910 (1969)). One can add that the Organization of Arab Petroleum Exporting Countries, founded in 1968 (781 UNTS 235), has its own standing tribunal for disputes relating to oil, which in its adjudication applies both international law and Islamic law. However, its activities have so far not been significant.

Regional courts for the protection of human rights **(157)** constitute a special category of courts. The pioneering European Court of Human Rights **(154)**, established under the European Convention for the Protection of Human Rights and Fundamental Freedoms of 1950 **(153)**, functioned in its first phase as an essentially part-time body until 1998 before being fundamentally restructured as a full-fledged permanent court in 1998. In the Western hemisphere the Inter-American Court of Human Rights **(165)** has been functioning since 1979. In Africa, the Banjul Charter **(143)** adopted by the Organization of African Unity, succeeded since 2001 by the African Union, does not provide for a human rights court. A protocol on the Establishment of an African Court of Human and Peoples' Rights was signed in 1998, but was not yet in force in 2004.

International criminal tribunals are a separate category of international judiciary in that, unlike the other international adjudicating bodies, they prosecute individuals **(81)** for violations of international law, and especially international humanitarian law **(353)**. Historically, African slave trade **(180)** mixed tribunals active in the 19th century were the first international criminal courts. In the 20th century, two *ad hoc* international military tribunals, one in Nuremberg (1945–1946) **(354)** and the other in Tokyo (1946–1948) **(355)** were established in the aftermath of World War II to try the major war criminals of Nazi Germany and Japan respectively. More recently, two specialized *ad hoc* international criminal tribunals were created by the UN Security Council (SC): the International Criminal Tribunal for the Former Yugoslavia, 1993 **(352)**, and the International Criminal Tribunal for Rwanda (ICTR), 1995 **(351)**. Both are still active, trying violators of international humanitarian law in their respective fields of jurisdiction. Finally, the most important and the first permanent international criminal tribunal was established by the SC as the International Criminal Court **(170)** in 1998. The Special criminal courts established in Sierra Leone in 2002 **(371)** and in Cambodia in 2004 are part international and part national institutions.

The proliferation of international judicial bodies raises a number of questions concerning the advisability of this development for the future of international law and the ICJ. First, there is the problem of possible conflicts of jurisdiction between judicial institutions, for example, between a regional court such as the ECJ and the global ICJ, but jurisdictional uncertainties may arise also between judicial bodies on the regional level. Concern has also been voiced that multiplication of international adjudicating bodies may threaten the integrity of universal international law and eventually lead to its fragmentation. On the other hand, it can be argued that the proliferation of various judicial bodies can contribute to strengthening the international rule of law, and clarifying and further developing international legal norms.

**307. International Centre for the Settlement of Investment Disputes.** The International Centre for the Settlement of Investment Disputes (ICSID) is an institution of international arbitration **(293)** between states **(127)** and foreign private enterprises, closely associated with the World Bank (International Bank for Reconstruction and Development, IBRD) and created by the Washington Convention of 1965 on the Settlement of Investment Disputes between States and Nationals **(175)** of Other States (575 UNTS 159), in force **(271)** in 1966, with more than 120 states parties in the early 2004. The function of the ICSID is to provide facilities for conciliation **(296)** and arbitration **(293)** of legal investment disputes between states and private foreign investors and its purpose is to encourage, by services of a neutral institution, a climate of mutual confidence between private foreign investors and host governments of developing countries, and thus promote the latter's economic development. Many bilateral investment treaties **(288)** binding states which are parties to the 1965 Convention provide for recourse to arbitration by the ICSID in cases of investment disputes.

The ICSID operates through standing panels of qualified conciliators and arbitrators, some of whom are appointed for five years by states parties and others are chosen for this term of years by the president of the IBRD. Arbitrators may be appointed also from outside. In practice, most arbitrators are appointed by the chairman of the Administrative Council of the ICSID at the request of the parties. The services of arbitrators are offered to states and their nationals after a state has joined the 1965 Convention. Consent to submit a dispute to the Centre must be in writing, whereupon the state of the national involved waives its right of diplomatic protection in respect of the dispute.

An arbitral tribunal of the Centre is made up either of a sole arbitrator or any uneven number, as agreed by the parties, and applies such rules of law as may be agreed by them, but in the absence of agreement it applies the law of the host state and relevant rules of international law. Thus, in practice, both municipal **(27)** and international law are used. The host state and the foreign investor may enter into an agreement whereby international law is to govern the case, in this manner "internationalizing" such agreement.

The arbitral bodies of the ICSID decide by a majority vote. An award may be interpreted by the tribunal at the request of either party. Revision is possible on the ground of discovery of fresh decisive evidence. An award can also be annulled by a committee on the usual grounds recognized in international arbitration, such as corruption, departure from a fundamental rule of procedure, or failure to state the reasons. The awards are legally binding and each state party to the 1965 Convention has the obligation to recognize them and enforce the pecuniary obligations imposed by an award within its territory **(228)** as if it were a final judgment of a court of that state. A party seeking recognition and enforcement of an award simply provides a competent court or other authority a certified copy of the award which becomes an enforceable executory title.

While states enjoy sovereign (state) immunity **(131)** within the context of the ICSID, the exact scope of such immunity is not a settled issue. Hence, enforcement and execution against a state that loses the case depends on the extent of such immunity granted by the state in which the execution is sought. Although the 1965 Convention confirms the existence of state immunity, it does not deal with the question of immunity from execution. A clause stipulating prior waiver of such immunity in a contract with a state is recommended by the ICSID to remedy the situation. In the United States (US) the Foreign Sovereign Immunities Act of 1976, as amended in 1978 (28 USC Sec. 1605(a)) removes immunity of a foreign state in actions for enforcement of an arbitral agreement, including that under the 1965 Convention, and declares as not immune from execution the property of a foreign state used in commercial activity (*jure gestionis*) in the US. In general, while the number of cases decided by the ICSID has been rather modest, its arbitrations have dealt with some interesting issues in the area of international economic law.

**308. International Commercial Arbitration.** International commercial arbitration is a legally binding resolution of private-law international commercial disputes by an impartial arbitrator or arbitrators deciding the dispute on the basis of the parties' agreement which ordinarily determines the choice of arbitrators, the venue, applicable law, language, and rules of the procedure. By agreeing to submit their dispute to commercial arbitration the parties waive their right to bring it before a national court. The private-law nature of international commercial arbitration distinguishes it from arbitration **(293)** between states **(127)** governed by public international law.

In the past two or three decades, international commercial arbitration has evolved as an accepted method of resolving international commercial disputes. A number of private or state-sponsored permanent arbitral institutes exist to offer their services for payment of a fee to clients preferring arbitration to adjudication by a national court. These institutes provide their organizational and administrative structure within which arbitral courts are set up for specific disputes. The International Court of Arbitration established in 1923 within the framework of the International Chamber of Commerce (ICC) in Paris is the oldest and most important institution in international commercial arbitration. Since its establishment, the International Court of Arbitration of the ICC has dealt with thousands of cases in all parts of the world. It functions according to the ICC Rules of Arbitration, revised over time to take account of the evolution of the growing arbitration practice. Currently, international commercial arbitration is governed by the ICC Rules of 1998 (36 ILM 1604 (1998)). Sessions of arbitral tribunals are held in some 40 countries every year, with arbitrators of many different nationalities hearing the cases and rendering final awards. The ICC International Court of Arbitration, made up of about 65 members from 55 countries supervises the arbitrations functioning according to the ICC Rules.

On the national level, there exist arbitral institutes, such as the American Arbitration Association in the United States and the London Court of Arbitration in the United Kingdom. In addition to general purpose arbitration institutes, there are specialized arbitration bodies to deal with disputes in specific areas such as, for example, maritime and various commodity disputes.

It is in the nature of international commercial arbitration to produce legal effects in more than one national jurisdiction, with potential problems in the area of recognition and enforcement of awards. The New York Convention on the Recognition and Enforcement of Foreign Arbitral Awards of 1958 (330 UNTS 38), in force for 134 countries in January 2004, sets forth provisions to remedy such problems. The European Convention on International Commercial Arbitration of 1961 (484 UNTS 349), with 29 parties, and the Inter-American Convention on International Commercial Arbitration of 1975 (14 ILM 336 (1975)) deal with similar matters within their respective regions. Awards against the losing party are enforced by national courts at the request of the winner. Under certain circumstances, such as invalidity of the arbitration agreement, irregular appointment of arbitrators, or error in the procedure, the state of forum may refuse recognition and enforcement of an award. Enforcement in disputes between states and private foreign investors is largely covered by provisions of the Convention of 1965 on the Settlement of Investment Disputes between States and Nationals of Other States (575 UNTS 159).

International commercial arbitration offers a number of advantages to business enterprises. Apart from a relatively low cost and a chance of a more speedy settlement, it allows them more flexibility as against litigation in a court. It also offers them a possibility to have their dispute decided by a tribunal that is potentially more impartial than a national court of either party. The possibility of choosing arbitrators who are not lawyers but experts in the required area may also encourage resort to commercial arbitration. All these reasons have contributed to a rapid expansion of international commercial arbitration in the era of rapidly progressing globalization of the world economy.

**309. International Court of Justice.** The International Court of Justice (ICJ) is one of the six principal organs of the United Nations (UN) and its principal judicial organ. Its seat is at the Peace Palace in The Hague, Netherlands. A successor of the Permanent Court of International Justice (PCIJ) **(320)**, the ICJ, popularly known as the "World Court," began its work in 1946. It functions on the basis of Chapter XIV of the UN Charter (Arts. 92–96) and its Statute which forms an integral part of the Charter. The Statute is supplemented by the Rules of Court, 1946, largely based—like most other provisions—on the Rules of the PCIJ. The Rules of the ICJ were amended in 1972 and thoroughly revised in 1978 (17 ILM 1286 (1978)) in order to simplify the proceedings and enhance their flexibility. Some revisions of the Rules were made in 2000. In addition, in 1968 the ICJ adopted a resolution concerning its non-binding Internal Judicial Practice (7 ILM 1395 (1968)), revised in 1976 (15 ILM 950 (1976)), subsequently articulated in 12 "Practice Directions" of 2002 (41 ILM 950 (2002)), as amended and further developed in 2004, and dealing, *inter alia*, with certain technical matters concerning the parties' pleadings, oral statements, and the Court's view that the parties should not nominate as judges *ad hoc* **(289)** persons who are acting as agent, counsel, or advocate in another case before the Court or have acted in that capacity in the three years preceding the date of the nomination. Similar direction applies to appearance as agent, counsel, or advocate of persons who until recently were members of the Court, judges *ad hoc* or higher officers of the Court.

Only states **(127)** may apply to and appear before the Court. All members of the UN are *ipso facto* parties to the Statute. Non-member states may become parties on conditions to be determined in each case by the General Assembly (GA) upon the recommendation of the Security Council (SC), a provision that, at this time, is not relevant because of the virtual universality of membership.

The ICJ is composed of 15 independent judges elected for a nine-year term with the possibility of re-election, with five judges elected every three years, at separate meetings, by the GA and—without the right of veto—of the SC. The judges must possess qualifications required in their respective countries for appointment to the highest judicial office, or be jurists of recognized competence in international law. They are elected from a list of persons nominated by the "national groups" in the Permanent Court of Arbitration (PCA) **(319)** or, if the state concerned is not represented in the PCA, by national groups appointed for this purpose by the government. Complex rules providing for a joint conference, made up of three members appointed by the SC and three by the GA, govern situations where seats on the Court remain unfilled after a third meeting of the two UN organs. A judge replacing another whose term of office has not expired holds office only for the remainder of his predecessor's term. The judges are elected as individuals regardless of nationality **(175)**, but no two of them may be nationals of the same state. A judge may be dismissed by a unanimous decision of the other members of the Court.

In its composition, the ICJ must as a whole assure the representation of the main forms of civilization and of the principal legal systems of the world. The permanent members of the SC, that is, China, France, Russia, the United Kingdom (UK), and the United States (US), normally have judges elected to the ICJ, but China did not have any national elected a judge in the period 1960–1984. Prior to 1960, a judge from the nationalist Republic of China in Taiwan had been sitting on the Court. In 1984 the first judge from mainland China was elected to the ICJ and took office in 1985. The ICJ elects its president and vice-president for three years, with a possibility of re-election. As of December 2004, the composition of the ICJ was as follows: president from China, vice-president from Madagascar, and judges from France, Sierra Leone, Russia, UK, Venezuela, Netherlands, Brazil, Jordan, US, Egypt, Japan, Germany, and Slovakia. The registrar is a Belgian national. Judges of the nationality of each of the parties ("national judges") retain the right to sit in the case. In addition, if a party before the Court does not have a judge of its nationality on the Court, it may appoint a judge *ad hoc* **(289)**. Although the ICJ has its seat at The Hague in on the Peace Palace funded by Andrew Carnegie before World War I, it may exercise its functions wherever it considers desirable. In 1997, for the first time in its history, the ICJ visited, at the invitation of the parties, the site of the disputed project of a Danube dam in the case of *Gabčíkovo-Nagymaros Project* (Hungary/Slovakia) (37 ILM 162 (1998)). As a rule, decisions are made by the full court, with a quorum of nine sufficing to constitute the Court. However, at the request of the parties a case may be heard and determined by a chamber **(295)**.

The ICJ has contentious **(297)** and advisory **(291)** jurisdiction. Contentious jurisdiction is governed by the fundamental principle that no state can be brought before the Court without its consent, as a rule express (special agreement of the parties; a jurisdictional clause of a treaty binding the parties, whereby one of them may refer the dispute to the ICJ; and under the optional clause **(317)**), but also implied, as in the rare cases of *forum prorogatum* **(301)**. In addition, in a sense, the ICJ has appellate jurisdiction resulting from provisions in a limited number of conventions providing for such jurisdiction, as for example, the Chicago Convention on International Civil Aviation of 1944 **(191)** which envisages appeals to the ICJ from the decisions of the Council of the International Civil Aviation Organization (ICAO). This happened once in the case concerning *Appeal Relating to the Jurisdiction of the ICAO Council* (India v. Pakistan) (1972 ICJ Rep. 46). Advisory jurisdiction is exercised by the ICJ pursuant to Art. 96 of the UN Charter on any legal question at the request of the GA, the SC, or a specialized agency so authorized by the GA.

As a judicial body, under Art. 38 of its Statute the ICJ decides disputes in accordance with international law, applying as sources **(36)** of this law, treaties **(40)**, international custom as evidence of a general practice accepted as law **(39)**, and the general principles of law recognized by civilized nations **(38)** meaning, in general, principles common to most or all national systems of law and general principles of international law. Furthermore, the ICJ applies judicial decisions **(22)** and the teachings of the most highly qualified publicists **(42)**, that is, scholars in international law, as "subsidiary means for the determination of rules of law." However, it must be emphasized that under an express provision of its Statute (Art. 59), the decision of the Court has no binding force except between the parties and in respect of that particular case. This means that—unlike the courts in the countries of the common-law system—the ICJ and, for that matter, other international tribunals, are not obliged to follow the doctrine of *stare decisis*, that is, the duty to follow its own previous decisions and, generally speaking, of all international tribunals, decisions of the court concerned and those of other tribunals of equal or greater authority. Yet, despite the absence of the *stare decisis* principle in international law, the ICJ, like its predecessor the PCIJ, has always had a strong tendency to rely upon its prior and PCIJ judgments and advisory opinions. Because of its high prestige, other international courts have also occasionally referred to pronouncements of the World Court, including in particular *obiter dicta*, that is, lesser propositions of law not connected with the principal issue, stated by the Court or by individual judges in their individual **(304)**, including even dissenting, opinions. It should be added that with the parties' consent, the ICJ has the power to decide a case *ex aequo et bono* **(13)**, that is, on grounds of justice and fairness, and other extra-legal considerations. So far the ICJ has not decided any case on this basis.

The proceedings before the ICJ in contentious cases are conducted pursuant to the provisions of the Statute (Arts. 39–64) and in the Rules of Court. They are conducted in English or in French, with everything written or said in one language being translated into the other. The proceedings are initiated either by the notification of the "special agreement" (*compromis*) of the parties or by a written application. Intervention **(311)** in the proceedings by other states is possible. To preserve the rights of either party the Court may indicate provisional measures **(322)**. Apart from the main proceedings on the merits, there are very often "incidental proceedings": requests for provisional measures; preliminary objections **(321)** to jurisdiction and admissibility; counterclaims; intervention in proceedings; special references to the Court; and discontinuance of cases. The parties are normally represented by agents and assisted by counsel and advocates. The proceedings consist of: 1. filing and exchanging written pleadings, that is, memorials, counter-memorials, and—if authorized by the Court (which, in order to expedite cases normally allows only one round of written pleadings)—replies and rejoinders (allowed by the Court in 2002 in the case of *Maritime Delimitation between Nicaragua and Honduras in the Caribbean Sea*, filed in 1999) and 2. oral pleadings, which are public unless the Court decides otherwise or the parties demand a closed session. After the oral phase of the proceedings the Court deliberates *in camera* and then delivers its decision at a public sitting. All questions are decided by a majority of the judges present; in the event of an equality of votes the president has a casting vote. The judgment must state the reasons on which it is based and must contain the names of the judges voting for and against the majority. Any judge is entitled to attach his individual opinion, separate or dissenting, or a declaration. Proceedings before the ICJ are very frequently affected by "preliminary objections" **(321)** raising questions of admissibility of the claim and/or jurisdiction of the Court.

The judgment of the ICJ is final and without appeal. However, in the event of a dispute as to the meaning and scope of the judgment the Court interprets it upon the request of any party. The request is made either by means of a special agreement between the parties or of an application by one or more of the parties. In 1950 the ICJ refused to interpret its judgment of 1950 in the *Asylum* case (Colombia v. Peru) (1950 ICJ Rep. 395); and, in 1999, its judgment of 1998 in the case concerning *Land and Maritime Boundary between Cameroon and Nigeria* (Cameroon v. Nigeria). In addition, in its judgment of 1985 (1985 ICJ Rep. 192) the Court did interpret the relevant portions of its *Continental Shelf* judgment of 1982 in the case between Tunisia and Libya, but found Tunisia's request for the revision of that judgment inadmissible. There have been three requests for revision, but all have been refused by the Court's judgments: namely, in addition to the above-mentioned request of Tunisia, the request of El Salvador in 2002 to revise the ICJ (Chamber) **(295)** judgment of 1992 in its dispute with Honduras; and the request of Yugoslavia in 2002 for a revision of the ICJ judgment of 1996 in the *Genocide* case (Bosnia and Herzegovina v. Yugoslavia).

Art. 94(1) provides that each member of the UN (practically speaking, "state") undertakes to comply with the decision of the ICJ in any case to which it is a party. The Court has no procedures for enforcing its decisions, but under Art. 94(2) failure to perform the obligations incumbent upon it under a judgment rendered by the ICJ entitles the other party to have recourse to the SC, which may, if it deems it necessary, make recommendations or decide upon measures to be taken to give effect to the judgment. These provisions have never been effectively implemented. While the UK did have recourse to the SC to enforce the provisional measures indicated by the ICJ in 1951 in the *Anglo-Iranian Oil Co.* (United Kingdom v. Iran), in which otherwise the Court declined jurisdiction in its judgment in 1952 (1952 ICJ Rep. 93), the obligation incumbent upon Iran was decreed by the Court not in a judgment but in an order, and it is not clear whether provisional measures indicated in an order of the Court are enforceable by the SC. An order may be made by the full Court or its president, vice-president, or a senior judge. In another case, a draft resolution of the SC calling for compliance with the ICJ judgment of 1986 in *Military and Paramilitary Activities in and against Nicaragua* (Nicaragua v. United States) (1986 ICJ Rep. 14) was vetoed by the US (25 ILM 1352 (1986)). Otherwise, this case was eventually discontinued by a Court's order in 1991. In general, the judgments of the ICJ have been complied with. Among the few exceptions have been: Communist Albania's refusal to pay the UK compensation in the *Corfu Channel* (United Kingdom v. Albania) case (1949 ICJ Rep. 4), an obligation apparently fulfilled by Albania following the fall of Communism in that country; Iceland's failure to comply in *Fisheries Jurisdiction* cases (United Kingdom v. Iceland and Federal Republic of Germany v. Iceland) (1974 ICJ Rep. 3); and Iran's noncompliance with the Court's judgment in the *United States Diplomatic and Consular Staff in Tehran* case (1980 ICJ Rep. 3). The case was eventually discontinued by a Court's order in 1981.

A disturbing phenomenon in cases before the ICJ, especially in the 1970s and 1980s, was the non-appearance of respondent states against which proceedings were instituted by application. Such conduct, unknown in the PCIJ, has occurred 10 times. Even some Western, ostensibly law-abiding, countries refused in some cases to appear before the Court: France in the *Nuclear Tests* cases (Australia v. France; New Zealand v. France) (1974 ICJ Rep. 253); Iceland in the above-noted cases; and the US, which refused to participate in the merits phase of the above-mentioned case of *Military and Paramilitary Activities* (Nicaragua v. United States) in 1986. Turkey did not appear before the Court in the *Aegean Sea Continental Shelf* case (Greece v. Turkey), but the ICJ declined jurisdiction in its judgment in 1978 (1978 ICJ Rep. 3). According to the ICJ rules, non-appearance of a party or failure to defend its case is no impediment to the Court's deciding in favor of the other party provided the Court is satisfied that it has jurisdiction and the claim is well founded in fact and law.

By 2004, that is, in approximately 58 years of the existence of the ICJ, more than 100 contentious cases had been brought before the Court and placed on its Court's List. However, this figure includes a number of parallel proceedings in identical disputes, cases ended by the ICJ judgments declining jurisdiction, cases of interpretation, and cases discontinued and removed from the List, altogether approximately some 25 cases. The ICJ had delivered some 80 judgments, mostly on merits, but also some on jurisdiction, preliminary objections, applications for interpretation or revision of a judgment, and applications for permission to intervene. Decisions on provisional measures are made in the form of orders. In addition to decisions in contentious jurisdiction, the ICJ has rendered 25 advisory opinions (two on basically the same issue, namely, the use of nuclear weapons in armed conflict). The request concerning *Legal Consequences of the Construction of a Wall in the Occupied Palestinian Territory* led to an advisory opinion in July 2004 (43 ILM 1009) and the case of *Avena and Other Mexican Nationals* (Mexico v. United States) resulted in a judgment in April 2004. In addition, 21 contentious cases (8 on the matter of the *Legality of Use of Force* brought by Serbia and Montenegro against eight Western European states) were pending before the Court.

Whereas in the 1970s not more than one or two cases at a time were on the ICJ docket, a marked and steady increase in the Court's workload has taken place since the 1980s and 1990s, with 10 contentious cases in 1990, 12 in 1996, and 21 pending or under deliberation in 2004, coming from all the continents and widely differing in content: territorial and maritime disputes, title to sovereignty, legality of use of force, charges of genocide, environmental matters, immunity of former high government officials from prosecution for war crimes, to name only a few. What is characteristic is the fact that most of the litigants before the Court are excolonial states, once reluctant to make use of the ICJ because of its alleged bias against them. African states represent the largest proportion of the Court's clients, making recourse to the ICJ to resolve disputes over unsettled boundary problems inherited from the colonial past. The consequences of the increase in the volume of cases before the ICJ, and in particular strains upon the Court's time and its modest budgetary resources, were the subject of the Court's response on these matters to the UN GA in 1998 (37 ILM 1466 (1998)).

While the ICJ has not played a major role in maintaining international peace and security, with many of the disputes submitted to it being of peripheral nature, its judgments and advisory opinions have made a significant contribution to clarification and even development of international law in a number of areas. The prospects for the Court in the new century appeared to be brighter as more countries, especially non-Western ones, were willing to accept its jurisdiction. At the same time, a debate has continued among international legal scholars over various ideas of reforming the ICJ, such as allowing standing to individuals **(164)**, the use of chambers in advisory proceedings and, of course, ways of strengthening the Court's potential for compulsory jurisdiction.

**310. International Tribunal for the Law of the Sea.** The International Tribunal for the Law of the Sea (ITLOS) is a permanent global judicial body established under Art. 287(1)(a) of the United Nations (UN) Convention on the Law of the Sea (LOS Convention) of 1982 **(264)** in accordance with Annex VI of the LOS Convention, which contains the Statute of the ITLOS. In addition, the Tribunal has adopted its Rules, amended in 2001, and Guidelines on Internal Judicial Practice. The ITLOS has its seat, with a registrar and other officers, in Hamburg, Germany (Annex VI Art. 1). It is composed of 21 independent members, with president and vice-president, elected by secret ballot by the states parties to the LOS Convention, for nine years on a staggered schedule, with a possibility of re-election and so as to ensure the representation of the principal legal systems and equitable geographical distribution. No two members may be nationals **(175)** of the same state, and there can be no fewer than three members from each geographical group as established by the UN General Assembly, namely, African states, Asian states, Eastern European states, Latin American and Caribbean states, and Western European and other states. A quorum of 11 members is required to constitute the Tribunal, but there is also, under the Statute (Art. 15), a possibility of forming special chambers **(295)**. The ITLOS has formed the following chambers: Chamber of Summary Procedure; Chamber for Fisheries Disputes; and Chamber for Marine Environment Disputes.

The Chamber of Summary Procedure, constituted annually, consists of five members and two alternates, with the president and vice-president of the ITLOS serving *ex officio*. The other two chambers consist of seven members each. In addition to the three chambers, the tribunal can form, at the request of the parties, a chamber for dealing with a particular dispute (Statute of ITLOS Art. 15(2)). The composition of the chamber is determined by the Tribunal, but with the approval of the parties. In 2000, at the request of Chile and the European Community (EC), the parties to the dispute concerning the conservation and the sustainable exploitation of swordfish stocks in the South-Eastern Pacific Ocean, the ITLOS formed, for the first time, a five-member special chamber to deal with this case (Case No. 7) (40 ILM 475 (2000). Disputes relating to activities in the deep seabed Area **(232)** are to be submitted to the Seabed Disputes Chamber of 11 judges; a quorum of seven is required. Members of the Chamber are selected by the Tribunal every three years, with a possibility of a second term. In addition, any party to a dispute before the Chamber may request it to form an *ad hoc* chamber composed of three members of the Seabed Disputes Chamber. The composition of an *ad hoc* chamber requires the approval of the parties to the dispute.

The ITLOS is open to states parties to the LOS Convention (Art. 291) and other entities that signed **(283)** the LOS Convention, including international organizations **(84)** (for example, the above-mentioned EC). In addition, entities other than states, even individuals **(81)**, may be parties before the Tribunal in any case expressly provided for in Part XI (the Area) of the LOS Convention or in any case submitted by virtue of a treaty **(288)** conferring jurisdiction on the ITLOS and accepted by all the parties to that case (LOS Convention Art. 291; ITLOS Statute Art. 20(2)).

The jurisdiction of the ITLOS in contentious cases comprises any disputes concerning the interpretation **(274)** and application of the LOS Convention and the Implementation Agreement of 1994 **(247)**, and any other disputes on matters specifically provided for in any other treaty that confers jurisdiction on the ITLOS. There are seven such multilateral treaties in force. It must be added, however, that by virtue of certain of the LOS Convention provisions on settlement of disputes (Part XV) there are limitations and exceptions to compulsory procedures entailing binding decisions, which apply also to the jurisdiction of the ITLOS (Art. 297). These restrictions exist because of sensitivity with regard to vital national interest and sovereign rights in certain categories of disputes, such as those concerning fisheries in the exclusive economic zone (EEZ) **(238)** and marine scientific research. Such matters are excluded from compulsory settlement procedures under the circumstances spelled out in detail in Art. 297 of the LOS Convention, but the dispute in question must be submitted to conciliation **(296)**. In addition, states have the option of not accepting the judicial or arbitral procedures under the LOS Convention, in respect to any or all of three categories of disputes, namely, disputes concerning military activities; disputes under consideration by the UN Security Council; and maritime delimitation disputes, as stipulated in detail in Art. 298 of the LOS Convention. So far, only a relatively small number of states have invoked, in dispute settlement, the optional exemption under this article. It should be noted that any dispute belonging to the categories referred to in Arts. 297 and 298 may, nevertheless, be submitted to the Tribunal or other dispute settlement procedure if the parties to the dispute so agree.

Furthermore, unless the parties otherwise agree, the Tribunal has mandatory jurisdiction in cases relating to the prompt release of vessels and crews under Art. 292 of the LOS Convention (the most common subject of the disputes before the ITLOS); and in cases relating to provisional measures **(322)** pending the constitution of an arbitral tribunal **(293)** under Art. 290(5) of the LOS Convention.

Like the International Court of Justice (ICJ), the ITLOS itself decides any question as to its jurisdiction (LOS Convention Art. 288(4)). The Tribunal may prescribe provisional measures to preserve the respective rights of the parties or to prevent serious harm to the marine environment. It may also indicate them in the above-mentioned situation under Art. 290(5) of the LOS Convention, as it was done for the first time in Cases No. 3 and 4, *Southern Blue Tuna* (New Zealand v. Japan; Australia v. Japan) in 1999. Under Art. 159(10) and Art. 191 of the LOS Convention, the Seabed Dispute Chamber of the ITLOS has also advisory jurisdiction **(291)**: it may give opinions at the request of the Assembly or the Council of the International Seabed Authority **(250).** In addition, the ITLOS as such may give advisory opinions in certain cases under treaties related to the purposes of the LOS Convention if the treaty in question specifically provides for submission to the ITLOS of a request for such opinion.

As before the ICJ, disputes are instituted either by written application or by notification of a special agreement. The procedure is spelled out in detail in the Statute and the Rules. The judgments are final and binding only between the parties and in respect to the particular dispute before the Tribunal. Third-party intervention in proceedings **(311)** is possible if that party proves having an interest of a legal nature. If the Tribunal grants a request for intervention, its decision in the dispute in question shall be binding upon the intervening state to the extent that the decision relates to matters in respect of which the intervention took place.

Since its creation, the ITLOS has heard a dozen cases, the first one (37 ILM 360 (1998), the *Saiga* (Saint Vincent and the Grenadines v. Guinea) (Cases Nos. 1 and 2), belongs to the most important decisions of the tribunal, involving such issues as extending customs jurisdiction into the EEZ (found impermissible); some aspects of hot pursuit **(246)**; and genuine link in the nationality of ships **(257)**. Most cases involved applications for prompt release of a detained vessel or its crew, or indication of provisional measures, as was done in the case (No. 10) of the *Mox Plant* (Ireland v. United Kingdom) involving Ireland's claim that a nuclear plant in the UK was a hazard to the marine environment. The Tribunal ordered provisional measures under the above-mentioned rule of Art. 290(5) of the LOS Convention (41 ILM 405 (2002)), whereupon the dispute was submitted to arbitration on the merits by an arbitral tribunal under Annex VII of the LOS Convention **(292)**.

The ITLOS belongs to one of the four categories of judicial and arbitral bodies envisaged by the LOS Convention (Art. 287), which states are free to choose in order to resolve disputes not settled by peaceful means of their choice, including a regional court, such as the European Court of Justice **(298)** to which the European Union (EU) members must submit their fishery disputes. The choice of one or more of these "compulsory" methods (which in practice are less used than the initial methods of the parties' own choosing) is made by means of a revocable written declaration deposited with the UN, but states need not choose the same category for all purposes. The other judicial and arbitral bodies that may be used are: the ICJ; arbitral tribunals under Annex VII of the LOS Convention; and special arbitral tribunals under Annex VIII. All of them apply international law, but the disputing parties may agree to request a decision *ex aequo et bono* **(13)**. If a state has not selected any of the four—and a number of them have not yet done so—it is deemed to have accepted arbitration under Annex VII.

**311. Intervention in the Proceedings.** Intervention in the proceedings is an institution in the procedure of international tribunals **(306)** whereby in certain circumstances and with the permission of the tribunal a state may intervene in a case between other states before the tribunal. Historically, the first instance of the possibility of intervention by third parties is a provision in the Hague Convention for the Pacific Settlement of International Disputes of 1899 (187 CTS 410), revised in 1907 (205 CTS 277). It related to an arbitration **(293)** procedure allowing intervention by third states which were parties to a treaty the interpretation of which was at issue in the proceedings. The institution of intervention was further developed within the framework of the Permanent Court of International Justice (PCIJ) **(320)** and subsequently the International Court of Justice (ICJ) **(309)**. In addition, intervention is admissible in some other international tribunals, such as the European Court of Justice **(298)** and the International Tribunal for the Law of the Sea **(310)**. In the ECJ intervention is available automatically (except in proceedings for preliminary rulings) to member states and institutions of the European Union (EU), and—under certain circumstances—to private persons, even individuals **(81)**.

According to the Statute of the ICJ, a state may intervene in a case between other states in two kinds of situation. First, under Art. 62, a state which considers that "it has an interest of a legal nature which may be affected by the decision in the case, may submit a request to the Court to be permitted to intervene." The other situation exists where, under Art. 63 of the ICJ Statute, a state requesting intervention is a party to a treaty the construction **(274)** of which is before the Court. All such states are notified of this situation by the Court's Registrar and have the right to request intervention, but if they use this right, the construction given by the judgment will be equally binding upon them.

The ICJ has been rather restrained in granting the right to intervene. In the PCIJ, intervention by Poland in the *Wimbledon* case (Great Britain, France, Italy and Japan v. Germany) (1923 PCIJ, Series A, No. 1) was the only instance of intervention. It concerned the interpretation of the Peace Treaty of Versailles between the Allied and Associated Powers and Germany, 1919 (225 CTS 188) and was based on Art. 63 of the Court's Statute, although the initial application had invoked Art. 62. The ICJ (Chamber) allowed Nicaragua intervention under Art. 62 in the case of *Land, Island and Maritime Frontier Dispute* (El Salvador/Honduras) (1990 ICJ Rep. 92); and by an order of the Court granted this right to Equatorial Guinea in the case of *Land and Maritime Boundary between Cameroon and Nigeria* (Cameroon v. Nigeria). (1996 ICJ Rep. 13). As far as intervention under Art. 63 is concerned, Cuba intervened in the *Haya de la Torre* (Colombia v. Peru) case (1951 ICJ Rep. 71) which involved the construction of the Havana Convention of 1928 on Asylum **(64)**. On the other hand, application for intervention was denied to: Malta in the *Continental Shelf* case (Tunisia/Libyan Arab Jamahiriya) (1981 ICJ Rep. 3); Italy in the *Continental Shelf* case (Libyan Arab Jamahiriya/Malta) (1984 ICJ Rep. 3); El Salvador (application under Art. 63) in the case of *Military and Paramilitary Activities in and against Nicaragua* (1984 ICJ Rep. 392); and, most recently in 2001, the Philippines in the case of *Sovereignty over Pulau Litigan and Pulau Sipadan* (Indonesia/Malaysia). In this case, involving sovereignty over two small islands off Borneo, the full Court ruled in its judgment that the Philippines' legal interest, namely its claim to sovereignty over North Borneo, was too general and did not relate to the subject matter of the case. Applications of five Pacific states in 1995 to intervene in an abortive case, in which New Zealand sought a re-examination of the *Nuclear Tests* judgment of 1974 (New Zealand v. France) (1974 ICJ Rep. 457), became moot after the Court's order dismissed New Zealand's request as not falling within the ruling of 1974.

**312. Iran–United States Claims Tribunal.** The Iran–United States Claims Tribunal (IUSCT) is a unique and perhaps the most significant arbitral body **(293)** in the history of modern claims arbitration. It was set up under the so-called Algiers Accords of 1981 (20 ILM 223 (1981)) which, through Algeria's good offices **(303)**, stipulated measures designed to resolve the crisis in relations between Iran and the United States (US) arising out of detention as hostages of 52 US nationals

**(175)**, namely diplomats **(68)** and consular officials **(57)**, at the US embassy in Tehran in 1979, and the subsequent freezing of Iranian assets by the US. The government of Algeria recorded the commitments that Iran and the US were willing to undertake in two declarations of the Accords in 1981: the General Declaration and the Claims Settlement Declaration, the latter instrument establishing the IUSCT as a mechanism for a third-party arbitration of claims between the two countries. Under the General Declaration, Iran agreed to release the hostages and in exchange the US promised to restore, insofar as possible, Iran's financial position to the state that had existed before the freeze of the Iranian assets. The US also agreed to terminate all legal proceedings in US courts involving claims of US nationals, individuals, and entities **(174)**, against Iran and to prohibit all further litigation based on such claims, and—the crucial objective—to bring about the termination of such claims through arbitration. The Claims Settlement Declaration provides therefore that as of the date of filing such claims with the Tribunal, claims referred to the IUSCT will be excluded from the jurisdiction of the courts of Iran, or of the US, or of any other court.

The IUSCT started its operations in the Peace Palace in The Hague in 1981 and then in 1982 moved to its own premises in The Hague. It consists of nine members, of whom three are appointed by each government and three selected from third countries by the six government-appointed members. The president of the Tribunal is elected from among the third-party arbitrators, but if no agreement can be reached on his appointment among the party-appointed arbitrators, the appointment is made by an "appointment authority" selected by the secretary-general of the Permanent Court of Arbitration **(319)**. In the latest appointment process, Iran challenged the appointment of the new president (an arbiter of Polish nationality) asserting doubts about his impartiality, but its challenge was rejected by the appointment authority, a former president of the International Court of Justice **(309)**.

The IUSCT has jurisdiction to decide claims of US nationals against Iran and of Iranian nationals against the US. In addition to these private contracts, expropriations, and other property rights claims, the Tribunal decides "official claims" between the two governments, relating to the purchase and sale of goods and services; disputes concerning return by the US of the property of the former Shah's family; certain claims between US and Iranian banking institutions; and disputes concerning the interpretation **(274)** or performance of the Algiers Declarations. However, the IUSCT has no jurisdiction over claims of the US and its nationals arising out of the seizure of the US embassy and the hostages in Tehran and out of the US counteraction to these events, as well as over claims arising under contracts specifically providing for the sole jurisdiction of the Iranian courts. All claims (except disputes of the two governments over the interpretation of the Algiers Declarations) had to be filed by 19 January 1982. Altogether there were about 1,000 claims for amounts of $250,000 or more, and 2,800 claims for amounts of less than $250,000. Claims belonging to the latter category were represented by the government of the national concerned and settled by a lump-sum agreement between the two governments, but the claims of the former category had to be presented by the claimants themselves. Iran's claim of $12 billion, involving undelivered, American-made, military equipment, was the largest claim before the Tribunal. According to the office of the secretary-general of the IUSCT the total number of cases finalized by award, decision, or order through September 2003 amounted to 3,935 cases, including 19 cases over interpretation or application of the Algiers Declarations; 72 cases of official claims of one government against the other; 960 large cases; and 2,884 claims of less than $250,000.

The IUSCT decides claims by one of three chambers, each with three members, or by the full Tribunal which hears particularly important questions referred to it by the chambers, and international law disputes between the two governments. Each government is represented by an Agent at the seat of the Tribunal, who also receives official communications directed to his government or nationals in connection with the proceedings. The expenses of the Tribunal are shared equally by the two governments. Under the Claims Settlement Declaration the Tribunal decides "on the basis of respect for law, applying such choice of law rules and principles of commercial and international law as [it] determines to be applicable, taking into account relevant usages of the trade, contract provisions and changed circumstances." This provision, and the Tribunal's opinion that the claims continue to be individual private claims not assumed by the state, testifies to the hybrid nature of the IUSCT which combines the features of arbitration between states, based on public international law, and arbitration between states and private persons. Both the appointment of arbitrators and the procedure of the Tribunal is governed by the 1976 arbitration rules of the United Nations Commission on International Trade Law (15 ILM 701 (1976)), with some modifications by the two governments and the Tribunal. The awards and other decisions of the IUSCT are final and enforceable against either government in courts of any country in accordance with its laws. The awards of the Tribunal may also be enforced under the multilateral New York Convention on Recognition and Enforcement of Foreign Arbitral Awards of 1958 (330 UNTS 38). Awards to the US and its nationals are enforceable out of a special "security account" of $1 billion, established by Iran from the frozen Iranian assets in the US, at the Settlement Bank of the Netherlands in the name of the Central Bank of Algeria. Iran was obliged to replenish this account once it fell below $500 million, which happened some 30 times until 1992. However, subsequently, Iran argued that no replenishment was necessary to satisfy the few remaining claims of US nationals against Iran.

By the turn of the century, the work of the IUSCT had practically reached its end, with only a few cases of claims by Iran remaining on its docket. Considering the continuing political conflict separating the two states and a tense climate of confrontation which at one time, in 1984, even led to an unprecedented physical assault upon the Swedish member of the Tribunal by his Iranian colleagues, the IUSCT was able to function efficiently, handing down a body of awards covering a wide range of problems of international commercial law and public international law. In the latter area, the Tribunal dealt with some fundamental issues, such as state responsibility **(128)** for injury to aliens **(144)**, especially expropriation **(145)** and expulsion **(146)**, as well as nationality of claims **(95)** in cases of dual nationality **(173)**. The work of the IUSCT, published in some 30 volumes of its Reports, constitutes a significant contribution to international arbitration and international law in general.

**313. Mediation.** Mediation is a diplomatic method of third-party peaceful settlement of disputes between states **(318)** whereby that party, with the agreement of the disputing states **(127)**, actively participates in the negotiations **(316)** by offering substantive suggestions concerning terms of settlement and trying to reconcile the opposite claims of the parties, and in general, providing assistance to the parties in order to help resolve the dispute **(299)**. Mediation goes beyond mere good offices **(303)** in that the mediator (a third state, an international organization **(84)**, or even an individual) instead of serving only as a go-between, directly assists the disputing states by discussing together with them the situation and offering concrete proposals in joint or separate meetings. Like good offices, mediation may not be regarded as an unfriendly act or interference in the affairs of other states.

Along with good offices, mediation is recognized by the Hague Convention for the Pacific Settlement of International Disputes of 1899 (187 CTS 410), revised in 1907 (205 CTS 277), as one of the recommended techniques of peaceful settlement. The pertinent rules codified in the Convention were subsequently includes in numerous treaties. Art. 33(1) of the Charter of the United Nations (UN) expressly includes mediation among other pacific means of settling disputes likely to endanger the maintenance of international peace and security. In actual practice, the record of mediation has been rather mixed. Among examples of successful mediation by major powers are the Tashkent mediation by the Soviet Union in the India-Pakistan round of war in 1966 and the United States Camp David mediation to end the state of war between Egypt and Israel in 1979. Most mediating activities have taken place under the auspices of the UN or a regional organization. Mediation is a rather sensitive technique in that it may jeopardize the relations between the mediating state and one or all of the disputants. On the whole, mediation has proved to be more successful in cases of less dangerous local disputes. It remains merely a mild third-party peaceful intervention in an international conflict, with the parties under no legal obligation to accept the proposal of the mediator.

**314. Mixed Arbitral Commissions and Tribunals.** These were *ad hoc* arbitral **(293)** tribunals or commissions established in relations between the Allies and the defeated states **(127)** under the

Peace Treaties ending World War I. The function of these bodies was: to settle claims of nationals **(175)** of the Allied and Associated Powers against Germany and its allies for damage caused by measures such as confiscation and requisitioning; to settle claims between individuals **(164)** resulting from pre-war obligations, largely processed through a clearing procedure; and to deal with claims of nationals of the defeated powers against the newly created states. Individuals as well as governments had standing before the mixed arbitral tribunals or commissions, that is, they could present their claims themselves.

Some 36 mixed arbitral tribunals were established under the treaties of: Versailles, 1919 (225 CTS 1880); Saint-Germain, 1919 (226 CTS 8); Neuilly, 1919 (226 CTS 332); Trianon, 1920 (6 LNTS 188); and Lausanne, 1923 (128 LNTS 11). They involved 14 European countries, Japan, and Siam (Thailand). In addition, a Germany–United States (US) Mixed Claims Commission **(315)** and a tripartite (US-Austria-Hungary) Commission were set up separately in 1922 since the US was not a party to any of those peace treaties. A German-Mexican Commission was also active. Following World War II, the Conciliation **(296)** Commission (in reality an arbitration commission) under the Peace Treaty with Italy, 1947 (49 and 50 UNTS) and the property commissions under the US-Japan Treaty of Peace of 1947 (136 UNTS 45) were similar to the mixed arbitral tribunals after World War I.

The mixed arbitral tribunals were made up of two national members appointed by the governments of the victorious and the defeated powers, respectively, and a neutral chairman chosen by mutual agreement who, in practice, largely determined the outcome of the adjudication **(306)**. The tribunals applied the relevant treaty provisions and the municipal law **(27)** appropriate under private international law (conflict of laws) rules **(32)**. The execution of awards involving debts was carried out according to the procedure of the debtor country. Judgments against states were executed under a clearing procedure or from proceeds of confiscated enemy property. The mixed arbitral tribunals of the post–World War I era were the busiest ever international tribunals. For instance, 20,000 claims were submitted before the Franco-German tribunal alone and some 10,000 before the Anglo-German tribunal. About 13,000 were settled by the German-US Mixed Claims Commission. However, many of these claims were disposed out of court. The activities of the tribunals were terminated in the early 1930s. Despite political difficulties, such as were encountered in Franco-German relations, the mixed arbitral tribunals made a valuable contribution to the development of international law, especially by the fact that they recognized to a certain degree the status of individuals before an international court, granting them the right directly to plead their cases before the tribunal.

**315. Mixed Claims Commissions.** A quasi-judicial method of settling international disputes **(299)** by a body of commissioners set up by a treaty **(288)** in order to decide on claims between nationals **(175)** of different states **(127)**; between states and nationals of another state; or between states themselves. In the 19th century only states had the right to file claims before mixed claims commissions. This changed in the 20th century when, under some treaties, individuals **(81)** obtained direct access to such commissions.

A mixed claims commission normally consists of two or more commissioners appointed in equal numbers by the governments concerned, with another, the umpire, co-opted by the commissioners or the governments. The institution of mixed claims commissions was initiated under the Jay Treaty of 1794 (52 CTS 243). Sometimes known simply as "mixed commissions," they became very common in the 19th century when some 80 such commissions were established. Among them, the best known are: the commissions set up to settle claims resulting from the Napoleonic wars; the United States (US)-Mexican claims commissions of 1868 which settled more than 2,000 claims; the US-Venezuelan commission; and other commissions settling claims in relations between the US or major European powers on the one hand, and Latin American countries on the other. The 19th-century mixed claims commissions were antecedents of the mixed arbitration tribunals **(314)** established in the aftermath of World War I. But still, in the inter-war period, mixed claims commissions were used in settling claims against Germany, and the two general claims commissions set up in relations between the US and Mexico in 1923 and 1924, became perhaps the best-known bodies of this kind. They dealt with some 6,000 claims, almost all of them by US nationals who alleged all kinds of injuries suffered in the conditions of the revolutionary turmoil in Mexico at that time. The US-Mexican claims commissions contributed a significant body of case law on state responsibility **(128)** for injury to aliens **(144)**. The law to be applied by the commission is ordinarily specified in the treaty which established such body. References are usually made to international law, justice, and equity **(13)**, or a similar formula.

After World War II the use of mixed claims commissions declined, with states resorting to lump-sum settlement agreements whereby one state agrees to pay another a lump sum in full satisfaction of the outstanding claims by the nationals of the latter against the former. The lump sum is then distributed to claimants by a national commission which normally applies international law in adjudicating the claims. The Iran–United States Claims Tribunal **(312)** has been perhaps the most outstanding body in the nature of mixed claims commission in the recent decades.

**316. Negotiation.** Negotiation is a diplomatic procedure whereby representatives of states **(127)** engage in discussing matters of mutual concern, including a dispute **(299)** between them, attempting to clarify and reconcile their divergent positions and resolve the dispute. Negotiation does not, in principle, directly involve any third parties, but is frequently an introduction to subsequent procedures of dispute settlement **(318)** with the participation of third parties. Diplomatic negotiations, bilateral or multilateral, are the oldest technique commonly used in order to settle a dispute by peaceful means. As a matter of fact, the bulk of international differences is settled by negotiations, with thousands of treaties testifying to the importance of this simplest technique of dispute resolution.

Under Art. 33(1) of the United Nations (UN) Charter, the parties to a dispute likely to endanger the maintenance of international peace and security should, first of all, seek solution by negotiation or some other peaceful means of their choice, listed in the Charter. The significance of negotiation as a flexible means of peaceful settlement is emphasized in a variety of resolutions of the UN General Assembly, and the obligation to negotiate in good faith and in a meaningful manner is implied in numerous treaties relating to the pacific resolution of disputes. It is also noted in *obiter dicta* of the International Court of Justice **(309)** in such cases as, *inter alia*, the *North Sea Continental Shelf* (Federal Republic of Germany/Denmark; Federal Republic of Germany/Netherlands) (1969 ICJ Rep. 3); and the advisory opinion **(291)** on the *Legality of the Threat or Use of Nuclear Weapons* (1996 ICJ Rep. 226). However, the obligation to negotiate in good faith does not necessarily entail an obligation to reach agreement, frequently constituting—as noted above—an antecedent to other peaceful methods of settlement. International law does not prescribe clear standards for determining the point in time at which negotiations can no longer lead to agreement, but—as held by the Permanent Court of International Justice **(320)** in the *Mavrommatis Palestine Concessions* (Greece v. Great Britain) (1924 PCIJ, Series A, No. 2)—the subject matter of a dispute should be clearly defined before the dispute can be submitted to adjudication **(306)**.

There is no agreement among international legal scholars on the question whether negotiation should be accorded special emphasis in international law as against the other methods of peaceful settlement. Those who do accord negotiation such priority perceive the advantages of negotiation as a flexible instrument better suited to deal with international disputes and, in general, conducive to compromise and desirable peaceful change **(279)** of the legal *status quo.* Other publicists contend that in contemporary international relations international law transcends the negotiation technique, developing institutionalized methods of settlement with the participation of impartial third parties, and in particular international tribunals, thus avoiding the disadvantages of negotiation which, more than other methods, inserts an element of subjectivity and may lack the moderating influence of third parties. Still, as demonstrated by international practice, negotiation continues to be the most common method in efforts to resolve differences between states in a peaceful way.

**317. Optional Clause.** This is a common term referring to a provision in a treaty **(288)**, normally a statute of the court, governing the jurisdiction of an international court, whereby a state **(127)** party to the treaty may at any time declare that it consents to the compulsory jurisdiction of the court. The optional clause is usually associated with the clause of Art. 36(2) of the Statute of the International Court of Justice (ICJ) **(309)**, but analogous clauses can be found, for example, in the treaties establishing the European Court of Human Rights **(154)**; and the Inter-American Court of Human Rights **(165)**, respectively. The rules of the more recently set up Court of Conciliation **(296)** and Arbitration **(293)** of the Organization for Security and Cooperation in Europe (32 ILM 557 (1993)) also provide for jurisdiction under an optional clause.

In the ICJ, the optional clause of Art. 36(2) of its Statute provides that the parties to the Statute may at any time declare that they recognize as compulsory *ipso facto* and without special agreement, in relation to any other state accepting the same obligation, the jurisdiction of the ICJ in all legal disputes **(299)** concerning: 1. the interpretation **(274)** of a treaty; 2. any question of international law; 3. the existence of a fact which, if established, would constitute a breach of an international obligation; 4. the nature or extent of the reparation **(118)** to be made for the breach of an international obligation. The acceptance of the Court's jurisdiction under the optional clause is effected by depositing a unilateral declaration with the Secretary-General of the United Nations (UN) which is registered **(281)** under Art. 102 of the UN Charter as an international agreement. Declarations made under the Permanent Court of International Justice (PCIJ) **(320)** system, which are still in force, are deemed to be acceptances of the compulsory jurisdiction of the ICJ for the period which they still have to run and in accordance with their terms. There were still six such declarations in 2004.

An optional clause declaration may be made unconditionally or on conditions of reciprocity, or for a certain time period. However, in practice all acceptances of compulsory jurisdiction of the ICJ under the optional clause are governed by the principle of reciprocity which applies to such acceptances either expressly or by implication. Consequently, the Court's jurisdiction is scaled down to the lowest common denominator of the undertaking common in the declarations of the two parties. As a result, each party, normally the respondent, may invoke a reservation to acceptance of compulsory jurisdiction of the ICJ **(323)** which is not stipulated in its own optional clause declaration but is included in the declaration of the other party, normally the applicant state. Hence, the Court's jurisdiction is limited to those categories of dispute which are not excluded by any state party to the proceedings, that is, to the extent that all the declarations coincide. It is important to note that under Art. 36(6) of the ICJ statute, in the event of a dispute as to whether the Court has jurisdiction, the matter is settled by the decision of the Court. Unlike the contentious jurisdiction of the ICJ based on an *ad hoc* special agreement or on a treaty provision, both of which are not limited with regard to the nature of the dispute, the Court's jurisdiction under the optional clause is expressly limited to "legal" disputes. This aspect of the ICJ jurisdiction is related to the theoretical distinction between "justiciable" (legal) and "non-justiciable" (political) disputes **(300)**.

The optional clause is the outcome of a compromise achieved by the drafters of the Statute of the PCIJ between the states advocating and those opposing compulsory jurisdiction. This compromise continues in the Statute of the ICJ. The expectations that a widespread acceptance of the optional clause will eventually lead to a *de facto* compulsory jurisdiction of the Court have not been fulfilled. As a matter of fact, the number of acceptances has diminished in terms relative to the number of states parties. Whereas during the PCIJ period 32 out of 52 signatories of the Statute accepted the optional clause, in 1955 the 32 acceptances represented 50 percent of the 64 states parties, and in 1991 the 53 declarations amounted to less than 30 percent of some 170 states parties. Following the end of the Cold War a number of states, including some former Communist countries, deposited declarations of acceptance, but in 2004 the total number of declarations under Art. 36(2) which had not lapsed or been withdrawn, including six declarations made under the Statute of the PCIJ, amounted to 64, that is, one-third of the UN members. The effectiveness of the optional clause has been further reduced by the states concerned about assuming commitments of uncertain duration, terminable upon notice immediately or in six months. Most importantly, it has been reduced by reservations to acceptance of compulsory jurisdiction **(323)**. While the automatic (self-judging) reservation **(294)** appears to be losing ground, numerous reservations of an amazing variety have reduced the scope of compulsory jurisdiction under the optional clause, especially in view of the reciprocal effects which such reservations have upon the ICJ jurisdiction, as illustrated, for example, in the case of *Certain Norwegian Loans* (France v. Norway) (1957 ICJ Rep. 9).

The denunciation by the United States (US) in 1985 (in force in 1986) of its optional clause declaration after 40 years (24 ILM 1742 (1985)), motivated by US dissatisfaction with the ICJ jurisdictional judgment in the case of *Military and Paramilitary Activities in and against Nicaragua* (Nicaragua v. United States) (1984 ICJ Rep. 392), was a serious blow to the Court's jurisdiction under the optional clause, but did not affect the Court's jurisdiction under numerous bilateral and multilateral treaties.

**318. Peaceful (Pacific) Settlement of International Disputes.** Peaceful or pacific settlement of international disputes **(299)** means resolution of disputes by peaceful means without recourse to the threat or use of force **(329)** and in such a manner that international peace and security are not endangered. As a general rule, international law governs disputes between states but, where appropriate, procedures governing such disputes apply also to disputes of states with international organizations **(84)** and those between such organizations. Exceptionally, disputes between states and private entities may apply some aspects of such procedures to their disputes.

The techniques of peaceful settlement may be either non-adjudicative, that is, by diplomatic methods, when the disputing states themselves agree on the terms of settlement, or adjudicative **(306)**, where a third party resolves the dispute by means of a legally binding decision which must be complied with by the parties. The process of settlement by diplomatic method may take the form either of direct negotiation **(316)** between the parties, without intercession by others, or it may be aided by a friendly third party interceding in resolving the dispute. Such intercession may vary in its involvement from "good offices" **(303)** to mediation **(313)**, and to the more formal technique of conciliation **(296)**. These three procedures, frequently combined with an examination of the facts of the dispute by means of a commission of inquiry **(305)**, cannot frequently be rigidly separated and merge in one process of attempts at a resolution of the dispute with the help of a friendly third party or parties. Both the United Nations (UN) and regional organizations have, on numerous occasions, been engaged in all these political methods of dispute resolution. Settlement of international disputes by international organizations is sometimes classified as a separate category of peaceful resolution. However, it is essential to bear in mind that all these techniques and procedures are only political processes, with no legal obligation of the disputing states to accept any suggested terms of settlement. It is mainly this feature that distinguishes all these methods from the other category of means of peaceful settlement, namely arbitration **(293)** and adjudication in all its forms in the strict sense of the term. In substance, both are judicial in the more inclusive meaning of the term; the award of an arbitration commission or tribunal or whatever its name and judgments of an international court or tribunal are equally binding upon the parties. It should be added that, apart from the case of very exceptional *ad hoc* tribunals and the International Criminal Court **(170)**, which try individuals (never states) for war crimes and crimes against humanity, international judicial bodies are not courts of criminal jurisdiction.

In the historical perspective of international law it was not until the turn of the 19th century that some limited and modest restraints—but not total prohibition—were hesitantly introduced upon resort to force as a means of resolving international disputes. The two Hague Peace Conferences of 1899 and 1907 were the first significant diplomatic efforts in this regard. The Convention for the Pacific Settlement of International Disputes of 1899 (187 CTS 410), revised in 1907 (205 CTS 277), and still in force, codified and developed various techniques for settling disputes, including arbitration within the framework of the Permanent Court of Arbitration **(319)**. The provisions of the Hague Convention were supplemented by numerous treaties **(288)** referring the parties to various methods of peaceful settlement, including conciliation, initiated by the "Bryan Treaties" in 1914.

The League of Nations Covenant, 1919, provided for a variety of procedures for peaceful settlement. Although the League could not prevent World War II, the UN Charter rules on the pacific settlement of disputes and the UN practices in this respect were based on and further developed in the light of the experience of the League of Nations. The creation by the League of Nations of the first permanent global international tribunal, the Permanent Court of International Justice **(320)** was a turning point in the history of international law. In 1928 the League's Assembly adopted the General Act for the Pacific Settlement of International Disputes **(302)**, an instrument that survived the League and was even revised in 1949, but is in force for only a few states and its validity has been questioned in today's world. More important was the adoption in 1928 of the General Treaty for the Renunciation of War (Pact of Paris or Kellogg-Briand Pact) **(330)** which, apart from banning resort to war, re-emphasized the duty to settle international disputes by peaceful means.

The contemporary position of international law in the matter of peaceful settlement of international disputes is predicated on the UN Charter. Under Art. 1(1), bringing about by peaceful means, and in conformity with the principles of justice and international law, adjustment or settlement of international disputes or situations which might lead to a breach of peace, is one of the major purposes of the UN. The duty of the member states to settle their disputes by peaceful means (Art. 2(3)) is one of the seven principles of the Organization, a principle that has become part of general (customary) international law **(39)**, and has been re-affirmed in various instruments, for example, in the UN General Assembly (GA) Friendly Relations Declaration of 1970 **(14)**. It is understood that this principle implies a positive obligation of disputing states to strive actively for a peaceful resolution of disputes by means of their choice. Chapter VI (Arts. 33–38) of the UN Charter sets forth the basic rules governing the role of the Organization, and especially of its Security Council (SC), in this area. Art. 33(1) lists negotiation, inquiry, mediation, conciliation, arbitration, judicial settlement as well as resort to regional agreements or arrangements, or other peaceful means as methods through which parties to a dispute, the continuance of which is likely to endanger the maintenance of international peace and security, should seek solution to the dispute. Under Art. 36(3) of the UN Charter, legal disputes should as a general rule be referred by the parties to the International Court of Justice (ICJ) **(309)**, which, however, is handicapped by lack of compulsory jurisdiction.

Apart from the ICJ, three other "principal organs" of the UN deal with peaceful resolution of disputes: the SC, the GA, and the Secretariat, through its head, the Secretary-General. For political reasons, the relatively clear division of power, envisaged by the Charter, in particular between the SC as an executive organ and the GA as a general forum for discussing any question, has not been maintained in practice, and both organs have dealt with international disputes, recommending solutions, although only the SC can adopt binding decisions in a dispute determined under Chapter VII of the Charter to be a threat or breach of peace, or an act of aggression **(325)**.

Chapter VII of the UN Charter governs the functions of the SC in the settlement of any disputes or "situations" which might lead to international friction or give rise to a dispute. However, the distinction between disputes and situations has been blurred in the practice of the SC. By a procedural vote (that is, one not subject to the veto), the Council decides whether or not to place a dispute or a situation on its agenda or to remove the dispute from it, but, if the parties fail to settle a dispute likely to endanger international peace and security, they are obligated to refer it to the SC (Art. 37). Under Art. 35, at any stage of such a dispute or situation, the SC may recommend appropriate procedures and make recommendations which, however, do not create a legal obligation. The GA may also discuss any question, including disputes brought by a party, and can make legally not binding recommendations (Arts. 10, 11, 14, 35), but no such recommendation may be made with regard to a dispute or situation which is being dealt with by the SC unless the SC so requests (Art. 12).

The Secretary-General has played a significant role in the settlement of numerous international disputes by his good offices and mediation either on his own initiative under Art. 99 of the UN Charter, which gives him the right to bring to the attention of the SC any matter which in his opinion may threaten the maintenance of international peace and security, or at the request of the SC, or the GA, or the parties themselves, or the regional organization concerned. In his Report on an *Agenda for Peace-Preventive Diplomacy, Peacemaking and Peace-Keeping* of 1992 (31 ILM 953 (1992)) the Secretary-General outlined the various courses of action and mechanisms that UN organs, irrespective of their formal competence, could use within the general context of settling or adjusting international disputes, decreasing tensions, and preventing armed conflict between states. The *Agenda* conceptualized all these actions and mechanisms into five categories: 1. preventive diplomacy, which includes such methods as good offices, inquiry ("fact-finding"), and confidence-building measures, all designed to ease tensions before they might result in conflict; 2. peacemaking, involving the peaceful means of settling disputes, but primarily negotiation and mediation; 3. peacekeeping **(334)**; 4. peace-building, involving building up support structures that will assist peace; and 5. peace enforcement irrespective of the parties' consent, based on the enforcement provisions of the collective security system **(327)** of the UN Charter.

Various regional organizations **(84)** have been active in pursuing non-adjudicative methods of peaceful settlement, either on their own or jointly with appropriate UN organs. It is a duty of states establishing such organizations to make every effort to achieve pacific settlement of local disputes through such arrangements or by such regional agencies before referring them to the SC which is obliged to encourage the development of such activities if consistent with the purposes and principles of the UN and without prejudice to the competence of the SC to deal with the disputes (Art. 52). Regional organizations have developed all sorts of mechanisms and procedures for settling disputes within their respective areas. Thus the European Convention for the Peaceful Settlement of Disputes of 1957 (320 UNTS 243), adopted under the auspices of the Council of Europe, provides for submitting legal disputes to the ICJ, and other disputes to conciliation or arbitration. In addition, various mechanisms for preventing and settling disputes exist within the Organization for Security and Cooperation in Europe (OSCE), and, in particular, its Convention on Conciliation and Arbitration of 1992 (32 ILM 557 (1993)), with a Court of Conciliation and Arbitration in Geneva. Within its framework, *ad hoc* conciliation commissions and arbitral tribunals decide disputes between parties to the Convention and between parties and non-parties. The OSCE has also been involved in various preventive diplomacy missions in the aftermath of the disintegration of Yugoslavia **(134)** and the Soviet Union **(133)**, including the supervision of elections in Bosnia and Herzegovina under the Dayton General Framework Agreement for Peace of 1995 (35 ILM 75, 170 (1996)). In the Western Hemisphere, the American Treaty for the Pacific Settlement of 1948 (the "Pact of Bogotá") (30 UNTS 55) sets forth all the traditional methods of peaceful settlement as mandated under Art. 23 of the Charter of the Organization of American States (OAS) of 1948 (119 UNTS 3) as amended in 1985, but in actual practice, the Council of the OAS and its appropriate mechanisms have played the major role in the settlement of disputes in the region. In Africa, the African Union, replacing in 2001 the Organization of African Unity established in 1963, created a Peace and Security Council as an organ with competence in prevention and resolution of disputes, supported by a number of subsidiary organs in its task of restoring security and stability in large portions of the continent. There are also subregional organizations involved, *inter alia*, in conflict resolution, of which the Economic Community of West African States is the best known for its peacekeeping and peacemaking missions in a series of conflicts in its region. In another African subregion, the Southern African Development Community has also developed elaborate structures for dispute resolution and even military enforcement measures authorized by the UN SC. Peaceful resolution procedures, including conciliation and arbitration are also envisaged within the framework of the Association of South East Asian Nations.

A variety of procedures for peaceful settlement of disputes exists in specialized agencies of the UN. For example, disputes within the World Trade Organization (WTO) are regulated by the elaborate Understanding on Rules and Procedures Governing the Settlement of Disputes (33 ILM 1226 (1994), constituting Annex 2 of the Marrakesh Agreement Establishing the WTO in 1994 (33 ILM 1125 (1994) and supplemented in 1997 by Rules of Conduct for this Understanding (36 ILM 477 (1997).

Of particular interest is the innovative system of dispute settlement under the UN Convention on the Law of the Sea of 1982 (LOS Convention) **(264),** set forth in great detail in Part XV (Arts. 279–299) of the Convention and in Annexes V-VIII. This system provides for flexible but, in most cases, compulsory procedures entailing binding decisions in cases where the parties fail to settle their dispute by a freely chosen peaceful means, including, *inter alia*, conciliation or submission of the dispute to a regional court, for example the European Court of Justice **(298)** in the case of the members of the European Union. Under Art. 287 of the LOS Convention the parties have the right, first, to settle any dispute by peaceful means of their choosing. If no agreement is reached, their dispute is submitted to one or more of the four means for the settlement of disputes which a state party chooses by means of a written declaration, when signing **(283)**, ratifying **(280)**, or acceding **(267)** to the LOS Convention, or at any time thereafter. These four methods are: 1. the International Tribunal for the Law of the Sea **(310)**; 2. ICJ; 3. an arbitral tribunal constituted in accordance with Annex VII **(292)** of the LOS Convention; and 4. a special tribunal constituted in accordance with Annex VIII **(324)**. If the chosen procedures differ, the dispute may be submitted only to arbitration under Annex VIII, unless the parties otherwise agree. However, there are certain exceptions from the obligation to submit disputes to one of the four mechanisms. Under Art. 297, only certain types of dispute with regard to the exercise by a coastal state of its sovereign rights **(125)** or jurisdiction **(87)**, as specified in detail in the Convention, are subject to compulsory settlement procedure. The same applies to certain disputes concerning marine scientific research and fisheries. In addition, there are certain optional exceptions which allow states to exempt certain types of sensitive disputes: maritime boundary delimitations, disputes involving historic bays **(234)** or titles, disputes concerning military or law enforcement activities, and disputes in respect of which the SC of the UN exercises its functions.

**319. Permanent Court of Arbitration.** This is a panel of international jurists, established at The Hague under the 1899 Convention for the Pacific Settlement of International Disputes (187 CTS 410), revised in 1907 (205 CTS 277), from which parties (states, international organizations, and even private legal persons, and individuals) can select arbitrators **(293)** for an *ad hoc* tribunal to adjudicate a dispute. The name "Permanent Court of Arbitration" (PCA) is somewhat misleading since, apart from a small permanent International Bureau with a Secretary-General, and a Permanent Administrative Council, the Hague Convention did not create a real court but merely a machinery for setting up arbitral tribunals when the need should arise. Each state party to the Convention nominates up to four "members of the PCA" potentially to serve as arbitrators for a renewable term of six years. States which agree to arbitration within the framework of the PCA, but cannot agree on the composition of the tribunal, follow further selection procedures stipulated in the Convention. In practice, the tribunals set up under the auspices of the PCA consist either of a sole arbitrator as, for example, in the celebrated *Island of Palmas* Arbitration between the United States (US) and the Netherlands in 1928 (2 RIAA 829); or of five members, as in the *North Atlantic Coast Fisheries* Arbitration between the US and Great Britain in 1910 (11 RIAA 173) and, recently, in the two-stage arbitration between Eritrea and Yemen in 1998:1. *Territorial Sovereignty and Scope of Dispute* (40 ILM 900 (2001)) and 2. *Maritime Delimitation* (40 ILM 983 (2001)). Under the PCA system, a five-member tribunal is suggested: each party appoints two arbitrators from the PCA panel (but each party may not choose more than one of its nationals), and the four select an umpire. If they cannot agree on the selection of the umpire, the selection is made by third parties, and for cases where even then no agreement is reached, the Convention provides for further complex selection procedures which ultimately may end in drawing lots to determine the person of the umpire. In practice, a three-member tribunal has been quite common. Awards are handed down on the basis of respect for law, but they can also be based on equity **(13)**.

Unless otherwise provided for in the parties' agreement (*compromis*), the provisions on arbitration procedure of the Hague Convention become operative, but more recently, in 1992, the PCA adopted Optional Rules for Arbitrating Disputes between Two States (32 ILM 572 (1993)), largely based on the rules of the United Nations Commission on International Trade Law used also in international commercial arbitration **(308)**. The PCA has also drafted optional rules for disputes between two parties of which only one is a state; disputes between international organizations **(84)** and states; and—an innovation—Optional Rules for Arbitration of Disputes Relating to Natural Resources and/or the Environment, 2001 (41 ILM 202 (2002)).

The PCA mechanism has proved useful in some very important cases in the first decades of the 20th century, but on the whole states were reluctant to agree in advance even to the relatively flexible PCA system. Altogether, 14 disputes used the PCA facilities before World War I and fewer in the inter-war period. A few cases were arbitrated under the PCA auspices in the early decades following World War II, but in general states did not make much use of the PCA mechanism. In recent years, however, there has been a revival of interest in the PCA and regional facilities of the Court have been established in South Africa and Costa Rica. In early 2004, 101 states were parties to the 1899 or 1907 Convention. It should be noted that parties in both inter-state disputes and disputes in which only one party is a state (or an international organization) have agreed to ask the PCA to serve as registry and provide other services. Interstate arbitrations included, in addition to the already noted two-stage arbitration between Eritrea and Yemen, the decision of the Eritrea-Ethiopia Boundary Commission of 2002 (41 ILM 1057 (2002)); the final award in the *Dispute Concerning Access to Information under Article 9 of the OSPAR Convention* (Ireland v. United Kingdom), 2003 (42 ILM 1118 (2003)), related to the *Mox Plant* case before the International Tribunal for the Law of the Sea **(310)** and involving access to information on pollution danger from the MOX (mixed oxide) plant in the Sellafield complex in the United Kingdom under the 1992 Convention for the Protection of the Marine Environment of the North-East Atlantic (the "OSPAR [Oslo-Paris] Convention) (32 ILM 1069 (1993)); two partial awards on *Prisoners of War* of the Eritrea-Ethiopia Claims Commission, 2003 (42 ILM 1056, 1083 (2003)); the award in the case of *Bank for International Settlements* over claims for compensation for shares formerly owned by the private claimants in the case; and the unusual case of *Larsen/Hawaiian Kingdom*, 2001, apparently intended by the claimants to highlight the 100th anniversary of the overthrow of the Hawaiian Kingdom. The arbitral tribunal ruled the case inadmissible by reason of the fact that the US was not a party and had not consented to the suit. In mid 2004 there were six cases pending in arbitrations in which the PCA served as the registry and offered other facilities: the continuing cases of the Eritrea-Ethiopia Boundary and Eritrea-Ethiopia Claims Commissions; the *Mox Plant* case (Ireland v. United Kingdom); the Belgium/Netherlands dispute concerning the so-called *Iron Rhine Railway Line;* the Netherlands/France dispute involving the application of the 1976 *Convention on the Protection of the Rhine against Pollution by Chlorides* (16 ILM 265 (1977)), with the *Additional Protocol of 1991*; and the case of the *Saluka Investments B.V.* v. *Czech Republic*, involving an arbitration between a Netherlands corporation and the Czech Republic.

The establishment of the PCA at the turn of the 19th century inspired plans and proposals for the creation of a permanent international tribunal which, in the course of time, culminated in the creation of the Permanent Court of International Justice **(320)**, succeeded in fact by the International Court of Justice (ICJ) **(309)**. As a matter of fact, the members of the ICJ are elected from a list of persons nominated by the "national groups" in the PCA (ICJ Statute Art. 5).

**320. Permanent Court of International Justice.** The predecessor of the International Court of Justice (ICJ) **(309)**, and the first permanently constituted global international tribunal, of general, albeit no compulsory, jurisdiction, the Permanent Court of International Justice (PCIJ) was established pursuant to Art. 14 of the Covenant of the League of Nations to settle disputes **(299)** between states **(127)** and give advisory opinions **(291)** on any dispute or question referred to it by the Council or the Assembly of the League.

Pursuant to Art. 14 of the Covenant, an Advisory Commission of Jurists drafted a Statute for the PCIJ which, following minor modifications, was approved by the League's Council and its Assembly in the Protocol of Signature **(283)** in 1920. The Statute, which in legal terms was a treaty **(288)** separate from the Covenant, entered into force in 1921, and the first session of the Court was held at its headquarters at The Hague in 1922. A Protocol of 1929, effective in 1936, revised the statute, the major amendments **(269)** dealing with inclusion of an article on advisory opinions. The PCIJ also adopted its Rules of Procedure. At one time, as many as 50 states were parties to the Statute, but the number declined as 13 states withdrew from it. Although the United States (US) signed the Protocols of 1920 and 1929, it never acceded **(267)** to the PCIJ Statute because of the Senate's refusal to ratify **(280)** them. The Soviet Union never joined the Statute.

In the years 1922 through 1940 the PCIJ delivered 32 judgments (including some non-merit judgments), the first being the judgment permitting intervention **(311)** by Poland in the *Wimbledon* case in 1923 (1923 PCIJ, Series A, No. 1) (Great Britain, France, Italy, and Japan v. Germany) which involved the freedom of navigation through the Kiel Canal **(252)**. The PCIJ ordered seven cases to be removed from the Court's List. The Court also gave 26 advisory opinions, perhaps the best known being the opinion on the *Customs Régime between Germany and Austria* (1931 PCIJ, Series A/B, No. 41, p. 37). Opinion was refused in the *Status of Eastern Carelia* case (1923 PCIJ, Series B, No. 5). The PCIJ issued some 200 "orders." Most (18) of the advisory opinions and 11 judgments dealt with disputes relating to the Versailles Peace Treaty with Germany, 1919, (225 CTS 188) and other post–World War I settlements. The activities of the PCIJ were interrupted in World War II by the German invasion of the Netherlands in May 1940. Following the war, the PCIJ was dissolved by the last meeting of the League of Nations Assembly in 1946. The functions of the Court were taken over by the ICJ which, while not being its legal successor, has in fact continued the activities of the PCIJ on the basis of the rules which are a virtual duplication of the Statute of the PCIJ. However, the PCIJ differed from the present Court in one major respect, namely, whereas the ICJ is one of the six "principal organs" of the United Nations (UN) and its Statute is an integral part of the UN Charter, the PCIJ, though commonly regarded as a League of Nations tribunal, was not an organ of the League, and only those states that ratified the Protocol of Signature of 1920 were bound by the Statute.

Subject to a few minor differences, the composition, structure, jurisdiction, and procedure of the PCIJ as well as the law to be applied and other rules, are closely copied by the ICJ and require no elaboration. It is essential to emphasize that, like its successor, the PCIJ did not have compulsory jurisdiction. What was needed in each case of contentious jurisdiction **(297)** was the parties' consent expressed either by an *ad hoc* special agreement of the parties or a clause in an existing valid treaty referring to the jurisdiction of the Court, or through the optional clause **(317)**.

Even though, unlike a national court, the PCIJ had no compulsory jurisdiction, its creation was a turning point in the history of international tribunals and international law institutions in general. Unlike the arbitral tribunals, whose experience otherwise contributed to its foundation, the PCIJ was a permanently constituted, global, judicial body with full-time, salaried judges, a registrar, largely public proceedings, and published records of pleadings, and other documentary evidence. The PCIJ developed judicial procedures, techniques, and practices which eventually provided a blueprint for the ICJ. At the same time, the first "World Court"—as the PCIJ and the ICJ are popularly called—made a positive contribution to the interpretation and development of substantive rules of international law, and through its cases built up a judicial tradition which continues in the work of its successor, the ICJ.

**321. Preliminary Objection.** This is an objection raised in the practice of international tribunals by a party to a dispute **(299)**, as a rule the respondent state **(127)**, whereby that party, in order to prevent the court from dealing with the merits of the case, requests the court to examine first and render a decision on a certain preliminary question or questions, distinct from the merits of the claim. In the Permanent Court of International Justice (PCIJ) **(320)** and the International Court of Justice (ICJ) **(309)** many preliminary objections have been resorted to—mainly in cases brought before the Court by application—since the PCIJ case of *Readaptation of the Mavrommatic Jerusalem Concessions* in 1927 (Greece v. Great Britain) (1927 PCIJ Series A, No. 11). Preliminary objections are also possible, *inter alia*, in the European Court of Justice **(298)** and the European Court of Human Rights **(154)**.

In the ICJ (Rules Art. 79(1)), preliminary objections, which are one category of "incidental proceedings," can be raised: 1. to the jurisdiction **(297)** of the Court; 2. to the admissibility of the application; or 3. in other matters. Objections to jurisdiction may be based on the respondent state's contention that the treaty conferring jurisdiction on the ICJ or the optional clause **(317)** declaration is no longer in force or is null and void, for example, in the case of *Preah Vihear* (Cambodia v. Thailand) (1961 ICJ Rep. 17); or that a reservation to acceptance of compulsory jurisdiction of the ICJ excludes the dispute in question, for example, in the case of *Certain Norwegian Loans* (France v. Norway) (1957 ICJ Rep. 17). Preliminary objections relating to the admissibility of an application include cases where the respondent state, without necessarily contesting the title to the Court's jurisdiction as such, alleges, in claims of the applicant state on behalf of its nationals **(95)**, lack of link of nationality **(175)** between the injured person and the applicant state, as in the case of *Nottebohm* (Liechtenstein v. Guatemala) (1953 ICJ Rep. 111), or claims of non-exhaustion of local remedies **(74)**, as in the case of *Interhandel* (Switzerland v. United States) (1959 ICJ Rep. 6). The third category ("other objections") may be based, for example, on the allegation that there exists no dispute between the parties because of the absence of negotiations **(316)**, as was the case in *Northern Cameroons* (Cameroon v. United Kingdom) (1963 ICJ Rep. 15). Normally, a preliminary objection is raised by the respondent state in cases of application by the applicant state, but a party other than the respondent state may also file an objection, as happened once in the history of the ICJ, namely, in the case of *Monetary Gold Removed from Rome in 1943* (Italy v. France, United Kingdom and United States) (1954 ICJ Rep.19).

Preliminary objections have been frequently raised before both the PCIJ and the ICJ. In the former Court, they were rejected in eight cases. In the latter, preliminary objections of respondent states contesting the Court's jurisdiction and, in some cases, admissibility of the application, have been a prominent feature of the proceedings before the ICJ; they have occurred some 40 times, but were rejected in most cases, including the United States (US) preliminary objections in the *Case Concerning Oil Platforms* (Iran v. United States) rejected in the Court's judgment in 1996. Incidentally, by its judgment (merits) in 2003 (42 ILM 1333 (2003)), the ICJ ruled that the retaliatory US Navy attacks against Iranian oil platforms in the Persian Gulf during the Iran-Iraq War in 1987 and 1988 did not violate the US-Iran Treaty of Amity, Economic Relations and Consular Rights of 1955 (284 UNTS 93) since, though constituting an unlawful use of force **(329)**, they did not adversely affect freedom of commerce in the relations between the parties

In cases where the respondent state, without formally filing a preliminary objection, simply failed to appear before the Court but informally apprised it of its objections, the ICJ would, on its own initiative, suspend the proceedings on the merits and would order consideration of the jurisdictional issue at large. The issues raised in preliminary objections are dealt with in a distinct phase of the proceedings, terminating in the Court's decision in the form of a judgment. The Court may either uphold an objection, thus dismissing the case, or reject it, or may rule that an objection does not possess, in the circumstances of the case, an exclusively preliminary character. In the last two mentioned situations the Court fixes the time limits for further proceedings. The relevant provisions of the Rules of Court (Art. 79) were recently amended with a view to expediting the procedure governing the filing of preliminary objections. While preliminary objections may be criticized as a device unduly hampering the jurisdiction of the ICJ, the Court must ensure that the preliminary objections procedure provides a safeguard for the principle of voluntary submission of disputes in the system of the contentious jurisdiction of the ICJ.

**322. Provisional Measures.** These are *interim* measures which, in urgent cases, an international tribunal may order in contentious proceedings **(297)** in order to preserve the respective rights of either party pending the tribunal's final decision, and to prevent any aggravation or extension of the dispute **(299)** or causing irreparable prejudice to such rights. Provisional measures, also known as *interim* measures of protection, are roughly equivalent to an *interim* injunction that a domestic court may issue pending the final determination of the case. Within the context of international tribunals **(306)**, provisional measures were already possible in the short-lived (1908–1918) Central American Court of Justice. Today, they are provided for in the respective constituent instruments of a number of international courts, such as, in addition to the International Court of Justice (ICJ) **(309)**, the European Court of Justice **(298)**, the European Court of Human Rights **(154)**, and the Inter-American Court of Human Rights **(165)**, and some lesser known international judicial, including arbitral, bodies. Moreover, international tribunals are believed to possess the power to grant provisional measures even in the absence of an express provision in the statute granting such power to the tribunal concerned. But the ICJ would not indicate any measures if the chances of the requesting state to win the case on the merits were slim.

Exactly what the legal effects of the Court's orders on provisional measures are is rather controversial, as analyzed by the ICJ in the below-discussed *LaGrand* case (Germany v. United States) (40 ILM 1069 (2001)). Following the rule on the interpretation of treaties found in Art. 33(4) of the Vienna Convention on the Law of Treaties **(288)** (1155 UNTS 331), the ICJ concluded that provisional measures were legally binding. Under Art. 41 of its Statute, the ICJ has the power to indicate, if it considers that the circumstances so require, any provisional measures which ought to be taken to preserve the respective rights of either party. If a case is brought to the Court by a special agreement, both parties may request provisional measures, as it happened in 1986 in the case of the *Frontier Dispute* (Burkina Faso/Mali) (1986 ICJ Rep. 554). Provisional measures are normally requested by the applicant state, but the Court may indicate, or rather order, them (Court Rules Art. 75) *ex officio* on its initiative. This has recently happened for the first time in two cases against the United States (US). First, in the above-noted *LaGrand* case involving the—otherwise US-admitted—charges by Germany that the US had not notified the LaGrand brothers awaiting execution in an Arizona prison of their right under the Vienna Convention on Consular Relations of 1962 (596 UNTS 261) **(56)** to contact German consular officials **(57)**, the ICJ issued a provisional measures order calling on the US to take "all measures at its disposal" to prevent the execution, and after the US failed to comply (the LaGrand brothers had been executed) the Court held that the US had breached the legally binding order of the Court. In the next case, *Avena and Other Mexican Nationals* (Mexico v. United States), in 2003, the ICJ ordered, at Mexico's request, provisional measures to the effect that the US "shall take all measures necessary" to ensure that the three Mexican nationals concerned are not executed pending final judgment (42 ILM 309 (2003)) which was handed down in April 2004.

A request for the indication of provisional measures has priority over all other issues before the ICJ. It constitutes a discrete phase of the case, leading, in general, to a decision within three weeks which is handed down in the form of an order read by the President of the Court at a public sitting. The urgent nature of *interim* measures of protection frequently conflicts with the principle that the Court's jurisdiction must be based on the parties' consent. In this respect, the ICJ has followed what is known as the "possibility test," as in the case of the *Military and Paramilitary Activities in and against Nicaragua* (Nicaragua v. United States) (1984 ICJ Rep. 392). In particular, if warranted by the circumstances, the Court indicates provisional measures as soon as it has been ascertained that an instrument or instruments submitted by the party concerned appears to provide a *prima facie* basis for the Court's jurisdiction (known as the "Lauterpacht test," after the name of Judge Elihu Lauterpacht). However, the order indicating provisional measures in no way prejudges the question of the Court's jurisdiction on the merits and leaves unaffected the parties' right to submit arguments in respect of such jurisdiction. *Interim* measures can also be indicated in cases of non-appearance of a party. Since frequently the question of provisional measures has political implications, for example in the parallel (now discontinued) cases of *Questions of Interpretation* **(274)** *and Application of the 1971 Montreal Convention* **(210)** *Arising from the Aerial Incident at Lockerbie* (United Kingdom v. Libya; United States v. Libya) (1998 ICJ Rep. 115) (37 ILM 587 (1998)), the Court must give notice of the measures indicated and the related decisions not only to the parties but also to the United Nations (UN) Secretary-General for transmission to the Security Council (SC).

The ICJ has received requests for provisional measures in some 35 cases (including parallel proceedings). It indicated such measures in less than half of these cases and—as noted above—ordered them *ex officio* in two cases, *LaGrand* and *Avena*. Among the other recent orders of the ICJ indicating provisional measures are: *Application of the Genocide Convention* **(155)** (Bosnia and Herzegovina v. Serbia and Montenegro) in 1993; and (by a unanimous decision) *Armed Activities on the Territory of the Congo* (Democratic Republic of the Congo v. Uganda) in 2000. Among the more recent requests rejected by the Court were orders in: the two parallel—now discontinued—*Lockerbie* cases (UK and US v. Libya); the above-noted *Genocide* case (the Court denying Bosnia and Herzegovina additional measures, 1993); the parallel cases, *Legality of Use of Force*, of Serbia and Montenegro against 10 North Atlantic Treaty Organization countries in 1999; the *Arrest Warrant of 11 April 2000* (Congo v. Belgium), 2000; and *Armed Activities on the Territory of the Congo* (*New Application*) (Congo v. Rwanda) in 2002.

In its Art. 41, the ICJ Statute uses the rather ambiguous term "indicate" rather than "order" provisional measures. Hence, it is not entirely clear whether the Court's orders "indicating" such measures are legally binding upon the parties. The General Act for the Pacific Settlement of International Disputes of 1928 **(302)** expressly stipulated their binding legal force. This position is supported by a general rule of international law enjoining the parties to a pending case to abstain from any act that would nullify the result of the tribunal's final judgment. However, this is not a generally held view.

In practice many respondent states, claiming that the ICJ lacked jurisdiction in the case, refused to comply with the court's provisional measures order. As noted above, in the recent *LaGrand* case the ICJ ruled that its provisional measures order was legally binding and that the US failed to comply with it. Similarly in the above-mentioned *Avena* case, the Court ordered that the US "shall" take all the necessary measures to ensure that the three Mexican nationals are not executed pending final judgment. Whether the SC has the authority to enforce such orders like judgments under Art. 94 of the UN Charter, is not clear. Nor was it settled in the *Anglo-Iranian Oil Co.* case (United Kingdom v. Iran) (1952 ICJ Rep. 93) when the issue was brought before the SC.

**323. Reservation to Acceptance of Compulsory Jurisdiction of the International Court of Justice.** This is a reservation which a state **(127)**, accepting the compulsory jurisdiction of the International Court of Justice (ICJ) **(309)** under the optional clause **(317)** of Art. 36(2) of the ICJ Statute, attaches to its declaration of acceptance, and which excludes a specific category or specific categories of dispute **(299)** from the Court's jurisdiction **(297)**. Historically, states have always been wary of submitting themselves to arbitration **(293)** or judicial settlement **(306)** in an all-inclusive fashion. Thus, for example, under the rules of the Permanent Court of Arbitration **(319)**, vital interests, honor, independence, or interests of other states were allowed to be excluded from the jurisdiction of an arbitral tribunal. Eventually, other types of reservation were added by states to rosters of such reservations. As far as the Permanent Court of International Justice (PCIJ) **(320)** is concerned, the Netherlands started the trend when in 1921 it excluded from the scope of its acceptance of the optional clause disputes which it had agreed to settle by other means of pacific settlement. On the whole, however, compared with the ICJ, there were not many reservations under the régime of the PCIJ. Among the reservations, the so-called domestic jurisdiction **(9)** reservation derived from Art. 15(8) of the Covenant of the League of Nations, which excluded disputes falling exclusively within the domestic jurisdiction of the accepting country, became quite frequent, primarily because of the automatic (self-judging) reservation **(294)** attached to it by the United States (US) in its acceptance of the optional clause in 1946.

The ICJ Statute (Art. 36(3)) allows two kinds of reservation: reservations relating to reciprocity and those relating to time. The former may be made on condition of reciprocity on the part of several or certain states, which means that until some other states have accepted the optional clause, the state making the reservation cannot be a respondent in any proceedings before the Court. Whereas no state has ever made a reservation of reciprocity in the meaning of Art. 36(3), a number of states have attached reservations relating to time, limiting the life of their respective declarations to a specific period, usually 5 or 10 years, with a possibility of tacit renewal. Many declarations reserve the right to be terminated by a simple notice taking effect after the lapse of a specific period of time or—quite frequently—immediately. Even if no termination notice was included in the acceptance of the optional clause, such acceptance may be withdrawn on reasonable notice, as ruled by the ICJ in the case of *Military and Paramilitary Activities in and against Nicaragua* (Nicaragua v. United States) (1984 ICJ Rep. 392). However, expiry of the declaration of one of the parties after the Court has been seised of a case does not deprive the Court of jurisdiction. Nor is the ICJ jurisdiction over a pending case affected by the withdrawal of acceptance by the state against which the proceedings are taking place.

Apart from the categories of reservations explicitly allowed by the ICJ Statute, a large variety of other reservations has been made by most states which accepted the optional clause, the number of reservations in a case reaching 11. These reservations have been recognized as valid by the ICJ, subject to the condition that they should not conflict with the Statute, as it appears to be the case of the automatic (self-judging) reservation. The most common is the reservation which excludes disputes which the parties are committed to submit to other means of peaceful settlement. Another fairly common reservation concerns disputes relating to matters which are "exclusively" or "essentially" within the domestic jurisdiction of the declaring state, as determined by international law (in a majority of the declarations) or—in case of an automatic (self-judging) reservation—as determined by the state depositing the declaration (Liberia, Malawi, Mexico, Philippines, and Sudan). Other reservations concern disputes: arising prior to a specific date; relating to situations originating in an armed conflict **(339)** or a collective security **(327)** or similar conflict situations for the specific purpose of which the other party appears to have made its declaration of acceptance of the optional clause; relating to certain aspects of the law of the sea **(254)**; between members of the British Commonwealth; and other exclusions, such as the so-called Vanderberg Amendment, which requires that all the treaty parties affected by a decision of the ICJ also be parties before the Court. This reservation was invoked by the United States (US) in the jurisdictional phase of the above-noted case of the *Military and Paramilitary Activities*. A US reservation concerning exclusion of Central American disputes was another legal basis unsuccessfully invoked by the US to contest the Court's jurisdiction in the same case.

The reservations to acceptance of the compulsory jurisdiction of the ICJ have considerably diminished the scope of the Court's contentious jurisdiction. In addition, their adverse effect is augmented by the condition of reciprocity which applies to all optional clause declarations and has the potential of reducing the Court's jurisdiction to the minimum common denominator of the acceptances in question. A reservation made by any party to a dispute may be invoked against it by the other party or parties which, by invoking the applicant state's reservation, can deprive the ICJ of jurisdiction, as happened in 1957 in the case of *Certain Norwegian Loans* (France v. Norway) (1957 ICJ Rep. 9). Similarly, the US had to withdraw its suit against Bulgaria in the case of *Aerial Incident of 27 July 1955* (United States v. Bulgaria), after Bulgaria, taking advantage of the principle of reciprocity, had invoked the US automatic (self-judging) reservation of domestic jurisdiction, even though the shooting down of a foreign (Israeli) airliner carrying US nationals could not in good faith be considered a matter of domestic jurisdiction.

**324. Special Arbitral Tribunals under Annex VIII of the Convention on the Law of the Sea of 1982.** These are arbitral tribunals in one of the four categories of compulsory procedures entailing binding decisions in disputes **(299)** over the application or interpretation **(274)** of the United Nations (UN) Convention on the Law of the Sea of 1982 (LOS Convention) **(264)**, the other three options available to the parties which have not reached settlement by means of their own choosing being: the International Tribunal for the Law of the Sea (ITLOS) **(310)**; the International Court of Justice **(309)**; and Arbitral Tribunals under Annex VII of the LOS Convention **(292)**. The tribunals in question are called "special" because under Annex VIII they can deal only with disputes concerning fisheries **(239)**; environmental protection **(255)**; marine scientific research; and navigation, including vessel-source pollution and pollution by dumping. As in the case of the other three categories, the choice to select the arbitral procedure under Annex VIII is made by means of a revocable written declaration deposited with the UN. Like the arbitral tribunals under Annex VII, special arbitral tribunals under Annex VIII are limited to states **(127)** and international organizations **(84)** as parties. A special tribunal for a specific case is composed of five members, with each party appointing two (but only one in each group may be a national of the party concerned), and a president, a national of a third state appointed by the parties. Failing agreement, the president is appointed by the UN Secretary-General, unless the parties agree upon some other individual. Arbitrators are selected preferably from four lists of experts drawn up and maintained, in each of the above-listed special fields of the law of the sea, respectively by the Food and Agricultural Organization (for fisheries), United Nations Environment Program; Inter-Governmental Oceanographic Commission (for research); and International Maritime Organization (for navigation including pollution from vessels and dumping). Like the other three categories of procedures entailing binding decisions, the special arbitral tribunals under Annex VIII apply international law or, with the parties' consent may decide *ex aequo et bono* **(13)**. Unless otherwise agreed by the parties, the award is final. The "compulsory" nature of special arbitral tribunals is subject to the same exclusions and optional exceptions under Arts. 297 and 298 of the LOS Convention as those applying to the ITLOS and the other compulsory procedures. By agreement of the parties a special arbitral tribunal under Annex VIII may also be used by them as a commission of inquiry **(305)**. Its findings become conclusive for the parties who then may agree to settle their dispute by any peaceful means **(318)** of their own choosing.

# Chapter VIII
# The Use of Force

**325. Aggression.** There exists no authoritative and legally binding definition of aggression, and what constitutes aggression is one of the most controversial issues in international law, debated since 1952 in the General Assembly (GA) of the United Nations (UN) for decades. At the San Francisco Conference on International Organization **(84)**, which founded the UN, the United States (US) successfully resisted attempts to elaborate a definition of aggression, mainly on the grounds that such a definition could never be comprehensive enough to encompass all cases of aggression or take into account the various circumstances of particular cases. In this regard, in 1950 President Harry S. Truman noted in his report to Congress that any definition of aggression would be "a trap for the innocent and an invitation to the guilty."

Two approaches to the definition of aggression emerged at the UN debate: an enumerative approach listing all acts constituting aggression and a general definition approach of one comprehensive formula. Following six years of work by the Special GA Committee on the Question of Defining Aggression, preceded by years of study by other GA committees, in 1974 the GA adopted, by consensus, the definition of aggression recommended in the report of the Special Committee. The definition, an annex to GA Resolution 3314 (69 AJIL 480 (1975)), adopted a mixed approach, with a general definition preceding a non-exhaustive list of specific acts of aggression by way of illustration. Patterned on Art. 2(4) of the UN Charter but explicitly limiting aggression to armed force and not including the threat of force, the GA Resolution 3314 defines aggression as "the use of armed force by a State **(127)** against the sovereignty **(125)** and territorial integrity or political independence of another State, or in any other manner inconsistent with the Charter of the United Nations." Among acts qualifying, regardless of the declaration of war **(338)**, as aggression, the GA definition includes in its Art. 3: (a). invasion or attack of the territory **(228)** of another state or military occupation **(363)** resulting from it, or any annexation **(194)** by the use of force; (b). bombardment of or any use of weapons against foreign territory **(228)**; (c). blockade **(326)** of ports or coasts; (d). an attack on the land, sea or air forces, marine, and air fleets of another state; (e). use of armed forces staying in foreign territory with the agreement of the receiving state, in contravention of the agreement; (f). allowing a state's territory to be used by another state for perpetrating acts of aggression against a third state; and (g). sending by or on behalf of a state armed bands, groups, or irregulars **(356)**, or mercenaries **(360)**, which carry out acts of armed force against another state of such gravity as to amount to the acts listed in items (a)–(f), or a substantial involvement of that state in such acts. This vague compromise over the content of "indirect aggression" is an attempt at reconciling the positions of those states which limited this concept to a state sending abroad armed bands to attack another state, and other states which widened the concept to include support of such bands and, in general, intervention in a civil war **(340)**. The acts enumerated in the GA definition are not exhaustive, and the Security Council (SC) may determine that other acts constitute aggression under the provisions of the UN Charter (GA Definition of Aggression Art. 4). However, in any case, the SC is not bound by the GA definition. No consideration of any nature may serve as justification for aggression and no territorial acquisition **(227)** or special advantage resulting from aggression is or shall be recognized **(106)** as lawful. The GA definition makes a distinction between a war of aggression and aggression as such; only the former is a crime against peace. Aggression gives rise to international responsibility **(128)** (Art. 5). This means that a war of aggression entails individual **(81)** criminal responsibility under international law while aggression (presumably its lesser forms) gives rise to state responsibility of the traditional kind, with an obligation of the aggressor state to make reparation **(118)**. The GA definition may not be construed as in any way enlarging or diminishing the scope of the UN Charter, including its provisions concerning cases in which the use of force is lawful (Art. 6). This provision presumably guarantees the right of self-defense **(335)** without, however, defining this right. While following the so-called priority principle, whereby the first illegal use of armed force **(329)** constitutes *prima facie* evidence of an act of aggression, the definition allows the SC to take into account the intent and purpose of the state resorting to force by concluding that in the light of all relevant circumstances, including insufficient gravity of the acts or their consequences, it would not be justified to determine that an act of aggression had been committed (Art. 2).

The definition of aggression was intended to clarify the concept of "act of aggression" referred to, but not defined, in Arts. 1 and 39 of the UN Charter. It appears, however, that the concept of "act of aggression" in Art. 39 is not entirely coterminous with that of the "use of force" under Art. 2(4) and the concept of "armed attack" under Art. 51 on self-defense. While providing some tests and criteria, the 1974 definition simply left a number of disputed points unanswered, meeting with a mixed reception by some states, including the US, which resisted the definition on the grounds that it did not reflect the existing customary law **(39)** and was not confirmed by practice. A major point of criticism of the definition was its adoption in Art. 7 of a double standard by virtually legalizing aggression in the name of the "right of self-determination" **(122)** and liberation from all forms of "alien domination" as understood in the GA Friendly Relations Declaration of 1970 **(14)**.

Despite its drawbacks, the GA definition of aggression of 1974 has had some effect upon the SC, which has made occasional references to it in its draft resolutions and other pronouncements. In the final analysis, the GA definition of aggression is not a legally binding instrument, and only the SC can authoritatively determine whether or not an act of aggression has taken place in a particular case, always provided that the SC action is not paralyzed by discord among its permanent members, as it was during the Cold War and—within a different international context—continues to be in the post–Cold War era.

The concept of aggression remains undefined in the new century. While the Rome Statute of the International Criminal Court (ICC) **(170)** includes the crime of aggression among "the most serious crimes of concern to the international community as a whole," the ICC can exercise its jurisdiction over aggression, granted to it in Art. 5 of the Rome Statute, only at some future date when the parties to the Statute, by amendment **(269)**, define the crime and set out the conditions under which the ICC shall exercise such jurisdiction. However, amendments may be proposed no sooner than seven years following the entry of the Statute into force **(271)**, that is, not until July 2009. It appears that states, and at this time especially the US, are not ready to bind themselves by a definition of aggression that may prove to hinder their freedom of action in some future contingency.

**326. Blockade, Pacific.** In traditional international law, the pacific blockade, to be distinguished from the belligerent blockade **(341)**, is a form of coercive measure short of war **(119)**, whereby a state **(127)** (or a group of states) bars access to the coasts of a state or part of it in order to prevent entry and exit of ships of the state under blockade. In the past, great powers, such as Great Britain and France, would resort to pacific blockade against weak states, sometimes acting jointly, to coerce the blockaded state into complying with their demands, as was done, for example, in 1902 when Great Britain, France, and Italy joined to blockade Venezuela in order to coerce it into honoring the debts owed by it to nationals **(175)** of those powers. In reaction to international protests **(44)** against the blockade, the blockading states proclaimed their action to be an act of war **(338)**, thus legally bringing about a state of war with Venezuela. Under the law of naval warfare **(361)**, this move allowed them to conduct searches of neutral **(362)** shipping. Whether a pacific blockade could be applied to ships of third states was a controversial matter, but eventually a rule emerged denying such right to blockading states.

By virtue of the ban on the use of force in international relations, introduced by the Charter of the United Nations (UN) in 1945 **(329)** and subsequently crystallized into a rule of customary international law **(39)**, pacific blockade without endorsement by the UN Security Council (SC) is unlawful. The definition of aggression **(325)** of 1974, drafted by the UN General Assembly, lists blockade among acts qualifying as aggression. A pacific blockade in the traditional meaning of the term must be differentiated from a blockade ordered or authorized by the SC as an enforcement measure executed on behalf of the UN within the context of the collective security system **(327)**, as was the case of the blockade by the United Kingdom of the then Portuguese port of Beira in Mozambique, an action which in 1966 was authorized by the SC as part of the enforcement measures against Southern Rhodesia. The 1962 "quarantine" of Cuba **(328)** by the United States was a *sui generis* case of measures short of war of questionable legality under international law.

**327. Collective Security System.** Collective security system is a generic term given to the centralized global system of international legal rules based on the Charter of the United Nations (UN) and conceived comprehensively to govern collective resort to force under the authority of the UN Security Council (SC) for the purpose of maintaining or restoring international peace and security. The collective security system is the corollary of the ban of the threat and use of force **(329)** in international relations (UN Charter Art. 3(4)). The SC, one of the six principal organs of the UN, is charged with primary responsibility for the maintenance of international peace and security (Art. 24(1)) and has exclusive decision-making powers concerning actions with respect to threats to the peace, breaches of the peace, and acts of aggression, as set out in Chapter VII of the Charter.

The centralized legal framework of the UN collective security system is an advance over that of the League of Nations. However, despite all the improvements, the UN collective security system has not been implemented as envisaged by the Charter. On the other hand, the UN has managed, sometimes in an imaginative way, to make positive contributions to maintaining security in an international system in which political realities allow only a limited application of collective security in a heterogeneous system of international politics. Whereas in the matter of the pacific settlement of international disputes **(318)** under Chapter VI of the Charter the SC may make only recommendations, in matters under Chapter VII (Action with respect to threats to the peace, breaches of the peace, and acts of aggression **(325)**) it has the power to make legally binding decisions (Art. 25) and take enforcement action against a delinquent state **(127)** or states. Obligations under the Charter prevail over any conflicting obligations in other international agreements.

Since the concepts of threat to the peace, breach of the peace, and act of aggression are not defined in the Charter, the first task of the SC is, in principle, to determine the existence of any of these situations (Art. 39). However, in practice the SC often proceeds to the substance of the case without discussing on what grounds its jurisdiction is to be based. This reluctance to make a clear determination under Art. 39 has been due to the desire to reach some compromise, or pure political expediency.

The concept of threat to the peace is not easy to define, and is the most extensive among the three concepts in Art. 39. Initially it was limited to threats to "international peace," but as early as 1948 the SC found the situation in the former Palestine mandate to constitute a threat to the peace. In the 1960s, internal political strife, and in particular that involving Southern Rhodesia after the unilateral proclamation of independence by the white minority regime, was found in 1965 by the SC to be a threat to the peace in a series of resolutions (especially Resolutions 217, 221, and 231). No determination of threat to the peace was made with regard to the mass murders committed by the Pol Pot regime in Cambodia. Since the 1990s, the SC has applied an increasingly generous construction

**(274)** of the concept of threat to the peace, going beyond the threat of force under Art. 2(4) to cover numerous chaotic situations of civil strife with frequent gross violations of human rights **(157)** amounting to a humanitarian catastrophe, on the rationale of possible adverse effects of such internal armed conflicts **(340)** upon other states. This approach was followed by the SC, first, in Resolution 688 (1991) which, *inter alia*, named Iraq's repression of the Kurds as a threat to the peace, and then, in a series of resolutions, beginning with Resolution 713 (1991) in respect to the mixed civil-international armed conflict and violations of international humanitarian law in the disintegrating Yugoslavia **(134)**. Similar determinations of threat to the peace were then made with regard to the conflicts in: Somalia (Resolution 733) in 1992; Liberia (Resolution 788) in 1992; the genocidal conflict in Rwanda (Resolution 955) in 1994; and in the complex conflict situations in Sierra Leone and the Congo where the UN peacekeeping operations **(334)** assumed features of enforcement under Art. VII of the Charter. At the same time, a widening of the SC jurisdiction through an extensive reading of the concept of threat to the peace took place in the 1990s within the context of the terrorist threat. Thus, Libya's initial failure to renounce terrorism and surrender the suspects in the 1988 Lockerbie bombing to the United States (US) or the United Kingdom (UK) was found by the SC to constitute a threat to international peace and security in 1992 (Resolution 748). Similarly, Sudan's failure to surrender suspects in an assassination attempt against Egypt's president was found to be a threat to the peace in Resolution 731 in 1992. The case of Haiti in 1991–1993 was rather unique in that the failure to reinstate what was ruled to be a legitimate government, accompanied by chaos and humanitarian crisis, was found in Resolution 841 to be a factor contributing to threats to international peace and security.

It is a testimony to the discord among the permanent members of the SC that despite many cases of inter-state violence since 1945, the SC determined only four times the existence of a breach of the peace under Art. 39, a concept that need not necessarily entail the used of armed force. The SC determined that a breach of the peace had occurred in: the case of the North Korean invasion of South Korea in 1950; Argentina's invasion of the Falkland Islands in 1982; the Iran-Iraq War (1980–1988), in which case the Council needed seven years to take note of one of the bloodiest armed conflicts in the post–World War II era; and Iraq's invasion of Kuwait in 1990 (Resolution 660). It is significant that a determination of "aggression" was made only against South Africa for its incursions into neighboring states (Resolutions 387 in 1976 and 568 in 1984) and against Israel, *inter alia*, in connection with Israel's bombing of the Palestine Liberation Organization headquarters in Tunisia in 1985 (Resolution 573 in 1985).

Once the SC has made a determination, it may, under Art. 40, "call upon"—a phrase interpreted by most commentators to mean "order"—the parties concerned to comply with certain provisional measures designed to stabilize the situation, such as cease-fire, withdrawal of troops, or other measures at its discretion. But it is less certain whether "calling upon the parties" entails a legal obligation to comply in the absence of a formal determination under Art. 39 or failure to cite Art. 40. In an ideal scheme of the UN Charter, enforcement action may be of two kinds: 1. measures under Art. 41 against the delinquent state which do not involve the use of armed forces, such as interruption of economic relations and means of communication, and the severance of diplomatic relations, and 2. military measures under Art. 42, including demonstrations (of force), blockade, and other operations. The SC may either order non-military measures binding under Art. 25 of the Charter (stipulating that the UN members agree to accept and carry out the decisions of the SC), or make non-binding recommendations—presumably under Art. 39—for voluntary measures of the same kind. Unlike the case of non-military enforcement measures, no state is legally obliged to take part in measures involving resort to armed force unless it has concluded a "special agreement" with the SC under Art. 43 on making available to the SC specific numbers and types of force, their degree of readiness and general location, and the nature of facilities and assistance to be provided. Since no such agreement has ever been concluded because of differences among the politically split permanent members of the Council, the provision of Art. 43 remains inoperative and measures under Art. 42 involving the use of armed force cannot be taken. The Military Staff Committee, an advisory body of the SC consisting of the chiefs of staff of the permanent members of the SC and responsible for the strategic direction of any armed forces placed at the disposal of the SC (Art. 47), remains inactive although during the Kuwait crisis of 1990–1991 it assisted the permanent members in coordinating their plans, a function given to it under SC Resolution 605 in 1990.

As a result of the failure to implement Art. 43, the SC can take action only under Art. 29 allowing it to establish subsidiary organs and under Art. 40 whereby it may call upon the parties to comply with any provisional measures, and order legally binding non-military enforcement measures under Art. 41. In addition, as discussed below, although the UN has not been able to implement its collective security system as envisaged in the Charter, it was determined to make at least some contribution to maintaining and restoring peace by authorizing states to use force if conditions for applying Arts. 39 and 42 were met (29 ILM 1560 (1990)). Such authorization of the use of military force—and request to all states to provide appropriate support for this action—is, of course, only a recommendation for the states willing to participate, but is legally binding for the delinquent state which cannot invoke self-defense **(335)** and is barred from resorting to countermeasures **(58)** against the participating states. Unlike the first Gulf crisis of 1990–1991, no authorization to "use all necessary means" to enforce compliance by Iraq with the Council resolutions, was issued by the SC. Hence, as discussed below, resort to military force by the US (and its "coalition") against Iraq in 2003 must be regarded as an unlawful use of force **(329)** under international law.

In addition, to use authorization for any voluntary enforcement by members states as a substitute for the inoperative enforcement mechanisms optimistically anticipated in 1945, the SC has developed wide-ranging "peacekeeping" **(334)** activities which in the past decade or so in a number of cases have amounted to *de facto* enforcement measures.

While the SC may, under the general voting rule, make decisions by a majority of at least 9 members out of 15, the Charter provides in Art. 27 that in non-procedural matters, which, of course, include those under Chapter VII (Action with respect to threats to the peace, breaches of the peace, and acts of aggression), the 9-vote minimum "shall" include the concurring votes of *the* permanent members. In decisions concerning pacific settlement of disputes (Chapter VI of the Charter) **(318)** a party to a dispute (but not parties in a situation where the dispute has been determined by the SC under Chapter VII to be a threat to the peace, breach of the peace, or act of aggression) shall abstain from voting. But a member of the SC which is a target of decisions under Chapter VII has no obligation to abstain and thus may cast a vote in its own case, which means that a permanent member of the SC may veto any decision that it does not like. Contrary to the wording of Art 27(3) of the Charter, a practice has developed in the Council whereby abstention of a permanent member (when otherwise the minimum affirmative nine votes are cast) is not regarded as a veto. Whether or not the absence of a permanent member is to be treated as abstention is not entirely clear although in the only case of this kind, in June 1950, the SC adopted a resolution on assistance to South Korea against the North Korean aggression in the absence of the Soviet delegate who happened to be boycotting the SC sessions in protest against the Council's refusal to seat the representation of the Communist government as the representation of China. Looking back at the history of the SC it is striking that whereas in the first 20 years the Soviet Union cast 106 vetoes the US never used its veto power in that period. However, in the period of 1966 to 2003 the roles were reversed, and whereas the Soviet Union, later Russia (which has hardly ever used the veto right) vetoed only 15 resolutions, the US cast as many as 76 vetoes through March 2003. The UK accounts for 32 vetoes; France for 18; and China (including the early vetoes cast by the representative of the nationalist government) only 5.

The decision-making powers of the SC are still extensive despite the absence in practice of the collective security mechanism under the Charter. Especially in the past decade or so, these powers have been exercised on a wide range of issues transcending the determination concerning threat or breach of peace or aggression. Thus, in the aftermath of the Gulf War in 1991 the SC made determination, *inter alia*, on such matters as delimitation of Iraq's border **(189)**; destruction of certain types of Iraq's weapons; compensation of the victims of Iraq's aggression; and—a significant action—the establishment in 1991 of the UN Compensation Commission, with a Fund, to deal with claims resulting from Iraq's invasion and occupation of Kuwait (30 ILM 864 (1991)).

This subsidiary organ of the SC combined the features of a political organ with those of an arbitration **(293)** claims commission common in international law. In addition, the SC established *ad hoc* war crimes tribunals for trying war criminals in the aftermath of the conflicts in Yugoslavia **(352)** and Rwanda **(351)**, and the Special Court for Sierra Leone **(371)** to prosecute perpetrators of war crimes in that country's bloody civil war.

Whether the basically political decisions of the SC are subject to judicial review by the International Court of Justice (ICJ) **(309)** with regard to their compatibility with international law is a difficult question. In the now discontinued parallel cases before the ICJ initiated by Libya against the US and the UK concerning *Questions of Interpretation and Application of the 1971 Montreal Convention Arising from the Aerial Incident at Lockerbie* (Libya v. UK; Libya v. US), Libya claimed that the UK and US demand to surrender the suspects in the Lockerbie bombing, and the resulting SC sanctions against Libya under Art. 41 were contrary to international law. However, the ICJ ruled in its judgment in 1992 that under Art. 103 of the UN Charter the obligations under the Charter (that is, the obligation to comply with the SC sanctions) prevailed over obligations under other treaties, in this case the above-mentioned Montreal Convention on aircraft sabotage **(210)**.

The General Assembly (GA) has no legal power to order enforcement measures and may only make recommendations (Arts. 10 and 11), but wherever there is a question on which action is necessary or if a dispute or situation is before the SC, the GA is not allowed to make any recommendations with regard to that dispute or situation unless the Council so requests (Art. 12(1)). During the Korean War, when the SC decision against the Chinese intervention was blocked by a Soviet veto in the fall of 1950, the GA, in order to assert what it considered its "secondary responsibility" for the maintenance of international peace and security, adopted the so-called "Uniting for Peace" Resolution (Resolution 377-V), whereby it resolved that in cases where the SC failed to exercise its primary responsibility (as a rule, in a veto situation), the GA must consider the matter immediately with a view to making recommendations for collective measures. Although the Soviet Union opposed this resolution as a violation of the UN Charter, in subsequent practice it took advantage of it as dictated by political expediency, as in response to the Anglo-French Suez invasion (and vetoes) in 1956.

During the Cold War the SC was able to order collective security measures not involving the use of force (Art. 41) only when there was a convergence of international political correctness among all the permanent members of the SC. The economic and commercial sanctions against the white minority regime of Southern Rhodesia (otherwise not recognized as a state **(116)** by the UN) in 1966–1979 and an arms embargo against South Africa (1977–1994) are the major cases. In addition, the SC managed to adopt a resolution condemning the illegal situation created by the proclamation of the Turkish Republic of Cyprus.

The post–Cold War era has witnessed a series of SC decisions within the collective security framework of Chapter VII, imposing economic and other sanctions under Art. 41 against a number of states in various regions of the world. The most comprehensive enforcement measures were undertaken in response to Iraq's invasion of Kuwait. The basic economic sanctions Resolution 661 (29 ILM 1325 (1990)), which followed the first SC resolution (Resolution 660) in reaction to the invasion (29 ILM 1323 (1990)), was complemented by Resolution 665 regarding shipping and the implementation of the economic sanctions (29 ILM 1329 (1990)) and Resolution 670 extending the economic sanctions to include air transport (29 ILM 1334 (1990)). In addition, Resolution 669 (29 ILM 1333 (1990)) established a sanctions committee charged with implementation of the sanctions and keeping the situation regarding foodstuffs in Iraq and Kuwait under constant review. It could also recommend to the SC President measures in response to requests for assistance under Art. 50 of the Charter by states whose economies were adversely affected by compliance with the sanctions against Iraq.

In another major case of SC enforcement measures under Art. 41 of the Charter, the complex Yugoslav **(134)** crisis, in which the UN and various international European organizations and bodies became involved in search of a peaceful solution (31 ILM 1421 (1992)), the SC adopted a large number of resolutions dealing with various aspects of the conflict (31 ILM 1427 (1992)). Of interest here is Resolution 713 (1991), *inter alia*, imposing an arms embargo upon all states of the former Yugoslavia, followed by Resolution 724 (1991) which, reiterating the measures of embargo, established a SC sanctions committee; Resolution 740 (1992) expressing concern over non-observance of the arms embargo; and Resolution 757 (1992) which imposed a trade embargo against the new Federal Republic of Yugoslavia (Serbia and Montenegro), except for the necessary food and medical supplies, ordered cutting off air links with it; and reduced diplomatic **(68)** and consular **(57)** staffs. Various maritime measures were also instituted to enforce these sanctions. In the latter stages of the conflict, the sanctions against Serbia and Montenegro were further tightened and territorially extended by resolution 820 (1993) to Serb-controlled areas of Bosnia and Herzegovina. The eventual negotiations led to the General Framework Agreement for Peace in Bosnia and Herzegovina, initialed in Dayton and signed in Paris in 1995 (35 ILM 75 (1996). The various enforcement measures against the former Yugoslavia and the new Federal Republic of Yugoslavia were progressively eased and then terminated by SC resolutions in 1996 (35 ILM 257, 259, 1561 (1996)). However, in the Kosovo crisis, the sanctions against Serbia and Montenegro were reimposed in 1998 (SC Resolution 1160) and subsequently lifted in 2001 (Resolution 1367).

In addition to the two major SC actions under Art. 41 against Iraq and Yugoslavia, the SC acted in a number of other situations. It imposed an arms embargo and other measures against Libya in 1992 (Resolution 748) for refusing to surrender the suspects in the above-noted Lockerbie bombing, but eventually, in 1998, they were repealed (Resolution 1192) after Libya had complied and handed them over for trial by a Scottish court especially set up in the Netherlands. Enforcement measures (*inter alia*, an embargo on export of diamonds) under Art. 41 were also ordered against Liberia in 1992 (Resolution 788), in 1995 (Resolution 985), and again in 2001 (Resolution 1343) (40 ILM 1024 (2001) in order to force Liberia to cease supplying the rebels of the Revolutionary United Front in Sierra Leone. In addition, in order to restrict the use of diamonds to finance internal conflicts in West Africa, in 2000 the SC ordered a worldwide embargo on purchase of rough diamonds from Sierra Leone (40 ILM 248 (2001). In another area of conflict in Africa, in the 1990s the SC adopted a number of resolutions designed to isolate the Union for the Total Independence of Angola rebels persisting in carrying on warfare against the Angolan government. In another part of the world, in 1993 and 1994, in an attempt to uphold the principle of democratic government in Haiti, the SC adopted a number of resolutions imposing selected economic sanctions upon the ruling military junta. These non-military measures were followed by the formation of a multinational force authorized by the SC (Resolution 940) to use all necessary means to enforce the departure of the junta. As demonstrated by the Haitian crisis of 2004, all these measures proved to be a failure. It might be noted that, as part of the anti-terrorist measures against terrorism, the SC imposed limited financial sanctions and an embargo on air communications against the Taliban government in Afghanistan.

Although military enforcement measures according to Art. 42 of the Charter have never been undertaken by the UN, the Organization has been able to uphold the idea of collective security by improvising two kinds of action which have been almost universally recognized as compatible with the Charter's system, even though not explicitly provided for in Chapter VII, namely, authorization to use force and peacekeeping operations. First, in the Korean War (1950–1953) and then in the Gulf War in 1991 the SC authorized member states to use force against the aggressor state. In the Korean conflict, the UN-sponsored action constituted an exercise in the right of collective self-defense **(336)** rather than a UN military action under Art. 42 of the Charter. In its resolutions, the SC recommended that member states assist the Republic of Korea in its defense against aggression from North Korea and that they place forces in a unified command under a US commander. While authorized by the SC to fly the UN flag, these forces were not, strictly speaking, UN forces. In the Gulf War, the SC Resolution 678 of November 1990 (29 ILM 1565 (1990)) authorized member states "to use all necessary means to uphold and implement resolution 660 (1990) [calling for the immediate and unconditional withdrawal of the aggressor from Kuwait] and all subsequent relevant resolutions and to restore international peace and security in the area." In the Iraq War of 2003, the US resorted to unilateral use of force against Iraq before any SC authorization resolution—which quite possibly might have been forthcoming—could be adopted. The resolutions of the SC, adopted after the invasion of Iraq, cannot be considered as expressing an *ex post* legitimation of the invasion. Taking account of this situation, they were simply motivated by humanitarian considerations and the desire to support Iraq's process of political transition toward a constitutional government based on credible elections.

In addition to invoking the dubious argument of self-defense, those very few international legal scholars and some writers not quite familiar with international law who asserted the legality of the US invasion of Iraq in 2003, based their case on the reasoning that the reference in SC Resolution 1441 of 2002 (42 ILM 250 (2003)) to "material breach" by Iraq of previous resolutions, including Resolution 687 of 1991 (30 ILM 846 (1991), "revived" the authorization of Resolution 678 of 1990 (29 ILM 1565 (1990)) which allowed individual states to use "all necessary means" (meaning in diplomatic language the use of military force) to liberate Kuwait and restore international peace and security in the area. According to this argument, Resolution 687 which set out the cease-fire terms with emphasis on elimination of Iraq's weapons of mass destruction and imposition of a weapons-monitoring régime, only suspended but did not terminate the authorization under Resolution 678. Allegedly, Resolution 687 had set up a post–Gulf War régime "in perpetuity," requiring, *inter alia*, that Iraq surrender its weapons of mass destruction and permit unobstructed verification. This whole argument is rejected by most international law scholars as, in essence, conflicting with the fundamental rule of contemporary international law that—apart from the right of self-defense **(335)**—only the SC has the right to authorize resort to force by states, and any response to a material breach of a SC resolution is within the exclusive competence of the Council itself. It is the SC, and not individual states, that is the party to the cease-fire agreement under Resolution 687. The fact that all Iraq-related resolutions of the SC from Resolution 687 to Resolution 1441 end with the phrase that the SC "decides to remain seized of the matter" is a reminder by the Council that it is the only authority to decide about the future course of action. Furthermore, the absence in Resolution 1441 of the phrase on using "all necessary means," included only in Resolution 678, makes it clear that the SC did not intend Resolution 1441 to be an automatic trigger for the use of force against Iraq. The reference in Resolution 1441 to "serious consequences" cannot be stretched to be read as an authorization to unilateral military action. It is also evident from the context of the reference in Resolution 1441 to material breach by Iraq of Resolution 687, that the Council's intent at the time was not, as yet, to endorse force, but to afford Iraq "a final opportunity to comply with its disarmament obligations" by setting up an enhanced inspection régime. Within its framework, Iraq was to provide the UN Monitoring, Verification and Inspection Commission (UNMOVIC), successor of the UN Special Commission, and to the International Atomic Energy Agency (IAEA) immediate, unimpeded, unconditional, and unrestricted access to all facilities and persons whom UNMOVIC or the IAEA wished to interview. Upon report by UNMOVIC or the IAEA of any material breach of obligations under Resolution 1441, the SC was to convene immediately. Possibly, such session would have authorized resort to force by the "all necessary means" formula.

Even if one accepts a revival of Resolution 678, the purpose of this resolution was to authorize the use of force solely for liberating Kuwait and restoring international peace and security, and this purpose had already been achieved in 1991. In addition, as demonstrated by the debates in the SC just prior to the invasion of Iraq, weapons of mass destruction were the focus of attention and concern of all in relation to Iraq. However, no such weapons were found either by UNMOVIC and the IAEA or subsequently by the US. As a result, the argument for the use of force based on the assertion of material breach by Iraq of its disarmament obligations under Resolution 687, with the consequent revival of authorization to use force on the basis of the revived Resolution 678, cannot be sustained, apart from the fact that the authorization is of limited scope, applying only to the eviction of Iraq from Kuwait, but not to invading it and changing the regime, however repugnant it might be.

In a number of situations, the SC authorized member states to use force in order to secure compliance by the delinquent state with the non-military sanctions. As early as 1966, the UK was authorized by Resolution 221 to search ships on the high seas **(245)** to verify the observance of the oil embargo against Southern Rhodesia. In the 1990s a similar authorization was granted to member states to verify compliance with the SC enforcement measures against Iraq and Yugoslavia, as well as Somalia, Haiti, Liberia, and Sierra Leone. In the course of such operations against Iraq and Yugoslavia several thousand ships were boarded and inspected by naval patrols of the participating states, but only a very small fraction of the vessels was found to smuggle the embargoed materials.

In addition to authorizing forcible verification of non-military sanctions under Art. 41 of the Charter, the SC, in an extensive interpretation **(274)** of the concept of threat to the peace, authorized military intervention in support of humanitarian operations, including the protection of safe havens, for example, the air strikes by the forces of the North Atlantic Treaty Organization (NATO) against Serb forces in Bosnia and Herzegovina. Military action was also authorized in situations of civil strife and breakdown of public order, as was the case of intervention in Albania in 1996 (Resolution 1101), East Timor in 1999 (Resolution 1264) (39 ILM 232 (2000)), and Haiti. It is a controversial issue whether SC Resolution 688 (which makes no reference to Chapter VII of the Charter, but recalls the domestic jurisdiction **(9)** provision of Art. 2(7)) condemning Iraq for the repression of the Kurds constituted a sufficient legal basis for the establishing by the US and the UK of "no-fly" zones in northern and southern Iraq in 1991 and 1992.

In some situations, and especially in the Yugoslav crisis, the SC authorization to use force was implemented by a regional organization, such as the Western European Union or a collective self-defense organization, such as the NATO. The implementation, by force if necessary, of the Dayton-Paris Agreement within the framework of the Implementation Force was entrusted to NATO (Resolution 1031). Finally, one should mention that following the unilateral use of force by NATO in the Kosovo crisis, by its Resolution 1244 in 1999, the SC authorized states and relevant international organizations **(84)** (in practice, NATO) to provide military support to the emerging administration of the province by UN administrators. Whether this authorization constituted an *ex post facto* legitimization of the breach of the UN Charter by NATO, is a highly controversial issue. Similar questions arise with respect to SC resolutions concerning the occupation **(313)** of Iraq by the US and its coalition after the invasion of Iraq in 2003.

Concerning peacekeeping as the other category of UN activity within the general ambit of the concept of collective security, one can briefly state here that it expanded into a wide-ranging and complex UN tool in the area of restoring international peace and security, often merging into enforcement action and thus making it difficult to distinguish the two concepts in actual practice.

To sum up, the UN collective security system has not been able to operate according to the scheme conceived in 1945 and articulated in Chapter VII. Despite that, with all its imperfections, the UN has, in many conflict situations, made a positive contribution to peace through its imaginative and persistent, though haphazard and sometimes improvised, operations. However, early in the new century the whole system of collective security devised in 1945 is in grave jeopardy brought about by actions of the superpower which seems to reject any subordination to the collective security rules and, openly proclaiming the strategy of preemptive or rather preventive action, follows the path of unilateralism, without any need of a "permission slip" from the multilateral security system it once helped establish. Such repudiation of the collective security system in today's interdependent world cannot be sustained in the long run, even by the superpower. It remains to be seen whether the events of 2003 were only a temporary setback for collective security or constituted a more profound repudiation of the foundations of contemporary international law governing the use of force in international relations.

**328. Cuban Quarantine.** This was a highly controversial new type of maritime blockade **(326)**, described by the United States (US) as a "quarantine" which, for a few weeks, was applied against Cuba by warships of the US, later joined by Argentina, Dominican Republic, and Venezuela, during the so-called "Cuban missile crisis" in 1962. The term "quarantine" was borrowed from international health regulations concerning detention or isolation of ships, people, animals, and plants on arrival at a port. An instance of interference with foreign vessels on the high seas **(245)**, the quarantine was designed to "interdict" on the high seas, "within a reasonable distance of Cuba," the delivery to that country of specified Soviet missiles and other offensive military equipment carried by vessels and other craft of whatever nationality **(257)**.

The US measures against Cuba were deliberately called "quarantine" because under traditional international law interference with foreign shipping would imply that the US action was a belligerent blockade **(341)**, that is, an act of war **(338)**. To avoid a dangerous precedent, the quarantine was not rationalized by the right of self-defense under Art. 51 of the United Nations (UN) Charter, but by a resolution of the Council of the Organization of American States acting on the basis of Arts. 6 and 8 of the Inter-American Treaty of Reciprocal Assistance (Rio Treaty) of 1947 (21 UNTS 77). Although the US justified this resolution as compatible with Chapter VIII of the UN Charter (Regional Arrangements), the resolution failed to obtain the authorization of the UN Security Council (SC) required under Art. 53(1) of the Charter. However, the SC did discuss the quarantine without condemning it or adopting any resolution on the subject. The US action was also criticized as a threat of force inconsistent with Art. 2(4) of the Charter and a violation of the principle of the freedom of the high seas **(242)**. However, some commentators, perhaps exaggerating the Soviet threat, argued that the propriety of the quarantine was not a legal issue since "the survival of state is not a matter of law."

Legally, the Cuban quarantine displayed features of both pacific and belligerent blockade. It was pacific to the extent that no state of war existed between the US and Cuba, neither party manifesting any belligerent intent and, in addition, no other state regarded the conflict as a war. On the other hand, the quarantine, exhibited features of a belligerent blockade in that it applied to vessels of third states. However, unlike a traditional international law blockade, the Cuban quarantine was not intended to blockade the coast of a state as such but only to interdict delivery of certain specific military equipment to Cuba. In addition, vessels *en route* to Cuba were subject to visit and search in an exception to the rule of the flag-state jurisdiction **(240)**, with possible resort to force, but were subject only to "custody" and not capture under the law governing contraband **(343)** in naval warfare **(361)**.

**329. Force, Illegal Threat or Use.** As defined in Art. 2(4) of the Charter of the United Nations (UN), illegal threat or use of force is "the threat or use of force against the territorial integrity **(228)** or political independence of any State **(127)**, or in any other manner inconsistent with the Purposes of the United Nations." This rule, a landmark in the history of international law, is recognized as part of general (customary) **(39)** international law binding all states, both members and nonmembers of the UN. It is also accepted that in its substance Art. 2(4) has acquired the status of a peremptory rule of international law, *jus cogens* **(24)**.

Unlike the previous attempts to restrict the use of armed force in international relations, namely, in the Covenant of the League of Nations, the Pact of Paris **(330)**, let alone in the first very modest attempt in Hague Convention II **(350)** on the Limitation of the Employment of Force for the Recovery of Contract Debts of 1907 (known as the Drago-Porter Convention) (205 CTS 233), the ban in the UN Charter covers not just war, but all threat or use of force in international relations, including such coercive measures short of war as reprisals **(119)** by means of armed force and any non-war hostilities and resort to armed force in violation of the Charter. Art. 2(4) does not mention such terms as "aggression" or "war," which means that such an imaginary case as a duel by mutual consent where neither side commits aggression is included within the sweeping range of the outlawry of force. Yet, the language of the Charter is not devoid of uncertainties which have not been entirely clarified by the Security Council (SC), a political organ rather than a judicial body concerned with a legal analysis of the Charter.

Art. 2(4) was given a more detailed though not necessarily clear meaning in the General Assembly Friendly Relations Declaration of 1970 **(14)** and analyzed in 1986 by the International Court of Justice (ICJ) in its judgment (merits) in *Military and Paramilitary Activities in and against Nicaragua* (Nicaragua v. United States of America) (1986 ICJ Rep. 14). The 1970 Declaration specifies, as threat or use of force, such categories as wars of aggression ("a crime against the peace"); propaganda for such wars; threat or use of force to violate international borders **(189)** or international lines of demarcation; reprisals by armed force; use of force in violation of the right of peoples to self-determination **(122)**; organizing armed bands for incursion into another state's territory; organizing, instigating, assisting, or participating in acts of civil strife or terrorist **(337)** acts in another state, or acquiescing in organized activities by a state in its territory directed toward the commission of such acts; and acquisition **(227)** of territory by the threat or use of force. The use of force in situations of an internal armed conflict **(340)** once generated a lot of controversy concerning the so-called wars of national liberation, an issue that by the turn of the century lost much of its intensity. The Declaration does not clarify whether illegal force means armed force only or—as claimed by many developing states—also economic and political pressures. However, the view prevails that the latter forms of coercion do not come under the prohibition of Art. 2(4) although under the circumstances they might become illegal intervention **(331)**. In the above-noted *Military and Paramilitary Activities* case the ICJ did not find the United States (US) economic sanctions against Nicaragua to be in breach of the principle of non-intervention.

Although the prohibition in Art. 2(4) might be interpreted **(274)** to mean that force used for purposes other than "the territorial integrity or political independence of any State," for example, for purposes of enforcing **(17)** international law or protecting human rights **(157)**, was legal, the predominant opinion is—and the Friendly Relations Declaration agrees—that the above-cited phrase should not be construed as restricting the concept of illegal use of force, and that Art. 2(4) should be interpreted broadly as prohibition of any resort to force, especially in the light of the phrase "or in any other manner inconsistent with the Purposes of the United Nations." Maintenance of international peace and security is listed in Art. 1(1) as the first among such purposes. This interpretation was endorsed in 1949 by the ICJ in the *Corfu Channel* case (United Kingdom v. Albania) (1949 ICJ Rep. 4) in which the Court, rejecting the United Kingdom argument that its action of minesweeping in the territorial sea **(262)** of Albania had threatened neither the territorial integrity nor the political independence of Albania, ruled that the British operation had violated the fundamental rule of the UN Charter on the prohibition of force. More recently, the ICJ judgment of 1986 in the above-mentioned *Military and Paramilitary Activities* case clarified a number of aspects of this rule within the context of the US intervention in Nicaragua.

Under the UN legal regime, which has crystallized into customary law **(39)**, the only exceptions to the prohibition of the use of force in relations between states are: self-defense, individual **(335)** and collective **(336)**; and collective security **(327)** enforcement action ordered or authorized by the SC, including enforcement action by a regional arrangement or agency with prior authorization by the SC. Arts. 53 and 107, which include the so-called enemy state clauses allowing the use of force without such authorization by a regional arrangement or agency against "renewal of aggressive policy" on the part of former enemy states in World War II, have long been obsolete. The use of force in humanitarian intervention **(332)** remains a controversial issue. One should add that in special circumstances, a limited resort to force is allowed under general international law by a warship or other authorized state ship **(265)** on the high seas **(245)** against a vessel suspected of piracy **(259)** or slave trade **(180)** and offering resistance; in response to an intrusion by a foreign military aircraft into the national airspace **(186)**; against foreign troops in a state's territory, refusing to withdraw after the state has revoked its consent to their presence; and in the case of a natural disaster in a foreign state's territory if that state is not able or willing to contain the danger threatening the intervening state.

The ban of force covers not only the use but also the threat of force, but the UN Charter does not provide guidelines clarifying the concept of threat. Generally speaking, a threat of force exists when a state expressly or by implication communicates its determination to resort to force in case of non-acceptance by the threatened state of its demands. An ultimatum traditionally constitutes the most explicit form of threat. It is a formal communication by a state to another state, demanding in an uncompromising manner that that state accept within an indicated, usually very short, deadline the terms indicated by the threatening state or face the use of force. Whether in less obvious situations threat of force is implied depends on the specific circumstances and may be difficult to ascertain. The purpose and intent of the threatening state are the decisive factors in qualifying a behavior as threat. For example, in the *Military and Paramilitary Activities* case the ICJ expressed the opinion that US military maneuvers near Nicaragua's borders did not constitute threat of force, and ruled the same in respect of the mere possession of nuclear weapons in its advisory opinion **(291)** on the *Legality of the Threat or Use of Nuclear Weapons* (1996 ICJ Rep.1). More generally, the ICJ ruled in that opinion that threatening to use force that would itself be unlawful, for example, to gain territory from another state, would be illegal. Hence, in order not to be unlawful, a declared readiness of a state to use force must involve a situation of the use of force in conformity with the UN Charter and, of course, the principles of necessity and proportionality.

Although the comprehensive ban on the use of force has had some modest restraining influence upon the behavior of states, in general there exists a gap between the ambitious letter of the law and actual international practice. Apart from the ever present impact of extra-legal, power consideration, the legal rules governing proscription of force suffer from inherent weaknesses, in particular the use by the law of imprecise and vague terms, such as force, aggression, and self-defense, which lend themselves to unilateral interpretation **(274)** in rationalizing a legally doubtful or dubious conduct. In addition, the sweeping ban on the use of force makes it formally impossible to resort to force in situations where the Charter's formalism conflicts with human rights and humanitarian considerations which at the time of the drafting of the Charter did not have today's major impact upon international law. The result is a tendency to depart from the rule of centralized decision making of the SC in situations of grave humanitarian crisis and undertake a regional enforcement action without the Council's authorization. How to deal with this problem is a major challenge to the UN system of regulating the use of force in international relations. In addition, there remains the fundamental weakness of the system that while international law proscribes violence, the law has not been able to develop effective procedures and institutions of compulsory peaceful settlement **(318)** of disputes **(299)** in order to prevent the resort to force by individual states.

**330. General Treaty for the Renunciation of War, 1928.** Known also as the Pact of Paris or Kellogg-Briand Pact, named after the United States (US) Secretary of State Frank Billings Kellogg and the French Foreign Minister Aristide Briand, this 1928 multilateral treaty **(288)** of indefinite duration, in force **(271)** 1929 (94 LNTS 57), on renunciation of war **(338)** as an instrument of national policy, condemns recourse to war for the solution of international controversies **(299)** and denounces war in relations between the states parties, and binds them to settle all disputes solely by peaceful means **(318)**. At the outbreak of World War II in 1939, 63 states were parties to the Treaty. It is still in force, with some 70 states parties, including the US and a number of new post–World War II states. While formally in force, the Treaty has, for all practical purposes, been superseded by the Charter of the United Nations (UN) and especially its comprehensive ban on the use of force **(329)**.

Although the Kellogg-Briand Pact could not prevent war, it still remains today as a historical landmark in international law in that it is the first international legal instrument condemning resort to war in international relations. However, the traditional right of self-defense **(335)** was not affected by the Pact. By renouncing war as an instrument of national policy, the Pact goes beyond the attempts of the League of Nations to cope with international violence, which had legal gaps that allowed resort to war under certain circumstances. The adoption of the Pact enabled the US, which was not a member of the League, to join in the general outlawry of war.

Initially, the renunciation of war by the Pact of Paris was legally binding only for its parties, but eventually its basic principles evolved into rules of general international law. In the aftermath of World War II, the Pact was invoked by the two major international military tribunals, at Nuremberg **(354)** and in Tokyo **(355)**, and national tribunals in trials of war criminals charged with crimes against peace. The shortcomings of the Pact of Paris, and in particular its ambiguous position on the legal status of armed measures short of war, such as reprisals **(119)**, which do not seem to be prohibited by the Pact, were in 1945 removed by the prohibition by the UN Charter of force and introducing in the Charter—however unworkable in practice—a machinery and procedures for enforcing this rule.

**331. Intervention.** While the legal meaning of the term "intervention" is rather vague, there seems to be consensus that intervention constitutes a dictatorial or other coercive interference by a state **(127)** or states in the internal or external affairs of another state in order to impose upon it a course of conduct desired by the intervening state. As a highly political concept, the term intervention has been used to describe all kinds of interference ranging from hardly discernible diplomatic pressure to armed intervention. It is the latter kind of intervention that, because of its open and dramatic character, can clearly indicate the fact of such interference; hence, the term "intervention" is often associated with the use of force in international relations. As a general rule, intervention is unlawful in international law and has been proclaimed so in numerous treaties **(288)** and resolutions of the United Nations (UN) General Assembly (GA) and other international instruments. Prominent among the GA resolutions is the Declaration on Inadmissibility of Intervention in the Domestic Affairs of States and the Protection of Their Independence and Sovereignty, adopted in 1965 by 109 votes to 0, with the United Kingdom (UK) abstaining because of the failure to define the terms used in the declaration. The Friendly Relations Declaration of 1970 **(14)**, which includes non-intervention among the basic principles of international law, prohibits intervention "for any reason whatever" and proclaims that "armed intervention and all other forms of interference or attempted threats against the personality of the State or against its political, economic and cultural elements, are in violation of international law." The implication is that an intervention to change the political system of the target state is unlawful. The UN Charter (Art. 2(7)) itself prohibits the UN to intervene in matters which are essentially within the domestic jurisdiction **(9)** of any state, but the range of such "domestic" matters has considerably narrowed in the course of time.

As elaborated in the International Court of Justice (ICJ) judgment on the *Military and Paramilitary Activities in and against Nicaragua* (Nicaragua v. the United States) (1986 ICJ Rep. 14), intervention in a foreign civil strife may assume a variety of forms, ranging from measures of an economic and political nature; through non-military support of opposition forces in another state, fighting the established government; to financial assistance and intelligence; and indirect support of a military character (sometimes described as "indirect aggression") through supply of weapons, equipment, training, and logistical support which, according to the GA, qualify as illegal threat or use of force; and finally, to direct military intervention using either the intervening state's armed forces or by organizing, tolerating, or dispatching irregular armed bands into the territory of the target state. Both situations qualify as armed attack or possibly aggression **(325)** and justify self-defense **(335)** measures. Intervention in a civil war ("non-international armed conflict") **(340)**, whether on the side of the established government or the insurgents, raises complex and controversial issues of the legality of resort to armed force and self-defense.

While intervention as such is prohibited by international law, there may arise exceptional circumstances justifying intervention in the affairs of another state. However, whether armed intervention is permissible at all, and if so, what kind of circumstances justify it, is a highly controversial matter. Despite reiteration in many instruments of the principle of non-intervention, state practice, including the conduct of states which have been most vocal in championing this principle, confirms the view that exceptions to it are possible. This was not uncommon during the Cold War era, and has continued thereafter.

Apart from the situation where intervention is justified in the exercise of the right of self-defense, the coercive nature of intervention implies the legality of intervention taking place at the genuine request and consent of the legitimate government of the inviting target state. Both the Security Council (Resolution 387) and the ICJ (in the above-noted *Military and Paramilitary Activities* case) have endorsed the legality of intervention at the invitation of the target government; the right to request intervention is inherent in the state's sovereign status. Intervention in a full-scale civil war is subject to special rules governing armed conflicts.

There have been numerous instances of lawful intervention by invitation, such as British and French interventions in various African countries and the Indian interventions in Sri Lanka in 1987 and the Maldives in 1988. However, as shown by the historical examples of Soviet intervention in Hungary in 1956, Czechoslovakia in 1968, and Afghanistan in 1979, invitation by a foreign government can be fabricated. United States (US) interventions in the Dominican Republic in 1963, in Grenada in 1983, and Panama in 1989, partly justified by alleged requests for assistance by the target state and the need to protect US nationals, were also of dubious legal validity.

The consent to foreign intervention may be given *ad hoc* or result from a treaty **(288)**, such as a treaty of guarantee allowing the guarantor state to intervene in order to protect the existing *status quo* in the state under guarantee. Thus, under Art. IV of the Treaty of Guarantee of 1960, Greece, Turkey, and the UK undertook as guarantors of the constitution of the newly independent Cyprus to consult together as to what action to take in the event of a breach of the Treaty. If concerted diplomatic action should not prove possible, the guarantor states reserved the right to take individual action with the sole aim of re-establishing the state of affairs created by the 1960 Treaty. In 1974, following a pro-Greece coup in Cyprus, Turkey, claiming to act under Art. IV of the Treaty, intervened militarily in Cyprus, but in the event this intervention went far beyond the limits of the Treaty of Guarantee and led to a division of Cyprus into two states already lasting more than 30 years.

Whether a forcible intervention to protect the intervening state's nationals **(175)** in an emergency abroad and secure compliance with the minimum standards of treatment of aliens **(144)** is lawful in international law is a controversial issue. Most developing countries categorically deny its legality as a breach of the prohibition of the use of force **(329)** and violation of the territorial integrity of the target state involved. On the other hand, Western states have occasionally intervened unilaterally to protect their nationals abroad in conditions of internal turmoil where the government proved unable or unwilling to guarantee their safety. Intervention to save nationals held as hostages, as was the case of the US-French-Belgian intervention in the Congo in 1978, the Israeli action in Entebbe, Uganda, in 1976 to free the mostly Israeli nationals of a hijacked **(199)** French airliner, and the abortive attempt by the US to rescue hostages in Iran in 1980, were also subject to criticism, mainly in Third World countries. In any event, intervention that masks the real motivation and objectives of the intervening state or exceeds the limits of necessity and proportionality cannot be regarded as lawful. Humanitarian considerations require that intervention to protect nationals abroad should be accepted as legal. It must be limited in time and restricted to cases where there is not just imminent threat to their property but mortal danger to their lives or threat of irreparable injury. In addition, it must be shown that the local authorities have failed to protect them in conformity with generally accepted standards of treatment and the intervening state's non-forcible means of protecting its nationals cannot reasonably, under the circumstances, be effective. The application of force by the intervening state must not conflict with the principle of proportionality.

Intervention to protect the intervening state's nationals abroad is related to and may overlap and merge with intervention to protect nationals of the target state. Such "humanitarian intervention" **(332)** in the strict sense of the term has absorbed the attention and resources of the international community confronted by humanitarian disasters in various regions of the world. Finally, it must be added that intervention by states acting individually must be distinguished from action amounting in fact to collective intervention, ordered or authorized by the competent organ of the UN.

**332. Intervention, Humanitarian.** Humanitarian intervention is the use of force by a state **(127)** or states in the territory **(228)** of another state in order to protect nationals **(175)** of that state, and possibly nationals of other states, from large-scale inhumane treatment and other severe violations of fundamental human rights **(157)** which "shook the conscience of mankind" and are committed or condoned by the authorities of that state, unable or unwilling to prevent them. Humanitarian intervention in this sense must be differentiated from intervention **(331)** to protect the intervening state's nationals abroad, which is sometimes included within the more general concept of humanitarian intervention.

The right to intervene on humanitarian grounds belongs to the most controversial issues in international law today. Even before the entry into force **(271)** of the prohibition of the use of force **(329)** in international relations, anchored in Art. 2(4) of the Charter of the United Nations (UN) in 1945, it was not a clearly established right under international law although it had been occasionally invoked in the 19th and early 20th centuries, especially on behalf of Christian minorities **(172)** in the Ottoman Empire. However, those interventions must be viewed within the context of the great powers' rivalry for influence in the decaying Ottoman Empire. Ostensibly for humanitarian reasons, an intervention could provide a convenient legal pretext for the pursuit of political rather than humanitarian interests.

Since 1945 the legality of humanitarian intervention has been questioned, in particular by developing countries, on the ground that, apart from constituting a violation of territorial integrity it could not be reconciled with the Charter's proscription of force. The International Court of Justice (ICJ) **(309)** itself held in *Military and Paramilitary Activities in and against Nicaragua* (Nicaragua v. the United States) (1986 ICJ Rep. 14) that the use of force could not be the "appropriate method" to ensure respect for human rights. On the other hand, and especially due to a growing emphasis on human rights in international law and in reaction to multiplying instances of massive and outrageous violations of such rights, inflicted by governments on their own population, arguments for the lawfulness of humanitarian intervention were growing in strength. Publicists, especially in the West, advocated the right to humanitarian intervention in extreme cases of violation in the absence of centrally ordered or authorized UN-sponsored measures. An additional argument was that forcible humanitarian intervention did not conflict with Art. 2(4) of the UN Charter since it was not used against the territorial integrity or political independence of any state and was not inconsistent with the UN purposes. The problem is, of course, which value, prohibition of the use of force or respect for human rights, should have priority.

In state practice, there have been very few, if any, situations where humanitarian intervention as such was solely invoked to justify military action by the intervening state. In its intervention in East Pakistan in 1971, allegedly to protect the Bengalis from oppression by the Pakistani government, India also invoked self-defense **(335)**, and its action, obviously motivated by political and strategic objectives, was condemned by a very large majority of the UN members. In Africa, Tanzania's intervention in Uganda in 1979, justified as a response to atrocities committed by the Ugandan government against its citizens, was not without ulterior motivations. Consequently, concern over abuse of the right of humanitarian intervention has not strengthened the legal basis of such intervention in international law.

Yet, it can be argued that extreme cases of gross violations of human rights, involving large-scale atrocities, could justify humanitarian intervention if this kind of use of force were strictly circumscribed in order to prevent abuse by the intervening state or states. Borrowing elements from the right of self-defense, the law of humanitarian intervention should meet a number of requirements. First, there would have to be proof of commission on a large scale or condoning by the target state of grave international crimes as defined in the Statute of the International Criminal Court (ICC) **(170)**. The overwhelming scope of such crimes would have to call for urgent and immediate action. Second, the intervening state should exhaust without success all reasonably practicable, non-forcible alternatives of action, including unsuccessful resort to the Security Council (SC). Third, states resorting to humanitarian intervention would have to observe the requirement of proportionality, concentrating on prompt relief of the affected population as the focus of intervention. Fourth, international humanitarian law **(353)** should be strictly observed. Fifth, the intervening state or states should give their advance consent to the jurisdiction of the ICJ **(297)** in cases of any claims by the target state or other concerned states, resulting from the intervention. Any alleged war crimes committed by the intervening force should be subject to the jurisdiction of the ICC or an *ad hoc* criminal tribunal.

From the point of view of the current status of the rules governing resort to force and of a reasonably justifiable regime of humanitarian intervention—if it is acceptable as lawful at all—the intervention by the North Atlantic Treaty Organization (NATO) in Kosovo without the authorization of the SC falls short of legality under international law. First of all, however desirable it would be, despite the growing emphasis on human rights, contemporary international law does not, as yet, admit exceptions to the peremptory rule (*jus cogens*) barring the use of force in international relations beyond the exceptions provided by the UN Charter. In 1999 the use of force in the name of humanitarian intervention without SC authorization was questioned both by the UN Secretary-General and the High Commissioner for Human Rights **(158)**, and a subcommission of the Human Rights Commission **(161)** adopted a resolution which found such intervention juridically unfounded under general international law. But even assuming that in exceptional cases the law admitted of humanitarian intervention, NATO's action in Yugoslavia failed to meet the suggested criteria of a lawful intervention. Specifically, except for some not quite convincing attempts at negotiating with Yugoslavia, NATO did not pursue the possibility of resorting to non-forcible measures before starting its bombing campaign and, except for a few isolated cases, did not provide documented proof of massive and widespread grave violations of international criminal law committed against the Albanian population, otherwise within the context of an inter-ethnic strife where both Serbs and Albanians committed such violations. Moreover, the NATO-forced withdrawal of the observers of the Organization for Security and Cooperation in Europe (OSCE), deployed under an agreement between the OSCE and Yugoslavia (38 ILM 24 (1999)), had made it easier for the Serbs to carry on their anti-Albanian measures including ethnic cleansing. However, it appears that the mass exodus of the Albanian population was, to a large extent, due to the NATO bombing campaign. Most importantly, contrary to the idea of humanitarian intervention as an action designed to bring urgent direct and immediate relief to the affected population, NATO's 78-day high altitude bombing campaign targeting the whole of Yugoslavia, with civilian losses among the Serbian population exceeding the number of Albanian victims of Yugoslav repression, did not bring much relief to the Kosovo Albanians, the ostensible beneficiaries of the intervention, for more than two months, only increasing the number of casualties. The alternative of a rapid ground campaign targeted directly at Kosovo would have been more reconcilable with the nature and objective of humanitarian intervention, and in the final analysis would have cost fewer casualties. All this raises doubts about the purely humanitarian considerations of the NATO intervention in Kosovo. As far as the UN is concerned, the SC rejected a draft resolution condemning the use of force against Yugoslavia by NATO; nor did it ever positively endorse it. The SC resolution adopted after the intervention (38 ILM 1217 (1999) cannot be regarded as an *ex post* legitimation of NATO's action. It might be added that, for its part, in April 1999, Yugoslavia instituted proceedings before the ICJ against 10 NATO countries taking part in the intervention, claiming violation by those countries of the rules governing resort to force and other obligations under international law (*Legality of Use of Force*, 1999). At the same time, Yugoslavia filed a request for provisional measures **(322)**, asking the Court to order the 10 respondent states to cease immediately their acts of force against Yugoslavia. In response, the Court ruled that it manifestly lacked jurisdiction **(297)** in the cases against the United States and Spain and accordingly removed them from its List. In the other eight cases (against Belgium, Canada, France, Germany, Italy, Netherlands, Portugal, and the United Kingdom) the ICJ refused to grant provisional measures because it lacked *prima facie* jurisdiction, but remained seised of those cases. The eight cases were still pending in 2004, but it appears that for pragmatic reasons and due to political changes in the country Serbia and Montenegro will abandon its suit.

The Kosovo crisis once again reflected the gap between emphasis on the increasing concern over human rights in international law and the reality of states committing violations of such rights invoking domestic jurisdiction **(9)** and sovereignty **(125)**. It also highlights the need to adjust the existing rules of international law in a way that would allow humanitarian crises to be solved without breaching the rules governing force in international relations. This remains one of the most daunting challenges confronting international law today.

**333. Just War Doctrine.** This is a doctrine of ancient origin which, for purposes of testing the legality of war **(338)**, made a distinction between just war (*bellum justum*) and unjust war (*bellum injustum*). Elements of the just war doctrine can be traced back to the writings of Cicero in the first century BC, but the doctrine was fully developed by Christian theologians, beginning with Saint Augustine at the turn of the fifth century. The conditions of just war were first formulated on the foundations of canon law by Raymund Peñaforte in the 13th century, followed by Saint Thomas Aquinas and other medieval Christian scholars. Their doctrine was eventually adopted and further developed by the classical writers on the law of nations in the 16th and 17th centuries, including Alberico Gentili (Gentilis) **(15)** and Hugo de Groot (Grotius) **(16)**. Generally speaking, according to the just war doctrine, to be just, a war must have a just cause and righteous intention. However, Christian scholars differed in their more specific formulation of the tests of just war. While all agreed that war in self-defense **(335)**, to punish wrongs, or to obtain reparation for a prior illegal act committed by the other side, were all just wars, there was no consensus on whether a war waged against pagans or heretics was to be regarded as just.

The problem with the concept of just war was that both Church scholars and classical publicists approached it from a subjective point of view, admitting the possibility of both sides of a conflict believing in good conscience in the justness of their cause. This approach made it impossible objectively to determine the legality of a war. As a matter of fact, while each state resorting to war would invoke its just cause, the just war doctrine could never become part of the evolving law of nations. Thus, eventually by the 18th century, the doctrine of just war had been discarded even in the theory of the law of nations. In an international system of sovereign **(124)** states **(127)** each state remained the sole judge of its cause and was entitled to decide whether to resort to war in the defense of its perceived vital interests. By the 19th century, international publicists **(42)** abandoned attempts to regulate the legality of war as such (*jus ad bellum*), focusing instead on the legality of the methods of warfare (*jus in bello*) **(353)**. Whether or not a war had a "just cause" was, in principle, irrelevant from the point of view of its legality as an instrument of a sovereign state's foreign policy.

It was not until the 20th century that scholarly attempts were made to revive the old distinction between just and unjust war. In a sense, the old doctrine of just war provided a doctrinal underpinning for restrictions to the right to resort to war, stipulated in the Covenant of the League of Nations in 1919 and the Pact of Paris of 1928 **(330)** on the renunciation of war as an instrument of national policy. Finally, in 1945, the Charter of the United Nations reestablished, as it were, in legal terms the doctrine of just war by making a fundamental distinction between legal and illegal recourse to force **(329)**. However, in an international heterogeneous system of sovereign states this distinction, which otherwise became part of general international law, continues to be as difficult to apply in practice as the classical distinction between just and unjust war.

**334. Peacekeeping.** Because of its evolution since the early and still continuing truce supervision operations in the first Arab-Israeli War in 1948 (United Nations Truce Supervision Organization, UNTSO) and on the India-Pakistani cease-fire line in Jammu and Kashmir in 1949 (United Nations Military Observer Group in India and Pakistan, UNMOGIP), the concept of the United Nations (UN) "peacekeeping" defies simple definition. However, in all its stages it has been based on the optimistic principle that the deployment of UN presence in areas of conflict, international, semi-international, or internal, can ease tensions between the hostile parties involved and eventually lead to a peaceful solution of the conflict.

The term "peacekeeping" does not appear in the UN Charter, and it is not entirely clear which of its provisions constitutes the legal basis for this kind of UN activity. However, one can identify a number of articles concerning the powers of the Security Council (SC), including those specified in Chapters VI (pacific settlement of disputes) **(318)** and VII (Action with respect to threats to the peace, breaches of the peace **(329)**, and acts of aggression) **(325)**, which could provide a legal basis for peacekeeping. They are, for example, Art. 29, on power to establish subsidiary organs; Art. 34, to investigate any dispute or situation; Arts. 37 and 38, to recommend procedures for settlement; Art. 39 to decide on measures to maintain (or restore) international peace and security; and Art. 40 to order provisional measures. Although a number of complex peacekeeping operations have been authorized under Chapter VII, Art. 42, which governs military action within the collective security **(327)** enforcement system, has, of course, never been invoked by the SC. The General Assembly (GA) may also establish subsidiary organs (Art. 22) and—like other UN organs, except the International Court of Justice (ICJ) **(309)**—entrust functions to the Secretary-General. The SC authorizes the deployment of a peacekeeping operation and determines its mandate, and the Secretary-General makes recommendations on the manner it is to be carried out. The mandate of a mission is usually extended for a period of six months. The Department of Peacekeeping Operations directs the operations in the field. Countries providing troops and equipment are compensated by the UN. While remaining members of their own respective national establishment, the personnel operate, under the control of the UN as an international force. UN peacekeeping forces stationed in a state **(127)** are governed by a status-of-forces agreement with the state concerned. A model of such agreement has been drafted by the UN Secretariat. In addition, the status of UN forces is regulated by the Convention of 1994 on the Safety of UN and Associated Personnel. It may be added in this context that, invoking Art. 16 of the Rome Statute of the International Criminal Court (ICC) **(170)** and at the insistence of the United States (US), the SC agreed to exempt for a year (extended for another year through 1 July 2004), from investigation or prosecution for any offenses relating to a UN operation, members of UN peacekeeping forces who are nationals of a state (including the US) not a party to the Statute of the ICC (Resolutions 1422 (2002) and 1487 (2003)) (41 ILM 1276 (2002); 42 ILM 1025 (2003)). While there has been some doubt on the matter, UN forces in situations of armed conflict, whether international **(339)** or internal **(340)**, actively engaged as combatants **(342)**, are subject to the rules of international humanitarian law **(353)**. The cost of peacekeeping operations is shared by all the members, with the GA apportioning them according to a special scale of assessments. Many countries make additional voluntary contributions. Member states providing, at the request of the Secretary-General, personnel, equipment, and other support for a mission, are reimbursed from the budget of the mission. As ruled in 1962 by the ICJ in its advisory opinion **(291)** on *Certain Expenses of the United* Nations (1962 ICJ Rep. 161), the costs of the UN peacekeeping operations constitute expenses of the Organization under Art. 17(2) of the UN Charter.

Apart from the above-noted truce supervision activities, the first UN peacekeeping operation, UN Emergency Force (UNEF I), 1956–1967, was established to supervise the withdrawal of British and French forces from the Suez Canal area and then monitor the armistice line between Egypt and Israel. Expanding a definition by a UN Legal Counsel, this kind of classical peacekeeping could be defined as actions involving the use of voluntarily provided military personnel to separate hostile parties in international conflict situations on the basis of the consent of all parties concerned and without resorting to armed force except in self-defense **(335)**. Subsequent peacekeeping operations involving international conflict included UNEF II (1973–1979), monitoring disengagement between Egypt and Israel and succeeded by a non-UN, US-sponsored observer force; the UN Disengagement Observer Force (UNDOF), 1974, Israel-Syria, still continuing; the UN Interim Force in Lebanon (UNIFIL), 1978, still continuing; the UN Iraq-Kuwait Observation Mission (UNIKOM), 1991–2003; the UN Iran-Iraq Military Observer Group, 1988–1991; the UN Aouzou Strip Observer Group, 1994, verifying withdrawal of troops in the territorial dispute between Chad and Libya; the UN Mission of Observers in Prevlaka, 1996–2002, monitoring the demilitarization of the Prevlaka Peninsula on the Adriatic; and, more recently, the UN Mission in Ethiopia and Eritrea (UNMEE), 2000, still continuing, verifying a cease-fire following the war between the two countries and demarcating the boundary **(189)**. The UN Good Offices Mission in Afghanistan and Pakistan, 1988–1990, and the UN Angola Verification Mission 1989–1991 supervised the withdrawal of Soviet troops from Afghanistan and Cuban troops from Angola, respectively.

The civil war in the Congo in the early 1960s, a portent of things to come in the 1990s, confronted the UN with problems of peacekeeping in the chaotic situation of a non-international armed conflict. The large-scale Congo operation (known after its French acronym as ONUC), 1960–1964, guided, after the Soviet veto in the SC, by the UN Secretary-General, demonstrated that, in situations of civil war, the UN force had to perform tasks that could be qualified as peace enforcement rather than peacekeeping. The structure of the forces also changed, including among the peacekeepers civilian police officers, specialists in administration, and other experts with the responsibility to restore normality and some semblance of governmental functions in the country. In Cyprus, the UN Peacekeeping Force in Cyprus (UNFICYP) (1964–) had the task of maintaining peace between the Greek and Turkish communities, first in the whole of the island, and then after the invasion by Turkey in 1974, along the boundary line south of the buffer zone imposed by Turkey. The UNFICYP continued to function in 2004 pending any future comprehensive political solution of the Cyprus question.

Since the 1990s, the nature of armed conflicts brought before the UN, has undergone major changes, with a proliferation of such conflicts within states threatening international peace and security. As a result, a great majority of UN peacekeeping operations, initially devised for conflict between states **(127)**, has been applied with mixed results to conflicts within states (or aspiring states); and peacekeepers, often working closely with relevant UN agencies and bodies and occasionally regional organizations **(84)**, have frequently found themselves facing complex situations within a hostile environment where the traditional distinction between peacekeeping and peace enforcement was blurred and a peacekeeping mission necessarily had to enforce peace and to undertake a variety of civilian peace-building tasks, including help in creating political institutions, reintegrating combatants into civilian society, humanitarian relief, supervision of elections, training of police, and the like. As analyzed in 1992 by the UN Secretary-General in his Agenda for Peace (31 ILM 953 (1992)) and defined in 2000 by a UN committee in a comprehensive review of the peacekeeping operations (39 ILM 1432 (2000)), peace building includes "activities undertaken on the far side of conflict to reassemble the foundations of peace and provide the tools for building on these foundations something that is more than just the absence of war." In a number of situations (Yugoslavia, Somalia, Rwanda, Sierra Leone, Côte d'Ivoire, Congo, Liberia), a peacekeeping operation set up first without reference to Chapter VII (collective security) **(327)** later obtained an explicit SC authorization under Chapter VII and specific actions were ordered directly under this Chapter.

Altogether there have been some 60 UN peacekeeping operations. In late 2004 the UN maintained 14 operations: UNTSO, UNMOGIP, UNFICYP, UNDOF, UNIFIL, UN Mission for the Referendum in Western Sahara, UN Observer Mission in Georgia, UN Interim Administrative Mission in Kosovo (UNMIK), UN Mission in Sierra Leone, UN Organization Mission in the Democratic Republic of the Congo, strengthened in 2003 by the deployment of an Interim Emergency Multinational Force in Bunia, in northeastern Congo; UNMEE; UN Mission of support in East Timor UNMISET; UN Operation in Côte d'Ivoire (UNOCI), and a large UN mission in Liberia; UN Stabalization Mission in Haiti (MINUSTAH); and UN Operation in Burundi (ONUB). The operations range in strength from a few hundred international and local staff to more than 15,000 of military and civilian peacekeepers. The total number of military personnel and civilian police exceeded 40,000 from some 90 countries, working with about 3,600 international and 7,000 local civilian staff. The total number of fatalities in all peacekeeping operations since 1948 has been approximately 1,800. In addition to peacekeeping operations, in 2004 there were 12 political and peacebuilding missions (Afghanistan, Guyana, Burundi, Central African Republic, African Great Lakes Region, Guatemala, Guinea-Bissau, Liberia, Middle East, Somalia, Tajikistan, and West Africa) with about 1,000 personnel. The North Atlantic Treaty Organization (NATO)–led International Security Assistance Force in Afghanistan is not a UN operation, but is explicitly authorized by the SC. Finally, one should add that in 2003 the SC (Res. 1500) established the UN Assistance Mission for Iraq (UNAMI), which for security reasons operated only outside of Iraq.

Among the many UN peacekeeping operations, some stand out as major, though not necessarily successful, undertakings because of their size, political importance, and legal implications as *de facto* enforcement actions under Chapter VII of the UN Charter. Perhaps the most complex of all were the various operations undertaken during the Yugoslav crisis in 1991–1995 and subsequently in Kosovo in 1999. Briefly speaking, following the establishment of the UN Protection Force (UNPROFOR) in 1992, a long series of SC resolutions adopted in response to the developments in the disintegrating Yugoslavia **(134)**, authorized UNPROFOR to take "all necessary measures" in self-defense to undertake a number of tasks: demilitarization of protected areas in Croatia; monitoring the Serb-controlled areas of Croatia, and demilitarization of the Prevlaka Peninsula. A special resolution, invoking Chapter VII of the Charter, called upon all states to take "all measures necessary" to facilitate delivery of humanitarian assistance. Following the adoption of the "no-fly" ban on military flights over Bosnia, further resolutions authorized member states to take such measures to ensure compliance with the ban. Under a special arrangement with the UN, NATO planes enforced the ban, and subsequently were used to protect—not always successfully—Muslim "safe areas" and other special exclusion zones, authorized, under Chapter VII, to use force in self-defense. Following the Croatian offensive which captured the Serb protected areas in Croatia, UNPROFOR was reorganized in 1995 into regional missions, with UNPROFOR to operate in Bosnia and the UN Confidence Restoration Operation in Croatia. In addition, the first-ever UN preventive peacekeeping force in Macedonia, the UN Preventive Deployment Force, authorized by the SC in 1992, was deployed in 1995 to monitor the Albania-Macedonia border in order to prevent any spillover of conflict into that new state. Following the 1995 Dayton-Paris General Framework Agreement for Peace in Bosnia and Herzegovina and related accords (35 ILM 75, 170 (1996)), UNPROFOR was replaced by the Implementation Force (renamed Security Force in 1996)), composed mainly of troops of NATO countries. However, the UN continued its operations designed to restructure the Bosnian police and assist in the return of refugees **(178)** and internally displaced persons, through its UN Mission in Bosnia and Herzegovina, taken over by the European Union in 2002. In addition, the Dayton Agreement established special international authorities, approved by the SC, with powers to implement the civilian aspects of the Agreement. However, the Dayton Agreement failed to include in the peace plan the problem of Kosovo, a region formally part of Serbia but with a very large Albanian majority. The ensuing Kosovo crisis of 1999 resulted in a NATO "humanitarian intervention" **(332)** and subsequent creation of the UNMIK, a still operating peacekeeping force of some 4,300 civilian police, 40 military personnel, 1,000 international, and 3,200 local civilian personnel.

The Kosovo as well as East Timor cases are two major examples of UN post-conflict involvement in peace building, and beyond that, performing important administrative functions amounting to international administration of a territory. The difference between the two is, however, that in the case of Kosovo the UN recognized the sovereignty **(125)** under international law of Serbia and Montenegro, limiting its involvement to securing substantial autonomy for the province. On the other hand, in the case of East Timor the comprehensive administration of the territory by the UN Transitional Administration in East Timor established by the SC under Chapter VII of the UN Charter, had the objective of total independence for East Timor, which was successfully achieved in 2002. However, the new state of Timor Leste still hosts the UNMISET, which is responsible for some major administrative functions and maintains a military component of about 3,500 personnel to ensure security.

In the Somalia crisis (1992–1994) the SC authorized a humanitarian intervention in the context of utter chaos in that disintegrating state. A small technical mission and then equally inadequate UN Operation in Somalia (UNOSOM I) proved unable to provide protection to humanitarian convoys in the conditions of anarchy and fighting between the warring factions. Consequently, the SC determined under Chapter VII that the situation constituted a threat to international peace and security and authorized the use of all necessary means to establish a secure environment for humanitarian relief operations. A large peacekeeping, mainly US, Unified Task Force was created, expanded into UNOSOM II, with a more extensive mandate to restore peace in Somalia. However, violence escalated to the point where the UN forces could not cope with the situation and the SC decided to terminate the mission. The Somali operation offers an extreme example of a situation that cannot be successfully controlled within the framework of the rules developed for UN peacekeeping operations and requires an unambiguous collective security enforcement action, assuming that an intervention in Somali-like conditions has any chance of achieving its objectives.

In Rwanda, in the midst of a civil war and because of the inability of the UN Observer Mission Uganda Rwanda to secure implementation of a prior peace agreement between the warring ethnic groups, the SC resolved to set up the UN Assistance Mission for Rwanda (UNAMIR), 1994–1996), which, however, was unable to prevent a full-scale genocidal war. As a result, the SC, acting under Chapter VII, decided to withdraw most of the UN contingents from Rwanda and authorized France to protect the population in a two-month operation until the UNAMIR could be reorganized and deployed in a protected zone. However, mass genocide in Rwanda had already occurred. Hence the UN operation in Rwanda must be considered as the major humanitarian failure of UN peacekeeping. In another part of the world, in Haiti, where the SC authorized the use of all means to enforce sanctions against the military junta to secure a democratic rule in the country, the UN operations, in concert with the SC-authorized regional organization, proved, despite a number of UN missions, a failure. In 2000 the UN Secretary-General recommended to the GA that the UN missions in Haiti should be terminated in view of continued political instability in Haiti. However, another major stabilization mission was established for Haiti in 2004. No effective UN mission was undertaken to prevent atrocities in Darfur, Sudan.

As demonstrated by a new crisis and anarchy in Haiti in 2004, the peacemaking and peacebuilding missions of the UN may encounter challenges that cannot be resolved in situations of organic political instability. In the final analysis, the success of UN peacekeeping depends on real commitment of all parties, both the countries assisted by the UN action and the contributing members of the Organization. Nevertheless, in most cases of the surprisingly large number of UN peacekeeping missions, the UN has been able to make a significant contribution to stabilizing situations of international conflict and—the main focus of UN peacekeeping today—internal political instability. From the international law point of view, perhaps the most significant conclusion is that the UN, and in particular the SC, have been able to devise a mechanism in order successfully to confront at least some peace-threatening situations despite the failure of the collective security arrangements of Chapter VII.

**335. Self-Defense.** As the major exception to the United Nations (UN) Charter's (Art. 2(4)) general prohibition of the use of force **(329)** in international relations, the right of self-defense, anchored in Art. 51 of the Charter, means the inherent right of states **(127)** of individual or collective **(336)** self-defense "if an armed attack occurs against a member of the United Nations." Although the Charter refers to "a Member," this formulation is generally interpreted **(274)** to mean any state. Under Art. 51, the right of self-defense terminates "as soon as the Security Council has taken measures necessary to maintain international peace and security," a provision interpreted to refer not just to a decision of the Security Council (SC) but an effective action by the UN in defense of the victim state. If the SC is unable to make any decision, as in the case of a veto by a permanent member of the SC (China, France, Russia, United Kingdom (UK), and United States (US)), the right of self-defense continues until the objective of repelling the attack is achieved. It appears that if the SC has adopted any measures, only the Council itself has the right to determine whether its measures have been adequate under the circumstances. As shown in 1982 by the action of the UK to recover the Falkland Islands conquered by Argentina and the collective eviction of Iraq from Kuwait in 1991, the right of self-defense continues to exist even following the completion of the hostile armed attack. Under Art. 51, measures taken by UN members in the exercise of the right of self-defense shall be immediately reported to the SC and shall not in any way affect the authority and responsibility of the Council to take at any time such action as it deems necessary in order to maintain or restore international peace and security. There is general agreement that the phrase "armed attack" in Art. 51 of the Charter must be understood as including not only a traditional invasion by regular armed forces but also gradual piecemeal infiltration and sending on behalf of the state of irregulars on a significant scale, that is, the attack must be more than provoking frontier incidents. The General Assembly's (GA) definition of aggression **(325)** treats such infiltrations as constituting a category of aggression, a view that is consistent with customary international law **(39)** and confirmed by the International Court of Justice (ICJ) **(309)** in its judgment in *Military and Paramilitary Activities in and against Nicaragua* (Nicaragua v. United States) (1986 ICJ Rep. 14). However, unless on a large scale, mere assistance to or training of rebels is not included within the concept of "armed attack" that would generate the right of self-defense of the target state. Such assistance may, however, be regarded as a threat or use of force **(329)**, or amount to intervention **(331)** in the affairs of another state, and entitles the target state to take appropriate countermeasures **(58)**. The relatively restrictive interpretation by the ICJ of the concept of armed attack, which in practice might exclude the right of self-defense of the target state, is not universally accepted. One can add that self-defense is not limited to defense against an attack on a state's territory **(228)**; it is also allowed to repulse attacks on the state's ships on the high seas **(245)** and in the course of legitimate innocent passage **(248)**. More controversial is the claim of self-defense to protect a state's nationals abroad by a military intervention **(331)**.

The inherent right of self-defense in accordance with Art. 51 arises for the attacked state also in response to a terrorist **(337)** attack, as recognized by the SC in its Resolution 1368 (40 ILM 1277 (2001)), adopted the day after the terrorist attacks on the US on 11 September 2001 and reaffirmed in Resolutions 1373 (40 ILM 1278 (2001)) and 1378 (41 ILM 505 (2002)) of 28 September and 14 November 2001, respectively. These resolutions provide, in effect, that the victim state of a terrorist attack has the right to bring to justice the perpetrators, with the implication that military action is permitted against states that are reasonably certain to aid, support, or harbor them. This was the generally recognized right of the US self-defense action against the terrorists whose territorial basis in Afghanistan and other support granted them by the government of that country were common knowledge. However, this reasoning and an implied authorization by the SC of anti-terrorist self-defense action cannot be applied to the US military intervention in Iraq in 2003 since no evidence was offered by the US of Iraq's aiding or harboring the perpetrators of the attacks on the US in September 2001.

In all cases, the right of self-defense is subject to the attacked state's duty to observe the principles of necessity and proportionality. The former requires that the target state be faced by a credible and imminent threat and has exhausted the means of peaceful settlement to prevent the conflict. The latter requires that the measures taken by it in self-defense must be proportional to the armed attack.

The wording of Art. 51 has generated a fundamental controversy over the scope of the right of self-defense in international law. In general, two approaches have been debated since 1945: the restrictive approach taking the wording of Art. 51 literally and the approach admitting anticipatory or preemptive (but *not* preventive) self-defense strictly circumscribed by certain conditions. In the prevailing restrictive interpretation the right of self-defense exists if and only if an armed attack *occurs*. This means, first, that no right of self-defense by armed force exists in response to a hostile action unless that action constitutes an *armed* attack. If it does not constitute such attack, then the target state is allowed self-defense only by coercive means short of armed force. Second, the restrictive interpretation of Art. 51 implies that the Charter does not allow anticipatory, preemptive (let alone—as discussed below—preventive) self-defense, that is, defense against an attack that the target state believes to be imminent. According to the extensive interpretation of Art. 51, the right of self-defense, including self-defense by armed force, is allowed not only against an armed attack but also against other violations of a state's fundamental rights. In addition, in a broad interpretation, Art. 51 does not exclude the right of anticipatory self-defense. In the age of nuclear confrontation during the Cold War, it was argued that anticipatory self-defense was admissible in the age of nuclear missiles when the target state could not risk destruction by waiting, like a "sitting duck," for the commencement of the aggressor's strike. In legal terms, the broad construction doctrine views the phrase "if an armed attack occurs" as merely one, albeit major, illustration of the otherwise existing natural or inherent right of self-defense in customary international law, including the right of anticipatory self-defense. However, this right of anticipatory self-defense may not transgress the limits circumscribed by international law and certainly does not include the right to a preventive war. In this regard reference is usually made to the celebrated *Caroline* incident in 1837 in relations between the US and Great Britain. In that incident, the British, claiming self-defense against raids by rebels on Canada's border with the US, who were supported by US nationals, destroyed in US territory a boat, the *Caroline,* supplying the Canadian rebels. Two US nationals were killed in the incident. In the ensuing diplomatic correspondence, the US Secretary of State Daniel Webster formulated the criteria of the legality of self-defense in customary international law. According to this test, accepted by the two disputing countries, a state claiming self-defense must show "a necessity of self-defense, instant, overwhelming, leaving no choice of means, and no moment for deliberation." In addition, the self-defense action must be proportionate to the severity of the attack and justified by the gravity of the danger. Now, while the *Caroline* formulation admits in principle the legality of the right of anticipatory self-defense, it limits the right of self-defense before an actual attack occurs to clearly proven cases of imminent attack. The *Caroline* test has been subsequently invoked in a number of situations. At the Nuremberg trial of the major Nazi war criminals, in connection with the German invasion of Norway in April 1940, the tribunal rejected Germany's claim of self-defense because of an allegedly imminent Allied landing in Norway and ruled that the situation had not met Webster's criteria of the *Caroline* case. Touching upon the controversy over the meaning of Art. 51, in its judgment in the case of *Military and Paramilitary Activities in and against Nicaragua* (Nicaragua v. United States) (1986 ICJ Rep.14) the ICJ admitted the existence in customary law **(39)** of an inherent right of self-defense, but did not find it necessary in the case to rule on the lawfulness of anticipatory self-defense. The ICJ left the matter open, but the prevailing opinion in the doctrine—at least at that time—was that anticipatory self-defense was inadmissible. Being based on imperfect, let alone arbitrary, judgment of individual states, it would easily lend itself to abuse and would conflict with the general spirit of the Charter's ban on the use of force. On the other hand, in most exceptional circumstances, especially when the very existence of the target state is involved and when an anticipated armed attack should turn out to have been really imminent, anticipatory self-defense under customary international law, if consistent with the *Caroline* criteria, could be considered legal or at least condoned by the international community as a justified resort to force. However, there are limits even to the broadly construed right of self defense under Art. 51 and, as later discussed, the new US doctrine of preemption (or, correctly, preventive, war) goes further than that, far transgressing the limits of the—otherwise still controversial under the Charter—extensively interpreted right to anticipatory self-defense in customary international law as circumscribed in the *Caroline* case. This doctrine seems to conflict with both traditional and contemporary international law.

Uncertainties over the scope of the right of self-defense are compounded by difficulties concerning an objective ascertainment of facts, including correct intelligence, which allows a state to invoke this right even when the legality of self-defense is rather dubious. Historical examples of aggressive action rationalized by the right of self-defense include, *inter alia*, the Soviet claims with regard to Hungary in 1956, Czechoslovakia in 1968, and Afghanistan in 1979. Self-defense was also invoked by Israel in its preemptive strike against its Arab neighbors in 1967 and in the case of the bombing of a nuclear reactor in Iraq in 1981. The US itself has used force in anticipatory self-defense, as in the air strikes in 1986 against Libya to forestall any future terrorist attacks sponsored by that country. Self-defense arguments were also invoked in the use of force against Panama and Sudan, and air strikes against Iraq prior to the war of 2003. However, it should be noted that in the Cuban missile crisis the US did not justify the quarantine **(328)** by self-defense arguments but by an action of a regional organization, out of concern that such a self-defense based legal interpretation of Art. 51 would establish a dangerous "precedent": it would have to be conceded to the Soviet Union against any US military threat, such as, for example, missiles in Turkey. The SC has, in general, followed a restrictive approach in interpreting Art. 51 and this position was clearly articulated by a unanimous condemnation of the Israeli action against Iraq in 1981. However, the SC, yielding to political considerations, failed to condemn Israel for its preemptive strike in 1967.

The issue of anticipatory self-defense became the subject of serious controversy after September 2001 and especially in connection with the US invasion of Iraq in 2003. Claiming that in an age of international terrorism and weapons of mass destruction the US could not afford waiting until attacked, the US proclaimed its new position on the strategy toward the terrorist threat. The National Security Strategy, published in 2002 (41 ILM 1478 (2002) (Introduction)) asserted the right of the US to use military force preventively against any country or terrorists group that was perceived as a potential threat to the security of the US and even if the time and place of the enemy attack remained uncertain. "America will act against such emerging threats before they are fully formed," stated the Strategy. This claim to self-defense establishes a very low threshold for triggering anticipatory self-defense, possibly based on faulty intelligence and going far beyond and stretching to indefinite limits the otherwise still controversial application of the pre-UN Charter traditional right of self-defense requiring clear evidence of an imminent threat, as articulated in the above-noted *Caroline* formulation. Under the new US strategy, the threat need not be imminent; probability and perhaps even possibility of an attack would be sufficient for a preventive action. Self-defense was invoked as one argument for the US military intervention in Iraq in 2003, the other argument being that resort to force had been authorized by past SC resolutions within the context of collective security **(327)**. Even if one assumes that the controversial extensive interpretation of Art. 51 allowing preemptive self-defense to forestall an imminent, that is, not actual, attack is admissible, such an interpretation simply does not fit the facts: there was no imminent threat; the SC-authorized teams of inspectors were searching, without restrictions, for weapons of mass destruction; no weapons were found by them or after the hostilities, by the US; nor did the inspectors discover any signs of preparations for an imminent attack by Iraq against the US or any other country. No state in the region alerted the SC of any threat by Iraq to international peace and security. Neither did the US present any proof of Iraq's harboring terrorist bases. One could argue that if such proof had been provided, the use of force against Iraq—like in 2001 against the Taliban in Afghanistan—might have been justified in terms of self-defense against terrorism, previously endorsed by the SC in its resolutions after September 2001. But in the case of Iraq, self-defense could not be invoked by the US as a rationale for its use of force.

The Strategy document does not make it clear whether other countries as well have the right to broadly conceived preventive self-defense. If other, especially major, states agreed with the US new concept of self-defense, this would practically be tantamount to a repudiation of the fundamental *jus cogens* rule as stipulated in Art. 2(4) of the UN Charter and—in a way—a return to the pre-Charter position of international law on the use of force in international relations. But it appears that a great majority of states still support the idea of a multilateral, UN-led, approach to the use of force. On the other hand, it is quite possible that an extensive interpretation of Art. 51, but still strictly within the limits of the *Caroline* test, will gain more support both in practice and in the doctrine of international law.

**336. Self-Defense, Collective.** Like the right of individual self-defense **(335)**, the right of "collective" self-defense is stipulated in Art. 51 of the United Nations (UN) Charter. It is an inherent right of a state **(127)** or group of states to come to the defense of another state against which an armed attack has occurred, until the Security Council (SC) has taken measures necessary to restore and maintain international peace and security. There is agreement among publicists **(42)**, confirmed by state practice, that the right of collective self-defense does not mean the exercise of individual self-defense by a group of states, but the right of states to come to the defense of a state under armed attack and entitled to individual self-defense under Art. 51. It should be noted that the term "collective" used in this article is somewhat misleading, suggesting the idea of "collective security" **(327)**, which is not the case in Art. 51. A state or states supporting by force of arms a state, victim of an armed attack, need not themselves be in a situation warranting individual self-defense although they may otherwise perceive a threat to their national security. In addition, as analyzed by the International Court of Justice **(309)** in its judgment in *Military and Paramilitary Activities in and against Nicaragua* (Nicaragua v. United States) (1986 ICJ Rep. 14), a state coming to the aid of a victim of armed attack may not use force against the aggressor unless the victim state itself declares that it has been attacked and requests military assistance. A prior treaty **(288)** may provide a legal basis for collective defense, such as the constituent treaty of the North Atlantic Treaty Organization, 1949 (34 UNTS 243) or some other mutual assistance agreement, such as the Inter-American Treaty of Reciprocal Assistance (Rio Treaty) of 1947 (21 UNTS 77). The right to enter into such collective defense alliances has never been questioned by the UN; the concept of collective self-defense itself was introduced into the Charter to fit the American system into the global security system of the UN. Among the relatively few instances of invoking the right of collective self-defense, one can mention the United States claims in the case of Vietnam, 1966, Nicaragua, 1981–1984, and following Iraq's aggression against Kuwait in 1990 in which case the allied action to liberate Kuwait was legally justified not only by the right of collective self-defense but also by the SC authorization to use force against Iraq within the framework of an *ad hoc* collective security arrangement. The legal criteria of the right of self-defense, including the controversies over the exact scope of this right (the meaning of armed attack, anticipatory self-defense, and so on), are also applicable to the exercise of the right of collective self-defense.

**337. Terrorism.** There is no consensus in the doctrine of international law and the practice of states **(127)** on how to define the phenomenon of terrorism. While certain specific acts of terror to advance a political cause are relatively easy to identify (aircraft hijacking, hostage taking, and the like), the concept of terrorism is too elusive and politically charged for a definition to encompass comprehensively all manifestations of terrorism. Naturally, the most vexing problem in defining terrorism is drawing a line distinguishing between terrorist activities on the one hand and, on the other, the struggle for independence by national liberation movements **(94)** and other groups, such as ethnic minorities **(172),** against governments in defense of their legitimate rights recognized in international law. The reports submitted to the Committee of the Security Council (SC), established to monitor implementation of Resolution 1373 of 2001 (40 ILM 1278 (2001)) in the aftermath of the September 2001 terrorist attacks upon the United States (US), revealed a wide divergence of views concerning the above-mentioned distinction.

Attempts at developing a generalized definition of terrorism date back to 1937, after the assassination in 1934 of the king of Yugoslavia and the French foreign minister prompted the League of Nations to adopt a Convention for the Prevention and Punishment of Terrorism, which, however, never entered into force **(271)**. In that abortive convention, terrorism, historically a term associated not with international terrorism but with the reign of terror in France during a period of the French Revolution, was defined in Art. 1(2) as "criminal acts against a State and intended or calculated to create a state of terror in the minds of particular persons or a group of persons or the general public." More recently, the Legal Committee of the United Nations (UN) General Assembly (GA) has been engaged in drafting a comprehensive convention on the elimination of terrorism. In addition, the GA and a number of UN specialized agencies, such as International Civil Aviation Organization (ICAO), International Maritime Organization, and International Atomic Energy Agency have been involved in the fight against terrorism, drafting since 1963 a dozen conventions designed to combat various specific forms of terrorist acts. Generally speaking, these global legal tools, 11 of which are in force, require the states parties to criminalize the offenses covered by the convention by severe penalties and either extradite **(75)** or prosecute the offenders. Four conventions have been adopted by the GA: 1. Convention on the Prevention and Punishment of Crimes against Internationally Protected Persons, Including Diplomatic Agents, 1973; 2. International Convention against the Taking of Hostages, 1979; 3. International Convention for the Suppression of Terrorist Bombings, 1987; and 4. International Convention for the Suppression of the Financing of Terrorism, 1999. A convention for the suppression of acts of nuclear terrorism was in the drafting stages in 2004. Eight conventions have been adopted by specialized agencies: 1. Convention on Offenses and Certain Other Acts Committed on Board Aircraft, 1963 (Tokyo Convention) **(229)**, in force 1969, 177 parties; 2. Convention for the Suppression of Unlawful Seizure of Aircraft, 1970 (Hague Convention) **(199)**, in force 1971, 17 parties; and the related Joint Statement of a number of European countries, US, and the United Kingdom (UK) on sanctions against countries sheltering air hijackers (17 ILM 1285 (1978); 3. Convention for the Suppression of Unlawful Acts against the Safety of Civil Aviation, 1971 (Sabotage Convention) **(210)**; 4. Convention on the Physical Protection of Nuclear Material, 1980; 5. Protocol on the Suppression of Unlawful Acts of Violence at Airports Serving International Civil Aviation, 1988 27 (ILM 627 (1988)), in force 1989, 142 parties, supplementary to the Montreal Convention, listed above at 3; 6. Convention on the Suppression of Unlawful Acts against the Safety of Maritime Navigation, 1988 (27 ILM 668 (1988)), in force 1992, 102 parties; 7. Protocol for the Suppression of Unlawful Acts against the Safety of Fixed Platforms Located on the Continental Shelf **(236)**, 1988 (27 ILM 685 (1988)), in force 1992, 95 parties; and 8. Convention on the Marking of Plastic Explosives for the Purpose of Detection, 1991 (30 ILM 726 (1991)), in force 1998, 104 parties. One should also mention the ICAO Declaration [not a treaty] of 2001 on Misuse of Civil Aircraft as Weapons of Destruction and Other Terrorist Acts Involving Civil Aviation (41 ILM 501 (2002)).

In addition to global agreements, there are a number of regional conventions on terrorism, *inter alia*, the Organization of American States (OAS) Convention to Prevent and Punish Acts of Terrorism Taking the Form of Crimes against Persons and Related Extortion that Are of International Significance, 1971 (27 UST 3949; TIAS No. 8413); the European Convention on the Suppression of Terrorism, 1977 (15 ILM 1272 (1976)), with the Agreement Concerning the Application of the Convention, 1979 (19 ILM 325 (1980)); the South Asian Association for Regional Cooperation (SAARC) Convention on Suppression of Terrorism, 1987; the Arab Convention for the Suppression of Terrorism, 1998; the Treaty on Cooperation among States Members of the Commonwealth of Independent States in Combating Terrorism, 1999; the Convention of the Organization of the Islamic Conference on Combating International Terrorism, 1999; the Organization of African Unity (OAU) Convention on the Prevention and Combating of Terrorism, 1999; and, the most recent, the OAS Inter-American Convention against Terrorism, 2002 (42 ILM 19 (2003)).

Apart from treaties, the UN measures to combat terrorism have included resolutions by the GA and the SC. The GA has adopted a series of resolutions condemning terrorism and suggested measures to eliminate all forms of terrorism from international relations. In a major resolution adopted by consensus in 1994 (Resolution 49/60), the annexed Declaration on Measures to Eliminate International Terrorism, supplemented by a declaration of 1996 in Resolution 51/210, condemned all acts of terrorism "in any circumstances unjustifiable whatever the considerations of a political, philosophical, ideological, racial, ethnic, religious or any other nature that may be invoked to justify them." The Declaration suggests three major elements for a definition of terrorism, referring to criminal acts; committed for political purposes; and intended or calculated to provoke a state of terror in the general public, a group of persons, or particular persons. It is the element of political motivation and goals that differentiates acts of terrorism from criminal acts which, while also spreading terror, are committed for common criminal motives. After the 11 September 2001 terrorist attacks on the US, the GA in its resolution 56/1 strongly condemned the attacks, calling for urgent action to enhance international co-operation in combating acts of international terrorism. The establishment in 1999 by the GA in Vienna of a terrorism prevention branch within the UN Office for Drug Control and Crime Prevention points to close analogies and connection between international terrorism and transnational organized crime. This fact was expressly noted in SC Resolution 1373 of 2001 (40 ILM 1278 (2001), adopted after the September attacks.

Already prior to September 2001, the SC had not only condemned all acts of terrorism as criminal and unjustifiable (in particular Resolution 1269 of 1999) but—significantly—recognized that international terrorism constituted a threat to international peace and security, a proposition articulated in 1992 in Resolution 731 relating to the Lockerbie terrorist bombing of 1988. This aspect of international terrorism was emphatically reaffirmed by the SC in its two resolutions adopted in reaction to the terrorist attacks in September 2001, Resolutions 1368 and 1373 (40 ILM 1277, 1278 (2001)). It is crucial that in both of these resolutions their preambles recognized and reaffirmed "the inherent right of individual **(335)** or collective **(336)** self-defense as recognized by the Charter of the United Nations." This allows the conclusion that a state, such as the US, which has been the target of a major terrorist attack, has the right to respond by armed self-defense measures under Art. 51 of the Charter. The SC thus recognized a state's right of self-defense also in case of an armed attack by transnational, non-state, actors, such as terrorist organizations. The problem is that, unlike states, such actors are not endowed with a territory **(228)** of their own. However, in any case, since they must operate from and be linked to a territorial basis in a state or states harboring and assisting them, the exercise of the right of self-defense by the target state against such state or states is justified under international law if the state concerned aids, supports or harbors, or acquiesces in the activities of international terrorists in its territory, and refuses requests of the target state to desist from such assistance and hand over the perpetrators. It is a recognized principle of international law, affirmed in the GA Friendly Relations Declaration of 1970 **(14)**, that a state is not allowed to support in its territory or acquiesce in activities of armed groups, including terrorists, whose purpose is to attack or commit terrorist acts in another state. SC Resolution 1368 holds accountable for terrorist acts not only the perpetrators, organizers, and sponsors of such acts but also their supporters. Reaffirming this resolution and Resolution 1189 of 1998, as well as the above-noted Friendly Relations Declaration of 1970, Resolution 1373 states that "every State has the duty to refrain from organizing, instigating, assisting or participating in terrorist acts in another State or acquiescing in organized activities within its territory directed towards the commission of such acts."

In the specific case of the September 2001 attacks, the US had a sufficient basis in international law for resorting to armed self-defense against the *de facto* **(110)** Taliban government of Afghanistan: there was credible proof linking the Afghanistan-based terrorist group to the attacks; the Taliban government openly harbored that group, refusing to desist from harboring it and surrender its leadership; the US right of self-defense was recognized by the SC to which the US reported its self-defense measures; and the SC continued to support the US in the matter. In addition to the SC, the GA and a number of international organizations **(84)** other than the UN, including European Union (EU), the North Atlantic Treaty Organization (NATO), and the OAS expressed their support for the US (40 ILM 1254 (2001)).

Since the Taliban government was otherwise engaged in a civil war **(340)** against the opposition Northern Alliance still controlling part of Afghanistan's territory, the US self-defense measures made it a *de facto* ally of the anti-Taliban opposition in the internationalized internal conflict in Afghanistan. The legal status under international law of terrorists and other individuals captured by the US in this armed conflict and transferred to Guantánamo became a subject of controversy, the major issue being which of them were entitled to the status of prisoner of war **(364)** and to what extent they should enjoy the protection of the Geneva Convention of 1949 **(349)** governing the status of prisoners of war.

The US self-defense action against the remaining terrorists has continued following the creation of a new government in Afghanistan, with that government's support of the anti-terrorist measures of the US. The allied International Security Assistance Force was fully endorsed by the SC (Resolution 1386 of 2001), which also welcomed the establishment of the new government in

Afghanistan and the continued anti-terrorist measures of the US and its allies in Afghanistan (Resolutions 1378 and 1383 of 2001 and Resolution 1401 of 2002). In addition, the SC adopted a number of resolutions calling upon states to intensify their efforts to combat terrorism and prevent and suppress all active and passive support to it. It should be added that in its second resolution after the September 2001 terrorist attacks, the SC, in its Resolution 1373 (40 ILM 1278 (2001)), established a Counter-Terrorism Committee of the SC, consisting of all its members, to monitor implementation of anti-terrorist measures by all states and transmit periodic (quarterly) reports on them to the SC according to a timetable set by the Committee. Many states submitted such reports, but, as noted by the SC in its Resolution 1456 of 20 January 2003 (42 ILM 510)), by that date 13 states had not submitted any reports and 56 were late in submitting further reports. By the end of 2003 only 83 states complied with the obligation to submit timely reports.

In the Afghanistan crisis, the US could rely at least on implied endorsement of its self-defense action by the SC. However, the argument of self-defense was not proven in the Iraq situation in 2003. Whether it would apply in any future situation depends on the specific circumstances of the case. Perhaps by failing to obtain in September 2001, at a psychologically favorable time, a generally phrased explicit SC authorization to use, within the framework of collective security, military force in self-defense against states supporting terrorist attacks, the US missed an opportunity to secure for itself a more solid legal base for its future anti-terrorist campaign.

**338. War.** "War," a term commonly used in traditional international law and still today in everyday language, but discarded in contemporary international legal terminology in favor of a more general notion of "international armed conflict" **(339)**, is a status or condition of armed hostility between two or more "belligerent" states. Although the distinction may sometimes be blurred, international war must be differentiated from civil or internal war **(340)** which in principle is not prohibited by international law albeit its conduct has been increasingly regulated by international humanitarian law **(353)** adapted to the nature of non-international armed conflict.

Whether under international law a state of war exists in a given case may be difficult to determine; there is no agreement in the doctrine on the definition of war, with various tests being suggested for its existence. Historically, a declaration of war—now a virtually obsolete act—by at least one state party, was the evidence that a state of war existed between the states involved even if no armed force was employed in the conflict. In World War II, most states that declared war on the Axis powers, including a number of Latin American states, and Turkey, which did not declare war on Germany until shortly before its end, did not actively participate in the hostilities. However, war could come into existence also through acts of armed force by a state or states against another state or group of states, with implied belligerent intent or even without it but treated as war by the other state or states. Apart from this subjective test, war exists irrespective of any disclaimer of belligerent intent by the states involved if the hostilities have assumed dimensions of large-scale regular warfare. This objective view became more common in the 20th century as states became engaged in hostilities disregarding any need for a formal declaration of war, prescribed by Hague Convention III Relative to the Opening of Hostilities of 1907 (205 CTS 263). Already before World War II and, as a rule, thereafter, numerous international armed conflicts, in effect *de facto* wars involving large-scale hostilities, took place without any declaration of war or even belligerent intent of one or both sides. As a matter of fact, Hague Convention III was adopted in reaction to Japan's attack on Russia without warning and before a formal declaration of war. The Convention required a declaration of war or an ultimatum with a conditional declaration of war. Examples of undeclared war in the first half of the 20th century include: Japan's aggression against China, begun in 1930; Italy's aggression against Ethiopia (Abyssinia) in 1935; the large-scale hostilities between the Soviet Union and Japan in 1938; Germany's and the Soviet Union's aggression against Poland in 1939; and the Soviet Union's against Finland in 1939.

Although state practice would vary, the opinion of international law writers was that if the outbreak of hostilities was followed by a declaration of war, legally the war commenced on the day of the declaration. But the United States' (US) position was that the war with Japan had commenced on the day of the Pearl Harbor attack and not the next day upon the declaration of war. After World

War II, the practice of declaring a state of war virtually fell into disuse and almost no declaration of war has taken place in the numerous armed conflicts of the post-war era, including the Korean War, 1950–1953; the Suez conflict of 1956; the Chinese-Soviet "border war" in 1962; the Indo-Pakistani rounds of conflict in 1961 and 1971; the war between China and Vietnam in 1979; the Falklands War between the United Kingdom and Argentina in 1982; and the Iran-Iraq War, 1980–1989, in which even diplomatic relations **(68)** were for quite a long time maintained during the war between the belligerents; Iraq's aggression against Kuwait in 1990 and the Gulf War of 1991; and the war with Iraq in 2003. The only cases of formal state of war were those between some Arab states and Israel. The Egypt-Israel and Jordan-Israel Peace Treaties of 1979 and 1994 respectively (18 ILM 362 (1974); 34 ILM 48 (1995)) expressly terminated the state of war between the states involved. But even in the new century some Arab states still claimed that a state of war existed between them and Israel. The virtual disappearance of the declaration of war from international practice led some publicists to suggest, especially in view of the prohibition of war by the United Nations (UN) Charter in 1945, let alone the pre–World War II General Treaty for the Renunciation of War of 1928 **(330)**, that the declaration of war was an obsolete institution and, otherwise, perhaps never a rule of international law. Yet, the International Military Tribunal at Nuremberg **(354)** invoked the violation by Germany of Hague Convention III among other treaty violations by that country in World War II. Thus, strictly speaking, Hague Convention III is legally in force for the 42 states, including the US, which are still parties.

The modern developments concerning the state of war have made it difficult to determine whether a state of war exists under the circumstances between states engaged in an armed conflict. If a conflict assumes large-scale dimensions, third states have the right to treat it as war in the traditional legal sense of the term and are entitled to declare neutrality **(362)** even though the contesting states continue to maintain a technically non-war status in their mutual relations. In fact, in a great majority of armed conflicts since 1945 such states have preferred not to consider themselves to be engaged in war in the traditional legal sense of the term.

Prior to the Covenant of the League of Nations, 1919, war was a legitimate instrument of policy of sovereign states. While the Covenant did not prohibit war altogether, the members undertook not to resort to it against a member that complied with an arbitral award **(293)** or a judicial decision **(306)**, to be made "within a reasonable time," or with the recommendation of a unanimous report of the League's Council, to be issued within six months after the submission of the dispute to the League. Thus the Covenant suffered from gaps that legally allowed a state to resort to war if it considered it to be a right tool of its policy. The General Treaty for the Renunciation of War of 1928 widened the League's partial ban into a total outlawry of war as an instrument of national policy. However, the limitations of the right to resort to war, imposed by the League of Nations Covenant and the above-noted General Treaty could not be clearly determined since no worldwide definition of war was available in international law and the emergence of *de facto* wars without a formal declaration made it difficult to determine when hostilities reached a stage constituting war. The UN Charter resolved this problem in Art. 2(4) without mentioning the term "war" or "aggression" by formulating a rule that banned not merely war but, more inclusively, the threat or use of force inconsistent with the purposes of the UN. Following the UN Charter and against the background of increasingly frequent "non-war" armed conflicts, international instruments, and especially those governing the conduct of hostilities ("international humanitarian law") began to refer to "armed conflict" irrespective of whether or not war in the traditional legal sense had been declared. "Armed conflict" also includes hostilities within a UN collective security **(327)** enforcement action under Chapter VII and, under the circumstances, a "peacekeeping" operation **(334)**. At the same time, the branding by the Nuremberg Tribunal of aggressive war as the gravest category of illegal use of force and a crime against peace was subsequently reaffirmed by the International Law Commission in 1950 and incorporated into the Draft Code of Offenses against the Peace and Security of Mankind in 1954. It has also been included in a number of UN General Assembly resolutions, and in particular the Friendly Relations Declaration of 1970 **(14)**. Prohibition of aggressive war has become a peremptory norm (*jus cogens*) **(24)**, but as yet no authoritative definition of aggression **(325)** has been developed in international law.

# Chapter IX
# International Humanitarian Law

**339. Armed Conflict, International.** A concept adopted in contemporary international law, which in addition to the traditional declared war **(338)** includes any armed clash between states **(127)** and applies to all cases of partial or total belligerent occupation **(363)** of foreign territory. The International Criminal Tribunal for the Former Yugoslavia (ICTY) **(352)**, in adopting a broad construction **(274)** of the concept of armed conflict in the *Tadić* case (Appeals Chamber) (35 ILM 32 (1996)), held that international humanitarian law **(353)** applied to an armed conflict (international or non-international) **(340)** as such, irrespective of whether or not actual fighting took place, from the initiation of the conflict "beyond the cessation of hostilities until a general conclusion of peace was reached."

Whereas the Hague Conventions of 1899 and 1907 **(350)** referred to "war," the term "armed conflict" has been used in more recent treaties regulating international humanitarian law, beginning with the four Geneva Conventions of 1949 **(349)**. This change in the terminology is due both to a proliferation of armed conflicts with no declaration of war, military interventions **(331)**, armed reprisals **(119)**, and other acts given as examples in the General Assembly definition of aggression **(325)** of 1974, and to the fact that the United Nations (UN) Charter outlaws not just war but, more inclusively, force. The concept of international armed conflict also encompasses any armed clash in which UN or regional peacekeeping **(334)** forces or forces authorized by the Security Council (SC) within the general context of collective security **(327)** are participating.

Whether the concept of international armed conflict applies to armed struggle against colonial domination was an important and controversial issue in the era of anti-colonial conflicts, but has lost much of its relevance in the post-colonial era. Contrary to the Western view on this issue, Third World countries considered wars of national liberation waged by national liberation movements **(94)** to be international armed conflicts even under customary law **(39)**. Pursuant to their position, the Third World countries succeeded in Protocol I of 1977 **(369)** to classifying such conflicts as international (Art. 1(4)). This provision was a major reason for the refusal of the United States (US) and some other Western states to become parties to the Protocol.

The concept of a classical international armed conflict involving only states as the traditional subjects of the law of war, began to break down in the latter decades of the 20th century when the distinction between international and internal conflicts would become blurred in complex and entangled conflicts involving states and subnational groups. The Yugoslav conflict of the early 1990s well illustrated such conflicts. It was not entirely clear whether and how long it was an internal conflict within a disintegrating Yugoslavia **(134)** or—and as of when—it became an international conflict between the rump Yugoslav state and the seceded republics. While the SC did not make a clear determination on the nature of that conflict, the ICTY, in the above-noted *Tadić* case, found the conflict to have both internal and international aspects; it was an armed conflict of a mixed nature.

Traditionally, international humanitarian law applied only to international armed conflicts, with civil wars basically governed by the municipal law **(27)** of the country concerned and insurgents frequently treated as common criminals. However, from the point of view of international humanitarian law, the distinction between international and non-international armed conflict has increasingly become less pronounced in an era of interdependence of states and under the impact of the human rights law **(160)**. Hence, the recent trend has been to gradually extend—where appropriate—the rules governing international armed conflicts to the conduct of hostilities in civil wars.

**340. Armed Conflict, Non-International.** In a more inclusive sense, the term "non-international armed conflict" may refer to any violent civil strife ranging from situations of relatively minor acts of politically motivated violence to a full-fledged civil war between the incumbent government and the insurgents, in its intensity comparable to an international armed conflict **(339)**. Incumbent governments have frequently viewed their political opponents resorting to acts of violence against the régime, including those in control of parts of the state's territory **(228)**, as criminals subject to penal sanctions under the law of the state concerned. Hence, historically, as a rule, governments, both the incumbent government in question and governments of third states, have been reluctant to grant insurgents (rebels) recognition of belligerency **(113)**, which act would admit that the ongoing civil war had assumed the dimensions of an international armed conflict in which the insurgents would have to be granted, by the recognizing government, the rights and obligations of lawful combatants **(342)** under the law of war, much more important than those under recognition of insurgency **(115)** and, in general, even a limited capacity of being a subject of international law **(85)**.

In the past, it was uncertain in customary international law **(39)** whether or not the traditional law of war applied also to civil wars which in the 20th century were becoming more frequent, ideologically motivated, and increasingly brutal, but virtually ignored by any humanitarian rules of war governing international conflicts. The fanaticism with which the Spanish Civil War (1936–1939) was waged prompted states to apply at least some fundamental humanitarian principles to internal armed conflicts, such as prohibition of targeting civilians and of attacking non-military objects, especially where the insurgents effectively controlled parts of the state's territory **(228)**, and their armed forces were under a responsible command and observed the rules of the law of war. Following World War II, this trend led to inclusion in the four Geneva Conventions of 1949 **(349)** of a common Article 3 which stipulated a certain minimum of safeguards for the protection of civilians, prisoners of war **(364)**, wounded and sick members of armed forces, and other victims of non-international armed conflicts. Article 3, considered to constitute a minimum yardstick for the treatment of such war victims, has been recognized as declaratory of customary law and fundamental general principles of humanity. It prohibits all violence against, and cruel treatment of war victims, outrages to dignity, and violation of due process of law in passing sentences and carrying out executions. It also mandates that the wounded and sick must be collected and cared for. In addition, it calls upon the parties to the four Geneva Conventions to endeavor to bring into force, by means of a special agreement, other pertinent provisions of these instruments. It should be added that the wording of Article 3 implies that it applies to any "armed conflict not of an international character" irrespective of its level of intensity and magnitude. Violence in Iraq following the formal termination of belligerent occupation by the United States and its Allies is also covered in Article 3.

Although Article 3 has been invoked and complied with in some of the many post–World War II non-international armed conflicts, and the International Committee of the Red Cross (ICRC), the crucial humanitarian non-governmental organization **(86)** offering services in armed conflicts, has been admitted—as required by Article 3—to perform its functions, the protection of non-combatants and individuals placed *hors de combat* proved—to say the least—inadequate in most cases of civil war. Consequently, in 1977 the Diplomatic Conference on the Reaffirmation and Development of International Humanitarian Law **(353)** adopted Protocol II (1125 UNTS 609) **(369)** which deals exclusively with non-international armed conflict, developing and supplementing Article 3 of the four Geneva Conventions. However, apart from the fact that Protocol I of 1978 considers wars of national liberation as a category of international armed conflict, Protocol II adopts a rather high threshold of application, by expressly providing that it shall not apply to "situations of internal disturbances and tensions, such as riots, isolated and sporadic acts of violence and other acts of similar nature." Such acts are not armed conflict under the Protocol (Art. 1(2)). This means that Protocol II applies only to full-scale civil wars between the government and—as laid down in Art. 1(1)—"dissident armed force or other organized armed groups which, under responsible command, exercise such control over a part of its territory as to enable them to carry out sustained and concerted military operations and to implement [the] Protocol." Notwithstanding this attempt at a definition, under the circumstances it may still be difficult to ascertain whether a given civil strife meets the threshold criteria of non-international armed conflict as defined in Protocol II. As demonstrated by the attitude of some Third World countries at the Conference of 1977, notably those affected by civil strife, states are reluctant to admit the existence in their territory of serious internal conflict fitting the definition of Protocol II, especially if other states do not insist on applying the rules of this treaty **(288)**. The gray areas, where the intensity of civil strife appears not to have reached the threshold indicated in Art. 3, have been under study by the ICRC and a United Nations (UN) committee on the protection of minorities

Generally speaking, the humanitarian principles of Article 3 have so far been mostly disregarded in the numerous internal armed conflicts of the recent decades and it remains to be seen whether the positive trend toward extending to civil wars the customary law prohibitions applicable to international armed conflicts will eventually assert itself to improve the humanitarian dimension of such non-international conflicts. It must be stressed that in recent international practice the concept of war crimes **(373)**, traditionally associated with international armed conflicts, has gradually been extended to internal armed conflicts, a development to which the case law of the International Criminal Tribunal for the Former Yugoslavia **(352)** and of the International Criminal Tribunal for Rwanda (ICTR) **(351)** has made a significant contribution. In addition, it should be noted that Art. 4 of the Statute of the ICTR implies that serious violations of Art. 3 common to the Geneva Conventions and of Protocol II are considered to be war crimes. It is also important that the Statute of the International Criminal Court **(170)** includes such violations in the concept of war crimes and provides a list of such crimes in Art. 8(2)(c)(e) of the Statute. Otherwise, despite the recent progress, international humanitarian law focuses mainly on international armed conflict and its rules must appropriately be adapted to situations prevailing in civil war.

**341. Blockade, Belligerent.** This is an institution of the law of naval warfare **(361)** whereby a belligerent's warships **(265)** block the access to the enemy coastline or part of the coastline in order to prevent entry and exit of vessels and aircraft of all states **(127)**. Under modern international humanitarian law **(353)**, a blockade designed solely to starve the civilian population is prohibited and the blockading power must allow supplies to reach the population through the intermediary of the designated protecting power **(368)** or a humanitarian organization such as the International Committee of the Red Cross, a non-governmental humanitarian organization **(86)** with headquarters in Geneva. A belligerent blockade must be distinguished from a blockade in peacetime, the so-called "pacific blockade" **(326)** which applies only to ships of the blockaded state. Such a blockade, once allowed in international law, is now unlawful unless authorized by the United Nations Security Council.

The institution of belligerent blockade dates back to the 16th century but became first regulated in 1856 by the rules of the Declaration of Paris **(344)** which, *inter alia*, lays down that to be legal and binding on neutral **(362)** states, a blockade must be declared, that is, notified to all states, and effective, that is, maintained by a naval force capable of carrying out the purpose of the blockade. It must be stressed that a neutral state whose ships run a blockade does not violate any laws of neutrality. However, a neutral blockade runner is liable to capture and condemnation by the captor's prize court **(365)**. In the prevailing opinion of publicists, insurgents **(115)** who are a party to a non-international armed conflict can blockade the coast under the control of the incumbent government if they possess the status of belligerency **(113)**.

As a result of profound changes in the conditions and means of naval warfare in the two World Wars (1914–1918 and 1939–1945), the traditional blockade maintained just off the coastline (the "close blockade") lost much of its importance and, as a major tool of economic warfare, was largely replaced by the so-called "long-distance blockade" covering vast and virtually unlimited expanses of the ocean and designed to force a total economic isolation of the enemy. Such a blockade was first initiated in 1915 by Great Britain and its allies. Initially declared to be only a belligerent reprisal **(370)** in response to Germany's declaration of an operational zone around Great Britain, in which all shipping would be subject to German attack, the blockade, joined by France, soon became a policy preventing any passage by sea to and from Germany. Although neutral states questioned the legality of the long-distance blockade on the grounds that it extended also to their coastlines and in many respects was not effective, eventually, and especially following the United States entry into the war in 1917, the opinion prevailed that such a blockade was lawful in naval warfare. World War II witnessed the application by the Allies of long-distance blockade against Germany. The blockading states devised complex arrangements designed to distinguish between *bona fide* neutral commerce and commerce ultimately destined for or originating in Germany. They introduced the system of the so-called navicerts (once used by England in the 16th century), which were certificates issued to neutral shippers by representatives of the blockading states in neutral countries, testifying that the cargo of the neutral vessel involved was not liable to seizure as contraband **(343)** and allowing the vessel and its cargo to proceed to its neutral destination.

**342. Combatants and Non-Combatants.** This is a fundamental distinction in international humanitarian law **(353)** between, on the one hand, individuals who are combatant members of the armed forces of a party to an armed conflict, international **(339)** or non-international **(340)**, and have the right to participate directly in hostilities and, on the other hand, civilians and non-combatant members of the armed forces, who normally have no such right and are not to be willfully attacked or injured. The distinction became an established principle of the law of war (today known as "international humanitarian law") by 1914 and was implied in the Regulations of Hague Convention **(350)** IV of 1907. However, in practice, the distinction between combatants and non-combatants is often not clear and to determine who has the status of combatant, a vital question for individuals captured in war, is one of the most vexing problems of international humanitarian law. Prior to World War II, while occasionally irregular forces **(356)** would take part in hostilities, wars were fought mainly by regular armies whose composition and structure were, as today, a matter of the domestic law of the belligerents (Regulations of the Hague Convention IV Respecting the Laws and Customs of War on Land of 1907, Art. 1(2)). Frequently, armies would include militias and, like in Great Britain, the Home Guard, within the organizational framework of national armed forces. Gradually, however, by the end of the 19th century other militias and volunteer corps, not forming part of the regular armed forces, gained combatant status. This was recognized in the Regulations of Convention IV (Art. 1) provided that four conditions were met by such irregular forces, as discussed below. Geneva Convention **(349)** III (prisoners of war) of 1949 added a fifth condition for irregular forces and, subsequently, when irregular forces became a standard feature of "national liberation wars," Protocol I of 1977 **(369)** (Art. 44) relaxed the requirements governing irregular forces under the Hague Regulations of 1907 and Geneva Convention III of 1949, and granted a more favorable treatment to irregular forces fighting for national liberation and against illegal belligerent occupation **(363)**.

It is international law, namely the Hague Regulations of the Hague Convention IV of 1907, Geneva Convention III Relative to the Treatment of Prisoners of War **(364)** of 1949, and Protocol I of 1977 that, complemented by customary law **(39)**, determine the categories of individuals who have the right to engage in hostilities and are entitled to be treated as prisoners of war upon capture. As a matter of fact, Geneva Convention III on prisoners of war approaches the legal status of combatants through the basically analogous status of prisoners of war.

Generally speaking, the combatant armed forces consist of regular and irregular forces. The former include, first of all, the organized regular forces, including paramilitary detachments, militias, and armed law enforcement agencies, and volunteers. The status of volunteers, especially the foreign ones, is not entirely clear. Under Art. 43(3) of Protocol I, incorporation of paramilitary or armed law enforcement agencies into a belligerent's armed forces must be notified to the other parties to the conflict. All these categories of regular forces must satisfy the following criteria: 1. being commanded by a person responsible for his subordinates to a party of a conflict, even if that party is represented by a government or authority not recognized by the adverse party, as, for example in World War II, armed detachments of those Allies whose territories were overrun by Germany; 2. having a fixed distinctive emblem recognizable at a distance; 3. carrying arms openly; and 4. conducting operations in accordance with the laws and customs of war. Foreign nationals may form part of a belligerent's forces. There is no express treaty provision, but members of regular armed forces should wear uniforms; customary law requires it. The second category of armed forces include 1. irregular forces, variously known as guerilla, resistance fighters, partisans, and the like; and 2. *levée en masse* **(357)**.

Noncombatants include 1. members of armed forces who, as a rule, do not take direct part in the hostilities (Hague Regulations Arts. 3 and 4(A)) and 2. civilians. By the former, the law means such persons as war correspondents accredited to the armed forces, supply contractors, civilian members of military aircraft crews, and the like. All these categories of noncombatants are entitled to treatment as prisoners of war. Medical personnel (except persons temporarily performing medical functions, such as hospital orderlies, nurses, and auxiliary stretcher bearers) and chaplains (Geneva Convention III Art. 33) enjoy a more favorable treatment in that they are not considered prisoners of war. They are entitled to all respect and protection, and must be allowed to perform their respective duties.

Civilians constitute the by far largest category of noncombatants. They are under the protection of international humanitarian law **(353)** unless proven to be unlawful combatants, such as saboteurs and spies **(372)**, in which cases they are liable to punishment by a military tribunal after a fair trial. Protocol I of 1977 (Art. 50(1)) defines a civilian as any person who does not belong to any of the combatant categories of the armed forces referred to in Art. 4A(1)(2)(3)(6) of Geneva Convention III (as described above) and Art. 43 of Protocol I. In case of doubt whether a person is a civilian, that person must be considered a civilian. The legal status of mercenaries **(360)** is a matter of some controversy.

Historically, the humanitarian aspects of the law of war placed emphasis on the protection of war victims, including civilians and individuals placed *hors de combat*, that is, members of armed forces no longer able to fight: prisoners of war; and the wounded, sick, and shipwrecked. The protection of civilian enemy aliens **(345)** found in the enemy's territory **(228)** at the outbreak of hostilities and of civilian population under belligerent occupation has been a subject of treaty rules since the Regulations of Hague Convention IV of 1907, and is now governed by very detailed provisions of Geneva Convention IV Relative to the Protection of Civilian Persons in Time of War, 1949. These Hague and Geneva rules include a few, rather vague, provisions designed to protect undefended localities and buildings and to prevent pillage; stipulate the duty to warn civilian population before commencing bombardment, to establish safety zones, and to afford protection to wounded and sick civilians (Geneva Convention IV Arts. 13–26). However, the problem of the protection of civilians who find themselves in the very theater of military operations was not seriously and in detail addressed until the 1977 Protocol I. The duty to protect civilians in time of an armed conflict was also reaffirmed by the Security Council in its Resolution 1299 of 1999 (39 ILM 1022 (2000)).

Against the background of the rapidly evolving military technology and methods of warfare in the 20th century, and an expansion of the concept of military objects, continuing in the new century, consensus eventually emerged to recognize four fundamental principles concerning protection of civilian population against the effects of hostilities. First, the principle of distinction mandates the duty at all times to distinguish between the civilian population and combatants and between civilian objects and military targets. Deliberate attacks, whether in land or aerial warfare, on civilian populations and targets, as such, are prohibited, as are also indiscriminate attacks, that is, attacks which are not directed at a specific military target. Second, the principle of proportionality requires that, while in modern warfare it is virtually impossible to avoid collateral damage, such incidental civilian damage must not be excessive in relation to the anticipated concrete and direct military advantage. Third, under the principle of precaution, parties to an armed conflict must take constant care to spare, in the conduct of military operations, civilian populations and civilian objects. Fourth, attacks on civilian population or civilians by way of belligerent reprisals **(370)** are prohibited. In addition to articulating in Arts. 48 and 51 the fundamental principles for the protection of civilian populations, Protocol I of 1977 (Arts. 52, 59–71) regulates in detail the protection of civilian objects, cultural objects, and places of worship; objects that are indispensable to the survival of the civilian population; the natural environment; and works and installations such as dams, dikes, nuclear power stations, and other potentially dangerous plants. It also deals with the protection of non-defended localities and demilitarized zones, civil defense, and relief in favor of the civilian population. Protocol II of 1977 relating to the protection of victims of non-international conflict includes analogous but much less detailed provisions on the protection of the civilian population.

In themselves, the principles which govern the protection of civilians in armed conflict cannot but be vague and even ambiguous, and even the elaborate definitions of such concepts as "attacks," "military objectives," or "indiscriminate" allow a wide latitude in their interpretation **(274)**. This points to the need for further development of international humanitarian law governing the distinction between combatants and noncombatants.

**343. Contraband.** A key concept in the traditional law of neutrality **(362)** and economic warfare at sea, the term "contraband" refers to goods that are prohibited by a belligerent to reach the enemy on the ground that they assist the enemy in the conduct of war **(338)**. While this concept of contraband can still be used in contemporary international practice, the collective security system **(327)** envisages employment of measures not involving the use of armed forces, which have been ordered or authorized by the United Nations (UN) Security Council (SC) against a state, under Chapter VII of the UN Charter. Among such measures under Art. 41 may be complete or partial interruption of economic relations with that state, including in particular imposition of an embargo on import of weapons and other military material. Within this context, proscribed materials which a state under UN sanctions attempts to acquire are analogous to the traditional contraband, and their interception, often at sea, has in a number of cases been authorized by the SC, as illustrated by the examples of embargoes against former Yugoslavia **(134)** and Iraq in the 1990s. Thus certain concepts and rules governing contraband under traditional international law are not entirely obsolete and can also be applied, where appropriate, to contraband in violation of UN collective security measures.

Historically, the status of contraband was among the subjects regulated by the Declaration of Paris Respecting Maritime Law of 1856 **(344)**, which established the principles that the neutral flag protected non-contraband enemy goods **(347)** and non-contraband neutral goods under an enemy flag were not liable to capture by the opposing party. The very nature of contraband suggests potential disagreement on the question of which articles are to be considered as contraband and thus subject to seizure. In this regard, state practice has developed a distinction between "absolute" contraband, meaning articles such as weapons, munitions, and the like, clearly of military character, and "conditional" or "relative" contraband, that is, dual-use articles, needed both in peace and war. It is evident that with an increasing impact of science and technology upon the conduct of war, the list of goods on the absolute contraband list must have included ever more items; also, many items were shifted from the free list to the rank of conditional contraband. As a result, in World War I the distinction between absolute and relative contraband broke down and in World War II hardly any article was not considered of use in the war effort.

In addition to the nature of goods, the enemy destination is the other essential feature of contraband. In this respect, state practice, at least since the 18th century, applied the test of ultimate destination of goods under the doctrine of the so-called "continuous voyage" or—more generally—continuous transportation. Under this doctrine a belligerent has the right to seize and condemn neutral goods, otherwise judged to be contraband, going from one neutral port ostensibly to another, if it can be proven that in reality the goods in question had an ultimate enemy destination by sea or by land. The doctrine of continuous voyage represented another restriction on the freedom of neutrals to trade with belligerents, but it soon became accepted as part of customary international law **(39)**. It was also applied by the United States Supreme Court in almost all cases of contraband or breach of blockade **(341)** in the American Civil War (1861–1865). In the British practice, the case of the German vessel the *Bundesrath* and other vessels seized in 1900 during the Boer War by the British navy on the grounds of carrying contraband to the Boer republics from German (neutral) ports via equally neutral Lourenço Marques (today Maputo) in Portuguese Mozambique, also points to the application of the doctrine of continuous voyage. In the two world wars of the 20th century the doctrine was applied to all kinds of goods deemed to be, in the captor's judgment, absolute or relative contraband.

**344. Declaration of Paris, 1856.** The first multilateral treaty **(288)** regulating some problems of the law of war, which established certain fundamental principles to govern maritime warfare **(361)** and neutrality **(362)**. The Declaration of Paris Respecting Maritime Law of 1856 (115 CTS 1) was adopted by the Congress of Paris following the Crimean War (1853–1856). Originally signed **(283)** by Austria, Great Britain, Prussia, Russia, Sardinia, and Turkey, it was eventually adhered to by almost all other maritime states, except the United States, which championed the complete abolition of captures at sea, and some Latin American states.

The principles adopted in the Declaration of Paris included: 1. abolition of "privateering," that is, naval warfare by private vessels under a commission ("letters of marque") issued by a state; 2. recognition that a neutral flag protects non-contraband **(343)** enemy goods and that non-contraband neutral goods carried under an enemy flag are exempt from capture; and 3. the rule that in order to be legally binding, a blockade **(341)** must be effective, that is, maintained by force sufficient to prevent access to the enemy coastline. The last-mentioned rule was eventually reiterated in the abortive Declaration of London, adopted by the London Naval Conference, 1908–1909 (3 AJIL 79 (1909)). In the course of time the principles of the Declaration of Paris acquired the force of general (customary) international law **(39)**, but the principle whereby a neutral flag protected non-contraband enemy goods was largely disregarded in the two world wars.

**345. Enemy Alien.** In the law of war the term "enemy alien" refers to a national **(175)** of an enemy state who finds himself in the territory **(228)** of a belligerent at outbreak of war **(338)**. Customary law requires that enemy aliens, but not the actual and potential members of the enemy armed forces, who become prisoners of war **(364)**, be granted a reasonable time to leave the belligerent's territory. The remaining enemy aliens may, at the discretion of the belligerent, be interned or left at liberty, subject to the duty of registration and other measures of control.

The protection of resident enemy aliens is now largely governed by the detailed provisions of the Geneva Convention **(349)** IV Relative to the Protection of Civilian Persons in Time of War, 1949, which includes such aliens **(144)** in a general category of the so-called "protected persons." Such persons are defined as "persons protected by the Convention who, at a given moment and in any manner whatsoever, find themselves, in case of a conflict **(339)** or occupation **(363)**, in the hands of a Party to the conflict or occupying Power of which they are not nationals" (Convention IV Art. 4(1)). Protocol I of 1977 **(369)** adds a few provisions relevant to the treatment of enemy aliens. The very elaborate provisions of Convention IV are designed to assure extensive humanitarian safeguards to enemy aliens, including the right to leave the territory. There are provisions on the treatment of non-repatriated persons, refugees **(178)**, conditions of internment, and transfer to another state. In addition, the Convention provides for assuring the full civil capacity of the interned enemy aliens. The provisions on the conditions of internment are most elaborate, including, *inter alia*, accommodation, hygiene, premises for religious services, religious freedom, canteens, air-raid shelters, food, clothing, medical services, recreation, including study, sports and games, working conditions, internees' committees, correspondence, relief shipments, discipline, treatment of escapees, and funeral allowances. During the two world wars of the 20th century, internment of aliens was practiced on a large scale. Some exchanges of enemy aliens took place through the intermediary of the International Committee of the Red

Cross, which is the key non-governmental international organization **(86)** in international humanitarian law **(353)**.

**346. Enemy Character.** This is a concept in the law of war, which qualifies as enemies not only the nationals, individuals **(175)** and entities **(174)** alike, of the enemy state but also enemy vessels and goods, and—under certain circumstances—nationals, vessels, and goods of neutral **(362)** states. There are no clear tests of enemy character in international law; each belligerent has discretionary power to determine such character. As a general rule, resident enemy nationals (enemy aliens) **(345)** are qualified as having enemy character, as are also corporations **(174)** incorporated or carrying on business in enemy territory or controlled by enemy nationals. In addition, enemy nationals residing in a neutral country are deemed to have enemy character for purposes of trading, as are also nationals of neutral countries who reside in enemy territory or carry on business there; if they enlist in the enemy's armed forces; or if they engage in hostile acts against the belligerent. Even nationals of the belligerent in question may become vested with enemy character if they find themselves in enemy territory.

Pending final judicial ruling, the enemy character of vessels is determined *prima facie* by the flag of the vessel. In addition, a neutral-flag but enemy-owned or controlled vessel acquires enemy character if it takes part in hostilities on the side of the enemy or forcibly resists a lawful exercise of the right to visit and search. The belligerent may disregard a pre-war reflagging of a ship from the enemy to a neutral flag if the transfer arrangement provides for repurchase of the vessel by the former owners upon the termination of the war. As illustrated by the Allies' non-recognition of transfer by Germany to the then still neutral Turkey of two cruisers early in World War I, transfer of title to a warship **(265)** or other public ship from the enemy to a neutral state is void in the eyes of the belligerent state which itself decides whether a ship has enemy character or not.

Ownership of the goods on board the vessel and, to a lesser extent, the trade relationship of the neutral state with the enemy, or enemy origin of the goods, are usually taken as tests of enemy character. But, unless proven to the contrary by neutral owners, all goods carried by enemy vessels are presumed to have enemy character. On the whole, however, since the rules governing the enemy character of the owners are not clear, state practice in the two world wars varied considerably, but the onset of total war eventually resulted in widening the scope of the concept of enemy character.

**347. Enemy Property.** This is public and private property owned by an enemy state or its nationals, both individuals **(175)** and corporations **(174)**, and situated in the belligerent state **(127)** at the outbreak of hostilities. This concept does not apply to enemy property in occupied territory **(228)**; its legal status is regulated by the law governing belligerent occupation **(363)**. International law rules governing enemy property developed mainly in the practice of the two world wars, but are not entirely clear or consistent. Public enemy property can be seized except for buildings belonging to diplomatic missions **(68)**. Until about the end of the 18th century the law allowed confiscation of all property belonging to private enemy subjects, but this practice was eventually discontinued by virtue of treaties **(288)** allowing enemy subjects and their property to be withdrawn when war broke out. It is not entirely clear whether such treaty rules have crystallized into customary law **(39)**. In the two world wars the belligerents refrained from confiscating enemy alien property, but eventually adopted measures which in fact were tantamount to seizure. Whether or not seized enemy property is to be returned to the owners in the absence of such obligation in the peace treaty, remains a disputed issue. In the aftermath of the two world wars, the peace treaties provided for compensating only nationals of the victorious states by the vanquished ones, and nationals of the latter could seek compensation only from their own respective governments. Thus, for example, the United States (US) War Claims Act of 1948 provided that owners of alien property seized during World War II would not be compensated. Among the alien property seized was General Aniline and Film Corporation which, while incorporated in the US was owned by a Swiss company, Interhandel, itself ultimately controlled by a German company, IG Farben. The recovery of the assets by Interhandel became the subject of a celebrated case before the International Court of Justice (ICJ) **(309)**, the *Interhandel* case (Switzerland v. United

States) (1959 ICJ Rep. 6). Incidentally, the ICJ held the claim inadmissible because of Interhandel's failure to exhaust the local remedies **(74)** in the US.

As far as ships are concerned, prior to World War I private enemy merchant vessels in the belligerent's waters were by comity **(6)** granted a limited period of time ("days of grace") during which they were allowed to leave. However, some states, anticipating outbreak of war, would lay an embargo on potential enemy's vessels. The matter had been regulated in 1907 by Hague Convention **(350)** VI Relative to the Status of Enemy Merchant Ships at the Outbreak of Hostilities, which called for allowing private enemy vessels to depart. However, this rule was disregarded by belligerents in both world wars. One may add that seizure of enemy civil aircraft does not appear to be contrary to international law.

**348. General Participation Clause.** Of historical significance, this is now an obsolete clause in early conventions **(288)** governing the conduct of hostilities, for example, in the pertinent Hague Conventions of 1899 and 1907 **(350)**, to the effect that a convention applies in war only if all the belligerents are parties to it. As a result, in the traditional law of war, even if one belligerent, however insignificant, was not a party, the convention did not apply to any of the belligerents regardless of whether or not they were contracting parties to the instrument in question. This unfortunate rule could be explained by the belligerents' concern for equal treaty restraints to be imposed upon each party to a war. Consequently, the belligerents' freedom of choosing methods and means of warfare could be limited only by customary rules of law which might or might not correspond to the conventional rules in question.

The general participation clause is abandoned in contemporary international humanitarian law **(353)**. It was expressly rejected already in the old 1929 Convention on prisoners of war, with regard of which the International Military Tribunal at Nuremberg **(354)** held in 1946 that the fact of the Soviet Union's not participating in that Convention did not permit Germany in its war against the Soviet Union to violate rules which, in any case, were declaratory of the accepted rules of customary international law **(39)**. The four Geneva Conventions of 1949 **(349)** uniformly provide in Art. 2(3) that if one of the belligerents is not a party to the convention in question, the belligerents remain bound by its provisions in their mutual relations and even in relations to a non-party belligerent, if the latter accepts and applies the convention in the armed conflict **(339)** in question. One should add that certain aspects of the now rejected general participation clause must not be confused with the principle of reciprocity, which allows a belligerent not to abide by the rules of warfare in relations with an adversary that patently and deliberately violates such rules.

**349. Geneva Conventions, 1949.** Sometimes referred to as "Red Cross Conventions," these are four treaties **(288)** of 1949 codifying, revising, and developing the rules of international humanitarian law **(353)** governing the protection of the victims of armed conflict **(339)**, including both members of armed forces and civilians. Drafted under the aegis of the International Committee of the Red Cross (ICRC), the most important non-governmental organization **(86)** in the area of international humanitarian law, and approved by a diplomatic conference in Geneva in 1949, these universally accepted conventions constitute the core codification of international humanitarian law. Convention I for the Amelioration of the Condition of the Wounded and Sick in Armed Forces in the Field (75 UNTS 31) builds upon and improves the original Geneva Convention of 1864 (revised in 1906 and 1929). Convention II for the Amelioration of the Condition of the Wounded, Sick, and Shipwrecked Members of the Armed Forces at Sea (75 UNTS 85) further develops the pertinent conventions of 1899 and 1907. Convention III Relative to the Treatment of Prisoners of War **(364)** (75 UNTS 135) replaces the old Geneva Convention of 1929 which, in turn, was preceded by the provisions on prisoners of war of the Hague Regulations, annexed to the Hague Convention **(350)** IV of 1907 and a similar Convention of 1899, respectively. Convention IV Relative to the Protection of Civilian Persons in Time of War (75 UNTS 297) is an innovative international instrument prompted by the genocidal atrocities committed, primarily by Nazi Germany, against civilian population, especially Jews, in occupied territories in World War II. Most of the principles and rules of the Geneva Conventions in the course of time crystallized into customary law **(39)**. On the other hand, new technological and political developments made it necessary to revise the

Conventions and adjust them to the more recent conditions of warfare. The two Protocols of 1977 **(369)** were designed with this objective in mind. More recently, the ICRC, jointly with a number of governments and the United Nations, has been involved in re-examining the Geneva Conventions in the light of the latest developments in modern warfare, focusing on such problems as determination of military objects in contemporary conflicts; protection of civilian population in air and missile bombardment; differentiation between combatants and non-combatants in the anti-terrorist campaign; and the extent of the application of human rights in this campaign.

**350. Hague Conventions, 1907.** The major codification of the traditional law of war **(338)** and neutrality **(362)** in the form of 10 conventions **(288)** adopted by representatives of 44 countries at the Second Hague Peace Conference in 1907 (205 CTS 216). Of the 11 war- or neutrality-related conventions adopted, 10 were ratified **(280)** and are still in force even though many of their provisions have become outdated. Convention XII on the Establishment of an International Prize Court never entered into force **(271)**. Conventions I and II did not deal with the law of war and neutrality.

The 10 conventions include: 1. Convention III Relative to the Opening of Hostilities (20 CTS 263); 2. Convention IV Respecting the Laws and Customs of War on Land, with Annex and Regulations (205 CTS 277), the most important of the Hague Conventions, in force for 43 states and replacing as between the contracting parties the Convention adopted at the First Hague Peace Conference in 1899 and still in force for 17 states; 3. Convention V Respecting the Rights and Duties of Neutral Powers and Persons in Case of War on Land (205 CTS 299); 4. Convention VI Relative to the Status of Enemy Merchant Ships at the Outbreak of Hostilities (205 CTS 305); 5. Convention VII Relative to the Conversion of Merchant Ships into Warships **(265)** (205 CTS 319); (6) Convention VIII Relative to the Laying of Automatic Submarine Contact Mines (205 CTS 331); 7. Convention IX Respecting Bombardment by Naval Forces in Time of War (205 CTS 345); 8. Convention X (revising Convention III of 1899) for the Adaptation to Maritime Warfare **(361)** of the Principles of the Geneva Convention [of 1864] (205 CTS 345); 9. Convention XI Relative to Certain Restrictions with Regard to the Exercise of the Right of Capture in Naval Warfare (205 CTS 367); and 10. Convention XIII Concerning the Rights and Duties of Neutral Powers in Maritime War (205 CTS 395). The United States is a party to the Hague Conventions except Conventions VI, VII, and VIII. However, to the extent that the law of the Hague Conventions is declaratory of customary law **(39)**, the rules of the Conventions are binding for the parties to an armed conflict **(339)**.

**351. International Criminal Tribunal for Rwanda.** An *ad hoc* international criminal court established in 1994 by the Security Council (SC) Resolution 955 (33 ILM 1598 (1994)) under Chapter VII (Action with respect to threats to the peace, breaches of the peace, and acts of aggression) of the United Nations (UN) Charter. The resolution was adopted by a vote of 13 in favor, 1 (Rwanda) against, and 1 (China) abstaining. The International Criminal Tribunal for Rwanda (ICTR), with headquarters in Arusha, Tanzania, was established for the sole purpose of prosecuting individuals responsible for genocide **(155)** and other serious violations of international humanitarian law **(353)** committed during the Rwandan civil war **(340)** in the territory of Rwanda, and Rwandan citizens responsible for genocide and other violations of this law, committed in the territory of neighboring states, between 1 January 1994 and 31 December 1994. The deadline for bringing indictments in the ICTR expired on 14 September 2004. The creation of the ICTR followed consideration by the SC of various UN reports indicating that genocide and systematic, widespread, and flagrant violations of international humanitarian law had been committed in Rwanda during the civil war between the Hutu-dominated government and the Rwandan Patriotic Front of Tutsi and moderate Hutu tribes. An international panel of eminent personalities estimated in its report (40 ILM 141 (2001)) that between 500,000 and 800,000 people, the vast majority of them Tutsi, were massacred in the spring of 1994.

The ICTR, set up in the year following the creation of another criminal court, the International Criminal Tribunal for the Former Yugoslavia (ICTY) **(352)**, functions pursuant to its Statute annexed to SC Resolution 955, and amended by SC Resolution 1329 in 2000, containing in Annex

II the amended articles of the Statute providing for expediting the trials by increasing the number of judges. In 1995 the ICTR adopted its (subsequently amended) Rules of Procedure and Evidence.

In most respects, the ICTR follows the provisions of the ICTY. The major exception is due to the nature of the conflict in Rwanda, which—unlike the mixed international-internal conflict in Yugoslavia—was a non-international armed conflict **(340)**. Like the ICTY, the ICTR has the power to prosecute individuals responsible for serious violations of international humanitarian law, and specifically for genocide and other crimes against humanity, and serious breaches of the laws of war. The definition of genocide follows that of the Statute of the ICTY. Specific crimes against humanity follow the list of such crimes in the ICTY, but, considering the nature of the Rwandan situation, they are acts committed "as part of a widespread and systematic attack against any civilian population on national, political, ethnic, racial or religious grounds" (Art. 3 of the ICTR Statute). With regard to war crimes **(373)**, Art. 4 of the Statute grants the Tribunal the power to prosecute persons, military and civilian, committing or ordering to be committed serious violations of Art. 3 common to the four Geneva Conventions of 1949 **(349)** and the additional Protocol II of 1977 **(369)**. As noted by the ICTR in the *Akayesu* judgment (37 ILM 1399 (1998)), in 1994 Rwanda was already a party both to the Geneva Conventions of 1949 and the two Protocols of 1977. Since 1994 these treaties were incorporated into and formed part of Rwanda's law and any violations of their rules could be tried before Rwandan courts. Furthermore, as noted by the Tribunal in the *Akayesu* case, the provisions of the common Art. 3 of the Geneva Conventions extended minimum standards of humanitarian protection to individuals affected by a non-international armed conflict and expressed fundamental principles of humanity, forming part of contemporary customary international humanitarian law. The protection of the common Article 3 was further developed with regard to non-international armed conflicts by Protocol II of 1977. The non-exhaustive listing, in Art. 4 of the ICTR Statute, of war crimes follows Art. 4(2) of this Protocol and in some respects also the common Article 3. It includes: violence to life, in particular murder, torture **(182)**, mutilation, or any form of corporal punishment; collective punishment; taking hostages; terrorism **(337)**; outrages against personal dignity, including rape and enforced prostitution and any form of indecent assault; pillage; passing sentences and carrying out executions without observing due process; and threats to commit any of the foregoing acts.

The organization of and principles to govern the functions of the ICTR follow that of the ICTY, but the latter's appeals chamber also serves the Rwandan tribunal. Until August 2003 the two tribunals had a common chief prosecutor (a Swiss national), but she was asked by the UN Secretary-General to step down amid controversies with the Rwandan government. She was succeeded by a Gambian national in September 2003.

Criticized, especially in its early year of operations, on grounds of mismanagement and inefficiency, the ICTR eventually restored its credibility as an international tribunal. As of March 2004 the ICTR had indicted over 70 suspects of whom 60 had been arrested. The trials of 13 had been completed; 12 defendants were convicted to sentences ranging from 12 years to life sentence, and 1 acquitted. The Appeals Chamber confirmed eight convictions and one acquittal. Eight trials involving 20 defendants were in progress and four appeals pending. Among the convicted individuals was the prime minister of Rwanda at the time of the genocide. Fourteen ministers and other high civilian officials and military commanders as well as church leaders, businessmen, journalists, and other members of educated segments of the Rwandan society were in custody in March 2004. Among the most significant decisions of the tribunal were judgments in the above-noted *Akayesu* case and the *Kambanda* case (37 ILM 1411 (1998)). The former case is important in that it produced the first guilty verdict by an international tribunal for the specific crime of genocide. The defendant, a mayor of a small town in Rwanda, was also convicted for direct public incitement to commit genocide and for crimes against humanity, including murder, extermination, torture, rape, and other inhumane acts. In the *Akayesu* case the Tribunal also ruled that rape and sexual violence, committed with the specific intent to destroy in whole or in part a particular group, targeted as such, also constituted genocide. In the *Kambanda* case, the defendant, Rwanda's prime minister during the period of mass atrocities and genocide, was also convicted for genocide, conspiracy to commit genocide, and complicity in that crime. Both defendants were sentenced to life imprisonment which is the highest penalty in the ICTR and the ICTY.

**352. International Criminal Tribunal for the Former Yugoslavia.** The International Criminal Tribunal for the Former Yugoslavia (ICTY) is an *ad hoc* international criminal court unanimously established in 1993 by the United Nations (UN) Security Council (SC) under Chapter VII (Action with respect to threats to the peace, breaches of the peace, and acts of aggression) of the UN Charter by resolution 827 (32 ILM 1203 (1993)) for the sole purpose of prosecuting persons responsible for serious violations of international humanitarian law **(353)** committed on the territory of the former Yugoslavia between 1 January 1993 and a date to be eventually determined by the SC upon the restoration of peace. As of March 2004 no such date had been determined. On the other hand, it is hoped that the ICTY will have concluded its work by 2007–2008. The Tribunal has its seat at The Hague and—as of March 2004—had some 1,240 staff members from 84 countries. Its working languages are English and French and it functions pursuant to the Statute as proposed by the UN Secretary-General in his Report to the SC (32 ILM 1163 (1993)) and approved by the Council. The judges, prosecutors, and their staff enjoy privileges and immunities under the UN Convention on the Privileges and Immunities of the UN of 1946 (1 UNTS 15) **(102)**. The Statute of the ICTY was amended by the SC in 2000 (Resolution 1329), the amended articles included in Annex I attached to the resolution. In 1994 the ICTY adopted its Rules of Procedure and Evidence (33 ILM 484 (1994)); a Directive on assignment of defense counsel (33 ILM 1581 (1994)); and Rules governing the detention of persons awaiting trial or appeal or otherwise detained on the authority of the Tribunal (33 ILM 1590 (1994)). The expenses of the ICTY are borne by the UN. From $10.8 million in 1994, the Tribunal's budget grew to $271.8 million in 2004–2005.

As noted in the Report of the Secretary-General, the Tribunal applies, in accordance with the principle of *nullum crimen sine lege* meaning that no act or omission is a crime unless qualified as such by the pre-existing law, those rules of international humanitarian law which are beyond any doubt part of customary law **(39)**. This approach eliminates the problem of adherence of some, but not all, states to specific conventions. Of particular relevance are: the Hague Convention IV of 1907 with its Regulations **(350)**; the four Geneva Conventions of 1949 **(349)**; and the Charter of the International Military Tribunal (IMT) of 1945 **(354)**. Accordingly, the Tribunal has jurisdiction to prosecute and try grave violations of international humanitarian law, as listed in the Geneva Conventions; the laws or customs of war as set forth in the Hague Convention IV; and crimes against humanity **(151)** and genocide **(155)**, as understood by the IMT. It should be borne in mind that in a number of its decisions, and especially in the *Tadić* case (35 ILM 32 (1990)), the ICTY concluded that the armed conflict in Bosnia and Herzegovina was an international armed conflict **(339)** between Bosnia and Herzegovina and the Federal Republic of Yugoslavia (the rump Yugoslavia) **(134)** also after the withdrawal of the Yugoslav armed forces from Bosnia and Herzegovina in May 1992, which forces retained overall *de facto* control over operations by Bosnian Serbs forces as its agents.

The definition of genocide in the ICTY Statute (Art. 4), a major category of crimes against humanity, in general, follows Art. II of the Genocide Convention and is the same as that in the future Statute of the International Criminal Court of 1998 **(170)**. Crimes against humanity include murder, extermination, enslavement **(180)**, deportation, imprisonment, torture **(182)**, rape, persecution on political, racial, and religious grounds, and "other inhumane acts." All such acts qualify as crimes against humanity when committed against any civilian population in both international and non-international **(340)** armed conflict. In its case law, for example, in the *Tadić* case (Judgment in sentencing Appeal, 2000) the ICTY view was that in law there was no distinction between the seriousness of a crime against humanity and that of a war crime **(373)** (39 ILM 635 (2000).

The competence of the ICTY *ratione personae*, that is, its personal jurisdiction, extends only to individuals. The concept of the criminal association or organization, as adopted by the IMT at Nuremberg, does not apply in the ICTY. In accordance with the general principles of responsibility of individuals under international law **(81)**, the Statute of the ICTY (Art. 7) is based on the principle of individual criminal responsibility. As a result, the plea of immunity of a head of state or the official capacity of the accused cannot be a defense; nor does it mitigate the punishment. A superior is not relieved of criminal responsibility if he knew or had reason to know that his subordinate intended to commit a criminal act or has committed it, and the superior fails to take the necessary and reasonable measures to prevent such acts or to punish the perpetrator. As a result, individuals throughout the whole chain of command from the highest political authority down to the individual members of the armed forces or civilians can be held liable for crimes. The superior order plea does not relieve an accused individual of criminal responsibility, but may be considered in mitigation of punishment.

The ICTY Statute provides for concurrent jurisdiction of the Tribunal and national courts, subject, however, to the primacy of the Tribunal which may at any stage of the proceedings formally request national courts to defer to its competence (Art. 9). The Statute recognizes the principle that a person shall not be tried twice for the same crime (*ne* or *non bis in idem*). However, after a trial before a national court a subsequent trial before the Tribunal is not precluded if the national court characterized the act as an ordinary crime or the proceedings in the national court were not impartial or were designed to shield the accused from international criminal responsibility, or the case was not diligently prosecuted. The extent of penalty imposed by a national court is taken into account in considering the penalty to be imposed by the Tribunal (Art. 10).

The ICTY consists of three organs: the Chambers, comprising two Trial Chambers and an Appeals Chamber; the Prosecutor; and a Registry (Art. 11). There are 16 permanent judges, elected for a four-year term, with possible re-election, by the UN General Assembly from a list submitted by the SC, taking due account of the adequate representation of the principal legal systems of the world. The judges elect a president who must be a member of the Appeals Chamber. To reduce the backlog of cases and expedite trials, the SC, by Resolution 1329 of 2000 amended the Statute to provide for a pool of 27 *ad litem* judges, appointed by the UN Secretary-General on the recommendation of the President of the Tribunal to sit only on one or several trials for a period of up to three years. As a result of the amendments of 2000 each Trial Chamber, which may be made up of up to three sections, consists of three permanent judges and up to six *ad litem* judges. The Appeals Chamber now has seven permanent judges, of whom five are from the permanent judges of the ICTY, and two from the 11 permanent judges of the ICTR **(351)**. These seven judges also constitute the Appeal Chamber of the ICTR. In both tribunals cases are heard and decided by five judges.

The Office of the Prosecutor, headed by a Chief Prosecutor appointed by the SC (with a possibility of re-election) for a term of 4 years, operates independently of the SC, of any state **(127)** or international organization **(84)**, and of the other organs of the Tribunal. Until August 2003, the Chief Prosecutor of the ICTY (a Swiss national) served also as the Chief Prosecutor of the ICTR. The Registry, headed by the Registrar (now a national of the Netherlands) is responsible for the administration and judicial support of the Tribunal.

Investigation and preparation of indictments are in the hands of the Office of the Prosecution, which, with the staff of some 400 lawyers and investigators, has the power to question suspects, witnesses, and victims; to collect evidence; and to conduct on-site investigation. Upon determination that a *prima facie* case exists, the prosecutor prepares an indictment and transmits it to a judge of a Trial Chamber who has the right to dismiss it. Upon confirmation of the indictment, the judge may, at the request of the prosecutor, issue arrest warrants and other orders required for the conduct of the trial. The Statute provides (Art. 21) for all guarantees of fair and expeditious trial, including, *inter alia*, providing counsel for indigent defendants; presumption of innocence; the right to adequate facilities and time to prepare defense; to examine adverse witnesses; the right not to be compelled to testify against oneself or to confess; and the right of appeal. In the Tribunal's Rules there are also provisions for the protection of victims and witnesses, including *in camera* proceedings. The hearings are normally public and the trial requires the physical presence of the accused. Drawing from both common law and civil law, the procedure in the ICTY makes an attempt at reconciling the adversarial system of examination and cross-examination with the inquisitorial method according to which evidence is normally collected in pre-trial proceedings, with the accused in the Tribunal's custody throughout the trial and appeal proceedings. There cannot be any trial *in absentia*; such a trial would be incompatible with Art. 14 of the International Covenant on Civil and Political Rights of 1966 **(166)**.

Judgments are rendered by a majority of the judges of the Trial Chamber. There is no death penalty, penal servitude, or fine. Penalties are limited to imprisonment, but the Chamber may order the return of any property and proceeds acquired by the convicted person. The longest penalty thus far has been 46 years in the conviction in 2001 of a Serbian general found guilty, *inter alia*, of genocide in the massacre of some 7,000 Muslims at Srebrenica in 1995. This *Krstić* case (40 ILM 1343 (2001)), now at appeal stage, was the first conviction by the ICTY on a charge of genocide. As of March 2004, there were 53 accused in custody, held in the ICTY detention unit at The Hague, and 22 arrest warrants had been issued against other suspects. Altogether, 94 accused had appeared in the proceedings before the ICTY, of whom 25 were at pre-trial stage; 8 were currently on trial (including former president of Yugoslavia Slobodan Milosević); 5 were awaiting Trial Chamber judgment or sentencing; and 46 had been tried, of whom 15 were still at appeal stage and 26 had received final sentence and were transferred to serve their sentences or were awaiting transfer. Sentences are served in a state that has signed an agreement with the SC indicating readiness to accept convicted individuals as prisoners who would serve their sentences in that state in accordance with its law. So far, such states have included Austria, Finland, Germany, Italy, Norway, and Sweden. It is the opinion of the UN Secretary-General that, given the nature of the crimes in question and the international character of the ICTY, sentences should not be served in the territory of the former Yugoslavia. Eight individuals had already served their relatively short sentences; two had been acquitted by the Trial Chamber; and three had been found not guilty by the Appeals Chamber. Five indictments were withdrawn. Pardon or commutation of sentence, pursuant to the law of the state in which the sentence is served, is possible. Upon notification of the Tribunal by the state concerned, the Tribunal decides the matter in accordance with the interests of justice and the general principles of law **(38)**. Under the Statute (Art. 29), states have the obligation to cooperate with the ICTY and comply without undue delay with any request for assistance or order issued by a trial chamber of the Tribunal, including assistance in apprehending suspects and surrendering them to the Tribunal.

Since its inception a decade ago, the ICTY has grown into the most important international criminal court since the IMT at Nuremberg and the International Military Tribunal of the Far East **(355)** just after World War II. Not only has the ICTY made an important contribution to the enforcement of international humanitarian law by trying perpetrators of war crimes and crimes against humanity in the international-internal armed conflict in Yugoslavia, but its adjudication has produced a sizable body of case law clarifying and developing various, hitherto never adjudicated, aspects of international humanitarian law and international criminal law in general. One can mention here detailed analyses of torture and rape as crimes against humanity and—the most important progressive contribution—propounding the principle that the concept of war crimes and principles of international humanitarian law apply also in situations of civil war.

**353. International Humanitarian Law.** International humanitarian law is the contemporary term used to describe the rules governing the protection of the victims, both combatants and noncombatants **(342)**, of international **(339)** and increasingly also non-international **(340)** armed conflict, and restricting for humanitarian reasons the methods and scope **(366)** of warfare and, in order to prevent unnecessary suffering, the use of especially harmful weapons **(367)**. The protection of international humanitarian law applies to all armed conflicts irrespective of whether the use of force in the situation is legal. A distinction is usually made between the law of land warfare and the law of naval warfare **(361)**. The law of air warfare—let alone the ballistic missiles warfare—is the least developed part of international humanitarian law. Traditionally, international humanitarian law, still sometimes referred to as the law in time of war **(338)**, *jus in bello*, encompassed such subjects as, *inter alia*, regulation of weapons and methods of warfare; protection of civilians during hostilities, individuals *hors de combat* (unable to fight); prisoners of war; wounded, sick, and shipwrecked members of armed forces; and treatment of civilian population in occupied territory. The law governing neutrality **(362)** developed as an essential complement of the rules designed to reconcile conflicts of interest between belligerents and third countries.

The rationale of international humanitarian law is that, while it has so far proved impossible to prevent war, international law ought at least to reduce and limit the suffering of individuals during an armed conflict. This humanitarian aspect of the law of war exhibits certain affinities with the law of human rights **(160)**, constituting, in a way, an extension of the protection of human rights during an armed conflict.

In addition to states **(127)**, subjects of international humanitarian law include insurgent groups (in an internal conflict); intergovernmental organizations, such as the United Nations (UN); and the International Committee of the Red Cross (ICRC), a non-governmental organization **(86)** which plays a vital role as an organization performing the functions of a "protecting power" **(368)** and constitutes the center of humanitarian relief in armed conflicts. The ICRC also takes part in drafting conventions governing international humanitarian law. As far as UN peacekeeping and other forces engaged in operations are concerned, the UN Secretariat issued a set of instructions on the observance of international humanitarian law in 1999 (38 ILM 1656 (1999)). It should be stressed that international humanitarian law binds all belligerents; it rejects the now historical "general participation clause" **(348)** found in some Hague conventions **(350)**.

In historical perspective, rudiments of legal rules enjoining a humane treatment of individuals in an armed conflict can be traced back to the teaching of the Church in medieval Europe and subsequently the classical doctrine **(21)** of the law of nations and of war in the 16th to 18th centuries. In the 18th and 19th centuries, customary laws of war continued to develop in state practice, especially since after the era of religious wars, relative absence of ideological fervor and the balance-of-power system of changing alliances exercised a certain moderating restraint upon the violence of war. War was considered and waged as a contest between armed forces of sovereign **(125)** states, with a limited objective to reduce the military capacity of the enemy. In the second half of the 19th century the customary rules **(39)** of the law of war began to be codified **(5)** and developed in a series of treaties, beginning with the Declaration of Paris of 1856 **(344)** regulating certain aspects of naval war and neutrality. An important development was the conclusion of the Geneva Convention of 1864 for the Amelioration of the Condition of Soldiers Wounded in Armies in the Field (129 CTS 361). Sponsored by Switzerland, this Convention, adopted at the initiative of Henri Dunant, the founder of the ICRC in 1863, was followed by the Declaration of St. Petersburg of 1868 (138 CTS 198) which prohibited the use of certain type of projectiles. The Convention of 1864 was eventually revised by the Geneva Convention of 1906 (202 CTS 144).

The First Hague Peace Conference of 1899 and especially the next one in 1907 are regarded as a landmark in the evolution of the traditional law of war. The 1899 Conference produced, *inter alia*, the Convention with Respect to the Laws and Customs of War on Land (187 CTS 429), subsequently revised at the 1907 Conference. Known in its 1907 version as Hague Convention IV Respecting the Laws and Customs of War on Land (205 CTS 277), this convention of 1907 (one of the several "Hague Conventions") was based on the instructions on the rules of war issued by the United States (US) during the American Civil War (1861–1865) and drafted by Francis Lieber. It has an annex with detailed Regulations which served as the major legal source of the law of war in both World War I and World War II and in part are still valid today. Naval warfare became the subject of Convention III of 1899, which adapted the principles of the original Geneva Convention of 1864 to sea warfare, and was subsequently revised in Hague Convention X of 1907. In addition, the 1899 Hague Conference adopted three Declarations. Two of them prohibited certain types of weapons, namely the expansive "dumdum" bullets, named after a British arsenal in a suburb of Calcutta (today Kolkata), which manufactured them, and projectiles whose purpose was the diffusion of asphyxiating and other deleterious gases. The third Declaration, on projectiles and explosives launched from balloons, is an early attempt at regulating air warfare.

The early treaties regulating the conduct of war restated and codified rules which had already crystallized into customary law or were subsequently recognized as such. However, it must be realized that those treaties governed only international armed conflicts. They were, and still are, based on a number of fundamental assumptions concerning the conduct of warfare which became part of customary law of war: that even in time of war the conduct of belligerents is subject to some rules of international law; that unnecessary suffering and superfluous injury must be avoided; that a fundamental distinction must be maintained between belligerents and neutral states, between combatants and non-combatants **(342)**, and between military and non-military objects; and that the laws of humanity and the "dictates of the public conscience "apply in cases not regulated by treaty. How to enforce compliance with the rules of the law of war was left to unilateral decision of the belligerent concerned. Belligerent reprisals **(370)** were a major method of enforcing compliance with the law.

The Hague Conventions were the climax of the traditional law of war. However, soon the onset of the modern destructive technology of warfare and the emergence of "total war" exposed them to very serious challenges, making many rules of the traditional law of war become inadequate or even obsolete. The process of undermining the traditional law started already in World War I, with unrestricted submarine warfare, the use of aircraft as a tool of combat, and resort to total economic warfare making the distinction between armed forces and the civilian population virtually meaningless. The decline of the Hague system culminated in the unprecedented destruction and atrocities of World War II fought for practically unlimited objectives until the total surrender of the enemy. However, the trials of war criminals, especially the International Military Tribunal at Nuremberg trial **(350)** of major war criminals of Nazi Germany and the Tokyo trial **(355)** of Japanese war criminals testified to the importance of such trials as a method of enforcing penalties for war crimes **(373)** and crimes against humanity **(151)**. The years following World War II witnessed, on the one hand, further rapid technological advances in the art of war, with nuclear weapons bearing the potential of making international humanitarian law irrelevant, and, on the other, continued incidence, despite the UN prohibition of force **(329)** of major, though only local, wars, and proliferation of internal armed conflicts, some of a mixed internal and international nature. They were often waged with disregard of fundamental principles of humanitarian law and did not fit the simple war-peace distinction of traditional international law, bringing about the decline of the traditional institution of neutrality. One vexing phenomenon has been a proliferation of new types of irregular forces **(356)** whose nature did not correspond to the traditional requirements of the law of war governing lawful combatants.

Yet, despite serious impediments in the application of the existing rules of the law of war, conventional law proceeded to develop in the 20th century. Following the experiences of World War I, the Geneva Protocol of 1925 (94 LNTS 65) outlawed chemical and bacteriological weapons. In addition, two conventions were adopted in Geneva in 1929, one on the treatment of prisoners of war (118 LNTS 343), whose law governed this problem in World War II, and the other, on wounded and sick soldiers (11 LNTS 303), replacing, as between the signatories, the Conventions of 1864 and 1906, respectively. Furthermore, the London Naval Treaty of 1930 (112 LNTS 65), with its Protocol of 1936 (173 LNTS 353) made a futile attempt to deal with the use of submarines against merchant vessels.

After 1945, as a result of the UN Charter's outlawry of force **(329)** in international relations, the question arose whether modern international law could still recognize the validity of a legal state of war with its corollary of continued applicability of the law of war to armed conflicts, a question of much relevance for the institution of neutrality. As shown by the concept of "armed conflict," used in modern international humanitarian law conventions, the view prevailed that the rules of the traditional law of war should apply on land and at sea, regardless of the legality of the use of force in the situation.

In the aftermath of World War II the four universally ratified **(280)** "Red Cross" Geneva Conventions of 1949 reaffirmed and greatly expanded the pre-war regulations. In 1977 they were supplemented by two Protocols **(369)** dealing with international and non-international armed conflict, respectively. However, these Protocols, though ratified by a majority of states, are not so widely accepted as the 1949 Conventions. The US and a number of other Western countries are not parties to the Protocols of 1977. A number of specialized conventions were also concluded prohibiting certain categories of weapons **(367)** and certain methods of warfare **(366)**. Among the former is the Convention of 1980 on Prohibitions and Restrictions on the Use of Certain Conventional Weapons which May Be Deemed to be Excessively Injurious or to Have Indiscriminate Effects, with four Protocols; and the Convention of 1997 on the Prohibition on the Use, Stockpiling and

Transfer of Automatic Personnel Mines and on Their Destruction. Certain prohibited methods of warfare are the subject of the 1954 Convention for the Protection of Cultural Property in Time of War and the 1977 Convention on the Prohibition of Military and Any Other Hostile Use of Environmental Modification Techniques. However, there are no treaties dealing with the question of the legality of the use of nuclear weapons in an armed conflict, the issue considered without any definitive answer in an advisory opinion of the International Court of Justice **(309)** in 1996. The legal aspect of air and ballistic missile warfare is a currently topical but not regulated issue of international humanitarian law. But it must be remembered that, especially in the areas not regulated by treaty, parties to an armed conflict are still bound by the principles of customary international law "as they result from the usages established between civilized nations, from the laws of humanity and the requirements of the public conscience," a phrase forming part of the so-called Martens Clause **(359)** of the Preamble to the Hague Convention IV of 1907.

The enforcement of compliance with the rules restraining inhumanity of war is a major challenge to international humanitarian law, not least in the numerous non-international armed conflicts proliferating in various regions, and especially in Africa. The scope of belligerent reprisals **(370)** has been limited under the Geneva Conventions of 1949 by the prohibition of such reprisals against individuals protected by the applicable Convention. Whether the extension of the prohibition to other protected persons in a combat zone, introduced by the 1977 Protocols, has become a rule of customary law is a disputed issue. Deterrence by the threat of and actual prosecution by national courts for war crimes under the principle of a broad, quasi-universal jurisdiction **(92)** and actual repression of such crimes by international courts have in the past decade or so become an increasingly important method of deterring war crimes and inducing compliance with the rules of international humanitarian law. A number of *ad hoc* courts have been established to deal with crimes committed in specific armed conflicts. The International Criminal Tribunal for the Former Yugoslavia and International Criminal Tribunal for Rwanda are the first such courts since the Nuremberg and Tokyo Tribunals just after World War II. The establishment of a mixed international and national Special Court for Sierra Leone **(371)** added another category of international criminal tribunal; similar courts are planned in the aftermath of other non-international armed conflicts. However deficient it may be, the traditional institution of the "protecting power" **(368)**, codified in the Geneva Conventions in 1949 and further developed in Protocol I of 1977, is also designed to secure compliance with international humanitarian law. Last, but not least, the ICRC, while formally only a non-governmental organization, has always played a crucial role in protecting victims of war, and its disclosures of violations by parties to an armed conflict have contributed to improving compliance with international humanitarian law.

International humanitarian law is perhaps the most sensitive part of public international law. By its nature, it is expected to be applied in situations charged with tension and emotions where in international armed conflicts sovereign rights of the parties are at stake and states are not always ready to accept restraints of the law hampering their freedom of action. The traditional law of war has evolved into a body of humanitarian rules which, however deficient they may be, repudiates the ancient maxim that *inter arma silent leges* (laws are silent in armed conflict) and imposes at least some restraints upon the conduct of belligerents to assure a modicum of protection of human rights in the daunting circumstances of an armed conflict, both international and increasingly non-international.

**354. International Military Tribunal at Nuremberg.** This international criminal tribunal was established on an *ad hoc* basis under the London Agreement of 1945 between the United States, United Kingdom, France, and the Soviet Union (later acceded to **(267)** by 19 states) for the Prosecution and Punishment of the Major War Criminals of the European Axis, with an annexed Charter which provided the basis of the Tribunal's jurisdiction (82 UNTS 279). The International Military Tribunal at Nuremberg (IMT) must be distinguished from many other tribunals in post-war Germany, trying other war criminals. Those tribunals were courts composed of judges from Allied countries or German courts established under Law No. 10 of the Allies' Control Council. Many trials of Nazi war criminals before local courts also took place in other European countries.

The IMT consisted of four members, each with an alternate, appointed by the individual original signatory states. The IMT Charter empowered the IMT to try and punish persons who, acting in the interests of the European Axis states, whether as individuals or as members of organizations, had committed: 1. crimes against peace; 2. war crimes **(373)**; or 3. crimes against humanity **(151)**, or had conspired to commit any of these categories of crime. Neither the official position nor the plea of superior orders was considered as freeing the defendants from responsibility, but the plea of superior orders might be considered in mitigation of punishment. The IMT was also granted jurisdiction to declare a group or organization criminal.

The IMT sat at Nuremberg in 1945–1946 and delivered its judgment in September–October 1946. Of the 22 major war criminals, 12 (including 1 *in absentia*) were sentenced to death; 3 to life imprisonment; 2 to 20 years; 1 to 15 years; and 1 to 10 years. Three defendants were acquitted. Of the six organizations indicted, the Gestapo, SS, and German General Staff were declared criminal.

The IMT has been criticized as a quasi-international court set up by the victorious powers, without any judge or prosecutor from a neutral **(362)** country, to try the crimes of the vanquished enemy. Its international character was questioned by arguments that it was a domestic court set up in Germany by the governments then exercising joint sovereign rights in occupied **(363)** Germany. There has also been a controversy concerning the retroactive effect of some rules of international law applied by the IMT. On the one hand, there is general agreement that the Tribunal's judgment regarding the traditional war crimes was well founded in international law under established rules providing for individual liability in such cases. On the other hand, the qualification of the crimes against peace, defined in the Tribunal's Charter as planning, preparing, initiating, or waging a war **(338)** of aggression **(325)** or in violations of treaties **(288)**, has been criticized by some jurists as contrary to the prohibition of the retroactive force of law. Most defendants were found guilty of this crime, and only one was found guilty under that head alone and sentenced to life imprisonment. It has been argued that although a war of aggression **(325)** was illegal under the General Treaty for the Renunciation of War of 1928 **(330)**, to which Germany was a party, that Treaty did not declare aggression a crime and did not impose obligations on the individuals responsible for aggression, that is, the aggressor state's leadership. One can argue, however, that already prior to World War II a number of League of Nations resolutions and international treaties, as quoted by the IMT, reflected the rule of customary international law **(39)** declaring aggression to be a crime.

The criticism of the Nuremberg judgment has been especially pronounced with regard to the crimes against humanity. Prohibition of these crimes had not been part of international law prior to World War II. Two of the accused war criminals were found by the IMT guilty solely of crimes against humanity. Under the Nuremberg Charter, criminal acts constituted a crime against humanity only if committed in execution of or in connection with a crime against peace or a war crime. In this sense, the scope of the crimes against humanity under the Nuremberg law was narrower than that of the crime of genocide under the Genocide Convention **(155)** adopted after the war in 1948.

It could be argued against the charges of retroactive law that no general rule of international law prohibited the Tribunal from applying such laws. Moreover, in view of the nature and magnitude of the crimes committed by the Nuremberg defendants, especially the crimes against humanity, it would not be reasonable to argue that failure to follow the principle of *nullum crimen sine lege*, that is, the principle that there is no crime without a law prohibiting it, constituted injustice inflicted upon the major Nazi war criminals who must have been aware of the criminal nature of their actions.

The law of the Nuremberg Tribunal established most important guidelines for the international law governing the use of force by states and responsibility of individuals **(81)** under international law for the crimes specified in the Nuremberg Charter. The Nuremberg principles were affirmed by the United Nations General Assembly in 1946 and by the International Law Commission in 1950. They have been universally recognized as part of the fundamental principles of contemporary general international law.

**355. International Military Tribunal for the Far East.** This international criminal tribunal was set up in 1946 on an *ad hoc* basis, by a special Proclamation of General Douglas MacArthur as Supreme Commander for the Allied Powers in the Pacific, in order to try and punish major Japanese war criminals. The Charter of the Tribunal closely resembled that of the IMT at Nuremberg **(354)** except that it did not provide for declaring criminal certain Japanese organizations and did not expressly exclude the right of appeal.

Composed of 11 judges representing the states at war with Japan, the Tokyo Tribunal tried 28 individuals in the years 1946–1948. All the defendants were found guilty, and seven of them who, in addition to other crimes, were found guilty of war crimes **(373)** were sentenced to death. Most of the defendants who were sentenced to terms of imprisonment were found guilty of crimes against peace only. It is noteworthy that the United States (US) Supreme Court ruled that the Tokyo Tribunal was not a court of the US, having been set up by General MacArthur acting as the agent of the states at war with Japan. It is for this reason that the Supreme Court held that it had no power to set aside the judgments of the Tokyo Tribunal. The criticism of this Tribunal's judgments focused on the same legal points as were raised with regard to the judgments of the IMT at Nuremberg.

**356. Irregular Forces.** "Irregular forces" is a term in international humanitarian law **(353)** referring to a category of combatants **(342)** consisting of individuals forming part of the armed forces of a party to an armed conflict, international **(339)** or non-international **(340)**, but not belonging to that party's regular forces and operating in or outside their own territory even if the territory is under occupation **(363)**. Participation of irregular forces had been known long before the term "guerrilla" originated in Spain to denote irregulars fighting Napoleon's army early in the 19th century. On the whole, however, prior to World War II, armed conflicts were fought by regular forces; any irregular fighters were normally treated as spies and saboteurs and were summarily dealt with by the other side. Under the Regulations of Hague Convention IV of 1907 **(350)**, which were drafted with an international conflict in mind, in order to be treated as combatants entitled to the status of prisoners of war **(364)**, militias and volunteers, whether organizationally part of the army or not, had to satisfy four conditions: 1. command by a responsible person; 2. fixed distinctive emblem; 3. carrying arms openly; and 4. compliance with the laws and customs of war. In fact, these conditions made irregular forces part of the regular army and proved to be completely unrealistic and incompatible with the guerilla warfare. They implied, for example, that members of irregular forces (resistance fighters, partisans, guerrillas) fighting Nazi Germany in occupied countries, and especially in Poland, Yugoslavia, and the Soviet Union, were practically denied the rights of lawful combatants and, as a rule, treated as common criminals, "bandits" in the occupier's terminology. Following World War II, Geneva Convention **(349)** III on prisoners of war, 1949, included in its definition of "prisoners of war," that is, combatants, "organized resistance movements" provided that they met the four conditions of the Hague Regulations of 1907 and belonged to a party to the conflict. However, the status of such resistance groups in occupied territories remained as precarious as before, except that Geneva Convention IV regulating protection of civilian persons paid lip-service to the problem, calling for humane treatment of persons under definite suspicion of activity hostile to the security of the occupying power.

In the years following the conclusion of the four Geneva Conventions of 1949 irregular forces became, as a rule, associated with guerrillas fighting "wars of national liberation" against "colonial domination," "alien occupation," and "racist regimes." Consequently, many Third World countries raised demands for a revision of the Geneva Conventions that would favor the legal status of such irregular combatants. As a result, at the Geneva Conference of 1974–1977, which adopted two Protocols **(369)** designed to update the Geneva law of 1949, the status of guerrillas was among the most controversial subjects. Eventually, Protocol I, apart from including "wars of national liberation" among international armed conflicts, adopted a compromise solution, set out in complex rules on "combatants and prisoners of war."

Included in the concept of armed forces are "groups and units which are under a command responsible for the conduct of its subordinates, even if [the party to the conflict] is represented by a government or an authority not recognized by the adverse party." In addition, such forces must be subject to an internal disciplinary system which, *inter alia*, must enforce compliance with the rules of international law applicable in armed conflict (Art. 43). The crucial Art. 44 is a compromise between demands for granting resistance fighters a more favorable treatment as combatants entitled to the status of prisoners of war, and concerns about preserving some distinctions between combatants and civilians at risk in guerrilla operations. Unlike Geneva Convention III, Art. 44 has no requirement of a distinctive sign and carrying arms openly, but stipulates that in order to promote the protection of the civilian population from the effects of hostilities, combatants are obliged to distinguish themselves from the civilian population while they are engaged in an attack or in a military operation preparatory to attack. This rule assumes that in guerrilla warfare most fighters are part-time combatants. At the same time, if such combatant fails to comply with the obligation to distinguish himself from the civilian population in such circumstances, he is subject to punishment by the other party to the conflict, but is not deprived of his status of combatant or prisoner of war. Recognizing that distinguishing oneself from the civilian population may be unrealistic in certain situations, such as guerrilla warfare in occupied territory, Protocol I further reduces the requirement of distinguishing oneself from civilians by stipulating that in such situations a combatant need not comply with this requirement, and may appear as a civilian and still retain his status as a combatant provided that he "carries his arms openly during each military engagement and during such time as he is visible to the adversary while he is engaged in a military deployment preceding the launching of an attack in which he is to participate" (Art. 4(3)). Failure to carry arms openly in these two situations results, in case of capture, in forfeiting the right to the prisoner of war status. But the combatant will still be entitled to protection otherwise accorded by Geneva Convention III to a prisoner of war tried and punished for any offenses he has committed.

In general, while the regulation by Protocol I of the status of the members of irregular forces is, despite its necessarily ambiguous concepts, an improvement over the traditional treatment of such forces, the Protocol has not been ratified **(280)** or even signed **(283)** by some countries, including the United States, which argues that Art. 44 of Protocol I offered protection neither to civilians nor to armed forces.

**357. *Levée en masse.*** This is an institution of the traditional law of war, of less importance in modern war, referring to the spontaneous taking up of arms on the approach of the enemy by inhabitants of a non-occupied territory who had not enough time to form themselves into regular army units. To be considered as lawful combatants **(342)**, entitled, if captured, to the status of prisoners of war **(364)**, the citizens participating in a mass rising against the invading enemy, must carry arms openly and respect the laws and customs of war, as laid down in Art. 4(A)(6) of Geneva Convention **(349)** III of 1949. There is no requirement of wearing any distinctive sign. When a *levée en masse* takes place, all men of military age can be treated by the enemy as prisoners of war even if they have laid downs arms and returned to their homes.

**358. Maritime War Zones.** Variously known as "defense zones," "war zones," "exclusion zones," or "operational zones," these are zones proclaimed by belligerents in maritime warfare **(361)**, in which they restrict or completely ban the movement of shipping. Legally, such zones are of dubious validity, considering that they impose limitations upon the traditional freedom of the high seas **(242)**. There are no treaties **(288)** sanctioning maritime war zones, but they were proclaimed as early as 1904 by Japan in its war with Russia. They were also introduced by belligerents on both sides in the two world wars (1914–1918, 1939–1945), in the Falklands War between Argentina and the United Kingdom in 1982, and in the Iran-Iraq War of 1980–1988. During the Iran-Iraq War, in 1986 the United States (US) proclaimed a unique variant of war zone, namely, a moving protective zone of five nautical miles (one nautical mile equals 6,080.20 feet or 1,853.25 meters) for each US naval unit in the Persian Gulf area. Though controversial, fixed exclusive zones have not met with much opposition in practice, and it appears that maritime war zones may eventually, in exceptional circumstances, become part of customary law **(39)**, on the condition, however, that their creation does not prejudice the belligerents' duties under international humanitarian law **(353)**; strictly meets the requirements of military necessity; observes the principle of proportionality; and gives due regard to the rights of neutral states **(362)**.

**359. Martens Clause.** A clause proposed by Fiodor F. Martens, the Russian delegate to the First Hague Peace Conference of 1899 and included in the Preamble to the Hague Convention II on the Laws and Customs of War on Land, 1899, and later restated in its substance in Hague Convention **(350)** IV of 1907. The Martens Clause has since been reiterated in a number of more recent international humanitarian law **(353)** conventions; invoked in national and international tribunals **(306)** and other international bodies; and cited in national manuals of military law. The Clause provides in substance that, as articulated in its original version—"[u]ntil a more complete code of the laws of war has been issued, the High Contracting Parties . . . declare that, in cases not included in the Regulations . . . the inhabitants and the belligerents remain under the protection and the rule of the principles of the law of nations, as they result from the usages established among civilized peoples, from the laws of humanity, and the dictates of the public conscience." Whether the "usages" considered as a category of international humanitarian law require—like customary law **(39)**—general and consistent practice is not clear.

Originally designed to protect civilian population under belligerent occupation **(363)**, the Martens Clause now applies to all armed conflict situations and occupies a central place in international humanitarian law. The rationale of the Clause is to provide a sort of residual legal protection to victims of war where the written law does not cover a specific situation. The 1949 Geneva Conventions **(349)** restate a version of the Clause in their denunciation **(287)** provisions (Arts. 63, 62, 142, and 158, respectively) in order to make sure that a party that denounces the Convention will continue to be bound by pertinent customary rules of international humanitarian law. In Protocol I of 1977 **(369)**, the original wording "usages" is replaced by "established custom" (Art. 1(2)). Protocol II (non-international armed conflicts) **(340)**) includes a shortened version of the Martens Clause, which lacks reference to customary law, stating merely in its Preamble that in cases not covered by the law in force, the human person remains under the protection of the principles of humanity and the dictates of the public conscience. To what extent the Martens Clause can be pertinent in considering the legality of the use of nuclear weapons remains an open question. While in its advisory opinion **(291)** on the *Legality of the Threat or Use of Nuclear Weapons* of 1996 (35 ILM 869 (1996)) the International Court of Justice **(309)** recognized that international humanitarian law did apply to nuclear weapons, it did not take a clear stand on the relevance of the Martens Clause for the legality of the use of such weapons.

**360. Mercenaries.** Historically, a common category of combatants **(342)**, mercenaries are nationals **(175)** of third states recruited for consideration (that is, compensation) to take direct part in hostilities in an international **(339)** or non-international **(340)** conflict. Customary law **(39)** as well as the Regulations of Hague Convention **(350)** IV of 1907 (and the corresponding provisions of the 1899 version) treat mercenaries and foreign volunteers as any other regular or irregular **(356)** combatants provided they abide by the laws and customs of war. However, more recently, in the 1960s and 1970s, the issue of mercenaries acquired a notoriety in connection with civil strife in a number of African countries, for example, the Congo, where (mostly white) mercenaries were normally recruited by the parties to civil wars. This practice was viewed by developing countries as harmful and hostile to the nation-building process in Africa. Since the institution of mercenaries became associated by those countries (with the support of the Communist bloc) with "neocolonialist" attempts at destabilizing new African states, the United Nations General Assembly in its Friendly Relations Declaration of 1970 **(14)** and the Organization of African Unity condemned the practice of hiring mercenaries. Accordingly, at the Geneva Conference on international humanitarian law of 1974–1977 they insisted—contrary to the fundamental principle of equality of treatment under international humanitarian law—to deny mercenaries (but not foreign volunteers) any rights as combatants. The resulting Art. 47(1) of Protocol I provides that a mercenary "shall not have the right to be a combatant or a prisoner of war." A mercenary is defined (Art. 47(2)) as any person "specially recruited locally or abroad in order to fight in an armed conflict; does in fact take a direct part in the hostilities; is motivated . . . essentially by the desire for private gain and, in fact, is promised by or on behalf of a Party to the conflict, material compensation substantially in excess of that promised or paid to combatants of similar ranks and functions in the armed forces of that Party; is neither a national of a Party to the conflict nor a resident of territory controlled by a Party to the conflict; is not a member of the armed forces of a Party to the conflict, and has not been sent by a state which is not a Party to the conflict on official duty as a member of its armed forces." This otherwise not entirely clear definition (one can ask, for example, how can a personal motivation essentially for gain be ascertained) and exclusion of mercenaries from the protection of international humanitarian law were largely determined by the specific context of the period, and in different political circumstances might be inconvenient even to its sponsors and disregarded in practice. It should be noted that in spite of the denial of any rights as combatants and prisoners of war and basically treated as common criminals, mercenaries are still entitled to "fundamental guarantees" of Art. 75 of the Protocol, including humane treatment in all circumstances without any discrimination.

**361. Naval Warfare.** The law governing naval (maritime or sea) warfare is the part of the international law of war, or, more generally, international humanitarian law **(353)**, which governs the conduct of hostilities at sea. The rules of sea warfare consist largely of customary law **(39)** and elementary considerations of humanity, with some aspects codified in treaties, beginning with the Declaration of Paris of 1856 **(344)**. The bulk of the traditional law of sea warfare was codified in seven of the Hague Conventions of 1907 **(350)**: Numbers VI, VII, VIII, IX, X, XI, and XIII. However, of these, only Convention VIII Relative to the Laying of Automatic Submarine Contact Mines (205 CTS 331) and parts of Convention VI Relative to Certain Restrictions with Regard to the Exercise of the Right of Capture in Naval War (205 CTS 367) and Convention XIII Concerning the Rights and Duties of Neutral Powers in Naval War (205 CTS 395) still retain relevance in the environment of the modern world. Convention X was eventually revised and substantially enlarged by Geneva Convention **(349)** II of 1949 for the Amelioration of the Condition of Wounded, Sick and Shipwrecked Members of Armed Forces at Sea, subsequently complemented by some provisions of Protocol I of 1977 **(369)**. Submarine warfare is subject to the London Protocol of 1936 (173 LNTS 352) formally still in force for 49 states, including the United States (US) and Russia, relating to the rules of submarine warfare against merchant vessels, which incorporated Part IV of the London Naval Treaty of 1930 for the limitation and reduction of naval armaments, terminated in 1936. The Protocol of 1936 is deemed to be declaratory of customary international law and its rules are of general validity. However, unrestricted submarine warfare against enemy merchant vessels was practiced by all belligerents in World War II. A number of naval powers have issued to their navies special manuals on the rules of naval warfare. For example, the US issued *The Commander's Handbook of Naval Operations*, 1995, with annotated supplements. The *San Remo Manual on International Law Applicable to Armed Conflicts at Sea*, 1995, is an attempt at revising and updating the law of maritime warfare.

In maritime warfare the objective of the belligerents is not only to overpower the adversary's naval force but also to establish control at sea and weaken the enemy economically by means of such acts of economic warfare as capture of merchant vessels and property of the enemy and—under certain circumstances—also of neutral **(362)** states. While these objectives have basically remained unchanged since 1907, the enormous technological advances in the missile and electronic age have made one question a continued validity of rules inherited from a different era. In addition, as a result of the prohibition of the use of force **(329)** by the United Nations (UN) Charter, a fundamental question arose whether contemporary international law could still recognize the legal state of war **(338)** with its corollary of rules of conduct in sea warfare and its relationship to the law of neutrality. On the whole, as illustrated by the Falklands War of 1982 and the Iran-Iraq War of 1980–1988, the view prevails that the laws of war and neutrality still apply where appropriate, regardless of the legality of the use of force in the situation. Furthermore, any naval operations taking place under the authority of the UN Security Council, such as those related to the enforcement of measures ordered under Art. 41 of the Charter, must comply with the rules of international humanitarian law in maritime warfare. The law of sea warfare has also had to be adapted to the revolutionary developments in the law of the sea **(254)** and in particular the expansion of coastal jurisdiction, with the consequent shrinking of the high seas **(245)** areas available to naval operations at war and simultaneous expansion of potentially neutral areas where belligerents are obliged to pay due regard to the rights (and duties) of neutral states. In general, however, the question whether and how to apply the rules of the traditional law of sea warfare in contemporary conditions remains a major challenge in the law governing the conduct of armed conflict.

There is a consensus that, however vague they may be, the fundamental principles of international humanitarian law, concerning in particular prohibited methods of warfare **(366)**, are also applicable to maritime warfare. Thus only military objects, such as enemy warships **(265)**, military aircraft, and military coastal installations may be lawfully attacked, that is, are legal under the law of naval warfare but not necessarily legal as part of the use of force in general. The more recent concerns relating to environmental protection **(197)** have added to these principles the obligation to avoid unnecessary damage to the environment. The treatment of enemy and neutral merchant vessels belongs to the most controversial issues in the law of naval warfare. In World War II, belligerents' merchant vessels were, as a rule, armed, and, as such, would be attacked as legitimate military targets. The modern view seems to be that, while foreign-flag merchant vessels may not be automatically attacked, if integrated into the enemy's war fighting effort they constitute military targets. Certain categories of vessels are exempt from attack. Here belong hospital ships; coastal rescue boats and other medical transport (otherwise exempt from capture under Geneva Convention II of 1949 and Protocol I of 1977); and vessels engaged in non-military scientific research, or on philanthropic or religious missions. Passenger ships with civilian passengers; vessels that have surrendered; and life boats and rafts are exempt under customary law. Vessels engaged in anti-pollution activities are a recent addition to this category. Under traditional customary law, small craft and coastal fishing boats are exempt from attack and capture, as thoroughly analyzed by the US Supreme Court in the case of the *Paquete Habana* and the *Lola* in 1900 (175 U.S. 677) and codified in Hague Convention XI. The status of neutral merchant vessels in sea warfare is the subject of Hague Convention XIII which is mostly declaratory of the customary law of its time. It is not clear to what extent its rules are still valid today. Generally speaking, neutral vessels may not be attacked unless engaged in "unneutral service." One can add that international practice seems to allow the cutting of submarine cables by belligerents.

The traditional law of naval warfare, as set forth in Hague Convention VIII, regulated the use of torpedoes and naval mines. In principle, its rules are still valid, but must be adjusted to the conditions of modern missile warfare and take account of the transformation of the jurisdictional zones in the oceans under the new law of the sea. Insofar as the methods of naval warfare are concerned, major issues are raised with respect to belligerent blockade **(341)** and the practice of establishing all kinds of maritime war zones **(358)**. Additional problems, by their nature not directly related to actual combat, concern, *inter alia*, the determination of enemy character **(346)** of merchant vessels; visit and search for contraband **(343)**; and capture and destruction of enemy and neutral vessels and goods.

**362. Neutrality.** The term neutrality refers to the legal status of a state **(127)** during an ongoing war **(338)** between third states, with respect to which that state adopts an attitude of impartiality toward the belligerents, which creates rights and duties between the neutral state and each of the belligerents. As illustrated, for example, by the posture of European states toward the American Civil War (1861–1865), neutrality can exist also in the case of a civil war where the state of belligerency **(113)** of the parties to such conflict is recognized by third countries concerned. Neutrality in relation to a particular ongoing war must be distinguished from the so-called "permanent neutrality" or "neutralization" **(97)**, associated with Switzerland and Austria.

Neutrality became part of the law of nations in the 17th century, but its more detailed rules did not crystallize until the 19th century. Apart from the neutralization of Switzerland in 1815, Belgium in 1831 (renewed in 1839), and Luxembourg in 1867, the Declaration of Paris of 1856 **(344)**, the policies of the major European powers with regard to the American Civil War, and especially the development of maritime trade, contributed to the evolution of the rules of neutrality, as codified in 1907 in the Hague Convention **(350)** V on neutrality in war on land (205 CTS 299) and Convention XIII on neutrality in naval warfare (205 CTS 395). The Declaration of London of 1909 concerning the prize law **(365)** never entered into force **(271)**. In addition, as late as 1928, eight states of the Western hemisphere adopted the Havana Convention on Maritime Neutrality (15 LNTS 187) to which the United States (US) is a party.

The traditional law of neutrality was designed to achieve a compromise between the interests of neutral states keen to continue unrestricted commercial relations with other states, including the belligerents, and the concerns of each belligerent striving to prevent any dealings of neutral states that would further the interests of the enemy. Under the rules of neutrality in land warfare, as codified in Convention V of 1907, belligerents are not allowed to use neutral territory **(228)** for war purposes. They may not open recruitment offices there, but, since the neutral rights and obligations are not vested in individuals but in states, a neutral state is under no obligation to prevent its nationals **(175)** or residents from going abroad and offering their services to a belligerent, as was done by Sweden which allowed several thousand volunteers to join Finland in its self-defense war against the Soviet Union, 1939–1940. While a neutral state as such, is barred from supplying war matériel and services to a belligerent, its nationals are allowed by international law to engage in such trade. A neutral state has the right—and a neutralized one the duty—to defend its neutrality by force of arms. Failure to do so authorizes the other belligerent to attack enemy forces on the neutral territory. Troops of any belligerent crossing the border **(189)** into a neutral state's territory must be interned by that state.

There is a close relationship between neutrality and the law of naval warfare. Under Hague Convention XIII of 1907, neutral waters are inviolate and belligerents are prohibited to engage in any hostilities there. However, an innocent passage **(248)** of a belligerent warship **(265)** and its prizes, that is, captured merchant vessels, does not compromise the rights of the neutral state concerned. A neutral state may allow a maximum of three belligerent warships to use its ports for reprovisioning and refueling for a maximum 24-hour stay. Only such repairs are permissible as are absolutely necessary to render the ship seaworthy without adding in any manner to its fighting capacity. The rights and duties of the neutral states in this respect were dramatically illustrated by the celebrated incident involving a German "pocket" battleship, the *Admiral Graf Spee,* granted by Uruguay 72 hours time to carry out repairs in Montevideo in World War II in 1939, but subsequently scuttled by its crew in Uruguay's waters. According to Hague Convention XIII, a neutral state has the duty to use "the means at its disposal" to prevent a fitting out or arming of a ship that might be used by a belligerent. This rule modified the "due diligence" clause of the US-British Treaty of Washington of 1871 (143 CTS 145) concerning the claims relating to operations of the Confederate cruiser the *Alabama* and some other ships built for the South in Great Britain. Under the traditional concept of unneutral service or hostile assistance, meaning any conduct on the part of a neutral vessel that furthers enemy interests (for example, apart from direct aid, operating under charter to the enemy, or transporting members of the enemy's armed forces or enemy nationals of military age), a belligerent's ship may stop a neutral vessel and remove persons improperly carried on board. In serious cases, the neutral vessel itself and its crew may be captured and the vessel condemned by a prize court.

A belligerent has two important rights with regard to neutral states: the right to visit and search neutral merchant vessels on the high seas in order to intercept contraband and the right to blockade enemy ports, thus preventing access to the enemy coast by neutral vessels. A belligerent ship may bring captured prizes into a neutral port only on the grounds of lack of seaworthiness, weather conditions, or shortage of fuel or provisions. Whether a belligerent may, in cases of urgent necessity, requisition a neutral ship on the high seas by virtue of the so-called right of angary, is a controversial matter.

The relatively clear rules of the law of neutrality became exposed to serious tests in both world wars of the 20th century which, as a result, brought about the decline of the institution of neutrality. Although non-belligerent states proclaimed neutrality, their status was repeatedly violated by belligerents both on land and at sea, beginning with the violation by Germany of Belgium's permanent neutrality in 1914. Numerous instances of such violations occurred at sea. Neutral states were harassed by belligerents of both sides; captured neutral vessels were destroyed or sunk without warning; neutral ports and coasts were blockaded; and other interference with neutral commerce became almost a routine procedure. Even more than World War I, World War II (1939–1945) witnessed wholesale violations of neutrality at sea, on land, and in the air **(186)**. Germany invaded neutral countries and violated Sweden's neutrality by pressuring that country to allow transit privileges to (unarmed) German troops and supplies to Norway in 1940–1945, and in 1941 to allow an armed German division to transit Sweden from Norway to Finland. Swiss airspace was repeatedly violated by both sides in the conflict. Insofar as neutral countries are concerned, it is believed by some that the US breached its neutral duties by supplying Great Britain with war matériel from US-owned arsenals. Until the US joined the war in December 1941 its posture had been that of "nonbelligerency" favoring one side rather than classical neutrality. However, such bias could be justified by Germany's unlawful resort to war in violation of the General Treaty for the Renunciation of War of 1928 **(330)**, an act of aggression **(325)** which exempted the neutral states parties to the Treaty from the duty of neutrality.

By the end of World War II it became evident that the traditional law of neutrality was virtually outdated. Apart from political considerations, this development can be attributed primarily to a rapid growth of military technology which changed the character of warfare, outpacing the restraints of the traditional rules protecting the rights of neutral states. The adoption of the total warfare policy was a further factor contributing to the decline of the institution of neutrality. Finally, the very *raison d'être* of the existence of the law of neutrality was put into question when in 1945 the Charter of the United Nations (UN) entered into effect, instituting a collective security system **(327)** in which, at least in theory, the attitude of impartiality toward belligerents, whether committing aggression or acting in self-defense **(335)**, became impermissible as contrary to the paramount idea of collective security. However, in practice, since the collective security system did not prove feasible and many states returned to the policy of ideologically motivated alliances, the assumption of the status of neutrality by individual states remained a possibility even though the traditional rules of neutrality themselves were in a state of chaos and uncertainty. There have been many armed conflicts since 1945, but nonbelligerent states have been reluctant formally to proclaim neutrality since such a unilateral act **(44)** would somehow imply legitimizing the ongoing war; would be detrimental to the economic and commercial relations of nonbelligerents; would hamper their legal and political standing; and would cause controversies and complications in the domestic legal system.

In the 21st century, the status of neutrality in international law has been in a state of legal limbo. Yet, it could not become altogether irrelevant or obsolete in an international political system characterized by the contradiction between the ideal law which denied it legitimate existence and the reality of numerous armed conflicts necessitating a distinction between belligerents and nonbelligerents. As a matter of fact, the Geneva Conventions of 1945 **(349)** on international humanitarian law **(353)** and other international instruments refer to the neutral status and, in general, accept the institution of neutrality as a fact in relations between states. But it is not clear which specific rules of the traditional law of neutrality are still relevant and in what circumstances they should be applied. Whereas some states may still employ the language of traditional neutrality as, for example, was done by the US and a number of other states invoking the rights of neutral states during the Iran-Iraq War of 1980–1988, other states may try to approach the issue of neutrality in terms of differentiating in treatment between belligerents abiding by the UN Charter's law (such as states acting in self-defense according to Art. 51 of the Charter or pursuant to the Security Council's authorization) and those resorting to illegal use of force.

**363. Occupation, Belligerent.** A type of military occupation in an international armed conflict **(339)** whereby before the end of hostilities a part of or the whole territory **(228)** of a state **(127)** is actually placed under the authority of a hostile army which exercises military authority according to the rules of international law. Belligerent occupation is a question of fact and is based on an actual and effective, albeit provisional, possession of territory. As stated in Art. 42 of the Regulations of Hague Convention **(350)** IV of 1907, a territory is considered occupied when it is "actually placed under the authority of the hostile army." It is an essential feature of belligerent occupation that sovereignty **(125)** over the occupied territory continues to be vested in the state whose territory is occupied. Invasion is normally a stage in military operations which precedes the taking of firm possession of the territory in question. Belligerent occupation as such need not, and in contemporary international law, may not, lead to acquisition of sovereignty. It must be distinguished from the now unlawful conquest **(194)** followed by annexation and transfer of sovereignty by means of a treaty of cession **(190)**, but sometimes by unilateral annexation resulting in subjugation.

The law of belligerent occupation was first codified and developed in the Regulations annexed to Hague Convention IV of 1907. Severely tested in World War I, the Hague rules on belligerent occupation were then completely disregarded in World War II by Nazi Germany, especially in the territories occupied in Eastern Europe where the subjugated populations were subjected to a systematic spoliation and rule of terror culminating in the policy of genocide **(155)** against the Jews, Gypsies (Roma), and other racial and ethnic groups. Most of the major war criminals before the International Military Tribunal at Nuremberg **(354)** were convicted for war crimes **(373)** connected with serious breaches of the rules of belligerent occupation. Serious crimes were also committed by Japan and—less-publicized violations—by the Soviet Union. The occupation of Germany in the aftermath of the war was a unique type of military occupation which was not in many respects an occupation of the traditional kind.

The experiences of World War II led to an expansion of the Hague law of belligerent occupation in respect to the treatment of civilian population by the 1949 Geneva Convention **(349)** IV Relative to the Protection of Civilian Population in Time of War, subsequently complemented by some provisions of Protocol I of 1977 **(369)**. However, in many ways the rules of 1949 and 1977, let alone the Hague Regulations of 1907, are clearly obsolete and require a thorough revision.

Among the numerous international armed conflicts in which all these rules were expected to be applied, two cases stand out: first, the occupation since 1967 by Israel of the Palestinian (formerly Jordanian) West Bank territories, the Gaza Strip, and parts of the Syrian Golan Heights; and, second, the occupation of Iraq by the United States (US) and the United Kingdom (UK), and some minor members of the coalition. The nature of Israeli occupation has raised some questions. On the other hand, both the occupying powers and the Security Council (SC) agreed that the occupation of Iraq was a belligerent occupation governed by the pertinent rules of international humanitarian law.

Invoking Art. 2(2) of Geneva Convention IV, providing, *inter alia*, that the Convention applies to occupation of the territory "of a High Contracting Party," Israel, apart from the argument of the longevity of the occupation, has asserted that the Convention applies only if sovereignty over an occupied territory was legally vested in the "state" displaced by the new occupying state; that, when captured by Israel in 1967, the West Bank and East Jerusalem were not under any contracting state's sovereignty and were not subject to the rules on belligerent occupation since, following the termination of the British mandate **(93)** and the lapse (or collapse) of the United Nations (UN) General Assembly (GA) partitioning plan in 1947 for the mandated territories of Palestine, the occupation and annexation of the West Bank and East Jerusalem by the Kingdom of Transjordan (one of the contracting parties to the Convention) in 1950, was recognized only by a very limited number of states. It must be noted here that in 1988 Jordan, motivated by the legal claim of the Palestinians' right to self-determination **(122)**, declared discontinuance of its administration of the above-mentioned Palestinian territories. This Statement concerning "disengagement from the West Bank and Palestinian self-determination" (27 ILM 1637 (1988)) amounted to a formal renunciation of Jordan's sovereignty over the Palestinian territories in favor of a future Palestinian state. Following the Jordanian statement, the Palestine National Council declared independence of "the State of Palestine" (27 ILM 1660 (1988)). Although this entity did not meet the requirements necessary for recognition as a state **(116)** and was not recognized as such by the international community, there was a consensus that the Palestine Liberation Organization possessed a limited international legal personality. The problem of the Gaza Strip, once also belonging to the mandated territory of Palestine, was left outstanding in Art. II of the Treaty of Peace between Egypt and Israel of 1979 (18 ILM 362 (1979)), but the Strip itself was left on the Israeli side of the boundary **(189)**. Concerning the status of the occupied Palestinian territories, an issue recently analyzed by the International Court of Justice (ICJ) **(309)** in its advisory opinion **(291)** of 2004 on *Legal Consequnces of the Construction of a Wall in the Occupied Palestinian Territory* (43 ILM 1009 (2004). Israel's position appears to be that, while claiming a *de facto* compliance with the provisions on belligerent occupation of the Geneva Convention IV, it does not consider itself to be bound by them *de jure* since the terrorists were not under any state's sovereignty prior to their annexation by Jordan and Egypt. The Israeli argument is rejected by the UN and its individual members, as well as by a large majority of international law commentators. Even the Supreme Court of Israel in a 2004 decision found that Israel was bound by Hague Convention IV of 1907 and Geneva Convention IV. Hence, Israel is legally obliged to observe the provisions of Convention IV concerning belligerent occupation, which under Art. 2(1) of the Convention apply to all cases of armed conflict except for certain less important regulations that cease to apply after a year. The rules of the Convention are binding despite the extended duration of the occupation. Nor do any new unilateral administrative policies of the occupying power change the status of an essentially belligerent occupation. A number of UN resolutions, both of the SC and the GA, have always stressed that the occupation of the Arab territories by Israel is subject to the rules of international humanitarian law governing belligerent occupation, and in particular Geneva Convention IV of 1949. On several occasions, SC resolutions have determined that all measures designed to change the legal status of the territories occupied by Israel in 1967, including the integration of East Jerusalem into Israel, as well as measures designed to change the demographic composition of those territories, have no legal validity. In addition, Israel's decision in 1981 to annex the Golan Heights (21 ILM 163 (1982)) was declared by the SC to be "null and void and without any international legal effect."

In the case of Iraq, there was no controversy concerning the nature of the occupation of that country. Both the UN SC and the US and the UK, and other members of the "coalition," agreed that the occupation was a belligerent occupation to which all the rules of international law governing such occupation must apply. These rules include, apart from international customary law, the Hague Regulations of 1907; Geneva Convention IV; and—as far as the UK and some other minor participants in the occupation are concerned—also Protocol I of 1977 to which the UK is a party. The occupation of Iraq governed by the régime of belligerent occupation imposes much more burdensome obligations and responsibilities (and perhaps even personal liability for breaches of such obligations) upon the US and the UK (the "occupying powers") than would have been the case of a SC-authorized deployment of "peacekeeping" and "peace-building" forces **(334)**, including all the UN administrative apparatus, as applied in the case of Kosovo and especially East Timor. While, of course, complying with the fundamental principles and rules of international humanitarian law, such a SC-mandated "occupation" would not be hampered by the many complex regulations applying to the traditional belligerent occupation régime. However, in the early days of the occupation, the US, concerned about preserving its freedom of action, rejected the SC-based legal framework. Hence in May 2003, SC Resolution 1483 (42 ILM 1016 (2003)), adopted under Chapter VII of the UN Charter, determined, without in any way legitimizing the invasion, that the US and the UK "as occupying powers under unified command (the 'Authority')" were bound to comply fully with their obligations under international law concerning belligerent occupation. The resolution requested the UN Secretary-General to appoint a Special Representative for Iraq who would report to the SC and coordinate, with the Authority, the humanitarian assistance and reconstruction activities. Whether such "reconstruction" activities could go beyond what was allowed under Art. 43 of the Hague Regulations of Convention IV is not clear. The resolution also expressed support for the formation by Iraqis, with the help of the Authority, of an Iraqi interim administration as a transitional administration run by the Iraqis until an internationally recognized **(114)** representative government was established by them and assumed the responsibilities of the Authority. The SC decided to review the implementation of Resolution 1483 within 12 months of its adoption, that is by 22 May 2004. Unfortunately, the first Special Representative of the UN for Iraq was among the 22 victims of the bombing of the UN headquarters in Baghdad. No new representative was appointed in 2004, but the deteriorating security situtation made it impossible to carry out the tasks of the UN Assistance Mission for Iraq (UNAMI) established by Resolution 1500 and extended for one year by SC Resolution 1557 in August 2004. On the other hand, the SC in its Resolution 1500 welcomed the creation by the Authority of the Governing Council of Iraq, and in October 2003 in Resolution 1511 determined that the Council was the Iraqi interim administration envisaged by the SC in its Resolution 1483. Resolution 1511 also authorized the formation of a multinational force for the maintenance of security and stability in Iraq, but did not define the relationship of such force to the belligerent occupation forces. No such force has as yet been established. Ultimately it appeared that the occupation of Iraq would continue to operate as a belligerent occupation until the occupying powers agreed to act under the authority of the SC or an internationally recognized sovereign government of Iraq assumed the responsibility of the Authority, a development that took place on 28 June 2004, thus formally ending the status of belligerent occupation of Iraq. However, the coalition troops remained in Iraq with the consent of the interim government.

Belligerent occupation results in a temporary military administration of the territory by the occupying power, but the laws of the occupied territory still apply, subject to the right of the occupying power to maintain order and the necessity to administer the territory in the interests of its inhabitants and for the occupying power's military needs. However, the precise content and scope of the occupier's competences in the legislative and administrative spheres is not certain. International humanitarian law requires that the inhabitants of the occupied territory be protected and accorded humane treatment in all circumstances. Geneva Convention IV and its Protocol I include a long list of guarantees of the inhabitants' rights, including, *inter alia*, respect for their honor, family rights, customs and religious practices, and private property. The law prohibits violence to the life and well-being of the persons under the power of the occupier: murder; torture **(182)**; corporal and collective punishment; reprisals **(370)** against civilians; humiliating and degrading treatment; taking hostages; discrimination on racial, religious, or political grounds; transfer or deportation; and requisitioning food and medical supplies to the detriment of the ordinary needs of the population. No coercion may be exercised against protected persons, in particular to obtain information, and any measure of brutality is prohibited, a provision violated by US inhumane treatment of Iraqi prisoners, especially in the Abu Ghraib prison in Baghdad. Protocol I provides for additional protective measures for women and children. Settlement of occupied territory by the occupier's own civilian population is illegal, as repeatedly held by the SC in reaction to Israel's state-sponsored and subsidized establishment of settlements in the occupied territories. It should be added that the duty to protect the civilian population in occupied territory obtains also in non-international armed conflicts.

It must not be overlooked that the population of the occupied territory has certain duties toward the occupying power. It is difficult to determine the exact scope of such duties and it is in particular not clear to what extent the population owes the duty of obedience to the occupying power and how such duty can be reconciled with the international law principle of self-determination of peoples **(122)**. It is also not clear to what extent the population of an occupied territory is released from the duty of obedience in reaction to severe breaches by the occupier of the law governing belligerent occupation. While it is accepted that, in reaction to denial by the occupying power of self-determination, the population in question is under international law entitled to resort to force, the exact scope and modalities of such resistance encounters difficult and very controversial problems in actual practice. In any case, however, the fundamental principles of international humanitarian law, including in particular the distinction between combatants and civilians must apply to both sides in such conflict. The occupying power has the right to punish individuals for armed resistance, but must observe the principles of necessity and proportionality. These requirements are well illustrated in the UN GA Report of the Secretary-General (Jenin Report), prepared in 2002 pursuant to a GA resolution of the 10th emergency session of the Assembly (41 ILM 1444 (2002)). The traditional law of belligerent occupation once permitted the death penalty, but such penalty does not appear permissible in today's international humanitarian law. One might add that the advisory opinion of the International ICJ on the *Legal Consequences of the Construction of a Wall in the Occupied Palestinian Territory* (45 ILM 1009 (2004)) clarified various aspects of the rights of the occupying power as against the population of the occupied territories.

The rules concerning the economic aspects of belligerent occupation are rather complex and, in certain areas, not clear. For example, it is not certain whether the occupying power has the right to exploit the natural resources of the territory under occupation, a question that arose in the past during the Israeli occupation of the Egyptian Sinai Peninsula. The problem became topical again in respect to the exploitation of the Iraqi oil fields under the belligerent occupation of the US and the UK. Very briefly, the already mentioned SC Resolution 1483 of 2003 established a Development Fund for Iraq to be disbursed for humanitarian purposes and reconstruction at the direction of the occupying powers' Authority in consultation with the Iraqi Governing Council. The Oil-for-Food Program was terminated and responsibility for the administration of any remaining activity of the program was transferred to the Authority. Except for 5 percent to be deposited into the Compensation Fund established by the SC in 1991 to settle claims against Iraq arising from its aggression against Kuwait and the Gulf War, all proceeds from the export sales of petroleum, natural gas, and petroleum products had to be deposited in the above-noted Development Fund for Iraq until an internationally recognized, representative government of Iraq was properly constituted. All these SC decisions mean that the US had no right in international law to dispose according to its will of the oil resources in occupied Iraq. Neither did the SC authorize the radical restructuring of Iraq's economic system, its investment and banking laws, and other reforms in fact carried out by the occupying powers.

The occupying power has the right to levy taxes and customs duties, and, as administrator of the immovable public property of the state is entitled to utilize but not to appropriate it. Movable public property that can be used for military operations can be appropriated. Confiscation, destruction, or damaging of cultural assets is prohibited, a subject regulated in detail by the 1954 Hague Convention for the Protection of Cultural Property in Time of War (249 UNTS 240). Private property may not be seized, except for movable property used for military purposes, but compensation must be paid upon the termination of the occupation and conclusion of the peace treaty.

The traditional legal rules governing occupation somehow do not fit contemporary conditions. In the past era of homogeneous politics and ideology, belligerent occupation was a relatively short episode in which the occupying power and its army had, as a rule, only purely military and security interests in the occupied territory. Today, as demonstrated by Iraq, the interests of the occupier can go far beyond the Hague Regulations mandate to ensure public order and safety for the time of a usually rather short and transient occupation, without changing the occupied country's laws and institutions unless they threatened the military and security interests of the occupying power. The policy of the occupation Authority in Iraq was a total transformation of the constitutional, legal, political, and economic system, which action is clearly contrary to the traditional rules on belligerent occupation. On the other hand, the above-mentioned Resolution 1483 of the SC, while expecting the occupying powers to comply with the Hague law and other traditional rules, did not seem to condemn the far-reaching reforms of the Authority transcending that law. In this respect, the inconsistency of Resolution 1483 seemed to be the product of a compromise in the SC between the US and the SC members opposing the US invasion.

Belligerent occupation may terminate in a number of ways. The territory may be liberated by the other side or a successful uprising of the population; or it may be returned to the lawful sovereign in accordance with the terms of the peace treaty. In less classical cases of belligerent occupation, such as the occupation of Iraq, belligerent occupation may end by a gradual formation of the government, which took place in Iraq; or by delegating the responsibilities of the occupying power to the SC, in which case the regulations governing belligerent occupation would, in principle, not apply.

**364. Prisoners of War.** Prisoners of war are individuals belonging to the armed forces of a party to an armed conflict, international **(339)** or non-international **(340)**, that is, combatants **(342)**, who have fallen into the power of the adverse party. In historical perspective, until about the Thirty Years War (1618–1648) prisoners of war were generally treated inhumanely and killed or sold into slavery, except that noble prisoners were often freed for ransom. In the 18th century the treatment of prisoners of war became more humane, and by the 19th century customary international law rules developed, requiring treatment of prisoners of war according to standards comparable to those applied to the armed forces of the detaining power. The Instructions issued in 1863 by the United States (US) government for the Union army during the Civil War (1861–1865), based on a draft by Francis Lieber, reflected this progress in humanization of warfare. By the outbreak of World War I, the treatment of prisoners of war was governed by customary law and the Regulations annexed to Hague Convention **(350)** IV of 1907 (or—for some states **(127)**—by the rules of the corresponding Convention of 1899). However, no enforcement procedures were envisaged in these treaties. After World War I, in 1929 more elaborate rules were developed in the Geneva Convention Relative to the Treatment of Prisoners of War (118

LNTS 343) which applied in World War II, except in relations between Germany and the Soviet Union. While in World War II there occurred some serious violations by Germany of the 1929 Convention in relation to prisoners of war of the Western Allies, in general the Western prisoners of war were treated relatively humanely and certainly much better than those from other countries. The treatment of the Soviet prisoners of war was uniquely brutal, in violation of the most fundamental rules of war and principles of humanity. The post-war trials of German and Japanese war criminals disclosed numerous cases of inhuman treatment of prisoners war by Germany and by Japan. It must be added that the Soviet Union also committed grave violations of the law of war protecting prisoners of war which were never brought to trial, including, *inter alia*, the notorious mass murder of thousands of Polish prisoners of war at Katyn in 1940, captured in 1939 by the Soviet Union in the joint Soviet-Nazi invasion of Poland.

Currently, the legal status of prisoners of war is governed by Geneva Convention **(349)** III of 1949 (75 UNTS 135) which is in force **(271)** for practically all states. Protocol I **(369)** of 1977 (on international armed conflict) **(339)**, additional to the Geneva Conventions, *inter alia*, developed rules concerning prisoners of war, dealing in particular with the status of combatants **(342)** belonging to irregular forces **(356)**. Some 160 states are parties to Protocol I, including the United Kingdom (UK), but not the US. To what extent the rules of international humanitarian law on prisoners of war are applicable to non-international armed conflicts **(340)** is an open question. Theoretically, such a conflict (internationalized by the participation of the US coalition) started in Iraq following the establishment there of the provisional government in June 2004. Protocol II **(369)** of 1977 (on non-international armed conflict), additional to the Geneva Conventions, includes a number of provisions to safeguard humane treatment of "persons deprived of their liberty for reasons related to the armed conflict, whether they are interned or detained," but does not employ the term "prisoner of war," apparently reserved only to prisoners in an international armed conflict.

The definition of prisoners of war in Convention III (Art. 4) allows the conclusion that the concept of persons entitled to treatment as such prisoners upon capture is that of combatants. This is confirmed in Protocol I stating that "any combatant, as defined in Article 43, who falls into the power of an adverse party shall be prisoner of war." Consequently, prisoners of war include captured individuals belonging to regular and irregular forces, including those who—like members of the free forces of the countries overrun by Germany in World War II—profess allegiance to a government or authority not recognized by the detaining power; various categories of civilians who accompany the armed forces; members of crews of merchant marine vessels and civil aircraft who otherwise, under international law, do not enjoy more favorable treatment; and members of a *levée en masse* **(357)**. In addition, treatment of prisoners of war applies to potential members of the armed forces of the occupied country and persons belonging to any category listed in Art. 4 who are interned in a neutral **(362)** state. Medical personnel and chaplains receive protection under Convention III, but are not considered as prisoners of war (Art. 33), except for persons temporarily performing medical functions who, according to Arts. 25 and 29 of Geneva Convention I (on wounded and sick soldiers), must otherwise be employed by the capturing state on their medical duties insofar as the need arises.

The rules of Geneva Convention III apply from the time a combatant is captured and until his final release and repatriation. If there is any doubt as to whether a captured person who committed a belligerent act is entitled to the status of prisoner of war, such person enjoys the protection of the Convention until such time as his status has been determined by a competent tribunal (Art. 5 and Protocol I Art. 45(1)). According to the US Department of the Army Field Manual on the law of land warfare, 1956, a board of not less than three officers constitutes such a tribunal. In addition, the Manual provides that persons held by the tribunal as not entitled to the prisoner-of-war status may not be executed, imprisoned, or otherwise penalized without further judicial proceedings. Substantially the same rule is articulated in Art. 45(2) of Protocol I which, in addition, requires representatives of the Protecting Power **(368)** to attend the proceedings.

If a person is determined by the above-mentioned tribunal not to be entitled to treatment as a prisoner of war (normally because he engaged in hostile or belligerent conduct against the detaining belligerent), he is still a "protected person" under Geneva Convention IV of 1949 Relative to the Protection of Civilian Persons in Time of War (75 UNTS 287). Spies **(372)** are not entitled to the status of prisoner of war. Saboteurs and other individuals who do not meet the conditions prescribed for recognition of irregular forces as combatants and who commit hostile acts against the adverse party are not treated as prisoners of war, and may be tried when apprehended.

In the Vietnam War, the US, concerned about the US captives in the hands of the North Vietnam-Vietcong, treated all captured enemies as combatants and thus entitled to the status of prisoners of war under Geneva Convention III to which the US and the two Vietnam states were parties. South Vietnam, which initially considered its citizens fighting in the Vietcong ranks as common criminals, was eventually persuaded by the US to treat them as combatants. On the other hand, North Vietnam did not observe the rules of the Convention, claiming that the US captives were war criminals **(373)**. There were no major problems concerning the status of Iraqi prisoners of war in the Gulf War of 1991 or—for that matter—in the war of 2003. However, the status of prisoners captured by the US and allied forces in Afghanistan in 2001–2002 became a subject of a rather confusing debate compounded by an ambiguous and inconsistent position of the US on this issue.

The military intervention by the US and its allies in Afghanistan took place in 2001 with an implied consent of the United Nations (UN) Security Council (SC) which had recognized the US right of self-defense **(335)** against international terrorism **(337)**. The intervention occurred after the extreme Islamic Taliban government of Afghanistan had refused to hand over the leaders of al Qaeda, an international Islamic terrorist organization, led by Osama bin Laden, which had established and built up its base for terrorist activities in Afghanistan with the connivance and support of the Taliban government. According to available evidence there was no reasonable doubt that al Qaeda had organized and directed the attacks upon the US in September 2001. The US self-defense action happened to take place at the time of the still ongoing, non-international armed conflict in Afghanistan between the incumbent Taliban government and anti-Taliban coalition of insurgent groups. Most of the territory of Afghanistan was under the control of the Taliban government which, however, was recognized **(114)** only by one or two states. Thus, the US action designed to destroy the terrorist infrastructure in Afghanistan and apprehend its leadership placed the US *de facto* on the side of the anti-Taliban insurgent forces still holding a small part of the territory of Afghanistan in the civil war in progress. While the US military intervention was the major incidental factor contributing to the overthrow of the Taliban régime, the US objectives were only partially achieved. The material infrastructure of the terrorists involved in the September 2001 attacks upon the US was largely destroyed, but the leadership of al Qaeda and its ally, the Taliban government, managed to escape. However, a few hundred prisoners captured directly by US forces or handed over to them by the newly installed friendly government in Kabul were detained by the US, with over 600 captives transferred to the US Guantánamo naval base, leased **(207)** from Cuba since 1903. A debate soon ensued over the legal status of the captives detained by the US.

The US intervention in Afghanistan internationalized a non-international armed conflict, at least insofar as the US and its allies are concerned. Hence, while the status of persons in the power of the adverse party in a civil war is not entirely clear, being governed by general and vague humanitarian principles, the status of those captured in an international armed conflict is regulated by detailed provisions of Geneva Convention III of 1949 in force for practically all the countries in the world, including Afghanistan and the US. However, neither the US nor Afghanistan are parties to Protocol I of 1977 which, with a view to improving the position of guerrilla fighters in a "national liberation war," provides for more indulgent rules governing the status of such irregular forces as combatants. However, it is doubtful that these relaxed rules of Protocol I have become binding as customary international law.

To determine the status of the captives detained by the US an initial distinction must be made between the rank-and-file fighters of the Taliban government, on the one hand, and other individuals fighting alongside them against the US forces on the other. They were primarily, though not exclusively, members of al Qaeda. Assuming that the Taliban rank-and-file fighters belonged to the category of "members of the armed forces" and were combatants meeting the four requirements of Art. 4(A)(2) of Geneva Convention III (command by a responsible person, fixed distinctive sign, carrying arms openly, and compliance with the laws of war), they would be entitled to treatment as prisoners of war upon capture (Art. 4(A)(1)). However, this does not prejudice the right of the detaining state (the US) in doubtful cases, such as, for example, suspicion of membership in a terrorist organization, to determine a suspect's status by a "competent tribunal" as stipulated in the already noted Art. 5. It is evident that proven members of a terrorist organization, just as members of other transnational criminal groups, such as drug traffickers, cannot be treated as prisoners of war. In legal terminology, it is misleading to use the term "war" to denote an anti-terrorist campaign and thus treat terrorists (and illicit drugs traffickers) within the legal framework of international humanitarian law. Under international law there cannot exist a relationship of "war" with a criminal group; members of such organizations, whether terrorists or drug dealers, are obviously not "combatants," lawful or unlawful. As a matter of fact, referring to the 11 September 2001 attacks as a "war crime" and to the terrorists as "unlawful combatants" can be construed as promoting common crimes, even of extraordinary magnitude, to the status of acts of war. Like piracy, terrorism is a crime particularly offensive and dangerous to the international community as a whole, and perpetrators are liable for their acts directly under international law and according to the principles of universality jurisdiction **(92).** It is the US position, as presented in the US response (41 ILM 1015 (2002)) to a request by the Inter-American Commission on Human Rights (41 ILM 532 (2002) for precautionary measures with regard of the Guantánamo detainees, that Art. 5 tribunals are not required where, as in the case of the Taliban detainees, there is no doubt about their status because they failed to meet at least two of the four criteria of Art. 4 of Convention III, in particular, the distinction from the civilian population (they certainly had no uniforms or distinguishing emblems); and conducting operations in accordance with the laws and customs of war. However, under the convention, even unlawful combatants, such as the Taliban, must be treated humanely. The position of the US on the legal status of al Qaeda members is the same as described in the above paragraphs, but should be based on sufficient proof of al Qaeda connection of individual detainees and determined by the tribunal under the Article 5 of Convention III.

As a general rule, under Convention III, should the tribunal hold an individual detainee not to be entitled to the prisoner-of-war status, further judicial proceedings must determine the criminal offense committed and the penalty to be imposed. If a detainee's status as a prisoner of war is confirmed by the tribunal, he enjoys all the privileges of a prisoner of war until his final release and repatriation. Mercenaries **(360)**, as defined in Protocol I, do not have any right to combatant or prisoner-of-war status. It is important to remember that SC Resolution 1390 of 2002 (41 ILM 511 (2002)), *inter alia*, condemned the Taliban for "using foreign mercenaries in hostile actions in the territory of Afghanistan."

Geneva Convention III lays down detailed rules mandating humane treatment of prisoners of war by the detaining power. When questioned on the subject, a prisoner of war is bound to give only his surname, first name or names, rank, date of birth, and serial number; he must not be forced to give information useful to his captors. Prisoners of war must at all time be protected, in particular against acts of violence and intimidation and against insults and public curiosity, such as, for example, displaying them on television screens, as was done by Iraq in the war of 2003. They may not be forced to confess alleged crimes or make statements against their own government. In all circumstances prisoners of war are entitled to respect for their persons and their honor. No prisoner of war may be exposed to the fire of a combat zone or used as a human shield to deter an attack by the adverse party. Prisoners of war may retain their personal effects and are entitled to the same maintenance and payment as the equivalent troops of the detaining power. Their labor may be utilized, but noncommissioned officers may only do supervisory work. Officers, if they request, must be allowed to work, but under no circumstances may they be compelled to work. The Convention stipulates detailed rules governing the work conditions; the prisoners' financial resources; their quarters, food, clothing, medical attention, recreation, correspondence, censorship, relief shipments, and the like. A special section of the Convention deals with penal and disciplinary sanctions. In this respect, the prisoners are, as a rule, subject to the same laws and regulations as those governing the armed forces of the detaining power. They may be tried by a military court unless trial by a civil court is permitted by the law in respect to the offense in question. The court must offer guarantees of independence and impartiality; the right of appeal is guaranteed. Prisoners may be tried for acts, including war crimes **(373)**, committed prior to capture, but even if convicted retain the benefits of the Convention. Recaptured escaped prisoners of war who rejoin their own forces are not liable to any punishment. Unsuccessful escape, even if repeated, is subject only to disciplinary penalties. Parole is permitted if allowed by the law of the prisoner's state. Wounded and sick prisoners must be sent back to their own country, but repatriation against the prisoner's will is prohibited. Special agreements between the opposing belligerents, known as cartels, were used in past wars to effect exchanges of prisoners of war and internees. Prisoners of war must be released and repatriated without delay after the cessation of hostilities. Repatriation of prisoners of war became a focus of serious controversy in the Korean War (1950–1953) when many North Korean and Chinese prisoners of war refused to return to their homes, with the resulting protracted stalemate in the armistice negotiations. In the Indo-Pakistani War of 1971, repatriation was delayed for several years by India, which threatened to hand over some Pakistani prisoners of war to Bangladesh for trial on charges of alleged genocide **(155)**. The dispute **(299)** found itself on the docket of the International Court of Justice **(309)**, but was withdrawn after the two states had settled it by negotiation **(316)**. In the numerous armed conflicts of the past few decades, the longest captivity was suffered by Moroccan prisoners of war captured by the Western Sahara insurgents (POLISARIO) and held in POLISARIO camps in Algeria for more than 25 years. Geneva Convention III regulates the activities of information bureaus and relief societies for prisoners of war, including the crucial role of the International Committee of the Red Cross whose delegates are accorded the same privileges, especially with regard to the right to visit prisoners' camps, as those granted to the Protecting Power **(368)**. Finally, one might add that many questions concerning the treatment of prisoners of war and the application of Convention III in contemporary practice have been examined and exhaustively analyzed in the awards of the Eritrea-Ethiopia Claims Commission in the aftermath of the war between these countries in 1998–2002 (42 ILM 1056, 1093 (2003)).

**365. Prize Courts.** A prize court is a domestic (municipal) **(28)** court of a belligerent state **(127)**, whose function is to adjudicate, according to international law, the lawfulness of prizes, that is, enemy or neutral **(362)** vessels, captured by the captor's state on suspicion of carrying contraband **(343)** or running a blockade **(341)**. If a prize court declared a vessel or its cargo or both to be a lawful prize, they were confiscated by the captor's state and could be sold, with the purchaser acquiring an internationally valid title, subject, of course, to the right of the condemned vessel's state to seek remedy in international law. Under international humanitarian rules, some categories of vessels are exempt from capture. They include, in addition to coastal fishing vessels (the subject of a celebrated leading case of the *Paquete Habana* and the *Lola* before the United States (US) Supreme Court (175 U.S. 677) in 1900), vessels engaged in religious, scientific, or philanthropic functions, hospital ships, and the more recently added category of vessels protected by the Convention and Protocol for the Protection of Cultural Property in Time of War of 1954 (249 UNTS 240, 258). In the practice of both world wars, captured enemy vessels were often destroyed, but contemporary humanitarian law **(353)** takes the position that such action should be an exceptional measure, and only after safeguarding the lives of passengers and crew and saving their personal effects and the ship's papers. In addition, enemy passenger vessels carrying only civilians may not be destroyed.

The prize courts apply rules of international law, customary **(39)** and conventional **(40)**. Among the latter are the Declaration of Paris of 1856 **(344)** and some of the Hague Conventions of 1907 **(350)** (or, for some relatively few states, of 1899), namely, Convention VI (enemy merchant ships at the outbreak of war); Convention VII (conversion of merchant ships into warships); Convention XI (restrictions of the right of capture); and Convention XIII (neutral powers in naval war). However, the "general participation clause" **(348)** seriously weakened the application of these Hague Conventions. The 1936 London Protocol on submarine warfare was largely disregarded by belligerents of both sides in World War II.

A prize court may be a purely judicial body, as was the case of British and US prize courts, or a mixed administrative-judicial court, as in continental European countries, Japan, and China, except that French prize courts were in their composition administrative bodies. In Great Britain and the US existing ordinary courts also had jurisdiction to function as prize courts in time of war; in other countries prize courts were *ad hoc* tribunals established at the outbreak of war. As a general rule, appeals from prize courts to a higher authority were possible.

The practice of adjudicating prizes originated as far back as the Middle Ages when it was included among the functions of the English Court of Admiralty which would decide whether a vessel and/or its cargo were liable to capture and condemnation as a lawful prize. Prize courts functioned in a number of countries during the two world wars of the 20th century. However, no such courts operated in the US in the two wars, having been activated last in 1899. But in World War I the US confiscated 100 German and Austrian ships which happened to lie in US ports and in World War II requisitioned, for future compensation, 80 "idle" enemy and neutral ships. The Soviet Union did not establish any prize courts. Claims between belligerents arising over captures are normally settled in the peace treaty; those between belligerents and neutrals are settled through negotiations **(316)** or arbitration **(293)**. In order to settle any disputes between states over alleged violations of international law by municipal prize courts (which occasionally displayed bias in favor of their state), a convention on establishing an international prize court with jurisdiction to hear appeals from municipal prize courts was adopted by the Hague Conference of 1907, but this Hague Convention XII never entered into force.

In terms of their war function, prize courts in World Wars I and II were tools of economic warfare against the enemy, keeping pace with the changing national prize law of the respective countries which gradually increased the severity of measures, such as expanding the concept of contraband and blockade, and other measures. Eventually, total warfare introduced new effective methods of isolating the enemy economically, such as the long-distance blockade, air warfare against merchant vessels, and all kinds of stringent controls imposed upon ships before they reached the high seas. All these measures considerably reduced the significance of prize courts in the conditions of modern total warfare, but did not make them entirely obsolete, as evidenced by the establishment of a prize court by Egypt in the first Arab-Israeli War in 1948.

**366. Prohibited Methods of Warfare.** These are methods of warfare which are intended or may be expected to cause superfluous injury or unnecessary suffering, or involve perfidy or breach of established rules of fairness in relation to the enemy. Motivated by humanitarian considerations, the prohibition of some methods of conducting hostilities (and of some weapons) **(367)** is designed to mitigate and restrain the brutality of warfare by trying to maintain a balance between military necessity and considerations of humanity and, however vague and deficient these prohibitions may be, to provide at least some standards for the use of military power in an armed conflict, both international **(339)** and non-international **(340)**. In this respect, certain general rules evolved in the customary law **(39)** of war before World War I and were codified in the Regulations annexed to Hague Convention **(350)** IV of 1907 Respecting the Laws and Customs of War on Land (or the corresponding provisions of the Convention of 1899). These basic rules dictate that in any armed conflict the right of the parties to choose methods and means of warfare is not unlimited and that superfluous injury and unnecessary suffering must be avoided.

Protocol I of 1977 **(369)**, which develops the rules of international humanitarian law **(353)** of the Geneva Conventions of 1949 **(349)** and the rules of the pertinent Hague Conventions, restates in Art. 35 these basic rules and, reflecting the rising concern of states **(127)** over the environment, adds the prohibition of methods and means of warfare which are intended or may be expected to cause widespread, long-term, and severe damage to the natural environment. Art. 55 reiterates this rule, with the emphasis on protecting the health and survival of the civilian population. However, it is not yet entirely certain whether the rule on the protection on the natural environment in warfare has already acquired the force of general (customary) international law. Otherwise, Protocol I elaborates in Part III on various aspects of methods of warfare, and Part IV focuses on the protection of the civilian population against the effects of hostilities. Here Protocol I restates the three basic rules which underlie the regulation of methods and means of warfare and are derived from the fundamental distinction between combatants and non-combatants: 1. distinction at all times between the civilian population and combatants and between civilian objects and military objectives (Art. 48); 2. precautions in attack to spare civilian populations and objects (Art. 57); and 3. proportionality, to be observed when attacking military targets can be expected to cause collateral civilian damage. To put it briefly, the rules prohibit attacking civilian objects for their own sake and mandate that when attacking military targets constant care must be taken to spare, as much as possible, civilians and civilian objects.

The basic principles and rules governing the methods of combat guide the still binding Regulations of the 1907 Convention IV. Among other restraints upon methods of combat, the Regulations prohibit attack on or bombardment of undefended localities and buildings (Art. 25), a provision further developed in Protocol I of 1977. Defended localities must be warned by the attacking force before the commencement of bombardment, except in the case of an assault (Art. 26). Distinctly marked hospitals and churches must be spared (Art. 27). Although there is no provision on permitting evacuation from a besieged locality, the commander of the investing force must make efforts to conclude an agreement for removal of the sick and wounded, children, and maternity cases, and medical and religious personnel. Taking hostages is strictly prohibited. Another institution of international humanitarian law, designed to protect a certain area by excluding it from military operations, are the so-called demilitarized zones established by the parties to the conflict. Such zones are addressed in detail in Art. 60 of Protocol I. Cultural, religious, and similar buildings must be spared and pillage is prohibited. More recently, the Hague Convention, with a Protocol, for the Protection of Cultural Property in the Event of Armed Conflict, 1954 (249 UNTS 215, 358), followed by the second Protocol in 1999 (38 ILM 769 (1999)), regulates in detail the protection of cultural property in armed conflict. There is growing consensus that the basic rules concerning the methods of combat and those governing the protection of civilians and civilian objects apply also in a non-international armed conflict. Unfortunately, as noted by the Security Council in Resolution 1296 of 2000 on the Protection of Civilians in Armed Conflict (39 ILM 1022 (2000)), civilians account for the vast majority of casualties in international and internal conflicts.

The Hague Regulations of 1907 prohibiting attacks on and bombardment of undefended localities became illusory already in World War I, and World War II witnessed large-scale destruction of civilian structures and whole cities, with very high civilian casualties. In many cases there was deliberate intent to disregard the restraints of humanitarian law, but otherwise it may be difficult to observe in the heat of battle the regulations of the law, especially in urban combat, let alone in air warfare where—as evidenced in practice—even the use of precision weapons does not exclude collateral civilian damage. In addition, such concepts as "military objective," "indiscriminate attack," or "precautionary measures," though defined in Arts. 42(2) and 51(4), or elaborated upon in Art. 57 of Protocol I, allow a margin of discretion to belligerents. In this regard, the International Committee of the Red Cross drew up a detailed list of military objectives, revised at 10-year intervals.

Among the methods of combat, air warfare occupies a unique position in terms of prohibitions of international humanitarian law in that it still remains an unregulated area of armed conflict. Even before the invention of aircraft, a Declaration, adopted in 1899 and renewed in 1907, prohibited the discharge of projectiles and explosives from balloons and by other methods of a similar nature. Strangely enough, though practically meaningless, this Declaration is still in force for some 30 states, including the United States (US) (36 Stat. 2439; TS 546). The wording of the Hague Regulations of Convention IV prohibiting the attack or bombardment of undefended localities by "any means whatever" would suggest prohibition of aerial bombardment. However, already in 1911–1912 Italy resorted to it in its war with Turkey and during World War I aircraft were increasingly used in warfare, including bombing civilian localities. Following World War I, a draft code of air warfare prepared in 1923 (17 AJIL Supp. 245 (1923)), was never ratified. Its distinction between legitimate bombardment of specific military targets and unlawful bombing in situations where it could not be carried out without indiscriminate injury to the civilian population proved to be meaningless even before World War II, as demonstrated by deliberate bombing by the *Luftwaffe* in the Spanish Civil War (1936–1939) and by the Japanese in China. In World War II unrestricted air bombardment, initiated by Germany and subsequently practiced on a much larger scale by the Allies, became a routine military operation. As in the case of unrestricted submarine warfare, the International Military Tribunal at Nuremberg did not charge the major German war criminals with indiscriminate use of air power against civilians; the other side resorted to the same method of warfare.

Since World War II aerial bombardment as a method of warfare has been used many times in various armed conflicts. The practice has shown that while the number of civilian casualties has been reduced as compared with World War II, owing to great strides in the technology of precision targeting of bombs and missiles, collateral damage is still unavoidable. But air warfare remains an unregulated, if legitimate, method in armed conflict. The Final Report to the Prosecutor of the International Criminal Tribunal for the Former Yugoslavia by the Committee Established to Review the NATO Bombing Campaign against the Federal Republic of Yugoslavia of 2000 (39 ILM 1257 (2000)) estimated the number of civilian casualties due to the bombing at approximately 500 killed and 820 wounded in 90 separate incidents. The Committee concluded in its report that those figures did not indicate that the North Atlantic Treaty Organization (NATO) might have conducted (in this "humanitarian intervention" **(332)**), a campaign aimed at causing substantial civilian casualties either directly or indirectly. The Committee concluded that there was no evidence of breaches of international humanitarian law, and never questioned the legality of the campaign.

In addition to the rules designed to protect civilians and civilian objects, the traditional law of war recognized that in the interest of all a certain amount of chivalry, fairness, and respect must prevail even in relations between hostile parties. This principle is also part of international humanitarian law **(353)** today. The relevant rules are spelled out in the Regulations of 1907, especially Arts. 23 and 24, and further developed in Protocol I of 1977 (Arts. 37–42). Briefly, resort to treachery or perfidy is prohibited. Perfidy is defined as "acts inviting the confidence of adversary to lead him to believe that he is entitled to, or is obliged to accord, protection under the rules of international law applicable in armed conflict, with intent to betray that confidence." Examples of perfidy include the feigning of the following: an intent to negotiate under a flag of truce or of a surrender; of an incapacitation by wounds or sickness; of civilian non-combatant status; and of protected status by the use of signs, emblems, or uniform of the United Nations (UN) or of neutral or other states not parties to the conflict (Hague Regulations Art. 23(b); Protocol I Art. 37(1)). However, ruses of war are not prohibited. Art. 37(2) of Protocol I defines them as "acts which are intended to mislead an adversary or to induce him to act recklessly but which infringe no rule of international law applicable in armed conflict and which are not perfidious because they do not invite the confidence of an adversary with respect to protection under that law." Examples of ruses are the use of camouflage, decoys, mock operations, and misinformation. In addition to acts of perfidy, prohibited methods of warfare include making improper use of the emblem of red cross, red crescent, or (as adopted by Iran) red lion and sun, or other internationally recognized protective emblems, signs, or signals, including the flag of truce and the protective emblem of cultural property. Unless authorized by the UN, the use of its emblem is also prohibited (Protocol I Art. 38). It is also illegal to make use of the flag or military emblems, insignia, or uniforms of a neutral state or—while engaged in attack or in order to shield or impede a military operation—of the enemy (Hague Regulations Art. 23; Protocol I Art. 39). A notorious case of using or rather abusing the enemy's uniforms occurred during the Battle of the Bulge in 1944 when German SS troops in US uniforms infiltrated behind the Allied lines. However, a US war crimes tribunal acquitted eight of the Germans after the war since they had not been captured in the act of violating the law of war and were not arraigned until after the cessation of hostilities. Improper use of the flag by a warship in order to disguise its national identity appears to be unlawful, but it was occasionally practiced in the two world wars.

It is also prohibited to order or to threaten that no quarter will be given, or to conduct hostilities on this basis (Hague Regulations Art. 23(d); Protocol I Art. 40). A belligerent also violates international humanitarian law if it attacks an enemy *hors de combat*, that is, when a member of the enemy force clearly intends to surrender or is incapacitated, or if he is already in the power of the adverse party (Hague Regulations Art. 23(e); Protocol I Art. 41). Under Art. 42 of Protocol I, airborne or parachute troops are not protected, but no person parachuting from an aircraft in distress may be made the object of attack during his descent. A parachutist must be given an opportunity to surrender unless it is apparent that he is engaging in a hostile act. However, this provision does not seem to be realistic. Unfortunately this may also be the case of rules governing other actual combat situations.

**367. Prohibited Weapons.** These are arms, projectiles, and other material used as a means of warfare, which are calculated to cause superfluous injury or unnecessary suffering. There are two general categories of prohibited weapons: weapons prohibited under the general definition without any specific ban of a particular weapon, and weapons specifically banned by treaty **(288)**. The idea that certain types of weapons should be prohibited dates back to the 19th century and soon became part of the general (customary) **(39)** international law of war. However, the general principles governing such prohibition were rather vague. As a result, no clear agreement emerged on the specific types of weapons whose use caused superfluous injury or unnecessary suffering and which therefore should be prohibited.

Prohibition by treaty, though only partially successful, has proved to be more useful in practice than general principles. On the whole, compliance with a ban on specific weapons has been better than with other rules of law, not least the rules governing the protection of non-combatants. The fact that a weapon is not specifically banned does not make it legal; in acquiring a new weapon, a party to an armed conflict is obliged to determine whether or not it is compatible with the general principles of international humanitarian law **(353)**.

Chronologically first to ban a specific weapon was the now outdated (but formally still in force for 17 states) Declaration of St. Petersburg of 1868 (138 CTS 297) banning the use of projectiles weighing less than 400 grams (14 ounces) which are either explosive or charged with inflammable substance. At the First Hague Peace Conference in 1899, a Declaration prohibited the use of the so-called dumdum bullets, named after an arsenal near Calcutta (now Kolkata) where they were produced, which expand or flatten easily in the human body. The ban on such bullets was generally complied with, but another declaration of 1899, the Hague Declaration on poisonous gases, was disregarded on a large scale in World War I when Germany resorted to chemical warfare, with consequent belligerent reprisals **(370)** by the Allies resorting to such warfare. On the other hand, the widely ratified Geneva Protocol of 1925 banning the use of poisonous gases, analogous liquids, materials, or devices, and of bacteriological weapons (94 LNTS 65) was, by a sort of tacit agreement, observed in World War II (unless one includes radiation produced by the atomic weapons among such prohibited materials) and eventually acquired the force of customary international law. The Hague Convention **(350)** VIII of 1907 Relating to the Laying of Automatic Contact Mines, which banned the laying of non-anchored contact mines not made harmless upon breaking loose from their moorings, and torpedoes still effective after missing their target, was, on the whole, disregarded in the two world wars.

After World War II, a number of important treaties banning the use of specific means of warfare have been adopted since the 1970s. The 1972 Convention on the Prohibition of the Development, Production and Stockpiling of Bacteriological (Biological) and Toxin Weapons and on Their Destruction (1015 UNTS 163), in force 1975, banned the use of such weapons for hostile purposes in an armed conflict. However, this Convention, in force for 144 states, including the United States (US), lacks realistic enforcement provisions. Protracted negotiations have so far failed to produce a verification system. In 2001 the US pulled out of these negotiations due to its concern over the effectiveness of the proposed Protocol to the 1972 Convention and over the intrusive nature of its inspection system which the US considered to be a threat to the proprietary rights of American pharmacological companies.

The use of chemical weapons in warfare is banned by the Convention of 1992 on the Prohibition of the Development, Production, Stockpiling and Use of Chemical Weapons and on Their Destruction (32 ILM 800 (1993)), open for signature **(283)** in 1993, in force 1997 and ratified by some 145 countries, including the US. The parties have 10 years (until 2007) to eliminate their chemical weapons stockpiles and their infrastructure. The Convention is enforced not only by reporting requirements but also by a system of short-notice inspections verifying the destruction of weapons, managed by the Organization for the Prohibition of Chemical Weapons established by Art. VIII of the Convention. Of related interest is the Convention on the Prohibition of Military or Any Other Hostile Use of Environmental Modification Techniques of 1977 (16 ILM 88 (1977)).

Land mines still kill or maim some 25,000 people every year. Their use is now banned by the (Ottawa) Convention of 1997 on the Prohibition of the Use, Stockpiling, Production and Transfer of Anti-Personnel Mines and on Their Destruction (36 ILM 1507 (1997), in force 1999, with more than 100 parties. However, such major producers and users of land mines, as the US, China, and

Russia, have refused to join the Convention, the US claiming a continued need to use land mines along the border **(189)** between North and South Korea. Employment of certain conventional weapons is prohibited by the Convention of 1980 on Prohibition or Restrictions in the Use of Certain Conventional Weapons Which May Be Deemed to Be Excessively Injurious or to Have Indiscriminate Effects (1342 UNTS 137), in force 1982, with more than 80 parties, including the US. This Convention, conceived as a framework agreement, is implemented by three annexed Protocols and a more recent Protocol of 1995. Protocol I on Non-Detectable Fragments bans the use of weapons, actually not yet developed, whose primary effect is to injure by fragments which in the human body escape detection by x-rays. Protocol II, as amended **(269)** in 1996 (35 ILM 1217 (1996), in force 1998 for more than 50 states, including the US, prohibits or restricts in international **(339)** and non-international **(340)** armed conflicts, the use of mines, booby traps, and other devices, but only if used indiscriminately, for example outside marked, fenced, or monitored areas. It should be noted that the above-mentioned Convention of 1997 totally bans the use of mines. Protocol III prohibits or restricts the use of incendiary weapons, and is designed to protect civilians and civilian objects from such air-delivered incendiary weapons as napalm. Protocol IV, 1995 (35 ILM 1218 (1996)), in force 1998, with some 50 parties, prohibits the use of blinding laser weapons.

The legality of the use of nuclear weapons is a highly controversial and difficult subject in international law, recently examined in the advisory opinion **(291)** of the International Court of Justice (ICJ) **(309)** of 1996 on the *Legality of the Threat or Use of Nuclear Weapons* (35 ILM 809, 1343 (1996)). However, the ICJ failed to reach a clear and definitive conclusion on this question. In the Cold War era, the very posture of the two nuclear superpowers confronting each other in the mutual "balance of terror" appeared to be predicated on the assumption of accepting the possibility of resort to nuclear weapons despite the fact that in 1961, for political motives, supporting the Third World countries, the Soviet Union voted for a Declaration of the United Nations (UN) General Assembly (GA) (Resolution 1653) which declared the use of nuclear weapons illegal. In the post–Cold War era any possible use of nuclear weapons in an armed conflict continues to remain the central issue of high politics. It appears that on this question, international law considerations would be likely to yield to dictates of national strategy and perhaps even the very survival of the state. In its advisory opinion of 1996, delivered at the request of the GA, the ICJ was asked to give its opinion on the question whether the threat or use of nuclear weapons was in any circumstances permitted under international law. Incidentally, the ICJ confirmed the competence of the GA to ask for an advisory opinion on the legality of the use of nuclear weapons, but in response to a similar request by the World Health Organization (WHO) for an advisory opinion on the *Legality of the Use by a State of Nuclear Weapons in Armed Conflict* the ICJ ruled in its advisory opinion that it had no jurisdiction to provide an answer to a request that did not relate to a question arising within the scope of the activities (UN Charter Art. 96(2)) of the WHO (1996 ICJ Rep. 66).

In examining the legality of the use of nuclear weapons, one must start, first of all, from the provisions of the UN Charter on any use of force, regardless of the category of weapons in question. Relevant are: Art. 2(4) prohibiting the threat or use of force **(329)** in international relations; Art. 51, on self-defense **(335)**; and Art. 42 on military enforcement action within the framework of the UN collective security system **(327)**. Thus, aggression **(325)** by means of a strategic nuclear first strike would clearly violate Art. 2(4), as would probably a pre-emptive nuclear strike in self-defense. A strategic second strike in self-defense would—at least in theory—be lawful, subject to the general requirements of necessity and proportionality. The legality of resort to tactical nuclear weapons would depend on the circumstances of the case. Concerning the threat to use nuclear weapons, the ICJ expressed the opinion that mere possession of nuclear weapons did not constitute "threat" to use force in breach of the UN Charter.

Second, like the use of other weapons, the use of nuclear weapons, both strategic and tactical, would require conformity with the principles of international humanitarian law. But, as also noted by the ICJ, in view of the unique characteristics of nuclear weapons their use in fact would be clearly irreconcilable with even the most rudimentary principles of international humanitarian law.

Neither customary law nor treaties contain any specific authorization for the threat or use of nuclear weapons. Nor does there exist any principle or rule of international law that would make the legality of a weapon, including nuclear weapons, dependent on a specific authorization. While there are a number of treaties banning possession, acquisition, manufacturing, and testing of nuclear weapons, they do not amount to a treaty ban on the threat or use of nuclear weapons as such. Nor are they prohibited by analogy to treaties banning poison gases and "all analogous . . . materials or devices." In addition, GA resolutions banning the use of nuclear weapons, like the 1961 Resolution 1653, adopted by a vote of 55 (mostly Third World countries) to 20 (Western countries), with 26 abstentions (mainly Latin American countries), cannot be considered as being declaratory of a customary rule of law specifically banning the use of nuclear weapons. Admitting the obvious truth that resort to nuclear weapons could scarcely be reconciled with international humanitarian law, the ICJ, still evenly divided, held by its president's casting vote that the threat or use of nuclear weapons would generally be contrary to the rules of international humanitarian law, but added that "in view of the current state of international law, and of the elements of fact at its disposal, the Court cannot conclude definitively whether the threat or use of nuclear weapons would be lawful or unlawful in an extreme circumstance of self-defense, in which the very survival of a State would be at stake." This inability of the ICJ to reach a definite conclusion on the question posed to it by the GA not only reflects divergent views of the judges, but also in a way testifies to the existence of a gap (*non liquet*) on perhaps the most sensitive point of international law. The ICJ added, however, that pursuit of negotiations in good faith on nuclear disarmament was an obligation of all states.

**368. Protecting Power.** This is an institution for enforcing compliance with the rules of international humanitarian law **(353)**, today regulated in Protocol I of 1977 **(369)** additional to the 1949 Geneva Conventions **(349)**, whereby a neutral or other state, not a party to the conflict and accepted by the adverse party, has agreed to carry out the functions of safeguarding the interests of the party, and in particular the protection of its nationals **(175)**, prisoners of war **(364)**, and civilians under the control of the enemy, and in general ensuring implementation of the rules of international humanitarian law.

The institution of protecting power was introduced in the Convention of 1929 on prisoners of war, and subsequently improved in the four Geneva Conventions of 1949, and further developed in Protocol I of 1977. According to these instruments each belligerent has the duty to designate, without delay, a "Protecting Power," and all belligerents must facilitate, to the greatest extent, the tasks of the Protecting Power's representatives or delegates, whose activities may not be restricted even in case of imperative military necessity, except as specifically otherwise provided for in the Geneva Conventions of 1949. Since the institution of Protecting Power and the performance of its functions is based on the consent of both sides to the conflict, a party's interests may not in fact be safeguarded by a Protecting Power, which may seriously weaken the enforcement of international humanitarian law. Each of the four Geneva Conventions provides for the institution of "substitutes for Protecting Power," whereby the parties may at any time agree to entrust the duties incumbent on the Protective Power to an impartial organization and in cases where protected persons (prisoner of war, wounded, sick, or shipwrecked member of the armed forces, or civilian victim of war) do not benefit from the activities of the Protecting Power or such organization, the belligerent state which detains them ("detaining power") must request a neutral state or an organization to undertake the functions of Protecting Power. If no such protection can be arranged, the detaining power must accept the Protecting Power services offered by a humanitarian organization, such as the International Committee of the Red Cross ICRC), the most important humanitarian non-governmental organization **(86)**. Protocol I of 1977 (Art. 5(3)) to the Geneva Conventions provides for the ICRC, without prejudice to the right of any other impartial humanitarian organization, to offer its good offices **(303)** to the parties with a view to the designation of a Protecting Power. Further provisions of the Protocol develop in more detail the parties' duty to accept an offer of the ICRC or any other impartial organization to act as a substitute for a Protecting Power.

During World War II Sweden and Switzerland acted as Protecting Powers for a number of belligerents. In the many regional armed conflicts after the war the institution of Protecting Power has been used only exceptionally. The states involved were concerned that consent to a designation of the Protecting Power might be construed as recognition **(106)** and, in general, were unwilling to negotiate agreements with the hostile party. As an example of refusal to consent to the appointment of a Protecting Power one can mention the refusal of India with respect to Pakistani prisoners of war in 1971. However, in the Falklands War of 1982 both sides agreed to appointing Protecting Powers: Switzerland for the United Kingdom and Brazil for Argentina. It may be added that Protocol I (Art. 5(5)(6)) expressly stipulates that the designation and acceptance of Protecting Powers does not affect the legal status of the parties to the conflict or of any territory, including occupied **(363)** territory, and that maintenance of diplomatic relations **(68)** is no obstacle to the designation of the Protecting Power.

On the whole, the functions of Protecting Powers and their substitutes, such as the ICRC, have been more extensive with respect to prisoners of war than with regard to wounded, sick, or shipwrecked members of armed forces. The effectiveness of the protection has largely depended on the readiness to cooperate and sincerity of the belligerent under whose control the protected persons concerned are held. While the ICRC has made a most significant contribution to ameliorating the condition of prisoners of war and other victims of armed conflict, states have been reluctant to use this leading humanitarian organization as a substitute Protecting Power.

**369. Protocols I and II, 1977.** Two treaties **(288)**, additional to the Geneva Conventions of 1949 **(349)**, adopted in Geneva by consensus by the Diplomatic Conference (1974–1977) on Reaffirmation and Development of International Humanitarian Law Applicable in Armed Conflicts. The two Protocols are based on the drafts prepared by the International Committee of the Red Cross (ICRC) pursuant to the distinction made by the Conference between international **(339)** and non-international **(340)** armed conflicts. Some 160 countries are parties to Protocol I, (1125 UNTS 3), including the United Kingdom, but not, among others, India, Indonesia, Iran, Iraq, Israel, Japan, Pakistan, and the United States. Also, a number of countries torn by civil strife have preferred not to join this Protocol.

Protocol I deals with the protection of victims of international armed conflict, developing in detail the rules of the Geneva Conventions of 1949 and the Regulations of Hague Convention **(350)** IV concerning the methods **(366)** and means **(367)** of warfare. Among the many subjects elaborated in Protocol I are: protection of wounded, sick, and shipwrecked, including very specific regulations governing medical transportation; status of combatants and prisoners of war; spies **(372)** and mercenaries **(360)**; protection of the civilian population and civilian objects against effects of hostilities; protection of war correspondents; and protection of works and installations containing dangerous forces, such as dams and nuclear power stations; and measures concerning the execution of the Geneva Conventions and the Protocol. In this regard, the Protocol (Art. 90) provides for the creation of an optional International Fact-Finding Commission **(305)** competent to inquire, at the request of a party to the conflict, into any alleged violations of the Conventions and the Protocol. However, states parties are bound by this provision only upon making a declaration accepting the competence of the Commission. Only a limited number of states have made such optional clause declarations.

Protocol II (1125 UNTS 609) relating to the protection of victims of non-international armed conflict, is a much shorter instrument than Protocol I. It is in force for 156 states (as of January 2004). The Protocol develops and supplements Art. 3 common to all four Geneva Conventions of 1949, but in substance applies only to full-fledged civil wars, leaving outside its regulation situations of internal disturbances and tension. Protocol II stipulates fundamental guarantees of humane treatment, including respect for honor, convictions, and religious practices of persons who do not take a direct part or who have ceased to take part in the hostilities. Other provisions address relatively briefly the treatment of wounded, sick, and shipwrecked, and the protection of the civilian population. On the whole, however, Protocol II greatly expands the protection under the common Art. 3 by, *inter alia*, banning collective punishment; taking of hostages; terrorism **(337)**; outrages to personal dignity; slavery **(180)**; and pillage. Special provisions govern the protection of children and interned and detained persons whose liberty has been restrained for reasons related to armed conflict. Prosecution and punishment of criminal offenses related to the armed conflict in question are designed to preserve fairness and due process of law. However, compared with the detailed rules of Protocol I on international conflict, Protocol II contains only a limited number of regulations, apart from the fact that the scope of its applicability is limited to internal conflicts reaching a rather high threshold of violence, a solution insisted upon by a number of less-developed countries whose societies are torn by internal strife which they are reluctant to subsume under the Protocol II concept of non-international armed conflict.

**370. Reprisals, Belligerent.** Belligerent reprisals are acts of retaliation in the form of otherwise unlawful conduct resorted to by a party to an armed conflict **(339)** against the enemy, as a means of inducing future compliance with the laws of war claimed by that party to have been violated by the enemy. Belligerent reprisals, that is, reprisals in time of war, must be distinguished from reprisals **(119)** in time of peace, more generally known in contemporary international law as countermeasures **(58)**.

In the traditional law of war, belligerent reprisals were universally recognized as a legitimate mechanism designed to coerce the enemy into desisting from serious breaches of the law of war. Historically, many instances of reprisals in war are on record, including such acts as maltreatment of prisoners of war (for example solitary confinement) or bombardment of undefended localities or civilian objects. In general, the experiences of the two world wars of the 20th century revealed that, instead of being a means of enforcing a legitimate conduct of hostilities, reprisals often degenerated into atrocities and cynical violations of fundamental principles of the law of war. Abuses of the right of belligerent reprisals occurred despite certain conditions governing resort to them under traditional law, reminding one of traditional reprisals in time of peace: ignored prior warning; decision to be taken by a superior political authority; observing the principle of proportionality; and terminating reprisals upon the enemy's ceasing the violations.

Attempts to restrict the scope of belligerent reprisals by limiting the range of permissible targets began before World War II, with the 1929 Convention relative to the treatment of prisoners of war **(364)** (118 LNTS 342). Following World War II, the four Geneva Conventions of 1949 **(349)** prohibited reprisals against protected persons and property in the power of a belligerent as well as reprisals by means of taking hostages, collective punishment, and terrorization of the population of the occupied territory. These rules soon became part of customary law **(39)** governing the conduct of hostilities. However, reprisals against civilians in a combat zone were not banned until Geneva Protocol I of 1977 **(369)** which specifically prohibited such reprisals against: the civilian population or civilians (Art. 51(6)); civilian objects (Art. 52(1)); cultural objects, the kind of reprisals already prohibited under Art. 4(4) of the Convention of 1954 for the Protection of Cultural Property in the Event of Armed Conflict (249 UNTS 215); objects indispensable to the survival of the civilian population (Protocol I Art. 54(4)); reprisals against the natural environment (Art. 55(2)); and against works and installations containing dangerous forces, such as dams and nuclear power stations (Art. 56(4)). Whether these wide-ranging prohibitions of belligerent reprisals have already become part of customary law is not certain. Some non-parties, including France and the United States, are opposed to the prohibitions of the Protocol, claiming that, lacking other effective measures against states violating international humanitarian law, the threat of taking reprisals may still be necessary to deter violations.

**371. Special Court for Sierra Leone.** This is an independent, part international and part municipal **(27)**, criminal court established in 2002 in Sierra Leone, with its seat in Freetown, with jurisdiction to try individuals bearing the greatest responsibility for the commission of crimes against humanity **(151)**, war crimes **(373)**, and other very serious violations of international humanitarian law **(353)**, as well as certain crimes under the law of Sierra Leone, all of which were committed in Sierra Leone during that country's decade-long brutal and vicious civil war (1991–2001). This conflict pitted the incumbent government forces against the rebels of the so-called Revolutionary

United Front (RUF) which became notorious for its grisly atrocities and impressing children into the ranks of its army. The war did not end until an intervention by regional and British troops, followed by the deployment of a United Nations (UN) peacekeeping force **(334)** of 17,000, managed to overcome the rebels, although sporadic violence continued in parts of Sierra Leone for some time.

The process of forming the Special Court started in 2000 when, at the request of the Sierra Leone government, the Security Council (SC) adopted Resolution 1315 (40 ILM 248 (2001)) requesting the Secretary-General to negotiate an agreement with Sierra Leone on creating a tribunal to try persons guilty of atrocities in the war. As a result, an agreement between the UN and Sierra Leone provided for the establishment of the Court according to a draft statute attached. A formal agreement was signed in 2002 and the Special Court for Sierra Leone (SCSL) started its functions by the end of that year.

The SCSL is a unique institution in that, first, unlike the International Criminal Tribunal for the Former Yugoslavia (ICTY) **(352)** and the International Criminal Tribunal for Rwanda (ICTR) **(351)**, it was not established by a SC resolution under Chapter VII of the United Nations (UN) Charter; it was granted jurisdiction not only over international crimes but also over specific offenses under the law of Sierra Leone; and its composition is of a mixed nature. The trial chamber consists of three judges, two of whom are appointed by the UN Secretary-General and one by Sierra Leone. Two of the five judges of the appeals chamber are also appointed by that country. The jurisdiction of the SCSL is limited to the prosecution of persons "who bear the greatest responsibility" for serious violations of international humanitarian law and the law of Sierra Leone. This excluded from prosecution a large number of grave offenders, leaving only some 20 to 25 individuals occupying leadership positions as suspects in the commission of the crimes. For practical reasons, the temporal jurisdiction of the Court includes only crimes committed since 30 November 1996, the date of one of the abortive peace agreements of the government with the RUF.

The subject matter of jurisdiction encompasses crimes against humanity, violations of the common Article 3 of the Geneva Conventions **(349)** and Protocol II of 1977 **(369)** on non-international armed conflict **(340)**, and other serious violations of international humanitarian law, such as deliberate attacks against civilians and peacekeeping forces and abduction and forced conscription of children under the age of 15. The principle of individual criminal responsibility is formulated in the Statute following similar provisions of the statutes of the ICTY and ICTR. Juvenile offenders (below the age of 18) must be treated with dignity and are to be rehabilitated and integrated into society. The Statute provides for the Rules of Evidence and Procedure of the ICTR to be applied in the proceedings of the Special Court, but, if needed, a rule may be changed according to the criminal procedure of Sierra Leone. The Statute guarantees a number of due process rights of the accused. Penalties are limited to imprisonment and—as the case may be—to forfeiture of property and proceeds acquired through crime. Unlike the ICTY and ICTR, which are funded from the regular UN budget, the SCSL is financed by voluntary contributions of UN members. Securing adequate funding appears to be, however, a major problem for the Court since its establishment.

The SCSL began its work by indicting seven men directly responsible for the atrocities of the war. However, the leader of the RUF (the chief perpetrator of the crimes) and two other notorious suspects had died before they could be prosecuted. An indictment was also issued against the former president of Liberia, in exile in Nigeria, accused of supporting the RUF in return for a share in Sierra Leone's diamonds. The model of a hybrid national-international criminal tribunal to try individuals on charges of war crimes and crimes against humanity was followed by Cambodia and was in consideration of Timor Leste.

**372. Spy in Wartime.** A spy in time of war is a person, whether a combatant or not, who acting clandestinely or on false pretenses, obtains or endeavors to obtain information in the zone of operations of a belligerent, with the intention of communicating it to the hostile party (Hague Convention **(350)** IV of 1907, Regulations Art. 29(1)). It is tacitly recognized, both in the customary law **(39)** of war and in treaty **(40)** regulations (Hague Convention IV Regulations Art. 29 and Protocol I of 1977 **(369)** Art. 46) that belligerents have the right to employ spies, and resort to espionage is not a breach of the law of war. Spies are punished not as violators of international law but of the municipal law of the belligerent concerned, in order to deter the practice of spying by rendering it as risky and ineffective as possible. An apprehended spy has no right to the prisoner-of-war status **(364)**, but is entitled to a fair trial and treatment according to the most fundamental principles of humanity. The regular penalty for espionage in wartime is death, regardless of whether or not the spy succeeds in obtaining information or conveying it to the enemy.

Since clandestine action is the characteristic feature of spying, it has to be ascertained by the belligerent concerned whether the suspect was wearing a uniform during his operations. Soldiers not wearing a disguise, who have penetrated into the zone of operations of the enemy for purposes of obtaining information, are not considered spies. Similarly, soldiers and civilians delivering dispatches to their own army or to the enemy are not treated as spies if they carry out their mission openly (Hague Convention IV Regulations Art. 29). Protocol I of 1977 reserves special treatment for those members of the armed forces who are residents of the occupied territory and gather information of military value within that territory. Such individuals are not considered to be engaged in espionage unless they do so through an act of false pretenses or deliberately in a clandestine manner. Moreover, they do not lose the right to the status of prisoners of war and may not be treated as spies unless captured while engaging in espionage (Art. 46(3)). Members of the armed forces who are not residents of the enemy-occupied territory and who are engaged in espionage there, do not lose the right to the status of prisoners of war. They may not be treated as spies unless they are captured before rejoining their own armed forces (Art. 46(4)). More generally, a spy who after rejoining his armed forces is subsequently captured by the enemy, must be treated as a prisoner of war and incurs no responsibility for his previous acts of espionage (Hague Convention IV Regulations Art. 31).

**373. War Crimes.** A category of international crimes entailing individual **(81)** criminal responsibility of the perpetrator directly under international law, war crimes can be broadly defined as violations of the law of war or—in today's terminology—international humanitarian law **(353)**. International practice includes within the concept of war crimes only serious violations and breaches of the laws of war, involving grave consequences for the affected victims. International prosecution and punishment of war crimes (and crimes against humanity **(151)**) are governed by special principles of international criminal law. Conspiracy, incitement, attempt at, as well as complicity in committing war crimes are also punishable. The official position of an accused person, including head of state or government, or a government official does not relieve such person of criminal responsibility or mitigate punishment. The fact that the criminal act was committed by a subordinate does not relieve his superior of criminal responsibility if he knew or had reason to know that the subordinate was about to commit such act or had done so, and the superior failed to prevent the offense or to punish its perpetrator. A superior order plea, that is, the fact that the offender acted pursuant to an order, is not a defense, but may be considered in mitigation of punishment. Here the test is whether or not a moral choice was possible for the offender in the circumstances of the case.

In the prevailing opinion, war crimes and crimes against humanity are not subject to any statute of limitations, that is, preclusion or barring of prosecution after the lapse of a specified period of time following the commission of the crime, a rule included in Art. 29 of the Statute of the International Criminal Court (ICC) **(170)**. The matter is of particular relevance for trials by municipal **(28)** courts in any of the states parties to the 1968 Convention on the Non-Applicability of Statutory Limitations to War Crimes and Crimes against Humanity (754 UNTS 73). Some 50 countries are parties to this Convention, including Germany. However, the United States (US) and the United Kingdom are among the countries opposing this Convention. Members of the Council of Europe are bound by a special European Convention of 1974 (13 ILM 540 (1974)) providing for non-applicability of the statute of limitations to war crimes and crimes against humanity. War crimes do not qualify as political offenses for purposes of extradition **(76)**.

The relevant body of the law on war crimes is constituted by both conventional **(40)** and customary **(39)** law, but it must be remembered that much of the conventional international humanitarian law is declaratory of otherwise binding customary law. This is in particular true of Hague Convention IV of 1907 with its Regulations **(350)**; the four Geneva Conventions of 1949 **(349)**; and the Charter of the International Military Tribunal at Nuremberg (IMT) of 1945 **(354)** and—to a lesser extent—the two Protocols of 1977 **(369)** to the Geneva Conventions of 1949. The Genocide Convention of 1948 **(155)** deals with a special category of crime of concern to the international community as a whole.

Historically, serious violations of the laws and customs of war were occasionally punished by belligerents even before the Hague Convention on the laws of war on land of 1899, replaced in 1907 (but still formally in force for a limited number of states) by Convention IV with annexed Regulations, of 1907, stipulated that there were certain serious offenses against the law of war for which individuals could be punished under the municipal law of a belligerent, in practice mainly offenders belonging to the armed forces of the other side of the conflict. However, none of the conventions regulating the conduct of hostilities designated offenses against laws of war as crimes punishable directly under international law. Individual criminal responsibility of individuals for violating, not just a rule of municipal law, but international law, was not yet an accepted part of the law of war. Apart from the generally unsuccessful attempts to try, by virtue of Arts. 228–230 of the Versailles Peace Treaty with Germany (225 CTS 188), suspected members of the German armed forces for war crimes committed—as alleged—in World War I, it was not until after unprecedented serious violations of laws and customs of war by Nazi Germany in World War II that the IMT at Nuremberg, followed by the Tokyo Tribunal trying Japanese war criminals **(355)**, instituted the principle of the criminal responsibility of individuals directly under international law and regardless of the official position of the accused.

Under Art. 6 of the Charter of the IMT at Nuremberg, the crimes under the jurisdiction of the IMT included three categories: crimes against peace; war crimes; and crimes against humanity. War crimes, that is, violations of the laws and customs of war (Art. 6(6)), included, but were not limited to: murder; maltreatment or deportation to slave labor or for any other purpose of civilian population of or in occupied territories; murder or maltreatment of prisoners of war **(364)** or persons on the seas; killing of hostages; plunder of public or private property; wanton destruction of cities, towns, or villages, or devastation not justified by military necessity. The listing of war crimes in the Statute of the IMT served as a model for the Tokyo Tribunal, and for many tribunals set up by the Allies in Germany to try other German war criminals, composed of judges from Allied countries, mainly the US. Trials of war criminals also took place before German courts under Law No. 10 of 1946 of the Control Council for Germany (Official Gazette No. 3, 1946). Many trials also took place in courts of the countries formerly under German occupation. Almost four decades later, in the 1990s, the institution of an *ad hoc* international criminal judiciary was revived to deal with gross violations of international humanitarian law in former Yugoslavia **(352)** and in Rwanda **(351)**. The Special Court for Sierra Leone (SCSL) **(371)**, expected to be followed by other, similar courts, can be considered as a variation of an *ad hoc* international criminal tribunal of a mixed international-national character. Finally, the idea of a permanent international criminal court to prosecute individuals for crimes against international law committed in peace time as well as in time of war, came to fruition with the establishment of the ICC in 1998.

Understandably, there exists no complete list of all war crimes. The most exhaustive roster of such crimes is found in Art. 8 of the ICC Statute and it can be considered as a reflection of the state of international humanitarian law on the subject. The relevant Art. 8 lists not only war crimes in international armed conflict but also those which are violations of customary and conventional law regulating non-international conflict, understood in the meaning of Protocol II of 1977 to include full-scale civil wars but not situations of internal disturbances and tension. The conceptual framework of Art. 8, which emerged from the conflicting positions of the negotiating **(316)** parties, distinguishes four categories of war crimes. Two of these refer to international and two to non-international conflict. A number of crimes appear in both categories, but there are some that are peculiar to civil-war situations.

The first category of war crimes in international armed conflict includes grave breaches of the Geneva Conventions of 1949 against protected persons or property; willful killing; torture or inhuman treatment, including biological experiments; willful causing of great suffering or severe injury; extensive destruction of property without military necessity, carried out unlawfully and wantonly; compelling a prisoner of war or other protected person to serve in the force of the hostile party; willfully depriving such persons of the right to fair trial; unlawful deportation or transfer or unlawful confinement; and taking hostages. Virtually identical listing can be found in the Statute of the ICTY (Art. 2). The second category of war crimes in an international armed conflict is constituted by "other serious violations of the laws and customs" applicable in such conflict, "within the established framework of international law," presumably including also such principles of international humanitarian law as necessity and proportionality. Whereas the Statute of the ICTY provides a non-exhaustive list of only five violations, the ICC Statute contains a long list of 26 "other serious violations," derived mainly from the pertinent prohibitory provisions of Protocol I of 1977 and earlier conventions. Such "serious violations" include: intentional attacks upon civilians and non-military objects and against personnel and equipment of humanitarian or peacekeeping **(334)** missions; intentional attacks in the knowledge that such action will cause incidental loss of life or injury to civilians or widespread long-term and severe damage to the environment; attacking undefended localities; killing or wounding combatants who surrendered at discretion; making improper use of flags; establishing a civilian settlement in occupied territory; deportation or transfer of the native population; intentional attacks upon hospitals and buildings dedicated to religious, scientific, cultural, and charitable purposes; subjecting persons to mutilation or unjustified medical experiments; treacherous killing or wounding of individuals of a hostile nation or army; declaring a no quarter policy; unjustifiably destroying or seizing enemy property; denying rights of actions in a court of law to nationals of the hostile party; compelling them to take part in war operations against their own country; pillaging and employing poison or poisonous gases, materials, or devices; employing dumdum bullets (hollow-nosed bullets that expand on impact, inflicting severe wounds, named after a suburb of Calcutta (Kolkata) where they were made), and weapons and projectiles causing superfluous injury; committing outrages against personal dignity; committing rape and other sexual violence; using protected persons as shields in military operations; intentionally attacking buildings, material, medical units and transport, and personnel, which have the distinctive emblem of the Geneva Conventions; intentionally starving civilians as a method of warfare; and conscripting children under the age of 15 years or using them to participate actively in hostilities.

Under the ICC Statute there are two categories of war crimes that apply to non-international armed conflict, most of which are parallel with those occurring in international conflicts. First (Art. 8(2)(c)), there are serious violations of Art. 3 common to the four Geneva Conventions, involving acts committed against protected persons, namely, any of the following acts: violence to life and person, in particular murder, mutilation, cruel treatment and torture **(182)**; outrages upon personal dignity; taking of hostages; and passing sentences and carrying out executions without previous court judgment with all judicial guarantees. The other category of serious violations of the laws and customs applicable in non-international armed conflicts, within the established framework of international law, comprises intentional attacks against the civilian population; against buildings, material, medical units and transport, and personnel, which have the emblem of the Geneva Conventions; against personnel and equipment of humanitarian or peacekeeping mission; or against hospitals and buildings dedicated to religious, cultural, scientific, or charitable purposes. Other war crimes encompass: pillaging; committing rape and other sexual violence; conscripting children under the age of 15 years or using them to participate actively in hostilities; displacement of the civilian population without imperative military reasons or the need for their security; treacherous killing or wounding of a combatant adversary; declaring a no quarter policy; subjecting persons to mutilation or unjustified medical experiments; and unjustifiably destroying or seizing the adversary's property.

Insofar as the mental element of war crimes (and other crimes involving individual responsibility) is concerned, a person is responsible and liable for punishment only if the act in question was committed with intent, that is, that person meant to engage in criminal conduct and to cause the consequences of such conduct, and with the knowledge of the act, that is, awareness that the consequences will occur in the ordinary course of events.

# Annex: Bibliography

## A. RESEARCH TOOLS: BIBLIOGRAPHIES, GUIDES, INDEXES

Beyerly, Elizabeth. *Public International Law: A Guide to Information Sources*. London: Munsell Publishing, 1991.

*George Washington Journal of International Law and Economics: Guide to International Legal Research*. Salem, N.H.: Butterworths Legal Publishers, 1990–.

Goedan, Juergen Christoph. *International Legal Bibliographies: A Worldwide Guide and Critique*. Translated from German by John E. Pickron. Ardsley, N.Y.: Transnational Publishers, 1991.

Harvard Law School Library. *Annual Legal Bibliography*. 21 vols. Cambridge, Mass.: Harvard Law School Library, 1961–1981.

*Index to Foreign Legal Periodicals* (quarterly). Chicago: American Association of Law Libraries.

*Index to Legal Periodicals* (monthly). New York: H. W. Wilson.

Max Planck Institute for Comparative Public Law and International Law. *Public International Law: A Current Bibliography of Books and Articles.* Berlin and Heidelberg: Springer, 1974– (semiannual). [By far the best and most comprehensive bibliography on international law.]

*For electronic resources:*

American Society of International Law. *Guide to Electronic Resources for International Law*. 3d ed. Edited by Marci Hoffman and Jill M. Watson. Washington, D.C.: American Society of International Law, 2003.

## B. ENCYCLOPEDIAS AND DICTIONARIES

Bernhardt, Rudolf, ed. *Encyclopedia of Public International Law.* 5 vols. Max Planck Institute for Comparative Public Law and International Law, Heidelberg. Amsterdam: Elsevier, 1992–2001.

Bledsoe, Robert L., and Boleslaw A. Boczek. *The International Law Dictionary.* Santa Barbara, CA: ABC-Clio, 1987.

Craig, Barker J., and John P. Grant, eds. *Parry & Grant Encyclopaedic Dictionary of International Law*. 2d ed. Dobbs Ferry, N.Y.: Oceana, 2003.

Fox, James R. *Dictionary of International and Comparative Law*. 2d ed. Dobbs Ferry, N.Y.: Oceana, 1997.

Kuehl, Warren F., ed. *Bibliographical Dictionary of Internationalists*. Westport, Conn.: Greenwood Press, 1983.

Lindbergh, Ernest. *International Law Dictionary: English/French/German*. New York: Oxford University Press, 2002.

Volger, Helmut, ed. *A Concise Encyclopedia of the United Nations*. Preface by Kofi Annan. Leiden, Neth.: Nijhoff, 2002.

## C. TREATY COLLECTIONS

### (1) General

League of Nations Treaty Series. *Treaties and International Engagements Registered with the Secretariat of the League*. 205 vols. 9 index vols. Geneva: League of Nations, 1920–1946.

Parry, Clive, ed. *Consolidated Treaty Series*. 231 vols. 10 index vols. Dobbs Ferry, N.Y.: Oceana, 1969–1981. [Contains treaties from 1648 to 1920.]

United Nations Treaty Series. *Treaties and International Agreements Registered or Filed and Recorded with the Secretariat of the United Nations*. New York: United Nations, 1946–. [By 2004, some 2,100 volumes had been published.]

### (2) United States

Bevans, Charles I., comp. *Treaties and Other International Agreements of the United States of America 1776–1949*. 13 vols. Washington, D.C.: Government Printing Office, 1968–1976.

*Treaties in Force: A List of Treaties and Other International Agreements of the United States in Force on January 1*. Annual. Washington, D.C.: Government Printing Office, 1941–.

*United States Treaties and Other International Agreements*. Annual. Washington, D.C.: Government Printing Office, 1950–.

NOTE: Treaties and Other International Acts Series (TIAS) has been issued singly in pamphlets by the Department of State since 1945. Before that, it was called Treaty Series (TS) or Executive Agreement Series (EAS), respectively.

### (3) Europe

*European Treaty Series*. Strassbourg: Council of Europe, 1950–.

*European Yearbook*. Leiden, Neth.: Nijhoff, 1952–. [Compiled by the Council of Europe, it also includes articles and documentation reviewing all the European organizations.]

## D. CURRENT AND RECENT PRIMARY SOURCE DOCUMENTATION

*International Legal Materials*. Bimonthly. Washington, D.C.: American Society of International Law, 1961–. [An indispensable research aid in international law, it reproduces official documents whenever possible. Foreign-language documents are translated. Includes, among other materials, treaties and major decisions of international courts.]

NOTE: Texts of selected major treaties can also be found in documents supplements of most casebooks. See also the following.

Brownlie, Ian, ed. *Basic Documents in International Law*. 5th ed. New York: Oxford University Press, 2002.

Weston, Burns H., ed. *International Law and World Order: Basic Documents.* 8 loose-leaf binders. Ardsley, N.Y.: Transnational Publishers, 1984–.

## E. DIGESTS

### (1) United States

Department of State, Office of the Legal Advisor. *Digest of United States Practice in International Law*. Washington, D.C.: Government Printing Office. [Conceived as an annual volume of current international law practice of the United States and, in a way, successor to Whiteman's *Digest* (see below), it appeared in 10 single volumes for the years 1973–1980 plus a cumulative index. It was followed by Lash's *Cumulative Digest* (see below).]

Hackworth, Green Haywood. *Digest of International Law*, 8 volumes. Washington, D.C.: Government Printing Office, 1940–1943.

Lash, Marian, ed. *Cumulative Digest of United States Practice in International Law, 1981–1988*. 3 vols. Washington, D.C.: Government Printing Office, 1993–1995.

Moore, John Bassett. *A Digest of International Law*. 8 vols. Washington, D.C.: Government Printing Office, 1906.

Murphy, Sean D., ed. *United States Practice in International Law*. Vol. 1, *1999–2001*. New York: Cambridge University Press, 2002.

Wharton, Francis. *A Digest of the International Law of the United States*. 3 vols. Washington, D.C.: Government Printing Office, 1886.

Whiteman, Marjorie M. *Digest of International Law*. 15 vols. (vol. 15, *General Index*). Washington, D.C.: Government Printing Office, 1963–1971.

### (2) Other Countries

*A British Digest of International Law*. London: Stevens & Sons.

## F. CASEBOOKS

Blakesley, Christopher L., Edwin B. Firmage, Richard F. Scott, and Sharon A. Williams, eds. *The International Legal System: Cases and Materials*. 5th ed. New York: Foundation Press, 2001. [Documents supplement.]

Blay, Sam, Ryszard Piotrowicz, and B. Martin Tsamenyi, eds. *Public International Law: An Australian Perspective*. Melbourne: Oxford University Press, 1997.

Carter, Barry E., Phillip R. Trimble, and Curtis A. Bradley, eds. *International Law.* 4th ed. New York: Aspen Publishers, 2003. [Documents supplement.]

Damrosch, Lori Fisler, Louis Henkin, Richard Crawford Pugh, Oscar Schachter, and Hans Smit, eds. *International Law: Cases and Materials*. 4th ed. St. Paul, Minn.: West Group, 2001. [Documents supplement.]

Dixon, Martin, and Robert Mccorquodale, eds. *Cases and Materials on International Law.* 4th ed. New York: Oxford University Press, 2003.

Dunoff, Jeffrey L., Steven R. Ratner, and David Wippman, eds. *International Law: Norms, Actors, Process: A Problem-Oriented Approach*. New York: Aspen Publishers, 2000.

Evans, Malcolm D., ed. *International Law*. New York: Oxford University Press, 2003.

Harris, D. J., ed. *Cases and Materials on International Law*. 5th ed. London: Sweet & Maxwell, 1998.

Janis, Mark W., and John Noyes, eds. *Cases and Commentary on International Law*. 2d ed. St. Paul, Minn.: West Group, 2001.

Ku, Charlotte, and Paul F. Diehl, eds. *International Law: Classic and Contemporary Readings*. 2d ed. Boulder: Lynne Rienner Publishers, 2003.

Steiner, Henry J., Detlev F. Vagts, and Harold Hongju Koh, eds. *Transnational Legal Problems: Materials and Text*. 4th ed. New York: Foundation Press, 1994. [Documents supplement.]

Weston, Burns H., Richard A. Falk, and Hilary Charlesworth, eds. *International Law and World Order: A Problem-Oriented Casebook*. 3d ed. St Paul, Minn.: West Group, 1997. [Documents supplement.]

## G. TEXTBOOKS AND TREATISES

American Law Institute, *Restatement of the Law – Third. The Foreign Relations of the United States*. 2 volumes. St. Paul, Minn.: American Law Institute Publishers, 1987.

Bederman, David J. *International Law Frameworks*. New York: Foundation Press, 2001.

Brierly, J. L. *The Law of Nations: An Introduction to the International Law of Peace.* 6th ed. Edited by Sir Humphrey Waldock. Oxford: Oxford University Press, 1963. [A classic, but needs updating.]

Brownlie, Ian, *Principles of Public International Law*. 6th ed. New York: Oxford University Press, 2003. [A major British treatise.]

Buergenthal, Thomas, and Harold G. Maier. *Public International Law in a Nutshell*. 2d ed. St. Paul, Minn.: West Publishing, 1990.

Cassese, Antonio. *International Law*. New York: Oxford University Press, 2001.

Chen, Ling-Chu. *An Introduction to Contemporary International Law: A Policy-Oriented Perspective*. 2d ed. New Haven, Conn.: Yale University Press, 2000.

Dixon, Martin. *Textbook on International Law.* London: Blackstone Press, 2000.

Epps, Valerie. *International Law for Undergraduates*. Durham, N.C.: Carolina Academic Press, 1998.

Glahn, Gerhard von. *Law among Nations: An Introduction to Public International Law.* 7th ed. Boston: Allyn and Bacon, 1996.

Hyde, Charles Cheney. *International Law Chiefly as Interpreted and Applied by the United States*. 3 vols. 2d rev. ed. Boston: Little, Brown, 1947. [A major American treatise in need of updating.]

Janis, Mark W. *An Introduction to International Law*. 3d ed. Boston: Little, Brown, 2003.

Levi, Werner. *Contemporary International Law: A Concise Introduction*. 2d ed. Boulder, Colo.: Westview Press, 1991.

Malanczuk, Peter. *Akehurst's Modern Introduction to International Law*. 8th rev. ed. London: Routlege, 2004.

Oppenheim, Lassa F. L. *International Law: A Treatise*. 2 vols. Vol. 1, *Peace*. 9th ed. 2 bks. Edited by Sir Robert Jennings and Sir Arthur Watts. London: Longman, 1992. Vol. 2, *Disputes, War, and Neutrality*. 7th ed. Edited by Hersch Lauterpacht. New York: McKay, 1952. [The best-known international law treatise.]

Shaw, Malcolm N. *International Law* 5th ed. Cambridge: Cambridge University Press, 2003. [A major British treatise.]

Verzijl, J. H. W. *International Law in Historical Perspective*. 12 vols. (vol. 12, *Index*). Alphen aan den Rijn: Sijthoff & Noordhoff, 1968–1998. [A monumental work by a Dutch scholar exploring in detail the historical roots of international legal rules.]

Wallace, Rebecca M. M. *International Law: A Student Introduction*. 3d ed. London: Sweet & Maxwell, 1997.

## H. SPECIALIZED STUDIES

Akashi, Kinji. *Cornelius van Bynkershoek: His Role in the History of International Law*. Leiden, Neth.: Nijhoff, 1998.

Alan, James. *Sovereign Statehood: The Basis of International Society*. London: Allen and Unwin, 1986.

Allott, Philip. *Eunomia: New Order for a New World*. Cambridge: Cambridge University Press, 1991.

——. *The Health of Nations: Society and Law beyond the State*. Cambridge: Cambridge University Press, 2002.

Amerasinghe, Chittharanjan F. *Jurisdiction of International Tribunals*. Leiden, Neth.: Nijhoff, 2002.

American Society of International Law. *Careers in International Law: A Guide to Career Paths and Internships in International Law*. Washington, D.C.: American Society of International Law, 2003.

Anaya, S. James. *Indigenous Peoples in International Law*. New York: Oxford University Press, 1996.

Arend, Anthony Clark. *Legal Rules and International Society*. New York: Oxford University Press, 1999.

Aust, Anthony I. *Modern Treaty Law and Practice*. Cambridge: Cambridge University Press, 2000.

Baslar, Kemal. *The Concept of Common Heritage of Mankind in International Law.* Leiden, Neth.: Nijhoff, 1998.

Bassiouni, M. Cherif., ed. *International Terrorism: A Compilation of UN Documents (1972–2001).* Ardsley, N.Y.: Transnational Publishers, 2001.

——, ed. *International Terrorism: Multinational Conventions, 1937–2001*. Ardsley, N.Y.: Transnational Publishers, 2001.

——. *Introduction to International Criminal Law*. Ardsley, N.Y.: Transnational Publishers, 2003.

Bassiouni, M. Cherif, and Edward M. Wise. *Aut Dedere Aut Judicare: The Duty to Extradite or Prosecute in International Law*. Leiden, Neth.: Nijhoff, 1995.

Bayevski, Anne F., ed. *The United Nations Human Rights Treaty System in the 21st Century*. The Hague: Kluver, 2000.

Becker, Joseph D. *The American Law of Nations*. Huntington, N.Y.: Juris Publishing, 2001.

Bederman, David J. *International Law in Antiquity*. New York: Cambridge University Press, 2001.

Bedjaoui, Mohammed. *International Law: Achievements and Prospects.* Leiden, Neth.: Nijhoff, 2002.

Bekker, Peter H. F. *World Court Decisions at the Turn of the Millennium*. Leiden, Neth.: Nijhoff, 2001.

Berg, Astrid. *Implementing and Enforcing European Fisheries Law*. Leiden, Neth.: Nijhoff, 1999.

Birnie, Patricia, and Alan Boyle. *International Law and the Environment*. New York: Oxford University Press, 2002.

Blackburn, Robert, and Jorg Polakiewicz. *Fundamental Rights in Europe: The ECHR and Its Member States, 1950–2000*. New York: Oxford University Press, 2002.

Boczek, Boleslaw A. *Historical Dictionary of International Tribunals*. Metuchen, N.J.: Scarecrow Press, 1994.

Boisson de Chazournes, Laurence, and Vera Gowlland-Debras, eds. *The International Legal System in Quest of Equity and Universality*. Leiden, Neth.: Nijhoff, 2001.

Bothe, Michael, and Thomas Dörschel, eds. *United Nations Peacekeeping: A Documentary Introduction*. The Hague: Kluver, 1999.

Bouchet-Saulnier, Françoise. *The Practical Guide to Humanitarian Law*. Translated by Laura Brav. Lanham, Md.: Rowman & Littlefield, 2001.

Bowett, D. W. *Self-Defence in International Law*. Manchester: Manchester University Press, 1958.

Boyle, Francis A. *The Future of International Law and American Foreign Policy*. Ardsley, N.Y.: Transnational Publishers, 1990.

Brownlie, Ian. *International Law and the Use of Force by States*. Oxford: Clarendon, 1963.

Caminos, Hugo, ed. *Law of the Sea*. Brookfield, Vt.: Ashgate, 2001.

Caron, David D., and John R. Crook. *The Iran–United States Claims Tribunal and the Process of International Claims Resolution*. Ardsley, N.Y.: Transnational Publishers, 2000.

Casanovas, Oriol. *Unity and Pluralism in Public International Law*. Leiden, Neth.: Nijhoff, 2001.

Cassese, Antonio. *International Criminal Law*. New York: Oxford University Press, 2003.

——. *Self-Determination of Peoples: A Legal Reappraisal*. New York: Cambridge University Press, 1995.

Castellino, Joshua, and Steve Allen. *Title to Territory in International Law: A Temporal Analysis*. Brookfield, N.Y.: Ashgate, 2003.

Chadwick, Elizabeth. *Traditional Neutrality Revisited*. Leiden, Neth.: Nijhoff, 2002.

Charlesworth, Hilary, and Christine Chinkin. *The Boundaries of International Law: A Feminist Analysis*. Huntington, N.Y.: Juris Publishing, 2000.

Cheng, Bing. *Studies in International Space Law*. New York: Oxford University Press, 1997.

Chesterman, Simon. *Just War or Just Peace? Humanitarian Intervention in International Law*. New York: Oxford University Press, 2001.

Churchill, Robin, and Vaughan Lowe. *The Law of the Sea*. 3d ed. Huntingdon, N.Y.: Juris Publishing, 1999.

Collier, John, and Vaughan Lowe. *The Settlement of Disputes in International Law: Institutions and Procedure*. New York: Oxford University Press, 1999.

Conforti, Benedetto. *The Law and Practice of the United Nations*. 2d rev. ed. Leiden, Neth.: Nijhoff, 2000.

Conforti, Benedetto, and Francesco Francioni. *Enforcing International Human Rights in Domestic Courts*. Leiden, Neth.: Nijhoff, 1997.

Crawford, James. *The International Law Commission's Articles on State Responsibility: Introduction, Text and Commentaries*. New York: Cambridge University Press, 2002.

D'Amato, Anthony. *International Law: Process and Prospect*. 2d ed. Ardsley, N.Y.: Transnational Publishers, 1995.

——. *International Law Sources: Collected Papers*. Leiden, Neth.: Nijhoff, 2004.

Degan, V. D. *Sources of International Law*. Leiden, Neth.: Nijhoff, 1997.

Dekker, Guido den. *The Law of Arms Control: International Supervision and Enforcement*. Leiden, Neth.: Nijhoff, 2001.

Denza, Eileen. *Diplomatic Law: Commentary on the Vienna Convention on Diplomatic Relations*. 2d ed. New York: Oxford University Press, 1998.

Detter, Ingrid. *The Law of War*. 2d ed. New York: Cambridge University Press, 2000.

Diederiks-Verschoop, I. H. Ph. *An Introduction to Space Law*. The Hague: Kluwer, 1999.

Dinstein, Yoram. *War, Aggression, and Self-Defence*. 3d ed. New York: Cambridge University Press, 2001.

Donner, Ruth. *The Regulation of Nationality in International Law*. Ardsley, N.Y.: Transnational Publishers, 1995.

Doswald-Beck, L., ed. *The San Remo Manual on International Law Applicable to Armed Conflicts at Sea*. New York: Cambridge University Press, 1995.

Duram, Helen, and Timothy L. H. McCormick, eds. *The Changing Face of Conflict and International Humanitarian Law*. Leiden, Neth.: Nijhoff, 1999.

Eggli, Ann Vibeke. *Mass Refugee Influx and the Limits of Public International Law*. Leiden, Neth.: Nijhoff, 2002.

Eiriksson, Gudmundur. *The International Tribunal for the Law of the Sea*. Leiden, Neth.: Nijhoff, 2000.

Eyffinger, Arthur, and Pieter H. Kooijmans. *The 1899 Hague Peace Conference: The Parliament of Man, the Federation of the World*. Leiden, Neth.: Nijhoff, 1999.

Fassbender, Bardo. *UN Security Council Reform and the Right of Veto: A Constitutional Perspective*. Leiden, Neth.: Nijhoff, 1998.

Fijnant, Cyrille, Jan Wouters, and Frederik Naert, eds. *Legal Instruments in the Fight against International Terrorism: A Transatlantic Dialogue*. Leiden, Neth.: Nijhoff, 2004.

Fox, Hazel. *The Law of State Immunity*. New York: Oxford University Press, 2002.

Franck, Thomas M. *The Empowered Self: Law and Society in the Age of Individualism*. New York: Oxford University Press, 1999.

——. *Recourse to Force: State Action against Threats and Armed Attacks*. New York: Cambridge University Press, 2002.

Frigessi di Rattalma, Marco, and Tullio Treves. *The United Nations Compensation Commission: A Handbook*. Leiden, Neth.: Nijhoff, 1999.

Gaebler, Ralph, and Maria Smolka-Day, eds. *Sources of State Practice in International Law*. Ardsley, N.Y.: Transnational Publishers, 2002.

Gardam, Judith, ed. *Humanitarian Law*. Adelaide, Austral.: University of Adelaide Press, 1999.

Grant, Thomas D. *The Recognition of States: Law and Practice in Debate and Evolution*. Westport, Conn.: Praeger, 1999.

Gray, Christine. *International Law and the Use of Force*. New York: Oxford University Press, 2000.

——. *Judicial Remedies in International Law*. Oxford: Clarendon, 1990.

Green, Leslie. *The Contemporary Law of Armed Conflict*. 2d ed. Huntington, N.Y.: Juris Publishing, 2001.

Grewe, Wilhelm G. *The Epochs of International Law*. Translated and revised by Michael Byers. Hawthorne, N.Y.: Walter de Gruyter, 2000.

Hannum, Hurst, ed. *Guide to International Human Rights Practice*. 3d ed. Ardsley, N.Y.: Transnational Publishers, 1999.

Harris, David J., and Stephen Livingstone, ed. *The Inter-American System of Human Rights*. Oxford: Clarendon, 1998.

Hartley, T. C. *The Foundations of European Community Law*. 4th ed. New York: Oxford University Press, 1998.

Higgins, Rosalyn. *Problems and Process: International Law and How to Use It*. New York: Oxford University Press, 1994.

Igarashi, Masahiro. *Associated Statehood in International Law*. Leiden, Neth.: Nijhoff, 2002.

Jennings, Robert. *The Acquisition of Territory in International Law*. Dobbs Ferry, N.Y.: Oceana, 1963.

Jones, John R. W. D. *The Practice of the International Tribunals for the Former Yugoslavia and Rwanda*. 2d ed. Ardsley, N.Y.: Transnational Publishers, 1999.

Joyner, Christopher C. *Governing the Frozen Commons: The Antarctic Regime and Environmental Protection*. Columbia, S.C.: University of South Carolina Press, 1998.

Kempees, Peter, ed. *A Systematic Guide to the Case Law of the European Court of Human Rights, 1960–1994*. 3 vols. The Hague: Kluver, 1996 (vols. 1–2); 1998 (vol. 3).

Kirgis, Frederic L., Jr. *International Organizations in Their Legal Setting*. 2d ed. St. Paul, Minn.: West Publishing, 1993.

Kish, John, and David Turns, eds. *International Law and Espionage*. Leiden, Neth.: Nijhoff, 1995.

Klabbers, Jan. *The Concept of Treaty in International Law*. Leiden, Neth.: Nijhoff, 1996.

——. *An Introduction to International Institutional Law*. New York: Cambridge University Press, 2002.

Knop, Karen. *Diversity and Self-Determination in International Law*. New York: Cambridge University Press, 2002.

Korman, Sharon. *The Right of Conquest: The Acquisition of Territory by Force in International Law*. New York: Oxford University Press, 1996.

Koskenniemi, Martti. *The Gentle Civilizer of Nations: The Rise and Fall of International Law, 1870–1960*. New York: Cambridge University Press, 2001.

Kuokkanen, Tuomas. *International Law and the Environment: Variations on a Theme.* Leiden, Neth.: Nijhoff, 2002.

Kwiatkowska, Barbara. *Decisions of the World Court Relevant to the UN Convention on the Law of the Sea: A Reference Guide.* Leiden, Neth.: Nijhoff, 2002.

Langholtz, Harvey, Boris Kondoch, and Alan Wells. *International Peacekeeping*. Leiden, Neth.: Nijhoff, 2004.

Långström, Tarja. *Transformation in Russia and International Law*. Leiden, Neth.: Nijhoff, 2003.

Laver, Roberto. *The Falkland/Malvinas Case: Breaking the Deadlock in Anglo-Argentine Sovereignty Dispute.* Leiden, Neth.: Nijhoff, 2001.

Le Goueff, Stepan, ed. *Satellite Regulation in Europe: Legal Texts and Materials*. Leiden, Neth.: Nijhoff, 2000.

Lee, Roy S. *The International Criminal Court: The Making of the Rome Statute.* Leiden, Neth.: Nijhoff, 1999.

Lim, C. L., and Christopher Harding, eds. *Renegotiating Westphalia: Essays and Commentary on the European and Conceptual Foundations of Modern International Law.* Leiden, Neth.: Nijhoff, 1999.

Maluwa, Tiyanjana. *International Law in Post-Colonial Africa*. Leiden, Neth.: Nijhoff, 1999.

McCaffrey, Stephen C. *The Law of International Watercourses: Non-navigational Uses.* New York: Oxford University Press, 2003.

McCoubrey, Hilaire, and Justin Morris. *Regional Peacekeeping in the Post–Cold War Era*. Leiden, Neth.: Nijhoff, 2000.

McDougal, Myres S., and F. Feliciano. *Law and Minimum World Public Order*. New Haven, Conn.: Yale University Press, 1961.

Merrils, J. G. *International Dispute Settlement*. 3d ed. New York: Cambridge University Press, 1999.

Merrils, J. G., and A. H. Robertson. *Human Rights in Europe*. 4th ed. Huntingdon, N.Y.: Juris Publishers, 2001.

Moir, Lindsay. *The Law of Internal Armed Conflict*. New York: Cambridge University Press, 2002.

Mrak, Mojmir, ed. *Succession of States*. Leiden, Neth.: Nijhoff, 1999.

Nanda, Ved P., and George (Rock) Pring. *International Environmental Law and Policy for the 21st Century*. Ardsley, N.Y.: Transnational Publishers, 2003.

Neff, Stephen. *The Legal Institution of War*. New York: Cambridge University Press, 2004.

———. *The Rights and Duties of Neutrals: A General History*. Huntington, N.Y.: Juris Publishing, 2000.

Nisuke, Ando, ed. *Japan and International Law: Past, Present, and Future*. Leiden, Neth.: Nijhoff, 1999.

Nordquist, Myron H., et al. *United Nations Convention on the Law of the Sea, 1982: A Commentary*. 4 vols. Leiden, Neth.: Nijhoff, 1985–1991.

Nowak, Manfred. *Introduction to the International Human Rights Régime*. Leiden, Neth.: Nijhoff, 2003.

Nussbaum, Arthur. *A Concise History of the Law of Nations*. Rev. ed. New York: Macmillan, 1953.

O'Connell, D. P. *State Succession in Municipal Law and International Law*. 2 vols. New York: Cambridge University Press, 1967.

Paust, J. J. *International Law as Law of the United States*. Durham: North Carolina University Press, 1996.

Provost, René, ed. *State Responsibility in International Law*. Brookfield, Vt.: Ashgate, 2002.

Ragazzi, Maurizio. *The Concept of International Obligations Erga Omnes*. New York: Oxford University Press, 1998.

Raic, David. *Statehood and the Law of Self-Determination*. Leiden, Neth.: Nijhoff, 2002.

Ratner, Michael, and Reed Brody, eds. *The Case of Augusto Pinochet in Spain and Britain.* Leiden, Neth.: Nijhoff, 2000.

Rayfuse, Rosemary Gail. *Non-flag State Enforcement in High Seas*. Leiden, Neth.: Nijhoff, 2004.

Reisman, Michael, ed. *Jurisdiction in International Law*. Brookfield, Vt.: Ashgate, 1999.

Reydams, Luc. *Universal Jurisdiction in International Law*. New York: Oxford University Press, 2002.

Rosenne, Shabtai. *The Law and Practice of the International Court, 1920–2004.* 4th ed. Leiden, Neth.: Nijhoff, 2004.

Rubin, Alfred P. *The Law of Piracy*. 2d ed. Ardsley, N.Y.: Transnational Publishers, 1998.

Rubino-Sammartano, Mauro. *International Arbitration: Law and Practice*. 2d ed. The Hague: Kluver, 2001.

Sadat, Leila Nadya. *The International Criminal Court and the Transformation of International Law: Justice for the Millenium*. Ardsley, N.Y.: Transnational Publishers, 2002.

Sands, Philippe. *Principles of International Environmental Law*. New York: Cambridge University Press, 2003.

Sands, Philippe, and Pierre Klein. *Bowett's Law of International Institutions*. 5th ed. London: Sweet & Maxwell, 2001.

Schabas, William. *Genocide in International Law: The Crime of Crimes*. New York: Cambridge University Press, 2000.

———. *An Introduction to the International Criminal Court*. New York: Cambridge University Press, 2001.

Schermers, Henry G., and Niels M. Blokker. *International Institutional Law: Unity within Diversity*. 4th rev. ed. Leiden, Neth.: Nijhoff, 2004.

Schreuer, Christopher H. *The ICSID Convention: A Commentary*. New York: Cambridge University Press, 2001.

Schweigman, David. *The Authority of the Security Council under Chapter VII of the UN Charter: Legal Limits and the Role of the International Court of Justice.* Leiden, Neth.: Nijhoff, 2001.

Scott, Shirley. *The Political Interpretation of Multilateral Treaties*. Leiden, Neth.: Nijhoff, 2004.

Sen, B. *A Diplomatic Handbook of International Law and Practice*. 3d ed. Leiden, Neth.: Nijhoff, 1988.

Shaw, Malcolm. *Title to Territory in Africa*. New York: Oxford University Press, 1986.

Simma, Bruno, ed. *The Charter of the United Nations: A Commentary*. 2d ed. New York: Oxford University Press, 2002.

Simpson, Gerry, ed. *The Nature of International Law*. Brookfield, Vt.: Ashgate, 2002.

Steiner, H., and P. Alston. *International Human Rights in Context*. 2d ed. New York: Oxford University Press, 2000.

Stuit, A. M., ed. *Survey of International Arbitrations, 1794–1989*. 3d ed. Leiden, Neth.: Nijhoff, 1990.

Talmon, Stefan. *Recognition of Governments in International Law*. New York: Oxford University Press, 1998.

Tanzi, Attila, and Maurizio Arcan. *The United Nations Convention on the Law of International Watercourses: A Framework for Sharing*. Leiden, Neth.: Nijhoff, 2001.

Tomuschat, Christian, ed. *Kosovo and the International Community*. Leiden, Neth.: Nijhoff, 2002.

United Nations. *Handbook on Environmental Law*. New York: United Nations, 2000.

——. *Handbook on the Peaceful Settlement of Disputes between States*. New York: United Nations, 1992.

——, ed. *Human Rights: A Compilation of International Instruments*. New York: United Nations, 2003.

——. *International Law as a Language for International Relations*. The Hague: Kluver, 1996.

——. *Report of the High-Level Panel on Threats, Challenges, and Change. A More Secure World: Our Shared Responsibility*. New York: United Nations, 2004.

Ünlü, Nihan. *The Legal Regime of the Turkish Straits*. Leiden, Neth.: Nijhoff, 2002.

Van Dijk, P., G. J. H. van Hoof, et al. *Theory and Practice of the European Convention on Human Rights*. 3d ed. The Hague: Kluver, 1998.

Volger, Helmut. *A Concise Encyclopedia of the United Nations*. Preface by Kofi Annan. Leiden, Neth.: Nijhoff, 2002.

Watts, Arthur. *The International Law Commission, 1949–1998*. 3 vols. New York: Oxford University Press, 2000.

Wheeler, Nicholas J. *Saving Strangers: Humanitarian Intervention in International Law.* New York: Oxford University Press, 2001.

White, Nigel D., ed. *Collective Security Law*. Brookfield: Ashgate, 2003.

# About the Author

**Boleslaw A. Boczek** (M.A., L.L.M., S.J.D., Jagiellonian University, Cracow; Ph.D. (Pol. Science), 1960, Harvard University) is Professor Emeritus of Kent State University where he taught international law and international organization courses for nearly 30 years. Prior to that he had served as a consultant to the United Nations and was on the staff of Harvard Law School as research associate for six years. For some time he was also a member of the Adjunct Faculty of Case Western University School of Law where he conducted a seminar in international organization. As a Visiting Professor and three-time Fulbright Senior Lecturer, he taught at universities in a number of foreign countries, including Belgium, Germany, Greece, Mexico, the Netherlands, Poland, and Switzerland. He was also a NATO Fellow in 1988. In addition, Professor Boczek presented papers at many scholarly conferences in the United States and overseas and has published extensively on various international law topics in professional journals in this country, including the *American Journal of International Law,* and overseas. He is the author of several books and monographs, including, among others, the classic *Flags of Convenience* (1962), *Taxation in Switzerland* (1976) and *Historical Dictionary of International Tribunals* (1994).

www.ingramcontent.com/pod-product-compliance
Lightning Source LLC
LaVergne TN
LVHW082021200926
848481LV00010B/2900